# ARCHIVES OF MARYLAND

## MUSTER ROLLS

AND

OTHER RECORDS OF SERVICE

OF

# MARYLAND TROOPS

IN THE

## AMERICAN REVOLUTION

1775–1783

PUBLISHED BY AUTHORITY OF THE STATE, UNDER THE DIRECTION
OF THE MARYLAND HISTORICAL SOCIETY

## CLEARFIELD

Originally Published as Volume XVIII of the *Archives of Maryland*
By the Maryland Historical Society
Baltimore, 1900

Reprinted with the Permission of the
State of Maryland through the Courtesy
of the Maryland Historical Society
Genealogical Publishing Co., Inc.
Baltimore, 1972

Reprinted for
Clearfield Company, Inc. by
Genealogical Publishing Co., Inc.
Baltimore, Maryland
1996, 2000

Library of Congress Catalogue Card Number 72-5687
International Standard Book Number: 0-8063-0519-3

*Made in the United States of America*

# PREFACE.

To The Maryland Historical Society:

*Gentlemen*:—We have the honor to submit the Eighteenth Volume of the Maryland Archives, containing the Records of Maryland Troops in the Continental Service during the War of the American Revolution, 1775–1783.

This publication of the muster rolls and other records of service of Maryland men in the war of the American Revolution was undertaken in March, 1897. The bravery and excellent reputation of the troops of the Maryland Line were such that their names deserved to be rescued from oblivion, while the services rendered by men of this State in the Flying Camp, German Regiment and other commands were also noteworthy.

A large number of Revolutionary papers were found in the possession of the Johns Hopkins University, to which institution they had been presented by the late Col. J. Thomas Scharf, formerly Commissioner of the Land Office. The custody of these papers was given the Society with authorization to copy and print such of them as should seem desirable. All lists in this work, without indication of source, are to be understood as a part of this collection. In December, 1896, the Society had purchased at auction in New York City a number of muster rolls, some of which had at one time been in Col. Scharf's possession. These are indicated by the letter M. In the Land Office of the State at Annapolis are a number of valuable Revolutionary papers. Some of these contained information duplicating that elsewhere obtained; but one of them, a Record of the soldiers in the Maryland Line from 1776 to 1780, is the most important single list in this work. It comprises over 6,000 names and is contained in three manuscript volumes. A list of those who served in the two battalions of select militia called out in 1781, was also obtained from the Land Office. We are indebted to the courtesy of the Maryland Society of the Sons of the American Revolution for permission to print the copy of the pay-roll of the Maryland Line 1781–83, which they obtained from the Land Office.

There are two plans for the preparation of a work of this kind: one, adopted by the State of Connecticut, to print the lists as found and give a general index of names, the other, adopted by the State of

Massachusetts, to put together all the information concerning each man and arrange all names in alphabetical order. We have adopted the former plan for several reasons; first, because this is a volume of Maryland Archives and, as such, should contain the lists as they are found; secondly, because we have no sufficient means at hand to enable us to identify or differentiate the persons of the same name found in different lists; and, thirdly, because for certain purposes it is interesting and useful to know who were associated in any command.

Doubtless, it will be found that the records are not absolutely complete. The wonder is rather that so many lists have been preserved through so many vicissitudes and opportunities of loss. We have sufficient information from what has been preserved, to give us the record of most of the Continental soldiers. Unfortunately, we have not found the rolls of those two companies who marched from Frederick County to the siege of Boston, but many of the records of the Independent companies are in our possession. The muster rolls of the Flying Camp are preserved, but no record of their service can be found. The records of the Maryland Line are quite complete. A chronological arrangement of the muster and pay-rolls has been adopted as far as possible. The rolls of certain special commands, such as Lee's and Pulaski's Legions, which it is difficult to fit into any chronological arrangement, are placed at the end of the work. It should be noted that the term " deserter," when used without the addition "to the enemy," merely signifies that the soldier was absent from his command without leave. The discipline of the Revolutionary armies was not strict, and many left the ranks, when they were needed at home, returning to the service after a few months.

After most of the volume was in type, certain muster rolls were secured too late to be inserted in their proper place in the volume. These are contained in an appendix.

The Committee deems it proper to record its indebtedness to Dr. Steiner, the Junior member of the Committee, for the large amount of time and labor bestowed by him in the preparation of the present volume. Acknowledgments are also due to Dr. F. E. Sparks, the Society's Archivist, for careful work in superintending details of verification and arrangement. Respectfully,

CLAYTON C. HALL,
HENRY STOCKBRIDGE,
BERNARD C. STEINER,
*Committee of Publication.*

BALTIMORE, 1900.

# TABLE OF CONTENTS.

# EARLY AND INDEPENDENT COMPANIES

1 January, 1776.

" Resolved, That this province be immediately put in the best state of defence.

Resolved, That a sufficient armed force be immediately raised and embodied under proper officers, for the defence and protection of this province.

Resolved, That 1444 men, with proper officers, be immediately raised in the pay and for the defence of this province.

Resolved, That 8 companies of the said troops, to consist of 68 privates each, under proper officers, be formed into a battalion.

Resolved, That the remainder of the said troops be divided into companies of 100 men each.

Resolved, That two companies of the said troops, to consist of 100 men each, be companies of matrosses, and trained as such."

14 January, 1776, Resolves were passed which authorized the troops to consist of a battalion of 9 companies, 7 independent companies, 2 companies of artillery and 1 company of marines. The officers were selected and their pay fixed. The Council of Safety was empowered to order these troops into Virginia, Delaware and Pennsylvania.

A Muster Roll of the Battalion of Regular Troops in the Service of the Province of Maryland and
First of that Part of the said Battalion stationed at Head Quarters at the City of Annapolis; to wit.

| | | | |
|---|---|---|---|
| William Smallwood, Esquire, | Colonel. | present. |
| Thomas Price, | " | Major. | " |
| Charles Wallace, | " | Paymaster. | " |
| Christr. Richmond, | " | Clerk to Colonel. | " |
| Dr. Michael Wallace, | | 1st Surgeon's Mate. | sick. |
| Joseph Marbury, | " | Quarter Master. | present. |
| Mr. Jacob Brice, | | Acting Adjutant. | " |

and of the 1st, 2nd, 3rd, 6th, 7th and 9th Companies as follows. Also the 4th and part of the 8th, stationed at Baltimore Town.

---

### FIRST COMPANY.

| | | | |
|---|---|---|---|
| Commd. Jany. 3d, 1776. | John Hoskins Stone, Captain. | sick. |
| " " " " | Daniel Bowie, 1st Lieut. | present. |
| " " " " | John Kidd, 2nd " | " [inst. |
| " " " " | Benjamin Chambers, Ensign. | resigned his comm. 3rd |

| RANK. | DATE OF ENLISTMENT. | NAMES. | | REMARKS. |
|---|---|---|---|---|
| Cadet | | William Courts | present | |
| " | | Henry Ridgely | " | |
| | Jan 30 | James Fernandis | | on detachment duty |
| | 24 | John Mitchell | " | |
| | | Samuel Jones | " | |
| | | Charles Smith | " | |
| | | Thos. Simpson | " | |
| | | James Sims, Sr. | absent | on furlough 23 May |
| | | Samuel Hanson | present | |
| | | Samuel McPherson | " | |
| Drum. | Mch 16 | Henry Walworth | sick | in barracks |
| Fifer | Apl 15 | Dennis Broderick | present | |
| Privates | Jan 24 | Andrew Ross Lindsay | | on detachment duty |
| | " | Andrew Green Sims | | on guard |
| | " | Thomas Norris | " | |
| | " | Ignatius Doyglass | " | |
| | " | William Smoot | | " " |

| RANK. | DATE OF ENLISTMENT. | NAMES. | | REMARKS. |
|---|---|---|---|---|
| Privates | Jan 24 | Edmund Cox | present | |
| | " | William Wheatly | " | |
| | " | John Boen | sick | in hospl |
| | " | John Hopson | present | |
| | " | John Adams | " | |
| | " | Thos. Way Connell | " | |
| | " | Joseph Cheatham | " | |
| | " | James Thompson | " | |
| | " | Samuel Thompson | " | |
| | " | John Plant | " | |
| | " | Thomas Smith | " | |
| | " | Jonathan Chunn | sick | and on furlough |
| | " | George Thomas | present | |
| | " | James Sims, Jr. | " | |
| | " | Samuel Wheatly | " | |
| | " | Bernard Nash | " | |
| | " | John Neal | " | |
| | " | Luke Matthew Sherburn | " | |
| | " | Samuel Luckitt | " | |
| | " | John Skipper | " | |
| | " | Thomas Burrows | " | |
| | " | Samuel Granger | " | |
| | " | Alban Smith | " | |
| | " | Edward Green | " | |
| | " | John Smith | " | |
| | " | John McPherson | " | |
| | " | Clement Edelen | " | |
| | " | Patrick Brady | | on guard |
| | " | Francis Sherhard | " | |
| | " | Samuel Kurk | " | |
| | " | Francis Green Baggott | | "     " |
| | " | Charles Green | " | |
| | " | Charles Griffin | | "     " |
| | " | John Ward | " | |
| | " | Richard Sheake | " | |
| | " | Edward Edelen | " | |
| | " | Saml. Hamilton | | "     " |
| | " | Francis Ware Luckett | " | |
| | 25 | Matthew Garner | " | |
| | 27 | Nathaniel Downing | " | |
| | " | Josias Miller | " | |
| | " | John Shaw | " | |
| | " | Edward Smith | " | |
| | " | John Norris | " | |
| | " | Joseph Jason Jenkins | " | |
| | " | James Hoge | | "     " |

| RANK. | DATE OF ENLISTMENT. | NAMES. | | REMARKS. |
|---|---|---|---|---|
| Privates | Feb  1 | Benjamin Gray | present | . |
|  | 2 | Richard Smith | " |  |
|  | 3 | John Smoot | " |  |
|  | 4 | William Clark | " |  |
|  | " | John Neary |  | on guard |
|  | 6 | Saml. Vermillion | " |  |
|  | " | Truman Hilton | sick | in barracks |
|  | 7 | Gilbert Garland |  | on guard |
|  | Mch  6 | Mark McPherson |  | "      " |
|  |  | M |  |  |

## SECOND COMPANY.

| Commd. | Jan 20th, '76, | Patk. Sims, Captain. | present |
|---|---|---|---|
| " | "   "   " | Benj. Ford, 1st Lieut. | " |
| " | "  3rd.  " | John Beans, 2nd  " | " |
| " | "   "   " | Henry Gaither, Ensign. | " |

| RANK. | DATE OF ENLISTMENT. | NAMES. | | REMARKS. |
|---|---|---|---|---|
| Cadet |  | John Burgis | present |  |
| " |  | Walter Cox | absent | on furlough 25 May |
| Serjt. | Feb 12 | John Richardson | present |  |
| " | Mch  7 | Peter Clarke | " |  |
| " | Feb 12 | Edward Spurrier | " |  |
| " | 3 | Alexius Conner | sick | in barracks |
| Corpl. | " | Michael Burgis | present |  |
| " | Jan 29 | Gazaway Watkins | " |  |
| " | " | John Elson | " |  |
| " | " | Henry Leek | " |  |
| Drum. | " | Benj. Lewis | " |  |
| Fifer | Feb  3 | Thos. Horson | " |  |
| Privates | Jan 28 | Jonathan Robinson |  | on detachmt. duty |
|  | Feb  7 | John Lindsay |  | on guard |
|  | 17 | Coxon Talbott |  | "      " |
|  | 7 | Lawrence Querney |  | "      " |
|  | Jan 29 | James Mitchell | " |  |
|  | 31 | Peter Gallworth | " |  |
|  | Feb 17 | Bozely Wright |  | "      " |
|  | 3 | Milburn Cox |  | "      " |
|  | " | John Willey | " |  |
|  | Apl  6 | James Adams | " |  |
|  | " | Hugh Tomlin | " |  |
|  | 8 | Amos Green | " |  |
|  | 9 | Christr. Brumbargher | " |  |

| RANK. | DATE OF ENLISTMENT. | NAMES. | | REMARKS. |
|---|---|---|---|---|
| Privates | Mch 7 | Thomas Simpkins | present | |
| | 11 | Elisha Everit | " | |
| | 5 | Willm. Skipper | " | |
| | Feb 14 | Willm. Heyder | " | |
| | 2 | Philip King | " | |
| | Mch 5 | Richd. Johnson | " | |
| | " | John Veach | " | |
| | Feb 1 | Patirck Nowlan | " | |
| | 9 | Moses McNew | " | |
| | 29 | Jacob Penn | " | |
| | 6 | James Byzch | " | |
| | 3 | Ben. Vermillion | " | |
| | Mch 22 | Richd. Lowe | " | |
| | Feb 8 | Robt. Nelson | " | |
| | 3 | Basil Ridgly | " | |
| | 20 | Michael Waltz | " | |
| | 23 | Willm. Evans | " | |
| | 8 | John Grant | " | |
| | Mch 6 | Thos. Connor | " | |
| | Jan 26 | John Russel | " | |
| | Mch 6 | John Edelin | " | |
| | Feb 3 | Danl. Rankins | " | |
| | Jan 28 | James Perry | " | |
| | Feb 3 | Richard Cox | " | |
| | 26 | Joseph Steward | " | |
| | 7 | Thomas Walsh | " | |
| | 3 | John Walker | " | |
| | Jan 31 | Edwd. Caine | | discharged 1 June |
| | Mch 11 | Chas. Burroughs | " | |
| | Jan 31 | Philip Jinkins | " | |
| | Mch 10 | Ben. Burroughs | " | |
| | Jan 28 | Francis Thompson | " | |
| | 29 | Francis Osburne | " | |
| | Feb 5 | Michael Barnitt | " | |
| | 13 | Paul Hagarty | " | |
| | 3 | Elias Perry | " | |
| | 29 | Veach Burgis | " | |
| | " | Jacob Holland | " | |
| | 3 | Middleton Marlow | " | |
| | " | John D. Lanham | " | |
| | " | John Mills | " | |
| | " | Thos. Perkins | " | |
| | " | Henry Lanham | " | |
| | 10 | Edward Blacklock | " | |
| | 6 | John Rodery | " | |

| RANK. | DATE OF ENLISTMENT. | NAMES. | REMARKS. |
|---|---|---|---|
| Privates | May 12 | Robt. Sapp | present |
| | 10 | Thos. Daws | " |
| Also— | | | |
| Privates | Mch 6 | Edmd. Carroll | sick |
| | Apl 19 | Edwd. Jones | present |

M

## THIRD COMPANY.

| | | | |
|---|---|---|---|
| Commd. Jan. 3d, 1776. | Barton Lucas, Capt. | present | |
| " " " " | Wm. Sterrett, 1 Lt. | | on furlough |
| " " " " | Alex. Roxburgh, 2 Lt. | " | |
| " " " " | Wm. Ridgely, Ensign. | " | |

| RANK. | DATE OF ENLISTMENT. | NAMES. | REMARKS. |
|---|---|---|---|
| Serjt. | Jan 20 | Peter Brown | present |
| " | 21 | James Burnes | " |
| " | 29 | Zacha. Tannahill | " |
| " | 30 | Levin Will Coxen | " |
| Corpl. | 31 | Saml. Hamiltone | " |
| " | Feb 3 | Benedict Woodward | " |
| " | Jan 29 | Benjn. Warner | sick   in barracks |
| " | Feb 3 | Zacha. Gray | "    "    " |
| Drum. | Jan 22 | Geo. Rex Leonard | present |
| Fifer | Apl 19 | Joshua Saffell | " |
| Privates | Jan 20 | John Cissell | at the magazine |
| | " | Zacha. Tilly | " |
| | " | Christopher Beal | on guard |
| | " | Leonard Watkins | " |
| | " | Thomas Scott | " |
| | " | Daniel McKay | " |
| | 22 | John Baker | " |
| | " | John Dunn | " |
| | " | Hugh Conn | " |
| | " | Robt. Lesache | " |
| | " | John Brown | " |
| | " | Benjn. Kelly | " |
| | " | Josias Connally | " |
| | 23 | Rhody Hously | " |
| | 26 | James Murphy | " |
| | 27 | George Knott | " |
| | " | John Enright | " |
| | " | Thos. Murray | " |

2

| RANK. | DATE OF ENLISTMENT. | NAMES. | | REMARKS. |
|---|---|---|---|---|
| Privates | Jan 29 | William Pearce | present | |
| | " | Charles Jones | " | |
| | 30 | Josiah Hatton | " | |
| | 31 | Richard Stone | " | |
| | Feb 3 | Samuel Ray | | on guard |
| | Jan 31 | George Hamiltone | " | |
| | Feb 3 | John Fleming | sick | in barracks |
| | " | John Wood | | deserted May 8th |
| | " | Richard Broekes | | on guard |
| | 5 | Zacha. Willing | | " " |
| | " | Richard Wade | | " " |
| | 7 | John Owings | present | |
| | 5 | Alex. Jackson | " | |
| | 8 | John Murphy | " | |
| | " | John Jackson | | dischd. 28th May |
| | 6 | John Flint | " | |
| | 13 | Abijah Buxtone | " | |
| | " | Nathan Peake | " | |
| | 2 | Timothy Collins | " | |
| | 3 | Jeremiah Owings | " | |
| | 13 | Joseph Barry | " | |
| | 17 | John Armstrong | " | |
| | Apl 11 | George Wright | " | |
| | Mch 10 | Philip Weller | " | |
| | Feb 8 | Amos Allen | " | |
| | 27 | John Hughes | " | |
| | 25 | Thos. Forguson | " | |
| | 7 | Obediah Sumers | absent | on furlough 16 May |
| | " | Absolam Stevenson | present | |
| | 20 | John Halsey | " | |
| | 16 | Thos. Windom | " | |
| | Mch 2 | James Smith | " | |
| | Jan 26 | George Evauns | " | |
| | Mch 10 | Thos. Shannen | " | |
| | Jan 22 | George Leadbarn | " | |
| | 27 | Michl. Catons | sick | in barracks |
| | 22 | James Hurdle | present | |
| | Apl 2 | Francis Cole | " | |
| | Feb 8 | Alex. Allen | " | |
| | 25 | Wm. Baker | " | |
| | Apl 17 | Garret Brinkenhoof | " | |
| | Jan 25 | John Rex Leonard | | |
| | Mch 10 | Bazil Jenkins | | |
| | Feb 2 | Bartholomew Finn | | |
| | " | Roddey Owings | | |

| RANK. | DATE OF ENLISTMENT. | NAMES. | | REMARKS. |
|---|---|---|---|---|
| Privates | Feb 17 | George Read | | disch 13 May |
| | May 14 | James Gardiner | | |
| | 18 | Patk. Collins | | in the black hole |
| | June 9 | Zachariah Hutchins (?) | present | |
| | | M | | |

## FOURTH COMPANY.

| | | | | |
|---|---|---|---|---|
| Commd. Jan. 3d, '76. | | Thomas Ewing, Captain. | | present |
| " " " " | | Joseph Butler, 1st Lieut. | | " |
| " " " " | | Vacant, 2nd " | | Joseph Baxter was elected by the Convention 2 Jan., 1776. Probably resigned. |
| " " " " | | Edward Pratt Ensign. | | present |

| RANK. | DATE OF ENLISTMENT. | NAMES. | | REMARKS. |
|---|---|---|---|---|
| Serjt. | Jan 8 | John Smith, 1st Serjt. | | present |
| " | " | John Toomy, 2d " | | " |
| " | 13 | Thomas Cunningham, 3d Serjt. | | " |
| " | 23 | Robert Morrow, 4th " | | " discharged 3d May |
| Corpl. | May 3 | George Hamelton, 1st Corpl. | | " |
| " | " | Robert Harvey, 2d " | sick | in hospital |
| " | 26 | Samuel McMellon, 3d " | | " " " |
| " | " | William McMellon, 4th " | | " " " |
| Drum. | 23 | Patrick Ivory | present | |
| Fifer | " | ——— Hired | | " |
| | 3 | John McGlaughlin, Corpl. | | " |
| | 20 | Vachel O'Legg | | " |
| | 18 | Richard Watts | | " |
| | 24 | Charles Pritchard | | " |
| | " | Levi Vezey | | discharged 31 May |
| | 22 | William Martin | | " |
| | 20 | Leonard Lion | sick | |
| | 29 | Nathaniel Cortland | present | |
| | 20 | Samuel Glasgow | | " |
| | 29 | William Baggott | | " |
| | 24 | William McGinnis | | " |
| | " | Thomas Hamelton | | " |
| | 27 | James Bennett | | discharged 29 April |
| | 18 | Edward Price | | " |
| | 27 | Thomas Haynon | | deserted 7th instant |
| | 20 | Robert Crafford | | " |
| | Jan 27 | Thomas Crafford | | " |

| RANK. | DATE OF ENLISTMENT. | NAMES. | | REMARKS. |
|---|---|---|---|---|
| Privates | Jan 18 | William Grimes | present | |
| | 24 | Dennis Turley | " | |
| | 29 | Patrick Reed | " | |
| | 24 | James Matthews | " | |
| | " | Charles Rieley | sick | in the hospital |
| | " | John Rieley | " | " " " |
| | 22 | Matthew Murry | present | |
| | 18 | John Herron | " | |
| | 22 | Thomas Hill | | discharged 26th April |
| | 29 | Michael Cady | " | |
| | 20 | Peter Burk | sick | in the hospital |
| | " | William Chaplin | present | |
| | 29 | John Price | " | |
| | 20 | John O'Neal | " | |
| | " | Richard Whealin | " | |
| | 29 | Thomas Holland | " | |
| | " | Thomas Mason | " | |
| | 22 | Neal Dearmond | " | |
| | " | William McCaulley | " | |
| | 29 | William Little | absent | on furlough |
| | " | Richard Carbury | present | |
| | 8 | Terrence Martin | " | |
| | 29 | John Gorden | " | |
| | 24 | Thomas Baker | | discharged 3d June • |
| | " | Samuel Wiltshire | " | |
| | 29 | Edward McKinzie | " | |
| | 22 | Valentine Smith | " | |
| | 24 | Edward Cosgrove | sick | in the hospital |
| | 29 | Thomas Wiseman | present | |
| | " | William Nixon | " | |
| | 24 | Edward Wright | sick | |
| | 22 | Andrew Warrick | present | |
| | 24 | Peter Smith | " | |
| | 29 | John Haney | absent | on furlough |
| | 8 | Thomas Donolan | present | |
| | 29 | Hugh Pugh | | deserted 19th instant |
| | 27 | William Parr | " | |
| | 24 | Patrick Baxter | " | |
| | 29 | Richard Doyle | " | |
| | 24 | John Cavender | " | |
| | " | Thomas McGuire | " | |
| | 27 | Samuel Thomas | sick | in the hospital |
| | 29 | James O'Lary | " | " " " |
| | June 3 | William McGlaughlin | present | |
| | May 31 | Samuel Goslin | " | |

| RANK. | DATE OF ENLISTMENT. | NAMES. | REMARKS. |
|---|---|---|---|
| Privates | Apl 26 | Joseph Mongomery | present |
| | May 3 | James Reed | " |
| | 8 | James Lamb | " |
| Also— | | | Signed |
| | | | Thos. Ewing Captain |
| | | Cornelius Murphy | |
| Drum. | | Thos. Roberts | |
| | | Wm. Preston | deserted |
| | | James Wills | |
| | | Michael Davis | |
| | | Thomas Jones | |
| | | Hugh Munroe | |
| | | Ralph Allison | |
| | | William Hart | |
| | | Wm. Luguard | |
| | | John Purtle | |
| | | Abraham Tennis | |
| | | Edward Freeman | |
| | | Francis Millner | |
| | | James Wells | refused |

## FIFTH COMPANY.

Nathaniel Ramsey, Captn.
Levin Winder, 1st Lieut.
Alexander Murray, 2nd Lieut.
Walker Muse, Ensign.

Elected by the Convention of Maryland, Jan. 2nd, 1776.*

## SIXTH COMPANY.

| | | | |
|---|---|---|---|
| Commd. Jan. 3d, '76. | | Peter Adams, Captain. | present |
| " " " " | | Nathl. Ewing, 1st Lieut. | " |
| " " " " | | Alex. Murray, 2d " | on furlough |
| " " " " | | John Jordan, Ensign. | " |

| RANK. | DATE OF ENLISTMENT. | NAMES. | REMARKS. |
|---|---|---|---|
| Serjt. | Jan 30 | Joseph Elliott | present |
| " | Feb 15 | Edward Edgerly | " |
| " | Jan 30 | Thomas McKeel | " |
| " | " | Thomas Dwyer | " |

*See Proceedings of the Conventions of Maryland, pp. 67, 68.

| RANK. | DATE OF ENLISTMENT. | NAMES. | | REMARKS. |
|---|---|---|---|---|
| Corpl. | Jan 22 | Danl. Dwigens | present | |
| " | " | Saml. Dwigens | " | |
| " | 30 | Jas. Rogan | " | |
| " | 23 | Danl. Floyd | " | |
| Drum. | Feb 15 | Robert Ross | " | |
| Fifer | Jan 22 | Chas. McKeel | | dischd. 7 June |
| Privates | " | John Clark | " | |
| " | " | Zacha. Nicholson | " | |
| " | " | Henry Covington | " | |
| " | " | Wm. Laighton | " | |
| " | " | Wm. McDaniel | " | |
| " | " | George Jackson | ' | |
| " | 23 | John Hatton | " | |
| " | " | Alex. Wright | " | |
| " | " | John Floyd | " | |
| " | " | Elijah Floyd | " | |
| " | " | Moses Floyd | " | |
| " | " | John McFadon | " | |
| " | " | Carbry Burn | " | |
| " | " | John McClain | absent | on furlough |
| " | 25 | John Johnson | present | |
| " | 26 | Jas. Kelly | " | |
| " | 30 | Willm. McGreger | " | |
| " | " | Thos. Fisher | " | |
| " | " | John Powell | " | |
| " | " | Joseph Pirkens | " | |
| " | " | Joseph Bootman | :: | |
| " | " | Hugh Wallace | " | |
| " | " | Willm. McDaniel, 2nd | " | |
| " | " | James Bell | " | |
| " | Feb 6 | Henry Clift | " | |
| " | " | Thos. Cooper | | on guard |
| " | 15 | Saml. McCubbin | | "    " |
| " | " | Wm. Glover | | "    " |
| " | " | John Bryan | " | |
| " | " | Wm. Holms | | "    " |
| " | " | Wm. Ray | " | |
| " | " | Thos. Laffy | " | |
| " | " | Jas. Kirk | " | |
| " | " | Wm. Leeson | " | |
| " | 22 | John Lowry | " | |
| " | " | John McClain, of Harford | " | |
| " | " | Alex. Fulton | " | |
| " | " | Jas. Craig | " | |
| " | " | Robert Man | " | |

| RANK. | DATE OF ENLISTMENT. | NAMES. | | REMARKS. |
|---|---|---|---|---|
| Privates | Feb 22 | Patk. Quigley | | in the black hole |
| | 24 | Wm. Locke | present | |
| | " | Wm. Nagle | " | |
| | " | John Lynch | " | |
| | " | Hugh McClain | " | |
| | " | Jas. Carmichael | " | |
| | " | Thos. Williams | | on guard |
| | " | John Kerby | | " " |
| | " | Jas. Gibson | " | |
| | " | Jno. Galway | " | |
| | " | Robt. Ritchie | sick | in barracks |
| | May 7 | Wm. Aitken | present | |
| | " | Hugh Galway | " | |
| | " | John Morrow | " | |
| | " | Geo. Dowling | " | |
| | " | Wm. Clark | | on detach. duty |
| | " | Wm. Temple | " | |
| | 20 | John Phelps | " | |
| | 7 | James Barkley | " | |
| | 15 | Crisenberry Clift | " | |
| | | M | | |

## SEVENTH COMPANY.

| | | | | |
|---|---|---|---|---|
| Commd. Jan. 3d, '76. | | John Day Scott, Capt. | present | |
| " " " " | | Thos. Harwood, 1 Lt. | " | |
| " " " " | | Thos. Goldsmith, 2 " | absent | on furlough |
| " " " " | | James Peale, Ensign. | present | |

| RANK. | DATE OF ENLISTMENT. | NAMES. | | REMARKS. |
|---|---|---|---|---|
| Cadet | | James Disney | absent | on furlough |
| Serjeant | Jan 20 | Saml. Barber | | disch. 23 May |
| " | " | Willm. Sands | " | on furlough recruit'g |
| " | Mch 9 | John Smith Selby | present | |
| " | Feb 15 | Thos. Gordon | " | |
| Corporal | 26 | Willm. Noyes | " | |
| " | 15 | Joshua Lamb | " | |
| " | " | Andw. Ferguson | " | |
| " | 25 | John Smith | absent | on furlough |
| Drummer | Jan 20 | John Meek | present | |
| Fifer | Feb 3 | Edward George | " | |
| Privates | Jan 20 | James Low | " | |
| | " | John Babb | " | |

| RANK. | DATE OF ENLISTMENT. | NAMES. | | REMARKS. |
|---|---|---|---|---|
| Privates | Jan 20 | Joseph Green | present | |
| | " | Willm. Austin | " | |
| | " | Joseph Anglain | " | |
| | " | Anthony Ryan | " | |
| | " | Nicholas Watkins | " | |
| | 22 | Richard White | " | |
| | " | Thomas White | absent | on guard |
| | " | Joseph Bassil | " | "    " |
| | 24 | Cephas Hoy | | on detachment duty at the magazine |
| | " | Hugh Armstrong | present | |
| | 27 | Ignatius Boon | " | |
| | " | Joseph Mattingly | " | |
| | 29 | Dennis Howley | " | |
| | " | John Jasper | absent | on guard |
| | " | Burgess Howard | sick | boarded out |
| | " | Francis Fairbrother | " | "    " |
| | " | Richard Rawlings | | confined in guard-house, to be disch., disch. 21 April |
| | Feb 1 | Henry Weedon | present | |
| | " | Charles Leech | sick | in barracks |
| | " | Thomas Mayo | present | |
| | 5 | John Ashton | " | |
| | 10 | Clement Barber | " | |
| | " | Joshua Naylor | sick | "    " |
| | " | Edward Lloyd Wales | | disch. 25 May |
| | " | Thomas Robinson | " | in barracks |
| | " | Thomas Weedon | present | |
| | 14 | Willm. Johnston | absent | on guard |
| | 15 | John Boothe | present | |
| | Mch 12 | Thomas Hamilton | " | |
| | Feb 15 | Joseph Matthews | " | |
| | 26 | Edward Murphy | " | |
| | 25 | Nicholas Gassaway | " | |
| | 26 | Charles O'Neale | sick | in barracks |
| | " | Peter Lawless | present | |
| | 28 | James Connery, (or Conway) | | disch. 23 May |
| | Mch 1 | Richd. Elwood | " | |
| | 5 | James Pope | " | |
| | " | Moses Paget | sick | in barracks |
| | 8 | Joseph Yater | " | "    " |
| | 9 | Willm. Watts | present | |
| | 11 | Joseph Orme | sick | "    " |
| | " | Dorset Hoy | present | |

| RANK. | DATE OF ENLISTMENT. | NAMES. | | REMARKS. |
|---|---|---|---|---|
| Privates | Mch 11 | John Harper | | disch. 9 May |
| | " | Francis Mitchell | present | |
| | " | John Carr | " | |
| | 8 | John Majors | " | |
| | " | Edward Edwards | " | |
| | Jan 24 | Dennis Kellis | " | |
| | Feb 12 | James McGill | " | |
| | 16 | John Hooper | | disch. |
| | Jan 29 | James Murphy | " | |
| | Mch 12 | James Ranter | " | |
| | Jan 21 | Nicholas Watkins | " | |
| | Feb 28 | Abraham Chapman | | disch. |
| | Mch 11 | Nathaniel O'Neale | " | |
| | " | James Devaun | " | |
| | " | William Sewell | " | |
| | Feb 15 | Wm. McKinsey | absent | making cloaths for company |
| | Apl 14 | John Nottingham | present | |
| | | Wm. Kinnick | " | |
| | | Elisha Richardson | sick | in barracks |
| | | Nicholas Ridgely | present | |
| | | John Swan | " | |
| | | M | | |

EIGHTH COMPANY.

Samuel Smith, Captain.              Joseph Ford, 2nd Lieut.
James Campbell, 1st Lieut.          Bryan Philpot, Ensign.

Elected by the Convention of Maryland, Jan. 2nd, 1776.*

A Copy of the Enlistment of the Eighth Company of the 1st Battalion of Maryland forces.  We whose names are hereto Subscribed do voluntarily Enlist ourselves Soldiers to Serve as Such during the present dispute between Great Britain & America unless Sooner discharged by Order of the Convention or Council of Safety of Maryland for the Time being hereby Subjecting ourselves to Such Rules & Regulations as are or shall be made by the Convention of Maryland for Regulating & governing the forces in the Pay of this Province, Witness our hands

* See Proceedings of the Conventions of Maryland, pp. 67, 68.

| 1776 | | 1776 | | Balto. Town, 1 Apl, 1776 |
|------|------|------|------|------|
| Jan 11 | Patrick Walsh | Jan 24 | John Rowan | A Roll of this Com-|
| " | Festus Burke | " | Adam Cramer | pany was returned the |
| " | John Rashe | 25 | Ludo. Taylor | —day of—but not be-|
| " | Dyonisius Hargreaves | 26 | Philip Hawkins | ing made out properly |
| " | Christian Closs | 27 | Samuel Percival | was returned. Since |
| 12 | Samuel Clark | " | Thomas Nowlan | which I have chang'd |
| " | Laurence Hutin | " | Jacob Plumly | some of the men or find-|
| " | John Cain | " | Gasper Clutter | ing it difficult to train |
| 13 | Andrew Yaeter | " | John Offield | them. |
| " | William Hopkins | " | Matthew Ritchie | |
| " | Robert Britt | " | Robert Ford | Sam. Smith |
| " | Joseph Crosbie | " | Francis Petty | |
| | | " | John Dill | |
| [Torn off.] | | " | Jerry Jones,  deserted | |

## NINTH COMPANY OF LIGHT INFANTRY.

Commd. Jan. 3rd, '76.  George Stricker, Capt.        present.
"      "      "      "     Thomas Smyth, Jr., 1st Lieut.   "
"      "      "      "     James Ringgold, 2nd       "    resigned 3d inst.
"      "      "      "     Hatch Dent, Jr., 3rd       "

| RANK. | DATE OF ENLISTMENT. | NAMES. | | REMARKS. |
|-------|--------------------|--------|--|----------|
| Cadet | | Richard Dorsey | present | |
| " | | Larkin Dorsey | " | |
| Serjt. | Jan 12 | Peter McNaughton | " | |
| " | 20 | John Good | " | |
| " | | David Giveny | " | |
| " | 26 | William Bruce | " | |
| Corpl. | Feb 4 | William McPherson | " | |
| " | Jan 20 | Adam Everly | " | |
| " | | Jacob Alexander | " | |
| " | 31 | Robert Chandler | sick | in hosp'l |
| Drum. | 28 | John Row | present | |
| Fifer | | Dennis May | " | |
| Privates | 20 | Jacob Gardner | " | |
| | 21 | Davall Stottlemeir | | on detach. duty |
| | " | Henry Miller . | " | |
| | " | Fredk. Keller | " | |
| | " | Alex. Nailor | " | |
| | " | Melcher Brobeck | | "    "    " |
| | " | John Mugg | | on guard |
| | " | Michael Hackethorn | " | |
| | " | Henry Young | " | |

| RANK. | DATE OF ENLISTMENT. | NAMES. | | REMARKS. |
|---|---|---|---|---|
| Privates | Jan 22 | Valentine Lynn | | on guard |
| | " | James Miller | | "      " |
| | " | John Heywood | | "      " |
| | " | William Tarrance | present | |
| | " | Andrew Hardy | " | |
| | " | Adam Bromcord | " | |
| | " | John Gerrish | " | |
| | " | Martin Kipheart | " | |
| | " | Michl. Curtz | " | |
| | " | Michl. Mullen | sick | in hospital |
| | " | Isaac Rice | present | |
| | " | Robert Tune | " | |
| | " | William Lynn | " | |
| | " | Michael Miller | " | |
| | " | William Witner | sick | in barracks |
| | " | John Glatz | present | |
| | " | Andrew Conslean | " | |
| | " | Fredk. Miles | sick | in hospital |
| | " | Nicholas Nailor | present | |
| | 25 | Alexander Boston | " | |
| | 26 | Thomas Byrn | . | drafted for Artillery |
| | " | Samuel Price | absent | on furlough 27 May |
| | " | Samuel Denny | present | |
| | " | Causamer Hill | " | |
| | " | John Hoofman | " | |
| | " | William Casbear | " | |
| | 27 | John McCabe | | discharged from the service 11 May, '76 |
| | 28 | George Hellmold | " | |
| | " | John Ross | " | |
| | " | Samuel Workman | " | |
| | " | Philip Kern | " | |
| | " | John Kasler | " | |
| | " | James Taylor | " | |
| | 29 | Jacob Grenewald | " | |
| | " | Frederick Myre | " | |
| | " | Jacob Harman | " | |
| | " | Peter Kline | " | |
| | " | Pacel Martin | " | |
| | " | Jacob Fisher | " | |
| | " | George Cretzinger | " | |
| | " | Willm. Smith | " | |
| | 31 | Stephen Fleehearty | " | |
| | " | George Morriner | " | |
| | " | George Kipheart | " | |

| Rank. | Date of Enlistment. | Names. | | Remarks. |
|---|---|---|---|---|
| Privates | Jan 31 | Henry Remsburg (?) | present | |
| | " | Peter Breat | " | ? |
| | " | Michael Deaver | " | |
| | Feb 8 | John Hite | " | |
| | " | James Beale | " | |
| | 10 | Solomon Cretzinger | " | |
| | " | Peter Myre | " | |
| | 12 | Basil Holland | " | |
| | Mch 4 | Levean Todd | " | |
| | 10 | Michael Haun | " | |
| | Apl 11 | John Taylor | sick | in barracks |
| | 17 | John Cobeth | | on guard |
| | June 7 | Notley Davis | present | |
| | June 10th, 1776. | M | Signed, | W. Smallwood. |

## Stationed at Baltimore Town—

Francis Ware, Lieutenant Colonel.                present.
Mordecai Gist, 2nd Major.                           "
Dr. Charles Frederick Wiesenthal, Surgeon.
Dr. William Augustus Dashiell, 2nd Surgeon's Mate.   absent.
And the 4th, 5th and 8th Companies.                  present.

M

---

1ST INDEPENDENT MARYLAND COMPANY. [CHARLES AND CALVERT COUNTIES.]

Rezin Beall, Capt.                     officers elected by the Con-
Bennet Bracco, 1st Lieut.                 vention of Maryland Jan.
John Halkerston, 2nd   "                  2nd, 1776.*
Daniel Jenifer Adams, 3rd Lieut.
Bennet Bracco, Capt.                   later list given in McSherry's
John Halkerston, 1st Lieut.               Hist. of Maryland.†
Thomas Beale,   2nd   "
Colmore Williams, 3rd   "

---

2ND INDEPENDENT MARYLAND COMPANY. [SOMERSET COUNTY.]

John Gunby, Capt.                      officers elected by the Con-
Uriah Forrest,   1st Lieut.               vention Jan. 2nd, 1776.‡
William Bowie,   2nd   "
Benjamin Brooks, 3rd   "

*Proceedings of the Conventions of Maryland, pp. 67, 68, 73, 93.
†McSherry's Hist. of Maryland, appendix A.
‡Proceedings of the Conventions of Maryland, pp. 67, 68, 73, 93.

MUSTER ROLL OF THE 3D MD. INDEPENDENT COMPANY, AUG. 20TH, 1776.
[WORCESTER COUNTY.]

| | | | | |
|---|---|---|---|---|
| John Watkins, | Captain. | Commd. Jan. 5th | present. |
| Moses Chaille, | 1st Lt. | "    "    " | absent, gone to be married. |
| Solomon Long, | 2nd " | "    "    " | present. |
| Ely Dorsey, | 3rd " | "    "    " | " |

| RANK | NAMES. | DATE OF ENLISTMENT. | REMARKS. | |
|---|---|---|---|---|
| Serjeant | Richard Grace | Jan 25 | present | |
| " | Solomon Jarvis | " | " | |
| " | Dixon Quinton | Feb 2 | absent | on furlough 12th inst |
| " | James Done | Apl 7 | " | "    "    29th June |
| Corpl. | Peter Hall | Jan 29 | present | |
| " | John Purdy | 25 | sick | in barracks |
| " | Josiah Cathell | Feb 5 | " | "    "    " |
| " | Littleton Johnson | 3 | present | |
| Drum. | John Morgan Jones | June 16 | " | |
| Fidler | William Jones | Mch 19 | " | |
| Privates | Richard Ayres | Feb 10 | " | |
| | Arthur McHenry | " | " | |
| | John McCormick | Apl 1 | absent | on furlough 12th |
| | John Williams | Feb 27 | present | |
| | Luke Lamb | 10 | sick | in the country |
| | James Truitt | 18 | " | at his mother's |
| | Joseph Johnson | 9 | present | |
| | Dennis Driskell | 5 | " | |
| | William Marchmont | 3 | sick | in the country |
| | Thos. Niember | 10 | present | |
| | James Cathell | 13 | " | |
| | John Brasher | 2 | absent | on furlough 10th |
| | Bennet Mason | Apl 29 | present | |
| | Robert Shipley | Feb 15 | " | |
| | Willm. Jarman | Mch 4 | " | |
| | James Hall | Feb 12 | " | |
| | Zadok Purnell | 7 | sick | at his mother's |
| | John Houston | 2 | present | |
| | James Crapper | 9 | " | |
| | John McQue | 3 | sick | in barracks |
| | Belitha Taylor | 5 | present | |
| | Levi Cathell | 13 | " | |
| | James Barber | Mch 11 | " | |
| | George Bishop | Feb 18 | sick | at his father's |
| | Philip Hall | 3 | present | |
| | John Shockley | Apl 8 | sick | in barracks |
| | Randall Smulling | Feb 13 | present | |
| | Solomon Taylor | 9 | " | |
| | Jesse Selby | Apl 28 | " | |

| Rank. | Names. | Date of Enlistment. | | Remarks. |
|---|---|---|---|---|
| Privates | Jesse Wright | Feb 21 | present | |
| | Thomas Donaldson | 24 | " | |
| | Zadock Timmons | 9 | " | |
| | Ephraim Stilley | " | | deserted 19 July |
| | Edward Coll | " | sick | in barracks |
| | John Freeman | Mch 12 | " | "    " |
| | Arthur Allen | Feb 9 | absent | on furlough |
| | Stephen Allen | " | " | "    " |
| | Kendall Hislup | 2 | present | |
| | Joseph Roan | 3 | " | |
| | Jas. White, (of Wm.) | 6 | " | |
| | Isaac Lone | 3 | " | |
| | Joshua Wheelton | 24 | " | |
| | Dunnick Dennis | Mch 9 | sick | in the country |
| | Robert Jarman | 28 | present | |
| | James Ayres | Feb 28 | sick | "    "    " |
| | Benj. Curtis | 10 | present | |
| | John Cottingham | 3 | " | |
| | Edwd. Maglamary | 13 | sick | "    "    " |
| | James White, (of J.) | 10 | present | |
| | Samuel Owings | 13 | " | |
| | Laban Teague | 9 | " | |
| | Laban Cathell | 13 | " | |
| | Kendall Smock | 3 | " | |
| | Francis Jester | " | " | |
| | Jacob Ardes | " | " | |
| | James Mason | 2 | " | |
| | Reuben Magee | 21 | " | |
| | Samuel Donaldson | Apl 15 | sick | "    "    " |
| | William Davis | 16 | present | |
| | Levin Davis | May 6 | | deceased 20 July |
| | Thomas Hayward | Feb 3 | absent | on furlough |
| | John Morris | Mch 12 | present | |
| | Levi Morris | 16 | sick | in barracks |
| | Wm. ——ton | Apl 17 | present | |
| | James Selby | 30 | " | |
| | Jarman Beatherd | Mch 18 | absent | on furlough |
| | Thos. Williams | Apl 15 | " | "    " |
| | George Truitt | Feb 2 | sick | at his father's |
| | Wm. Cowley | 14 | " | "    "    " |
| | John Franklin | 8 | present | |
| | Saml. Truitt | Apl 1 | " | |
| | James Nelson | Feb 10 | " | |
| | Wm. Cahoon | 3 | " | |
| | Zachariah Bishop | 8 | " | |
| | Walter Ives | 17 | " | |

| RANK. | NAMES. | DATE OF ENLISTMENT. | REMARKS. | |
|-------|--------|--------------------|----------|---|
| Privates | Elisha Baker | Mch 16 | absent | on furlough |
|  | Thos. Lendall | Apl 21 | present | |
|  | Danl. Wheelton | Feb 24 | " | |
|  | Willm. Digman | 3 | " | |
|  | George Jarman | Apl 5 | " | |
|  | Willm. Streets | Feb 9 | " | |
|  | Jesse Gray | May 16 | | deserted 30 June |
|  | Lambert Purnell | 7 | sick | at his mother's |
|  | Robert Holston | June 30 | present | |
|  | Thos. Newman | May 20 | " | |
|  | George Roberson | June 1 | " | |
|  | John Donaldson | Feb 3 | " | |
|  | Abram Smith | May 1 | " | |
|  | John Nicholson | June 9 | " | |
|  |  |  | Signed J. Watkins, Capt. | |

M

MUSTER ROLL OF THE 4TH INDEPENDENT MARYLAND COMPANY.
[TALBOT COUNTY.]

Muster Roll of the 4th Independent Company of Maryland Regular Troops, September, 1776.

| Commissd. Jan. 5th, 1776. | James Hindman, Capt. |
|---|---|
| "      "     "     " | Archibald Anderson, 1st Lieut. |
| "      "     "     " | Edward Hindman, 2nd    " |
| "      Mch. 7th, " | William Frazier,    3rd    " |

| | DATE OF ENLISTMENT. | | SERJEANTS. | DATE OF ENLISTMENT. | |
|---|---|---|---|---|---|
| Thomas Hall | Jan 20 | deserted 28 July | Peter Hardcastle | Jan 26 | |
| James Morgan | " | | John Miller | 22 | enlisted as corporal |
| William Martindale | 28 | | | | |
| | | | CORPORALS. | | |
| Perdue Martindale | Jan 28 | | Clement Cannon | Jan 23 | enlisted as a private |
| James Orrell | 26 | | | | |
| Levin Frazier | Feb 11 | enlisted as a private | | | |
| | | | DRUM AND FIFE. | | |
| James Mead | Mch 16 | | John Williams | | |
| | | | PRIVATES. | | |
| Bryan Sinnett | | | William All | Feb 3 | |
| John Emory | Jan 26 | | Richard Snook | " | |

## PRIVATES.

| DATE OF ENLISTMENT. | | |
|---|---|---|
| David Thatcher | Jan 28 | |
| Nathan Harrington | " | |
| Peregrine Evans | Feb 19 | |
| Lawrence Connerley | Jan 25 | |
| John Fleming | | |
| Joshua Chippey | 28 | |
| Humphry Spencer | Feb 2 | |
| Henry Stapleford | 15 | |
| Solomon Harris | 5 | |
| John Millington | 15 | |
| Robert Ferguson | 19 | |
| Thomas Brown | Jan 20 | |
| James Burgess | 24 | |
| Henry Higgins | 26 | disch. 28 July |
| Richard Caton | 29 | |
| William Blanch | Feb 4 | |
| Stephen Bryan | | |
| Hambleton Warren | 19 | |
| Reuben Jeffers | Jan 28 | |
| James Devereux | 29 | |
| James Todd | Feb 7 | |
| John Hughes | Jan 25 | missing 27 Aug. on Long Island |
| Thomas Camper | 26 | |
| Jacob Jeffers | 28 | |
| James Robinson | Feb 6 | |
| John Humbey | 8 | |
| Charles Moore | 12 | deserted 3 Aug. |
| Henry Martin | Jan 20 | enlisted as corporal |
| Peter Bromwell | 22 | |
| James Ray | 23 | |
| Robert Ellis | " | |
| Francis Hazledine | 25 | |
| Samuel Giles | 28 | |
| Daniel Higgins | 29 | |
| Gilbert Burgess | Feb 12 | |
| Andrew Hughes | Jan 20 | |
| Richard McDaniel | 23 | |
| Richard Besswick | 25 | |
| Peter Jeffers | 27 | |
| Thomas Barker | Feb 5 | left on Long Island 29 Aug. |

| DATE OF ENLISTMENT | | |
|---|---|---|
| James Coburn | Jan 31 | |
| Edward Welch | 30 | |
| Benjamin Crisp | " | |
| Jonathan Valiant | Feb 5 | |
| John Hopkins | 2 | |
| Nathan Madding | | |
| John Ryan | 6 | |
| Nathan Duling | Jan 25 | |
| Daniel Richardson | Feb 12 | |
| Lambert Robinson | Jan 20 | |
| Job Barnes | " | |
| Thomas Colvert | 25 | |
| William Smith | 29 | |
| James Watts | 20 | |
| David Priestley | 23 | |
| William Pitts | 25 | |
| William Tarr | Feb 2 | |
| Delahay Duling | Jan 26 | |
| Joseph Merchant | 28 | missing 27 Aug. Long Island |
| Thomas Davis | 27 | |
| Russel Armstrong | 25 | |
| Henry Gates | . | |
| John Foster Leverton | 28 | |
| Joseph Jackson | " | |
| Thomas Lumley | " | |
| Philemon Porter | 25 | |
| John Smith | 28 | |
| William Beauver | Feb 2 | |
| William Bratchee | 12 | |
| Ben. Worthington | Jan 22 | |
| Thomas Buckley | 24 | |
| Thomas Start | 25 | |
| Richard Sampson | Feb 8 | |
| William Jenkins | Jan 22 | |
| James Jones | " | |
| John O'Bryan | 23 | |
| William Woods | 28 | |
| George McNamara | 26 | deserted 3 Aug. |
| William Kenney | | |
| Nicholas Farewell | | |
| Thomas Burgess | | |
| Charles Cooper | 25 | |

### PRIVATES.

| DATE OF ENLISTMENT. | | DATE OF ENLISTMENT. | |
|---|---|---|---|
| Thomas ——— | | Ezekiel Abbott | Jan 23 deserted 3 Aug. taken again 5 Aug. dead |
| John Buckley | Jan 24 | | |
| John Masterson | 28 | | |
| John Garrott | Feb 10 | | |
| Matthew Hardikin | Jan 23 | John Dobson | 31 |
| Thomas Connerly | 25 | John Sweeney | Feb 1 |
| William Burgess | " | Thomas Liles | 2 |
| William Melony | " | Stephen Byram | 6 |
| Robert Heffernon | 30 | John Murphy | 7 |
| Josias Murdoch | 31 deserted | | |

Names in the above list, without date of enlistment, are taken from a roll published in the "Pennsylvania Magazine of History and Biography," January, 1898, page 503. Stephen Bryan is, perhaps, Stephen Byram, and Thomas ——— is, perhaps, Thomas Connerly.

---

### 5TH INDEPENDENT MARYLAND COMPANY. [ST. MARY'S COUNTY.]

| | |
|---|---|
| John Allen Thomas, Captain. | officers elected by the Convention Jan. 2nd, 1776.* |
| John Steward, 1st Lieut. | |
| John Davidson, 2nd " | |
| Henry Neale, 3rd " | |

---

### MUSTER ROLL OF THE 6TH INDEPENDENT MARYLAND COMPANY. [DORCHESTER COUNTY.]

| | | | |
|---|---|---|---|
| Commissd. Jan. 5th, 1776. | Thomas Woolford, Capt. | | present. |
| "       "   "   " | John Eccleston, | 1st Lieut. | " |
| "       "   "   " | Hooper Hodson, | 2nd " | " |
| "       Mch. 2nd, 1776. | Lilburn Williams, | 3rd " | " |

| DATE OF ENLISTMENT. | NAMES. | | REMARKS. |
|---|---|---|---|
| Feb 20 | John Gray | present | |
| " | Willm. Woolford | " | |
| Jan 20 | Hugh McKinley | sick | in barracks |
| Apl 2 | John Linch | | dischd. 29th June |
| Feb 26 | Hooper Hodson | present | |
| 20 | William Watts | " | |
| 23 | Jas. McCollester | " | |
| 7 | Edwd. McFading | | dischd. 10th inst |
| Mch 15 | Richd. Frazier | " | |
| 4 | Peter Taylor | " | |

\* Proceedings of the Conventions of Maryland, pp. 67, 68, 73, 93.

3

| DATE OF ENLISTMENT. | NAMES. | | REMARKS. |
|---|---|---|---|
| Aug 10 | Hugh Walworth | present | |
| Feb 20 | Thomas Howell | " | |
| Jan 25 | Richard Wood | " | |
| " | John Martin | " | |
| 26 | John Callihorn | " | |
| " | Samuel Ash | sick | in the country |
| " | John Watkins | " | in barracks |
| 27 | Chris. Minges | absent | on furlough |
| 28 | Thomas Gaines | sick | in barracks |
| 27 | John Murphy | present | |
| 29 | Jacob Hustone | " | |
| " | Edward Flin | " | |
| " | Wm. Compton | " | |
| 1 | Patk. Farren | sick | "      " |
| " | William Cole | present | |
| 2 | Lawrence Hughes | sick | "      " |
| 4 | Lawrence Fitzpatrick | present | |
| " | Barney Maloy | sick | in the country |
| " | William Thom | present | |
| " | Samuel McCracking | sick | "   "   " |
| 8 | Daniel Norris | present | |
| " | Samuel Rones | sick | in barracks |
| Feb 15 | George Nest | present | |
| " | William Lee | " | |
| 26 | John Malone | " | |
| " | Joseph Read | " | |
| Mch 2 | Hugh Kelly | " | |
| " | Michl. Conner | " | |
| " | Daniel Brophy | " | |
| 7 | John Welsh | " | |
| Feb 21 | Edward Hodson | " | |
| " | Nathan Wright | sick | in the country |
| " | Edmond Garoughty | | dischd. 10th August |
| 23 | John Dunn | present | |
| " | Deweast Downing | " | |
| " | Jonathan Price | " | |
| Mch 21 | Ephm. Wheelar | " | |
| 11 | Patrick Rach | sick | in barracks |
| 12 | John Basset | present | |
| Feb 20 | Thos. Grayham | " | |
| " | Luke Cox | " | |
| " | Solomon Tylor | " | |
| " | Thomas Bayley | " | |
| " | Robert Ruarke | " | |
| " | William Smith | " | |
| " | Matthew Hayard | " | |

| DATE OF ENLISTMENT. | NAMES. | | REMARKS. |
|---|---|---|---|
| Feb 20 | Charles Foxwell | sick | in the country |
| " | Samuel North | present | |
| " | Miles Shehern | " | |
| " | Calib Joy | " | |
| " | Daniel Dinet | " | |
| " | William Mann | " | |
| " | Philip Hodge | " | |
| 23 | William Dingle | " | |
| " | Francis Noble | sick· | in barracks |
| " | John Hayward | present | |
| " | John Caffey | " | |
| " | Edward Hardikin | " | |
| 26 | Matthew Colbert | | deceased 8th June |
| Mch 3 | J—— Sherren | " | |
| 4 | William ——lihay | " | |
| " | Thomas Harrison | " | |
| 5 | Edward Williams | " | |
| 4 | William Killinough | " | |
| 9 | Thomas Saunders | " | |
| 14 | Isaac Southard | " | |
| Feb 24 | Levin Prichard | " | |
| " | Joseph Staplefort | " | |
| " | Spencer Saunders | " | |
| 25 | John Noble | " | |
| 26 | Richardson Gamble | " | |
| Mch 1 | James Sulivain | " | |
| " | Patrick Caton | " | |
| 7 | John Keron | " | |
| 4 | Patrick Connorly | " | |
| 15 | Denniss —— | " | |
| 19 | William Hale | sick | in the country |
| 21 | Hooper Elliot | present | |
| 28 | John Martin, (of Dorset) | " | |
| " | Thomas Hayard | " | |
| " | James Andrew | absent | on furlough |
| Apl 1 | Samuel Spencer | present | |
| 8 | William Hays | sick | in barracks |
| " | James Urey | present | |
| 9 | Jeremiah Andrew | " | |
| May 2 | Robert Skinner | " | |
| 7 | James Haney | " | |
| 9 | Thomas Hart | " | |
| Apl 3 | Richard Bush | " | |
| May 27 | Absolum Comini | " | |
| July 20 | Robert Henderson | " | |
| 26 | William Becks | " | |

| DATE OF ENLISTMENT. | NAMES. | | REMARKS. |
|---|---|---|---|
| July 13 | James Dolly | present | |
| 20 | John Stevens | absent | on furlough |
| " | Robert Smith | present | |
| " | Benjamin Deshield | sick | in barracks |
| Aug 10 | William Andrew | present | |

Signed, Thomas Woolford, Capt.

M              Aug. 19th, 1776.

---

7TH INDEPENDENT MARYLAND COMPANY.   [QUEEN ANNE'S AND KENT COUNTIES.]

Edward Veazy, Capt.                     officers elected by the
William Harrison, 1st Lieut.            Convention Jan. 2nd,
Samuel Turbutt Wright, 2nd Lieut.       1776.*
Edward DeCourcy, 3rd Lieut.

---

Officers of the two Rifle Companies that served before Boston in 1775.

Capt. Michael Cresap               Capt. Thomas Price
1st Lieut. Thomas Warren           1st Lieut. Otho Holland Williams
2nd Lieut. Joseph Cresap           2nd Lieut. John Ross Key.†
Ensign Richard Davis

NOTE.—Early artillery companies will be found under the heading of Artillery Rolls.

* Proceedings of the Conventions of Maryland, pp. 67, 68, 73, 93.
† McSherry's Hist. of Maryland, appendix A.

## FLYING CAMP.

### RESOLVES OF CONTINENTAL CONGRESS.

3 June, 1776.

" Resolved, That a flying camp be immediately established in the middle colonies; and that it consist of 10000 men ; to complete which number,

Resolved, That the colony of Pennsylvania be requested to furnish of their militia 6000, Maryland, of their militia 3400, Delaware government, of their militia 600.

Resolved, That the militias be engaged to the first day of December next, unless sooner discharged by Congress."

### RESOLVES OF THE MARYLAND CONVENTION OF JUNE, 1776.

25 June, 1776.

" Resolved unanimously, That this province will furnish 3405 of its militia, to form a flying camp, and to act with the militia of Pennsylvania and the Delaware government in the middle department; that is to say, from this province to New York inclusive, according to the request of the Congress in their resolutions of the 3d day of this instant June."

These companies were to serve within said limits until 1 December, 1776, unless sooner discharged by Congress. None were to be compelled to serve out of said limits or beyond 1 December. They were to be arranged in 4 battalions and 1 company, each battalion consisting of 9 companies. Warrants were to be issued, by the President of the Convention, to the persons appointed by the Convention, to enroll the non-commissioned officers and privates. A captain was to enroll 30, a lieutenant 20, and an ensign 16 men. Enrollments, even if not completed, were to be returned to the Convention, or Council of Safety, by July 20th. If any enrollments were not complete, the Convention, or Council of Safety, could commission the persons to whom the warrants were directed or any other persons, as would best promote the service. Enrollments were to be of those who voluntarily offered themselves. All who enrolled were to sign the following enrollment: " We the subscribers, do hereby enroll ourselves to serve as militia of Maryland in the middle department, that is to say, from this province to New York inclusive, until the first day of December next, unless sooner discharged by the honourable Congress according to the resolutions of the Convention of Maryland, held at Annapolis the 21st day of June, 1776."

The order adopted in arranging the Flying Camp Companies is that of the Convention of Maryland in the election of the officers of said companies, 29 June, 1776. After each County's name, the names of the officers of the companies for such County, elected by the Convention, are given. See Proceedings of the Conventions of Maryland, p. 176.

St. Mary's County.

Capt. Uriah Forrest  
1 Lt. Wm. Bond  

2 Lt. Moses Tabbs  
Ensign Edward Mattinly *

A List of men enrolled by Capt. Uriah Forrest, Lieut. Wm. Bond, Lieut. Moses Tabbs and Ensign Mattingley, to compose one company in Col. Thomas Ewing's Battalion for the Flying Camp. Mustered, examined and passed July 28th, 1776, by Ign. Fenwick, Jr.

| | | | |
|---|---|---|---|
| Geo. Armstrong | Thos. Shircliff | William Rock | Wm. Adams |
| Chas. Lewellin | Jo. Bradshaw | Jere. Allstone, | Jo. Adams |
| Ign. Simms, Jr. | James Bramhall | (Allstan) | Robt. McClannon, |
| Saml. H. Briscoe | Thos. Davie | Alex. Shanks | (McClelland) |
| Wm. J. Hager | Luke Cusick | Ign. Knott | Wm Hendry |
| John Maddox | Jesse Herbert | Thos. Bridgitt | John Christopher |
| John McKoy, | Thos. Martin | Wm. Moles | Richard Hindmore |
| (McKay) | Richard Bullock | Joseph Long | Joseph Alvey |
| Edw. Spalding | Jesse Jordan | John Bond, Jr. | Ign. Watkin, |
| Geo. Elms | Wm. Hebb | Moses Adams | (Wathen) |
| Edw. Marshall | Joshua Ellis | John Baker | John Fields |
| Fran. Watkin | Gabriel Williams | Enoch Sanders | Richard Weakley, |
| Edward White | John Moore | John Price, Jr. | (Weaklin) |
| John Bramhall | Richard Gardiner | Henry Horn Carter | John C. Watkin, |
| Auston Howard | Saml. Jordan | Wm. Howard | (Wathen) |
| Matthew Shanks | James Jordan | Wm. Burnett | John Hughs |
| Charles Jones | Chas. Bond | Thos. Cook, Jr. | Thos. Cahill |
| Wm. Ennis | Justinian Weeden, | Enoch Adams | John Holland |
| Thos. Bartcly | (Wheeden) | Richard Morris | John Compton |
| Elias Baily | Wm. Cheseldine | Wm. Johnstone | Thos. Biggs |
| Robert Shanks | Reubin Craig | Wm. Carpenter, Jr. | Rich. E. Gatton, |
| Jesse Dennis | Thos. Wood | Richard Kerbey | (Gadden) |
| James Tear | Wm. Coode | Thos. Haywood | Joseph Johnstone |
| James Melton | Joseph Dailey | Thos. Files | John Graves |
| Jesse Tennison | | | |

Enlisted by Lieut. Wm. Bond, July 3rd, 1776. Reviewed and passed by John H. Briscoe, July 12th, 1776.

Gerard Cheseldine.

*Proceedings of the Conventions of Maryland, p. 176.

CHARLES COUNTY.

Capt. Thomas Hanson
1 Lt. George Dent
2 Lt. Samuel Jones
Ensign William Adams

Capt. Belain Posey
1 Lt. Henry Boarman
2 Lt. John Forbes
Ensign Gerard Fowke*

---

Enrolled by Thos. Hanson.　Passed by Saml. Hanson, Jr., July 19th, 1776.

Paul Parker
William Hanson
Joseph Simms
Whorton Qualls
John Nelson
William Cox
David Dyal
Thomas Jordan
Penner Nelson
Edward Wilmon

William Donnollon
Samuel Leach
Thomas Gaugh
Thomas Milstead
Wilson Gray
Jesse Evans
Alexander Evans
William Rippith
Alexander Swan
John Worder

Hezekiah Dunington
Richard Thompson
William Henry
Joseph Timms
Francis Wier
Edward Pearson
Richard Fowke
Thomas Harrison
Isaac Steuart
Henry Mudd

---

Townly Ratcliff　　　John Adlow Clements, of Joseph

Gentlemen :—The above is the enrollment of two men, one of which I was defective when I waited on you the 5th inst. and the other, Viz. John Adlow Clements, enrolled in the place of a certain Bayne Smallwood whom I have returned to you, by erasing whose name and adding the other you'll greatly Oblige

Gentlemen Your Mt. Obt. St.

Sunday, 11th of August, 1776.　　　Geo. Dent, of John.

---

Enlisted by Samuel Jones.　All, except John Hatchen and Samuel Chandler, passed by Will. Harrison July 27th, 1776.

Samuel Elgin
Jacob Johnson
Richard Clinscales, (Clink-
　scales)
John Brawner
Joseph Manning
George Speake

Thomas Goley, (Goaley)
Elijah Clark
James Scott
Ignatius Luckett
Samuel Maddox
Noah Maddox
John Hatchen

John Franklin
George Gray
Charles Riggin
William Wapels, (Waple)
John Philops, (Phillips)
Samuel Chandler
William Franklin

* Proceedings of the Conventions of Maryland, p. 176.

Enrolled by Wm. Adams.  Passed by Wm. Harrison, July 25th, 1776.

| | | | |
|---|---|---|---|
| Joseph Mcant | Walter Sutherland | John Fitzgerald | Richard Elgin |
| Thos. Patterson | Thomas Ashford | Zachariah Davis | John Carvoll |
| Aaron Maddox | Antipas Coltart | Michael Notaire | Wm. Johnson |
| Samuel Adams | Thos. Perry | Walter Coomes | John C. Coomes |

Enlisted by Capt. Belain Posey.  Reviewed by John Marshall, July 8th, 1776.

| | | |
|---|---|---|
| Joseph Taylor, (Talor) | Henry Duggins | Samuel Hodskin,(Hodgkins) |
| John Posey | Baker Wathen | Hezekiah Cooksey |
| John Aushur | George Mountgomery | Clement Boarman |
| Thos. Andrew Dyson | John Williams | John Simmons |
| Richard Ferrell | Francis Edilen | Gilferd Minetree |
| John Mudd | Zeph. Swann | John Burnett |
| Thomas Maccan | Ledstone Smd. Cooksey | Jacob Dixson |
| Joseph Boarman | Gerrard Johnson | William Robertson |
| Daniel Barron | Gustavous Burch | John Wilder Wood |
| Thomas Barron | Thomas Suit, (Sute) | Joseph Thompson |
| Benjamin Mudd | Henry Boarman, Jr. | |

#### ADDITIONAL MEN.

| | | |
|---|---|---|
| Alexander Weakling | Basill Swann | Paul Minitree |
| Wm. S. Compton | James Swann, Jr. | William Layman |
| Benj. Postin | St. Larence Posey | Ignatius Martin |
| Benjamin Cox | James Cox | Thomas Posey |

Last man enrolled July 27th, 1776.

Enlisted by Henry Boarman.  Mustered and passed by J. Hawkins, July 18th, 1776.

| | | |
|---|---|---|
| Henry Miles | Richard Blanford | Francis Wathan |
| Thomas Ozburn | Henry Miles, of Joseph | Ignatius Beaven |
| Samuel Daily | James Downing | James Montgomery |
| Leonard Smith | Joseph Philbert | Walter Glasgow |
| Charles Beaven | Francis Wathan, of Barton | Henry Luckett |
| James Keech | John Bowling | Richard Smith |
| Edward Miles Smith | Matthew Johnson | |

Enlisted by Lieut. Forbes.  Passed by J. Hawkins, July 20th, 1776.

| | | |
|---|---|---|
| William Burroughs | Gladden Hunt | John Dent |
| Richard Beavan | Thomas Tyser | Gerrard Davies |

George Walls
William Walls
William Anderson
William Whitely
John Robertson

Zeph. Burroughs
Perry Michall
Richard Kinnick
Jesse Edwards
George Harrison

William Woodburn
Robert Spicknall
James Greer
Luke Gardiner
Leonard Hickey

## CALVERT COUNTY.

Capt. John Brooke
1 Lt. Frederick Skinner

2 Lt. Nathaniel Wilson
Ensign James Somerville *

Enlisted by Captain John Brooke. Passed by Alex. Somervill, July 25th, 1776.

Richard Everitt
John McKenney
Absolam Games
Thomas Gray
John Hungerford
Edward Denton

Richard Gray
Wm. Brinkley
William Gardener
Basil Hellen, (drummer)
John Baker

Wm. Price
Stephen Hutchings
Ellis Dixon
John Tucker
Walter Bowen, (Bawen)

Enlisted by Capt. John Brooke. Passed by Joseph Wilkinson, July 26th, 1776.

James Hellen
Thomas Everett
Absolum Greaves
Nathl. Cullember
Thomas Hardesty,
 (son of Jos.)

Richard Hudson
Clement Hutchins
Nathaniel Simmons
Benjamin Harvey
John Baptis Delafrany

William Marques
John Morris
Benjamin Parran
George Ireland

Enlisted by Frederick Skinner. Passed by Benjamin Mackall, 4th, August 23rd, 1776.

Ignatius Blanford
Joseph Blanford
John Boon
Henry Wood
William Wilson
Arthur Skinner
Thomas Rice

Kilman Lisby
Joseph Briant
Thomas Gwin
James Clerke
Archibald Edmondson
John Sanders

John Younger
James Lawrence
John Grimes
John Stevens
John Ramsay, Jr.
John Prout

William McDaniel, a man enlisted by Frederick Skinner, is not present, but am of Opinion upon being examined will certainly pass as effective. Benj. Mackall, 4th.

* Proceedings of the Conventions of Maryland, p. 176.

Enlisted by Nathaniel Wilson. Passed by Benj. Mackall, 4th, August 23rd, 1776.

| | | | |
|---|---|---|---|
| George Young | Rich. Allen | John Cullenber | James Stewad |
| Robert Games | John King | Joseph Crook | Jono. Wedge |
| Arron Abell | Cuthbirt Abell | Leonard Moore | Adam King |
| Benson Biles | Jereh. Wood | Saml. Ashcom | William Evans |

Enlisted by Nathaniel Wilson. Passed by Joseph Wilkinson, August 31st, 1776.

| | |
|---|---|
| Samuel Day | Arthur Hall |
| Thomas Stone | Benjamin Johns |

Enrolled by Ensign James Somervill. Passed by Alex. Somervill, July 25th, 1776.

| | | |
|---|---|---|
| George Gray | Bazil Newton | Joseph Davis |
| William Baker | Henry Newton | Joseph Bruden |
| James Greaves Avis | | |

Enrolled by Ensign James Somervill. Passed by Jos. Wilkinson, July 26th, '76.

| | | |
|---|---|---|
| Jesse Day | Richard Marshall | Roger Howard |
| James Simmons | Thomas Hardesty | Elisha Quarey |
| John Wells | John Burkett | Joseph Deale |

### PRINCE GEORGE'S COUNTY.

| | |
|---|---|
| Capt. John Hawkins Lowe | Capt. Robert Bowie |
| 1 Lt. John Magruder Burgess | 1 Lt. Benjamin Brooks |
| 2 Lt. William Duvall | 2 Lt. William Dent Beall |
| Ensign Horatio Clagett | Ensign Colmore Beans, resigned and William Shircliff appointed July 6th, 1776, by the Convention |

| | |
|---|---|
| Capt. Alexander Howard Magruder | 2 Lt. Benjamin Contee |
| 1 Lt. William Sprigg Bowie | Ensign Alexander Truman* |

Enrolled by Capt. John H. Lowe. Reviewed and passed by John Addison, July 13th, 1776.

| | | |
|---|---|---|
| Walter Bayne | Samuel McSwain | Willian Worren |
| Lenard Lacklin | Samuel Hambleton | Josias Bayne |
| Philip Locker | David Burtin | Thomas D. Marlow |

* Proceedings of the Conventions of Maryland, pp. 176, 177.

James Penny
John Willson
Henry Wade
George Wade
Thomas Jenkins
John White
Richard Pickrell

John Masters
Osburn Talburt
Eli Lanham
Abraham Russill
Darby Mullowny
Benjamin Talburt
John Worren

Josua Sissill
John Hoggins
David Bently
John Sherwood
Elias Lanham
James Locker
James Lowe

---

Enrolled by Lieut. John M. Burgess.    Reviewed and passed by John Addison, Lieut. Col. of the Lower Battalion, July 20th, 1776.

John Taylor
Thomas Mitchell
James Hinds
John Miller
Nathan Lowe
Wm. Tuell
Samuel Warner

Andrew Ogden
Richard B. Edelen
William Orde
Edward Longly
James Clemons
William Long
James Jarboe

John Williams
Solomon Write
Jacob Miller
James Ball
John Marlowe
Walter Dyer

---

Enrolled by Lieut. William Duvall.    Passed the 18th of July, 1776, by John Addison, Lieut. Col. of the Lower Battalion.

Benjamin Jonson
John Macdaniel
William Shugar
Joseph Hoppes
William Gilpin
Ebenezar Athy
Samuel Morris

James Kidwell
James Miles
George Jinkens
George Boswell
Ignatious Gilpin
Ignatious Howard
Edward B. Smith

John Conner
Bassil Hatten
Notly Ford
Walter Power
Bayne Smallwood
George Daymond

---

Enrolled by Ensign Horatio Clagett.    Reviewed and passed by John Addison, July 15th, 1776.

Butler Edelen Stonestreet
Zacharias Meek Wade
Elijah Kidwell
Smallwood Aeton
Henry Hannon
John Lay
Ralph Clements

John Clements
Thomas Willcoxon
Wm. Smallwood Wynn
Henry Aeton
John Vinson
Peter Oard
Jacob Miller

Ledstone Smallwood
James Johnson
Walter Dyar
William Berrey
John Marlow
George Newman

A Return of Capt. Bowie's Muster Roll.   Part of the Flying Camp.
Made by Lt. Brooke, Lt. Beall and Ensign Shircliff.

| Names | When enrolled | By whom | Place of nativity | Highth | No. guns | Ages | Remarks |
|---|---|---|---|---|---|---|---|
| Charles Mitchell | July 6 | B. Brooks | Maryland | 5.5 | 1 | 18 | Brown hair, fair skin |
| William Berk | 10 | do | P. G. County | 5.4 | | 17 | |
| Wm. Anderson | 8 | do | do | 5.10 | 1 | 22 | |
| Benj. Duvall | 12 | do | do | 5.10½ | 1 | 16 | |
| Andrew Millar | 17 | do | do | 5.11 | 1 | 25 | |
| Nathan Mitchell | " | do | do | 6. | 1 | 20 | |
| Wm. Hutcheson | " | do | do | 5.6 | 1 | 25 | |
| James Hardie | " | do | do | 5.10 | 1 | 24 | |
| John Dew | 25 | do | do | 5.9 | 1 | 20 | |
| Edward Mitchell | 20 | do | do | 5.6 | 1 | 22 | |
| Thomas Johnson | Aug 8 | do | England | 5.10 | 1 | 35 | |
| William Roberts | 20 | · do | do | 5.6 | | 23 | |
| Joseph.Williams | " | do | P. G. County | 5.8 | | 48 | |
| John James | July 25 | do | do | 5.4 | | 25 | |
| Thos. Simpson, Jr. | 16 | William Shircliff | Chas. County | 6. | 1 | 17 | |
| Thomas Owen | " | do | do | 6.¼ | 1 | 23 | |
| Basil Bowman, (Bazil S. Boarman) | 14 | do | do | 6.3 | 1 | 19 | |
| John F. K. Sanders | 16 | do | do | 5.11 | | 20 | |
| Walter Macatee | 17 | do | do | 6.¼ | 1 | 21 | |
| Thomas Sanders | " | do | do | 5.8½ | 1 | 18 | |
| John Wallace | 16 | do | do | 5.8½ | | 21 | |
| Roger Simms | " | do | do | 5.8½ | | 21 | |
| Mark Norriss | " | do | do | 5.7¼ | 1 | 17 | |
| James Deven | 13 | do | do | 5.10 | | 20 | |
| William Spalding | 17 | do | do | 5.6½ | | 17 | |
| Wm. Boomar, (Boarman) | 12 | do | do | 5.4½ | 1 | 16 | |
| John Fisher | 17 | do | Germany | 5.6½ | 1 | 25 | |
| Thos. Simpson, Sr. | 16 | do | Chas. Co. | 6. | 1 | 25 | |
| Joseph Shutliff, (Shiercliff) | " | do | do | 5.11 | 1 | 22 | |
| Chas. Sewele, (Sewall) | 12 | do | do | 5.10 | 1 | 22 | |
| Leonard Edelen | 15 | do | P. G. County | 5.8 | 1 | 22 | |
| Jeremiah Atchuson, (Atchison) | 27 | Capt. Bowie | do | 5.8 | 1 | 18 | |
| George Edelen | " | do | do | 5.7½ | | 17 | |
| Thomas Roby | Aug 3 | do | do | 5.5½ | | 17 | |
| Wiseman Clagett | July 17 | do | do | 5.9 | 1 | 23 | |
| Greenbury Simpson | 16 | do | do | 6.¼ | 1 | 27 | |
| Saml. Busey | 20 | do | do | 5.6 | 1 | 31 | |
| William Mud | Aug 3 | do | do | 5.4 | 1 | 19 | |

| Names | When enrolled | By whom | Place of nativity | Highth | No. guns | Ages | Remarks |
|---|---|---|---|---|---|---|---|
| John Macclane | July 17 | Capt. Bowie | P. G. County | 5.8 | 1 | 31 | |
| Thomas Webster | Aug 4 | do | Scotland | 5.5 | | 42 | |
| Edward Kaine | July 16 | Wm. D. Beall | England | 5.5 | | 20 | Fair complexion, brown hair |
| Thomas Drown . | 18 | do | do | 5.7 | | 25 | Dark hair, fair complexion, much pocked |
| John Hurley | 19 | do | Ireland | 5.6 | | 25 | Well made with dark hair, fair complexion |
| Edward Jenkerson | " | do | England | 5.11 | | 40 | Red hair, brown complexion |
| Peter Phealean | " | do | do | 5.8 | | 26 | Black hair, fair complexion |
| John Mantle | 20 | do | do | 5.6 | | 20 | Brown hair, fair complexion, very well made |
| James Phillips | 22 | do | do | 5.6 | | 22 | Black hair, yellow complexion |
| William Harriss | " | do | do | 5.7 | | 21 | Black hair, fair complexion |
| Jeremiah Cooke | 29 | do | Maryland | 5.4 | | 18 | Black hair, brown complexion |
| John McDonnald | 30 | do | do | 5.8 | | 20 | Brown hair, brown complexion |
| Thomas Fitzsimmons | Aug 4 | do | England | 5.3½ | | 21 | Black hair, brown complexion |
| Th omas Gordon | " | do | Scotland | 5.2½ | | 19 | Brown hair, brown complexion |
| Joseph Coewn (?) | 9 | do | Maryland | 5.5 | | 25 | ditto, ditto |
| James Olive | " | do | England | 5.7 | | 18 | Brown hair, fair complexion |
| John McDonnald | 18 | do | do | 5.6 | | 33 | Brown hair, brown complexion |
| Thomas Lann | 4 | Capt. Bowie | Maryland | 5.4 | | 16 | |
| Basil Ray | July — | do | do | 5.8 | 1 | 22 | |
| George Older | 21 | do | do | 5.10 | | 24 | |
| Elijah Coe | 22 | do | do | 6. | 1 | 25 | |
| Philip Pindle, (Pindell) | Aug 1 | do | do | 5.9 | 1 | 18 | |

Enlisted by Alexander Howard Magruder. Reviewed by Jos. Sim, Col. of the 11th Battalion, Prince George's County, August 21st, 1776.

| NAMES. | WHEN ENROLLED. | NAMES. | WHEN ENROLLED. |
|---|---|---|---|
| Robert Baden | July 3 | Wm.T., (or F.), Greenfield, (Cadet) | July 18 |
| Jeremiah Baden | " | William White | " |
| Thos. Wm. Sasser | " | William Sasser | " |
| Edward Mullan | 4 | Edwd. Stephens | " |
| Henry Bean | " | John White | " |
| John Sollers | " | Maryland Beaven | July 20 |
| Isaac Barnett | 9 | John Watson | 25 |
| Randolph Marlow | 10 | Benjamin Rawlings | " |
| John Downing | " | John Rawlings | Aug. 1 |
| Hugh Stephens | 15 | William Mayhew | " |
| John Young | 18 | Bryan Mayhew | 5 |
| Benj. Paggatt | " | Thomas Lane | 19 |
| Thomas Bean | " | Leonard White | " |
| | | Put on List after viewed by the Colonel | |
| Peter Dayley | July 23 | Joseph Bumford, (Fifer) | July 12 |
| Charles Leech | " | Blk. Boy Gim, (Drummer) | 14 |

Raised by Alex. Trueman, Ensign, for Capt. Magruder's Company. Passed by Jos. Sim, Prince George's County, August 21st, 1776.

| NAMES. | WHEN ENROLLED. | NAMES. | WHEN ENROLLED. |
|---|---|---|---|
| Thomas Baden | July 3 | Wilson Cage, (or Caye) | July 8 |
| Elijah Rawlings | 4 | Nevitt Rawlings | 4 |
| Thomas Cohoe | " | William Burnes | 20 |
| John Mills | 5 | John West | 2 |
| Benjamin Ellis | 6 | Samuel Grover | 3 |
| William Teanneclift | 8 | Jonathan Weeden | 5 |
| Leonard Hickey | 7 | John Bean | 4 |
| Richard Jones | " | George Naylor | " |

## ANNE ARUNDEL COUNTY.

Capt. Edward Norwood
1 Lt. Samuel Godman
2 Lt. John W. Dorsey
Ensign Richard Talbott
Capt. Edward Tillard
1 Lt. Samuel Lloyd Chew
2 Lt. John Sprigg Belt
Ensign John Gassaway, resigned and John Kilty appointed by the Convention, July 5th, 1776.

Capt. Daniel Dorsey
1 Lt. Joseph Burgess
2 Lt. John Lorah. Must be John O'Hara, who resigned and James Howard appointed by the Council of Safety, July 24th, 1776. It is printed Lorah in the Journal of the Convention, but it must be a mistake.
Ensign Michael Burgess
Capt. James Disney

<table>
<tr><td>1 Lt. Henry Ridgely</td><td>Capt. Thomas Hammond</td></tr>
<tr><td>2 Lt. Jonathan Sellman</td><td>1 Lt. Thomas Mayo</td></tr>
<tr><td>Ensign Edward Spurrier</td><td>2 Lt. Joshua Merriken</td></tr>
<tr><td></td><td>Ensign Andrew Hammond*</td></tr>
</table>

## Enlisted by John Worthington Dorsey.  Passed by John Dorsey, July 22nd, 1776.

| | | |
|---|---|---|
| Jonas Smart | Patrick Robinson | Michael O'Conner |
| Richard Sparks | Moses Petcock | Joseph Tearn |
| Charles Harvey | Petticoat Earp | Dennis O'Hario |
| William Ridgway | Mathew Boys | Robert Archibald |
| George Bennette | Mark Halfpenny | Robert Burgoone |
| John Hood | James Logey | Lawrence Greyer |
| Samuel Partridge | | |

## Enlisted by Rich. Talbot.  Passed by John Dorsey, July 22nd, 1776

| | | |
|---|---|---|
| Ignatius Davis | Cornelius Mattox | Hanbury Jones |
| William Phelps | Edw. Bennette | Chas. Sewell |
| William Jones | Thomas Weston | Thos. Bland |
| Alex. Scott | Robert Gainer | James Fosh |
| Mich. Gladman | Charles Chapman | Ely Hyatt |
| Bartholemew MacDonald | | |

## CAPT. TILLARD'S MUSTER ROLL, 1776.

Enrolled by Edw. Tillard.  All of Maryland except Joseph Jee of England.  Returned the Council of Safety, July 10th.

| SOLDIERS' NAMES. | HIGHT. | SOLDIERS' NAMES. | HIGHT. | SOLDIERS' NAMES. | HIGHT. |
|---|---|---|---|---|---|
| Jacob McSeney, (Macceney) | 5. 10 | Richard Dennisson, (Denison) | 5. 7½ | Geo. Parker | 5. 7½ |
| Steph. Allingham, (Allenjem) | 5. 11 | Geo. Simmons | 5. 5 | Henry Powell | 5. 8½ |
| Caleb Conner | 5. 9 | Willm. Dove, Jr. | 5. 8 | John Battee | 5. 4 |
| John Miles | 5. 9 | Thomas Taylor | 5. 9 | Wm. Brashears | 5. 5 |
| Robert Day | 5. 10 | Saml. White | 5. 6½ | Richard Sansberry | 5. 6 |
| Willm. Simmons | 5. 7 | Charles Watkins | 5. 7 | James Frazier, (Fraser) | 5. 7 |
| John Stone | 5. 6 | Isaac —— (Jones ?) | 5. 9 | | |
| Edwd. Cowley, (Crowley) | 5. 6 | Jacob Sollars | 5. 3 | Isaac Lansdale | 5. 7 |
| Willm. Parrett, (Parratt) | 5. 6 | Willm. Wells | 5. 6½ | Fardinan Battee | 5. 5 |
| | | | | Joseph Jee | 5. 6½ |
| John Deale | 5. 8 | Philip Davis | 5. 6½ | Wm. Cowley | 5. 6 |

*Proceedings of the Conventions of Maryland, p. 177.

Enrolled by S. Chew.  All of Maryland.  Enrolled the 25th July and returned the Council of Safety.

| SOLDIERS' NAMES. | HIGHT. | SOLDIERS' NAMES. | HIGHT. | SOLDIERS' NAMES. | HIGHT. |
|---|---|---|---|---|---|
| David Furganson, (Ferguson) | 5. 11 | Willm. Roberts | 5. 6 | Benj. Childs | 5. 6½ |
| John Grames | 5. 7 | John Morgan | 5. 4 | Richard Camden, (Cambden) | 5. 8 |
| John Giddings | 5. 8 | Orrell, (Oriel), | | Nathan Wells | |
| Peter Gardiner, (Gardner) | 5. 2 | Marr | 5. 8 | James Bowie | |
| Joseph Crandle, (Cramdale) | 5. 5 | Lovely, (Lovedy), Hinton | 5. 6 | John Gardner, (Gardiner) | 5. 9 |
| Willm. Nowell | 5. 10½ | Solomon Tayler | 5. 7 | Abraham Chapman | 5. 4 |
| Robert Sollars | 5. 2½ | Henry Roberts | 5. 10 | | |
| | | John Souvener, (Scrivner) | 6. 1 | | |

Enrolled by J. Belt.  All of Maryland except James Johnson of Scotland, and Thomas Tophouse of England.

| | | | | | |
|---|---|---|---|---|---|
| Joseph Crasby | 5. 8½ | John Slack | 5. 3½ | Willm. Williams | 5. 3½ |
| Willm. Ray | 5. 6 | John Galwith | 5. 4½ | James Johnson | |
| John Smith | 5. 5½ | John White | 5. 4½ | Henry Lamboth | 5. 7 |
| Humphry Menchon | 5. 2 | Willm. McNorton | 5. 7½ | Thomas Tophouse | 5. 2 |
| Zadock Brashears | 5. 8½ | Willm. Collins | 5. 6 | Willm. Everett | 5. 4½ |

Enrolled by J. Kilty.  All of Maryland.

| | | | | | |
|---|---|---|---|---|---|
| John Lavy | 5. 6½ | Zachariah Turner | 5. 6½ | John Everitt | 5. 4 |
| Thomas Stone | | | | | |

Enlisted by Capt. Edward Tillard.  Passed by Rich. Harwood, Jr., July 16th, '76.

| | | | |
|---|---|---|---|
| Isaac Jones | Wm. Miles | Robert Welsh | Danl. Skelly |

A List of men enlisted by Joseph Burgess for the Flying Camp.  Passed July 20th, 1776.

| | | | |
|---|---|---|---|
| Rich. Burgess | Wm. Edge | Ely Barnes | Joseph Hobbs |
| Philip Barnes | Joshua Burgess | John Leason | Samuel Stoner |
| Elijah Barnes | James Higgins | John Nuton | John Knock |
| Benj. Whips | George Sturt | John Rickords | Wm. Shedbolt |
| Jacob Jarvis | Wm. Wood | Edw. Purdy | Charles Dorsey |

### Enlisted by Michael Burgess.    Passed by Col. Hyde, July 20th, 1776.

| | | | |
|---|---|---|---|
| Vachel Dorsey | Jacob Lavely | Vachel Stevens, | Joseph Webb |
| Richd. Johnson | Wm. James | son of Benjamin | Daniel Brown |
| James Carwin | Thos. Price | John Jimson, | Henry Ireland |
| Patrick Stoaks | Thos. Gaither | (or Jenison) | John Frost |
| Math. Wilson | | Aquilia Barnes | |

### Enrolled by Capt. James Disney, Jr.    Passed by Col. Richard Harwood, July 13th, 1776.

| | | | |
|---|---|---|---|
| Richard Ricketts | Gassaway Watkins | Isaac Jones | Isaiah Cheney |
| Stephen Watkins | John Watkins | Benjamin Jones | Benj. Phelps |
| Richard Disney, Jr. | Thomas Latten | Richard Jones | Basil Barry |
| Robert Davis | John Thomas | William Nicholason | Jacob Barry |
| Vincent Lusby | John Watts | Richard Jones, | Samuel Watts |
| William Holliday | Snowden Taylor | (barber) | Chaney Williams |
| John Hopper | Richard Robinson | William Nichols | Joseph Williams, Jr. |
| Thomas King | William Williams | Thomas Baldwin | Willliam Rear |

### Enrolled under Henry Ridgely, Jr.    Passed by Col. J. Carvil Hall, Aug. 26th, 1776.

| | | | |
|---|---|---|---|
| Thomas Pattan | John Waters | Thomas Williames | George McIntoch |
| Edward Hearn | Edward Moyston | Patrick Burke | Benjamin Penn |
| Thomas Millard | Thomas Grinall | George Robinson | Joseph Bennett |
| Henry Hall | Jacob Ryan | John Molony | Samuel Levy |
| George Morfitt | Richard Harrison | John Graitwood | James Warwick |

### Enlisted by Edw. Spurrier.    Passed by Thomas Dorsey, July 20th, 1776.

| | | | |
|---|---|---|---|
| John Wells | Charles Hunt | James White | Charles Fenton |
| Robert Mark | Nathan Ryan | Mathew Daley | John Benson |
| Charles Ashmore | Wm. Reynolds | Thos. McCauley | Richard Page |
| Richard Biddle | Thos. Reynolds | Zachariah McCauley | John Linsey, |
| | | | (or Linday) |

### Enlisted by Thomas Mayo.    Last man enlisted July 20th, 1776.

| | | | |
|---|---|---|---|
| Edward Marshall | Nicho. Brewer | James Evans | Wm. Langly |
| Wm. Humphreys | Benjamin Miller | Thos. Moss | Joseph Jacobs |
| Nathaniel Shepherd | Jas. Davidson | Wm. Sally | Charles Mattox |
| Thos. Fairbrother | Wm. McCartin | Nathnl. Hall | Stephen Grymes |
| Wm. Grimes | Nathl. Grimes | Edward Jefferson | John Brown |

4

FREDERICK COUNTY—LOWER DISTRICT. [MONTGOMERY COUNTY.]

| | | |
|---|---|---|
| Capt. Edward Burgess | Capt. Leonard Deakins | Capt. Benjamin Spyker |
| 1 Lt. John Gaither | 1 Lt. Thomas Nowland | 1 Lt. Greenbury Gaither |
| 2 Lt. Thaddeus Beall | 2 Lt. Elisha Williams | 2 Lt. Richard Anderson |
| Ensign Thomas Edmondson | Ensign John Griffith, re-signed and Dennis Griffith appointed by the Council of Safety, Oct. 2nd, 1776. | Ensign Nicholas Scybert* |

A List of Capt. Edward Burgess' Company of Militia in the Lower District of Frederick County, viz:

Edward Burgess, Capt.  
Thomas Edmonston, 1st Lieut.  
Alexander Estep, 2nd Lieut.  
Zephaniah Beall, Ensign.

*Nathan Orme  
*Richard Weaver Barnes  
*Charles Gartrell  
*Alexander Lazenby  
Edward Harden  
*Zachariah Aldridge  
*Samuel Beall White  
*Nathan Waters  
*Benjamin Fitzjarrald  
*Gilbert Bryan  
*Nathan Musgrove  
*James Burgess  
*Benjamin Burgess  
Arthur Legg  
*Thomas Freeman  
John Sheekels,(or Shukels)  
ᵏJohn Ray  
*Shadrech Penn, (Peen)  
*Zephaniah Browning  
*George Fryback  
*John Hanson Wheeler  
*Samuel Wheeler  
*Thomas Culver  
*Henry Lazenby  
*Jeremiah Beall  
John Harding  
*Samuel Taylor Orme  
*Thomas Wallis  
*John Lashyear, (Layzare)  
Reson Hollon

Alexcious Simms  
Thomas Nichols  
Laurance Hurdle  
William Crow  
Lenard Wood  
Saml. Carter  
Thomas Beall  
Kinsey Hanee  
Joseph Gartrell  
*John Geehan, (or Guhan)  
James Hurvy  
Edward Trout  
Samuel Solamon  
William Hopkins  
*Miles Mitchell  
*Thomas Wood  
*Charles Maccubin Reynolds  
*Joseph Estep  
*John Tuckker  
Jeremiah Ferrell  
Samuel Purnal  
Thomas Sheekels,(Shukels)  
Thomas Gittings  
Archibald Hoskinson  
Alexander Barratt  
Owen Haymon  
Alexander Edmonston Beall  
John Beaden  
Alexander Tucker

John Wilcoxen  
Richard Burgess  
John Fryback  
Daniel Lewis  
John Ryan  
Benj. Tucker  
Wevour Waters  
Morris Brashears  
Obed Willson  
Stephen Gatrell  
James Beall, (of Roger)  
John Elwood  
James Carter  
Josiah Harding, (Harden)  
Henry Clark  
John Nichols  
Alexander Robert Beall  
William Garten  
Solomon Dickerson  
William Young Conn  
Marthew Lodgeade  
Leaven, (Leven), Beall  
John Ferrell  
William Hicke  
Dennis Marhay  
John Crook  
Samuel Taylor  
William Blackburn  
Richard Nicholasson

* Proceedings of the Conventions of Maryland, p. 177.

Lower District of Frederick County, to wit:—

I do hereby certify that I have at sundry times reviewed eighty-seven of the men as above enrolled by Capt. Edward Burgess, for the service of the Flying Camp; but that, two, to wit: Obed Wilson and Henry Clarke, who are on the said List, are reported by Capt. Burgess to be effective, able bodied men; and in my opinion and judgment the whole number so reviewed, is composed of effective men and fit for military duty.  Given under my hand this 7th Day of August, 1776.

John Murdock.

[Names with a star prefixed are those who were enlisted by Capt. Burgess, July 12th, 1776.]

---

Enrolled by Capt. Leonard Deakins.  Reviewed and passed by Richard Crabb and Francis Deakins, Frederick County, July 13th, 1776.

| | | |
|---|---|---|
| Lloyd Beall | William Draper | Thomas Stewart |
| Zachariah Askey | Henry Allison | John Stewart |
| William Lanham | Leonard Hagon | William Walker |
| Richard O'Daniel | Charles Mahoney | James McCulloch |
| David Green | John Baptis Gauff | William Lovet |
| John Taylor | James Gauff | Jessee Woodward |
| Thomas Lightfoot | John Yates | Nathan Wilson |
| James McDeed | Jacob Veatch | Robert Wilson |
| Samuel Spycer | William Longley | Edward Jinkings |
| Bartholomew Edelin | Dennis Griffith | William Hays |

---

Enrolled by Capt. Benj. Spyker.  Reviewed and passed by Will. Deakins, Jr., Frederick Co., July 29th, 1776.

| | | |
|---|---|---|
| 1 Zachariah Rily | 11 John Smith | 21 John Reynolds |
| 2 John Gorman | 12 Archibald Trail | 22 William Holland |
| 3 John McDavid | 13 Nathan Green | 23 Allan Mackabee,(Mockbee) |
| 4 Edward Northcrafft | 14 John Currington | 24 Francis Downing |
| 5 Neil Dogherty | 15 William Murphy | 25 James Wilson |
| 6 Michael Stanly | 16 Joseph Crawly | 26 Thomas Love |
| 7 William Carlin | 17 Edward Goodwin | 27 Thomas Knowlar |
| 8 Peter Hoey, (Hoy) | 18 Timothy Maclamary | 28 Abraham Booker |
| 9 Strutton Hazel | 19 John Turner | 29 Joseph Penny |
| 10 Henry Burton | 20 William Glory | 30 John Wilson |

Enlisted by Greenbury Gaither. Reviewed and passed by Will. Deakins, Jr., Fredk. Co., July 29th, 1776.

1 Nathan Trail
2 James Artis
3 Aaron Wood
4 John Keemer
5 William Leitch
6 William Baitson, (Bateson)
7 Charles Saffle
8 Nicholas Gaither
9 Lodowick Davis, (Davies)
10 Bennett Herd
11 Richard Short
12 Thomas Chattell, (Chattle)
13 John Haymond Nicholls
14 Richard Cooke
15 Lewis Mullican
16 James Pelly
17 Eli Smith
18 John Collins
19 William Lowry
20 Osborn West

---

Enrolled by Richd. Anderson.  Passed by R. Crabb, Aug. 5th, 1776.

Henry Mackee, (Mackey, Makee)
Michael Rily, (Riley)
Walter Nichols, (Nicholl)
Edward Waker
Thomas Malloon
John Gaskin
Robert Drake

Patrick Carroll
Thomas Wise
William House
Leven Kersey
William Jerbo
John Lowry
John Langton

John Evans
Henry Atchison, (Atchingson, Hutchingson)
John Madding
Robert Rickets
Zachariah Evans
Benjamin Holland

---

Enrolled by Nich. Scybert.  Passed by R. Crabb, Aug. 5th, 1776.

Geor. Sybert, (Scybert)
Nathan Roberts
Stephen Harper
John Cook
Joseph Ross
Patrick Murphy

George Heater
Dennis Clary
Richard Kisby
Michael Carter
Thomas Sheppart
William Pack

John Cavenor, (Caverner, Cavernor)
Philip Hindon
Stephen Warman
George Heathman

---

FREDERICK COUNTY—MIDDLE DISTRICT. [FREDERICK COUNTY.]

Capt. Philip Meroney
1 Lt. Elisha Beall
2 Lt. John Hellen
Ensign William Beatty, Jr
Capt. Jacob Good
1 Lt. John Baptist Thompson

2 Lt. John Ghiselin
Ensign John Smith
Capt. Peter Mantz
1 Lt. Adam Grosh
2 Lt. Peter Adams
Ensign John Richardson *

* Proceedings of the Conventions of Maryland, p. 177.

List of Capt. Philip Maroney's Company in the Flying Camp, Aug. 5th, 1776.  Reviewed and passed by Charles E. Griffith, August, 1776.

Garah Harding
William Jacobs
John McCrery
Daniel Shehan
John Churchwell
George Holliday
George Hill
William Gilmour,
    (Gilmore), deserted
Patrick Murphy
Francis Quynn
Samuel Wheeler
John Shank
James McKinzie
Thomas Gill
William Calvert
John McClary
William Skaggs
John Marshall
Bennett Neall
John Test
Thomas Kirk, Jr
Ninion Nichols, (Nickols)
William Cash
James Burton
Thomas Bayman
Thomas Hillery
James Beall, (Ball)
John Brease, (Breeze)
Patrick Scott
William McKay, (McKoy)
Zadock Griffith
Henry Meroney

Henry Clements
Thomas Fenly, (Finley)
James McCormack Beall,
    deserted
Patrick Connan
Chas. Philpott Taylor
James Lowther
Henry Barkshire, deserted
John Maynard
James Beckett
James Tannehill
John Miller
James Bryant
Michael Arran
Jacob Barrack
John Donack
James Kelam
George McDonald
James Hutchcraft
Jacob Holtz
Henry Smith
Richard Wells
Elisha Rhodes
Paul Boyer
Samuel Busey
John Kenneday
William Chandler
William Hilton
Warran Philpot
Christopher Wheelen
James Buller
John Jones

James Carty
John Hutchinson
Luke Barnet
William Barnitt
Samuel Silvor
Edward Salmon
James McCoy
John Sehom
Robert McDonald
Richard Tongue
Herbert Shoemaker
John Myer
Richard Fletcher
Joseph McAllen
Thomas Harrison
John Alsop
Charles Dullis
Joshua Pearce
Jacob Rhodes
George Kelly
William Louden
Christian Smith
Frederick Beard
Henry Fisher
James Hudson
Michael Hale
John Rite, deserted
William Byer
Francis Freeman
John Cash
William Hollings
Jacob Burton

---

Frederick County, July the 27th, 1776.

I hereby certify that I have this day received Twenty Two men for the Flying Camp which were enrolled by Lieutenant Elisha Beall which appeared to me, to be able bodied men, Two of which he intended for Capt. Meroney, as Witness my hand the day abovesaid.

Jos. Wood, Jr.

Enrolled by Capt. Jacob Good, Lieut. John Battis Thompson, Lieut. John Ghiselin and Ensign John Smith. Reviewed and passed by Baker Johnson, July 20th, 1776.

| | | |
|---|---|---|
| Christeen Clisce | Henry Miller | Joseph McCracken |
| George Obalam | Ludwick Mober | William Linch |
| Tobias Hammer | Peter Giddy | John Toughman |
| George Rice | Jacob Horine | Edward Pegman |
| Philip Fletcher | Philip Pepple | John Wart |
| Martin Fletcher | Daniel Means | Michael Dodson |
| Christeen Gobble | Henry Brawner | Benj. Norris |
| Adam Keller | Patrick Money | George Bonagal |
| John Dwyre | John Money | George Ettleman |
| John Billow | Peter Penroad | James Vaughan |
| John Chamberlin | James Campbell | Wm. Brown |
| William Trace | Leonard Macatee | Geo. Spunogle |
| Jacob Freeman | Thomas Anderson | Peter Weaver |
| James Collins | Jacob Bearae | George Free |
| Thomas White | Philip Jacob | Daniel McTier |
| Charles Freind | William McClane, | Patric McIntire |
| James Estup | (McClame) | Danl. McIntire |
| John O'Bryan | Peter Havclay | Danl. Merfey |
| John Wimer | Philip Cenedey | Thomas Adams |
| George Gobble | Patrick Deneley | John Sill |

The 16 men last above mentioned are enrolled by the above officers, but did not appear at the review. I am informed they are able bodied and effective.

B. Johnson.

---

Enrolled by Capt. Jacob Good, Lieut. John Baptis Thompson, Lieut. John Ghiselin and Ensign John Smith, for the Flying Camp. Reviewed and passed by Col. Charles Beatty, July 20th, 1776.

| | | |
|---|---|---|
| Anthony Thomas | John Duncan | Danl. Benning |
| Matthew King | Saml. Hamilton | John Robertson |
| Joseph McClaine | William Price | George Carroll |
| David Jones | Henry Fanslar | John Henderson |
| John Harrison | William Boe | Patrick White |
| Fettea Stuffle | Jacob Martin | John Test |
| Jacob Ridingour | Jonathan McDonall | Robert McLeod |
| George Benter | Zachariah Ward | Wm. Drome |
| Joseph Ray | John Slagel | Wm. Brinsford |

The five men last above mentioned are enrolled by the above officers, but did not appear, at the review. I am informed they are able bodied and effective.

C. Beatty.

List of men enrolled in Capt. Mantz's Company.  Passed by C. Beatty, July 13th, 1776.

William Richardson
John Shelman
Andrew Loe
Henry Bear
Andrew Wolf
John Kellar
John Martin
Andrew Speak
Charles Smith
John Newsanger,
          (Neswangher)
John Gombare, Jr
Jacob Bayer
George Siegfried
Jacob Stevens
William Mills
Mathias Overfelt
David Eley
Henry Smith
John Smith
Peter Bell
John Twiner
John Netsley
Geo. Mich. Hawk
John Conrad
Joseph Pinnall, (Pannell)
Frederick Kallenberger
Valentine Brunner
John Foster
Mich. Cramer
Laurence Myers

John Bennett
John Gisinger
Peter Snowdenge,
          (Snowdeigel)
John Striser
Henry Myer
John Shenk
John Smith, dyer
Jos. Williams
Philip Flack
John Hendrickson
Peter Fine
Wm. Hendrickson
Dennis Realley
Thomas Smith
Jacob Carnant
John Snider
John Lock
Saml. Yaulet
James Adams
Peter Walts
Henry Huffman
Jacob Crapell, (Creppell)
Mathew Rudrieck
Christ. Stanley
Thomas Stanley
Chr. Kallenberger
Jacob Kern
George Hower
David Nail

George Tennaly
Jonathan Jones
Frederick Heeter
Rudolph Morolf
John Redenour
John Mouer, (Mourrer)
John Dutterer
Martin Heckentom
Abraham Boucher, (Bucher)
Philip Bowman
George Stoner
Henry Hulsman
Henry Grose
George Plummer
Peter Wagoner
Thomas Tobiry
Philip Aulpaugh
Jacob Shade
Henry Teener
Henry Berreck
John Baker
Daniel Hinds
Henry Hinds
George Boyer
Joseph Shame
Michael Baugh
Nicholas Becketh,
          (Beckwith)
Jacob Bowman
Andrew Ringer

---

We the subscribers, do hereby Certify that Capt. Peter Mantz had his Complyment of Men Inrolled for the Flying Camp on the 1st Day of July, 1776.      Witnesseth

Adam Fischer,
Nicholas Tice,
Nicholas White.

·I do hereby Certify that the Above Adam Fischer, Nicholas Tice and Nicholas White are men of Credit and may be depended on.

C. Beatty.

Frederick Town, July 13th, 1776.

Gentlemen:

Capt. Mantz informs me that his Company will be ready to march by the 20th of this Instant if he can be supplied with canteens, camp kettles and a few guns. Therefore I hope you will send up some money by the bearer hereof in order to purchase the guns and canteens for they may be had here for the cash. No camp kettles are to be had here, therefore hope you will give orders concerning them and to what place he is to march and you will greatly oblige

Yr Humble Servant,

C. Beatty.

To the Honourable Council of Safety for Maryland.

[Capt. Mantz' Company was ordered to Leonardtown and from there to Philadelphia where it arrived Aug. 23rd.*]

Frederick County.

At the request of Lt. John Hellen, I have this day Reviewed and Passed twelve able bodied effective men for the Flying Camp. I also Reviewed and Passed, on the 14th Instant, twenty four effective men for the Flying Camp for Ensign Wm. Beatty, Jr., eight of which he requests may be appropriated for Lt. John Hellen's Warrant. Given under my hand this 20th day of July, 1776.

Joseph Wood, Jr.

### FREDERICK COUNTY—UPPER DISTRICT. [WASHINGTON COUNTY.]

Capt. Aeneas Campbell
1 Lt. Clement Hollyday
2 Lt. John Courts Jones
Ensign David Lynn
Capt. John Reynolds
1 Lt. Moses Chapline
2 Lt. Christian Orndorff

Ensign Nathan Williams
Capt. Henry Hardman
1 Lt. Daniel Stull
2 Lt. Peter Contee Hanson, resigned and Jona. Morris appointed by the Council of Safety, August 7th, 1776.
Ensign John Rench †

Enrolled by Capt. Aeneas Campbell. Reviewed and passed by Major Francis Deakins, July 18th, 1776.

*Md. Archives XII, 239.     † Proceedings of the Conventions of Maryland, p. 177.

John Moxley
Levi Walters
George Hoskins
William Frankline
William Davis
John Gillam, (Gillum)
Henry Beeding, (Beading)
Michael Hagan
Daniel Moxley
George Gentile, (Gentle)
William Dixon
Mark Chillon

Martin Kiezer
Shedereck Locker
John Steel
James Williams
Samuel Lintridge, (Lentarage)
Benjamin Osburn, (Ozenburn)
William Veatch
William Lucas, (Luckas)
Charles Byrn, (Burn)
William Housley, (Owsley)

Notley Talbot, (Talbort)
John Martin, (Martain)
Charles Hoskins
Barton Lovelass, (Charles Lovless)
Grove Tomlin, (Tamlane)
William Stallings, (Stalion)
Thomas Gillam, (Gillum)
John Henry
Richard Lewis
Aeneas Campbell, Jr, cadet

---

Enrolled by Capt. Campbell.    Passed by Maj. John Fulford.

James Raidy
John Williams

John Compton
Peter Boardy

William Poland
Cornelius Harling

---

Enrolled by 1st Lieut. Clement Hollyday.    Passed by Maj. Francis Deakins, July 25th, 1776.

Josh. Harbin
Charles Lucas, (Luckas)
John Ellis

Stephen Gentile
Joseph Beeding
Philip Sulivane

John Ferrell
Patrick Rine
Benjamin Ellit

---

Enrolled by 1st Lieut. Clement Hollyday.    Passed by Col. Wm. Lucket, Aug. 8th, 1776.

Ignatius Maddox
William Carroll
John Snowden Hooke
Richard Sarjeant, Jr.

James Weakley
George Kingston
John Simpson Aldridge
Charles Thomas Philpot

Jeremiah Fulsome
John Heart
Edward Cane

---

Enrolled by 2nd Lieut. John Courts Jones.    Reviewed and passed by Thomas Johns, Frederick County, July 22nd, 1776.

Robert Beall Crafford
Philip Tracy
Henry Jones
Thomas Chappell
Jacob Mills
Hezekiah Speake
Walter Raley, (Raleigh)

Zephaniah Mockbee
John Higdon, Jr
William Lewis
Henry Allison
Nathan Thompson
James Glaze
Archibald Chappell

Hugh Elder
Arthur Carns
William Windham
Samuel Busey
Alexander Adams
Lewis Peak, (Speake)
Stephen West

Enrolled by Ens. David Lynn. Passed by Maj. Francis Deakins, July 25, 1776.

| | | |
|---|---|---|
| Thomas Owen | William Briggs | Daniel Ferguson |
| John Jeans | Francis Kitely | John Self |
| William Lamar | Nathaniel Glaze | William Oliver |
| William Thompson | Peter Hardesty | John White |
| Stephen West | Thomas Barrett | Abraham Chapman |

Enlisted by Capt. John Reynolds, Frederick Co., July 18th, 1876. Passed by Joseph Smith.

| | | |
|---|---|---|
| William Walker | Wm. Patrick | Edward Brown |
| Moses Hobbins | Archibald Mullihan | Henry Coonse |
| John Ferguson | Edward Pain | George Deale |
| Wm. Bradford, volunteer | Wm. Coffeeroth | Benedict Eiginor |
| Jacob Hosler | John Wade | Edward Dumatt |
| Thomas Fowler | Thomas Stogdon | Daniel Murphey |
| John Been | Silus Tomkins | Ludowick Kiding |
| David Grove | John Class | Christopher Curts, (Cortz) |
| Thos. Bissett | John Hurley | Henry Knave |
| Wm. Messersmith | Thomas Pitcher | Thomas McKoy, D. S. T. |

Enlisted by Moses Chapline, July 24th. Passed by Joseph Smith.

| | | |
|---|---|---|
| Henry Saftly | James Nowles, D. S. T. | William Baumgartner |
| John Berry | Edward Nowles | George Baumgartner |
| Rinear Bennett | Thomas Barrett, D. S. T. | Teeter Waltenback |
| Francis Thornbourgh | Christian France | James Thompson |
| Peter Seaburn | Jacob Weisong | George Reynolds |
| Thomas Sands | Joseph Finch | Philip Wyonge |
| James Cunningham | John Hood | Allexander Sparrow |

Enlisted by Lieut. Christn. Orndorff, July 20th. Passed by Joseph Smith.

| | | |
|---|---|---|
| Christian Weirich | Joseph Emrich | Nicholas France |
| Nicholas Weirich | Jacob Brunner | Thomas Wilkins |
| Peter Loar | Edward Kerny | George Flick |
| Jacob Long | Nathaniel Linder | George Bowersmith |
| Nicholas Pinkely | Hermon Consella | Robert Wells |
| Mathias Wolf | Nicholas Hasselback | John Walker |
| John Randle | Philip Loar | Garrett Closson |
| Michael Edelman | | |

Enlisted by Ensign Nathan Williams.  Passed by Joseph Smith, July 25th, 1776.

Basill Williams
Simon McClane
Joseph Carrick
John Peirce Welsh
John McKenny
Benjamin Dye
Jacob Forsythe
Edward Garner, D. S. T.

Joseph Moor
Laurance Williams
Bennett Madcalf
Ephraim Skiles
John Powell
Michael Cortz
Clement Howard
John Teeter

Jacob Teeter
William Fanner
John Iden
William Kerney
John Eove, (Cove?)
Jacob Linder
Rodger Dean
James Stewart

---

Capt. Henry Hardman's Return, made July 19th, 1776.  Passed by Henry Shryock, July 19th, 1776.

Chs. White
Francis Frumantle
Daniel Matthews
James Jordon
George How
Thomas West
Jno. Kirk
Maurice Baker
Daniel Cline
Jno. Newman
Jno. Brown
Livie Jones
Thomas Fish
John Lindsey
Jno. Troxel
Jno. Collins
Thos. Smith
Chas. Feely
Abm. Miller
George Colley
Jno. Mowen
Martin Rickenbaugh
Pat. Ryley
Robert English
James Crale
Jno. Stoner
Jacob Hirsh
Jno. Bemhart
Jno. Grant
Thos. Robison

James Duncan
Peter Haines
Phil. Brugh
Peter Fiegley
Chr. Neal
George Fiegley
Phil. Brener
Abm. Troxel
Samuel Sprigg
Barny Riely
John Closs
Peter Digman
Chn. Berringer
Thomas McGuyer
Paul Shley
Wm. Crale
James Martin
Danl. Fisher
Phil. Flack
James Green
Isaac Hardey
Wm. Casey
Saml. Smith
Wm. Wallis
Thos. Jones
Danl. Henderson
John Ward
George Morrison
Chr. Hart

Jno. Welsh
Jno. Moor
Jno. Aim
Jno. Barry
Stephen Preston
Rhd. Noise
Mathias Houks
Stephen Rutlidge
William Davis
Thomas Collins
William Divers
Chr. Metts
Danl. Wicks
Jno. Dicks
Jacob Storam
Saml. Richardson
Conomus Acre
Daniel Carty
Rhd. Morgon
Wm. Campian
Isaac Barnet
Chr. Fogely
Michael Pote
George Rismel
Chr. Alinger
Peter Splise
Chr. Walker
John Hager
Jas. Munn

### BALTIMORE COUNTY.

Capt. Zachariah Maccubbin
1 Lt. Thomas Yates, promoted to a Captaincy and John Christie appointed 1 Lt. by the Council of Safety, August 5th, 1776.
2 Lt. John Christie, promoted 1 Lt. and Thomas Lingan appointed 2 Lt. by the Council of Safety.
Ensign Thomas Lingan, promoted 2 Lt. and William Wilmot appointed Ensign by the Council of Safety.
Capt. John E. Howard

1 Lt. Thomas Lansdale
2 Lt. William Riley
Ensign Robert Morrow
Capt. James Young
1 Lt. James Bond
2 Lt. John Smith
Ensign James Toole
Capt. John Stevenson, resigned and Thomas Yates appointed Capt.
1 Lt. Edward Oldham
2 Lt. James Ogleby
Ensign Joseph Lewis *

---

Enlisted by Zachariah Maccubin. Reviewed and passed by Thos. Jones, July 20th, 1776.

| | | |
|---|---|---|
| Joseph Britten, | Charles Griffen, (Griffin) | William Limebarker |
| Basil Geoghegan | William Dunsyre | Mathew Skiffington |
| John Phinnimore | John Oaram | John Thompson |
| John Coale | Henry Young | Luke West |
| Thomas Robinson | Michael Carnee | Mathew Moore |
| John Cooke | Hugh Lynch | George Bailey |
| Thomas McDaniel | Thomas Cummins | Joseph Weston |
| Edward Puntany | Christopher Fells | Bartholomew Donohue |
| Isaac Hall | Hugh Paulton | James Howard |
| Thomas Griffen, (Griffin) | Jacob Wilderman | James Griffith |

---

Enlisted by John Christie. Passed by Thos. Jones, July 25th, 1776.

| | | |
|---|---|---|
| John Tuder | Thomas Kenny | Lewis Wise |
| Thomas Fox | Benjamin Quine | Roberson Wood |
| John White | Peter Millar | Edward Smith |
| Edward Kersey | Thomas Mahany | William Bailey |
| Charles Burnett | Joshua Bond | Benjamin Furlong |
| George Price | Francis Ward | Nathan Biggs |
| Michael Martin | John Lennox | |

---

Enlisted by William Wilmott. Passed by John Cradock, August 14th, 1776.

| | | |
|---|---|---|
| Edward Chenoweth | George Allen | Edward Traisey |
| William Harriman | James Lawrence | John Hosel |
| Henry Middleton | Jacob Knight | Edward Parrish |
| Joseph Welch, (Welsh) | Hugh Gainer | Richard Hood |
| Richard Cole, (Coale) | Charles Kelley | John Hood |
| Thomas Chenoweth | Daniel McIntire | |

* Proceedings of the Conventions of Maryland, p. 177.

Enlisted by John E. Howard, of Baltimore County. Passed by William Hyde, Baltimore Town, July 17th, 1776.

John Caldwell
Thomas Haley
Nathan Griffith
Barney McLaughlin
Patrick Welsh
George Griffith
John Hamilton
Benj. Bank
White Wilson
Darby Murphey

Nicholas Clark
John Davis
George Pattington
Malcolm McFee
Greenbury Griffith
Robert Smetherest
Nicholas Griffith
Nicholas Rim
James Griffith
Thomas Murphey

George Fullum
John Talbott
John Neal
Abraham Tennes
Jacob Yater
Gabril Wilson
John Clark
Joseph Muller
Thomas McLain
Daniel Lacey

Enlisted by Thomas Lansdale, of Baltimore County. Passed by Thomas Jones, 2nd Major Baltimore Town Battalion, July 20th, 1776.

John Van Zandt
John Coleing
Thomas Murphey
William Marriott
William Adams
Richard Clarke
Richard Burke

Patrick Newgin
Jacob Rawlings
Tobias Wilson
Edward Holebrooke
William Drewitt
Nehemiah Lunn
Jacob Stowie

James Wells
Lawrence Connelly
Daniel Smyth
Benjamin R. Talbot
Thomas Barney
Hugh Moore

Enlisted by Wm. Reily. Reviewed and passed by Thos. Jones, July 26th, 1776.

Knotliff Taylor
Jacob Hooper
James Fitzgerald
Timothy Tate
Dennis Doyle
Fergus Lee

Timothy Mahony
John Murphy
Edward Parish
John McMahon
William Sollers
Edward Reedy

Thomas Watson
James Meloy
John McFall
Nicholas Corbley
James Grey

Enlisted by Wm. Reily. Reviewed and passed by Wm. Hyde.

Joseph Hoy

Edward Palfrey

Florence Mahony

Enlisted by Robert Morrow of Baltimore County. Passed by Thomas Jones, July 20th, 1776.

John Murphey
John Noyes
Thomas Stephens,
  (Stephen)
Hugh Oneal
Alexander Burke, (Burk)

Job Lewis
David Fahay
Stephen Shelmerdine
Edward Young
Jehu Bowen
James Bowen

Philip Norwood
Cornelius Conner
Samuel Adams
Samuel Adams, 2d
William Schooling

A List of Men Enrolled by Capt. Jas. Young, Lieut. Jas. Bond, Lieut. John Smith and Ensign James Tool. To Compose one Company in Col. Thos. Ewing's Battalion for the Flying Camp. August, 1776.

| Names. | By Whom Enlisted. | Where Enlisted. | When Enlisted. | Size. | Age. | Place Nativity. | Remarks. |
|---|---|---|---|---|---|---|---|
| CADETS. | | | | ft. in. | | | |
| Stephen Dorsey | Capt. Jas. Young | Harford Co. | July 7 | 5 9¾ | 18 | America | dark hair |
| Joshua Brown | Lieut. Bond | " " | 9 | 5 9¼ | 20 | " | light colored hair |
| John Allinder | " " | " " | 7 | 5 6½ | 19 | " | light colored hair |
| Wm. Osborne, (Osbourn) | " " | " " | " | 5 2½ | 21 | " | short black hair |
| Thos. Gouldsmith | " " | " " | " | 5 3 | 18 | " | short light hair |
| William Bunting | " " | " " | " | 5 6¼ | 34 | England | short black hair |
| SERGEANTS. | | | | | | | |
| John Poe, 1st | Capt. Jas. Young | Baltimore Co. | " | 5 8 | 22 | America | long black hair |
| Thomas Hill, 2nd | " " | " " | " | 5 6¼ | 27 | Ireland | long black hair |
| Benj. Hipwells, 3rd | Ensign Tool | " " | 5 | 5 9 | 23 | " | long black hair |
| David Smith, 4th | Lieut. Smith | Harford Co. | 15 | 5 8 | 20 | America | light colored hair |
| CORPORALS. | | | | | | | |
| John Burk, (Bourk), 1st | Capt. Jas. Young | Baltimore Co. | 6 | | | | |
| Jereh. Sullivan, (Swillivan), 2nd | " " | " " | 5 | 5 7 | 32 | Ireland | short black hair |
| Jas. Gordon, 3rd | " " | " " | 7 | 5 9¼ | 19 | " | short light hair |
| Thos. Sullivan, (Swillivan), 4th | " " | " " | " | 5 7 | 27 | " | much pock marked |
| DRUMMER. | | | | | | | |
| Thomas Cole | " " | Harford Co. | " | 5 2 | 25 | England | short black hair |
| FIFER. | | | | | | | |
| Francis Herd, (a servant) | Lieut. Smith | " " | 15 | 5 6 | 20 | America | short curled hair |
| PRIVATES. | | | | | | | |
| Edward Higman | Capt. Jas. Young | Baltimore Co. | July 5 | 5 3¼ | 18 | England | black hair, scar on his cheek |
| William Ryan | " " | " " | " | 5 7¼ | 26 | America | black hair, sandy complexion |
| James McMaken, (Makin) | " " | " " | " | 5 2½ | 34 | Ireland | short light hair |
| John McCann | " " | " " | " | 5 1¼ | 29 | | long black hair |

| Names. | By Whom Enlisted. | Where Enlisted. | When Enlisted. | Size. ft. in. | Age. | Place Nativity. | Remarks. |
|---|---|---|---|---|---|---|---|
| PRIVATES. | | | | | | | |
| Robert Curtis | Capt. Jas. Young | Baltimore Co. | July 5 | 5 3¼ | 28 | England | light hair |
| Nicholas McAvoy | " | " | " | 5 0½ | 41 | Ireland | short hair, full face |
| Henry Evans | " | " | " | 5 1 | 20 | " | short black hair, round face |
| John Dannitz | " | " | 7 | 5 2 | 28 | Germany | black hair, pock marked |
| William Collins | " | " | " | 5 1½ | 26 | Ireland | black hair |
| Anthony Grimes | " | " | 5 | 5 5¼ | 26 | England | sandy hair, pock marked |
| William Gradey, (Gready) | " | " | 7 | 5 4 | 30 | Ireland | sandy complexion |
| Orrise Patty | " | " | 5 | 5 8 | 25 | America | short black hair |
| Abraham Jarman | " | " | 7 | 5 5¼ | 21 | " | short black hair |
| Thomas Proctor | " | " | " | 5 5¼ | 20 | " | sandy hair |
| Wm. Appleby | " | Harford Co. | " | 5 6¼ | 24 | " | black curled hair |
| Wm. Price | " | " | " | 5 3 | 26 | England | full faced |
| Edward Murphey | " | " | " | 5 8 | 25 | Ireland | short black hair and stoppage |
| Richard Hackett | " | " | " | 5 4 | 28 | England | black hair   [in his speech |
| Nicholas Rylie, (Reiley) | " | Baltimore Co. | " | 5 3½ | 27 | Ireland | sandy complexion |
| David Galvin | " | " | " | 5 5 | 25 | " | black hair |
| Terrence Grimes | " | " | " | 5 7½ | 30 | " | black hair, scar on his left cheek |
| Benjamin Yarnall | " | " | " | 5 10¼ | 28 | England | pock marked |
| George Childs | " | " | " | 5 3 | 21 | Ireland | full faced |
| Rengard Jackson | " | Annapolis | " | 5 3 | 21 | " | black hair |
| David Phillips | " | Baltimore Co. | " | 5 8 | 24 | America | short hair, pock marked |
| George Berry | " | " | " | 5 5 | 17 | " | short hair |
| Wm. Swillivan | " | " | " | 5 6 | 29 | " | long hair |
| Wm. Goodson | Lieut. Bond | " | " | 5 6¾ | 21 | " | sandy complexion |
| Benj. Wilson | " | " | " | 5 2½ | 18 | | short black hair |
| Saml. Quay, (Qua) | " | " | " | | | | |
| Anthony Potter | " | " | " | | | | |

| Names. | By Whom Enlisted. | Where Enlisted. | When Enlisted. | Size. (ft. in.) | Age. | Place Nativity. | Remarks. |
|---|---|---|---|---|---|---|---|
| PRIVATES. | | | | | | | |
| James Quay, (Qua) | Lieut. Bond | Baltimore Co. | July 7 | 5 6 | 18 | | sandy hair |
| John Gill | " | " | " | 5 2½ | 31 | | light colored hair |
| Jas. Mehaney, (Mahoney) | " | " | " | 5 1 | 18 | Ireland | short black hair |
| James Barns | " | " | " | 5 5 | 18 | America | sandy complexion |
| James Groves | " | " | " | 5 4 | 19 | | short curled hair |
| Hugh Deiver, (Devier) | Lieut. Smith | Harford Co. | July 15 | 6 1½ | 24 | | black hair |
| William Rice | " | " | " | 5 9¾ | 38 | England | sandy hair |
| Michael Meloy | " | " | " | 5 5 | 26 | Ireland | straight hair |
| Robert Stevenson | " | " | " | 5 7¾ | | America | sandy complexion |
| Lawrence Connoway, (Conaway) | " | " | " | 5 3¾ | 20 | Ireland | black hair |
| Patrick Tiarny | " | " | " | 5 4¾ | 28 | Ireland | sandy complexion, black hair |
| Patrick Fowler | " | " | " | 5 4½ | 21 | " | sandy hair |
| Jas. Hannah, (Hanna) | " | " | " | 5 8½ | 23 | " | thin visage |
| Peter Donnavon, (Donavan) | " | " | " | 5 5 | 28 | " | thin visage |
| William King | " | " | " | 5 8 | 31 | America | sandy complexion |
| Joseph Whiteflatt | " | Baltimore Co. | " | 5 4 | 50 | England | curled hair |
| David Collins | " | " | " | 5 2 | 21 | Ireland | full faced |
| John Carney | " | " | " | 5 4 | 25 | " | sandy complexion |
| Pat. McDonald | " | Harford Co. | " | 5 7½ | 23 | " | black hair |
| James Smith | " | " | " | | | America | short black hair |
| Chas. O'Neale | " | " | " | | | " | sandy hair |
| Wm. Jordon | Ensign Tool | Baltimore Co. | July 5 | 5 5 | 40 | America | long black hair |
| Jas. Benny | " | " | " | 5 7½ | 21 | " | short black hair |
| John Blakney, (Blackney) | " | " | " | 5 6 | 26 | Ireland | long black hair |
| John Carr | " | " | " | 5 3 | 20 | Germany | short black hair |
| Wm. Vandike, (Vandyke) | " | " | " | 5 8½ | 38 | America | full faced, black hair |
| James Currye, (Corry) | " | " | " | 5 6 | 29 | America | sandy complexion |
| | " | " | " | 5 6½ | 20 | Ireland | fair complexion |

| Names. | By Whom Enlisted. | Where Enlisted. | When Enlisted. | Size. ft. in. | Age. | Place Nativity. | Remarks. |
|---|---|---|---|---|---|---|---|
| PRIVATES. | | | | | | | |
| George Stibbonds Comer, (Colman) | Ensign Tool | Baltimore Co. | July 5 | 5 6½ | 35 | England | short curled hair |
| Peter Daulton | " | " | " | 5 6½ | 29 | Ireland | sandy complexion |
| Thomas Tallon | " | " | " | 5 4 | 25 | " | full faced, pitted with smallpox |
| Daniel Key, (Keay) | " | " | " | 4 11 | 29 | England | sandy complexion |
| Arthur Shane, (Shean) | " | " | " | 5 5¼ | 20 | America | long light colored hair |
| Hugh Gwin | " | " | " | 5 5 | 20 | Ireland | short curled hair, pitted with |
| John Love | " | " | " | 5 7 | 41 | Scotland | sandy complexion [smallpox |
| Thomas Moffitt, (Moffatt) | " | " | " | 5 10 | 22 | Ireland | black hair |
| John Smith | " | " | " | 5 7¼ | 38 | America | short hair |
| James Ryan | " | " | " | 5 7 | 30 | Ireland | fullfaced |
| George Betson, (Bettson) | " | " | " | 5 4¼ | 16 | America | short hair |
| Jacob Stroup, (Straup) | " | " | " | 5 5 | 20 | " | black hair |
| Michael Boyd | " | " | " | 5 4½ | 32 | Ireland | sandy complexion |
| Joseph Smith | " | " | " | 5 5½ | 36 | America | short curled hair |
| William Garrett | " | " | " | 5 5 | 40 | England | black hair |
| Peter Jennett, (Jannett) | Capt. Jas. Young | " | " | 5 5 | 21 | Ireland | long brown hair |
| Nicholas McGeaugh, (McGaw) | Lieut. Smith | " | 15 | | | | |
| James Casey | Capt. James Young | | 7 | | | | |
| John Rodgers | " | | " | | | | |
| John Walters, (Watters) | " | | | | | | |
| William Barns, (James Barnes?) | Lieut. Bond | | | | | | |
| William Sandiant | " | | | | | | |
| Bartholomew Downey (Dawney), absent | Ensign Toole | | 5 | | | | |
| Michael Ulence, absent | " | | " | | | | |
| Thomas Stevenson | " | | " | | | | |
| John Waller | | | | | | | |
| John Brown | | | | | | | |
| James Bryan, (James Ryan?) | | | | | | | |

[The last eleven names are on the Muster Roll of July, 1776, but not on that of August, 1776.]

Enlisted by Capt. Thomas Yates. Reviewed and passed by Thomas Jones, 2nd Major of the Baltimore Town Battalion, July 18th 1776.

*Patrick Sheehan
*Valentine Kizer, (Kiser)
*John Rieley
*Robert Gregory
*Richard Cumings, (Cummins)
*Joseph Fisher
*John Roach, (Reach)
*John Lindiff
*William Lawrence
*Thomas Crafford, (Crayford
*Edward Willson
*Daniel O'Brien, Serjt.

*Edward Dulany
*Timothy Driskill
*William Saylers, absent
Jeremiah Driskill
Jacob Shanley
Michael Hart
Larrons Keenan
Richard Mansel, (Mansal)
Charles Lovett
Thomas Johnson
John Selly
*Francis Milner
Robert How
Joseph Darlington

William Green
James Walker
*William Peach
*Benjamin Heritage
*Martin Hynes
Timothy Sheehan
John McDearmett
John Murrey
Roger Deland
*John Barnett
*William Collins, absent
*James Wright,      "
*Joseph Grey,       "

[Names with a star prefixed are those who were passed by M. Gist, July 5th, 1776.]

Enlisted by Lieut. Edward Oldham. Passed by Thomas Bond, July 19th, 1776.

John Jeffreys
Nicholas Day
Charles Sweiney
Steven Torrell, (Forrell)
John Dunnevan
Henry Kagen

Richard Smith
William Forgeson
William Eaton
Stephen Body
John Hipkins
Isaac Hanson

John Shipley
John Miller
Nathan Fitspartrick
James Ryant
Henry Henderson
Anthony Cummins

Enlisted by James Ogleby. Reviewed and passed by John Cradock, August 15th, 1776.

John Minney
Isaac Willson
Thomas Ward
Robert Gilhampton
John Smith
Charles Loud
George Hinley
John Kelly

Moses Rutter
Robert Cowell
Thomas Rutter
Timothy Carty
Joseph Hown
David Harriman
William Meadows

Timothy Shawnesey
John Wills
Philip Bailey
Richard Rollings
Thomas Kelley
John Smith
Samuel Baxter

Enlisted by Ensign Lewis. Reviewed and passed by William Hyde.

Nathl. Twining
James Norris
Toal McCollester
Rich. Donavan
James Kemp
Joseph Smith

Roger Dellin
Charles Kelley
Samuel Baxter
John Mining
Robt. Gilhampton

Thomas Ward
John Smith
Isaac Wilson
John Barnett
Manna Roe

---

## HARFORD COUNTY.

Capt. Aquila Paca
1 Lt. John Beedle Hall
2 Lt. Michael Gilbert
Ensign John Patterson

Capt. Bennet Bussey
1 Lt. Joshua Miles
2 Lt. Azabel Hitchcock
Ensign Aquila Amos *

---

Enrolled by Capt. Paca. Reviewed and passed by Jas. Carvel Hall, July 24th, 1776.

Isaac Johnson
James Thomas
Thomas Stevenson
Barney Haney
Jas. Allen
Job Bennington
Joseph Glyn
Aquila Lee Jones
William Robinson
Jacob Dozens
Isaac Dozens
Wm. Gray Dozens
Ephraim Collins

Reese Jones
Edward Morris
William Saunders
John Morris
John Collins
Wm. Brucebanks
Cornelius Akins
Thomas Younger
Isaac Giant
Jonathan Walker
Thomas Welsh
John Clarke
Thomas Dusft, (or Dufft)

Thomas McDaniel
John Loney
Alexander Nolstone
Michael Barry
William Duly
John O'Neal
Amatio Taylor
William Durham
Alexander Admiston
Jas. Willson
Michael Morris
Matthew Snodey

---

Enrolled by Lt. J. B. Hall. Passed by Aquilla Hall, Aug. 5th, 1776.

Joab Murphey
William Hart
Stephen Crouch
William Logan
John Brackenridge
James McKnight
John Ryan

Charles Williams
Isreal Combest
Michael Mullen
Nicholas Brady
George Stewart
Leven Dorsey
Thomas Harrod

Edward Low
William Hassett
James Hurley
John Walker
Phillip Peiken, (or Pictern)
Alexander Edmonston

* Proceedings of the Conventions of Maryland, pp. 177, 178.

Enrolled by Capt. Bennet Bussey.  Passed by Thos. Bond July 20th, 1776.

Grafton Preston
John Clayton, (Clyton)
Robt. Ogle
Ewd. Johnson
Wm. Greenhill,(Green Hill)
Wm. Preston
Isaac Akeright, (Aksright)
James Mathews
Michael Carr
Francis Williams

Thomas Hinks
James Moore
Robt. Carlile, (Carlisle)
Simon Howard, (Froward)
John Steel
Thos. Able
Lawrence Hynds
Wm. Cooper
John Toole
Wm. Howe

Bartho. Finn, (Firm)
Arch. McNear
James Cox
Godfrey Woolmore
William Miles
James Smith
Benj. Rhoads
Edw. Freeman
Denis Clancey

Enrolled by Capt. Bennett Bussey.  Reviewed and passed by Thos. Jones, 2d Major of the Balt. Town Battalion of Militia.

Ambrose Timmons

Thomas Lacy

Enrolled by 1st Lieut. Joshua Miles.  Passed July 27th, '76.

James Nelson
Michael McNeile
Thomas Slatry
James Mays
Bartholomew Downs
Henry Shane
John Rogers

James Moore
Denis Clancy
Patrick Doran
William Gaddis
Laurence Hinds
Thomas Godfrey
John Downey

John Condron
Hugh McMillen
John Dennis
Valentine Stratford
John Tapier
John Spencer

Enrolled by Lieut. Asell Hitchcock, Jr.  Passed by Asell Hitchcock, July 25th, 1776.

Thos. James
Wm. Cunningham
Wm. Wright
Asell Rockwell
Wm. Rutledge
Wm. Night
Wm. Condron

Richard Hopkins
Saml. Baxley
John Garrett
Andrew Craven
Jos. Wood White
Claudius Jamison
Chas. Porter

Saml. Hodgskins
Martin Scary
Jonathan Cunningham
John Lyon
Noah Reaves
Patrick Norton

Enrolled by Ensign Aquila Amos.  Passed by Thos. Bond, July 25th, 1776.

Mordicai Amos
Joshua Amos
William Gash
Richard Burk
George Gardner, (Garder)

Winstone Smith
Barney Devine
John Roberts
John Miles
Daniel Darby

Samuel Peacock
John Catherwood,(Carthwood)
John O'Donel
Nathan Smith
John Long

## CECIL COUNTY.

Capt. Joshua George
1 Lt. William Veazey
2 Lt. John Stockton
Ensign Richard Bird

Capt. Walter Alexander
1 Lt. Andrew Porter
2 Lt. Harman Arrants
Ensign George Hamilton *

### CAPT. JOSHUA GEORGE'S COMPANY.

Reviewed and passed by John D. Thompson, Lieut. Col. 18th Battalion, Cecil County, 18th August, 1776.

| | | |
|---|---|---|
| John Etherington | James Lawrenson | George Boyce |
| James Hays | Joseph Veazey | John Dennis |
| Thomas Parsley | William Ford | James Kimble Price |
| Henry McGahan | John McCoole | William McWilliams |
| Isaac Money | Augusteen H. Ensor | Bassett McClarey |
| Joseph Kirk | Thomas Campbell | Tile Belew |
| Henry Maulden | Silvester Latham | Richard Hays |
| Jeremiah Lanchaster | James Brown | Charles Elexson |
| Ephraim Lee, (or See) | Aron Latham | Daniel Wilson |
| William Husler | Richard F. Elwood | Richard Harrison |
| James Conner | Noble Veazey | Robert Walmsley, (Walmley) |
| Joseph Hukins | Michael Morrison | John Hurley |
| William Patterson | Archibald Lemon | James Mansfield |
| Daniel Daley | William Richardson | John Pemberton |
| Jesse Comegys | Henry Campbell | Benomi Currier |
| Joseph Moss | Robert S. Scott | James Beverly |
| Garrett Othoson | John Baker | Andrew Mitchell |
| John Ryland | James Hussa | John Bailey |
| Augusteen Can | Slyter Bouchell | Daniel McCurdey |
| Jonathan Comegys | Nathl. Dawson | George McNamarr |
| John Cox | William Sears | John McCurdey |
| John Jaraliman | Samuel Money | David McCurdey |
| Ephraim Cooper | Ephraim Price | William Garrott |
| Benjamin Serverson | Noble Price | Joseph Haltham |
| William Hall | Edward Savin | Edward Furner |
| John Nowland. | Marlow Taylor | David Marr |
| James Middlecut | Joseph Terry | Evin Hughes |
| James Smith | James Wroth | John McCoy |
| Gilbert Nowland | Johnson Braddock | |

Cecil County, July 16th, 1776.

I have mustered Twenty men Enrolled by Mr. William Veazey, First Lieutenant of a Company of Militia to be raised in Cecil County to make part of the Flying Camp, and do hereby certify that they are a parcel of able bodied effective men. Given under my hand the day and year above.
Jno. D. Thompson,
Lieut. Col. 18th Batt.

* Proceedings of the Conventions of Maryland, p. 178.

Cecil County, July 20th, 1776.

I hereby certify that I have mustered Twenty men Enrolled by Mr. John Stockton, Jr., Second Lieutenant of a Company of Militia to be raised in Cecil County to make part of the Flying Camp, and that they are a parcel of able bodied effective men. Given under my hand the day and year above.

Jno. D. Thompson,
Lieut. Col. 18th Batt.

---

Cecil County, July 29th, 1776.

Sirs—Mr. Richard Bird has Enrolled Sixteen men, part of Capt. George's Company, Three of which did not appear at the time the others met to be mustered and passed. The other Thirteen are able bodied effective men. The whole of Mr. Bird's men will in a day or two be mustered and passed. As Capt. George is anxious to go to Annapolis to get Directions, it is thought not necessary to detain him for the few remaining. In a few days a Roll of the whole will be transmitted to you. I am Sirs Your very Humb. Servt.

Jno. D. Thompson.

To The Honourable The Council of Safety of Maryland.

---

Enrolled by Capt. Walter Alexander. Passed by Col. Charles Rumsey, July 24th, 1776.

| | | |
|---|---|---|
| William Alexander | Joseph Dawson | John McClintock |
| Christopher Rutledge | James Cavinder | Joseph Beath, (Bath) |
| Jonathan Mullins | Kenniday Bay | Stephen McConnel |
| William Kite | Alexander Work | Patrick Robison |
| Edward Martin, (Martain) | Robert Evans | John Denney |
| Robert Ray | James Cochran | James Smith |
| John Patterson | Abraham Holms | Thomas Quail |
| Thomas Doyl | Ezekiel Alexander | William Conway |
| Phineas Harvey | James Alexander | John Mills |
| Thomas Owens | Robert Longwill | John Davidson |
| Gregry Pearce | | |

---

Enrolled by 1st Lieut. Andrew Porter. Reviewed and passed by Elihu Hall, of Elisha, July 27th, 1776.

| | | |
|---|---|---|
| John Tibbs | James Conner, (Connor) | Stephen Right |
| Edward Gallinough | William Creaighton, | Daniel Linsey |
| William Mackey | (Creaghton, Creaton) | Dinish Smith |
| Stephen Mahoney | John Tower | James Quigley |
| Roger Daugherty | Patrick McFaden | William Beard |
| John Barry | John Duffy | Solomon Collins |
| John Smith | John Campbell | Michael McCasker |
| George Carlin, (Carlon) | Frances Farrel | |

Enrolled under Harman Arrants.  Reviewed and passed by Charles Rumsey, August 3rd, 1776.

Richard Hodgson
Edward Donoly
Johnandrew Strikeingburg
James Wallace
Jesse Price
Robert Hemphill
Nathan Phillips

Thomas Bricen
Levi Veazey
William Beek
Samual Lewis
Calab Donoly
Henry Beedlee
James Sapington

William Grace
Jonathan Richardson
Thomas Citely, (Ceitly)
John Rickets
William Jonson
Michael Smith

Enrolled by Ensign Hamilton.  Reviewed and passed by Thomas Hughes, Lieut. Col. 30th Battalion, July 25th, 1776.

| Names. | When enrolled. | Names. | When enrolled. |
|---|---|---|---|
| John Hamilton, Jr | July 1 | Samuel Payenter | July 22 |
| Thomas Baker | 4 | Thomas Halluran | " |
| Joseph Talen | 9 | David Emmitt | 18 |
| Simon Gibney | 15 | Patt Shiels | " |
| Patt Downey | 17 | John Emmitt | 25 |
| James Doogan | 18 | Thomas Dixson | " |
| Samuel Davis | " | John Cunningham | " |
| Hugh May | 22 | Nathan Bennett | " |

KENT COUNTY.

Capt. Isaac Perkins
1 Lt. Abraham Falconer
2 Lt. Jesse Cozden
Ensign James Henry

Capt. Thomas Smyth
1 Lt. James Williamson
2 Lt. Nathaniel Kinnard
Ensign Josiah Johnson*

Enlisted by Capt. Isaac Perkins.  Reviewed and passed by Wm. Henry, July 17th, 1776.

Benjamin Burchinall
John Williams
William Apsley
William Mann
John Phillips
Abednegoe Jackson
John Rollison
William Dauherty
Denniss Hurley
David Newell

Benjamin Everitt
Conrod Whiteman
David Tulley
Nathaniel Herring
Adam Laurence
Froggitt Tillard
Augusteen Spencer
James Butcher
John McKinney
Daniel Knock

Joseph Greenwood
John Lynch
Richard Kennard
John Pearce
David Crane
Daniel Turner
Thomas Norman
Edward Stewart
William Jones
Samuel Sinnett

* Proceedings of the Conventions of Maryland, p. 178.

Capt. Perkins assures me that he had his Company full on the 5th Day of this Inst.

William Henry.

------

Enlisted by Lieut. Abraham Falconer. Reviewed and passed by William Henry, July 19, 1776.

Daniel Ahern
Benj. Roberts
William Hunter
George Burch
Benj. Pharow
Benj. Garland, (or Gavland)
Joseph Morris
Robert Little
Danl. Toas Massy
Jeremiah Collins

James Ragan
Michael Thomas
Daniel Mulcahy
Nazareth Freeland
Love Alley, (or Alby)
Wm. Herring
James Wise
Ebenezar Costillo
John Walls, Jr.
Wm. Walls, Jr.

------

Enlisted by Lieut. Jesse Cosden, July 4th, 1776. Reviewed and Passed by Wm. Henry, July 13th, 1776.

Lambert Boyer
William Hammon
John Cosden
Cornelius Comegys
John Finley
John Woodall
Matthew Smyth
Hartley Sapington
Wm. Smith
Saml. Eades

Daniel Sevell, (or Serell)
Edwd. Wm. Johnson
John Smith
Wm. Wiltshier
James Reyley
William Hill
James Green Wood
Johnson Brooks
Joshua Vanzant
James Copper

------

Enrolled by Lieut. James Williamson, July 10th, 1776. Reviewed and passed by Edward Worrell, July 29th, 1776. Part of the Company of Capt. Thos. Smyth, Jr.

Thomas Punny
James Wilson
James Dunn, Jr
William Hynson
Charles Scott
John Holder
John Rolph

Charles Scoone
Owen Whaland
Thomas Rolph
Frogget Younger
John Hughes
Caleb Catlin
Thomas Ridiford

Anthony Dunn
Stephen Kindle
James Saunders
Daniel McConnican
John Phillips
James Carmichael

Enlisted by Lieut. Nathaniel Kinnard, Jr.  Reviewed and passed by William Henry, July 22nd, 1776.

| | |
|---|---|
| William Foreman | Richard Lane |
| Francis Lamb | Phillip Reed |
| Joseph Howard | Wm. Foster |
| Charles Jones | Wm. Kinnard |
| John Punney | Francis Armstrong |
| John Sillivin | John Curtain |
| Wm. Giant | Benj. Connerwey |
| Stephin Giant | Isaac Smith |
| Anguish McDonnold | Thomas Knimptum |
| Benj. Jones | John Husselton |

Enlisted by Ensign Josiah Johnson.  Reviewed and passed by William Henry, July 27th, 1776.

| | |
|---|---|
| George Tolson | Thomas Jones |
| George Foard | Morriss Marrah |
| William Meeks | John Rosse |
| Robert Meeks | Henry Truelock, Jr. |
| George Scone | Daniel Donnowin |
| Theophilius Lowmuth, (or Lowmuch) | William Jones |
| John Patten, (or Tatten) | William Dugan |
| George Connor | Nathan Brooks |

## QUEEN ANNE'S COUNTY.

| | |
|---|---|
| Capt. John Dean | Capt. John Dames |
| 1 Lt. John Hawkins | 1 Lt. Thomas Lane Emory |
| 2 Lt. John Neville | 2 Lt. Sam'l Wright Thomas |
| Ensign Samuel Earle | Ensign John Jackson * |

## CAPT. JOHN DEAN'S COMPANY.

From 1 to 30, inclusive, enrolled by Capt. John Dean and passed by Jno. Seney July 13th, from 31 to 55, inclusive, enrolled by 1st Lt. John Hawkins and passed by James Kent July 8th, from 56 to 75, inclusive, enrolled by 2nd Lt. John Neville and passed by Jno. Seney July 17th, and from 76 to 86, inclusive, enrolled by Ensign Samuel Earle and passed by Th. Wright, Col. of the 20th Batt. of Militia, July 18th, 1776.

* Proceedings of the Conventions of Maryland, p. 178.

1 Joseph Foreacres
Joseph Turner
John Arno
William Knotts
John Delanaway
Matthew Peters
Samuel Connaway
John Holding
William Dudley
William Comegys
William Ascott, (Arscott)
John Wells
Solomon Price
Thomas Clymer,(Clymore)
Edward Coppage
William Spry
Solomon Phillips
James Ryan
Joseph Smyth, (Smith)
Robert Kenniford
James Lawrence
John Cole
Jacob Walters
Joseph Elliott
Samuel Green
Griffin, (Griffith), Oliver
John Clemmonds
Christr. Simmonds
Wm. Clark, of Wm.
Charles Bryne
31 Edward Pickering,
   (Pickorine)

Jonas Daugherty,
   (Dehorty)
Daniel Daugherty,
   (Dehorty)
James Gould Sparkes
James Hamilton,
   (Hambleton)
Wm. Deford
Charles Deford
Joseph Wright
Lodman Downes
James Lawrence
John Williams
Thomas Meredith,
   (Meradith)
Matthew Griffith
James Kersey, (Cearsey)
Thomas Tarr
William Parkes
James Meredith,(Meradith)
Wm. Caulker, (Corker)
James Burk
Benj. Moore, (More)
James Gould
Wilson Boone
Wm. Rogers
Wm. Hendley, (Henley)
Edward Taylor
56 Wm. Price
Richard Wells
Wm. Wallace
George Bostick

Thomas Burchinall
John Rolph
Thomas Rolph
Wm. Rolph
John McHannah
James Hudson Greaves
John Clark
Claudius Sylvester
James Lawrence
Richard Nabb
John Cannon
John Emory Hall
Thomas Devorix
James Baggs
Thomas Holmes
Charles Keene
76 Edward Holdson, (Holson)
John Taylor
Wm. Morgan
James Williams
Thos. Meredith O'Bryon
James Reed
Nathaniel Tucker
Matt. Brown Chambers
Benj. Blunt
Elias McConakin, (McCon-
   nikin, McConnican)
Thos. Chambers

---

## CAPT. JOHN DAMES' COMPANY.

### Passed by John Seney, July 25th, 1776.

John Godwin
Charles Scrivner
Joseph Rediew
John Gormon
William Larey
John Smith
James Clayland, Jr
Thomas Davis, Jr
Christopher Yewell
Edward Loyd
Joseph Rigbey

John Laurence
James Macy Slaughter
William Holding
Rob't Hannah,(or Mannah)
Pay, (or Pery), Ashford
William Sevill
John Hargadine
James Butler, Sr.
John Bennett
Acquilla Downes
Samuel Bowlsover

James Tool
Daniel Saunders
Nathan Baker
Charles Jinkins
Thomas Yewell
Peter Cockey
John Yewell
John Weedon
Joseph Rodness
Samuel White
Thomas Murphy

Elisha Nabb
James Barnes
Samuel Blunt
John Chace
John Baxter
John McConikin
John Meridith
John Bennett
Benjamin Teakle
John Sherwood
William Emory
Nathan Emory Clements
Samuel Emory
Elias Jeffers
John Mansfield
William Greenwood
Benjamin Tolson
John Barnard

Thomas Jackson
John Thorn
Jacob Seth
Edward Thomas
Samuel Legg
Joseph Jackson
John Grimes
John Newell
David Newell
John Kemp
Thomas Bailey
John Crouch
William Robinson
James Brown
William Sillivant
Benjamin Holdine
Thomas Betts
Thomas Parfit

Robert Scrivener
John Jonson
James Cook
George May
Thomas Dailey
James Robinson
Thomas Malone, (or Malom)
Charles Dimond
Benjamin Blunt
William Osburn
Thomas Felick
Philip Kinnimon
James Harris
William Shields
John Phillips
Aaron Sanders
Edward Williams

---

## TALBOT COUNTY.

Capt. Greenbury Goldsborough
1 Lt. Woolman Gibson, son of John

2 Lt. John Thomas
Ensign Perry Benson*

---

### CAPT. GREENBURY GOLDSBOROUGH'S COMPANY.

Reviewed and passed by Chris. Birckhead, Col. of the 4th Battalion of Militia, July 27th, 1776.

William Goldsborough
Thomas Skinner
James Bracco
Jonathan Gibson
Robert Newcomb
Joseph Newnam
Risdon Newnam
Jarman, (or Jerman), Cade
Isaac Lewis
James Austin
Jonathan Floyd
Peter Meagher
John Crowder
Wm. Ozbun, (Ozbon)
Christopher Bruff
Isaac Steuart, (Stuart)

Robert Bond
Thomas Knapp
Ephraim Small
Jonathan Small
Roger Kelly
Jonathan Woods
John Sewell
John Warren
Thos. Coleman
Saml. Pritchet
William Bent
William Knight
John Mears
Thomas Simmons
John Mills
John Holland

\* Proceedings of the Conventions of Maryland, p. 178.

John Empson
Richard Pounder
William Shields
Andrew Steuart, (Stuart)
Hugh Sherwood
William Ray
Jacob North
William Ozbun, (Ozbon)
John Start
James Barber
Henry Winstandley
David Fitzpatrick
John Ray
George Parrott
John Parrott
James Ashcroft, (Ashcraft)
Stephen Harrison
William Powell
Thomas Hill
James Fairbanks
Philemon Ward
George Garey
Joseph Nowels
Richard Lunderkin, (Lundergin)
John Woolcutt
James Shields
Solomon Harris

John Shawhane
William Winstandley
Thomas Maquay
William Bryan
John Hewey
Joseph Sewell
Oakley Haddaway
Thomas Lambden Haddaway
Thomas Rolinson, (Rolingson)
Andrew Oram
John Samuels
Daniel Willis
John Dorgin
George Sanxton
Wm. Fitzpatrick
John Atkins
John Warner
Ephraim Maquay
James Farguson
Henry Oldfield
Solomon Horney
John Green
Robert Steuart, (Stuart)
Edward Jones
Henry Davis
Vachel Savere
John Tibby

My part of the Company was complete Friday the 19th July, 1776.

Greenbury Goldsborough.

## CAROLINE COUNTY.

Capt. Zabdiel Potter, unable to raise a company, resigned and was appointed Surgeon's Mate by the Council of Safety. As his successor the Council of Safety appointed Jos. Richardson.

1 Lt. Thomas Wyer Lockerman

2 Lt. Levin Handy
Ensign Philip Casson, resigned
Capt. Philip Fiddeman
1 Lt. Henry Downes
2 Lt. John Reynolds
Ensign Thomas Mason *

Enlisted by Capt. Richardson. Passed by Wm. Richardson, Aug. 31st, 1776.

*Proceedings of the Conventions of Maryland, p. 178.

Andrew Price
Thomas Comerford
Massy Fountain
John Webb
William Brown
John Kanahan
Edward Hardin
Perry Gannon
Alex. Robbs
Cornelius Morris
Hughett Conner
Wm. Walker
John Hobbs
Ellis Thomas
John Diragin, (Duregin)

John Needles
William Hobbs
John McKinney
Silah Parrott
Michal Walker
John Hughs
Robert Thomas
Zebdiah Billitor
Thomas Vaine
John Vaine
John Ford
James Tanner
Benj. Caulk
William Cook
Zadock Harvey

---

Enrolled by Thomas Wynn Loockerman.   Last man enrolled July 17th, 1776.

Jarvus, (or Jervis), Willis
John Carter
John Turner
John Cohee
Robert Waddle
James McQuallity
Thomas Scoudrick

William Allcock
John Ritchee, (Richee)
William Sharp
William Cooper
Samuel Hopkins
Elijah Tylor, (Tyler)
Elijah Clark

John Thomas
William Clark
Henry Willis
Andrew Willis
Joseph Thomas
John Ryan

---

Enrolled by Lieut. Levin Handy. Reviewed and passed by William Hopewell, Aug. 4th, 1776.

William Foster
John Froume, sick
William Willin
George Handy
George Martin
Thomas Merrill

John Selby Martin
John Reed
James Haven
William Dorman
John Benston
Isaac Broughten

Isaac Duncan
Fradrick Barnicassle
Charles Roach
Jesse Parker
William Hosier
Charles Richardson, Aug. 2nd.

---

No enlistments of Capt. Philip Fiddeman's Company found.   The company was raised, however, and marched to Philadelphia.   See Md. Arch., XII, pp. 225, 234, 251, 258.

## DORCHESTER COUNTY.

Capt. Thomas Burk                          2 Lt. John Lynch
1 Lt. Berkit Falcon                        Ensign James Woolford Gray *

---

Enrolled by Thomas Burke.    Passed by Thom. Muse and Robt.
Harrison, Aug. 8th, 1776.

Thos. Bourke, Capt.                John Lynch, 2nd Lieut.
Birket Falcon, 1st Lieut.          James W. Gray, 3rd Lieut.

James Ridgaway
Henry Pritchett
John Jones
Adam Smith
Isaac Cordery
John McGraw
John Hooper
Matthew Anderson
James Kelly
Thomas Hill
Joseph Travers
Lewis Pickron
John Eliason
Matthew Handley
Caste Williams
Valentine Arnett
Solomon Jones
Charles Ffooks
Ezekiel Hooper
Wm. Collins, Tay'.
Matthew Bright
Hooper Evans
Thomas Hooper
Wm. Wilson
Thomas Watson
George Branigan
John Redington
Emanuel Nicholson
John Brown
John Clary
Stephen Stubbs
Thomas Roberts
David Cullin
John Burriss
James Dickson, deserted
*Thomas Aires, (Ayres)
Kimbral Follin

George Procter
James Ingram
Barnaby Current
Michael Mullin
John Mitchell
John Vinson
Wm. Hubbard
Charles Strong
Wm. Man
John Wiley
Thomas Bartlet
David Kirk
Wm. Sanders
Elijah Bright
John Bourk
Whittington Walace
Bryan Sweeny
William Rogers
Thomas Cook
Samuel Stanford
Thompson Bright
William Moore
*Hugh Walworth
Thomas Keene
Wm. Mills
Wm. G. Goutee
Caleb Busick
James Fraizer
George Murphy
Levin Lane
John Cummins
Henry Sutton
Jos. Shehawn
*John Bradly, deserted
*Robert Reynolds, deserted
*John Penn, deserted

*Morris, (or Mores), Lane
*Thomas Nowland, (Noland)
*Martin Dorsey
*James Murphy
*John Bailey
*John Talbott
*Daniel Coffee
*Wm. Morrane, (Moren)
*Wm. O'Harr, (O'Harra)
*Henry Bright
*John Dick
*Michael Berry, (Barry)
John Priday
*Peter Laughlain,
    (Laughlanhon)
*William Collins
*John Connley, (Conley)
*Thos. Dawling, (Dowling)
*Jeremiah Connell
*John Shaw
*Geo. Burrell
*Spencer Sibra, (Sebree)
Thomas McCann
John McGuyar
Thomas Nubry
John Swan
Hugh McCall
Abel Germier
Thomas Marshall
Peter Marshall
Edward Ingram
Joseph Insley, absent
Anthony Fleetwood, absent
*Henry Harrington, deserted
*Geo. Childs, deserted
*Thomas Jones, deserted

* Proceedings of the Conventions of Maryland, p. 178.

I hereby certify that I enrolled the six men here last mentioned, and that they have since deserted.    John Lynch.

[Names with a star prefixed are those who were enlisted by Lt. John Lynch, July 12th, 1776.]

A company in Cecil County, Capt. John Oglevie, 1st Lt. Joseph Tanner, 2nd Lt. Elisha Rodgers, Ensign James Boggs, enrolled July 25th, 1776, for the Flying Camp and offered to the Council of Safety. For the complete list of the names of the men in this company see Md. Arch., XII, 132.

## PROCEEDINGS OF THE MARYLAND CONVENTION.

10 September, 1776.

"The president laid before the convention a letter and several resolutions from the honourable the president of the congress, of the third day of this instant, which was read and thereupon the convention taking the same into consideration,

Resolved, That the commanding officers of the several battalions of militia in Prince George's, Frederick, Anne Arundel, Baltimore, Harford, Cecil, Kent, Queen Anne's and Caroline Counties, be requested to call their battalions together as soon as possible, and that the field officers of the said Counties, respectively, select companies of volunteers as follows, to wit: Prince George's one, Frederick three, that is, one in each district thereof, Anne Arundel two, Baltimore two, Harford two, Cecil three, Kent two, Queen Anne's two, and Caroline one; that each company consist of 68 privates, 4 sergeants, 4 corporals, one drummer, and one fifer, under the command of a captain, two lieutenants and an ensign."

(Officers to be recommended by the field officers or the committee of observation of each county).

" That the said companies be enrolled until the first day of December next, unless sooner discharged by congress, and receive continental pay from the day of enrollment.

That the companies of militia so to be raised be enrolled in the counties and districts where they are directed to be raised as aforesaid, and not of inhabitants of other counties or districts.

That if any company of militia shall offer themselves, they shall be allowed to go into the service under their present officers; or if the present officers of any company, with a considerable number of their company, offer to go shall be able to fill up the number by enrollment of others, such company may march under such officers."

FREDERICK COUNTY—MIDDLE DISTRICT. [FREDERICK COUNTY.]

Vallentine Creager, Capt.
Phillip Smith, Jr., 1st Lieut.

George Need, (Neet), 2nd Lieut.
John Parkinson, (Pirkinson), Ensign

Serjeants.

Solomon Bentley, 1   Josiah Hedges, 3
Aquilla Carmack, 2   Christian Cumber, 4
Joseph Allsop, Drummer

Corporals.

John Brattle, 1        Charles Menix, 3
Solomon Rowlins, 2   John Link, 4
Peter Trux, (Trucks), Fifer

Thomas Edison
Christian Smith
George Dotts
Jacob Bostion
Matthias Andess
John Springer
Oliver Linsey
Ludwick Moser, (Mouser)
James Silver
Michael Fox
George Burrawl, (Burrol)
Jacob Barrick, (Barrack)
Jonothan Beard
Christopher Cooper
Patrick Daugherty,
(Daugérty)
Jacob Holtzman
Peter Lickliter
John Mortt
William Slick
Thomas Tumbleson,
(Tombleson)
Adam Russ
Jacob Weyant, (Wicant)

John Ciferd
James Cammell, (Campbell)
Henry Decamp
James Buckhannon,
(Buchanan)
Peter Heveron
Jacob Rignall, (Rignell)
Edward Hossilton
John Smith
Laurence Stull
Samuel Hulse
William Weier
James Smith
Joseph Smith
Thomas Parkinson,
(Pirkinson)
Henry Fogle
Henry Fox
Frederick Hardman
John Waggoner
Adam Waggoner
Adam Simmon, (Simon)
George McDonald
Henry Clice, (Clise)

Thomas Nailor, (Nalor)
George David
Henry Reich
Patrick Dayley
James Branwood
Thomas Cook
Philip Greenwood
Robert Sellers, (Sellors)
John White
David Barringer
Patrick Rowin
George Serjeant
Peter Dick
Cornelius Downey
William From
George Younger
Lodwick Woller, (Wooler)
Daniel Moore
Evan Morris
William Preston
Robert Parson
John Langley
Daniel Bryan
Jacob Ringer

We, the Subscribers, Delegates in Convention for Frederick County, do hereby certify that

Valentine Cregar was appointed Captain.
Philip Smith,    1st Lieut.
George Need,    2nd    "
John Pirkinson, Ensign, of the

Company of Militia directed to be raised in Frederick County, and that they have embodied their Company and marched therewith to the Camp at New York, but that no Commissions have as yet issued.

October 3rd, 1776.
Upton Sheredine,
Chris. Edelen,
Adam Fischer.

---

A company in Montgomery County under Capt Richard Smith, 1st Lt. Walter White 2nd Lt. Thomas Hayes, Ensign Thomas Sprigg, enrolled for the Flying Camp Sept. 19th, 1776. For the complete list of the names of the men in this Company see Md. Arch. XII, 352.

---

A company from Harford County under Capt. Robert Harris, 1st Lt. William Cole, 2nd Lt. Benjamin Scott, Ensign James Steele, enrolled for the Flying Camp, arrived at Philadelphia Nov. 2nd, 1776. Warrant issued by the Council of Safety Sept. 23rd, 1776, to Harris to raise this company. For the complete list of the names of the men in this Company see Md. Arch. XII, 435.

---

Capt. Daniel Clapsaddle, 1st. Lt. Frederick Nicodemus, 2nd Lt. David Harvy, Ensign Matthias Hickman, were commissioned by the Council of Safety Sept. 26th, 1776, officers of a company enrolled for the Flying Camp in Washington County.

---

CAPT. CLAPSADLE'S RETURN. GUNS, ETC , 1776.

An Account What Was Taken By the Enemy at Fort Lee On the Armies Retreat from that Place, [Nov. 20th, 1776,] of the Continentle Property From Captn. Daniel Clapsadle's Company, viz. 14 Tents, 14 Camp Cittles, 30 Canteens, 49 Habersacks, 6 Blankets, 1 Rifle, 2 Muskes & 2 Bayonets, 8 Belts, 31 Tommehocks, 3 Bouches and 4 Horns.
Daniel Clapsadle, Capt.

A List Guns, &c delivered to Mr. Robert Gowers, Dec. 6, 1776. Per his receipt at Philadelphia, 47 Guns, 31 Bay$^{ts}$, 34 Belts, 19 Tomahawks, 53 Blankets, 24 Haversacks, 62 Pouches, 34 Powder-Horns, 9 Rifles, 1 Drum-Sticks & Sling.
Daniel Clapsadle, Capt.

---

A company in Cecil County, enrolled for the Flying Camp, under Capt. Samuel Evans, 1st. Lt. Henry Dobson, 2nd Lt. Thomas Ramsay,

Ensign Wm. Steuart, marched to Philadelphia Oct., 1776. The officers were commissioned by the Council of Safety Sept. 28th, 1776.

---

A company in Cecil County, enrolled for the Flying Camp, under Capt. James Maxwell, 1st Lt. John Hartshorne, 2nd Lt. William Johnstone, Ensign Adam Glascow, commissioned Oct. 3rd and ordered to Philadelphia Oct. 15th, 1776, by the Council of Safety.

---

A company in Frederick County, enrolled for the Flying Camp, under Capt. Andrew Hynes, 1st Lt. Isaac McCrackin, 2nd Lt. Ezekiel Cox, Ensign John Jacobs, commissioned Oct. 12th and ordered to Philadelphia Oct. 15th, 1776, by the Council of Safety.

---

A company in Harford County, the Harford Greens, enrolled for the Flying Camp, under Capt. Francis Holland, 1st Lt. John Carlile, 2nd Lt. William Young, Ensign Robert Morgan, commissioned Oct. 15th, 1776, by the Council of Safety. This company marched to Philadelphia Oct. 23rd, 1776.

---

### Applications from Col. Richardson's Regiment.

| | | |
|---|---|---|
| 1st Lt. Hawkins | Capt. | St. Jones |
| "   "   Porter | " | "  Maslin |
| 2nd "  Cosden | " | "  Ridgeway |
| Adjt. Robt. Campbell | " | "  Skinner |
| 1st Lt. Saml. Thomas | " | "  Needles |
| 2nd "  Johnson | " | "  Gibson |
| "   "   Handy | " | "  Alexander |
| "   "   Burk | " | "  Gold |
| "   "   Lynch | " | "  Cole, a good officer and a prisoner |
| 3rd "  Gray | " | "  Catlin, back |
| Ensign Henry | " | Privates James Hacket, a prisoner and |
| "   Moore | Lt. |     good soldier |
| "   Mason | " | George Handy, to be promoted |
| "   Benson | " | Oakly Haddaway, ditto |
| Qr. Mastr. Edmondson | | John Reed,        ditto, bad |
| | | Benjamin Roberts, ditto, 2nd Lt. |

Gentlemen :

I have acted sometime past as Ensign to Capt. Evans of the Maryland Flying Camp, and having an inclination of continuing in the Service co'd I be appointed to a First Lieutenancy in the same Company with Thomas Ramsay, for which I apply. Captain Evans will give you my Character and if it is such that you can intrust me with such an Office Shall gladly accept it and acknowledge it as a favor done.

Gentlemen,

| | |
|---|---|
| To the Gentlemen, Commissioners | Your obt. Hble. Servt. |
| from Maryland for appointing | Wm. Stewart, |
| Officers in the Standing Army. | 4 December, 1776. |

---

Philadelphia, December 7th, 1776.

Gentlemen :

We beg Leave to Recommend to your Honours for an Ensign's Commission in the Company now Recruiting by Captain Andrew Hynes, Mr. Richard Donovan as he has served in said Company when in the service of the Last Maryland Flying Camp as first Serjeant, in which office he availed himself in his duty in such a sort as to Merit a more worthy Recommendation, We are Gentlemen

Your Honours Most Obedt.

| | |
|---|---|
| To the Honorable | huml. servants, |
| The Commissioners | Andrew Hynes. |
| For the State of Maryland. | Ezekiel Cox. |

## MUSTERS OF MARYLAND TROOPS.

### "MARYLAND LINE."

RESOLVES OF CONTINENTAL CONGRESS, 16 SEPTEMBER, 1776.

"Resolved, That 88 battalions be inlisted as soon as possible, to serve during the present war, and that each state furnish their respective quotas in the following proportions, . . . . . . Maryland 8 battalions."

RESOLVES OF MARYLAND CONVENTION, 9 OCTOBER, 1776.

"Resolved, That the 8 battalions required by congress to be raised by this state, exceeds its just quota, . . . . That this state, desirous of exerting the most strenuous efforts to support the liberties and independence of the United States, will therefore use its utmost endeavours to raise the 8 battalions required, (including the troops already raised and in the service of the United States), as soon as possible.

That four commissioners be appointed to repair to the camps in the Jerseys and New York, and there obtain a list of such of the officers in the regular troops and flying camp from this state, now in the service of the United States, as are willing to engage in the service during the war; and also to enlist or cause to be enlisted all or every of the said regular troops or flying camp militia in the service of the United States during the war, continuing the regular battalion and forming the independent companies into a battalion, and filling both up according to the continental establishment; and the said commissioners, or any three of them, may also fill up such of the blank commissions sent to this convention by congress, as may be immediately necessary for the officering of the said corps; but in filling up the said commissions they are required not to introduce into the corps of the now regulars, any officer other than such as are of those regulars, nor into the corps which may be formed of the flying camp militia, any officer not now an officer in the said regulars or flying camp."

RESOLVES OF MARYLAND CONVENTION, 11 NOVEMBER, 1776.

"Resolved, That this Convention adjourn . . . . And that the said Council of Safety be and are fully empowered to take and pursue all measures that they shall think necessary or proper for raising, completing, and equipping the 8 battalions resolved by this convention to be raised for the Continental service, agreeable to the resolves of this convention."

### RESOLVES OF CONTINENTAL CONGRESS, 27 JUNE, 1776.

" Resolved, That six companies of riflemen, in addition to the three companies now at New York, be raised, and the whole regimented ; and that a commission be granted to captain Stevenson, to be colonel of the said regiment of riflemen, which is to be enlisted for three years, unless sooner discharged by Congress; the men to be allowed a bounty of ten dollars; and that Moses Rawlins be lieutenant-colonel, and Otho Holland Williams, major of the said regiment: That four companies of riflemen, for the said regiment, be raised in Virginia, and two in Maryland."

(Rawlings became colonel about 1 January, 1777.)

### RESOLVES OF CONTINENTAL CONGRESS, 9 OCTOBER, 1778.

" Resolved, That if any of the states in which col. Moses Rawlins shall recruit for his regiment shall give to persons enlisting in the same, for three years, or during the war, the bounty allowed by the state, in addition to the continental bounty, the men so furnished, not being inhabitants of any other of the United States, shall be credited to the quota of the State in which they shall be enlisted."

### RESOLVES OF CONTINENTAL CONGRESS, 23 JANUARY, 1779.

" Resolved, That col. Rawlings and such of the officers of his corps as shall be appointed by the commander-in-chief, forthwith recruit three companies of that corps to the full complement: That the volunteers be inlisted for the war, and ordered to repair to Fort Pitt."

Colonel Moses Rawlings' Rifle Regiment was originally raised in Maryland and Virginia as Stephenson's Maryland and Virginia Rifle Regiment, and reorganized in 1777 as one of the 16 additional Regiments.

## MUSTERS OF MARYLAND TROOPS, VOL. I.

| NAMES. | RANK. | TIME OF SERVICE. Enlisted. | Discharged. | REMARKS. |
|---|---|---|---|---|
| | | **FIRST REGIMENT.** | | |
| Allen, Barna. | private | 10 Dec 76 | 16 Augt 80 | prisoner |
| Austin, Robt. | id | 25 Mar 77 | 10 May 80 | died |
| Adams, John | Copr | 10 Dec 76 | | |
| | reduced | 1 Jany 78 | 6 March 78 | deserted |
| Allison, Thomas | private | 10 Dec 78 | 16 Augt 80 | prisoner |
| Allen, Alexander | id | id | 27 Dec 79 | discharged |
| Angleir, Joseph | id | id | 9 March 77 | dead |
| Armstrong, Hugh | id | 10  id | 2 July 77 | deserted |
| Austin, James | id | 21 May 77 | | never joined |
| Adams, James | Corpl | 10 Dec 76 | 13 Sept 77 | missing |
| Allen, William | private | 20 May 78 | 3 Sept 78 | died |
| Adams, Adam | id | 16 May 78 | 1 Nov 80 | present |
| Athey, Ebenezer | id | 4 June 78 | 5 April 79 | discharged |
| Adams, John | id | 1 June 78 | id | id |
| Allen, Jesse | id | 18 May 78 | 20 Feby 79 | id |
| Atchison, Jeremiah | id | 30 May 77 | 23 Sept 78 | died |
| Adams, Ignatius | id | 9 May 79 | 1 Nov 80 | present |
| Atchison, say Hutchinson, Wm. | id | 31 May 79 | | see H. record Book |
| Alvey, Josiah | id | 24 May 79 ' | | |
| Arnold, Wm. | Drum | Joined 1 Jany 80 | | |
| | | | 1 Nov 80 | present |
| Adams, Peter | Lt. Col. | | | |
| | Lt. Col. Comt. | | 1 Augt 79 | |
| Arvin, Ananias | private | 10 June 79 | 8 Augt 80 | deserted |
| | | **SECOND REGIMENT.—*Beginning January* 1778.** | | |
| Andrew, Jeremiah | Corpl | | 2 Oct 78 | dead,  paid |
| Andrew, James | id | 10 Jany 77 | 10 Jany 80 | discharged, paid |
| Aspin, Thomas | private | 15 Augt 77 | 1 Nov 80 | serving in Armons as farrier, paid |
| Allender, John | id | | do | discharged |
| Angles, John | id | not mustered since | | |
| Allen, Solomon | private | do | | |
| Anderson, Arc. | Corpl | .10 Dec 76 | promoted to 3 Regt. | |
| | Major | 10 June 77 | | |
| Abbot, Geo., 9 mo. | private | 20 May 78 | 1 Nov 80 | present |
| Arnet, Thomas | id | | time out | discharged |
| Alvey, John | id | 10 June 79 | 1 Nov 80 | present |
| Abdel, Jacob | id | 9 May 79 | in May 79 | deserted |
| Austin, Henry | id | 14 April 78 | 16 Augt 80 | missing |

## MUSTERS OF MARYLAND TROOPS, VOL. I.

| NAMES. | RANK. | TIME OF SERVICE. Enlisted. | Discharged. | REMARKS. |
|---|---|---|---|---|

THIRD REGIMENT.—*Beginning* 77.

| NAMES. | RANK. | Enlisted. | Discharged. | REMARKS. |
|---|---|---|---|---|
| Alexander, James | pt | 22 Mar 77 | 29 Sept 80 | discharged, off Rolls |
| Appleby, Wm. | pt | | 15 March 78 | deserted |
| Appleby, Jno. | id | | | below joined |
| Armstrong, Geo. | Lieut Capt | 10 Dec 76 | | |
| Armsworthy, Baptist | pt | 22 April 77 | 16 Augt 80 | missing |
| Adams, Wm. | pt | 27 April 77 | 29 April 79 | deserted |
| Allen, William | ⎰ private ⎱ Corporal ⎱ Sergt | 15 Feby 78 1 June 79 | ⎱ 16 Aug 80 | prisoner |
| Allison, James | Lieut | | | |
| Andrews, Joshua out July 78 | private | 2 May 77 | | deserted |
| Adams, Richard out July 78 | id | 22 Augt 77 | | id |
| Arnold, Thomas | id | 2 June 77 | Augt 77 | died |
| Aschum, Samuel out Augt 80 | Corpl | 10 March 77 | Augt 78 | off Rolls |
| Anderson, John reenlisted | private id | 1 June 78 20 Feby 77 | 10 March 80 28 Feby 80 18 Augt 80 | time expired deserted |
| Adamisell, John | id | | 26 Oct 77 | died |
| Allen, John | id | 20 April 78 | Dec 78 | off Rolls |
| Allibon, Thomas | id | 15 April 78 | 16 Augt 80 | missing |
| Adams, John | id | 3 Mar 78 | 1 Nov 80 | present |
| Adams, Thomas | id | 22 April do | 9 Dec 78 | |
| Alvey, Travers | id | 28 April do | 1 Nov 80 | present |
| Assom, John | Corpl | 19 Feby 78 | 28 Mar 79 | discharged |
| Alvey, Thomas Green | private 1 Feb 79 Corpl | 24 April 78 | wounded | furlowed |
| Adams, Nathaniel | private | 22 May 78 | 18 Oct 78 | |
| Adams, Thomas | id | 25 April 78 | | |
| Anderson, William | id | 23 April 78 | | |
| Adams, James | id | | | |
| Armstrong, James July &c. must. 80 | Drum | | 16 Augt 80 | missing |

## MUSTERS OF MARYLAND TROOPS, VOL. I.

| NAMES. | RANK. | TIME OF SERVICE. Enlisted. | Discharged. | REMARKS. |
|---|---|---|---|---|

### FOURTH REGIMENT.—*Beginning Dec.* 1777.

| NAMES. | RANK. | Enlisted. | Discharged. | REMARKS. |
|---|---|---|---|---|
| Adamson, George[1] | private | 27 Dec 76 | 16 Augt 80 | missing |
| Aaron, Moses | id | | Jany 78 | left out the rolls |
| Adams, Mark | id | | Dec 77 | drafted for sea |
| Adamson, Alexander[2] | Drum | | 16 Aug 80 | missing |
| Anderson, Daniel[3] | private | | 1 Nov 80 | present |
| Allender, Joshua[4] | id | paid June mus. 80 | | time expired |
| Adams, William[5] | Lieut | 10 Dec 76 | Augt 78 | resigned |
| Allcock, Martin[6] | private | | 16 Aug 80 | missing |
| Adams, Richard[3] | id | 12 Feby 78 | 17 May 78 | deserted |
| Allen, Richard[4] | id | 11 Jany 78 | 1 May 78 | do |
| Aldham, Danl[2] | id | 21 Apl 78 | July 80 | do |
| Allman, William[4] | id | 19 May 78 | } July 80 | do |
| | Corpl | 1 Dec 79 | | |
| Austin, Isaac[1] | private | | 16 Aug 80 | missing |
| joined May & June must. 80 | | | | |
| Arnold, Christopher | pt | paid | | R. see Chr. Onnel |

### RAWLINGS' REGIMENT.

| NAMES. | RANK. | Enlisted. | Discharged. | REMARKS. |
|---|---|---|---|---|
| Austin, James | Drum | 17 Augt 76 | 20 Dec 76 | deserted |
| Allexander, Mathw. | Sergt | 28 July do | | |
| Andrews, William | private | 18 do do | | paid |
| | Corpl | 1777 | | |
| Arnot, T. D. | pt | 17 Augt 76 | | |
| Alexander, John | id | | | |
| Allinger, Stepn. | id | | | |
| Aitzil, Jacob | id | | | |
| Adams, Jacob | id | 5 Feby | | |
| Adams, Jacob | id | 9 June | | |

### FIRST REGIMENT.

| NAMES. | RANK. | Enlisted. | Discharged. | REMARKS. |
|---|---|---|---|---|
| Brown, Peter | Lieut | 10 dec 76 | 10 July 77 | resigned |
| Britt, Robert | Sergt | | 1 Nov 80 | present, forage |
| | | 1 Jany 80, 2 m Sergt | | [Dep. |
| Bennett, George | Corpl | | missg. | 11 Sept 77 |
| Basil, John | pt | | 27 Dec 79 | discharged |
| Brown, John | id | 19 May 77 | 21 Jany 78 | deserted |
| Bruce, William | Lieut | 10 Dec 76 | 6 July 78 | appd. Adjt. |
| | Capt | 1 Augt 79 | | |

[1] Oldham's.  [2] Norwood's.  [3] Godman's.  [4] Selman's.  [5] Bowie's.  [6] Burgess'.  (These are names of captains of companies.)

## MUSTERS OF MARYLAND TROOPS, VOL. I.

| NAMES. | RANK. | TIME OF SERVICE. Enlisted. | Discharged. | REMARKS. |
|---|---|---|---|---|
| Brady, Patrick | Sergt | 10 Dec 76 | 12 Oct 78 | reduced |
| | | | 27 Dec 79 | discharged |
| Broderick, Dennis | fifer | 10 Dec 76 | | |
| fife major | | 1 Apl 77 | deserted 78 | Wilmington |
| Buxton, Abijah | private | 10 Dec 76 | 27 Dec 79 | discharged |
| re-enlisted | mustr. | June 80 | 1 Nov 80 | present |
| Booth, John | pt | do | 8 Sept 78 | died |
| Burrows, Thomas | id | do | 4 Apl 77 | id |
| Bond, William | id | 1 Feby 77 | 17 Apl 77 | deserted |
| Beanes, J. H. | Capt | 10 Dec 76 | 2 Dec 77 | resigned |
| Brown, William | pt | | 24 June | deserted |
| Boon, John | Corpl | 26 May 77 | | |
| | Sergt | 1 July 79 | 26 Mar 80 | discharged |
| | Ensign | 14 March 80 | | |
| | Lieut | | | |
| Boon, Ignatius | pt | 10 Dec 76 | | |
| | Sergt | 1 Dec 77 | 27 Dec 79 | discharged |
| Beall, Christopher | do | do | do | do |
| Brown, John | do | 14 Apl 77 | | deserted |
| Bulley, William | do | 10 June 77 | 16 Aug 80 | prisoner |
| Blanford, Igs. | pt | 21 June 77 | time out | discharged |
| | Corpl | 1 July 79 | | |
| | Sergt | 12 Dec 79 | | June 80 |
| Bailey, Robert | do | 2 June 77 | 3 Augt 80 | deserted |
| Basford, William | do | 10 Dec 76 | 27 Dec 79 | discharged |
| Booth, John | do | do | 27 Nov 77 | deserted |
| Bootman, Joseph | do | do | 7 Feby 77 | dead |
| Basil, Daniel | fife | 10 Apl 77 | 1 Nov 80 | present |
| Baker, William | pt | 10 Dec 76 | | dead or deserted |
| Butler, Jacob | id | id | 20 Mar 77 | died |
| Babbs, John | id | id | 13 Dec 79 | discharged |
| Baker, John | id | 3 May 77 | 10 Aug 80 | deserted |
| Baker, Joseph | id | 27 Mar 77 | dead or deserted | |
| Bromgart, Adam | id | 28 May 77 | 9 Oct 77 | deserted |
| | | joined 9 April 79 | | |
| Burgess, Vachl. | Corpl | | | |
| | Ensign | 17 Apl 77 | | |
| | Lieut | | 22 Aug 79 | resigned |
| Brown, William | pt | 3 Apl 77 | | dead or deserted |
| | Sergt | 10 May 77 | May 80 | discharged |
| Bartley, Thomas | Corpl | 17 Mar 77 | prisr. 12 May 79, joined Aug 79 | |
| | Sergt | 20 Oct 77 | reduced 10 Feby 78, Sergt 7 Mar 78 | |
| | pt | 29 Mar 77 | reduced 5 Nov 79, Sergt again, discharged 21 Mar 80 | |

## MUSTERS OF MARYLAND TROOPS, VOL. I.

| NAMES. | RANK. | TIME OF SERVICE. Enlisted. | Discharged. | REMARKS. |
|--------|-------|----------------------------|-------------|----------|
| Burch, Francis | pt | 29 Mar 77 | 29 Mar 80 | discharged |
| Barbar, Clemt. | id | 10 dec 76 | 27 Dec 79 | id |
| Barber, Saml. | Adjt | 5 May 77 | resigned July 6, 78 | |
| Bell, Lawson | pt | 4 Jany 78 | 27 Dec 79 | transferred, discharged 1 Apl 80 |
| Baker, John | pt | 3 May 78 | paid | Sickann's |
| Briscoe, Philip | id | 3 June 78 | 5 April 79 | discharged |
| Brissington, Abra. | | 17 May 78 | dead or deserted | |
| Bivens, Luke | pt | 4 May 78 | May 80 | invalids |
| Burnes, Michael | id | 9 May 78 | 4 Dec 78 | deserted |
| Barclay, James | | | June 78 | deserted |
| Butler, John | id | 4 June 78 | 1 Sept 78 | died |
| Bateman, George | id | 5 ditto | 9 mo. out | |
| re-enlisted 5 April 79—8 Jany 80 discharged | | | | |
| Burton, Francis | | 3 May 78 | | |
| Buchanan, John | Drum | 9 May 79 | 1 Nov 80 | present |
| Bassett, Peter | pt | 20 June 79 | 30 June 80 | deserted |
| Boarman, Thomas | | 15 June 79 | 16 Augt 80 | prisoner |
| Bagley, Sam'l | | 5 July 79 | do | missing |
| Button, Thomas | | 30 May 79 | 12 Dec 79 | deserted |
| Brookbank, James | | 5 July 79 | dead or deserted | |
| Berry William | | | 27 July 80 | do |
| Brookbank, Jno. | | 31 July 79 | 1 Nov 80 | present |
| Bryant, James | Fife | 24 Nov 78 | do | do |

SECOND REGIMENT.—*Beginning with the Muster Rolls for January,* 1778.

| NAMES. | RANK. | Enlisted. | Discharged. | REMARKS. |
|--------|-------|-----------|-------------|----------|
| Briscoe, John H. | Sergt | | 1 Jany 78 | resigned |
| Bostwick, Richard | Corpl | 4 Mar 77 | 10 June 80 | discharged |
| Brown, Thomas | pt | 27 Jany 77 | 4 Nov 79 | died |
| Burgess, Thomas | id | 1 Jany 77 | 10 Aug 79 | died of wounds received at Stony Point |
| Brewer, Richard | pt | | 23 Jany 78 | deserted |
| Blades, John | id | 10 Mar 77 | 28 Jany 80 | prisoner war |
| Bush, Richard | id | | 12 Feby 79 | died |
| Burk, Levy, (or Burch) | id | 10 Dec 76 | | |
| | Corpl | June 80 | 1 Nov 80 | present |
| Beaver, William | pt | | 10 Jany 80 | discharged |
| Bradley, John | fifer | 13 Jany 77 | paid depreciation | |
| | pt | 1 Jany 80 | 23 March 80 | prisoner |
| Bettis, Jacob | id | 29 Dec 76 | 29 Dec 79 | discharged |
| Brewer, Thomas | Sergt | 7 Aug 77 | | |
| add. to Corpl | | 1 June 78 | 1 June 80 | discharged |
| | Sergt | 1 Feby 80 | | |

## MUSTERS OF MARYLAND TROOPS, VOL. I.

| NAMES. | RANK. | TIME OF SERVICE. Enlisted. | Discharged. | REMARKS. |
|---|---|---|---|---|
| Broughton, Joshua | pt | | 31 Dec 79 | died |
| Bryan, Charles | id | | 10 Jany 80 | time out while on furl. |
| Barret, James | id | | ditto | discharged |
| Buckley, Daniel | id | 28 Feby 76 | 1 Nov 80 | present |
| Beall, Charles | id | | 10 Jany 80 | discharged |
| Boles, William | | | 1 May 80 | died |
| Boyles, Daniel | pt | 10 Dec 76 | Mar 79 | transferred to Invalids |
| | | | 5 May 80 | discharged |
| Bayley, John | id | | | struck off |
| Brady, James | id | | 22 Jany | deserted |
| Baldwin, James | id | | | struck off |
| Belamy, John | id | Entered on the other side | | |
| Beck, Osborne | id | | 10 Jany 80 | discharged |
| Burgess, James | id | 1 Jany 79 | 10 Jany 80 | discharged |
| Buckley, Thomas | id | 20 Feby 78 | 1 Nov 80 | present |
| | Sergt | 1 Feby 80 | | |
| Bandy, John | pt | 25 Feby 78 | 78 | died wounds |
| Bryan, John | pt | 1 Aprl 78 | 78 | died |
| Brookes, William | id | 13 Feby 78 | 1 Nov 80 | present |
| Burch, Joseph | id | 28 Feby 78 | Corpl 1 Feby 80 | |
| | Corpl | 15 May 78 | private 25 Oct 80 | |
| Corporal 1 April 79 | pt | 1 Mar 78 | 1 Nov 80 | present |
| Brookshear, James | id | 25 Aprl 78 | | time out, discharged |
| Bramble, Eton | id | 1 May 78 | 1 July 78 | deserted |
| Burnes, Zekiel | id | 23 April 78 | 16 Aug 80 | killed |
| Bramble, Hackett | id | 4 May 78 | 1 Nov 80 | present |
| Bellows, Isaac | id | 15 May 78 | dead or deserted | |
| Bishop, Thomas | id | 4 Mar 78 | 1 Nov 80 | present |
| Boarman, Daniel | id | 20 Jany 78 | July 80 | deserted |
| Baldwin, John | id | 19 Aprl 78 | 20 April 78 | do |
| Ball, Richard | id | 5 Aprl 78 | 15 Aprl 78 | do |
| Brathwait, Wm. | id | 1 May 78 | } 1 Nov 80 | present |
| | Corpl | 1 Mar 80 | | |
| Burns, John | pt | 20 do do | Mar 80 | died |
| Boon, Foster | id | 28 May 78 | 8 Mar 79 | discharged |
| Battingly, Stanley | id | 31 May 78 | 3 April 79 | do |
| Bell, Thomas | id | 24 do | do | do |
| Biggs, Thomas | id | 4 April 78 | do | do |
| Barnes, James | id | 29 May 78 | do | do |
| Burris, Norm. | id | 30 May 78 | do | do |
| Brown, Thomas[1] | id | | 10 Jany 80 | do |

[1] Dent's

## MUSTERS OF MARYLAND TROOPS, VOL. I.

| NAMES. | RANK. | TIME OF SERVICE. Enlisted. | TIME OF SERVICE. Discharged. | REMARKS. |
|---|---|---|---|---|
| Butt, Zachariah | id | 28 Mar 78 | 16 Aug 80 | missing |
| Butt, Baruch | id | 3 April 78 | 1 Nov 80 | present |
| Browning, William | id | 6 June do | Mar 80 | prisoner war |
|   Priso. Mar 80 | | | | |
| Beck, Amos | id | 10 do do | 16 Augt 80 | missing |
| Brannon, James | pt | 8 Mar 77 | 8 Mar 80 | discharged |
| Boyland, Andrew | id | 20 May 78 | 3 Aprl 79 | discharged |
| Batson, James | id | do do | July 79 | time out, discharged |
| Byrne, Charles | id | | 16 Augt 80 | killed |
| Boyes, Alexander | id | 8 May 78 | 21 Jany 79 | discharged |
| Baker, John | id | 25 ditto | 26 Dec 78 | deserted |
| Butts, Thomas | Drum | 8 April 78 | 1 Nov 80 | present |
| Butts, Edward | fifer | 28 Mar do | } 1 Nov 80 | present |
| | private | 1 July 79 | | |
| Bennet, Frederick | Fifer | 26 do do | 1 Nov 80 | do |
| Bramble, William | pt | | 3 April 79 | do |
| Barrett, Danl. | id | | } | |
|   Joined 9 May 79 | Corpl | 1 May 80 | } 16 Aug 80 | missing |
| Brown, Solomon | pt | | 19 June 79 | deserted |
|   1st muster June 79 | | | | |
| Blanford, Richard | id | 13 June 79 | 16 Augt 80 | missing |
| Bramble, David | id | 7 do | 1 Nov 80 | present |
| Brooks, Thomas | id | 8 July 79 | 22 July 79 | deserted |
| Brashears, Igns. | id | 18 Jany 77 | 18 Jan 80 | discharged |
| Boyd, Thomas | Ensn | 27 Oct 79 | | |
| | Licut | June 80 | | |
| Brittenham, Solo. | fifer | 1 April 80 | 16 Aug 80 | missing |
| Bellemy, John | pt | | 1 Nov 80 | present |
| Buttons, Levin | id | 5 April 80 | do | do |
| Bramble, Levin | id | 16 July 80 | do | do |

### THIRD REGIMENT.—*Beginning* 77.

| | | | | |
|---|---|---|---|---|
| | Ensn | 27 May 78 | | |
| Baldwin, Henry | Sergt | 26 Feby 77 | | |
| | qr. mast. | | | |
| Bridges, Richard | pt | 9 Mar 77 | 1 Nov 80 | present |
| Bate, Thomas | id | 21 June 77 | | not heard of, |
| Branwood, James | id | | taken on S. Island 22 Augt | |
| Banney, James | id | | 2 Nov 78 | to Invalids } |
| | | | 5 Nov 79 | discharged } |
| Blakney, (or Blake), Jno. | id | | 19 July 80 | deserted |
| Burnes, James | id | | } 1 Nov 80 | |
| | Corpl | 1 June 79 | } | |
| | Sergt | 1 Sept 79 | } deserted about the 15 Mar 81 | |

## MUSTERS OF MARYLAND TROOPS, VOL. I.

| NAMES. | RANK. | Enlisted. | Discharged. | REMARKS. |
|---|---|---|---|---|
| Brookes, Benja. | Capt | 10 Dec 76 | | |
| Brown, Thomas | Corpl | 1 Jany 77 | 1 Nov 80 | present |
| Bennett, Jesse | pt | 5 Apl 77 | 1 May 79 | deserted |
| Butterworth, Jos. | id | | 16 Aug 80 | missing |
| Bray, Joseph | id | 28 do do | 1 Feb 80 | |
| Burnett, Thomas | id | 13 May 77 ⎫ | 16 Aug 80 | prisoner Camden |
| out May 78 | Sergt | 15 Mar 78 ⎬ | | |
| Sergt July 80 | Nov 78 Corpl | ⎭ | | |
| Beard, William | pt | 29 June 77 | 19 Dec 78 | died, Invalid Corps Sept. 11, 78 |
| Bloyds, Daniel | id | 19 Aprl 77 | 4 July 80 | deserted |
| Burris, William | id | 18 Aug do | 20 Dec 77 | died |
| Barkers, James | id | 18 Sept do | 14 July 78 | deserted |
| Barker, William | id | 6 Augt do | 16 Augt 80 | missing |
| Burris, George | id | 9 Sept do | 2 Jan 78 | died |
| Bailey, John | Lieut | | 18 Nov 79 | resigned |
| Bailey, Joseph | Serg & pt | 21 May 77 ⎫ 10 Oct do ⎬ | | furd. 5 Augt 78, never returned |
| Byass, James | pt | 1 Jany 77 | 1 Nov 80 | present |
| Beaver, Martin | id | 9 May 77 | served time out |
| Breakley, John | id | 2 July 77 | do do do |
| Benn, Whidd'r | id | 8 Aug 77 | 1 Nov 80 | present |
| | Corpl | 15 Feby 78 | | |
| Bush, Francis | pt | | Aug 80 | deserted |
| Bryan, Daniel | id | | 7 Dec 77 | died |
| Brice, Jacob | Capt B. Insp. | 10 Dec 77 1 May 78 | | |
| Bronely, John | pt | 3 April 77 | | |
| | Sergt | 3 Oct 77 | 16 Augt 80 | prisoner |
| Brearly, George | pt | 27 June do | not heard of | |
| Brown, James | id | 21 July do | Dec 78 | died |
| Brown, John | id | | 1 Nov 80 | present |
| Burns, Hugh | id | 4 May 77 | | |
| | Corpl | 20 May 78 | 16 Augt 80 | prisoner |
| Barber, John | pt | | do do | missing |
| Boston, John N. | id | 28 April 77 | | deserted |
| Brady, Michael | id | 27 July do | 23 July 78 | do |
| Butler, Richard | id | 16 Nov 77 | 1 Nov 80 | present |
| Baker, John | id | 10 April 77 | 21 Feby 80 | time expired |
| Bidgood, William | id | | 28 Feby 78 | deserted |
| Bolton, Richard | id | | 15 Oct 79 | do |
| joined 27 April, 78 | | | | |
| Best, James | id | | 27 Oct 78 | died |

MUSTERS OF MARYLAND TROOPS, VOL. I.

| NAMES. | RANK. | TIME OF SERVICE. | | REMARKS. |
| | | Enlisted. | Discharged. | |
| --- | --- | --- | --- | --- |
| Burk, Peter | pt | 1 Oct 78 | 1 Jan 80 | off rólls |
| | Corpl | | | |
| Bicknall, Esau | pt | | dead or deserted | |
| Byars, John | id | Know nothing of him | | |
| Bartholomew, Ben | Adjt | | Mar 78 | cashiered |
| Barrett, John | pt | 25 April 78 | 18 Augt 80 | deserted |
| Bartley, Thomas S. | id | do  do | 16  do  do | missing |
| Bachilor, Thomas | id | 26 do  do | know nothing of him | |
| Burns, David | pt | 25 April 78 | 16 Aug 80 | missing |
| Bryan, John | id | taken by prior enlistment, re-enlisted in State Regt. | | |
| Blissell, Edward | id | 27 April 78 | time out | discharged |
| Bullock, Jesten. | id | 24 ditto | | dead, time unknown |
| Blunderwill, John | id | 30 ditto | 18 Oct 78 | dead |
| Bailey, John B. | id | 24 ditto | | |
| Brown, William | Sergt | 24 Feby 78 | 4 June 78 | deserted |
| Butler, George | do | 28 April 78 | 20 June 78 | ditto |
| Bradley, James | pt | 3 April 78 | 14 Aug 78 | ditto |
| Buttery, Thomas | id | 16 May 78 | 16 Aug 80 | killed |
| Brown, Basil | id | 9 April 78 | 1 Nov 80 | present |
| Brown, George | id | 23 do  do | do | do |
| Bowers, Thomas | id | | 12 Sept 78 | died |
| Brett, John | id | | 21 Jan 80 | deserted |
| Bray, Joseph | id | see the other side | | |
| Bingley, Alexander | id | 13 May 78 | 1 Nov 80 | present |
| Barnhouse, Rodolph | id | 1 June 78 | 4 Aug 79 | discharged |
| Branson, Thomas | id | 25 do do | 30 Oct 78 | do |
| Burch, Zacharh. | id | 26 May 78 | 1 Nov 80 | present |
| Bean, Leonard | id | 29 do  do | do | do |
| | 1 Jany 80, Corpl | | | |
| Blake, George | pt | 9 June 78 | 24 Nov 78 | deserted |
| Brown, William | id | 23 April 78 | know nothing of him | |
| Barry, William[1] | id | do  do | do | do |
| Bellwhight, Sam'l[2] | id | do  do | 1 Nov 80 | present |
| Bachilor, William | id | 27 do  do | Sept | dead |
| Beaver, John | id | 1 June 78 | 13 Feby 79 | discharged |
| Boardman, Rob't | id | 1 May 78 | Dec 79 | deserted |
| Brand, Gabriel | pt | 5 June 78 | 1 Nov 80 | present |
| Bean, John | id | do  do | ditto | ditto |
| Bird, Thomas | id | do  do | ditto | ditto |
| Boyd, Benjamin | id | 8 May 78 | ditto | ditto |
| Byalls, Peter | id | 9 do  do | 23 Mar 80 | prisoner |

[1] Griffith's.                    [2] Jones'.

MUSTERS OF MARYLAND TROOPS, VOL. I.

| NAMES. | RANK. | TIME OF SERVICE. Enlisted. | Discharged. | REMARKS. |
|---|---|---|---|---|
| Bullock, John | pt | | April and May | time expired |
| Blair, John | id | 15 Jany 79 | 1 Nov 80 | present |
| Berry, Isaac | fife | 10 May 78 | know nothing of him | |
| Brickstake, Roger | pt | | 16 Augt 80 | missing |
| joined 17 June 79 | | | | |
| Batson, George | id | 1 Dec 76 | | time out 1 Dec 79 |
| 1 muster May 79 | | | | |
| Bullen, John | id | | | |
| 1 muster May 79 | | | Sept 79 | deserted |
| Bowie, Matthew | id | 18 May 79 | Feby 80 | id |
| Buccard, Peter | id | 5 Sept 77 | 1 Oct 80 | present |
| Barry, William[1] | id | | 16 Augt 80 | missing |
| Bailey, Thomas | id | 3 May 77 | 1 Nov 80 | present |
| joined 15 Sept 79[2] | | | | |

FROM OCTOBER MUSTERS, 1780, AND JULY, &C.

| NAMES. | RANK. | Enlisted. | Discharged. | REMARKS. |
|---|---|---|---|---|
| Bailey, James | Drum | 7 Mar 80 | 1 Nov 80 | present |
| Buckley, John | pt | 7 Jan 80 | do | do |
| Blower, James | id | 3 Mar 80 | do | do |
| Berry, William | fife | | July 80 | deserted |
| Busby, Christopher | pt | | 16 Augt 80 | missing |
| Bolton, William | id | | do　do | killed |

FOURTH REGIMENT.—*Beginning December,* 1777.

| NAMES. | RANK. | Enlisted. | Discharged. | REMARKS. |
|---|---|---|---|---|
| Beach, John | Drum M. | 1 May 77 | 1 Nov 80 | present |
| Barrett, Joshua[3] | pt Sergt | 18 Dec 76 } 1 June 79 } | 16 Augt 80 | missing |
| Bowen, Samuel | pt | | 10 Sept 78 | discharged |
| Baulk, Benjamin | do | 19 Dec 76 | 19 Dec 79 | ditto |
| Branmon, Caleb[4] | do | | 25 May 80 | time expired |
| Barrow, James | id | | 15 June 78 | discharged |
| Bannerman, Jno. | id | 1 May 77 | | |
| Bates, John[5] | id | | 1 Nov 80 | present |
| Bostwick, Thomas | id | 12 Jan 77 | 12 Jan 80 | discharged |
| Bredding, John | id | | 16 Augt 80 | missing |
| Bond, Joshua | id | | ——— 76 | |
| Begley, George[6] | id | 9 May 77 | 16 Augt 80 | prisoner |
| Boyd, Edward | id | | 1 April 78 | deserted |
| Brown, John | id | | 1 dec 77 | discharged |
| Bidwell, Richard[7] | id | 6 Dec 76 | 6 Dec 79 | do |

[1] Late Smith's.　[2] Brooks'.　[3] Oldham's.　[4] Norwood's.　[5] To Selman's, Godman's.
[6] Lansdale's.　[7] Sellman's.

## MUSTERS OF MARYLAND TROOPS, VOL. I.

| NAMES. | RANK. | TIME OF SERVICE. Enlisted. | TIME OF SERVICE. Discharged. | REMARKS. |
|---|---|---|---|---|
| Bowen, Jehu[1] | Ensn | | 16 Oct 78 | remov'd to Mary'd Dragoons |
| Banks, Charles | pt | | 21 May 79 | died |
| Bransby, William | id | | 26 Feby 78 | deserted |
| Brown, Christopher | id | 19 July 77 | July 80 | ditto |
| Beach, John | Drum M. | 1 May 77 | see above | D. Major |
| Buttoridge, John | pt | | Jan 78 | left out the Rolls |
| Dec 77 sea service | | | | |
| Bowie, Wm. Sprigg[2] | Capt | | | left out of Roll |
| Berry, John | pt | 5 Aug. 77 | July 80 | discharged |
| Brown, James | id / Drum / Fife M. | 19 May 77 / 1 June 78 / 1 June 80 | 16 Augt 80 | missing |
| Bradley, George | Corpl | 29 May 77 | 1 Nov 80 | present |
| Burgess, Joseph[3] | Capt | 10 Dec 76 | 17 Nov 78 | died |
| Belt, John Sprigg | Lieut / Capt | do do / 15 Dec 77 | | |
| Baker, William | pt | 7 April 77 | 1 Nov 80 | present, (deserted,so say Capt Belt) |
| Badham, Edward | id | | 15 April 78 | deserted |
| Bardmore, John | id | | Feby 78 | left out Rolls |
| Bowdon, Arthur | id | 17 April 77 | 17 April 80 | time expired |
| Blackwell, Hugh | id | 2 April 77 | April&May 79 | not heard of |
| Bloice, Abraham | id | 11 Augt 77 | Dec 79 | deserted |
| Brown, Isaac,[4] joined from Sellman's | | 26 Dec 77 | see Isaac Brown below | |
| Booth, William | pt | 21 Jan 78 | 14 Sept 78 | transd. 4 Pens. Regt. |
| Britt, Thomas[1] | id | 19 Jan 78 | 19 May 80 | deserted |
| Burn, Michael,[5] joined Oldham's 1 June 79 | id | 26 April 78 | July 80 | ditto |
| Bond, James | pt | 27 April 78 | 9 Jan 80 | ditto |
| Blower, John[6] | id | 9 May 78 | 23 Jan 80 | ditto |
| Brown, Isaac | pt / Corpl | 26 Feby 77 / 1 Nov 78 | 26 Feby 80 | time out |
| Barnett, John[7] | pt | 5 May 78 | 16 Augt 80 | missing |
| Bright, William | id | | | |
| From Capt. Brown's Ary. | | 1 April 78 | 1 Nov 80 | present |
| Batteast, John | pt | 25 April 78 | May 79 | deserted |
| Bardeu, William | id | 2 May 78 | April 80 | left out |

[1] Spurrier's.　[2] Bowie's.　[3] Burgess'.　[4] Lansdale's.　[5] Norwood's.　[6] To Sellman's, Lansdale's, April, 78.　[7] Sellman's.

## MUSTERS OF MARYLAND TROOPS, VOL. I.

| NAMES. | RANK. | TIME OF SERVICE. Enlisted. | Discharged. | REMARKS. |
|---|---|---|---|---|
| Bowler, Peter[1] | pt | 27 April 78 | 1 Nov 80 | present |
| Barraclift, John[2] | id | 9 May 78 | Sept 80 | deserted |
| Bryan, Thomas | id | 8 May 78 | 5 May 80 } | ditto |
|  |  |  | July 80 } | ditto |
| Bates, Roland[3] | id | 15 May 78 | July 80 | ditto |
| Brown, John[2] | pt | 21 April 78 | Dec 21 1780 | discharged |
| Brown, Thomas[4] | id | 6 Sept 77 | 1 May 80 } | deserted |
| prs'r 22 Augt, joined 23 June 78 | | Corpl 1 Jan 80 | July 80 } | ditto |
| Brown, Robert | pt | 23 Feby 78 | { 14 May 80 } | ditto |
| prs'r 22 Augt 77, joined 23 June 78 | | | { July 80 } | ditto |
| Bermingham, Patrick[5] | id | 20 May 78 | 16 Augt 80 | missing |
| Boshibea, Joseph | id | 22 Jan 78 | 1 Nov 80 | present |
| Brisington, Philip[1] | id | 1 April 78 | see below |  |
| Butler, Joseph[6] | id | 28 May 78 | 16 Aug 80 | missing |
| Bushell, Peter[7] | id | 18 April 77 | 18 April 80 | discharged |
| pris'r 22 Aug 77, joined 10 Aug 80 | | | | |
| Balff, Edward[1] | pt | 1 Aug 78 | 9 June 80 | deserted |
| Brown, Luke[7] | id | 1 July 77 | July 79 | ditto |
| Brishington, Philip,[1] | id | 1 April 78 | 16 Augt 80 | missing |
| Enlisted in So. Caro. with the enemy | | | | |
| Ballamy, John[7] | pt | 27 May 79 } |  |  |
|  | joined | 24 Sept 80 } | 1 Nov 80 | present |
| Byrne, Michael | pt | see Michael Burn, Norwood's Compy. | | |
| Joined 1 June 79 | | | | |
| Brown, Richard[5] | id |  | 16 Augt 80 | missing |
| Mus'd June 79 | | | | |
| Belford, Jeremiah[6] | id | 8 May 79 | Jan 80 | deserted |
| Bowen, Robert | fifer | 16 do do | 16 Augt 80 | missing |
| Bentley, Thomas[8] | pt | 23 Oct 79 | 2 Jan 80 | deserted |
| Late Godman's | | | | |
| Bowser, Samuel | id | 18 May 77 | 18 Mar 80 | discharged |
| Joined 1 Nov 79 | | | | |
| Bailey, Joseph[7] | id | left out Oct. 1780 | | |
| Joined May & June mus. 80 | | | | |
| Bailey, Philip | pt | 16 April 80 | 1 Nov 80 | present |
| Burgess, Joshua | Ensign | 14 Mar 80 | | |

[1] Reily's, late Bowie's.   [2] Godman's.   [3] Norwood's.   [4] Lansdale's.   [5] Sellman's.
[6] Burgess', June, 78.   [7] Oldham's.   [8] Belt's.

MUSTERS OF MARYLAND TROOPS, VOL. I.

| NAMES. | RANK. | TIME OF SERVICE. Enlisted. | TIME OF SERVICE. Discharged. | REMARKS. |
|---|---|---|---|---|
| | | RAWLINGS' REGIMENT. | | |
| Buller, Patrick | pt | 18 Aug 76 | 27 Dec 76 | deserted |
| Barnes, Richard | pt | 8   do | 18  do | ditto |
| Baker, Charles | pt | 29  do | 9 Aug 79 | discharged |
| Burton, Joseph  3 | pt | July 76ʳ | | |
| Batten, Wm. | Sergt | 76 | | |
|   promd. to Sergt 79 | | | | |
| Burton, Joshua | pt | | 1 July 79 | discharged |
| Burk, John | pt | | | |
| Baker, Charles | pt | | | |
| Bush, Dennis  3 | Sergt | | 21 July 79 | do |
| Beatty, William | pt | | | |
| Becraft, John | | | 1 July 79 | do |
| Brown, George | | | 9 Aug 79 | do |
| Bean, Gilbert | | | 4 Sept | deserted |
| Bedinger, Daniel | Corpl | | 9 Aug 79 | discharged |
| Burch, Benjamin | Sergt | | | |
| Balman, Thomas | pt | | 9 Aug 79 | do |
| Brown, John | do | | | |
| Brannan, George | do | | do  do | do |
| Barnes, James | do | | do | do |
| Burgess, Edward  1 yr. | do | | 1 July 79 | do |
| Berry, Zachariah | do | 6 May 78 | | |
| Barnett, John | Sergt | | | |
| Bean, John | pt | 4 April 78 | | |
| Blair, Samuel | do | 1   do | | |
| Bierley, Jacob | do | 6   do | | |
| Brooks, Benjamin | do | 29  do | | |
| Beall, William  6 mo. | do | 8 Feby 79 | | |
| Burnsides, John  6 mo. | pt | 19 May 79 | | |
| Brunt, Edward  do | do | 13 do  79 | | |
| Brown, William  do | do | 2 April 79 | | |
| Barnett, Robert  do | do | 24 Mar 79 | | |
| Bair, Peter  do | do | 7 Mar 76 | | |
| Beall, Thomas | Capt | 25 July 76 | | |
| | | FIRST REGIMENT. | | |
| Cosgrove, Edward | pt | 10 Dec 76 | 23 Jan 80 | joined |
| Cann, Ingram | do | do | 27 Dec 79 | discharged |
| Crosbey, Joseph | do | do | 30 April 77 | deserted |
| | | joined 3 June 79 | deserted | 6 July 79 |
| Clary, William | pt | 17 Feby 77 | | |
| Clancy, John | do | 5 Mar | April 80 | prisoner |

## MUSTERS OF MARYLAND TROOPS, VOL. I.

| NAMES. | RANK. | TIME OF SERVICE. Enlisted. | Discharged. | REMARKS. |
|---|---|---|---|---|
| Carvin, Thomas | pt | 9 May | 4 Oct 77 | missing |
| Chaney, John | do | 14 Feb | 10 May | deserted |
| Chaney, Richard | do | 10 Dec 76 | | |
| Chunn, Jonathan | do | do | 6 Mar 77 | died |
| Callahan, (or Cullanan) Jno. | do | do | 22 Augt 77 | prisoner |
| | | joined 28 July 78 | | discharged 27 Dec 79 } |
| Chaplin, William | pt | 10 Dec 76 | 6 Mar 78 | deserted |
| Clements, John | do | 21 Feby 77 | 22 Feby 80 | discharged |
| Coe, Richard | Sergt | | 22 Feby 79 | appd. Q. M. |
| | | | 27 Dec 79 | discharged |
| Coe, Milburn | Corpl | | do | do |
| Coe, Hezekiah | pt | | 31 Nov 77 | died |
| Courts, William | Lieut | 10 Dec 76 | 17 April | promd. 2d Regt. |
| Chapman, Henry | pt | 11 Mar 77 | June | died |
| Clark, William | do | 10 Dec 76 | July 77 | deserted |
| Connor, Thomas | do | do | 27 Dec 79 | discharged |
| Carmichael, James | do | do | 10 July 77 | do |
| Cramphur, James | do | 14 Feby 77 | 25 April 79 | do |
| Capshort, Martin | do | | not joined | |
| Corbett, Jacob | do | 2 Mar 77 | 2 Mar 80 | discharged |
| Chapman, William | do | 29 do do | 28 do do | ditto |
| Cox, Edmond | Sergt Q. M. | 10 Dec 76 19 July 77 | | dismissed 3 October 1778 |
| Connally, John | pt | 10 July 76 | 17 Dec 77 | deserted |
| Cullis, John | do | 12 feby 77 | prisoner | Jan 25 80 |
| Callahan, John | do | 10 April 77 | 18 July | deserted |
| Cronan, John | do | 23 feb 77 | 23 feb 80 | discharged |
| Clements, James | do | 28 do do | 28 do do | do |
| Clements, Henry | do | 16 April 77 | time out | discharged |
| Corbett, Patrick | do | 13 Mar 78 | 25 feb 79 | deserted |
| Currill, John | do | 2 April 78 | feb 79 | died |
| Chapman, Thomas | do | 3 May 78 | 1 Nov 80 | present |
| Caile, David | do | 10 June 78 | do do | do |
| Coombs, William | do | 6 do do | 5 Aprl 79 | discharged |
| Clark, Thomas | do | 24 April 78 | June 80, off rolls, left out June 80 | |
| Connelly, John | do | 2 Mar 78 | 3 Aprl 79 | deserted |
| Casser, William | | 28 Apl 78 | July 79 | not heard of |
| Cheney, John | do | 10 Feb 78 | 10 Sept | discharged |
| Chinn, Samuel | | | 17 do 78 | died |
| Cooley, Robert | do | 20 May 78 | 6 Oct 78 | do |
| Cooley, Joseph | do | 8 Jan 79 | 1 Nov 80 | present |
| Cooley, James | do | 20 do | 5 April 79 | discharged |
| Carroll, John | do | 12 May 78 | July 79 | deserted |
| Carroll, John, Jnr. | | 17 May 78 8 Jan 79 } | 1 Nov 80 | present |

## MUSTERS OF MARYLAND TROOPS, VOL. I.

| NAMES. | RANK. | TIME OF SERVICE. Enlisted. | Discharged. | REMARKS. |
|---|---|---|---|---|
| Closs, Christian | | 10 Dec 76 | 16 Aug 80 | deserted |
| Coleson, John | | 24 Jan 78 | 10 Feby 79 | do |
| Collard, James | fife | 1 Dec 78 | 1 Nov 80 | sick Maryd. |
| Campton, Edward | Ensn | 12 April 79 } | | |
| | Lieut | 1 Aug 80 } | | |
| Cooley, Mordecai | private | 26 April 79 | 16 Aug 80 | missing |
| Cormine, John | pt | 20 June 79 | 16 Aug 80 | missing |
| Coombs, Nicholas | do | 11 Sept 79 | 1 Nov 80 | present |
| Clements, William | do | do do | do | do |
| Congleton, David | do | | 13 Jan 80 | deserted |
| Cotting, Peter | do | 30 June 80 | | do |
| Crist, John | do | | 30 June 80 | do |
| Carpenter, Hump'y | do | June 80 | 16 Aug 80 | prisoner |
| Cole, Michael | do | Mar 80 | 1 Nov 80 | present |
| Cregan, Dennis | | 14 May 78 | 26 April 80 | to Invalids |
| | joined 1st Regt. | | 14 July 81 | per Invalid Ret. |

### SECOND REGIMENT.—*Beginning January*, 1778.

| NAMES. | RANK. | TIME OF SERVICE. Enlisted. | Discharged. | REMARKS. |
|---|---|---|---|---|
| Crisps, Benjamin | pt | 4 Mar 77 | 25 dec 79 | discharged |
| Campher, Thomas | do | 3 do do | 1 Nov 80 | present |
| Calvert, Eleakim | do | 27 May 77 | 10 Jan 80 | discharged |
| Cooksey, John | do | 8 do do | do do | do |
| Connely, Laurence | do | 4 Mar 77 | May 80 | do |
| Conner, John | Drum | | | out of Rolls 1777 |
| Cavender, Patrick | pt | | 16 Aug 80 | missing |
| Connally, Thomas | Corpl | | 15 May 78 | deserted |
| Cunningham, Jno. | pt | 30 dec 76 | 5 Jan 79 | discharged |
| Carly, Lawrence | do | 9 feb 77 | 16 Aug 80 | missing |
| Carleton, Richard | do | | | out of Rolls Dec 77 |
| Connally, Michael | do | { 1 June 77 | } 1 Nov 80 | present |
| | Corpl | { 1 May 80 | } | |
| Campbell, Peter | Sergt | | 16 Mar 78 | deserted |
| Crips, Nathaniel | pt | 12 Jan 77 | 1 Nov 80 | present |
| Cato, William | do | | } 1 Nov 80 | do |
| | Sergt | 1 Jan 80 | } | |
| | pt | 15 Sept 80 | } | |
| Christopher, John | pt | 28 July 77 | 1 Nov 80 | prisoner |
| must. Jan 78 left out Feby in. in April 78 | | | 16 Aug 80 | prisoner |
| Cole, William | pt | } 1 Jan 79 | 10 Jan 80 | discharged |
| | Corpl | } | | |
| Cheshire, Thomas | pt | | | off Rolls Dec 77 |
| Carr, Solomon | do | | | do do |
| Crawford, Jacob | Sergt | | | |

## MUSTERS OF MARYLAND TROOPS, VOL. I.

| NAMES. | RANK. | TIME OF SERVICE. Enlisted. | Discharged. | REMARKS. |
|---|---|---|---|---|
| | q. mr. | 11 Feb 79 | | |
| | Ensign | 26 Jan 80 | 10 Jan 80 | discharged |
| | Lieut | | | |
| Cross, Joseph | Sergt | 11 Feby 77 | do do | do |
| Cross, Samuel | pt | 10 Jan 77 | do do | do |
| Christian, John | do | | 12 feb 78 | died |
| Cain, John | do | | | off Rolls Dec 77 |
| Conner, Michael | Sergt | | 1 Feb 78 | discharged |
| Cromey, Andrew | pt | 3 April 77 | 1 Nov 80 | present |
| Carroll, John | do | | 21 May 78 | deserted |
| Cators, Patrick | Sergt | | reduced to the ranks 15 Jan, | |
| | | 8 may 78, deserted | | |
| Courts, William | Lieut | | | |
| Carroll, Jeremiah | pt | | | struck off Jan 78 |
| Cain, Hugh | do | 18 Mar 78 | 16 Aug 80 | missing |
| Carroll, Bryan | do | 1 Mar 78 | 1 Nov 80 | present |
| Cole, John | do | 27 Dec 77 | Mar 79 | died |
| Cantewell, William | do | 4 feb 78 | Mar 80 | deserted |
| Connegin, John | do | | see McConnegan | |
| Cooksen, Peter | do | | 19 May 78 | deserted |
| Cornish, John | do | 27 April 78 | 79 | dead |
| Collins, Jacob | do | 12 May 78 | 1 Dec 79 | transfd. to Invalids |
| Claridge, Henry | do | 6 do do | Oct 80 | |
| Chamberlain, Jonas | do | 20 do do | 16 Aug 80 | missing, once a |
| Coatney, William | do | 25 April 78 | 12 Jan 80 | deserted [Corpl |
| Cairy, Patrick | do | 20 May 78 | 1 Nov 80 | present |
| Cosfield, Luke | pt | 20 May 78 | Jan 79 | struck off |
| Conner, David | do | 23 April do | sick Mary'd Invalid war | |
| Citizen, Morris | do | 4 May 78 | 1 Nov 80 | present |
| Crooke, Joseph | do | 28 May 78 | 79 Feby | not heard of |
| Clark, Charles | do | 30 May 78 | 3 April 79 | discharged |
| Clark, Joseph | do | | Jan 79 | struck off |
| Conner, Patrick | do | Mar 77 | 1 Nov 80 | present |
| Crating, John | do | | Jan 79 | struck off |
| Clark, Igns. | do | 30 May 78 | 3 April 79 | discharged |
| Compton, Alexd. | Sergt | 1 Jan 77 | 10 Jan 80 | do |
| Chard, John | pt | 26 Jan 77 | left out Aprl Rolls 80, time out | |
| Chatland, William | do | 17 Mar 77 | sick Maryd., 1 Nov 80 | |
| Cook, Benjamin | do | 1 May 78 | | |
| | Corpl | 12 Oct 78 | Jan 79 | struck off |
| Cutler, William | pt | 5 June do | 1 Nov 80 | present |
| Cusick, Michael | do | | 18 Dec 78 | deserted |
| Cope, John | do | 20 May 78 | 10 Oct 78 | died |
| Craft, James | do | do do | 24 dec 78 | discharged |

## MUSTERS OF MARYLAND TROOPS, VOL. I.

| NAMES. | RANK. | TIME OF SERVICE. Enlisted. | Discharged. | REMARKS. |
|---|---|---|---|---|
| Cornish, Constant | pt | do   do | 3 April 79 | discharged |
| Code, William | do | do   do | do   do | do |
| Clarke, William | do | 3 April 78 | 16 Aug 80 | prisoner |
| Current, James | do | 25 May 78 | 26 dec 78 | deserted |
| Clark, William | do | do   do | Jan 79 | time out |
| Champhin, John | do | do   do | 26 Dec 78 | deserted |
| see John Camphin on the other side | | | | |
| Connely, Michael | do | do   do | Mar 79 | discharged |
| Cooper, Charles | do | 4 Mar 77 | | returnd pd. by Denny |
| prisr. 25 Mar 80 | | | | |
| Cowsway, Solomon | do | 20 May 78 | 24 dec 78 | discharged |
| Collins, James | Sergt | 24 dec 76 | 10 Jan 80 | discharged |
| Conway, James | pt | | Feby 80 | died |
| Cathel, James | do | | 12 dec 79 | discharged |
| Cook, Benjamin | Corpl | | } | off Rolls |
| taken by prior Enlistment | | | | |
| Cox, Emund [1] | Sergt | 15 Mar 79 | } 1 Nov 80 | present |
| | private | 1 Jan 80 | } | |
| | Sergt | 1 April 80 | } | |
| reduced again 1 Sept 80 | | | | |
| Chisley, Robert | Lieut | | | |
| | Capt | | | |
| Carnes, Benjamin | pt | 11 June 79 | 1 Nov 80 | do |
| Campin, John | do | 19 do do | do   do | } do |
| Joined 25 Oct 80 | Corpl | 1 Jan 80 | } | |
| Cooly, George | pt | April 80 | ditto | ditto |
| Copeland, William | Drum | | ditto | do |
| | June 80 | | | |
| Corsey, Hampton | do pt | 24 Mar 80 | do   do | do |
| Collings, William | do | 6 April 80 | 16 Aug 80 | missing |
| Collins, James | do | | | |
| left out June Rolls 79 | | | June 79 | left out Rolls |
| Conner, William | do | | 1 Nov 80 | present |

### THIRD REGIMENT.—*Beginning* 77.

| | | | | |
|---|---|---|---|---|
| Coomes, Richard | Sergt | 10 May 77 } | | |
| private 25 May 79 | Sergt | 18 June 78 } May | | discharged |
| Crismond, Leonard | fife | 3 Feby 77 | left out Mar 80, time expired | |
| Clarke, George, or Jno. | pt | 16 do do | do   do | |
| Clements, Henry | do | 28 do do } | time expired 28 feb 80 | |
| | Corpl | 1 Augt 77 } | | |
| | Sergt | 1 June 79 } | promoted to be Ensign | |

[1] Williams's.

## MUSTERS OF MARYLAND TROOPS, VOL. I.

| NAMES. | RANK. | TIME OF SERVICE. | | REMARKS. |
|---|---|---|---|---|
| | | Enlisted. | Discharged. | |
| Carr, John | Ensn | | | |
| Conn, Robert | pt | } 10 Jan 78 | 1 June 79 | deserted |
| | Corpl | | | |
| Collins, Thomas | pt | | 16 Augt 80 | missing |
| Carty, Martin | do | | Dec 77 | deserted |
|    Joined June 79 | | | | |
|    left out Nov 77 | | | | |
| Childs, George | do | } Jan 77 | | |
| | Corpl | } 1 April 78 | } 1 Nov 80 | present |
| Callahan, John | pt | 11 May 77 | see Retahan | |
| Clark, Peter | Lieut | July 79 | | resigned |
| Cockran, George | pt | | 1 Nov 80 | present |
| Coffer, James | do | 28 Jan 77 | 1 Jan 80 | deserted |
| Cullip, William | do | | June 79 | left out the Roll |
| Clinch, John | do | | | deserted |
|    out April 78 | | | | |
| Cooenah, Thomas | do | 20 Mar 77 | 16 Aug 80 | missing |
| Collins, John | do | 3 May do | 3 May 80 | dischd. by Maj. |
| Children, John, (or Wm.) | do | do do | do do | do [Anderson |
| Cummins, Ephram | do | | 10 Jan 78 | deserted |
| Connally, Francis | do | 18 Sept 77 | 4 Nov 77 | do |
| Callahan, Daniel | do | 6 Aug do | 5 Mar 78 | do |
| Cooender, Charles | do | } 15 feb 78 | 31 Dec 79 | do |
| | Corpl | | | |
| | Sergt | | | |
| Conner, James | pt | | 16 Aug 80 | missing |
| Carter, James | do | 10 Jan 77 | 10 Jan 80 | discharged |
| Campbell, William | do | | July 78 | struck off |
| Collins, Jno., (Griffith) | do | | 16 Aug 80 | missing |
| Cooper, Charles | Drum | 20 Aprl 77 | mustd. dead May 78 | |
| | | | 16 Nov 77 | died Invalid corps |
| Cockran, Owen | pt | 12 May 77 | | |
| Clancy, Daniel | do | 15 June 77 | 1 Nov 80 | present |
| Crouch, Joseph | do | 10 April 77 | | |
| Crouch, John | pt | 10 April 77 | 1 Feby 80 | discharged |
| Connelly, Patrick | do | 31 Aug 77 | 16 Aug 80 | deserted |
| Conner, John | do | 20 April do | 20 do do | do |
| Crauford, Robert | do | 2 July do | 16 do do | missing |
| Callahan, Samuel | do | 2 Jan 77 | | |
| Crosby, James | do | 1 Mar 77 | 14 do do | deserted |
| Chaphey, John | do | | | do |
|    mus. Nov 77 | | | | |
| Carr, John | do | 24 Nov 77 | 1 Nov 80 | present |
| Cockey, Peter | Ensn | 10 April 77 | Feby 79 | died |

## MUSTERS OF MARYLAND TROOPS, VOL. I.

| NAMES. | RANK. | TIME OF SERVICE. | | REMARKS. |
|---|---|---|---|---|
| | | Enlisted. | Discharged. | |
| Clagett, Horatio | Lieut | 10 Dec 76 | Capt. 10 Oct 77 | |
| Colter, Antipas | Sergt | 2 April 77 | 2 April 80 | time expired |
| Clark, John | pt | nothing known of him | | |
| did not appear upon the Rolls till Dec 79 then mustd. deserted | | | | |
| Carroll, William | pt | | 20 Jany 79 | discharged |
| Cullomine, John | do | jd. 1 April 78 | 28 June 78 | killed |
| Carney, Edward | do | 28 April 78 | | |
| missing Monmouth 28 June 78, left out Jan & Feb 80, joined 26 July 79 | | | | |
| Clark, John | pt | 6 Feb 78 | Aug 78 | struck off |
| out Aug 78 | | | | [sion |
| Cheser, Bennett | do | 26 April 78 { 10 July 83, discharged on pen-{ Jan & Feb 80, transferred to In-valids | | |
| Collins, George | do | do   do | 15 June 81 | discharged |
| Coyle, Samuel | do | 3 April 78 | 1 Nov 80 | present |
| Joined Oct 80 | | | | |
| Cheek, Nathaniel | do | 12 feb 77 | 1 April 79 | discharged |
| Cox, William | do | 24 Jan 78 | 26 May 78 | deserted |
| Craig, John | do | 5 May 78 | joined Oct Rolls 80 | |
| Cassiday, Allen | do | 1 April 78 | 18 Aug 80 | deserted |
| Cassidy, Barney | do | 20   ditto | 16 Aug 80 | killed |
| Cox, John | do | 17   ditto | 28 April 80 | to Invalids, died 5 Sept 80 |
| Cooley, Joseph | pt | 16 April 78 | 16 Nov 78 | deserted |
| Cissell, Barton | do | 27   ditto | } 1 Nov 80 | present |
| musd. Corpl July 1780 | Corpl | 15 Jan 79 | } | |
| Chrispin, Alexander | pt | 18 Feb 78 | 16 Aug 80 | missing |
| Clements, Charles | do | 17 April 78 | 1 Nov 80 | present |
| Clemons, David | do | | | } |
| joined Feby Mar 79 | | | 21 June 80 | } deserted |
| Carter, Luke | do | 19 May 78 | 1 Nov 80 | present |
| Carpenter, John | do | 23   ditto | 4 April 79 | discharged |
| Cushman, James | do | 31   ditto | ditto | ditto |
| Carter, Justenian | do | 25   ditto | 11 Aug 78 | died |
| Carter, Jesse | do | 14   ditto | June 78 | deserted |
| Carr, William | do | 2 June 78 | 18 Aug 80 | do |
| Cullinane, Dennis | do | 28   ditto | 1 Feby 79 | discharged |
| Cook, Jeremiah | do | 28 Feby 77 | 31 Jan 80 | do |
| Culling, James | do | 25 April 78 | May 79 | left out the Rolls |
| Carthew, Edmund | do | do   do | 3 feb 80 | deserted |
| Clagett, John | do | do   do | 1 Nov 80 | present |
| Cooke, Richard | do | 24 May 78 | 16 Aug 80 | missing |
| Cowen, Thomas | do | 30 June 78 | 22 Jan 80 | deserted |
| Cannum, William | do | 1 June 78 | 13 Feby 79 | discharged |

## MUSTERS OF MARYLAND TROOPS, VOL. I.

| NAMES. | RANK. | TIME OF SERVICE. | | REMARKS. |
|---|---|---|---|---|
| | | Enlisted. | Discharged. | |
| Conway, Laurence | pt | 1 June 78 | 13 Feby 79 | discharged |
| Clements, Mark | do | 16 Mar 78 | 16 Aug 80 | missing |
| Coonehan, Thomas | do | 19 do do | 5 Jan 80 | deserted |
| Cavender, Charles | do | 28 April 78 | see Sergt. Cavender | |
| Clarke, Thomas [1] | do | 4 June 78 | 1 May 79 | died |
| Clark, Thomas [2] | do | | 1 Nov 80 | present |
| Jan 79 | Sergt | | | |
| pt. reinlisted 5 Mar 79 | | | | |
| Conner, John Clagett | pt | no account of him   last must. in 80 | | |
| joined 5 May 79 | | | | |
| Carrier, Thomas | do | 11 May 79 | 16 Aug 80 | missing |
| Chilmans, George | do | 23 April 79 | ditto | ditto |
| Carey, Richard | do | no account of him   musters in 80 | | |
| 1st must. Oct 79 | | | | |
| Collier, William | do | 3 June 78 | 15 Sept 82 | discharged |
| 1st must. Oct 79 | | | | |
| Carlton, Thomas | do | | Dec 79 | struck off |
| must. Oct & Nov, left out Dec Roll 79 | | | | |
| Cissill, John B. | Corpl | 15 Jan 79 | see the other side, Barton | |

### FROM OCTOBER ROLLS, 1780.

| | | | | |
|---|---|---|---|---|
| Carty, John | Drum | | 1 Nov 80 | present |
| Carr, Hezeka. | fife | 1 June 80 | do | do |
| Clark, Zacha. | Drum | | do | do |
| Cardiff, Thomas | pt | 4 feb 80 | do | do |
| Creamer, James | do | | do | do |
| Crauford, James | do | | do | do |
| Courts, John | do | 7 feb 80 | 16 Aug 80 | missing |
| Cunningham, Joseph | do | | do | do |
| Cissall, Nicholas | do | | do | do |
| Cooke, William | | | 7 dec 78 | discharged from Invalids |

### FOURTH REGIMENT.

| | | | | |
|---|---|---|---|---|
| Cromwell, Thomas [3] | Lieut | 20 May 77 | 10 Dec 79 | resigned |
| Clark, Richard | Sergt | 6 dec 76 | } 6 Dec 79 | discharged |
| | pt | 12 May 78 | | |
| Clark, Michael | pt | 7 Dec 76 | 16 Aug 80 | missing |
| Cavanaugh, William | do | | 9 July 78 | deserted |
| Cord, Roger [4] | Corpl | | 1 Aprl 78 | do |
| Craig, George | pt | 3 Aprl 77 | | joined |
| Clark, William | do | | 15 June 78 | discharged |

[1] Baly's.        [2] Brooke's.        [3] Oldham's.        [4] Norwood's.

## MUSTERS OF MARYLAND TROOPS, VOL. I.

| NAMES. | RANK. | TIME OF SERVICE. Enlisted. | Discharged. | REMARKS. |
|---|---|---|---|---|
| Cullimane, Jerema. | pt | | 28 July 79 | dead |
| Craig, John[1] | Corpl | } | 1 Nov 89 | present |
|     Oct 80, mustd. as private | } | | | |
| Craine, Michael | Drum | } | } June 78 | musd. not heard of |
| | private | } 1 Aug 78 | | |
| Crutchley, Benjamin | do | Jan 77 | 12 Jan 80 | discharged |
| Cypress, William | do | 1 ditto | 12 Jan 80 | ditto |
| Crosby, John[2] | Corpl | } 6 April 77 | } 1 Nov 80 | present |
| | private | } 1 Sept 78 | | |
| Chew, Richard[3] | Sergt | } | | |
| | Ensign | } | | |
| Cantwell, Richard | pt | | 24 June 80 | deserted |
| Coland, John[4] | Sergt | 5 dec 76 | 1 Nov 80 | present |
| Collins, Timothy[2] | Corpl | 19 feb 77 | } 12 feb 80 | time expired |
|     to Lansdale's 22 May 78 | Sergt | 11 feb 78 | | |
| Chatterton, John | pt | 6 dec 76 | 6 dec 79 | discharged |
| Corsey, Charles | do | | dead or deserted | |
| Cloney, John | do | 20 Aug 77 | 13 dec 79 | deserted |
| Carvin, James | do | 4 dec 76 | 10 dec 79 | discharged |
| Cooper, James[3] | do | 19 ditto | 5 feb 79 | to Invalids |
| Cook, Henry | do | 3 Jany 77 | 3 Jan 80 | discharged |
| Cain, (or Kain), Michael | do | 28 May 77 | 28 May 80 | ditto for inability |
| Crabb, Jeremiah | Lieut | | 1 April 78 | resigned |
| Chamberlain, Ben. | pt | 27 April 77 | 1 Nov 80 | present |
| Colegate, John[5] | Ensign | } | } 1 May 80 | resigned |
| | Lieut | } 4 Aug 78 | | |
| Clark, James | Sergt | } 25 Mar 77 | } | |
| | S. Major | } 10 feb 78 | } 25 Mar 80 | time expired |
| Carter, William | pt | 29 July 77 | 1 Nov 80 | present |
| Carroll, Joseph | pt | 9 Aug 77 | 9 Aug 80 | discharged |
| Clark, Richard | do | 14 April 77 | 14 April 80 | do |
| Callahan, William | do | 24 Mar 77 | 1 April 79 | deserted |
| Chadwick, William | do | 5 April 77 | 5 April 80 | discharged, same person, see Shadwick |
| Congleton, William[6] | do | 17 Mar 78 | Aug 78 | died |
| Conner, William, (or Jas.) | do | 21 April 78 | 25 Mar 79 | deserted |
| Cregan, Lawrence[7] | do | 26 do do | 16 Aug 80 | missing |
| Cathagin, Annanias[2] | do | 22 Apl 78 | 1 Nov 80 | present |
| Cross, Charles[3] | do | 3 do do | } 1 Nov 80 | present |
|     Reduced 13 Oct 80, (Sellman's) | Corpl | 1 June 80 | } | |

[1] Godman's.  [2] Lansdale's.  [3] Sellman's.  [4] Spurrier's.  [5] Burgess'.  [6] Oldham's.  [7] Norwood's.

## MUSTERS OF MARYLAND TROOPS, VOL. I.

| NAMES. | RANK. | TIME OF SERVICE. Enlisted. | Discharged. | REMARKS. |
|---|---|---|---|---|
| Cruell, John | pt | 24 April 78 | 1 Sept 78 | discharged |
| Cole, Joseph[1] | do | 1 April 78 | 5 Jan 80 | deserted |
| Smith's late Spurrier's. | | | | |
| Craig, John | do | 6 May 78 | 17 May 80 | do |
| Catchsides, Abm. | do | do  do | 1 Nov 80 | present |
| Crosby, George[2] | do | 17 feb 78 | 1 April 80 | deserted |
| (Riely's late | | | | |
| Crosby, Richard | do | 25 Mar 78 | 16 Aug 80 | missing |
| Craig, John | do | 6 May 78 | 1 Nov 80 | present |
| Joined Oct 80 | | | | |
| Cain, Edward | do | 1  do do | 16 Aug 80 | missing |
| Cummins, Richard[3] | Corpl | 6 dec 76 | 6 dec 79 | discharged |
| Cail, Robert | pt | 11 May 78 | dead or deserted | |
| Cappock, Simons[4] | do | 14  do do | 16 July 79 | died |
| Clinton, Thomas[5] | do | 1 July 78 | 1 Nov 80 present | } to Godman's and promoted to fifer 1 Aug 78 |
| Crampton, James[6] | do | 19 May 78 | 15 Nov 78 | to invalids |
| Chivers, Andrew | do | 18 May 78 | 30 June 80 | deserted |
| Cupit, John | do | 13 May 78 | 3 Sept 79 | do |
| Carroll, Dennis[1] | do | 21 May 78 | 1 April 80 | do |
| Coleman, Michael[2] | do | 16 April 78 | 10 Jan 78 | do |
| Callahan, Michael | do | 5 do  do | 1 Nov 80 | present |
| Chevick, John[7] | do | 12 May 78 | July 80 | present |
| Burgess', June 78 | | | | |
| Clinton, Thomas[8] | fife | see above, Lansdale's Co. | | |
| Godman's, July 78 | | | | |
| Cain, Robert[3] | pt | 11 May 78 | dec 79 | deserted |
| Caton, William[2] | do | 15 June 79 | April 80 | to invalids |
| Cheney, Richard[3] | do | | Nov 79 | deserted |
| Colegate, Asaph[5] | do | 29 feb 80 | 1 Nov 80 | present |

### FROM INVALIDS' RETURN.

| | | | | |
|---|---|---|---|---|
| Conner, Dennis | Sergt | 4 Aug 80 | 27 May 79 | discharged |

### RAWLINGS' REGIMENT.

| | | | | |
|---|---|---|---|---|
| Colman, John | pt | 16 July 76 | | |
| Crockett, John | do | 28 Aug 76 | | |
| Callender, John | do | 17 July | 11 July 79 | discharged |
| Chinea, Adam S. | do | 1 Aug 76 | | |
| Cooper, John | do | 17 ditto | 9 Aug 79 | discharged |
| Corbett, Jesse | do | 15 ditto | | |

[1] Lt. Smith's.   [2] Riley's.   [3] Oldham's.   [4] Norwood's.   [5] Lansdale's.   [6] Sellman's.
[7] Burgess'.   [8] Godman's.

## MUSTERS OF MARYLAND TROOPS, VOL. I.

| NAMES. | RANK. | TIME OF SERVICE. Enlisted. | Discharged. | REMARKS. |
|---|---|---|---|---|
| Cartrell, John | pt | 8 Oct 76 | | |
| Cooper, William | do | 15 July 76 | 15 July 79 | discharged |
| Campbell, Pat. | do | 10 Oct 76 | 20 Oct 76 | deserted |
| Crawford, Jno. | Sergt | | 1 July 79 | discharged |
| Cartrill, William | pt | | 9 Augt 79 | do |
| Collins, John | do | | | |
| Collins, Patrick | do | 9 Aug 76 | 9 Aug 79 | do |
| Cardonis, Jno. | do | 25 Mar | | |
| Conwell, Arthur | do | | 9 Oct 79 | do |
| Cockran, Jno. | do | | | |
| | Corpl | 1 Sept | | |
| Cockindall, Elijh. | pt | 1 Oct 77 | | |
| Craig, Thomas | do | Aug 76 | | |
| Cravin, Jeremiah | | | 9 Aug 79 | do |
| Chinworth, Jno. | Sergt | | 9 Aug 79 | discharged |
| Chinworth, Arthur | Corpl | | do | do |
| Crumm, Adam | pt | | 1 July 79 | do |
| Carly, Dennis | do | | | |
| Coone, Adam | do | | 15 July | killed |
| Crawford, Robt. | Corpl | 2 Oct | | |
| Connally, Wm. | pt | 18 Mar | | |
| Carmichael, Jno. | do | 28 ditto | 6 April | discharged |
| Connally, Philip | do | 6 April | | |
| Cunningham, Thos. | do | 15 do | | |
| Carpenter, Chrisn. | do | 12 Aug | | |
| Cooper, Jno., 6 Mo. | Sergt | | | |
| Clark, Jos.,    ditto | pt | | | |
| Christie, Jas.,   do | do | | | |
| Craig, Saml.,   do | do | | | |

### FIRST REGIMENT.

| NAMES. | RANK. | Enlisted. | Discharged. | REMARKS. |
|---|---|---|---|---|
| Dignam, Christn. | pt | 10 Dec 76 | 21 Jan 78 | deserted |
| Devine, Dennis | do | do | 1 Nov 80 | present |
| Davis, William | do | 29 April 77 | | |
| Davis, Richard | do | 24 Jan 77 | | |
| Douglass, Igns. | Sergt | 20 Feby 77 | 25 Dec 79 | discharged |
| Downing, Natl. | pt | 10 Dec 76 | 27 do do | ditto |
| Dyer, Jonathan | do | 26 Mar 77 | 13 July 80 | deserted |
| Daly, James | do | 10 Dec 76 | 24 May 77 | do |
| Dewell, Thomas | do | 7 Apl 77 | | |
| Dutton, Notley | do | 29 Mar 77 | see below | |
| Devaun, James | do | 10 Dec 76 | 27 dec 79 | discharged |
| Donovan, Jeremh. | do | 22 Apl 77 | 17 Dec 77 | deserted |

## MUSTERS OF MARYLAND TROOPS, VOL. I.

| NAMES. | RANK. | TIME OF SERVICE. Enlisted. | Discharged. | REMARKS. |
|---|---|---|---|---|
| Dugan, Danl. | pt | 1 Apl 77 | | deserted |
| Downes, James | do | 8 ditto | | do |
| Davis, William | do | 10 Mar 77 | 20 Apl 77 | died |
| Downing, Saml. | do | 16 do | 16 Mar 80 | discharged |
| Dunn, Dennis | do | 18 Mar 78 | 3 dec 78 | deserted |
| Dawkins, Charles | Sergt | 25 Aprl 78 | 1 Nov 80 | present |
| Dodson, John | pt | 5 feb 78 | 11 June 78 | discharged |
| Davidson, James | do | 20 April 78 | 25 Jan 80 | prisoner |
| Dohorty, Jesse | do | 7 May 78 | | |
| Denny, Peter | do | 20 May 78 | 30 Aug 78 | deserted |
| Davis, Enus | 9 mos. do | 21 ditto | 5 April 79 | discharged |
| Dutton, Thomas | do do | 5 June 78 | 1 Nov 80 | reinlisted |
| Dutton, Notley | 3 yrs. do | 29 Mar 78 | 24 May 79 | discharged |
| Delozier, Wm. | 9 mos. do | 4 June 78 | 14 Feby 79 | ditto |
| Dunning, Dennis | pt | 17 dec 78 | 1 Nov 80 | present |
| | Drum | 1 April 79 | | |
| Davaun, Michael | pt | | Feby 79 | discharged |
| Donovan, (or Dennis), Paul | do | 9 June 79 | 8 July 79 | deserted |
| Dixon, John | | 28 Aprl 79 | 1 Nov 80 | present |
| Denear, Francis | | 8 June 79 | do | do |
| Ducey, William | | do | July 79 | deserted |
| Devorah, Butes | | 29 do | 1 Nov 80 | sick |
| Dortch, William | | 25 June 80 | do | present |
| Dixon, Hanry | | 7 feb 80 | do | do |
| Doyle, Martin | Corpl | | 3 Aug 80 | deserted 8 feby 81 discharged |

### SECOND REGIMENT.

| NAMES. | RANK. | Enlisted. | Discharged. | REMARKS. |
|---|---|---|---|---|
| Devereaux, Jno.,(or James) | Sergt | | 10 Jan 80 | discharged |
| Devinns, Emanl. | pt | | 12 dec 79 | ditto |
| Dawson, William | do | | 10 Jan 80 | ditto |
| Duel, Charles | do | | 14 June 80 | deserted |
| Dent, Hatch | Capt | 17 Apl 77 | | resigned |
| Duvall, Saml. | pt | | 10 Jan 80 | discharged |
| Duvall, Joseph | do | 4 feb 77 | 4 feb 80 | ditto |
| Dowling, James | do | | 10 Jan 80 | ditto |
| Dyer, Edward | Lieut ⎱ B. Q. Master ⎰ Capt ⎰ | 10 April 77 ⎱ Jany 79 ⎰ | | |
| Dyer, Thomas | pt | 22 Jany 77 | time elaps'd, | left out Rolls |
| | Sergt | 1 May 78 | | Jany 80 |
| Drake, Richard | pt | 27 April 77 | Jan 79 | left out |
| Davis, William | Corpl | | 9 Sept 78 | died |
| Dayly, James | pt | | 29 dec 77 | ditto |

## MUSTERS OF MARYLAND TROOPS, VOL. I.

| NAMES. | RANK. | TIME OF SERVICE. Enlisted. | Discharged. | REMARKS. |
|---|---|---|---|---|
| Davidson, John | Capt<br>Major | } 10 dec 76 } | | |
| Duling, (or Duley), Nathl. | pt | | 10 Jan 80 | discharged |
| Dean, Edward | do | 16 May 78 | feb 80 | ditto |
| Dulany, James | do | 24 Jan do | July 80 | ditto |
| Deal, Noble | do | 14 feb do | 1 July 78 | deserted |
| Dorsey, Elie | Capt | 10 dec 76 | left out of the musters Mar 79, | |
| | | not having assigned any cause for his absence since Sept 78 | | |
| Day, John | pt | 2 April 78 | 18 June 79 | deserted |
| Draper, John | do | 10 May 78 | Jan 79 | discharged, being |
| Daily, Thomas | do | 16 ditto | 27 Oct 79 | died  [a servant |
| Drury, Robt. B. | do | | 3 April 79 | discharged |
| Dent, George | do | 25 May 78 | ditto | ditto |
| Drury, Joseph | do | 24 ditto | ditto | ditto |
| Davidson, Geo. | do | 6 July 78 | 23 feb 79 | ditto |
| Dennis, Dunick | do | | 12 dec 79 | ditto |
| Dent, John | do | 20 May 78 | 78 | died in Town |
| Devin, James | do | 14 ditto | 3 April 79 | discharged |
| Debora, Jacobus | do | | } | |
| | fife | 1 Mar 79 | | |
| | private | 1 Mar 80 | } 1 Nov 80 | present |
| Dailey, John | pt | | 17 June 79 | deserted |
| 1st mus. June 79 | | | | |
| Duvall, Edward | Lieut<br>Capt | 17 Aprl 77 | } 16 Augt 80 | killed Camden |
| Dowes, William | pt | 8 June 79 | never joined | |
| muster Nov 79, never appeared | | | | |
| Denston, John  June 80 | pt | | 1 Nov 80 | present |
| Dusky, Jonathn.  June 80 | do | sick Maryland, 1 Nov 80 | | |

### THIRD REGIMENT.—*Beginning* ——

| NAMES. | RANK. | Enlisted. | Discharged. | REMARKS. |
|---|---|---|---|---|
| Deale, John | pt | 13 feb 77 | 1 Jan 78 | deserted |
| Dolton, Peter | do | | 16 Augt 80 | missing |
| Dunkin, John | do | | 19 July 80 | deserted |
| Donovan, Peter | do | 22 April 77 | 28 April 80 | discharged |
| Donaldson, Phil. | do | 3 May 77 | 8 Nov 79 | deserted |
| Duvall, Isaac | Ensn<br>Lieut | } | | |
| Dudley, Joseph | pt | | 26 Sept 80 | ditto |
| Dixon, George | do | 27 April 77 | 1 Nov 80 | present |
| Dillon, William | do<br>Corpl | 1 May 77<br>1 April 79 | } 1 Nov 80 | } ditto |
| Deaver, John | Lieut | 10 Dec 76 | 8 April 79 | resigned |

## MUSTERS OF MARYLAND TROOPS, VOL. I.

| NAMES. | RANK. | TIME OF SERVICE. | | REMARKS. |
|---|---|---|---|---|
| | | Enlisted. | Discharged. | |
| Dommit, William | pt | 8 Sept 77 | 7 July 78 | deserted |
| Downey, Dennis | do | ⎰ 13 Mar 77 | ⎱ Dec 79 | struck off |
| left out Dec Roll 79 | Sergt | ⎱ 10 Oct 77 | ⎰ April 80 | discharged |
| Dyer, John | pt | Jan 77 | 1 Nov 80 | present |
| Doyer, Peter | do | | 7 dec 79 | died |
| Duvall, George | pt | 12 Jan 77 | 12 Jan 80 | discharged |
| Dollison, James | do | | Augt 80 | deserted |
| Draper, Thomas | do | | | do |
| Denshon, James | Corpl | 30 Mar 77 | ⎱ Sept 78 | discharged |
| private Sept 78 | Sergt | 1 Mar 80 | | |
| Denton, James | pt | 30 June 77 | 18 Augt 80 | deserted |
| Deaver, Aquilla | do | 14 May 77 | 1 Nov 80 | present |
| Dean, George | do | 26 Nov 77 | 18 Oct 79 | deserted |
| Dyer, Walter | Sergt | 26 June 77 | 26 Jan 80 | promoted |
| Dunnington, Wm. | pt | 6 April 77 | Re-enlisted again | |
| Daily, Philip | do | | 31 mar 78 | discharged |
| Dashiell, Wm. | Surgn | | 5 dec 80 | died at Baltimore |
| Denwood, Levin | Mate | (see 7th Regt. Surgeon) | | |
| Dutton, George | pt | 25 April 78 | June 78 | deserted |
| Ducater, Jno. | do | 24 ditto | 5 feb 79 | died |
| Davis, Jno. | do | 13 May 78 | 16 Aug 80 | killed |
| Dolby, Daniel | do | | 12 July 80 | deserted |
| Joined 22 July 78 | | | | |
| Dyer, James | do | 22 May 78 | | . |
| Davis, Jno., (Bailey) | do | 28 April 78 | 16 dec 78 | died |
| Dunn, Thomas | do | do | 1 June 79 | discharged |
| Dennis, Edward | do | 27 do | 1 Nov 80 | prisoner |
| Dailey, Patk. | do | 30 do | 1 Jan 80 | off the Rolls |
| Davis, Edward | do | 28 May 78 | 16 Augt 80 | missing |
| Dimsey, Luke | pt | 19 May 78 | 1 Nov 80 | present |
| Dennison, Jas. | do | 3 June 78 | May 79 | time expired |
| Daken, James | do | 29 May 78 | not musterd. 1780 | |
| Daniel, Jno. Natl. | do | 20 ditto | 16 Augt 80 | missing |
| Dent, Jno. | do | 1 May 77 | not musterd. 1780 | |
| Deaver, William | do | 1 July 78 | ditto   ditto | |
| Day, Jacob | do | 14 May 78 | 1 Nov 80 | present |
| Driver, John | do | 12 May 78 | 27 Jan 80 | deserted |
| Dean, John | do | ⎰ not mustered 1780 | | |
| first must. feb 79 | | ⎱ | | |
| Downey, John | do | | 10 dec 79 | deserted, (joined Sept 79) |
| Dorsey, Joshua | do | not mustered 1780 | | . |
| 1st must. July 79 | | | | |

## MUSTERS OF MARYLAND TROOPS, VOL. I.

| NAMES. | RANK. | TIME OF SERVICE. Enlisted. | Discharged. | REMARKS. |
|---|---|---|---|---|

### FROM OCTOBER MUSTER, 1780.

| | | | | |
|---|---|---|---|---|
| Derrington, Francis | pt | on the Roll for Oct 80, left out Nov 80 | | |
| Drudges, Thomas | do | 2 feb 80 | 1 Nov 80 | present |
| Dunnington, Jer. | do | left sick at Salsbury, Aug 80 | | |
| Demay, John | do | | 16 Aug 80 | missing |
| Dunington, Wm. | do | | 1 Aug 80 | deserted |
| Douglass, James | do | | 16 Aug 80 | killed |
| Drury, John | do | | do | missing |
| Davids, C. W. | Sergt | 77 | 83 deserted from Invalids | |
| Dugan, Paul Md. list. | | 1 April 77 | 26 Aug 80 discharged, Invalids | |
| Dewire, James | | 26 April 80 to Invalids 1 Sept 82, retired on pension | | |

### FOURTH REGIMENT.—*Beginning December, 1777.*

| | | | | |
|---|---|---|---|---|
| Drishell, Jeremiah[1] | pt | 6 Dec 76 | | |
| Dunnevan, (or Dunnegan), John | do | 28 June 77 } | | |
| Joined again Oct 80 | | | | |
| Delany, Edward | do | 16 dec 76 | 16 dec 79 | discharged |
| Dunster, John[2] | do | | 1 June 79 | to Invalids |
| 22 Aprl 80 musd. in Invalids to have joined his Regt., not so 1 Nov 80 | | | | |
| Dorsey, Nicholas | Lieut | 17 April 77 | 10 Nov 78 | resigned |
| Denbugh, Wm.[3] | pt | | | deserted |
| Dye, William | do | detained in Maryland March 1778 | | |
| Dodson, Michael[4] | do | { 20 April 77 | | |
| | Corpl | { 1 Nov 78 } | 20 April 80 | discharged |
| | pt | { 15 June 79 } | | |
| Downes, William[5] | do | 19 Aug 77 | 16 Aug 80 | missing |
| Dorhorty, Francis | do | | 26 Feb 78 | deserted |
| Davis, Thomas[6] | do | 7 Mar 77 | 16 Aug 80 | missing |
| Dawson, James | do | 20 Aug 77 | June 79 | left out Roll, joined and discharged 23 Feby 81 |
| Duffey, Michael | do | 25 July 77 | transfd. to Invalids 1 dec 78, 15 Sep 82 dischd. | |
| Doran, Barnaba[2] | do | | 16 Aug 80 | missing |
| Doyall, Thomas[7] | do | 4 feb 78 | 1 Nov 80 | present |
| Dohorty, Arthur[2] | do | 30 April 78 | Sept 80 | deserted |
| Deliazon, Peter[8] | do | 21 do | 1 Nov 80 | present |
| Smith's, late Spurrier's | | | | |
| Darling, Robert[9] | do | 25 do | do | do |
| · to Belt's, joined June 79 | | | | |

[1] Oldham's. [2] Norwood's. [3] Godman's. [4] Lansdale's. [5] Spurrier's. [6] Burgess'. [7] Bowie's.
[8] Lt. Smith's. [9] Belt's.

## MUSTERS OF MARYLAND TROOPS, VOL. I.

| NAMES. | RANK. | TIME OF SERVICE. Enlisted. | Discharged. | REMARKS. |
|---|---|---|---|---|
| Daffin, James | Sergt | 8 April 78 | 1 Nov 80 | present |
| Dwyer, Thomas[1] | Drum | 16 Mar 78 | | |
| Riely's late Bowie's | private | 1 June 78 | 3 July 80 | deserted |
| Durnor, Thomas[2] | do | 10 Jan 78 | 16 Aug 80 | missing |
| Dennison, Patk. | do | 4 June 78 | 20 Jan 80 | deserted, joined |
| Dougherty, John[3] | do | | | |
| prisoner 22 Aug 77, joined 22 July 78 | | | 20 dec 78 | do |
| Dougherty, Edward[4] | pt | 13 May 78 | | |
| | Corpl | 1 Aug 79 | | |
| | Sergt | 1 Jan 80 | 1 Nov 80 | present |
| Davis, John | pt | 6 dec 76 | | |
| prisr. 22 Aug 77, joined 23 June 78, Corpl 6 dec 79, Sergt 1 Jan 80. July 80 deserted | | | | |
| Dease, Michael[5] | pt | 30 Aprl 78 | 5 July 80 | deserted |
| Dowen, Nicholas | do | 11 May 78 | 23 June 79 | ditto |
| Denmass, Wm.[6] | fifer | 22 April 78 | 11 June 80 | ditto |
| Burgess', June 78 | | | | |
| Derry, Michal[5] | pt | | | |
| Lt. Smith's, Sept 78 | | | | |
| from Col Stewart's Pennsa. Regt. | | to Pennsa. Line, 28 July 79 | | [Regt. |
| Durbinn, John | pt | 6 Sept 78 | 3 May 79 | transfd. to Hazen's |
| Dorsey, Charles | do | 19 feb 77 | | |
| | Corpl | 1 July 79 | 19 Feby 80 | discharged |
| Devire, Darby[1] | pt | 3 May 78 | 16 Aug 80 | missing |
| Deane, Francis[7] | fifer | 2 Sept 79 | dead or deserted | |
| Drowns, Robert[1] | Drum | 28 Aug 79 | left out after April 80 | |
| | private | Mar 80 | | |
| Dean, John[2] | Major | 11 Mar 78 | | |
| Douglass, William[8] | fife | | 1 Nov 80 | present |
| mus. May & June 80 | | | | |

### RAWLINGS' REGIMENT.

| NAMES. | RANK. | Enlisted. | Discharged. | REMARKS. |
|---|---|---|---|---|
| Denniston, James | Drum | 17 Aug 76 | | for war |
| Dytche, Peter | pt | 27 July 76 | | |
| Devenport, Adam | do | | 9 Aug 79 | discharged |
| Davis, Levi | | | | |
| Davoir, Cornelius | | | 9 Aprl | deserted |
| Dewist, Francis | | | | |
| Dowdon, James | | | | |
| Debrular, John | | | 9 Augt 79 | discharged |
| Dennis, Henry | | | | |
| Davis, Joseph | pt | | ditto | ditto |
| Davis, David | do | | 6 July | do |
| Deacon, Pierce | do | 13 Aprl 79 | | |
| Denaho, John | do | 7 May | | |
| Davis, James | do | 27 Mar | | |

[1] Riely's. [2] Oldham's. [3] Godman's. [4] Lansdale's. [5] Lt. Smith's. [6] Burgess'. [7] Selman's. [8] Spurrier's.

8

## MUSTERS OF MARYLAND TROOPS, VOL. I.

| NAMES. | RANK. | TIME OF SERVICE. Enlisted. | Discharged. | REMARKS. |
|---|---|---|---|---|

### FIRST REGIMENT.

| NAMES. | RANK. | Enlisted. | Discharged. | REMARKS. |
|---|---|---|---|---|
| Elliott, Thomas | pt | 10 dec 76 | 27 dec 79 | discharged |
| Edwards, Edward | do | do | 1 Nov 80 | present |
| Eadlin, John | do | do | 27 dec 79 | discharged |
| Ewing, Nathanl. | Capt | do | 16 Mar 79 | resigned |
| Edelin, Clement | Sergt | do | 27 Dec 79 | discharged |
| Evans, William | pt | do | 27 Nov 77 | deserted |
| Enwright, John | do | do | 15 Aprl 77 | ex. for A.Hughes |
| Eadlin, Edward | do | do | 27 Dec 79 | discharged |
| Eltham, John | do | 28 feb 78 | } 16 Aug 80 | prisoner |
|  | Corpl | 27 feb 80 | | |
| Ellicott, Edward | pt | 13 May 78 | 1 Nov 80 | present    [son |
| Everett, Elisha | do | 12 Mar 78 | 18 Aprl 79 | exchd. for Jeffer- |
| Ennis, George | | | 10 June 78 | deserted |

### SECOND REGIMENT.—*Beginning with the Muster Rolls for January,* 1778.

| NAMES. | RANK. | Enlisted. | Discharged. | REMARKS. |
|---|---|---|---|---|
| Ewing, Samuel | P. M. | 17 April 77 | 1 July 80 | deserted |
| Edgerly, Edward | Adjt | } 3 April 77 | } | |
|  | Lieut | 27 May 78 | | |
| Emmory, John | pt | 3 May 77 | Mar 80 | discharged |
| Ellis, Robert | do | 4 Mar 77 | 14 April 79 | deserted |
| Ellis, Barnard | do | | Jan 78 | left out |
| Evans, Peregrine | do | 10 Jan 77 | } 1 Nov 80 | present |
| Sergt 10 Jany 80 | Corpl | 1 May 78 | | |
| Ewing, James | Lieut | 17 April 77 | | |
| Eccleston, John | Capt | } 10 dec 76 | } | |
| June 79 mustered pd. | Major | 10 dec 77 | | |
| Easom, Bartholm. | pt | } 18 May 78 | } 1 Nov 80 | present |
|  | Corpl | 1 July 80 | | |
| Easom, Joseph | pt | ditto | 1 July 78 | deserted |
| Everitt, Joseph | do | 28 May 78 | 18 Dec 78 | discharged |
| Ellis, Michael | fife | 3 Nov 78 | 1 Nov 80 | present |
| Elbon, Mathew[1] | pt | 4 May 79 | 16 Aug 80 | missing |
| First must. July 79 | | | | |
| Elbon, Nathanl. | do | 14 June 79 | 1 Nov 80 | present |
| Eddy, James[2] | see James Ady | | | |
| First must. July 79 | | | | |
| Ervine, Abram | see Irvine | | | |

### THIRD REGIMENT.—*Beginning* 1777.

| NAMES. | RANK. | Enlisted. | Discharged. | REMARKS. |
|---|---|---|---|---|
| Edwards, John | Sergt | | | |
|  | Sergt. Major | 11 Aug 77 | 28 Aug 78 | } Comy. Dept. |
| transfd. to Comy. dept. | | 28 Aug 78 | | |

## MUSTERS OF MARYLAND TROOPS, VOL. I.

| NAMES. | RANK. | TIME OF SERVICE. Enlisted. | Discharged. | REMARKS. |
|---|---|---|---|---|
| Ecort, Godfrey | pt | 9 May 77 | dead or deserted | |
| Elliott, Robert | do | 2 April 77 | ditto    ditto | |
| Evans, Thomas | do | 1 Jan 77 | 1 Nov 80 | present |
| English, William | do | 8 Mar 78 | 6 Sept 79 | deserted |
| Evans, William | do | | 16 May 78 | dead |
| Elliott, Thomas | do | 1 June 78 | 18 Aug 80 | joined |
| Edelin, Basil | Corpl | 27 May 78 | discharged, time out | |
| Edelin, George | do | 30 May 78 | 13 feb 79 | discharged |
| Edelin, Henry | do | ditto | | |
| rein. 12 feb 79, 14 feb 79 furld. | | | } April and May 79, left out | |
| English, James | F. Major | 1 May 79 | 16 Aug 80 | prisoner |
| English, Samuel | pt | must. Oct and Nov 79. | | Struck off Dec 79, left out Dec Roll 79 |

### FOURTH REGIMENT.—*Beginning Dec.,* 1777.

| NAMES. | RANK. | Enlisted. | Discharged. | REMARKS. |
|---|---|---|---|---|
| Eaton, William[1] | pt | | April 78 | left off the Rolls |
| Ellis, John[2] | do | 23 Aug 77 | 3 Jan 79 | deserted |
| Elliott, Samuel[3] | do | 3 Oct 77 | 3 Oct 80 | discharged |
| Ennis, Thomas[4] | do | 14 May 77 | 14 Mar 80 | ditto |
| Ellis, William[2] | pt | 24 Jan 78 | 1 nov 80 | present |
| Eyre, John[5] | do | } 18 April 78 } 14 May 80 | | deserted |
| | Corpl | } 1 June 78 } | | |
| Evins, Edward[2] | pt | 24 feb 78 | 1 nov 80 | present |
| Evins, William | do | 26 ditto | ditto | ditto |
| Edwards, Thomas[6] | Sergt | 20 Jan 78 | } 1 Nov 80 | ditto |
| out May and June 80 | Q.M.Sergt | 1 May 80 | } | |
| Eades, Thomas[7] | pt | 6 may 78 | 16 Aug 80 | missing |
| Ellwood, Richard | do | 3   do | do | do |
| Easton, John[3] | do | 12   do | do | do |
| Emanuel, Peters[6] | do | 21 Aprl 78 | 4 Nov 78 | deserted |
| Eyles, Samuel[9] | do | 6 July 78 | 11 May 80 } July 80 | do   do |
| England, (or Ingle), Wm., or Ingle[2] | do | 8 May 79 | 1 Nov 80 | present |

### RAWLINGS' REGIMENT.

| NAMES. | RANK. | Enlisted. | Discharged. | REMARKS. |
|---|---|---|---|---|
| Eaton, William | pt | | 9 Aug 79 | discharged |
| Evans, John | Corpl | | | |
| Earls, Richard | Drum | | | |
| Eakins, Archd.   6 mo. | pt | 4 May 79 | | |
| Eakins, Solomon   do | do | 9 April 79 | | |
| Ellis, Thomas   do | do | 6 Mar 79 | 4 May 79 | deserted |

[1] Oldham's.   [2] Lansdale's.   [3] Sellman's.   [4] Spurrier's.   [5] Norwood's.   [6] Burgess'.
[7] Riely's.   [8] Lt. Smith's.

## MUSTERS OF MARYLAND TROOPS, VOL. I.

| NAMES. | RANK. | TIME OF SERVICE. Enlisted. | Discharged. | REMARKS. |
|---|---|---|---|---|
| | | **FIRST REGIMENT.** | | |
| Flora, Jacob | pt | 10 Dec 76 | 1 Nov 80 | present |
| Floharty, Stephen | | 10 Dec 76 | | } |
| | Corpl | 1 Aug 79 | 27 dec 79 | } discharged |
| Fairbrother, Francis | do | 10 Dec 76 | | hospital |
| Fitzsimmons, Henry | | 13 Mar 77 | 22 Aug | prisoner } |
| | | 17 April 78, joined | 13 Mar 80 | discharged } |
| Fulton, Alexander | pt | | 27 dec 79 | ditto |
| Flemming, Jno. | do | 10 dec 76 | 20 Nov 77 | died |
| Ford, Joseph | Capt | 10 dec 76 | | resigned |
| Fernandis, Jas. | Lieut | do | | |
| | Capt | | 15 July 79 | resigned |
| Francois, John | pt | 1 Jan 78 | 1 Nov 80 | present |
| Franklin, Thos. | do | 2 feb 78 | 1 Nov 80 | sick Jersey |
| Fowler, Henry | do | 23 May 78 | 5 April 79 | discharged |
| Fresh, Stephen | do | 20 do | 6 July 79 | deserted |
| joined 20 Sept 79 | | 1 Nov 80 | | present } |
| Fowler, Joseph | pt | 20 Jan 78 | 1 Nov 80 | do |
| Ford, Archd. . | do | 30 May 78 | 14 Feby 79 | discharged |
| Fisher, William | do | 17 do | 1 Nov 80 | present |
| Flint, James | do | 1 June 79 | 4 Jan 80 | deserted |
| Fishwater, Ben. | Corpl | 1 June 79 | } | |
| | Sergt | June 80 | } 1 Nov 80 | present |
| Fowler, Jonathan | pt | 22 April 79 | 16 Aug 80 | missing, joined |
| Ford, John | Mu'n | June 80 | 12 Aug 80 | deserted |

### SECOND REGIMENT.—*Beginning Jany.*, 1778.

| NAMES. | RANK. | Enlisted. | Discharged. | REMARKS. |
|---|---|---|---|---|
| Finch, George | pt | 8 Jan 77 | 10 Jan 80 | discharged |
| Finlason, George | do | 2 Aprl 77 | 1 Nov 80 | present |
| Ferguson, Robt. | do | 18 do | 1 April 79 | discharged |
| Fowler, William | do | nothing known of him 78 Jan | | |
| French, Martin | do | 10 Jan 77 | 10 Jan 80 | discharged |
| Foumel, William | do | | July 80 | sick Jersey |
| Freeman, Jacob | do | | 10 Jan 80 | discharged |
| Faulkner, Amos | do | | 25 June 78 | deserted |
| Flynn, Edward | Corpl | | 22 Jan | ditto |
| Forman, Jacob | pt | } June 80 | 16 Aug 80 | missing |
| | Corpl | } | | |
| Ford, Hezekiah | Sergt | } | | |
| | Ensign | } 1 Sept 77 | | |
| | Lieut | } first muster June 79 | Adj., 10 June 79 | |
| Frazier, Hobart | pt | 1 feb 78 | 1 July 78 | deserted |
| Foxwell, Charles | do | | do | do |

## MUSTERS OF MARYLAND TROOPS, VOL. I.

| NAMES. | RANK. | TIME OF SERVICE. Enlisted. | Discharged. | REMARKS. |
|---|---|---|---|---|
| Fowler, John | pt | 4 April 78 | April 78 | struck off |
| left out of must. for April 78 | | | | |
| Frederick, Bennet | fife | 27 Mar 78 | | see B |
| Fipps, Thomas | pt | 6 May 78 | 1 Nov 80 | present see |
| Phips in letter P | | | | |
| Farrill, James | pt | 25 Mar 78 | 1 Nov 80 | present |
| Farrill, Thomas | do | 2 do | 7 dec 79 | deserted |
| Fricker, John | do | 13 do  Corpl., 1 mar 79 | | dead or deserted |
| Fitzpatrick, Lawrce. | do | 29 Aprl 78 | 27 feb 79 | deserted } |
| private 1 Nov 78 | Corpl | | | |
| Fitzgerald, Jas. | pt | 3 do | 1 Nov 80 | present |
| Forly, William | do | 13 May 78 | do | do |
| Fenwick, Francis | do | 29 do | 3 Aprl 79 | discharged |
| French, Stephen | do | 25 do | do | do |
| Farrand, Patk. | do | | 10 Jan 80 | do |
| Freeman, Francis | do | do | 1 Nov 80 | present |
| Flanegan, Henry | do | | 3 Aprl 79 | discharged |
| Fulsom, John | do | | 1 Nov 80 | sick  Maryd. |
| Fergusson, Jno. | do | 1 Aprl 79 | 16 Aug 80 | prisoner |
| Franklin, Edwd. | do | | 10 Jan 80 | dischd., joined 4 May 79 |

### THIRD REGIMENT.—*Beginning* 1777.

| NAMES. | RANK. | TIME OF SERVICE. Enlisted. | Discharged. | REMARKS. |
|---|---|---|---|---|
| Franklin, Francis | pt | 23 Aprl 77 | | dead or deserted |
| Florence, Lewis | do | 17 do | | do |
| Farmer, Samuel | Ensign | | | |
| | Lieut | | 16 Aug 80 | wounded prisoner |
| Farmer, Nathl. | Sergt | | Mar 79 | left out the Roll |
| Fleming, Richard | pt | | 15 Mar 78 | deserted |
| Flanagan, Wm. | fifer | 6 Aprl 77 | } 2 Aprl 80 | time expired |
| | private | 5 May 79 | | |
| Fuller, William | pt | | 20 Jan 79 | discharged |
| Farence, Owen | do | 6 Aprl 77 | 7 May 80 | died |
| Forrest, Uriah | Major | 10 Dec 76 | Lt. Col. | |
| Ferren, Philip | pt | 20 April 78 | | off Rolls |
| French, Randolph | do | 27 do | feb 79 | discharged |
| Farding, John | do | do | Nov 78 | struck off |
| Furnor, Edward | do | 19 Jan 78 | 1 Nov 80 | present |
| Fleeton, William | Sergt | 30 Mar 78 | 29 May 78 | taken prior En- |
| Fernand, Andrew | pt | 10 do | 1 Nov 80 | present  [list. |
| Forbus, John | do | 2 Sept 77 | 16 Aug 80 | missing |
| Fairburn, Wm. | do | 76 | do | prisoner |
| Fain, Michael | do | 14 April 77 | May 79 | out the Roll |
| Fell, Christopher | do | | July 78 | to Invalids |

## MUSTERS OF MARYLAND TROOPS, VOL. I.

| NAMES. | RANK. | TIME OF SERVICE. Enlisted. | Discharged. | REMARKS. |
|---|---|---|---|---|
| Foster, James | pt | 28 May 78 | 1 Nov 80 | present |
| Fields, Joseph | do | 2 do | May 79 | out the Rolls |
| Fields, George | do | 20 April 78 | 23 Mar 80 | prisoner |
| Francis, Alexander | do | 26 May do | 1 Nov 80 | present |
| Fraim, John | do | 8 June 78 | June 79 | left out the Rolls |
| Freeman, Richard | do | 5 do | 1 Nov 80 | present |
| Farn, Patrick Joined 17 Jan 79 | pt | 3 May 78 | 27 Jan 80 | deserted |

### FROM OCTOBER MUSTERS, 1780.

| | | | | |
|---|---|---|---|---|
| Franklin, Wm. R. | pt | 15 April 80 | 1 Nov 80 | present |
| Ferril, John | do | 2 feb 80 | do | do |
| Freemoult, Robert | | 6 Oct 78 | 11 June 83 | dismissed on furlough |
| Fagan, Charles | | 16 do 79 | 29 Oct 79 | deserted |

### FOURTH REGIMENT.—*Beginning December*, 1777.

| | | | | |
|---|---|---|---|---|
| Fowler, James[1] | pt | 28 Jan 77 | 10 Sept 78 | discharged |
| Frisby, William | do | | Oct 79 | deserted |
| Finely, Coleman[2] | do | | 3 May 78 | do |
| Feraby, Richard[3] | do | 26 May 77 | 1 Nov 80 | present |
| Fitzgerald, James[4] | Sergt pt | } 12 Feby 77 } 1 Jan 79 } | 12 feb 80 | discharged |
| Flinn, Fredk. | do | 4 May 77 | 16 Aug 80 | missing |
| Flaharty, James | do | 16 feb 77 | 16 feb 80 | discharged |
| Ferrell, James[5] | Sergt pt Sergt | 12 feb 77 15 Aug 78 30 Sept 78 | 12 feb 80 | discharged |
| Fosh, James | pt | | 2 April 78 | deserted |
| Flannery, Christ. | pt | 12 Aug 77 | 16 Aug 80 | missing |
| Fell, Edward | do | 26 do | 5 Nov 78 | discharged |
| Frazier, William | do | 14 Mar 77 | 14 Mar 80 | do |
| Frewen, Richard[6] | do | 20 April 77 | Jan 80 | deserted |
| Fox, John | pt | | 10 April 78 | deserted |
| Filley, William[7] | do | 12 April 78 | 10 Jan 80 | do |
| Fitzpatrick, Bryan[2] | do | 6 May 78 | 16 Aug 80 | missing |
| Flanagan, William[8] | do | 7 May 78 | 18 Jan 80 | prisoner |
| Farrell, James[2] | do | 5 do | 27 April 79 | discharged |
| Ford, Robert[4] | Sergt private | 23 April 78 } 1 Jan 80 } | April 80 | died |
| Fisher, Joseph[1] prisoner 22 Aug 77 Joined 16 July 78 | Corpl | 16 dec 76 | 16 Dec 79 | discharged |

[1] Oldham's.  [2] Norwood's.  [3] Godman's.  [4] Lansdale's.  [5] Spurrier's.  [6] Burgess'.  [7] Bowic's.
[8] Sellman's.

## MUSTERS OF MARYLAND TROOPS, VOL. I.

| NAMES. | RANK. | TIME OF SERVICE. Enlisted. | Discharged. | REMARKS. |
|---|---|---|---|---|
| Foy, John[1] | pt | 10 May 78 | 16 Aug 80 | missing |
| Foisdell, Stafford[2] | Drum | 16 April 78 } | 1 Nov 80 | present |
|  | pt | 1 July 78 } | | |
| Fountain, Peter[3] | do | 15 May 78 | do | do |
| French, John[4] | do | 13 do 79 } | 16 Aug 80 | missing |
|  | Corpl | 1 June 80 } | | |
| Fenwick, Richard[5] | pt | 9 July 79 } | 1 Nov 80 | present |
|  | Corpl | 1 April 80 } | | |
| Follet, Benjamin[2] | Drum | 11 feb 80 | do | do |
| Fitzgerald, Jno. | pt | | 26 Oct 80 | deserted |
| Joined June mus. 80 | | | | |
| Folliott, Joseph | fifer | 16 April 80 | 1 Nov 80 | present |
| Fossett, Robert | pt | | 16 Aug 80 | missing |

### RAWLINGS' REGIMENT.

| NAMES. | RANK. | Enlisted. | Discharged. | REMARKS. |
|---|---|---|---|---|
| Farmer, John | pt | 27 July 76 | | |
| Ford, John | Corpl | Aug 76 | 3 Aug 79 | discharged |
| France, Peter | pt | | 9 do | do |
| Firth, Robert | Corpl | 28 May 79 | | |
| Furguson, Jas. | do | Aug 76 | 19 Aug 79 | discharged |
| Fleming, Thos. | pt | do | | |
| Flinn, Thomas | Sergt | 20 Mar | | |
| Ferguson, Alex. | pt | 4 Jany | | |
| Finnegan, Paddy | do | 12 Mar | | |
| Forsyth, John | Sergt | | | |
| Fardo, Wm. L. | pt | Aug 76 | 9 do | do |
| Fox, Balser | do | | 30 Sept | deserted |

### FIRST REGIMENT.

| NAMES. | RANK. | Enlisted. | Discharged. | REMARKS. |
|---|---|---|---|---|
| Gaither, Henry | Lieut | 10 dec 76 } | | |
|  | Capt | 17 April 77 } | | |
| Georgehagan, John | Sergt | do | 10 April 77 | promoted |
| Griffith, James | pt | 25 Mar 77 | 25 Mar 80 | discharged |
| Grover, I. Mason | do | 14 feb 77 | 1 July 78 | Corpl 24 feb 80 discharged |
| Green, John | do | 21 Mar 77 | 6 Mar 78 | deserted |
| Green, William | do } | | 11 Jan 80 | discharged } |
| joined 6 May 79 | Corpl } | | | |
| Gibney, David | pt | 10 dec 76 | | deserted |
| Gwynn, James | do | 19 April 77 | 16 Aug 80 | prisoner |
| Gassaway, Nicholas | Sergt | 10 dec 76 | 17 April | promoted |
| Gray, Benjamin | pt | do | 27 dec 79 } | discharged |
| reinlisted for war | | 80 | 1 Nov 80 } | present |
| Gosnell, Saml. | do | do | | deserted |

[1] Lansdale's.  [2] Riely's.  [3] Burgess'  [4] Belt's.  [5] Spurrier's.

## MUSTERS OF MARYLAND TROOPS, VOL. I.

| NAMES. | RANK. | TIME OF SERVICE. Enlisted. | Discharged. | REMARKS. |
|---|---|---|---|---|
| Gee, Joseph | Drum | 7 April 77 | April 80 | time out |
| Glasgow, Saml. | Corpl | 10 Dec 76 | 17 July 77 | deserted |
| Green, Amos | pt | do | | |
| Green, Richard | do | 21 April 77 | 25 Dec 77 | 1 Nov 80, do |
| Gorman, John | do | 3 June 77 | Jan 80 | prisoner |
| Gailand, Gilbert | do | } 10 dec | 14 feb | Corpl 13 Sept |
| | Sergt | } 10 June 77 | | |
| Greenwalt, James | pt | 21 Mar 77 | } Mar 80 | discharged |
| | Corpl | 1 Aug 78 | } | |
| | Sergt | | } | |
| Gough, Charles | pt | 21 Mar 77 | Jan 80 | prisoner |
| Gutrick, William | do | | dead or deserted | |
| Garner, Mathew | Sergt | 10 dec 76 | } | |
| | Ensign | | } 5 Mar 78 | resigned |
| Garton, James | pt | 12 May 78 | 15 July 80 | deserted |
| Gordon, Thomas | Qt. Mr. | joined 5 July 78, reduced 22 feb 79, | | |
| | | | | discharged 18 dec 79 |
| Ganina, Abm. | pt | 14 Mar 78 | 1 Nov 80 | present |
| Gattau, Richard | do | 10 June 78 | } do | do |
| | Corpl | 1 July 80 | } | |
| Gates, Leonard | pt | | do | do |
| Gardiner, John | do | 1 June 78 | 16 Aug 80 | missing 5 April 79 |
| Gates, William | do | 4  do | 5 April 79 | discharged |
| Garner, Thomas | do | 17 do | | struck off |
| Garvey, William | do | 28 Aprl 78 | 2 June 78 | missing |
| Gatton, Sulvester | | 4 Oct 78 | 1 Nov 80 | present |
| Green, Saml. | do | 9 Jan 79 | do | do |
| Green, John | | do | do | do |
| Galloway, Hugh | do | 10 dec 76 | 15 Mar 79 | deserted |
| Griffin, William | fifer | 19 Jan 79 | 16 aug 80 | prisoner |
| Glashen, Hendry | pt | 25 feb 79 | } | |
| | Drum | 1 July 79 | } 1 Nov 80 | present |
| Gee, George | | 8 May 79 | July 79 | deserted |
| Grooms, Emanuel | pt | 10 dec 76 | 27 dec 79 | discharged |
| Gordon, George | Sergt | 11 feb 80 | 16 Aug 80 | prisoner |
| Glover, Thomas | pt | 14 feb 80 | 1 Nov 80 | present |

### SECOND REGIMENT.

| NAMES. | RANK. | Enlisted. | Discharged. | REMARKS. |
|---|---|---|---|---|
| Garnett, Andrew | fifer | 1 Jan 77 | 1 Nov 80 | present |
| Gollihigh, Wm. | pt | | 3 Sept 79 | deserted |
| Gallaway, Joseph | Corpl | | 10 Jan 80 | discharged |
| Gorman, John | do | | 20 Jan 78 | deserted |
| Gray, Jacob | do | 4 Mar 77 | 1 Nov 80 | present |
| Giles, Samuel | do | do | 14 April 79 | discharged |

## MUSTERS OF MARYLAND TROOPS, VOL. I.

| NAMES. | RANK. | TIME OF SERVICE. Enlisted. | Discharged. | REMARKS. |
|---|---|---|---|---|
| Gray, Joseph | Corpl | | 28 feb 78 | died |
| Gassaway, Jno. | Lieut | } 17 April 77 } | | |
| | Capt | } 2 April 80 } | | |
| Guibard, Thomas | pt | | 16 July 80 | |
| Musd. as Sergt between April and June | | | Discharged as such | |
| Griffin, John | pt | 1 Jan 77 } | | |
| Joined April Mus. Roll 78 | | | } 10 Jan 80 | discharged |
| Gold, William | pt | 20 feb 78 | 1 Nov 80 | present |
| Griffin, Mack | do | 1 Jan 78 | do | do |
| Griffin, Nathan | do | do | do | do |
| Galloway, Charles | do | 16 May 78 | Nov 79 | not heard of |
| Gray, Richard | do | 28 Jan 78 | 15 dec 78 | dead |
| Grinnel, Stephen | pt | 29 May 78 | 3 April 79 | discharged |
| Godthart, Barton | do | 30  do | do | do |
| Goodyer, Edward | do | 1 do | feb 80 | not heard of |
| Garner, Henry | do | 6 July  do | 4 April 79 | discharged |
| Giles, John | do | 9 May  do | 18 July 78 | died |
| Garner, Abel | do | 20 do | 3 April 79 | discharged |
| Grace, William | do | 25 do | Mar 79 | do |
| Grishill, Jno. | do | do | 78 | dead |
| Garish, William | do | do | 26 Dec 78 | deserted |
| Gooster, Reubin | do | 27 dec 78 | 1 Nov 80 | present |
| Gray, James | do | 24  do 76 | | returned |
| Galworth, Gabl. | do | | 10 Jan 80 | discharged |
| Gardiner, Richd. | Sergt | | 18  do | do |
| Gale, John | Lieut | 10 April 77 } | | |
| first mus. June 79 | Capt | 10 dec 77 } | | |
| Grace, Richard | Lieut | } never joined | | |
| 1 mus. June 79 | Capt | } | | |
| Green, Henry | pt | 26 April 79 | 1 Nov 80 | present |
| Galloway, James | do | | Nov 79 | not heard of |
| Gassaway, Henry[1] | Ensn | 26 Jan 80 | | |

### THIRD REGIMENT.—*Beginning* 77.

| NAMES. | RANK. | Enlisted. | Discharged. | REMARKS. |
|---|---|---|---|---|
| Gordon, Thomas | pt | 22 Jan 77 | 28 Jan 80 | taken prisoner |
| Gladson, William | pt | 28 May 77 | 28 Jan 80 | discharged |
| Gilpin, William | do | do feb do | 21  do | do |
| Glasgow, Walter | do | 13 May 77 | 16 Aug 80 | missing |
| Grant, Samuel | Sergt | | 15 May 78 | deserted |
| Gouger, Joseph | pt | | Mar 79 | left out the Roll |
| Green, Henry | do | 23 April 77 | 15 Mar 78 | deserted |
| Gills, John | do | 4 dec 76 | 1 Nov 78 } | transfd. to Invalids |
| | | | 4 dec 79 } | discharged from do |

[1] Gale's.

## MUSTERS OF MARYLAND TROOPS, VOL. I.

| Names. | Rank. | Enlisted. | Discharged. | Remarks. |
|---|---|---|---|---|
| Geary, Richard | pt | | dead or deserted | |
| Garnett, Francis | do | 10 Aug 77 | April 78 | struck off |
| Gassaway, Nich. | Ensn<br>Lieut | } 17 April 77 } | | |
| Gorsuch, Thomas | Drum | 3 June 77 | 1 Nov 80 | present |
| Griffith, Saml. | Capt | | 12 Aug 78 | resigned |
| Griffith, Chas. | Lieut | | 19 May 77 | do |
| Gavin, Michl. | pt | 5 Jan 77 | 5 Jan 80 | discharged |
| Galloway, Marsl. | Drum | 27 June 77 } | | |
| | pt | 4 May 78 } | } 1 nov 80 | present |
| George, Edward | } do | } | } 16 Aug 80 | prisoner |
| Drum Major | } | } 1 Aug 78 | } April 85 | returned |
| Gainer, Jno. | pt | 11 May 77 | 16 Aug 80 | missing |
| Garrett, John | do | 28 feb 77 | 28 feb 80 | time expired |
| Gilpin, Igs. | do | | 2 July 78 | deserted |
| Garrett, Leonard | pt | 25 feb 77 | 29 feb 80 | time expired |
| Gorman, Hugh | do | | July 78 | struck off |
| Gist, Mordicai | Col | 10 dec 76 | | |
| Gadrick, Philip | pt | 28 Aprl 78 | June 78 | deserted |
| Graves, James | do | 15 May 78 | do | discharged |
| Gordan, William | do | 20 Mar 78 | 1 Nov 80 | present |
| Goodwin, James | do | } | } | } |
| present Oct Roll 80 | | } | 1 Nov 80 | } present |
| Greenwell, Robt. | Sergt | | 9 Jan 79 | discharged |
| Gill, John | pt | 21 May 77 | 1 feb 79 | do |
| Exchg. and joined 22 July 78 | | | | |
| Gregory, William | pt | 13 May 78 | Corpl 1 Nov 79, 16 Aug missing | |
| Gordon,(or Jordon),William | do | | do | do |
| Goldsbury, Henry[1] | do | 14 May 78 } | | |
| reinlisted 18th Nov 78 | | } 1 Nov 80 | present | |
| Goldsmith, Notley | pt | 28    do | 4 April 79 | discharged |
| Geoghegan, Anthy. | Drum | 20 Mar 78 | 1 Nov 80 | present |
| Grace, Jesse | pt | 25 April 78 | do | do |
| | | | 17 April 81 | discharged |
| Gibson, John | do | 20    do | do | do |
| Gardiner, Richd. | do | 24    do | not mustd. in 80 | |
| Griffiths, John | do | 18 May 78 | 1 Nov 80 | present |
| Gorrell, Abm. | do | 1 June 78 | time out, discharged | |
| Grant, Richard | do | 11 Jan 78 | 13 feb 79 | do |
| Green, Isaac | do | 2 June 78 | 1 Nov 80 | present |
| Gask, William | do | | 14 feb 79 | discharged |
| Glascoe, William | do | 12 April 78 | 1 Nov 80 | present |
| Gordon, John | Drum | 15 June 79 | 1 Nov 80 | present |

[1] Deaver's.

## MUSTERS OF MARYLAND TROOPS, VOL. I.

| NAMES. | RANK. | TIME OF SERVICE. Enlisted. | Discharged. | REMARKS. |
|---|---|---|---|---|
| | | OCTOBER MUSTER, 1780. | | |
| Goldsborough —— | | see Henry Goldsborough | | |
| Goldsborough, Chs. | pt | 2 feb 80 | 1 Nov 80 | present |
| Goddard, John | do | do | do | do |
| Gates, William | do | 13 Mar 80 | do | do |
| Grant, James | do | | 16 Aug 80 | missing |
| | | FOURTH REGIMENT.—*Beginning Dec'r*, 1777. | | |
| Gregory, Robt.[1] | Corpl | 7 dec 76 | 1 dec 79 | dischd. pt. 20 feb 79 |
| Godfrey, Thomas | pt | | Dec 77 | drafted for sea |
| Gilhamton, Robt. | do | do | 16 Aug 80 | missing, joined & |
| Godman, Saml. | Capt | 10 dec 76 | left out | [died 1 Oct 81 |
| Gainer, Hugh[2] | pt | Dec 76 | 1 Nov 80 | present |
| Gray, James | do | do | dec 79 | discharged |
| Garth, James | do | 5 Jan 77 | 1 Nov 80 | present |
| Glorey, William | do | | 16 May 78 | discharged |
| Garvin, John[3] | do | 20 Nov 77 | 1 Nov 80 | present |
| Goodall, Elias | do | | April 78 | left out |
| Gassaway, Henry[4] | Sergt | | 6 dec 79 | discharged |
| promoted Ensign 2d Regiment | | | | |
| Greenwell, Jesse | pt | | feb 78 | died of his wounds |
| Griffith, George[5] | Sergt | 14 July 77 | 23 June 79 | deserted |
| Gibson, Joseph[6] | do | 1 April 77 | 7 dec 79 | discharged |
| Gill, Hugh[7] | pt | 19 Aug 77 | 19 Aug 80 | do |
| Green, James[8] | do | 27 Jan 78 | 16 Aug 80 | missing |
| Guarn, Hugh[1] | do | 28 dec 76 | 28 dec 79 | discharged |
| Gray, Thomas | Drum | 15 April 78 } | 1 Nov 80 | present |
| | pt | 1 June 78 } | | |
| Gollier, John[n] | do | 26 April 78 | 16 Aug 80 | missing |
| Gentils, John[2] | do | 5 feb 78 | 3 July 78 | deserted |
| Gaiffin, Michael | do | 18 May 78 | 16 Aug 80 | missing |
| Gray, Robert[4] | do | 2 do | 1 Nov 80 | present |
| Goldsborough, Jno.[9] | do | 25 April 78 | Sep 80 | deserted |
| Smith's, late Spurrier's | | | | |
| Glaswey, Pat. | do | 25 April 78 | Corpl 1 Apl 80, 16 Aug 80 mis- | |
| Gordon, Thomas[10] | do | 27 do | 14 Aug 79 | deserted     [sing |
| Rieley's, late Bowie's | | | | |
| Getcomb, John | do | 5 May 78 | 5 Sept 78 | discharged |
| Gamble, William[1] | do | 20 do | | discharged, see below |
| Gardiner, Alexd.[8] | do | 16 April 78 | 1 July 80 | deserted |
| Gummy, Peter[9] | fifer | 17 June 78 | 1 Jan 80 | deserted |

[1] Oldham's.   [2] Godman's.   [3] Lansdale's.   [4] Selman's.   [5] Lt. Spurrier's.   [6] Bowie's.   [7] Burgess'.
[8] Norwood's.   [9] Lt. Smith's.   [10] Riely's.

## MUSTERS OF MARYLAND TROOPS, VOL. I.

| NAMES. | RANK. | TIME OF SERVICE. | | REMARKS. |
|---|---|---|---|---|
| | | Enlisted. | Discharged. | |
| Garrish, Francis[1] | pt | 18 May 78 | 17 May 80 | deserted |
| Gamble, William[2] | do | 26 July 78 | May 79 | discharged |
| Gainford, Mathias | do | 18 May 79 | July 80 | deserted |
| Gwinn, John[3] | Corpl | | | |
| musd. Feby 78 | Sergt | 1 July 79 | 1 Nov 80 | present |
| Gorman, John[1] | pt | 27 Aug 79 | 16 Aug 80 | missing |
| Glinn, James[2] | do | | 1 Nov 80 | present |
| joined 17 Mar 80, transfd. from the Virginia Troops 1 dec 79 | | | | |
| Goff, Richard[4] | pt | 2 feb 80 | July 80 | deserted |
| Gray, James[5] | do | 17 April 80 | 1 Nov 80 | present |
| | | | | { same person before mentioned, discharged and reinlisted supposed |

### RAWLINGS' REGIMENT.

| | | | | |
|---|---|---|---|---|
| Gratsinger, John | | pt | | |
| Gordon, John | | do | 27 May 79 | |
| Grimes, David | | do | | |
| Gowarn, Brian | | do | 11 Mar | |
| Glass, Andrew | | do | 31 April | |
| Green, John | | do | 17 July | |
| Glass, Anthony | | do | 31 Mar | |
| Godfrey, Jno. | 6 mo. | do | 15 feb 79 | |
| Guthrey, Wm. | do | do | 2 Mar | |
| Gault, James | do | do | 12 do | |
| Gibson, John | do | do | 10 do | |
| Gullion, John | do | do | 1 Mar | |
| Gullion, Jeremh. | do | do | 23 do | |
| Germing, Wm. | | do | | |
| Guthry, William | | Lieut | 19 Feb 79 | |

### FIRST REGIMENT.

| NAMES. | RANK. | Enlisted. | Discharged. | REMARKS. |
|---|---|---|---|---|
| Hardy, Thos. Dent | Lieut | 19 July | 6 July 78 | resigned |
| Heron, John | Corpl | 10 dec 76 | 6 Mar 78 | deserted |
| Horson, Thomas | Drum | do | 27 dec 79 | discharged |
| Hiltzhimer, Franz } say Kelsimer | pt | do | do | do |
| Hannagan, Brian | do | do | | exd. in 77 |
| Hargraves, Dennis | do | do | 10 feb 77 | died |
| Higgins, Dennis | do | 15 feb 77 | 11 Sept 77 | missing |
| Howe, Walter | do | 18 do | 11 Jan 80 | discharged |
| Helmes, John | do | 1 feb | do | do |
| Howard, Joseph | do | 9 May 77 | 1 Nov 80 | present |

[1] Riely's.    [2] Oldham's.    [3] Godman's.    [4] Lansdale's.    [5] Lt. Hanson's.

## MUSTERS OF MARYLAND TROOPS, VOL. I.

| NAMES. | RANK. | TIME OF SERVICE. Enlisted. | Discharged. | REMARKS. |
|---|---|---|---|---|
| Hoye, Cephas | pt | 10 dec 76 | | never joined |
| Hanson, Saml. | Ensn | | 7 dec 77 | resigned |
| Hamilton, Saml. | Sergt | do | 11 July 78 | joined Comy. |
| Harrod, John | pt | do | 13 Mar 79 | deserted  [Dept. |
| Hartlove, John | do | do | 16 Aug 80 | missing |
| Hanson, Saml. | Ensn | 24 July 77 | } 1 Aug 78 | Qt. Mr. |
| Q. M. | Lieut | 1 Aug 79 | | |
| Heywood, John | pt | | 25 July 77 | deserted |
| Hughes, Henry | do | | 1 April 80 | do |
| Harwood, Thomas | Capt | 10 dec 76 | 10 June 77 | resigned |
| Hilleary, Rignal | Ensn | do | } | |
| | Lieut | 27 May 78 | | |
| Hutchinson, R. G. | pt | 18 feb 77 | | |
| Hutchinson, Saml. | do | do | 11 feb 80 | time expired, dis- |
| Hale, Thomas | do | 11 Mar | 16 Aug 80 | missing  [chgd. |
| Hopkins, A. H. | pt | 6 Mar 77 | Jan & feb 80, left out musr. | |
| Holmes, William | do | 10 dec 76 | 27 dec 79 | discharged |
| Hamilton, Thos. | do | do | 6 Mar 78 | deserted |
| Holsey, John | do | do | | |
| Hughes, John | do | do | exchanged for R. Baily | |
| Heldmole, Geo. | do | do | 31 Oct 77 | deserted |
| Hennen, Thos. | do | do | | |
| Huling, Thos. | do | 24 April 77 | 27 May | deserted |
| Hogg, James | do | 10 Dec 76 | 27 dec 79 | discharged |
| Howard, Benja. | do | 3 Mar 77 | 2 Mar 80 | do |
| Hubbard, Hanson | do | 25  do | 3 May 80 | do |
| Hanan, Henry | do | 27 May 77 | } 1 Jan 80 | promoted Sergt. |
| | Corpl | 1 June 79 | | |
| Hall, Elisha | Ensn | | 22 Aug 77 | prisoner |
| | Lieut | 27 May 78 | | |
| Howby, Dennis | pt | 10 Dec 76 | 28 May 77 | deserted |
| Hamilton, Geo. | | do | 21 April | ex. R. Green |
| Howsman, Tho. | | 1 April 77 | 3 April 79 | deserted |
| Harding, Robt. | do | 10 May 77 | Sept 79 | transferred to } Invalids |
| | | | 18 Mar 80 | discharged |
| Hickey, Leond. | do | 10 dec 76 | } reduced | } 27 July 80 de- |
| | Corpl | 3 June 78 | } 5 Nov 79 | } serted |
| Hughes, Andrew | pt | 18 April 77 | 18 Aug 80 | missing |
| Hebb, Jesse | Sergt | 8 Mar 77 | 10 July 77 | discharged |
| Hagarthy, Paul | pt | 10 dec 77 | 27 dec | do |
| Horrill, Jas. | do | 2 April 77 | | |
| Howard, Thos. | Surgn. Mate | 1 April 78 | 79 | resigned |

## MUSTERS OF MARYLAND TROOPS, VOL. I.

| NAMES. | RANK. | TIME OF SERVICE. Enlisted. | Discharged. | REMARKS. |
|---|---|---|---|---|
| Havers, Jno. | pt | 12 Jan 78 | 18 July 80 | deserted |
| Humpton, Wm. | pt | Mar 78 | 16 Aug 80 | missing |
| Hennesey, Edwd. | do | 21 May 78 | 4 April 79 | Ex. for Edwd. Jefferson |
| Hunter, Thos. | do | 25 feb 78 | 10 Sept 80 | discharged |
| Harrington, Wm. | do | 8 May 78 | 1 Nov 80 | present |
| Hanington, Richd. | | 5 June 78 | 5 April 79 | discharged |
| Hanington, Levin | | do | do | do |
| Howell, John | | 12 May 78 | 20 June 79 | deserted |
| Hutton, Lance. | | 11 June 78 | 16 Aug 80 | prisoner |
| | Corpl | 1 Jan 80 | | |
| Hanson, Robt. | | 25 Mar 78 | | |
| Hynes, John | pt | 5 June 78 | 15 Sept 79 | deserted |
| Hudson, Thos. | do | 16 May 78 | 28 feb 79 | discharged |
| Hunt, James | do | 20 do | 14 do | do |
| Hickey, Fran. | do | 2 do | do | do |
| Hardy, George | do | 5 June 78 | 5 April 79 | do |
| Higdon, Wm. | do | 5 April 79 | 1 Nov 80 | present |
| Harding, Jno. | do | 30 Mar 79 | 1 Aug 80 | deserted |
| Holland, Wm. | do | 9 May 79 | 16 do | missing |
| Hughes, Wm. | do | 17 do | 1 Nov 80 | present |
| Horrell, Jno. | do | 17 June 79 | do | do |
| Hall, Joseph | do | 1 do | do | do |
| Hannon, Jno. | do | 22 May 79 | do | do |
| Harding, A. | | 10 June 79 | see A. A. Arvin | |
| Howard, Stephen | | 21 do | 16 Aug 80 | missing |
| Harry, Thomas | do | 20 feb 80 | do | prisoner |
| Hoskins, Rand. | do | 2 feb 79 | 1 Nov 80 | present |
| Hagan, Raphael | Corpl | | 16 Aug 80 | prisoner |
| Harris, Silvester | pt | | 10 do | deserted |
| Hart, William | do | | 16 do | prisoner |

### SECOND REGIMENT.—*Beginning Jan., 1778.*

| NAMES. | RANK. | TIME OF SERVICE. Enlisted. | Discharged. | REMARKS. |
|---|---|---|---|---|
| Hopkins, John | pt | 1 Jan 77 | 10 Jan 80 | discharged |
| Hughes, Andrew | do | 7 April 77 | Jany 79 | died in Hosptl. |
| Howard, James | do | | Jan 78 | struck off |
| Hardikin, Edward | Sergt | | 10 Jan 80 | discharged |
| Holder, Kemp, | pt | | do | do |
| Holder, John | do | | do | do |
| Hazell, Philip | Sergt | 22 Mar 77 | 9 Sept 78 | died |
| Head, John | Drum | 15 Jan 77 | | |
| Hasser, John | pt | | 15 Mar 78 | discharged |
| Hamilton, George | do | | 3 April 79 | deserted |

## MUSTERS OF MARYLAND TROOPS, VOL. I.

| NAMES. | RANK. | TIME OF SERVICE. Enlisted. | Discharged. | REMARKS. |
|---|---|---|---|---|
| Hawkins, Philip | pt | | 10 Jan 80 | discharged |
| Hill, Richard | Corpl | | do | do |
| Hatcher, Igns. | pt | | do | do |
| Hughes, John | Corpl | sick Maryd. ⎫ | | |
| reduced to | pt | 1 June 78 ⎭ | 1 Nov 80 | present |
| Henly, Roger | do | | 10 Jan 80 | discharged |
| Hardman, John | Lieut | 10 April 77 ⎱ | died 31 Aug 1780 of wounds | |
| | Capt | 2 April 80 ⎰ | recd. at Battle of Camden | |
| Hayward, Thomas | Corpl | | | |
| Harding, John | pt | | 16 Aug 80 | prisoner |
| Howell, Thomas | fifer | | 15 May 78 | deserted |
| Hart, Thomas | pt | | 16 Aug 80 | killed |
| Hughs, Lawrence | do | | 8 feb 79 | deserted |
| Harrison, Tho. | do | 2 Mar 76 | 1 Nov 80 | sick Maryd. |
| Harris, Solomon | do | 14 Aug 79 | 16 Jan 80 | discharged |
| Holeston, William | do | | 19 June 78 | deserted |
| Henry, Adam | do | 1 Jan 78 | 16 Aug 80 | missing |
| Harper, William | do | 19 Mar 78 | 9 Jan 79 | died |
| Harper, Richard | do | do | 1 Nov 89 | present |
| Hays, Bartholo. | do | do | 1 July 78 | deserted |
| Hall, John | do | 18 do | 24 Jan 79 | died |
| Hill, James | do | 4 Jan 78 | 1 Nov 80 | present |
| Heaney, John | do | 3 April 78 | do | do |
| Harmer, Jos. | do | 12 May 78 | 15 Sept 80 | deserted |
| Holliday, Geo. | do | 9 Oct 77 | 9 Oct 80 | discharged |
| Horsefield, Jos. | do | 20 May 78 | 1 Nov 80 | present |
| Hagarthy, Geo. | do | 12 do ⎱ | | |
| | Sergt | 1 Jan 80 ⎰ | do | do |
| Hobbs, Thomas | pt | 28 May 78 | do | do |
| Howard, John | do | 25 feb 78 | do | do |
| Howard, Leond. | do | 23 May 78 | 3 April 79 | discharged |
| Hill, Edward | do | 29 do | 2 dec 78 | died |
| Howell, John | do | | 3 April 79 | deserted |
| Hughston, Jacob | do | | 1 Nov 80 | present |
| Hillyer, W. P. | do | 30 do | 16 Aug 80 | prisoner |
| Hayle, Anthony | do | 8 June 78 | do | do |
| Hall, George | pt | | 4 June 79 | deserted |
| Hughes, Samuel | do | 19 May 78 | 1 Nov 80 | sick in Maryd. |
| Hughes, Henry | do | 20 do | 21 feb 79 | discharged |
| Hodibuck, Conrad | do | 25 do | 16 Aug 80 | killed |
| Hugill, Joseph | do | do | 1 Nov 80 | present |
| Hill, Abner | do | 20 do | 78 | died fishkill |
| Holmes, Thomas | do | do | time out, discharged | |
| Hubbard, Charles | do | do | 78 | died fishkill |

## MUSTERS OF MARYLAND TROOPS, VOL. I.

| NAMES. | RANK. | TIME OF SERVICE. Enlisted. | Discharged. | REMARKS. |
|---|---|---|---|---|
| Haslip, William | do | 24 May 79 | 18 Sept 79 | discharged |
| Hooper, Abram | do | 1 July 79 | 1 Nov 80 | present |
| Haire, James | do | 1 June 79 | do | do |
| Hayes, Vachel | do | 30 July 79 } killed at | } missing | |
| | Drum | | } 16 Aug 80 } | |
| Hayes, Luke | pt | 22 June 79 | 1 Nov 80 | present |
| Haynie, Ezekiel | S. M. | 1 Aug 79 } | | |
| | Surgn | } | | |
| Horsfield, Luke | pt | | 16 Aug 80 | prisoner |
| Harris, James | do | 17 April 80 | 1 Nov 80 | present |
| Hackett, Joshua | do | | 16 Aug 80 | missing |

### THIRD REGIMENT.—*Beginning* 77.

| | | | | |
|---|---|---|---|---|
| Hatkerston, Robt. | Sergt | 5 feb 77 | 9 Jan 80 | discharged |
| Hamilton, William | Drum | 5 May 77 | 1 Nov 80 | present |

### SMALLWOOD'S REGIMENT.

| | | | | |
|---|---|---|---|---|
| Hewin, John | pt | 2 feb 77 | 16 Aug 80 | prisoner Camden |
| Musd. as Sergt. Aug 80, says he got from the British in feb 80, never joined afterwards | | | | |
| Horner, Robt. | pt | 5 feb 77 | no acct. of him | |
| Hopewell, Jno. | do | 19 do | 21 feb 80 | discharged |
| Hall, Fredk. | do | 11 May 77 | 10 Jan 78 | deserted |
| Harrison, Joseph | pt | 14 April 77 | 14 April 80 | discharged |
| Hardie, James | Sergt | | | |
| Hammond, Joseph | pt | | 28 Aug 78 | deserted |
| Hood, (or Wood), John | do | | | |
| Head, William | do | 3 May 77 | April 78 | struck off |
| Hall, William | do | 3 June 77 | 1 Aug 78 | deserted |
| Holder, John | do | 8 Sept 77 | 9 Nov 79 | do |
| Hudson, John | do | do | 28 Jan 78 | do |
| Hayley, John | do | 20 May 77 | 16 April 80 | discharged |
| pt 1 June 79 | Corpl | October 78 | | |
| Hood, Edward | pt | 1 Jan 77 | 1 Nov 80 | present |
| Hazlewood, Jacob | do | | Mar 79 | left out the Roll |
| Hughes, John | do | 5 dec 76 | 16 Aug 80 | missing |
| Hart, Zacha. | Sergt | 20 June 77 | | |
| Hoole, Joseph | pt | 4 Sept 77 | 16 Aug 80 | killed |
| Husey, James | do | 1 do | July 78 | deserted |
| Heney, Barna. | do | 1 April 77 } | } 16 Aug 80 | do—joined |
| | Corpl | 20 May 78 } | | |
| | private | 1 July 79 } | | |
| Holloway, Jno. | do | | feb 78 | died |
| Hannagin, Bri. | | | 11 Sep 77 | prisoner |

## MUSTERS OF MARYLAND TROOPS, VOL. I.

| NAMES. | RANK. | TIME OF SERVICE. Enlisted. | Discharged. | REMARKS. |
|---|---|---|---|---|
| Hough, John | private | Nov 77 joined | | |
| Howard, John | Corpl pt | } 1 June 78 | Aug 78 | struck off |
| Hughes, Saml. | do | | | |
| pt 15 July 79 | Corpl | } 23 May 78 | | |
| Howard, Thomas | pt | | 10 Jan 78 | died |
| Hilton, Samuel | do | | 15 do | do |
| Hagarthy, Dennis | do | | 1 June 78 | discharged |
| Harpur, Francis | do | 5 April 78 | | |
| Hughes, James | pt | 25 April 78 | Aug absent wo. leave, never [joined |
| Haydon, John | do | do | | |
| Hoskins, John | do | 20 do | 16 Aug 80 | missing |
| Hart, William | do | 6 feb 78 | | |
| Holmes, John | do | 30 April 78 | do | do |
| Howard, Austin | do | do | 1 Nov 80 | present |
| Hall, Richard | do | 21 do | do | do |
| Harley, Henry | do | 25 do | 16 Aug 80 | missing |
| Holt, William | do | 23 do | 14 Oct 78 | discharged |
| Henry, Elias | pt | } 4 May 78 1 Oct 80 | 1 Nov 80 | present |
| mustered ——— | Sergt | | | |
| Harley, Edward | pt | 5 May 78 | do | do |
| Howard, William | Corpl pt | 24 feb 78 31 Oct 78 | feb 79 | discharged |
| Hatfield, Edward | do | 27 April 78 | 1 Nov 80 | present |
| Harris, William | do | | do | do |
| Higdon, Thomas | do | 7 Mar 78 | do | do |
| Hines, Henry | do | do | do | do |
| Hopkins, Francis | do | 9 do | do | do |
| Hood, Richard | do | 9 May 78 | 16 Aug 80 | missing |
| Hurst, Phineas | do Sergt | 25 do 18 Jan 79 | } 1 Jan 80 | deserted |
| Hoskins, Zepha. | pt | 30 May 78 | 14 April 79 | discharged |
| Harris, Josias | do | 26 do | 1 Nov 80 | private |
| Joined 3 Aug 78 musd. Sergt 1 Oct 80 | Corpl | 5 May 79 | | |
| Hines, Peter | pt | 2 June 78 | 18 Aug 80 | deserted |
| Holloway, William | fifer | | 27 Oct 80 | deserted |
| Harper, Stephen | pt | 25 April 78 | 1 Nov 80 | present |
| Holbrook, James | do | 27 do | do | do |
| Hardey, Elias | do | 25 do | do | do |
| Hackett, James | do | 20 May 78 | 1 Jan 80 | deserted |
| Hamilton, Jno. | do | 22 Apl 78 | 1 Nov 80 | present |
| Hair, Robert | do | 1 June 78 | | |
| Hardman,(or Harding),Jno. | do | 20 April 78 | 16 Aug 80 | missing |

## MUSTERS OF MARYLAND TROOPS, VOL. I.

| NAMES. | RANK. | TIME OF SERVICE. Enlisted. | Discharged. | REMARKS. |
|---|---|---|---|---|
| Harris, Joseph | pt | | | |
| Hennis, John | do | 4 June 78 | 26 Sep 80 | deserted |
| Hall, William | do | 14 May 78 | 26 Nov 78 | do |
| Harris, Thomas | do | | 31 dec 79 | do |
| Hall, Frederick | do | 11 May 77 | dead or deserted, Capt. Baldwin say he deserted on ye way to S. ward | |
| deserted 10 Jan 78, joined 25 Mar 79 and was on the Rolls to April 80 | | | | |
| Hays, Levin | Sergt | 10 dec 76 | | |
| Hines, Michael | pt | | May 79 | deserted |
| Handly, Thomas | do | 4 Jan 78 | 16 Aug 80 | missing |
| Howard, Peregrim | do | 9 May 79 | 1 Nov 80 | present |
| Howard, Charles | Sergt | do | do | do |

### FROM OCTOBER MUSTER, 1780.

| NAMES. | RANK. | Enlisted. | Discharged. | REMARKS. |
|---|---|---|---|---|
| Haslip, John | pt | | do | do |
| Holland, Daniel | do | 10 Mar 80 | 16 Aug 80 | |

### FOURTH REGIMENT.—*Beginning Dec., '77.*

| NAMES. | RANK. | Enlisted. | Discharged. | REMARKS. |
|---|---|---|---|---|
| Hall, Josias C. | Col | 10 Dec 76 | | |
| Hamilton, Jno. | P. M. | 1 Aug 77 | | |
| | Ensn | 27 May 78 | | |
| | Lieut | 11 June 79 | | |
| Hanson, Isaac | Qr. M. | 1 May 77 | | |
| | Ensn | 8 Nov 79 | | |
| | Lieut. d | 15 Dec do | | |
| | Q. Mr. | | | |
| Hood, James | Q. M. S. | 1 May 77 | 20 Aug 78 | assd. Comy. 2d B. |
| | Corpl | 5 Mar 77 | | |
| Howard, J. E. | Major | 10 Dec 76 | | |
| | Lt. Col. | | | |
| | Lieut. Col. Comd· | | | |
| Harding, Daniel [1] | pt | 30 May 77 | Jan 80 | discharged |
| private Sept 79 | Corpl | 1 April 78 | | |
| Harp, Reice | pt | | 1 Mar 78 | died |
| Herwell, Thomas | do | 8 dec | 8 dec 79 | discharged |
| Hinks, Thomas | do | 6 do | 6 do | do |
| Hood, John [2] | Sergt | 24 April 77 | 24 April 80 | time expired |
| Hanes, John | pt | | June 80 | deserted |
| Houspan, Jno. C. [3] | do | | 25 May 80 | time expired |
| Hessey, John H. | do | 13 May 77 | do | do |
| | | | 13 May 80 | discharged |
| Holland, Thomas | do | 19 Apl 77 | 1 Mar 80 | struck off |

[1] Oldham's.  [2] Norwood's.  [3] Belt's.

## MUSTERS OF MARYLAND TROOPS, VOL. I.

| NAMES. | RANK. | TIME OF SERVICE. Enlisted. | Discharged. | REMARKS. |
|---|---|---|---|---|
| Hatfied, Edward[1] | pt | | 1 Jan 80 | discharged |
| Harvey, Charles | do | 1 Jan 77 | 1 Nov 80 | present |
| | Sergt | 1 dec 79 | | • |
| Hamilton, J. A.[2] | Ensn | 10 dec 76 ⎫ | | |
| | Lieut | 1 feb 78 ⎬ | | |
| | Capt | ⎭ | | |
| Hickory, Jno. | pt | 25 May 77 | 16 Aug 80 | missing |
| Hyde, John | do | 13 feb 77 | 1 Nov 80 | present |
| Hedge, William[3] | do | 6 dec 76 | 2 Jan 80 | deserted, joined |
| Harley, Jeremh. | pt | | 1 Jan 78 | died    [again |
| Hatton, Thomas | do | 4 Aug 77 | 16 Aug 80 | missing |
| Hall, William[4] | do | 29 May 77 | 29 May 80 | discharged |
| Hilland, Mark[5] | do | | 1 April 78 | deserted |
| Harris, Richard[6] | do | 13 Aug 77 | 13 Aug 80 | discharged |
| Hitland, Henry | do | 18 do ⎫ | 16 do | prisoner |
| | Corpl | 1 July 79 ⎬ | | |
| | Sergt | 10 Feby 80 ⎭ | | |
| Hipsley, Jos. | pt | | 25 Jan 78 | deserted |
| Hinon, Nichs. | do | 22 April 77 | 22 April 80 | time expired |
| Heltinhead, Jno. | do | 19 Aug 77 | Dec 79 | deserted |
| Hartshorn, Jno. | Adjt | 25 Jan 78 ⎫ | | |
| | Lieut | 21 May 79 ⎭ | | |
| Hoops, Adam | do | from Hazin's Regt., 15 dec 79 ⎫ | | |
| exchanged with Lieut. Lewis 3 Nov 76 | | | | ⎭ |
| Hull, William[7] | pt | 8 Jan 78 | | |
| Howell, John | do | 21 do | 1 Nov 80 | present |
| Harding, Thomas | do | 25 do | June 79 | discharged |
| Hagan, Andw. | do | 12 feb 78 | 16 Aug 80 | missing |
| Hickey, Thomas[8] | do | 26 Aprl 78 ⎱ | 2 Jan 80 | deserted |
| | Corpl | 1 do 79 ⎰ | | |
| Hackett, John | pt | 26 Apl 77 | 1 June 79 | to Invalids |
| | | | 11 July 83 | or Furlough dismd. |
| Holden, Jos. | do | 6 May 78 | 28 feb 80 | deserted |
| Huddleston, Th.[7] | do | 2 — 78 | June 79 | discharged |
| Howe, William | do | 21 April 78 | 1 Nov 80 | present |
| Hollyday, Isaac[9] | do | 2 May 78 ⎫ | do | do |
| | fifer | 1 Aug 78 ⎬ | | |
| (Smith's, late Spurrier's) | private | 31 July 79 ⎭ | | |
| Hooper, Jeremh. | do | 4 April 78 | 6 Oct 78 | died |
| Hudson, William | pt | 2 May 78 | 3 June 79 | to Invalids, 17 Sept 79 |
| Hennis, Joseph[8] | do | 20 feb 78 | | [deserted |

[1] Godman's.    [2] Lansdale's.    [3] Spurrier's.    [4] Riely's.    [5] Bowie's.    [6] Burgess',
[7] Selman's.    [8] Norwood's.    [9] Lt. Smith's.

## MUSTERS OF MARYLAND TROOPS, VOL. I.

| NAMES. | RANK. | TIME OF SERVICE. Enlisted. | Discharged. | REMARKS. |
|---|---|---|---|---|
| Hamilton, Geo.[1] | pt | 2 June 78 | Dec 79 | deserted |
| Hals, John | do | 20 May 78 | 8 Nov 78 | died |
| Hellam, Thomas[2] | do | 16 do | 1 April 79 | deserted |
| Hynes, Isaac[3] | do | 18 do | 10 Nov 78 | died |
| Hailey, Thomas[4] | do | 6 dec 76 | 6 dec 79 | discharged |
| prisoner 22 Aug 77, joined 23 June 78 | | | | |
| Horam, Saml.[5] | Drum | 4 April 78 | see Samuel Oram | |
| Hindes, Jacob | pt | 30 do | 1 Nov 80 | present |
| Hodges, John[6] | do | 14 May 78 | 16 Aug 80 | missing |
| Harpham, Robt. | do | 18 do | do | prisoner |
| | Corpl | 1 Aug 79 | | |
| | Sergt | 1 June 80 | | |
| Hyner, Joseph | pt | 20 feb 78 | 20 Dec 78 | deserted |
| Harvey, Richd.[7] | do | 28 Aug 78 | June 79 | do |
| Hall, John[4] | do | 19 Apil 79 | 11 Oct 80 | do |
| | Corpl | 1 April 80 | | |
| Handley, Philip[7] | pt | 2 Sept 79 | 16 Aug 80 | missing |
| Hatton, John[9] | do | 26 Oct 79 | July 80 | deserted |
| Hay, John | do | 5 do | 16 Aug 80 | missing |
| Hailey, Thomas[4] | do | 11 feb 77 | 11 feb 80 | discharged |
| to serve till 11 feb 80 in the room of Tobias Wilson discharged 6 Dec 79 | | | | |
| Hood, James[8] | Corpl | 5 Mar 77 | 5 Mar 80 | discharged |
| Hudson, Robt.[9] | pt | | July 80 | deserted |
| Joined June mus. 80 | | | | |
| Harris, Thomas[10] | pt | | 16 Aug 80 | missing |
| Hull, Nathl. | do | | 1 Nov 80 | present |
| Hall, Tobias | | 8 Oct 77 | 2 Mar 78 | died |

### RAWLINGS' REGIMENT.

| NAMES. | RANK. | TIME OF SERVICE. Enlisted. | Discharged. | REMARKS. |
|---|---|---|---|---|
| Harrison, Kinsey | pt | | 9 Aug 79 | discharged |
| Howe, John | Corpl | 22 July 76 | | |
| Howard, J. B. | pt | 24 Sept 76 | 2 April 77 | do |
| Hogans, Roger | do | | | |
| Helms, Geo. | | | 9 Aug 79 | do |
| Hains, Peter | do | | do | do |
| Harkenson, Josiah | | 1 feb 79 | 1 July 79 | do |
| | S. Maj. | | | |
| Hays, Gabriel | Q.M.Sergt. | 6 May | 10 July do | do |
| Hart, William | pt | 18 April | | |
| Horsfield, Thos. | | 28 May | Corpl | 14 Dec |
| Hays, John 1 yr. | | | 1 July 79 | discharged |

[1] Oldham's.    [2] Norwood's.    [3] Godman's.    [4] Lansdale's.    [5] Lt. Smith's.    [6] Burgess'.
[7] Riely's.    [8] Lt. Lee's.    [9] To Oldham's, Belt's.    [10] Selman's.

## MUSTERS OF MARYLAND TROOPS, VOL. I.

| NAMES. | RANK. | TIME OF SERVICE. Enlisted. | Discharged. | REMARKS. |
|--------|-------|----------|------------|----------|
| Howe, Daniel | fife | 6 Mar | | |
| Hazlewood, Jacob | pt | | 9 Aug 79 | do |
| Hill, Thomas | do | 5 feb | | |
| Haggarty, Nic. | Corpl | 12 Mar | | |
| Holland, Francis | pt | 4 June | | |
| Haney, Michael | do | 15 April | | |
| Herbert, William | pt | 20 May | | |
| Hansford, William | do | 26 Oct | | |
| Hannah, Jno.    6 mo. | | | | |
| Harbeson, Wm. | do | | | |
| Hays, Alex. | do | | | |
| Hall, Sam. | do | | | |
| Hurn, Henry | do | | | |
| Harbeson, Rob. | do | | | |
| Hum, Daniel | do | | 8 April 79 | killed |
| Halfpenny, Isaac | pt | | | |

### FIRST REGIMENT.

| NAMES. | RANK. | Enlisted. | Discharged. | REMARKS. |
|--------|-------|-----------|-------------|----------|
| Ivory, Patrick | Drum | 10 Dec 76 | 12 feb 79 | deserted 19 dec 79, joined 20 May 79 |
| Johnson, Vincent | pt | 10   do | 11 Sep 77 | killed |
| Jordon, John | Lieut | 10   do | | |
| | Capt | 1 June 79 | | |
| Jenkins, Jason | Corpl }  Sergt } | 1 Mar 79 | 27 dec 79 | discharged |
| Jenkins, George | pt | 20 feb 77 | 20 feb 80 | do |
| Jackson, John | do | not musd. | after July 79 (in Invalids, died 21 dec 79) |
| Jenkins, Edward | pt | 22 Mar 77 | 22 Mar 80 | discharged |
| James, John | do | 6 April do | 16 Aug 80 | missing |
| Jenkins, Phil. | do | 10 dec 76 | 16 Sept 78 | prisoner 27 dec 79 discharged |
| Jackson, Thomas | do | 1 Mar 77 | 1 June 77 | dead |
| Johnson, William reinlisted | Corpl | 10 dec 76 | 27 dec 79 | discharged |
| Jasper, John | pt | do | 22 Jan 78 | deserted |
| Jones, William | Drum | 18 Mar 77 | 21   do | do, joined 22 March, from to by D. Major |
| Ingleton, Thomas | pt | do | 18 Mar 80 | discharged |
| Joyce, William | do | 2 May 78 | 1 Nov 80 | present, see 3d Regt. |
| Jacobs, Zachariah | | | | discharged |
| Jenkins, Thomas | do | 20   do | 5 April 79 | do |
| Jeckett, William | do | 15 Aug 78 | 7 dec 78 | |

## MUSTERS OF MARYLAND TROOPS, VOL I.

| NAMES. | RANK. | TIME OF SERVICE. Enlisted. | Discharged. | REMARKS. |
|---|---|---|---|---|
| Jefferson, Edward | pt | 4 April 79 | | |
| | | left out June 80, 18 July deserted | | |
| Johnson, Archd. | pt | 23 May 79 } | 1 Nov 80 | present |
| Sergt 15 June 80 | Corpl | 1 Jan 80 } | | |
| Irons, (or Iams), John | pt | 3 June 79 | do | do |
| Jenkins, Isaac | pt | 5 May 79 | 16 Aug 80 | missing |
| Irvine, Edward | do | 11 July 79 | 1 Nov 80 | present |
| Jenkins, Joseph | do | 1 do | do | do |
| Jones, Isaac | do | 1 Aug 79 | do | |

SECOND REGIMENT.—*Beginning with the Muster Rolls for Jany., 1778.*

| NAMES. | RANK. | TIME OF SERVICE. Enlisted. | Discharged. | REMARKS. |
|---|---|---|---|---|
| Johnson, Robert | | | 19 Mar 81 | discharged |
| Iiames, Thomas | Sergt | 10 Jan 77 | 1 Jan 80 | discharged |
| Issabel, Robt. | Drum | 10 feb 76 } | | |
| | Sergt | 10 Jan 80 } | | |
| Jeffers, Reubin | pt | 27 Jan 77 | 10 Jan 80 | discharged |
| Jeffers, Jacob | do | 11 Mar 77 | do | do |
| Jeffers, Peter | do | 15 do | do | do |
| Irvin, Abm. | do | 17 feb 77 | 11 June 79 | prisoner war |
| Jones, James | do | | Mar 78 | died |
| Jacobs, Henry | do | Dec 76 } | 1 Nov 80 | present |
| | fifer | 1 Jan 80 } | | |
| Jones, Neile | pt | 16 Nov 77 | do | do |
| Jones, Joseph | do | 6 feb 77 | do | do |
| Innis, John | do | 28 July 77 | 16 Aug 80 | prisoner |
| Johnson, Robt. | do | 19 Mar 78 | 1 Nov 80 | present |
| Jennings, Wm. | do | 78 | discharged from Hospital Dec 78 | |
| Joel, John | do | 21 Jan 78 | Corpl | July deserted |
| Jones, John | do | 5 April 78 | 16 Aug 80 | prisoner |
| Jenkins, William | do | 1 June 78 | 1 Nov 80 | present |
| Jackson, Abed | do | 25 May 78 | 3 April 79 | discharged |
| Jackson, James | Corpl | 29 Jan 77 | Sergt 1 Aprl 80, 1 Nov 80 present | |
| Jones, David | pt | 1 feby 78 | | do    do |
| | Corpl | do 79 | | |
| Jones, Lewis | pt | 6 July 79 | 23 feby 79 | discharged |
| Jones, Aaron | do | 20 May 78 | 17 feby 79 | died |
| Insley, Robert | do 9 mo. | | 31 Jan 79 | dead |
| Insly, Naboth | do | | 3 April 79 | discharged |
| Insly, John | do | | do | do |
| Insly, David | do | | do | do |
| Insly, Abram | do | 26 July 79 | 1 Nov 80 | present |
| Johnson, John | do | 9 June do | 22 July 79 | deserted |
| Johnson, William | do | | 1 Nov 80 | present |

## MUSTERS OF MARYLAND TROOPS, VOL. I.

| NAMES. | RANK. | TIME OF SERVICE. | | REMARKS. |
|---|---|---|---|---|
| | | Enlisted. | Discharged. | |

### THIRD REGIMENT.—*Beginning* 77.

| NAMES. | RANK. | Enlisted. | Discharged. | REMARKS. |
|---|---|---|---|---|
| Jones, Samuel | Lieut | 10 Dec 76 | } 11 feb 80 | resigned |
| | Capt | 6 Aug 77 | | |
| Irvin, Mathias | pt | 21 May 77 | May 80 | discharged |
| Jeffers, Thomas | Corpl | | 1 Oct 79 | do |
| Jones, Lewis | pt | 21 feb 77 | 21 feb 80 | time expired |
| Jones, Cuthbert | Drum | 4 Aprl 77 | } 4 Aprl 80 | discharged |
| | pt | 4 June 78 | | |
| Jordon, Justian. | do | 18 Apl 77 | | |
| red'd to pt 25 May 79 | Sergt | 2 April 78 | | |
| Jones, John | pt | | | [ex. for Jno. Pasgrove |
| Jones, Thomas | do | 20 Jany 77 | 1 June 78 | 11 Virginia Regt. |
| Jones, William | do | 8 Aug do | 16 Aug 80 | missing |
| James, John | Ensn | 1 Jan 77 | } 11 Jan 80 | resigned |
| | Lieut | 10 April 77 | | |
| Jones, Thomas | pt | | 1 Oct 80 | present |
| Jones, Job | Drum | | | |
| Johnson, Richard | pt | | 27 April 78 | discharged |
| Johnson, Benj. | Fife | 10 June 78 | } 1 Nov 80 | present |
| | pt | 1 feb 79 | | |
| Jones, Thomas | do | 1 Mar 78 | do | do |
| | Corpl | 1 April 80 | | } |
| Johnson, Benj. | pt | | 16 Aug 80 | missing |
| James, Walter | do | 30 June 78 | time out, discharged | |
| Jones, Richard | do | 5 do | do | do |
| Jones, Joseph | do | 14 May 78 | 16 Aug 80 | missing |
| Jones, Philip | do | 20 May 78 | | |
| Jamison, John | Sergt | 14 April 79 | to Invalids, dischd. 7 Nov 80 } June 79 left out the Roll | |
| Jeames, Walter | pt | 30 June 78 | time out, discharged | |
| Johnson, Barnard | fifer | 18 feb 78 | | |
| Jackson, William | pt | 25 Aprl 78 | | |
| Jacob, Zacha. | do | 13 May 78 | 1 Nov 80 | present |
| Johns, James | do | 25 dec 76 | | |
| 1 must. Mar 79 mustered | discharged | 28 Dec 79 | | |
| James, Walter | pt | | time out, discharged | |
| Jordon, Jestenian | do | 25 May 79 | (see J. Jordon, Sergt.) | |
| Jones, Lewis | fife | 5 Aprl 79 | Dec 79 | died |

### JULY, &c., MUSTERS, 1780.

| NAMES. | RANK. | Enlisted. | Discharged. | REMARKS. |
|---|---|---|---|---|
| Johnson, Henry | Sergt | | 26 July 80 | deserted |
| Jones, James | Drum | | 16 Aug 80 | missing |
| Jenkins, Richd. | | 1 Sept 77 | 12 feb 81 | discharged |

## MUSTERS OF MARYLAND TROOPS, VOL. I.

| NAMES. | RANK. | TIME OF SERVICE. Enlisted. | Discharged. | REMARKS. |
|---|---|---|---|---|

### FOURTH REGIMENT.—*Beginning Dec., 77.*

| NAMES. | RANK. | Enlisted. | Discharged. | REMARKS. |
|---|---|---|---|---|
| Johnson, Abm.[1] | pt | | 26 Sept 78 | died |
| Inch, John | do | | 22 Dec 77 | missing |
| Johnson, Jos.[2] | do | 1 Mar 77 | 1 Nov 80 | present |
| Johnson, Miles[3] | do | 6 Jan 77 | 6 Jan 80 | discharged |
| Jenkins, Jos.[4] | do | 1 Jan 77 | 8 do | do |
| Jameson, Adam | do | 25 July 77 | 1 Nov 80 | present |
| Jefferies, David[5] | do | | Jan 78 | left out the Roll |
| James, William[6] | Corpl | 11 April 77 | | |
| | pt | 29 Mar 79 | } 1 Nov 80 | present |
| Jerriott, James | do | 11 April 77 | 16 Aug 80 | missing |
| Isaacs, Isaac | do | 18 Aug 77 | 18 do | discharged |
| Jackson, Anth. | do | 10 Mar 77 | Sept 79 to Invalids, 25 Apl 80 [discharged | |
| Jones, Joseph | do | | Jan 78 | left out the Roll |
| Jacobs, Robinson[1] (Smith's, late Bowie's) | do | 13 Aprl 78 | 16 Aug 80 | missing |
| Innis, Thomas[7] waited on Maj. Morris (with orders Jan 79) | do | 12 Mar 77 | } feb 78 | left the Roll |
| Jessup, Thomas (Riely's, late Bowie's) | pt | 26 April 78 | 1 Nov 80 | present |
| Jones, Joseph[8] | do | 28 do | 15 June 78 | discharged |
| Jones, Samuel[1] | do | 19 May 78 | 16 Aug 80 | missing |
| Jacks, Richard[8] Joined 26 Sept 79 | do | 28 do | July 80 | deserted |
| Johnson, John[7] | do | 8 do | 1 Oct 80 | present |
| Joseph, John | pt | 21 April 78 | 4 Nov 78 | deserted |
| James, Francis[3] | do | | 26 feb 80 | do |
| Joace, William | do | | 1 Nov 80 | present |
| Johnson, John | do | 1 Jan 80 | 16 Aug 80 | missing |

### RAWLINGS' REGIMENT.

| NAMES. | RANK. | Enlisted. | Discharged. | REMARKS. |
|---|---|---|---|---|
| Iron, John | pt | 24 Aug 76 | reinlisted into 1st M. R. | |
| Jones, Joshua | do | 23 July do | 12 Nov 76 | ex. another |
| Johnson, Jno. M. | do | 23 do | | |
| Jeans, Joseph | do | | | |
| | Sergt | 1 Oct 79 | | |
| Jordan, John | pt | 3 May 79 | | |
| Jackson, John | do | | | |
| Jarmy, William | do | 1 Mar | | |
| Islman, Michl. | 6 mo. | 31 Mar 79 | | |

[1] Norwood's.　[2] Godman's.　[3] Selman's.　[4] Spurrier's.　[5] Bowie's.　[6] Burgess'.
[7] Lt. Smith's.　[8] Riely's.

## MUSTERS OF MARYLAND TROOPS, VOL. I.

| NAMES. | RANK. | TIME OF SERVICE. Enlisted. | Discharged. | REMARKS. |
|---|---|---|---|---|

### FIRST REGIMENT.

| NAMES. | RANK. | Enlisted. | Discharged. | REMARKS. |
|---|---|---|---|---|
| Kernan, Barna. | pt | 10 Dec 76 | 19 July 77 | died |
| Keen, John | do | 28 Jan 77 | | deserted |
| King, Philip | do | 10 dec 76 | 22 Jan 78 | do |
| Kelly, James | do | do | 22 Aug 77 | prisoner, 27 dec 79 [discharged |
| Kelly, John | do | do | | Riely, see R |
| Kennady, Tho. | do | | | deserted |
| Keener, Lawrce. | do | 22 Mar 77 | | do |
| Kirby, John | do | 10 dec 76 | 22 Aug | prisoner |
| Kelly, Dennis | do | 1 April 77 | 28 Mar 80 } | present |
| reinlisted 10 Apl 80 | Corpl | June 80 | 1 Nov 80 } | |
| King, Adam | pt | 27 Mar 77 | | |
| Keech, Saml. | do | 10 dec 76 | 10 April 77 | died |
| Kellow, William | do | 1 June 78 } | | |
| Sergt 1 Jan 80 | Corpl | 1 Aug 79 } | 1 Nov 80 | present |
| Knott, James | pt | 22 May 79 | pris. Jan 80 | struck off |
| Kephart, Martin | do | | 27 dec 79 | discharged |
| King, Thomas | do | Aprl 79 | 1 Nov 80 | present |
| Francis, Keltrimer | see letter H | | | |

### SECOND REGIMENT.—*Beginning Jan.,* 78.

| NAMES. | RANK. | Enlisted. | Discharged. | REMARKS. |
|---|---|---|---|---|
| Knott, James | pt } | | | |
| Knott, Jeremh. | do } | | dead or deserted | |
| Kinsey, David | do } | | | |
| Kersey, Daniel | do | 24 Jan 78 | 16 Aug 80 | missing |
| Kilby, Thomas | pt | 20 Aprl 78 } | 16 Aug 80 | prisoner |
| Corpl 1 feb 80 | Sergt | 1 July 80 } | | |
| Keephart, Ad. | pt | 12 Jan 78 | 1 Nov 80 | present |
| King, George | do | 21 do | | |
| Knight, Jacob | do | 19 May 78 | 1 Nov 80 | present |
| Kearnes, James | do | 29 do | 1 Oct 80 | do |
| Killman, Edwd. | do | 20 do | 1 Nov 80 | do |
| Killegan, Jas. | do | 9 May 79 | do | do |
| Knight, George | do | | 1 Oct 80 } | do |
| left out June Roll 79 | | | | |

### THIRD REGIMENT.—*Beginning* 77.

| NAMES. | RANK. | Enlisted. | Discharged. | REMARKS. |
|---|---|---|---|---|
| King, Isaac | pt | | | |
| Kelly, William | do | 15 May 77 | 15 Mar 78 | deserted |
| Kersey, Brian | do | | | |
| Kelly, Hugh | do | 18 July 78 | to Invalids 16 Sept 78 died |

## MUSTERS OF MARYLAND TROOPS, VOL. I.

| NAMES. | RANK. | TIME OF SERVICE. Enlisted. | Discharged. | REMARKS. |
|---|---|---|---|---|
| Kimble, Stephen | pt | 1 April 77 | June Muster 82 | |
| Kelly, George | do | 1 July 77 | prior Enlistment | |
| Knight, Thos. | do | 25 April 78 } | | |
| | Fifer | 1 July 78 } | | |
| Kelly, Hugh | pt | 18 April 78 | see above | |
| Kennedy, Wm. | do | 25 do | Sep 78 | struck off |
| Kelly, Patrick | do | 20 do | 29 June 78 | deserted |
| Kenedy, Michl. | do | 23 do | 6 feb 80 | to Invalids |
| musd. in Invalids joined former Regt, not joined 1 Nov 80 | | | | |
| Kelly, James | pt | ditto | 16 Aug 80 | missing |
| King, Henry | Sergt | 25 May 78 } | | |
| Comy. Dept. | | Oct 78 } Comy. Dept. | | |
| King, Jeremiah | pt | 22 do } | | |
| | Corpl | 14 Aug 78 } 14 April 79 | | dischd. |
| Kidwell, Benj. | pt | 26 May 78 | 1 Nov 80 | present |
| Kelly, Michael | do | 25 Apl 78 | 28 Sept 79 | deserted |
| Kirk, William | do | 20 do | May 79 | left out the Roll |
| Keith, Duncan | do | } 1 July 79 | | |
| | Corpl | } | | |
| Kennedy, Wm. | pt | | 1 Nov 80 | present |
| Kiggan, Jno. | do | 12 May 78 } | | |
| | Corpl | 1 July 79 } | | |
| S. Major | Sergt | 1 Jan 80 } 16 Aug 80 | | prisoner |
| Kennedy, Michael | pt | 28 April 78 | | |
| Kendall, Sam. | do | 26 May 79 | | |
| Kennedy, Thomas | do | 4 June 79 | 1 Nov 80 | present, see [Thomas Cannady |

### FROM OCTOBER MUSTER, 1780.

| | | | | |
|---|---|---|---|---|
| Kernall, Wm. | pt | | ditto | ditto |

### FOURTH REGIMENT.—*Beginning Dec., 77.*

| | | | | |
|---|---|---|---|---|
| Kelly, Richard [1] | pt | 4 June 77 | 4 Mar 79 | deserted |
| Kelly, John | do | 1 dec 76 | 15 Nov 78 | do |
| Kenney, Thomas [2] | do | | Dec 79 | discharged |
| Kilty, John | Lieut | | | |
| Knox, Jno. [3]    O. S. | pt | 1 Jan 77 | 1 Nov 80 | present |
| Bowie's (see Jno. Knox 7 Regt.) | | | | |
| Kenney, Jno. [4] | pt | | Jan 78 | left out |
| sent to shipping | | | | |
| Kelly, Matthew [5] | do | 4 May 77 | 22 Apl 80 | time expired |

[1] Oldham's.        [2] Godman's.        [3] Spurrier's.        [4] Bowie's.        [5] Burgess'.

## MUSTERS OF MARYLAND TROOPS, VOL. I.

| NAMES. | RANK. | TIME OF SERVICE. Enlisted. | Discharged. | REMARKS. |
|---|---|---|---|---|
| Kennedy, David | pt | | Jan 78 | left out the Roll |
| Kidd, John | do | 25 Aug 77 | 1 Nov 80 | present |
| Keats, Thomas[1] | do | 28 Jan 78 | do | do |
| | Corpl | 1 Feb 80 | | |
| | Sergt | 1 March 80 | | |
| Kelly, Mathew[2] | pt | 29 Jan 78 | 16 Aug 80 | missing |
| King, William[1] | do | 25 April 78 | 1 Nov 80 | present |
| Knight, John[3] | fife | 26 May 78 | do | do |
| King, John[4] | pt | 18   do | 25 Jan 80 | prisoner |
| Knight, John[5] | do | 23 feb 79 | 1 Oct 80 | present |
| Kennedy, James[5] | do | 22 May 79 ⎫ | | |
| | Corpl | 1 feb 80 ⎬ | | |
| pt 1 Sept 80 | Sergt | 1 June 80 ⎭ | 1 Nov 80' | do |
| Kelly, Edward[6] | pt | 18 Nov 79 | April 80 | discharged |

### RAWLINGS' REGIMENT.

| NAMES. | RANK. | Enlisted. | Discharged. | REMARKS. |
|---|---|---|---|---|
| Kann, John | pt | July 76 | | |
| Kimboll, Josias | do | 2 Oct | | |
| Kirby, Patk. | do | 76 | | |
| Kemp, James  3 | do | | | |
| Knight, David | | | 15 Sep 79 | discharged |
| Kelly, James | | | | |
| Kirk, Edward | | | | |
| King, James | do | 21 Mar | | |
| Kerr, Robt.   6 mo. | Sergt | | | |
| Kean, Danl.   do | | Mar | | |
| Kean, James   do | | do | | |
| Kelly, Edward  do | | do | | |

### FIRST REGIMENT.

| NAMES. | RANK. | Enlisted. | Discharged. | REMARKS. |
|---|---|---|---|---|
| Leeke, Henry ⎱ | Sergt | 17 April 77 | 10 dec 79 | discharged |
| pt 10 December 76 ⎰ | | | | received a discharged afterwards |
| Logan, Charles | pt  ˙ | 10 Dec 76 | 6 Mar 77 | deserted |
| Leaf, Robert | do | 30 Jan 77 | | never joined |
| Lewis, Benjamin | do | 10 dec 76 | 10 April 77 | died |
| Lowden, Michael | do | do | 16 Aug 80 | prisoner |
| Lanham, Jno. | do | do | 27 dec 79 | discharged |
| Langley, William | do | | 3 June 77 | deserted |
| Linn, Valen | do | do | 27 dec 79 | discharged |
| | Corpl | 12 Apl 77 | 11 Oct 77 | joined in July 78, reduced 15 Sept 78 |

[1] Selman's.   [2] Bowie's.   [3] Lansdale's.   [4] Oldham's.   [5] Riely's.   [6] Belt's.

## MUSTERS OF MARYLAND TROOPS, VOL. I.

| NAMES. | RANK. | TIME OF SERVICE. Enlisted. | Discharged. | REMARKS. |
|---|---|---|---|---|
| Little, Richard | pt | 19 Apl 77 | 12 Aug 77 | prisoner |
| Leadburn, Geo. | do | 10 dec 76 | do | do prisr. 16 Aug 80 |
| reinlisted 1 musr. June 80 | | | 27 dec 79 | discharged |
| Lucus, William | pt | 1 feb 77 | 21 Jan 78 | deserted |
| | | | 27 dec 79 | discharged, re- [inlisted } |
| Luckett, Saml. | Sergt | 10 dec 76 | 27 dec 79 | discharged |
| Luckett, F. Ware | Corpl | do | 16 April 78 | died |
| Lomax, John | pt | 6 June 77 | Jan 80 | prisoner |
| Long, Thomas | do | 10 July 77 | 20 Aug 77 | deserted |
| Layman, Wm. | Ensn Lieut | 10 April 77 | 4 June 79 | resigned |
| Lowe, James | Sergt | 10 dec 76 | 3 Oct 77 | reduced |
| Lowe, Richard | pt | do | | never joined |
| Lidington, Peter | do | 8 May 77 | 1 feb 79 | transferred to Invalids |
| Lamb, Joshua | Corpl Sergt | 10 dec 76 1 Aug 77 | 27 dec 79 | discharged |
| Lowe, James | pt | 10   do | 1 Mar 80 | deserted |
| Lewis, Jonathan | do | 5 June 78 | 1 Nov 80 | |
| Luffer, John | do | 17   do | do | present |
| Lawrence, Joshua | do | 19 feb 78 | | |
| Loveless, Elisha | do | 22 May 78 | 16 Jan 79 | dead |
| Lawson, Michl. | do | 5 June 78 | 5 April 79 | discharged |
| Lanham, Richard | do | do | do | do |
| Lynch, John | Corpl | 10 dec 76 | April 79 | do |
| Lock, William | do | do | 23 May 78 | deserted |
| Land, William | pt | 1 feb 77 | May 80 | transferred to Invalids } |
| | | | 16 Oct 80 | discharged } |
| Lindsey, Theops. | do | 2 June 79 | pris. Jan 80 | |
| Lasher, John | do | 3 May 79 | June 80 | deserted |
| Luckett, David | Ensn | 26 Jan 80 | | |
| Lewis, Joseph | Musn | June 80 | 16 Aug 80 | missing |

### SECOND REGIMENT.—*Beginning Jany., 1778.*

| NAMES. | RANK. | TIME OF SERVICE. Enlisted. | Discharged. | REMARKS. |
|---|---|---|---|---|
| Lowe, J. Tolson | Sergt Ensn | 26 Jan 80 | 10 Jan 80 | discharged |
| Langford, Elijaha | pt | 1 Jan 77 | do | do |
| Lloyd, Michl. | do | do | 1 Nov 80 | present |
| London, William | do | | 1 Mar 78 | discharged |
| Long, Solomon | Capt | 10 dec 76 | 4 June 78 | resigned |

## MUSTERS OF MARYLAND TROOPS, VOL. I.

| NAMES. | RANK. | TIME OF SERVICE. Enlisted. | Discharged. | REMARKS. |
|---|---|---|---|---|
| { Summers, Obad. | | | | see S |
| { Smith, Robt. | | | | do |
| Lettman, William | pt | | | killed Eutaw |
| Laws, William | do | 18 May 77 | 1 Nov 80 | present |
| Leonard, James | do | 20 Jan 77 | 20 Jan 80 | discharged |
| Lucas, John | Sergt | 14 do | 14 do | do |
| reduced to pt 27 Aug | | | | |
| 78 reappd. | do | 27 Sept 78 | | |
| Lindsay, James | Corpl | 10 feb 77 | | |
| reduced to pt 16 feb 79 | Corpl | 3 Aprl 79 | 10 feb 80 | do |
| Lane, Bartholw. | pt | | 10 Jan 80 | do |
| Lynch, Barney | do | | 11 June 78 | deserted |
| Lucas, Basil | Sergt | | 10 Jan 80 | discharged |
| Launders, Geo. | pt | 29 Aprl 78 | 1 Nov 80 | present |
| Lucas, John | do | 15 May do | do | do |
| Laws, George | do | 2 June do | do | do |
| Lynch, John | do | | 4 June 79 | deserted |
| Lord, Henry | do | 4 May 78 | 1 Nov 80 | present |
| Laine, Solomon | do | 20 do | 3 Apl 79 | discharged |
| Laine, Levin | do | do | do | do |
| prisr. 8 Jan 80 | | | | |
| Levingston, Henry | do | 10 June 78 | | |
| Langrell, Asquith | do | | 3 Aprl 79 | do |
| Lucas, James | do | 10 Jan 80 | | discharged |
| | Sergt | 25 Dec 79 | | deserted |
| Lovelet, Benja. | pt | | Apl & May 79 | deserted |
| Lyles, Zacha. | pt | 11 June 79 | 1 Nov 80 | present |
| Lord, Levin | do | 26 May 79 | do | do |
| Lee, William | do | 10 June do | do | do |
| Land, Richard | do | Aprl 80 | do | do |

THIRD REGIMENT.—*Beginning* 77.

| NAMES. | RANK. | Enlisted. | Discharged. | REMARKS. |
|---|---|---|---|---|
| Lawler, David | pt | 5 feb 79 | 16 Aug 80 | missing |
| Lacey, Stephen | do | 7 Aprl 77 | | |
| Lynch, William | do | 1 Jan 77 | 1 Oct 80 | present |
| Love, John | do | do | 1 Nov do | do |
| Lilly, William | do | do | | |
| not heard of since 4 June 78, joined Smith's Compy. May 79 | | | | |
| Lowe, John | Corpl | 1 May 77 | Sergt 2 feb 80 time expired | |
| Lauglane, Mark | pt | see Mack MacLaughlin | | |
| Lawler, John | Corpl | 1 July 77 | 7 July 78 | deserted |
| Lyon, Jacob | Sergt | 1 June 79 | to Invalids Sept 5 81 died | |
| Lassell, Alex. | pt | 2 May 77 | April & May 79 | left out the |
| Lyles, Henry | Lieut | | | [Roll |

## MUSTERS OF MARYLAND TROOPS, VOL. I.

| NAMES. | RANK. | TIME OF SERVICE. Enlisted. | Discharged. | REMARKS. |
|---|---|---|---|---|
| Long, Thomas | Corpl | | | |
| | pt | 15 feb 78 | } 1 Nov 80 | present |
| Leach, James | do | | | |
| Lynch, John | do | 7 April 78 | | |
| Lee, John [1] | do | 25  do | 20 July 80 | deserted, joined |
| Luff, Thomas, (or Jno.) | pt | 9 Mar 78 | 16 Aug 80 | missing, sup- [posed killed |
| Lucast, Peter | fife | 30 April do | do | do |
| Leonard, Hugh | do | 3  do | 17 May 78 | deserted |
| Lynn, Thomas | do | | 8 June 78 | do |
| Layman, Jeremh. | do | 4 May 78 | | Corpl 5 June 79 |
| Layman, Garliner | do | 31  do | July 80 | deserted, rein- [listed 10 Nov 78 |
| Lee, John [1] | do | 15  do | 1 Nov 80 | present |
| Lyon, Isaac | do | 19  do | do | do |
| Looney, Thomas | do | 1 Aprl 78 | 16 Aug 80 | missing |
| Lee, Joseph | do | 5 June 78 | 5 Dec 78 | died |
| Lewis, Thomas | do | do | 1 Nov 80 | present |
| Longest, Danl. | do | 20 Mar 78 | 14 April 80 | to Invalids Sept 15 82 dischd. |
| Lowes, Henry | do | 4 June 78 | 9 Sept 80 | deserted |
| Larner, John  joined feb 79 | do | | | |
| Larey, Danl.  joined feb 79 | do | | | |
| Lavender, Jno. | do | 19 May 79 | feb 80 | died |
| Lewton, Thomas | do | 11  do | 28 Sept 79 | deserted |

### FROM OCTOBER MUSTERS, 1780.

| | | | | |
|---|---|---|---|---|
| Lawler, Michael | pt | 1 Jan 80 | 1 Nov 80 | present |

### FOURTH REGIMENT.—*Beginning Dec., 77.*

| | | | | |
|---|---|---|---|---|
| Logie, James [2] | Sergt | Dec 76 | } | |
| | do M. | 1 Aug 77 | } agrees to serve to the end of | |
| Oldham's Asst. | F. M. | 10 Feby 80 | | [James Warder's time |
| Lewis, Charles | Corpl | 18 dec 76 | 18 Jan 80 | discharged |
| | Sergt | 1 June 78 | | |
| Lewis, Nicholas | pt | 13 Jan 77 | 13 Jan 80 | do |
| Lawler, David [3] | Corpl | 12 April 77 } | 12 April 80 | do |
| | pt | 29 Sept 78 } | | |

[1] Smith's.  [2] Oldham's.  [3] Norwood's.

## MUSTERS OF MARYLAND TROOPS, VOL. I.

| NAMES. | RANK. | TIME OF SERVICE. Enlisted. | Discharged. | REMARKS. |
|---|---|---|---|---|
| Lewis, Joseph | Lieut | exchd. with Lieut. A. Hoops from Hazen's Regt. | | |
| Lennox, John[1] | pt | Corpl 1 dec 79 | Sept 80 | deserted |
| Lynch, Hugh | pt | 13 April 77 | 13 Aprl 80 | discharged |
| Lansdale, Thomas | Capt Major | 10 dec 76 | | |
| Lucas, John[2] | Sergt pt | 9 dec 77 | July 80 | deserted |
| Leavley, Jacob[3] | Corpl pt | 23 feb 77 } 13 Aug 80 } | 23 feb 80 | discharged |
| Lake, William | do | 8 Jan 77 | 5 July 80 | deserted |
| Lindsay, Jno. | do | 23 dec 76 | 16 Aug 80 | missing |
| Lilly, William[4] | do | see William Filly | | |
| Lloyd, Thomas | do | | Jan 78 | left out the Roll |
| Leamon, William[5] | Sergt | 22 April 77 | 22 Apl 80 | time expired |
| Lynch, John | pt | 5 Aug 77 | 1 Nov 80 | present |
| Lucas, James | pt | 18 Aug 77 | Mar 79 | deserted |
| Loveday, Thomas | fife M. | 10 feb 78 | | do |
| Lee, Parker[6] | Ensn Lieut | 1 Jan 78 16 Oct 78 | | |
| Lawler, John[2] | pt | 16 Jan 78 | June 78 transfd. to 10th Virga. | |
| Lewis, Edward | do | 7 feb 78 | 17 May 78 | deserted [Regt. |
| Ludford, Henry[1] | do | 24 Mar 78 | 1 June 80 | do |
| Levie, Alexander[7] | do | 22 April 78 | 1 Nov 80 | present |
| Longdon, Thomas[8] | do | 8 do | Sept 80 | deserted |
| Smith's, late Spurrier's | | | | |
| Lynch, Robt. | do | 15 do | 1 Nov 80 | present |
| Lamal, (or Lamie), William | do | 21 do | 15 Sept 78 | deserted |
| Lawrence, James | do | 25 do | 3 June 79 | to Invalids, 5 Oct 80 deserted |
| Leary, Daniel | do | 7 May 78 | 4 Jan 80 | May & June 80 |
| discharged by furlough, man in his place | | | | |
| Corpl 27 do, private 20 Oct 79 | | | | |
| Lindiff, John[9] | Sergt Sergt. M. | 1 May 80 | | } 16 Aug 80 priso- |
| prisr. 22 Aug 77, joined 16 July 78, Qr. M. Sergt. 20 Aug 78 | | | | } [ner |
| Lieuty, John | pt | 19 May 78 | Sep 80 | deserted |
| Leary, Daniel[8] | do | 11 do | 4 Jan 80 | do |
| Lyons, William[1] | do | 2 Nov 78 | 20 dec 78 | do |
| Leary, Michael[8] | do | 28 Jan 77 } | 8 Jan 80 } | do |
| prisr. 27 Aug 77, joined 24 July 78 | Corpl | 1 Nov 79 } | | |
| Lions, William[10] | pt | 13 June 78 | 10 Aprl 79 | discharged |

| | | |
|---|---|---|
| [1] Godman's. | [2] Selman's. | [3] Spurrier's. [4] Bowie's. [5] Burgess'. |
| [6] Norwood's. | [7] Lansdale's | [8] Lt. Smith's. [9] Oldham's. [10] Riely's. |

## MUSTERS OF MARYLAND TROOPS, VOL. I.

| NAMES. | RANK. | TIME OF SERVICE. Enlisted. | Discharged. | REMARKS. |
|---|---|---|---|---|
| Lister, Charles | pt | 2 May 78 | 16 Aug 80 | missing |
| Lunn, John[1] | do | | July 80 | deserted |
| London, John[2] | do | 6 Oct 79 | 16 Aug 80 | missing |
| Lester, John[3] to Oldham's | pt | 14 Sept 79 | July 80 | deserted |

### RAWLINGS' REGIMENT.

| NAMES. | RANK. | TIME OF SERVICE. Enlisted. | Discharged. | REMARKS. |
|---|---|---|---|---|
| Lovely, Thomas | fife | 21 Aug 76 | | |
| Lynch, Daniel | pt | 2 July | 28 Nov 76 | deserted |
| Layard, George | do | 16 Aug | 12 dec 76 | do |
| Livistone, John | do | | 9 Aug 79 | discharged. |
| Lemon, Patk. | do | | 13 May 79 | do |
| Lacey, John | do | | 9 Aprl 79 | deserted |
| Lewis, Lewis | do | | do | do |
| Lewis, Lawrence | do | | 15 Mar | do |
| Lockhart, Jno. | do | 10 Mar | | |
| Linley, James  6 mo. | Corpl | | | |
| Larimore, David  do | pt | | | |
| Lanham, Nehimh. | | | | |

### FIRST REGIMENT.

| NAMES. | RANK. | TIME OF SERVICE. Enlisted. | Discharged. | REMARKS. |
|---|---|---|---|---|
| Mudd, Richard | Sergt | | 7 Jan 82 | discharged |
| McKeel, Thomas | Ensn | 10 dec 76 | | never served |
| McKoy, Alexander | fifer | 4 Aprl 77 | 14 July 77 | died |
| McGinnis, Willian | pt | 14 dec 76 | 12 Aug 77 | deserted |
| Mitchell, James | do | do | 16 Aug 80 | missing |
| McCain, —— | do | do | 10 Aprl 77 | Virga. |
| McDaniel, Roger | do | 5 Mar 77 | June 80 | deserted |
| Mason, Thomas | do | 23  do | | never joined |
| Muse, Walker | Lieut | 10 dec 76 | Capt. 10 June 77 | |
| Mitchell, Jno. | do | do | | |
| | Capt | 15 July 77 | | |
| Marlow, Middlen. | Sergt | | 27 dec 79 | discharged |
| Mitchell, Francis | pt | 10 dec 76 | 27  do | do |
| Martin, Hezek. | do | | | never joined |
| Mills, John | do | | 10 June 77 | discharged |
| McCallister, Arch. | Lieut | 17 April 77 | B. Capt. | 24 Sept 79 |
| Mattingly, Jos. | pt | 10 dec 76 | | |
| | Sergt | 24 May 77 | 27 dec 79 | discharged |
| McKensey, Wm. | pt | 10 dec | 20 April 77 | died |
| McDonough, Wm. | do | 5 Apl 77 | | never joined |
| Monroe, Danl. | do | 3 May 77 | 20 May 80 | discharged |
| Mackay, Thos. | do | 19 Aprl 77 | 11 Sept | taken prisoner |

[1] Lt. Colgate's.    [2] Belt's.    [3] Oldham's.

## MUSTERS OF MARYLAND TROOPS, VOL. I.

| NAMES. | RANK. | TIME OF SERVICE. Enlisted. | Discharged. | REMARKS. |
|---|---|---|---|---|
| McCoy, John | Sergt | 10 dec 76 | Aug 78 | joined forage |
| Miller, Michael | pt | do | 22 Aug | [Dept. |
|  |  | joined | 15 Sept 78 | present 1 Nov 80 |
| McKean, MacMal. | do | do | 24 feb | exchanged for J. Shout |
| Mathews, Jos. | pt | 10 dec 76 | 13 Aug 78 | deserted |
| McCarty, Jesse | do | do | 24 May | do |
| McLane, Jno. | Corpl | O. S. | 27 dec 79 | discharged |
| McLane, Hugh | pt | 10 dec 76 | 25 Aprl 79 | do |
| Murray, Mathew | do | do | 15 Apl 78 | deserted |
| McNew, Moses | do | do | 31 Aug 80 |  |
|  |  | joined 18 Oct 80 | 1 Nov 80 | present |
| Mire, Frederick | pt | 10 dec 76 | 27 dec 79 | discharged |
| May, Dennis | fifer | do | 22 Aug 77 | prisoner |
| McCormick, Richd. | pt | 18 Mar 77 | 18 Sept 77 | missing |
| McPherson, Sam. | Lieut | 10 dec 76 | Captain | 7 April 80 |
| McPherson, Mark | Sergt | do | 27 dec 79 | discharged |
|  | Ensn | Lieut |  |  |
| Mudd, Martin | Sergt | 10 May 77 | 24 Sept 78 | died |
| Martin, Ignatius | pt | 18 Mar 77 | 27 Aug 77 | do |
| Mudd, Thomas | do | 14 Aug 77 | 18 Oct 77 | discharged |
| Murray, Alexr. | Capt. | 10 Dec 76 | 10 June | resigned |
| Miller, Josiah | Corpl | do | 27 dec 79 | discharged |
| Mayhew, Thos. | pt | do | Exchd. for L. Hickey |  |
| Majors, Jno. | do | 4 feb 78 | 16 Aug 80 | prisoner |
| Mitchell, Jno. | do | 28 do 77 | 17 dec 77 | deserted |
| Meek, Jesse | do | 4 Mar 77 | June 80 left out, not heard of |  |
| Malcomb, Tho. | do | 5  do | 17 dec 77 | deserted [Nov 80 |
|  |  | joined 1 Aprl 78 | 7 Mar 80 | discharged |
| McNamara, Benja. | pt | 10 Mar 77 | never joined |  |
| McCarty, James | do | 25 feb 77 | 26 feb | deserted |
| Mitchell, Igns. | do | 16 May 77 | 16 May 80 | discharged } |
|  | Sergt | 1 Aug 77 | 25 July 78 | promoted } |
| Maynadier, Hy. | Surgn. Mate |  |  |  |
| Millston, Barker | pt | 9 Oct 77 | 1 Jan 78 | deserted |
| Morrison, Wm. | do | 17 Sept 77 | 17 Sept 80 | discharged |
| Moire, Peter | do | 3 May 78 |  |  |
|  | Corpl | 1 Mar 80 | 16 Aug 80 | missing |
| McNamara, Darley | pt | 7 May 78 | do | do |
| Marsh, Benja. | do | 10 June 78 | 23 Mar 80 | prisoner |
| Mudd, Richard | do | 6 Jan 79 | 6 Jan 80 | discharged |
|  | Corpl | 1 Jan 80 |  |  |
| McCaul, Wm. | do | 1 Sept 79 | 1 Nov 80 | present |
| Martindale, Jno. | pt | 4 May 78 | 16 Aug 80 | missing } |
|  | Fife Major | 1 July 80 |  |  |

## MUSTERS OF MARYLAND TROOPS, VOL. I.

| NAMES. | RANK. | TIME OF SERVICE. Enlisted. | Discharged. | REMARKS. |
|---|---|---|---|---|
| Miller, Jacob | pt | 4 June 78 | 28 feb 79 | discharged |
| Martin, Lond. | do | 1 do | 14 do | do |
| May, Richard | do | 23 May 78 | 5 April 79 | do |
| Mudd, Bent. | do | 9 feb 79 } | } | |
| | Sergt | 1 July 80 } | 1 Nov 80 | present |
| McNaughton, Peter | do | 10 dec 76 | · do | do |
| Morrison, Jno. | fifer | 9 April 78 | do | do |
| McCormick, Jno. | do | 1 Oct 77 | do | do |
| Moore, Francis | pt | 25 April 79 | | |
| Medcalf, Richd. | do | 6 Mar 78 | | |
| McCoy, Hugh | pt | 15 May 79 | 16 Aug 80 | missing |
| Moran, Azell | do | 14 June 79 } | | |
| | Drum | 1 Aug 79 } | 21 Aug 80 | do |
| Miles, Walter | pt | 1 Sept 79 } | 1 Nov 80 | present |
| | Corpl | 1 Jan 80 } | 1 April 83 | discharged |
| Medcaff, Robt. | pt | June 80 | 12 Aug 80 | deserted |
| Millet, George | pt. mus'd | do | 16 Aug 80 | missing |
| Millstead, Jno. | do | 1 feb 80 | 1 Nov 80 | present |
| Menitry, Gueld'd | | 29 Jan 80 | do | do |

SECOND REGIMENT.—*Beging. with the Muster Rolls for January,* 1778.

| NAMES. | RANK. | TIME OF SERVICE. Enlisted. | Discharged. | REMARKS. |
|---|---|---|---|---|
| Marshall, Wm. | Surgn. Mate | | | removed to hos- |
| Moore, Hezekiah | Qr. M. S. | 3 June 77 | | promoted [pital |
| Mead, James | Drum M. | 15 Aug 77 | 1 Nov 80 | present |
| Miller, John | | 4 Mar 77 } | | |
| O. S. | Sergt | } | 10 Jan 80 | discharged |
| Martin, Robt. | Corpl | | do | do |
| Masterson, Jno. | pt | do | do | do |
| Murphy, James | do | | 1 June 78 | died |
| McDonald, Stephn. | do | | 14 feb 78 | deserted |
| McLaughlan, Wm. | do | 1 Sept 77 | 1 Nov 80 | present |
| Moser, Cruise, | pt | 6 Jan 77 | 16 Aug 80 | killed |
| McGraw, Christ. | Drum | 1 Aprl 77 | · 1 Nov 80 | present |
| McAndrew, Pat. | pt | | 28 Jan 78 | deserted |
| Mason, Caleb | Corpl | | 10 Jan 80 | discharged |
| Miles, John | pt | | do | do |
| Mahoney, Clemt. | do | | 22 Jan 78 | in Hospt., time expired |
| Joined April Muster Roll 78 | | | 1 April 80 | 10 Jan 80 dis-charged |

Mitchell, Henry    Corpl Sergt. 1 Aug 78, reducd to pt. 27 Aug 78, Sergt. 27
10 Jany 80 discharged    [Sept 78

| McNemara, Pat. | pt | | 10 Jan 80 | discharged |
| Malone, Andrew | do corpl | 1 Feb 78 | do | do |

## MUSTERS OF MARYLAND TROOPS, VOL. I.

| NAMES. | RANK. | TIME OF SERVICE. Enlisted. | Discharged. | REMARKS. |
|---|---|---|---|---|
| Mason, James | pt | | 12 dec 79 | discharged |
| More, William | do | 17 Mar 77 | 16 Aug 80 | prisoner |
| Murphy, Anthy. | do Sergt | 1 Jan 80 | do | deserted |
| Magragh, Jno. | pt | | 1 April 80 | do |
| McHendricks, James | do | | 10 Jan 80 | discharged |
| | Corpl | 20 July 78 | | |
| Murphy, Michael | pt | | 7   do | deserted |
| Martin, John | do | | 22 Jan 78 | do |
| Maloy, Michael | do | | do | do |
| Maynard, Peter | do Corpl | 1 feb 80 | 16 Aug 80 | do |
| Marlow, Saml. | pt | | 29 Sept 79 | discharged |
| Mentges, Chrisn. | do | 18 feb 77 | 18 feb 80 | do |
| Melvin, Peter | do | 4 do | 1 Nov 80 | present |
| Mockbee, Wm. | pt | | Nov 80 | not heard of |
| Martin, John | do | 12 feb 77 | 16 Aug 80 | prisoner |
| Maloy, Barney | do | | 1 Nov 80 | present |
| McCalmont, Jas. | Surgn | 1 Jan 78 | 10 June 79 | resigned |
| Moore, Reubin | pt | 27 dec 77 | 1 Nov 80 | present |
| Moore, William | do | do | do | do |
| Mann, William | do | 30 Mar 78 | joined again 12 Sept 79, 1 Nov 80 present ㅠ |  |
| McFarlen, James | do | | 19 May 78 | deserted |
| Miller, James | do | 10 April 78 | | |
| Murphey, James | do | 18 Mar 78 | 20 July 78 | died |
| McDugle, Jno. | do | 21 April 78 | 1 July 78 | died |
| McConneken, Jno. | do | 6   do | do | do |
| Matthews, Saml. | do | 28   do | | |
| McAdams, Jno. | do | 15 Jan 78 | Sergt 10 Jan 80, 1 Nov 80 present |  |
| McDonald, Alex. | do | 11 Mar 78 | 17 July 80 | deserted |
| McGee, John | do | 29 Jan 78 | 8 Mar 79 | discharged |
| Matthews, Thos. | do | 26 feb 78 | 18 June 79 | deserted |
| Magraugh, Jas. | do | 18   do | 1 Nov 80 | present |
| McCay, Henry | do | 16   do | 15 Aprl 78 | deserted |
| McGraw, John | do | 2 May 78 | 18 Oct 78 | died |
| Mulhulland, Arthur | do | 13   do | 1 Nov 80 | present |
| Morgan, Johnson | do | 22 April 78 | 25 July 78 | died |
| McCarty, Thimothy | do | 9 May 78 | 17 July 80 | deserted |
| McCoy, William | do | 30 April 78 | 16 Aug 80 | prisoner |
| McKenney, Jno. | do | | dec 78 | deserted |
| Mattingley, Thos. | pt | 31 May 78 | 3 April 79 | discharged |
| Mattingley, Phil. | do | do | do | do |
| Mackey, Jacob | do . | 1 June 78 | do | do |
| Metcalf, Jno. | do | do | 15 July 78 | died |
| Mansell, James | do | | 4 Aug 79 | deserted |

## MUSTERS OF MARYLAND TROOPS, VOL. I.

| NAMES. | RANK. | TIME OF SERVICE. Enlisted. | Discharged. | REMARKS. |
|---|---|---|---|---|
| Maxwell, Wm. | pt | | 12 Nov 78 | deserted |
| Miles, Fredk. | do | 25 April 78 | 1 May 81 | discharged |
| | Corpl | 10 Jan 80 | 1 Nov 80 | present |
| Mason, James | pt | 29 May do | 1 Oct 80 | ditto |
| Mathews, Wm. | do | 1 June 78 | Nov 80 | not heard of, afterwards joined Invalids |
| Murphy, Jno. | do | 3 May 78 | 2 April 79 | deserted |
| Manning, Hy. | do | | 1 Aprl 80 | discharged |
| McKean, Levin | do | 20 do | 3 April 79 | do |
| Mitchell, Levin | do | do | do | do |
| Moxey, Gregory | do | do | 24 dec 78 | do |
| Medlicutt, Jas. | do | 25 do | 26 do | deserted |
| Mahood, Jno. | do | do | Mar 79 | discharged |
| McCurdy, Jno. | do | do | do | do |
| McClarey, Bassel | do | do | 26 dec 78 | deserted |
| McCallister, Jos. | do | 28 do | 24 do | discharged |
| Marlow, Butler | do | | 10 Jan 80 | do |
| Malone, Jno. | do | | 20 June 79 | deserted |
| Meglamery, Edwd. | do | | 1 do 80 | discharged |
| McCormick, Mathew | do | 30 do 79 | 16 Aug 80 | prisoner |
| Moore, Richd. | pt | | 15 Nov 79 | deserted |
| Morain, Jno. | do | 3 Aug 79 | 1 Nov 80 | present |
| Martin, Joseph | do | 22 May 79 | 22 July 79 | deserted |
| Mason, Caleb | Ensn | 26 Jan 80 | 16 Aug 80 | killed Camden |
| Mitchell, Richd. | pt | 20 Mar 80 | 1 Nov 80 | present |
| Mie, Thomas | do | May 78 | do | do |

### THIRD REGIMENT.—*Beginning 77.*

| NAMES. | RANK. | TIME OF SERVICE. Enlisted. | Discharged. | REMARKS. |
|---|---|---|---|---|
| Marbury, Jos. | Capt | 10 dec 76 | | |
| Mudd, Henry | Corpl | 21 May 79 | | |
| McCanh, Jos. | do | 5 Aprl 77 | | |
| McNorton, Wm. | do | 16 May 77 | all out November 77 | |
| Maddox, Notly | do | 18 feb 77 | | |
| McPherson, A. | do | 9 May 77 | dec 77 | died |
| Molohon, Wm. | Lieut | 10 Dec 76 | 1 July 78 | resigned |
| McMullen, Timo. | Corp | do | | |
| or McMahon | Sergt | 7 Sep 77 | joined in Carolina from Pennsylvania | |
| | Sergt. Mt. | 28 Aug 78 | | |
| Mansfield, Jas. | fife | | 1 Mar 79 | discharged |
| Manning, Wm. | pt | | 15 Mar 78 | deserted |
| McLaughlin, Nic. | do | 11 May 77 | 1 Nov 80 | present |
| Morton, James | do | do | 21 Sep 80 | deserted |
| Mileter, Pat. | do | 25 Mar 77 | 25 Mar 80 | discharged |

## MUSTERS OF MARYLAND TROOPS, VOL I.

| NAMES. | RANK. | TIME OF SERVICE. Enlisted. | Discharged. | REMARKS. |
|---|---|---|---|---|
| McDonald, Arch. | pt | 6 May 77 | 28 Aug 80 | deserted |
| Manger, Nic. | Lieut | 20 feb 77 | Capt. | |
| McCay, John | Corpl | 1 Aprl 77 | 1 April 80 | discharged |
| Mattehannan, Wm. | pt | 2 Aug do | | |
| Martin, Phil. | do | 4 do | | |
| Murray, James | Sergt pt | 20 June 77 | | Aprl & May 79 left out the |
| McGuire, Michl. | pt | 1 April 77 | | [Rolls |
| Menton, Danl. | do | | 1 Nov 80 | present |
| Martin, Michl. | do | 12 Jan 77 | 12 Jan 80 | discharged |
| McLamar, Timoy. | do | do | do | do |
| Morris, Thomas | do | | 16 Aug 80 | missing |
| McGuire, Jas. | do | 10 do | 5 Jan 80 | discharged |
| McGuire, Jno. | Sergt | 26 Mar 77 ⎫ | | |
| | Sergt. Major | 26 Sept ⎬ | | promoted Ensign |
| | Adjt | 28 Mar 78 ⎭ | | |
| Morris, Michl. | pt | 7 July 77 | 25 Jan 78 | died |
| Manfield, Robt. | do | 15 April 77 | 1 May 78 | to Invalids |
| Mercer, Jno. | do | 10 Mar 77 | 10 Mar 80 | discharged |
| Murphy, Danl. | do | | June 79 | left out the Roll |
| McDermot, Tho. | do | 12 Jan 78 | | |
| McGee, Hugh | do | 28 do | 14 April 78 | deserted |
| Morris, Jno. | Sergt | | 20 May 80 | discharged |
| McDaniel, Elisha | Corpl | | 12 Dec 77 | died |
| Minning, Jno. | pt | 30 Oct 77 | 1 Dec 79 | deserted |
| McCann, Jno. | do | 21 July 77 | dec 77 | do |
| | | | 20 Aug 80 | do |
| McMullen, Jas. | do | | April 78 | struck off |
| Morrow, Wm. | do | 25 April 78 | | |
| Murphy, Chs. | pt | 17 April 78 | | |
| | Corpl | 1 Sept 79 | | |
| | Sergt | 1 Jan 80 | | |
| Maires, Saml. | pt | 21 do | Sept 79 | struck off |
| Morgan, Richd. | do | 22 do | Oct 78 | died |
| Mackey, Tho. | do | 20 do | Jan 80 | struck off |
| Magson, Mard. | do | do | do | do |
| McKim, Ben. | do | | 1 do | time expired |
| McGee, William | do | 20 Apl 78 | 1 Nov 80 | present |
| McGee, Charles | do | 28 do | do | do |
| McAtee, Leond. | do | 26 do | 19 feb 79 | discharged |
| McAtee, Thomas | do | do | do | do |
| Main, David | do | 2 Mar 78 | | |
| | Corpl | 1 July 78 | 16 Aug 80 | prisoner |
| Mingo, Jos. | pt | 22 April 78 | | |
| Mumford, Chs. | do | | 20 Jan 79 | discharged |

## MUSTERS OF MARYLAND TROOPS, VOL. I.

| NAMES. | RANK. | TIME OF SERVICE. Enlisted. | Discharged. | REMARKS. |
|---|---|---|---|---|
| Moyland, Dens. | pt | | 19 dec 79 | deserted |
| Moses, Jacob | do | | 1 Oct 80 | present |
| Morris, Jno. | do | 14 do | 1 Nov 80 | do |
| Morgan, Jereh. | do | 16 May 78 | 14 Oct 78 | died |
| McCalley, Jno. | do | 19 do | 4 April 79 | discharged |
| McCartney, Edwd. | do | | June 78 | do |
| McCummert, Michl. | pt · | 30 April 78 | | |
| McDonah, Michl. | do | 30 May 78 | 30 Oct 79 | deserted |
| McDonald, Wm. D. | Sergt | | 1 Nov 80 | present |
| Matthews, Jno. | pt | 11 June 78 | do | do |
| McCarty, Wm. | do | 30 do | 16 Aug 80 | missing |
| Mayhew, Thomas | do | 20 July 78 | 23 Jan 79 | discharged |
| Mayhew, Jona. | do | do | reinlisted | see below |
| Mullens, Timy. | do | 19 May 78 | 16 Aug 80 | missing |
| McMillion, Wm. | Sergt | | June 79 | out the Roll |
| Mahugh, Jona. | pt | 9 Jan 79 | 1 Nov 80 | present |
| May, Joseph | do | 4 June 78 | 16 Aug 80 | missing |
| Mobley, Thomas | do | 5 do | 12 April 79 | discharged |
| McLaughlan, Mark | do | 20 Mar 77 | 1 Nov 80 | present |
| McCloud, Hugh | do | 5 Jan 77 | 5 Jan 80 | discharged |
| Murray, John | do | 7 feb 79 | to Invalids, dismissed or fur- } lough July 11th, 1783 } | |
| Murnet, Michl. | do | 30 April 78 | do | do |
| Miller, John | do | | 6 feb 80 | to Invalids |
| Moore, Matthew | do | 18 May 78 | 1 Nov 80 | present |
| Monghon, Pat. | do | 23 April 79 | | |
| Matthews, Geo. | do | 11 May 79 | | |
| Mandewitt, Phil. | do | 28 Nov 79 | 4 Jan 80 | deserted |
| Mills, John | Corpl | 27 Mar 80 | 1 Nov 80 | present |
| McFarlane, Alex. | pt | | do | do |

### OCTOBER MUSTER, 1780.

| NAMES. | RANK. | Enlisted. | Discharged. | REMARKS. |
|---|---|---|---|---|
| Mitchell, Wm. | pt | 15 feb 80 | 1 Nov 80 | present |
| Mattingly, Chs. | do | | do | do |
| Mohan, Patk. | do | | 16 Aug 80 | missing, see |
| Monghon, (or) Mahorn | | | | [above |

### FOURTH REGIMENT.—*Beginning December, 1777.*

| NAMES. | RANK. | Enlisted. | Discharged. | REMARKS. |
|---|---|---|---|---|
| McAllester, Joel [1] | Sergt | 8 dec 76 | 8 dec 79 | discharged |
| Mason, John | pt | 6 do | do | deserted |
| McKenny, Robt. | do | 30 Jan 77 | 30 Jan 80 | discharged |

[1] Oldham's.

## MUSTERS OF MARYLAND TROOPS, VOL. I.

| NAMES. | RANK. | TIME OF SERVICE. Enlisted. | Discharged. | REMARKS. |
|---|---|---|---|---|
| Murphey, Jno. | pt | | | deserted |
| McGain, Pat. | do | | feb 78 | do |
| Mansell, Richd. | do | 7 dec 76 | | } |
|    pt 1 June 78 | Sergt | 1 Aprl 78 | 26 Oct 80 | } do |
| Merino, Charles | pt | 19 Jan 77 | 19 Jan 80 | discharged |
| McNeall, Jno.[1] | Corpl | Exchanged for Thomas Potts | | } |
| | | 20 May 77 | 20 May 80 | dischd., reinlisted } |
| Murphey, Cornes. | pt | 7 Apl 77 . | 1 Nov 80 | present |
| Murphey, Tho.[2] | do | dec 76 | Jan 80 | deserted |
| Mumford, Robt. | do | | 15 June 78 | discharged |
| Moore, Mathew[2] | do | 76 | 1 Nov 80 | present |
| Menchim, Humpry. | do | 1 May 77 | do | do |
| Moreton, Joshua | do | feb 77 | July mus. 79 | died Maryland |
| McDaniel, Thos. | do | 8 Jan 77 | } | |
| | Corpl | 1 Aprl 80 | } July 80 | deserted |
| Miller, William | pt | | | see the other side |
| McIntire, Danl. | pt | | 1 Nov 80 | present |
| Martin, John | do | | | |
| Murphey, David[4] | do | | 3 May 78 | deserted |
| Mathews, John, (or Wm.) | do | 16 May 77 | 10 Jan 80 | do |
| McDermot, Owen | do | 19 do | 1 Oct 80 | present |
|   reinlisted —— | | | | |
| McCarty, Jere. | do | 25 do | Apl & May 79 | left out |
| McIntosh, Geo.[5] | do | | } 10 Aprl 80 } | do the Roll } |
| | Corpl | 26 dec 77 | } | } |
| | private | 31 Oct 78 | } | } discharged } |
| McKenzie, Brice· | pt | 6 dec 76 | 6 dec 79 | do |
| Murphey, Pat. | do | 6 Jan 77 | 6 Jan 80 | do |
|   reind., entd. below | | | | deserted Oct 80 |
| Marshall, Edwd. | do | | | |
| Moyston, Edwd. | do | 6 dec 76 | 6 dec 79 | discharged |
| Marks, John[2] | do | 30 May 77 | 14 May 80 | do |
| Morton, Vachel | do | 1 feb 77 | 1 feb 80 | do |
| Murphey, Thos. | do | 9 feb 77 | 1 Nov 80 | present |
| Manwaring, Chs. | do | | 30 June 78 | died |
| McAway, Chas.[6] | do | 18 Aug 77 | 1 Nov 80 | present |
| Mattinson, Danl. | do | 10 feb 77 | 13 feb 80 | discharged |
| Mallows, Robert[7] | do | 10 Apl 77 | 10 Apl 80 | time expired, 20 |
| Millions, (or Miller), Wm.[8] | pt | 25 July 77 | } | [Apl 80 dischd. |
| | Corpl | 1 April 79 | } 17 July 80 | discharged |
|   to Riely's Co. & promd. to Sergt | | 1 July 79 | | |

[1] Norwood's.    [2] Spurrier's.    [3] Godman's.    [4] Lansdale's.    [5] Sellman's.
[6] Bowie's.    [7] Burgess'.    [8] Riely's.

## MUSTERS OF MARYLAND TROOPS, VOL. I.

| NAMES. | RANK. | TIME OF SERVICE. Enlisted. | Discharged. | REMARKS. |
|---|---|---|---|---|
| Mustin, Richard | pt | 27 Mar 77 | | |
| | Corpl | 1 Apl 78 | 1 Mar 80 | time expired |
| | pt | 1 feb 79 | 1 April 80 | discharged |
| McCormick, Jno. | do | 1 Aug 77 | Aprl & May 79 | not heard of |
| Malone, Conner | pt | | Jan 78 | left out the Roll |
| McAway, Thomas | do | 18 Aug 77 | dec 79 | deserted, joined |
| Murphey, John[1] | do | 17 Jan 78 | 16 Aug 80 | missing |
| Miller, John[2] | do | 12 feb 78 | June 78 | left out |
| Madden, Chris.[3] | do | 27 Apl 78 | 7 Aug 79 | deserted |
| Mathias, James[4] | do | 3 do | 1 Nov 80 | present |
| McCormick, Thos.[1] | do | 6 May 78 | 23 Jan 80 | deserted |
| Maxwell, Richd.[5] Smith's, late Spurrier's | do | 3 do | 23 Oct 78 | died |
| McGlachlan, Corns. | do | 4 do | 13 dec 79 | deserted |
| McCarty, James[6] | do | 31 Mar 78 | | |
| Riely's, late Bowie's | Corpl | 1 Mar 80 | 16 Aug 80 | prisoner |
| | Sergt | 1 May 78 | | |
| Murry, John[7] | pt | 1 May 80 | dec 79 | deserted |
| McKew, Thomas | do | 19 do | 1 June 79 | discharged |
| Morton, Archl. | do | 26 June 78 | June 80 | do |
| McDonald, Jos.[8] | do | 11 May 78 | | |
| | Corpl | 1 Oct 78 | | |
| | private | 1 Mar 79 | 16 Aug 80 | prisoner |
| | Corpl | 1 Aug 79 | | |
| McGinity, Pat.[8] | pt | 30 Mar 78 | do | missing |
| McLone, James[4] prisoner 22 Aug 77, Joined 23 June 78 | do | 6 dec 76 | do | do |
| Murphy, Timoy. | pt | 16 May 78 | 1 Nov 80 | present |
| Montgomery, Alex.[5] | Sergt | 19 do | | |
| | pt | 21 feb 79 | July 80 | deserted |
| McKinley, Jas. | do | 22 May 78 | 15 feb 80 | do |
| McMillion, Hugh | do | 13 do | | |
| | Corpl | 1 Sept 78 | 1 Nov 80 | present |
| | Sergt | 1 July 79 | | |
| Miles, John[9] May and June Roll 80, deserted time not known | pt | 17 May 78 | July 80 | deserted |
| Morris, William | pt | 28 May 78 | 16 Aug 80 | missing |
| McAway, Stephen[10] | do | 7 June 79 | 15 May 80 | deserted |
| Merican, Edwd.[7] | do | 11 Aug 79 | 28 dec 79 | do |
| Murphy, Pat.[1] | do | | 14 Oct 80 | do |

[1] Sellman's.  [2] Bowie's.  [3] Norwood's.  [4] Lansdale's,  [5] Smith's.
[6] Riely's.  [7] Oldham's.  [8] Godman's.  [9] Burgess'.  [10] Belt's.

## MUSTERS OF MARYLAND TROOPS, VOL. I.

| NAMES. | RANK. | TIME OF SERVICE. Enlisted. | Discharged. | REMARKS. |
|---|---|---|---|---|
| McKenny, Lawr.[1] | pt | | 16 Aug 80 | missing |
| Marwood, Andrew[2] | do | | Oct 80 | deserted |
| McKnight, Jno. | do | 23 feb 79 | 1 do | present |

### RAWLINGS' REGIMENT.

| NAMES. | RANK. | Enlisted. | Discharged. | REMARKS. |
|---|---|---|---|---|
| McCartny, Jere. | pt | 29 feb 79 | | |
| McKann, Jno. | Sergt | 2 Aug 76 | | deserted |
| McGowan, Ben. | pt | 22 do | 12 Nov 76 | do |
| McCulloch, Wm. | do | 6 July | | |
| McCann, Pat. | do | 22 Aug | | |
| Morton, Jos. | do | 2 do | 18 feb 77 | died |
| McBride, Jno. | do | | | |
| McCreary, Thos. | | | 17 Aug | deserted |
| Marlow, Wm. | do | | | |
| McMachen, Peter | do | | | |
| Mitchell, Conrad | do | | 6 July 79 | discharged |
| McVay, James | do | | 10 June | deserted |
| Markwell, Wm. | do | | 8 Mar 80 | discharged |
| McBride, Jno. | fife | | | |
| Magruder, Enoch   1 yr. | Sergt | | | |
| McAttee, Saml. | pt | | 1 Aug 79 | do |
| Marlon, John   1 yr. | do | | | |
| Morgan, Jno. | pt | | 8 May | deserted |
| McKenny, Rodk. | do | | | |
| McCartny, Peter | do | 11 April | | |
| Mains, Francis | do | 28 Mar | | |
| McKinny, Felix | do | 1 May | | |
| McAdams, Alixd. | do | 3 April | | |
| Mains, George | do | 10 do | | |
| Miller, David | do | 5 do | | |
| McClean, Lackn. | do | 7 do | | |
| Murphy, Michl. | do | 16 Oct | | |
| McCoy, Eneas | do | 8 April | | |
| McDonald, Jno.   6 mo. | | 1 mar 79 | | |
| McMahan, Peter | do | | 10 June | do |
| McKinsie, Thos. | do | | | |
| McFarren, Walter | Drum | | | |
| McCord, Saml. | pt | 30 mar | | |
| McGuire, Pat.   6 mo. | | 12 mar | | |
| McGlaughland, J. 6 mo. | | 30 do | | |

[1] Spurrier's.

[2] Hoop's.

## MUSTERS OF MARYLAND TROOPS, VOL. I.

| NAMES. | RANK. | TIME OF SERVICE. Enlisted. | Discharged. | REMARKS. |
|---|---|---|---|---|

### FIRST REGIMENT.

| NAMES. | RANK. | Enlisted. | Discharged. | REMARKS. |
|---|---|---|---|---|
| Nixon, William | pt | 10 dec 76 | 16 Mar 78 | deserted |
| Nicholls, Becket | do | 24 Jan 77 | | never joined |
| Naylor, Alexr. | Sergt | 10 dec 76 | | transferred |
| Nicholson, Nichl. | pt | do | 27 dec 79 | discharged } |
|   reinlisted 15 April | Sergt | | 1 Nov 80 | present } |
| Naylor, Nicholas | do | | | |
| | Q. M. S. | Corpl 10 Dec 76 | | |
| Nayry, John | Sergt | 10 June | 1 Nov 80 | present } |
|   time out 1 Jan 80, reinlisted 11 Mar 80 | | | | |
| Neagle, William | pt | 10 Dec 76 | 4 feb 77 | dead |
| Nash, Barnard | do | do | 17 Mar 77 | do [charged |
| Neale, John | do | do | | Sergt 25 July 78, 27 dec 79 dis- |
| Nithington, Jere. | do | 28 feb 77 | 20 feb 80 | discharged |
| Nolan, Patk. | do | 10 dec 76 | 27 dec 79 | do |
| Noyes, William | S. Major | do | do | do |
| Neale, Thomas | pt | 4 May 78 | 1·Nov 80 | present |
| Nelson, John | Ensn | 26 Jan 80 | | |

### SECOND REGIMENT.—*Beginning Jany.*, 1778.

| NAMES. | RANK. | Enlisted. | Discharged. | REMARKS. |
|---|---|---|---|---|
| Noble, William | pt | | 29 Aprl 78 | deserted |
| Norton, George | do | 1 Mar 77 | 8 Mar 80 | discharged |
| Nutt, George | do | 10 Jan 77 | 10 Jan 80 | do |
| Noble, John | do | | 1 do | do |
| | Sergt | 1 June 78 | | |
| Nesbitt, Richd. | pt | 11 May 78 | 7 Mar 79 | deserted |
| Nickleson, Henry | pt | 4 Aprl 78 } | | |
| | Corpl | 10 Jan 80 } | 1 Nov 80 | present |
| Nickleson, Steph. | pt | 18 do } | 16 Aug 80 | prisoner |
| | Corpl | 1 feb 79 } | | |
| | Sergt | 10 Jan 80 } | furlough | |
| Newton, William | pt | 10 dec 76 | 1 Nov 80 | present |
| Nienbar, Thomas | do A.S. | | June 80 } | discharged |
| | | | 20 May 80 } | |
| Noble, Martin | do | 26 June 79 | 16 Aug 80 | missing, died of wounds |

### THIRD REGIMENT.—*Beginning* 77.

| NAMES. | RANK. | Enlisted. | Discharged. | REMARKS. |
|---|---|---|---|---|
| Newnan, Wm. | pt | 18 Aprl 77 | 1 Jan 80 | deserted |
| Nevill, Philip | do | 12 May 77 | | |
| Nowland, John | do | | 26 Jan 79 | to Invalids } |
| | | | 18 July 81 | deserted } |
| Neall, Charles | do | 26 April 78 | | |

## MUSTERS OF MARYLAND TROOPS, VOL. I.

| NAMES. | RANK. | TIME OF SERVICE. Enlisted. | TIME OF SERVICE. Discharged. | REMARKS. |
|---|---|---|---|---|
| Nailor, Joshua | pt | 30 Mar 78 | | |
| | Sergt | 24 Oct 78 | 16 Aug 80 | prisoner |
| Norris, John | pt | 29 May 78 | 4 Aprl 79 | discharged |
| Nunan, John | do | 1 July 78 | 6 dec 78 | deserted |
| Nisbet, Barney | do | 25 April 78 | 16 Aug 80 | missing |
| Nisbit, Charles | do | 30  do | 1 Aprl 79 | discharged |
| Nicholls, Sael | do | 11  do | 11 Aprl 81 | do |
| Neagle, Morris | do | | 16 Aug 80 | prisoner |
| | | continued to the end of the war | | |
| Nonan, William | do | | see above | |
| Nott, Nathanl. | Corpl | | 16 Aug 80 | prisoner |

### FOURTH REGIMENT.—*Beginning December, 77.*

| NAMES. | RANK. | Enlisted. | Discharged. | REMARKS. |
|---|---|---|---|---|
| Nujant, Pat.[1] | pt | 15 dec 76 | 16 dec 79 | discharged |
| Norris, Philip[2] | do | | 31 Oct 78 | died |
| Nelson, John | do | | 22 May 80 | discharged |
| Norwood, Edwd. | Captain | 10  do | 29 Sept 78 | left the service |
| Newton, Thomas[3] | pt | | 3 May 80 | deserted |
| Noland, Patk. | do | | 25 dec 79 | discharged |
| | reinlisted | 15 Aug 80 | 29 Aug 80 | died |
| Naylor, Joshua[4] | Corpl | 1 Aug 77 | 20 May 80 | discharged |
| Nash, Chrisn. | pt | | Jan 78 | left out the Roll |
| Nicholson, Anthy.[5] | do | 6 Aug 77 | feb 79 | dead |
| Nicholl, Archd.[6] | do | 10 feb 78 | Aug 80 | deserted |
| Nicholson, Geo. | do | 7 Mar 78 | 16 Sept 79 | died |
| Nuttall, Joseph[7] | do | 14 Aprl 78 | 3 June 79 | to Invalids |
| Smith's, late Spurrier's | Joined 17 April 81 | | | discharged |
| Norton, Lawrence[8] | do | 21 Aprl 78 | July 80 | deserted |
| Riely's, late Bowie's | | | | |
| Noland, Thomas[2] | do | 23  do | 16 Aug 80 | missing |
| Nelson, Richd.[9] | do | 20 May 78 | | |
| Nason, Saml.[8] | do | 20 Aprl 78 | 5 Sept 78 | discharged |
| Nowland, James[3] | do | 18 Nov 78 | | |
| | Corpl | 1 July 79 | 16 Aug 80 | missing |
| | Sergt | 1 April 80 | | |
| Newcomb, Robt.[1] | pt | 25 April 78 | dec 79 | deserted |
| Needham, Wm. | Sergt | 3 June 79 | 1 Nov 80 | present |
| Nicholls, Edward[10] | pt | 21 May 79 | 20 May 80 | deserted |
| | | | July 80 | do |
| Nicholls, Jos. | do | | 1 Nov 80 | present |

[1] Oldham's.　　[2] Norwood's.　　[3] Godman's.　　[4] Bowie's.　　[5] Burgess'.　　[6] Lansdale's
[7] Smith's.　　[8] Riely's.　　[9] Selman's.　　[10] Belt's.

## MUSTERS OF MARYLAND TROOPS, VOL. I.

| NAMES. | RANK. | TIME OF SERVICE. Enlisted. | Discharged. | REMARKS. |
|---|---|---|---|---|
| | | | | |

### RAWLINGS' REGIMENT.

| NAMES. | RANK. | Enlisted. | Discharged. | REMARKS. |
|---|---|---|---|---|
| Norris, Ben. | Corpl | 20 July 76 | | |
| Nailor, Isaac | pt | | 9 Aug 79 | discharged |
| Neale, Joseph | | 5 feb | | |

### FIRST REGIMENT.

| NAMES. | RANK. | Enlisted. | Discharged. | REMARKS. |
|---|---|---|---|---|
| Ofield, John | pt | 10 dec 76 | 1 Jan 80 | discharged |
| Owings, John | do | do | 6 Mar 78 | deserted |
| Oneal, John | do | do | 24 May 77 | do |
| Ostrow, William | do | 17 June 77 | 1 Oct 79 | |
| did not return to his furlough, discharged by G. Smallwood 20 April 80 | | | | |
| Oneal, John | pt | 11 April 78 | 23 Jan 80 | deserted |
| Owings, Joseph | do | 5 June 78 | feb 79 | discharged |
| Owings, Saml. | do | mustered | joined | 1 April 80 |

### SECOND REGIMENT.—*Beginning January Muster*, 1778.

| NAMES. | RANK. | Enlisted. | Discharged. | REMARKS. |
|---|---|---|---|---|
| Ormond, Wm. | pt | | 13 June 78 | discharged |
| O'Boyle | | see Boyles | | |
| Orm, William | Corpl | | 10 Jan 80 | do |
| Orm, Moses | pt | | do | do |
| Outterbridge, Leod. | do | 1 May 78 | 1 Nov 80 | present, 25 April 81 discharged |
| Oaster, (or Ostend), Henry | do | 14 April do | see H. Austin | |
| O'Bryan, Jno. | do | 4 Mar 77 | 16 Aug 80 | deserted |
| Orme, Joseph | do | | | |
| Owings, Saml. | do | | } | |
| | Corpl | 3 Oct 78 | } 10 Jan 80 | discharged |

### THIRD REGIMENT.—*Beginning 77.*

| NAMES. | RANK. | Enlisted. | Discharged. | REMARKS. |
|---|---|---|---|---|
| Owings, Arthur | Sergt | private | 15 Aug 78 | |
| Osmond, John | pt | 17 May 77 | 1 Nov 80 | present |
| Osborn, William | do | 15 Aug 77 | 24 Jan 78 | died |
| O'Connell, Wm. | do | 21 April do | 6 do | do |
| Ogden, James | do | | | |
| Owens, John | do | 11 Mar 78 | dec 78 | do |
| Overcreek, Jos. | do | 4 June 78 | 16 Aug 80 | missing |
| Oram, Cooper | do | 30 April 78 | | |
| Oliver, Nicholas | pt | May 79 | struck off | |

## MUSTERS OF MARYLAND TROOPS, VOL. I.

| NAMES. | RANK. | TIME OF SERVICE. Enlisted. | Discharged. | REMARKS. |
|---|---|---|---|---|
| FOURTH REGIMENT.—*Beginning December,* 77. | | | | |
| Oneil, Hugh[1] | pt | 1 dec 76 | 15 Nov 78 | deserted |
| Owings, James | do | do | 1 dec 79 | discharged |
| O'Conner, Dennis[2] | Sergt | | Aug 78 | left out |
| O'Keiff, Constantine | pt | | June 78 | mustered not heard of |
| Oram, John[3] | do | | 13 April 80 | discharged |
| Onnell, Christopr. | do | | 12 Jan 80 | do |
| Oldham, Edward | Lieut | 10 dec 76 | Capt. 20 May 77 | |
| O'Donnally, Thos., (or Timy.)[4] | pt | | 31 Jan 78 | deserted |
| O'Quinn, Danl.[5] | do | 2 April 77 | 1 Nov 80 | present |
| O'Hara, George[6] Riely's, late Bowie's | do | 6 May 78 | 1 April 79 | deserted |
| Oram, Saml.[7] | Drum | 7 April 78 | 1 Nov 80 | present |
| RAWLINGS' REGIMENT. | | | | |
| O'Hara, Patk. | pt | | | |
| FIRST REGIMENT. | | | | |
| Peake, Nathan | | | | [expired 17 Nov 82 certified by Ensign B. Burgess that his time of service |
| Pearce, Ezekiel | pt | 10 dec 76 | 12 May 79 | prisr., dischd. 27 dec 79 |
| Parr, William | pt | do | 16 Sept | missing, deserted |
| Plant, John | Corpl | do | 1 July 78 | appd. a Sergt. |
| Pearce, Joshua | pt | do | | |
| Paine, George | do | 1 Mar 77 | 18 Mar 80 | discharged |
| Phillips, William | do | 8   do | 12 Mar 77 | deserted |
| Pearce, John | do | | 7 Sept 80 | discharged |
| Pindall, Nicks. | do | 3 feb 77 | 31 July 79 | died |
| Parkinson, Jno. | do | 7 Mar | 16 Aug 80 | prisoner |
| Phillips, John | do | 15 Mar | do | missing |
| Porter, Charles | Sergt | 10 dec 76 | 17 April | promoted |
| Powel, John | pt | do | | |
| Peck, Nathl.   reinlisted | do | do | 1 Nov 80 | present |
| Palmer, Anthy. | do | 8 feb 77 | 27 dec 79 | discharged |
| Peale, James | Lieut | 10 dec 76 | | |
| | Capt | | 1 June 79 | resigned 2 June 79 |
| Price, Edward | pt | do | 20 Mar 77 | deserted |
| Posey, James | do | 18 feb 77 | | |
| Posey, Benja. | do | 9 Mar 77 | 7 Mar 80 | discharged |

[1] Oldham's.   [2] Norwood's.   [3] Godman's.   [4] Spurrier's.   [5] Burgess'.   [6] Riely's.
[7] Smith's.

## MUSTERS OF MARYLAND TROOPS, VOL. I.

| NAMES. | RANK. | TIME OF SERVICE. Enlisted. | Discharged. | REMARKS. |
|---|---|---|---|---|
| Pope, James | pt | 10 dec 77 | 22 April 77 | for J. Donovan 3 Regt. |
| Pike, James | do | 21 Mar 77 | 21 Mar 80 | discharged |
| Priest, John | do | 27 April 77 | 11 Sept 77 | missing |
| Paine, Jerem. | do | 10 Mar 77 | 2 Aug 77 | died |
| Pringle, John | do | 6 feb 78 | 16 Aug 80 | missing. |
| Powell, Joseph | do | 7 May 78 | 19 Aug 80 | deserted |
| Phelps, Benja. | | 20 April 78 | 27 Oct 78 | dead |
| Poling, William | | 21 May 78 | 1 Oct 80 | present |
| Penn, John | pt | 16  do | 28 feb 79 | discharged |
| Penn, Stephen | do | do | do | do |
| Posey, Bennett | do | 5 June 78 | 5 April 79 | do |
| Proctor, Charles | do | 29 May 78 | 3 Nov 78 | dead |
| Proctor, Walter | do | 22 Aprl 78 | 10 Mar 79 | do |
| Perrie, John | do | | 1 Aprl 80 | deserted |
| Perrie, Simon | do | 12 May 78 | 1 Nov 80 | present |
| Price, John | pt | 6 May 78 1 June 79 | } 16 Aug 80 | prisoner |
| | 1 July 80 Corpl | joined — | | |
| Pennuwell, Chas. | pt | 2 July 79 | Sept 79 transfd. to 2 Regt. | |
| Phearson, Jos. | | 5 July | Jan 80 | prisoner |
| Parsons, William | | | 29 Nov 79 | deserted |
| Pain, John | 1 musr. | June 80 | | Artillery |
| Pherson, William | | 22 June 79 | 1 Nov 80 | present |
| Purdy, John | Sergt | | see 2d Regt. | |
| Phillips, William | pt | 1 May 78 | do  do | |
| Praul, Edward | Lieut | 1 Jany 77 } | | |
| | Capt | 10 June do } | | |
| Price, Benja. | pt | | 1 Nov 80 | present |

### SECOND REGIMENT.

| NAMES. | RANK. | Enlisted. | Discharged. | REMARKS. |
|---|---|---|---|---|
| Price, Thomas | Col | 10 dec 76 | 30 April 80 | resigned |
| Price, John | Q. M. | | | |
| | again Sergt | 10 Jan 80 | | |
| Pitts, William | Sergt. M. | 15 Sept 77 } | 1 Nov 80 | present |
| joined feby musr. reduced to pt | | 27 Aug 78 } | left out of musr. for Sept 78 | |
| Porter, Philemon | do | | | |
| | . Corpl | 1 Jan 78 | 10 Jan 80 | discharged |
| Powers, Thomas | pt | 8 Mar 77 | 17 July 80 | deserted |
| Pallet, James | do | 19  do | 16 Aug 80 | do |
| Price, Benja. | Lieut | 10 Apl 77 | Capt. 1 July 79 | |
| Perkle, Jacob | pt | | | |
| Parrot, Chrisr. | Sergt | | 10 Jan 80 | discharged } |
| reinlisted in service to take up deserts till Aug 80 by Col. Forrest | | | | } |

## MUSTERS OF MARYLAND TROOPS, VOL. I.

| NAMES. | RANK. | TIME OF SERVICE. Enlisted. | Discharged. | REMARKS. |
|---|---|---|---|---|
| Payn, Benjamin | pt | | 10 Jan 80 | discharged |
| Powell, William | do | | do | do |
| Purdy, John | Sergt | | 4 Mar 78 | deserted |
| Pickeron, John | pt | 13 feb 78 | 1 Nov 80 | present |
| Peters, Joseph | do | 9 May 78 | 18 July 78 | dead |
| Pritchard, James | do | 15 do | | do |
| Parker, John | do | 18 Aprl 78 | April 80 | transfd. to Invalids |
| Preston, And. | do | 19 May do | 4 July 79 | died |
| Philips, John | do | 24 feb 78 | 15 April 78 | deserted |
| Pennington, Jno. | do | | Sept 78 | died |
| Phillips, William | do | 1 May 78 | } 16 Aug 80 | deserted |
| | Corpl | 1 Jan 80 | | |
| Phillips, Henry | pt | 16 do | 1 Nov 80 | present |
| Payne, Barny | do | 29 do | 3 Aprl 79 | discharged |
| Purtle, Robert | pt | 25 May 78 | | time out, discharged |
| Prather, Zach. | do | 1 do | } 1 Nov 80 | present |
| | Sergt | 10 Jan 80 | | |
| Pagram, William | pt | 2 June do | 16 Aug 80 | prisoner |
| Plummer, Cupid | do | 1 Aprl do | 1 Nov 80 | present |
| Plummer, Obe. | do | do | do | do |
| Pierce, Aquilla | do | 4 do | do | do |
| | Drum | | | |
| Pierce, Danl. | pt | 18 do | do | transferred |
| Parsley, Edwd. | do | 25 May 78 | 26 dec 78 | deserted |
| Pew, Humphrey | Corpl | | } 10 Jan 80 | discharged |
| | Sergt | 20 Sept 78 | | |
| Phillips, David | pt | 19 Mar 77 | 12 Sept 78 | deserted |
| Pollard, Kinsey | do | 20 May 78 | 78 | died |
| Patton, John | do | do | 3 April 79 | discharged |
| Perry, Charles | do | | Mar 79 | do |
| Purchass, Wm. | do | 15 Aug 79 | } 1 Nov 80 | present |
| | Corpl | 1 May 80 | | |
| | pt | 31 Oct 80 | | |
| Pennywell, Chas. | do | 2 July 79 | 24 Nov 79 | deserted |
| Penney, John | do | Aprl 80 | 1 Nov 80 | present |
| Phips, Thomas | do | 6 May 78 | 4 May 81 | discharged |

Brought from letter F

### THIRD REGIMENT.—*Beginning* 77.

| NAMES. | RANK. | Enlisted. | Discharged. | REMARKS. |
|---|---|---|---|---|
| Pearson, Edward | pt | 13 May 77 | 8 May 80 | discharged |
| Pratt, William | Corpl | 1 April 77 | } 2 Aprl 80 | time expired |
| | Sergt | 15 Mar 78 | | |
| Phillips, David | pt | | 18 Aug 80 | deserted |
| Price, William | do | | Nov 77 | do |

## MUSTERS OF MARYLAND TROOPS, VOL. I.

| NAMES. | RANK. | TIME OF SERVICE. | | REMARKS. |
| | | Enlisted. | Discharged. | |
| --- | --- | --- | --- | --- |
| Paton, John | pt | | 15 Mar 78 | deserted |
| Pepper, Josep | do | 11 May 77 | 1 Nov 80 | discharged |
| Purdie, Edwd. | do | 5 Mar 77 | 16 Aug 80 | missing |
| Procter, Richd. | do | 4 June do | 1 Nov 80 | present |
| Peck, Joshua | do | 6 Aprl do | dec 79 | deserted |
| Pitman, John | do | 10 Jan do | 12 Jan 80 | discharged |
| Parry, John | Corpl | 4 Sept 77 | | |
|     pt 1 Sept 78 | Sergt | 21 June 78 | } 28 Aprl 79 | deserted |
| Pope, James | pt | 10 dec 76 | | |
| Parriott, Is. | do | | 4 Aug 77 | died |
| Pike, Thomas | do | 24 Nov 77 | 1 Sept 78 | deserted |
| Parriott, Wm. | do | | | do |
| Price, Thomas | pay M. | Lieut | 11 feb 80 | |
| Patrick, George | pt | 25 Mar 78 | 18 Aug 80 | |
| Pickard, John | do | 26 Aprl 78 | 1 Mar 79 | discharged |
| Price, William | do | do | Jan 80 | struck off |
| Parker, Danl. | do | 20 do | June 78 | deserted |
| Pasgrove, (or Pascoe), John | Sergt | 6 feb 78 | 15 July 78 | do |
| Poole, Benja. | pt | 3 April 78 | 1 Nov 78 | discharged |
| Prigg, Charles | pt | 9 Aug 77 | 1 Oct 79 | to Invalids |
| Petmore, Richd. | do | 12 May 78 | 16 Aug 79 | deserted |
| Pendergast, Jno. | do | 27 April 78 | 1 Nov 80 | present |
| Pendleberry, Marmd. | do | 21 do | 16 Aug 80 | missing |
| Preston, Stephen | do | 21 May 78 | do | do |
| Powell, John | Drum | 13 do | 2 do | deserted |
| Pike, William | pt | 5 June 78 | 16 do | missing |
| Pennock, Jona. | do | do | do | do |
| Pennington, Jno. | do | 29 May 78 | do | do |
| Peters, William | do | 25 June 78 | 1 Nov 80 | present |
| Perrin, Philip | do | 20 April 78 | 16 Aug 80 | missing |
| Pinnuch, Jona. | do | 9 Jan 79 | see above | |
| Peterkin, Philip | Sergt | | 20 Aug 80 | deserted, pt.when |
| Preston, Saml. | pt | | | [deserted |
| Price, John | do | transferred to 1st Regt. by prior right | | |
| Parmer, Thomas | do | 21 May 79 | 22 dec 79 | transferred to In- |
| | | | 21 June 80 | deserted [valids |

FOURTH REGIMENT.—*Beginning December, 77.*

| Pindell, Richd. | Sergn. Mate | | | |
| | Sergn. | 11 Nov 77 | | |
| Purcell, William[1] | pt | 6 Aug 77 | 16 Aug 80 | |
| Philips, John | do | | 24 feb 80 | deserted |

[1] Norwood's.

## MUSTERS OF MARYLAND TROOPS, VOL. I.

| NAMES. | RANK. | TIME OF SERVICE. Enlisted. | Discharged. | REMARKS. |
|---|---|---|---|---|
| Patterson, Wm. | pt | Jan 78 | | Excd. for P. Doran |
| Parrish, Edward[1] | Corpl | | | |
| | Sergt | 1 June 79 | 8 dec 79 | discharged |
| Penn, John | pt | | 10 dec 77 | died |
| Prior, William[2] | do | 30 May 77 | 1 Nov 80 | present |
| Prudent, Thomas | do | 4 Mar 77 | 11 June 80 | deserted |
| Popham, Samuel[3] | do | | 1 Aprl 78 | transfd. to Artill- |
| Petterfer, William[4] | do | | 28 May 78 | discharged [ery |
| Powell, John[5] | do | | feb 78 | left out the Roll |
| Potts, Thomas[6] | Corpl | ⎫ | | Waggoner Wil- |
| Joined Lansdale's | private | ⎬ | | [mington |
| Oldham's | private | ⎭ 1 June 78 | | Sept 79 not heard of |
| Price, Daniel[7] | pt | | 16 Aug 80 | missing |
| Pringle, Thomas | do | 15 April 78 | 6 May 80 | deserted |
| | fife | | | [lough |
| Purnell, Stephen[6] | pt | 3   do | 25   do | destd. on fur- |
| Perry, Francis[2] | do | 18 Mar 78 | 27   do | deserted |
| to Col. Hall's Co. | | | | |
| Peach, William[3] | Sergt | 2 Aug 77 | ⎫ | |
| | pt | 31 Oct 79 | ⎭ 22 April 80 | deserted |
| Smith's, late Spurrier's, afterwards upon showing cause, discharged | | | | |
| Powell, Peter[8] | pt | 11 May 78 | 15 Aprl 79 | deserted |
| Picker, William[9] | do | 23 feb 78 | 1 Nov 80 | present |
| Riely's, late Bowie's | | | | |
| Page, John[1] | do | 27 Aprl 78 | 16 Aug 80 | missing |
| Paine, Anthy.[9] | do | 1 May 78 | 25 Jan 80 | deserted |
| Patterson, Robt.[1] | do | 10   do | 10 dec 79 | |
| Pheasant, Sam.[2] | do | 8 Mar 78 | June 80 | dischd. finding |
| Pike, James[3] | Sergt | 16 Aprl 78 | ⎫ | [substitute |
| | pt | 1 Aug 78 | ⎭ 22 dec 79 | deserted |
| Pike, John | fifer | 27 Jan 78 | ⎱ July 80 | do |
| | pt | 12 May 80 | ⎰ | |
| Polston, Emanuel[8] | pt | 29 April 78 | 30 July 78 | died |
| Parker, Jerrold[6] | do | 19 May 78 | 1 Nov 80 | present |
| Preston, Grafton[9] | do | 1 June 78 | 1 Mar 79 | discharged |
| Prior, John[10] | do | 3 April 80 | 1 Nov 80 | present |

### RAWLINGS' REGIMENT.

| | | | | |
|---|---|---|---|---|
| Pritchard, Sam. | Corpl | 23 July 76 | 10 Mar 77 | died |
| Power, Saml. | pt | 17 Aug 76 | 19 Aug 79 | discharged |
| Pike, Hutchen | do | 21   do | 19 feb 77 | do |

[1] Godman's.   [2] Lansdale's.   [3] Sellman's.   [4] Spurrier's.   [5] Burgess'.   [6] Norwood's.
[7] Oldham's.   [8] Lt. Smith's.   [9] Riely's.   [10] Lt. Hanson's.

11

## MUSTERS OF MARYLAND TROOPS, VOL. I.

| NAMES. | RANK. | TIME OF SERVICE. Enlisted. | Discharged. | REMARKS. |
|---|---|---|---|---|
| Pritchard, Wm. | pt | 23 July | | |
| Parker, George | | 16 April 79 | | |
| Palmer, Jacob | | 5 May | | died Nov 80 per Certificate of Adamson Tannaker |
| Pierce, Edward | Corpl | | 22 Sept 79 | discharged |
| Phillips, George | pt | 20 Mar | | |
| Proser, Danl. | do | 10 May | | |
| Pinks, Jas.    6 mo. | do | 23 April | | |

### FIRST REGIMENT.

| | | | | |
|---|---|---|---|---|
| Quarney, Lawce. | pt | 10 dec 76 | 27 dec 79 | discharged |
| Quay, James | id | | 16 July 79 | killed Stoney [Point |
| pay commences 15 feb 78 | | | | |

### SECOND REGIMENT.

| | | | | |
|---|---|---|---|---|
| Quick, Jno. | pt | | | |
| | Sergt | 1 Jan 80 | 1 Nov 80 | present |

### THIRD REGIMENT.—*Beginning* 77.

| | | | | |
|---|---|---|---|---|
| Quiggins, Henry | pt | 30 May 77 | 16 Aug 77 | killed |
| Quiggins, John | do | do | Corpl. 1 Aug 78 | |
| Quinland, Jas. | do | 5 April do | 16 dec 78 | deserted |
| Quynn, Joseph | do | 20 May 78 | 1 Nov 80 | present |

### FOURTH REGIMENT.

| | | | | |
|---|---|---|---|---|
| Queen, Jno.[1] | Corpl | | | see Gwinn |

### RAWLINGS' REGIMENT.

| | | | | |
|---|---|---|---|---|
| Quinn, Patk. | pt | 15 Oct 76 | 1 Jan 77 | deserted |

### FIRST REGIMENT.

| | | | | |
|---|---|---|---|---|
| Ritchie, Mathew | pt | 10 dec 76 | 6 Mar 78 | deserted |
| Rogers, William | do | do | 16 Aug | prisoner |
| Ryan, Michael | do | 4 feb 77 | 11 Jan 80 | discharged |
| Rolls, William | do | 7 June 77 | June 77 | deserted from Invalids |
| Reed, Thomas | do | 10 dec 76 | 11 Sept 77 | missing |
| Roxburgh, Alex. | Capt | do | 1 April 80 | Major of 7 Regt. |
| Read, John | pt | do | 27 dec 79 | discharged |
| Reese, Henry | do | 14 April 77 | July 80 | to 7th Regt. |
| Rankin, Danl. | do | 10 dec 76 | 27 dec 79 | discharged |

[1] Godman's.

## MUSTERS OF MARYLAND TROOPS, VOL. I.

| NAMES. | RANK. | TIME OF SERVICE. Enlisted. | Discharged. | REMARKS. |
|---|---|---|---|---|
| Roberts, Zacha. | Corpl | 31 Mar 77 servg. Q. M. Dept., 2 May 80 dis- | | [charged |
| Ridgely, William | Lieut | 10 dec 76 | | |
| Ricketts, Vincent | pt | do | 1 Nov 80 | present |
| S. Major 10 Aug 1780 | Corpl | 1 Jan 80 | Sergt. Sept 80 | |
| Robertson, Thos. | pt | do | 27 dec 79 | discharged |
| Rash, John | do | do | | |
| Ray, Samuel | do | do | Mar 10 | dead |
| Ridgely, Bazil | Ensn | 17 April Corpl from 10 dec 75, resigned 7 dec 77 | | |
| Ricketts, John | pt | 22 Mar 77 | | |
| Reynolds, James | do | 12 April 77 | Oct 4 | missing |
| Robertson, Michl. | do | 26 Mar 77 | | |
| | Q. M. Sergt. 26 Mar 80 | | | discharged |
| Rigg, Charles | pt | 29 Mar 77 | 1 feb 79 | Corpl. 28 Mar 80 [discharged |
| Ryan, Anthy. | do | 10 dec 76 | 20 Mar 77 | deserted |
| Robinson, Jno. | pt | 10 dec 76 | 16 Aug 80 | prisoner |
| Richardson, Elisha | do | 23 April 77 | 27 dec 79 | discharged |
| Riely, Charles | do | 10 dec 76 | 3 May 77 | ex. for J. Baker |
| Richmond, Chr. | pay M. | 1 Jany 77 | | |
| | Lieut | 27 May 78 | Capt. Oct 81 | |
| Riely, John | pt | 10 dec 77 | 22 Jan 78 | deserted |
| Roberts, Richd. | do | 23 April 78 | Aug 78 | dead |
| Roberts, William | do | 1 May 78 | 1 July 80 | joined, 1 Nov 80 [present |
| Russell, Henry | do | 29   do | 1 feb 79 | died |
| Roberson, Charles | do | 10 June 78 | 1 Nov 80 | present |
| Roby, John | do | 13 May 78 | } reinlisted | |
| | prisoner | Jan 80 | } 9 Jan 82 | discharged |
| Roberts, William | fifer | 4 May 78 | 16 Aug | prisoner |
| Rady, James | pt | 3 Mar 78 | 8 July 79 | deserted |
| Rady, Laurence | do | 7 feb 78 | do | do |
| Reynolds, Jno. | do | 14 do | 1 Nov 80 | present |
| Riely, Patk. | do | | 16 Aug 80 | prisoner |
| Rollins, Chs. | do | 11 Aprl 79 | 31 Aug 80 | deserted |
| Reynolds, Robt. | do | 3 June 79 | 1 Nov 80 | present |
| Robey, Joseph | do | 14 June 79 | } 25 Sept 80 | died |
| | fifer | 1 Oct 79 | } | |
| Rose, William | pt | 10 June 79 | | |
| | Sergt | 14 Aug 79 | | |
| | S. M. | 25 dec 79 | 1 Nov 80 | present |
| Rowe, Robert | pt | see 2nd Regt. | | |
| Ryan, Mathew | do | transferred to Invalids 15 Jan 78, see 2nd | | [Regt. |

## MUSTERS OF MARYLAND TROOPS, VOL. I.

| NAMES. | RANK. | TIME OF SERVICE. Enlisted. | Discharged. | REMARKS. |
|---|---|---|---|---|

### SECOND REGIMENT.

| NAMES. | RANK. | Enlisted. | Discharged. | REMARKS. |
|---|---|---|---|---|
| Robertson, Lambert | pt | 4 Mar 77 | 10 June 80 | discharged |
| Richardson, Danl. | do | 27 Jan 77 | do | do |
| Ray, James | do | 4 Mar 77 | do | do |
| Revell, Randall | Sergt | | do | do |
| Read, Obadiah | pt | | 16 Jan 78 | deserted |
| Rones, Samuel | do | | 17 do | do |
| Roly, Silvester | do | | | do |
| Riggan, Timy. | do | | | do |
| Ray, Joseph | do | 24 dec 76 | 1 Nov 80 | present |
| Rawlings, Jona. | do | | 16 Aug 80 | prisoner |
| Rowe, Robert | do | | 12 dec 79 | discharged |
| Ryan, Matthew | do | | 15 Jan 78 | 13 June 78 dis-[charged |
| Read, John | Ensn | 10 Apl 77 | 12 April 79 | resigned |
| Read, James | pt | 4 do 78 | May 80 | deserted |
| Rigg, George | do | 16 Mar 78 | 10 Jany 80 | do, 16 Aug 80 [prisoner |
| Robinson, Nathl. | do | 20 Aprl 78 | 29 Aprl 78 | deserted |
| Richardson, Edwd. | fifer | 6 May 78 | 20 feb 79 | discharged |
| Rider, James | pt | 15 May 78 | 24 dec 78 | do |
| Richards, Thomas | do | 23 feb 78 | 13 Aprl 78 | transferred to |
| Richy, William | do | 22 Aprl 78 | know nothing of him [Gist'sCo. | |
| Rawn, Patk. | do | 5 May 78 | 1 Nov 80 | present |
| Riswick, Jos. | do | 30 do | 3 April 79 | discharged |
| Randall, David | do | 24 do | do | do |
| Riely, (or Riney), Jonathan | pt | 25 April 78 | 3 April 79 | discharged |
| Ryan, John | do | 1 Jan 77 | feb 80 | prisoner |
| Rolls, Richard | do | 18 May 78 | | |
| | fifer | 1 July 79 | 16 Aug 80 | prisoner |
| Read, William | pt | 20 May 78 | 79 | discharged |
| Riggs, Andrew | do | 10 feb 78 | 1 Nov 80 | present |
| | | | 10 feb 81 | discharged |
| Runien, Henry | do | | 1 June 79 | deserted |
| Ratcliff, Robt. | do | 28 Aug 79 | | do |
| | Nov Roll 79, never appeared | | | |
| Robertson, Jno. | do | June 80 | 16 Aug 80 | prisoner |
| Roberson, David | do | | 24 do | deserted |

### THIRD REGIMENT.

| NAMES. | RANK. | Enlisted. | Discharged. | REMARKS. |
|---|---|---|---|---|
| Reeder, Hezekiah | Lieut | 14 Mar 77 | 9 feb 78 | resigned |
| Roberts, Thomas | Corpl | 2 June 77 | 18 June 78 | died |
| Reynolds, Charles | pt | 22 May 77 | 9 Jan 80 | discharged |

## MUSTERS OF MARYLAND TROOPS, VOL. I.

| NAMES. | RANK. | TIME OF SERVICE. Enlisted. | Discharged. | REMARKS. |
|---|---|---|---|---|
| Ridgely, Henry | Capt | | | |
| Roland, Patk. | pt | | 13 Mar 80 | deserted, 19 Aug [80 deserted |
| Rock, Oliver | Sergt | 23 feb 77 | 23 feb 80 | discharged |
| Reed, James | pt | 23 Aprl 77 | June 78 | dead |
| Richardson, Edwd. | do | 1 feb 77 | 1 Nov 80 | present |
| Rue, William | do | 13 Sept 77 | 14 July 78 | deserted, joined |
| Richardson, Wm. | do | | 1 Nov 80 | present |
| Roberts, John | pt | 10 Jan 77 | 10 Jan 80 | discharged |
| Roberts, John | Sergt | 3 Jan 77 } | | time expired |
|   left out Jan & feb 80, time expired | | | | |
| Ridgely, Saml. | Corpl | 17 April 77 } | | |
| | Sergt | | } 16 Aug 80 | prisoner |
| Richards, John | pt | Jan 80 | | present, struck off |
| | Sergt | July 1780 | 10 feb 80 | discharged |
| Rowe, William | pt | 16 Aug 77 ) | | |
|   private 1 July 78 | Corpl | 15 Mar 78 } | | |
|   do    1 June 79 again | do | 1 April 79 ) | 1 Nov 80 | present |
| Reveley, Francis | Lieut | 15 April 77 | | |
| Richards, Paule | pt | 1 Jan 78 | do | do |
| Relahan, Jno. | do | 11 May 77 | do | do |
| Ramsey, Nathanl. | Lt. Col. | 10 dec 76 | | |
| Riely, John | pt | 25 April 78 | 28 Aug 80 | deserted |
| Readon, Patk. | do | 28    do | July 78 | struck off |
| Robb, John | do | 23    do | 16 Aug 80 | missing |
| Reewark, Jas. | do | 25    do ) | | joined |
| Rae, Barny | do | do } | | Nov 80 out |
| Richardson, Jno. | do | 22    do ) | | |
| Rock, Edward | Corpl | | | |
| | pt | 1 April 78 | June 78 | struck off |
| Rock, John | do | 26 April 78 | | present |
| Rock, William | pt | 26 April 78 | 1 Nov 78 | present |
| Rutter, Thomas | do | 16 Jan 78 | dec 78 | died |
| Robertson, Wm. | do | 3 feb 78 | 14 July 78 | deserted |
| Roads, Jeremiah | do | 31 May 78 | 1 Nov 80 | present |
|   reinlisted 17 feb 79 | | | 17 feb 82 | discharged |
| Rains, Adam | do | May 78 | 1 Nov 80 | present |
|   joined 2 Aug 78 | | | | |
| Ragan, Morris | do | 21 do | 19 Oct 79 | deserted |
| Russell, Thomas | do | 16 do | | |
| Roberson, Thomas | do | 3 do | July 80 | do |
| Ryan, Nathan | do | 8 April 78 | | |
| Reidy, William | do | | Oct 78 | struck off |
| Riely, James | do | 10 June 78 | 1 Nov 80 | present |
|   rein. 17 Nov 78 | | | | |

## MUSTERS OF MARYLAND TROOPS, VOL. I.

| Names. | Rank. | Enlisted. | Discharged. | Remarks. |
|---|---|---|---|---|
| Reynolds, Benedt. | pt | 28 July 78 | time out, discharged | |
| Robertson, John | do | 2 May 78 | 1 Nov 80 | present |
| Roberts, Edward | do | 10 June 78 | 16 Aug 80 | missing |
| Reynolds, Richard | fifer | 20 May 78 | 10 Dec 78 | died |
| Redding, William | do | | | |
| Rowlings, Benedict Joined Sept 79 | do | 18 June 78 | 18 June 81 | discharged |

### FOURTH REGIMENT.

| Names. | Rank. | Enlisted. | Discharged. | Remarks. |
|---|---|---|---|---|
| Ridgely, Revely[1] | Sergt | | 11 Nov 77 | resigned |
| Riely, John[1] | pt | 1 dec 76 | 1 Nov 80 | present |
| Ragan, James | do | 17 dec 76 | 16 dec 79 | discharged |
| Riding, Henry | do | 1 April 78 | 1 Nov 80 | present |
| Riding, Henry | do | 11 Jany 77 | June 80 | deserted |
| Ramsey, Henry,[2] | do | 3 April 77 | 1 Nov 80 | present |
| Reynald, Tobias | do | | 24 May 80 | discharged |
| Rolls, William | do | | 1 May 81 | discharged |
| Riely, William[3] | Lieut | 10 dec 76 | Capt. 15 Oct 77 | |
| Rowland, William[4] | pt | 23 April 77 | 1 Mar 80 | discharged |
| Reedy, Thomas | do | | 2 April 78 | deserted |
| Rawlings, Jacob reduced 9 Dec 77 | Sergt | 6 Mar 77 | } 6 Mar 80 | discharged |
| Rowley, John[5] | do | 1 June 79 | | |
| Reading, John[1] | pt | 7 June 77 | 14 May 80 | do |
| to Oldham's | do | 4 April 77 | } 16 Aug 80 | prisoner |
| Ray, David[6] | Sergt | 8 dec 79 | | |
| Rowe, James[7] | pt | 14 Mar 77 | 14 Mar 80 | discharged |
| Robinson, Hugh | Sergt July 78 musd. sick Hospl., to be left out till joins | | | |
| | pt | 12 April 77 | | |
| Corpl 1 April 79 | Corpl | 1 April 78 | } 12 April 80 | time expired |
| Rigney, Michl. | pt | 10 Oct 78 | | |
| Ross, John | do | 10 July 77 | 12 Sept 79 | deserted |
| Robinson, Peter 30 Jany joined | Surgn. Mate 7 Mar 78 | | April 78 | left out |
| Richardson, Robt.[6] | pt | 7 feb 78 | 1 Nov 80 | present, joined [Oct 80 |
| Roads, William[6] | do | 2 feb 78 | } 15 May 80 | deserted |
| | Corpl | do | | |
| Norwood's | private | 1 April 79 | } 16 Aug 80 | missing |
| Raynard, Jno. C. | do | 23 April 78 | 27 May 80 | do |
| Roberts, Joseph[3] | do | 1 Mar 77 | 1 Nov 80 | present |
| Rogers, Joseph[4] | do | 17 Mar 78 | 29 dec 79 | deserted |
| Ringrose, James[5] | do | 7 May 78 | | |

[1] Oldham's.  [2] Norwood's.  [3] Godman's.  [4] Lansdale's.  [5] Selman's.  [6] Bowie's.  [7] Burgess'.

## MUSTERS OF MARYLAND TROOPS, VOL. I.

| NAMES. | RANK. | TIME OF SERVICE. Enlisted. | Discharged. | REMARKS. |
|---|---|---|---|---|
| Radley, John[1] | private | 5 May 78 | | |
| | Corpl | 1 April 79 | } 1 Nov 80 | present |
| | Sergt | 1 Mar 80 | | |
| Rorke, Michl.[2] | pt | 26 July 78 | 2 Mar 79 | discharged |
| Redman, Thomas[3] | do | 27 Aprl 78 | 1 Nov 80 | present |
| Hoops', late Norwood's, | | | | |
| Reynolds, Benedict[1] | do | 1 Nov 80 prest., 28 July 78 | | enlisted |
| Russell, John[4] | do | 7 July 79 | 1 Nov 80 | present |
| Rose, James | do | 21 Aug 79 | 24 feb 80 | deserted |

### RAWLINGS' REGIMENT.

| NAMES. | RANK. | Enlisted. | Discharged. | REMARKS. |
|---|---|---|---|---|
| Rose, Isaac | Corpl | 1 Aug 76 | | |
| | Sergt | Nov 77 | } 9 Aug 79 | discharged |
| Ross, Ruben | pt | 20 July 76 | 11 July 79 | do |
| Rowland, Henry | do | 20 Sept | 2 Sept 79 | do |
| Rigdon, John | do | 6  do | | |
| Riely, James | do | do | 17 dec 76 | deserted |
| Russell, Nichs. | do | | 9 Aug 79 | discharged |
| Rankins, Wm. | do | 11 Aprl 79 | 26 July | do |
| Reed, John | Q. Mr. | | | |
| Richards, Wm. | Sergt | | 31 July 79 | discharged |
| Roof, Peter   1 yr. | pt | | 9 Aug 79 | do |
| Riely, John | do | 21 Aprl 79 | | |
| Ryan, James | do | 26 June | | |
| Rock, John | do | 26 Mar | | |
| Rudolph, Jacob | do | 23 Mar | | |

### FIRST REGIMENT.

| NAMES. | RANK. | Enlisted. | Discharged. | REMARKS. |
|---|---|---|---|---|
| Stillwell, Obadiah | Sergt | 10 dec 76 | 27 dec 79 | discharged |
| Splavin, Timothy | pt | do | 6 Mar 78 | deserted |
| Spillard, Mathew | do | do | | do |
| Smith, Peter | do | do | 27 dec 79 | discharged |
| reinlisted | | | 1 Nov 80 | present |
| Smith, Joseph | do | 6 April 77 | | |
| Sapp, Robert | do | 16  do | | deserted |
| Smoot, William | Sergt | 10 dec 76 | 27 dec 79 | discharged |
| Smith, Alvin | pt | do | 5 Mar 77 | died |
| Smith, Richard | do | do | 27 dec 79 | discharged |
| Shea, Daniel | do | do | do | do |
| Sergeant, William | do | do | 6 Mar 78 | deserted |
| Smith, William | do | do | 1 Nov 80 | present |

[1] Riely's.        [2] Godman's.        [3] Hoops'.        [4] Oldham's.

## MUSTERS OF MARYLAND TROOPS, VOL. I.

| NAMES. | RANK. | TIME OF SERVICE. Enlisted. | Discharged. | REMARKS. |
|---|---|---|---|---|
| Smith, James | pt | 22 feb 77 | 22 feb 80 | discharged } |
|  | Corpl 1 Jan 78 |  | Sergt July 79 | } |
| Shirvin, Charles | pt |  | 29 Sept 78 | dead |
| Smith, John | Sergt | 10 dec 78 | 14 Aug 78 | Forage Dept. |
| Skipper, William | pt | 22 feb 77 |  | deserted |
| Sullivan, John | do | 8 Mar |  | never joined |
|  | prisr. | Jany 80 |  |  |
| Simmes, James | Q. Lieut | 17 April 77 |  |  |
| Sewel, William | pt | 10 dec 76 | 27 dec 79 | discharged |
| Smith, Valentine | do | do | May 80 | transferred to In-[valids |
| Smith, John<br>Dichd. the 27 dec 79 | } do | do | 14 dec 82 | discharged |
| Strap, Jacob | do | 24 feby 77 | 24 Jan 80 | do |
| Seward, David | do | 21 May 77 | 11 Sept | missing |
| Slack, John | pt | 22 Mar 77 | 23 Mar | deserted |
| Shepard, Francis | Sergt | 10 dec 76 | 27 dec 79 | discharged |
| Smith, John | Corpl | do | do | do |
| Sheridan, Thomas | pt | 6 Mar 77 |  |  |
| Skepper, John | do | 10 dec 76 | Aug 77 | died |
| Simms, Ignatius | do | 19 May 77 | 17 July 79 | do |
| Smith, Charles | Lieut | 10 dec 76 | 10 feb 80 | resigned |
| Sewall, Clement | Sergt | 4 Mar 77 | 14 Sept | promoted |
| Shaw, John | pt | 10 dec 76 | 1 feb 80 | discharged |
| Simpson. Thomas | do | 28 May 77 } |  |  |
|  | Corpl | 1 Aug 77 } | 5 Jan 80 | discharged |
| Steel, Elisha | pt | 24 feb 77 } |  |  |
|  | fifer | 1 Aug 77 } | 20 feb 80 | do, as pt. |
| Stone, John H. | Col. |  | 1 Aug 79 | resigned |
| Sim, Patk. | Lt. Col. |  | 20 June 77 | do |
| Sterritt, William | Major |  | 16 dec 77 | do |
| Swann, Barton | pt | 7 Sept 77 | 20 Sept 78 | died |
| Sanders, Thomas | do | 25 Oct 77 | 16 Aug 80 | prisoner |
| Shaw, Alex. | O. Soldr., joined 4 dec 77, furloughed June 80 |  |  |  |
| Spykes, William | pt | 3 Mar 78 | 1 Nov 80 | present |
| Sutherland, Wm. | do | 6 Jan 78 | July 79 | not heard of |
| Smith, William | do | 9 Mar 78 | 1 Nov 80 | present |
| Simmons, Danl. | do | 15 April 78 | Corpl. 5 Nov 79, 16 Aug 80 |  |
|  | Sergt | 1 Jan 80 |  | [prisr. |
| South, Alexander | pt | 9 May 78 | 18 Aug 80 | missing |
| Savoy, Philip |  | 20 May 78 | 25 Jan 80 | prisoner |
| Smith, Joseph |  | 11 do |  |  |
| Sherivenor, Jno. |  | 1 do |  |  |
| Salsbury, Thomas |  | 14 feby 78 | feb 79 | died |

## MUSTERS OF MARYLAND TROOPS, VOL. I.

| NAMES. | RANK. | TIME OF SERVICE. Enlisted. | Discharged. | REMARKS. |
|---|---|---|---|---|
| Smith, Nathl. | | 13 Mar 78 | July 79 } May 80 | died |
| Sheridan, John　3 | | 6 Mar 77 | 2 Mar 80 | discharged |
| Scott, Charles | | 28 May 78 | 1 Nov 80 | present |
| Scott, Joshua | | 27　do | do | do |
| Saunders, Bennett | | 4 June 78 | 5 Aprl 79 | discharged |
| Skiffington, Roger | | 19 Jan 78 | 16 Aug 80 | missing |
| Spalding, Wm. | pt | | 26 Nov 78 | dead |
| Snilling, John | do | 1 Aprl 78 | 12 Sept 80 | joined |
| Smith, John | do | 24　do | 1 Nov 80 | present |
| Stallings, Thomas | do | 1 May 79 | 1 Jan 80 | transferred to In- |
| Simms, Edward | Ensn | 11 Sept 79 | 7 feb 80 | resigned　[valids |
| Smoot, William | do | 26 Jan 80 | | |
| Souther, Valenn. | Musn. | June 80 | 14 Aug 80 | deserted |
| Smith, Anthy. | | | 16　do | prisoner |
| Smith, John | | 24 Jan 80 | 16 Aug 80 | missing |
| From 7th Regiment | | | | |

### SECOND REGIMENT.

| NAMES. | RANK. | TIME OF SERVICE. Enlisted. | Discharged. | REMARKS. |
|---|---|---|---|---|
| Steward, John | Major | 17 April 77 | | |
| Sampson, Richd. | Sergt | 6 Sept 77 | 10 Jan 80 | discharged |
| Sinnett, Bryan | Corpl | 8 Jan 77 } | | |
| | Sergt | 1 Jan 78 | } 10 Jan 80 | discharged |
| Spencer, Humpy. | private | 4 Mar 77 } | | |
| 　Sergt 1 May 80 | Corpl | 10 Jan 80 | } 1 Nov 80 | present |
| Stevens, Levi | pt | 8 Jan 77 | 10 Jan 80 | discharged |
| Spencer, Jos. | do | 10 April 77 } | | |
| 　Q. M. S.　. | Sergt | 10 Jan 80 | } 1 Nov 80 | present |
| Smook, Richd. | pt | 10 dec 76 | 1 May 80 | discharged |
| Shipley, Robt. | do | 30 Jan 77 | 1 Nov 80 | present |
| Sanders, Spencer | do | Aug 79 | discharged having got a man in [his place | |
| Stevens, Benja. | do | | 10 Jan 80 | discharged |
| Spicer, Levin | do | | 15 Mar 78 | deserted |
| Scott, Charles | do | see the other side, C. Scott Corpl. | | |
| Sharp, Henry | do | | | |
| Skinner, Robt. | do | | | |
| Sute, Jesse | Sergt | 20 Jan 77 } | | |
| 　Sergt June 80, reduced to pt 7 Oct 79 | | | } 1 Nov 80 | present |
| Shotten, James | do | 18 May 77 | entd. below on the other side | |
| Spicknall, Mathew | Sergt | | 10 Jan 80 | discharged |
| Spalding, Aron | pt | 1 Jan 77 } | | |
| 　Musd. as Sergt for May & June 80 | | | } 1 Nov 80 | present |
| Sweeney, Richd. | pt | 1 Sept 77 | 16 Aug 80 | killed |

## MUSTERS OF MARYLAND TROOPS, VOL. I.

| NAMES. | RANK. | TIME OF SERVICE. Enlisted. | Discharged. | REMARKS. |
|---|---|---|---|---|
| Smith, John | pt | | 10 Jan 80 | discharged |
| Summers, Oba. | Sergt | | 20 April 80 | joined |
| Smith, Robert | pt | 13 April 77 | 1 do | discharged |
| Sears, John | Sergt | | 10 Jan 80 | do do |
| Sterling, Isaac | pt | 10 Jan 77 | do | do |
| Slocome, Solomon | do | | 27 May 78 | deserted |

Joined June musr. 78, joined 24 Sept 80, afterwards J. Davidson & deserted to
[Enemy

| NAMES. | RANK. | Enlisted. | Discharged. | REMARKS. |
|---|---|---|---|---|
| Southerland, Alex. | pt | | 10 Jan 80 | discharged |
| Saunders, Jno. | do | | 15 feb 78 | died |
| Smith, John | do Sergt. 10 Jan 80, 16 Aug 80 killed | | | |

reduced 8 Oct 79 to pt, Corpl 1 June 78, Sergt. 10 Sept 78

| NAMES. | RANK. | Enlisted. | Discharged. | REMARKS. |
|---|---|---|---|---|
| Spalding, Henry | pt | do 77 | 10 Jan 80 | discharged |
| Summers, Thomas | do | | do | do |
| Shoebrook, Philip | do | 26 feb 78 | 13 June 78 | do |
| Smith, Henry | do | 17 Jan 78 | | |
| Smith, James | do | do | 1 Nov 80 | present |
| Scott, Charles | do | 10 dec 76 | Corpl. 15 May 78 | |
| Swaney, James | do | 78 | 2 June 79 | died |
| Smoot, William | do | 3 May 78 | 23 dec 78 | deserted |

Sergeant 10 July 78

| NAMES. | RANK. | Enlisted. | Discharged. | REMARKS. |
|---|---|---|---|---|
| Sammon, John | pt | 13 April 78 | 1 Nov 80 | present |
| Sanders, James | do | 24 do | Oct 80 | deserted |
| Spicer, John | do | 20 May 78 ⎱ 21 Aug 80 | | do |
| | Corpl | 1 feb 80 ⎰ | | |
| Scoot, Isaac | pt | 20 April 78 | 1 Nov 80 | present |
| Smith, Levi | do | 26 feb 78 | 13 May 78 | deserted |
| Schean, Daniel | do | 10 do | 15 April 78 | do |
| Schean, James | do | 29 April 78 | | sick Maryland |
| Shovell, John | do | 9 do | 1 Nov 80 | present |
| Spraigh, (or Spray), John | Corpl | 24 do | 16 Aug 80 | prisoner |
| | pt | 1 Nov 78 | fifer 1 June 79 | |
| Sergeant, Thomas | do | 24 April 78 | 20 Nov 78 | died |
| Slone, Charles | do | 13 May 78 | 1 Nov 80 | present |
| Stone, Joseph | do | 29 do | 3 April 79 | discharged |
| Stone, John | do | 25 do | do | do |
| Smith, John | do | 24 do | do | do |
| Senner, John | do | 29 do | 25 dec 78 | died |
| Strickland, Jos. | do | 24 do | 3 April 79 | discharged |
| Snow, Charles | do | 16 do | Oct 80 | died |
| Smee, Thomas | do | 1 June do | see T. Mee | |
| Smith, Anthy. | do | 15 April do | 1 Nov 80 | present |

Joined June 79

| NAMES. | RANK. | Enlisted. | Discharged. | REMARKS. |
|---|---|---|---|---|
| Scriviner, Robt. | . do | 4 ditto | do | do |
| | Sergt | 1 feb 80 | | |

## MUSTERS OF MARYLAND TROOPS, VOL. I.

| NAMES. | RANK. | TIME OF SERVICE. Enlisted. | Discharged. | REMARKS. |
|---|---|---|---|---|
| Saunders, Thomas | pt A. S. | | 10 Jan 80 | discharged |
| Standley, Roger | pt | 20 May 78 | 10 Oct 78 | died |
| Stanton, Mathew | do | do | 3 April 79 | discharged |
| Smith, David | do | 10 Mar 78 | 1 Nov 80 | present |
| Savin, Edward | do | 25 May 78 | 26 dec 78 | deserted |
| Stanton, Mathew | do | 20    do | | |
| Shottin, James | pt | | 16 Aug 80 | missing |
| Simpson, Charles | Corpl | | | |
|   reduced to | pt | 1 Jan 79 | } feb 80 | died |
| Suite, Edward | do | 8 July 79 | | |
|   1 musr. Augt | Corpl | 1 feby 80 | } 1 Nov 80 | present |
| Sullivan, Mark | pt | 26 June 79 | 16 Aug 80 | missing |
| Stokes, Thomas | do | 21    do | 1 Nov 80 | present |
| Slade, John | do | 16 May 79 musr. | Nov Roll 79 | never appeared |
| Sappington, Thomas | | 3 Aug do | 4 Sept 79 | deserted |
| Sears, John | Ensn | 26 Jan 80 | | |
| Stoaks, John | pt | | 16 Aug 80 | missing |
| Sails, Gabriel | do | 4 June 80 | 14    do | deserted |
| Saunders, Robt. | do | | | sick Maryland |
| Summers, Oba. | Sergt | | | see L |
| Smith, Robt. | pt | | | do |

### THIRD REGIMENT.

| NAMES. | RANK. | TIME OF SERVICE. Enlisted. | Discharged. | REMARKS. |
|---|---|---|---|---|
| Swann, Alexr. | pt | 16 feb 77 | 16 Aug 80 | missing |
| Swann, Basil | do | 18 Mar 77 | Jan 78 | struck off |
| Smith, William | do | 21 April 77 | do | do |
| Sanders, John | do | 10 June 77 | 15 July 79 | to Invalids |
| Smith, John[1] | Lieut | 10 Dec 76 | Capt. | |
| Sheriden, Bartholm. | Sergt | exchanged into Congress Regt. | | |
| Silk, William[2] | pt | | Mar 79 | left out the Rolls |
| Stainger, Fortunatus | do | 11 June 77 | 16 Aug 80 | missing |
| Stanley, William | do | 11 May 77 | 1 April 79 | transferred to Invalids |
| | | | May 80 | discharged |
| Sears, Noah | do | 3 Jany 77 | 1 Nov 80 | present |
| Southall, Jos. | do | 1 Aprl 77 | do | do |
| Smith, James | do | 16    do | 16 Aug 80 | missing |
| Sheridan, James | do | 14 feb 77 | Jan 79 | transferred to Invalids, dismissed on Furlough 11 July 83 |
| Skepper, Isaac | do | 24 June 77 | April 78 | struck off |
| Smoot, Thomas | Sergt | 23 April 77 | 29 Aug 78 | discharged |
| Spry, Joseph | pt | 9 Sept 77 | Jan 78 | struck off |

[1] Marbury's.    [2] Smith's.

## MUSTERS OF MARYLAND TROOPS, VOL. I.

| NAMES. | RANK. | TIME OF SERVICE. Enlisted. | Discharged. | REMARKS. |
|---|---|---|---|---|
| Swann, John | pt | | 1 April 79 | discharged |
| Stevenson, Jno. | do | | Aug 80 | deserted |
| Stringer, Joseph | do | Jan 77 | Dec 79 | struck off |
| Dec Roll 79 left out | | | 14 April 80 | discharged } |
| Stanley, Thomas | do | | 19 feby 79 | deserted |
| Strong, John | do | 3 April 77 | Dec 78 | do |
| Short, Edward | do | 2 do | 16 Aug 80 | missing |
| Slade, John | do | | 3 feb 78 | dead |
| Stallings, Thomas | do | | 15 Jan 78 | discharged |
| Stallings, Jacob | do | | do | do |
| Smith, Edwd. Miles | Q. M. S. | | 16 Mar 80 | time expired |
| Smith, Leonard | pt | 18 Mar 77 | 11 Mar 80 | |
| Smith, John | do | 1 Jan 77 | } 16 Aug 80 | prisoner |
| | Corpl | 1 Jan 79 | } | |
| Swain, John | pt | 8 Sept 77 | } | deserted |
| deserted 1 mus., joined feby 1778 | | | } | |
| Sappington, Thomas | S. Mate | | | |
| Sutton, Edward | pt | 25 Mar 78 | 3 July 80 | do |
| Sanders, John | do | 25 April 78 | 16 Aug 80 | missing |
| Stroud, William[1] | do | 15 do | 18 do | deserted |
| Sullivan, James | do | 4 Mar 78 | 21 Aug 79 | do |
| Spalding, William | do | 30 do | Feby 79 | discharged |
| Shink, Joseph | do | 2 May 78 | 24 feb 79 | died · |
| Scriables, Jeremh. | do | 29 April 78 | 14 Oct 78 | do |
| Spraggs, John | do | 28 do | 6 Mar 79 | do |
| Spalding, George | do | 1 May 78 | 19 feby 79 | discharged |
| Sullivan, Patk. | Corpl | April 78 | } June 79 | out the Roll |
| | private | 1 Sept 78 | } | |
| Scantling, Thomas | do | 2 May 78 | 16 Aug 80 | missing |
| Swann, Leonard | do | 3 do | 1 Nov 80 | present |
| Suffolk, Richd. | do | | do | do |
| Shell, Richard | do | | 27 Jan 80 | deserted |
| Sadler, Humphy | do | | 30 Aug 78 | died |
| Smith, Saml. | do | | 28 do | deserted |
| Shirley, George | do | 31 May 78 | 24 do | died |
| Smart, Richd. | do | 25 do | 4 April 79 | discharged |
| Sanders, John | fifer | | 16 Aug 80 | missing |
| Speak, Thomas | pt | 20 Aprl 78 | April & May 79 left out Rolls |  |
| Joined 22 Aug 78 | | | | |
| Smith, Josias | do | 2 June 78 | do | do |
| Joined 22 Aug 78 | | | | |
| Sears, James | pt | 20 April 78 | | |

[1] Smith's.

## MUSTERS OF MARYLAND TROOPS, VOL. I.

| NAMES. | RANK. | TIME OF SERVICE. | | REMARKS. |
|---|---|---|---|---|
| | | Enlisted. | Discharged. | |
| Self, John | pt | 25 April 78 | 28 Sept 79 | discharged |
| Sugars, William | do | do | | |
| Smith, Matthew | do | 24 May 78 | | |
| Smith, Levin | do | 5 June 78 | 20 Oct 78 | died |
| Simms, James | Sergt | pt | | |
| Joined Oct 78 | pt | June 79 | 21 Sept 79 | do |
| Steel, Joseph | do | 10 June 78 | 16 Nov 78 | do |
| Still, John | do | 4   do | see below | |
| Smith, Henry | do | 13 May 78 | Nov 80 | out |
| Smith, Joseph | do | 3 June 78 | 16 Aug 80 | missing |
| Joined and Discharged 13 Aug 81 | | | | |
| Swails, Robert | Sergt | | feby 79 | discharged |
| Still, James | | 18 Nov 78 | 1 Nov 80 | present |
| Sullivan, Thomas | pt | } | 2 feb 80 | deserted |
| Joined 18 June 79 | | | | |
| Scott, John | do | Joined Sept 79 | | |
| Scoot, William | do | Musd. Oct & Nov, left out dec 79 | | |

### FROM OCTOBER MUSTER, 1780.

| | | | | |
|---|---|---|---|---|
| Scott, John | Drum | 13 Aprl 80 | 1 Nov 80 | present |
| Swann, William | do | do | do | do |
| Simmes, Jesse | Corpl | 20 Mar 80 | 1 Nov 80 | present |

### FOURTH REGIMENT.—*Beginning December,* 77.

| | | | | |
|---|---|---|---|---|
| Smith, Samuel | Lt. Col. | 10 April 77 | | |
| Smith, William[1] | Sergt | 28 Jan 77 | feb 79 | died |
| Spencer, William | pt | 24  do | 14 Jan 80 | discharged |
| Shean, Patk. | do | 1 dec 76 | } 16 Aug 80 | prisoner |
| | Corpl | 1 Sept 79 | | |
| Smith, John | pt | 6 dec 76 | do | do |
| Smith, John, 2d | do | | 18 June 79 | deserted |
| Shean, Timothy | do | 7   do | 16 Aug 80 | missing |
| Smith, Joshua | do | 14 Jan 77 | 14 Jan 80 | discharged |
| Smith, James[2] | do | | 8 July 79 | deserted |
| Smith, Daniel | do | | 3 May 78 | do |
| Scott, Alexr.[3] | Sergt | | dec 79 | time expired |
| Skiffington, Mathias | do | | 16 Aug 80 | missing |
| | private | 28 April 78 | | |
| Sollers, William | do | | 10 April 80 | deserted |
| Smith, Edward | do | 1 April 77 | 1   do | discharged |
| Sansberry, Richd. | do | | 14 dec 79 | do |

[1] Oldham's.    [2] Norwood's.    [3] Godman's.

## MUSTERS OF MARYLAND TROOPS, VOL I.

| NAMES. | RANK. | TIME OF SERVICE. | | REMARKS. |
|---|---|---|---|---|
| | | Enlisted. | Discharged. | |
| Stedds, Richd. | private | | 28 April 80 | discharged |
| Smith, James[1] | Lieut | | 20 June 79 | resigned |
| Sowall, Charles | do | | 17 Nov 77 | do |
| Smothers, Robt. | Corpl | 1 May 77 | 1 May 80 | discharged |
| Smith, William | Drum | 1 Mar 77 | 1 Nov 80 | present |
| Sinklair, Andrew | pt | | 14 June 78 | discharged |
| Sellman, Jona.[2] | Capt | 10 dec 76 | | |
| Shercliff, Wm. | Lieut | do | feb 78 | resigned by Roll |
| of Field &c. | | | | signed by Sam. Smith, Lt. Col. |
| Skally, Danl. | Corpl | 6 dec 76 | 6 dec 79 | discharged |
| Stockett, Henry | fifer | 6 dec 76 | ⎫ | |
| | Fife Major | 1 July 78 | ⎬ 6 dec 79 | discharged |
| Spurrier, Edward[3] | Lieut | 10 dec 76 | ⎫ | |
| | Capt | 21 May 78 | ⎬ | |
| Shelmerdine, Steph. | Lieut | ditto | 10 Dec | resigned |
| Street, George | pt | 6 dec 76 | Sept 80 | deserted |
| Simmons, John | do | 1 feb 77 | 16 Aug 80 | prisoner |
| Stewart, Robert | do | 12 Jan 77 | 1 Nov 80 | present |
| Sheain, Arthur | do | | 3 Aug 78 | discharged |
| Sewell, John | do | 5    do | 5 Jan 80 | time expired, discharged |
| Simms, Thomas | do | 3 April 77 | 22 April 80 | deserted |
| Joined 19 feb 80 | | | | |
| Smith, Thomas | do | 26 July 77 | ⎫ 1 Jan 80 | supposed dis- |
| | | 26 Jan 77 | ⎬ | [charged |
| Sprigg, Thomas[4] | do | | | |
| Stokes, Patk.[5] | do | | April 78 | left out the Roll |
| Sterne, John | do | | | |
| Stewart, Richd.[6] | do | 23 feb 78 | 10 July 78 | deserted |
| Steenson, John[1] | do | 19 Jan 78 | 26 April 78 | do |
| Smith, John[2] | do | 22  do | 10 July 78 | do |
| Street, James | do | 17  do | 16 dec 79 | do |
| Street, Samuel[7] | fifer | 31 Mar 78 | July 80 | do,    joined |
| Scroggy, Francis | pt | 25 April 78 | 16 Aug 80 | missing |
| Stacy, Robert[1] | do | 27  do | 1 Nov 80 | present |
| to Lansdale's Co., joined | do | | | |
| Silver, James[1] | | 9 May 78 | 16 Aug 80 | missing, joined |
| Smith, Labs. C.[2] | do | 11  do | 1 Nov 80 | present |
| Simmons, Thomas[8] | do | | | |
| Smith's, late Spurrier's | | | | |
| Salbott, William[9] | do | 27 April 78 | | |
| Riely's, late Bowie's | | | | |

[1] Lansdale's.    [2] Sellman's.    [3] Spurrier's.    [4] Bowie's.    [5] Burgess'.
[6] Godman's.    [7] Norwood's.    [8] Lt. Smith's.    [9] Riely's.

## MUSTERS OF MARYLAND TROOPS, VOL. I.

| NAMES. | RANK. | TIME OF SERVICE. Enlisted. | Discharged. | REMARKS. |
|---|---|---|---|---|
| Staid, Thomas | pt | 27 April 78 | 1 Nov 80 | present |
| Smith, Humphy. | do | 5 May 78 | 27 Aug 78 | discharged |
| Simmons, John[1] | pt | 20 May 78 | Corpl. 10 Feby 80 ⎱ | |
| | pt | 1 May 80 | ⎰ | deserted |
| Simmes, James | do | 10 June 78 | Dec 78 | discharged |
| Smith, Thomas | do | 16 May 78 | 1 Nov 80 | present |
| Smith, Elijah | do | 22 April 78 | 2 April 80 | |
| | | 9 July 78 | | |
| Smith, John[2] | do | 29 May 78 | 1 Mar 79 | discharged |
| Stewart, James[3] | do | 1 July 78 | 1 Oct 80 | present |
| | | deserted in Mar 81, Capt. Ewing | | |
| Shoemaker, Jacob[4] | pt | 9 Aug 78 | ⎱ 26 Jan 80 | promoted to be |
| | Sergt | 1 Mar 79 | ⎰ see forwd. | [Ensign |
| Stevens, William[1] | pt | 6 May 78 | feby 78 ⎱ | left out the Roll |
| | | | July 79 ⎰ | do |
| Stovely, James[4] | do | 1 Mar 79 | 15 May 80 | deserted |
| | | | July 80 | do |
| Smith, Jno., (Tayler)[1] | do | 14 do | Jan & feb 80 | absent with leave |
| | | | Mar 80 | left out |
| Slye, Robert[5] | do | 7 July 79 | 17 Jan 80 | deserted |
| Shulmear, Peter[6] | do | 23 do | 16 Aug 80 | missing |
| Swiney, Dennis | do | | do | do |
| Smith, Reubin[7] | do | 24 Oct 79 | 1 Nov 80 | present |
| Smith, Nathan[6] | Ensn | 18 Nov 79 ⎱ | | |
| | Lieut | 14 feb 80 ⎰ | | |
| Shoemaker, Jacob | Ensn | 26 Jan 80 ⎱ | | [wounds |
| | Lieut | 14 feb 80 ⎰ | 1780 prisoner and died of his | |
| Shadwick, William | pt | 5 April 77 | 5 April 80 | time expired |
| Stead, William[1] | do | | 16 Aug 80 | missing |
| Joined June mus. 80 | | | | |
| Spilliard, Mathew | do | | do | do |
| Joined June mus. 80 | | | | |

### RAWLINGS' REGIMENT.

| NAMES. | RANK. | Enlisted. | Discharged. | REMARKS. |
|---|---|---|---|---|
| Sanders, Joshua | Sergt | 17 July 76 | | died |
| Smith, Thomas | pt | 29 do | 21 July 79 | discharged |
| Scarriat, Thomas | do | 22 do | | |
| Scott, Joseph | do | 18 do | 20 dec 76 | deserted |
| Stafford, John | do | 17 Sept | | |
| Sadler, John | do | 13 Nov | do | do |
| Shephard, Jona. | do | July | | |
| Shaw, Basil | | 5 April 79 | Sergt. 27 July 79 | |

[1] Oldham's.   [2] Lansdale's.   [3] Lt. Smith's.   [4] Riely's.   [5] Hoops'.   [6] Sellman's.   [7] Belt's.

## MUSTERS OF MARYLAND TROOPS, VOL. I.

| NAMES. | RANK. | TIME OF SERVICE. Enlisted. | Discharged. | REMARKS. |
|---|---|---|---|---|
| Smith, Wm.   3 | | | 9 Aug 79 | discharged |
| Soaker, James   3 | | | 21 July do | do |
| Stephens, John   1 yr. | | | 9 Aug | do |
| Such, George | Sergt | 14   do | | |
| Shaw, William | pt | 11 Mar | | |
| Shocknesey, Thos. | do | 15 Mar | | |
| Stackpole, Jas. | do | 24 April | | |
| Shafer, Adam   6 mo. | | 25 Mar | | |
| Stacks, John | | | | |
| Starr, William | do | 2 Sept 76 | 17 Jan 77 | deserted |

### FIRST REGIMENT.

| NAMES. | RANK. | TIME OF SERVICE. Enlisted. | Discharged. | REMARKS. |
|---|---|---|---|---|
| Taylor, John | Sergt | 10 dec 76 | 77 | deserted |
| Taylor, John | pt | do | June 80 | do |
| Taylor, Ludowk. | do | do | 15 Mar 78 | do |
| Timmons, William | do | 4 Mar 77 | 10 Mar | do |
| Thomas, George | do   · | 10 dec 76 | 7 Mar 77 | died |
| Turner, Thomas | do | 1 feb 77 | 22 Jan 78 | deserted |
| Towzey, Thomas | do | 12 April 77 | 12 April 80 | discharged |
| Thompson, Saml. | do | 10 dec 76 | 10 April 77 | died |
| Tucker, William | do | 18 feb 77 | } 18 feb 80 | do |
| 25 Dec 79 | Corpl | 20 dec 79 | } | |
| Taylor, James | pt | 24 Mar | | deserted same mo. |
| Taylor, Aquilla | do | 10 dec 76 | 1 Jan 78 | dead |
| Tomling, Hugh | do | do | 27 dec 79 | discharged |
| Thomson, James | Sergt | do | do | do |
| Talbot, Coxon | pt | do | 23 May 77 | died |
| Thomson, Francis | do | do | 27 dec 79 | discharged   } |
| reinlisted mustered | | June 80 | 1 Nov 80 | present   } |
| Timms, Joseph | pt | 25 Oct 77 | } | |
| | Corpl | | } 14 Sept 80 | discharged |
| Thackerel, Rezin | pt | 27 April 78 | 16 Aug 80 | missing, killed |
| Thomson, Charles | do | 5 June 78 | 5 April 79 | discharged |
| Timms, Edward | do | 11 feb 78 | 1 Nov 80 | present |
| Taylor, William | do | 26 April 78 | do | do |
| Thomson, Richd. | do | 1 June 78 | 21 Oct 78 | died |
| Taylor, John | do | 9 mo. | 5 April 79 | dischd. |
| Timmons, Wm. | do | 21 Sept 79 | June 80 | left out, deserted |
| Tucker, John | do | 9 feb 80 | left out | October 80 |
| Tucker, John | pt | 21 feb 80 | 1 Nov 80 | present |
| Thomas, William | do June must. 1780 | | 16 Augt | missing |
| Tippet, Notley | do | | 1 Nov 80 | present |

## MUSTERS OF MARYLAND TROOPS, VOL. I.

| NAMES. | RANK. | TIME OF SERVICE. Enlisted. | Discharged. | REMARKS. |
|---|---|---|---|---|

SECOND REGIMENT.—*Beginning with the Muster Rolls for Jany.*, 1778.

| NAMES. | RANK. | Enlisted. | Discharged. | REMARKS. |
|---|---|---|---|---|
| Thatcher, David | Corpl / pt | 22 April 77 } 19 June 79 | 10 Jan 80 | discharged |
| Thompson, Benja. | do | 10 Jan 77 | do | do |
| Tharp, Jacob | do | Aprl & May 79 to Invalids, 31 May 80 died | | |
| Tull, John | do / Corpl | } 12 Sept 78 | 10 Jan 80 | discharged |
| Thomas, Hezeka. | Sergt | 10 Jan 77 | do | do |
| Tarleton, Jeremha. | pt / Corpl | do 1 June 78 } | do | do |
| Thomas, Stanhope | pt | 7 April 77 | do | do |
| Taylor, William | do | | do | do |
| Towland, William | do | 1 Jan 77 | 1 Nov 80 | present |
| Thompson, William | | | Jan 78 | Lt. Dragoons |
| Thompson, William | Drum | | July 80 | Hosptl.,supposed [dead |
| Taylor, Edward | pt | | 1 Nov 80 | present } |
| Thoroughgood, Jno. | do / Corpl | } 1 July 78 | 1 Jan 80 | discharged } |
| Tiler, Edward | pt / Corpl | 10 Jan 78 15 May 78 | } 10 Jan 80 | do |
| Thompson, Bennitt | pt | 20 July 77 | 1 July 78 | dead |
| Thompson, Charles | do | | do | deserted |
| Taylor, Thomas | do | 19 Mar 78 | | |
| Thompson, Thomas | do | 2 April 78 | 1 April 80 | do |
| | | | joined & 4 dec 80 | discharged |
| Tate, John | S. Mate | 10 May 78 | | resigned |
| Trego, James | pt | 20 April 78 | 78 | died Dansbury |
| Thompson, Lambert | do | 12 Jan 78 | 1 Nov 80 | present |
| Tutton, William | do | 30 do | 1 Aprl 79 transfd. to Invalids } 4 Jan 83 discharged on pen- } [sion |
| Turner, Abram | do | 24 May 78 | 30 Sept 78 | died |
| Thomson, Barthola. | do | | 1 Nov 80 | present |
| Turner, William | do | 20 do | feb 80 | deserted |
| Tayler, John | do | 20 Mar do | 1 Nov 80 | present |
| Thomas, Joseph | do | 25 May 78 | | discharged |
| Tayler, John | do | do | Mar 79 | do |
| Thorougood, John | Sergt | 1 Jan 80 | 1 Nov 80 | present |

THIRD REGIMENT.—*Beginning 77.*

| NAMES. | RANK. | Enlisted. | Discharged. | REMARKS. |
|---|---|---|---|---|
| Taylor, Snowden | pt | | 6 Dec 79 | discharged |
| Thompson, Natha. | do | 19 Apr 77 | | |
| out April 78, joined May | | | | |

12

MUSTERS OF MARYLAND TROOPS, VOL. I.

| NAMES. | RANK. | TIME OF SERVICE. Enlisted. | Discharged. | REMARKS. |
|---|---|---|---|---|
| Tarance, Owen | pt | 6 April 77 | | see Farance |
| Turner, Richd. | do | 26 do | | |
| | Corpl | 16 Mar 78 | } 16 Aug 80 | prisoner |
| | Sergt | 29 Augt 78 | | |
| Turbott, John | pt | | } 23 feb 80 | discharged |
| | Corpl | Oct 78 | | |
| Taylor, Robert | pt | 15 Jan 77 | 15 Jan 80 | do |
| reinlisted, see forward | | | | |
| Taylor, Thomas | do | 12 do | 12 do | do |
| Tenfield, Richd. | do | do | do | do |
| Toole, Thomas | pt | | | |
| Twyford, Wm. | do | 5 Nov 77 | 22 dec 77 | died |
| Tippits, Peter | do | 25 May 77 | 1 Nov 80 | present |
| Tucker, Thomas | do | 2 Sept 78 | transferred to Invalids 11 feb 80 | deserted } |
| Tarry, James | do | 25 April 78 | 22 Mar 80 | prisoner |
| reinlisted | | | joined | |
| Truman, John | Sergt | 30 do | promoted 80 | |
| Thomas, James | pt | 1 May do | 1 Nov 80 | present |
| | Drum | 4 June 78 | | |
| | private | 11 June 79 | | |
| Thompson, Ignats. | do | 13 do | | |
| or Athanatus | Corpl | 14 Aug 78 | } do | do |
| Q. M. Sergt. 1 March 80 | Sergt | 1 Jan 80 | | |
| Turner, John | pt | 23 May 78 | do | do |
| reinlisted 15 Jan 79 | | | | |
| Tibbles, Robert | do | 18 do | 12 dec 78 | deserted |
| Taylor, Griffith | do | 20 April 78 | 1 Nov 80 | present |
| Taylor, John | do | 1 June 78 | 13 feby 79 | discharged |
| Tarman, Henry | do | 5 do | Aug 79 | deserted |
| rein. 17 Nov 78 | | | (Jesse Suits) | |
| Trigg, Samuel | do | 6 Jan 78 | 1 Nov 80 | present |
| Tasker, Richard | do | 27 May 78 | 1 Nov 80 | do |
| reinlisted | | | | |
| Tawman, Henry | do | 17 Nov 78 | | |
| Tillert, Samuel | do | | 20 Jan 79 | discharged |
| Townley, Henry | do | 4 June 78 | 16 Aug 80 | missing } |
| | | | joined | |
| Thomas, Thomas | do | 13 May 78 | | |
| Tedford, John | do | 12 do | | |
| Tragasskiss, Jacob | pt | | 16 Aug 80 | missing |

## MUSTERS OF MARYLAND TROOPS, VOL. I.

| NAMES. | RANK. | TIME OF SERVICE. Enlisted. | TIME OF SERVICE. Discharged. | REMARKS. |
|---|---|---|---|---|

### FROM OCTOBER MUSTER, 1780.

| NAMES. | RANK. | Enlisted. | Discharged. | REMARKS. |
|---|---|---|---|---|
| Turner, Leonard | pt | | 1 Nov 80 | present |
| Trusky, Samuel | do | | do | do |
| Trusty, John | do | | do | do |
| Taylor, Robert | do | | do | do |
| Thomson, Joseph | do | 1 April 80 | do | do |
| Thomas, Thomas | do | | do | do |

### FOURTH REGIMENT.—*Beginning Dec.,* 1777.

| NAMES. | RANK. | Enlisted. | Discharged. | REMARKS. |
|---|---|---|---|---|
| Twineing, Natha.[1] | Ensn | 29 feb 77 | } 1 June 79 | resigned |
|  | Lieut | 20 Nov 77 | | |
| Tood, Benjamin | Sergt | | June Roll 78 | left out |
| Townshend, Wm.[2] | pt | | Jan 80 | deserted |
| Tidings, Caleb[3] | do | 1 July 77 | } 1 July 80 | time expired |
|  | Corpl | 31 Oct 78 | } 16 May | discharged |
|  | Sergt | 1 dec 79 | | |
| Taylor, John[4] | pt | | 26 feb 78 | deserted |
| Turner, Samson | do | | 1 Mar 78 | discharged |
| Turner, Thomas[5] | do | 14 Aug 77 | 1 Nov 80 | present |
| Tracey, Thomas | do | | 25 Jan 78 | deserted |
| Tompson, Lawce. | do | 7 do | 1 Nov 80 | present |
| Troy, John[1] | do | 23 Mar 78 | 9 July 78 | deserted |
| Tiser, James[2] | do | 26 April 78 | Jan 80 | do |
| Thomas, John[6] | pt | 4 May 78 | 16 Aug 80 | missing |
| Topping, Peter | do | do | 1 Nov 80 | present |
| Thornby, Joseph[7] | do | 17 April 77 | 16 Aug 80 | missing |
| prisr. 22 Aug 77, joined 23 June 78 | | | | |
| Taylor, John[8] | do | 4 May 78 | do | do |
| Tree, Thomas | do | 12 July 79 | do | do |
| Tumberson, Evan[1] | do | Dec 76 | 1 Nov 80 | present |
| Tipling, Isaac | | | 16 Aug 80 | missing |

### RAWLINGS' REGIMENT.

| NAMES. | RANK. | | Enlisted. | Discharged. | REMARKS. |
|---|---|---|---|---|---|
| Thomson, John | Sergt | | 15 July 76 | | |
| Tress, Peter | pt | | 76 | | |
| Tracy, Charles | do | 1 yr. | | 1 July | discharged |
| Trust, Peter | do | 3 | | | |
| Trotten, Lowden | Corpl | | | | |
| Thomson, Chas. | | 1 yr. | | do | do |
| Treviss, John | pt | | | | |
| Taylor, William | do | | | | |

[1] Oldham's.  [2] Norwood's.  [3] Selman's.  [4] Spurrier's.  [5] Burgess'.
[6] Godman's.  [7] Lansdale's.  [8] Riely's.

## MUSTERS OF MARYLAND TROOPS, VOL. I.

| NAMES. | RANK. | TIME OF SERVICE. Enlisted. | Discharged. | REMARKS. |
|---|---|---|---|---|
| Thompson, Thomas | 1 yr. | | 9 Aug | |
| Tryar, And. | Sergt | | 1 July 79 | discharged |
| Twinch, George | Drum | | | |
| Terring, Wm. M. | Fifer | | 15 do | do |
| Tannehill, Josiah | Adjut | 1st do | | |

SECOND REGIMENT.—*Beginning January,* 1778.

| | | | | |
|---|---|---|---|---|
| Uncles, Benja. | pt | 11 April 77 | 11 April 80 | discharged |

THIRD REGIMENT.—*Beginning* 77.

| | | | | |
|---|---|---|---|---|
| Urquhart, Andw.  Out Nov 77 | pt | 3 July 77 | | |

FIRST REGIMENT.

| | | | | |
|---|---|---|---|---|
| Vermillion, Saul | pt | 10 dec 76 | 12 Mar 77 | deserted, joined |

SECOND REGIMENT.—*Beginning Jan.,* 78.

| | | | | |
|---|---|---|---|---|
| Vaughan, Wm. | pt | | 5 May 81 | discharged |
| Valient, Jonathan | pt | 11 Mar 77 | 10 Jan 80 | discharged |
| Vaughan, William | do | 6 May 78 | 1 Nov 80 | present |
| | | | 6 May 81 | discharged } |
| Vincent, John | do | 1 ditto | do | do |
| Vautier, Danl. | do | 2 April 78 | do | do |
| Varlow, Stephen | do | 10 June 78 | do | do |
| Vickers, John | do | | 20 Mar 80 | deserted |

THIRD REGIMENT.—*Beginning* 77.

FOURTH REGIMENT.—*Beginning Dec.,* 77.

| | | | | |
|---|---|---|---|---|
| Vansant, John[1] | pt | 6 dec 76 | 1 Nov 80 | present |
| Vergen, John[2] | Sergt | | | |

FIRST REGIMENT.

| | | | | |
|---|---|---|---|---|
| White, Jona. | | wounded 25 April 81 Camden, 29 Sept furld. by Genl. Smallwood, 29 Sept 81 to be settled with to that time full pay | | |
| Winder, Levin | Capt | 10 dec 76 | Major 17 April 77 | |
| Wheelan, Martin | pt | do | 24 May 77 | deserted |
| Watkins, Leonard | do | do | | |
| Wilson, John Fred. | do | 4 feb 77 | | |
| Wilson, John, Jr. | do | 21 do | | |

[1] Lansdale's.

[2] Burgess'.

## MUSTERS OF MARYLAND TROOPS, VOL. I.

| NAMES. | RANK. | TIME OF SERVICE. Enlisted. | Discharged. | REMARKS. |
|---|---|---|---|---|
| Wheatly, Samuel | Corpl | 10 dec 76 | 22 Aug 77 | prisr. war |
| Whilling, Thomas | pt | do | 6 Mar 78 | deserted |
| Ward, Ignatius | do | 10 feb 77 | 11 feb 80 | discharged |
| Welstead, William | do | 10 dec 76 | 27 dec 79 | do |
| Weller, Philip | do | do | do | do |
| Wheatley, William | Corpl | do | 28 June 78 | killed |
| Walker, John | pt | | | |
| | Corpl | 1 Oct 77 | 27 dec 79 | discharged |
| Wood, William | pt | | 19 Aug 77 | died |
| Watkins, Nichs. | Corpl | 10 dec 76 | 27 dec 79 | discharged |
| | Sergt | 18 April 77 | | |
| Walker, William | pt | 14 Mar 77 | 27 Nov 77 | deserted } |
| | | joined and deserted again 6 Augt 78 | | |
| Wise, Thomas | do | 26 do | 26 Mar 80 | discharged |
| Wyndham, Thomas | Corpl | 10 dec 76 | 27 dec 79 | do } |
| reinlisted 10 Jan 80 | Sergt | 10 Jan 80 | 1 Nov 80 | present |
| Watts, Richard | pt | 10 dec 76 | | |
| Willshire, Samuel | do | do | 24 May 77 | deserted |
| Watkins, Nicholas | Corpl | do | 10 dec 79 | discharged |
| Wiseman, Thomas | pt | do | 17 Aug 80 | deserted |
| Ward, Ignatius | do | 11 feb 77 | | see above |
| Waters, Richard | Lieut | 10 April 77 | Capt. 7 April 80 | |
| Wallace, Hugh | pt | 10 dec 76 | | |
| Wellman, Jacob | do | 7 Mar 77 | | |
| Wellman, William | do | do | 22 Aug 77 | prisoner |
| Whelen, Richard | do | 10 dec 76 | 3 June 77 | Exd. Jno. Gorman |
| Williams, Thomas | do | do | | |
| | Corpl | 1 Aug 77 | redd. 10 feb 78 } discharged | |
| | | left out of musr. taken in April 80 | | |
| Wallace, Michael | Surgeon | 10 dec 76 | | resigned |
| Warfield, Walter | S. Mate | 27 Nov 77 | 28 feb 79 | |
| Williams, John | pt | 11 May 78 | 16 Aug 80 | missing |
| Weston, Thomas | do | 9 do | 1 Nov 80 | present |
| Williams, Jno., Jr. | do | 24 April 78 | 31 Aug 80 | deserted |
| | | Joined 10 Oct 80 | | |
| Williams, John | do | 20 April 78 } | | |
| musr. Oct 80 | | 5 April 79 } 1 Nov 80 | | present |
| Wright, Alexr. | do | 9 June 78 | | |
| Ward, George | | 10 June 78 | 1 Nov 80 | present |
| Woodard, Jesse | do | 6 do | 5 April 79 | discharged |
| Welch, George | do | 16 do | do | do |
| Wade, Lanct. | do | 4 do | do | do |
| Ward, Thomas | do | 20 May 78 | 14 feb 79 | do |
| Williams, John | Gist | | | |

## MUSTERS· OF MARYLAND TROOPS, VOL. I.

| NAMES. | RANK. | TIME OF SERVICE. Enlisted. | Discharged. | REMARKS. |
|---|---|---|---|---|
| Walker, John, Jr. | pt | 12 Sept 79 | 1 Nov 80 | present |
| Whitticer, Francis | do | 15 May 80 | 16 Aug 80 | prisoner |
| West, Alexr. | do | mr. June 80 | 1 Nov 80 | present |
| West, John | fifer | | 16 Aug 80 | missing |
| White, Jonathan | pt | 12 dec 79 | 1 Nov 80 | present |
| Willing, Littleton | pt | | 16 Aug 80 | prisoner |

SECOND REGIMENT.—*Beginning with the Musr. Rolls for Jan.,* 78.

| NAMES. | RANK. | Enlisted. | Discharged. | REMARKS. |
|---|---|---|---|---|
| Woolford, Thomas | Lt. Col. | 17 April 77 | | |
| Welch, John | pt | | 23 dec 78 | discharged |
| | | Joined Mar 80 | | |
| Worthington, Ben. | do | 4 Mar 77 | 16 Aug 80 | missing |
| | | | dec 78 | deserted |
| joined musd. Mar 79 | | No Land | dec 79 | do again |
| Wright, Nathan | Sergt | 10 Jan 80 | | discharged |
| Walker, Thomas | Corpl | | 22 Jan 78 | deserted |
| Worring, John | pt | | | |
| Wall, Patk. | do | | 24  do | do |
| Wright, John | do | 24 dec 76 | 24 dec 79 | discharged |
| White, James | Sergt | | 10 Jan 80 | do |
| Waymore, Thomas | pt | | | |
| Joined 18 April 79 | | | 1 April 80 | do |
| Wheeler, William | do | | 10 Jan 80 | do |
| Winset, Raphl. | do | | do | do |
| Wheatley, Henry | do | 15 Mar 77 | 15 Mar 80 | do |
| Wright, Jesse | do | 1 Aug 77 | 1 Nov 80 | present |
| Walker, Edward | | | 22 Jan | deserted |
| Wisely, Benja. | do | 4 feb 77 | June 79 | transferred to In-valids |

4 Nov 79 joined again, 4 feb 80 discharged, memorandum, he deserted 25 Oct 79

| NAMES. | RANK. | Enlisted. | Discharged. | REMARKS. |
|---|---|---|---|---|
| Williams, Sullivan | Lieut | 10 April 77 | Capt. 17 April 77 | |
| Wheeler, Nathl. | pt | 1 Jan 77 | 16 Aug 80 | prisoner |
| Welsh, John[1] | pt | 5 April 78 | | |
| B. Price's Co. | fifer | | | |
| Welsh, John | pt | | 16 Aug 80 | missing joined |
| Woolford, William | Ensn | 17 April 77 | Lieut. 11 April 79 | |
| Webster, Thomas | pt | 24 dec 76 | 16 Aug 80 | killed |
| Waters, Richard | S. M. | 7 May 78 | | |
| Williams, David | pt | 12 April 78 | 1 Nov 80 | present |
| | fifer | 1 Nov 78 | | |
| Wheatley, Wm. | pt | 20 April 78 | do | do |

[1] B. Price's.

## MUSTERS OF MARYLAND TROOPS, VOL. I.

| NAMES. | RANK. | TIME OF SERVICE. Enlisted. | Discharged. | REMARKS. |
|---|---|---|---|---|
| Wilson, William | pt | 19 May 78 | 16 Aug 80 | killed |
| Wingate, Andw. | do | 1 do | 1 Nov 80 | present |
| Wall, William | do | 15 do | 1 July 78 | deserted } |
| Joined and discharged by Col. Forrest 22 Aug 80 | | | | |
| Williams, Cassitee | do | 16 do | 16 Aug 80 | missing |
| Joined Aug 79 | | | | |
| Welsh, James | pt | 28 April 78 | 28 June 78 | killed Battle Monmouth |
| Warlough, John | do | 20 May 78 | 16 May 80 | deserted |
| Winsett, James | do | 29 do | 3 April 79 | discharged |
| Wheatly, John | do | do | do | do |
| Wise, Thomas | do | 25 do | 3 April 79 | do |
| Wheatley, Sylvt. | do | 16 do | 16 Aug 80 | missing |
| Woodbarn, Jona. | do | 1 June 78 | 3 April 79 | discharged |
| Wells, Martin | do | 24 May 78 | | do |
| Williamson, Alex. | do | do | Sept 78 | do |
| Williams, John | Corpl | | 10 Jan 80 | do |
| Wood, Thomas | do | 20 do | 1 Nov 80 | present |
| White, Edward | pt | 18 Mar 78 | } 1 Nov 80 | present } |
| | Corpl | July 80 | } depreciation twice recd. | |
| Whood, John | pt | 5 June do | 16 Aug 80 | missing |
| Woodward, John | do | 20 May do | do | do |
| Wall, Jesse | do | 20 do | 3 April 79 | discharged |
| Wall, David | do | do | do | do |
| Wilson, Danl. | do | 9 feb 78 | 1 Nov 80 | prisoner |
| Wills, George | do | 25 May 78 | 26 dec 78 | deserted |
| Wright, William | do | 20 do | 3 Aprl 79 | discharged |
| Wright, Saml. | do | do | 24 dec 78 | do |
| Wallis, Thomas | do | | do | do |
| Wood, John | fifer | 2 June 78 } | | |
| | private | 1 Mar 79 } | | |
| | fifer | 1 Aprl 79 } | 1 Nov 80 | present |
| Warfield, Walter | Surgn | 10 June 79 } | | |
| Surgeon's Mate of 6 M. R. | | 1 April 78 } | | |
| Welch, Thomas | pt | 8 May 79 | 1 Nov 80 | present |
| 1 mus. July 79 | | | | |
| Wilkinson, Jno. | do | | 16 Aug 80 | missing |
| do Aug 79 | | | | |
| Wake, Richd. | fifer | 25 do } | | |
| | pt | 1 Oct 79 } | 26 dec 79 | deserted |
| Wilson, James | do | 14 June 79 | 1 Nov 80 | present |
| Wimberry, Thos. | do | 10 Mar 80 | do | do |
| 1 mus. Jan 80 | | | | |
| Waters, York | do | June 80 | do | do |
| | | | 4 June | discharged } |

## MUSTERS OF MARYLAND TROOPS, VOL. I.

| NAMES. | RANK. | TIME OF SERVICE. | | REMARKS. |
| | | Enlisted. | Discharged. | |
|---|---|---|---|---|
| Winn, John | pt | | 16 Aug 80 | prisoner |
| Ward, Peter | do | 20 Mar 80 | do | killed |
| Wait, Thomas | pt | 16 May 80 | 1 Nov 80 | present |
| Willing, William | pt | | 1 Nov 80 | present |
| Whitcomb, Notley | do | 15 June 80 | 18 Aug 80 | discharged |

### THIRD REGIMENT.—*Beginning* 77.

| NAMES. | RANK. | TIME OF SERVICE. | | REMARKS. |
| | | Enlisted. | Discharged. | |
|---|---|---|---|---|
| Wright, Richard | Corpl | 14 Aprl 77 } | 24 Sept 79 | died |
|   Nov & Dec 78 | Sergt | | | |
| Williams, Jeremiah | pt | 15 Mar 77 | 15 Mar 80 | discharged |
| Wildman, Edward | do | 23 April 77 | 10 dec 79 | deserted |
| Wright, William | do | 15 do | 20 Nov 77 | died |
| Williams, David | do | 22 June 77 | 27 Sep 79 | deserted & musd. |
|   prisr. 11 Sep 77, joined 18 June 78 | | | | deserted in Aug 1780 |
| Welch, Patk. | do | | | |
|   not heard of since 4 June 78, Joined | | | | |
| Watkins, William | do | May 79 | | |
|   said to be dead May musr. 78 | | | | |
| Wood, John | do | 28 April 77 | 28 April 80 | discharged |
|   Excd. & joined 22 July 78 | | | | |
| Wells, Edmund | do | 28 Aug 77 | 11 Mar 77 | deserted |
| Wire, James | do | 25 April 77 | | |
| Wilmot, William | Lieut | 10 dec 76 | · Capt. 15 Oct 77 | |
| Walker, Robert | pt | 14 April 77 | 1 Nov 80 | present |
| Whittaker, (or Whit- | fifer | 17 do | 16 Aug 80 | missing |
|   comb), Thos. | pt | musr. feb 78 | | |
| Wood, Thomas | do | 10 July do | 3 April 78 | died |
| Williams, Osborn | Ensn | 18 Mar 77 | | |
| Wright, Thomas | pt | 13 May do | 16 Aug 80 | missing |
| Wayton, John | Sergt | 7 May do | 1 Jan 80 | off the Roll |
| Watkins, Peter | pt | 8 Sept 77 | 10 feb 78 | died |
| Weathersby, Thos. | pt | 9 Sept 77 | Jan 78 | off Roll |
| Walls, Sutton | do | do | 6 Jan 78 | died |
| Weathersby, Jas. | do | do | 78 off Rolls | |
| Webb, John | do | was discharged 1 April 79 | | |
|   Jan 78 absent wth. leave | Sergt | 10 June 77 | procuring a man in his place | |
|   pt 23 May, April Roll 78 | | | | |
| Whittaker, Francis | pt | 12 Jan 77 | 12 Jan 80 | discharged |
| Woolford, Michl. | do | 5 May 77 | 1 Nov 80 | present |
| Wilson, James | do | 12 Jan 77 | 12 Jan 80 | discharged |
| Wade, James | do | 2 June 77 | 16 Aug 80 | missing |
| Wilmot, Fredk. | do | 12 feb 77 | 1 Nov 80 | present |
| Watson, Thomas | do | 1 Jan 77 | 16 Aug 80 | missing<br>joined } |

## MUSTERS OF MARYLAND TROOPS, VOL. I.

| NAMES. | RANK. | TIME OF SERVICE. | | REMARKS. |
|---|---|---|---|---|
| | | Enlisted. | Discharged. | |
| Walker, John | pt | 1 Aprl 77 | | |
| | Corpl | 5 Oct do | } 16 Aug 80 | joined |
| | pt | 8 April 78 | | |
| Wilder, Henry | do | 12 Aug do | 19 June 78 | deserted |
| Woodthey, John | do | 20 Aprl do | 12 feb 78 | died |
| Woodley, Jonathan | do | 9 June 77 | 11 Mar 78 | deserted |
| Whittle, Robert | Corpl | | | |
| Joined 5 May 79 | pt | | | |
| White, John | do | 28 Aprl 77 | time expired | |
| | | | 30 April 80 | discharged } |
| Wilson, William | do | 24 May 77 | 1 Nov 80 | present |
| Whiteley, William | do | 27 Mar 77 | 1 May 80 | discharged |
| Whitmore, Stephen | do | off Rolls Jan 78 | | |
| by J. Lowe's certificate was enlisted 20 feb 77 | | | | |
| Wilcox, James | | | 10 Mar 80 | died |
| out Aug 78, Joined 5 May 79 | | | | |
| Wells, Jno.[1] | do | 21 April 78 | May 79 | left out the Rolls |
| Welsh, John | pt | 6 feb 78 | 16 Aug 80 | missing } |
| | | | 1 Nov 80 | present |
| Joined 20 July 79, left sick at pluckemain, Jersey, in April 80 | | | | |
| Willingham, Jno. B. | pt | 13 May 78 | feb 79 | discharged |
| Williams, Zepha. | do | 2   do | 16 Aug 80 | killed |
| Wild, James | do | 14 Apl 78 | do | missing |
| Wort, (or Word), Richard | do | | June 78 | transferred to Invalids |
| Whitmore, Stephen | do | | | |
| out Aug 78 | | | | |
| Wedding, John | do | 25 May 78 | 23 Sep 78 | died |
| Warring, William | do | do | 15 Mar 79 | discharged |
| Windham, George | do | 25 April 78 | 1 Nov 80 | present |
| Wade, Edmund, (or) | } | | | |
| Edward | } do | 24  do | | Guard |
| Watkins, James | do | 2 June 78 | } 16 Aug 80 | prisoner |
| | Corpl | 1 July 79 | | |
| Wilder, Henry | pt | | dec 78 | deserted |
| Joined Oct 78 | | | | |
| West, William | do | 5 June 78 | 1 Nov 80 | present |
| rein. 9 Jan 79 | | | | |
| Williams, John | do | 14 April 78 | do | do |
| Wood, Jno.[2] | do | 26 Jan 77 | do | do |
| Wilson, Barnaby | do | 9 May 78 | do | do |
| Windberry, George | do | 5 June 78 | May 79 | time expired |
| Wood, Dorsey | do | 11 May 78 | 24 dec 78 | discharged |
| Wilkinson, Wm. | do | 3 Mar 78 | 1 Nov 80 | present |

[1] Smith's.                                                     [2] Claggett's.

## MUSTERS OF MARYLAND TROOPS, VOL. I.

| NAMES. | RANK. | TIME OF SERVICE. Enlisted. | Discharged. | REMARKS. |
|---|---|---|---|---|
| Williams, John | pt | 20 feb 79 | 3 Mar 79 | deserted |
| Whight, Tarance | do | 3 Sept 78 | 1 Nov 80 | present |
| 1st musr. June 79 | | | | |
| Wilson, John | do | 1 July 79 | 5 Jan 80 | deserted |

FROM OCTOBER MUSTER, 1780, & JULY, &C.

| NAMES. | RANK. | Enlisted. | Discharged. | REMARKS. |
|---|---|---|---|---|
| Williams, Charles | pt | 27 Mar 80 | 1 Nov 80 | present |
| Windley, John | do | | | |
| Wilson, Barney | fifer | | 16 Aug 80 | prisoner |
| Windley, Benja. | pt | | | |
| White, Saml. B. | do | 2 April 78 | 1 Nov 80 | present |
| (from B. 3 Regt.) | | | | |
| Watson, Thomas | | | 15 Nov 83 | discharged |

FOURTH REGIMENT.—*Beginning Decr., 77.*

| NAMES. | RANK. | Enlisted. | Discharged. | REMARKS. |
|---|---|---|---|---|
| Winstanly, Francis[1] | pt | 15 dec 76 | 29 June 78 | deserted or gone to Invalids, deserted from Invalids 11 June 81 |
| Williams, Thomas | do | | 10 Sept 78 | discharged |
| Wells, John[2] | Corpl | | 1 Nov 80 | present |
| joined private | 1 Aug 78 | | | |
| West, Fredk.[2] | pt | | feb Roll 78 | died Baltimore |
| Welsh, John | do | | 1 Aug 80 | discharged |
| Wright, John | do | 4 Aug 77 | 16 do | missing |
| joined 16 Aug 79 | | | | |
| Webster, John[2] | do | | July 80 | deserted |
| do | | | | |
| Warden, James | do | Sergt. 1 April 78 } dec 79 | | dischd. |
| | pt | 1 Mar 79 } | | |
| Ware, John | do | | 16 Aug 80 | missing |
| Williamson, Robt. | do | | June 78 | not heard of |
| Williamson, Thos. | do | | do | do |
| Wilderman, Jacob[4] | Corpl | pt. 28 Aug 78 } 13 April 80 | | dischd. |
| | Sergt | 1 Jan 79 } | | |
| Welch, Joseph | pt | | 16 Aug 80 | missing |
| Wood, Robertson | pt | 1 Jan 77 | 1 Nov 80 | present |
| Welch, Thomas | do | 3 Mar 77 | 3 Mar 80 | discharged |
| Wilson, Tobias[5] | Sergt | 11 feb 77 | 6 dec 79 | dischd., Thos. Hailey to serve the remainder his time |
| Wood, Thomas | pt | 13 do | 1 Nov 80 | present |
| Wright, Edward | do | 26 July 77 | do | do |
| Wallingsford, Jas.[6] | do | 6 Jan 77 | 6 Jan 80 | dischd. |
| Watkins, Stephen | do | 15 July 77 | 20 May 80 | do |

[1] Oldham's.    [2] Norwood's.    [3] Spurrier's.    [4] Godman's.    [5] Lansdale's.    [6] Selman's.

## MUSTERS OF MARYLAND TROOPS, VOL. I.

| NAMES. | RANK. | TIME OF SERVICE. Enlisted. | Discharged. | REMARKS. |
|---|---|---|---|---|
| Webb, Jos.[1] | Sergt | | 11 feb 78 | died |
| Wood, William[2] | pt | 20 dec 76 | 20 dec 79 | dischd. |
| Wheland, Jno., or Geo.[1] | do | 9 Aug 77 | 10 dec 79 | deserted |
| Warwick, James[3] | do | 6 Jan 77 | 6 Jan 80 | dischd. |
| Warwick, Wm.[2] | do | 20 May 77 | 20 April 80 | do |
| | Corpl | 20 feb 78 | | |
| | pt | 1 April 78 | 1 Mar 80 | time expired |
| Williams, Thomas | do | 16 April 77 | July 80 | deserted |
| left out June 78, joined 1 June 78 | | | | |
| Walker, John[4] | do | | | see Riely's below |
| Bowie's, Mar 78 | | | | |
| Waldron, Joseph[5] | do | 20 April 78 | Sept 80 | deserted |
| Williams, John | do | 29 do | 22 Nov 78 | do |
| Wiggins, James[6] | do | 20 Mar 78 | 16 Aug 80 | prisoner |
| Lansdale's, April 78 | | | | |
| Willis, John[7] | do | 6 dec 76 | 6 dec 79 | dischd. |
| Smith's, 78 | | | | |
| Williams, Wm. | do | 13 May 78 | 16 Aug 80 | missing |
| Wilkerson, John[8] | do | 13 Mar 78 | | |
| Riely's, late Bowie's | | | | |
| Walker, John[9] | do | | 16 Aug 80 | do |
| Whitehouse, Jos.[9] | do | 5 May 78 | 1 Nov 80 | present |
| Wheeler, James[8] | pt | 1 May 78 | 16 Aug 80 | missing |
| Whitehouse, Sam.[9] | do | | 10 April 79 | dischd. |
| Whitecotton, James[6] | do | 29 do | 4 Mar 79 | deserted |
| Williams, Jereh. | do | 3 do | 16 Aug 80 | missing |
| | Corpl | 1 June 80 | | |
| Williams, John | pt | 16 May 78 | 4 Oct 78 | joined |
| Williams, Jarvis[3] | do | 17 do | 1 Nov 80 | present |
| Walker, John[3] | do | 29 Jan 78 | June 78 | left out |
| Welch, John[2] | do | 6 July 78 | 11 May 80 | deserted |
| | | | July 80 | do |
| Wilmington, Jos. | do | | 1 Nov 80 | present |
| Joined Oct 78 | | | | |
| Williams, John[3] | do | 16 | 16 Aug 80 | missing |
| mus. June 79 | | | | |
| Willshire, John[6] | do | 18 June 79 | 15 Jan 80 | deserted |
| Wood, Jacob[10] | do | 25 May 78 | 2 July 80 | do |
| Wood, James[11] | do | 3 feb 80 | 1 Nov 80 | present |

[1] Spurrier's.  [2] Burgess'.  [3] Selman's.  [4] Bowie's.  [5] Norwood's.  [6] Lansdale's.
[7] Smith's.  [8] Riely's.  [9] Godman's.  [10] Hoops'.  [11] Lt. Hanson's.

## MUSTERS OF MARYLAND TROOPS, VOL. I.

| NAMES. | RANK. | TIME OF SERVICE. Enlisted. | Discharged. | REMARKS. |
|---|---|---|---|---|
| | | **RAWLINGS' REGIMENT.** | | |
| Watson, Abram | pt | 26 Aug 76 | | |
| Wilson, William | do | 20 April 79 | | |
| Williams, Alexr. | do | | 15 July 79 | discharged |
| Whireley, David | 1 yr. do | | 1 July 79 | deserted |
| Wade, George | do | | 1 July | do |
| Wilson, Helbriath | do | | | |
| Weedon, Jonathan | do | | 15 May 79 | do |
| | | Joined 17 Nov 79 | | |
| Watts, James | pt | | 15 July 79 | killed |
| Williams, Andrew | 1 yr. | | 6    do | discharged |
| White, John | Corpl | 11 April 79 | | |
| Whilmon, Jno. | Drum | 17 Mar | | |
| Wallenberg, F. | Corpl | | | |
| Willyard, Henry | Drum | | | |
| White, Jas. | 6 mo. pt | 11 Mar | | |
| Wannaker, B. | 6 mo. | | 8 April 79 | killed |
| Woodman, Jno. | do | 25 June | | |
| | | **FIRST MARYLAND REGIMENT.** | | |
| Yeator, Joseph | pt | 10 dec 76 | 16 Aug 80 | prisoner |
| | | **SECOND REGIMENT.** | | |
| Yates, Richard | pt | 17 Mar 78 | 15 Sept 78 | died |
| Yates, James | do | 29    do | 3 April 79 | dischd. |
| | | **THIRD REGIMENT.** | | |
| Young, John | pt | 20 April 77 | | |
| out July 78 | | | | |
| Yarnall, Benja. | do | 26 Jan 77 | | |
| | | **FOURTH REGIMENT.**—*Beginning Dec., 77.* | | |
| Young, Benja.[1] | Sergt | | 8 dec 79 | dischd. |
| Joined Hoops' Co. | | | | |
| Young, John[2] | pt | 14 May 78 | 1 Nov 80 | present |
| | | **RAWLINGS' REGIMENT.** | | |
| Young, Peter | 1 yr. | | | |
| Young, John | | 19 Mar 79 | | no Land |

[1] Godman's.    [2] Norwood's.

## MUSTERS OF MARYLAND TROOPS, VOL. II.

### "MARYLAND LINE."

---

#### RESOLVES OF CONTINENTAL CONGRESS, 25 MAY, 1776.

" Resolved, That one battalion of Germans be raised for the service of the United Colonies."

#### RESOLVES OF CONTINENTAL CONGRESS, 27 JUNE, 1776.

" The committee to whom it was referred to devise a mode of raising the German battalion, voted on the 25th of May last, brought in their report, which was taken into consideration : Whereupon,

Resolved, That four companies of Germans be raised in Pennsylvania and four companies in Maryland, to compose the said regiment: That it be recommended to the convention, or in their recess, to the council of safety of Maryland, immediately to appoint proper officers for, and direct the inlistment of, the four companies to be raised in that colony :.

That the said companies be inlisted to serve for three years, unless sooner discharged by Congress, and receive bounty, pay, rations, and all other allowances equal to any of the continental troops : That the said companies, when raised, be formed into a battalion, under the command of such field officers as Congress shall appoint : That the rank of the captains of the said companies be regulated as Congress shall hereafter direct."

#### RESOLVES OF THE MARYLAND CONVENTION OF JUNE, 1776.

6 July, 1776.

" Resolved, That this province will raise . . . . four companies of Germans, according to the requisitions of Congress in their resolutions of the 27th day of June last.

That . . . two of the said companies of Germans be raised in Baltimore county, . . . . and two of the companies of Germans be raised in Frederick county. That each of the companies of Germans consist of one captain, two lieutenants, one ensign, four sergeants, four corporals, one drummer, one fifer, and seventy-six privates."

#### RESOLVES OF CONTINENTAL CONGRESS, 17 JULY, 1776.

" Resolved, That Nicholas Hauseigger be colonel ; George Stricker, lieutenant-colonel ; Ludewick Wiltner, major of the German battalion.

Resolved, That another company be added to the German battalion: That David Welper be appointed captain of said company."

CONTINENTAL CONGRESS,

25 September, 1776.

"The committee appointed to settle the rank of the captains and subalterns in the German battalion, reported the same as follows, which was agreed to:

Captains, Daniel Burkhart, Philip Graybill, George Hubley, Henry Fister, Jacob Bonner, George Kaports, Benjamin Weiser, William Keyser, and David Woelpper.

First-lieutenants, Frederick Rolwagen, John Lora, Peter Boyer, Charles Bulsel, William Rice, Jacob Kotz, Jacob Bower, Samuel Gerock, and Bernard Hubley.

Second-lieutenants, George Hawbacker, Christian Meyers, John Landenberger, Michal Bayer, George Schaeffer, Adam Smith, Frederick Yeiser, William Ritter, and Philip Schrawder.

Ensigns, John Weidman, Martin Shugart, Christian Helm, Jacob Crummet, Jacob Cramer, Paul Christman, Christopher Godfrey Swartz, and John Landenberger."

The German Regiment was regarded as one of the additional 16 Regiments raised under Resolutions of Congress 27 December, 1776.

---

## MUSTERS OF MARYLAND TROOPS, VOL. II.

| NAMES. | RANK. | TIME OF SERVICE. Enlisted. | Discharged. | REMARKS. |
|---|---|---|---|---|
| **5TH MARYLAND REGIMENT.** | | | | |
| Ayres, John[1] | pt | 22 Mar 1777 | 7 Mar 80 | time expired |
| Anderson, James[2] | do | 24 June 77 | April 7— | left out |
| Allen, James | do | 8 July 77 | 1 Nov 80 | present, paid |
| Austin, Harris | fife | 25 July | 1 Jany | private, left out of Rolls |
| Ayres, Thomas[3] | pt | 17 dec 76 | 1 Nov 80 | present |
| Ayres, James[4] | do | 10 dec 76 | 10 dec 79 | time out |
| Q. M. Sergt. 1 Mar 79 | Sergt | 9 July 77 | | |
| Alexander, Wm.[5] | Lieut | 10 dec 76 | 27 Aug 77 | died |
| Allen, Gilbert | pt | 20 Augt 77 | 16 Aug 80 | missing |
| Armstrong, Jno.[6] | do | 10 Mar 77 | 23 Mar 80 | prisoner |
| Ayres, William[5] | do | | June 78 | left out |
| Abel, John[7] | do | 8 June 78 | Augt 78 | not heard of |

[1] Dean's.    [2] Hawkins'.    [3] Lynch's.    [4] Handy's.    [5] Johnson's.
[6] Emory's.    [7] Lt. Hamilton's.

## MUSTERS OF MARYLAND TROOPS, VOL. II.

| NAMES. | RANK. | TIME OF SERVICE. Enlisted. | Discharged. | REMARKS. |
|---|---|---|---|---|
| Allen, Emanual[1] | Lieut | 6 May 78 | 16 Aug 80 | missing, paid |
| Arnett, William[2] | do | 6 June 78 | Feby 79 | died |
| Austin, Joseph[1] | do | 10 June 78 | Jany 80 | prisoner war |
| Andrews, Jno.[3] | do | 1 Jany 79 | 1 Nov 80 | present |
| Adair, William[4] | do | 27 May 79 | 16 Augt 80 | missing |

### 6TH MARYLAND REGIMENT.

| | | | | |
|---|---|---|---|---|
| Ahern, William[5] | pt | 15 May 78 | 16 Aug 80 | missing |
| Allen, Robert[6] | Sergt | 25 Jany 77 | 10 Jany 80 | discharged |
| Ashbox, Jacob | pt | 30 April 78 | April & May 79 | mustd. not |
| Ambler, George[7] | do | 4 April 77 | | [heard of |
| Ayers, Fredk. | do | 19 May 78 | 16 Aug 80 | killed |
| Allen, Jacob[8] | do | 3 April 77 | 16 Aug 80 | prisoner |
| Atkinson, Wm. | do | 28 Aprl 77 | 16 Aug 80 | missing |
| Arris, James[9] | do | 1 July 78 | | |
| Armstrong, Alex.[6] | pt | 9 June 78 | 14 March 79 | discharged |
| Armstrong, Thomas | do | 9 June 78 | 14 Mar 79 | discharged |
| Armstrong, Robert[9] | do | 2 May 78 | 16 Aug 80 | prisoner |
| Andeton, William[10] | do | 23 May 78 | 10 March 79 | deserted |
| Askins, Zacha. | Sergt | | 13 Sept 80 | deserted |
| Anderside, Wm. | pt | 26 Mar 78 | 16 Aug 80 | missing |
| Armstrong, John | do | | 1 Nov 80 | present. |
| Mus. 1780 | | | | |

### SEVENTH REGIMENT MARYLAND TROOPS.

| | | | | |
|---|---|---|---|---|
| Adams, D. Jenifer | Major | 10 dec 76 | 1 June 79 | resigned |
| Anderson, Richard | pt | 10 dec 76 | 5 July 78 | discharged |
| | Qr. Master | 27 June 77 | | |
| Adams, Peter | Lt. Col. | | | |
| Annis, Benjamin[11] | pt | 1 April 77 | 1 April 80 | discharged |
| Anderson, Richd.[12] | do | 10 dec 76 | See Richd. Anderson above | |
| Anderson, Richd. | Lieut | 10 dec 76 | | |
| | Capt | 28 dec 77 | | |
| Aaron, Michael[13] | pt | 6 dec 76 | 13 dec 76 | deserted |
| Acre, Cronamus | pt | 7 dec 76 | 8 dec 79 | discharged |
| Ash, or Nash, Edmund[14] | do | 9 May 77 | See Edward Nash | |
| Allsop, John | pt | 4 Augt 77 | 1 Aug 80 | discharged |
| Ainsworth, Robt.[15] | do | 19 April 77 | | off Rolls 77 |
| Armstrong, George | do | 12 June 77 | 13 July 77 | deserted |
| Anderson, John,[16] joined 10 Aug 78 | } do | | Augt 78 | to invalids, from thence discharged 5 feby 80 |

[1] Handy's.   [2] Ensign Jones'.   [3] Johnson's.   [4] Lynch's.   [5] Ghiselin's.
[6] Dobson's.   [7] Beall's.   [8] Chapline's.   [9] Williams'.   [10] Miles'.
[11] Jones'.   [12] Grosh's.   [13] Morris'.   [14] Bayly's.   [15] Reynolds'.   [16] Deam's.

## MUSTERS OF MARYLAND TROOPS, VOL. II.

| NAMES. | RANK. | TIME OF SERVICE. Enlisted. | Discharged. | REMARKS. |
|---|---|---|---|---|
| Asshwell, Wm. | pt | | 16 Augt 80 | missing |
| Adams, Danl. Jen. | Major | 10 Dec 76 | See above | |
| Adams, William | Ensign | | | |
| | Lieut | 14 April 78 | | |
| Adams, Nathaniel[1] | pt | 23 feb 78 | 20 Aug 79 | deserted |
| Ashmore, John[2] | do | 6 June 78 | 1 Nov 80 | present |
| Abbott, Thomas[3] | do | 30 May 78 | 6 March 79 | discharged |
| Allsop, Joseph[4] | do | 8 June 78 | 30 March 79 | discharged |
| Armond, Abell[5] | do | 7 June 78 | 1 July 80 | deserted |
| Able, Cuthbert[6] | Sergt | 1 feb 80 | 1 Nov 80 | present |

### GERMAN REGIMENT.

| NAMES. | | RANK. | TIME OF SERVICE. Enlisted. | Discharged. | REMARKS. |
|---|---|---|---|---|---|
| Arrings, Levy to 1 Jany 81 | 3 | pt | | 1 Aug 80 | present |
| Ashly, James W. L. to 1 Jany 81 | | pt | 25 April 78 | do | do |
| Alexander, Jacob do | 3 | Sergt | 1 feb 78 | do | do |
| Armstrong, John | 3 | | | 26 July 79 | discharged |
| Abel, John | 3 | | | 20 do | ditto |
| Arnold, George | 9 | | | 22 March 79 | ditto |
| Amersley, John | | See John Hammersley | | | |
| Aberly, Leonard | | | | 2 dec 78 | ditto |

### 5TH REGIMENT MARYLAND TROOPS.

| NAMES. | RANK. | TIME OF SERVICE. Enlisted. | Discharged. | REMARKS. |
|---|---|---|---|---|
| Bennett, Thomas[7] | pt | 30 Mar 77 | 3 April 80 | discharged |
| Bromel, Robert | do | 10 dec 76 | 16 Aug 80 | missing |
| Boxly, David | do | 9 July 77 | 1 Nov 80 | present |
| | fifer | 15 Aug 78 | | |
| Buckley, John | do | 3 Nov 77 | 20 Nov 78 | deserted |
| Benton, Mark[8] | Lieut | 20 feb 77 | 1 June 79 | resigned |
| Burk, James | pt | 3 April 77 | April 78 | left out |
| | Corpl | 1 Feby 78 | | |
| Brinsfield, George | pt | 5 Aug 77 | 13 Oct 78 | discharged |
| Brooks, Lawrence[9] | Sergt | 4 July 77 | 13 Oct 78 off Rolls,to Invalids } |
| | | | 10 Aug 81 | discharged } |
| Bright, James | pt | 14 June 77 | March 80 | left out |
| | | | 14 May 80 | discharged by Col. Forrest |
| Benton, John | do | 6 June 77 | April 78 | left out |
| Barrick, John | do | 7 Mar 77 | ditto | ditto |

[1] Bayly's.  [9] Jones'.  [3] Spyker's.  [4] Morris'.  [5] Beatty's.
[6] Lamar's.  [7] Dean's.  [8] Hawkins'.  [9] Lynch's.

## MUSTERS OF MARYLAND TROOPS, VOL. II.

| NAMES. | RANK. | TIME OF SERVICE. Enlisted. | Discharged. | REMARKS. |
|---|---|---|---|---|
| Branffield, John | pt | 17 dec 76 | 16 Aug 80 | missing |
| Barry, John | do | do | 1 Nov 79 | deserted |
| Baetts, Samuel | do | 13 Nov 77 | 28 June 78 | missing |
| Burns, William | do | 19 Jan 78 | April 78 | left out |
| Benson, Perry[1] | Lieut | 10 Dec 76 ⎰ | | |
| | Capt | 11 Mar 78 ⎱ | | |
| Birk, Nathaniel | pt | 14 Jan 77 | 10 Jan 80 | discharged |
| Barrett, Nicholas | do | 10 Feby 77 | 7 feb 80 | do |
| Blades, James | do | 31 Mar 77 | 16 Aug 80 | missing |
| Barnes, George | do | 20 May | | off Rolls |
| Byron, Thomas[2] | do | 13 feb 77 ⎰ Corpl 1 Oct 77 ⎬ Sergt —— ⎱ | 16 Aug 80 | missing |
| Burnett, Charles[3] | do | 27 Jany 77 | 17 July 78 | died |
| Bernard, John[4] | do | 28 do | 15 July 78 | died |
| Burnett, John | Corpl | 14 Aug 77 ⎰ pt 17 July 78 ⎱ | 1 Nov 80 | present |
| Bowser, Samuel | pt | 18 Mar 77 | 1 June 79 | transferred to 4th [Maryland Regt. |
| Burns, Thomas | pt Corpl pt | 18 Mar 79 ⎰ 8 Nov 78 ⎬ 12 Jan 80 ⎱ | January 80 | present |
| Bryan, Luke | pt | 15 Mar 77 | 16 Mar 80 | discharged |
| Bird, Richard | Lieut Capt | 10 May 77 ⎰ 1 June 79 ⎱ | | |
| Bantham, Perie[5] | pt | 23 Feby 79 | 1 Nov 80 | present |
| Bay, Kennedy | pt | 6 dec 76 | 6 Sept 80 | deserted |
| Brown, James | pt | 6 do 76 | 16 Aug 80 | missing, see Depreciation account |
| Blanch, William[6] | Corpl pt. | 15 Aug 78 | Jany 80 | present |
| Boyd, Samuel | private | 23 April 78 | 15 June 78 | discharged |
| Brinsfields, George[2] | do | see Brinsfield, Geo. Hawkins Co., the other | | [side |
| Benny, John | do | 2 April 78 | Aug 78 | died |
| Burgan, Joshua[5] | do Corpl | 30 May 78 ⎰ 10 July 78 ⎱ | 19 Oct 78 | died |
| Bryan, John | pt | 4 May 78 | 6 Sept 80 | deserted |
| Bradley, James | do | 29 May 78 | May 79 | died, time not off Rolls [known |
| Bendon, Thomas | do | | | |
| Barruch, James | do | 6 June 78 | 18 Nov 78 | died |
| Boone, John | do | 8 June 78 | Aug 78 | not heard of |
| Birh, Nathaniel[7] | do | 1 April 78 | see N. Burk | Hund |
| Brent, John | do | 14 May 78 | 16 Aug 80 | missing |

[1] Handy's.   [2] Johnson's.   [3] Emory's.   [4] Gray's.   [5] Lt. Hamilton's.
[6] Ensign Jones',   [7] Lynch's.

13

## MUSTERS OF MARYLAND TROOPS, VOL. II.

| NAMES. | RANK. | TIME OF SERVICE. Enlisted. | Discharged. | REMARKS. |
|---|---|---|---|---|
| | fifer | 1 Oct 79 | | |
| Blackam, George[1] | pt | 1 May 78 | 1 Nov 80 | present |
| Bending, Thomas | do | 6 June 78 | Aug 78 | not heard of |
| Brown, John | do | 6 June 78 | 2 July 78 | deserted |
| Barrow, James[2] | do | 16 June 78 | 16 Aug 80 | missing |
| Biles, William | pt | 6 June 78 | 1 Mar 79 | discharged |
| Bentley, Samuel | do | 6 June 78 | 1 Aug 78 | died |
| Beck, Alexander[3] | do | 4 Mar 78 | Nov 79 | died |
| Burns, Michael | do | 4 April 78 | Nov 79 | died |
| Blunt, Benjamin[1] | do | 12 June 78 | May 79 | not heard of |
| Burrough, John | do | 1 June 78 | July 78 | left out |
| Burrough, Zacha. | do | 1 June 78 | ditto | ditto |
| Birh, Jeremiah[4] | do | 4 June 78 | 28 June 79 | deserted |
| Bowser, Thomas | do | 4 June 78 | 1 Nov 80 | present |
| Bailey, James | pt | 27 April 78 | 16 Aug 80 | missing |
| | Corpl | 12 June 79 | | |
| | Sergt | | | |
| Bowen, Abraham | pt | 14 May 78 | 1 Nov 80 | present |
| Bailey, Mark[5] | do | 2 April 77 | 1 Jany 80 | deserted |
| Bantham, John[6] | do | 18 June 77 | 1 Nov 80 | present |
| Barrett, Solomon[7] | do | 19 June 79 | 1 Nov 80 | present |
| Bateman, Nathl.[4] | do | May 79 | 1 Nov 80 | present |
| Bryan, William[8] | do | | last muster January 80 | |
| Brown, Solomon | do | | do | |
| Bradshaw, James | do | | 1 Nov 80 | present |
| Beachbeach, Benja. | do | | 16 Aug 80 | missing |
| Bryan, George[9] | pt | | Sept 77 | taken by prior [enlist. |

### SIXTH MARYLAND REGIMENT.

| NAMES. | RANK. | Enlisted. | Discharged. | REMARKS. |
|---|---|---|---|---|
| Boyer, Lambert[10] | Lieut | 7 Aprl 77 | 12 Oct 77 | resigned |
| Buller, James | pt | 23 Aug 77 | 15 Aug 80 | discharged |
| Broughton, Wm. | do | 20 Aug 78 | last muster Jany 80 | |
| Boyle, Robert | do | 19 May 78 | Mar 79 | left out |
| Boward, Valentine | do | 5 May 78 | 16 Aug 80 | missing |
| Burk, James | pt | 16 May 78 | 1 Nov 80 | present |
| Boward, Leonard | do | 17 May 78 | 1 Nov 80 | present |
| Beanes, Colmore | Surg. Mate | 25 June 77 | 12 Oct 77 | resigned |
| Bradley, John[11] | pt | 5 feb 77 | 5 feb 80 | discharged |
| Brady, Thomas | do | 16 April 77 | last muster Jany 80 | |
| Bithel, John | pt | 1 June 77 | } 1 Nov 80 | present |
| | Corpl | 1 Jany 79 | | |

[1] Handy's.   [2] Ensign Jones'.   [3] Johnson's.   [4] Hawkins'.   [5] Emory's.   [6] Lt. Hamilton's.   [7] Benson's.   [8] Lynch's.   [9] Dean's.   [10] Ghiselin's.   [11] Dobson's.

## MUSTERS OF MARYLAND TROOPS, VOL. II.

| NAMES. | RANK. | TIME OF SERVICE. Enlisted. | Discharged. | REMARKS. |
|---|---|---|---|---|
| Bullin, Thomas | pt | 18 May 77 | last muster Jany 80 | |
| Beavan, Charles[1] | Ensign | 28 July 77 | | paid |
| | Lieut | 26 Jany 78 | July 80 | resigned |
| Wales, Edward L. | Sergt | 8 Mar 77 | } 1 Jany 78 | resigned |
| | Ensign | 17 Mar 77 | } | |
| Boulton, Richard | pt | 24 Aug 77 | 24 Aug 80 | discharged |
| Ballard, Richard | do | 10 Jany 78 | 3 July 79 | deserted |
| Beale, Wm. D.[2] | Capt | 10 Dec 76 | | |
| Bruff, James | Lieut | 20 feb 77 | Capt. 8 Sept 81 | |
| Buchan, William | Sergt | 20 June 77 | 16 May 80 | discharged |
| Bayley, Seth | Corpl | 16 Aprl 77 | } 16 Aug 80 | prisoner |
| | pt | 1 June 78 | } | |
| Baldwin, Wm. J. | pt | 5 feb 78 | 16 Aug 80 | missing |
| | Sergt | 5 feb 79 | Sergt. Major | |
| Blake, Michael | pt | 24 April 78 | June mus. 78 | left out the Roll |
| Batton, Hugh | do | 20 May 78 | Aug 79 | died |
| Body, Robert | do | 21 do | 16 Aug 80 | killed |
| | fifer | 1 July 78 | | |
| Brown, John[3] | Corpl | 5 dec 76 | 30 Sept 80 | to Invalids |
| 22 Mar 79 Sergt., reduced pt. 29 Mar 79, again Sergt. 25 April 79 | | | | |
| Beveren, Thomas | pt | 5 dec 76 | 16 Aug 80 | prisoner |
| Buyers, James | do | 30 do 76 | 30 dec 79 | discharged |
| Booth, Edward[4] | Sergt | 16 Jan 78 | 1 Nov 80 | present |
| Sergt Oct do | pt | Jany 79 | | |
| Boyle, James | do | 17 Jan 77 | 16 Aug 80 | killed |
| Barker, William[5] | do Sergt. 21 July 77, pt. 1 July 78, 16 May 80 discharged | | | |
| now Miles' | | | | |
| Boe, William | do | 14 Mar 77 | 16 Aug 80 | prisoner |
| | pt | 12 May 78 | 1 April 79 | discharged |
| Beall, John[6] | do | 1 July 78 | 1 April 79 | discharged |
| 1 July 78 joined | | | | |
| Baker, Peter | do | 1 July 78 | 1 April 79 | do |
| 1 July 78 joined | | | | |
| Binehart, Andrew | do | 1 July 78 | see Richard, Andrew | |
| 1 July 78 joined | | | | |
| Bradley, Cornel[7] | do | 10 June 78 | 14 Mar 79 | discharged |
| 1 must. June 78 | | | | |
| Blackburn, Thos.[1] | do | 1 June 78 | 3 Sept 78 | discharged |
| Brown, John | do | 1 June 78 | 1 April 79 | do |
| Backett, Isaac[2] | do | 22 May 78 | 1 Nov 80 | present |
| 1 must. Jany 78 | | | | |
| Banfield, James[3] | do | 28 dec 76 | 28 dec 79 | discharged |
| Joined June 78 | | | | |

[1] Trueman's.    [2] Beall's.    [3] Hynes'.    [4] Harris'.    [5] Chapline's.    [6] Ghiselin's.    [7] Dobson's.

## MUSTERS OF MARYLAND TROOPS, VOL. II.

| NAMES. | RANK. | TIME OF SERVICE. Enlisted. | Discharged. | REMARKS. |
|---|---|---|---|---|
| Bowers, George[1] | pt | 1 May 78 | 1 Nov 80 | present |
| Barrett, John rein. 23 dec 78 | do | 30 do | 17 Aug 80 | deserted |
| Batman, Thos. | do | 4 June 78 | 4 feb 79 | discharged |
| Birk, Richard | do | 18 May 78 | 26 dec 79 | deserted |
| Brannan, Timothy[2] | pt | see O'Brannon of Hynes' Company | | |
| Burns, Simon[3] | do | 7 May 78 | 20 dec 79 | deserted |
| Burness, Benjamin | do | 23 May 78 | 17 July 80 | do |
| Burk, Garret | do | 8 May 78 | 22 feb 79 | do |
| Bradley, John | do | 16 May 78 | 17 July 80 | do |
| Brown, John[1] | do | 15 June 78 | 25 June 78 | do |
| Billop, Henry[3] | do | 8 April 79 | 1 Nov 80 | present |
| Bowler, Aaron[4] joined 21 Sep 79 | do | | last muster Jany 80 | |
| Brazenton, Thos.[5] | do | 25 Aug 79 | 16 Aug 80 | missing |
| Bare, Thomas | do | 2 Sept 79 | 1 Nov 80 | present |
| Bome, Barthw.[4] | do | | do | ditto |
| Bumgardner, George Oct Roll 1780 | do | 26 feb 80 | do | ditto |
| Brockett, Richard | do | | do | ditto |
| Burch, Benja. | | | | see below |
| Buller, Thomas | do | | 21 Aug 80 | deserted |
| Baker, Abram | do | | 17 July 80 | ditto |
| Burch, Benja. | do | 18 Jany 80 | 16 Aug 80 | missing |

### SEVENTH MARYLAND REGIMENT.

| NAMES. | RANK. | TIME OF SERVICE. Enlisted. | Discharged. | REMARKS. |
|---|---|---|---|---|
| Bryan, Richard[6] | Corpl pt | 16 Mar 77 } 31 May 78 } | 16 Mar 80 | discharged |
| Bush, John | pt | 13 April 77 | 25 May 77 | deserted |
| Barrett, Williams | pt Corpl | 17 Mar 77 } 30 Sept 78 } | 17 Mar 80 | discharged |
| Bowden, Thos.[7] | pt | 16 feb 77 | 16 feb 80 | discharged |
| Brown, Daniel | do | 30 May 77 | 13 Sept 77 | deserted |
| Brindley, Michael | do | 2 April 77 | 4 Oct 77 | killed G. Town |
| Brown, Zebulon[8] | do | 5 June 77 | March 78 | off Rolls |
| Barnicloe, Thos. | do | 1 Nov 77 | Mar 78 | off Rolls |
| Bryan, John[9] joined 11 Aug 78 | do | 10 June 77 | 1 Nov 80 | present |
| Bryant, James[10] | do | 13 April 77 | 13 April 80 | discharged |
| Bernig, (or Bercning), Danl. | do | 6 dec 76 | 1 Nov 80 | present |
| Broderick, Dennis July 78 returned | do | 6 feb 77 | 16 Aug 80 | missing |

[1] Lt. Williams'.  [9] Harris'.  [3] Miles'.  [4] Trueman's.  [5] Norris'.
[6] Jones'.  [7] Grosh's.  [8] Spyker's.  [9] Stull's.  [10] Morris'.

## MUSTERS OF MARYLAND TROOPS, VOL. II.

| NAMES. | RANK. | TIME OF SERVICE. | | REMARKS. |
|---|---|---|---|---|
| | | Enlisted. | Discharged. | |
| Bailey, Patrick | pt | 18 Mar 77 | 9 June 77 | deserted |
| Bryant, John | do | 20 Mar 77 | 22 Aug 77 | prisoner |
| Birk, Michael | do | 1 April 77 | 30 June 80 | deserted |
| joined 11 Aug 78 | | | | |
| Bryant, Daniel | do | | 7 Jan 80 | discharged |
| Berry, John | do | 6 April 77 | June 78 | off Rolls |
| Brown, William | do | 6 April 77 | July 77 | off Rolls |
| Bayley, Mountjoy | Capt | 3 dec 76 | 14 Sept 78 | resigned |
| Beatty, William | Lieut | 10 dec 76 | | paid |
| | Capt | 14 Sept 78 | | |
| Beall, Lloyd | do | 10 April 77 | | paid |
| Baker, Joel[1] | pt | 19 dec 76 | 1 June 79 | Corpl. 26 Jany [dischd. |
| Birk, John | do | 10 May 77 | 11 Sept 77 | prisoner |
| Brady, James | do | 5 May 77 | Sept 78 | deserted |
| Joined June 78 | | | | |
| Bleas, Joseph | do | 28 May 77 | 16 Aug 80 | missing |
| Bracco, James | Ensign | 10 Feby 77 | 3 jan 80 | resigned |
| | Lieut | 28 dec 77 | | |
| Brooks, Jacob[2] | pt | 1 April 77 | 3 May 79 | deserted |
| Burges, John | do | 12 April 79 | April 80 | discharged |
| Bomgardner, Wm. | pt | 2 May 77 | 8 May 80 | do |
| joined 4 June 78 | | | | |
| Botts, Joseph | do | 11 May 77 | 1 Nov 80 | present |
| Burrill, John | do | 10 July 77 | 12 July 77 | deserted |
| Barney, Moses[3] | Corpl | 1 Aug 78 | 1 Nov 80 | present |
| from Sergt reduced to pt 3 Sept 78 | | Sergt | 1 April 80 | |
| Benson,(or Penson), Edmund | pt | | Feby 78 | off Rolls |
| Boone, Richd. | do | 8 feb 77 | 1 Nov 80 | present |
| | | | | claimed by R. B. Boone |
| Barnes, Benja.[4] | do | 31 jany 78 | March 79 | not heard of |
| from Hazen's in Room of Wm. Monk | | | | |
| Brown, Joshua[5] | do | 23 Aprl 78 | 1 Nov 80 | present |
| Banks, James | do | 23 April 78 | May 78 | off Rolls |
| Barlow, John[1] | do | 4 Mar 78 | 18 May 78 | deserted |
| Burgess, Josias[6] | do | 20 Aprl 78 | 1 Nov 80 | present |
| Bedder, James | do | 25 April 78 | 1 Nov 80 | present |
| Beckett, Humpy. | do | 24 May 78 | 1 Nov 80 | present |
| Bulger, Danl. | do | 5 June 78 | March 79 | discharged |
| Biggs, Benja. | do | 11 April 78 | 16 Aug 80 | missing |
| Bruff, Wm. | do | 24 April 78 | 1 Nov 80 | present |
| | Corpl | May 80 | | |

[1] Bayly's.  [2] Reynolds'.  [3] Deams'.  [4] Spyker's.  [5] Grosh's.  [6] Jones'.

## MUSTERS OF MARYLAND TROOPS, VOL. II.

| NAMES. | RANK. | TIME OF SERVICE. Enlisted. | Discharged. | REMARKS. |
|---|---|---|---|---|
| Bryan, Richard | pt | See above | | |
| Burn, Elijah[1] | pt | 12 May 78 | 20 Aug 78 | discharged |
| Beaven, Thos. | do | | March 79 | not heard of |
| Bower, Boston[2] | do | 1 June 78 | 1 April 79 | discharged |
| Baker, Boston | do | 2 June 78 | 1 April 79 | discharged |
| Barnett, Daniel[3] | do | 11 Aprl 78 | 1 Nov 80 | present |
| Brannan, Lawrce.[4] | do | 22 Aprl 78 | 14 May 79 | private |
| | Corpl | 18 June 78 | | |
| | Sergt | 1 Jany 80 | 16 Aug 80 | missing |
| Burton, John | pt | 20 April 78 | 16 Aug 80 | missing |
| Briggs, Wm.[2] | do | 6 June 78 | 30 Mar 79 | discharged |
| Brown, George | do | 21 April 78 | 16 Aug 80 | missing |
| Broughton, Adam[5] | do | 20 July 78 | 9 April 79 | discharged |
| Blades, William | do | 20 July 78 | 9 April 79 | ditto |
| Bissill, Assa | do | 20 July 78 | 9 April 79 | do |
| Bizel, Abram[3] | do | 12 Oct 78 | 16 Aug 80 } | |
| | fifer | 1 Nov 78 | } | missing |
| Buck, George[6] | pt | 19 May 78 | 26 April 79 | prisoner, 1 Nov |
| 8 Aug 79 exchanged | | | | 80 present |
| Bowles, Martin | } do | 30 April 78 | 26 Aug 80 | deserted |
| in Provost Mar 79 | } | | | |
| Berry, James[3] | do | 12 July 78 | 30 Mar 79 | discharged |
| Bedford, Thomas[7] | do | 14 Aug 79 | 16 Aug 80 | missing |
| Bryant, Patrick[3] | do | not mustered since Feby 80 | | |
| Morris', 10 Feby 80 | | | | |
| Bryan, Thomas[8] | do | | 27 Aprl 80 | deserted |
| Mason's, Mar 80 | | | | |
| Brown, Thomas[9] | do | | 19 June 80 | ditto |
| Beall's, Mar 80 | | | | |
| Buxton, Abijah[7] | do | 14 Jan 80 | 1 Nov 80 | present |
| Black, Francis[6] | do | | 16 Aug 80 | missing |
| Beatty's, Mar 80 | | | | |
| Blair, John[10] | pt | 2 April 80 | 1 Nov 80 | present |
| Blake, Martin[7] | pt | 29 May 80 | 16 Aug 80 | missing |
| Brooks, Charles[3] | pt | | do | do |
| Barnett, Jesse[11] | fifer | 24 April 80 | 1 Nov 80 | present |
| Brooks, John[6] | pt | | 1 July 80 | deserted |

### GERMAN REGIMENT.

| | | | | |
|---|---|---|---|---|
| Bough, (or Buck), Geo. | pt | | 1 Aug 80 | |
| to 1 Jan 81 | | | | |
| Bauswell, Saml. | | | 22 Nov 80 | deserted, joined |
| did not appear on Rolls till 80 | | | | in 81 |

[1] Spyker's.   [2] Stull's.   [3] Morris'.   [4] Bayly's.   [5] Grosh's.   [6] Beatty's.   [7] Anderson's.
[8] Mason's.   [9] Beall's.   [10] Lynn's.   [11] Jones'.

## MUSTERS OF MARYLAND TROOPS, VOL. II.

| NAMES. | RANK. | TIME OF SERVICE. Enlisted. | TIME OF SERVICE. Discharged. | REMARKS. |
|---|---|---|---|---|
| Backer, Peter[1] | | | 15 July 79 | discharged |
| Benner, Michael | | | 17 do do | do |
| Bender, (or Painter), Henry | | | 12 Oct 79 | do |
| Bishop, Jacob | | | 26 July 79 | do |
| Betzhover, Jacob | | | do | do |
| Beam, Philip | Corpl | 30 July 75 | 24 do | do |
| Baylor, Danl. | | 5 Aug 75 | do | do |
| Bower, John | | 23 July 75 | 24 do | do |
| Brown, John | fifer | 21 July 75 | do | do |
| Brieger, John | Corpl | | 17 July | do |
| Brodbech, Michael | pt | paid from 1 Nov 79 to 1 Aug 80 pst. | | |
| to 1 Jany 81 | | | | |
| Bantz, George | | | 22 Mar 79 | discharged |
| Burk, John, (or Jas.) | Corpl | | 24 July 79 | do |
| Beam, Conrad | | 26 July 75 | do | do |
| Bennett, John | | | | |
| Bates, Philip | | | 22 Mar 79 | do |
| Bowerd, Michael | | | 16 July 79 | do |

### FIFTH MARYLAND REGIMENT.

| NAMES. | RANK. | TIME OF SERVICE. Enlisted. | TIME OF SERVICE. Discharged. | REMARKS. |
|---|---|---|---|---|
| Crawford, James | Qr. Mr. | 14 Oct 77 | 20 Sept 79 | resigned |
| Cleary, John | Qr. Mr. Sergt. | 10 Aprl 77 | 20 July 77 | dead |
| Crawford, James | do | 20 July 77 ⎱ dismissed | | served full 79 |
| | Qr. Mr. | 14 Oct 77 ⎰ | | |
| Carmick, Robert[2] | fifer | 30 Mar 77 | 16 Aug 80 | missing, joined R. |
| Colfield, Francis[3] | pt | 3 May | 1 Nov 80 | present |
| Callahan, Thomas | pt | 10 May | April 78 | left out |
| Carroll, John | do | 18 June | ditto | do, joined R. |
| Condon, William | do | 10 May 77 | | last muster Jany 80 ⎱ discharged May 80 by Col. Forrest ⎰ |
| Cross, Robert | fifer | 19 Mar 77 ⎱ | | |
| | pt | 1 Jan 78 ⎬ R | | paid |
| | fifer | 20 Aug 78 ⎰ | | |
| Clary, John | Sergt | 4 dec 76 | 10 April 77 | Q. M. Sergt., Apl 78 left out |
| See John Cleary above, quere if not the same person | | | | |
| Craig, Michael[4] | Corpl | 20 Jan 77 | 16 Aug 80 | missing |
| Cannon, Thomas | pt | 28 Aug 77 | April 78 | left out |
| Carroll, John | do | 22 Jan 78 | 1 Nov 80 | present |
| Carter, John[5] | Corpl | 7 dec 76 | 1 April 77 | private, 6 dec 79 dischd. |
| Catlin, Thomas[6] | Sergt | 8 feb 77 | 8 Jan 80 | discharged as Sergt. |
| | pt | 11 Aug 78 | | |

[1] Myers'.    [2] Dean's.    [3] Benson's.    [4] Lynch's.    [5] Handy's.    [6] Johnson's.

## MUSTERS OF MARYLAND TROOPS, VOL. II.

| NAMES. | RANK. | TIME OF SERVICE. Enlisted. | Discharged. | REMARKS. |
|---|---|---|---|---|
| Catlin, B. Caleb | Corpl | 28 Jan 77 | Sergt. 7 June 77, out April 78 | |
| Connady, John | pt | 20 feb 77 | April 78 | left out |
| Connel, Patrick | do | 28 do } | 79 | left out |
| | Sergt | 4 May 79 } | | |
| Connely, Daniel | Corpl | 12 Jan 77 | pt. 30 Sept | June 78 left out |
| Chaires, John[1] | Sergt | 28 Jan 77 | 12 Jan 80 | discharged |
| Collins, William[2] | pt | 22 Sept | 30 Dec 77 | died |
| Covington, Henry | do | 10 dec 76 } | 12 Jan 80 | discharged |
| | Corpl | 1 July 79 } | | |
| Cosden, Jesse | Capt | 10 dec 76 | 7 dec 77 | resigned |
| Couch, Charles[3] | Corpl | 27 Jan 77 | 1 Nov 80 | present |
| 1 musr. April 78   must. Sergt Oct 80 | | | | |
| Conner, James, Sr. | pt | 4 Dec 76 | 4 dec 79 | time expired |
| Conner, James, Jr. | do | 3 dec 76 | 5 dec 79 | do  [valids |
| Conner, James, the 3d | do | 10 April 77 | Oct mus. 80 transferred to In- } | |
| | | | 1 Nov 83 discharged on pen- } | |
| Cann, Augustine | do | 8 dec 76 | 1 Nov 80 | present   [sion |
| Carman, James | do | 21 feb 77 | 16 Aug 80 | missing |
| Chritchets, William[4] | do | 21 July 77 | 14 Jan 78 | deserted |
| Joined April 78 | | | | |
| Chritchets, Benja. | do | 21 July 77 | 16 Aug 80 | missing |
| Joined April 78   must. Sergt Oct Roll 80 | | | | |
| Coheall, James[3] | do | 6 June 78 | Augt 78 | not heard of |
| Coffee, Daniel[5] | do | 17 dec 76 | 16 Aug 80 | missing |
| 1 mustr. Jany 78 | | | | |
| Collins, James | do | 18 Jan 77 } | 16 Aug 80 | missing |
| 1 mustr. June 78 | Corpl | 1 April 79 } | | |
| Cooke, Moses | pt | 2 June 78 | 1 Mar 79 | died |
| Clift, James[6] | do | 14 May 78 | May 79 | died, time unknown |
| Camble, Dunk | do | 6 June 78 | 1 Mar 79 | discharged |
| Connolly, John | do | 5 May 78 | Feby 79 | mustrd. not heard of |
| Cooke, Moses | do | 29 May 78 | July 79 | left out |
| Connally, John | do | 15 May 78 | 6 June 78 | deserted |
| Conner, George[7] | do | 1 Jan 77 | 16 Aug 80 | missing |
| Caves, John | do | 26 May 78 | Nov 79 | died |
| Conner, Hugh[8] | do | 9 feb 77 | 16 Aug 80 | missing |
| now Gray's | 1 musr. June 78 | | | |
| Casley, William | do | 9 June 78 | 16 Aug 80 | missing |
| Clarke, William | do | | July 78 | left out |
| Chandler, John[9] | pt | 19 June 78 | last muster Jany 80 | |
| 1 musr. June 78 | | | | |
| Carney, Thomas | do | 13 May 78 | 1 Nov 80 | present |

[1] Emory's.          [2] Gray's.          [3] Lt. Hamilton's.          [4] Ensign Jones'.
[5] Lynch's.          [6] Handy's.          [7] Johnson's.          [8] Hawkins'.

## MUSTERS OF MARYLAND TROOPS, VOL. II.

| NAMES. | RANK. | TIME OF SERVICE. | | REMARKS. |
|---|---|---|---|---|
| | | Enlisted. | Discharged. | |
| Carr, Mathew | pt | 6 June 78 | 2 July 79 | deserted |
| Callahan, Dennis[1] | do | 6 June 78 | 19 Mar 79 | discharged |
| Callahan, Cornelius | do | 10 June 78 | 30 June 79 | deserted |
| Collins, Benja. | do | 20 May 78 | 6 July 78 | deserted |
| Caldwell, Charles | do | 16 May 78 | June 79 | left out, not heard of for 11 mo. |
| Corker, John[2] | do | 15 Jan 77 | 16 Aug 80 | missing |
| now Gray's | Joined 12 June 78 | | | |
| Cox, John[1] | do | 27 July 77 | June muster 79 not heard of [for 11 mo. | |
| Joined 18 Aug 78 | | | | |
| Clancy, Michael[2] | do | 4 June 79 | } 15 Nov 79 | died |
| 1 mustr. June 79 | Sergt | 1 Aug 79 | } | |
| | pt | 13 Sept 79 | } | |
| Clancy, Michael, Sr. | fifer | 14 June 79 | 16 Aug 80 | missing, joined [Regt. |
| 1st muster June 79 | | | | |
| Clark, Richard[4] | pt | | 5 dec 79 | discharged |
| Joined in June 79 | | | | |
| Crouch, Amos[5] | do | 7 July 79 | 16 Aug 80 | missing |
| | drum | 1 Sept 79 | | |
| Conydon, Edward | pt | 1 Sept 79 | last mustr. Jan 80 | |
| Connolly, Thomas[4] | do | | do do | |
| joined 1 Oct 79 | | | | |
| Civill, William[6] | do | 4 April 79 | 1 Nov 80 | present |
| Benson's, late Dean's | | | | |
| Conner, Dennis | | | mustered Oct 80 Sept deserted | |
| Chairs, John | Ensign | | | |

### SIXTH REGIMENT.

| NAMES. | RANK. | TIME OF SERVICE. | | REMARKS. |
|---|---|---|---|---|
| Corkery, William[7] | pt | 31 Mar 78 | 10 July 80 | deserted |
| Coughlan, Michael | do | 14 May 78 | last muster Jany 80 | |
| Carroll, John | do | 18 May 78 | 22 dec 79 | deserted |
| Chambers, William | | 5 May 78 | 1 Nov 80 | present |
| Charlton, J. W. | Paymr | 22 April 77 | 1 Oct 78 | resigned |
| Cardiff, Patrick[8] | pt | 1 Aug 77 | 16 Aug 80 | prisoner } |
| | fifer | 1 May 78 | ditto drum major 1 May 78 } | |
| Conner, William | pt | 2 feb 77 | 5 feb 1780 | discharged |
| Cahoe, Thomas[9] | do | 29 July 77 | 1 Nov 80 | present |
| Conner, Cornelius | do | Dec 76 | 21 Jan 80 | discharged |
| Coleman, William[10] | do | 2 Aug 77 | 2 Aug 80 | discharged |
| Carney, Patrick | do | 11 May 77 | 16 Aug 80 | missing |
| Cleaver, Benja. | do | 14 feb 78 | 1 Nov 80 | present |

[1] Emory's.    [2] Handy's.    [3] Lynch's.    [4] Gray's.    [5] Hawkins',
[6] Benson's.    [7] Ghiselin's.    [8] Dobson's.    [9] Trueman's.    [10] Beall's.

## MUSTERS OF MARYLAND TROOPS, VOL. II.

| NAMES. | RANK. | TIME OF SERVICE. Enlisted. | Discharged. | REMARKS. |
|---|---|---|---|---|
| Curwell, Peter | pt | 12 May 78 | 16 Aug 80 | killed |
| Coir, Michael | do | 11 May 78 | 16 Aug 80 | killed |
| Collins, Charles | do | 1 May 78 | 16 Aug 80 | prisoner |
| Crail, James[1] | do | 6 dec 76 | 78 June mustr. | left out |
| deserted 30 April 77, joined 1 Sept 1777 | | | | |
| Carlin, Wm. | do | 9 dec 76 | 9 dec 79 | discharged |
| Claward, Abram | do | 20 feb 77 | last muster Jany 80. | |
| Collins, George | do | 18 June 77 | 6 June 82 | present |
| Cannon, Patrick[2] | do | 6 Aug 77 | 16 Aug 80 | missing |
| Connally, Michael[3] | do | 28 May 77 | 1 Nov 80 | present |
| Q. M. S. 3 July 78 | Sergt | 3 Nov 77 | | |
| delivd. to | | as Sergt Oct 78, reduced to private 21 Sept 80 | | |
| Coyn, Donn | pt | 21 May 77 | last mustr. Jany 80 ⎱ | |
| | | discharged by G. Lineder, joined again —— ⎰ | | |
| Chaplain, Moses[4] | Capt do | 10 Dec 76 ⎱ 7 Oct 77 | | resigned |
| now Miles' | Capt | 20 feb 77 ⎰ | | |
| Clarke, David | pt | 7 Mar 77 | 16 Aug 80 | missing |
| Crowder, Saml. | pt | 7 May 77 | 3 July 79 | deserted |
| Crozier, John[5] | do | 10 June 78 | 16 Aug 80 | killed |
| 1 mustr. June 78 ⎱ | | | | |
| rein. 23 dec 78 ⎰ | | | | |
| Campbell, John | do | 24 May 78 | 1 Nov 80 | present |
| 1 mustr. June 78 ⎱ | | | | |
| rein. 23 dec 78 ⎰ | | | | |
| Cachey, Hector | do | 9 June 78 | do | do |
| 1 mustr. June 78 ⎱ | | | | |
| rein. 23 dec 78 ⎰ | | | | |
| Carroll, William | do | 9 June 78 | 14 Mar 79 | discharged |
| 1 mustr. June 78 | | | | |
| Church, Abram[6] | do | 12 May 78 | 1 Nov 80 | present |
| Cusick, Christopher | do | 30 May 78 | do | do |
| Coyle, Michael[6] | do | 28 April 78 | 16 Aug 80 | missing |
| Collen, Michael | do | 30 April 78 | 16 Aug 80 | do |
| Clifford, William | do | 10 June 78 | 1 April 79 | discharged |
| Courts, Christopher | do | 1 June 78 | do | do |
| Coventree, Jacob | do | 22 May 78 | feb 79 | mustered time expired |
| Callaghan, Joseph | do | 29 May 78 | 30 May 79 | deserted |
| Clanahan, Robert | do | 30 May 78 | 1 Nov 80 | present |
| Cray, John | do | 22 May 78 | 29 June 78 | deserted |
| Collins, Edward[7] | do | 23 May 78 | 1 Nov 80 | present |
| Connard, Thos.[1] | do | 9 April 78 | 10 July 78 | deserted |

[1] Hynes'.    [2] Laurence's.    [3] Harris'.    [4] Chapline's.
[5] Dobson's.    [6] Lt. Williams'.    [7] Miles'.

## MUSTERS OF MARYLAND TROOPS, VOL. II.

| NAMES. | RANK. | TIME OF SERVICE. Enlisted. | TIME OF SERVICE. Discharged. | REMARKS. |
|---|---|---|---|---|
| Cooney, Laughlan | pt | 20 April 78 | 26 April 78 | deserted |
| Craven, Andrew[1] | do | 23 June 78 | 22 Mar 79 | discharged |
| Cooke, William[2] | do | 1 June 78 | 16 Aug 80 | missing |
| 1 mustr. Augt 78 | | | | |
| Condrone, John[1] | do | 1 Aug 78 | 8 Jan 79 | died |
| Collard, William[3] | do | | 16 Aug 80 | prisoner |
| 1st muster July 79 | | | | |
| Crime, Michael[4] | do | | 1 Nov 80 | present |
| 1st muster July 79 | Fifer | 14 Oct 79 | | |
| Class, Michael[5] | pt | 27 Augt 79 | 17 Oct 79 | deserted |
| Carter, Noah[6] | Drum | 22 dec 79 | 1 Nov 80 | present |
| Cahoe, Thos., Jr. | do | | do | do |
| Oct Muster 1780 | | | | |
| Carey, Edward | pt | | Sept 80 | missing |
| Cole, William | do | 3 Oct 80 | 1 Nov 80 | present |

### SEVENTH REGIMENT.

| NAMES. | RANK. | Enlisted. | Discharged. | REMARKS. |
|---|---|---|---|---|
| Churchill, John[7] | pt | 10 Jan 77 | May 77 | off Rolls |
| Crail, William | do | 18 May 79 | 1 Nov 80 | present |
| Joined the 31 April 79 | | | | |
| Carter, Timothy | do | 12 April 77 | 11 April 80 | discharged |
| Joined 21 July 78 | | | | |
| Carter, Michael[8] | do | 14 April 77 | 4 Oct 77 | missing |
| Calihart, Frederick | do | 6 May 77 | June 78 | off Rolls |
| Crowley, Dennis | Drum | 18 May 77 | 16 Aug 80 | missing |
| | pt | 1 Aug 77 | | |
| Cole, William | do | 10 May 77 | 12 April 78 | deserted |
| | Corpl | 1 Oct 77 | | |
| Coleman, John | pt | 18 June 77 | 16 Aug 80 | missing |
| Clary, Dennis | Corpl | 1 April 77 | | |
| retd. 16 July 78 | Sergt | 1 Jany 80 | 1 April 80 | discharged |
| Christian, John[9] | Sergt | 22 May 77 | Oct 77 | off Rolls |
| Conroy, Hugh | pt | 10 June 77 | 22 Aug 77 | prisoner |
| Collins, James[10] | Sergt | 6 dec 76 | 2 April 80 | discharged |
| reinlisted | | | | |
| Connally, James | Drum | 14 April 77 | June 78 | off Roll |
| Carroll, George | pt | 6 dec 76 | 8 dec 79 | discharged |
| Cooke, William | do | 8 Jan 77 | 25 May 79 | deserted |
| Carty, James | do | 9 Jan 77 | 16 Aug 80 | missing |
| Conner, Thomas | pt | 3 feb 77 | Jany 78 | off Rolls |
| Cooke, Thomas | do | 1 Mar 77 | 16 Aug 80 | missing |

[1] Miles'.　　[2] Hynes'.　　[3] Trueman's.　　[4] Lt. Williams'.　　[5] Norris'.
[6] Jacobs'.　　[7] Grosh's.　　[8] Spyker's.　　[9] Stull's.　　[10] Morris'.

## MUSTERS OF MARYLAND TROOPS, VOL. II.

| NAMES. | RANK. | TIME OF SERVICE. Enlisted. | Discharged. | REMARKS. |
|---|---|---|---|---|
| Casey, Peter[1] | pt | 28 Mar 77 | 16 Aug 80 | missing |
|  | Corpl | 19 Oct 78 } | | |
|  | pt | 20 June 80 } | | |
| Clacker, Ghehoikin | pt | 6 April 77 | 9 June 77 | deserted |
| Carter, Richard | do | 5 Sept 77 | 16 Aug 80 | missing |
| Carroll, Patrick[2] | do | 4 dec 76 | 11 Sept 77 | prisoner |
| to Anderson's | | | | |
| Cunningham, Peter | do | 5 dec 76 | 1 Oct 80 | present |
| Carnant, Jacob | do | 6 dec 76 | 1 Nov 80 | present |
| Crosby, Joseph | do | 6 dec 76 | 8 dec 76 | deserted |
| Carroll, William | do | 21 Jan 77 | 2 Feby 77 | deserted |
| Connally, Patrick | do | 28 May 77 | 2 April 80 | discharged |
|  | Sergt | 20 Mar 77 } | | |
| Cofforth, William[2] | Fifer | 26 dec 77 } 1 Nov 80 | | discharged |
| from Reynolds' Co. | F. Major | 27 Jan 78 } | | |
| Cunningham, James[3] | Corpl | 25 June 77 | 1 July 80 | deserted |
| Cofforth, Conrad | Fifer | 20 Mar 77 | May 80 | discharged |
| Cahill, David | pt | 24 April 77 | 20 April 80 | do |
| Connelly, William | do | 18 April 77 | Jany 80 | prisoner War |
| Coatney, Anthony | do | 20 May 77 | May 80 | deserted |
| Casey, William | do | 30 May 77 | | |
| Joined 21 Nov 77 | | | | |
| Chamberlain, John | pt | 6 June 77 | 6 June 77 | deserted |
| Callahan, Barthw.[4] | do | 7 dec 76 | 7 dec 79 | discharged |
| | | appeared at Annapolis 25 April 89 | | |
| Clarke, Arthur | do | | 1 Nov 80 | present |
| Connally, Laurence | do | | 28 June 78 | missing |
| Curran, Robert | do | | Feby 78 | off Rolls |
| Clarke, John[5] | pt | 4 May 78 | June 79 | dead |
| Cross, James | pt | 21 April 78 | 5 July 80 | deserted |
| Copes, John | do | 9 May 78 | 1 Mar 79 | discharged |
| Can, Nicholas[2] | do | 6 Jan 78 | Nov 78 | off Rolls |
| Cox, Mathew | do | 4 Mar 78 | 16 April 78 | deserted |
| Chesire, John[6] | Sergt | 11 Jany 78 | | } |
| | | Joined again and on 18 June 81 killed at 96 | | } |
| Coleby, John | pt | 30 April 78 | March 80 | prisoner War |
| Coventry, Charles | do | 6 June 78 | 16 Mar 79 | discharged |
| Craine, Henry | do | 6 June 78 | 16 Mar 79 | dischd., joined |
| Corner, Thomas[7] | do | | 1 Mar 79 | do |
| June, Spyker's | | | | |
| Class, Martin[8] | do | 9 June 78 | do | do |

[1] Anderson's.    [2] Bayly's.    [3] Reynolds'.    [4] Deams'.
[5] Spyker's, Grosh's.    [6] Jones'.    [7] Spyker's.    [8] Stull's.

## MUSTERS OF MARYLAND TROOPS, VOL. II.

| NAMES. | RANK. | TIME OF SERVICE. Enlisted. | Discharged. | REMARKS. |
|---|---|---|---|---|
| Crow, Adam | pt | 28 April 78 | 1 Nov 80 | present |
| Colgain, William | do | 22 April 78 | 11 Sept 80 | deserted |
| Campbell, Isaac | do | 29 June 78 | Dec 79 | off Rolls |
| Carpenter, Mathew | do | 18 April 78 | 1 April 79 | deserted |
| Cummings, Wm. | do | 23 April 78 | 1 Nov 80 | present |
| Joined 2 Aug 79 Clarke, Richd.[1] | do | 24 April 78 | Nov & Dec 78 | dead |
| Campbell, Nichs. | do | 21 April 78 | Jany 79 | dead |
| Crowley, Darby[2] | do | 25 feb 78 | 22 June 80 | joined |
| Carney, Thomas | do | 3 April 78 | 20 May 80 | deserted |
| | Corpl | 18 June 78 | | |
| Cypher, John[1] | pt | 5 June 78 | 30 Mar 79 | discharged |
| Campbell, John | do | 8 June 78 | 30 Mar 79 | discharged |
| Cox, Clarkeson[3] | do | 7 June 78 | 11 April 79 | discharged |
| Clarke, William[4] | do | | 11 Jan 79 | transd. to 2nd [Md. Brigade |
| 2d Nov 78 Grosh's Cassady, Mathew[1] | pt | | 16 Aug 80 | missing |
| Oct 78 Md. Morris' Carey, William[3] | do | 21 May 78 | 16 Aug 80 | missing |
| Christopher, Thos. H. | do | 20 May 78 | 1 Nov 80 | present |
| Chitham, Aquilla | do | May 78 | } do | do |
| | Sergt | 1 May 80 | | |
| Cox, Ezaiah | pt | 1 Mar 79 | 5 Mar 79 | deserted |
| Chandler, James[5] | do | 1 Mar 80 | 8 May 80 | deserted |
| Cowling, George[1] | do | 22 Jan 80 | 16 Aug 80 | missing |
| Calbart, Simon[6] | do | 24 Jan 80 | 1 Nov 80 | present |
| Carey, Owen[7] | Corpl | 1 feb 80 | 80 do | do |
| Mch 80 Lamar's Carey, Michael[7] | Drum | 10 feb 80 | do | do |
| do Lamar's Compton, Igns.[8] | do | 1 April 80 | do | do |
| Curren, James[9] | do | 8 feb 80 | do | do |
| Caton, William[10] | do | 30 Mar 80 | 16 Aug 80 | missing |
| Carr, Stephen[6] | do | 12 April 80 | Nov 80 | present |
| Clancy, Edwd.[1] | fifer | 4 April 80 | do | do |
| Cochran, John[8] | pt | | do | do |
| Clements, James | do | | do | do |
| Clarke, Saml. | do | | do | do |

[1] Morris'.   [2] Bayly's.   [3] Beatty's.   [4] Grosh's.   [5] Jones'.
[6] Anderson's.   [7] Lamar's.   [8] L. Beall's.   [9] Mason's.   [10] Lynn's.

## MUSTERS OF MARYLAND TROOPS, VOL. II.

| NAMES. | RANK. | TIME OF SERVICE. Enlisted. | Discharged. | REMARKS. |
|---|---|---|---|---|

### GERMAN REGIMENT.

| NAMES. | RANK. | Enlisted. | Discharged. | REMARKS. |
|---|---|---|---|---|
| Cahill, Timothy to 1 Jan 81 | pt | 27 May 78 | 1 Aug 80 | present |
| Caufman, Jacob to do | do | 21 Aprl 78 | do | do |
| Cole, Benjamin to 1 Jan 81 | do | 20 May 78 | do | do |
| Crothorn, George to 1 Jan 81 | do | 2 April 77 | do | do |
| Curley, Owen | mustrd. dest. Pay roll 1 Aug 80 | | | deserted, joined again |
| Croft, (Kraft), William | Corpl | | 26 July 79 | discharged |
| Cole, John | Sergt | | 24 do | do |
| Cronise, Henry | | | 24 do | do |
| Croft, John | | | 24 July 79 | discharged |
| Clifton, Thomas | | | 26 do | do |
| Cambler, (or Gambler,) Michael | pt | | 1 Aug 80 pst. & 1 Jany 81 paid | |
| Casner, Christopher to 1 Jany 81 | do | | do | do |
| Crower, Rudolph | | | 15 July 79 | discharged |
| Cowley, Michael | | | 14 Aug 79 | do do |
| Champness, Chs. | | | 1 Aug 80 | to Invalids |
| Cromer, (or Cramer), Jacob | | | 20 July 79 | discharged |
| Crush, Michael | see Michael Grosh | | | |
| Cline, John | see Kline | | | |

### FIFTH REGIMENT.

| NAMES. | RANK. | Enlisted. | Discharged. | REMARKS. |
|---|---|---|---|---|
| Dean, John[1] | Capt | 10 dec 76 | 16 Nov 77 | prisoner taken F. Washington |
| Downs, Lodman | Corpl | 28 Jan 77 | 1 Sept 77 | promoted Sergeant |
| | pt | 11 Jan 78 | } | |
| | Sergt | 1 Jan 79 | } 5 Feby 80 | discharged |
| Dawson, Andrew | pt | 11 July 77 | 16 Aug 80 | missing |
| Dennison, William | do | 10 dec 76 | April 79 | deserted |
| Davis, Griffith[2] | Sergt | 4 May 77 | } | |
| | pt | 12 June 79 | } | |
| | Q.M.Sergt. | 24 dec 79 | } | |
| Deford, Jesse | pt | 24 June | last muster Jany 80 | |
| Davis, (Daves or Davis), William | do | 30 June | April 78 | left out |
| Dyal, John[3] | do | 4 June 77 | July 78 | off Rolls |

[1] Dean's.  [2] Hawkins'.  [3] Lynch's.

## MUSTERS OF MARYLAND TROOPS, VOL. II.

| NAMES. | RANK. | TIME OF SERVICE. Enlisted. | Discharged. | REMARKS. |
|---|---|---|---|---|
| Dawson, John[1] | Sergt | 9 Mar 77 } | | |
| | pt | 29 May 79 } | 6 Mar 80 | discharged |
| Dean, Thomas[2] | do | 22 Mar 77 | 15 July 78 | died |
| Denson, Isaac | do | 10 dec 76 | 22 May 78 | died |
| Dorsey, John | Sergt | 23 feb 78 | | |
| Dawson, Joseph[3] | pt | 15 Jany 78 | | joined |
| 1 mustr. April 78 | | | | |
| Doyle, James | do | 2 Jan 77 | Sept 80 | joined |
| Davis, Philemon[4] | do | 26 April 78 | discharged 16 May 80 | |
| to Hawkins', 1 mustr. April 78 | | | | |
| Deford, John[5] | do | 8 Mar 78 | 10 Oct 79 | died |
| Deford, Joseph[5] | do | 8 Mar 78 | | |
| Corpl Oct Muster 80 | | | | |
| Downey, Alex.[3] | do | 28 May 78 | 1 Mar 79 | discharged, reinlisted again } |
| Muster again Sept Roll 78 | | | | |
| Davy, Edward | do | 30 May 78 | Aug 78 | not heard of |
| Doblin, Edward | do | 6 June 78 | Aug 78 | not heard of |
| Danks, John[6] | do | 28 April 78 | 25 June 78 | deserted & Sept 1 deserted |
| 1 mustr. Jany 78 | | | | |
| Dean, Elijah | pt | 15 May 78 | | joined R. |
| Doran, Michael[1] | do | 1 June 78 | 1 Nov 80 | present |
| 1 muster June 78 | | | | |
| Dun, Patrick | do | 6 May 78 | feb 79 | not heard of |
| Dickeson, John[4] | do | 12 May 78 | last muster Jan 80 | |
| Duhague, John[1] | do | 5 May 78 | 1 Nov 80 | present |
| 1 mus. June 78 | | | | |
| Dyers, (or Duis), George[7] | do | 28 April 78 | last muster Jany 80 | |
| Dimond, Charles | do | 4 June 78 | 19 Mar 79 | discharged |
| Dice, (or Dues), James | do | 12 June 78 | Jany 80 | prisoner war |
| Downey, John[8] | do | 25 April 78 | 1 Nov 80 | present |
| Dapson, James[2] | do | 4 May 78 | 6 July 78 | deserted |
| Dohorty, Barney[8] | do | 14 June 79 | 1 Sept 79 | to Invalids |
| 1 must. June 79 | | | | |
| Dee, (or Dean), Elijah | do | 11 May 78 | 1 Nov 80 | present |
| 1 mus. July 79 | | | | |
| Durgan, Patrick[8] | do | 13 June 79 | 21 Nov 79 | died |
| Durgan, James | do | 16 June 79 | 1 Nov 80 | present |
| | Fifer | 1 Aug 79 | | |
| Downey, Dennis | pt | | | |
| Darah, John[9] | pt | 1 Nov 80 | | present |
| joined 7 April 79 | | | | |
| Dowling, Roger[10] | do | 16 June 79 | do | do |
| Dutch, Mathias[11] | do | 30 April 79 | last muster Jany 80 | |

[1] Handy's.  [2] Emory's.  [3] Lt. Hamilton's.  [4] Johnson's.  [5] Hawkins'.  [6] Lynch's.  [7] Bird's.  [8] Benson's.  [9] Beall's.  [10] Lt. Williams'.  [11] Norris'.

## MUSTERS OF MARYLAND TROOPS, VOL. II.

| NAMES. | RANK. | TIME OF SERVICE. Enlisted. | Discharged. | REMARKS. |
|---|---|---|---|---|

SIXTH REGIMENT.

| NAMES. | RANK. | Enlisted. | Discharged. | REMARKS. |
|---|---|---|---|---|
| Donnally, Patrick[1] | pt | 22 July 77 | 22 July 80 | discharged |
| Donovan, Richd. | Ensign | 10 Dec 76 | 17 April 77 | Adjutant |
|  | Adjt | 17 April 77 |  | |
|  | Lieut | 1 April 78 | 16 Aug 80 | killed |
| Dobson, Henry[2] | Capt | 10 dec 76 | | |
| Donnelly, Caleb | pt | 20 May 78 | 1 Nov 80 | present |
| Day, Samuel[3] | pt | 23 May 77 | | last muster Jan 80 |
|  |  | discharged by Col. Forrest 14 May 1780 | | |
| Delon, (or Dolon), Peter | do | 14 Oct 77 | 16 Aug 80 | prisoner |
|  | Corpl | 1 Aug 79 | | |
|  | Sergt | 22 dec 79 | | |
| Duvall, Benja.[4] | pt | 4 dec 76 | | last muster Jany 80 |
|   private 6 July 79 | Sergt | 1 Mar 78 | | |
| Dunster, Peter | pt | 10 Jany 77 | 16 Aug 80 | killed |
| Dickason, Wm. | do | 27 feb 77 | | last muster Jany 80 |
| Duffy, Terrence | do | 5 May 77 | | |
| Dominick, Benja. | do | 19 May 78 | 1 Nov 80 | present |
| Donovan, Danl.[5] | do | 9 feb 77 | | last muster Jany 80 |
| Dennis, Basil[6] | do | 22 April 77 | do | do |
| Dougherty, Michael[7] | Lieut | 14 June 77 | 12 April 79 | cashiered |
| Delany, Nicholas | pt | 24 Jany 78 | 16 Aug 80 | missing |
| Durgan, Anthony[1] | pt | 13 June 78 | Dec 79 | absent wt. Leave |
| Dugan, Edward[2] | do | 25 May 78 | 10 Sept 78 | died |
|   1 muster June 78 |  |  |  | |
| Delefraney, John B.[3] | do | 1 June 78 | 30 Nov 78 | died. |
| Davis, John[4] | do | 19 feb 77 | wounded and discharged by | |
|   Joined June 78, mustered March Roll 79 |  |  | Genl. Arnold 25 Aug 78. | |
| Davett, Henry[8] | pt | 22 April 78 | last muster Jany 80 | |
| Davis, Robert | do | 28 April 78 | 1 Nov 80 | present, discharg- [ed 1 May 81 |
| Dailey, Patrick | do | 1 June 78 | April 79 | deserted |
|   rein. 24 dec 78 |  |  |  | |
| Duvall, Richd.[5] | do | 30 Mar 78 | 1 Nov 80 | present |
| Duley, Saml.[6] | do | 20 April 78 | 20 May 78 | deserted |
| Durham, William | do | 28 April 78 | 1 Nov 80 | present |
| Davis, Samuel[8] | do | 27 Mar 78 | April 78 | deserted, joined R. |
| Doran, Patrick[9] | Corpl | 4 April 78 | 1 Nov 80 | present |
|   1 mustr. Aug 78 | Sergt | 19 Nov 78 | | |
| Dorsey, Levin[10] | pt | 31 Aug 79 | 17 Oct 79 | deserted |
| Dunbar, Saml. | do |  | 17 July 80 | deserted |
|   1 muster Sept 79 |  |  |  | |

[1] Ghiselin's.　　[2] Dobson's.　　[3] Trueman's.　　[4] Beall's.　　[5] Hynes'.
[6] Laurence.　　[7] Harris'.　　[8] Lt. Williams'.　　[9] Miles'.　　[10] Norris'.

## MUSTERS OF MARYLAND TROOPS, VOL. II.

| NAMES. | RANK. | TIME OF SERVICE. Enlisted. | Discharged. | REMARKS. |
|---|---|---|---|---|
| Denoon, John | drum | 1 Mar 80 | 1 Nov 80 | present |
| Oct Mus. 80 | | | | |
| Davis, Henry | pt | | do | do |
| Devericks, James | do | | do | do |
| joined 16 Sept 80 | | | | |
| Davis, Richard | do | | 1 Oct 80 | do |
| Doyle, John | do | | 16 Aug 80 | missing |
| Decorn, John | do | | 16 Aug 80 | missing |

### SEVENTH REGIMENT.

| NAMES. | RANK. | Enlisted. | Discharged. | REMARKS. |
|---|---|---|---|---|
| Denny, Robert | pt | 10 dec 76 | | |
| | Qr. Master | 30 April 77 | | |
| | Py.Master | 27 June 77 | | |
| | Lieut | 3 Jany 80 | | |
| Donnally, Patrick | Adjt | 13 April 77 | | |
| | Ensign | 28 May 78 | | |
| | Lieut | 7 Oct 79 | | |
| Dixon, Richard[1] | pt | 1 April 77 | 28 Mar 80 | discharged |
| Dowling, James[2] | pt | 26 Jany 77 | | |
| | Corpl | 8 June 77 | | private 1 Nov 1780 |
| 1 Jany 80 Sergt | Sergt | 1 Nov 77 | | |
| | pt | 6 Aug 77 | | |
| Day, Francis | pt | 8 Aprl 77 | 27 Oct 78 | died |
| | Corpl | 1 May 77 | | |
| Denn, Edward | pt | 14 April 77 | 8 Mar 78 | decd. |
| Davis, Thomas[3] | Corpl | 20 April 77 | 16 Aug 80 | missing |
| | pt | 25 dec 77 | | |
| Driver, James | pt | 20 April 77 | 16 Aug 80 | missing |
| | Corpl | 1 Mar 80 | | |
| | pt | 1 June 80 | | |
| Delanaway, John | pt | 21 May 77 | 16 Aug 80 | missing |
| Davis, William[4] | do | Q. M. 77 | 2 Mar 80 | discharged |
| Dixon, William | do | 10 June 77 | 1 Jany 80 | deserted |
| Doyle, Hugh[5] | Sergt | 6 dec 76 | 9 dec 79 | discharged |
| 4 May 79 private | | | | |
| Donovan, William | pt | 7 Jany 77 | Sept 77 | off Rolls |
| Dillon, James | do | 5 feb 77 | | feby 78 off Rolls |
| Joined Jany 78 | | | | |
| Duley, William | do | 24 Mar 77 | 16 Aug 80 | missing |
| Dixon, John | do | 3 April 77 | 31 July 77 | deserted |
| Darby, John[6] | do | 8 Aug 77 | Sept 77 | off Rolls |
| Dailey, (or Delany), Jno. | do | 1 Sept 77 | 6 July 80 | deserted |

[1] Jones'.    [2] Grosh's.    [3] Spykers'.    [4] Stull's.    [5] Morris'.    [6] Miles'.

## MUSTERS OF MARYLAND TROOPS, VOL. II.

| NAMES. | RANK. | TIME OF SERVICE. Enlisted. | TIME OF SERVICE. Discharged. | REMARKS. |
|---|---|---|---|---|
| Deane, Roger[1] | pt | 5 dec 76 | July 78 | off Rolls |
| Devitt, George | do | 11 Jan 77 | 1 Nov 80 | present |
| Downey, Cornelius | do | 15 Jan 77 | 28 June 78 | killed at Monmouth |
| | Corpl | Sept 77 | | |
| Dorman, Thomas | pt | 9 feb 77 | 28 Mar 80 | prisoner War |
| Duffey, John | do | 8 May 77 | 16 Aug 80 | missing |
| Donent, John | do | 28 April 77 | 28 April 80 | discharged, appld. 26 May 1789 } |
| Duncan, Robert | do | 7 Aug 77 | 1 Nov 80 | present |
| Davis, John | do | 4 Aug 77 | 16 Aug 80 | missing |
| Dennison, John | do | 26 Nov 77 | 16 Aug 80 | missing |
| | Corpl | 19 Oct 78 | | |
| | Sergt | 1 Jan 80 | | |
| Denny, Saml. | Sergt | | 2 Mar 81 | discharged |
| Dixon, John | pt | 17 Nov 77 | 25 Oct 80 | deserted |
| Donavan, Wm.[2] | do | | 17 Mar 77 | do |
| Denny, Saml.[3] | do | 27 Mar 78 | 1 Nov 80 | present |
| | Corpl | 1 Jan 80 | | |
| | Sergt | 1 April 80 | discharged 2 Mar 81 | |
| Davidson, Allen[4] | fifer | 24 dec 77 | 8 feb 78 | deserted |
| Davidson, James[5] 1 muster April 78 | Sergt | | May 78 | off Rolls |
| Davidson, Luke | pt | 27 dec 77 | 8 feb 78 | deserted |
| Downs, Richd.[6] | do | 6 June 78 | 16 Mar 79 | discharged, reinlisted July 80 |
| Dodd, James[2] | do | 6 June 78 | 15 feb 79 | discharged |
| Dailey, John[7] | do | 6 May 78 | May 80 | deserted |
| Davis, Evans[4] | do | 18 May 78 | 16 Augt 80 | missing |
| Davis, Samuel[1] | do | 9 May 78 | 1 Nov 80 | present |
| | Sergt | 1 June 80 | | |
| Dodson, Wm.[4] | pt | 13 June 78 | 30 Mar 79 | discharged |
| Duncan, Jessee[2] 1st muster Joined 20 July 78 | Sergt | | 5 Jan 79 | discharged |
| Dove, John[5] Field & Staff Q. M. 16 April 80 | Sergt | 1 May 78 | | |
| Disheroon, Thos. | pt | | 10 feb 79 | died |
| Delany, John[8] | do | 7 feb 79 | 2 June 80 | deserted |
| Denwood, Levin | Surgeon | 3 Oct 79 | | |
| Donaldson, Wm.[4] | pt | | Jany 80 | prisoner War |
| Devenish, George[9] | do | | 16 Aug 80 | missing |
| Dawson, (or Davison), John[10] | do | | 16 Aug 80 | missing |

[1] Bayly's.  [2] Deams'.  [3] Grosh's.  [4] Morris'.  [5] Beatty's.
[6] Jones'.  [7] Stull's.  [8] Hardman's.  [9] Lamar's.  [10] Mason's.

## MUSTERS OF MARYLAND TROOPS, VOL. II.

| NAMES. | RANK. | TIME OF SERVICE. Enlisted. | Discharged. | REMARKS. |
|---|---|---|---|---|

### GERMAN REGIMENT.

| NAMES. | RANK. | Enlisted. | Discharged. | REMARKS. |
|---|---|---|---|---|
| Dyer, James | Invalid | 1 May 77 | | 5 May paid |
| Dalton, John | pt | 1 June 77 | 1 Aug 80 | present |
| Dunkin, James | | | 16 July 79 | discharged |
| Dretch, John | | | 20 July 79 | do |
| Danruth, Godlb. | | | 30 do 79 | do |

### FIFTH MARYLAND REGIMENT.

| NAMES. | RANK. | Enlisted. | Discharged. | REMARKS. |
|---|---|---|---|---|
| Edmondson, Sam. | Q. M. | 10 dec 76 | 14 Oct 77 | resigned |
| Ellis, Richard[1] | private | 15 Mar 77 | 16 Aug 80 | missing |
| Emory, Richard | Capt | 10 dec 76 | 27 dec 77 | resigned |
| Emory, Gideon[2] | 1 Lieut | 14 feb 77 | | |
| Evans, Thomas | pt | 28 April 77 | July 78 | off Rolls |
| | | | 6 Jan 81 | discharged |
| Engram, Wm. | do | 18 May 77 | see William Ingram | |
| Elfry, Godfrey[3] | do | 20 Jan 77 | 12 Jan 80 | discharged |
| Eaton, Richard[4] | do | 10 dec 76 | 10 dec 79 | time expired |
| Ellery, Dennis[5] | do | 30 May 78 | Aug 78 | not heard of |
| Edgerly, Wm.[1] | do | 29 May 78 | time out Mar 79 left out | |
| Ewbanks, Jona.[6] | do | 13 do do | 2 July 78 | deserted |
| Ewbanks, Richd. | do | 9 May 78 | do do | do |
| Edwards, Burton[7] | do | 6 May 78 | 11 April 79 | do |
| Evans, John[5] | do | 27 April 79 | 1 Oct 80 | present |
| Eccleston, Jervis[8] | do | 16 June 79 | do do | do |

### SIXTH MARYLAND REGIMENT.

| NAMES. | RANK. | Enlisted. | Discharged. | REMARKS. |
|---|---|---|---|---|
| Evans, William[9] | pt | 21 July 77 | 12 Oct 78 | deserted |
| deserted 20 Aug 77, joined 25 May 78 | | | | |
| Evans, Benja. | pt | 28 April 78 | 31 Oct 79 | died |
| Elliott, Joseph[10] | do | 11 May 78 | 1 Nov 80 | present |
| Ellms, George[11] | fife | 14 Oct 77 | do do | do |
| | fife Major | 18 feb 78 | | |
| Etheridge, Jno. | pt | 2 Mar 78 | 16 Nov 79 | died |
| Estep, Alexander[12] | Lieut | 20 feb 77 | 13 Oct 77 | resigned |
| Elleary, (or Hilleary), John | pt | 10 Jan 77 | 1 Nov 80 | present |
| Elliott, John[13] | do | 21 April 77 | do | do |
| Evans, Richard | do | 1 May 77 | Jan 80 | present |
| | | | 1 May 80 | discharged |

[1] Lynch's.    [2] Emory's.    [3] Cosden's.    [4] Ensign Jones', Benson's.    [5] Lt. Hamilton's.
[6] Handy's.    [7] Hawkins'.    [8] Benson's.    [9] Ghiselin's.    [10] Dobson's.
[11] Trueman's.    [12] Beall's.    [13] Laurence's.

## MUSTERS OF MARYLAND TROOPS, VOL. II.

| NAMES. | RANK. | TIME OF SERVICE. Enlisted. | Discharged. | REMARKS. |
|---|---|---|---|---|
| Egan, Patrick[1] | pt | 21 do do | 1 Nov 80 | present |
| Elvin, John[2]  9 | do | 2 June 78 | 14 Mar 79 | discharged |
| Everett, Richard[3]  9 | do | 1 June 78 | 1 April 79 | do |
| English, Saml.[4]  9 | do | 3 do do | do | do |
| Eddleman, Michl.[5]  3 | do | 8 Mar 77 | 10 dec 77 | 9 Mar 80 |
| | | | | discharged |
| Ellis, Thomas  9 | do | 3 June 78 | 22 Mar 79 | dischd. |
| Ellis, Brion | do | | 16 Aug 80 | prisoner |

### SEVENTH MARYLAND REGIMENT.

| NAMES. | RANK. | TIME OF SERVICE. Enlisted. | Discharged. | REMARKS. |
|---|---|---|---|---|
| Evans, John[6] | pt | 16 Jan 77 | Mar 78 | off Rolls |
| Evans, John[7] | Sergt | 1 April 77 | 2 Mar 80 | resigned |
| | 5 Jan 80 Sergt Major | | | |
| Early, Benja.[6] | pt | 6 June 78 | 16 Mar 79 | discharged |
| Edwards, Saml.[8] | do | 19 May 78 | 26 May | deserted |
| Ellison, Richard[9] | do | 2 May 78 | 26 May 79 | died |
| Easter, Nichs. | pt | . | 26 April 81 | dischd. |

### GERMAN REGIMENT.

| NAMES. | RANK. | Enlisted. | Discharged. | REMARKS. |
|---|---|---|---|---|
| Elliott, Benja. | 1 mus. desd. P. R. | | 1 Aug 80 | deserted |
| Eissell, John  3 | | | 11 Aug 79 | discharged |
| Ellsperger, Wolfgn. | | | 16 July 79 | do |
| England, Benja. | Drum | | do | do |
| Elsing, Paul | | | 30 July 79 | do |
| Etnier, John | | | 26  do | do |
| Ensey, Jas. | | | 10 Oct 79 | do |
| Etter, Jacob | Corpl | | 15 July 79 | do |
| Engellee, (or) Angel, Peter | | | 14 Aug 79 | do |
| Engle, Bartel | | | 6 Aug 79 | do, died |

### FIFTH MARYLAND REGIMENT.

| NAMES. | RANK. | Enlisted. | Discharged. | REMARKS. |
|---|---|---|---|---|
| Frazier, William[10] | 1st Lieut | 10 dec 76 | | |
| Foster, Rigby | pt | 30 May 77 | 1 Nov 80 | present |
| Friend, James | do | 7 Aug 77 | 1 Jany 80 | do |
| | | | | discharged Augt 80 |
| Freeland, (or Freeman), John[11] | do | 3 May | | |
| Joined 1 April 79 | Joined again 20 March 80 | | | |
| Foster, William[12] | Sergt | 15 dec 76 | pt. 1 April 77, Corpl. 1 Nov, |
| | | | Sergt. 1 Oct 79, 16 Augt 80 missing |

[1] Harris'.  [2] Dobson's.  [3] Trueman's.  [4] Lt. Williams'.  [5] Miles'.  [6] Jones'.
[7] Spyker's.  [8] Grosh's.  [9] Beatty's.  [10] Dean's.  [11] Hawkins'.  [12] Handy's.

## MUSTERS OF MARYLAND TROOPS, VOL. II.

| NAMES. | RANK. | TIME OF SERVICE. Enlisted. | Discharged. | REMARKS. |
|---|---|---|---|---|
| Ferguson, James | Corpl | 7 April 77 | 10 Jan 80 | discharged |
| Foreman, William[1] | Sergt | 13 dec 76 | | |
| | Sergt. Major | 1 Jan 79 | | |
| Flynn, Bryan | pt | 13 Mar 77 | 16 Aug 80 | missing |
| Foreman, Perry | do | 3 feb 77 | April 78 | left out |
| Freely, Charles | do | 8 dec 76 | 16 Aug 80 | missing |
| to Hamilton's or Comd. feby 80 | | | | |
| Finoughty, Thomas[2] | do | 10 March 77 | 5 April 78 | deserted |
| Finley, George[3] | do | 14 Jan 77 | 12 Jan 80 | discharged |
| prvt 1 April 79, Corpl April 78 | | | | |
| Farrell, William[4] | pt | 4 Mar 77 | 1 Nov 80 | present |
| 1st muster 78 | | | | |
| Floid, Joseph,[5] | do | 13 Jany 78 | drum. 15 Aug 78, 10 Jan 80 dischd. | |
| Joined April 78 | | | | |
| Fullom, John[1] | do | 17 Mar 77 | 1 Nov 80 | present |
| Hugou's, 1 muster April 78 | | | | |
| Flowers, Edward[6] | do | 30 Mar 78 | 16 Aug 80 | missing |
| 1 muster April 78 | | | | |
| Fairbanks, Johns[4] | do | 1 June 78 | 15 Aug 80 | died |
| Fields, Michael[6] | do | 23 April 78 | 12 Aug 78 | deserted |
| Foster, Stephen | do | 2 June 78 | Inlisted with Genl. Palaskey | |
| Fountain, William[7] | pt | 13 June 78 | Oct 78 | died |
| Forson, George | do | 20 May 78 | Feby 79 | heard of |
| Farrowfield, John | do | 20 May 78 | July 78 | off Rolls |
| Fitzgerald, Thomas | do | 12 May 78 | Feby 79 | not heard of |
| Foster, Mark[5] | do | 15 May 78 | 1 Nov 80 | present |
| Foster, Nathaniel | do | 30 May 78 | Jan 80 | present |
| Ford, George[1] | do | 13 May 78 | 15 Aug 78 | joined |
| Fremly, Thomas[7] | do | 19 June 78 | 1 Nov 80 | present |
| 1st muster June 78 | | | | |
| Ford, Ash | do | 25 May 78 | April & May 79 not heard of | |
| 1st muster June 78 | | | | |
| Freeland, John | do | | July 78 | off Rolls |
| 1st muster June 78 and July 78 | | | | |

### Sixth Maryland Regiment.

| Fouts, Jacob | Corpl | 15 Aug 77 | Augt 78 | off Rolls |
|---|---|---|---|---|
| Ford, Benja. | Major | 20 Feby 77 ⎫ | | |
| | do Col. | 17 April 77 ⎬ | | |
| | do Col. Comt. | ⎭ | | |

[1] Johnson's.    [2] Emory's.    [3] Cosden's.    [4] l.t. Hamilton's.    [5] Ensign Jones'.
[6] Lynch's.    [7] Handy's.

## MUSTERS OF MARYLAND TROOPS, VOL. II.

| NAMES. | RANK. | TIME OF SERVICE. Enlisted. | Discharged. | REMARKS. |
|---|---|---|---|---|
| Finlow, Daniel[1] | pt | 12 May 78 | Jany 80 | present |
| Finton, Abram | do | 18 May 78 | Aug 78 | off Rolls |
| Freeman, Jeremiah[2] | do | 15 July 77 | do | do |
| Felton, Thomas[3] | do | 3 March 77 | 7 May dischd. by Col. Forrest | |
| Fitzsimmons, Thos. | do | 10 Jan 77 | 10 Jan 80 | discharged |
| Faup, Benja. | | 5 May 78 | (see Phap, Benjamin) | |
| Fox, Anthony[4] | Sergt | 20 April 77 | Jany 80 | present } |
| | | | 21 April 80 dischd. by Col. Howard } | |
| Fitzpatrick, Bars.[5] Chaplin's, now Miles' | pt | 22 July 77 | 7 Mar 79 | died |
| Finacy, William[6] 78 1 July Joined | pt | 1 July 78 | Dec 79 | absent without leave |
| Fullam, Michl. 78 1 July Joined | do | 1 July 78 | 1 April 79 | discharged |
| Finacy, John 1 July 78 Joined | do | 1 July 78 | Dec 78 | do |
| Furwott, John Peter[7] | do | 29 Apr 78 | 1 Nov 80 | present |
| | Sergt | 1 June 78 | | |
| Flick, George | pt | June 78 | 1 April 79 | discharged |
| Farrance, Nichs. | do | 22 April 78 | do | do |
| Foster, Jona.[8] | do | 20 May 78 | Jany 80 | present |
| Ford, William | do | 19 May 78 | 16 Aug 80 | missing |
| Ford, John[9] | do | 28 Aprl 78 | 16 Aug 80 | prisoner |
| Fitzgerald, Timothy[1] Joined for 3 years 23 dec 78 | do | 11 July 78 } | 1 Nov 80 | present |
| Fairfield, Thomas | pt | 12 June 78 | 10 July 78 | deserted |
| Filbert, Joseph[2] (See the Letter P). | Corpl | 30 May 78 | 1 Nov 80 | present |
| Freely, William[10] Joined 2 Aug 78 | pt | 17 June 77 | 1 Jany 80 | present |
| Force, Joseph[11] | do | 1 June 79 | 1 Jan 80 | do |
| Frost, Silvester[2] 1 muster Oct 79 | do | 15 Sept 77 | 1 Jan 80 | do |
| Flack, James[12] | Sergt | 23 April 79 | 1 Nov 80 | do |
| Fuller, William | pt | | do | do |

### SEVENTH MARYLAND REGIMENT.

| | | | | |
|---|---|---|---|---|
| Ford, George[13] | Corpl | 3 Mar 77 | 3 Mar 80 | discharged |
| | Sergt | 1 Nov 77 } | | |
| | pt | 21 Sept 78 } | | |

| | | | | |
|---|---|---|---|---|
| [1] Dobson's. | [2] Trueman's. | [3] Beall's. | [4] Laurence's. | [5] Chapline's. |
| [6] Ghiselin's. | [7] Lt. Williams'. | [8] Miles'. | [9] Hynes'. | [10] Harris'. |
| [11] Somerville's. | [12] Jacobs'. | [13] Jones'. | | |

## MUSTERS OF MARYLAND TROOPS, VOL. II.

| NAMES. | RANK. | TIME OF SERVICE. Enlisted. | Discharged. | REMARKS. |
|---|---|---|---|---|
| Fitzgerald, Benja.[1] | pt | 11 feb 77 | 1 Nov 80 | present |
|  | Corpl | 30 Sept 78 |  |  |
|  | Sergt | 1 June 80 |  |  |
| Finch, Joseph | pt | 28 Mar 77 | 28 Mar 80 | discharged |
| Fogwell, George[2] | Sergt | 16 Jan 77 | 23 Jan 78 | deserted |
|  | pt | 26 July 78 |  | [Comd. |
| Farran, John[2] | Sergt | 20 April 77 | Oct 78 | deserted from |
| Fisher, Henry | pt | 24 July 77 | Feb 78 | off Rolls |
| Fletcher, Richd.[4] | do | 14 July 77 | 24 Oct 77 | died |
|  | Corpl | 1 Sept 77 |  |  |
| Fletcher, Phillip[5] | fifer | 20 dec 76 | 4 dec 79 | discharged |
| 4 June 78 Joined |  |  |  |  |
| Fox, John | pt | 21 Mar 77 | Jany 80 | prisoner War |
| Farrell, John[6] | pt | 3 dec 76 | 5 Jan 80 | discharged |
| Furguson, John | do | 6 dec 76 | Feby 78 | off Rolls |
| Joined Sept 77 |  |  |  |  |
| Frogget, Richard | do | 17 Mar 77 | 22 Mar 80 | discharged |
| Fitzgerrald, Michael | do | 28 May 77 | 16 Aug 80 | missing |
| Joined 21 July 78 |  |  |  |  |
| Farado, Absalam | do | 16 Nov 77 | 1 Nov 80 | present |
| Fitzgerald, Jeremiah[7] | do | 1 April 77 | do | do |
| Fullam, George[8] | Sergt |  | 6 dec 79 | discharged |
|  | Q.M.Sergt. | 1 July 77 |  |  |
| Fowler, John | pt |  | 22 Aug 77 | prisoner |
| Fummer, John Mths. | pt | 8 feb 77 | 1 Nov 80 | present |
| Flannigan, Richd.[4] | do | 27 Jan 78 | May 78 | off Rolls |
| Fren, Andrew[9] | do | 30 dec 77 | 8 feb 78 | deserted |
| Fillson, James[2] | do | 25 May 78 |  | deserted from } Hospital time unknown } |
| Fubbard, Francis[3] | do |  | July 78 | off Rolls |
| Fitzgerald, William[4] | do | 1 June 78 | 1 Mar 79 | discharged |
| Fisher, Abram | do | 1 June 78 | 1 April 79 | discharged |
| Felmott, Dorus | do | 21 April — | 1 Nov 80 | present |
| Fitzgerald, Nichs. | do | 2 May 78 | 1 Nov 80 | present |
| Fickle, Benja.[5] | Sergt | 6 April 78 | } |  |
|  | Ensign | 26 Jan 80 | } Promoted |  |
| Foster, Moses[5] | pt | 23 April 78 | 1 Nov 80 | present |
| Filson, Saml. | do | 18 Apr 78 | do | ditto |
|  | Sergt | 16 dec 79 |  |  |
| Fortune, William[10] | pt | 3 June 78 | Jan 80 absent without leave, } 30 June deserted } |  |

[1] Beall's.    [2] Grosh's.    [3] Spyker's.    [4] Stull's.    [5] Morris'.
[6] Bayly's.    [7] Reynolds'.    [8] Deams'.    [9] Beatty's.    [10] Anderson's.

## MUSTERS OF MARYLAND TROOPS, VOL II.

| NAMES. | RANK. | TIME OF SERVICE. Enlisted. | Discharged. | REMARKS. |
|---|---|---|---|---|
| Fitzgerald, Henry[1] | pt | 20 July 78 | 9 Aprl 79 | discharged |
| Fennel, Edward[2] | do | 23 June 78 | dec 79 | died |
| Flanning, John[1] | fifer | 26 July 79 | 6 July 80 | deserted |
| Flaharty, Stephen | pt | 27 dec 79 | 1 Nov 80 | present |
| from 1 Regt.   Mustered Sergt July 80 | | | | |
| Fernan, Dennis | | See Dennis Fernan | | |

### GERMAN REGIMENT.

| | | | | |
|---|---|---|---|---|
| Fennell, John | pt | 21 May 78 | 1 Aug 80 | present |
| Ferrins, Henry | fifer | 16 May 78 | do | do |
| Folliot, John | | Joined 10 Oct 79 | do | prst., stop. F. S. |
| Fisher, Henry | pt | 1 April 78 | do | prst. |
| Fulham, Charles | | 23 April 78 | do | prst. |
| Fleming, Patrick | | | 9 Aug 79 | discharged |
| Franklin, John | do | 4 Mar 78 | 1 Aug 80 | prst., dischd. 4 Mar 80 |
| Frymiller, Jacob | | | 15 July 79 | discharged |
| Frantz, Abram | | | 19 ditto | ditto |
| Frey, Bernard | Corpl | | 26 do | do |
| Fleck, John | | | 26 do | do |
| Fisher, Philip | | | 26 do | do |
| Filler, Fredk. | | | 26 do | do |
| Finch, David | | | 7 Aug 79 | do |
| Forney, James | | | 26 July do | do |
| Fisher, Philip | | | 24 do | do |
| Fitzpatrick, Philip  9 mo. | | | 29 Mar 79 | do |

### FIFTH MARYLAND REGIMENT.

| | | | | |
|---|---|---|---|---|
| Gould, James[2] | Ensn | 20 May 77 ⎫ | | |
| Q. M. 20 Sept 79 | Lieut | 11 Mar 78 ⎭ | | |
| Gilling, Thomas | pt | 19 May | | |
| Gorman, John | do | 4 Sept | 16 Aug 80 | missing |
| Gray, W. James[4] | 1 Lieut | 10 Dec 76 ⎫ | | |
| | Capt | 26 dec 77 ⎭ | | |
| Gilby, Henry | pt | 18 feb 77 | 1 Nov 80 | present |
| Gother, John | do | 23 feb 77 | do | do |
| Gray, James | do | 1 Sept 77 | 16 Aug 80 | missing |
| Gibson, Jonathan[5] | Lieut | 10 dec 76 ⎫ | | |
| Capt 1 May 1780 | P. M. | 25 feb 79 ⎭ | | |
| Garey, George | Corpl | 4 feb 77 ⎫ | | |
| | Sergt | 1 July 79 ⎭ | 4 Feby 80 | discharged |

[1] Grosh's.    [2] Morris'.    [3] Hawkins'.    [4] Lynch's.    [5] Handy's.

## MUSTERS OF MARYLAND TROOPS, VOL. II.

| NAMES. | RANK. | TIME OF SERVICE. Enlisted. | Discharged. | REMARKS. |
|---|---|---|---|---|
| Gill, William[1] | pt | 6 Mar 77 | 1 Jan 80 | present |
| Gully, John | pt | 9 do | 21 Mar 78 | died |
| Griffith, Saml. | do | | 16 Aug 80 | missing |
| Joined 1 April 78 | Sergt | 1 Mar 80 | | |
| Garrett, William[2] | Corpl | | | June 78 left out |
| 1st muster Aprl 78 | | | | |
| Geeting, John[3] | pt | 1 Mar 78 | 1 Jan 80 | present |
| 1st muster April 78 | | | | |
| Griffin, Elisha[4] | pt | | 10 June 78 | discharged |
| 1st muster June 78 | | | | |
| Griffin, Moses | do | | 10 June 78 | do |
| 1st muster June 78 | | | | |
| Gow, William | do | 29 May 78 | 16 Aug 80 | missing |
| | Corpl | 1 April 79 | | |
| Gibson, John[3] | pt | 29 May 78 | 1 Mar 79 | discharged |
| Grenage, William | pt | 18 May 78 | 1 Jan 80 | present |
| Goady, William | do | 6 June 78 | do | do |
| Gelon, John[5] | do | 6 June 78 | | |
| Gray, William | do | 21 Aug 77 | 1 Jan 80 | present |
| Gaad, Robert | do | 6 June 78 | | off Rolls, time out |
| Goldby, John | do | 6 June 78 | Feby 79 | not heard of |
| Gannan, William | do | 6 June 78 | | off Rolls |
| Rein. 19 feb 79 | | | | |
| Graves, Moses[6] | do | 6 May 78 | Nov 78 | died |
| Grindage, James | do | 25 May 78 | 1 Jan 80 | present |
| Glaudstone, Nathl. | do | 14 May 78 | Augt 78 | mustered not heard of |
| Garrett, Enoch[3] | do | 4 June 78 | 18 Aug 78 | died |
| Goodburn, Francis[7] | do | 25 May 78 | 16 Aug 80 | missing |
| 1st muster Jan 78 | Sergt | 1 Mar 80 | | |
| Gray, John | pt | 19 June 78 | dec 78 | not heard of |
| 1st muster June 78 | | | | since 18 June 78 |
| Greenwood, William | do | 4 June 78 | 1 Mar 79 | discharged |
| Gothard, Thomas[8] | pt | 4 May 78 | 16 Aug 80 | missing |
| 1st muster June 78 | Corpl | 1 July 79 | | |
| George, James | pt | 18 May 78 | | 28 June 79 de- |
| 1st muster June 78 | Joined dec 78 | | | serted |
| Gosgraves, Thomas | pt | | | June 78 transfd., never joined |
| 1st muster June 78 | | | | |
| Goodburn, Francis | do | | | Transfd. to Handy's Co. see |
| 1st muster June 78 | | | | other side |
| Graves, Jonas | pt | | | 16 Aug 80 missing |
| 1st muster June 78 | Joined Sept 79 | | | |

[1] Emory's.  [2] Lt. Hamilton's.  [3] Handy's.  [4] Lynch's.
[5] Ensign Jones'.  [6] Johnson's.  [7] Bird's.  [8] Hawkins'.

## MUSTERS OF MARYLAND TROOPS, VOL. II.

| NAMES. | RANK. | TIME OF SERVICE. Enlisted. | Discharged. | REMARKS. |
|---|---|---|---|---|
| Gouldsparks, Jas. | pt | 4 June 78 | 24 dec 78 | discharged |
| Garnett, Benja. | Ensn | 13 Aug 78 } | | |
| dischd. 23 Sept 79 | Lieut | 13 Oct 78 } | | |
| Gregory, James[1] | pt | 14 June 79 | | |
| Joined 17 Mar 80 | | | | |
| Gamble, Abraham[2] | do | 21 June 79 | 1 Nov 80 | present |
| Games, Francis[3] | | 30 April 79 | do | do |
| Gill, John | pt | | 16 Aug 80 | missing |

### SIXTH MARYLAND REGIMENT.

| NAMES. | RANK. | Enlisted. | Discharged. | REMARKS. |
|---|---|---|---|---|
| Ghiselin, John[4] | Capt | 20 June 77 | 1 June 79. | resigned |
| Greenwood, James | Drum | 4 May 77 | 1 Nov 80 | present |
| Gibson, John | pt | 22 Aprl 77 | 16 Aug 80 | prisoner |
| Grantham, Henry | do | 5 May 77 | 16 Aug 80 | missing |
| Gahagan, James | do | 20 April 78 | 30 Oct 78 | deserted |
| Geoghegan, John | Ensn | 29 feb 77 | 20 Jan 78 | resigned |
| Greaden, Robert[5] | pt | 3 Mar 77 | 1 Jan 80 | present |
| Greaves, Absalom[6] | Corpl | 23 Mar 77 } | 1 Jany 80 | do |
| | Sergt | 28 May 78 } | | |
| George, William | pt | 25 Aug 77 | 1 Nov 80 | present |
| Graham, Moses | do | 4 June 77 | do | do |
| Greaves, Isaac[7] | do | 4 Aprl 78 | do | do |
| Garnett, Pero. | do | 15 May 78 | 6 Oct 78 | discharged |
| Griffith, Stephen[8] | do | 6 dec 76 | Aprl & May 79 | left out |
| | Corpl | 1 Nov 77 | | |
| Galliher, John | pt | 8 July 77 | 1 Jan 80 | present |
| Gregory, Benja.[9] | do | 24 April 77 | do | ditto |
| | | 27 April 80 | discharged by Col. Howard | |
| Gordon, John | pt | 30 Sept 77 | July 78 | unfit for service |
| Gridley, Martin[4] | | 1 July 78 | 10 Oct 78 | died |
| 1 July 78 Joined | | | | |
| Greenwood, Milburn | pt | 20 Aprl 77 | July 78 | supposed dead |
| German, Thomas[5] | do | 25 May 78 | | |
| 1 must. June 78   15 Oct 79 Joined | | | 16 Aug 80 | prisoner |
| Garrish, Edward | do | 2 June 78 | 16 Aug 80 | do |
| 1 mustr. June 78 | | | | |
| Grover, John[6] | do | 1 Jan 78 | 16 Aug 80 | prisoner |
| | Drum | 26 Aug 78 | | |
| Gardner, William | pt | 1 June 78 | 1 April 79 | discharged |
| Games, Francis | do | 1 June 78 | feby 79 | left out |
| Garrehan, James[8] | do | 1 Jany 80 | | present |

[1] Benson's.   [2] Hugou's.   [3] Bird's.   [4] Ghiselin's.   [5] Dobson's.
[6] Trueman's.   [7] Beall's.   [8] Hynes'.   [9] Laurence's.

## MUSTERS OF MARYLAND TROOPS, VOL. II.

| NAMES. | RANK. | TIME OF SERVICE. Enlisted. | Discharged. | REMARKS. |
|---|---|---|---|---|
| Grinnard, Paul[1] | pt | 4 May 78 | 16 Aug 80 | missing |
| Gory, Daniel[2] | do | 13 Sept 79 | 16 Aug 80 | do |

### SEVENTH MARYLAND REGIMENT.

| NAMES. | RANK. | Enlisted. | Discharged. | REMARKS. |
|---|---|---|---|---|
| Grunby, John | Col | 10 dec 76 | | |
| Grosh, Adam[3] | Capt | 10 dec 76 | 30 Mar 80 | resigned |
| 8 June 79 | Major | | | |
| Griffith, Richard | pt | 1 Aprl 77 | Sept 77 | out of the Rolls |
| Gee, Richard[4] | do | 23 Aprl 77 | 1 Nov 80 | present |
| Gordon, Peter | do | 30 May 77 | Mar 78 | off Rolls |
| Gilmore, William[5] | do | 6 dec 76 | 11 dec 76 | deserted |
| Green, David[6] | Sergt | 4 dec 76 | } 5 Jan 80 | discharged |
| | Sergt. M. | 4 June 77 | } | |
| | Ensign | | | |
| Green, Robert | Sergt | 8 Jan 77 | 4 Jan 80 | discharged |
| Green, Cuthbert | pt | 8 Jan 77 | 17 feb 78 | died |
| Gibbons, William | do | 15 Jan 77 | July 78 | off Rolls |
| Gardner, George | do | 26 Nov 77 | 28 Jan 80 | deserted |
| Goodwin, Henry[7] | do | 1 July 77 | April 78 | off Rolls |
| Green, George | do | 11 July 77 | 15 July 77 | deserted |
| Griffith, Danl.[8] | Corpl | } | | |
| 15 Mar 79 | pt | } | | |
| 1 June 79 | Sergt | } | 16 Aug 80 | missing |
| Goodfrey, Wm. | Drum | | 7 Sept 77 | discharged |
| Gaskin, Wm. | pt | | 21 June 80 | deserted |
| Green, Samuel[3] | do | 28 Mar 78 | June 78 | off Rolls |
| Grant, John[5] | do | 20 feb 78 | Jany 80 | prisoner of War |
| 1 mustr. April 78 | | | | |
| Gilligan, John[9] | do | 6 April 78 | 16 Aug 80 | missing |
| Depreciation issued to Gen. Williams formerly of the Rifle Corps | | | | |
| Geary, Saml. | pt | 27 April 78 | 1 Nov 80 | present |
| Gordon, Joseph[9] | do | 30 April 78 | 16 Aug 80 | missing |
| Graham, John | do | 26 April 78 | 13 Aug 78 | deserted |
| Gearrish, Sampson[4] | do | | 1 Mar 79 | discharged |
| Grieg, Harvy[10] | do | 5 May 78 | 3 Oct 78 | died |
| Gahort, Jacob | do | 1 June 78 | 1 April 79 | discharged |
| Gandy, Jacob[5] | do | 4 June 78 | Jan 80 | deserted |
| | Corpl | 27 Oct 78 | | |
| Guize, John | pt | 8 June 78 | 30 Mar 79 | discharged |
| Givens, Ezekiel[11] | do | 11 June 78 | 11 April 79 | discharged |
| Green, Joseph[3] | do | 20 July 78 | 20 dec 78 | do |
| Green, David | Ensn | 26 Jan 80 | | |
| Green, Robert | do | | do | |

[1] Miles'.  [2] Norris'.  [3] Grosh's.  [4] Spyker's.  [5] Morris'.  [6] Bayly's.
[7] Reynolds'.  [8] Deams'.  [9] Jones'.  [10] Stull's.  [11] Beatty's.

## MUSTERS OF MARYLAND TROOPS, VOL. II.

| NAMES. | RANK. | TIME OF SERVICE. Enlisted. | Discharged. | REMARKS. |
|---|---|---|---|---|

### GERMAN REGIMENT.

| | | | | |
|---|---|---|---|---|
| Gaul, Richd. | Sergt | 16 May 78 | 1 Aug 80 | prst. |
| Grosh, Michael | pt | 1 Jany 77 | do | do |
| Grupp, John | | | 26 July 79 | discharged |
| Getig, George | | | do do | do |
| Gavan, Francis | | | do do | do |
| Gould, Edward | Mustd. sick | | 1 July 79 | |
| Gantner, Adam | | | 20 July 79 | discharged |
| Grunlin, (or Quinlin), Corns. | | Mustd. | killed at New Town July 79 | |
| Grice, Peter | see Peter Kruise | | | |
| Gambler, Michael | see Cambler | | | |

### 5TH REGIMENT.

| | | | | |
|---|---|---|---|---|
| Hindman, James | Col | 10 dec 76 | 4 April 77 | resigned |
| Hollyday, Clement | Pay Mr. | do | 25 feb 79 | resigned |
| Hindman, John | Surgeon | do | 13 Jan 78 | do |
| Hooper, E. William | Mate | 15 July 77 | 28 April 78 | do |
| Harrington, Nathan[1] | pt | 10 dec 76 | | |
| | Sergt | 1 Sept 77 | 1 feb 80 | discharged |
| Hill, William | pt | 23 July 77 | | |
| | Sergt | 26 Sept 77 | | |
| | pt | 29 Sept 78 | | |
| Houlder, John | do | 30 Mar 77 | 16 Aug 80 | prisoner |
| Halfpenny, Andrew | do | 27 April 77 | April 78 | left out |
| Harris, John[2] | do | 20 July 77 | 1 Nov 80 | present |
| Hawkins, John | Capt | 20 feb 77 | | |
| Hussey, Saml.[3] | pt | 19 May | 1 June 80 | present |
| | | | May 80 | discharged |
| Holland, John | do | 14 June | 15 Aug 79 | discharged by Capt. |
| Joined dec 78 | | | | Hawkins |
| Hall, James | do | 19 May | 1 Jan 80 | present |
| Handy, Levin | Capt | 10 dec 76 | | |
| Harrison, John[4] | pt | 12 Mar 77 | April 78 | left out |
| Hugou, B. Thomas[5] | 2d Lieut | 10 dec 76 | | |
| Herron, William | pt | 20 Jan 77 | 1 Oct 80 | present |
| Herron, John | do | 4 April 77 | April 78 | left out |
| Hanna, Robert[6] | do | 22 Jan 77 | 12 Jan 80 | discharged |
| Hillman, Wm.[7] | do | 10 dec 76 | do | do |
| Joined 20 Nov 78 | | | | |
| Hinds, James | do | 13 April 77 | 1 Jan 80 | present |
| Handy, George[8] | Ensn | 17 April 77 | 28 Aug 78 | resigned |
| | Lieut | 10 May 77 | | |

[1] Dean's, Benson's.  [2] Hamilton's.  [3] Hawkins'.  [4] Handy's.
[5] Johnson's.  [6] Emory's.  [7] Gray's.  [8] Cosden's, Bird's.

## MUSTERS OF MARYLAND TROOPS, VOL. II.

| NAMES. | RANK. | TIME OF SERVICE. Enlisted. | Discharged. | REMARKS. |
|---|---|---|---|---|
| Hadley, James | pt | 14 Jan 77 | April 78 | left out |
| Hindsley, Solomon | do | 9 feb 77 | 1 Jan 80 | present |
| Hamilton, George | Lieut | 10 dec 76 | } | |
| | Capt | 25 Jan 78 | } | |
| Hartley, John[1] | pt | | June 78 | left out |
| 1st mustr. April 78, out June 78 | | | | |
| Hart, Richard | pt | | June 78 | taken prisoner |
| 1st mustr. April 78 | | | | |
| Hailey, Daniel | do | 9 Mar 78 | | |
| Harper, Hezekiah | do | 28 feb 78 | 1 Jan 80 | present |
| Hughes, Thomas[2] | do | 7 July 77 | 6 July 78 | deserted |
| Hall, John[3] | do | 14 June 78 | | |
| Hobee, Thomas[4] | do | 2 June 78 | Aug 78 mustered not heard of, see the other side | |
| Hansfield, George[5] | do | 19 June 78 | Aug 78 | not heard of |
| 1st muster June 78 | | | | |
| Hurley, Josiah | do | 6 June 78 | feby 79 | died some months |
| Harvey, Zadock[5] | do | 5 May 78 | | [since |
| Horney, William[2] | do | 12 May 78 | Nov 80 present | |
| Hull, John | do | 12 May 78 | } | |
| | fifer | 1 April 79 | } | |
| Hughey, John, or Jona. | pt | 12 May 78 | Feby 79 | not heard of |
| Horney, Thomas[6] | do | 6 June 78 | 20 Mar 79 | discharged |
| Hawkins, James | pt | 12 May 78 | Feby 79 | died |
| Horney, John | pt | 6 June 78 | 20 Mar 79 | discharged |
| Harris, Perry | do | 6 June 78 | 2 Sept 78 | do |
| Harris, Joseph[1] | do | 4 June 78 | 1 Mar 79 | discharged |
| Hilton, Benjamin | do | 22 May 78 | | deserted |
| Mustr. Sept 78 | | | | |
| Harper, Richard | pt | 4 April 78 | 8 Aug 78 | died |
| Harwood, Nathl. | do | 22 April 78 | 10 June 78 | to Invalids |
| Holland, John | do | 4 June 78 | 8 June 78 | deserted |
| Harper, Hezekiah[2] | do | 18 April 78 | 1 Jan 80 | present |
| 1st muster June 78 | | | | |
| Hamthon, Thos. | do | 25 May 78 | 1 Oct 80 | present |
| 1st muster June 78 | | | | |
| Harper, Anthony | do | July 78 | | left out the Rolls |
| 1st mustr. June 78 & July 78 | | | | |
| Hayes, Thomas | pt | | do     do | |
| 1st muster June 78, out July 78 | | | | |
| Hall, John[4] | pt | 4 June 78 | June 79 | died |
| Hukins, John | do | 5 May 78 | 16 June 78 | deserted |

[1] Johnson's.          [2] Handy's.          [3] Lt. Hamilton's.
[4] Hawkins'.          [5] Lynch's.          [6] Ensign Jones', Benson's.

## MUSTERS OF MARYLAND TROOPS. VOL. II.

| NAMES. | RANK. | TIME OF SERVICE. Enlisted. | Discharged. | REMARKS. |
|---|---|---|---|---|
| Hodgson, John | pt | 28 April 77 | | dischd. 28 April 80 |
| 1st muster June 78 | Joined 11 Oct 78 | | | |
| Hargedine, John[1] | pt | 28 feb 78 | 16 Aug 80 | missing |
| 1st muster June 78 | fifer | 15 Aug 78 } | | |
| | pt | 1 Sept 79 } | | |
| Hines, Thomas | do | 15 May 78 | 25 Feby 79 | discharged |
| Heath, Charles | do | 21 April 78 | 18 Aug 78 | died |
| Hill, James[2] | do | | 16 Aug 80 | missing |
| 1st muster Mar 79 | | | | |
| Hobbee, Thomas[3] | pt | 30 June 79 | 16 Aug 80 | missing |
| Joined 20 Mar 80 | | | | |
| Harris, Arthur | Ensn | 27 Aug 79 | | paid |
| Hewit, Henry[3] | pt | 17 April 79 | | |
| 1st mustr. 12 dec 79 | | | | |
| Hobbs, John[4] | do | 12 Mar 80 | | |
| Hopkins, Thomas | do | 13 feby 80 | 1 Nov 80 | present |
| Higdon, George | do | | 1 Oct 80 | do |
| Hanagan, Charles | do | | 1 Nov 80 | do |
| Hadin, George | do | 12 feb 80 | | paid |
| Hudson, Solomon | do | | 1 July 80 | deserted |
| Hudson, Asariah | do | | 1 July 80 | do |
| **SIXTH REGIMENT.** | | | | |
| Hailey, Michael[5] | pt | 20 Apl 77 | 12 April 79 | died |
| Hills, Charles | do | 21 April 78 | 1 Nov 80 | present |
| | Corpl | 5 Feby 80 | | |
| Hall, John | pt | 15 May 78 | 16 Aug 80 | prisoner |
| | Corpl | Oct 80 | | |
| Holland, Gabriel | pt | 30 Aprl 78 | 1 Jan 80 | present |
| Hayes, William | do | 15 Aprl 78 | 10 Aug 80 | deserted |
| Hagarthy, Andrew[6] | Drum | 13 Mar 77 | 1 Jany 80 | present |
| Higgins, Saml. | pt | 7 feby 77 | June 78 | to Invalids, } |
| | | | | full pay to 1 Aug 80 } |
| Harris, William[7] | pt | 10 Jany 77 | | |
| reinlisted | | | | |
| Hollyday, John, Sr. | pt | 21 April 78 | 16 Aug 80 | killed |
| Hollyday, John, Jr. | pt | 21 April 78 | 1 Nov 80 | present |
| Hart, Richard | do | 10 Mar 78 | Oct 78 | deserted |
| Hynes, Andrew | Capt | 10 dec 76 | 1 Mar 79 | resigned |
| Harst, Jacob | pt | 8 dec 76 | 16 Aug 80 | prisoner |
| Hamilton, Mathew | do | 10 dec 76 | 10 dec 79 | discharged |
| Harris, Robert[8] | Capt | 10 dec 76 | 9 Nov 77 | quit the Service |

[1] Emory's.  [2] Handy's.  [3] Hawkins'.  [4] Lynch's.
[5] Ghiselin's.  [6] Dobson's.  [7] Beall's.  [8] Harris'.

## MUSTERS OF MARYLAND TROOPS, VOL. II.

| NAMES. | RANK. | TIME OF SERVICE. Enlisted. | Discharged. | REMARKS. |
|---|---|---|---|---|
| Hooper, Abram | pt | 18 feb 77 | Jan 80 | present |
| Haymond, Owen[1] | Ensn | 19 April 78 | 28 June 78 | killed |
|   now Miles' | Lieut | 10 dec 77 | | |
| Hodges, Richard | pt | 1 July 77 | Jan 80 | present |
| Hannon, Patrick | do | 9 Aug 77 | 1 Aug 80 | deserted |
| Hanson, Rezin[2] | do | 6 June 78 | } 23 July 80 | ditto |
| | Corpl | 1 Sept 78 | | |
| Haisty, James | pt | 19 June 78 | 28 June 78 | left out |
|   Joined 10 June 78 | | | | |
| Hart, John[2] | do | 2 June 78 | 1 Jan 80 | present |
|   1st muster June 78 | | | | |
| Howe, James[4] | do | 1 June 78 | 1 Aprl 79 | discharged |
| Hall, William[6] | do | 13 May 78 | 16 Aug 80 | prisoner |
| | Corpl | 1 July 78 | | |
| Harvey, William | pt | 3 June 78 | 1 Aprl 79 | discharged |
| Henny, Michael | do | 4 June 78 | do | do |
| Hawley, William[6] | do | 31 dec 76 | 1 Jan 80 | present |
|   Joined Jan 79 | | | | |
| Hamilton, Saml. | Ensn | 27 May 79 | July 80 | resigned |
| Halley, William | pt | | 16 Aug 80 | missing |
|   Oct Musters 1780 | | | | |
| Henry, Peter | pt | | 1 Nov 80 | present |
| Hatwell, Henry | do | | 16 Aug 80 | prisoner |
| Housely, John | do | 10 April 80 | 1 Nov 80 | present |

### SEVENTH REGIMENT.

| NAMES. | RANK. | Enlisted. | Discharged. | REMARKS. |
|---|---|---|---|---|
| Housley, William[7] | Sergt | 31 Jan 77 | 22 Aug 77 | prisoner |
| Harrison, Richd. | Drum | 9 Mar 77 | 1 Jan 80 | present } |
| | | | 22 feby 80 | |
| Hart, Joseph | pt | 1 Mar 77 | 1 Mar 80 | discharged |
| | Corpl | 1 June 78 | | |
| | Sergt | 30 Sept 78 | | |
| Hutchinson, Nichs.[8] | pt | 16 Jan 77 | 12 Jan 80 | discharged |
| Holden, Thomas | do | 1 Aprl 77 | 22 Aug 77 | prisoner |
| Hudson, John | do | 3 April 77 | 3 April 80 | discharged |
| Hall, John[9] | do | 20 April 77 | July 78 | off Rolls |
| Hand, Thomas | do | 23 April 77 | 11 Sept 77 | missing |
| Hare, Thomas | do | 21 April 77 | 27 Aprl 80 | discharged |
| Hollyday, Robt., or Thos. | do | 14 July 77 | Aprl & May 80 | left out of the Rolls |
| | Corpl | 16 Nov 77 } | | |
|   Corpl 4 Oct 78 | pt | 20 Mar 78 | | |

[1] Chapline's.　　[2] Ghiselin's.　　[3] Dobson's.　　[4] Trueman's.　　[5] Lt. Williams'.
[6] Daugherty's.　　[7] Jones'.　　[8] Grosh's.　　[9] Spykers'.

## MUSTERS OF MARYLAND TROOPS, VOL. II.

| NAMES. | RANK. | TIME OF SERVICE. Enlisted. | Discharged. | REMARKS. |
|---|---|---|---|---|
| Harvey, James | pt | 16 June 77 | 1 July 80 | deserted |
| Hardcastle, Peter | Sergt | 10 dec 76 | | |
| | Ensn | 10 feb 77 | | |
| | Lieut | 30 Nov 77 | | |
| Heritage, Thomas[1] | pt | 3 Aug 77 | 11 Sept 77 | missing |
| Howe, George[2] | pt | 5 dec 76 | 13 April 80 | discharged |
| July 78 returned | | | | |
| Hower, George | pt | 6 Aprl 77 | 31 July 77 | deserted |
| Harrison, William | do | 1 Jan 77 | Jan 78 | off Rolls |
| Henderson, Danl. | do | 7 Aprl 77 | 30 Mar 78 | discharged |
| Helmn, Balss.[3] | do | 6 dec 76 | 17 dec 76 | deserted |
| Hays, Thomas | do | 7 Jan 77 | 16 Aug 80 | missing |
| Hoster, Jacob | do | 21 Jan 77 | Jan 79 | deserted |
| Hall, Thomas | do | 16 feb 77 | | off Rolls |
| Hewlet, John | pt | 26 feb 77 | | do |
| Joined 10 Aug 78 | | | | |
| Hutchcraft, James | do | 6 Jan 77 | April 80 | deserted |
| Horn, Patrick, or John, | do | 28 May 77 | 22 May do | do |
| Hullet, William[4] | do | 5 June 77 | 25 Oct 80 | do |
| Hall, Joseph[5] | do | 16 Aug 80 | | missing |
| Fifer Oct 77 | F. Major | 1 Sept 77 | | |
| Holden, Habikuk | pt | | 16 Aug 80 | missing |
| Joined 10 Aug 78 | | | | |
| Heberly, Fredk. | do | | Feby 78 | off Rolls |
| Haynes, John | do | | 17 May 77 | deserted |
| Hoy, Patrick | do | | 7 dec 79 | discharged |
| Howard, William[6] | do | 8 May 78 | 21 May 78 | deserted |
| Head, George[7] | do | 30 dec 77 | 8 feb 78 | deserted |
| Ham, James[8] | do | 3 May 78 | 8 July 80 | do |
| Hurdle, Lawrence | do | 11 May 78 | 1 Nov 80 | present |
| Hooper, Robert | do | 6 June 78 | 16 Mar 79 | discharged |
| Holtzman, Henry[6] | Sergt | 11 May 78 | 26 Mar 1780 | discharged by |
| | pt | 20 Sept 79 | | Genl. Smallwood |
| Hill, Ebenezer[9] | pt | | July 78 | off Rolls |
| Hutton, William[1] | do | 23 Aprl 78 | 12 Sept 78 | deserted |
| Howell, Thomas | do | 25 Aprl 78 | 78 | off Rolls |
| Heister, Nichs. | do | 24 Aprl 78 | 1 Nov 80 | present |
| Hartley, Robert | do | 29 May 78 | 19 June 78 | deserted |
| Hopkins, John[2] | do | 16 May 78 | 19 dec 78 | died |
| Hammond, William | do | 11 May 78 | April 79 | ditto |
| Hutton, William | do | 20 May 78 | Nov & Dec 78 | ditto |

[1] Stull's.      [2] Morris'.      [3] Bayly's.      [4] Reynolds'.      [5] Deams'.
[6] Grosh's.      [7] Beatty's.      [8] Jones.'      [9] Spyker's.

## MUSTERS OF MARYLAND TROOPS, VOL. II.

| NAMES. | RANK. | TIME OF SERVICE. Enlisted. | Discharged. | REMARKS. |
|---|---|---|---|---|
| Hannagan, Patrick | pt | 9 June 78 | 16 Aug 80 | missing |
| Hill, John | do | 8 June 78 | 30 Mar 79 | discharged |
| Hunt, Jacob | do | 13 June 78 | 1 Nov 80 | present |
| Hearty, Fredk. | do | 13 June 78 | 1 Nov 80 | do |
| Hayes, Levin | do | 30 June 78 | 30 Mar 79 | discharged |
| Holloway, John[1] | Corpl | 18 May 78 | } 8 April 79 | deserted |
| | pt | 1 Jany 79 | | |
| Humphrys, Thos.[2] | do | 20 July 78 | 22 feb 79 | discharged |
| Hopkins, William | do | 20 July 78 | 2 Mar 79 | do |
| Hammond, Edward | do | do | 9 April 79 | do |
| Holt, William | do | 29 June 78 | 9 April 79 | do |
| Hutchins, Caleb[1] | do | 11 May 78 | 18 April 79 | deserted |
| Hovington, Thomas[3] | do | 27 feb 79 | 11 April 79 | do |
| Hardman, Henry | Capt | 10 dec 76 | } | |
| | Major | 1 June 79 | } | |
| Hillman, William | pt | | Sept 80 | |
| Heading, John | do | 10 June 79 | 1 Nov 80 | present |
| Hall, Daniel[2] | do | 9 July 79 | 1 Nov 80 | do |
| Hunt, Thomas | do | 2 July 79 | 19 Mar 80 | to Invalids |
| Holson, Edward[4] | See Oldstone | | 1 July 80 | deserted |
| Hoye, Thomas[5] | pt | 25 April 78 | 1 Nov 80 | present |
| Hagan, Leonard[4] | do | 2 feb 79 | do | do |
| Joined 9 May 80 | | | | |
| Hurley, William | do | 22 feb 80 | do | do |
| Hill, Henry[6] | do | | | |
| Hampton, William[8] | do | 31 Jan 80 | 1 Nov 80 | present |
| Hagan, Walter[7] | do | 1 feb 80 | do | do |
| Hagan, Leonard | do | 1 Jany 80 | 1 Oct 80 | R. paid |

### GERMAN REGIMENT.

| NAMES. | RANK. | Enlisted. | Discharged. | REMARKS. |
|---|---|---|---|---|
| Hutchcraft, Thos. | Drum | 16 May 78 | 1 Aug 80 | present |
| Hazelip, Richd. | pt | 1 April 78 | do | do |
| Halfpenny, Thos. | do | 22 April 78 | do | do |
| Hartman, Michael | do | 15 May 78 | do | do |
| Hammersly, (or Amersly), Jno. W. | mustrd. deserted on P. R. | | 1 Aug 80 | |
| Haller, F. William | | | 18 July 79 | discharged |
| Harley, John | | | 30 July do | do |
| Hook, Joseph   3 | Corpl | | do | do |
| Herring, Henry | | | 24 do | do |
| Hull, Casimer | | | 26 do | do |
| Haseligh, Jacob | | | 1 Aug 80 | present |

[1] Beatty's.  [2] Grosh's.  [3] Dove's.  [4] L. Beall's.  [5] Lamar's.  [6] Jones'.  [7] Mason's.

15

## MUSTERS OF MARYLAND TROOPS, VOL. II.

| NAMES. | RANK. | TIME OF SERVICE. Enlisted. | Discharged. | REMARKS. |
|---|---|---|---|---|
| Hazlewood, Thos. 9 mo. | | | 20 Mar 79 | discharged |
| Heffner, Jacob | | | 12 Oct 79 | do |
| Hose, Jacob | Sergt | | 26 July 78 | do |
| Hochshield, John | Corpl | | 24 do | do |
| Hockett, Jonathan | | | 25 Aug 79 | deserted |
| Heron, John | Sergt | 12 Aug 75 | 24 July 79 | discharged |
| Hewer, or Hoover, Peter | | | 12 Oct 79 | do |
| Hemerick, (or Emerick), Peter | | | 24 July 79 | do |
| Hatfield, John | | | 26 July 79 | do |
| Hain, Henry | Ensn | | | resigned |
| Hile, Conrad | See Conrad Stoyle | | | |
| Hoover, Jacob | | | 12 Oct 79 | discharged |
| Hughes, James | pt | | 1 Aug 80 | present |
| Hausman, Conrad | | | 26 July 79 | discharged |
| Haninghouse, Dedrick | | | do | do |

### FIFTH REGIMENT.

| NAMES. | RANK. | Enlisted. | Discharged. | REMARKS. |
|---|---|---|---|---|
| Jones, Thomas[1] | Ensn | 20 feb 77 | 13 Oct 78 | resigned |
| Joyse, Thomas | pt | 22 Mar 77 | Aug 78 | off Rolls |
| Johnston, Jacob[2] | do | 20 May | 16 Aug 80 | missing |
| Johnston, John | do | 27 May | 1 Oct 79 | transferred to Major |
| Jordan, John | do | 10 Augt | 1 Oct 80 | present    [Lee's |
| Mustered Q. M. Oct 80 | | | | |
| Johnson, Thomas[3] | Corpl | 2 Jan 77 | } 12 April 79 | deserted |
| | pt | 4 April 78 | | |
| Jones, Benjamin[4] | do | 26 dec 76 | Aug 78 | off Rolls |
| Jones, Aaron | do | 1 Jan 77 | 1 Nov 80 | present |
| Johnson, Josiah | Capt | 10 dec 76 | 1 Nov 78 | Invalids |
| Mustered Jan 79 absent, sick since Sept 1777 | | | left out April & May muster 79 | |
| Jones, Jacob[5] | Ensn | 20 feby 77 | 27 Jan 78 | resigned |
| Jordan, John | pt | 15 feb 77 | July 78 | left out |
| Ingram, Abraham[6] | Sergt | 25 Jan 77 | 16 Jan 80 | discharged |
| Jenkins, Joseph | pt | 16 Mar 77 | 16 Mar 80 | do |
| Jenkins, Samuel | do | 18 feb 77 | 1 Oct 79 | transferred, not heard of since |
| Jeffers, Richard | do | 2 Aug 77 | 7 Mar 79 | deserted & 6 Jan. 80 discharged |
| Jeffers, William | do | 5 Mar 77 | 16 feby 80 | discharged |
| | fifer | 1 Feby 79 | | |
| | pt | 1 Sept 79 | | |

[1] Dean's.　　[2] Hawkins'.　　[3] Lynch's.　　[4] Handy's.　　[5] Johnson's.　　[6] Emory's, Gray's.

## MUSTERS OF MARYLAND TROOPS, VOL. II.

| NAMES. | RANK. | TIME OF SERVICE. Enlisted. | Discharged. | REMARKS. |
|---|---|---|---|---|
| Ingram, William | pt | 18 Mar 77 | 18 July 80 | deserted |
| Joined 1 May 79 | | | | |
| Johnson, Nichols[1] | pt | 27 May 77 | 27 Mar 80 | discharged |
| Joined 20 May 78 | | | | |
| James, William[2] | do | | 17 Mar 78 | deserted |
| 1st muster April 78 | | | | |
| Jones, Thomas[3] | pt | 10 Mar 78 | | |
| | Corpl | 1 April 78 | | |
| | Sergt | 1 June 78 | 1 Nov 80 | present |
| Jones, Benjamin | pt | 1 April 78 | 16 Aug 80 | missing |
| | Drum | 1 May 79 | | |
| | pt | 1 June 79 | | |
| Jones, Richard[1] | do | 2 June 78 | 1 Jan 80 | present |
| rein. 19 Feby 79 | | | | |
| Jones, John[2] | do | 2 June 78 | 16 June 78 | deserted |
| Impy, Michael[4] | pt | 4 June 78 | 19 Mar 79 | discharged |
| Johnson, Robert | pt | 8 June 78 | Dec 78 mustrd. not heard of since 18 June 78 | |
| Johnson, Mason | pt | 14 May 78 | July 78 | left out |
| Jones, James[5] | pt | 4 June 78 | 5 Jan 80 | deserted |
| Johnson, Abram[6] | pt | | 15 July 78 | deserted |
| 1st mustr. June 78 | | | | |

### SIXTH MARYLAND REGIMENT.

| NAMES. | RANK. | Enlisted. | Discharged. | REMARKS. |
|---|---|---|---|---|
| Jacob, Jesse | Sergt | 23 July 77 | 1 Nov 80 | present |
| Jacobs, George | Ensn | 20 feb 77 | | |
| | Lieut | 14 July 77 | | |
| Jackson, John[7] | pt | 16 May 77 | Sept 80 | sick Virginia, pst. |
| Ireland, George[8] | Lieut | 20 feb 77 | 3 Oct 78 | resigned [Oct 80 |
| Jenkins, Francis | Sergt | 9 June 77 | 1 Jan 80 | present |
| | pt | 20 April 78 | 16 May 80 | discharged |
| Johnston, Thomas[9] | Corpl | 11 Jan 77 | 11 Jan 80 | ditto |
| | pt | 1 Oct 79 | | |
| Jones, Thomas | pt | 24 Aprl 77 | 16 Aug 80 | deserted |
| Jacobs, Jno. Jeremh.[10] | Lt. Pay Mr. | 1 Oct 78 | | |
| Johnson, John[11] | pt | 22 Aprl 78 | 1 Jan 80 | present |
| Jenkins, Jehu | do | 20 May 78 | Aprl & May 79 | not heard of |
| 1st must. June 78 | | | | |
| Javers, Daniel[12] | do | 23 May 78 | 1 Nov 80 | present |
| Johnson, George | do | 19 May 78 | 16 Aug 80 | missing |
| Johnson, John | do | 4 June 78 | 16 Aug 80 | do |

[1] Ensign Jones'.  [2] Johnson's.  [3] Lynch's.  [4] Handy's.  [5] Hawkins'.  [6] Emory's.
[7] Dobson's.  [8] Trueman's.  [9] Beall's.  [10] Hynes'.  [11] Lt. Williams'.  [12] Miles'.

## MUSTERS OF MARYLAND TROOPS, VOL. II.

| NAMES. | RANK. | TIME OF SERVICE. Enlisted. | Discharged. | REMARKS. |
|---|---|---|---|---|

### SEVENTH REGIMENT.

| | | | | |
|---|---|---|---|---|
| Jones, Jno. Courts[1] | Lieut | 10 dec 76 ⎫ | | |
| | Capt | 28 dec 77 ⎭ | | |
| Johnson, James | pt | 10 feb 77 ⎫ 11 feb 80 | | discharged |
| | Corpl | 1 July 77 ⎭ | | |
| James, John | pt | 10 feb 77 | May 78 | off Rolls |
| Jenkins, Thomas[2] | do | 15 dec 76 | 6 Jan 80 | discharged |
| to Beatty's Co. | Sergt | 24 feb 78 | | |
| Justice, Charles[3] | pt | | 17 May 77 | deserted |
| Jones, James, or John[4] | do | 16 May 78 | 1 Jany 80 | present |
| Johns, John[5] | do | 21 May 78 | 1 Nov 80 | do |
| Jones, Dennis | do | 5 May 78 | 13 June 79 | deserted |
| Jones, William | do | 28 April 78 | 1 April 79 | do |
| Jones, William[6] | do | 20 May 78 | May 79 | died |
| Jones, Samuel[2] | do | 6 June 78 | 29 June 79 | deserted |
| Johnson, Simon | do | 13 April 78 | 25 June 78 | do |
| Johns, James[6] | pt | 30 June 78 | 30 Mar 79 | discharged |
| Jarvis, Cato[4] | do | 18 May 78 | 9 April 79 | do |
| Isham, Joshua[7] | Drum | | 1 Nov 80 | present |
| James, Thomas[8] | pt | 13 May 78 | 16 Aug 80 | prisoner |
| Jackson, John[4] | do | 12 June 79 | 8 dec 79 | discharged |

### GERMAN REGIMENT.

| | | | | |
|---|---|---|---|---|
| Jones, Charles | Sergt | 7 June 78 | 1 Aug 80 | present |
| Johnson, William | Sergt | 16 May 78 | 1 do | do |
| Jacquett, Danl. | do | | 26 July 79 | discharged |
| Johnston, James | no pay from Sep 79 | | 1 Aug 80 | mustrd. dest. |

### FIFTH MARYLAND REGIMENT.

| | | | | |
|---|---|---|---|---|
| Keach, Ebenezer[9] | pt | 9 Sept 77 | April 78 | off Rolls |
| Kennedy, Saml[10] | Corpl | 1 April 77 | do | do |
| | Sergt | 12 April 77 | sick in Maryland pr. cert. Dep. | |
| Kelly, David | pt | 20 feb 77 | 1 Nov 80 | present [acct. |
| Kent, Stephen[11] | do | 7 Mar 77 | 30 Mar 80 | deserted |
| King, Levin[12] | Ensn | 20 feb 77 | 8 Nov 77 | resigned |
| Kelty, William | S. Mate | 28 April 78 ⎫ | | |
| | Surgeon | 1 April 1780 ⎭ | | |
| Kincaid, John[13] | pt | | Aug 78 | not heard of |
| 1st muster April 78 | | | | |
| Kincaid, Peter | do | 4 May 78 | 1 Nov 80 | present |
| Kidney, Michael[14] | pt | 20 May 78 | do | do |

[1] Jones'.  [2] Bayly's.  [3] Deams'.  [4] Grosh's.  [5] Stull's.
[6] Morris'.  [7] Lynn's.  [8] Beatty's.  [9] Hawkins'.  [10] Lynch's.
[11] Johnson's.  [12] Emory's.  [13] Hamilton's.  [14] Handy's.

## MUSTERS OF MARYLAND TROOPS, VOL. II.

| NAMES. | RANK. | TIME OF SERVICE. Enlisted. | Discharged. | REMARKS. |
|---|---|---|---|---|
| Kinnahan, John[1] | pt | 6 June 78 | 1 Nov 80 | present |
| Joined 2 Oct 80 | | | | |
| Kerby, Nathaniel | pt | 6 June 78 | feby 79 | mustr. not heard |
| Knowland, Lucas[2] | do | 22 May 79 | Jan 80 | present      [of |
| Kelson, George[3] | do | 2 April 79 | 1 Nov 80 | present |
| Kelly, William | do | do | do | do |
| | Drum | Oct 80 | | |
| King, Charles | pt | | 16 Sept 80 | deserted |

### SIXTH REGIMENT.

| NAMES. | RANK. | Enlisted. | Discharged. | REMARKS. |
|---|---|---|---|---|
| Kennick, William[4] | Sergt | 12 feb 77 | | |
| | Sergt Major | 12 Sept 77 } 12 feb 80 | | discharged |
| Kach, John[5] | pt | 16 July 77 | 16 May 80 | discharged |
| Kersey, Edward | pt | 21 April 78 | 1 Jan 80 | present |
| Knight, Isaac | do | 19 May 78 | 4 April 79 | transferred to In- |
| Kerrick, Joseph[6] | pt | 21 Jan 77 | 24 Aug 80 | deserted   [valids |
| reduced 9 Aprl 79 | Corpl | 3 Aug 78 | | |
| Corpl 1 Sept 79 | | | | |
| King, Francis | pt | 26 feb 77 | 1 Jan 80 | present |
| | Corpl | 10 April 79 | | |
| Kattakan, Joseph[7] | pt | 18 April 77 | Mar 78 | left out |
| Kearns, James | do | 8 July 77 | 1 Jan 80 | present |
| Kelly, Patrick[8] | Corpl | 29 Mar 77 | | |
| | pt | Aug 78 | Sept 78 | left out |
| Kearns, Thomas | do | 14 dec 76 | | |
| Joined July 79 | | | | |
| Keough, William | pt | 20 Mar 77 | | |
| Kennedy, William[9] | do | 11 June 78 | 15 Oct 78 | died |
| Heidley, Henry[10] | do | 8 June 78 | 8 Mar 79 | time expired |
| 1st muster June 78 | | | | |
| Kirshaw, William[4] | do | 1 June 78 | 1 April 79 | time expired, } mustr. Hos- } pital 1 Nov 78 } |
| Kelly, Thomas[11] | pt | 22 April 78 | 17 June 78 | discharged |
| Kernan, Martin | do | 22 May 78 | 3 Jan 79 | do |
| Kernan, Michael[11] | pt | 18 May 78 | 16 Aug 80 | missing |
| Knave, Henry[12] | pt | 16 feb 77 | 1 Jan 80 | present, dischd. 12 feb 80 |
| Kelly, Edward[6] | do | 21 April 78 | 26 April 78 | deserted |
| Koik, Benja. H.[13] | Fifer | 6 Mar 77 | 24 Aug 80 | do |

[1] Ensign Jones'.   [2] Lynch's.   [3] Handy's.   [4] Trueman's.   [5] Beall's.
[6] Hynes'.   [7] Harris'.   [8] Chapline's.   [9] Ghiselin's.   [10] Dobson's.
[11] Lt. Williams'.   [12] Miles'.   [13] Jacobs'.

## MUSTERS OF MARYLAND TROOPS, VOL. II.

| NAMES. | RANK. | TIME OF SERVICE. Enlisted. | Discharged. | REMARKS. |
|---|---|---|---|---|
| | | SEVENTH REGIMENT. | | |
| Kinney, John[1] | Corpl | 13 April 77 | Aug 77 | left out of the |
| Kelly, Thomas[2] | pt | 30 dec 76 | 16 Aug 80 | missing    [Rolls |
| Joined 22 Mar 80 | | | | |
| Keefe, Thomas | pt | 10 Jan 77 | 1 Nov 80 | present |
| | drum | 16 feb 79 | | |
| Knowland, Michael | pt | 1 April 77 | 1 April 80 | discharged |
| Kelly, Thomas[3] | do | 15 Aug 77 | 7 Sept 78 | deserted |
| Keland, James[4] | Corpl | 7 dec 76 | 16 Aug 80 | missing |
| | pt | 2 dec 77 | | |
| Knox, John | do | 2 Sept 77 | joined from Pennsylvania Line |
| Joined 1 May 78 | | | | [in 1782 |
| Kelly, Daniel[5] | do | 21 Jan 77 | July 77 | off Rolls |
| Kelly, George | do | 14 Mar 77 | April 80 | discharged |
| Joined May 77 | | | | |
| Keys, Patrick | do | 19 Jan 77 | 3 June 79 | deserted |
| Joined June 78 | | | | |
| Kelly, George[6] | do | 22 May 77 | 22 June 77 | do |
| Kinsey, Samuel[7] | Lieut | 8 dec 76 | | |
| Kennedy, Thomas | pt | | 16 July 77 | discharged |
| Kinchley, Morgan[1] | do | 6 June 78 | 16 Aug 80 | missing |
| Kindle, William[8] | do | 25 April 78 | 1 Nov 80 | present |
| King, John | do | 28 April 78 | 1 Nov 80 | do |
| Keen, William[5] | do | 17 April 78 | 25 June 78 | deserted |
| Kinsee, George[4] | do | 4 June 78 | Nov 78 | left off the Rolls |
| Keitley, Francis[9] | do | 30 June 78 | 1 Nov 80 | present |
| Kelly, James[10] | do | 14 feb 80 | do | do |
| | Corpl | 1 May 80 | | |
| King, John | pt | 25 April 78 | 25 April 81 | discharged |
| Kenny, William[11] | do | 22 Jan 80 | 9 July 80 | deserted |
| | | GERMAN REGIMENT. | | |
| Kruise, Peter | | | 24 July 79 | discharged |
| Kuntz, Philip | | | 15    do | do |
| Kibber, John | | | 26    do | do |
| Keyer, Keiser, Mathias | | | 26    do | do |
| Kelly, Patrick | Corpl | 24 July 76 | 24    do | do |
| Kendrick, John | | | July 79 | deserted |
| Kline, or Cline, John | | | 12 Oct 79 | discharged, appeared 5 May, |
| Keplinger, Chresn. 9 mo. | | | 22 Mar 79 | do    [1789 |

[1] Jones'.    [2] Grosh's.    [3] Spyker's.    [4] Morris'.    [5] Bayly's.    [6] Reynolds'.
[7] Deams'.    [8] Stull's.    [9] Lynn's.    [10] Mason's.    [11] L. Beall's.

## MUSTERS OF MARYLAND TROOPS, VOL. II.

| NAMES. | RANK. | TIME OF SERVICE. Enlisted. | Discharged. | REMARKS. |
|---|---|---|---|---|
| Kettle, Abram | pt | 3 April 79 | 1 Aug 80 | prst. |
| Keyser, Jacob | Sergt | 13 feb 79 | do | do |
| Kettle, Daniel | | 1 Nov 79 | do | do |
| Kerns, Francis | pt | 1 June 78 | 1 Aug 80 | present |
| Koons, Peter | do | do | | do |
| Keephart, Geo. | pt | 13 feb 78 | do | do |
| Kershner, Michael | | 16 July 79 | | discharged |
| Kline, Jacob | | | 26 do | do |
| Kentz, Jacob | | | 30 do | do |
| Kaufman, Jacob | See John Caufman | | | . |

### FIFTH MARYLAND REGIMENT.

| NAMES. | RANK. | TIME OF SERVICE. Enlisted. | Discharged. | REMARKS. |
|---|---|---|---|---|
| Lawrence, James[1] | pt | 30 May 77 | 1 Nov 80 | present |
| Lofman, Benjamin | do | 6 Aug 77 | 1 Jan 80 | do |
| Lyon, John | Corpl private } | 13 May | 8 May 80 | discharged |
| Lynch, John | Capt | 10 dec 76 | | |
| Lord, Andrew[2] | pt | 8 Aug 77 | 23 Mar 80 | prisoner |
| Lomax, Theops.[3] | do | 31 Mar 77 | 16 Aug 80 | missing |
| Lucas, John[4] | do | 7 Sept 77 | 1 Nov 80 | present |
| | Corpl | Oct 80 | | |
| Lloyd, Joseph | do | 22 Sept 77 | 1 Jan 80 | do |
| Linex, James[5] | Sergt | 13 Jan 77 | | |
| pt 2 Sept 78 | | | | |
| Corpl 1 Nov 78 } pt 30 June 79, pt 19 April 78 | | | | private |
| | Sergt | 1 June 78 | 12 Jany 80 | discharged as |
| Lewis, Richard[6] | pt | | 1 Feb 80 | dead or deserted |
| 1st mustr. April 78 | Corpl | 15 June 78 | | |
| Lawrence, William | pt | Aug 78 | 16 Nov 79 | to Invalids, discharged |
| Lawrence, David[7] | do | 12 Jan 77 | May 79 | not heard of |
| 1st mustr. April 78 | | | | |
| Lowrey, James[7] | do | 1 Mar 78 | | |
| 1st mustr. April 78 | | | 2 Jan 81 | discharged |
| Loe, Henry | do | 1 Mar 78 | | [with Genl. Palaskey } |
| 1st mustr. April 78 Nathan Duley of 2nd Regt. asserts that Low never enlisted } | | | | |
| Lord, Henry[2] | pt | 2 June 78 | | |
| Lowry, John[7] | do | 6 June 78 | 1 Mar 79 | discharged |
| Lee, Jeremiah | pt | 19 May 78 | See below | |
| Ledenham, Nathl.[8] | do | 6 June 78 | Feby 79 | deserted |
| Layton, Jehu[3] | do | 4 June 78 | 19 Oct 78 | died |

[1] Hawkins'.  [2] Lynch's.  [3] Johnson's.  [4] Emory's.
[5] Cosden's, Gray's.  [6] Lt. Hamilton's.  [7] Handy's.  [8] Ensign Jones',

## MUSTERS OF MARYLAND TROOPS, VOL. II.

| NAMES. | RANK. | TIME OF SERVICE. Enlisted. | Discharged. | REMARKS. |
|---|---|---|---|---|
| Longfellow, Thos.[1] | pt | 4 June 78 | 16 Aug 80 | missing |
| Lee, Jeremiah[2] | do | 19 May 78 | 1 Oct 80 | present |
| 1st mustr. July 79 | | died some short time after this says Capt. Benson | | |
| Lahea, William[3] | pt | | 16 Aug 80 | missing |
| Linthicum, Francis | | | 16 Aug 80 | missing |
| Lilly, Robert | pt | | Sept 80 | deserted |

### SIXTH MARYLAND REGIMENT.

| NAMES. | RANK. | Enlisted. | Discharged. | REMARKS. |
|---|---|---|---|---|
| Lowther, James[4] | pt | 23 Aug 77 | 24 Nov 78 | deserted |
| Lintridge, Saml. | pt | 26 April 78 | 25 June 79 | do |
| Laukin, John[5] | do | 21 feb 77 | 1 July 79 | deserted |
| Joined 15 April 79 | Joined Aug 79 | | | |
| Linian, Darby | pt | 13 May 77 | 1 Jan 80 | present |
| Lock, George | do | 11 feby 78 | do | do |
| Linsey, Oliver[6] | pt | 5 dec 76 | } 5 Dec 79 | time expired |
| | Corpl | 13 Aprl 77 | | |
| Lawrence, Levin | Capt | 1 Aprl 77 | 1 Aprl 78 | resigned |
| Long, Joseph[7] | pt | 16 Aprl 77 | 1 Nov 80 | present |
| Longden, Joseph[4] | do | 13 June 78 | 17 Jan 80 | deserted |
| Loud, George | do | 1 July 78 | 1 June 79 | do |
| 1 July 78 Joined, rein. | | | | |
| Lee, Dudley | pt | 1 July 78 | 1 Aprl 79 | dischgd., reinlisted |
| 1 July 78 Joined | | | | |
| Litt, Daniel | pt | 1 July 78 | 1 April 79 | discharged |
| Love, John[8] | pt | 28 May 78 | 1 Nov 80 | present |
| 1st muster June 78, rein. 22 dec 78 | | | | |
| Leonard, Adam[9] | pt | 3 June 78 | 4 feb 79 | discharged |
| Layzer, Adam | do | 30 May 78 | 1 April 79 | time out, dis- |
| 1st muster June 78 | | | | charged |
| Lewis, William[10] | do | 3 May 78 | 4 feb 79 | discharged |
| Lawless, John[9] | do | 11 May 78 | May 78 | deserted |
| Lincoln, John[11] | do | 27 April 79 | 1 Nov 80 | present |
| Loyce, Peter | do | 9 May 79 | 1 Jan 80 | do |
| Linn, John | Lieut | 1 June 79 | 1 Nov 80 | do |
| Longley, James | pt | | 16 Aug 80 | prisoner |

### SEVENTH MARYLAND REGIMENT.

| NAMES. | RANK. | Enlisted. | Discharged. | REMARKS. |
|---|---|---|---|---|
| Love, William[12] | pt | 11 feb 77 | 11 Feb 80 | discharged |
| Lowe, William | do | 17 feb 77 | Mar 78 | off Rolls |
| Lamar, William | Ensn | 14 feb 77 | } | |
| Acting Q. Mr. July 78 5 July Lt | 28 dec 77 | | | |

[1] Handy's.    [2] Benson's.    [3] Hawkins'.    [4] Ghiselin's.    [5] Beall's.    [6] Hynes'.
[7] Chapline's.    [8] Dobson's.    [9] Lt. Williams'.    [10] Trueman's.    [11] Lt. Norris'.    [12] Jones'.

## MUSTERS OF MARYLAND TROOPS, VOL. II.

| NAMES. | RANK. | TIME OF SERVICE. Enlisted. | TIME OF SERVICE. Discharged. | REMARKS. |
|---|---|---|---|---|
| Linn, David[1] | Lt | 10 dec 76 ⎫ | | |
| | Capt | 22 May 79 ⎭ | | |
| Lewis, Basil | pt | 6 dec 76 | July 77 | off Rolls |
| Lynch, Patrick | do | 6 feb 77 | 1 Jan 80 | present |
| Life, Robert[2] | do | 6 dec 76 | 18 April 77 | deserted |
| Lynch, Patrick | do | 22 May 77 | 22 May 80 | discharged |
|   Joined 22 May 80 | | | | |
| Lochlin, Michael | pt | 17 Nov 77 | 16 Aug 80 | missing |
| Lee, Thomas[3] | pt | 18 May 77 | 1 May 80 | deserted |
| Lard, William | do | 3 June 77 | Dec 77 | off Rolls |
| Lawson, Ralph[4] | do | | feb 78 | do |
| Lee, Timothy[5] | do | 18 Jan 78 | 12 feb 78 | deserted |
| Lingo, Thomas[6] | do | | Aug 78 | dead |
|   1st muster June 78 | | | | |
| Lister, Joshua[7] | do | 22 May 78 | 1 Nov 80 | mustrd. Hosptl. Annapolis |
| Lieth, Alexander[7] | do | | 1 Mar 79 | discharged |
| Longfellow, Andw.[8] | do | 20 July 78 | 12 feb 79 | do |
| Lowry, John[6] | do | 28 April 78 | 16 Aug 80 | missing |
| Leonard, Robert[9] | do | 9 Aug 79 | 16 Aug 80 | do |
| Leakins, William | do | 20 Aug 79 | 1 Nov 80 | present |
| Lee, Joseph[6] | do | 21 feb 80 | 16 Aug 80 | missing |
| Larry, William[10] | do | 15 feb 80 | 11 Sept 80 | deserted |
| Love, David[11] | Sergt | 8 Sept 79 | 1 Nov 80 | present |
| Loveday, John[10] | pt | 20 April 80 | do | do |

### GERMAN REGIMENT.

| NAMES. | RANK. | TIME OF SERVICE. Enlisted. | TIME OF SERVICE. Discharged. | REMARKS. |
|---|---|---|---|---|
| Lecrose, John | pt | 12 Mar 80 | 1 Aug 80 | present |
| Larmore, Thomas | do | | 7 Aug 79 | ⎱ prst., dischgd., |
| | | | 1 Aug 80 | ⎰ reinlisted 30 mar |
| Lago, Charles | pt | 1 April 80 | 1 Aug 80 | present [80, present |
| Lowe, Jacob | Sergt | Aug 76 | 1 Aug 80 | prst., dischgd. 21 |
| Leithusier, George | | | 22 July 79 | discharged [feb 81 |
| Larantz, Fredk. | | | 15 do | do |
| Lorantz, Vendel | | | 20 July | do |
| Ladder, John | Sergt | | 9 Aug 79 | discharged |
| Lewis, William | do | | 16 July 79 | do |
| Locker, Fredk. | | | 9 Aug 79 | do |
| Lantz, Martin | | | 15 July 79 | do |
| Ludwick, Leonard | | | 24 do | do |
| Lawrey, Galfried | | | 1 Oct 79 | do |

[1] Morris'.    [9] Bayly's.    [3] Reynolds'.    [4] Deams'.    [5] Beatty's.    [6] Jones'.
[7] Spyker's.    [8] Grosh's.    [9] Anderson's.    [10] Lynn's.    [11] Lamar's.

## MUSTERS OF MARYLAND TROOPS, VOL. II.

| Names. | Rank. | Time of Service. Enlisted. | Discharged. | Remarks. |
|---|---|---|---|---|

### Fifth Maryland Regiment.

| Names. | Rank. | Enlisted. | Discharged. | Remarks. |
|---|---|---|---|---|
| McKey, William | Q. M. Sgt. | 14 Oct 77 | 1 feb 79 | ¦to Hide department |
| | | | 14 April 80 | discharged |
| Mead, James | Drm. Major | 10 dec 76 | transffd. 11 June 77 | |
| McQuay, Thomas[1] | pt | 10 Mar 77 | 1 Jan 80 | present |
| | | | 8 Mar 80 | discharged } |
| Maddin, Nathan | do | 10 dec 76 | do | do |
| Murphy, John | Corpl | 15 Sept 78 | | |
| | Sergt | 1 April 79 | | |
| | pt | 20 April 77 | | |
| | Sergt | 24 feb 80 | | |
| McCone, Thomas | pt | 13 Jan 77 | Aprl 78 | left out |
| Moreland, Henry[2] | Corpl | 22 May | | |
| | pt | 1 Aprl 79 | } was carried home by Lt. Benton and detained in May till time out | |
| Meconican, Elias | Corpl | 6 June | 1 Jan 80 | present |
| | pt | 1 feb 78 | 16 May 80 | discharged |
| Mills, Edward | do | 24 July | 15 Aug 78 | died |
| McBride, James[3] | pt | 20 feb 77 | 22 May 78 | discharged |
| Murray, Mathew | do | 17 feb 77 | 25 June 78 | deserted |
| Mills, John[4] | pt | 11 Mar | | |
| to Bird's | Sergt | 10 May | } July 79 | Forage department |
| | pt | 16 Aug 79 | 18 feb 80 | discharged |
| McDaniel, John[5] | do | 30 Jan 77 | 10 Jan 80 | discharged |
| McDaniel, Anguish | Corpl | 1 Jan 77 | 12 Jan 80 | do |
| McHalsey, or Halfey, Ben. mustd. Sept 78 | pt | 6 Jan 77 | | |
| Morgan, William[6] | Sergt | 23 Jany 77 | April 78 | left out |
| Markey, William | do | 4 dec 76 | 14 Oct 77 | Q. Mr., left out |
| Magee, Josiah | do | 29 July 77 | 1 Jan 80 | present [Aprl 78 |
| | Corpl | 12 Jan 80 | 16 May 80 | discharged |
| Murphy, Thomas | do | 16 Jan 77 | | |
| | Sergt | 22 dec 77 | } 12 Jan 80 | discharged |
| Murphy, James | Corpl | 16 Jan 77 | dec 78 | left out, unfit for duty |
| | | | 16 Jan 80 | dischgd. from Invalids |
| Miles, Thomas | pt | 25 Aprl 77 | | |
| | Corpl | 10 Sept 77 | } 16 Aug 80 | missing |
| | Sergt | 1 Nov 78 | | |
| McDermot, Michael | pt | 20 Mar 77 | | |
| | Corpl | 22 dec 77 | } 5 Aprl 77 | deserted |
| Melles, William | pt | 18 July 77 | 29 feb 78 | died |

[1] Dean's.     [2] Hawkins'.     [3] Lynch's.     [4] Handy's.     [5] Johnson's.
[6] Emory's.

## MUSTERS OF MARYLAND TROOPS, VOL. II.

| NAMES. | RANK. | TIME OF SERVICE. Enlisted. | Discharged. | REMARKS. |
|---|---|---|---|---|
| Moore, Robert | pt | 9 Mar 77 | Sept 78 | not heard of |
| Mitchel, Saml. | do | 10 dec 76 } | | |
| | Corpl | 22 Oct 78 } | 12 Jan 80 | discharged |
| McLane, John | pt | 18 feb 77 | 3 Aprl 80 | do |
| Moore, Smith[1] | 2d Lieut | 10 dec 76 | 10 May 77 | resigned |
| Murphy, Edward | pt | 23 dec 76 | 20 dec 79 | discharged |
| Marrough, James | do | 14 Jan 77 | 13 dec 79 | do |
| Morrindon, Michael[2] | Corpl | 13 Mar 77 | 13 Mar 80 | do |
| 1st muster April 78 | Joined as private 16 May 79 | | | |
| Marr, David | Drum | 8 dec 76 | | |
| McWilliams, Wm.[3] | pt | 6 dec 76 | 6 dec 79 | discharged |
| McKinsey, Wm.[3] | Drum | | Aug 78 | off Rolls, to Invalids |
| 1st muster April 78, out Aug 78 | | | 16 May 79 | discharged |
| McDonald, Danl.[4] | pt | 30 June 78 | 15 Mar 79 | deserted 21 Jan |
| 1st muster April 78 | | | | 80 desertd. |
| Maloney, Wm.[5] | pt | 3 May 77 } | 29 Aug 78 | deserted |
| Joined April 78, to Emory's Co. | | | | |
| Mason, Arthur[3] | pt | 22 April 77 | 1 Jan 80 | present |
| | | | 25 Aprl 80 | discharged |
| McIntosh, John[3] | do | 4 June 78 | 30 Sept 78 | died |
| Massey, Jesse | do | 9 June 78 | Aug 78 | not heard ot |
| McFarlin, Charles[6] | pt | | | never joined |
| 1st muster June 78, out July 78 | | | | |
| Madding, Sampson | pt | 20 May 78 | 1 Mar 79 | discharged |
| Mooney, William | do | 2 June 78 | | inlisted with Genl. Palaskey |
| McGinney, Solomon[3] | do | 15 May 78 | 11 Aprl 79 | deserted |
| McKernal, Thomas | do | 5 feb 78 | 1 Oct 80 | present |
| Mason, John | do | 4 June 78 | 1 Mar 79 | discharged |
| Mann, Jesse | do | 16 May 78 | 1 Nov 80 | present |
| McDonald, Charles | do | 19 May 78 | 6 June 78 | deserted |
| Murphey, Wm. | pt | 15 May 78 | Feby 79 | not heard of |
| Murphey, John | do | 10 June 78 | 1 July 78 | deserted |
| McCarty, Thomas[4] | do | 22 Aug 77 | 21 feb 80 | deserted |
| Murray, James | pt | 2 June 78 | 16 Aug 80 | missing |
| rein. 16 dec 79 | | | | |
| McKay, Isaac | pt | 4 June 78 | 26 Mar 79 | discharged |
| McKay, John | do | 4 April 78 | 1 Nov 80 | present |
| | | | 14 feb 82 | discharged |
| Murray, William | pt | 22 Aprl 78 | 1 Jan 80 | present |
| mustd. Sept 78, reinlisted Dec 79 | | | | |
| Morgan, Thomas[3] | pt | 25 May 78 | 1 Nov 78 | died |
| 1st muster June 78 | | | | |

[1] Cosden's.   [2] Hamilton's.   [3] Handy's.   [4] Johnson's.   [5] Hawkins'.   [6] Lynch's.

## MUSTERS OF MARYLAND TROOPS, VOL. II.

| NAMES. | RANK. | TIME OF SERVICE. | | REMARKS. |
|---|---|---|---|---|
| | | Enlisted. | Discharged. | |
| Merryfield, Josiah[1] | pt | 6 May 78 | 21 June 79 | deserted |
| 1st mustr. June 78 | | | | |
| Mansfield, George[2] | do | 19 June 78 | 1 Mar 79 | discharged |
| 1st mustr. dec 78 | | | | |
| Medley, Thomas[3] | pt | 10 dec 78 | 17 June 79 | deserted |
| Moore, Benjamin[2] | do | 23 Jan 77 | 9 Jan 80 | discharged |
| Joined 1 May 76 | | | | |
| McQuay, Martin[4] | pt | 2 June 79 | 1 Jan 80 | present |
| 1st muster June 79 | | | | |
| Miorley, Dennis | pt | 7 June 79 | 1 Nov 80 | do |
| 1st mustr. June 79 | | | | |
| McLemare, Wm. Cooke | pt | 6 July 79 | | |
| | drum | 1 Aug 79 | | |
| | pt | 1 Oct 79 | 1 Oct 80 | present |
| Marshall, William | do | 27 April 80 | | paid |
| Murphey, Thomas | pt | | 16 Aug 80 | missing |

### SIXTH MARYLAND REGIMENT.

| NAMES. | RANK. | Enlisted. | Discharged. | REMARKS. |
|---|---|---|---|---|
| Miller, Henry[5] | Sergt | 30 July 77 | 1 Jan 80 | present |
| Meeks, Thomas[6] | do | 21 July 77 | do | do |
| | | | 4 April 80 | discharged |
| McDonald, John | pt | 4 Sept 77 | 17 Aug 80 | deserted |
| Mondle, George | do | 4 April 78 | 1 Nov 80 | present |
| Mathews, Robert | do | 15 May 78 | do | do |
| McManis, Henry | do | 12 May 78 | 16 July 78 | deserted |
| McLeod, Robert | do | 2 May 78 | 16 Aug 80 | missing |
| McKinsey, Thomas | do | 2 May 78 | 5 Mar 79 | transferred, not |
| Miles, Joshua[7] | Lieut | 3 Aprl 77 | | [heard of |
| | Capt | 10 Oct 77 | 18 May 79 | resigned |
| Monks, James | pt | 6 feb 77 | 21 Aug 80 | deserted |
| Muldroh, Robert | do | 3 feb 77 | 19 Oct 78 | died |
| Mellone, William | pt | 17 May 77 | 16 Aug 80 | killed |
| McLiney, (or McLenchey), | | | | |
| James | do | 20 feb 77 | 1 Jan 80 | was present |
| pt 1 Jan 79 | Corpl | 1 Nov 77 | 5 feb | discharged |
| Milburn, Nicholas | pt | 22 Aprl 78 | 1 Nov 80 | present |
| Mason, John | do | 9 May 78 | 10 Aug 80 | deserted |
| Miles, John[8] | Corpl | 2 June 77 | 1 Jan 80 | was present |
| Mahanny, Thomas | pt | 14 Oct 77 | 1 Nov 80 | present |
| Martin, Michael | pt | 14 Oct 77 | 1 Jan 80 | was present |
| Moses, Francis | pt | 3 April 78 | | |
| Joined 30 Jan 79 | | | | |

[1] Hawkins'.      [2] Hamilton's.      [3] Johnson's.      [4] Lynch's.
[5] Ghiselin's.      [6] Afterwards Somerville's.      [7] Dobson's.      [8] Trueman's.

## MUSTERS OF MARYLAND TROOPS, VOL. II.

| NAMES. | RANK. | TIME OF SERVICE. Enlisted. | Discharged. | REMARKS. |
|---|---|---|---|---|
| Markell, John[1] | Lieut | 17 April 77 | 15 Aug 77 | resigned |
| Mantle, John reinlisted | Sergt | 10 Jan 77 | | |
| Moren, William Joined 20 feb 79 | pt | 24 feb 77 | | |
| Moren, Patrick | pt | 24 feb 77 | 1 Jan 80 24 feb 80 | was present discharged |
| McKindly, Wm. | do | 11 feb 78 | 16 Aug 80 | killed |
| McCrackin, Isaac[2] | Lieut | 10 dec 76 | 12 Nov 77 | resigned |
| McCreary, John | Ensn | 20 feb 77 | 7 Aug 77 | discharged |
| Moran, Edmond | Sergt Q. Mr. Lieut | 5 dec 76 17 April 77 21 May 79 | } 15 July 80 | dismissed the Service |
| Maxwell, John | pt Corpl Sergt | 1 Jan 77 16 May 77 1 Aug 77 | } 5 May 79 | died |
| McKirk, Benja. | Drum | 6 Mar 77 | See B. H. Kirk | |
| McConnell, John | fifer | 19 May 78 | Nov dec 78 | left out |
| Morgan, Richard | pt | 5 dec 76 | 5 dec 79 | discharged |
| Morgan, Benjamin | pt | 4 Jan 77 | 1 Nov 80 | present |
| Marshall, John | do | 13 Jan 77 | 1 June 79 | to Invalids |
| McCalleb, Patrick | do | 13 Jan 77 | 17 Aug 80 | deserted |
| Marshall, Robert[2] | do | 5 Mar 77 | 1 Jan 80 5 Mar 80 | was present discharged } |
| McNaiton, Wm. | do | 17 Aug 77 | 4 June 78 | deserted |
| Maunders, Thos. | do Corpl | 23 April 78 20 Jan 80 | 16 Aug 80 | prisoner |
| McCray, Henry[3] | Sergt | 22 Aug 77 | 10 June 80 | discharged |
| McDonald, Martin | pt | 10 Aug 77 | April & May 79 | mustrd. not heard of |
| Mong, Richard | do | 22 April 77 | 1 Jan 80 22 April 80 | present discharged } |
| Mitchell, John[4] Mustd. 11 Sept 77 | Sergt Joined 14 mar 78 pt | 26 May 77 4 July 78 | | |
| Moulan, Richd. | Corpl | 26 April 77 | 1 Jan 80 25 April 80 | present discharged |
| McCan, Michael | pt | 5 June 77 | 1 Nov 80 | present |
| Murray, Thomas[5] | pt Sergt pt | 10 feb 77 1 May 77 20 Aug 77 | } 16 Aug 80 | prisoner |
| Martin, William | do Corpl | 29 April 77 1 June 78 | 1 Nov 80 | present } |

[1] Beall's.    [2] Hynes'.    [3] Laurence's.    [4] Harris'.    [5] Chapline's.

## MUSTERS OF MARYLAND TROOPS, VOL. II.

| NAMES. | RANK. | TIME OF SERVICE. Enlisted. | Discharged. | REMARKS. |
|---|---|---|---|---|
| Mathews, Thomas | pt | 22 Mar 77 | 1 Jan 80 | was present |
| Mooney, Patrick | do | 3 April 77 | 16 Aug 80 | missing |
| Mahoney, Edward | do | 8 Mar 77 | 1 Jan 80 | was present } |
| | | | 8 Mar 80 | discharged |
| McDonehough, Jno.[1] | pt | 1 July 78 | 24 Nov 78 | deserted |
| 1 July 78 Joined | | | | |
| Marr, Paul | | 1 July 78 | 9 Jan 79 | do |
| 1 July 78 Joined | | | | |
| McNeale, Wm. | pt | 1 July 78 } | | |
| 1 July 78 Joined | Corpl | 1 dec 78 } 1 Nov 80 | | present |
| rein. 2 dec 78 | | | | |
| McConnell, Saml.[2] | Sergt | 10 June 78 | 1 Nov 80 | present |
| Joined June 78 | pt | 11 May 79 | 9 June 81 | discharged |
| Sergt 1 July 79 | | | | |
| McMullin, Danl. | Sergt | 10 June 78 | 1 April 79 | deserted |
| 1st mustr. June 78 | | | | |
| rein. 22 dec 78 | | | | |
| Maxwell, James | pt | 1 June 78 | 1 Nov 80 | present } |
| 1st mustr. June 78 | } Corpl | 1 Aug 79 | | |
| rein. 22 dec 78 } | | | | |
| McKenny, James[3] | pt | 1 June 78 | 25 Oct 78 | died |
| McKay, John Alexr.[4] | do | 5 May 78 } 1 Nov 80 | | present |
| | Corpl | 1 July 78 } | | |
| McDonald, Allen | pt | 28 April 78 | April & May | 79 left out |
| McCoy, James | pt | 3 June 78 | 17 dec 78 | died |
| Myers, Adam | do | 3 June 78 | 1 April 79 | discharged |
| Mong, Adam | do | 30 May 78 | 1 do | do |
| McKinley, Archibld. | do | 3 June 78 | 1 May 79 | deserted |
| McCullough, Saml. | do | 4 June 78 | 1 April 79 | do |
| reinlisted 23 dec 78 | | | | |
| Malcome, Hugh | pt | 30 May 78 | 1 April 79 | discharged |
| McFaddon, John | do | 1 June 78 | 4 feb 79 | do |
| McLaughlin, Hugh | do | 30 May 78 | 4 feb 79 | do |
| Marshall, John | do | 1 June 78 | 1 Nov 80 | present |
| rein. 20 Dec 78 | | | | |
| McLaughlin, Wm. | pt | 18 May 78 | 27 June 79 | deserted |
| May, George[5] | do | 7 May 78 | Feby 79 | do |
| Murphy, Hugh | do | 8 July 78 | 17 Mar 79 | do |
| Moore, William[6] | pt | 20 April 78 | 16 Aug 80 | missing |
| Morris, James[6] | do | 6 June 78 | 16 Aug 80 | missing |
| Mills, Benjamin | do | 1 May 78 | 1 Jan 80 | present |
| Mathews, William | do | 3 June 78 | 1 Oct 80 | do [heard of |
| Murphy, William | do | | 10 Aug 80 | transfd., not |

[1] Ghiselin's.   [2] Dobson's.   [3] Trueman's.   [4] Lt. Williams'.   [5] Hynes'.   [6] Miles'.

## MUSTERS OF MARYLAND TROOPS, VOL. II.

| NAMES. | RANK. | TIME OF SERVICE. | | REMARKS. |
|---|---|---|---|---|
| | | Enlisted. | Discharged. | |
| McCleery, Patrick[1] | pt | 9 May 78 | May 78 | deserted |
| Miles, Joshua[2] | do | 16 June 78 | 1 April 79 | discharged |
| Malone, Hugh[3] | do | | 1 Jan 80 | present |
| 1st muster July 79 | | | | |
| Murdock, William | Ensn | 6 Sept 79 | | |
| McFadgin, Abram[4] | pt | 11 Aug 79 | 17 Oct 79 | deserted   [Kill |
| May, John[3] | do | 25 Sept 79 | Sept 30 | Hospital Fish |
| Mullin, Patrick[4] | do | 21 May 77 | 1 Jan 80 | was present |
| Martin, John | pt | 10 feb 80 | 1 Nov 80 | present |
| Oct mustr. 80 | | | | |
| Moorman, Thos. | do | 28 Mar 80 | 16 Aug 80 | prisoner |

### SEVENTH REGIMENT.

| NAMES. | RANK. | Enlisted. | Discharged. | REMARKS. |
|---|---|---|---|---|
| Maddox, Walter[5] | fifer | 9 Mar 77 | 28 June 78 | killed at Mon- |
| | pt | 1 Mar 78 | | mouth |
| McGurck, James | do | 6 April 77 | 6 April 80 | discharged |
| Maybury, Benja.[6] | Sergt | 10 dec 76 | July 78 | off Rolls |
| | pt | 1 July 77 | | |
| Mahaney, Thos., (or James) | Corpl | 30 dec 76 | 27 Mar 78 | deserted |
| McMullin, James | pt | 10 Jan 77 | 3 April 79 | do |
| Mahoney, Danl. | pt | 26 Jan 77 | 12 Jan 80 | discharged |
| Murray, John | do | 6 April 77 | 12 April 80 | do |
| McManis, Thomas[7] | do | 4 June 77 | 12 May 80 | do |
| Marquis, William | pt | 24 May 77 | 12 May 80 | do |
| Miller, Joseph, (or Joshua) | do | 31 May 77 | 4 May | deserted |
| McDonald, John | do | 15 Aug 77 | 7 Sept 78 | ditto |
| Monk, William | do | 15 Aug 77 | 31 Jan 78 | to Congress Regt. for Benjamin Barnes |
| Meek, Francis[8] | pt | 10 dec 76 | 26 dec 79 | discharged |
| | Sergt | 6 May 77 | | |
| Mahoney, Saml.• | Corpl | 22 April 77 | Oct 77 | off Rolls |
| Joined Sept 77 | | | | |
| Mahoney, Michael | pt | 22 April 77 | 22 Aug 77 | missing |
| Medler, Boston | drum | 2 feb 77 | 1 Nov 80 | present |
| | drum Major | 1 May 80 | | |
| Medler, Jacob | pt | 12 April 77 | May 78 | off Rolls |
| Moore, John | do | 22 Mar 77 | May 79 | to Invalids, joined |
| Murray, Laurence | pt | 27 May 77 | June 80 | deserted |
| Mathews, William | do | 25 April 77 | Sept 77 | off Rolls |
| Minn, John | do | 3 May 77 | 4 Mar 79 | deserted |
| | Corpl | 1 Oct 77 | Joined May | |
| | pt | 10 Sept 78 | | |

[1] Williams'.    [2] Miles'.    [3] Trueman's.    [4] Norris', formerly Harris'.    [5] Jones'.
[6] Grosh's.    [7] Spyker's.    [8] Stull's.

## MUSTERS OF MARYLAND TROOPS, VOL. II.

| NAMES. | RANK. | TIME OF SERVICE. Enlisted. | Discharged. | REMARKS. |
|---|---|---|---|---|
| Mans, William | pt | 21 Aprl 77 | | |
| Joined July 78 | Corpl | 16 May 79 | | |
| Mails, John | pt | 30 June 77 | | |
| Mason, Thomas | Lieut | 10 May 77 | | |
| | Capt | 8 June 79 | | |
| Morris, Jonathan | Lieut | 2 dec 76 | | |
| | Capt | 28 dec 77 | | |
| Maguire, Thomas[1] | Sergt | 7 dec 76 | 7 dec 79 | discharged |
| | pt | 1 July 77 | | |
| Malm, Andrew | Corpl | 5 Jan 77 | | |
| from Sergt | pt | 7 Oct 78 | 6 Oct 80 | joined |
| Murrough, John | Corpl | 5 Jan 77 | Aug 77 | off Rolls |
| Morrison, George | pt | 8 dec 76 | 4 April 77 | died |
| Murphey, Patrick | do | 5 Jan 77 | 22 Aug 77 | prisoner, off Rolls June 78 |
| Manyan, Patrick | do | 18 feb 77 | 4 feb 80 | discharged |
| Mahoney, Patrick | do | 10 Mar 77 | Nov 77 | off Rolls |
| | Corpl | 1 Sept 77 | | |
| Murray, Edward | pt | 13 Mar 77 | 9 July 80 | deserted |
| McCloud, Edwd. | do | 18 Mar 77 | 31 July 77 | do |
| Maloney, Thomas | do | 23 Mar 77 | 16 Aug 80 | missing retd. & Invalided |
| Miles, Murphey | do | 6 Aprl 77 | 16 Aug 80 | missing |
| Mitchell, Francis | do | 7 Aprl 77 | 1 July 80 | |
| | | | 3 day of Aug 80 | discharged |
| Maguire, John | pt | 8 Aprl 77 | July 77 | off Rolls |
| Mooney, Patrick | do | 15 Aug 77 | 8 July 80 | deserted |
| 25 July 79 Joined | | | | |
| Murdock, Benja. | Ensn | 17 April 77 | 12 April 79 | resigned |
| | Lieut | 28 dec 77 | | |
| McDonald, George[2] | Sergt | 21 Jan 77 | 11 June 78 | deserted |
| McKinney, John | pt | 6 dec 76 | 22 Mar 77 | do |
| McDonald, Robert[2] | do | 11 feb 77 | | |
| Moore, John | do | 15 Aug 77 | 1 Nov 80 | present |
| Myers, John George[3] | Sergt | 9 May 77 | 4 Oct 77 | missing |
| | pt | 1 Sept 77 | | |
| Majors, Charles | do | 12 April 77 | June 80 | deserted |
| Mullet, William | do | 5 June 77 | See William Hulet | |
| Myers, Christopher | pt | 16 July 77 | 1 Nov 80 | present |
| McGuire, Danl. | do | 9 April 77 | 9 April 77 | deserted |
| Merrit, William[4] | Corpl | | 19 June 79 | discharged |
| Maloney, James | pt | | dec 77 | off Rolls |

[1] Morris'.    [2] Bayly's.    [3] Reynolds'.    [4] Deams'.

## MUSTERS OF MARYLAND TROOPS, VOL. II.

| NAMES. | RANK. | TIME OF SERVICE. Enlisted. | Discharged. | REMARKS. |
|---|---|---|---|---|
| Mooring, William | pt | | 9 dec 77 | discharged |
| McLaughlin, John | | | 1 Nov 80 | present |
| McManis, Barney | pt | | 18 Aug 80 | died |
| Mortimer, John | do | | 16 Aug 80 | missing |
| | fifer | 7 Sept 77 | | |
| McFaul, James | pt | | 8 dec 79 | discharged |
| Miller, Thomas | do | | | |
| Murphey, Michael | | | 16 Aug 80 | missing |
| Miller, Thomas | pt | | | [leave |
| Miller, Philip | Ensn | 17 Aprl 77 | 19 Sept 77 | left the Regt.wo. |
| Messar, John[1] | pt | 15 Mar 78 | April 78 | off, exchd. for Jas. |
| 15 Mar 78 in the place of James McMullin | | | | McMullin |
| Mathews, James[2] | pt | 13 April 78 | Oct 78 | dead |
| McGreary, Alex.[3] | pt | | 26 April 78 | deserted |
| 1st mustr. April 78 | | | | |
| McDonald, Michael[4] | pt | 23 Mar 78 | 28 Jan 80 | deserted |
| 1 Sept present | | | | |
| McNabb, Charles[5] | Sergt | 7 June 78 | 1 Nov 80 | present |
| Moore, Andrew | pt | 29 Mar 78 | do | ditto, died |
| | | | | 15 Mar 81 |
| Moran, William | pt | 6 June 78 | 10 dec 79 | discharged |
| Monro, John | do | 2 May 78 | 5 June 79 | deserted |
| Mullen, Dennis[2] | pt | 30 May 78 | 16 Aug 80 | missing |
| Mullen, Michael[6] | Sergt | 30 Aprl 78 | | |
| Joined 2 Oct 78 | pt | 12 Oct 78 | 13 dec 78 | deserted |
| Mathews, Richd. | do | 20 May 78 | 16 Aug 80 | missing |
| Manage, James[6] | pt | 1 May 78 | 9 Sept 80 | joined |
| McCormick, Andrew | do | 24 April 78 | 1 Mar 79 | deserted |
| Monro, Barny | pt | 20 April 78 | 1 Nov 80 | present |
| McNally, John[3] | do | 2 April 78 | 1 Nov 80 | do |
| Morris, Evan[4] | do | 12 Mar 78 | 17 Mar 78 | deserted |
| Morris, Saml.[3] | do | 3 June 78 | 20 feb 79 | discharged |
| McDonald, John | do | 30 June 78 | do | do |
| Maddin, Nathl.[1] | Sergt | 28 Oct 78 | 30 April 79 | deserted |
| | pt | 20 feb 79 | | |
| McLane, Enoch[7] | Sergt | 6 May 78 | 1 Nov 80 | present |
| Macum, John | pt | 11 May 78 | 16 Aug 80 | missing |
| Moad, William | do | 2 April 78 | Joined 26 Oct 80 | |
| McVay, David[1] | do | 26 April 79 | 5 July 80 | deserted |
| McMurray, Jeremh. | pt | 14 April 79 | 13 Sept 79 | do |
| Maxwell, John | do | 1 June 79 | 1 Nov 80 | present |

[1] Grosh's.  [2] Spyker's.  [3] Morris'.  [4] Bayly's.  [5] Jones'.  [6] Stull's.  [7] Beatty's.

## MUSTERS OF MARYLAND TROOPS, VOL. II.

| NAMES. | RANK. | TIME OF SERVICE. Enlisted. | Discharged. | REMARKS. |
|---|---|---|---|---|
| McDanald, James[1] | pt | 23 June 78 | 23 Mar 80 | prisoner of the |
| Joined 2 Nov 79 | | | | Guards |
| Murphey, Joseph[2] | pt | Mar 79 | 16 Aug 80 | missing |
| McCulloch, John[1] | pt | 15 feb 80 | 16 Aug 80 | do |
| Mick, John[2] | pt | 1 feb 80 | 1 Nov 80 | present |
| McGuire, Peter | do | | 16 Augt 80 | missing |
| Morris, Cornelius | do | 8 feb 80 | 1 Nov 80 | present |
| Mills, John[3] | pt | do | do | |
| Murray, Thomson[4] | do | 12 feb 80 | 12 July 80 | deserted |
| McLean, Arthur[5] | Sergt | 10 feb 80 | 1 Nov 80 | present |
| Mattingly, Joseph | pt | 3 feb 80 | do | do |

### GERMAN REGIMENT.

| NAMES. | RANK. | TIME OF SERVICE. Enlisted. | Discharged. | REMARKS. |
|---|---|---|---|---|
| Michael, Henry | | 26 July 79 | | discharged |
| Michael, John | Corpl | | 16   do | do |
| Mongaul, Fredk. | | 21   do   75 | 24   do | do |
| Miller, John | mustr P.R. 28   do | | 1 Augt 80 | deserted |
| Miely, Jacob | | | 11 Aug 79 | discharged |
| Miller, Jacob, Jr. | | | 20 July 79 | do |
| McColough, Lewis | | | 24   do | do |
| Mummart, William | pt | | 1 Aug 80 | present |
| Miller, Jacob, Sr. | | | 20 July 79 | discharged |
| Martin, Henry | pay drawn from 1 Nov 79 | | | |
| Maunsel, Wm. | first muster Aug 80 | | 22 Nov 80 | deserted |

### FIFTH MARYLAND REGIMENT.

| NAMES. | RANK. | TIME OF SERVICE. Enlisted. | Discharged. | REMARKS. |
|---|---|---|---|---|
| Nichols, Nicholas[6] | pt | 18 Jan 77 | 10 Jan 80 | discharged |
| North, Jacob[7] | Corpl | 28 June 77 | 1 Jan 80 | was present |
| | Sergt | June 78 | | |
| Nabb, Richard[8] | Sergt | 26 Jan 77 | 12 Jan 80 | discharged |
| 1st muster April 78 to Bird's | | | | |
| Nicholson, John[9] | pt | 25 feb 78 | 1 May 79 | prisoner, transfd. |
| Hawkins & Joined 15 Aug 79 | | | | to Invalids in 1780 |
| Newcome, Robert[7] | pt | 1 Mar 78 | 1 Aug 78 | deserted |
| 1st muster Aprl 78 | | | | |
| Newman, Jesse[8] | pt | 4 June 78 | 1 Mar 79 | discharged |
| Newman, William | do | 4 June 78 | Aug 78 | not heard of |
| Nabb, Joseph[10] | do | 6 May 78 | 1 Nov 80 | present |
| Nevell, Robt. | do | 18 May 78 | July 78 | left out |
| Nailor, William | do | 25 Aprl 78 | 1 Nov 80 | present |

[1] Morris'.  [9] Mason's.  [3] Lamar's.  [4] Anderson's.  [5] Lynn's.
[6] Dean's.  [7] Handy's.  [8] Lt. Hamilton's.  [9] Johnson's.  [10] Handy's, Gray's.

## MUSTERS OF MARYLAND TROOPS, VOL. II.

| NAMES. | RANK. | TIME OF SERVICE. Enlisted. | Discharged. | REMARKS. |
|---|---|---|---|---|
| Nicks, John[1] | pt | 18 feb 80 | 16 Aug 80 | missing |
| Nevill, Saml. | do | | 20 July 80 | deserted |
| 1st muster Mar 80 | | | | |

### SIXTH MARYLAND REGIMENT.

| NAMES. | RANK. | Enlisted. | Discharged. | REMARKS. |
|---|---|---|---|---|
| Nelson, John | Sergt | 10 May 77 | July 78 | mustered resigned |
| Noland, Michael[2] | pt | 2 feb 77 | 1 Jan 80 | was present |
| Made prisoner in Jan 80 and exchanged the last of same year | | | | 1 feb 80 |
| Newton, Basil[3] | pt | 17 Mar 77 | do | do |
| Norris, Jacob[4] | Ensn | 15 May 77 | | |
| | Lieut | 26 Jan 78 | | |
| Nash, Joseph[5] | pt | 3 May 77 | 16 Aug 80 | prisoner |
| | drum | 1 May 79 | | |
| Nave, Henry[6] | pt | 16 feb 79 | See Henry Knave, Miles' Co. | |
| Nash, Thomas[8] | pt | 1 June 78 | 1 April 79 | discharged |
| Nowell, James | pt | 1 June 78 | 1 Nov 80 | present |
| | fifer | 3 Sept 78 | | |
| Nicholls, John[6] | pt | 16 June 78 | 16 Aug 80 | missing |
| Neagle, James[7] | do | 18 June 79 | 1 Jan 80 | was present |

### SEVENTH MARYLAND REGIMENT.

| NAMES. | RANK. | Enlisted. | Discharged. | REMARKS. |
|---|---|---|---|---|
| Nicholls, Thomas[8] | pt | 29 Mar 77 | 1 feb 78 | discharged |
| Nabb, Charles[9] | pt | 2 May 77 | 8 May 80 | do |
| Norton, John[10] | pt | 16 Nov 77 | 26 Aprl 79 | prisoner |
| Newton, or Luton, Joseph[11] | do | 2 May 77 | 1 Aug 77 | dead |
| Nash, Edward | pt | 9 May 77 | Nov 77 | off Rolls |
| Newell, William[12] | Sergt | | 4 Oct 77 | killed |
| Nayse, Richard | pt | | feb 78 | off Rolls |
| Newman, John[10] | pt | 1 June 78 | 1 April 79 | discharged |
| Nick, William[11] | pt | 5 May 78 | 16 Aug 80 | missing |
| Norman, Basil[13] | pt | 6 June 78 | 1 Nov 80 | present |
| Niblet, William[14] | pt | 15 May 78 | do | do |
| Nicholas, John[15] | do | 29 June 78 | 9 April 79 | discharged |
| Nichols, John Mc.[14] | pt | 28 June 78 | 15 Mar 79 | do |
| Neighbours, John[16] | pt | 28 Jan 80 | 16 Aug 80 | missing |
| Nowland, Michael | pt | See Knowland | | |

### GERMAN REGIMENT.

| NAMES. | RANK. | Enlisted. | Discharged. | REMARKS. |
|---|---|---|---|---|
| Neving, William | | | 1 July 79 | missing |
| Nevitt, John | | musterd. deserted | 13 Nov 80 | deserted |

---

[1] Handy's.   [2] Dobson's.   [3] Trueman's.   [4] Laurence's.   [5] Chapline's, now Miles'.
[6] Miles'.   [7] Norris'.   [8] Jones'.   [9] Spyker's.   [10] Stull's.   [11] Bayly's.
[12] Deams'.   [13] Anderson's.   [14] Beatty's.   [15] Grosh's.   [16] Mason's.

## MUSTERS OF MARYLAND TROOPS, VOL. II.

| NAMES. | RANK. | TIME OF SERVICE. Enlisted. | Discharged. | REMARKS. |
|---|---|---|---|---|

### FIFTH MARYLAND REGIMENT.

| NAMES. | RANK. | Enlisted. | Discharged. | REMARKS. |
|---|---|---|---|---|
| O'Bryan, M. Thos.[1] | Sergt | 19 May 77 | 1 Jan 80 | was present |
|  | pt | 21 May 78 | 3 May 80 | discharged |
|  | Sergt | 1 June 78 |  |  |
| Owens, James[2] | pt | 1 Jan 77 | do | do |
| Oglesby, Charles[3] | pt | 2 Aprl 77 | 1 Aprl 80 | discharged |
| Olephant, Thomas[4] | pt | 28 July 77 | 23 April 78 | died |
| Outerbridge, Stephen[2] | do | 15 May 78 | Sept 80 | deserted |
| O'Bryan, Joseph[1] | do | 4 June 78 | 19 June 78 | deserted |

### SIXTH MARYLAND REGIMENT.

| NAMES. | RANK. | Enlisted. | Discharged. | REMARKS. |
|---|---|---|---|---|
| Oram, Peter[5] | pt | 12 Jan 77 | 12 Jan 80 | discharged |
| O'Mullen, Patrick[6] | pt | 21 May 77 | See Mullen, Patrick |  |
| O'Branan, Timothy | pt | 21 May 77 | April & May 79 transfrd., not heard of Nov 80 | |
| O'Hara, John | pt | 29 Aug 77 | 15 June 78 | deserted |
| Owens, Stephen[7] 1st muster June 78 | pt | 16 May 78 | 1 Nov 80 | present |
| O'Hara, Arthur[8] | pt | 6 May 78 | 1 Jan 80 | was present |
| Orchard, William[9] | pt | 17 May 79 | 16 Aug 80 | missing |
| Owens, James Oct mustr. 80 | do | | 14 Sept 80 | deserted |

### SEVENTH MARYLAND REGIMENT.

| NAMES. | RANK. | Enlisted. | Discharged. | REMARKS. |
|---|---|---|---|---|
| Osband, John[10] Joined 22 July 78 | pt | 14 Aprl 77 | 26 May | deserted |
| Owens, William[11] | pt | 17 Jan 77 | 10 Mar 78 | do |
| Oliver, John | pt | 15 Nov 77 | 16 Aug 80 | missing |
| O'Neale, Patrick[12] | do | 5 Aprl 77 | 1 Jan 80 | was present |
|  | Sergt | 1 Sept 77 |  |  |
|  | pt | 26 dec 77 |  |  |
| O'Neale, Patrick[13] Joined | do | | June 80 | deserted |
| Oldstone, Edward[10] | pt | 13 Aprl 78 | 1 July 80 | do |
| Orme, Charles[14] | do | 6 June 78 | 1 Nov 80 | present |
| Osborn, William | pt | 6 June 78 | 16 Aug 80 | missing |
| O'Ph——, Stephen[15] | do | 14 June 80 | See Stephen Flaharty | |

### GERMAN REGIMENT.

| NAMES. | RANK. | Enlisted. | Discharged. | REMARKS. |
|---|---|---|---|---|
| O'Quin, Richd. | | | 1 Sept 82 | dischd. Invalids [dispd. |

[1] Hawkins'.   [2] Handy's.   [3] Johnson's.   [4] Emory's.   [5] Hynes'.   [6] Harris'.
[7] Dobson's.   [8] Lt. Williams'.   [9] Norris'.   [10] Grosh's.   [11] Bayly's.   [12] Reynolds'.
[13] Deams'.   [14] Jones'.   [15] Morris'.

## MUSTERS OF MARYLAND TROOPS, VOL. II.

| NAMES. | RANK. | TIME OF SERVICE. Enlisted. | Discharged. | REMARKS. |
|---|---|---|---|---|

### FIFTH MARYLAND REGIMENT.

| NAMES. | RANK. | Enlisted. | Discharged. | REMARKS. |
|---|---|---|---|---|
| Pierce, John | Surgeon | 13 Jan 78 | | |
| Purdy, Joseph | drumMajor | 11 June 77 | 1 Nov 80 | present |
| Powers, Charles[1] | pt | 27 July 77 | April 78 | left out |
| Proctor, John | pt | 30 Mar 77 | 16 Aug 80 | missing |
| Price, Nicholas[2] | pt | 4 Sept | | |
| Pryday, John[3] | pt | 17 dec 76 | 16 Aug 80 | missing |
| Peters, Joseph | do | 16 Jan 77 | 1 Mar 79 | discharged |
| Porters, William | do | 18 feb 77 | 1 Mar 80 | deserted  [ment |
| Paul, Thomas[4] | Sergt | 27 April 77 | 1 Aug 79 | Commss. Depart- |
| | | | 27 April 80 | discharged |
| Pounder, Richard | Corpl | 6 dec 76 | pt. 1 April 77 | |
| | Corpl | 1 April 79 | 16 Aug 80 | missing |
| Poole, James[5] | pt | 1 feb 77 | 1 Nov 80 | present |
| Philips, Elijah[6] | do | 10 dec 76 | 12 Jan 80 | discharged |
| Philips, Jacob | do | 10 dec 76 | do | do |
| Parkfield, Wm. | do | 4 Sept 77 | 1 April 78 | discharged |
| Philips, John[7] | do | 5 feb 77 | 5 feb 80 | do |
| | Corpl | 1 April 79 | | |
| Philips, Stephen[8] | Sergt | 25 April 77 ⎫ | | |
| 1st muster April 78, Sergt 1 April 79 | | | | |
| | pt | July 78 ⎭ | 25 April 80 | discharged |
| Pennington, Robert | pt | 10 feb 77 | 1 Nov 80 | present |
| Pennington, George | pt | | 22 feb 80 | deserted |
| Powell, John[5] | pt | 2 Mar 78 | | |
| Proctor, Daniel[2] | do | 15 May 78 | 1 Mar 79 | discharged |
| Pierce, George[4] | pt | 28 April 78 | | |
| Joined 1 April 80 | drum | 1 Aug 78 | 16 Aug 80 | missing |
| Peters, Gabriel | pt | 8 April 78 | 1 Nov 80 | present |
| Payne, John[5] | do | 15 feb 77 | do | do |
| Mustrd. Sergt. reduced 26 April 79 sick Braskinridge | | | | |
| Pilkinton, Michael | pt | 3 June 78 | 21 Jan 80 | joined |
| Poney, Edward | do | 2 June 78 | 1 Mar 79 | discharged |
| Mustrd. again Sept 78 | | | | |
| Powell, John[4] | pt | 19 June 78 | 1 Jan 80 | was present |
| Price, John | do | 1 June 78 | May 79 | discharged |
| Powell, James[2] | do | 5 May 78 | 15 Aug 78 | died |
| Poor, Philip[9] | pt | 7 July 79 | 1 Nov 80 | present |
| Pendergrast, William | Lieut | 29 Oct 79 | | paid |

[1] Dean's, Benson's.   [2] Hawkins'.   [3] Lynch's.   [4] Handy's.   [5] Johnson's.
[6] Emory's.   [7] Cosden's.   [8] Lt. Hamilton's.   [9] Lynch's, or Dower's.

## MUSTERS OF MARYLAND TROOPS, VOL. II.

| NAMES. | RANK. | TIME OF SERVICE. Enlisted. | Discharged. | REMARKS. |
|---|---|---|---|---|

### SIXTH MARYLAND REGIMENT.

| NAMES. | RANK. | Enlisted. | Discharged. | REMARKS. |
|---|---|---|---|---|
| Parsons, William[1] | pt | 20 April 77 | 16 Aug 80 | missing |
| Parsons, John | pt | 28 May 77 | 16 Aug 80 | killed |
| deserted 20 dec 77 | Joined 25 May 78 | | | |
| Pack, James | pt | 29 April 78 | 4 Oct 78 | died |
| Philip, William[2] | Corpl | 13 Mar 77 | | |
| | Sergt | 1 Nov 77 | 15 feb 78 | died |
| Palmer, Samuel[3] | Corpl | 5 April 77 | 1 Jan 80 | was present |
| | | | 5 April 80 | discharged |
| Pattron, William | pt | 9 May 78 | 8 Aug 80 | deserted |
| | fifer | 1 June 78 | | |
| Price, Stephen[4] | pt | 9 June 78 | 1 Nov 80 | present |
| Q. Mr. Sergt. 1 July 80 | Corpl | 10 Nov 77 | | |
| Pinnox, Isaac | pt | 29 June 77 | | [not known |
| deserted 4 Nov 77 & Joined 1 May 78 | | | Mar 79 | diedTrenton,time |
| Palmer, Michael[5] | pt | 31 May 77 | 16 Aug 80 | missing |
| Phillips, Saml.[2] | Sergt | 9 June 78 | 13 Sept 80 | deserted |
| 1st muster June 78, rein. 22 dec 78 | | | | |
| Price, Thomas[6] | pt | 12 June 78 | 18 Aug 78 | died |
| 1st muster June 78 | | | | |
| Perry, John[7] | pt | 16 May 78 | 16 Aug 80 | missing |
| Pound, John | Corpl | 4 May 78 | 18 Aug 80 | deserted |
| Corpl Oct 80 | pt | 1 Nov 79 | | |
| Piper, Joseph[6] | do | 27 Mar 78 | April 78 | deserted |
| Pome, Barthw.[8] | pt | probably never joined | | |
| 1st muster July 79 | | | | [lids |
| Phap, Benjamin[8] | do | 5 May 78 | 30 Sept 80 | transferd.to Inva- |
| Parran, Thomas | Surgeon | 11 Aug 78 | July 80 | resigned |
| Purdy, Edward | pt | 5 feb 80 | 1 Nov 80 | present |
| Oct Muster 80 | | | | |
| Purdy, John | | 20 feb 80 | do | do |
| Purdy, Henry | | 5 feb 80 | do | do |
| Pierce, John | | | 16 Aug 80 | missing |
| Pierce, Saml. | | | 16 Aug 80 | do |
| Pindell, Philip | | | 16 Aug 80 | do |
| Philbert, Joseph | Corpl | 30 May 78 | 1 Nov 80 | present |
| Peny, William[9] | pt | 6 July 77 | 6 Aug 80 | do |
| | Corpl | 10 Oct 77 | | |
| | pt | 1 June 78 | | |

[1] Ghiselin's.   [2] Dobson's.   [3] Beall's.   [4] Harris'.   [5] Chapline's, now Miles'.
[6] Lt. Williams'.        [7] Miles'.   [8] Trueman's.   [9] Laurence's.

## MUSTERS OF MARYLAND TROOPS, VOL. II.

| NAMES. | RANK. | TIME OF SERVICE. Enlisted. | Discharged. | REMARKS. |
|---|---|---|---|---|

### SEVENTH MARYLAND REGIMENT.

| | | | | |
|---|---|---|---|---|
| Parran, Thomas | S. Mate | 18 April 77 | 11 Aug 78 | Surgeon of 6 Regt. |
| Parker, William[1] | pt | 16 Jan 77 | 12 Jan 80 | discharged |
| Purnell, Saml. | do | 11 feb 77 | 9 feb 80 | do |
| Porter, Charles | Ensign | 17 April 77 ⎫ | | |
| | Lieut | 28 dec 77 ⎬ | | |
| Enlisted to be Second Lieut | | 7 July 77 ⎭ | 19 feb 80 | discharged |
| Philips, George[2] | pt | 18 Mar 77 | Joined 25 July 79 | |
| Pinder, John | pt | 4 April 77 | April 78 | off Rolls |
| Parker, John | pt | 4 April 77 | April 78 | off Rolls |
| Pinctly, John[3] | fifer | 2 feb 77 | feb 78 | off Rolls |
| Poke, William | pt | 3 May 77 | Oct 77 | off Rolls |
| Peacock, Neale[4] | do | 24 dec 76 | 1 Nov 80 | present |
| Philpot, Charles[5] | Sergt | 4 dec 76 | 4 dec 79 | discharged |
| Powell, John | Corpl | 5 dec 76 | 4 Oct 77 | killed |
| Porter, John | pt | 19 dec 76 | 22 dec 76 | deserted |
| Pike, William | pt | 22 feb 77 | 31 July 77 | do |
| Parmer, Nathl. | pt | 15 Nov 77 | 16 Aug 80 | missing |
| Pinckley, Michael[6] | pt | 2 May 77 | 1 May 80 | discharged |
| Pumphry, John | pt | | 16 Aug 80 | missing |
| Preston, Thomas | pt | | 1 June 80 | deserted |
| Price, Robert | pt | | | Hospital Annapolis |
| Pasterfield, Thomas[2] | pt | 16 May 78 | July 78 | off Rolls |
| Pollard, William[1] | pt | 30 April 78 | Sept 79 | not heard of |
| Prangley, William | pt | 19 May 78 | 1 Nov 80 | present |
| Price, James | pt | 29 Mar 78 | 30 Mar 79 | deserted |
| Peace, John[2] | Corpl | 28 April 78 | 1 Nov 80 | present |
| Sergt. Major May 80, 16 May 79 Sergt. and M. S. 2 Mar 80 | | | | |
| Paine, George[4] | pt | 13 June 78 | 30 Mar 79 | discharged |
| Pennywell, Radcliffe[2] | pt | 20 July 78 | 9 April 79 | ditto |
| Parris, John | pt | 20 July 78 | 20 dec 78 | deserted |
| Pepper, Elijah[7] | pt | 20 May 78 | 1 Nov 80 | present |
| Peacock, Thomas | pt | 16 Mar 79 | do | do |
| Pugh, Thomas[2] | pt | 2 July 79 | | |
| 20 Sept 79 Transferred | | | | |
| Penn, Michael[7] | pt | | 1 Nov 80 | present |
| Mar 80 Lt. Beall's | | | | |

### GERMAN REGIMENT.

| | | | | |
|---|---|---|---|---|
| Polhouse, Thomas | Corpl | 1 Nov 78 | 1 Aug 80 | present |
| to 1 Jan 81 | | | | |
| Proctor, Thomas | | 4 May 78 | do | do |
| to 1 Jan 81 | | | | |

[1] Jones'.   [2] Grosh's.   [3] Stull's.   [4] Morris'.   [5] Bayly's.   [6] Reynolds'.   [7] Beall's.

## MUSTERS OF MARYLAND TROOPS, VOL. II.

| NAMES. | RANK. | TIME OF SERVICE. Enlisted. | Discharged. | REMARKS. |
|---|---|---|---|---|
| Pointer, William | | | 13 Nov 80 | deserted |
| Porter, Robert | pt | May 78 | Aug 80 | present |
| to 1 Jan 81 | | | | |
| Painter, Henry | See Henry Bender | | | |

### FIFTH MARYLAND REGIMENT.

| | | | | |
|---|---|---|---|---|
| Quain, John[1] | pt | 15 May 77 | | |

### SEVENTH MARYLAND REGIMENT.

| | | | | |
|---|---|---|---|---|
| Quynn, Timothy[2] | pt | 30 Mar 77 | 16 Aug 80 | missing |
| 21 July 78 Joined | | | | |
| Quinley, Levin[3] | pt | 4 May 78 | dec 79 | deserted |
| Quinton, William | pt | | 1 Nov 80 | present |
| 1 Oct 80 joined | | | | |

### GERMAN REGIMENT.

| | | | | |
|---|---|---|---|---|
| Quier, Henry | | | 26 July 79 | discharged |

### FIFTH MARYLAND REGIMENT.

| | | | | |
|---|---|---|---|---|
| Richardson, William | Col | 10 Dec 76 | | |
| Ryan, Gilbert[4] | pt | 13 July 77 | | |
| Rogers, Robert[1] | pt | 1 May 77 | | |
| Ried, Philip[5] | Ensn | 20 feb 77 | | |
| | Lieut | 13 Oct 78 | | |
| Ross, Bathw. | pt | 30 June 77 | May 79 | not heard of |
| Ryan, Robert[6] | do | 10 feb 77 | 7 feb 80 | discharged |
| Ray, William | do | 11 Mar | 16 April 78 | Sergt., 5 May dead, April 78 left out |
| Richardson, Charles | do | 17 Mar | 17 Mar 80 | discharged |
| Raisin, William[7] | Corpl | 10 Jan 77 | | |
| Reily, John[8] | pt | 18 feb 77 | 2 Sept 78 | died |
| Reancifer, John[9] | Sergt | 8 Jan 77 | July 78 | left out |
| Roster, William | pt | 13 Jan 77 | April 78 | do |
| Ryan, James[10] | pt | | 16 Aug 80 | missing |
| 1st muster April 78 to Bird's | | | | |
| Redding, Thomas | pt | 5 June 77 | } 1 Jan 80 | was present |
| | Corpl | 4 Nov 78 | } | |
| | pt | 18 June 79 | | |
| Richie, John[6] | pt | 5 dec 76 | do | do |
| 1st muster 78 | | | | |
| Reynolds, Thomas[3] | pt | 15 June 78 | Mar 79 | discharged |

[1] Hawkins'.    [2] Grosh's.    [3] Morris'.    [4] Dean's.    [5] Lynch's.    [6] Handy's.
[7] Johnson's.    [8] Emory's.    [9] Cosden's.    [10] Hamilton's.

## MUSTERS OF MARYLAND TROOPS, VOL. II.

| NAMES. | RANK. | TIME OF SERVICE. | | REMARKS. |
| | | Enlisted. | Discharged. | |
| --- | --- | --- | --- | --- |
| Richards, Stephen[1] | pt | 13 May 78 | | |
| Sick at Annapolis | | | | |
| Ryall, John[2] | pt | 6 June 78 | 20 Mar 79 | discharged |
| Rumford, William[3] | pt | 5 June 78 | 16 Aug 80 | missing |
| | Sergt | 6 Mar 80 | | |
| Richardson, Thomas[4] | pt | 28 May 78 | 16 Aug 80 | missing |
| Joined 12 Aug 79 | | | | |
| Reordon, John | pt | 4 June 78 | 28 June 79 | deserted |
| Ryan, Michael[5] | pt | 1 Aprl 79 | 10 Jan 80 | discharged |
| Rankin, Robert[6] | pt | 5 May 79 | 16 Aug 80 | missing |
| 1 muster June 79 | | | | |
| Reynolds, Thomas[4] | pt | 10 May 79 | 16 Aug 80 | do |
| Reynolds, James | pt | 30 Mar 79 | 1 Nov 80 | present |
| Ross, Thomas | pt | | | |
| Reason, William | Ensn | 26 Jan 80 | | |

### SIXTH MARYLAND REGIMENT.

| NAMES. | RANK. | TIME OF SERVICE. | | REMARKS. |
| | | Enlisted. | Discharged. | |
| --- | --- | --- | --- | --- |
| Riely, Patrick[7] | Corpl | 3 May 78 | 15 Aug 80 | deserted |
| | pt | 6 Oct 78 | | |
| Rowen, Christopher | pt | 15 Aug 77 | 2 July 79 | deserted |
| Ridley, Drew | pt | 25 Aprl 78 | 10 Aug 80 | do |
| Rogers, Michael[8] | pt | 18 May 77 | | |
| Robertson, Saml. | pt | 27 May 78 | Sept 80 | missing |
| Rigby, William[9] | Sergt | 29 April 77 | } | |
| | Q.M.Sergt. | Jany 79 | } 30 April 80 | discharged |
| Rayne, William[10] | pt | 24 feb 78 | 27 Sept 78 | died |
| Reason, Jacob | pt | 13 Aprl 78 | 29 Jan 79 | died |
| Robinson, William[11] | pt | 30 dec 76 | 30 dec 79 | discharged |
| Rawlings, Solomon | pt | 5 dec 76 | 5 dec 79 | do |
| Reardon, John[12] | pt | 27 dec 76 | 16 Aug 80 | missing |
| Rochester, Abram[6] | do | 10 June 78 | dec 79 | absent without leave |
| 1st muster June 78, 23 dec 78 reinlisted | | | | |
| Balston, Joseph | pt | 9 June 78 | 1 Nov 80 | present |
| 1 muster June 78, rein. 23 dec 78 | | | | |
| Rawlings, Benja.[9] | pt | 1 June 78 | 1 Aprl 79 | discharged |
| Ryan, Hugh | pt | 1 June 78 | 15 dec 79 | died |
| rein. 1 Jany 79 | | | | |
| Ralph, William[10] | pt | 24 April 78 | 1 Jan 80 | was present |
| 1st mustr. June 78 | | | | |
| Battican, James[12] | pt | 18 April 78 | See Hattakan, Joseph | |
| Roach, James[13] | do | 4 May 78 | 1 Aug 80 | deserted |

[1] Handy's.      [2] Ensign Jones'.      [3] Johnson's.      [4] Hawkins'.      [5] Dean's.
[6] Lynch's.      [7] Ghiselin's.      [8] Dobson's.      [9] Trueman's.      [10] Beall's.
[11] Hynes'.      [12] Harris'.      [13] Miles'.

## MUSTERS OF MARYLAND TROOPS, VOL. II.

| NAMES. | RANK. | TIME OF SERVICE. | | REMARKS. |
| | | Enlisted. | Discharged. | |
|---|---|---|---|---|
| Rork, John | pt | 19 May 78 | 30 June 79 | deserted |
| Reynolds, William | do | 3 May 78 | 3 Mar 79 | discharged |
| Rinehart, Andrew[1] | do | 1 July 78 | 1 April 79 | do |
| Reason, John, or James[2] rein. 9 Nov 78 | pt | 24 June 78 | 1 Jan 80 | was present |
| Robertson, Robert | pt | 24 Aprl 78 | 16 Aug 80 | missing |
| Rattican, Peter[3] | do | 1 July 78 | 1 Jan 80 | was present |
| Rockhole, Hasael[4] | pt | 4 Nov 79 | 1 Nov 80 | present |
| Rice, Robert | pt | 30 April 78 | do | do |
| Rowland, Jacob[2] Joined 19 Aug 78 | pt | 27 June 77 | do | do |
| Beaves, Noah[4] | Corpl | 27 July 78 | 1 May 79 | discharged |
| Roe, William[5] 1st mustr. Aug 79 | pt | | 14 Sept 80 | deserted |
| Rice, William[6] | pt | 14 Aug 79 | 1 Nov 80 | present |
| Richardson, John Oct Roll 1780 | drum | | 16 Aug 80 | missing |

### SEVENTH REGIMENT.

| NAMES. | RANK. | TIME OF SERVICE. | | REMARKS. |
| | | Enlisted. | Discharged. | |
|---|---|---|---|---|
| Ross, Alexander[7] | pt | 11 feb 77 | 1 Nov 80 | present |
| Ramsey, Charles | do | 17 Mar 77 | 17 Mar 80 | discharged |
| Read, Christopher[8] | do | 15 May 77 | July 78 | off Rolls |
| See a certificate in Read's depreciation acct. | | | 5 May 80 | discharged |
| Rotherford, John | pt | 15 May 77 | 15 May 80 | do |
| | Corpl | 1 April 78 | | |
| | Sergt | 4 Oct 78 | | |
| Riely, Patrick[9] | Corpl | 4 dec 76 | 1 Nov 80 | present |
| | pt | 15 July 78 | | |
| Riely, Barney | do | 12 dec 76 | 22 Aug 77 | killed |
| Ragan, Darby | do | 1 Aprl 77 | 4 Oct 77 | missing |
| Riggs, John[10] | drum | 5 dec 76 | 8 dec 79 | discharged |
| | D. Major | 4 June 77 | | reinlisted |
| Riley, Walter | pt | 5 dec 76 | 4 Oct 77 | killed |
| Ringer, Andrew Joined Sept 77 | do | 6 dec 76 | 1 July 80 | deserted |
| Robertson, Isaac | pt | 21 Nov 77 | 8 April 79 | do |
| Reynolds, John | Capt | 10 dec 76 | | |
| Rodwell, Godfrey[11] | Sergt | | Sept 77 | off Rolls |
| Reynolds, Francis | pt | | 1 Nov 80 | present |
| Rowell, William[12] to Grosh's, reinlisted | do | 24 Mar 78 | 4 May 79 | |
| | | | 16 Aug 80 | missing |

[1] Ghiselin's.  [2] Hynes'.  [3] Harris'.  [4] Miles'.  [5] Jacobs'.  [6] Norris'.
[7] Jones'.  [8] Spyker's.  [9] Morris'.  [10] Bayly's.  [11] Deams'.  [12] Anderson's.

## MUSTERS OF MARYLAND TROOPS, VOL. II.

| NAMES. | RANK. | TIME OF SERVICE. Enlisted. | Discharged. | REMARKS. |
|---|---|---|---|---|
| Roe, Obediah[1] | pt | 9 May 78 | July 78 | off Rolls |
| Rosstell, Joseph[2] | do | 12 Jan 78 | 8 feb 78 | deserted |
| Riely, John[3] | do | 25 April 78 | 20 feb 80 | do |
| Russell, Aron | do | 30 May 78 | 30 Sept 78 | died |
| Rimington, John | do | 6 June 78 | 16 Mar 79 | discharged |
| Read, James[4] | do | 19 May 78 | Aug 79 | not heard of |
| Ryan, Patrick | do | 22 Apri 78 | 16 July 80 | deserted |
| Joined | | | | |
| Read, William[5] | do | 5 May 78 | 16 Aug 80 | missing |
| Rochford, Edward | do | 23 April 78 | 27  do | deserted |
| Riggs, William[1] | do | | 11 Jan 79 | transferrd. to 2d Md. Brigade |
| Row, John | do | 20 July 78 | 9 Apri 79 | discharged |
| Ricketts, Andrew | do | 13 May 79 | 16 Aug 80 | missing |
| Roberts, Horatio[6] | do | 2 feb 80 | 16 Aug 80 | do |
| Roxburgh, Alexr. | Major | 1 Apri 80 | | promoted from 1st Regt. |
| Riggs, John[6] | fifer | 6 May 80 | 1 Nov 80 present, see J. Riggs } of Bayley's } |
| Reese, Henry | pt | 14 Apri 77 | do | do |

### GERMAN REGIMENT.

| NAMES. | RANK. | TIME OF SERVICE. Enlisted. | Discharged. | REMARKS. |
|---|---|---|---|---|
| Roach, (or Rock), John | drum | 2 Mar 78 | 1 Aug 80 present & 1 Jan 81 | |
| Rider, William to 1st Jan 81 | | 12 May 78 | do     do   [paid | |
| Ronenberger, Chas. to 1st Jan 81 | | 6 June 80 | do     do | |
| Ritmire, Michael to 1st Jan 81 | pt | 1 feb 80 | do     do | |
| Riely, Conrad | | | 24 July 79 | discharged |
| Rummelson, Wm. | Sergt | | 16   do | do |
| Robinson, Edward | | | 20 July do | do |
| Robinson, Andrew | | | do | do |
| Raybert, Chs., or Chrisr. | | | 26 July 79 | do |
| Ruppert, Jacob | | | 15 July 79 | discharged |
| Rittlemeyer, George | | | 11 Aug do | do |
| Rumfell, Henry | | | 28 July do | do |
| Regalman, George | | | 12 Oct 79 | do |
| Ricknagle, Jacob | | | 26 July 79 | do |
| Richards, John | | Mustrd. sick at Windsor 1 July 79 | | |
| Raver, Christr. | | | 26 July 79 | discharged |
| Riely, Bernard | | | 6 Nov 80 | deserted |

[1] Grosh's.    [2] Beatty's.    [3] Jones'.    [4] Morris'.
[5] Bayly's.    [6] Mason's.

## MUSTERS OF MARYLAND TROOPS, VOL II.

| NAMES. | RANK. | TIME OF SERVICE. Enlisted. | Discharged. | REMARKS. |
|---|---|---|---|---|
| | FIFTH MARYLAND REGIMENT. | | | |
| Smyth, Thomas | Major | 10 Dec 76 | | |
| Spratbrow, Wm.[1] | Sergt.Major 10 April 77 | | | [Forage Depart. |
| | Sergt.Major 1 Nov 77 | | 1 feb 79 | transferred to |
| Shaw, Dennis[2] | Sergt | 21 July 77 | Dec 78 | not heard of |
| Start, Moses[3] | pt | 18 Jan 77 | 16 Aug 80 | missing |
| Mustd. Sergt. Oct. 80 | | | | |
| Saunders,(or Launders), John | do | 30 Mar 77 | 22 Mar 80 | discharged |
| St. Clair, William | do | 13 Jan 77 | 16 Aug 80 | missing, joined |
| Saunders, William[4] | do | 30 Mar 77 | | |
| to Hamilton's | Corpl | 21 feb 80 | 30 Mar 80 | discharged |
| Scoudrick, Charles | do | 20 July 77 | 16 Aug 80 | missing |
| Mustd. Corpl Oct 80 | | | | |
| Slaughter, Philip | fifer | 10 Jan 77 | April 78 | left out |
| Scoudrick, Thomas | pt | 13 July 77 | 1 Nov 80 | present |
| Mustd. Corpl Oct 80 | | | | [reason assigned |
| Swany, Thomas | do | 30 Mar 77 | feb 80 | struck off, no |
| Skinner, Thomas[1] | Lieut | 20 feb 77 | 10 dec 77 | resigned |
| Smith, Jonathan | pt | 10 dec 77 | 1 Jan 80 | was present |
| | fifer | 20 Aug 78 | May 80 | discharged |
| Stableford, Taylor[2] | pt | 30 July | do | do |
| Smith, Levi | pt | 19 July | | |
| | Corpl | 20 Oct 78 | | |
| | Sergt | 1 Aprl 79 | 1 Nov 80 | present |
| Seth, Jacob | Sergt | 15 Aug 77 | | |
| | pt | 1 July 78 | 20 Aug 80 | discharged |
| Stoakes, Peter[5] | 2d Lieut | 13 June 79 | 24 Aug 78 | resigned |
| Stevens, Robert | pt | 12 April 77 | 16 Aug 80 | missing |
| Sullivan, James | pt | 10 Sept 77 | Jan 79 | not heard of for 8 mos. |
| Samuels, John[6] | do | 10 feb 77 | April 78 | left out |
| Smyth, Daniel | do | 2 April | 1 Nov 80 | present |
| Stephenson, John | do | 20 May | April 78 | left out |
| Sullivan, William | do | 27 July | 1 Nov 80 | present |
| Swift, Gideon | do | 4 Sept | April 78 | left out |
| Sutton, Abram[7] | do fifer | 10 dec 76 | | [of Lee's Division |
| | F. Major | 10 feb 79 | 16 Aug 80 | missing, afterwards |
| Stone, (or Scone), George | pt | 14 Jan 77 | 1 Nov 80 | present |
| | Corpl | 80 | | |
| Strickenburgh, Andw. John | pt | 23 April 77 | dec 78 | left out |
| Sturges, Thomas | do | 5 July 77 | July 78 | do |
| Stinson, William[8] | 2d Lieut | 14 feb 77 | 1 Nov 77 | resigned |

[1] Hawkins'.    [2] Dean's.    [3] Benson's.    [4] Hamilton's.
[5] Lynch's.    [6] Handy's.    [7] Johnson's.    [8] Emory's.

## MUSTERS OF MARYLAND TROOPS, VOL. II.

| NAMES. | RANK. | TIME OF SERVICE. Enlisted. | Discharged. | REMARKS. |
|---|---|---|---|---|
| Sharpt, (or Tharp), Danl. | pt | 18 feb 77 | 22 May 78 | discharged |
| Stewart, Thomas | pt | 16 July 77 | | |
| Sheavers, Danl. | pt | 26 Mar 77 Joined again | desd. 26 Jany 80 and never joined | |
| Smith, John[1] | pt | 23 Jan 77 | 1 Nov 80 | present |
| pt 1st Nov 78 | Corpl | 27 July 78 | | |
| Sharon, Frederick | do | 8 Jany 80 | do, 8 Jany 80 | discharged |
| Smith, James[2] | pt | 5 dec 76 | 19 May 79 | do |
| 1st mustr. April 78 | | | | |
| Sinnett, Nicholas | pt | | June 78 | left out |
| Small, Jonathan[3] | pt | 10 feb 77 | 14 feb 80 | discharged |
| 1st mustr. April 78 | | | | |
| Sullivan, Perry[4] | pt | 2 April 77 | 1 Nov 80 | present |
| 1st mustr. April 78 | | | | |
| Sappington, Thos.[2] | pt | 1 June 78 | do | do |
| reinlisted | Sergt | 19 June 78 | | |
| Stockett, Thomas | pt | 9 May 78 | 10 April 79 | deserted |
| rein. 16 Jan 79 | | | | |
| Swift, David | pt | 6 June 78 | 1 Mar 79 | discharged |
| pt Dec 78 | | | | |
| Sullivan, Darby | pt | | Augt 78 | not heard of, see Darby Sullivan below |
| Swain, John | pt | 8 June 78 | Aug 78 | mustd. not heard of |
| Shorter, Roger[5] | pt | 21 Aprl 78 | 1 Nov 80 | present |
| 1st mustr. June 78 | | | | |
| Sharp, William[6] | pt | 29 May 78 | 1 May 81 | discharged |
| Oct mustr. 80 | Corpl | | | |
| Silvester, Thomas[7] | pt | 20 May 78 | 21 Aug 78 | died |
| Stewart, Andrew | pt | 20 May 78 | 16 Aug 80 | missing, 1 Aug 81 dischgd. |
| Satchell, James | pt | 8 May 78 | Feby 79 | not heard of |
| Summers, Solomon | do | 6 May 78 | 1 Nov 80 | present |
| Sullivan, Darby[3] | do | 6 June 78 | 15 Sept 79 | died |
| 1 Sept 78 to Hamilton's Co. | | | | |
| Sherwood, Hugh[8] | pt | 6 June 78 | July 78 | discharged |
| Saunders, George[4] | do | 23 May 78 | 1 Nov 80 | present |
| Sidner, Joseph | pt | 6 June 78 | 15 Jan 80 | joined |
| Shove, John[7] | do | 4 June 78 | 19 Mar 79 | discharged |
| Samuel, William | do | 4 June 78 | do | do |
| Sevell, William | do | 4 June 78 | See William Sewell below | |
| reinlisted | | | | |

[1] Cosden's.  [2] Lt. Hamilton's.  [3] Ensign Jones', Benson's.  [4] Johnson's.
[5] Lynch's.  [6] Benson's.  [7] Handy's.  [8] Ensign Jones'.

## MUSTERS OF MARYLAND TROOPS, VOL. II.

| NAMES. | RANK. | TIME OF SERVICE. Enlisted. | Discharged. | REMARKS. |
|---|---|---|---|---|
| Scott, James | pt | 4 June 78 | July 78 | left out |
| Scudder, Jesse[1] | do | 17 Aprl 78 | 2 July 79 | deserted |
| 1st muster June 79 | | | | |
| Smith, William | pt | 3 June 78 | | |
| Sewell, William[2] | do | 4 April 79 | | See Civill, William, Letter G R |
| Stallings, Thos.[3] | pt | 1 May 79 | 11 Nov 79 | transferred, not |
| 1st muster June 79 | | | | heard of since |
| Surton, Robert[1] | pt | 1 dec 79 | 30 Oct 80 | died |
| Joined 1 dec 79 | Mustr. Sergt Oct roll 80 | | | |
| Stoddart, William | Lieut | | | |

### SIXTH MARYLAND REGIMENT.

| NAMES. | RANK. | Enlisted. | Discharged. | REMARKS. |
|---|---|---|---|---|
| Somerville, James[4] | Lieut | 20 feb 77 } | 16 Aug 80 | wounded |
| | Capt | 1 June 79 } | | |
| Shean, Patrick | pt | 19 May 78 | 1 Jan 80 | was present |
| Speak, Nathaniel | do | 23 Aprl 78 | do | do |
| Smith, William[5] | do | 10 feb 77 | 26 Aprl 79 | prisoner war |
| Sappington, Thos. | do | 3 feb — | 12 June 78 | deserted |
| Shehey, Edward | pt | 17 May 77 | 1 Nov 80 | present |
| Swift, John[6] | pt | 12 Aug 77 | Oct 80 | discharged |
| Smith, Benjamin[7] | pt | 16 July 77 | 1 Jan 80 | was present |
| Stephens, William | pt | 23 June 77 | 2 July 79 | deserted |
| Sharpless, Robert | pt | 28 feb 78 | 1 Nov 80 | present } |
| | Corpl | 5 feb 79 | | |
| Simmons, Noble | pt | 11 feb 78 | 2 July 78 | died |
| Spyers, William[8] | pt | 8 Mar 77 | Dec 78 | do |
| Sharer, Michael | do | 10 July 77 | 1 Jan 80 | was present |
| deserted 13 Oct & Joined 13 April 78 | | | 16 May 80 | discharged by } Col. Forrest } |
| Scott, Benjamin[9] | Lieut | 10 dec 76 | 21 Sept 78 | resigned |
| Swanton, Peter | pt | 8 July 77 | 16 Aug 80 | missing |
| Stevenson, Alexr. | Drum | 1 Jany 77 | 1 Nov 80 | present |
| Smith, John[10] | Lieut | 10 dec 76 } | | |
| | Capt | 9 Nov 77 } | | |
| Sparrow, Alexr. | pt | 17 dec 76 | 20 dec 79 | discharged |
| | Corpl | 6 April 79 | | |
| Smith, Thomas[4] | pt | 1 July 78 | 1 June 79 | deserted |
| 1 July 78, rein. 3 Sept 78 pt | | | | |
| Summers, John[6] | pt | 10 June 78 | 1 Nov 80 | present |
| 1st mustr. June 78, rein. 6 Sept 78, Joined 15 Aug 79 | | | | |
| Scott, James | pt | 10 June 78 | 14 Mar 79 | discharged |
| 1st mustr. June 78 | | | | |

[1] Hawkins'.   [2] Dean's, Benson's.   [3] Lynch's.   [4] Ghiselin's.   [5] Dobson's.
[6] Trueman's.   [7] Beall's.   [8] Hynes'.   [9] Harris'.   [10] Chapline's, now Miles'.

## MUSTERS OF MARYLAND TROOPS, VOL. II.

| NAMES. | RANK. | TIME OF SERVICE. | | REMARKS. |
|---|---|---|---|---|
| | | Enlisted. | Discharged. | |
| Stalcob, Henry | pt | 10 June 78 | 14 Mar 79 | deserted |
| 1st mustr. June 78 | | | | |
| Stonestreet, William | pt | 1 April 78 | 1 Nov 80 | present |
| 1st mustr. June 78 | | | | |
| Spencer, George[1] | do | 6 June 78 | 1 Jan 80 | was present |
| 1st muster June 78 | | | | |
| Smith, John[2] | do | 5 dec 76 | | |
| Joined June muster 78 | | | | |
| Sullivan, Lawrence[3] | pt | 14 May 78 | | |
| Joined Oct 78 | | | | |
| Sloop, Joseph | pt | 16 May 78 ⎫ | 1 Nov 80 | present |
| | drum | 1 Aug 78 ⎬ | | |
| | pt | Oct 80 ⎭ | | |
| Sponk, Jacob | do | 4 May 78 | 1 Jan 80 | was present |
| Sloop, John | do | 2 May 78 | 3 Aug 78 | died |
| Simkins, William | pt | 2 June 78 | 1 April 79 | discharged |
| Slately, Michael | pt | 11 May 78 | time expd., discharged April 79 | |
| Spoutman, Francis | pt | 1 June 78 | 1 Aprl 79 | discharged |
| 1st mustr. June 78 | | | | |
| Sweney, Owen[4] | pt | 23 May 78 | 16 Aug 80 | missing |
| Suel, James | pt | 25 May 78 | 1 Nov 80 | present |
| Smith, Elias[2] | pt | 28 Aprl 78 | 1 Jany 80 | was present reinlisted |
| Shipley, Saml.[4] | pt | 3 June 78 | 22 Mar 79 | discharged |
| Stewart, Saml. | fifer | 11 June 78 | 1 Jany 80 | was present reinlisted |
| Smith, John | pt | 4 June 78 | do | do |
| Series, John[5] | pt | 11 May 79 | June 79 | absent wo. Leave |
| Smith, Thomas[6] | pt | 30 June 77 | 1 Nov 80 | present |
| 1st mustr. July 79 | | | | |
| Shugert, Peter[3] | pt | 30 Aprl 79 | 1 Nov 80 | do |
| Solomon, David[6] | pt | | 16 Aug 80 | prisoner |
| 1st mustr. 21 Sept 79 | | | | |
| Sevink, Abraham | pt | | 1 Nov 80 | present |
| Joined 21 Sept 79 | | | | |
| Stanley, Michael[7] | pt | 17 May 79 | do | do |
| Joined Sept 79 | | | | |
| Sanders, Danl.[3] | pt | 27 Aprl 79 | 16 Aug 80 | missing |
| Smith, Thomas[7] | do | 10 Aug 79 | 1 June 80 | was present |
| Smith, William | Sergt. Mate | 1 Feby 80 | | |
| Stern, George | pt | | 1 Nov 80 | present |
| Oct mustr. 1780 | | | | |

[1] Beall's.  [2] Hynes'.  [3] Lt. Williams'.  [4] Miles'.  [5] J. Jacobs'.  [6] Trueman's.  [7] Norris'.

MUSTERS OF MARYLAND TROOPS, VOL. II.

| NAMES. | RANK. | TIME OF SERVICE. Enlisted. | Discharged. | REMARKS. |
|---|---|---|---|---|
| Stewart, James | pt | 8 Jan 80 | 1 Nov 80 | present |
| Slackhouse, John | pt | 2 April 80 | do | do |
| | | 2 April 83 | discharged | |
| Sinester, Thomas | pt | | do | do |
| Shoemaker, Michael | pt | | do | do |
| Speake, Joseph | pt | | 16 Aug 80 | prisoner |
| Sowers, Michael | pt | 6 Mar 80 | 16 Aug 80 | prisoner |
| Smith, William | pt | | 10 Aug 80 | deserted |

### SEVENTH MARYLAND REGIMENT.

| NAMES. | RANK. | TIME OF SERVICE. Enlisted. | Discharged. | REMARKS. |
|---|---|---|---|---|
| Shoulder, Nicholas[1] | Drum | 7 dec 76 | Sept 77 | out of the Rolls |
| Seveny, James | pt | 10 April 77 | 8 May 77 | deserted |
| Smith, James | do | 2 April 77 | 1 Nov 80 | present |
| Skinner, James John | Lieut | 7 July 77 | | |
| Spyker, Benjamin | Capt | 10 Dec 76 | 12 May 79 | resigned |
| Smith, Isaac[2] retd. 16 July 78 | pt | 20 April 77 | | |
| Stoops, Andrew retd. July 78 | pt | 29 May 77 | | |
| Satterfield, Wm. Joined 2 Feby. | pt | 7 June 77 | | |
| | Corpl | 25 dec 77 | | |
| | Sergt | 1 Mar 80 | 16 Aug 80 | missing |
| Smith, William | pt | 7 May 77 | 16 Aug 80 | do |
| Shean, Dennis | do | 15 Aug 77 | 13 Sept 80 | discharged |
| Shaw, John | do | 15 Aug 77 | July 78 | Invalid |
| | | | 18 June 1781 | discharged |
| Stull, Daniel | Capt | 10 dec 76 | 14 Sept 78 | resigned |
| Seburn, John[3] | pt | 26 April 77 | May 80 | discharged |
| Simms, James[4] | pt | 7 dec 76 | 9 dec 76 | deserted |
| Storrom, Jacob | do | 8 dec 76 | 7 dec 79 | discharged |
| Smith, John | do | 24 Jany 77 | Jany 80 | do |
| | | | 19 Jany | mustered |
| Swain, Richard | do | 14 April 77 | June 79 | off Rolls |
| | Corpl | 1 Jan 78 | | |
| Sullivan, John | pt | 15 April 77 | 9 June 77 | deserted |
| Simpkins, Charles | do | 1 Sept 77 | 1 Nov 80 | present |
| Sullivan, Philip[5] Joined April 78 | Corpl | 4 dec 76 | | |
| Stewart, John | pt | 3 dec 76 | 22 Aug 77 | prisoner, never |
| Shaver, John | do | 3 dec 76 | | [retd. |
| | fifer | 1 Sept 77 | | |
| | pt | 26 dec 77 | Sept 78 | deserted |

[1] Grosh's.     [2] Spyker's.     [3] Stull's.     [4] Morris'.     [5] Bayly's.

## MUSTERS OF MARYLAND TROOPS, VOL. II.

| NAMES. | RANK. | TIME OF SERVICE. Enlisted. | Discharged. | REMARKS. |
|---|---|---|---|---|
| Scott, Patrick | pt | 5 dec 76 | 16 Aug 80 | killed |
| Joined June 78 | | | | |
| Stricker, John | do | 6 dec 76 | 6 dec 79 | discharged |
| Joined 22 Aug 77 | | | | |
| Stewart, Thomas | do | 6 dec 76 | 4 Oct 77 | killed |
| Shaver, Andrew[1] | pt | 4 May 77 | 3 May 80 | discharged |
| Scott, James | pt | 30 May 77 | June 77 | deserted |
| Scofield, William | do | 28 June 77 | 30 June 77 | do |
| Stapleton, Richard[2] | Corpl | | | |
| | Sergt | 1 June 78 | | [dischd. |
| Joined 23 July 78 | pt | 10 feb 79 | Sergt 1 June 79, 8 dec 79 | |
| Shanley, Jacob | pt | 14 dec 76 | | |
| reduced to pt 8 Nov 78 | Corpl | 1 Oct 77 | | [Invalids |
| | Sergt | 28 dec 77 | 31 Oct 79 | transferred to |
| Stevens, John | pt | 10 feb 77 | Nov 77 | off Rolls |
| Stewart, William | do | 12 Jan 77 | Jan 78 | off Rolls |
| Smith, John[3] | do | 28 Mar 78 | 12 Aug 78 | deserted |
| Sheerlock, Salathiel[4] | do | 24 dec 77 | 8 feb 78 | do |
| Sanson, Luke[5] | do | 21 April 78 | | |
| Joined Oct 80 | | | | |
| Spigman, John | do | 30 April 78 | 16 Aug 80 | missing |
| Sly, William | do | 30 April 78 | 16 Aug 80 | do |
| mustd. Corpl July 80 | | | 30 April 81 | discharged |
| Satchwell, Thomas | pt | 6 June 78 | 8 May 80 | deserted |
| Sargood, John | do | 22 April 78 | 8 May 80 | do |
| Swanwick, Thos. | do | 8 June 78 | 16 Aug 80 | missing |
| Sullivan, Thos.[6] | do | 11 May 78 | 6 July 80 | deserted |
| Salegh, Nichs.[7] | do | 18 May 78 | 16 Aug 80 | missing |
| Stonbreak, Valen. | do | 2 May 78 | | deserted |
| Shaver, Peter | do | 1 June 78 | 1 April 79 | discharged |
| Stallings, Abram.[8] | do | 20 May 78 | 1 Nov 80 | present |
| to Lynch's Co. | drum | 26 July 78 | | |
| Shoemaker, Peter | pt | 17 May 78 | 16 Aug 80 | killed |
| Smith, Aquilla[3] | do | 2 June 78 | 1 Nov 80 | present |
| | | | 2 June 81 | discharged |
| Smith, William | do | 19 May 78 | 24 Mar 78 | deserted |
| Sewell, John[8] | do | 8 June 78 | | |
| | Corpl | 25 Aug 78 | | |
| | Sergt | 27 dec 79 | 16 Aug 80 | missing |
| Short, James | pt | 30 June 78 | Jan 80 | deserted |
| Slater, Barthw.[9] | pt | 20 July 78 | 20 dec 78 | do |

[1] Reynolds'. 　[2] Deams'. 　[3] Bayly's. 　[4] Beatty's. 　[5] Jones'.<br>[6] Spyker's. 　[7] Stull's. 　[8] Morris'. 　[9] Grosh's.

## MUSTERS OF MARYLAND TROOPS, VOL. II.

| NAMES. | RANK. | TIME OF SERVICE. | | REMARKS. |
| | | Enlisted. | Discharged. | |
| --- | --- | --- | --- | --- |
| Stockley, John | pt | 20 July 78 | 6 Jan 79 | discharged |
| Sanky, John[1] | do | 16 May 78 | 13 May 79 | died |
| Stevens, Peter[2] | do | 19 May | 1 Nov 80 | present |
| | Corpl | 1 dec 79 | - | |
| Smith, Danl. | pt | 27 Jan 80 | do | do |
| Sizland, William[1] | pt | 6 Aug 80 | | missing |
| Mar 80 Beatty's | retd. per Cert. of Major Brice & Genl. Gist | | | |
| Stone, Cuthbert[3] | pt | | 1 Nov 80 | present |
| June 80 Jones' | | | | |

### GERMAN REGIMENT.

| NAMES. | RANK. | TIME OF SERVICE. | | REMARKS. |
| | | Enlisted. | Discharged. | |
| --- | --- | --- | --- | --- |
| Smitherd, John | pt | 24 April 78 | 1 Aug 80 | present |
| Shively, John | pt | 1 Mar 78 | do | do |
| Smith, Michael | drum | 28 April 78 | do | do |
| Smith, James | Corpl | 1 Aprl 78 | do | do |
| Silver, George | pt | 30 March | do | do |
| Smith, Christion | Mustd. pt | | 1 Aug 80 | deserted |
| Smith, Mathias | pt | 19 May 78 | 1 Aug 80 | present |
| Shoemaker, S. Fredk. | Corpl | 8 May 78 | do | do |
| Slite, (or Fite), James | | 13 Aprl 78 | do | do and 1 Jany 81 |
| Stanton, John | | 4 May 78 | do | do    [paid |
| Smith, Robert | Mustd. pt | | 1 Aug 80 | deserted |
| Settlemeyer, Chr. | | | 20 July 79 | discharged |
| Stauffer, George | Sergt | | 29    do | do |
| Smith, John | | | 12 Oct 79 | do |
| Sealors, Alexander | | | 9 Aug 79 | do |
| Shrayock, John | | | 20 July 79 | discharged |
| Slreiter, Joseph | | | 16    do | do |
| Slife, John | | | 20    do | do |
| Stanly, Christr. | Sergt | | do | do |
| Shotts, John | | | 24    do | do |
| Shoemaker, Michael | | . | do | do |
| Studer, Philip | | | do | do |
| Smith, (or Smithly), Philip | | | 12 Oct 79 | do |
| Smith, John | | | 10 Aug 79 | do |
| Strome, Henry | | | 17 July 79 | do |
| Shark, John | | | | died |
| Sollers, Frederick | Sergt | | 28 July 79 | discharged |
| Shutz, Jacob | | | 14 Aug 79 | do |
| Shrayer, Mathias | | | 1 Oct 79 | do |
| Smith, Henry | | | 25 Aug 79 | do |
| Shaffer, John | | | 19 July | do |

[1]Beatty's.          [2]Anderson's.          [3]Jones'.

## MUSTERS OF MARYLAND TROOPS, VOL. II.

| NAMES. | RANK. | TIME OF SERVICE. | | REMARKS. |
|---|---|---|---|---|
| | | Enlisted. | Discharged. | |
| Snider, John | | | 24 July | discharged |
| Stonebraker, Adam | | | 26 do | do |
| Shaffer, Adam | | 21 July | 20 do | do |
| Switzer, Fredk. | | | 16 do | do |
| Smithly, (or Smith), John | | | 12 Oct do | do |
| Statler, Henry | | | do | do |
| Stoner, Michael | | | do | do |
| Stoyle, Conrad | See Hoyle | | 20 July do | do |
| Selwood, William | | 15 April 80 | 1 Aug 80 | present |
| Selas, Andrew | | 22 May 80 | do | do |

### FIFTH MARYLAND REGIMENT.

| NAMES. | RANK. | Enlisted. | Discharged. | REMARKS. |
|---|---|---|---|---|
| Taylor, William[1] | pt | 29 June 77 | April 78 | left out |
| Thomas, Allen | do | 22 July 77 | 1 Jany 80 | was present |
| Tylea, Benjamin[2] | do | 24 June 77 | April 78 | left out |
| Taft, Joseph | do | do | 1 Jan 80 | was present |
| | Corpl | 1 June 78 | | |
| | Sergt | 12 Jan 79 | } 16 May 80 | discharged |
| Townshend, Benja.[3] | do | 4 feb 77 | } 1 Nov 80 | present |
| | pt | 1 Aug 78 | | |
| Tullock, William | do | 25 Mar | April 78 | left out |
| Taylor, Joshua | do | 7 July | | |
| | Corpl | Oct 80 | } 1 Nov 80 | present |
| Thompson, Henry | pt | 5 Sept | April 78 | left out |
| Thompson, Cornelius[4] | do | 26 Mar 77 | 1 Nov 80 | present |
| Tullis, Litchfield[5] | do | 30 Jan 77 | 27 July 78 | discharged |
| Toomey, John | do | 6 April | 1 Jan 80 | was present |
| | | | 8 May 80 | discharged |
| Thompson, Benja.[6] | do | 8 feb 77 | 20 June 79 | deserted |
| Turner, John[7] | do | 29 May 78 | May 79 | not heard of |
| Tucker, Anthony[3] | do | 7 May 78 | 1 Nov 80 | present |
| Thomas, Richard[4] | do | 4 June 78 | 20 Mar 79 | discharged |
| Tanner, John | do | 24 April 78 | Nov 78 | died |
| Twiner, Spintlo[2] | do | | July 78 | left out |
| 1st mustr. June 78, out July 78 | | | | |
| Terrett, William[2] | pt | 5 Jany 78 | 1 Jany 80 | was present |
| 1st mustr. June 78 | | | | |
| Terrier, Charles | do | 30 April 78 | 16 Aug 80 | missing |
| 1st mustr. June 78 | | | | |
| Thomas, Isaac[7] | do | 5 May 78 | 1 Oct 79 | deserted |

[1] Dean's.  [2] Hawkins'.  [3] Handy's.  [4] Johnson's.
[5] Emory's.  [6] Cosden's.  [7] Lynch's.

## MUSTERS OF MARYLAND TROOPS, VOL. II.

| NAMES. | RANK. | TIME OF SERVICE. Enlisted. | Discharged. | REMARKS. |
|---|---|---|---|---|

### SIXTH MARYLAND REGIMENT.

| NAMES. | RANK. | Enlisted. | Discharged. | REMARKS. |
|---|---|---|---|---|
| Thompson, John[1] | pt | 2 June 77 | 1 Jan 80 | was present |
| | | | 2 June 80 | discharged |
| Trainer, Patrick | pt | 20 May 78 | 16 Aug 80 | prisoner |
| Tuff, John | do | 5 May 78 | 10 May 79 | died |
| Tillard, Edward | Major | 20 feb 77 | | |
| | Col | | | |
| Tidley, Edward[2] | pt | 12 Mar 77 } 1 Nov 80 | | present |
| | Corpl | 1 Sept 78 } | | |
| Truman, Alexr. | Capt | 10 dec 76 | | |
| Taylor, Robert[3] | pt | 22 feb 78 } | | |
| mustr. Sergt Oct 80 | Corpl | 1 June 78 } 1 Nov 80 | | present |
| Thomas, George | pt | 16 May 78 | July 80 | deserted |
| Turner, Richd.[4] | pt | 24 Aug 77 | 24 Aug 80 | discharged |
| Taylor, Benjamin[5] | do | 23 May 77 | 1 Nov 80 | present |
| Turnbridge, Saml. | D. Q. M. Sergt | 1 July 77 | 17 June 78 | discharged |
| Taymon, Benja.[1] | pt | 1 July 78 | | dead or deserted |
| 1st July 78 Joined | | | | |
| Taggart, John[2] | pt | 10 June 78 | 14 Mar 79 | discharged |
| 1st mustr. June 78 | | | | |
| Tuhton, (or Tuchstone), Christopher | pt | 24 May 78 | 1 Nov 80 | present |
| 1st mustr. June 78, rein. 22 dec 78 | | | | |
| Thompson, Nathl.[6] | pt | 13 May 78 } | | |
| | Corpl | 1 July 78 } | | |
| Taylor, James[7] | pt | 20 May 78 | 1 Aug 80 | deserted [valids |
| Tancard, Thomas[8] | do | 28 April 78 | 8 April 79 | transferrd to In- |
| Thomas, John[7] | do | 28 April 78 | feby muster 79 | died at Fish Kill |
| Taylor, George[6] | pt | 27 April 79 | 1 Nov 80 | present |
| Tuyger, Danl.[9] | pt | | 1 Jan 80 | was present |
| 21 Sept 79 Joined | | | | |
| Thomas, John[6] | pt | 7 Aug 79 | 1 Nov 80 | present |

### SEVENTH REGIMENT.

| NAMES. | RANK. | Enlisted. | Discharged. | REMARKS. |
|---|---|---|---|---|
| Tabbs, Barton | Surgeon | 10 April 77 | 3 Oct 79 | resigned |
| Taylor, James[10] | pt | 30 dec 76 | 13 Sept 77 | deserted & 26 |
| Joined again | | | | May 78 dischgd |
| Turner, Nathl. | pt | 30 dec 76 | 5 Jan 80 | discharged |
| Taylor, Thomas | pt | 13 Mar 77 | 3 May 80 | do |
| Taylor, William[11] | do | 17 April 77 | 26 April 80 | to Invalids |

[1] Ghiselin's.  [2] Dobson's.  [3] Beall's.  [4] Lawrence's.  [5] Harris'.
[6] Lt. Williams'.  [7] Miles'.  [8] Hynes'.  [9] Trueman's.
[10] Grosh's.  [11] Spyker's.

## MUSTERS OF MARYLAND TROOPS, VOL. II.

| NAMES. | RANK. | TIME OF SERVICE. Enlisted. | Discharged. | REMARKS. |
|---|---|---|---|---|
| Townshend, Joseph | pt | 9 May 77 | 1 April 80 | died |
| Tutwiller, Jonathan[1] | Sergt | 4 dec 76 | 7 dec 79 | discharged |
| Joined June 78 | | | | |
| Thoupe, Richard[2] | pt | 20 May 77 | 4 Oct 77 | died |
| Thompson, John | do | 9 June 77 | Dec | deserted |
| Thompson, Jeremiah[3] | Sergt | 8 Aug 77 | | deserted |
| Taylor, William | pt | | 1 Nov 80 | present |
| Joined Oct 80 | | | | |
| Townshend, Aaron[4] | do | 20 April 78 | 9 Oct 78 | died |
| Townshend, Wm. | do | 2 May 78 | 1 Nov 80 | present |
| | | | 24 April 81 | discharged |
| Thompson, Jeremiah[5] | pt | 20 Jan 78 | 8 Feby 78 | deserted |
| Thompson, William[6] | do | 5 May 78 | July 79 | deserted |
| Tongue, Robert | pt | 6 June 78 | 16 Aug 80 | missing |
| Turner, Solomon | | | 12 May 81 | |
| Tucker, John[6] | pt | 6 June 78 | 16 Aug 80 | missing |
| Toomy, Dennis | do | 29 April 78 | 8 May 80 | deserted |
| Turner, John[7] | pt | 6 May 78 | 1 Nov 80 | present |
| Trendall, Michael[8] | pt | 20 April 78 | 16 Aug 80 | missing |
| Turner, John[1] | do | 8 May 78 | Nov & dec 78 | dead |
| Taylor, Saml. | do | 20 May 78 | 2 June 78 | deserted |
| Turner, Solomon[9] | do | 2 Mar 78 | 16 Aug 80 | missing } |
| | | | 12 May 81 | discharged } |
| Tanner, Thomas | pt | 22 April 78 | 16 Aug 80 | missing |
| Tomlinson, Zadock[1] | pt | 8 June 78 | 30 Mar 79 | discharged |
| Taylor, Saml.[9] | Fifer | 22 April 78 | | |
| Joined Oct 80 | | | | |
| Taylor, John[7] | pt | 20 July 78 | 23 Nov 78 | died |
| Thomason, Ezekiel[5] | do | 3 June 78 | 16 Aug 80 | missing |
| Townshend, James | pt | Left with Baron Stuben when the Troops } marched Southward } | | |
| Tanckard, Wm.[10] | pt | | 16 Aug 80 | missing |
| Turnon, Dennis[1] | pt | 1 feb 80 | 16 Aug 80 | missing, joined |
| Taylor, Richard | pt | 6 feb 80 | 1 Nov 80 | present |

### GERMAN REGIMENT.

| NAMES. | RANK. | TIME OF SERVICE. Enlisted. | Discharged. | REMARKS. |
|---|---|---|---|---|
| Timblin, John | pt | 28 Aprl 78 | 1 Aug 80 | present |
| Tawney, Fredk. | not on any musters | | | |
| Truck, John | Sergt | 24 July 79 | | discharged |
| Taylor, William | | | 12 Oct 79 | do |
| Tite, James | See James Stite | | | |

---

[1] Morris'.    [2] Reynolds'.    [3] Deams'.    [4] Spyker's, Grosh's.    [5] Beatty's.
[6] Jones'.    [7] Grosh's.    [8] Stull's.    [9] Bayly's.    [10] Lynn's.

| NAMES. | RANK. | TIME OF SERVICE. Enlisted. | Discharged. | REMARKS. |
|--------|-------|------------|-----------|---------|
| **FIFTH MARYLAND REGIMENT.** | | | | |
| Valliant, James[1] | pt | 14 Mar 77 | 14 Mar 80 | discharged |
| Vallient, John | do | 14  do | do | do |
| Vallow, John[2] | do | 1 Mar 78 | 1 Oct 80 | present |
| Vincent, Benjamin[2] | do | 22 May 79 | 1 Oct 79 | deserted |
| **GERMAN REGIMENT.** | | | | |
| Vaughan, Cornelius | pt | 21 May 78 | 1 Aug 80 | present |
| Vincent, William | do | 15 May 78 | do | do |
| Vatchle, John | | | 24 July 79 | discharged |
| Veatch, Abram | | | 22 Nov 80 | deserted |
| **FIFTH MARYLAND REGIMENT.** | | | | |
| Woulds, James | Adjt | 16 Mar 77 } | | |
| | Ensn | 27 May 78 } 23 Sept 79 | | resigned |
| Warfield, John[4] | 2d Lieut | 10 May 77 | 7 Nov 77 | do |
| Willis, Andrew | pt | 17 feb 77 | 14 feb 80 | discharged |
| Willis, Jarvis[5] | Corpl | do | 14 feb 80 | do |
| Woods, Zadock | pt | 31 May 77 | Aprl 78 | left out |
| Warren, John | pt | 28 April 77 | 12 Oct 79 | discharged |
| Worner, William[6] | do | 10 May | April 78 | left out |
| Worner, Solomon | do | do | do | do |
| Williams, Henry | Corpl | 3 May | 2 April 78 | discharged |
| Welch, John[3] | pt | 25 feb 77 } | | |
| | Corpl | 16 April 77 } reduced 10 Sept 77 | | |
| | pt | 1 Aprl 78 } 25 feb 80 | | discharged |
| Walls, M. John[7] | Ensn | 20 feb 77 | 13 Oct 78 | resigned |
| Williams, John | pt | 21 Mar 77 | April 78 | left out |
| Wilson, John | do | 1 Jan 77 | 1 Jan 80 | discharged |
| Ward, Mathew[2] | D. fife | 20 Aprl 77 | 3 Nov 79 | died |
| Warner, Arbuckle[1] | pt | 21 feb 77 | 2 Sept 80 | do |
| Willoughby, William | do | 29 Jan 77 | 31 Mar 79 | deserted |
| Wright, Nathanl. | pt | 18 July 77 | 1 Jan 80 | was present |
| | | | 1 Aug 80 | off the Rolls |
| Welsh, Patrick | pt | 10 May 77 | 27 Oct 78 | to Invalids } |
| | | | 13 May 80 | discharged } |
| Williams, Thomas[8] to Bird's | pt | 6 Aprl 77 | 5 feb 80 | do |
| Woodfind, Thos.[9] 1st mustr. April 78 | pt | | 1 Oct 78 | to Invalids |
| | | | 23 feb 79 | discharged |
| Willis, Daniel[10] 1st mustr. April 78 | Drum | 9 feb 77 | 16 Aug 80 | missing } |
| | | | | joined } |

[1] Emory's.  [2] Johnson's.  [3] Lynch's.  [4] Dean's.  [5] Williams'.
[6] Hawkins'.  [7] Handy's.  [8] Cosden's, Birds.  [9] Lt. Hamilton's.  [10] Handy's, Bird's.

## MUSTERS OF MARYLAND TROOPS, VOL. II.

| NAMES. | RANK. | TIME OF SERVICE. Enlisted. | Discharged. | REMARKS. |
|---|---|---|---|---|
| Walsh, David[1] | pt | | 1 feb 79 | deserted 24 May do |
| 1st mustr. April 78 | | | | |
| White, Joseph | pt | 6 Aprl 78 | 16 Aug 80 | missing |
| Williams, James[2] | pt | 1 June 78 | 5 Nov 78 | died |
| 1st muster June 78 | | | | |
| Wilson, George[3] | pt | 29 May 78 | depreciation issued twice | } |
| | | | 1 Oct 80 | present |
| | | | 5 May 81 | discharged } |
| Waters, Abraham | pt | 20 May 78 | 29 July 78 | died |
| Woolcott, William[4] | pt | 7 May 78 | | |
| Wright, William | pt | 4 May 78 | 1 June 79 | discharged |
| Winterbottom, John[5] | pt | 6 June 78 | 23 Mar 79 | do |
| Williams, Simon | pt | 15 May 78 | feb 79 | not heard of |
| Wilson, David[1] | pt | 4 Mar 78 | 1 Nov 80 | present |
| reinlisted 1 dec 79, mustered present 1 Oct 80 | | | | |
| Wittington, Benja. | pt | 14 May 78 | Augt 78 | not heard of |
| Witeman, Conrod[1] | pt | 14 Aprl 78 | 1 Mar 79 | discharged |
| White, Joseph[6] | pt | 8 Aprl 78 | 1 Jan 80 | was present |
| 1st muster June 78 | | 1 feb 79 | | |
| | Sergt | 16 Aug 79 | | |
| Whittington, Joseph | pt | | July 78 | left out |
| 1st muster June 78 | | | | |
| Watts, Solomon[7] | pt | 2 May 78 | June 79 | died |
| Williams, Thos. | pt | 9 June 78 | 19 Mar 79 | discharged |
| Wright, Coursey | pt | 20 Aprl 78 | 19 June 78 | deserted |
| Ward, William[8] | pt | 1 July 78 | 28 feb 79 | discharged |
| Wilkinson, John[9] | pt | 17 May 79 | 1 Nov 80 | present |
| 1st muster June 78 | Sergt | 1 Aug 79 | | |
| Wallis, John[9] | pt | 4 July 79 | 1 Jan 80 | was present |
| | | | 8 May 80 | discharged by Col. Forrest |
| Wheller, Philip | | | 16 Aug 80 | missing |
| Oct Muster 80 | | | | |
| Wilson, George | | | 5 May 81 | |

### SIXTH MARYLAND REGIMENT.

| | | | | |
|---|---|---|---|---|
| Warrior, Daniel[10] | fifer | 5 May 78 | 1 Oct 80 | present |
| reduced to fife 8 Aug 79 | Drum M. | 1 April 79 | | |
| drum Major 2 Sept 79 | | | | |
| Williams, O. H. | Col | 10 dec 76 | | |

[1] Johnson's.   [2] Lt. Hamilton's.   [3] Lynch's.   [4] Handy's.   [5] Ensign Jones'.
[6] Handy's, Bird's.   [7] Hawkins'.   [8] Emory's.   [9] Benson's.   [10] Ghiselin's.

## MUSTERS OF MARYLAND TROOPS, VOL. II.

| NAMES. | RANK. | TIME OF SERVICE. Enlisted. | Discharged. | REMARKS. |
|---|---|---|---|---|
| Wright, Benja.[1] | Ensn | 14 June 77 | | |
| | Lieut | 1 Jan 78 | 28 Nov 78 | absent wo. Leave |
| Westwood, William | pt | 26 June 77 | 1 Nov 80 | present |
| Wailes, Edward[2] | Ensn | See Letter B | | |
| Woodam, Robert[3] | pt | 17 feb 77 | 16 Aug 80 | killed |
| Windle, Jonathan | do | 24 Aprl 78 | 1 Nov 80 | present |
| Woods, David | do | 4 May 78 | 16 Aug 80 | killed |
| Watson, James | do | 21 May 78 | 4 feb 79 | discharged |
| Wright, James[4] | Sergt | 5 dec 76 | June must. 78 | left out |
| | S. Major | 28 June 77 | | |
| Wiltz, Benjamin | pt | 30 dec 76 | 30 Dec 79 | discharged |
| | Sergt | 7 Sept 77 | | |
| Welch, William | Sergt | 2 Aprl 77 | 10 Jan 80 | do |
| reduced | pt | 20 Oct 77 | | |
| Williams, Nathan[6] | Lieut | 10 dec 77 | 16 Aug 80 | killed |
| Ward, William | pt | 22 Aug 77 | 16 Aug 80 | missing |
| Woods, Joseph[6] | pt | 6 Mar 77 | 16 Aug 80 | killed |
| Walker, Saml.[7] | | 2 May 1777 | | |
| | Sergt | 25 Nov 77 | | |
| | pt | 19 Nov 78 | 16 Aug 80 | missing |
| Williams, Thos.[8] Joined 1 July 78 | pt | 1 July 78 | Feby 79 | left out |
| Willis, John[3] 1st muster June 78 | pt | 3 April 78 | 1 Nov 80 | present |
| Wice, Peter[9] | pt | 3 June 78 | 4 Aprl 79 | discharged |
| Wolf, Peter | pt | 3 June 78 | 1 Aprl 79 | do |
| Watson, James | do | 1 June 78 | | |
| Whelan, Laurence D. rein. 12 feb 79 | do | 13 June 78 | } Oct 78 } 26 feb 79 | deserted do |
| Ward, Zachariah | pt | 5 May 78 | 21 Jan 79 | deserted |
| Welsh, William | pt | 11 May 78 | 7 July 78 | do |
| Waters, John | pt | 3 April 78 | 23 Aug 78 | died |
| Watkins, Leonard[10] | Sergt | 2 May 78 | 1 Jan 80 | present |
| | | | 11 May 80 | discharged |
| Walker, Edward | pt | 16 May 78 | 16 Aug 80 | missing |
| Welsh, David[4] | pt | 4 June 78 | 1 April 79 | discharged |
| Wooling, Richard | pt | 4 June 78 | 1 April 79 | do |
| Wooling, Mason Joined 9 Oct 78 | pt | 4 June 78 | 23 Oct 78 | died |
| Welch, William[2] 1st mustr. July 79 | pt | | 16 Aug 80 | prisoner |

[1] Dobson's.   [2] Trueman's.   [3] Beall's.   [4] Hynes'.   [5] Laurence's.
[6] Harris'.   [7] Chapline's, now Miles'.   [8] Ghiselin's.   [9] Lt. Williams'.   [10] Miles'.

## MUSTERS OF MARYLAND TROOPS, VOL. II.

| NAMES. | RANK. | TIME OF SERVICE. Enlisted. | TIME OF SERVICE. Discharged. | REMARKS. |
|---|---|---|---|---|
| Wood, Joseph | pt | | 13 Nov 79 | deserted |
| 1st muster July 79 | | | | |
| Wirey, Michael[1] | Fifer | 12 May 79 | 1 Nov 80 | present |
| Williams, Benja. | pt | | do | do |
| Oct mustr. 80 | | | | |
| Wright, Absolom | do | 20 Mar 80 | 16 Aug 80 | missing |

### SEVENTH REGIMENT.

| NAMES. | RANK. | TIME OF SERVICE. Enlisted. | TIME OF SERVICE. Discharged. | REMARKS. |
|---|---|---|---|---|
| Wright, Thomas[2] | pt | 4 feb 77 | 3 feb 80 | discharged |
| Winstanley, Francis | do | 8 Aprl 77 | 9 April 77 | deserted |
| Warner, Samuel[3] | Sergt | 25 Mar 77 | feb 78 | off Rolls |
| Watkins, Solomon | pt | 29 Mar 77 | July 78 | off the Rolls |
| Ward, William[4] | pt | 18 April 77 | Mar 78 | off Rolls |
| | | | May 80 | time out |
| Williams, John | Sergt | 19 May 77 | 8 May 80 | discharged |
| Wright, Edward | Ensign | 1 Mar 77 | 7 Oct 79 | resigned |
| | Lieut | 28 dec 77 | | |
| Wells, Valentine[5] | pt | 27 Mar 77 | April 78 | off Rolls March |
| Wilson, James | do | 7 Aprl 77 | May 78 | off Rolls |
| Williams, Elisha | Capt | 10 dec 76 | 28 Nov 78 | resigned |
| Webb, William[6] | pt | 7 Jan 77 | 9 June 77 | deserted |
| Walker, Edward[7] | do | 19 dec 76 | 22 dec 76 | do |
| Wright, Edward | do | 20 Aprl 77 | 16 Aprl 80 | time out, dis-charged |
| Joined again | | | | |
| Watkins, Gassaway | Ensign | | | |
| | Lieut | 1 May 77 | | |
| Warner, John[8] | Corpl | 13 July 77 | 20 Oct 77 | died |
| Woods, James | pt | 24 Aprl 77 | 27 Aug 78 | do |
| Welch, Mark | pt | 2 June 77 | July 78 | off Rolls, transferred to Invalids } |
| Warrent, James | pt | 26 June 77 | Mar 79 | not heard of |
| Winkfield, James[9] | pt | | 16 Sept 77 | deserted |
| Ward, Thomas | do | | 16 Aug 80 | missing |
| Wood, William | do | | 17 May 77 | deserted |
| Wykell, or Vycall, Adam[4] | do | 2 July 77 | 2 July 80 | discharged |
| 1st muster June 78 | | | | |
| Whalor, Ignatius Mitchell[2] | pt | 25 feb 78 | 1 Nov 80 | present |
| Mustr. John Apl & May roll, Sergt May 80 | | | | |
| Wheelor, Thomas[10] | pt | 23 April 78 | Oct 78 | died |
| White, Thomas | do | 17 Mar 78 | 16 Aug 80 | missing } |
| | | | 1 Mar 81 | discharged } |
| | | | | depreciation recd. twice } |

| | | | | |
|---|---|---|---|---|
| [1] Norris'. | [9] Jones'. | [3] Grosh's. | [4] Spyker's. | [5] Stull's. |
| [6] Williams'. | [7] Bayly's. | [8] Reynolds'. | [9] Deams'. | [10] Spyker's, Grosh's. |

## MUSTERS OF MARYLAND TROOPS, VOL. II.

| NAMES. | RANK. | TIME OF SERVICE. Enlisted. | Discharged. | REMARKS. |
|---|---|---|---|---|
| Wedge, William[1] | pt | 14 Mar 78 | 1 Nov 80 | present |
| Walter, Mathew[2] | do | 27 dec 77 | 8 feb 78 | deserted |
| Wastfalling, Danl. | do | 27 dec 77 | 8 feb 78 | do |
| Whatmore, Robert[3] | do | 19 May 78 | 8 July 80 | deserted |
| White, James | do | 20 May 78 | 1 Nov 80 | present |
| Wizer, Michael | do | 1 June 78 | 16 Aug 80 | missing |
|  |  |  | 1 June 81 | discharged } |
| Whaling, Lawrence[4] | pt | 13 May 78 | 1 Sept 78 | deserted |
| Walker, Charles[5] | pt |  | 1 Mar 79 | discharged |
| June Spyker's |  |  |  |  |
| Wildman, William | do | 2 May 78 | 1 June 78 | deserted |
| Waltman, Michael[6] | do | 16 Apl 78 | 1 Nov 80 | present |
| to Morris' |  |  |  |  |
| Wheatley, George | do | 9 June 78 |  |  |
| Woltmon, Nicholas | do | 26 Aprl 78 | 10 July 78 | deserted |
| Wharton, William[6] | do | 28 May 78 | 16 Aug 80 | missing |
| Wolters, Ephriam[7] | do | 4 May 78 | Dec 79 | deserted |
| Wilson, Daniel[4] | do |  | 11 Jan 79 | transferrd. to 2 Md. Brigade |
| White, Peter | do | 20 July 78 | 20 Dec 78 | deserted |
| Wheley, Zadock | fifer | 20 Oct 78 | June 79 | off Rolls |
|  | pt | 1 Mar 79 | Joined 82 |  |
| Webb, John[2] | pt | 4 May 78 | 1 Nov 80 | present |
| Whipple, William | do |  | 9 Sept 80 | deserted |
| Williams, Benja.[4] | do | 9 June 78 | 15 Aprl 80 | paid |
| to Grosh's | Fifer | 11 feb 79 | Joined 82 |  |
| Weagle, George[6] | pt | 9 Jan 78 | 9 Mar 79 | discharged |
| Weeks, Benjamin[8] | do | 20 Aug 79 | 16 Aug 80 | missing |
| Wilson, William[9] | do | 6 feb 80 | 16 Aug 80 | do |
| Wedge, Samuel[2] | do | 2 feb 80 | 16 Aug 80 | do |
| Williams, Gabriel[10] | Sergt | 6 feb 80 | 1 Nov 80 | present |
| Worslick, William | pt |  | 16 Aug 80 | missing |

### GERMAN REGIMENT.

| | | | | |
|---|---|---|---|---|
| Wilstock, Henry | pt | 1 Nov 79 | 1 Aug 80 | present |
| to 1 Jan 81 |  |  |  |  |
| Wade, John | do | 4 May 78 | do | do |
| to 1 Jan 81 |  |  |  |  |
| Williams, Danl. | do | 9 June 80 | do | do |
| to 1 Jan 81 |  |  |  |  |
| Welty, John |  | 17 July 78 | do | do |

| | | | | |
|---|---|---|---|---|
| [1] Bayly's. | [2] Beatty's. | [3] Jones'. | [4] Grosh's. | [5] Spyker's. |
| [6] Stull's. | [7] Morris'. | [8] Anderson's. | [9] Lynn's. | [10] Mason's. |

## MUSTERS OF MARYLAND TROOPS, VOL. II.

| NAMES. | RANK. | TIME OF SERVICE. Enlisted. | Discharged. | REMARKS. |
|---|---|---|---|---|
| Wright, Saml. | pt | 3 June 80 | 1 Aug 80 | present |
| Walker, John | do | 10 Aprl 80 | do | do |
| Woolford, Thomas | do | 15 May 78 | do | do |
| Williams, Joseph | | | 22 July 79 | discharged |
| Weaver, Michael | | | 26 do | do |
| Waggoner, Chrisr. | | | 12 Oct 79 | do |
| Witsinger, Ludk. | | | 20 July | do |
| Wink, Jacob | | | 1 June 80 | present |
| Wilhelme, George | | | 17 July 79 | discharged |
| Wagoner, Jacob | | | 24 do | do |

### FIFTH MARYLAND REGIMENT.

| | | | | |
|---|---|---|---|---|
| Yoe, Thomas[1] | pt | 4 June 78 | 19 Mar 79 | discharged |
| Yoe, Joseph, (or Robert) | do | 8 June 78 | | |
| pt 1st May 79 | Sergt | 1 July 78 | 1 Oct 79 | deserted |
| Yewell, C. Solomon[2] | pt | 4 June 78 | | |
| Young, Thomas[1] | pt | 6 June 79 | 1 Jan 80 | now present |

### SIXTH MARYLAND REGIMENT.

| | | | | |
|---|---|---|---|---|
| Young, Samuel[3] | pt | 22 Apr 78 | 1 Nov 80 | present |
| Young, John[4] | do | 10 Mar 77 | do | do |
| | Corpl | 1 dec 79 | | |
| Young, Henry[5] | pt | 1 July 78 | feb 79 | left out |
| 1st July 78 joined | | | | |
| Young, Daniel[4] | pt | 1 June 78 | 21 Nov 78 | died |
| Young, Godhed | do | 2 Aug 78 | 23 Aug 80 | to Invalids |
| Joined 21 Sept 79 | | | | |

### SEVENTH MARYLAND REGIMENT.

| | | | | |
|---|---|---|---|---|
| Yates, John[6] | Corpl | 15 Aprl 77 | | |
| | Sergt | 7 June 77 | | |
| | Q.M.Sergt. | 1 Aug 77 | 16 Aprl 80 | discharged |
| Young, Thomas[7] | pt | 4 June 77 | July 78 | Invalids |
| Young, William | do | 15 Aug 77 | 1 Nov 80 | present |
| Yoe, Thomas | Drum | 26 Sept 77 | Sept 80 | discharged |
| Younger, George[8] | pt | 8 Mar 77 | | off Rolls |
| Yates, Robert[9] | Corpl | 15 dec 76 | 6 Jan 80 | discharged |
| | Sergt | 1 Aprl 78 | | |
| Yost, George[10] | Drum | 4 May 77 | 20 May 80 | discharged |
| York, William[11] | pt | 12 July 78 | 14 Sept 78 | died |

[1] Hawkins'.  [2] Emory's.  [3] Dobson's.  [4] Trueman's.
[5] Ghiselin's.  [6] Grosh's.  [7] Spyker's.  [8] Morris'.
[9] Bayly's.  [10] Reynold's.  [11] Stull's.

MUSTERS OF MARYLAND TROOPS, VOL. II.

| NAMES. | RANK. | TIME OF SERVICE. Enlisted. | Discharged. | REMARKS. |
|---|---|---|---|---|
| | | GERMAN REGIMENT. | | |
| Yakely, Michael | | | 17 July 79 | discharged |
| | | SEVENTH REGIMENT. | | |
| Zacharius, Fredk.[1] | pt | 4 June 78 | 30 Mar 79 | discharged |
| | | GERMAN REGIMENT. | | |
| Zimmerman, John | | | 12 Oct 79 | discharged |

SOLDIERS WHO HAVE NOT RECEIVED DEPRECIATION AND PAY UPON INSUFFICIENT CERTIFICATES.

| | |
|---|---|
| Abel Ormond | Certificate of John Dove |
| John Waller | pt 2nd Regt., recd. depreciation twice |
| Thomas James | deserted, 5 mos. pay recd. by Dove |
| Joseph Southall | twice depreciation      Mr. Rose |
| Joseph Bray | do      do |
| Chrisr. Beall | do      do      Crawford |

Settled for by Mr. Crawford in final Settlements

[1] Morris'.

# SUPPLEMENTARY GERMAN REGIMENT PAPERS.

## GERMAN REGIMENT.

Roll of Capt. Henry Fister's Company.   In the German Battalion.
Commd. by Col. Nicholas Hussecker. 1776.

Lieut. Charles Balzel
" Michael Bayer
. Ensign Jacob Grommet
Serjt. John Balzel, recommended
by the Major & Capt.
" Philip Shroop
" Philip Shopper

Sergt. George Wintz
Corpl. George Hoover
" Fredk. Wilhite
" Jacob Tudderow
" Jacob Low
Drummer John Heffner

### Privates

Henry Delawter
Henry Hawk
Fredk. Mittag
Jacob Fantz
Peter Copple
Jacob Kuntz
John Ridenhour
Willm. Snider
Adam Froshour
Christn. Sheafer
Leonard Everley, absent
John Wachtel, Dis. 24 July
George Studdlemier
Philip Colour
Valentine Shotter
Henry Ziegler
Jacob Tabler
Mathias King
Jacob Miller
Philip Isingminger
John Leather
Henry Hildebrand
Anthony Miller
Jacob Farber
Michael Moser

### Privates

Ludwick Visinger
Jacob Hammer
Martin Watkins
Nicholas Frye
Jacob Weaver
Jacob Eggman
John Beckerson
George Clinton
Christopher Slender
Michael Beiker
Anthony Hamilton
Jacob Sheafer
Adam Charles
Abraham Fettie
John Imfeld
George Shrantz
Adam Smeltzer
John Bird
Gottlieb Klein
Peter Graff
John Ringer, absent
Jacob Croumer
Philip Stouder
Peter Hoover

### Privates

Peter Americk
Conrad Houseman
John Klein
Henry Hain
Jacob Kurtz
John Zimmerman
Henry Smith
Adam Gentner
Henry Cronies
Leonard Ludwick
John Snider
Henry Herring
Peter Kuntz
Justinius Hogshield
Edward Robertson
John Shatz
Michael Stiener
John Able
Michael Shoemaker
Frederick Henninghouse
Thomas Polehouse
Bartle Engel
John Klein
John Miller, absent

Pay Roll of Capt. Michael Bayer's Company in the German Regiment, Continental Troops in the United States. Commanded by Lt. Col. Ludwick Weltner. For the months of July, August, September and October, 1779.

| NAMES. | REMARKS. | NAMES. | REMARKS. |
|---|---|---|---|
| | | Privates | |
| Capt. Michael Bayer, (Boyer) | | Ludwick Wesinger | Dischd. July 20 |
| Sergt. —— —— | Promoted Aug. 1st | Rudolph Marolf | "        "  " |
| "    —— —— | Dischd.    "  9th | Jacob Miller, Jr. | "        "  " |
| "    —— —nley | "    July 20th | John Abel | "        "  " |
| Corpl. —— Polehouse | Promoted Aug. 1st | Adam Gantner | "        "  " |
| "    —k Shoemaker | "    "  " | Jacob Miller, Sr. | "        "  " |
| "    —rew Robinson | Dischd. July 20th | Jacob Cramer | "        "  " |
| "    John Hoshield | "    "  24th | Leonard Ludwick | "        "  24 |
| "    John Shotz | "    "  " | Michael Shoemaker | "        "  " |
| Drum. Thomas Hatchcraft | | Peter Emerick | "        "  " |
| "    Henry Ferrins | | Henry Herring | "        "  " |
| Privates | | Michael Moser | "        "  " |
| Thomas Mahony | | Henry Cronise | "        "  " |
| George Kepphard | | Phillip Fisher | "        "  " |
| Peter Kuntz | | John Snider | "        "  " |
| Abraham Kettle | | John Wachtel | "        "  " |
| Henry Fisher | | Phillip Strider | "        "  " |
| John Foliott | Joined Oct 10th | Jacob Riggnagle | "        "  26 |
| Owen Curley | | Casemar Hill | "        "  " |
| Charles Fullim | | Conrad Housman | "        "  " |
| James Johnson | | Michael Stoner | "    Oct 12 |
| —— Wade | | William Taylor | "        "  " |
| —— Mallady | | John Zimmerman | "        "  " |
| —— ——rd | | John Cline | "        "  " |
| —— —— —— | Deserted Augt 25th | Peter Hewer | "        "  " |
| Edward Robinson | Dischd. July 20 | Bartle Engle | Died Aug 6 |

Muster Roll of Capt. Geo. P. Keeport's Compy. of the First German Battalion Continental Troops. Commanded by Colonel Nichs. Husacker. Philadelphia, Sept. 19th, 1776.

| ENLISTED. | NAMES. | ENLISTED. | NAMES. |
|---|---|---|---|
| 1776 | | 1776 | |
| July  8 | George P. Keeports, Capt. | July 15 | Jacob Smith, 1st Serjt. |
| 12 | Saml. Gerock, 1 Lt. | 30 | Henry Speck, 2nd " |
| " | Willm. Ritter, 2 " | Aug. 19 | John Keener, 3rd Serjt. |
| " | John Lindenberger, Ensign | " | Christn. Kearns, 4th " |

| ENLISTED. | NAMES. | | ENLISTED. | NAMES. |
|---|---|---|---|---|
| 1776 | | | 1776 | Privates |
| July 15 | George Cole, | 1st Corpl. | Aug 7 | Jacob Stein |
| 19 | Fredk. Moppes, | 2nd " | 8 | John Schorcht |
| 21 | Ulrich Linkenfetter, | 3rd ". | 9 | Christn. Lichte |
| " | Philip Bitting, | 4th " | 10 | George Schesler |
| 15 | Benja. England, Drummer | | " | Danl. Fuhrman |
| | Privates | | 11 | Henry Traut |
| " | Michael Brubacher | | " | Jacob Schütz, |
| " | Michael Grosh | | 14 | Peter Hahn |
| 17 | Michael Dochterman | | 19 | George Miller |
| " | Christn. Settlemires | | 25 | Peter Anckle |
| 20 | Peter Kries | | 5 | Jacob Wink |
| 21 | Jacob Koefflich | | " | Danl. Boehler |
| " | Adam Markel | | 12 | John Harring |
| " | David Streib | | 18 | John Franken |
| " | Joseph Carrol | | July 15 | John Cole |
| " | David Levy | | 21 | Adam Schaeffer |
| " | Willm. Trux | | " | Mathias Schreier |
| " | John Capes | | " | Conrad Reitz |
| " | John Trux | | " | John Brown |
| 28 | Jacob Bigler | | " | Fredk. Mongoal |
| Aug 1 | Jacob Burk | | 23 | John Bauer |
| 3 | John Weller | | 26 | Conrad Boehm |
| 5 | Gotfried Loure | | 28 | John Miller, sick |
| " | Jacob Wagner | | 30 | Phillip Boehm |
| 6 | Peter Bast | | " | John Smith |

Roll of Capt. William Heyser's Company.  Dated October 23rd, 1776.

William Heyser, (Keyser), Captain.       Adam Smith, 2nd Lieut.
Jacob Kottz, 1st Lieut.                  Paul Christman Ensign.

| SERGEANTS. | CORPORALS. | DRUMS. & FIFES. |
|---|---|---|
| David McCorgan, (recomd. by Maj. & Cap.) | Andrew Filler | George Gittin, Drum |
| Jacob Hose | Phillip Reevenach | Jacob Gittin, Fife |
| Daniel Taquet, (or Jaques) | Barnard Frey | |
| Jacob Miller | William Lewis | |

| Privates | Privates | Privates |
|---|---|---|
| Peter Sheese, Deserted | John Smith | James Duncan |
| Henry Stroam " | Michael Weaver | John Breecher |
| Adam Stonebreaker | Jacob Belsoover | Fredk. Switzer |
| John Fogle | John Rothe | Jacob Fowee, Deserted |
| Jacob Klien | Wentle Strayly | Thomas Burney, " |
| George Miller | John Flick | John Itnier |
| Phillip Fisher | John Mettz, Deserted | Phillip Greechbaum |
| Jonathan Hecket | Henry Michael | Jacob Bishop |
| Henry Tomm | George Riggleman, | Alex. Sailor |
| Jacob Hoover | Deserted | Martin Pifer, Deserted |
| Michael Cambler | Nicholas Baird | Peter Gittin |
| George Harmony | John Hottfield, Deserted | Frances Myers |
| Thomas Clifton | Jacob Greathouse, " | Melcher Benter |
| Micgael Boward | George Buch | Tobias Friend, Deserted |
| Henry Wagner | Stuffle Reever | Jacob Heefner, " |
| John Crafft | George Wise | John Smithley, " |
| John Shoemaker, Deserted | John Michael | Everheart Smith |
| Mathias Gieser | John Robertson | Godfrey Young |
| Mathias Dunkle | Adam Lieser, Deserted | Frederick Locher |
| Frederick Filler | Robt. Hartness, " | Michael Yeakly |
| Christian Sides, Deserted | Henry Benter | James Furnier |
| John Kibler | John Armstrong | Henry Queer |
| Stuffle Wagner | Simon Fogler | Henry Statler, Deserted |
| Jacob Heefner | Jacob Grass | John Cropp |
| Conrod Hoyle | Phillip Smithly, Deserted | |
| Balsor Fisher | George Wilhelm | |

Pay Roll of Lt. Col. Weltner's Company in the German Regt. of the Continental forces of the United States. Commanded by Lt. Col. Ludwick Weltner, for the months July, August, Sept and Oct, 1779.

| NAMES. | REMARKS. | NAMES. | REMARKS. |
|---|---|---|---|
| Capt. Philip Shrawder | | Privates | |
| Serjt. William Lewis | Disd. July 16th | Michael Gambler | |
| "  Jno. Danl. Jacquet | "    "    26th | James Ashley | |
| "  Jacob Hose | "    "    " | William Pointer | |
| Corpl. James Smith | Promd. Aug 1st | Jacob Mosen | |
| "  John Michael | Disd. July 16th | Jonathan Hackett | Deserted Aug 25th |
| "  John Brucher | "    "    17th | Henry Straam | Disd. July 17th |
| "  Adam Stonebraker | "    "    26th | James Duncan | "    "    16th |
| "  Bernard Fry | "    "    " | George Wilhelm | "    "    17th |
| Drum. Moses McKinsey | | Melcher Benner | "    "    " |
| "  Joshua McKinsey | | Fredrik. Schwidzer | "    "    16th |

| NAMES. | REMARKS. | NAMES. | REMARKS. |
|---|---|---|---|
| Privates | Dischd. July 17th | Privates | Dischd. July 26 |
| Michael Yockley | "      " | John Etnier | "      " |
| Conrod Hoyle | "      20th | Jacob Bishop | "      " |
| John Fliet | "      26th | Chris. Raver | "      " |
| Fredrik. Filter | "      " | Philip Fisher | "      " |
| Michl. Weaver | "      " | Fredk. Locker | "      Aug. 9 |
| James Forney | "      " | Alex. Taylor | "      " |
| Jacob Beltzhoover | "      " | Patrick Fliming | "      " |
| John Groop | "      " | George Regliman | "      Oct. 12 |
| George Getting | "      " | Henry Stalter | "      " |
| John Hatfield | "      " | Christopr. Waggoner | "      " |
| Henry Michael | "      " | John Smith | "      " |
| Thomas Clifton | "      " | Henry Benter | "      " |
| John Craft | "      " | Philip Smithly | "      " |
| Francis Gavin | "      " | Jacob Heefner | "      " |
| Jacob Kline | "      " | John Smithly | "      " |
| John Kebler | "      " | Jacob Haver | "      " |
| Mathias Keiser | "      " | Henry Quier | "      July 29 |
| John Armstrong | "      " | | |

## A Roll of Capt. Philip Graybell's Company.   1776.

### ENLISTED BY CAPT. GREYBELL.

Ferdinand Lorentz
Philip Miller
Henry Millberger, (Millberger)
Jacob Freymiller,(Frymiller)
James Cappelle, (Caple)
John Rick
Lorentz Kneary
Jacob Etter
Peter Baker
Rudolph Crower
Adam Rohrbach, (Rohhbaugh)
Rowland Smith
John Shriock, (Shryock)
William Rommelsem, Serjt.
Jacob Striter
Martin Lantz
John Hearly, (Harley)
Wilfgang Ettsperger
Christopher Regele,(Regle)

Frederick Wm. Haller
John Moore
Wendell Andrews, (Andreas)
Michael Kearshner
Wolfgang Ettzinger
John Shaffer
David Mumma, (Muma)
Abraham Frantz
Frederick Weger
Henry Hartman
Wendel Lorentz
Jacob Hartenstein, (Hardenstein)
William Altimus
Jacob Burke
Jacob Kintz, (Keintz)
George Rittlemyer
Philip Kautz
Jacob Myer, (Myers)

John Shlife
John Machenheimer, Sjt.
George Stauffer, Corpl.
Gottlieb Danroth
Lorentz Danroth
Henry Decker
Jacob Hoffman
Charles Zarrell
Charles Charles
Joseph Procter
Joseph Braeter
Christian Apple
George Myers, (Myer)
Henry Willsdaugh
George Lighthauser, (Leithauser)
Joseph Smith
Henry Wilstock
Henry Rumfeld
George Hyatt, Fifer

18

### ENLISTED BY LIEUT. JOHN LOHRA, (LORAH).

Thomas Kimmel,(Kemmell) Frederick Heller, Serjt.    Michael Growley
Anthony Miller          Andrew Gorr, (Gore)          Frederick Sollers, Corpl.
Joseph Hook             William Speck, Corpl.        Nicholas Frey
Jacob Miley             Henry Hargeroder, (Herge-
Jacob Miller                roder)

### ENLISTED BY LIEUT. CHRISTIAN MYERS.

Jacob Kerns, (Kearns)      John Welty          Fredk. Downey, (Tawney)
Simon Rinehart, (Reinhart) John Summers        William Cunius, (Cunnius)
Mathias Boyer,(Byer),Corpl. Michael Huling     James Smith
Jacob Ruppert             John Eyssell         Peter Finley, Drummer
Nicholas Keyser           William Litzinger, Serjt.

### ENLISTED BY ENSIGN MARTIN SHUGART.

John Smith                William Kraft        Henry Smith
John Bartholomew Deitch,  Joseph Williams      John Stricker, Cadet
   (Dych)                 Henry Spengle        Peter Segman

A List of Recruits belonging to the German Regiment. Commanded by Lieut. Colonel Weltner. White Plains, Sept. 5th, 1778.

| NAMES. | TIME OF SERVICE. | NAMES. | TIME OF SERVICE. |
|---|---|---|---|
| John Kendrick | 3 yrs | Samuel Barts | War |
| James Champness | War | Mathias Smith | do |
| George Buch | 3 yrs | William Rider | do |
| Adam Mussler | do | William Malinia | do |
| William Vincent | do | Benj. Cole | do |
| Stephen McGrough | do | Timothy Cahill | do |
| William Neving | War | Robert Smith | do |
| James Woolford | 3 yrs | Cornelius Vaughan | do |
| James Stiles | War | James Murphy | do |
| Peter Batolomey | do | Christian Castner | do |
| Richard Hazlip | 3 yrs | William Pope | do |
| Robert Porter | do | John Fennell | do |
| William Mummard | War | Jacob Kauffman | 3 yrs |
| Hugh McKoy | do | Thomas Proctor | do |
| John Ammersley | do | Richard Gaul | do |
| John Stanton | do | John Shively | do |
| John Bennet | do | Thomas Halfpenny | do |
| John Roach | do | William Johnston | do |
| Benj. Elliott | do | John Richards | do |
| Cornelius Quinlin | 3 yrs | Albert Hendricks | 9 mos |
| Philip Fitzpatrick | 9 mos | Philip Bates | do |
| Francis Carns | 3 yrs | George Arnold | do |
| Charles Jones | War | Adam Mattrit, fifer | War |

| NAMES. | TIME OF SERVICE. | NAMES. | TIME OF SERVICE. |
|---|---|---|---|
| Michael Smith, drummer | War | James Dyer | 3 yrs |
| John Malady | do | Henry Fisher | do |
| Thomas Mackall | do | Jacob Alexander | do |
| Charles Fulham | do | Christian Kepplinger | 9 mos |
| John Hughmore | do | Philip Hinkel | do |
| Thomas Hutchcrofft | do | Thomas Polehouse | do |
| John Wade | do | Abraham Miller | do |
| Alexander Smith | do | Bernhard Ridenhour | do |
| Frederick Shoemaker | do | Levy Aaron | 3 yrs |
| James Johnston | do | Moses McKinsey | do |
| Casimir Hill | 3 yrs | Joshua McKinsey | do |
| Thomas Mahony | do | Jacob Moser | do |
| John Smadern | do | Richard O'Quin | War |
| Jacob Dolton | do | James Ashley | do |
| John Timhen | do | James Smith | do |
| Michael Hardman | do | Thomas Rowlands | 9 mos |
| Henry Ferrins | do | George Bantz | do |

| NAMES. | TIME OF SERVICE. | REMARKS. |
|---|---|---|
| Thomas Hazelwood | War | on Furlough |
| Richard Hopkins | 9 mos | died 7 July |
| Christn. Mumma | do | Died July 27th, '78 |
| William White | War | Was a Deserter from Carolina |
| James Connoway | 3 yrs | Ditto of Col. Chambers |
| Thomas Holdup | War | Ditto of Carolina |
| Mathias Custgrove | 3 yrs | Deserted |
| John Waldon | do | ditto |
| Andrew Shuler | War | ditto |
| John Stout | do | ditto |
| Robert Barnet | do | sick, absent |
| George Kephard | 3 yrs | Deserted |
| Edward Connoly | do | Taken by the Virginia Artillery |
| Frederick Stone | do | Given up to the Laboratory |
| John Weeguel | do | Left at Frederick Town |

The number of Officers in the four Maryland Companies belonging to the German Regiment:

| 1 Lieut. Colonel | Number of Sergeants and Rank and File: |
|---|---|
| 1 Captain | 13 Sergeants |
| 4 Lieutenants | 8 Drums and fifes |
| 2 Ensigns | 221 Rank and file. |

MISCELLANEOUS.

| | | | |
|---|---|---|---|
| Jacob Myers, Discharged | 20 July | Peter Bartholomay | |
| Henry Smith, " | 15 Aug | Albert Henricks | |
| David Mumma, " | 20 July | Thos. Mahoney | |
| Corpl. Wm. Krofft, " | 26 " | Chris. Mummard | |
| John Emersly | | Thos. Machall | |
| Adam Musler | | Jas. Tomey, Discharged July 26 | |
| John Henrick | | John Viebler | |
| Stephen McGraw | | John Weegul | |
| Hugh McCaw, (or Koy) | | | |

---

ENLISTMENTS FOR 3 YEARS, ALL IN CAPT. MICHAEL BAYER'S COMPANY.

Edward Bairford, Enlisted June 19th, 1780. Joined the Regiment at Northumberland

Michael Rightmyer, (Right Myer), Enlisted Feb. 1st, 1780

Charles Lago, Enlisted April 1st, 1780

Dineas Doron, (Dinnis Dorah), Enlisted June 26th, 1780

George Silver, Enlisted March 31st, 1780

John Rogers, " April 10th, 1780

John Nevet, " April 13th, 1780

---

Annapolis, 1st April, 1785.

Copy, to Joseph Howell,

       I have now to Address you upon a very serious subject. When we were so earnest about obtaining the Muster Rolls of the German Regiment, it was on a suspicion that several frauds had been committed upon this State, with respect to Depreciation. The State of Maryland passed an Act of Assembly granting Depreciation to all Officers and Soldiers of the Quota of that State, who had served three years in the Continental Army, consequently, that part of the German Regiment which was called the four Companies of Maryland, having served faithfully; became entitled to receive the same.

    The event of an examination with the Muster Rolls of 1779 and 1780 has shewn that our suspicions were not without foundation, for, of two hundred and sixty who have received Depreciation, there are forty seven, as by the List enclosed; who are not upon the Maryland Musters. Twelve of the forty seven are upon the Pennsylvania Musters, and the other thirty five not found Mustered in 1779 in any of the Rolls of the Regiment. For the thirty five, however, Discharges were procured, purporting that the Person mentioned in each of them served three years faithfully, and were for the most part discharged by Capt. Bunner in the Month of July, 1779. I have enclosed one of the Discharges which has the appearance of having been written at a much later date than what is expressed in it. We can trace out the Persons who presented them here and obtained the Certificates, but we want to find out whether Capt. Bunner, whose signature is to the greatest part of them, really did sign them, or not—there has been a most villainous combination somewhere and it has been excited by a knowledge that the State, for want of regular Musters, generally issued upon Discharges.

Now if *Bunner* is within your reach, I shall esteem it a favor if you will take another Man of Credit along with you, and enquire of *him* whether the Signature on the Discharge, (Charles Kees, now sent, is *his*—if he avows it, I shall be obliged to you for your Deposition, and that of the person with you, that he acknowledged it, which Deposition, with all the forms of Office, please to transmit to me. If, on the Contrary, Bunner denies it to be his, please to inform him of so much of these transactions as you may chuse to disclose, and obtain his affidavit, setting forth that he did not sign the same, or any of the Discharges, in the names of those, or any of them, on the enclosed List. I need not caution you about using your utmost address in endeavouring to lay open this Scene of Iniquity. Your own love of Justice, and the public Station you fill; will, I dare say, be sufficient incentives to your exertion in this dark business.

Pray has the State of Pennsylvania granted Depreciation to their three year's Men Discharged before the 10th of April, 1780; if it has, and continues to issue, it will be proper that the Comptroller should see the list I send, to examine it with his issues. Be pleased to procure the favor of Mr. Nicholson to furnish such remarks as may be necessary and transmit them to me as soon as possible.

Yrs.
C. Richmond.

List of Certificates fraudulently obtained from State of Maryland in the names of Soldiers of the German Regiment.

| NAMES. | SUMS. | TO WHOM DELIVERED. | REMARKS. |
|---|---|---|---|
| Vendel Andrews | 56, 16, 9 | John Miller, per order | Not on any musters, 1779 |
| William Basht | 57, 17, 0 | John Randall, for Stauffer | ditto |
| Charles Charrell | 57, 5, 3 | Jacob Myers p. order | ditto |
| James Calhoun | 62, 13, 11 | ditto | ditto |
| Frederick Charrell | 58, 10, 1 | John Miller | P. Boyer's Pennsylva. Co. |
| Timothy Conn | 56, 13, 11 | J. Randall for Stauffer | Not on any musters, 1779 |
| Thomas Cammell | 56, 11, 0 | ditto | ditto |
| Peter Finley | 63, 5, 3 | John Miller | ditto |

| NAMES. | SUMS. | TO WHOM DELIVERED. | REMARKS. |
|---|---|---|---|
| Andrew Goar | 56, 19, 8 | John Miller | Not on any musters, 1779 |
| George Hensell | 56, 18, 9 | Jacob Myers | Hubley's Co., Pennsylva. |
| Henry Hargrader, (or Hergood) | 58, 14, 5 | John Miller | Shrawder's Co., ditto |
| George Hyatt | 63, 18, 10 | ditto | Not on any musters, 1779 |
| John Hart | 63, 16, 2 | ditto | P. Boyer's Co.,Pennsylva. |
| Philip Helter | 58, 5, 9 | ditto | Shrawder'sCo.,Pennsylva. |
| George Hartsell | 56, 13, 11 | J. Randall, for Stauffer | Not on any musters, 1779 |
| Michael Hausman | 57, 2, 5 | ditto | ditto |
| Michael Jackell | 56, 8, 2 | William Lewis | ditto |
| Nicholas Johnson | 57, 1, 0 | J. Randall, for Stauffer | ditto |
| William Kumius | 58, 1, 7 | Jacob Myers | ditto |
| Nicholas Keyser | 56, 13, 11 | John Miller | ditto |
| Charles Keys, (or Kees) | 56, 16, 9 | J. Randall, for Stauffer | ditto |
| William Kemp | 56, 19, 8 | ditto | ditto |
| Jacob Levy | 58, 11, 4 | David Levy | Rice's Pennsylvania Co. |
| Nicholas Lines | 56, 16, 9 | J. Randall, for Stauffer | Not on any muster, 1779 |
| Henry Lane | 56, 13, 11 | ditto | P. Boyer's Pennsylva. |
| Anthony Miller | 57, 8, 3 | George Stauffer | Not on any muster, 1779 |
| Henry Mielberger | 57, 5, 6 | ditto | ditto |
| John Moore | 56, 16, 9 | John Miller | ditto |
| Joshua Procter | 57, 2, 7 | ditto | ditto |
| Peter Sigman | 58, 5, 10 | Jacob Myers | ditto |
| Joseph Smith | 56, 13, 11 | George Stauffer | ditto |
| John Shultz | 56, 9, 7 | John Miller | ditto |
| Nicholas Stover | 62, 4, 5 | ditto | Bunner's Co., Pennsylva. |
| Henry Spengel | 56, 15, 4 | ditto | Not on any musters, 1779 |
| James Smith | 56, 12, 6 | ditto | ditto        [nia |
| Peter Shrover | 57, 8, 4 | J. Randall, for Stauffer | Bunner's Co., Pennsylva- |
| Valentine Shultz | 79, 11, 10 | ditto | Not on any musters |
| George Shriver | 58, 5, 9 | ditto | ditto |
| Jacob Smith | 77, 2, 2 | Himself | ditto |
| Frederick Tawney | 57, 10, 1 | John Miller | ditto |
| Frederick Weiger | 58, 14, 9 | Jacob Myers | ditto |
| Michael Yewling | 57, 19, 1 | John Miller | ditto |
| John Zeigler | 56, 16, 9 | J. Randall, for Stauffer | ditto |
| John Miller | 80, 5, 4 | Himself | Mustered Deserted |

## DISCHARGES.

John Zeigler, Corporal in Capt. Boyer's Company, German Regiment.

Served 3 years.  Discharged July 21st, 1779.

Wilhelm Kemp, Private in Capt. Myers' Company, German Regiment.

Served 3 years.  Discharged July 23rd, 1779.

Peter Shrover, Private in Capt. Christian Myers' Company, Served 3 yrs. Dis. July 29th, 1779.

Valentine Shultz, Serjt. in Capt Baltzel's Co. Served 3 yrs. Dis. Aug. 13th, 1779.
Michael Hatman, Private in Capt. Christian Myers' Co. 3 yrs. Dis. July 17th, 1779.
George Hartzell,    "    in Capt. Baltzel's Co. 3 yrs. Dis. July 19th, 1779.
George Shriver,    "    "    "    "    "  3 yrs. Dis. Aug. 11th, 1779.
Thomas Cammell,    "    "    "  Charles Baltzel's Co. 3 yrs. Dis. July 17th, 1779.
Henry Lane,    "    "    "    "    "    "    "    "  July 19th, 1779.
William Basht,    "    in Capt. Boyer's Co. 3 yrs. Dis. Aug. 5th, 1779.
Nickolas Johnson,    "    in Capt. Charles Baltzel's Co. 3 yrs. Dis. July 24th, 1779.
Timothy Conn,    "    "    "    "    "    "    "    "    "  July 19th, 1779.
Michael Hausman,    "    in Capt. Boyer's Co. 3 yrs. Dis. July 25th, 1779.
Nickolas Limes,    "    in Capt. Charles Baltzel's Co. 3 yrs. Dis. July 21st, 1779.
Charles Kees,    "    "    "    "    "    "    "    "    "    "    "    "

All the above discharges were given at Camp Wyoming, except Schultz's and Shriver's at Camp Tioga. Each is signed by Jacob Bunner, Capt, Commanding the German Regt. Depreciation certificates were issued Dec. 5th, 1783, to all the above.

---

Wyoming, July 21st, 1779.

This is to certify that the Bearer, Charles Kees, a Private in the German Regiment in Captain Charles Baltzel's Company, Served three years as a good Soldier from the time of his Inlistment he is hereby Discharged from the same.

Whome it may         ⎧ Depce. C. R.
     Concern           ⎪   Given under my hand the Day and
Depreciation Certificate issued ⎨ Date above written
     the 5th Decem. 1783.    ⎪        Jacob Bunner, Capt.
          C. Richmond    ⎩   Commanding the German Regt.
               Aud. Genl.

---

Philadelphia.

Personally appeared before me, William Adcock Esq., one of the Justices for the City and County of Philadelphia, Joseph Howell, Jr., Asst. Commissioner of Accounts, and John Phelan, Asst. to the Commissr. of Accounts, and made solemn Oath, that the annexed Certificate and discharge of Charles Kees was presented by them to Jacob Bunner, late a Captain in the German Regiment, and Acknowledged by him, the said Jacob Bunner, to be his Signature, and they do further swear, that the said Jacob Bunner did acknowledge to have signed nearly all the discharges that were given to the Soldiers of said Regiment, which discharges were given them on, or about, the time that is expressed in the

discharge of Charles Kees, and further sayeth not.  Sworn and subscribed this tenth day of May, 1785.

Sworn this 10th day of
May, 1785
Before Willm. Adcock.    (Seal)

Joseph Howell, Jr.,
John Phelan.

---

Comptroller Genl.'s Office,
May 17th, 1785.

Sir:

I have received yours of the 5th Inst. and have examined and com-
pared it with my Returns.  This State, adhering to the recommenda-
tions of Congress, makes up depreciation for none of the Troops discharged before the 10th April, 1780; and, altho I find in your List of the
German Regiment, that the State of Maryland hath settled with a number of the same name as those which have been settled with here, such
as Nicholas Stover, John Hart, George Hensil and some others, yet they
were not the same men, but have been imposters, (very probably), with
discharges dated in 1779 in these men's names who continued in the
Army until 1780, and some of them till the end of the war, there is, however, none of those who continued till after April, 1780, per your list, which
have been settled here.  I am much obliged by the list of Settlements
with Hartley's Regiment, or, as we called it, the 11th Pennsylvania Regiment, for it was incorporated therewith in 1779.  Of the list you gave
me, the following persons had been previously settled with here and
received their depreciation, viz—John Burgess, Corpl., John Barber,
Sergt., James Beal, Private, Jeremiah Ferrall, Sergt., & Willm. Marquis,
Private, the rest of them I have marked off in my Rolls as settled by the
State of Maryland, and shall not adjust their Accounts here.  Joseph
Hyner, only, of Moylan's Regiment, had been settled with, by this State,
of all those upon your list, the residue I shall take care not to settle with.
If there is any other communication which I have here omitted to make,
please let me know.  I have the person, who I think is at the bottom of
the nefarious proceeding you have been fortunate enough to detect,
bound over for an attempt of almost a similar nature here.

I am with great respect
Sir
Your Most Obedt. Servant,
Jno. Nicholson.

C. Richmond Esq., Audt. Genl.
State of Maryland.

## MUSTERS OF MARYLAND TROOPS, VOL. III.

"MUSTER ROLLS."

NAMES LEFT OUT, &C.

## MUSTERS OF MARYLAND TROOPS, VOL. III.

| NAMES. | RANK. | TIME OF SERVICE. Enlisted. Discharged. | REMARKS. |
|---|---|---|---|

THIRD REGIMENT.

Men left out of the Alphabet, being off the Rolls to the last of Oct., 77.

| | | | |
|---|---|---|---|
| Adam, Argent | | 22 Augt | prisoner |
| Arnold, Thomas | | | died in Augt |

Capt. Jones Comy. Muster for Octobr. & November, 79.   Recruits entered and mustered Deserted &c. as follows:

| | | | |
|---|---|---|---|
| Arding, Benja. | | 19 June | deserted |

FOURTH REGIMENT.—*Dec. Roll*, 1777.

| | | | | |
|---|---|---|---|---|
| Allen, Robt. | | 8 July | 17 Aug | deserted |

FIFTH REGIMENT.

Non Commissioned Officers and Soldiers of the 5th Maryland Regiment left out of the Roll Feby., 1778.

| | | | | |
|---|---|---|---|---|
| Andrews, Joseph | | 17 Sept | 4 Oct 77 | missing |
| | | | 22 July 78 | joined |
| Akers, Michael | | 17 dec 76 | 10 June 77 | deserted |
| Atkins, Jno. | | 16 Jan 77 | 15 April | died |
| Abbot, John | | 12 May 77 | 20 Sept 77 | deserted |
| Alford, William | | 31 dec 76 | 25 Mar 77 | do |
| Alexander, Jno. | | 14 Jan 77 | 24 Jan | do |
| Abbott, John | | 12 May 77 | 20 Sept 77 | deserted |

SIXTH REGIMENT.

Non Comd. Officers and Soldiers of the Sixth Regiment left out before the Muster 1 June, 1780.

| | | | | |
|---|---|---|---|---|
| Ashman, Charles | | 7 Mar 77 | | Hospital Oct 77, not heard of |
| Anguish, Alexr. | | 19 May 77 | | 30 May 77 |
| Ambross, Patk. | | 1 July 77 | | transferred to Col. Chambers |
| Anderson, John | | 29 Aug 77 | | Hosptl. Oct 77, not heard of |
| Adams, William | pt | 28 June 77 | 19 May 78 | deserted |
| Addlemon, Michael | do | 8 Mar 77 | 10 Dec 77 | do |
| Allen, William | do | 3 May 79 | 25 July | do |

## MUSTERS OF MARYLAND TROOPS, VOL. III.

| NAMES. | RANK. | TIME OF SERVICE. Enlisted. | Discharged. | REMARKS. |
|---|---|---|---|---|

### LEFT OUT OF MUSTERS THIRD REGIMENT.

| NAMES. | RANK. | Enlisted. | Discharged. | REMARKS. |
|---|---|---|---|---|
| Buzzard, Leighton | | 26 Jan | 15 May | died |
| Baker, Thomas | | 19 June | 11 Sept | missing |
| Branwood, Jas. | Taken Staten Island 22 Aug | | | |
| Bonoday, Jas. | | | 17 May | deserted |
| Baker, James | | | 11 June | do |
| Bajaint, Thos. | | | 11 Sept | prisoner |
| Breslor, Edward[1] | | | 12 dec | deserted |
| Bay, Charles | | | 4 Oct | killed |
| Berry, William | | | do | missing |
| Brady, Michael | | | 11 Sept | taken |
| returned & entered | | | | |
| Beveridge, Jno. | | 3 April | 21 April | deserted |
| Bryan, Danl. | | | 28 July | do |

### FOURTH REGIMENT.

| NAMES. | RANK. | Enlisted. | Discharged. | REMARKS. |
|---|---|---|---|---|
| Burk, Patk. | | 6 dec 76 | 1 feb 77 | do |
| Bonnett, Thos.[2] | | 22 Mar 77 | 25 April 78 | do |
| Bray, John[3] | | 6 feb 78 | 10 July 78 | do |
| Bosick, Joseph | | 19 May | 30 May | do |
| Burk, Thomas | | 1 Sept | 12 Oct | deserted |

### FIFTH REGIMENT.

Non Commissioned Officers and Soldiers of the Fifth Maryland Regiment, left out of the Rolls February, 1778.

| NAMES. | RANK. | Enlisted. | Discharged. | REMARKS. |
|---|---|---|---|---|
| Bassicks, Richd. | | 10 dec 76 | 22 Aprl 77 | transferred |
| Bromell, Peter | | do | 26 June 77 | died |
| Bryan, (or Byron), Stephen | | do | 22 Aprl 77 | transferred |
| Buckly, Thomas | | do | 14 Jan 78 | deserted |
| Brayly, William | | 13 Jan 77 | 22 Aug 77 | prisoner |
| Burgess, Thomas | | 10 dec 76 | 22 April 77 | transferred |
| Blanch, William | | do | 1 Sept 77 | taken by prior Enlistment |
| Brown, Aaron | | do | 30 Aug 77 | deserted |
| Bryan, O. John | | 1 Sept 77 | 27 Nov 77 | do |
| Byrom, Michael | | 1 June 77 | 12 Sept 77 | died |
| Benton, James | | 24 do | 21 dec 77 | do |
| Barry, Michael[4] | Sergt | 17 dec 76 | 12 April 77 | do |
| Bryan, John | | 22 feb 77 | 25 Aug 77 | deserted |
| Brown, John | | 4 do | 11 feb 77 | do |
| Beldock, Edward | | 10 Jan 77 | 17 Mar 77 | do |

[1] Lt. Smith's.        [2] Norwood's.        [3] Riely's.        [4] Lynch's.

## MUSTERS OF MARYLAND TROOPS, VOL. III.

| NAMES. | RANK. | TIME OF SERVICE. Enlisted. | Discharged. | REMARKS. |
|---|---|---|---|---|
| Bennit, Robt. | | 1 Mar 77 | 4 Mar 77 | deserted |
| Benston, John | | 18 Mar | 20 April | dead |
| Bennett, Jno. | | 10 Jan 77 | 1 July 77 | died |
| Brannon, Jno. | | 16 Mar | 15 April | deserted |
| Burns, Thomas | | 7 Sept | 20 Sept | missing |
| Bailey, Mark | | 2 Aprl | 10 July 77 Joined 21 June | deserted } |
| Brown, John | | 10 Mar 77 | 20 Mar 77 | deserted |

SIXTH REGIMENT.

| NAMES. | RANK. | Enlisted. | Discharged. | REMARKS. |
|---|---|---|---|---|
| Brown, James | | 1 May 77 | 15 Oct 77 | transferred |
| Buchan, William | Sergt | Error see Roll | | |
| Brawton, Mathew | | 2 Mar 78 | 24 April 78 | |
| Bruff, Edward | | 24 July 77 | 15 Oct 77 transferred to Marines | |
| Beall, James | pt | 6 dec 76 | 11 dec 76 | deserted |
| Branfield, James | pt | 28 dec 76 | 28 feb 78 | deserted |
| | | | musd. joined June 78 | |
| Bates, Henry | do | 11 dec 76 | 22 Aug 77 | missing |
| Bradley, Thos. | do | 14 Jan 77 | prior Inlistment | |
| Brodericks, Richd. | do | 21 do | 13 April 77 | deserted |
| Bramwood, Jas. | do | 5 dec 76 | 17 Aug 77 | transferred |
| Brawner, Jacob | do | 7 do | 5 Mar 77 | do |
| Baker, James | Sergt | 14 Oct 77 | 25 Jany 78 | died |
| Bates, John | pt | do | 1 April 78 | do |
| Barlsom, Anthy. | do | 28 April 79 | 6 May | deserted |
| Bryan, Peter | do | 1 June 79 | 5 June 79 | do |

LEFT OUT OF MUSTERS THIRD REGIMENT.

| NAMES. | RANK. | Enlisted. | Discharged. | REMARKS. |
|---|---|---|---|---|
| Clark, George | | | 4 Oct | killed Ger. Town |
| Carey, Richard | | | 23 Aug | deserted |
| Chambers, Wm. | | | 11 Sept | missing |
| Coalman, Mathew[1] | | | prior Enlistment | |
| Coalman, Saml. | | | 4 Oct | killed |
| Cole, J. B. | Sergt | | do | do |
|   5th Compy. | | | | |
| Clark, James | | | 7 May | deserted |
|   6th Compy. | | | | |
| Causins, Peter | | | 4 October | killed |
| Cunningham, John | | | 2 June | deserted |
| Croane, Timothy | | | 8 July | died |
| Crosby, James | | | 4 Oct | taken |
|   returned & entered | | | | |

[1] Brooks'.

## MUSTERS OF MARYLAND TROOPS, VOL. III.

| NAMES. | RANK. | TIME OF SERVICE. | | REMARKS. |
|---|---|---|---|---|
| | | Enlisted. | Discharged. | |
| Cork, Ralph | | 6 June | | deserted |
| Cowan, William | | 6 Aug | | do |
| Cluff, John | | 10 May | | drowned |
| Cudwick, Lewis | | 13 Oct | | deserted |
| Cassidy, Hugh | | 11 Aug | | do |
| Crawford, Jno. | | 8  do | | do |

Collins, John, of the 3d Maryland Regt., discharged 3d May, 1780 by Major Anderson.

### FOURTH REGIMENT.

| NAMES | RANK | Enlisted | Discharged | REMARKS |
|---|---|---|---|---|
| Cullen, John | | 22 Oct 77 | 28 Nov | died |
| Cain, John | | 13 Aug | 20 Aug | deserted |
| Curtis, William | | 15 June | 28 July | do |
| Campbell, James | | 17 Aug | 27 Aug | do |
| . Cole, Henry | | 3 feb | 29 July | prisoner or deserted |

### FIFTH REGIMENT.

Non Commissioned Officers and Soldiers of the Fifth Maryland Regiment, left out of the Rolls February, 1778.

| NAMES | RANK | Enlisted | Discharged | REMARKS |
|---|---|---|---|---|
| Cleary, John | | 10 April 77 | 20 July 77 | dead |
| Connelly, Laurence | | 10 dec 76 | 22 April 77 | transferred |
| Cooper, William | | 10 June 77 | 20 dec 77 | died |
| Chilton, William | | 13 July 77 | 4 Nov 77 | do |
| Cooper, Charles | | 10 dec 76 | 22 April 77 | transferred |
| Critchets, William | | 21 July 77 | 14 Jan 78 | deserted |
| | | | April 78 | joined |
| Critchet, Benja. | | do | do | do  do |
| Chisholm, William[1] | Sergt | 18 May 77 | 20 July 77 | deserted |
| Certain, William | | 1  do | 18 June | discharged |
| Chambers, Mathew Brown | | 25 July 77 | 9 dec | died |
| Clarke, John | | 9 Sept | 17 Jan 78 | do |
| Crosby, Joseph | Corpl | 15 Jan 77 | reduced 16 April | |
| | | | 3 May 77 | deserted |
| Collins, James | | 18 do | 22 Aug 77 | prisoner |
| Craine, Lawrence | | 6 April 77 | do | do |
| Coffee, Daniel | | 17 dec 76 | 11 Sep 77 | do |
| Cousins, Edwd. | | 20 feb 77 | 21 Aug 77 | died |
| Condon, William | | 13 do | 4 Oct 77 | missing |
| Connor, Ambrose | | 7 April 77 | 15 April 77 | discharged |
| Connor, George | | 1 Jan 77 | 28 Jan 78 | deserted |
| | | | 8 June 78 | joined |
| Crook, Martin | | 11 Mar 77 | 6 dec 77 | died |

[1] Hawkins'.

## MUSTERS OF MARYLAND TROOPS, VOL. III.

| NAMES. | RANK. | TIME OF SERVICE. Enlisted. | Discharged. | REMARKS. |
|---|---|---|---|---|
| Crouch, Arthur | | 22 May 77 | 20 July 77 | died |
| Coombs, William | | 25 | 5 Aug 77 | do |
| Clayland, James | | 18 feb | 18 April | discharged |
| Cox, Mathew[1] | | 16 Jan 77 | 11 Sep 77 | prisoner |
| Cox, John | | 27 July | 1   do | deserted |
| | | | Joined Aug 78 | |
| Corker, John | | 15 do | 25 Mar | deserted |
| Clements, Jno. | | 20 Jan 77 | 1 Oct 77 | taken by prior Enlistment |
| Conner, Hugh | | 9 feb 77 | 1 April 77 | deserted |

### LEFT OUT OF SIXTH REGIMENT.

| NAMES. | RANK. | Enlisted. | Discharged. | REMARKS. |
|---|---|---|---|---|
| Concella, Andw. | Corpl | 30 July 77 | 20 Sept 77 | deserted |
| Conner, Hugh | | 23 Aug 77 | Mar 78 | left out |
| Cole, Thomas | Sergt | 15 June 77 | 2 April 78 | died |
| Clark, Charles | Sergt | 10 Jan 77 | 15 Oct 77 transferred to Marines | |
| Carr, Nicholas | | 28 April 77 | 1 Sept 77 transferred to Invalids | |
| Catlin, James | | 7   do | 15 Oct 77 | do    to Marines |
| Collins, Thomas | | 5 dec 76 | 13 April 77 | deserted |
| Crail, James | pt | 7   do | 30   do | do |
| | | | 28 feb 78 | joined |
| Clarss, Francis | do | 30   do | 27 Nov 77 | deserted |
| Collins, John | do | 28 June 77 | 28 July 77 | do |
| Colon, John | do | 9 May 78 | 29 May 78 | deserted |
| Connally, Jno. | do | 5 June 79 | 21 June | do |

### LEFT OUT OF MUSTERS THIRD REGIMENT.

| NAMES. | RANK. | Enlisted. | Discharged. | REMARKS. |
|---|---|---|---|---|
| Doun, James | pt | | 28 Jan 81 | discharged |
| Hartley's Regt. | | | | |
| Dalziell, Thomas | | 28 feb | 23 June | deserted |
| Dorsey, Martin | | prior Enlistment | | |
| Dearlove, James | | 3 June | 22 Aug | killed or taken |
| Drury, Thomas | | | 10 feb | discharged |
| Dalby, Daniel | | | 4 Oct | missing |
| Joined 22 July | | | | |
| Dowling, John | | | 28 May | deserted |

### FOURTH REGIMENT.

| NAMES. | RANK. | Enlisted. | Discharged. | REMARKS. |
|---|---|---|---|---|
| Davis, William | | 25 Mar | 5 April 77 | deserted |
| Douch, William | | 28 do | 12   do | do |
| Donnavan, Jno. | | | 25 Nov 77 | deserted |
| Dick, Hart. | | 6 dec 76 | 1 feb 77 | do |

[1] Cosden's.

## MUSTERS OF MARYLAND TROOPS, VOL. III.

| NAMES. | RANK. | TIME OF SERVICE. Enlisted. | Discharged. | REMARKS. |
|---|---|---|---|---|
| Dickett, Jno. | | 16 feb 78 | 13 Mar 78 | deserted |
| Donald, George | | 27 May | 2 June | do |
| Ducasy, John | | 26 May | 30 May | do |
| Davey, Thomas | | 30 June | 26 July | do |

### FIFTH REGIMENT.

Non Commissioned Officers and Soldiers of the Fifth Maryland Regiment left out of the Rolls February, 1778.

| | | | | |
|---|---|---|---|---|
| Devereaux, James | | 10 dec 76 | 22 April 77 | transferred |
| Dicks, George | | 30 Mar 77 | 4 Oct 77 | missing |
| Dwer, William | | 10 dec 76 | 22 April 77 | transferred |
| Davis, Philemon | | 27 July 77 | wounded and | gone home |
| Dixon, John | Corpl | 1 feb 77 | 24 April 77 | deserted |
| Davise, John | | 16 May 77 | 1 July 77 | do |
| Davise, Joseph | | do | 20 Oct 77 | do |
| Deoran, James | | 14 Jan | 23 dec 77 | died |
| Dunn, Jno. (D. F.) | | 10 dec 76 | 15 April 77 | discharged |
| Daniels, Jacob | | 10 Jan 77 | 29 Jan 78 | do |
| Dellen, Theobald | | 3 feb 77 | 28 Sept 77 | deserted |

### SIXTH REGIMENT.

| | | | | |
|---|---|---|---|---|
| Delany, James | Corpl | 21 April 77 | 21 Jan 78 | deserted |
| Davis, John | | 19 feb 77 musd. again | 7 Mar 78 June 78 | |
| Darrough, Jno. | | 16 feb 78 | 24 April 78 | |
| Davis, John | Corpl | 5 dec 76 | 21 April 77 | deserted |
| Davis, John | pt | 12 feb 77 | 14 feb 77 | do |
| Davis, William | do | 22 July 77 | 1 Jan 78 | Hospital, not heard |
| Dixon, Richard | pt | 15 July 79 | 12 Aug | deserted    [of |

### FOURTH REGIMENT.

| | | | | |
|---|---|---|---|---|
| Evans, Thomas | | 9 Oct | 21 Nov | deserted |

### FIFTH REGIMENT.

Non Commissioned Officers and Soldiers of the Fifth Maryland Regiment left out of the Rolls Febry., 1778.

| | | | | |
|---|---|---|---|---|
| English, Danl. | | 10 Aug | 17 Jan | died |
| Edwis, Richard | | 22 May 77 | 20 July 77 | discharged |

### LEFT OUT OF THE SIXTH REGIMENT.

| | | | | |
|---|---|---|---|---|
| Edwards, Wm. | | 4 Aug 77 | 1 April 78 | died |
| English, Wm. | pt | 10 dec 76 | 28 feb 78 | deserted |
| Ervine, David | do | 8 May 79 | 8 July | do |

## MUSTERS OF MARYLAND TROOPS, VOL. III.

| NAMES. | RANK. | TIME OF SERVICE. | | REMARKS. |
|---|---|---|---|---|
| | | Enlisted. | Discharged. | |

### LEFT OUT OF MUSTERS THIRD REGIMENT.

| | | | | |
|---|---|---|---|---|
| Ferrall, Jere | | | 28 Jan 81 | discharged |
| Hartley's Regt. | | | | |
| Farwell, James | pt | | do | do |
| Hartley's Regt. | | | | |
| Flaid, James | | | 11 Sept | missing |
| Frost, James | | | 15 Oct | deserted |
| Farris, Francis | | | 13 May 79 | do |

### FOURTH REGIMENT.

| | | | | |
|---|---|---|---|---|
| Fitzburn, James | | 8 April | 10 April 77 | deserted |

### FIFTH REGIMENT.

Non Commissioned Officers and Soldiers of the Fifth Maryland Regiment left out of the Rolls February, 1778.

| | | | | |
|---|---|---|---|---|
| Floyd, Joseph | Corpl | 13 Jan 78 | 14 Jan 78 | deserted |
| | | | April 78 | joined |
| Foard, John | | 5 dec 76 | 15 Jan 77 | dead |
| Fromee, John | | 7  do | 28 April | died |
| Floyd, Saml. | | 4 feb 77 | 2  do | do [Enlistment |
| Floyd, John | | 29 May 77 | 24 Sep 77 | taken by prior |

### SIXTH REGIMENT.

| | | | | |
|---|---|---|---|---|
| Feely, William | | 17 June 77 | 4 Nov 77 | |
| Fisher, Danl. | pt | 7 dec 76 | 11 Sept 77 | died |
| Flemming, Jno. | do | 5 Mar 77 | 24 feb 78 | do |
| Farthing, Robt. | do | 10 July 77 | 27 May 78 | died |

### LEFT OUT OF MUSTERS THIRD REGIMENT.

| | | | | |
|---|---|---|---|---|
| Glasgow, Walter | | 13 May | 23 June | deserted |
| Gardner, John | | | 19 June | do |
| Grantt, James | | | 22 Aug | taken |
| Griffin, Darby | | | 12 June | deserted |
| Goodwin, James | | | left out January Roll 78 | |
| Joined April 78 | | | | |
| Griffith, Thomas[1] | | 26 Mar 78 | 27th | deserted |
| Gee, George | | | 4 July | do |

### FOURTH REGIMENT.

| | | | | |
|---|---|---|---|---|
| Grace, William | Drum | | 25 Nov 77 | deserted |
| Goodchild, Wm.[2] | | 12 feb 78 | 13 May 78 | do |

[1] Lt. Armstrong's.          [2] Lansdale's.

## MUSTERS OF MARYLAND TROOPS, VOL. III.

| NAMES. | RANK. | TIME OF SERVICE. Enlisted. | Discharged. | REMARKS. |
|---|---|---|---|---|
| Gibbs, John | | 26 April | 2 May | deserted |
| Granade, Jno. | | 18 May | 24  do | do |
| Grilliot, Jos. | | 26 April | 4   do | do |
| Girte, Chrisr. | | 4 July | 14 Aug | do |
| Glenn, James | | Joined 1 Jan 80 | 15 Jan 80 | do |

### FIFTH REGIMENT.

Non Commissioned Officers and Soldiers of the Fifth Maryland Regiment left out of the Rolls February, 1778.

| NAMES. | RANK. | Enlisted. | Discharged. | REMARKS. |
|---|---|---|---|---|
| Gadd, Thomas | | 12 July 77 | 4 Oct 77 | missing |
| Grace, John | | 30 Mar 77 | 25 June 77 | died |
| Gray, William | | 21 Aug 77 | 4 Oct 77 | missing |
| | | | | Joined 22 July 78 |
| Gibney, Simon | | 24 dec 76 | 29 Jan 77 | deserted |
| Gray, Joseph | | 12   do | 12 Mar | discharged |
| Githin, Robt. | | 1 feb 77 | never joined Regt. | |
| Gurney, (or Gumey), Jno. | | 29 May 77 | 2 Jan 78 | died |
| Gormely, Joseph | | 22   do | the same day | deserted |
| Guist, George | | 24 Mar | 23 April 77 | transferred |
| Gill, William | | 13 Jan 77 | 1 feb 77 | taken by Civic |
| Gray, Thomas | | 2 May 79 | 13 June 79 | deserted [power |
| Glann, Saml. | | 18 Jan 77 | 15 May 77 | discharged |

### SIXTH REGIMENT.

| NAMES. | RANK. | Enlisted. | Discharged. | REMARKS. |
|---|---|---|---|---|
| Greenwood, Michl. | | 20 April left sick in Phila. | | not heard of |
| Garland, James | | 15 Aug 77 | 18 Oct 77 | died |
| Gorman, Jno. | | 21 May 77 | 15 July 77 | |
| Graham, Alexr. | | 12 July 77 | 2 feb 78 | |
| Gallaspie, John | | 18 July 77 | 28 July 77 | deserted |
| Gregory, Saml. | | 3 May 77 | 6 feb 78 | died |
| Gatreen, John | pt | 5 dec 76 | 21 Jan 77 | do |
| Grosman, Sol. | do | 6   do | 9 Mar 77 | deserted |
| Gallagan, Jno. | do | 7 Jan 77 | 28 feb 78 | do |
| Gannon, John | do | 6 June 77 | 15 Nov 77 | do |

### LEFT OUT OF MUSTERS THIRD REGIMENT.

| NAMES. | RANK. | Enlisted. | Discharged. | REMARKS. |
|---|---|---|---|---|
| Hanson, Saml.[1] | Sergt | 10 May 77 | promoted 24 July 1st Regt. 1777 | |
| Horner, Robt. | | | 10 Aug | died |
| Harrison, Thomas | | | 4 Oct | killed |
| Hannah, Miles | | | do | do |

[1] Marbury's.

MUSTERS OF MARYLAND TROOPS, VOL. III.

| NAMES. | RANK. | TIME OF SERVICE. Enlisted. | Discharged. | REMARKS. |
|---|---|---|---|---|
| Heart, William | | | | prior Enlistment |
| Hay, John | | | 9 Sept | deserted |
| Hindmore, Richd. | | | 11 feb 77 | died |
| Hollyday, Jno. | | | 2 do | deserted |
| Hough, John | | | 19 June | do |
| returned & entered | | | | |
| Henis, James | | | 12 do | do |
| Hulet, John | | | 22 Aug | taken |
| Harris, William | | | | left out January Roll 78 |
| Joined April 78 | | | | |
| Hois, Thomas | | | 25 April | deserted |

FOURTH REGIMENT.

| | | | | |
|---|---|---|---|---|
| Hunt, Charles[1] | | 6 dec 76 | 1 feb 77 | died |
| Harris, William | | 19 Aug 79 | 27 Aug 77 | deserted |
| Hall, Tobias | | 27 May 77 | 1 July 77 | do |
| Haggerty, Peter[2] | | 30 Jan 78 | 19 Mar 78 | do |

FIFTH REGIMENT.

Non Commissioned Officers and Soldiers of the Fifth Maryland Regiment left out of the Rolls February, 1778.

| | | | | |
|---|---|---|---|---|
| Higgins, Danl. | | 10 dec 76 | 30 Aug 77 | deserted |
| Hopkins, John[3] | | do | 22 April 77 | transferred |
| Hodgdon, (or son), John | | 28 April 77 | 22 Sept 77 | deserted |
| Hills, Edward | | 5 Aug | 4 Oct | prisoner |
| Hughes, Jacob | | 14 July | 5 Nov 77 | died |
| Howell, John | | 17 feb 77 | 4 May 77 | discharged |
| Harding, Edwd. | | 1 Sept 77 | 1 feb 78 | died |
| Handy, George[4] | Sergt | 4 dec 76 | 17 April 77 | transferred |
| Hughes, John | do | 7 do | | not joined Regiment |
| Harrison, Stephen | | 6 do | 16 Aug 77 | deserted |
| Hamilton, Robt. | | 12 do | 12 Mar | discharged |
| Humphreys, Thos. | | 1 April 77 | 17 Aug | deserted |
| Hughes, Thos. | | 7 July | 4 Oct | prisoner |
| | | | 5 May 1778 returned | |
| Haynes, Joseph | | Inlisted and discharged same day | | |
| Hamilton, Jno. | | 6 June 79 | 13 June 79 | deserted |

SIXTH REGIMENT.

| | | | | |
|---|---|---|---|---|
| Hoffman, John[5] | Sergt | 14 July 77 | 31 Mar 78 | died |
| Hayes, John | | 15 Aug 77 | Mar 78 | left out |

[1] Selman's.   [2] Bowie's.   [3] Dean's.   [4] Handy's.   [5] Ghiselin's.

19

## MUSTERS OF MARYLAND TROOPS, VOL III.

| NAMES. | RANK. | TIME OF SERVICE. Enlisted. | Discharged. | REMARKS. |
|---|---|---|---|---|
| Harris, Walter | | 6 Aug 77 | Mar 78 | left out |
| Haverin, Peter | | 9  do | deserted same day | |
| Herron, Charles[1] | Sergt | 20 April 77 | 30 Sep 77 | transferred |
| Hauge, John | pt | 10 dec 76 | 15 Oct 77 | do |
| Hawley, Wm. | | 1 Jan 77 | 13 Oct Hospital, not heard of } Joined Jany 79 | |
| Hennsey, Jno. | | 1 April 77 | 10 April 77 | |
| Haynes, Lawce. | | 20 Jan 77 | 26 May 77 | |
| Heath, John | do | 12 July 77 | 2 feb 78 | deserted |
| Hanson, Robt. | | 17 April 77 | 4 June 78 | |
| Hannagan, Jno. | | 9 June 77 | 4 Oct 77 | missing |
| Harmon, Geo. | Sergt | 5 dec 76 | 11 Sept 77 | do |
| Hewitt, Elijah | | 1 feb 77 | 22 Aug 77 | prisoner |
| Harvey, James | Drum | 5 dec 76 | 16 dec 77 | died |
| Hickey, William | pt | 5 dec 76 | 13 April 77 | deserted |
| Henderson, Jno. | do | 6  do | 27 Nov 77 | do |
| Hurley, John | do | 14 Jan 77 | 13 April 77 | do |
| Hunter, Nathl. | do | 24 Jan 77 | 22 May 77 | do |
| Hailey, Thomas | do | 29 Jan 77 | 25 Aug 77 | do |
| Hamilton, Thos. | do | 27 June 77 | 27 July 77 | do |
| Hardy, Isaac | do | 5 dec 78 | 22 Aug 77 | prisoner |
| Hunt, John | Sergt | 15 May 77 | 15 dec 77 | died |
| Hottle, Jacob | pt | 10 July 77 | 26 Nov 77 | discharged |
| Hurdle, Robt. | do | 9 June 77 | 13 Mar 78 | by Govr. Maryd. discharged |

### LEFT OUT OF MUSTERS THIRD REGIMENT.

| | | | | |
|---|---|---|---|---|
| Jordan, William | | | 4 Oct | killed |
| Johnston, John | | | 22 Aug | taken |

### FOURTH REGIMENT.

| | | | | |
|---|---|---|---|---|
| Joseph, John | | 19 May | 25 May | deserted |

### FIFTH REGIMENT.

Non Commissioned Officers and Soldiers of the Fifth Maryland Regiment left out of the Rolls Feby., 1778.

| | | | | |
|---|---|---|---|---|
| Johnson, Nichs. | | 27 May | 3 Sept 77 | deserted |
| | | | 20 May 78 | joined |
| Jenkins, William | | 10 dec 76 | 14 Jan 78 | deserted |
| Jones, Edward | | 10 feb 77 | 13 Mar 77 | died |
| Jenkins, Chas. | | 9 dec 76 | 22 Aug 77 | prisoner |

[1] Lawrence's.

## MUSTERS OF MARYLAND TROOPS, VOL. III.

| NAMES. | RANK. | TIME OF SERVICE. Enlisted. | Discharged. | REMARKS. |
|---|---|---|---|---|

### LEFT OUT OF MUSTERS THIRD REGIMENT.

| | | | | |
|---|---|---|---|---|
| King, William | | | 3 feb 77 | |
| Kelly, George | | | prior Enlistment | |
| Kingston, Geo. | | | left out January Roll 78 | |

### FOURTH REGIMENT.

| | | | | |
|---|---|---|---|---|
| Kennady, Robt. | | 19 Aug — | 27 Aug 77 | deserted |
| Killing, Jno.[1] | | 19 Mar 78 | 9 May 78 | do |
| Keiff, Patk. | | October and November in Goal | | |

### FIFTH REGIMENT.

Non Commissioned Officers and Soldiers of the Fifth Maryland Regiment left out of the Rolls Feby., 1778.

| | | | | |
|---|---|---|---|---|
| Kemper, Thomas | | 10 dec 76 | 22 April 77 | transferred |
| Kelly, James | Sergt | 2 Jany 77 | 16 May 77 | died |
| Kempton, Thos.[2] | | 5 dec 76 | 25 Mar 77 | deserted |

### SIXTH REGIMENT.

| | | | | |
|---|---|---|---|---|
| Kelly, William[3] | Sergt | 26 April 77 | 11 Sept 77 | missing |
| Kelly, John | pt | 17 feb 77 | 24 April 77 | died |

### LEFT OUT OF MUSTERS THIRD REGIMENT.

| | | | | |
|---|---|---|---|---|
| Lawler, James | | 4 feb | 12 feby | died |
| Lockett, Richd. | | 10 April | 11 Sept | deserted |
| Lattlemore, Anda. | | | 19 June | do |
| Lewis, Richard[4] | Sergt | | 15 Jan 78 | do |

### FOURTH REGIMENT.

| | | | | |
|---|---|---|---|---|
| Levermore, Peter | | 7 May | 12 May | deserted |

### FIFTH REGIMENT.

Non Commissioned Officers and Soldiers of the Fifth Maryland Regiment left out of the Rolls Feby., 1778.

| | | | | |
|---|---|---|---|---|
| Lysought, Jno. | | 17 dec 76 | 3 Aug 77 | deserted |
| Lastly, Joseph | | do | 10 June 77 | do |
| Lowrey, Chrisn. | | 28 Jan 77 | 20 May 77 | do |
| Lee, Thomas | Sergt | 5 dec 76 | 28 dec 76 | died |
| Laythrum, Sylvester | | 7 March | never joined | |
| Lawrence, Jno. | | 23 Jan | 5 Aug 77 | died |

[1] Riely's, late Bowie's.    [2] Cosden's.    [3] Harris'.    [4] Brice's.

## MUSTERS OF MARYLAND TROOPS, VOL. III.

| NAMES. | RANK. | TIME OF SERVICE. Enlisted. | Discharged. | REMARKS. |
|---|---|---|---|---|
| | | **SIXTH REGIMENT.** | | |
| Non Commissioned Officers and Soldiers Sixth Regiment. | | | | |
| Long, Chris. | Sergt | 18 April 77 | 21 Nov 77 | deserted |
| Lloyd, Thomas | do | 8 May 77 | 14 Jan 78 | do |
| Lockwood, Stephen | | 21 May 77 | 2 feb 78 | do |
| Lewis, William | | 26 Aug 77 | 2 feb 78 | do |
| Lancaster, John | pt | 1 Jan 77 | 11 Sept 77 | missing |
| Larkin, Anthy. | do | 25 July 77 | 7 Aug 77 | deserted |
| Lewes, James | do | 8 Jan 77 | 15 dec 77 | died |
| Letchworth, Jos. | Sergt | 21 June 77 | 3 April 78 | do |
| Lewis, Enoch | pt | 2 Mar 77 | 15 Oct 77 | deserted |
| Lukart, Fredk. | do | 5 May 79 | 25 May | do |
| Land, Jas. | do | 21    do | 21 June | do |
| | | LEFT OUT OF MUSTERS THIRD REGIMENT. | | |
| Magness, Wm. | | | 28 Jan 81 | discharged |
| Hartley's Regt. | | | | |
| McCant, Jos. | | | taken Staten Island 22 Aug | |
| Maddox, Notley | | | 16 Sept | died of wounds |
| Miller, William[1] | | 10 April | 10 June | deserted |
| Mullinoux, Wm. | | | 22 Aug | prisoner |
| May, Peter | | | 27 Aug | deserted |
| Moses, Jacob[2] | | | missing Staten Island 22 Augt | |
| Missett, Lawrence | | | do Brandywine 11 Sept | |
| McCloud, Hugh | | | 4 Oct | missing |
| McNash, Mathw. | | | 11 Sept | taken |
| McIntire, Alexr. | | | | died in June |
| Million, John[3] | | | left out January Roll 78 | |
| McDonald, Martin[2] | | | do    do    do | |
| McGinnis, Robt. | | | 13 July | deserted |
| Miller, John | | | 13 May 79 | do |
| | | FOURTH REGIMENT. | | |
| Marsh, Thomas[4] | Sergt | 14 July 77 | 5 Jan 78 | died |
| Martin, Wm. | | | 25 Nov 77 | deserted |
| Marfee, Michl.[5] | | | 16 Sept | do |
| McGuire, Philemon[6] | | 22 Mar 77 | 4 April 77 | died |
| Millard, Thomas | | 6 dec 76 | 12 April 77 | do |
| Murphy, James | | 12 Nov 77 | 15 Nov 77 | deserted |
| Missick, Lawrence | | 23 April 77 | 30 April 77 | do |
| Mowberry, Geo. | | 6 Mar 78 | 15 May 78 | do |
| Moore, Jno.[4] | | 19 May 79 | 15 June 79 | do |
| May, Francis | | 24 April | 30 May | do |
| Martin, James | | 1 July | 3 Aug | do |

[1] Ridgely's.    [2] Griffith's.    [3] Brice's.    [4] Oldham's.    [5] Spurrier's.    [6] Lansdale's.

MUSTERS OF MARYLAND TROOPS, VOL. III.

| NAMES. | RANK. | TIME OF SERVICE. | | REMARKS. |
|---|---|---|---|---|
| | | Enlisted. | Discharged. | |

### FIFTH REGIMENT.

Non Commissioned Officers and Soldiers of the Fifth Maryland Regiment left out of the Rolls Febry., 1778.

| NAMES. | RANK. | Enlisted. | Discharged. | REMARKS. |
|---|---|---|---|---|
| McCarty, Danl. | | 30 Mar 77 | 17 June 77 | died |
| Martin, Henry | | 4 Jan 77 | 14 feb 77 | do |
| Malsny, William | | 3 May 77 | 28 June 77 | deserted |
| | | | 11 April 78 | joined again |
| Masters, William | | 5 July 77 | 18 July 77 | deserted |
| McMahon, Francis | Sergt | 17 dec 76 | 14 June 77 | do |
| McKinsey, John | | 2 Jany 77 | 29 Oct 77 | died |
| Morsell, John | | 10 Mar 77 | 10 Aug 77 | do |
| Morton, Benja. | | 20 dec 76 | 2 Oct 77 | deserted |
| McGaw, Nichs. | | 2 Jan 77 | 17 feb 77 | died |
| McCarson, Jno. | | 16 Jan 76 | 26 Jan 77 | deserted |
| McMahon, Jno. | | 10 dec 76 | 10 feb 77 | do |
| McLaughlin, Philip | | 4 feb 77 | 7 Mar 77 | do |
| Mason, Arthur | | 22 April 77 | absent without leave, returned | |
| McCarty, Thomas | | 13 feb | 22 Aug | prisoner ⎱ |
| | | | 22 July 78 | joined   ⎰ |
| McClarty, George | | Damn him he deserted 15 April 77 | | 7 Jan 77 Enlisted |
| Moore, William | | 20 feb 77 | 10 May 77 | transferred |
| Meredith, James | | 16 Jan | 1 April 77 | discharged |
| Malcolm, Thomas | | 1 feb | 6    do | died |
| Meryfield, Josiah | | Inlisted and Discharged same day | | |
| Monroe, Finley | | 19 July | 4 Oct 77 | prisoner |

### LEFT OUT OF SIXTH REGIMENT.

| NAMES. | RANK. | Enlisted. | Discharged. | REMARKS. |
|---|---|---|---|---|
| McCoy, John | | 15 Aug 77 | 1 June 78 | discharged |
| McEvoy, Patk. | | 4 Sept | 13    do | do |
| McDonald, Wm. | | 30 Augt | deserted same day | |
| McDonough, Thos. | pt | 20 April 77 | 21 Jan 78 | deserted |
| McDonald, Thos. | | 7 Mar 77 | 23 Sept 77 | do |
| Martin, Charles | | 5 May 77 | 2 feb 78 | do |
| Murphy, Thomas | | 21 April 77 | 10 Juiy 77 | |
| Moran, William | | 17 June 77 | 25 May 78 | |
| Main, Henry | | 27 April 77 | 11 Sept 77 | missing |
| Moland, James | | 1 Aug 77 | | killed German Town |
| Mitz, Chris. | Sergt | 5 dec 76 | 3 July 77 | deserted |
| Massey, William | pt | 15 Jan 77 | 4 Oct 77 | killed |
| Morgan, Richd. | | | | |
| Moorcraft, Wm. | do | 9 dec 76 | 9 Mar 77 | deserted |
| Martin, Thomas | do | 17 Jan 77 | 14 feb 77 | do [heard of |
| McCarty, Florence | do | 28 April 77 | 1 Jan 78 | Hospital, not |

## MUSTERS OF MARYLAND TROOPS, VOL. III.

| NAMES. | RANK. | TIME OF SERVICE. Enlisted. | TIME OF SERVICE. Discharged. | REMARKS. |
|---|---|---|---|---|
| McKey, John | pt | 3 April 77 | 12 dec 77 | deserted |
| McDonald, James | | 1 June 77 to Oct 77 | | discharged |
| | reind. | 12 May 78 | 1 June 78 | deserted |
| Mitchell, Jno. | pt | 25 June 79 to July 79 | | do |
| McDonald, Jno. | do | 15 May 79 | 20 Nov 79 | do |

LEFT OUT OF MUSTERS THIRD REGIMENT.

| | | | | |
|---|---|---|---|---|
| Neagle, Morrice | | | 4 Oct | prisoner |

FOURTH REGIMENT.

| | | | | |
|---|---|---|---|---|
| Newthall, Thos. | | | 15 dec 77 | discharged |
| Nivin, Patk. | | 7 May | 20 May | deserted |
| Neil, John | | 26 Oct | 20 Nov | d |

FIFTH REGIMENT.

Non Commissioned Officers and Soldiers of the Fifth Maryland Regiment left out of the Rolls Feby., 1778.

| | | | | |
|---|---|---|---|---|
| Nixon, Robt. | pt | 1 Sept 77 | 14 Jan 78 | dead |
| Notts, John | | 12 dec 76 | 26 dec 76 | deserted |
| Norman, Thomas | | 4 Jan 77 | 16 April 77 | deserted |
| Norman, Richd. | | 26 feb 77 | 20 July 77 | do |

SIXTH REGIMENT.

| | | | | |
|---|---|---|---|---|
| Noaksworth, John | | 30 Aug | deserted same day | |

LEFT OUT OF MUSTERS THIRD REGIMENT.

| | | | | |
|---|---|---|---|---|
| Owens, John[1] | | | 13 July | deserted |

FIFTH REGIMENT.

Non Commissioned Officers and Soldiers of the Fifth Maryland Regiment.

| | | | | |
|---|---|---|---|---|
| Ormond, William[2] | | 27 feb 77 | 1 July 77 | deserted |
| O'Hara, William | fifer | 4 dec 76 | 22 Nov 77 | died |
| Oar, John | | 14 Jan 77 | 24 Jany | deserted |

LEFT OUT OF SIXTH REGIMENT.

| | | | | |
|---|---|---|---|---|
| Okey, John | | 11 April 78 | 4 June 78 | |

LEFT OUT OF MUSTERS THIRD REGIMENT.

| | | | | |
|---|---|---|---|---|
| Prarey, John | | | 4 Oct | prisoner |
| Primer, Henry | | | 12 dec | deserted |
| Peggs, Henry | | | 15 Mar 77 | do |
| Peacock, Robert | | | 4 Oct | missing |
| Potter, John | | | 8 Aug | deserted |

[1] Dorsey's.          [2] Lynch's.

MUSTERS OF MARYLAND TROOPS, VOL. III.

| NAMES. | RANK. | TIME OF SERVICE. Enlisted. | Discharged. | REMARKS. |
|---|---|---|---|---|

### FOURTH REGIMENT.

| | | | | |
|---|---|---|---|---|
| Patterson, Levin | | 18 May | 25 June | deserted |
| Oct & Nov 79 | | | | |
| Pascall, Peter | | 22 May | 1 June | do |
| Pound, Edward | | 22 Aug | 5 Sept | do |

### FIFTH REGIMENT.

Non Commissioned Officers and Soldiers of the Fifth Maryland Regiment left out of the Rolls Feb., 1778.

| | | | | |
|---|---|---|---|---|
| Pitts, William[1] | | 10 dec 76 | 10 May 77 | transferred |
| Pratt, Jno. | Corpl appd. 30 Mar 77 | | 27 Nov 77 | died |
| Paine, Robert | | 5 May 77 | 22 Sept 77 | deserted |
| Paul, Lewis Griffith | | 9 July | 7 dec | died |
| Payne, William | | 12 Jan 77 | 17 Jan 77 | deserted |
| Plowman, Philemon | | 10 Sept 77 | 30 Jan 78 | do |
| Pritchett, Peter | | do | 4 Oct 77 | missing |
| Price, Levin | | 14 July | 25 July | deserted |
| | | | 5 May 78 | returned |
| Payne, John[2] | Sergt | 15 feb 77 | 7 June 77 | detained by Civil |
| | | | 8 June 78 | joined    [power |
| Pigman, John | | 10 Jan 77 | 22 April 77 | deserted |
| Parfoot, Thomas | | 21 Jan | 2 April | died |
| Parrumore, Thos. | | 1 Aug | 13 Aug 77 | deserted |
| Potster, Peter | | 19 dec 76 | 6 April 77 | died |
| Paul, William | | 8 Jan 77 | 12   do | do |
| Payne, Saml. | | 10 May 79 | 13 June 79 | deserted |

### SIXTH REGIMENT.

| | | | | |
|---|---|---|---|---|
| Plumly, Jacob | Corpl | 20 July 77 | 20 Sept 77 | deserted |
| Patterson, Peter | | 20 April 77 | 18 Mar 78 | do |
| Philips, Abram | | 5 May 77 | 9 Aug 77 | shot for desertion |
| Pennox, Isaac | | 27 June 77 | 4 Nov 77 | |
| Page, George | pt | 17 feb 77 | 17 Mar 77 | sick Hospital, never joined |
| Phillips, William | Sergt | 1 Nov 77 | 15 feb 78 | died |
| Peters, William | | Was in a Consperacy in So. Carolina | | and was sent off |
| | | from the Army | | |

### SIXTH REGIMENT.

Non Commissioned Officers and Soldiers Sixth Regt.

| | | | | |
|---|---|---|---|---|
| Quixall, Thomas | | 15 Aug 77 | 19 dec 78 | deserted |

[1] Dean's.                [2] Johnson's.

## MUSTERS OF MARYLAND TROOPS, VOL. III.

| NAMES. | RANK. | TIME OF SERVICE. Enlisted. | Discharged. | REMARKS. |
|---|---|---|---|---|
| | LEFT OUT OF MUSTERS THIRD REGIMENT. | | | |
| Reland, Mathew | Appears taken as a servant | | | |
| Ricketts, William | | | 16 Mar | deserted |
| Rooker, James | | | 22 Aug | missing |
| Ryan, James | | | | deserted |
| Rockhold, T.[1] | Sergt | | 22 Aug | taken |
| Richmond, Nathl. | | | do | do |
| Rock, John | | 21 feb | 19 May 78 | deserted |
| Reevin, Stephen | | | 12 June 79 | do |
| Ryan, Timothy | | | 15 Aug | do |
| | FOURTH REGIMENT. | | | |
| Ridgely, Doctor Fredk. | appd. Surgeon 4th Regt. 1777 by Assembly | | | |
| Ringrose, James[2] | | 7 May 78 | 31 May 78 | deserted |
| Rich, Samuel[3] | | | 10 July 78 | do |
| Redweads, Jos. | | 14 Sept | 26 Sept | do |
| Reeves, Jos.[4] | | 20 May 79 | 2 June 79 | do |

### FIFTH REGIMENT.

Non Commissioned Officers and Soldiers of the Fifth Maryland Regiment left out of the Rolls Feby., 1778.

| NAMES. | RANK. | Enlisted. | Discharged. | REMARKS. |
|---|---|---|---|---|
| Reily, William | | 8 Aug 77 | 30 Aug 77 | deserted |
| Reily, Patk. | | 7 feb 77 | 12 Mar 77 | died |
| Ready, Michael | | 4 Jan 77 | 25 April 77 | transferred |
| Ray, William | Sergt | 16 April 77 | 5 May 77 | died (11 Mar pt.) |
| Roberts, Henry | | 5 dec 76 | 5 dec 76 | deserted |
| Ryan, John | | 7   do | 7 April 77 | died |
| Richardson, Geo. | | 13 feb 77 | 16 Aug | deserted |
| Roche, Thomas | | 23 April 77 | 30 July 77 | died |
| Rea, William | | 8 Jan 77 | 11 Sept 77 | missing |
| Roster, Thomas | | 12   do | 30 April 77 | died |

### LEFT OUT OF SIXTH REGIMENT.

| NAMES. | RANK. | Enlisted. | Discharged. | REMARKS. |
|---|---|---|---|---|
| Reeves, John | pt | 15 July 77 | 16 Mar 78 | died |
| Rooks, John | | 31   do | deserted same day | |
| Railey, Hugh | | 24 April 77 | 31 May 78 | deserted |
| Reah, John | | 5 May 77 | 17 June 77 | |
| Rutherford, Jas. | | 23 Mar 78 | 4 June 78 | |
| Raidy, Edmd. | pt | 6 dec 76 | 9 feb 77 | died |
| Reidy, Michael | do | 5   do | 1 Sept 77 | deserted |
| Ronderberk, John | do | 18 Jan 77 | 9 Mar 77 | do |
| Robertson, John | do | 15 feb 77 | 3 Aug 77 | do |
| Reily, Miles | do | 24   do | 13 April 77 | do |
| Rowland, Jacob | do | 27 Jan 77 | 27 July 77 | do |

[1] Brice's.          [2] Selman's.          [3] Burgess'.          [4] Oldham's.

## MUSTERS OF MARYLAND TROOPS, VOL. III.

| NAMES. | RANK. | TIME OF SERVICE. Enlisted. | Discharged. | REMARKS. |
|---|---|---|---|---|
| | | LEFT OUT OF MUSTERS THIRD REGIMENT. | | |
| Smith, Bagwell | | Enlisted 30 April 81 for 3 yrs. by Cert. of J. Bordley of Waters' Co. | | |
| Stewart, Chas. | | Artillery, has lost his papers | | |
| Swann, Basil | | | 10 Aug | died |
| Smith, William | | | 11 Sept | missing |
| Sockett, Richd. | | | do | deserted |
| Shields, William | | | 10 May | do |
| Swain, John[1] | | | 8 Sept 77 | do |
| | | | Joined feb 78 | |
| Sweeny, Edward | Sergt | | 17 April | do |
| Sherry, William | | | 4 Oct | killed |
| Spence, John | | | 4 Aug | deserted |
| Shell, Richd.[2] | | 7 feb 78 | 19 May 78 | do |
| Smith, Joseph | | | 25 June | do |
| Sappington, Thos. | | | 5 do | do |
| Smith, John | | | 24 Sept | do |
| | | FOURTH REGIMENT. | | |
| Scott, William | | 19 May | 26 May 77 | deserted |
| Smith, William | | 7 Jan 78 | 1 April 78 | do |
| Sothoren, Anthy. | | 26 April | 1 May | do |
| Sicard, Anthy. | | 24 do | 6 June | do |
| Soap, Jno. | | 2 Aug | 18 Aug | do |
| | | FIFTH REGIMENT. | | |

Non Commissioned Officers and Soldiers of the Fifth Maryland Regiment left out of the Rolls February, 1778.

| NAMES. | RANK. | Enlisted. | Discharged. | REMARKS. |
|---|---|---|---|---|
| Sampson, Richd. | | 10 dec 76 | 11 June 77 | transferred |
| Snooks, Richd. | | do | do | do |
| Spencer, Humphrey | | do | 22 April 77 | do |
| Small, Jona. | | 10 feb 77 | 14 Jan 78 | deserted |
| Stuart, Thomas | | 17 do | do | do |
| Smyth, John | | 30 Mar 77 | 17 July 77 | died |
| Sutton, Ab. | | 22 do | 22 Mar | taken by M.Page |
| Shoudon, Thomas | | 10 Aug | 10 Aug 77 | discharged |
| Sutton, Richd. | Corpl | 12 feb 77 | reduced April 16 | |
| | | | 4 July 77 | deserted |
| Sullivan, John | | 14 do | 15 July 77 | deserted |
| Smith, Thomas | | 2 Jan 77 | 18 Mar 77 | do |
| Saxey, Geo. | | 16 May | 19 July | discharged |
| Smith, John[3] (D. F.) | | 16 Jan 77 | 1 April 77 | do |

[1] Lt. J. Deaver's.  [2] Marbury's.  [3] Emory's.

MUSTERS OF MARYLAND TROOPS, VOL. III.

| NAMES. | RANK. | TIME OF SERVICE. Enlisted. | Discharged. | REMARKS. |
|---|---|---|---|---|
| Shelton, Jno. | | 17 Jan | 10 April | died |
| Stewart, Charles | | 6 June 77 | 6 dec 77 | do |
| Smyth, Joseph | Corpl | 17 March | 25 Aug 77 | do |
| Smith, John[1] | fifer | 16 Jan 77 | See Smith, Jno., 1st man Emory's | |
| Slocum, Solomon | | 25  do | 10 May 77 | discharged |
| Simmond, Wm. Fitz. | | 10 May 77 | 20 July 77 | do |
| Stevens, George | | 8 Mar | 8 April 77 | do |
| Southerland, David | | 14 feb 77 | 16 Sept 77 | deserted |
| Shelly, John | | 1 Jan | 28 Sept | discharged |
| Stevens, Geo. | | 8 Mar | 8 April 77 | do |
| Silvey, Jacob | | 14 Jan 77 | 4 Aug 77 | died |
| Smyth, John | | 10 May 79 | 14 June 79 | deserted |

SIXTH REGIMENT.

| NAMES. | RANK. | Enlisted. | Discharged. | REMARKS. |
|---|---|---|---|---|
| Steers, John | | 6 feb 77 | 1 April 77 | |
| Sullivan, Owen | | 8 July 77 | 5 Mar 78 | |
| Sullivan, Thomas | | 28 April 77 | 18 Sept 77 | |
| Smith, John | pt | 5 dec 76 | 24  do | deserted |
| | | | June 78 | joined |
| Solomon, Saml. | pt | 5 dec 76 | 13 April 77 | deserted |
| Swainey, Roger | pt | 9  do | 21 do | do |
| Staunton, Peter | do | 15 Jan 77 | 21 do | do |
| Swartzell, Henry | do | 23 Jan 77 | 24 Sept 77 | do |
| Story, Robert | do | 22 feb 77 | 3 Mar 77 | do |
| Sharer, Michael | do | 11 July 77 | 13 Oct 77 | do |
| Shokey, Abram | do | 10 Mar 77 | 3 Sept 77 | do |
| Stratton, Mack | do | 10 July 77 | 11 Sept 77 | missing |
| Sax, Richard | do | 23 May 77 | 4 Oct 77 | killed |
| Smith, Thomas | do | 14 Oct 77 | 1 Nov 77 | deserted to |
| Saund, Thomas | do | 17 May 79 | 8 July 79 | deserted [Enemy |
| Smith, Alex. Lawson | Capt | 13 July 1776 | | |

FOURTH REGIMENT.

| NAMES. | RANK. | Enlisted. | Discharged. | REMARKS. |
|---|---|---|---|---|
| Torny, Patk. | | 6 Mar 78 | 15 May 78 | deserted |
| Talbott, William[2] | | | 2 Aug 78 | died |
| Thompson, James | | 10 Nov | 19 Nov | deserted |
| Tawson, James | | 26 Oct | 8 Nov | do |
| Thompson, James | | 14 Aug 77 | 20 Aug 77 | do |

[1] Emory's.          [2] Riely's.

## MUSTERS OF MARYLAND TROOPS, VOL. III.

| NAMES. | RANK. | TIME OF SERVICE. Enlisted. | Discharged. | REMARKS. |
|---|---|---|---|---|

### FIFTH REGIMENT.

Non Commissioned Officers and Soldiers of the Fifth Maryland Regt. left out of the Rolls Feby., 1778.

| | | | | |
|---|---|---|---|---|
| Thornton, Harry | | 28 Jan 77 | 29 May 77. | discharged |
| Thomas, Michael | | 26 May | 24 Aug 77 | died |

### SIXTH REGIMENT.

| | | | | |
|---|---|---|---|---|
| Taggart, Danl. | | 8 feb 77 | 9 Oct 77 | deserted |
| Tipton, Francis | | 2 May 77 | 15 July 77 | |
| Tugby, John | | 15 July 77 | 28 Oct 77 | died |
| Tracy, William | | 26 feb 78 | 13 May 78 | |

### SEVENTH REGIMENT.

Doctor Tabbs appd.   Surgeon 7th Regt. the 29th Mar., 1777 by Assembly

### FIFTH REGIMENT.

| | | | | |
|---|---|---|---|---|
| Usher, John | | 3 feb 77 | 15 Mar 77 | died |
| Vandyke, Wm. | | | 28 Jan 77 | deserted |
| Vinestreet, Jno. | | 26 July | 19 Dec | died |

### LEFT OUT OF MUSTERS THIRD REGIMENT.

| | | | | |
|---|---|---|---|---|
| Williams, David | | | 11 Sept | missing |
| Joined 18 June 78 | | | | |
| Wattson, Edward | | | 4 Oct | killed |
| Wallis, Richard | | 17 May | 11 Sept | do  or taken |
| Wilkes, Charles | | | 19 June | deserted |
| Walker, William | | | left out January Roll 78 | |
| Watts, Richard | | | do    do | do    do |
| Webber, William | | | do | do    do |
| Wright, Danl.[1] | | 24 Mar 78 | 17 May 78 | deserted |

### FOURTH REGIMENT.

| | | | | |
|---|---|---|---|---|
| Wright, Jno.[2] | | Musd., deserted in the musr. for June 79 | | |
| Webb, John | | 14 May | 10 June 79 | deserted |
| Wright, Charles | | 17 April | 2 June | do |
| Williams, Jno. | | 8 Nov | 17 Nov | do |
| Wilton, Jno. | | 1 Oct | 2 Nov | do |
| Williams, John | | 24 Aug | 10 Sept | do  [reason |
| Welch, Thomas | | Musd. feb 80 | Mar 80 | left with. assg. any |
| Lee's Legion | | | | |

[1] Lt. Deaver's.          [2] Riely's.

## MUSTERS OF MARYLAND TROOPS, VOL. III.

| NAMES. | RANK. | TIME OF SERVICE. Enlisted. | Discharged. | REMARKS. |
|---|---|---|---|---|

### FIFTH REGIMENT.

Non Commissioned Officers and Soldiers of the Fifth Maryland Regiment left out of the Rolls February.

| NAMES. | RANK. | Enlisted. | Discharged. | REMARKS. |
|---|---|---|---|---|
| Willington, John | | 10 dec 76 | 22 April 77 | transferred |
| Worthington, Benja. | | do | do | do |
| White, John | | 18 June 77 | 23 Oct 77 | deserted |
| Williams, James | | 3 May 77 | 20 May | discharged |
| Williams, Nathan | | 3 May | 22 May | do |
| Welsh, Patk. | | 2 Jan 77 | 30 Mar 77 | died |
| Wilson, Mathew | | 17 dec 76 | 16 feb 77 | deserted |
| Williams, Morgan | | 9 feb 77 | 20 April 77 | transferred |
| Williams, Jno. | | 10 feb | 15 feb | deserted |
| Wilkerson, Geo. | | 7 April 77 | 11 Sept | killed |
| Williams, John | | ·17 feb 77 | 15 April | deserted |
| Waggoner, Joseph | | 5 May 79 | 13 June 79 | do |
| Williams, Thomas | | 11 June 79 | do | do |
| Wood, John | | 8   do | do | do |
| Williams, George | | 6   do | do | do |

### SIXTH REGIMENT.

| NAMES. | RANK. | Enlisted. | Discharged. | REMARKS. |
|---|---|---|---|---|
| Woodward, Richard | | 14 Sept 77 | 26 Jan 78 | died |
| Woods, John | | 16 Jan 77 | 2 Mar 77 | deserted |
| White, Wood Jos. | | 12 July 77 | 2 feb 78 | |
| Webber, George | | 18   do | do | |
| Welch, Nichs. | | 14 April 77 | 24 April 77 | |
| Withers, James | | 25 May 77 | 21 feb 78 | died |
| Wilson, John | pt | 6 dec 76 | 11 dec 76 | deserted |
| Wilson, Richd. | do | 4 Jan 77 | 5 Mar 77 | do |
| Williamson, Ben. | do | 8   do | 3 Aug 77 | do |
| Whitman, Henry | do | 2 May 77 | 22   do | prisoner |
| Wade, Augustin | do | 12 feb 77 | 13 June 78 | discharged |
| Wright, Jas. | Sergt Maj. | 21 June 77 | 22 Aug 77 | prisoner |

### LEFT OUT OF MUSTERS FIFTH REGIMENT.

| NAMES. | RANK. | Enlisted. | Discharged. | REMARKS. |
|---|---|---|---|---|
| Yoe, Thomas | | 18 Mar | 10 May 77 | discharged |

## MISCELLANEOUS MARYLAND LINE PAPERS.

### FIRST REGIMENT.

I hereby certify that Thomas Hutson was drafted in the year 1778 to serve nine months in Continental Army, which time he served in my Company in the First Maryland.   Given at Annapolis Nov. 5th, 1783.

Henry Gaither, Capt.

### SECOND REGIMENT.

A Roll of John Eccleston's Company in the 2nd Maryland Regiment.   Commanded by Col. Thomas Price.

John Eccleston, Capt.              John Gale, 1 Lieut.
John Ridd, Ensign.

| | | |
|---|---|---|
| Nathan Wright | James Murphy | Hugh Caine |
| John F. Lowe | Spencer Sanders | Reuben Moore |
| James Collins | Patrick Cavender | John Bandy |
| Edward Hardikin | John Lynch | Adam Henry |
| Randle Revle | George Hall | John Bryan |
| Jeremiah Andrew | John Flanagan | Daniel Kersey |
| James Andrew | John Crockett | James Delaney |
| Samuel Owens | Thomas Sanders | John Sammon |
| Charles Scott | Richard Rollins | David Williams |
| Edward Armstrong | William Nuton | William Goald |
| Richard Isable | Jacob Tharp | William Hillman |
| John Conner | Charles Moore | William Moore |
| Nathan Duley | Robert Skinner | Bryan Carroll |
| Benjamin Stevens | Silvester Ryley | John Cole |
| Levin Spicer | Obidiah Read | Thomas Buckley |
| Soloman Harriss | William Beaver | Henry Smith |
| Kemp Holder | Daniel Haly | Charles Pennerwell |
| John Blades | Timothy Riggin | James Smith |
| Jeremiah Carroll | John Martin | Peter Cahoon |
| Levy Burke | Robert Smith | John McAdams |
| Elijah Lankford | Darby Carter (?) | William Brooks |
| Richard Bush | James Pritchard | Joseph Burch |
| Samuel Roans | Henry Sharpe | John Pickeron |
| Joseph Gray | Edward Dean (?) | William Man |
| John Holder | Wm. Cantwell | Thomas Colvert |

Charles Foxwell
Barthw. Cook Hays
Thomas Thompson
James Read
John McConnakin.
James McFarrin
William Harper
Richard Harper
Thomas Taylor

Philip Strobrook, (or Shobrook)
Robert Johnson
Jonathan Wiltshire
James Donnelly
Thomas Kelley, (or Kelby)
William Wheatley
Isaac Scott
James Trego
Nehemiah Ellensworth

William West, (alias Gill)
Ezekiel Burnes
John McDougle
Edward Scott
Henry Turner, Vagrant
John Cornish
James Sanders
Noble Dean

Return of Recruits and Substitutes received and inlisted in Frederick County for the Second Maryland Regiment. Commanded by Colonel Thomas Price. 1778.

### RECRUITS.

John Hart        Feb 18
George King       "   28
John Joel         "    "
Alex. McDonald  Mch 12

James Ferrell  Mch 24
Charles Parker   "   28
Jas. Fitzgerald  Apl 3

John Haney          Apl 6
John Shovell
Lawrence Fitzpatrick "  29

### SUBSTITUTES.

John Day
John Holden
Nicholas Moss
John Baldwin
John McKinney
John Parker
Wm. Richey
Johnsey Morgan
John Spray
Daniel Vantier
Charles Stone
Thomas Daley
Arthur Mullholland
Jacob Knight
Andrew Preston
Thomas Sarjent

Wm. Courtney
David Conner
Henry Oyster
Roger Landers
Wm. McKoy
Wm. Braithwait
James Shehan
Thomas Brown
Wm. Phillips
James Eddy
Wm. Stephens
John Burns
Wm. Forbey
Patrick Carey
Jones Chamberlin

Thomas Ferrell
John McGraw
Patrick Raven
Timothy McKarty
George Hegerty
John Draper
James Henessey
James Harmer
Richard Nisbett
John Fricker
Luke Horsefield
Wm. Alinder
James Welch
James Horsfield
John Waller

### OLD SOLDIERS.

John Wright
Thomas Webster

Hugh Kelly
John Martin

Thomas Summers
Bartley Laine

Revd. James Armstrong served in the 2nd Md. Brigade from Nov., 1778, to Apl. 1780.

COMPANIES IN THE THIRD MARYLAND REGIMENT.

Muster Roll of Capt. Horatio Claggett's Co. in the 3rd Md. Regt.
Under Command of Major Anderson, for December, 1779.

FIFTH COMPANY.

| | | |
|---|---|---|
| Capt.      Horatio Ciaggett | Commd. Oct 10th, 1777 | |
| 1 Lieut. Osburn Williams | Commd. Apl 12th, 1779 | resigned |
| 2   "     Nicholas Gassaway | "       "   17th, 1777 | sick, absent |

| RANK. | NAMES. | DATE OF ENLISTMENT. | TIME. | REMARKS. |
|---|---|---|---|---|
| Serjt. | Antipas Coltart | 23 Apl 77 | 3 yrs | |
| " | Jno. Morriss | | War | |
| Corpl. | Josias Harriss | 26 May 78 | 3 yrs | |
| " | Duncan Keith | | War | |
| Drum. & Fife } | Jno. Sanders | | " | |
| Privates | James Jones | | " | |
| | Jno. Forbus | | " | |
| | Edwd. Davis | | " | |
| | William West | 9 Jan 79 | 3 yrs | |
| | Jno. Garrett | 28 Feb 77 | " | |
| | Jno. McCann | | War | |
| | Robt. Whittle | | " | |
| | Alex. Crispin | | " | |
| | Patk. Fane | | " | |
| | Jno. Robertson | | " | |
| | James Willcox | | " | |
| | Benj. Johnson | | " | |
| | Richd. Tasco | | " | |
| | Thos. Evins | | " | |
| | Jno. Anderson | 25 Feb 77 | 3 yrs | |
| | Jno. Beam | 9 Jan 79 | " | |
| | Richd. Cook | 8 "   " | " | |
| | George Brown | 28 Apl 78 | " | |
| | Jona. Pemnick | 9 Jan 79 | " | |
| | Thos. Higdon | | War | |
| | Isaac Lyan | | " | |
| | Jno. Wood | | " | |
| | Wm. Glasgow | 16 May 78 | " | |
| | Jno. Driver | | " | sick, present |
| | Richd. Suffolk | | " | "      " |
| | Saml. Hughes | | " | "      " |
| | Francis Hopkins | | " | on Fatigue |

| RANK. | NAMES. | DATE OF ENLISTMENT. | TIME. | REMARKS. |
|---|---|---|---|---|
| Privates | Zach. Burck, (or Burch) | 26 May 78 | 3 yrs | on Command |
| | Jno. White | 28 Apl 77 | " | "      " |
| | Mark McGlocklain | | War | "      " |
| | James Riley | 17 Nov 78 | 3 yrs | "      " |
| | Jona. Mahugh | 9 Jan 79 | " | "      " |
| | Alex. Frances | | War | "      " |
| | Steph. Priston | | " | "      " |
| | Henry Homs,(or Horns) | 7 Mch 78 | 3 yrs | "      " |
| | Leo. Swann | 3 May " | " | "      " |
| | Wm. Fairburn | | War | "      " |
| | Richd. Shell, (or Stull) | | " | "      " |
| | Wm. Whitely | 29 Mch 77 | 3 yrs | "      " |
| | Wm. Flanagin | 9 April 77 | " | "      " |
| | Esau Buknell | | War | "      " |
| | Peter Tippitts | | " | "      " |
| | Wm. Willson | | " | "      " |
| | Benj. Kidwell | | " | furlough  4 Jan 80 |
| | Basil Brown | | " | "       "    " |
| | Chas. Clements | | " | "       "    " |
| | Wm. Dunington | | " | sick Hospl. |
| | Jno. Minning | | 3 yrs | deserted  1 Dec 79 |
| | Jno. Conner | | War | "    17   " |
| | Philip Mandwell | | " | "     4 Jan 80 |

Jan. 19th, 1780. Mustered Capt. Clagett's Company as specified in the above Roll.

T. Brice, Maj. Brig.

Roll of Capt Wm. Wilmot's Company in the 3d Regt. December, 1779.

### SIXTH COMPANY.

| | | | | |
|---|---|---|---|---|
| | Wm. Wilmot, Captain | Comd. 15 Oct '79 | | |
| | Isaac Duvall, Lieut. | "  12 Apl '79 | | on furlough |

| RANK. | NAMES. | DATE OF ENLISTMENT. | TIME. | REMARKS. |
|---|---|---|---|---|
| Serjt. | Wm. Allen | | War | |
| Corpl. | John Turbott | 12 Feb 77 | 3 yrs | |
| " | John Keegan | | War | |
| " | Whedon Benn | | " | |
| Fifer | Isaac Barry | | " | sick, absent |
| Drum. | John Gordon | | " | |
| Privates | John Clegett | 25 Apl 78 | 3 yrs | |
| | Jacob Moses | | War | |
| | Wm. Sugars | | " | |
| | Saml. Bellwhite | | " | |

| RANK. | NAMES. | DATE OF ENLISTMENT. | TIME. | REMARKS. |
|---|---|---|---|---|
| Privates | John Pendergrast | | War | |
| | Danl. Martin | | " | |
| | Thos. Watson | | " | |
| | John Stephenson | | " | |
| | Edmd. Carthew | | " | |
| | John Williams | | " | |
| | Mark Clements | | " | |
| | Thos. Robinson | | " | |
| | Wm. Browne | | " | |
| | Wm. Jones | | " | |
| | Thos. Russell | | " | |
| | James Dollison | | " | |
| | James Byass | | " | |
| | George Windham | 25 Apl 78 | 3 yrs | |
| | George Fields | | War | on Command |
| | John Gibson | 30 Apl 78 | | "      " |
| | Michl. Mumner | | " | "      " |
| | Mar—— —— | 5 May 77 | 3 yrs | "      " |
| | Jesse Grace | 25 Apl 78 | " | "      " |
| | John Roberts | 10 Jan 77 | " | "      " |
| | Peter Byall | | War | "      " |
| | Michl. Woolford | | " | "      " |
| | James Connor | | " | on Guard |
| | Mamd. Penderberry | | " | "      " |
| | John Hailey | 3 May 77 | 3 yrs | sick, present |
| | James Sayers | | War | on furlough |
| | Godfrey Acort | | " | " |
| | Jas. Holebrooke | | " | " |
| | Michl. Martin | 10 Jany 77 | 3 yrs | dischd. 12 Jan 80 |
| | Timy. McNemara | | " | "      " |
| | George Duvall | | " | "      " |
| | Thos. Taylor | | " | "      " |
| | John R——an | | " | "      " |
| | Richd. T——ield | | " | "      " |
| | Fras. Whitaker | | " | "      " |
| | James Wilson | | " | "      " |
| | James Johns | 26 Dec 77 | " | "   28 Dec 79 |
| | Thos. Coonehan | | War | deserted 5 Jan 80 |
| | John Wilson | | " | "      " |
| | Thos. Adams | 25 Apl 78 | 3 yrs | sick Hospl. Yellow Springs 11 Jan 79 |
| | Edwd. Wade | " | " | "  Albany 20 July 79 |
| | Nathan Ryan | | | "   "   16 Oct 79 |

19 Jan., 1780. Mustered Capt. Wilmot's Company as specified in the above Roll.   T. Brice, Major Brigade.

20

Muster Roll of Capt.-Lieut. Armstrong's Co. in the 3d Regt. December, 1779.   Commanded by Major Archibald Anderson.

G. Armstrong, Capt.-Lieut.    Commd. 12 August, 1778.

| RANK. | NAMES. | DATE OF ENLISTMENT. | TIME. | REMARKS. |
|---|---|---|---|---|
| Serjt. | John Trueman | | War | |
| " | Richd. Turner | | " | |
| " | Phinchas Hurst | | | deserted 1 Jan 80 |
| " | Athantius Thomson | 12 May 78 | 3 yrs | Corpl. until appt. as Serjt. 1 Jan 80 |
| Corpl. | Thos. Alvey | | War | on Command |
| " | Wm. Dillin | | " | |
| Drum. & fife | } Barney Johnson | | " | recruiting |
| Privates | Thos. Luff | | " | |
| | John Collins | 3 May 77 | 3 yrs | |
| | Wm. Rock | 7 May 78 | War | |
| | Auston Howard | | " | |
| | Travis Alvey | | " | |
| | Edward Harley | 17 May 78 | 3 yrs | |
| | Luke Carter | | War | |
| | Henry Gouldsborou | 18 Nov 78 | 3 yrs | |
| | Jeremiah Rhodes | 10 Oct 78 | War | |
| | Richard Hall | | " | |
| | John Holmes | | " | |
| | Perrygreen Howard | | " | |
| | Mathew Moore | | " | |
| | Justinian Jourdan | 8 Apl 77 | 3 yrs | |
| | George Collins | 26 Apl 78 | " | |
| | William Children | — May 77 | " | |
| | Bennett Chesser | | War | |
| | Jacob Tragasskiss | | " | |
| | Wm. Ridding | | " | |
| | John Scott | | " | |
| | Baptis Armesworthy | | " | |
| | John Blair | 15 Jan 77 | 3 yrs | |
| | James Foster | | War | |
| | Wm. Magee | | " | |
| | Chas. Magee | | " | |
| | John Adams | | " | |
| | Thos. Carrier | | " | |
| | John Rock | 20 Apl 78 | 3 yrs | |
| | James Thomas | | War | on Command |
| | Richd. Aris | | " | "    " |
| | John B. Cissell | 15 Jan 79 | 3 yrs | "    " |
| | Cuthbert John,(or Jones) | 4 Apl 77 | " | "    " |

| RANK. | NAMES. | DATE OF ENLISTMENT. | TIME. | REMARKS. |
|---|---|---|---|---|
| Privates | Valentine Murray | 14 May 78 | 3 yrs | on Command |
| | John Morriss | 14 Apl 78 | " | " " |
| | Mathew Bowie | | War | " " |
| | Elias Henry | 4 Apl 78 | 3 yrs | on furlough |
| | Gerbiner Lemmon | 10 Nov 78 | " | sick |
| | Thos. Lavender | | War | sick Hospital |

Kimbels Farm, 19 Jan., 1780.   Mustered Capt.-Lieut. Armstrong's Company as specified in above Roll.   T. Brice, Major Brigade.

Muster Roll of the Major's Co. in the 3d Regt. Commd. by Major Anderson, for December, 1779.

Ensign & Paymaster Thos. Price   Commissioned officer

| RANK. | NAMES. | DATE OF ENLISTMENT. | TIME. | REMARKS. |
|---|---|---|---|---|
| Serjt. | Jas. Burnes | | War | Furloughed |
| Corpl. | Geo. Childes | | " | |
| " | Chas. Murphy | | " | |
| Drum. & fife | } Thos. Knight | | " | Furlough |
| Privates | John Lee | | " | |
| | John Love | | " | |
| | Wm. Strowd | | " | |
| | Patk. Millater, (or Mittater) | | " | |
| | Jos. Harrison | 14 Apl 77 | 3 yrs | |
| | Robt. Haires | 19 Jan 79 | " | |
| | Wm. Anderson | | War | |
| | Geo. Patrick | | 3 yrs | |
| | Peter Donovan | 22 Apl 77 | " | |
| | Forts. Stringer | | War | |
| | Arthur Owens | | " | |
| | Isaac King | 19 Jan 77 | 3 yrs | |
| | John Barrett | | War | |
| | John Harden | | " | |
| | James Renark | | " | on Furlough |
| | Wm. Jordan | | " | |
| | Henry Towers | 14 Jan 78 | 3 yrs | " " |
| | Thos. Barkly | | War | " " |
| | Francis Harper | | " | " " |
| | Nichs. McLaughlin | | " | " " |
| | Philip Perrin | | " | " " |

| Rank. | Names. | Date of Enlistment. | Time. | Remarks. |
|---|---|---|---|---|
| Privates | John Sanders | | War | on Furlough |
| | Thos. Eliott | | " | " " |
| | David Philips | | " | " " |
| | Peter Dotton | | " | " " |
| | James Terry | | " | " " |
| | John Duncan | | " | " " |
| | Wm. Lilly | | " | " " |
| | Edwd. Carney | | " | " " |
| | Thos. Collins | 23 Mch 77 | 3 yrs | " " |
| | John Robb | | War | " " |
| | Wm. Barry | | " | " " |
| | Wm. Linch | | " | " " |
| | Patk. Roland | | " | " " |
| | Thos. Allibon | | " | " " |
| | James Morton | 9 May 77 | 3 yrs | " " |
| | Thos. Mackey | | War | " " |
| | Nathl. Thompson | 19 Apl 77 | 3 yrs | " " |
| | Dennis Moyland | | War | deserted 19 Dec |
| | Wm. Price | | " | on Command |
| | Duke Mayson, (or Magson) | | " | " " |
| | Peter Hines | 19 Jan 79 | 3 yrs | " " |
| | James King | | | " " |
| | Jno. Welch | | | sick, absent |
| | Jno. Richardson | | War | absent |
| | John Wood | 23 April 77 | 3 yrs | sick, absent |
| | James Alexander | 22 Mch | " | " " |
| | Wm. Kennedy | | War | on Command |

19 Jan., 1780.    Mustered Major Anderson's Company as specified in the above Roll.                    T. Brice, Maj. B.          *

---

### FOURTH REGIMENT.

Muster Roll of Capt. Alexander Lawson Smith's Company, including part of the Companies belonging to the Regiment of Lt. Col. Moses Rawlings, being a part of the 11th Virginia Regiment commanded by Col. Daniel Morgan, Lt. Col. Febiger and Lt. Col. Nicholas, during 1777 and afterward being a part of the 4th Maryland Regiment commanded by Col. Josias Carvel Hall.

From Rolls for June, July, 1777, Col. Morgan, Sept., 1777, Lt. Col. Febiger, Oct., 1777, Lt. Col. Nicholas, Jan., 1778 to Jan., 1779 inclusive, Col. Hall.

* Thomas Olvie, Corporal in 3rd Md. Regt., May 25th, 1779.

| Capt. | Alex. Lawson Smith | Commissd. | | on furlough June and July '77, |
|---|---|---|---|---|
| | | July 13th '76 | | Feb '78 and Nov 15th '78, Dec '78, Jan '79 |
| Lieut. | Wm. Bradford | | | on furlough Jan and Feb '78, resigned April 3rd '78 |
| " | Adamson Tannahill | | | (last appears on Roll of July '77) |
| " | Elijah Evans | | | (last appears on Roll of Oct '77) |

| RANK. | NAME. | TIME. | DATE OF ENLISTMENT. | REMARKS. |
|---|---|---|---|---|
| Serjt. | John Thompson | 3 yrs | | (last appears on Roll of July '77) |
| " | Matthew Alexander | " | | deserted Oct 7th '77 |
| " | Joshua Saunders | " | | at Hospital Oct '77, (last appears on Roll of Oct '77) |
| " | Isaac Rose | " | | appt. 1 June '77, sick at New Hackensack Oct '78 |
| " | John Stafford | " | | Corpl. until Jan '78, appt. Corpl. 1 June '77 |
| " | John Chinneth, (Chineth) | " | | (first appears on Roll of Jan '78), at Hospital Jan to March 15th '78, at Hospital at Peeks Kill June to July 18th '78 |
| Corpl. | John Howe, (How) | " | | (last appears on Roll of July '77) |
| " | Wm. Andrews | " | | appt. 1 July '77, at Hospital June and July '77, with Gen. Scott Sept '78 |
| " | John Ford | " | | with Baggage at Chads Ford June 6th '78, sick at New Castle June to July 24th '78 |
| " | James Ferguson | " | | Capt. Thos. Bell's Company |
| " | Arthur Chinneth, (Chineth) | " | | (first appears on Roll of Jan '78), at Hospital Jan to 15 March '78, on detach. with Capt. Lynch Apl '78 |
| Fifer | Thos. Lovely | " | | promoted to Fife Major 10 Feb '78, reduced from Fife Major 1 July '78 |
| Drummer | John McBride | " | | Capt. Richard Davis' Company |
| Privates | Reuben Ross | " | | Hosp. Sept '77 Oct '77 |
| | Thomas Smith | " | | |
| | Samuel Power | " | | fur. March '78, at Hosp. Peeks Kill July 18th and Aug '78 |
| | Abraham Watson | " | | fur. Jan '78, deserted when on furlough Feb 1st '78 |
| | John Callender | " | | |
| | James Dennison | " | | Hosp. Sept '77 to Feb '78 |
| | John Cooper | " | | |
| | John Debruler | " | | Hosp. June & July '77 |

| Rank. | Names. | Time. | Date of Enlistment. | Remarks. |
|---|---|---|---|---|
| Privates | Chas. Baker | 3 yrs | | fur. March '78, detach. Col. Pope Apl '78 |
| | Henry Rowland | " | | fur. March '78, waiter Sept '78, fur. Nov 15th '78–Feb '79 |
| | Wm. Cooper | " | | Hosp. June & July '77 |
| | Wm. Cattrill, (Cattrell) | " | | |
| | John Irons | " | | Hosp. June and July '77 |
| | Josias Kimble, (Kimbal) | " | | Black River Hosp. June & July '77, Hosp. Nov, Dec '78, died Jan 1st '79 |
| | Patk. Quinn | " | | sick and present July '78 |
| | John Leviston | " | | |
| | David Knight | " | 28 Aug '77 | Hosp. Sep & Oct '77, with Baggage Chad's Ford June 6th '78 |
| | Thos. Harris | " | 21 Aug '77 | missing 11 Sept '77 |
| | John Collins | " | 25 Aug '77 | Hosp. Jan '78, (last appears on Roll of Jan '78) |
| | John Cotman | " | | (last appears on Roll of July '77) |
| | John Crockett | " | | (last appears on Roll of July '77) |
| | Wm. McCullough | " | | Waggoner, (last appears on Roll of July '77) |
| | Thos. Dearmott | " | | (last appears on Roll of July '77) |
| | Patrick McCann | " | | (last appears on Roll of July '77) |
| | Jesse Corbett, (Corbit) | " | | at Hospital June and July '77, (last appears on Roll of July '77) |
| | John Wilson | " | 20 Mch '78 | Brunswick Hosp. July 6th '78–Feb '79 |
| | Wm. Pritchard | " | | dead June 18th '77 |

### CAPT. PHILIP GRIFFITH'S COMPANY.

| Rank. | Names. | Time. | Date of Enlistment. | Remarks. |
|---|---|---|---|---|
| Privates | Joshua Burton | 3 yrs | | |
| | Patk. Lemon | " | | on Detachment with General Woodford Apl '78, Waiter Sept '78 |
| | John Carr | " | | (last appears on Roll of July '77) |
| | John Johnston | " | | (last appears on Roll of July '77) |
| | Peter Dyche | " | | (last appears on Roll of July '77) |
| | Joseph O'Neill | | | joined July '78 |

### CAPT. RICHD. DAVIS' COMPANY.

| Rank. | Names. | Time. | Date of Enlistment. | Remarks. |
|---|---|---|---|---|
| Privates | John Bourke | 3 yrs | | on Detachment with Col. Pope Apl '78, died at Monmouth Plains June 28th '78 |
| | Patk. Kerby, (Kirby) | " | | (last appears on Roll of July '77) |

| RANK. | NAMES. | TIME. | DATE OF ENLISTMENT. | REMARKS. |
|---|---|---|---|---|
| Privates | Jona. Shepperd, (Shephard) | 3 yrs | | on furlough June and July '77, (last appears on Roll of July '77) |
| | John Cochran | " | | (first appears on Roll of Jan '78), sick in Quarters Jan '78, on furlough Jan 17th '79 |
| | Henry Dennis | " | | (first appears on Roll of Jan '78), on Detachment with Col. Pope Apl '78 |
| | Elijah Cochindall | " | | (first appears on Roll of Jan '78), at Hospital Feb to Mch 15th '78 |
| | Wm. Markwell | " | | (first appears on Roll of Jan '78), on Detachment with Capt. Lynch Apl '78. |

## CAPT. THOS. BELL'S COMPANY.

| RANK. | NAMES. | TIME. | DATE OF ENLISTMENT. | REMARKS. |
|---|---|---|---|---|
| Privates | Adrian Devenport | 3 yrs | | at Peeks Kill Hospital June to July 18th '78 |
| | Wm. Batten | " | | |
| | Peter Trust | " | | wagoner Oct '77, sick in Quarters Feb and Mch '78, absent with leave June 3rd '78, returned to service August '78 |
| | Patk. Collins | " | | under guard Sept '77 |
| | John Hopwood | " | | joined Mch 15th '78, transferred to Rollins' Regt. Nov 18th '78 |
| | Robt. Parrs | " | Aug 28 '77 | deserted Sept 1st '77 |

May 18th, 1778. Isaac Hind, of Ann Arundel County, a substitute, received by Saml. Godman, Capt. in 4th Md. Regt.

## FIFTH REGIMENT.

James Murphy—Queen Anne's County, enlisted in 1777 in the Fifth Maryland Regiment. He lost a leg in the Service.

## SIXTH REGIMENT.

Pay Roll of Capt. Andrew Hynes' Company for the extra Month's Pay.

Capt. Andrew Hynes          1st Lieut. John T. Jacobs

| RANK. | NAMES. | RANK. | NAMES. |
|---|---|---|---|
| Serjt. | John Maxwell | Privates | Daniel Donovan |
| " | Benj. Wilk | | Benj. Moran |
| Corpl. | John Brown | | Patrick McCaleb |
| " | —liver Linday | | John Marshall |
| " | Stephen Griffey | | Abraham Cloward |
| Fifer | Benj. H. Kirk | | James Bryers |
| Privates | William Welch | | Francis King |
| | William Carlin | | William Spyers |
| | Solomon Rollins | | Joseph Kirk |
| | Jacob Hearse | | Robert Marshall |
| | Richard Morgan | | |
| | | M. | |

Pay Roll of Capt. Robert Harris' Company for the extra Month's Pay.

1st Lieut. Benj. Scott          2nd Lieut. Michael Dougherty

| RANK. | NAMES. | RANK. | NAMES. |
|---|---|---|---|
| Serjt. | Michael Connelly | Privates | Timothy Brannon |
| Corpl. | Richard Moland | | Joseph Woods |
| " | Stephen Price | | Peter Swanton |
| Fifer | Alex. Stephenson | | James Rattican |
| Privates | Nicholas Delany | | Dominick Coyn |
| | Abraham Hooper | | James Kearns |
| | Michael McCann | | Charles Ashman |
| | James Boyle | | Wm. Hawly |
| | John Reardon | | Benj. Taylor |
| | Patk. O'Mullan | | Wm. Anderson, deserted |
| | Patk. Eagon | | |
| | | M. | |

## COMPANIES OF THE 7TH REGIMENT.

### Inlistment of Capt. Frederick Deam's Company, 7th Regt.

| 1776. | | 1776. | |
|---|---|---|---|
| Dec. 10th | Fredrick Hoperly | Dec. 11th | William Bune |
| | Thomas Preston | | Jerimiah Thomson |
| | Mathew Turner | | Godfrey Rodwall |
| | Patrick Hay | | Habycuck Holden |

| 1776. | | 1777. | |
|---|---|---|---|
| Dec. 14th | Thomas Miller | Jan. 1st | Joseph Miller |
| | Arther Clark | | Jno. Chaterlon, (Chaterton ?) |
| | Alexander Mubary | | Jno. Stephens |
| | Patrick O'Neal | | Jno. Tarings |
| | George Fullum | | Wm. Ashwall |
| | Jno. Noice | | Robert Price |
| 15th | Richard Jackson | 5th | Jno. Lee |
| | Richard Noice | | Robert Calvert |
| | James Kelly | | Jno. Pumphry |
| 16th | Jessy McCarty | | Wm. Dickman |
| 17th | Wm. Moring | | Edmund Godfrey |
| 19th | Wm. Wood | 7th | Peter Smith |
| | Daniel McQuire | | Neal McCrue |
| | Jno. Fowler | | Wm. Merritt |
| | James Murphy | | Jno. Slyser |
| | Exicael Solomon | 14th | Robt. Stewart |
| | Dennis Doice | 16th | Robert Lawsin |
| 21st | Richard Boone | | Wm. Caskin |
| | Francis Reynolds | | Wm. Godfrey |
| | Moses Barney | | Wm. Dennerivay |
| 23rd | Daniel Griffin | | Charles Chester |
| 24th | Jno. Duffy | | Barney Keener |
| | Dennis Dougherly, (Dougherty?) | 17th | Wm. Newvall |
| | Stephen Slups | | James McFall |
| 25th | Edward Benson | 19th | Thos. Simmons |
| | Cornelius Sullivan | | Jno. Jones |
| | Daniel Larry | | Jno. Moran |
| | Barney McMannis | 23rd | David Evans |
| 26th | William Taylor | | Jno. Keysey |
| 27th | Jno. Mallimore | 28th | Richd. Stepleton |
| | James Ringfield | | Thos. Thomson |
| | John Hains, (or Hairs) | | Danl. Rief |
| | Jacob Shadley | | Jno. Anderson |
| 27th | Thos. Ward | Feb 4th | Bradley Killyham |
| | John Melony | | Joseph Hall |
| | John McClockling | | Richard Viceman |
| | Michael Murphy | | |

---

Muster Rolls of Capt. Jona. Morris' Co. in the 7th Md. Regt.
Commanded by Col. John Gunby, Apl 1778–July 1779.

| Capt. | Jona. Morris | Commissd. | on furlough 7 Feb '78, |
|---|---|---|---|
| | | Dec 28th 1777 | on command Oct '78, |
| | | | on furlough 27 Feb '79 |
| 1st Lieut. | Thos. Mason | Apl 17th 1777 | on furlough 2 May '78, |
| | | | on command Jan '79 |
| 2nd " | Benj. Murdoch | July 4th 1777 | on furlough 24 Dec '78, |
| | | | (last appears on Roll of Mch '79) |

| RANK. | NAMES. | TIME. | WHEN ENLISTED. | REMARKS. |
|---|---|---|---|---|
| Serjt. | James Collins | 3 yrs | | sick and absent June '78, absent on leave Feb '79, on command Mch '79, recruiting June & July '79. Light Corps |
| " | Jona. Tootwiler, (Tutwiller) | " | | pris. 22 Aug '77, joined 23 July '78 |
| " | *Andw. Mallen, (Mallon) | " | | reduced 7 Oct '78, absent with leave Feb '79. Scout |
| " | Hugh Doyl | " | | Orderly to the sick |
| " | Benj. Fickle | War | 6 April, '78 | |
| Corpl. | Richd. Swine | 3 yrs | | sick Sept 78–Mar 79, (last appears on Roll of Mch '79) |
| " | *Patk. Riley,(Reyley) | " | | reduced to Priv. 15 July '78, under guard Sept and Oct '78, sick at Newinsor June and July '79 |
| " | John Sewell | " | | (first appears on Roll of Sept '78) |
| " | Peter Casey | " | | enlisted as a private, promoted 19 Oct '78, absent 4 Nov '78, in service June '79 |
| " | Jacob Gandy | 9 mos | 30 June '78 | on furlough 17 Jan '79–Aug '79 |
| Drum. & Fife | Philip Fletcher | 3 yrs | | desert. July 3d, '77, returned to the service 4 June '78 |
| " | *Abraham Stallions | War | 20 May '78 | enlisted as a private, sick and present Sept '78, transferred 1 Nov '78, (last appears on Roll of Oct '78) |
| " | Allen Davidson | | 24 Dec '77 | deserted 8 Feb '78 |
| " | James Conoly | 3 yrs | | sick and absent Apl and May '78, (last appears on Roll of May '78) |
| " | Abram Bizel, (Bissel) | War | 12 Oct '78 | enlisted as a private, promoted 1 Nov '78, on furlough 17 Jan '79 |
| Privates | *Richd. Carter | 3 yrs | | Orderly for the sick Sept '78 and Feb '79, absent without leave Oct '78 and Mch '79, sick at Middle Brook June '79 |
| | Jacob Storm (Storum, Storrum) | " | | wagoner Jan '79, absent July '79 |
| | *Wm. Duly | " | | Light Corps |
| | *Danl. Benning | " | | sick F. Kills 16 Sept '78, in service Jan '79 |
| | *James Carty | " | | |
| | Thos. Maguire | " | | sick at Fish Kills Jan '79, at Hospital Feb and Mch '79 |

| RANK. | NAMES. | TIME. WHEN ENLISTED. | REMARKS. |
|---|---|---|---|
| Privates | *Neal Peacock | 3 yrs | Orderly to the sick Sept and Oct '78, absent with leave Feb '79, returned to the service Mch '79 |
| | *Patk. Lynch | " | |
| | *Chas. Symkins | " | sick at Fish Kills 16 Sept '78, sick in camp Feb and Mch '79, in service June '79 |
| | Cronomus Acre | " | |
| | George Carroll | " | Light Corps |
| | Danl. Bryant, (Bryan) | " | sick Valley Forge June '78, in service Oct '78 |
| | *Ed. Murry | " | absent with leave Feb '79 |
| | *Thos. Cook | " | Commissary's Guard Sept '78, sick and absent Jan '79, sick in quarters Feb '79, sick in camp Mch '79, sick June '79, sick at Pluckimin July '79 |
| | *John Knox, (Nox) | " | prisoner 4 Oct '77, joined 1 May '78, sick at Middle Brooke June '79 |
| | Patrick Mannan, (Manyan) | " | waiter, on furlough June and July '79 |
| | *John Dailey | " | omitted Feb and Mch '78 |
| | *Thos. Maloney | " | absent without leave Oct '78, returned to service Mch '79 |
| | *James Keelan, (Keeland) | " | Light Corps |
| | *John Grant | " | omitted 20 Feb–1 Apl '78, sick and absent Apl '79, in service Oct '78, Light Troops July '79 |
| | *John Fox | " | Scout, sick at Valley Forge June '78, in service Oct '78, sick in camp Jan '79, sick at Brunswick Feb–June '79 |
| | Patk. Murphy | " | sick and absent May '78, (last appears on Roll of May '78) |
| | Patk. Mooney | " | absent without leave 25 May '78, returned to service 25 July '79 |
| | John Smith | " | waiter |
| | *Miles Murphy | " | Scout, Light Corps |
| | *Wm. Donnalson, (Donoldson) | . | Scout, sick at Fish Kills 16 Sept '78, in Hospital Oct 78, in service July 79 |
| | John Berry | " | sick and absent Apl and May '78, (last appears on Roll of May '78) |

| Rank. | Names. | Time. | When Enlisted. | Remarks. |
|---|---|---|---|---|
| Privates | *Daniel Barnett | 3 yrs | 11 Apl '78 | Orderly to Flying Hospital Sept and Oct '78 |
| | *Nichs. Cammel, (Cambell) | " | 21 | sick at Fish Kills 16 Sept and Oct 78, sick at Albany Jan '79, at Hospital Feb and Mch '79, sick June and July '79 |
| | Wm. Jones | " | 20 May '78 | sick in Flying Hospital 4 Sept and Oct '78, dead May '79 |
| | Levin Quinley | " | 4 | sick at Cossels or Kerrels Ferry June '78–Aug '79 |
| | John Hopkins | " | 16 | sick at Prinstown June '78, sick at Fish Kills 16 Sept '78, in service Oct '78, sick at Brunswick Dec '78, dead 19 Dec '78 |
| | Ephm. Wootters | War | 4 | sick in Flying Hospital 27 July '78, Oct '78 and Jan '79–Aug '79 |
| | Jas. Thos. Read | 3 yrs | 19 | wagoner, absent Sept and Oct '78, Feb '79–July '79, not heard of July 79 |
| | *Even. Davis, (Davice) | " | 18 | sick in Flying Hospital 8 Aug '78– Apl '79, on command June '79 |
| | Richd. Clark | " | 24 April '78 | sick at F. Kills 7 Sept and Oct '78, (last appears on Roll of Mch '79) |
| | John McNalley | War | 2 | |
| | Moses Foster | " | 23 | absent without leave Oct '78 |
| | Saml. Filson, (Felson) | " | 18 | |
| | John Turner | " | 8 May '78 | sick in Flying Hospital Sept and Oct '78, (last appears on Roll of Oct '78) |
| | Wm. Hammon | " | 11 | waiter, sick at Fish Kills 8 Oct '78–Jan '79, in Hospital Feb and Mch '79, dead May '79 |
| | *Peter Shoemaker | 3 yrs | 17 | sick at camp Jan '79, sick at Brunswick Feb '79, in Hospital Mch '79 |
| | Simon Taylor | " | 20 | deserted 2 June '78 |
| | Wm. Hutton | " | " | sick 22 Aug, Sept and Oct '78, (last appears on Roll of Oct '78) |
| | George How, (Howe) | " | | Light Corps, pris. 22 Aug '77, joined 23 July '78 |
| | *Dennis Brodricks | " | | pris. 22 Aug '77, joined 23 July '78 |

| RANK. | NAMES. | TIME. | WHEN ENLISTED. | REMARKS. |
|---|---|---|---|---|
| Privates | Patk. Ryon, (Ryan) | 3 yrs | 22 Apl '78 | deserted 17 Oct '78 |
| | *Francis Mitchel | " | | Apl, May and June '78 omitted, absent without leave Oct '78, returned to service Feb '79, sick at Summersett June '79, sick at Pluckimin July '79 |
| | *James Bryan | " | | (first appears on the Roll of Sept '78) |
| | *Michael Burk | " | | sick at Fish Kills 5 Oct '78–Jan '79, in the Hospital Feb and Mch 79, in service July '79 |
| | George Pain, (Peign, Payne) | 9 mos | 30 June '78 | dischd. 30 Mch '79 |
| | *Jacob Hunt | " | " | on furlough 17 Jan '79 |
| | Zadoch Tombleson | " | " | sick in camp Feb '79, dischd. 30 Mch '79 |
| | Wm. Briggs | " | 6 June '78 | dischd. 30 Mch '79 |
| | Saml. Morris | " | 30 June '78 | dischd. 28 Feb '79 |
| | Francis Keetley, (Kelley) | " | " | transferred 11 Oct '78 |
| | Joseph Alsop | " | " | dischd. 30 Mch '79 |
| | Fredk. Zacharias | " | " | absent without leave Oct '78, dischd. 30 Mch '79 |
| | *Wm. Fortune, (Fourtune) | 3 yrs | " | on furlough 17 Jan '79, returned to service July '79 |
| | *George Brown | " | 21 Apl '78 | |
| | James Short | 9 mos | 30 June '78 | on furlough 17 Jan–Aug '79 |
| | Elisha McDonnald | " | " | dischd. 28 Feb '79 |
| | James Johns | " | " | sick in camp Oct '78, in service Jan '79, dischd. 30 Mch 79 |
| | Levin Hays | " | " | sick in camp Feb '79, dischd. 30 Mch '79 |
| | John Hill | " | " | dischd. 30 Mch '79 |
| | John Guise, (Guice) | " | " | " " |
| | *Patk. Hanagan, (Hennigan) | 3 yrs | 9 June '78 | sick Fish Kills Sept '78, on furlough 17 Jan '79 |
| | John Cypher, (Sypher) | 9 mos | 30 June '78 | dischd. 30 Mch '79 |
| | John Cammell, (Campbell) | " | " | " " |
| | Wm. Dodson | " | " | sick in Flying Hospital 7 Sept and Oct '78, dischd. 30 Mar '79 |
| | *Fredk. Harty | " | " | sick at F. Kills 16 Sept '78, in service Oct '78, on furlough 17 Jan '79 |

| RANK. | NAMES. | TIME. | WHEN ENLISTED. | REMARKS. |
|---|---|---|---|---|
| Privates | George Kinser | 9 mos | 30 June '78 | joined Virginia, (only appears on Roll of Sept '78) |
| | *Matthew Casaday | 3 yrs | | (first appears on Roll of Oct '78), on furlough 17 Jan '79 |
| | James Berry | 9 mos | | (first appears on Roll of Jan '79), dischd. 30 Mch '79 |
| | Edward Fennel, (Finnell) | 3 yrs | 23 June '78 | sick at Chester Jan–Aug '79 |
| | Alex. McGrary | | | deserted 26 Apl '78 |

Mustered at Wilmington May 22nd, '78 at Valley Forge June 1st, '78, at White Plains July 26th, '78, at Fish Kills Oct. 4th and Nov. 2nd, '78, at Middle Brook Feb. 2nd, Mch. 3rd and Apl. 3rd, '79, at Smith's Clove July 3rd, '79, and at Buttermilk Falls Aug. 14th, '78.

[Unless otherwise stated the service was from March, '78 to Aug., '79.

A star prefixed to any name indicates re-enlistment for during the war.

Jacob Gandy and James Short re-enlisted for 3 yrs., Gandy re-enlisted Oct. 27th, '78.]

---

Muster Roll of Capt. Beatty's Co. in the 7th Regt. June to Dec., 1779.

---

| Commissd. 14 Sept., 1778 | Wm. Beatty, Capt.    Joined 11 June '79 |
| | David Lynn, 1st Lt.    Promoted 10 June '79 |
| "    14 Sept., 1778 | Gassaway Watkins, Lieut. |

| RANK. | NAMES. | TIME. | WHEN ENLISTED. | REMARKS. |
|---|---|---|---|---|
| Serjt. | Chas. Philpot | 3 yrs | 4 Dec '76 | dischd. 5 Dec '79 |
| " | Robt. Green | " | 8 Jan '77 | dischd. 4 Jan '80 |
| " | Robt. Yates, (Yeats) | " | 8 Jan '77 | dischd. 6 Jan '80 |
| Drum. | Josh. Eshome | War | | |
| Corpl. | Thos. Carney | " | | on furlough Dec |
| " | John Denison | " | | |
| " | Joel Baker | 3 yrs | 19 Dec 76 | |
| Fife. | Abm. Stallions | War | | |
| Privates | John Alsop | 3 yrs | 4 Sept '77 | |
| | Andw. Ringer | War | | on commd. |
| | Jos. Hutchcraft | " | | on furlough Dec |

| RANK. | NAMES. | TIME. | WHEN ENLISTED. | REMARKS. |
|---|---|---|---|---|
| Privates | John Stricer | 3 yrs | 2 Dec '76 | dischd. 6 Jan, 1780 |
| | Wm. Reed,(Read) | War | | sick at Fish Kill |
| | Absalom Fardo | " | | on commd. |
| | Aquila Smith | 3 yrs | 2 June '78 | |
| | Saml. Jones | War | | |
| | Saml. Davis | " | | on furlough |
| | Thos. Dorman | " | | on commd. |
| | Michl. McLochlin | " | | on guard |
| | Michl. McDonnold | " | | desert. 12 Aug '79, but present in Dec. |
| | Michl. Fitzjarld, (Fitzgerald) | " | | on commd. |
| | Patt. Scott | " | | |
| | John Olliver | " | | |
| | Robt. Dunken | " | | on commd. |
| | John Davis | " | | sick, present |
| | Darby Crowley | " | | on guard |
| | Nathl. Adams | " | | on commd. |
| | John Dickson, (Dixon) | " | | on furlough Dec, on commd. |
| | Peter Cunningham | | | on commd. |
| | John Duffey | " | | |
| | John More, (Moor) | " | | |
| | John Burton | " | | sick Camp |
| | Patt. Hoarn, (Horan) | 3 yrs | 22 May '77 | on furlough |
| | Sol. Turner | " | 12 " '78 | on commd. |
| | George Gardiner | War | | on commd. |
| | Thos. Hays | " | | |
| | Patt. Connelly | 3 yrs | 2 Apl '77 | on guard |
| | George Kelley | " | 14 Mch '77 | on commd. |
| | Richd. Froggat | " | 17 " '77 | |
| | Wm. Wedge | " | 2 May '78 | sick Camp |
| | Francis Kitely | War | | on commd. |
| | John Ferrel | 3 yrs | 6 Dec '76 | dischd. 6 Jan, 1780 |
| | Edwd. Wright | " | 20 Apl '77 | on commd. |
| | Jos. Blaze | War | | sick Camp |
| | John Hulett | " | | on commd. |
| | Jacob Carnant | " | | on commd. |
| | George Devit | " | | on commd., on furlough Dec |
| | Wm. Nick | " | | on commd., on furlough Dec |
| | Nathl. Palmer, (Parmer) | " | | on commd. |
| | Thos. Tanner | " | | on commd., Dec sick, present |
| | Patt. Lynch | 3 yrs | 22 May '77 | on commd. |

| RANK. | NAMES. | TIME. | WHEN ENLISTED. | REMARKS. |
|---|---|---|---|---|
| Privates | John Devorant, (Durrant) | 3 yrs | 21 Apl '77 | on commd., waggoner |
| | Larry Brannan | War | | hospl. 3 June '79 |
| | Patt. Key | " | | deserted " " " |

Voluntary Enlistments in the 7th Md. Regt.  To serve three years.

| NAMES. | WHEN ENLISTED. | NAMES. | WHEN ENLISTED. |
|---|---|---|---|
| John Parsons | Feb 15 1780 | John Dawson | Feb 29    1780. |
| Thomas Kelly | "   25   " | Baptiste Désormeaux | "   11      " |
| James McDonnold | "   13   " | Joseph Ferrol | June 8        " |
| Joseph Lee | "   21   " | Wm. Leary,(Larrey) | March 12    " |
| William Lislend | "   29   " | John Boulanger | Feb 11      " |

Voluntary Enlistments for 3 years, Dec. 3rd, 1776.

Darby McNamarra                         Terrence Duffey

MARYLAND ACTS, OCT., 1777.

"An ACT for recruiting the quota of troops of this state in the American army, and furnishing them with cloathing and other necessaries.

Whereas an enlistment of volunteers on bounty is the most eligible mode to furnish two thousand men for recruiting our quota of the American army ;

*Be it enacted, by the General Assembly of Maryland,* That the said two thousand men be apportioned amongst the several counties, according to the number of militia in each county . . . . . .

*Be it enacted,* That every recruit, at the time of his enlistment shall have his choice of the regiment or company in which he will serve, provided such regiment or company be not full, and if full, he may choose any other regiment or company, which shall be entered against his name, and returned to the officer appointed to receive such recruit.

*And be it enacted,* That the recruits aforesaid shall be carried by the recruiting officers respectively before the lieutenant of the county in which such recruits are raised, to pass muster," . . . . .

A List of Recruits passed by James Brice, Lieut. of Annl. County.

| | | |
|---|---|---|
| James Clark | Gifford Minitree | Antoine Pomairol |
| John McLane | Pheltr. Souther | John Cope |
| Benj. Gray | Nathan Peak | Andrew White |
| George Leadbourn | George Gordon | Peter Cutong |
| Francis Thompson | Joseph Ford | John Neary |
| Germain Poulain | Jean Laravier | Wm. Ferguson |

A List of the Men recruited agreeable to an Act of the General Assembly Entitled, "An Act for recruiting the Quota of Troops of this State &ca," who have been passed by James Brice, Lieut. of Annl. County.

| NAMES OF RECRUITS. | COUNTRY. | TIME WHEN PASSED. |
|---|---|---|
| Adam Henry | Scotland | 31st Dec, 1777 |
| Willm. Sutherland | America | 8th Jan, 1778 |
| Joseph Fowler | England | 12th |
| Willm. Lund | | |
| Willm. Parsons | | |
| John Havers | | |
| John Franceway | France | |
| Roger Skiffington | Ireland | |
| John McAdams | America | |
| John Galvin | Ireland | 17th |
| Robert Purdell | America | 19th |
| John Coulston | England | |
| John Hughs | | 9th Feby |
| Jonathan Wiltshire | England | 10th |
| John Headwood | Ireland | 12th |
| James Quay | America | 14th |
| Daniel Colbert | Ireland | 25th |
| John Dodson | | 27th |
| Lawrence Riley | | |
| Philip Shobrook | | |
| John Eltham | | 28th |
| John Baxter | | |
| Richard Brannum | | |
| James Riley | | 5th March, 1778 |
| Robert Medcalfe | England | 7th |
| William Smith | America | 9th |
| Brian Carroll | do | 12th |
| William Sykes | England | 20th |
| John Williams | do | |
| Hugh Cain | | 24th |
| David Jones | | 30th |

21

| NAMES OF RECRUITS. | COUNTRY. | TIME WHEN PASSED. |
|---|---|---|
| John Steel | | |
| Edward White | | |
| James Millar | England | 8th April |
| William Jennings | do | 9th |
| John Neale | Ireland | 11th |
| Samuel Smith | do | |
| Thomas Clark | England | |
| John Wilbey | Ireland | |
| Henry Nicholson | America | 12th |
| Aquila Pearce | do | |
| Robert Scriviner | do | |
| Edward Hanasy | Ireland | 22nd May |
| William Smith | | 9th |
| Nathan Smith | | |
| Philip Savory | | 19th |
| Silvester Gaither | | 30th Sept |
| William Jenkins | France | " |
| John Stanton | | 18th Nov |
| Anthony Nowry | | " |

Voluntary enlistment of John Grover, Jan. 28th, 1778.

A Return of Recruits for the Continental Army. Passed by Charles Beatty, Esq., Lieut. of Fredk. Co.   March 10th, 1778.

| WHEN PASSED. | NAMES OF THE RESPECTIVE RECRUITS. | WHEN PASSED. | NAMES OF THE RESPECTIVE RECRUITS. |
|---|---|---|---|
| 1778 | | 1778 | |
| Jan 6 | Nicholas Karr | *Feb 19 | John Holland |
| * 12 | Lambert Thompson | 20 | John Grantt |
| * " | Adam Keepheart, (Kephart) | * 21 | John Garvis, (Jarvis) |
| * 21 | Daniel Bowman | * 23 | Patrick Ofalvey, (Ofarling) |
| * 28 | Thomas Gill | * " | Thomas Richards |
| * | James Houston | " | Nathaniel Adams |
| * 29 | George Holliday | * 24 | John Philips |
| * | William Tuten | * 25 | Thomas Matthews |
| *Feb 3 | John Magee, (McGee) | " | Darby Crowley |
| * " | Richard Gray | * " | John Howard |
| * 11 | John Hildrop | 27 | George Gibhart |
| * " | Daniel Shahan, (Schean) | " | Cosomer Hill |
| * 16 | Henry Mackey | * " | Levy Smith |
| 17 | John Hamilton | 28 | Rosalius Lett |
| * 18 | James McGraw | | James Lett |
| | John McDonald | Mar 2 | Solomon Turner |

| WHEN PASSED. | NAMES OF THE RESPECTIVE RECRUITS. | WHEN PASSED. | NAMES OF THE RESPECTIVE RECRUITS. |
|---|---|---|---|
| 1778 | | 1778 | |
| * Mar 2 | William Tallawer, (Tollaver) | * Mar 4 | Thomas Bishop |
| 3 | Matthew Cox | 5 | William Atkinson |
| " | Jacob Alexander | 6 | Michael McDonald |
| 4 | John Barlow | * 10 | Thomas Roberts |

[Names with a star prefixed are those who were enlisted for the Second Maryland Regiment.]

A List of Recruits passed by the Lieut. of Frederick County as Part of the Quota of said County.

| DATE. | NAMES. | DATE. | NAMES. |
|---|---|---|---|
| 1778 | | 1778 | |
| Mch 12 | Evan Morris | Apl 9 | James McCabe |
| 24 | Alexander McGarey | 10 | John Schevel |
| 28 | William Wedge | 10 | Frederick Stein |
| 28 | John Smith | 14 | Edward Connelly |
| Apl 2 | Thomas Mahoney | 17 | Henry Jones |
| 3 | Thomas Carney | 18 | Samuel Filson |
| 6 | Benj. Fickle | | |

Chas. Beatty, Lieut. of Fredk. Co.

### RESOLVES OF CONTINENTAL CONGRESS, 26 FEB., 1778.

"Resolved, That the several states hereafter named be required forthwith to fill up by draughts from their militia, or in any other way that shall be effectual, their respective battalions of continental troops. . . . .

Maryland—8 battalions including the German Regiment."

### MARYLAND ACTS, MARCH, 1778.

"An ACT to procure troops for the American army.

Whereas it has been represented by congress as absolutely necessary to use the most vigorous exertions to bring a powerful army into the field the ensuing campaign, and it appearing to this assembly to be the indispensable duty of this state to adopt the most effectual means to attain that end,

*Be it therefore enacted, by the General Assembly of Maryland,* That two thousand nine hundred and two men be raised, including the two artillery companies already marched to camp, and such volunteers as have been already obtained by recruiting ; and that one hundred and sixty men being deducted for the said two artillery companies, the remaining two thousand seven hundred and forty-two men be apportioned among the several counties, according to the number of militia in each county.

Out of which number, so apportioned, each county shall have a deduction for all able bodied men heretofore enlisted in virtue of the act, entitled, An act for recruiting the quota of troops of this state, in the American army, and furnishing them with cloathing and other necessaries.

*And be it enacted,* That every idle person above eighteen years of age, who is able bodied and hath no fixed habitation, nor family, nor any visible method of getting an honest livelihood, and who may be adjudged by the lieutenant of the county, or any field officer, to come properly under the above description of a vagrant, shall from and after such adjudication, be considered as a soldier enlisted, and have it in his choice, whether he will serve for nine months, or enlist for three years or during the war.

*Provided nevertheless,* That the governor and council shall have full power and authority, . . . . to discharge any person adjudged a vagrant, if in their judgement such person does not answer the above description.

*And be it enacted,* That no British prisoner or deserter, nor any convict, until his original term of service is expired, shall be enlisted or deemed a proper recruit, nor any servant whatever, until emancipated and set at liberty

*And be it enacted,* That all recruits, in virtue of this or the before recited act, shall be carried before the lieutenant of the county or some field officer in which the recruits are or shall be raised, to pass muster "

---

DORSET COUNTY, 1778.

John Pennington—a substitute

---

A List of Substitutes furnished under the Act, entitled, "An Act to procure Troops for the American Army," passed in March Session, 1778.  Anne Arundel County.

| NAMES OF SUBSTITUTES. | COUNTRY. | WHEN PASSED. | TERM. | TO WHOM DELIVERED. |
|---|---|---|---|---|
| Daniel Simmons | America | 15th Apl, 1778 | 3 yrs | Col. Stone |
| William Berry | England | 16th | " | " |
| Jacob Myers | Ireland | 16th | " | " |
| Joseph Cole | England | | " | Col. Smith |
| Thomas Byfield | " | 22nd | War | Col. Stone |
| Richard Roberts | | 24th | 3 yrs | " |
| Rezin Thackarel | America | 27th | War | " |
| William McCall | England | | " | " |
| Robert Beard | Scotland | 28th | 3 yrs | John Enwright for Pulaski |
| Jesse Doltrey | America | 11th May | " | Col. Stone |
| Joseph Smith | " | | War | " |
| John Jenkins | Wales | 25th April | " | " |
| Edward Tame | England | 12th May | 3 yrs | " |
| Michael Burn | " | 13th | War | " |
| Edward Elliott | " | | " | " |
| Alexander South | " | | " | " |
| Abram Brissington | Free Negro | 18th | 3 yrs | " |
| Benjamin Ritchie | Scotland | 18th | War | John Enwright for Pulaski |
| John Scott | | 2nd | 3 yrs | |
| Luke Burn | | 6th | " | |
| Joseph Smith | | | " | |
| Thomas Chapman | | | " | |
| Charles Snow | | | " | |
| Thomas Weston | | 16th | " | |
| John Bannon | | 4th | War | |
| John Kahoe | | | " | Jno. Enwright for Pulaski |
| John Braithwaite | | | 3 yrs | " " |
| Thos. Bennington | | 15th | War | " " |
| Negro Anthony | | 30th April | " | |
| Owen Brannon | | 3d May | 3 yrs | " " |
| Peter Moore | | 6th | " | |
| Joseph Wedon | | | War | |
| John Williams | | 8th | 3 yrs | |
| Wm. Harrington | | | " | |
| Joseph Powell | | | " | |
| Thos. Neil | | | War | Col. Stone |
| Darby Macnamara | | | | |
| Wm. Hampton | | 9th | 3 yrs | |
| George Richardson | | | War | Jno. Enwright for Pulaski |
| Patrick Burke | | | " | |
| John Scriviner | | 20th | 3 yrs | |
| Wm. Robarts | | | " | |
| Thos. Robinson | | 3rd | " | |
| John Thomas | | 5th | War | |
| John Williams | | | " | |

| Names of Substitutes. | When Passed. | Term. | To Whom Delivered. |
|---|---|---|---|
| Wm. Stevens | | War | |
| Peter Topping | 15th May, 1778 | " | |
| John Johnson | 16th | " | |
| John Williams | | " | |
| Isaac Hind | 18th | " | |
| John Fox | 19th | " | |
| John Parraclift | 9th | " | |
| Wm. Bellison | 11th | " | |
| Robert Patterson | 12th | 3 yrs | |
| John Eassen | | War | |
| Edmund Crow | 18th | 3 yrs | |
| Samuel Dixon | | War | |
| Gerrard Parker | 19th | " | |
| Joseph Butler | 20th | 3 yrs | |
| Stepn. Nicholson | 24th April | " | |
| Daniel Pearce | 24th | 3 yrs or War | Capt. L. Williams |
| Benjamin Phelps | | " | Lt. James Peale |
| Benjamin Gravels | | " | "      " |
| William Taylor | 2nd May | " | "      " |
| Charles Ivory | | " | Capt. L. Williams |
| Obed. Plummer | | " | "      " |
| Cupit Plummer | | " | "      " |
| Willm. Roberts | 4th | " | |
| John Murphy | 10th | " | |
| James Davidson | 16th | " | Lt. James Peale |
| Francis Burton | 19th | " | |
| Joseph Waldrum | 20th April | 3 yrs | |
| Edward Cooper | 21st | War | |
| John Page | | " | |
| Michael Burn | 26th | " | |
| James Tiser | | " | |
| Lawrence Cragon | | " | |
| John Hackett | | " | |
| John Gollicor | | " | |
| Robert Stacey | | " | |
| Thomas Hickey | | " | |
| Christopher Madden | | " | |
| Jacob Hynes | 28th | " | Lt. Edward Spurrier |
| Michael Dace | 30th | | |
| John Sullivan | 4th May | " | Lt. Edward Spurrier |
| Dennis Clancey | | " | |
| Thomas Jesap | 5th | " | |
| Cornelius McLaughlin | 5th | " | |
| Thos. McCormack | 6th | " | |
| Jesse Dority | | 3 yrs | |

| NAMES OF SUBSTITUTES. | WHEN PASSED. | TERM. | TO WHOM DELIVERED. |
|---|---|---|---|
| Abram Catcherside | 7th May, 1778 | War | |
| Richd. Maxwell | | " | |
| Joseph Whitehouse | | " | |
| Thomas Bryan | | " | |
| John Wilson | 9th | " | |
| Peter Powell | 11th | " | |
| Joseph Roberts | | " | |
| Joseph McDannell | | " | |
| John Williams | 13th | " | Capt. Saml. Griffith |
| Rolen Bates | 14th | " | |
| Michael Monks | | " | |
| John Young | 15th | " | |
| Arthur Donaghey | | " | |
| Richd. Jenkins | 16th | " | |
| Daniel Leary | 18th | " | Ben Todd, (Recruiting |
| Robert Harpham | | " | [Serjt.) |
| John King | | " | Lt. Edward Spurrier |
| Robert Derling | | " | |
| Simon Cappock | | " | |
| Jarvis Williams | | " | |
| Samuel Rich | | " | |
| Samuel Jones | 19th | " | |
| Thomas Hillum | | " | Ben Todd, (Recruiting |
| William Lee | 20th | 3 yrs | [Serjt.) |
| James Thomas | | War | John Enwright for Pulaski |
| Dennis Carroll | | " | |
| James McKenley | | " | |

## A List of Substitutes furnished by the Companys Classed.

| NAMES. | WHEN PASSED. | TERM. | TO WHOM DELIVERED. |
|---|---|---|---|
| Joseph Follitt | 30th May '78 | 3 yrs | Enwt. for Pulaski |
| William Hall | | War | Serjt. Gordon |
| Joseph Quynn | | 3 yrs | same |
| Joseph Jones | | do | same |
| Dorsey Wood | | 9 mos | same |
| Israel Strum | 2nd June | 3 yrs | same |
| Saml. Fowler | | 9 mos | same |
| Lewis Francis | | 3 yrs | same |
| Benj. Gundun | | do | same |
| Lewis Luairn | | do | same |

| NAMES. | WHEN PASSED. | TERM. | TO WHOM DELIVERED. |
|---|---|---|---|
| Jona. Lewis | | 3 yrs | Serjt. Gordon |
| Easy Nichols | 10th June '78 | do | Lt. Clarke |
| William Joice | | 9 mos | Serjt. Gordon |
| David Caghill | | 3 yrs | same |
| Benj. Marsh | | 3 yrs | same |
| Abram Turner | | 9 mos | same |

Thos. Weems, he expected to go as an offr. wth. the Draughts as there was no drats. he was sent on board one of the Galleys, first having paid the money he rec'd into the treasury.—by Governor and Council.

### ANNE ARUNDEL COUNTY RECRUITS AND SUBSTITUTES.

| | |
|---|---|
| Substitutes Under the Act to Procure Troops for the American Army | 117 |
| Recruits. The Act for Recruiting the Quota of Troops of this State | 50 |
| Substitutes furnished by the Companys | 16 |
| 4 Substitutes passed by Col. Dorsey's certifs. not retd. | 4 |

A List of Substitutes Passed by the Lieut. of Frederick County as Part of the Quota of Said County Agreeable to the Late Act of Assembly.

| DATE WHEN PASSED. | NAMES. | TIME OF SERVICE. | REGIMENT. |
|---|---|---|---|
| 1778 | | | |
| April  2 | John Day | 3 yrs | Col. Thomas Price |
| 13 | Nicholas Myss | 3 yrs | Ditto |
| 18 | John Baldwin | 3 yrs | Ditto |
| 18 | John McKinney | War | Ditto |
| 18 | John Parker | War | Ditto |
| 20 | Michael Hardman | 3 yrs | German Regt. |
| 21 | Henry Fisher | 3 yrs | Ditto |
| 21 | Nicholas Cammel | 3 yrs | Gunby's Regt. |
| 21 | George Brown | 3 yrs | Ditto |
| 22 | John Dalton | 3 yrs | German Regt. |
| 22 | John Houlden | War | Col. Thos. Price's |
| 22 | Patrick Wryon | War | Col. Gunby's |
| 22 | William Richey | War | Col. Thos. Price's |
| 22 | Thomas Halfpenny | 3 yrs | German |
| 22 | Johnsey Morgan | 3 yrs or War | Price's |
| 23 | Moses Foster | War | Gunby's |
| 23 | Charles Fulham | War | German |
| 24 | Richard Clark | 3 yrs | Gunby's |
| 24 | Richard Haylip | 3 yrs | German |
| 24 | John Hamilton | War | Ditto |

| DATE WHEN PASSED. | NAMES. | TIME OF SERVICE. | REGIMENT. |
|---|---|---|---|
| 1778 | | | |
| April 24 | John Spray | War | Price's |
| 24 | John Smatter | 3 yrs | German |
| 24 | Stephen McGraw | 3 yrs | Ditto |
| 25 | Joseph Weigle | War | Ditto |
| 25 | Drue Reddley | War | Gunby's |
| 25 | James Ashley | War | German |
| 25 | John Walton | 3 yrs | Ditto |
| 25 | William Mummert | 3 yrs | Ditto |
| 25 | William Cartney | War | Price's |
| 27 | James Murphy | War | German |
| 27 | Henry Oyster | War | Price's |
| 27 | Timothy Cahill | War | German |
| 27 | John McNaley | War | Gunby's |
| 27 | John Hammersly | War | German |
| 27 | Richard Keen | 3 yrs | Gunby's |
| 27 | Thomas Holdup | War | German |
| 28 | James Welch | War | Price's |
| 28 | Charles Hills | 3 yrs | Col. Williams' |
| 28 | Moses McKinsey | 3 yrs | German |
| 28 | Joshua McKinsey | 3 yrs | Ditto |
| 28 | John Temblin | 3 yrs | Ditto |
| 28 | William Molnix | War | Ditto |
| 29 | Roger Landers | War | Price's |
| 29 | James Pack | War | Col. Williams' |
| 29 | Steven Stevenson | 3 yrs | Gunby's |
| 30 | Adam Mushler | 3 yrs | German |
| 30 | Gabriel Holland | War | Williams' |
| 30 | Simon Johnson | War | Gunby's |
| 30 | William McCoy | War | Price's |
| 30 | Samuel Hottenstein | 3 yrs | German |
| May 1 | Wm. Braithwaite | War | Price's |
| 1 | John Shively | 3 yrs | Williams' |
| 1 | Thomas Brown | War | Price's |
| 1 | William Philips | 3 yrs | Ditto |
| 1 | Richard Quin | War | German |
| 2 | James Dyer | 3 yrs | Ditto |
| 2 | Robert McCland | 3 yrs | Williams' |
| 2 | Thomas Hazlewood | War | German |
| 2 | John Malady | War | Ditto |
| 3 | Patrick Riley | 3 yrs | Williams' |
| 4 | James Eddy | War | Price's |
| 4 | George Boogher | 3 yrs | German |
| 4 | William Norris | War | Ditto |
| 5 | John Megraw | War | Price's |

| DATE WHEN PASSED. | NAMES. | TIME OF SERVICE. | REGIMENT. |
|---|---|---|---|
| 1778 | | | |
| May 5 | Thomas Ferrell | War | Price's |
| 5 | Patrick Rawen | War | Ditto |
| 5 | William Nicks | 3 yrs | Gunby's |
| 5 | John Wade | War | German |
| 5 | Daniel Woriew | War | Williams' |
| 5 | John Tuff | War | Ditto |
| 5 | Henry Grantham | War | Ditto |
| 5 | William Whit | War | German |
| 6 | John Twiner | War | Gunby's |
| 6 | James Champnis | War | German |
| 6 | Andrew Shuler | War | Ditto |
| 7 | Robert Barnett | War | Ditto |
| 7 | John Stanton | War | Ditto |
| 8 | Jona. Cunningham | War | Gunby's |
| 9 | Timothy McCarty | War | Price's |
| 10 | Jacob Kaufman | 3 yrs | German |
| 11 | William Hamon | War | Gunby's |
| 11 | Daniel Barnett | War | Ditto |
| 11 | James Hennisy | War | Price's |
| 11 | Henry Holtzman | War | Gunby's |
| 12 | Jacob Moser | 3 yrs | German |
| 12 | Mathias Cosgrove | 3 yrs | Ditto |
| 12 | Hugh Moore | War | Ditto |
| 13 | John Fricker | War | Price's |
| 13 | Charles Slone | War | Ditto |
| 13 | Thomas Macrell | War | German |
| 14 | Lawrence Whalin | War | Gunby's |
| 14 | Michael Coughlan | 3 yrs | Williams' |
| 14 | James Stite | War | German |
| 15 | Robert Porter | 3 yrs | Ditto |
| 15 | Robert Mathews | 3 yrs | Williams' |
| 15 | James Connoway | 3 yrs | German |
| 15 | John Drapier | War | Price's |
| 15 | Thomas Wolfred | 3 yrs | German |
| 16 | Richard Gaul | 3 yrs | Ditto |
| 16 | Thomas Daley | 3 yrs | Price's |
| 16 | Wm. Ahearn | 3 yrs | Williams' |
| 16 | Wm. Johnson | 3 yrs | German |
| 16 | James Burk | 3 yrs | Williams' |
| 16 | John Jones | 3 yrs | Gunby's |
| 17 | George Hagerty | War | Price's |
| 17 | Adam Madern | War | German |
| 17 | George Gardner | 3 yrs | Gunby's |
| 17 | Peter Shoemaker | 3 yrs | Ditto |

| DATE WHEN PASSED. | NAMES. | TIME OF SERVICE. | REGIMENT. |
|---|---|---|---|
| 1778 | | | |
| May 18 | Joseph Branner | 3 yrs | German |
| 18 | John Carroll | War | Williams' |
| 18 | John Bennett | War | German |
| 19 | Thomas Hutchcraft | War | Ditto |
| 19 | Samuel Davis | War | Gunby's |
| 19 | Patrick Shean | War | Williams' |
| 19 | Robert Boyle | War | Ditto |
| 19 | Arthur Mulholland | War | Price's |
| 19 | Samuel Edwards | 3 yrs | Gunby's |
| 19 | William Nevin | War | German |
| 19 | Andrew Preston | War | Price's |
| 19 | Jacob Knight | War | Ditto |
| 19 | Mathias Smith | War | German |
| 19 | William Forbey | War | Price's |
| 19 | Hugh McCoy | War | German |
| 20 | Peter Barttomew | War | Ditto |
| 20 | Robert Smith | War | Ditto |
| 20 | Christian Casner | War | Ditto |
| 20 | William Rider | War | Ditto |
| 20 | Cornelius Vaughan | War | Ditto |
| 20 | John Burns | War | Price's |
| 20 | James Smith | War | German |
| 20 | John Fannell | War | Ditto |
| 20 | Benjamin Cole | War | Ditto |
| 20 | Henry Ferrence | War | Ditto |
| 20 | William Vincent | 3 yrs | Ditto |
| 20 | Patrick Trainer | War | Williams' |
| 20 | Luke Horsefield | War | Price's |
| 20 | William Allender | War | Ditto |
| 20 | Patrick Cary | War | Ditto |
| 20 | Jonas Chamberlin | War | Ditto |
| 20 | James Johnson | War | German |
| 20 | Abraham Stallings | War | Gunby's |
| 20 | William Pope | War | German |
| 20 | John Stout | War | Ditto |
| 20 | Joseph Horsefield | War | Price's |
| 20 | Michael Smith | War | German |
| 20 | John Woler | War | Price's |
| 20 | William Prangley | War | Gunby's |
| 20 | Alexander Smith | War | German |
| 20 | Benjamin Ellott | War | Ditto |
| 20 | Charles Jones | War | Ditto |
| 20 | John Richards | War | Ditto |
| 20 | Samuel Fletcher | War | Ditto |

| Date When Passed. | Names. | Time of Service. | Regiment. |
|---|---|---|---|
| 1778 | | | |
| May 20 | Dennis Waylon | War | Gunby's |
| Apl 21 | Saml. Lintridge | War | |
| 23 | D——— —onner | 3 yrs | |
| 24 | Thomas —rejent | 3 yrs | |
| May 11 | Richard Misbett | War | |
| 12 | Joseph Harmor | War | |
| 14 | Isaac Bellows | War | |
| 19 | William Stevens | War | |
| Apl 29 | James Shehon | | |
| 23 | Benj. Evans | 3 yrs | |
| 27 | William Chambers | 3 yrs | |
| May 18 | Thomas Burk | War | |
| Apl 20 | William Broughton | 3 yrs or War | |
| 20 | Daniel Vantire | War | |
| 22 | John Gibbons | War | |
| May 12 | Henry McManis | War | |
| 15 | William Hays | War | |
| 15 | John Hall | War | |
| Apl 21 | John Roach | | |

A List of Substitutes Furnished by the Different Battalions After their being Classed in Order for the Draught.   Frederick County.

| Date When Passed. | Names. | Time of Service. | Regiment. |
|---|---|---|---|
| 1778 | | | |
| May 29 | James Obryan | War | German |
| June 1 | George Loux | 9 mo | Col. Williams' |
| 1 | Francis Kerns | 3 yrs | German |
| 1 | Christopher Keplinger | 9 mo | Ditto |
| 2 | Michael Fullam | 9 mo | Williams' |
| 2 | Thomas Williams | 9 mo | Ditto |
| 2 | Christian Mummaw | 9 mo | German |
| 2 | George Arnold | 9 mo | Ditto |
| 2 | Philip Hinkle | 9 mo | Ditto |
| 2 | Thomas Polhouse | 9 mo | Ditto |
| 2 | George Bontz | 9 mo | Ditto |
| 2 | Acquila Smith | 3 yrs | Gunby's |
| 2 | Henry Young | 9 mo | Williams' |
| 3 | Barnard Ridenour | 9 mo | German |
| 3 | Abraham Miller, Jr. | 9 mo | Ditto |

| DATE WHEN PASSED. | NAMES. | TIME OF SERVICE. | REGIMENT. |
|---|---|---|---|
| 1778 | | | |
| June 3 | Albert Hendrickson | 9 mo | German |
| 3 | Philip Beattys | 9 mo | Ditto |
| 3 | Nathan Speake | 3 yrs | Williams' |
| 3 | William Fortune | 9 mo | Gunby's |
| 3 | Samuel Morris | 9 mo | Ditto |
| 3 | Charles McNabb | War | Ditto |
| 3 | Jacob Hommer | 9 mo | Ditto |
| 4 | Jacob Gandy | 9 mo | Ditto |
| 4 | George Kinser | 9 mo | Ditto |
| 4 | Frederick Lokerias | 9 mo | Ditto |
| 4 | William Todd | War | Ditto |
| 5 | John Sifer | 9 mo | Ditto |
| 6 | Reson Hanson | 3 yrs | Williams' |
| 6 | William Finacy | 9 mo | Ditto |
| 6 | Daniel Lett | 9 mo | Ditto |
| 6 | Thomas Rowlands | 9 mo | German |
| 6 | John Finacy | 9 mo | Williams' |
| 6 | Philip Fitzpatrick | 9 mo | German |
| 6 | William Ridge, (Cooper) | 9 mo | Gunby's |
| 6 | Samuel Jones | 3 yrs | Ditto |
| 6 | James Dodd | 9 mo | Ditto |
| 8 | Thomas Swannick | 3 yrs | Ditto |
| 8 | John Newman | 9 mo | Ditto |
| 8 | John Cammell | 9 mo | Ditto |
| 8 | John Sewell | War | Ditto |
| 8 | Zadock Tomlinson | 9 mo | Ditto |
| 8 | Joseph Alsop | 9 mo | Ditto |
| 8 | John Hill | 9 mo | Ditto |
| 8 | John ——ise | 9 mo | Ditto |
| 5 | William Jones | 9 mo | Williams' |
| 6 | William McNeal | 9 mo | Ditto |
| 6 | David Boulton | 9 mo | Ditto |
| 6 | James Heasty | 9 mo | Ditto |
| 6 | Dudley Lee | 9 mo | Ditto |
| 6 | Teter Baker | 9 mo | Ditto |
| 6 | John Bell | 9 mo | Ditto |
| 8 | Thomas Smith | 9 mo | Ditto |
| 8 | Paul Marr | 9 mo | Ditto |
| 9 | William Kennedy | War | Ditto |
| 9 | John McDonnagh | 9 mo | Ditto |
| 9 | Richard Hobson | 9 mo | German |
| May 28 | John Kendrick | 3 yrs | Ditto |
| June 9 | Martin Gridler | 9 mo | Williams' |
| 12 | William Mefford | 9 mo | Gunby's |

| DATE WHEN PASSED. | NAMES. | TIME OF SERVICE. | REGIMENT. |
|---|---|---|---|
| 1778 | | | |
| June 9 | Andrew Renhard | 9 mo | Williams' |
| 13 | Joseph Lougdon | War | Ditto |
| 13 | Anthony Durgan | 3 yrs | Ditto |
| 13 | Wm. Robt. Howe | 9 mo | Ditto |
| 13 | Frederick Harty | 9 mo | Gunby's |
| 13 | George Pain | 9 mo | Ditto |
| 13 | William Doddson | 9 mo | Ditto |
| 13 | Jacob Hunt | 9 mo | Ditto |
| 13 | Benjamin Tarman | 9 mo | Williams' |
| 13 | James Aires | 9 mo | Ditto |

A List of the Men's Names Enlisted by the Officers Mentioned, and Passed by me.

| DATE. | OFFICERS' NAMES. | MEN'S NAMES. | TIME OF SERVICE. |
|---|---|---|---|
| 1778 | | | |
| May 27 | Capt. Montjoy Baily | John Smith | 3 yrs |
| June 9 | Capt. Jon. Morriss | Peter Hangin | 3 yrs |
| May 26 | Capt. Adam Grosh | James Feilson | 3 yrs |
| 26 | Lieut. Edwd. Dyer | Patrick Crawley | War |
| June 15 | Capt. Jno. Ghiselin | John Brown | 3 yrs |
| 23 | Ditto | John Timly | 3 yrs |
| 23 | Capt. Jona. Morriss | Edwd. Fennell | War |
| 23 | Ditto | William Lyons | War |
| 18 | Ditto | James Mullings | War |
| 23 | Ditto | James McDonald | War |
| May 10 | Thomas Porter taken up as a Vagrant by Serjt. Benj. Fickle, & Delivered to Capt. Jona. Morriss. | | |
| May 2 | Thomas Bowl taken up as Ditto by Wm. Bently & Jno. Wood who was Enlisted by an Officer in Col. Hartley's Regt. Penna. & taken away. | | |

A List of Deserters taken up and Brought before the Lieutenant of Frederick County who were Committed to the Public Goal of said County.

| DATE. | NAMES. | REGIMENT OR COMPANY. |
|---|---|---|
| 1778 | | |
| Apl 19 | Jacob Haifley | German Regiment |
| 22 | Peter Peterson | Williams' ditto |
| 23 | Adam Goodeberger | Capt. Weaver's Co., Penna. Troops |
| 23 | Lodowick Mackeman | "    Westfield's  "   Va.    " |
| 23 | Hugh Riley | 6th Md. Regt. |
| 25 | William Smith | Col. Rawlings |
| 25 | Conrod Michael | Ditto |
| 25 | Lawrence Fitzpatrick | Col. Price's |
| 25 | John Johnson | 6th Maryland Regt. |
| 25 | John Langly | Col. Hartley's Penna. Troops |
| 26 | John Malone | Col. Thompson's    ditto |
| 27 | John Charles | "   Thuston's Va.   do |
| 25 | Samuel Barts | Georgia Regt. |
| 25 | William McNamara | Baltimore Fort |
| 21 | John Braswell | 4th North Carolina Regiment |
| May 7 | Robert Sapp | 1st Md. Regt. |
| 18 | Samuel Brotner | Col. Thuston's Va. Troops |
| Apl 25 | Forrest McCatchen | "   Hartley's Penna. do |

Chas. Beatty, Lieut. of Fredk. Co.

A List of Draughts and Substitutes under the Command of Capt. Charles Williamson.

DRAUGHTS.

Wm. Dare
James Weems, (of John), now at Camp
Thomas Man

Benj. Askew
John Smith
Benj. Johns, (of Benjamin)

SUBSTITUTES.

Benj. Johns, (of Absolum)
Martin Wells, (of Martin)
Recruit Randall Wright
   do    John Grover
Joseph Shukland
John B. Dela'Franey
David Randall
Richard Calbut
Basil Hellen
Francis Games
Richard Everit
Wm. Kirshaw
Daniel Young
James Nowell
Thomas Blackburn

Richard Hame
Alexander Williamson
3 years        sent to Camp with Lt. Clark
ditto           with Capt. Truman's Sergt.
9 months
James McKenny
James Lawrence
Wm. Gardner
Thomas Nash
Hugh Ryon
Wm. Thomas—Vagrant
James Charlton
John King          } Deserters
Wm. Scott

June 14th, 1778        Benjamin Mackall, Lieut. of Calvert Co.

Prince George's County, June 15th, 1778.

| Lt. | George Dyer | a draft | Charles Jenings | a draft |
|-----|-------------|---------|-----------------|---------|
| Serjt. | Josiah Gordon | " " | John Wilson | " " |
| | Chrisr. Beall | a deserter from 2nd Md. Regt. | | |
| | George Inness | a substitute to serve for three years | | |
| | Thos. Beall, son of Thomas | " | " | " nine months |

Muster Roll of Capt. John Kershner's Compy. Guarding the Prisoners of War. Fort Frederick June 27th, 1778. (1777–1778.)

| Capt. | John Kershner | Privates | Michael Kernam, | Dischd. 17 May |
|-------|---------------|----------|-----------------|----------------|
| Lieut. | Jno. McLaughlin | | Danl. Kemmer | |
| " | Peter Backer | | Adam Coon, | Dischd. 5 June |
| Ensign | Wm. Conrod | | Jacob Adams | " 6 " |
| Serjt. | Luke Sholly | | Jno. Fiche | |
| " | Martain Phipher | | Goodhert Tressel, | Deserted 2 " |
| " | David Wolgamot | | Christiain Kirgery | |
| " | George Fanglar | | James Flack | |
| Drum. | John Oster | | George May, | " 2 June |
| & Fife. | Peter Lighter | | Chris. Shock, | Dischd. 19 " |
| Corpl. | Jacob Craver | | Jno. Robinson | |
| " | Jacob Barnt | | Jacob Geerhert, | " 5 " |
| " | Peter Conn | | David Fosney | |
| " | John Conn, Dischd. 21 June | | Richd. Menson | |
| Privates | Michael Hartly | | Peter Oster | |
| | George Stuart | | Thos. McCullim | |
| | George Hudson | | Casper Snider | |
| | Jno. Shriber | | Peter Rough | |
| | Elias Reeter | | Mathw. Williams | |
| | George Carter | | Wm. Allin | |
| | Abraham Bower | | Abraham Feeter | |
| | Martain Harry, (or Narry) | | John Augusteen, | Deserted 26 May |
| | Andrew Miller, Dischd. 8 June | | Jacob Rorer, | Dischd. 20 May |
| | Peter Haflegh | | Peter Sybert | |
| | Fredk. Craft | | Michl. Spesser | |
| | Henry Tyce | | Fredk. Deefhem, (or Deefherr) | |
| | Adam Sydey, Dischd. 8 June | | Fredk. Shackler | |
| | Jacob Binkler | | Phillip Criegh, | Dischd. 14 June |
| | Abraham Troxal, Jr. | | David Wirley, | " 5 " |
| | Jacob Ridenour | | Christiain Nockey, (or Hockey) | |
| | Peter Adams | | Jacob Tysher | |
| | Abraham Leedy | | | |
| | Jno. Gable | | | |

J. Kershner, Capt.

Return of Substitutes, Drafts and Vagrants from St. Mary's County.
June 10th, 1778.

| WHEN ENTERED. | NAME. | TIME OF SERVING. | WHEN ENTERED. | NAME. | TIME OF SERVING. |
|---|---|---|---|---|---|
| 1778 | | | 1778 | | |
| Apl 20 | Patrick Kelly | 3 yrs | May 28 | Notley Goldsmith | 9 mo |
| 30 | Wm. Spalding, son of Jas. | 9 mo | 25 | Stephen French | do |
| 20 | Wm. McGee | 3 yrs | 25 | John Stone | do |
| 28 | Charles McGee | War | 25 | Robert Swales | do |
| 24 | John Duncaster | 9 mo | 29 | Barnard Pane | do |
| 27 | Edmd. Barton Cissell | 9 mo | 29 | Stephen Greenwell | do |
| 26 | John Rock | 3 yrs | 29 | John Wheatley | do |
| 30 | John Holmes | 3 yrs | 29 | Joseph Stone | do |
| 30 | Austin Howard | 3 yrs | 29 | Thomas Jarboe | do |
| 26 | Benj. Chesher, run off | War | 29 | Robert Greenwell | do |
| May 4 | Bennet Cox, vagrant, deserted | 9 mo | 29 | John Senior | do |
| | | | 29 | James Wimseld | do |
| 13 | John Bapt. Willingham | 9 mo | 30 | Edward Barton Godart | do |
| Apl 21 | Thos. Green Alvey | 3 yrs | 25 | Geo. Dent | do |
| 24 | Justinian Bullock | 3 yrs | 26 | Notley Tippett | do |
| 30 | John Blundull | 3 yrs | 29 | Peter Richie | do |
| May 4 | Elias Henry | 3 yrs | 30 | Norman Bouroughs | do |
| Apl 24 | John Bapt. Baley | 3 yrs | June 1 | Jonathan Woodburn | do |
| 21 | Richard Hall | 3 yrs | May 29 | Edmund Hill | do |
| 28 | Travers Alvey | 3 yrs | 25 | Thomas Branson | do |
| May 2 | Joseph Shanks | War | 28 | Joseph Crook | do |
| 2 | Zephaniah Williams | War | 28 | Benj. Dailey | do |
| 1 | James Thomas | 3 yrs | 13 | James Graves | do |
| Apl 25 | Henry Harley | 3 yrs | Apl 27 | Rudolph French | do |
| 26 | George Collings | 3 yrs | 23 | John Fields | do |
| 23 | Wm. Holt | 3 yrs | 26 | Leod. McAtee ⎱ vagrants or | do |
| May 5 | Edwd. Harley | 3 yrs | 26 | John McAtee ⎰ deserters | do |
| Apl 27 | John Farden | 3 yrs | May 1 | George Spalding | do |
| 29 | Jeremiah Scraher | 3 yrs | Apl 26 | Wm. Rock | 3 yrs |
| 22 | Thos. Curtis | War | May 14 | Justinian Carter | do |
| 28 | John Spragu | 3 yrs | 16 | Henry Causey | do |
| May 13 | Athas. Thomson | 3 yrs | Apl 20 | John Morris | do |
| Apl 30 | John Truman | War | May 14 | Henry Gouldsburry | 9 mo |
| May 26 | Jeremiah Morgan | 9 mo | 2 | Silvester Wheatley | 3 yrs |
| 23 | John Turner | do | 19 | Luke Carter | War |
| 23 | John Blair | do | Apl 4 | Thos. Biggs | 9 mo |
| 23 | John Carpentor | do | May 16 | Henry Philips | 3 yrs |
| 25 | Edward Smith | do | 14 | Ignatius Downs | do |
| 25 | Leonard Branson | do | 19 | John McCalley | 9 mo |
| 25 | Abednigo Jackson | do | 31 | Garbiner Lemmon | do |
| 27 | Edward McKarteney | do | 31 | Geo. Shirley | do |

22

| WHEN ENTERED. | NAME. | TIME OF SERVING. | WHEN ENTERED. | NAME. | TIME OF SERVING. |
|---|---|---|---|---|---|
| 1778 | | | 1778 | | |
| May 31 | Jeremiah Rhoades | 9 mo | May 30 | Danl. Friend, a ship carpenter, a draft | 9 mo |
| 31 | James Coachman | do | | | do |
| 30 | Jessee Chiveral | do | 25 | Jesse Carter | do |
| 23 | David Johns | do | June 1 | Jacob McKey | do |
| 29 | John Norris | do | 1 | John Medcalf | do |
| 28 | James Foster | do | 1 | John Barton Drury | do |
| 23 | Bennett McLeland | do | May 31 | Thos. Mattingley | |
| 22 | Nathan Adams | do | 31 | Philip Mattingley | |
| 22 | Jeremiah King | do | 31 | Stanley Battin | |
| 22 | James Dyer | do | | Joseph Johnston | do |
| 25 | Henry King | do | | Joseph Smith | do |
| 25 | Thomas Wise | do | | John Jones | do |
| 25 | Richard Smart | do | | James Barnes | do |
| 28 | Smith Mahoney | do | | Jonathan Riney | do |
| 25 | Robert Turtle | do | June 10 | Rudolph Barnchouse, (Barnhouse) | do |
| 28 | Thomas More | do | | | |
| 30 | James Yates | do | 10 | Joseph Moore | do |
| 30 | Zepheniah Hoskins | do | 10 | Phineas Hurst | do |
| 30 | Joseph Fields | do | 10 | Michael Fields | 3 yrs |
| 23 | Leonard Howard | do | | James McBride | do |
| 30 | Ignatius Clark | do | 10 | William Spalding, a draft | |
| 30 | Charles Clarke | do | | Benj. Morgan, a draft | |
| 30 | Joseph Reswick | do | | Benj. Thomson, a deserter from the Continental Army. | |

A List of Recruits, Substitutes and Draughts Furnished in Charles County by Vertue of an Act of Assembly for procuring Troops for the Continental Army, &c., passed 1778.   Sept 11th, 1778.

### VOLUNTAIR.
Saml. Hanson, of Walter.

### RECRUITS.

Thomas Franklin
Henry Dickson

Thomas Salsbury
Benj. Jon. Biggs

William Garvey
Stephin Fresh
Peter Dennis
John Helmsley
Francis Coffer
Simon Perrie
Dennis Pearson
John Morrison

#### SUBSTITUTES FOR 3 YEARS.
George Ward
John Martindale
Martin Doyai
Perry Patterson
Henry Russell
William Poland
Samuel Owings
Charles Scott

Charles Robertson
George Ennes
Leonard Gates
Thos. G. Hinds
Charles Clements
William Glasgoe
Leonard Bean
Isaac Lyon

## SUBSTITUTES DURING THE WAR.

John Perrie
Dennis Cragain

Abraham Garceny
John Hinds

John Hardin

## SUBSTITUTES FOR 9 MONTHS.

Richard E. Gattin
Randolph Hoskins
Hezekiah Patterson
John Penn
William Higoon

Bennit Mudd
Benjamin Green
William Lovless
Stephin Penn

Adam Adams
Jeremiah Parsons
Robert Coley
Benjamin Tasker

## FURNISHED BY CLASSES FOR 9 MONTHS.

Emanuel Goomes
Walter Procter
John Williams
Michael Lawson
Jacob Miller
Thomas Mahew
Benjamin Pryor
Elias Lovless
Josias Smith
Hewit Johnson
Francis Hicky
James Murrey
William Killow
John G. Gardiner
Acton Robey
Matthew Smith
Jonathan White
James Hunt
Benjamin Rollings
Raphael Hagan

John Taylor
Isaac Rollings
John B. Mills
Joseph Owings
Matthew Johnson
Samuel Chinge
Richard May
Levine Smith
Joseph Drurey
Thomas Dutton
Philip Briscoe
George Bateman
Henry Fouler
James Devin
Bennet Posey
Charles Procter
George Walker
Samuel Thompson
Thomas Hudson
Jesse Allin

Samuel Green
Jesse Woodward
William Griffin
Joseph Bradshaw
John Carroll
John Carroll, Jr.
William Coombes
Richard Mudd
William Gates
Ebinezer Athey
Robert Tharlkill
John Wedding
Joseph Philbert
James Coley
Joseph Coley
Basil Wheeler
Richard Thompson
John Hughes
Bennit Sanders

## DRAUGHTED AND JOINED THE ARMY.

Leonard Martin
Enious Davice
Silvester Gatten
William Delozior
Lancelot Ward

Francis Posey
Benj. Wright, (Fined by
    Court Martial)
John Butler

William Warrin
Thomas Ward
John Adams
George Welch

## DRAUGHTS WHO HAVE NOT JOINED THE ARMY.

George Higgs
Edward Flurry

Ignatius Baggott
Philip Morland

Matthew Kidwell
Richard Carroll

**Frans. Ware, Lieut. of Chas. Co.**

## MUSTER AND PAY ROLLS FOR 1780.

### MARYLAND ACTS—NOV., 1779.

"An ACT for recruiting the quota of troops of this state in the American army.

Whereas an enlistment of volunteers on bounty is the most eligible mode to furnish fourteen hundred men for recruiting our quota of the American army;

*Be it enacted, by the General Assembly of Maryland,* That the said fourteen hundred men be apportioned amongst the several counties according to the number of militia in each county.

*And be it enacted,* That every recruit, at the time of his enlistment, shall have his choice of the regiment or company in which he will serve, provided such regiment or company be not full, and if full, he may chuse any other regiment or company not being full, which shall be entered against his name.

*And be it enacted,* That the recruits aforesaid shall be carried by the recruiting officers respectively before the lieutenant, or any field officer, of the county in which such recruits are raised, to pass muster."

---

Sir:

Bladensburgh, February 22nd, 1780.

Inclos'd you have certificates for Eleven men authenticated by Mr. Christopher Lowndes. The men comes under the command of Serjeant Mantle who makes the number mentioned. I have three or four others who, not being certify'd, is obliged to remain behind. If your Excellency thinks proper Serjeant Mantle & Wm. Harriss will return, as their presence with me is very essential. No doubt your Excellency will think proper to cloth the recruits immediatly, it being a part of their Bounty.

I have the Honor to be

N. B. The Serjeant brings 14 Men
˙1 of which is not Certify'd owing to the freshes. W. D. B.

Your Excellency's
Most Obedient
Humble Serviant
Wm. D. Beall.

To His Excellency
Thomas Sim Lee, Esq.

A Return of Recruits Passed by Joshua Beall, Lieut. P. G. Cty.

| WHEN PASSED. | NAMES. | WHERE BORN. | AGE. | TIME OF SERVICE. |
|---|---|---|---|---|
| | Passed by Jos. Beall. | | | |
| 1780 Feb. 14th | John Dacorne | France | 28 | 3 yrs or during War |
| " | John Dupre | " | 36 | " " " |
| March 15th | John Ballard | Mty. Co. | 18 | " |
| " | Saml. Gold | " | 16 | " |
| | Passed by Col. John Addison. | | | |
| | John Hughes | | | during War |
| | Passed by Col. Barton Lucas. | | | |
| Jan. 7th | Richd. Harris | | | |
| 27th | William Harris | | | 3 yrs or during War |
| | Passed by Lt. Col. Abraham Boyd | | | |
| Feb. 19th | Joseph Sabolle | | | 3 yrs or during War |
| " | John Armstrong, Jr. | | | " " " |
| " | Henry Purdy | | | " " " |
| " | Edward Purdy | | | " " " |
| Jan. 31st | John Mantle | | | |
| " | John Armstrong, Sr. | | | |
| Feb. 12th | John Martin, Jr. | | | " " " |
| " | John Purdy, son of Henry | | | " " " |

Men enrolled in Charles County by Capt. Joseph Marbury and Lieut. Samuel Hamelton. Capt. Marbury's Company, 3rd Md. Regt. 1780.

Peter Sanquehart
Michael Lavigne
Julius Mercer
James Armstrong
John Scott
Francis Dunington
Wm. Hamelton
Frederick Hall

John Hughs
Jesse Semms, (Simmes)
Willm. Gates
Wm. Robertson Franklin
John Boucher Haislope
Thomas Thompson
William Conner
John Bapt. Mills

Joseph Thompson
William Swann
Benj. Steuart
*James Steuart
*John Richards
*William Fuller
*James Langly
*Samuel Clarben

[Names prefixed by a star are those who were enlisted by Lt. Hamelton.]

Baltimore, March 2nd, 1780.

Men recruited by Samuel Chester and delivered to Capt. Samuel Farmer of the 3rd Md. Regt.

| | | |
|---|---|---|
| James Douglass | John Smith | James O'Bryan |
| James Cromer | Thomas Cardof, (Cardiff) | John Buckley |
| Thomas Hoopper,(Hooper) | James Grant | Zachria Clark |
| Adam Sheets | James Ryan | Richard Walls |
| Barney McCarren | Lucas Ives | James Hilton } Deserted. |
| James Dunavan | Robert Gatting, (Gathing) | James Penman } |
| | George Sawyer | |

### Samuel Chester's Recruits.  Passed by Thos. Sollers.

| | | |
|---|---|---|
| James Steel | George Watson | William Bolton |
| Samuel True | James Robinson | Patrick Moran |

Men Inlisted in Fredk. Town for the 7th Md. Regt. from Jan. until April, 1780.

| | | | |
|---|---|---|---|
| Henry Jones | deserted | George Hiland | gone to Camp |
| John Cockran | now in Fredk. | Hugh Kelley | ditto |
| John Parsons | ditto | Stephen Flaherty | ditto |
| John Aghern | deserted | Thos. Brown | ditto |
| Wm. Cocks | now in Fredk. | Michl. Pinn | ditto |
| Baptiste Desormaux | deserted | Francis Black | ditto |
| Alex. Sterling | gone to Camp | John Ross | ditto |
| John Newland | ditto | John Williams | in Fredk. |
| Michael Ceary | ditto | Joseph Kelsey | gone to Camp |
| James Burns | ditto | Wm. Leary | ditto |
| James McDonnold | in Fredk. | John Boulonger | deserted |
| John Dawson | ditto | Francis Williams | ditto |
| Abijah Buxton | gone to Camp | Thos. Corter | deserted & in Balto. goal |
| Henry Ostwabt | ditto | | |
| James Allen | in Fredk. | John Smith | deserted |
| John Reiley | gone to Camp | Wm. Chamberlain | ditto |
| George Cowland | ditto | Wm. Mais | in Fredk. |
| Thos. Burns | ditto | James Clements | deserted |
| James Chandler | ditto | James Brooks | ditto |
| Joseph Lee | ditto | John Brooks | in Fredk. |
| Thos. Kelley | ditto | Saml. Wedge | gone to Camp |
| Wm. Leseland | ditto | Joseph Murphy | { in McCullum's place, gone to Camp |
| Wm. Kenney | ditto | | |
| Simon Colibert | ditto | John Williams | |
| Nicholas Hutchinson | in Fredk. | Jessey Barnet | |
| James Kelley | gone to Camp | Peter Outhouse | |
| John Mick | ditto | John Riggs | |
| David McCulloch | ditto | John Murphy | |
| Owen Ceary | ditto | | |

List of Recruits enlisted for during the war and Deserters enlisted for during the war from Kent Co., Apl. 6th, 1780.

| RECRUITS. | | ENLISTED BY ENSIGN SEARS. | | | |
|---|---|---|---|---|---|
| Ezekiel Clifton | John Riley | Peter Ward | Mch 20, '80 | | War |
| Wm. Simmons | Thos. Sappington | Richard Mitchel | " | " " | " |
| Robert Streights | Philip Hustons | Richard Ballard | " 23, | " | 3 yrs |
| Wm. Jones | John Mackay | | | | |
| Jas. Richardson | Nathan Harper | DESERTERS. | | | |
| Benj. Gilbert | Solomon Askins | David Welch | not joined '82 | | |
| John Frawney | Wm. Smyth | Mark Bailey | | | |
| Robt. Redgrave | Emanuel Berry | Saml. Druley | " | ' " | |
| Saml. Wilson | Nathan Teat | Henry Roberts | | | |
| James Clifton | Chas. Delany | | | | |
| Thos. Johnson | Joseph Savory | | | | |
| John McCay | Joseph Donohoo | | | | |
| | Patk. Reding | | | | |

Sergeant John Lindiff's Recruits. Passed by Thos. Sollers. (April 11th, 1780)

| | | |
|---|---|---|
| Charles Thompson | Pharo Flinn | Daniel Lacey |
| Matthias Kees | Francis Anthony Stooncloser | Thomas Jones |
| Patrick Murphey | Matthias Spillard | James Simson |
| William Snow | Philip James | |

Men passed by Thos. Rutter, Baltimore County. (April 11th, 1780)

| | | |
|---|---|---|
| James Carman | Robert Tayler | Dennis Heiggens |
| Barney McCarnan | James Killey | James McLaughlin |
| James Donovan | Daniel Holland | James Welsh |
| John Handley | William Ray | William Hall |
| James Waldon | Thos. Colen | Thos. Roynorld |
| Willm. Doughlas | John Hughs | Richard Waller |
| John Larance | John Smith | Joshua Rogers |
| James Bayliss (?) | James Duglas | George Duvaull (?) |
| Thos. Harrison | John Barkley | John Trustee |
| John Fuller | Andrew Marwood | Michel Noles |
| Thomas Ryon | William Joyce | James Croford |
| Richard Goffer | Robert Hutson | James Brannan |
| Barnett Francher (?) | James Wood | Thos. Gore |
| James O'Brian | | |

2 men passed for William Towson and lost their names.

A List of Recruits and Deserters Passed by Thomas Sprigg, Lieut. of Washington County, April 22nd, 1780.

| | | |
|---|---|---|
| Felix Snider | Daniel Cline | Josep Clay |
| Henry Shepherd | Thomas McDaniel | John Kennear |
| Charles Girdler | William Allin | Thos. Williamson |
| Saml. Richardson | Anthony Byrne | John Patterson |
| Volintine Claper | William Simson | Jno. Casper Merser |
| James M'Clain | John Sickley | Allener Ratherford |
| Jacob Gregory | Martin Smith | Patrick Mellan |
| Jno. Row | Gedeon Walker | James Waddle |
| Jno. Hood | Henry Ross | James Harvey |
| Richard Allsy | James Draden | Jno. Hackett |
| Thomas Gillham | John Snider | Richd. Brockle |
| James Acklin | Balser Borett | George Flack |
| Joseph Smith | Jno. Smith | Fredk. Snyder |
| Paul Lappin | Henry Shaw | Balser Fox |
| Martin Smith | Wm. McFaron | Reuben Tedre |
| John Chambers | Thomas Evans | Fredk. Ream |
| John Brown | Wm. McDonald | Michl. Gambler |
| John Kenny | John Tyler | Jeremiah Shehan |
| John Farrol | Timothy Troy | Indian George |
| Saml. Guilman | James Neale | James Paupin |
| Patrick Collins | Charles McKensley | |

MARYLAND ACTS—JUNE, 1780.

"An ACT to procure recruits to complete the battalions of this state in the service of the United States, and to raise an additional regiment, if necessary.

Whereas it has been represented by congress, and by letters from general Washington and the committee of co-operation, that it is absolutely necessary to bring a powerful army into the field this campaign ; and it appearing to this general assembly their indispensable duty to make the most vigorous exertions to recruit the quota of troops of this state :

*Be it therefore enacted, by the General Assembly of Maryland,* That fourteen hundred men be forthwith raised, and that the same be apportioned among the several counties. . . . Out of which number, so apportioned, each county shall have a deduction for all able bodied men heretofore enlisted in virtue of the act passed at November session, seventeen hundred and seventy-nine, entitled, An act for recruiting the quota of troops of this state in the American army.

*And be it enacted,* That the lieutenant of the county, and the several field officers, together with the commissioners of the tax in each county, are hereby required, to meet . . . on the fifteenth day of July next, to class all the property last assessed in their respective counties into as many equal classes as there may be men wanted for such county, and each class shall, within ten days thereafter, find an able bodied recruit to serve during the war, or take up a deserter enlisted to serve during the war.

*And be it enacted,* That all recruits, raised in virtue of this act, shall be carried before the lieutenant of the county, or some field officer in which the recruits are or shall be raised, to pass muster.

*And,* Whereas this assembly has proposed to the commander in chief to raise a regiment of five hundred and thirty one men, to join the army in lieu of the militia required from this state :

*Be it enacted,* That the governor and council shall have full power and authority, upon notice that the commander in chief accepts the. proposal, to order the following proportions of the said number of five hundred and thirty one men, to be raised by the several counties (in addition to the number by the first part of this act apportioned) . . . . . and the governor and council shall appoint such officers as they may think proper and necessary to command such regiment, and the first five hundred and thirty one men which are raised shall be incorporated into a regiment and forthwith sent forward to join the army under the commander in chief."

---

"An ACT to expedite the raising an additional battalion of regulars.

Whereas his excellency general Washington and the committee of co-operation have thought proper to accept the proposal made by the legislature of this state, to raise an additional battalion of regulars in lieu of the two thousand two hundred and five militia, at first requested to be furnished by this state, provided the same be raised so as to reach the place of rendezvous by the last of July, and it is thereupon become necessary to expedite the raising the said battalion :

*Be it enacted, by the General Assembly of Maryland,* That the lieutenants and field officers of the respective counties, shall immediately on receipt of this act, and of the acts of assembly passed this session, entitled, An act to procure recruits to complete the battalions of this state in the service of the United States, and to raise an additional regiment, if necessary, and the supplement thereto, at furthest, on or before the fifteenth day of this instant July, proceed to class all property in their respective counties, agreeable to the directions of said acts, into as many classes as there are men wanted to complete said battalion or regiment, and shall forthwith give notice to each class; and if recruits be not procured or deserters taken up within eight days after such class hath notice, shall proceed to order out the militia, agreeable to the directions of this act, and the recruits obtained or the deserters taken up shall forthwith be sent forward to the head of Elk, or other place of rendezvous, and put under the care of proper officers to be appointed by the governor and council, who are to march them with all expedition to head quarters, or such other place of rendezvous as may be directed by the commander in chief."

John Clare, Jr., enlisted July 12th, 1780, by virtue of an "Act to procure Recruits to complete the Battalions &c."

A Roll of the Men Furnished by the Classes of Prince George's County for filling up the Old Regiments, 1780.

| Substitutes' Names. | Age. | Where Born. | Substitutes' Names. | Age. | Where Born. |
|---|---|---|---|---|---|
| George Stephins | 35 | England | Banks Webb | 16 | Native |
| Walter Watson | 19 | Native | Roger Mulloy | 22 | England |
| Henry Conley | 21 | do | Dinnis Tramel | 17 | Native |
| Wilkerson Greegsby | 20 | do | Andrew McGinnis | 21 | Ireland |
| William Jones | 16 | do | John Auber | 35 | England |
| James Wilson | 20 | Scotland | Jonn. Chubb | 18 | Native |
| Robert Avery | 28 | England | Jessey Cole | 18 | do |
| Isaac Berry | 19 | do | John Spencer | 40 | Scotland |
| John Moore | 20 | do | George Ryan | 19 | England |
| John Rumbald | 18 | Native | Thos. Walls | 35 | Native |
| Thos. Pingston | 31 | England | John Gregory | 29 | England |
| John Deacon | 21 | do | | | |

| Recruit's Name. | Age. | Where Born. | Recruit's Name. | Age. | Where Born. |
|---|---|---|---|---|---|
| George Campbell | 36 | Ireland | Joseph Kellee | 20 | Native |

Sir :

The above is a Roll of the men furnished by the Classes for filling up the Old Regiments, together with Two men I recruited, for which I was obliged to pay three thousand pounds each. As some of those classes neglected furnishing Substitutes, I had employed men to recruit, but finding that the extraordinary pay I was oblige to advance to them, and the exorbitant Bounty I should be oblige to give for recruits, (especially after the Virginians began to give such extravagant Bounties for men to serve only 18 Months), would far exceed the 15 pr. Ct., I therefore thought it most prudent to desist from employing persons to recruit, till I received your farther orders on that head. When, on receiving your letter relative to the peoples bringing in Wheat at Sixty Dollars pr. Bushell in Lieu of the Substitutes or money I advertised them thereof, and allowed them four weeks for so doing. The time is now expired, and neither wheat nor money brought in. I am therefore now about issuing warrants to the Sheriff for distressing all those who have not complied with the Law, or your orders respecting the grain.

I am Sir,

Your Most Obedient Servt, Jos. Beall.

Lt. P. G's. Cty.

His Excy. Thos. Sim Lee.

---

Dorchester County Recruits and Deserters. July 25th, 1780.

RECRUITS FROM DORCHESTER COUNTY AS THEIR QUOTA OF THE REGIMENT EXTRAORDINARY TO BE RAISED BY THE STATE.

| | | |
|---|---|---|
| Pope Connon | Ephraim Game | Barton Edwards |
| Henry Flannagan | Alex. Hughs | Jesse Forough |
| James Murray | Joseph Button | John Mills, Jr. |
| John Hobb | Constantine Wright | Benton Harriss |
| George Still | Owen Day | Levin Culver |
| John Dunn | Isaac Henderson | Richard Bounds |
| Robinson Ross | James Lord | |

DESERTERS FROM THE CONTINENTAL ARMY ENLISTED TO SERVE DURING THE WAR.

| | | | |
|---|---|---|---|
| Thomas Thompson | not joined '82 | James Dulany | not joined '82 |
| William Noble | do | James Ruark | joined |
| Isaac Scott | do | Stephen Culver | not joined |

RECRUITS ENROLLED AND PASSED IN CONSEQUENCE OF AN ACT OF ASSEMBLY
PASSED NOV. SESSION, 1779.

Patrick Bryan
Thomas Wyatts, (Waytts)
James Harris
Levin Button          These sent forward to the Army some time past
William Willen        by Capt. W. Woolford, Lt. 2nd Md. Regt.
David Robson, (Robinson)

John Carter           Deserters sent with Capt. Woolford to appear be-
Henry Causey          fore the Governor and Council to determine whether
Daniel Oliver         they are to continue in the Army or be discharged.
Laban Bramble
Gabriel Sales   for three years.        Henry Hooper, Lt. Dr. Co.

Recruits and Deserters from Balto. County.   Furnished under the
Acts to procure Recruits &c. and for raising an Additional &c.

| | | |
|---|---|---|
| James McGill | Patk. Connelly | Joseph Ablewhite |
| Edwd. Hawkins | James Bickham | John Fallen |
| Jas. Breaman | Thos. Higgenbotham | Patrick Kelley |
| John Pratten | John Jones | John Casey |
| Emanuel Farrara | John Hedgely | John Bennitt |
| Peter Walkletts | Anthony Flan | John Kildray |
| John Bolton | George Lynton | Bartholony McDono |
| Edwd. Dews | George Vernon | James Brown |
| Chas. Bolchlob | Thos. Murphey | Giles Powell |
| Wm. Mason | Jeremiah Sullivan | Peter McGuire |
| John Adams | Anthony Jackson | James Adams |
| Marane Ore | Thos. Eckister | John Hartford |
| Isaac English | Thos. Arthus | Wm. Wheeler |
| John McKinney | Thos. Theston | Chas. Burchfield |
| John Fre-Ladner | George Orridge | Richd. Biddle |
| John Ryan | Wm. Watkins | Samuel Gray |
| John Anderson | Lazarus Higgs | Michl. Doren |
| Wm. Collis | Christr. Shubut | Thos. Smith |
| Edwd. Evans | Wm. Aggis | Wm. Hamilton |
| Francis Barbett | John Higgins | Wm. Murphey |
| David Brian | Jas. Robinson | Wm. Tolbott |
| Peter Jones | John West | Thos. Smith |
| Simon Mackanary | Thos. Hall | James Walter Honee |
| Daniel King | John Brown | Andrew Russell |
| Samuel Chappel | Chas. Hales | Thos. Fisher |
| John Hamilton | Chas. Byrne | Alex. Hamilton |
| Wm. Smith | Thos. Nuth | George Dawe |
| John Blackburn | Henry Crook | Wm. Worthington |
| John Johnson | | |

| Wm. Snow | a deserter from the 4th Regt. |
| Josh. Nichols | "      "      "      " |
| Lewis Martin | "      "      " Balt. Matrosses |
| Wm. Johnson | "      "      " 2nd Md. Regt. |
| John OBryan | "      "      " 12th Va.   " |
| John Philips | "      "      " Balt. Matrosses |
| John Perry | " |

A List of Recruits raised in Montgomery County to make good her quota in the Continental Army.

### RECRUITED BY CAPT. LLOYD BEALL.

| | | | |
|---|---|---|---|
| Richd. Taylor | Thompson Murray | Peter McGuire | Andrew McMahone |
| Edwd. Clancey | Dennis Ternen | Igns. Crumpton | Henry Hughes |
| John Loveden | John Worsley | Wm. Quintum | Henry Hill |
| Wm. Hurley | James Amley | Richd. Downes | Wm. Lewden |
| Cornels. Morris | John Davis | Phil. Sullivain | Wm. Caton. |

### PASSED BY COL. ORME.

| | | | |
|---|---|---|---|
| James Moland | Alex. West | Wm. Westlick | Stephen Carr |
| John West | Wm. Glover | John Crague | Joseph Ferrill |

### RECRUITED BY ROBT. GREEN.

| | | |
|---|---|---|
| John Nabers | Willm. Hempstone | Leonard Hagan |

### RECRUITED BY DAVID GREEN.

| | | |
|---|---|---|
| Walter Hagan | Joseph Mattanly | George Devonshire |

### RECRUITED BY WILLIAM JENKINS.

Horatio Roberts

### RECRUITED BY CAPT. BASIL ROBERTS.

| | | | |
|---|---|---|---|
| Richd. Bond | John Walten | Michael Coale | John Tucker |

### RECRUITED BY CAPT. BEALL.

| | | |
|---|---|---|
| Charles Brooke | John Toplin | Daniel Devine |
| Joseph Sucksberry | James Curren | John Blair |

### RECRUITED BY CAPT. GAITHER.

| | | |
|---|---|---|
| Umphrey Carpenter | Thomas Jordan | Francis Whitekar |

PASSED BY MAJOR OWEN.

| | | | |
|---|---|---|---|
| Joseph Law | James Blower | John Ballett | Thomas ——— |
| Wm. Mitchell | James Campbell | James Doncaster | Christopher Onerah |

### 1ST 30 FOR THE EXTRA REGMT.

| | | |
|---|---|---|
| 1 Thomas Pendor | 19 Thomas McBride | Partrick Riley |
| 2 James Bigwood | William Quinton, | John Butcher |
| 3 George Clarke | a deserter | John Robins |
| 4 John Higgins | 21 Thomas Maddin | Robert Ferrell |
| 5 John Pickering | 22 John Buller | John Jones |
| 6 William Stewart | 23 Partrick Smith | Elijah Clarke |
| 7 Daniel Bulger | 24 Richard Downes | John Freeman |
| 8 John McGuire | 25 John Smith | Anthony Wedge |
| 9 Edward Daw | 26 Partrick Cavenough | William Groves |
| 10 William Cox | 27 Thomas Shears | Thomas Elliss |
| 11 John Maginnis | 28 John Ahair | Thomas Matthews |
| 12 James Barrow | 29 Thomas Pennifield | Stephen Fennell |
| 13 Joseph Floyd | 30 Richard Kisby | John Tucker, a deserter |
| 14 John Harvey | 20 John McCoune, in Place | Thomas Burch |
| 15 Jesse McCarty | of Wm. Quinton | Charles Reynolds |
| 16 Henry Crane | Richd. Whiley | Timothy McLamar |
| 17 William Curtin | James North, dead | John Clayton |
| 18 John Whealand | | |

A List of Recruits and Deserters procured by the Lieut. & Field Officers of Queen Ann's County for the Regiment Extraordinary raised by the State of Maryland, July, 1780.   Nov. 4th, 1780.

| | | |
|---|---|---|
| Thomas Yewell | John West Tate | John West |
| George Duncan | Benjamin Lee | Joseph Paggat |
| Edward Legg | Richard Gemmeson | James Baver |
| Charles White | Edward Vickers | Lambert Phillips |
| Job Sylvester | Elijah Barn | John Hickins |
| Robert Legg | John Oliver | Richard Murphy |
| Thomas Gadd | William Carter | Timothy Connor |
| William Aller | John Moore | Edward Dominie |
| Daniel Dulany | | |

Thomas Fox, deserted before he joined the Regt.

David Willon } deserters taken up enlisted for 3 years but enlisted { Joined
Thomas Trew }        during the war                                          { not " 1782

Joseph Crouch, deserter enlisted during the War                            do

James Chittendon, deserter taken up and deserted again                     do

William Terrett } deserters enlisted during the War                        { Joined
Benj. Loftsman }                                                           {   do

Valentine Saint Tee, deserted before he joined the Regt.

William Hemsley,
Lieut. of Queen Ann's County.

## A Return of Recruits enlisted in Harford County.    1780

| DATE OF ENLISTMENT. | NAMES OF RECRUITS. | IN WHAT REGT. ENLISTED. | THE TERM OF ENLISTMENT. |
|---|---|---|---|
| | John McDonal | 1st Md. Regt. | 3 years |
| | Aaron Winfrey | | 3 years |
| July 17 | Moses Williams | New Regt. | during the War |
| " | Thomas Blunder | " " | " |
| " | Christopher Seemer | " " | " |
| " | William Chapman | " " | " |
| 24 | William Wilson, (deserted since Enlistment) | " " | " |
| 16 | Edward Freeman | " " | " |
| 13 | James Scott | " " | " |
| " | Edward Burgess | 1st Md. Regt. | " |
| 17 | Dennis Downs | New Regt. | " |
| 25 | Joseph McNamarra | " " | " |
| 28 | William Lytle | " " | " |
| " | Nathanl. Sullavin | " " | " |
| 31 | Andrew McCune | " " | " |
| 29 | James Jordon | " " | " |
| 25 | James McDonal | " " | " |
| 31 | John Lewin | " " | " |
| Aug. 1 | James Sullavin | " " | " |
| " | Wm. Bowden | " " | " |
| " | James Phillips | " " | " |
| 3 | Daniel Darby | " " | 3 years |
| 28 | John Park, (broke Goal and made his escape) | " " | during the War |
| | Thomas Beaver | " " | |
| | John Garreguies | 8th Md. Regt. | during the War |
| | William Gloury | James Fitz Gerrald | |
| | Francis McClane | Thomas Smith | |
| | John Butler | John Cooley | |
| | Peter Scott | James Jackson | |
| | Michl. Daugherty | William Lowry | |
| | James O'Brian | Thomas Duff | |

## A Return of Deserters taken up in Harford County.

| DESERTERS' NAMES. | REGT. DESERTED FROM. | TERM OF ENLISTMENT. |
|---|---|---|
| George Kelley | Cicil County | during the War. |
| James Neagle | 6th Regt. | ditto |
| Adam Smith | Virginia Troops | ditto |
| Robert Hair | 3d Md. Regt. | ditto |

| DESERTERS' NAMES. | REGT. DESERTED FROM. | TERM OF ENLISTMENT. |
|---|---|---|
| John Park | New Regt. | during the War. |
| Thos Hanan, (1st Desertion) | 1st Md. Regt. | ditto |
| John Roberts | Capt. Chesney's Co., 7th Md. | ditto |
| Thomas Aval | Delaware Regt. | ditto |
| Solomon Watson | ditto | ditto |
| Thomas Bryan | ditto | ditto |
| John Connally, (Conoly) | the Artillery | |
| Thomas Knight | Pennsylvania Troops | |
| Samuel Wetheral | 1st Md. Regt. | |
| Daniel King | Balto. Co. | |
| Thomas Night | 3rd Md. Regt. | ditto |
| John Lynch | ditto | ditto |
| Roger Cord | 4th    ditto | |
| Edward Hawkins | New Regt. | |
| William Lock | 1st Md. Regt. | |
| James Wilson | Congress Regt. | |

| | | |
|---|---|---|
| John Sampson | Thos. Connoway | James O'Bryan, (2nd desertion) |
| Thomas Simmons | James Kirk | |
| David Grant | James Harris | John King |
| John Ofield | Wm. Wathington | John Cooney |
| Thos. Renalds | Thos. Hanan, (2nd desertion) | William Wilson |
| Thos. Archer | Edwd. Freeman | Peter Hammer |
| Thomas Jones | Thos. Hanan, (3rd desertion) | John White |
| Nathaniel Bass | James Fitz Gerrald, (1st desertion) | John Lampert |
| Jas. O'Bryan, (1st desertion) | | James White |

Aug. 4th, 1780.                    Richd. Dallam, Lt. Harford County.

A List of Men from Frederick.   Return of Men sent to Annapolis by Capt. William Beatty.   Delivered by Col. Baker Johnson 28th Aug., 1780.

| DATE OF ENLISTMENT. | MEN'S NAMES. | | DATE OF ENLISTMENT. | MEN'S NAMES. | |
|---|---|---|---|---|---|
| July 18 | Adam Shate | | Aug 1 | Edward Rylet | |
| 25 | Philip Fisher | | 7 | Henry Lancaster | Not marched for want of their pay. |
| Aug 5 | John Babbs, (followed the 1st Troops) | Marched. | 14 | Barnaby Kelly | |
| | | | 15 | John White | |
| | | | 21 | Edward Smith | |
| 8 | William Elkins | | July 25 | Morris McMahon | Deserted. |
| 10 | John Wells | | 27 | Walter Burk | |
| 16 | Jacob Blyth | | Aug 6 | George Kinsey | |
| 21 | John Saunders | | 9 | Rowland Baker | |

A List of Recruits Names whose Inlistments or Dates thereof
I never Obtain'd.

| | | |
|---|---|---|
| James McLean | John Jackson | John Mills |
| John Patterson | Dudley Lee | Alliner Rutherford |
| Anthony Weaver | George Jennings | Cornelius Bulger |
| John Wooden | John Dayley | James Lee |

W. Beatty, Lt. Fredk. Co.

A List of Deserters taken up in Frederick County, October 9th, 1780.

| | |
|---|---|
| John McDaniel | Deserted from Annapolis, belonging to one of the old Regiments. |
| John Walton | Deserted from Annapolis, belonging to the ——— |
| Thomas Ellis | Deserted from the New Regt. at Chester, past from Montg. Co. |
| William Simpson | Deserted from Annapolis, sent from Washington. |
| Thomas Hand | Known by several to belong to the Maryland Line and When first Taken Acknowledged it, but now Denies and Refuses to tell to what Regiment he belongs. |
| William Hays | Acknowledges he is a Deserter, it is known that he Enlisted in Baltimore County, when first Taken said he Marched with the Militia from Baltimore, then said he belonged to the Virginia Line and now says he belongs to the Pennsylvania Line. |

List of Recruits and Deserters in Cecil Co.  Oct. 16th, 1780.

Recruits Sent to Chester Town.

| | | |
|---|---|---|
| John Banbury | Wm. Sterling | John Toole |
| John Hurley | Saml. Hamilton | David Garner |
| James Thomas | Peter Munford | Wm. Mahoney |
| James Hayes | Thomas Baker | Wm. Walker |
| John Toulson | Benj. Mayberry | Wm. Jefferson |
| Chas. Shirkey | Patk. McDonald | James Crozier |
| Joseph Neighbours | Amos Davis | John Shirley |
| Wm. Smith | Peter Carberry | James Needs,    a recruit |
| George Plumley | James Brown | John Robinson,    " |
| John Young | James Maffitt | Richard Gillespie,    " sick |
| Nathl. Jones | Morris McMahon | in Cecil Co. |
| John Tunstill | Robert Clark | Ephraim Hendrickson, a recruit |

George Keller } Delivered by James Creswell, a recruiting Officer of this Co., to
John Campbell } Lieut. John Hamilton.

23

### Deserters Sent to Chester Town.

Wm. Arno
Wm. McGreagor
John Corlet, a deserter, deserted
Wm. Lock    } deserters taken up in Harford Co. for two of the Classes
James Kelly  }        of this Co. and delivered to Col. Dallam
John Brown, a recruit, deserted same day he enlisted
John Boyd,    "        "    few days after he enlisted
Wm. Tucker, a recruit, deserted
Felix O'Nail,    "        "

---

### Return of the Recruits in Caroline County, Oct. 17th, 1780.

Charles Fitzgarral        Wm. Fitzgarral        William Earl Hill

William Whiteley, Lt.

---

### A List of Recruits from and Deserters taken up in Somerset County. Oct. 20th, 1780.

John Carter                John Mitchel
Saml. Furrow               Chas. Revel
James Huet                 Levin Abbet
Levi Reese                 Abel Amoss, deserter, not joined '82
Barnaby Case               Wm. Rhoads }
Edwd. Blake                John Stevens } deserters belonging to
Salathiel Carmine          Wm. Evans  }   the Delaware State

---

### Recruits, Washington County.

1780  October 19th  James Smith        November 10th    Elisha Robinson

---

Muster Roll of the late Sixth Maryland Regiment, now the Fourth Company of the Second Battalion of Colonel Williams' Regiment of Infantry, serving in the Southern Army of The United States for the Month of October, 1780.

---

Captain Dobson                     Lieut. Lynn

| NAMES. | DATE. | WAR. | 3 YEARS. | REMARKS. |
|---|---|---|---|---|
| Serjeants | | | | |
| Jesse Jacobs | | I | | |
| James Flack | 28 April '79 | I | | |
| John Mantle | | I | | |
| Saml. McConnell | 10 June '78 | | I | |
| Edward Booth | | | I | |
| Patrick Doran | | I | | Furlough |
| Peter Fervott | | I | | On Guard |
| Wm. McNeil | | I | | On Guard |
| Joseph Philbert | 30 May '78 | | I | |
| John Alex. McKey | | I | | On Comd. Light Infantry |
| William Martin | | I | | On Furlough Maryland |
| Robert Taylor | | I | | Recruiting |
| Corporals | | | | |
| Edward Teadly | | I | | |
| James Maxwell | | | I | |
| John Young | | I | | |
| Peter Sugars | | I | | |
| Robt. Sharpless | | I | | Sick Absent Hillsborough |
| John Bethell | | I | | Sick Monmouth N. Jersey |
| Charles Hill | | | | Comd. Light Infantry |
| Drum. & Fifers | | | | |
| Alex. Stephenson | | I | | |
| James Greenwood | | I | | |
| John Denoon | | I | | |
| Thos. Cahoe, Jr. | | I | | |
| George Stumm | | I | | |
| James Steward | | I | | |
| Edward Purdy | | I or I | | |
| Noah Carter | | I | | |
| Rank & File | | | | |
| Thos. Simister | | I | | |
| Wm. Rice | | I | | |
| Harry Billop | | I | | |
| Benj. Williams | | I | | |
| Joseph Elliott | | I | | |
| John Summers | | I | | |
| Isaac Beckell, | | I | | |
| (or Beckett) | | | | |
| Michl. McCann | | | | |
| Wm. Westwood | | I | | |
| Patrick Egan | | I | | |
| Chris. Cusick | | I | | |
| Nich. Milburn | | I | | |
| Saml. Young | | I | | |

| NAMES. | DATE. | WAR. | 3 YEARS. | REMARKS. |
|---|---|---|---|---|
| **Rank & File** | | | | |
| Hecter Cackey | | I | | |
| Wm. Harris | | I | | |
| John Hously | | I | | |
| Caleb Donelly | | I | | |
| George Montle | | I | | |
| Stephan Owens | | I | | |
| Robt. Clenchan, | | I | | |
| (or Clenehan) | | | | |
| Wm. Chambers | | I | | |
| Edmond Collins | | I | | |
| John Marshall | 20 Dec '78 . | | I | |
| Joseph Sloop | May '78 | | I | |
| Wm. George | | I | | |
| Michl. Crime | | I | | |
| Michl. Wirey | | I | | |
| James Devericks | | | | |
| John Dorough | | I | | |
| John Campbell | | I | | |
| John Ellery | | I | | |
| John Holliday, Jr. | | I | | |
| Moses Graham | | I | | |
| Asel Rockhold | | I | | |
| John Purdy | 20 Feb '80 | I | | |
| John Armstrong | | I | | |
| Jona. Windle | 24 Apl '78 | | I | |
| Wm. Durham | | I | | |
| Timy. Fitzgerald | 22 Dec '78 | | I | |
| John Elliott | | | I | |
| John Stackhouse | | | I | |
| Michl. Shoemaker | | I | | |
| Thomas Bare | | I | | |
| George Taylor | | I | | |
| John Wells | | I | | |
| Wm. Cole | | | | Joined, Recruit 3 October '80 |
| Robert Davis | 28 April '78 | | I | |
| John Thomas | | I | | |
| John Lincoln | | I | | |
| James Nowell | | I | | |
| Benj. Dominick | | I | | |
| Henry Davis | | | | |
| George Bowers | 1 May '78 | | I | |
| John Jackson | | I | | |
| Abraham Church | 30 May '78 | | I | |
| Wm. Moran | | | | |

| NAMES. | DATE. | WAR. | 3 YEARS. | REMARKS. |
|---|---|---|---|---|
| Rank & File | | | | |
| Wm. Stonestreet | | 1 | | |
| James Burk | | 1 | | |
| George Bomgardner | | 1 | | |
| Peter Henecy | | | 1 | |
| Mich. Connelly | | 1 | | |
| Thos. Mahanny | | 1 | | |
| Thomas Smith | | 1 | | |
| Bartle Bome | | 1 | | On Guard |
| Henery Purdy | 5 Feb '80 | 1 or | 1 | do    do |
| John Love | 22 Dec '78 | | 1 | do    do |
| Robert Matthews | 15 May '78 | | 1 | do    do |
| Abraham Swink | | 1 | | do    do |
| Richard Duvall | | 1 | | do    do |
| Thomas Cahoe, Sr. | | 1 | | do    do |
| John Martin | 10 Feb '80 | | 1 | do    do |
| John May | | 1 | | Hospital Fish Kills |
| Richard Brockell | | 1 | | do    Annapolis |
| Edward Shehee | | 1 | | do    Hillsborough |
| Benj. Taylor | | 1 | | do    do |
| Chris. Touchstone | | 1 | | do    do |
| Mich. Rogers | | 1 | | do    do |
| Mich. Stanley | | 1 | | do    do |
| James Sewell | | 1 | | do    do |
| Joseph Ralston | 23 Dec '78 | | 1 | On Command, Detach. |
| Joseph Long | | 1 | | On Command, Gen. Smallwood |
| Benj. Moran | | 1 | | do    do    Detach. |
| Leonard Boward | | 1 | | Fatigue |
| Benj. Cleaver | | 1 | | Artificer Roan Oak |
| Jacob Rowland | | 1 | | Waiter on Mr. J. Jacobs,  Md. |
| Isaac Greaves | | 1 | | do    do Capt. Somervile, do |
| Thomas Kearnes | | 1 | | do    do Genl. Gates |
| Robert Rice | | | 1 | Waggoner |
| William Fuller | | 1 or 1 | | do |
| Daniel Javins | | 1 | | Furlough, Maryland |
| Godfrey Young | | 1 | | Transfd. to Invalids Corps 23 Oct '80 |
| Roger Dowlin | | 1 | | Sick Albany |

Camp Hillsborough, North Carolina, Nov. 1st, 1780. Mustered then the Late Sixth Maryland Regiment now the fourth Company in Second Battalion of Col Williams' Regiment.

John Davidson, B. Inspt.

Muster Roll of the Maryland Corps in the Service of the U. States, Commanded by Captain Thomas Beall for the Months of Jan., Feb., March, April, May, June, July, Aug., Sept. and Oct. 1780.

| | |
|---|---|
| Commissd. | Thomas Beall, Capt., absent. Dismissed the Service Aug. 14th, 1780.* |
| " | Adamson Tannehill, Capt., April 1st, 1778. |
| " | Elijah Evans, Lieut., Aug. 8th, 1776, absent. |

| RANK. | NAMES. | TIME OF SERVICE. | REMARKS. |
|---|---|---|---|
| Serjt. | Joseph Jeanes | War | |
| " | Basil Shaw | " | |
| " | George Twinch | " | Appd. April 25th, '80 |
| " | Jonathan Weden | " | " Aug. 10th, '80 |
| " | Wm. Batten | " | Reduced June 22nd, '80 |
| " | Benj. Burch | " | |
| Corpl. | Elisha Cockindall | " | Appd. Apl. 10th, '80 |
| " | John Brown | " | " May 1st, 80 |
| " | Thomas Horsfield | " | |
| " | Loudon Trotter | " | |
| Drum. | George Twinch | " | Prom'd. Apl. 25th, '80 |
| & Fife. | Jno. McBryde | " | |
| " | Thos. Lovely | " | Absent with leave |
| " | Danl. Howe | " | |
| Privates | James Denniston | " | |
| | Patrick Quinn | " | |
| | Henry Dennis | " | |
| | Saml. Martin | 3 yrs | Absent |
| | Elisha Cockindall | War | |
| | Patrick O'Harra | " | Deserted July 1st, '80 |
| | John Stacks | " | |
| | Thomas McKinsy | " | |
| | Dennis Carty | " | |
| | James Kilty | " | On Command |
| | Jacob Aitzil | " | |
| | Edward Kirk | " | |
| | John Jordon | " | |
| | Roderick McKinney | " | |
| | Jonathan Weeden | " | Promoted Aug. 10th, '80 |
| | William Hart | " | Absent |
| | John Riley | " | |
| | John Brown | " | Promoted May 1st, '80 |
| | John McKann | 3 yrs | Dischd. May 3rd, '80 |
| | James Cunnigham | War | Joined July 15th, '80, absent |

* Pennsylvania Archives, Vol. XI, Second Series, page 602.

| RANK. | NAMES. | TIME OF SERVICE. | REMARKS. |
|---|---|---|---|
| Privates | Jonathan Shepherd | War | |
| | Thomas Craigg | " | |
| | Wm. Beatty | " | |
| | Richard Hoggins | " | |
| | Nehemiah Lanham | " | |
| | George Parker | " | |
| | Wm. Marlow | " | |
| | John Burk | " | |
| | Wm. Wilson | " | |
| | Levy Davis | " | Deserted Aug. 20th, '80 |
| | Jacob Palmer | " | |
| | Francis Dewist | " | |
| | John Gordon | " | |
| | Robert Fyrth | " | |
| | Kilbreth Wilson | " | |
| | Thomas Fleming | " | |
| | John Treviss | " | |
| | Wm. Tayler | " | |
| | Jacob Adams | " | On Command |
| | John Gratsinger | " | |
| | Thomas Hill | " | |
| | Joseph Neale | " | |
| | Wm. Jarmey | " | Deserted Sept. 30th, '80 |
| | Zachariah Berry | " | On Command |
| | Pierce Deacon | " | |
| | James Dowden | " | |

Pittsburgh July 13th, 1781.   Then Mustered the Mary'd. Corps as Specified in the Above Roll.

J. Crawford, Lt. & Adjt. 8th Pennsa. Regt.

I do Swear that the within Muster Roll is a true State of the three Companies of the Mary'd. Corps without fraud to the United States or any Individual According to the best of my Knowledge.

Sworn before me this 13th day of July, 1781.

Before me

Jno. Gibson, Col. Comdt. F. Pitt.

---

That Part of Capt. Joseph Marbury's Company of Infantry belonging to the Maryland Line, which is Ordered to Fort Pitt.   Aug., Sept., Oct., Nov. and Dec., 1780.

| Serjeants | Privates | Privates |
|---|---|---|
| Basil Shaw | John Gordon | James Dowden |
| George Twinch | Nicholas Welch | Edward Kirk |
| Corporal | Robert Firth | John Traviss |
| John Brown | Thomas McKinsey | George Parker |
| Drummer | William Wilson | Francis Dewist |
| John McBryde | Daniel How | William Batton |
| Privates | Zachariah Berry | Joseph Neal |
| Thomas Hill | Rhodk. McKinsey | William Marlow |
| Thomas Flemming | | |

Return of Officers and Men of the 1st Company who were in Service from the First of August, 1780 to the first January, 1781.

William Reiley, Capt.　Retired 1 Jan., '83.
Lieut. William Adams
Ensign Henry Clements

| Serjts. | | Corpls. |
|---|---|---|
| Levi Smith | | Abraham Bowin |
| John Wilkerson | | John Smith |
| James Collins | | Fife. |
| Drum. | | Joseph Nabb |
| William Ferrell | | |

| Privates | Privates | Privates |
|---|---|---|
| James Holmes | James Doyl | Emanuel Allen |
| John Bantham | Solomon Summers | George Dyace |
| Thomas Carney | Anthony Weaver | Wm. Horney |
| Paul Lappin | Valentine Clapper | Saml. Richardson |
| Henry Gilby | Perrigrine Sullivan | John Mills |
| Aaron Jones, (or Jonas) | David Wilson | George Kelvin (?) |
| John Andrew | Roger Shorter | Cornelius Thompson |
| James Allen | Thomas Gilliam | Thomas Bowzer |
| John Downey | John Fulham | George Jinnings |
| James Owings | Stafford Fosdale | Danl. Brumiger |
| William Hill | William Sivill　. | Thomas Elliot |
| Jervis Eccleston | Augusten Cann | John Hurley |
| Wm. St. Clair | Benj. Loftman | John McKay |
| Thomas Ayers | Thomas Frimley | John Carrol |
| John Hull | Alexander Downey | James Bayless |
| Charles Girdler | | |
| 3d April. | | W. Adams, Lt. |

Return of the Names Commissioned and Non Commissioned Officers and Privates of the 2nd Company wch. have been in the Service from 1st Aug., Year '80 to the 1st Jan., '81.

Mark McPherson, Ensign

| Serjts. | | Serjts. |
| --- | --- | --- |
| Thomas Edwards | | John Gwinn |
| John Colein | | Charles Harvy, Transferred |
| Hugh McMillan | | to Maryland |
| | John McNight, Fifer | |

| Privates | Privates | Privates |
| --- | --- | --- |
| Richard Farraby | William Hedge | William Pecker |
| Peter Topping | William Carter | Edward Evans |
| Emal. Cathajane | Michal Clark | Elijah Smith |
| James Gray | Joseph McAntee | Henry Reading |
| Joseph Johnson | Adam Jamison | Evan Tumbleston |
| Willm. Ingle | Thomas Slade | Matthew Moore |
| Jeriah William | John Lynch | Chrisr. McWay |
| Michael Calihorn | Daniel O'Quinn | Henry Ramden |
| Thomas Murphy | Asaph Colegate | Thos. Richardson |
| John Kidd | John King | John Blades |
| Hugh Gainor | John Hyde | John Lucas |
| Conrod Smith | John Berryman | James Due |

M. McPherson, Lieut.

A Return of the Commd., Non Commissd. Officers & Privates Names of the 3rd Company who have Been in the Service since 1st of Aug., till 1st of Jan., 1781.

John Sprig Belt, Capt.  Retired 1 Jan., '83
Henry Baldwin, Lieut.

| Serjts. | | Drummer |
| --- | --- | --- |
| Fras. MaGauran | | Daniel Warrier |
| Jesse Jacobs | | Fifer |
| Jas. Deverex | | Alex. Stevenson |

| Privates | Privates | Privates |
| --- | --- | --- |
| John Carson, promoted | John Nicholson | James Erwin |
| Serjt. Mch., 1781 | John Wade | Jno. Nevitt |
| James Ashly, promoted | Chr. Cusack | Geo. Bowers |
| Corpl. since Augt., 1781 | Jas. Steward | Daniel Kettle |
| Nichs. Milburne, ditto | John Armstrong | Abm. Kettle |
| Saml. Young, ditto | Wm. Stonestreet | Joseph Eliott |
| Richard Dewall | Joshua McKinsey | Moses McKinsey |
| Benj. Williams | Paul Greenard | Wm. Cooke |
| Michl. McCann | Jno. Holloday | Corns. Vaughan |
| Wm. Silwood | Thos. Hutchcraft | Matthew Dyche |

Privates
Michael Smith
Thos. Larmore
Absolum Wright
Fras. Karns
Wm. Ryder
John Hall
George Taylor

Privates
Henry Billop
George Mauntle
Saml. Boswell
Elias Smith
Chas. Jones
John Eliott

Privates
Moses Graham
John Stanton
Michael Hardman
Geo. Bumgardner
Chrisr. Smith
Benj. Clever

Henry Baldwin, Lt.

---

### 1st Maryland Regt.

Return of Officers and Men in the 4th Company who were in Service from the first of August, 1780, to the first of January, 1781.

James Woolford Gray, Capt.
Regnal Hilleary, Lieut.

---

Serjts.
John Reeder
Larrance Branham
Corpl.
Walter Howe

Drum.
Anthony Gohegan
Fife.
Robert Cornick

Privates
John Moore
Jas. Kelley
Humphry Beckell,
  (or Beckett)
John Hamilton
Samuel Gray
George Dixon
Thomas Jones
Wm. Derrington
Chas. Ormer
Richard Taskò
Wm. McGee
John Wells
Neal Peacock
Travers Alvey
Dudley Lee
Michl. Pilkoston
Michl. Woolford
Phillip Savoy

Privates
Joseph Jenkins
George Foard
Chas. McGee
James Byus
Matthew Moore
Zachariah Clark
John Dyar
Austen Howard
Joshua Pierce
John Love
Willm. Mitchell
John Lee
Francis Hopkins
Edward Erving
John Fransway
Luke Demsey
Christopher Semore
John Craig
Edward Furrener

Privates
Levin Abbitt
Luke Carter
John Appleby
Joseph Southall
John Lewin
John Buckley
Matthew Carty
John Gorman
John Ashmore
John Gorden
Emanuel Farrara
Hezekiah Carr
John Jerviss
John Onions
Andrew Russell
Edward Evans
James Thomas
Charles Murphy

J. W. Gray, Capt.

Camp James Island, April 4th, 1783.

Return of Commissioned and Non Commissioned Officers & Privates of the 5th Company who were in Service from 1st Aug., '80, to 1st Jan., '81, now serving in the 5th Company, 1st Maryland Regiment.

Benj. Price, Capt.
Willm. Rasin, Lieut.
Saml. Edmiston, Ensign

Serjts.
Willm. A. Needham
John Quick
Patrick Doran
Thomas Buckley
Corpls.
Issachar Mason
Henry Nicholson

Drummer
Thomas Hawson
Fifers
Jas. Greenwood
Danl. Bassell
Thomas Butt
Fredk. Bennett

| Privates | Privates | Privates |
|---|---|---|
| Thos. Pennifield | Levi Lord | William Jones |
| Jesse Wright | John Moore | John Branson |
| Richard Kisbey | Thomas Ellis | John Ashberry |
| Willm. Carter | Richard Wiley | Lambert Philips |
| Joseph Rhea | Leonard Holt | Charles White |
| Bennet Shirley | Thomas Pendor | Patrick Reilley |
| Francis Lang | Jeremiah French | Thomas Wember |
| Willm. Toland | Francis Freeman | Edward Holland |
| William Cox | William Fitzgerald | Enoch Ennis |
| George Craggs | Charles Fulham | Abm. Catchesides |
| Stephen Fennell | James Baber | Jacob Blake |
| John Frawney | Alexander Levi | Joseph Barton |
| William Manley | George Duncan | James Huett |
| Rhode Woodland | Willm. Moore | James Knott |
| William Hope | Willm. Nuton | James Smith |
| John Ennis | Thomas Gadd | Job Sylvester |
| John West | William Hicks | Edward Kersey |
| Henry Mansfield | William Shirley | Henry Jacobs |
| Benjamin Kearns | Peter Degazoone | William Lee |
| Charles Fitzgerald | | |

Ben. Price, Capt.

6TH COMPANY, 1ST MD. REG'T.

A Return of the Officers and Soldiers who were in the Service From the 1st of Aug. '80 to the 1st of Jan. '81.

Loyd Beall, Lieut.
Philip Hill,  "

---

| Serjts. | | Corpls. |
| --- | --- | --- |
| Stephen Fluharty | | William Bruff |
| Samuel Fillson | | George Field |
| Charles McNabb | | Pett. Stephens |

| | Fifer | Drum. | |
| --- | --- | --- | --- |
| | Benj. Williams | Bosston Medler | |

| Privates | Privates | Privates |
| --- | --- | --- |
| George Devatt | Michael Curtis | William Casey |
| Saml. Clarke | Fredk. Harty | Pett. McGwire |
| Zedk. Whaylay | Willm. Mann | Theops. Lincey |
| Wm. Hillman | Jno. McA Nally | Benj. Massh |
| Alexander Ross | Wm. Quinton | Jno. Armstrong |
| George Buck | Jno. Twiner | Henry Townley |
| Josa. Lesster | Luke Sampson | Geor. Hamillton |
| Robert Duncan | Chas. Clements | Jno. Hullett |
| Absm. Fardo | Moses Foster | Paull Roan |
| Darly Crowley | Richard Gae | Edwd. Crossgrove |
| Wm. Linkins | Jno. Mansfield | Wm. Ellkins |
| Jno. Knox | Jno. Mills | Jno. Fullford |
| Jno. Ryan | Wm. Niblett | Wm. Taylor |
| Elijah Pepper | Saml. Wedge | Wm. Phearson |
| Neal Morris | Lar. Harman | Jos. Phearson |
| Jno. Loveday | Chas. Simpkins | |
| Joseph Blasse | Wm. Craill | |

Thos. Beatty, Lt.

---

### 1st Maryland Regiment.

A Return of the Commissd., Non Commisd. Officers and Privates Names of the 7th Company who have been in Service Since the 1st of August, '80 till the 1st of January, '81.

---

Samuel McPherson, Capt. Lt. and Adjt.
Edmund Compton, Lieut.
John Brevitt, Ensign.  Promoted to Lieut. Sept. 20th, 1780.

---

| Serjts. | Corpls. |
| --- | --- |
| William Collis | Wm. Braithwate |
| Humphrey Spencer, (dead) | Bartholomew Essom |
| Robert Scrivner | Drummer |
| Aaron Spaldin | John Head |
| | Fifer |
| | Andrew Garnett |

Privates
John Bradey
Daniel Bulger
Isaac Grieves
Aquilla Pierce, deserter
Philip Fitzpatrick
John Haney
William Gould
Hampton Coarsey
Henry Greene
John Welch
Roger Launders
Michael Lloyd, deserter
Charles Cooper
James Mason
John Gregory
Thomas Waite
John Alby
Peter Melvin
Wm. Moore
James Willson, deserter

Privates
John Robins
John Buckhannan
James Ferrell
Abram Irvin
David Bramble
Thomas Campher
William Purchase
John Taylor, deserter
Adam Kephart
Jacob Knight
William Laws
Michael Casner
Richard Blansford
James Harris, deserter 1781
Solomon Brittinham
John Dennison
William Glorey
John Sommers
Benj. Gaither, deserter 1781
Robert Streets

Privates
Joseph Donnoho
William Moore
William Rice
William Mathews, deserter
Charles Sickle
Thomas Bare
Patrick Rowing
William Jones, deserted to
    the British
Thomas Porters
Lambert Thompson
Joseph Hewkill
John Sammon
William Groves
Cathael Carmile
Pat. Cavanough
Richard Biddle
James Bigwood
Daniel Jervais

Saml. McPherson, Capt.

A List of the Officers and Soldiers of the 8th Company of the Maryland Line who were in Service from the first of August, 1780, until the first of January, 1781.

James Winchester, Lieut.    Nicholas Gassaway, Lieut.

Serjt.
Peter McNaughtan
Corpls.
Benjamin Prior
George Childes

Drummer
Thos. Gossage
Fifer
John Martindale

Privates
Peter Smith
John Kerr, (dead)
Richard Hall
John Adams
John Bailey
Peter Bocard
Michael Lawler
Basil Brown
Thomas Kennedy
John Brown

Privates
Samuel Hambleton
William Lilley
Patrick Molohon
John Williams
Thomas Thomas
Charles Goldsbury
Alexander Francis
Peregrine Howard
Richard Procktor
Samuel Harper

Privates
Edward Hammon
Barnard Wilson
Benj. Steward
Noah Sears, (dead)
Frederick Wilmott
Thomas Clark
Benjamin Boid
James Thomas
Samuel Callehan
John Osburn

| Privates | Privates | Privates |
|---|---|---|
| Henry Lowers, | William Sax | William Nailor |
| (or Sowers) | Darby McNemar | William Joice, |
| Richard Butler | David Cail | (or Joiel) |
| Josep Hall | Stephen Fresh | John Brookbank |
| Amas Green | Michael Miller | John Irons |
| Francis Demar, | William Poland | Jacob Flora |
| deserter | John Jackson | William Clarey |
| Wm. Horrington | Ignatius Adams | Francis Fairbrother |
| Abijah Buxton | Jonathan Fowler | John Anderson |
| Abraham Gaseney | | |

J. Winchester, Capt.

A List of the Commissd. and Non Commissd. Officers and Privates who were in the Service of Maryland from the 1st of August, 1780, to the 1st of Jan., 1781, Light Infantry Company, 1st Maryland Regiment.

Frances Reveley, Lieut.
John T. Lowe, Ensign.

Serjts.
Stephen R. Price
Chas. Runnenberg
Archibald Johnson

Corpl.
John Folden
D. and F.
Benj. H. Kerrick
Michael Clansey

| Privates | Privates | Privates |
|---|---|---|
| John Lynch | Michael Wierey | James Collard |
| Andrew Crummy | Robert Clanahan | Richard Mitchell |
| John Thomas | William McGlouchlin | James Managee |
| Wm. Sullivan | Daniel Buckley | Joseph Jones |
| John Burnett | Patrick Dennison | James Jackson |
| George Pearce | Jacob Myers | Henry Fisher |
| Rigby Foster | Barrack Butt | Livey, (or Leiry), Burck |
| Daniel Smith | James Wood | Thomas Evans |
| Robinson Ross | Henry Crane | Jacob Moses |
| John McCan | John Harrell | James Keelan |
| Charles Scott | William Jinkins | Joseph Botchabey |
| Edward Roberts | Richard Haislip | Edward Vickers |
| Michael Waldman | Joseph Sloop | James Crozier |
| James Ruarck | Bartholomew Thompson | John Delany |
| William Roberts | Reubin Smith | George Saunders |
| John Roach | John Walker | John Smallwood |
| Joseph Long | John Haidon | |

April 1st, 1783.

Frances Reveley, Capt.

## A List of Men in Service 1 Aug., 1780 to 1 Jan., '81.

| RANK. | MEN'S NAMES. | WHEN ENLISTED. | TERM OF SERVICE. | WHEN DISCHARGED. | REGT. |
|---|---|---|---|---|---|
| | Henry Dixon | 8 Feb '79 | 3 years | 8 Feb '81 | |
| | Leonard Swan | " | " | 2 May '81 | |
| | George Brown | | " | 24 Apl '81 | |
| | Zadock Harvey, (or Haney) | | " | 1 May '81 | |
| | Samuel Owens | 1777 | War | | |
| | James Kelly | | " | | |
| | Thomas Baily | | " | | |
| | Jno. Snelling | | 3 years | 2 Aug '81 | |
| | Thos Hovington | | | | Col. Ramsay |
| | Able Arman | | | | " " |
| | Francis Thompson | | | | " " |
| | John B. Haislope | | " | died 11 Sept '82 | |
| | Lazarus Higgs | 26 July '80 | " | | |
| | Notley Whitcomb | | | | Matross |
| | Jno. Hurdle, (or Hundle) | | | | |
| | Matthew McMackin | | " | 1 Sept '81 | Matross |
| | John Robertson | | | 2 Apl '81 | |
| | Andrew Lord | | | | |
| | Randal Hoskins | | " | 8 Jan '82 | |
| Corpl. | Richard Gadden | | " | 26 Apl '81 | |
| | John Claggett | | " | 25 " " | |
| | Dennis Trammel | | " | 31 May '83 | |
| Corpl. | Leonard Bean | | " | 12 Apl '81 | |
| Serjt. | Josias Harris | | " | 25 " " | |
| | John Milstead | | War | | |
| | Jeremiah Rhodes | 1 May '78 | 3 years and 9 months | 17 Feb '82 | 3d Md. Regt. |
| | Wm. Dillon | | | 2 May '82 | |
| | John Howard | | | July '81 | |
| Serjt. | Thos. Harrison | | | " " | |
| | Aaron Simmons | | | " " | |
| Corpl. | James Daffin | 5 Apl '78 | 3 years | 5 Apl '81 | 4th Md. Regt. |
| | Richard Taylor | 26 Feb '80 | " | 6 May '83 | |
| | John McDonald | | | | Roxburgh's Detachment |
| Corpl. | Wm. Sharpe | | " | 1 May '81 | 5th Regt. |
| Pt. | Stephen Hancock | July '80 | War | | |
| Serjt. | Joseph Philbert | 2 June '78 | 3 years | 2 June '81 | 2d Regt. |
| Pt. | Elias Hardy | | " | 25 Apl '81 | |
| Pt. | Wm. Wilkinson | | " | 3 Mch '81 | |

| Rank. | Men's Names. | When Enlisted. | Term of Service. | When Discharged. | Regt. |
|---|---|---|---|---|---|
| Pt. | Henry Philips | | 3 years | 1 May '81 | |
| Pt. | Thomas Summers | 1776 | War | | |
| Pt. | Michael McGuire (?) | | " | 1 Sept '82 | at his request being unfit for duty |
| | Saml. Hamilton | | " | | Winchester's Company |
| Serjt. | Jas. Dyar | | | 6 Jan '83 | German Regiment |
| | John Kildee | . | " | | |
| | Wm. Aggis | 26 July '80 | " | | |
| | Ths. Arthus | 25    " | " | | |
| | Joseph Ablewhite | 28    " | " | | |
| | Jas. Adams | 31    " | " | | |
| | John Bolton | 18    " | " | | |
| | Jno. Butler | 12 Sept  " | " | | |
| | Js. Brown | 29 July  " | " | | |
| | Js. Brannon | 15    " | " | | |
| | John Blackburn | 22    " | " | | |
| | Francis Barbett | 20    " | " | | |
| | David Bryan | 20    " | " | | |
| | John Bennett | 30    " | " | | |
| | Chs. Byrne | 28 | " | | |
| | Jas. Bickham, Jr. | 24 | " | | |
| | Wm. Dunkin, (or Demkin) | 29 Mch '81 | 3 years | | |
| | John Casey | 28 July '80 | War | | |
| | Pat. Connelly | 24 | " | | |
| | Chs. Chinchfiell | 2 Aug '80 | " | | |
| | Michael Doren | 2    "    " | " | | |
| | Edwd. Dewes | 15 July '80 | " | | |
| | George Daw | 14 Aug '80 | " | | |
| | William Richardson | | | | 7th Md. Regt. |

## MUSTER AND PAY ROLLS FOR 1781.

"*Resolved*, That such of the sixteen additional regiments as have not been annexed to the line of some particular state, and all the separate light corps of the army, both of horse and foot, and also the German battalion, be reduced on the 1st day of January next: that the non-commissioned officers and privates in those several corps, be incorporated with the troops of their respective states, and that such of them as do not belong to any particular state, be annexed to such corps as the commander in chief shall direct.

That the regular army of the United States, from and after the 1st day of January next, consist of 4 regiments of cavalry or light dragoons ; 4 regiments of artillery ; 49 regiments of infantry, exclusive of colonel Hazen's regiment, hereafter mentioned ; 1 regiment of artificers :

That the several states furnish the following quotas, viz. . . . . . . . . Maryland, 5 regiments of infantry :

That the states shall select from the line of the army a proper number of officers to command the several regiments to them respectively assigned, taking notice that no new appointment is to be made of a higher rank than that of a lieutenant-colonel commandant :

And whereas, by the foregoing arrangement, many deserving officers must become supernumerary, and it is proper that regard be had to them :

*Resolved*, That from the time the reform of the army takes place, they be entitled to half pay for seven years, in specie, or other current money equivalent, and also grants of land at the close of the war, agreeably to the resolution of the 16th of September, 1776."

"An ACT to draught the non-commissioned officers and privates of the regiment extraordinary into the battalions of the quota of this state, and to recal the commissioned officers of the said regiment.

WHEREAS congress have recommended to this state to reduce the number of their regiments in the continental service, and the commander in chief has most earnestly called upon this state to complete the number of men in said battalions without delay: And whereas it is

24

deemed impracticable to comply with said requisition, so as to have the quota of men in the field at the time required, without draughting the non-commissioned officers and privates of the regiment extraordinary.

*Be it therefore enacted, by the General Assembly of Maryland,* That the non-commissioned officers and privates of the regiment extraordinary be draughted into the old battalions of the quota of this state in the continental service, and that the field and commissioned officers of said regiment be recalled.

*And be it enacted,* That the said field and commissioned officers shall be reimbursed the extraordinary expence they may have incurred, and over and above the pay that may be due to them at the time of their discharge, shall receive one year's pay, deducting therefrom the money and value of the cloathing and other necessaries by them received; provided always, that lieutenant-colonel Alexander Lawson Smith, of the said regiment extraordinary, do hold the rank of lieutenant-colonel, as a supernumerary officer of this state in the continental service, he having resigned his commission in the continental service for the purpose of accepting the command of the said regiment, and being entitled in course to the rank of lieutenant-colonel."

---

Arrangement of the Maryland Line in 5 Regts., January 1st, 1781.

| RANK. | NAMES. | WHEN COMMISSIONED. | RANK. | NAMES. | WHEN COMMISSIONED. |
|---|---|---|---|---|---|

### 1ST REGIMENT.

| RANK. | NAMES. | WHEN COMMISSIONED. | RANK. | NAMES. | WHEN COMMISSIONED. |
|---|---|---|---|---|---|
| Col. | Otho H. Williams | 1st Jan '77 | 16 Lieut. | James Ewing | 27 May '78 |
| Lt. Col. | Uriah Forrest | | 21 do | James J. Skinner | 14 Sept do |
| Major | John Eccleston | 10 Dec do | 26 do | Isaac Duvall | 12 Apl '79 |
| 1 Captain | Thomas Lansdale | 1 Jan do | 31 do | John Hamilton | 1 June do |
| 6 do | Jona. Sellman | do do | 36 do | Willm. Woolford | 11 Sept do |
| 11 do | John Hawkins | 20 Feb do | 41 do | Patrick Danelly | 7 Oct do |
| 16 do | Edwd. Prall | 10 June do | 46 do | Willm. Raison | 26 Jan '80 |
| 21 do | Willm. Riely | 15 Oct do | 51 do | Joshua Burgess | 14 Mch do |
| 26 do | John S. Belt | 15 Dec do | 56 do | Hezekiah Ford | 16 Aug do |
| 31 do | Christn. Orendorff | 1 Apl '78 | 61 do | John Nelson | 1 Jan '81 |
| 36 do | Richd. Bird | 1 June '79 | 1 Ensign | John T. Lowe | 26 Jan '80 |
| 41 do | Geo. Armstrong | 11 Feb '80 | 6 do | Edward M. Smith | do do |
| 1 Capt.Lt. | Lloyd Beall | 8 June '79 | 11 do | Saml. Edmiston | 1 June do |
| 6 do | Jno. J. Jacobs | 16 Aug '80 | Surgeon | Richard Pindell | |
| 11 Lieut. | William Lamar | 15 Nov '77 | Mate | Ezekiel Hayne | |

| RANK. | NAMES. | WHEN COMMISSIONED. | RANK. | NAMES. | WHEN COMMISSIONED. |
|---|---|---|---|---|---|

## 2ND REGIMENT.

| RANK. | NAMES. | WHEN COMMISSIONED. | RANK. | NAMES. | WHEN COMMISSIONED. |
|---|---|---|---|---|---|
| Col. | John Gunby | 17 Apl '77 | 17 Lieut. | Christr. Richmond | 27 May '78 |
| Lt. Col. | John E. Howard | 11 Mch '79 | 22 do | George Jacobs | 14 Sept do |
| Major | John Dean | do do | 27 do | John Carr | 12 Apl '79 |
| 2 Capt. | Benj. Brookes | 1 Jan '77 | 32 do | William Adams | 8 June do |
| 7 do | Alex. Trueman | do do | 37 do | Nicholas Gassaway | |
| 12 do | Jonathan Morris | 14 Apl do | 42 do | Arthur Harris | 26 Oct do |
| 17 do | Walker Muse | 10 June do | 47 do | Thomas Price | 11 Feb '80 |
| 22 do | William Wilmot | 15 Oct do | 52 do | William Murdoch | 1 Apl do |
| 27 do | John Jordan | 20 Dec do | 57 do | Zedekiah Moore | 10 Sept do |
| 32 do | Wm. Beatty | 14 Sept '78 | 62 do | Mark McPherson | 1 Jan '81 |
| 37 do | Thomas Mason | 8 June '79 | 2 Ensign | Jacob Crawford | 26 Jan '80 |
| 42 do | John Gassaway | 2 Apl '80 | 7 do | William Smoote | do do |
| 2 Capt.Lt. | Adam Hoops | 15 Dec '79 | 12 do | James Arthur | 17 June do |
| 7 do | Edward Dyer | 10 Sept '80 | Surgeon | Walter Warfield | |
| 12 Lieut. | Jno. A. Hamilton | 1 Feb '78 | | | |

## 3RD REGIMENT.

| RANK. | NAMES. | WHEN COMMISSIONED. | RANK. | NAMES. | WHEN COMMISSIONED. |
|---|---|---|---|---|---|
| Lt. Col. Commd. | Peter Adams | 1 Aug '79 | 13 Lieut. | James Gould | 11 Mch '78 |
| Major | John Steward | 17 Apl '77 | 18 do | James Winchester | 27 May do |
| do | Henry Hardman | 22 May '79 | 23 do | Philip Read | 13 Oct do |
| 3 Capt. | Henry Dobson | 1 Jan '77 | 28 do | John Hartshorne | 21 May '79 |
| 8 do | Joseph Marbury | do do | 33 do | Rignal Hillary | 15 July do |
| 13 do | Lilburne Williams | 17 Apl do | 38 do | Philip Hill | |
| 18 do | Robert Chesley | 10 June do | 43 do | Wm. Pendergast | 29 Oct '79 |
| 23 do | John Smith, (6th) | 9 Nov do | 48 do | Henry Baldwin | 11 Feb '80 |
| 28 do | James W. Gray | 26 Dec do | 53 do | David Luckett | 7 Apl do |
| 33 do | Edward Spurrier | 21 May '79 | 58 do | Walter Dyer | 15 Sept do |
| 38 do | Benj. Price | 1 July do | 63 do | Nathan Wright | 1 Jan '81 |
| 43 do | Richd. Waters | 7 Apl '80 | 3 Ensign | John Boone | 26 Jan '80 |
| 3 Capt.Lt. | Henry Lyles | 11 Feb '80 | 8 do | John Trueman | do do |
| 8 Lieut. | Francis Revely | 15 Apl '77 | Surgeon | Levin Denwood | |

| RANK. | NAMES. | WHEN COMMISSIONED. | RANK. | NAMES. | WHEN COMMISSIONED. |
|---|---|---|---|---|---|

## 4TH REGIMENT.

| RANK. | NAMES. | WHEN COMMISSIONED. |
|---|---|---|
| Lt. Col. Commd. | Thos. Woolford | |
| Major | Levin Winder | 17 Apl '77 |
| do | Alex. Roxburgh | 7 Apl do |
| 4 Capt. | John Lynch | 1 Jan '77 |
| 9 do | Jacob Brice | do do |
| 14 do | Henry Gaither | 17 Apl do |
| 19 do | John C. Jones | 20 Sept do |
| 24 do | Richd. Anderson | 15 Nov do |
| 29 do | George Hamilton | 25 Jan '78 |
| 34 do | David Lynn | 22 May '79 |
| 39 do | John Mitchell | 15 July do |
| 44 do | Jona. Gibson | 1 May '80 |
| 4 Capt.Lt. | Saml. McPherson | 7 Apl '80 |
| 9 Lieut. | Nicholas Mangers | 15 Apl '77 |
| 14 Lieut. | James Simmes | 27 May '78 |
| 19 do | Peter Hardcastle | 14 Sept do |
| 24 do | Benj. Garnett | 13 Oct do |
| 29 do | Wm. Trueman Stoddert | 21 May '79 |
| 34 do | Elihu Hall | 1 Aug do |
| 39 do | Levache de Vaubrunne | |
| 44 do | Nathan Smith | 15 Dec '79 |
| 49 do | Edmd. Compton | 18 Feb '80 |
| 54 do | Joshua Rutledge | 1 May do |
| 59 do | John Brevett | 20 Sept do |
| 64 do | John McCoy | 1 Jan '81 |
| 4 Ensign | Robt. Halkerston | 26 Jan '80 |
| 9 do | Henry Gassaway | do do |
| Surgeon | William Kilty | |

## 5TH REGIMENT.

| RANK. | NAMES. | WHEN COMMISSIONED. |
|---|---|---|
| Lt. Col. Commd. | Benj. Ford | |
| Major | Archd. Anderson | |
| do | John Davidson | 1 Jan '81 |
| 5 Capt. | Wm. Dent Beall | 1 Jan '77 |
| 10 do | John Smith, (3rd) | do do |
| 15 do | Edward Oldham | 20 May do |
| 20 do | Horatio Clagett | 10 Oct do |
| 25 do | John Gale | 10 Dec do |
| 30 do | Perry Benson | 11 Mch '78 |
| 35 do | James Somervill | 1 June '79 |
| 40 do | William Bruce | 1 Aug do |
| 45 do | Edward Edgerly | 10 Sept '80 |
| 5 Capt.Lt. | Thos. B. Hugou | 1 May '80 |
| 10 Lieut. | James Bruff | 7 Oct '77 |
| 15 Lieut. | Archd. McAllister | 27 May '78 |
| 20 do | Gassaway Watkins | 14 Sept do |
| 25 do | Jacob Norris | 26 Nov do |
| 30 do | John Lynn | 1 June '79 |
| 35 do | Saml. Hanson | 1 Aug do |
| 40 do | Thomas Rowse | |
| 45 do | Robert Denny | 3 Jan '80 |
| 50 do | Benj. Fickle | 19 Feb do |
| 55 do | Roger Nelson | 15 July do |
| 60 do | Thomas Boyd | 1 Jan '81 |
| 65 do | John Sears | do do |
| 5 Ensign | Henry Clements | 26 Jan '80 |
| 10 do | Adam Jamison | 1 June do |

OFFICERS ENTITLED TO PROMOTIONS IN THEIR OWN REGIMENTS PREVIOUS TO
JAN. 1st, 1781.

Wm. Pendergast when Appd. a Vacancy 5th Regt.
Wm. Raison             do         do
Edmd. Compton 18 Feb, Smith's resignation
Benj. Fickle      19 do Porter's dismission
Jos. Burgess when 1st Appd. a Vacancy
David Lucket 7 Apl. Roxburgh's promotion
William Murdoch 1 Apl. Bevin's resignation
Jos. Ruttledge 1 May when 1st Appd. a Vacancy
Roger Nelson 15 July Moran's dismission
H. Ford 16 Aug. Duvall's death
Zed. Moore 10 Sept. Hardman's    do
John Brevett 20 Sept. Shoemaker's do
Walter Dyer 15 Sept. Farmer's    do

The above Officers have Ensigns Commissions on the 1st Jan., 1781,
but entitled to Lieutenancy on the dates specified.

SUPERNUMERARIES IN THE LATE 7 REGIMENTS JAN. 1st, '81.

| | | | |
|---|---|---|---|
| Col. | Josias Carvel Hall | 1 Jan '77 | late 4th Regt. |
| Lt. Col. Comd. | Nathl. Ramsey | | do 3rd do |
| Lt. Col. | Edward Tillard | | do 4th do |

OFFICERS OF THE MARYLAND ARTILLERY SUPERNUMERARY.

| | | |
|---|---|---|
| Richard Dorsey, Captain | Jacques Baques, 1st Lieut. | James McFadon,  1st Lieut. |
| Wm. Brown,  do | Nicholas Rickets,  do | Isaac Rawlings,  2nd  do |
| Ebenezer Finley, Capt. Lt. | Young Wilkinson,  do | John Cheviar,  do |
| James Smith,  do | Clement Skerrett,  do | John Carson,  do |
| Robert Wilmot, Lieut. | | |

OFFICERS IN THE MARYLAND PART OF THE RIFLE REGIMENT
SUPERNUMERARY JANY., 1st, 1781.

| | | | | |
|---|---|---|---|---|
| Capt. Thomas H. Luckett | 1 Jan '77 | Capt. | Reazin Davis | 27 July '80 |
| do  Adamson Tannehill | Dec '78 | Lt. | Elijah Evans, claims | |
| do  James Lingan | do | | Captaincy | 10 Apl '78 |

OFFICERS IN THE MARYLAND PART OF THE GERMAN REGIMENT
SUPERNUMERARY JANY. 1st, 1781.

| | | | | |
|---|---|---|---|---|
| Lt. Col. Lodwick Weltner | 9 April '77 | Capt. | Michael Bayer | 25 May '78 |
| Capt. Charles Baltzel | 10 May do | Lt. | Martin Shugart | |
| do  Christian, (or Christo- | | do | Jacob Gromath | 4 Jan '78 |
| pher), Mayers | 12 Mch '78 | do | David Morgan | 8 April do |

Ensign Jacob Reybold, 24 July '78
Surgeon's Mate Alexr. Smith, August '78.

### OFFICERS IN THE MARYLAND PART OF COL. NATHANIEL GIST'S REGT.

| | |
|---|---|
| Maj. Nathaniel Mitchell | Capt. Joseph Smith |
| Capt. John Gist | do   Joseph Britain |

There are many other officers not included here who raised their Companies in & went from the State of Maryland into the Continental Line who come under the same description with those above enumerated therefore upon Application the expediency of admitting their Claims must necessarily come under Consideration.

W. Smallwood, M. G.

---

Capt. Murdoch's Company of the Md. State Regiment.   15 M. '81.

---

| | | |
|---|---|---|
| John Reader, Serjt. | George Stevens | John Carter |
| John Auber, D. Maj. | Walter Watson | Samuel Scott |
| Ezekiah Crowson, Fifer | William Jones | John Rumwill |
| Chas. Revelle, Drummer | Roger Maloy | John Jones |
| Joseph Greer | Wilkinson Gregsby | Henry Connolly |
| William Manly | George Ryon | Thomas Pingston |
| Edward Hinths | Richard Biddle | John Walker, Serjt. |
| Thomas Smith | Samuel Furrow | John Moore |
| Hugh Burns | Salithiel Carmin | Banks Webb |
| Jeaneth Crowd | Levy Reese | Abram Barker |
| Henry Mansfeld | James Hewitt | |

---

MARYLAND ACTS—OCT., 1780.

"An ACT to procure recruits.

WHEREAS this general assembly are earnestly called upon by several requisitions from congress, and letters from general Washington, to recruit the quota of troops of this state :

*Be it enacted, by the General Assembly of Maryland,* That one thousand men be forthwith raised to serve in the regiments of this state in the continental service for three years, if not sooner discharged, by an equal assessment on all property within this state.

*And be it enacted,* That the lieutenant of each county shall, as soon as may be after notice of this act, divide and apportion all the property last assessed in his county, . . . . into classes of sixteen thousand pounds each, . . . . and each class shall, within twenty days after classing as aforesaid, find an able bodied recruit, between sixteen and forty-five years old, to serve for three years, if not sooner discharged, and the same recruit deliver to the lieutenant of the county, to be by him passed.

*And be it enacted,* That any able bodied slave, between sixteen and forty years of age, who voluntarily enters into the service, and is passed by the lieutenant, in the presence and with the consent, and agreement of his master, may be accepted as a recruit.

*And be it enacted,* That the lieutenants aforesaid, and the field and commissioned officers of the militia in each county, shall, within five days after the expiration of the said twenty days, meet . . . . and shall proceed to examine whether each class hath found a proper effective recruit according to this act, and if any class hath not found such recruit, . . . . they shall cause lots to be cast . . . . and the person to whose lot it shall fall shall be from thenceforth, to every intent and purpose, considered as an enlisted soldier, to serve until the tenth day of December seventeen hundred and eighty-one, in the quota of this state of the continental troops, . . . . but if such person shall, within twenty days thereafter, provide a good and sufficient recruit, to serve until the said tenth day of December in his stead, he shall be discharged ; or if he shall at any time afterwards find a good and sufficient recruit in his stead, to serve for three years unless sooner discharged, he shall be discharged.

*And be it enacted,* That all recruits raised in virtue of this act shall be carried before the lieutenant of the county in which the recruits are or shall be raised, to pass muster, . . . . but no imported convict who hath not served his full term of seven years, or British deserter, shall be passed as a recruit within this act.

*And,* for the discovery of deserters, and the punishment of those who entertain, harbour, or conceal them,

*Be it enacted,* That if, after the first day of March next, any free male person shall entertain, harbour, or conceal, any deserter, knowing him to be such, such person shall, upon such conviction, be considered as an enlisted regular soldier for the term of three years, and may be taken as such by any officer of the Maryland line ; and if any free male person, convicted as aforesaid, shall be the father of such deserter, or of or above forty-five years of age, or unfit for the service, he shall furnish an able-bodied recruit for the war, and deliver him to the lieutenant of his county within ten days after conviction, and in case of neglect shall be liable to pay thirty-five pounds in specie, or the value thereof, to the lieutenant of his county, . . . . and if any female, the mistress of any family, shall entertain, harbour, or conceal, any deserter, and shall be thereof convicted as aforesaid, she shall furnish and deliver an able bodied recruit as aforesaid, or be liable to the payment of the same penalty as aforesaid, . . . . and if any person, liable to such penalty for not procuring a recruit as aforesaid, shall be unable to pay the same, the lieutenant of the county may commit such person, for any time not exceeding six months, to the work-house or goal of his county, there to be kept to hard labour."

A List of Recruits furnished in Caroline County agreeable to an Act of Assembly passed Oct., 1780.

### SUBSTITUTES.

| | | |
|---|---|---|
| Handy Handly | Henry Fisher | Jacob Branton |
| Tom Potts | James Fisher | Wm Miers. |

### DRAFTS.

| | | |
|---|---|---|
| Allemby Millington | Matthias Noland | Edmond Lunceford |
| Elijah Jump | Nathan Batchelor | Roger Connelly |
| John Jones | Hezekiah Wheelar | Jonathan Greenhugh |
| Richard Chance | | |

Wm. Whiteley, Lt. Caroline Co., Apr. 16th, 1781.

### VOLUNTARY ENLISTMENTS OF

| | | | | |
|---|---|---|---|---|
| William Standley | Dorchester County | April 18th '81 | three years |
| Nathan Ross | "        " | "   11th '81 | "      " |
| Charles Dean | "        " | "   23d '81 | "      " |
| John Riley   for the 6th Regt., Col. O. H. Williams, Aug 26th '81 | | | "      " |

A Return of the Recruits, Draughts and Substitutes in Ann Arundel County under the Act to procure Recruits passed October Session, 1780.

| NAMES. | TIME. | | TO WHOM DELIVERED. |
|---|---|---|---|
| Chas. Alexander | 3 years | Recruit | Col. Adams |
| William Barry | until 10th Dec | Draught | |
| Samuel Fowler | do | do | |
| Willm. Potter | 3 years | Recruit | Capt. Trueman |
| William Elliott | 'til 10th Dec | Draught | |
| Wm. Woodward, Jr. | do | do | |

| NAMES. | TIME. | | TO WHOM DELIVERED. |
|---|---|---|---|
| John Newton | 3 years | Recruit | Capt. Trueman |
| Adam Musler | do | do | Lt. John Sears |
| Levy Moody | do | do | Col. Adams |
| Richard Moss | 'til 10th Dec | Draught | |
| Johns Meek | do | do | |
| John Winterburn | 3 years | Recruit | same |
| John Britton | do | do | same |
| Thomas Horn | do | do | Capt. Trueman |
| James Wallingsfort | 'til 10th Dec | Substitute | same |
| Benjamin Combly | do | Draught | |
| William Spicer | do | do | |
| William Lovitt | do | do | |
| Charles Pennington | do | do | |
| Isaac Jones | do | do | |
| Thomas Atkinson | do | do | |
| Willm. Palmour | do | Substitute | Col. Adams |
| Thomas Hannen | 3 years | Recruit | Lt. Jas. Jno. Skinner |
| Nathan Moss | 'til 10th Dec | Draught | |
| Paul Phillips | do | do | |
| Machael Mundus | 3 years | Recruit | Capt. Trueman |
| John Fitgency | 'til 10 Dec | Draught | |
| Aaron McKenzie | do | do | |
| John Davis | 3 years | Recruit | same |
| Nichs. Selby | 'til 10 Dec | Draught | |
| Alex. Cockburn | 3 years | Recruit | same |
| Gideon Walker | do | do | Col. Adams |
| Thomas Hawkins | 'til 10 Dec | Draught | |
| Robert Folger | 3 years | Recruit | Capt. Trueman |
| Francis Read | do | do | same |
| Willm. Appingstall | do | do | same |
| James Humphries | do | do | same |
| Michael Smith | do | do | same |
| Charles Onion | 'til 10 Dec | Draught | |
| Willm. Beachman | do | do | |
| Misail Deavour | do | do | |
| John Jordan | War | Recruit | same |
| Jno. Brown, (Shoem.) | 'til 10 Dec | Draught | |
| Edwd. Dorsey, of Caleb | do | do | |
| James Portland | do | do | |
| James Beachgood | do | do | |
| Pascho Isleck | do | Substitute | same |
| Chas. Williams | 3 years . | Recruit | same |
| John Griffis, Jr. | 'til 10 Dec | Draught | |
| Thos. Batterson, (Negro) | do | Substitute | Col. Adams |
| Adam Allen | do | Draught | |
| John Collins | do | do | |

| NAMES. | TIME. | | To Whom Delivered. |
|---|---|---|---|
| Thomas Gordon | 3 years | Recruit | Col. Adams |
| Thomas Tongue | 'til 10 Dec | Draught | |
| Ferdinando Battee, Jr. | do | Substitute | same |
| Jono. Brashears | do | Draught | same |
| Andrew Hoofman | 3 years | Recruit | Maj. Steward |
| Samuel Wood | 'til 10 Dec | Draught | |
| Jno. Birkhead | do | do | |
| Nathnl. Robt. Harnsbury | 3 years | Recruit | same |
| Thomas Hawkins | do | do | Col. Adams |
| Caleb Tydings | 'til 10 Dec | Substitute | same |
| George Collins | do | Draught | |
| Richard Foggitt | do | Substitute | Capt. Mitchell |
| William French | do | Draught | |
| James Davidson | do | Substitute | Col. Adams |
| Aaron Stevenson | 3 years | Recruit | same |
| John Dâds | 'til 10 Dec | Draught | |
| John Cowman | do | do | |
| Wm. Summerland | do | do | |
| Isaiah Williams | 3 years | Recruit | Capt. Trueman |
| James West | do | do | same |
| David Stewart | 'til 10 Dec | Draught | |
| Thomas Moffitt | do | Substitute | Col. Adams |

No draughts for Classes 86 and 87, there not being any Militia in the Classes.                    James Brice,
    The Draughts are ordered to Annapolis.    Lieut. of A. A. Co.

Talbot County, to Wit—

A List of persons Draughted to serve until the tenth day of December, 1781, in the quota of this State of the Continental Troops. May 1st, 1781.

| PERSONS' NAMES. | COMPANY. | BATTALION. | CLASS. |
|---|---|---|---|
| James Collison | Bayside | 36 | 1 |
| John Duling | Sword in Hand | 4 | 2 |
| Richd. Hopkins, Jr. | Hearts of Oak | 38 | 3 |
| Thomas Cooper | Bayside | 38 | 4 |
| Wm. Jones, Jr. | Broad Creek | 38 | 5 |
| George Townsend | United | 38 | 6 |
| Thomas Wrightson | do | 38 | 7 |
| Anthony Kerby | Hearts of Oak | 38 | 9 |
| Joseph Leonard | do | 38 | 10 |

| PERSONS' NAMES. | COMPANY. | BATTALION. | CLASS. |
|---|---|---|---|
| Henry Delahay, Jr. | Oxford | 38 | 11 |
| Richard Standfield | Miles River | 38 | 12 |
| Charles Sherwood | do | 38 | 13 |
| Solomon Plummer | Wye | 4 | 14 |
| James Kinnard | do | 4 | 15 |
| James Kendrick | Volunteer | 4 | 16 |
| Alex. Anderson | do | 4 | 17 |
| Nathan Foster | do | 4 | 18 |
| Thomas Ozmond | Hand in Hand | 4 | 19 |
| Robt. Frampton | do | 4 | 20 |
| James Price, Sr. | Sword in Hand | 4 | 22 |
| Greenberry Goldsborough | Oxford | 38 | 23 |
| William Mardary | 2 Volunteer | 4 | 24 |
| Capt. Richd. Bruff | Union | 4 | 25 |
| George Poney | do | 4 | 26 |
| John Robt. Saml. Coffree | do | 4 | 27 |
| Robert Kemp | Third Haven | 4 | 28 |
| Samuel Jenkins | do | 4 | 29 |
| Jonathan Clash | do | 4 | 30 |
| John Harrison, Jr. | Oxford | 38 | 31 |
| James Plowman, Jr. | Hand in Hand | 4 | 33 |
| Wm. Rakes | 2 Volunteer | 4 | 34 |
| Richard Easley | Oxford | 38 | 35 |

(32 Draughts)        Chrisr. Birckhead, Lieut. T. County,
                                                    May 7th, 1781.

Talbot County, to Wit—
A List of Recruits who have enlisted to serve three years in the quota of this State of the Continental Troops.

| NAMES OF THE RECRUITS. | WHEN ENLISTED. |
|---|---|
| Thomas Jones | March 20th 1781 |
| John Brown | "    30th 1781 |
| Allin Townsend | April 11th 1781 |

May 7th, 1781.        Christr. Birckhead, Lieut. Talbot County.

A Return of the Men Draughted in Worcester County, May the first, 1781.

| | | |
|---|---|---|
| Thomas Handley | William Conner | Kendal Taylor |
| Adkins Dennis | Isaac Boston | Elisha Long |
| Henry Corckwell | William Marshall | Edward Bishop |
| Alexander Porter | Henry Ayrs | Isaac Marshal |
| William Butler | William Cowley | Ruben Cropper |
| Daniel Eashom | Richard Sturgis | Isaac Brillingham |
| Edward Cropper | Midleton Harmon | Levi Powell |
| Jesey Brattan | John Ewens, of Jushua | Levi Cropper, of Natl. |
| John Gray | Elias Penewell | John Brevard |
| William Handy | John Johnson | Seth Hutson |
| William Jones | Levin Newton | James Mumford |
| George Turner | | |

Joseph Dashiell, Lieut.

KENT COUNTY RECRUITS. [ALL ENLISTED FOR THREE YEARS.]

| | | |
|---|---|---|
| Henry Williams | William Brada | John Gleen |
| Henry Harris | Daniel B. Bayley | Jacob Jefferies |
| James Bryne | James Reynolds | William Taylor |
| Reubin Elbon | William Grace | James Wilson |
| John Collins | Richard Green | Augustine Bryan |
| William Lynes | Abraham Reynolds | Thomas Farmer |
| William Wilson | Smyth Bagwell | Edward Chambers |
| James Shepperd | John Thomas | Shadrick Sap |
| George Finley | Ishmael Wroth | John Starkey |
| William Dunkin | John Harris | Absolom Scott |
| Richard Dolvin | William Guggon | Richard Demby |
| William Elbon | James Chambers | Class 18 drafted May 5 |
| Thomas Wood | Timothy Conner | |

Agreeable to the assessment we made out thirty-nine Classes of sixteen Thousand pounds each & every Class, (except one), has furnished a recruit for three years according to the above list. The deficient Class was drafted on the fifth day of May & I hope that a recruit for three years will be produced for that Class. Alexander Boys passed by Class No. 35, we discovered was subject to fits; who we have since discharged, the Class agreeing to pay their proportion to the State. The said Boys having received but a small sum.

W. Bordley.

May 16th, 1781.

RESOLVES OF CONTINENTAL CONGRESS—31 MAY, 1781.

" Whereas the British king, regardless of the rights of mankind, and of the United States in particular, continues the ravages of war with relentless fury ; . . . . and whereas the deficiency of the continental regular lines, makes it absolutely necessary to call forth a respectable body of militia, till those lines be completed ; . . . . It is also earnestly recommended to the state of Maryland, immediately to raise, arm, equip and accoutre for the field, two battalions of infantry, consisting of nine companies of 64 rank and file each ; and a corps of cavalry of 64 troopers ; . . . . And it is further recommended . . . . to cause the said troops, as soon as raised, . . . . to be marched . . . . to such place or places as the commander-in-chief shall direct, to remain in the service for and during the space of three months, . . . . unless sooner discharged by Congress or the commander-in-chief, and to be subject to the orders of the commander-in-chief."

MARYLAND ACTS—MAY, 1781

"An ACT to raise two battalions of militia for reinforcing the continental army and to complete the number of select militia.

WHEREAS it hath been earnestly recommended by congress to call forth two battalions of militia in this state, for the purpose of aiding and assisting our friends, now actually invaded, in the southern states, and this present general assembly have thought it reasonable and necessary to comply with the said recommendation :

*Be it therefore enacted, by the General Assembly of Maryland,* That thirteen hundred and forty effective men, to compose the non-commissioned officers and privates of two battalions of militia, to be officered according to the resolutions of congress of the third and twenty-first days of October last, be immediately raised in this state, in manner hereafter directed, to act in conjunction with the continental army until the tenth day of December next.

*And be it enacted,* That the said two battalions be apportioned upon and raised in the several counties, according to the number of militia in each county.

*And be it enacted,* That proper persons shall be appointed in each county by the governor and council, to procure the said number of militia men on or before the 16th of July next, by voluntary enrollment, . . . . and where several persons are appointed to recruit in any county, he that shall procure the highest number of recruits exceeding twenty, shall be entitled to a commission as lieutenant . . . . and he that shall procure the next highest number of recruits exceeding ten, shall be entitled to a commission of an ensign in one of the companies of said battalions.

*And be it enacted,* That the governor and council shall be and are hereby authorised and requested to appoint fit and proper officers out of the Maryland line, not engaged in actual service the present campaign, down to captains inclusive, to command the said battalions and companies, . . . . and if such officers cannot be had, then to appoint such officers as may be wanted out of those best qualified,

*And,* Whereas there are many idle and disorderly persons in the several counties in this state, who pursue no visible means to obtain an honest subsistence, but spend their time in such a manner as to render no service to the community by which they are protected :

*Be it enacted,* That every such free male idle person above sixteen years of age, and who is able bodied and effective, and hath no family, nor any visible method of getting an honest livelihood, and who may be adjudged by the lieutenant of the county to come under the above description of a vagrant, shall, from and after such adjudication, be considered as a soldier enlisted, and shall have it in his choice whether he will serve until the tenth of December, or enlist for three years or during the war ; . . . . provided that no person who hath served in the continental army as a regular soldier, and hath been discharged, shall be deemed a vagrant under this act.

*And be it enacted,* That in case the number of militia be not procured in the several counties by voluntary enrollment, or by enrolling vagrants in manner as above mentioned, on or before the sixteenth day of July next, it shall and may be lawful for the lieutenant of the county, . . . . to call together the field officers of each county respectively, and cause the militia in their respective counties . . . . to be distributed into as many classes as men may be wanted, and each class shall, within five days, find a recruit to serve until the tenth day of December next, or . . . . shall cause such class as doth not find a substitute . . . to be draughted, and two persons to be selected therefrom by lot, and such person of the two as the lieutenant . . . . shall direct and appoint, shall be deemed a militia man enrolled to serve until the tenth day of December next, and shall accordingly march, unless he find a substitute, to be approved by the lieutenant . . . . within five days after such appointment shall be notified unto him ; and any nonjuror who shall voluntarily enlist and serve, or if draughted or procured as a substitute shall serve during the time aforesaid, such nonjuror shall be restored to all the rights and privileges of a free citizen of this state without exception.

*And be it enacted,* That the said recruits and militia men, draughted or otherwise procured to go in the above battalions, shall be subject to the continental articles of war; and all freemen, although blacks or mulattoes, who are not deemed vagrants or enlisted as such, shall be taken into the militia and be subject to a draught as above directed.

*And be it enacted,* That where any three persons, to be appointed by the governor and council as herein before directed, shall enlist the whole number of men wanted for that county before the sixteenth of July next, if the number be equal to that of a full company, to consist of seventy-four non-commissioned officers and privates, such persons shall be entitled to commissions as captain, lieutenant, and ensign."

---

List of Recruits & Substitutes for Queen Ann's County procured under the Law for raising Recruits passed at the October Session, 1780.

| RECRUITS. | TERM OF ENLISTMENT. | SUBSTITUTES. | TERM OF ENLISTMENT. |
|---|---|---|---|
| John Barnaby | 3 years | Nathaniel Bailey | 9 months |
| Edward Bartlett | do | James Cockrill | 3 years |
| John Smallwood | do | John Harriss | do |
| SUBSTITUTES. | | James Smith | do |
| Thomas Harriss | do | John Holland | do |
| Jacob Collins | do | Charles Nabb | 10 December |
| Samuel Hadley | 10 December | George Penfold | do |
| James Harriss | do | George Belfast | 3 years |
| Thomas Berry | do | George Ellas | do |
| Daniel Keitch | 9 months | Philip Russell | do |
| Thomas Burk | 10 December | | |
| Arnold Longfellow | do | | |

DRAUGHTS.

| | | |
|---|---|---|
| Thomas Long | Charles Devons, (subject to fits) | Samuel Osburne |
| Thos. Ford | Jonathan Briley | Sabret Huxter |
| Joseph Dobson | Thomas Chambers | William Clark, |
| William Hollingsworth | David Huxter, (subject to fits) | (shoe maker) |
| William Whitaker | John Jerman | John Cohee |
| Benj. Greenage | Jeremiah Davenport | William Tarbutton |
| Richard Ratcliff | Robert Cockleton, | Joseph Badger |
| | (servt. to Mr. Forman) | |

William Hemsley,

June 11th, 1781.          Lieut. of Queen Ann's County.

Port Tobacco, 2nd Sept., 1781.

Dear Col.

The enclosed are Exact Lists of the draughts and Substitutes draughted &c. for this County the present year. I Judge you Will be amazed to See Such a number Discharged, therefore have Noted against their Respective Names, the Causes that Rendered it Necessary. There are Also Several that are So debilitated by Sickness that they are Not able to March at present, and a few Sculkers that I have Not been able as yet to git hold off, tho have made use of the most probable means for that purpose, and hope in a few days to accomplish it. Please Lay the Lists Before the Honorable the Governor and Council and Oblige

Dr. Sir

Your Respectfull Huml. Servt.,

Frans. Ware.

To Col. John H. Stone, Annapolis.                    *

---

Return of the drafts from Charles County who were drafted the 11th and 12th June, 1781.

| Names of Drafts. | In Service or Not. | Names of Drafts. | In Service or Not. |
|---|---|---|---|
| Charles Willett | Service | Levi Clinkscales | Service |
| Benjamin Shaw | do | Nellson Johnson | do |
| Jese Warder | do | William Glassgow | do |
| Joseph Newberry | do | Charles Athey | do |
| John Ensy Clements | do | William Lary | do |
| Lawrence Simpson | do | Notley Whitcombe | do |
| James Wright | do | Gerrard Wood | do |
| Roger Posey | do | Thomas James | do |
| Francis McCann | do | Benj. Calbert Johnson | do |
| Walter Brooke | do | Chas. Beavin, (sick) | |
| Allison Maddox | do | Caleb Thomas, (small pox) | |
| James Dunning | do | Thomas Hill, (Flux) | |
| James Anderson | do | Joseph Pagett, (Lame) | |
| John Lowrie | do | Alex. Wallace | |
| John Stone Hunt, enlisted | do | Jediah Waters, (Lame) | |
| for 3 years | | Elias Rawlings | |
| Barton Wathen | do | Wm. Boarman, (small pox) | |

---

Return of the drafts from Charles County who were drafted the 27th July, 1781.

*Names of draughts excused or discharged are not printed.

| Names of Drafts. | In Service or Not. | Names of Drafts. | In Service or Not. |
|---|---|---|---|
| Thomas Gillsim | Service | Ignatius Montgomery | Service |
| Walter Warren Hannon | do | Barton Beall | do |
| Nicholas Miles | do | Charles King | do |
| Matthew Smoot | do | James Taylor | do |
| William Lovelin | do | Benedict Clements | do |
| Matthew Brooke | | Henry Proctor | do |
| David Davis | do | Ignatius Stuart | do |
| John Boswell | do | Thomas Elliott | do |
| John Butler | do | James McDaniel | do |
| Henry Butler | do | Richard Robey | do |
| William Oliver | do | Thomas Davis | do |
| Hezekiah Elgin | do | Zechariah Posey | do |
| Lancelot Chunn | do | William Neale | do |
| Jese Davis | do | James Warrington | do |
| Harrison Elgin | do | John Huntington, (sick) | |
| George Maddox | do | Richard Meeke, (at sea) | |
| Charles McDonald | do | John Newberry, (sick) | |
| Samuel Dent | do | Joseph Owens, (sick) | |
| George Hudson | do | Richard Brown | |
| William Coombe | do | Joseph Beavin, (sick) | |
| Joshua Steuart | do | Edward Miles | |
| George McNess | do | Nicholas Hagan | |
| Hezekiah Mudd | do | Samuel Wright, (sick) | |
| William Clinkscales | do | Henry Clements    since enrolled himself | |
| William Dorton | do |     a Substitute in P. G. Co. & joined the | |
| John Clements | do |     Army | |

Dorchester County, June 28th, 1781.

Sir :

 I have sent fourteen draughted Militia Men under the Care of Lieut. Hugh McGuire, procured under a late Act of Assembly, to serve in the Continental Army untill the 10th Day of December next.   A List of their Names you have inserted below—several of them have been Waterman & seem very desirous of serving on board some of our Barges, particularly Peter Harrington, Job Hubbert, Roger Tregoe & Anthony Tall, Jr.   I have desired Mr. McGuire to apply to your Board to satisfy him for transporting the draughted Men to Annapolis

I have the Honour to be

Sir yr. very hble. Servt.,

Henry Hooper.

His Excellency the Governor—Dorchester County in Council.

| John Wheeler | Ezekiel Whitchocks | Roger Trego |
| Nehemiah Lingard | Job Hubbert | Peter Herrington |
| John Dicks | Willm. Procter, Jr. | John Booth |
| Samuel Hurst | Nathan Busick | Willm. Dickinson |
| Levin Thomas | Anthony Tall, Jr. | |

## Arrangement of the Maryland Line July, 1781.

| RANK. | NAMES. | WHEN COMMISSIONED. | PROMOTIONS SINCE JANY. 1ST, '81. |
| --- | --- | --- | --- |
| | | 1ST REGIMENT. | |
| 1 Col. | Otho H. Williams | 1 Jan '77 | |
| 2 Lt. Col. | John Steward | 19 Feb '81 | vice Forrest, resigned |
| 2 Major | John Eccleston | 10 Dec '77 | |
| 4 Capt. | Jonathan Sellman | 1 Jan do | |
| 13 do | Edward Prall | 10 June do | |
| 18 do | William Reily | 15 Oct do | |
| 23 do | John S. Belt | 15 Dec do | |
| 28 do | Christn. Orendorff | 1 Apl '78 | |
| 32 do | Richd. Bird | 1 June '79 | |
| 37 do | Geo. Armstrong | 11 Feb '80 | |
| 42 do | Lloyd Beall . | 19 Feb '81 | vice Lansdale, promoted |
| 45 do | Thos. B. Hugou | 1 June do | do Hawkins, resigned |
| 5 Lieut. | William Lamar | 15 Nov '77 | |
| 9 do | James Ewing | 27 May '78 | |
| 14 do | Jas. Jno. Skinner | 14 Sept do | |
| 18 do | Isaac Duvall | 12 Apl '79 | |
| 22 do | John Hamilton | 1 June do | |
| 26 do | William Woolford | 11 Sept do | |
| 35 do | William Raison | 26 Jan '80 | |
| 40 do | Joshua Burgess | 14 Mch do | |
| 45 do | Hezekiah Ford | 16 Aug do | |
| 54 do | John T. Lowe | 20 Jan '81 | vice Jacobs, resigned |
| 55 do | Edward M. Smith | 19 Feb do | do Beall, promoted |
| 57 do | Samuel Edmiston | 14 Mch do | do Danelly, resigned |
| 59 do | John Trueman | 16 do do | do Nelson, killed |
| 1 Surgeon | Richard Pindell | | |
| 1 Mate | Ezekiel Hayne | | |
| | | 2ND REGIMENT. | |
| 2 Col. | John Gunby | 17 Apl '77 | |
| 1 Lt. Col. | John E. Howard | 11 Mch '79 | |
| 3 Major · | John Dean | do do | |
| 5 Capt. | Alex. Trueman | 1 Jan '77 | |
| 9 do | Jonathan Morris | 14 Apl '77 | |

| RANK. | NAMES. | WHEN COMMISSIONED. | PROMOTIONS SINCE JANY. 1ST, '81. |
|---|---|---|---|
| 14 Capt. | Walker Muse | 10 June '77 | |
| 19 do | William Wilmot | 15 Oct do | |
| 24 do | John Jordan | 20 Dec do | . |
| 33 do | Thomas Mason | 8 June '79 | |
| 38 do | John Gassaway | 2 Apl '80 | |
| 43 do | Adam Hoops | 16 Mch '81 | vice Brooks, promoted |
| 44 do | Samuel McPherson | 25 Apl '81 | do Beatty, killed |
| 1 Capt. Lt. | Edward Dyer | 10 Sept '80 | |
| 6 Lieut. | John A. Hamilton | 1 Feb '78 | |
| 10 do | Christopher Richmond | 27 May do | |
| 23 do | William Adams | 8 June '79 | |
| 27 do | Nicholas Gassaway | | |
| 31 do | Arthur Harris | 26 Oct '79 | |
| 36 do | Thomas Price | 11 Feb '80 | |
| 41 do | William Murdoch | 1 Apl do | |
| 46 do | Zedekiah Moore | 10 Sept do | |
| 50 do | Mark McPherson | 1 Jan '81 | |
| 56 do | Jacob Crawford | 20 Feb do | vice Jacobs, resigned |
| 58 do | Willm. Smoote | 16 Mch do | do Hoops, promoted |
| 65 do | James Arthur | | do Carr, resigned |
| 2 Surgeon | Walter Warfield | | |

### 3RD REGIMENT.

| RANK. | NAMES. | WHEN COMMISSIONED. | PROMOTIONS |
|---|---|---|---|
| 1 Lt. Col. Comd. | Peter Adams | 1 Aug 79 | |
| 4 Major | Henry Hardman | 22 May do | |
| 7 do | Thomas Lansdale | 19 Feb '81 | vice Steward, promoted |
| 1 Capt. | Henry Dobson | 1 Jan '77 | |
| 6 do | Joseph Marbury | do do | |
| 10 do | Lilburn Williams | 17 Apl do | |
| 15 do | Robert Chesley | 10 June do | |
| 20 do | John Smith, (6th) | 9 Nov do | |
| 25 do | James W. Gray | 26 Dec do | |
| 29 do | Edward Spurrier | 21 May '79 | |
| 34 do | Benjm. Price | 1 July do | |
| 39 do | Richd. Waters | 7 Apl '80 | |
| 2 Lieut. | Francis Revely | 15 Apl '77 | |
| 7 do | James Gould | 11 Mch '78 | |
| 11 do | James Winchester | 27 May do | |
| 15 do | Philip Reed | 13 Oct do | |
| 20 do | John Hartshorne | 21 May '79 | |
| 24 do | Rignal Hillary | 15 July do | |
| 28 do | Philip Hill | | |
| 32 do | William Pendergast | 29 Oct '79 | |
| 37 do | Henry Baldwin | 11 Feb '80 | |

| Rank. | Names. | When Commissioned. | Promotions Since Jany. 1st, '81. |
|---|---|---|---|
| 42 Lieut. | David Lucket | 7 Apl '80 | |
| 47 do | Walter Dyer | 15 Sept do | |
| 51 do | Nathan Wright | 1 Jan '81 | |
| 60 do | John Boone | 12 Apl do | vice Lyles, resigned |
| 3 Surgeon | Levin Denwood | | |

### 4th Regiment.

| | | | |
|---|---|---|---|
| 2 Lt. Col. Comd. | Thomas Woolford | | |
| 1 Major | Levin Winder | 17 Apl '77 | |
| 5 do | Alex. Roxburgh | 7 do '80 | |
| 2 Capt. | John Lynch | 1 Jan '77 | |
| 7 do | Jacob Brice | do do | |
| 11 do | Henry Gaither | 17 Apl do | |
| 16 do | John Courts Jones | 20 Sept do | |
| 21 do | Richd. Anderson | 15 Nov do | |
| 26 do | George Hamilton | 25 Jan '78 | |
| 30 do | David Lynn | 22 May 79 | |
| 35 do | John Mitchell | 15 July do | |
| 40 do | Jonathan Gibson | 1 May '80 | |
| 3 Lieut. | Nichs. Mangers | 15 Apl '77 | |
| 8 do | James Simmes | 27 May '78 | |
| 12 do | Peter Hardcastle | 14 Sept do | |
| 16 do | Benjm. Garnett | 13 Oct do | |
| 19 do | Wm. Truman Stoddert | 21 May '79 | |
| 29 do | Levache de Vaubrunne | | |
| 33 do | Nathan Smith | 15 Dec '79 | |
| 38 do | Edmd. Compton | 18 Feb '80 | |
| 43 do | Joshua Rutledge | 1 May '80 | |
| 48 do | John Brevett | 20 Sept do | |
| 52 do | John McCoy | 1 Jan '81 | |
| 61 do | Robert Halkerston | 25 Apl do | vice McPherson, promoted into 2nd Regt. |
| 63 do | Henry Gassaway | 12 May do | vice Hall, resigned |
| 4 Surgeon | William Kelty | | |

### 5th Regiment.

| | | | |
|---|---|---|---|
| 3 Lt. Col. Comd. | Benj. Ford | | |
| 6 Major | John Davidson | 1 Jan '81 | |
| 8 do | Benj. Brookes | 16 Mch do | vice Anderson, killed |
| 3 Capt. | Wm. Dent Beall | 1 Jan '77 | |
| 8 do | John Smith, (3rd) | do do | |
| 12 do | Edwd. Oldham | 20 May do | |
| 17 do | Horatio Clagett | 10 Oct do | |
| 22 do | John Gale | 10 Dec do | |

| RANK. | NAMES. | WHEN COMMISSIONED. | PROMOTIONS SINCE JANY. 1ST, '81. |
|---|---|---|---|
| 27 Capt. | Perry Benson | 11 Mch '78 | |
| 31 do | James Somervill | 1 June '79 | |
| 36 do | William Bruce | 1 Aug do | |
| 41 do | Edward Edgerly | 10 Sept '80 | |
| 4 Lieut. | James Bruff | 7 Oct '77 | |
| 13 do | Gassaway Watkins | 14 Sept '78 | |
| 17 do | Jacob Norris | 26 Nov do | |
| 21 do | John Lynn | 1 June '79 | |
| 25 do | Saml. Hanson | 1 Aug do | |
| 30 do | Thomas Rowse | | |
| 34 do | Robert Denny | 3 Jan '80 | |
| 39 do | Benj. Fickle | 19 Feb do | |
| 44 do | Roger Nelson | 15 July do | |
| 49 do | Thomas Boyd | 1 Jan '81 | |
| 53 do | John Sears | do do | |
| 62 do | Henry Clements | 25 Apl do | vice McAllister, resigned |
| 64 do | Adam Jamison | 1 June do | do Hugou, promoted into 1st Regt. |

### RECRUITS FROM PRINCE GEORGE'S COUNTY, JULY 13th, 1781.

| NAMES OF RECRUITS. | COUNTRY. | AGE. | WHEN ENLISTED. | TIME OF SERVICE. | REMARKS. |
|---|---|---|---|---|---|
| Terence Duffe | Ireland | 40 | Feb 23 | 3 years | Pennsylvania, sent to Annapolis |
| Chas. Hickie | ditto | 44 | 23 | ditto | ditto    ditto |
| Thos. Hammond | Native | 16 | Apl 28 | ditto | ditto |
| Allen Burrell | England | 38 | May 25 | ditto | ditto |
| Aquilla Clements | Native | 16 | 14 | ditto | ditto |
| James Lyles | ditto | 18 | | during war | At Annapolis as per Certificate from Col. Adams |
| Richard Jones | England | 24 | May 9 | 3 years | |
| Robert Robinson | Native | 36 | 19 | ditto | Sent to Annapolis |
| John Jones | England | 27 | 21 | ditto | ditto |
| Wm. McPherson | Native | 16 | 23 | ditto | ditto |
| James Clements | ditto | 21 | 25 | ditto | ditto |
| Wm. Marlow | ditto | 16 | 25 | during war | ditto |
| Alexander Steel | ditto | 18 | 26 | 3 years | ditto |
| James Jackson | ditto | 21 | 28 | ditto | ditto |
| Philip Grahame | ditto | 32 | 28 | ditto | ditto |

| NAMES OF RECRUITS. | COUNTRY. | AGE. | WHEN ENLISTED. | | TIME OF SERVICE. | REMARKS. |
|---|---|---|---|---|---|---|
| James Kelly | Native | 28 | May 29 | | 3 years | Deserted |
| Wm. Harrison | ditto | 44 | | 30 | ditto | Sent to Annapolis |
| Thomas Felton | England | 39 | June | 4 | ditto | Maryland, sent to Annapolis on furlough |
| Walter Bean Small-wood | Native | 18 | | 5 | ditto | Sent to Annapolis on furlough |
| John Merry | ditto | 23 | May 28 | | ditto | Sent to Annapolis |
| John Connely | ditto | 18 | June | 5 | ditto | ditto   on furlough |
| John Hickson | ditto | 16 | | 5 | ditto | ditto   "    " |
| John Keitch | ditto | 44 | | 5 | ditto | ditto   "    " |
| John Smith | ditto | 16 | | 18 | ditto | |
| John Anderson | Scotland | 44 | | 9 | ditto | |
| Willm. Allbright | German | 33 | | 12 | during war | |

## DRAFTS FROM THE CLASSES FOR FILLING UP THE QUOTA OF MEN FROM PRINCE GEORGE'S COUNTY.

### PERSONS DRAFTED.

William Hardacre
William Fraser
James Card
John Ryon, of Joseph
Thos. Mobberly
Edward Atchinson
Thomas Swain
John Ranter
William Walker
John Mitchell
Thomas Sadler
Saml. Hutchinson

Joseph Mockbee
Josias Beanes
Thomas Wood
Mathew Clubb
Isaac Jones
William Clarkson
Nicholas Lowe
John King
James Tannihill
James Smith
Zacha. Tilley

John Letman
Saml. Evans
Thomas Whitehead
Zachariah Wilson
Negro Absolom
Daniel Brodie
William Turnor
Charles Shaw
Jacob Aldridge
Ninian Edmonson
Thomas King

### SUBSTITUTES.

Jereh. Leitch
Caleb Davis
Butler Marlow
James Wood

Thos. Keadle
John Spires
Zadock Riston

James Jones
Benj. Duvall, of Elisha
Richard Tyler

Recruits raised in Dorchester County pursuant to a late Act of Assembly for raising Two Battalions in this State.

| RECRUITS' NAMES. | DATE OF ENROLLMENT. | RECRUITS' NAMES. | DATE OF ENROLLMENT. |
|---|---|---|---|
| | | UPPER BATTALION | |
| Wm. Harrington, (absent) | 9 July '81 | Elisha Stack, (absent, not sworn) | 14 July '81 |
| Aaron Perry, (during War, absent) | 12 " | Andrew Kerven, (absent) | 18 " " |
| John Huffington, (3 years, with Capt. Gray) | " " | David Foxwell | 23 " " |
| Foster Hooper | " | Wm. Valient, (absent, adjudged) | 11 " " |
| Wm. Pritchett | " " | Elijah Lyons, (absent, adjudged) | 12 " " |
| John Willen | " " | Potter Shehee, (absent, not sworn) | " " " |
| John Stinnett | " " | George Buly, (sick, absent, not sworn, no enrollment) | |
| John Watkins | " " | David Meddiss | 12 July '81 |
| Thomas Smith | " " | Salady Standley | " " " |
| David Murray Stewart | " " | Frederick Johnson | " " " |
| Philemon Timmons | 13 " | John Dean | 13 " " |
| John Briley | 12 " | John Hambleton | " " " |
| John Greenwood | " " | John White | " " " |
| James Taylor | " " | Amos Griffith | " " " |
| Andrew Bramble | " " | William Covey | 16 " " |
| Joseph Rose | " " | | |
| Levin Collins | " " | | |
| Moses Morelake | " " | | |
| | | LOWER BATTALION. | |
| John Dobson | 9 July '81 | Richard Harrington, 3 yrs. | 16 July '81 |
| Robert Burress | " " " | Levin Harrington, " | " " " |
| James Driver | 10 " " | George Williams | 23 " " |
| Abel Garner | | Godfrey Sullener | 16 " " |
| Aaron Vinson | 9 " " | William Harper | 11 July '81 |
| Matthew Navey | 10 " " | Joseph Harper | " " " |
| Jacob Tucker | " " " | Richard Hayes | " " " |
| Thomas Morgan | " " " | John Willis | " " " |
| Benjamin Fletcher | " " " | William Procter | 14 " " |
| William Roberts | " " " | David Davis | " " " |
| Henry Harper | " " " | Levin Ross | 16 " " |
| Timothy Langrell | Robert Meekins | John Stevens | |
| Aaron Mitchell, (als. Newberry) | John Matkins | James Busick | |
| Absolom Goostree | David Jones | Thomas Owens | |
| | | FOR THE CORPS. | |
| Charles Sickle, (3 yrs.) | 16 July '81 | Robert Johnson | 14 July, '81 |
| Daniel Blake | 17 " " | Wm. Murphy | 16 " " |
| Levi Johnson, (absent, adjudged) | 14 " " | Joseph Insley | " " " |
| Charles Horner | 23 " " | Levin McGraw | " " " |
| Francis Insley | 14 " " | Adams Foxwell | " " " |

July 24th, '81.               John Goldsborough, Dor. Co.

A Return of Draughts and Substitutes sent from St Mary's Co. under the Act of May Session to join the Troops at Annapolis.

### SUBSTITUTES.

| | | | | | |
|---|---|---|---|---|---|
| James Adams Substituted 28 July '81 | | | Edward Harley | Substituted 1 Aug '81 | |
| John Jennings | 31 | " " | Igns. Griffin | 2 | " " |
| Joseph Kerby | 31 | " " | Walter Buckler | 5 | " " |
| Igns. Adams | 23 | " " | Barnard Pain | 31 July '81 | |
| William Kirkpartrick | 26 | " " | Moses Adams | 31 | " " |
| Thos. Curtis | 26 | " " | Peter Jarboe | 31 | " " |
| Joseph Wimsott | 27 | " " | Edwd. Hasil | 1 Aug.'81 | |
| Igns. Pain | 28 | " " | Joseph Brown | 2 | " " |
| John Madox | 28 | " " | William Pike | 2 | " " |
| Joseph Reswick | 28 | " " | John Norris | 2 | " " |
| John Dent Suit | 28 | " " | John Greenwell | 2 | " " |
| Baptis Gough | 29 | " " | Thos. Wise | 5 | " " |
| Elisha Burrowes | 30 | " " | Cuthb. Jones | 12 | " " |
| Charles Gough | 31 | " " | | | |

### DRAUGHTS.—All draughted 27 July, '81.

| | | |
|---|---|---|
| Joseph Newton | Charles Attwood | Nicholas Goldsbury |
| Henry Briscoe | Jeremiah Hazel | Igns. Brion |
| Edward Monark | Solomon Dixon | William Adams |
| Jeremiah Herbert | Henry Norris | Bennet Anderson |
| Struton Edwards | Robert Jarboe | Igns. Mattingly |
| Igns. Howard | John King | William Pratt |
| Arnold Norris | Charles Tawney | Nathaniel Kahil |
| Zacha. Newton | Charles Cole | |

Caroline County, 13th Aug., 1781.

Your Excellency & Honours:

Inclosed you have a list of our Recruits and Drafts those that are excused are marked and likewise those that have run, which I shall send forward as soon as we can Ketch them: I thought it most expedient to send these forward and not to wait for those that have deserted. There is five enlisted for three years which Compleats our Quota of the last Springs Drafts, whose inlistments I have sent forward.

I am your Excellency & Honours

Most Obedt. Humble Servt.

William Whiteley.

P. S.

If you are in want of Officers for the Drafts, there is a young man amongst them by the name of George Dawson, if you think him Capable

Shou'd be glad you would give him an Ensign's Commission. There is a man by the name of Gideon Longfellow who is a Recruit for this County and has since gone to Queen Ann's County and there entered as a Substitute for a Class, therefore beg you'll please to have him entered for this County.                                    W. W.

---

A List of Recruits and Drafts belonging to Caroline County.

RECRUITS TO THE 10TH DEC.

| | | |
|---|---|---|
| James Darnell | Thoms. Baxter | Negro Dick, (run) |
| James Williams | John Baxter | John DeRoachbroom |
| Leven Minner | William Wales | Aaron Jester |
| Charles Cornish | Charles Wheelar | Gidian Longfellow |
| William Jones | William Barcoss | |

DRAFTS TO THE 10TH DEC. NEXT.

| | | |
|---|---|---|
| Richard Browning | Thomas Clarkson, (run) | John Manning |
| Henry Harnaman | John Blades, (sick) | George Jewell, (sick) |
| Thomas Lane | William Eagle | Levy Chance, (run) |
| John Prouce | John Smith, (sick) | Wm. Hutson, (run) |
| Daniel Conner | Rich. Smith, of Ralph,(run) | Nathan Smith, (run) |
| Ansell Vallient | Thos. Matthews, (run) | George Dawson |
| Thomas Jackson, (run) | Garey Leverton | Roger Connelly |
| John Brown | Barth. Jadwin, (sick) | Nathan Batchelor, (run) |
| Hooper Hutson | John Hutson | Allemby Millington, (run) |
| John Fowler | Henry Emmerton | Robert Hobbs, (run) |
| Walter Edgell | | |

A LIST OF THE RECRUITS FOR THREE YEARS.

| | | | |
|---|---|---|---|
| George Carney | Solomon Sulivane | Robert Blood | Cornish Friend |
| | Thomas Crompton | | |

Wm. Whiteley,
14th August, 1781.

---

Chester Town, Kent County, Aug. 23rd, 1781.

Sir :

I have lately received several Letters from you, two of which relate to the forwarding the recruits to Annapolis, those raised in consequence of the Law passed last October, have been long since at Annapolis, & that part of the Law empowering the Lieutenants to excuse any indigent person drafted, who has a wife & children, we have nothing to do with, having hired recruits for three years. Your appointment as purchaser of cloathing I have received with an enclosed Law to seize all articles suitable for that purpose. The dificulty of purchasing without anything to purchase with, must be very apparent to your Excellency & to seize those articles from merchants, who have very few goods, and nothing else to depend on, will prove their ruin ; yet I am fully convinced of the necessity of supplying the Soldiery with cloathing; & was it in my power to forward this business with any degree of propriety, I would undertake it, notwithstanding I am of opinion that Lieutenants of Counties are very improper persons to execute Laws of this Nature. Should you think it necessary to have seized, the few goods in our Town, you will please to appoint some other person for that purpose, as I am already fully employed. I have enclosed a list of the recruits obtained by virtue of the Law passed last Session, & have engaged Capt. Kemp to carry them to Annapolis in his Vessel from our Town, the drafted men are endeavouring to procure substitutes which I will send with all possible dispatch, those who do not get recruits may be very dificult to collect, a few of them are poor men with Families. The 27th battalion have furnished their proportion of select militia, the 13th battalion is Classed for the purpose of Drafting. Mr. George Hanson who was appointed collector of horses refused to Act, he being Lieut. in the troop of Light Horse, had not time to execute the Law. On his refusal, I appointed Capt. George Hartshorn who has been very unsuccessful, he has brought for examination about six horses, & tells me that the nonjurors have not horses fit for the purpose. I have done all in my power to spur him to execute the Law with dispatch & have requested him to call on the commissioners for their direction. I am apprehensive that I shall not be able to send all the recruits agreeable to my list, some of them being in the Country without permission.

I am Sir with respect yr.

hble. Servt.

To His Excellency                                        W. Bordley.
   Thos. Sim Lee, Esq.

---

Kent County.   A List of Recruits.   [Enlisted for 3 yrs.]

| | | |
|---|---|---|
| Charles Ogilsby | William Grant, (during | Samuel Whitehouse, (dead) |
| John Pearce | the War) | Nicholas Smith |
| William Caulk, (during | Daniel Norris | Peregrine Reed |
| the War) | John Kelly | Beal Thomas |

Samuel Binn
Hugh Pearce
Daniel Herrin
Starling Thomas
Thomas Frasier
James McDoal
John Perkins

William Paul
Nathan Basnett
William Hall
James Kelly
Henry Thomas
Simon Beck
John Lesley
William Bogue

Edward Kelly
George Jones
George Thomas
James Hininbottom
Wm. John Lessenby
James Griffith
Daniel Ashley

---

Talbot County. August 30th, 1781.

A List of Persons draughted to raise two Battalions of Militia to reinforce the American Army, to serve 'till the 10th of December, 1781.

---

William Willoby
William Harrisson, of James T. P.
Wm. Lambden
Wm. Haddaway
Wm. Higgins
Danl. Winterbottom
John Blades
Thomas Blades
John Kerby
Joseph Robinson
Richd. Spencer
Joseph Hopkins, of Benja.
John Sewell
Edward Markland
Joseph Norwood
Richard Start
Robert Robinson
Robert Hopkins

Richd. Smith
Wm. Lane
Richd. Beswick
Thomas Chapman
Francis Baker
Jonathan Cheesley
Isaac Faulkner, Jr.
Levy Faulkner
Robert Hefferson
Hynson Faulkner
James Morris
George Brown
John Morgan
John Watson, of Benona
Cloudsberry Austin
Thos. Nilghbours, of Saml.
Charles Allen
Wm. Troth, Jr.
James Tilghman

William Whittocks
Wm. Catrop
Joseph Neal
Richard Adley
James Kearse
Isaac Cox, Jr.
James Berry, Jr.
John Cooper
Bristol, (a free negro)
Wm. Brinn
James Akers
John Merrick
Thos. Hilsby, of Wm.
Saml. White
Wm. Chaplin

John Holt
John Crowder
Spindilow, (a free negro)

Chrisr. Birckhead, Lieut. T. County.

---

A List of Recruits, Vagrants and Draughts raised in Washington County under the Act for raising two Battalions of Militia, &c.

| When Enlisted. | Recruits. | When Enlisted. | Recruits. |
|---|---|---|---|
| Aug 24 | John Fisher | Aug 18 | William Newell |
| "  14 | Philip Mustersbaugh | "  " | Francis Gavin |
| "  " | Jacob Keeson | "  " | Tiller Younger |

| WHEN ENLISTED. | RECRUITS. | WHEN ENLISTED. | RECRUITS. |
|---|---|---|---|
| Aug 14 | William Mount | Aug 20 | Joseph Martin |
| " 15 | Balser Young | " 18 | Philip Nogle |
| " " | William Clifford | " 20 | Elijah Wright |
| " " | Samuel Larrymor | " " | Patrick Owens |
| " 16 | Peter Boret | " " | Basil Lakin |
| " 17 | Wm. Allen | " 21 | Peter Fry |
| " 15 | Wm. Allen, (deserted) | " 22 | George Shaver |
| " 17 | Thomas Wright | " " | Nathl. Prutzman |
| " " | Peter Cramer | " 23 | Christr. Ninor |
| " 18 | Peter Aley | " 24 | Adam Miller |
| " " | William Elkison | " " | John Bumgardner |
| " 10 | Melchor Wickart | " 18 | Joseph Hoskins |
| " 12 | Simon Liedy | " 21 | William Lewis |
| " 10 | Danl. Hoover | " 22 | Martin Bringman |
| " 14 | Michl. Leatherman | " 24 | John Long |
| " 15 | Geo. Valentine | " " | Lodowk. Smith |
| " 18 | Frederick Snyder | " 25 | Hugh McGlaughlan |
| " " | Nicholas Cline | " 27 | Wm. Haney |
| " 24 | Jacob Weaver | Sept 5 | John Russell |
| " " | Richard Higgins | " " | Samuel Wycoff, Jr. |
| " " | Andrew Barranger | " " | Andrew Rude |
| " 27 | John Beard | " " | Isaac Dobson |
| Sept 5 | William Rugles | " " | Benj. Howard, (deserted) |
| " " | John McNiel | | |
| " " | Philip Anthony | | Vagrants. |
| " " | John Flat | Aug 17 | Casper Reed |
| " " | Henry Bray | | |
| " " | Philip Ward | | Draughts. |
| " " | Cornelius Cock, (or Coch) | Aug 18 | Frederick Kinstry |
| " " | Daniel Pearce | " " | Michael Hammon |
| | Arthur Boyes, a Recruit for during the War | | |

Muster Roll of the late Capt. Beatty's Company under command of Lt. W. Lamar, in the 1st Maryland Regiment Serving in the Southern Army of the United States, made this — Day of August, '81. [For Jan., Feb., Mch., Apl., May, June and July, '81.]

| NAMES. | DATE OF ENLISTMENT. | PRESENT IN JULY. | REMARKS. |
|---|---|---|---|
| Serjeants | | | |
| Enoch McLean | | present | |
| Samuel Denney | 2 March '78 | | Dischd. 2 Mch '81 |
| Arthur McLean | 10 Feb '80 | " | |

| NAMES. | DATE OF ENLISTMENT. | PRESENT IN JULY. | REMARKS. |
|---|---|---|---|
| Serjeants | | | |
| Cuthbert Able | 1 Feb '80 | | A. F. M. Jan–July |
| Stephen Flaharty | | | In Hospital 19 June and July |
| David Love | 8 Sept '80 | | Lt. Infantry, transfd. 12 Mch |
| Benjamin Fitzgerald | Oct '79 | absent | Recruiting in Md. Jan–July |
| Samuel Filson | | " | "    "    " |
| Moses Barney | | " | "    "    " |
| Gabl. Williams | 6 Feb '80 | " | "    "    " |
| Igns. Wheeler | | " | "    "    " |
| Aquilla Cheatham | | " | "    "    " |
| Samuel Davis | | " | "    "    " |
| Ch. McNabb | | " | "    "    " |
| Owen Carey | 1 Feb '80 | | Light Infantry, dead Mch '81 |
| John Scott | 9 July '80 | present | State Regt., joined 12 Mch '81 |
| Corpls. | | | |
| Wm. Bruff | | | |
| Peter Stephans | | | On guard. |
| James Kelley | | | Light Infantry, transferred 12 Mch '81 |
| John Falling | | " | State Regt., joined 12 Mch '81 |
| Drum. & Fifes | | | |
| John Riggs | 6 May '80 | | Light Infantry, transferred |
| Jesse Barnett, (or Barrett) | | " | [12 Mch '81 |
| Abram Stallings | | " | |
| Saml. Taylor | | | Dead, June '81 |
| Edward Clancey | | " | |
| Joshua Ishome | | absent | Recruiting in Md. Jan–July |
| Michael Carey | | " | ditto        ditto |
| Thos. Wingate | 26 Oct '80 | | P. War, 25 April |
| Privates | | | |
| Zadock Whaley | | present | On guard |
| Peter Outhouse | | " | |
| Michl. Curtis | | " | |
| Alexander Ross | | " | |
| Jos. Mattingly | | " | On guard |
| Jon. Hadan | | " | |
| Robt. Dunkin | | " | |
| Chas. Simpkins | | " | Sick, July |
| John Loveday | | " | |
| Richd. Taylor | | " | On guard |
| Danl. Smith | | " | |
| Jon. Maxfield | | " | |
| Igns. Cumpton | | " | Sick, July |
| George Devit | | " | Sick, July |
| Thos. Peacock | | " | |

| NAMES | DATE OF ENLISTMENT. | PRESENT IN JULY. | REMARKS. |
|---|---|---|---|
| Privates | | | |
| Absolum Fardo | | present | |
| Leonard Hagan | 1 Jany '80 | " | |
| Elijah Pepper | | " | On guard |
| Wm. Hurly | | " | |
| Luke Simpson | | " | |
| Stephen Carr | | " | |
| Jacob Hunt | | " | |
| Walter Hagan | 1 Feby '80 | " | |
| Wm. Leakin | | " | |
| George Buck | | " | |
| Christian Myers | | " | |
| John Twiner | | " | |
| William Young | | " | |
| Wm. Quinton | | " | On guard |
| Wm. Hamston | 31 Jany '80 | " | On guard |
| Saml. Clark | | " | |
| James Managa | | " | Deserted Jan, returned to Service 14 May |
| Lawre. Hurdle | | | Genl. Smallwood, July |
| Henery Reese | | | Waiter Major Roxburgh, July |
| Wm. Crail | | | Waiter Capt. Mason, July |
| Jacob Carnant | | | Lt. Infantry Jan, transfd. 12 Mch |
| John Ashmore | | do | do |
| James White | | do | do |
| Humphry Beckett | | do | do |
| Michl. Waltman | | do | do |
| Neal Peacock | | do | do |
| John More | | do | do |
| John W. Loclen | | do | dead March |
| Chas. Ormes | | do | transfd. 12 Mch |
| Bazel Norman | | do | transfd. 12 Mch |
| Wm. Mann | | | Waiter to Capt. Anderson Deserted Feb, returned to Service 17 May. In Hospl. 19 June and July |
| Fredk. Harty | | | Lt. Infantry Jan, transfd. 12 Mch |
| Saml. Garcy | 27 Apl '78 | do | do |
| John O'Bryan | | do | dead 25 April |
| Josiah Burgess | 19 Apl '78 | do | transfd. 12 Mch |
| Simon Colbert | | do | deserted Feb |
| James McDonnel | | present | Waggoner Jan–July |
| Cornelius Morris | | " | do    July |
| John Mills | | " | do    Jan–July |
| James Smith | | " | do    July |
| Partrick Riley | | " | do    do |

| NAMES. | DATE OF ENLISTMENT. | PRESENT IN JULY. | REMARKS. |
|---|---|---|---|
| Privates | | | |
| Willm. Niblet | | present Waggoner July | |
| Dorest Felmot | 5th May '78 | do | Dischd. 5 May |
| Moses Foster | | B. Smith, July | |
| Richard Gee | | Orderly Hosptl. July | |
| Daniel Hall | | ditto    ditto | |
| Joshua Lester | | ditto    ditto | |
| Barney Munrow | | Hosptl. 16 June and July | |
| Andrew Mallen | | do    15 March and July | |
| Cuthbert Stone | | Lt. Infantry.  Hosptl. July | |
| Wm. Kindle | 25 Apl '78 | Discharged 25 April | |
| Nichls. Fitzjarold | 2 May '78 | Lt. Infantry, dischd. 2 May | |
| Joseph Gordan | 1  do '78 | do    do    1  do | |
| Soloman Turner | 12 do '78 | do    transfd. 12 March | |
| John King | 25 Apl '78 | do    do    do | |
| Nichls. Hearty | 24 do '78 | Discharged 24 April | |
| Willm. Townsend | | do    May | |
| Aquilla Smith | 2 June | do    2 June | |
| Adam Crow | 28 Apl '78 | Discharged 28 April | |
| Thomas Hay | 25 do '78 | do    25  do | |
| Joshua Brown | 23 do '78 | do    23  do | |
| John McNalley | | P. War, 25 April | |
| James Current | | do    do | |
| John M. Funner | | do    do | |
| Willm. Prangley | | do    do | |
| Willm. Comming | | do    do | |
| John Webb | | do    Feby | |
| James Dowlen | | do    25 April | |
| Richd. Boon | | Killed 15 March | |
| John Cockran | | do    do | |
| Geo. Phillips | | Dead March | |
| Andrew More | | Killed 15 March | |
| John Meeks | | do    do | |
| Francis Kitely | | do    25 April | |
| Willm. Wedge | | Dead March | |
| Michael Penn | | Deserted April | |
| Thos. Christopher | | do    March | |
| John Jones | | do    15  do | |
| James Brooke | | do    January | |
| Thos. Keeff | | do    15 March | |
| Willm. Mode | | do    February | |
| Daniel Barnet | | do    January | |
| James Clemonts | | do    22 June | |
| William Taylor | | do | |
| Daniel Benning | | do    January | |

| NAMES. | DATE OF ENLISTMENT. | PRESENT IN JULY. | REMARKS. |
|---|---|---|---|
| Privates | | | |
| Philip Sulivan | | Orderly in Hosptl. July | |
| William Casey | | In Hospital July | |
| Francis Reynolds | | do do | |
| Joseph Botts | | do do | |
| —ar'y. Fitzjarold | | do do | |
| Jon. Blair | | do | Wounded March |
| David McVey | | present | |
| Willm. Hellman | | " | |

I do swear that the within Muster Roll is a true State of the Company under my Command. W. Lamar, Lt.

The following members of the 3rd, 4th and 5th Maryland Regiments received from Robert Denny, in Bills of Credit and in Specie, pay due them for the present Campaign. 3rd Regt., Augt. 28th, 1781.

### 1ST COMPANY, 3RD REGIMENT.

**Serjts.**
George Fields
Jno. Coolin
Jesse Suite
Robt. Scrivener
Chas. Jones

**Corpls.**
Peter Byall
Jos. Phearson
Joel Baker
Theo. Lindsay
Jona. Foster

**Drummers**
Wm. Stewart
Wm. Smith
Moses McKinsey
Joshua McKinsey

**Privates**
Benj. Smith
Jno. Holder
Jno. Hullett
Wm. Jefferies

**Privates**
Jno. Connolly
Elijah Neall
Jno. Jones
James West
Nath. Hawthorn
Jno. Newton, Sr.
Jno. Newton, Jr.
John Robey
W. B. Smallwood
Aqa. Clements
James Nott
Mattw. Kelly
Jno. Fullford
Wm. Newbury
Jno. Overman
Saml. Smith
John Brown
Patk. Mallone
Thos. Archer
Robt. Hornsbury
Jno. Beaumont
Basset McCleary
Richd. Hayes
Jno. Welsh

**Privates**
James Lowry
Andw. Lord
Handy Handley
James Russell
James Evans
Thos. Larramore
Henry Wilstock, (or Witstock)
Jesse McKinsey
Alex. Cockburn
Luke Merryman
Richd. Haslip
Francis Purcell
Jos. Austin
George Bough
Thos. Sheridan
Jos. Crouch
Patt. McKinsey
Levy Moody
Jacob Doyne
Christr. Smith
Robt. Robertson
Wm. Harrison
Matthias Sipher

Privates
Garrett Welsh
Jas. Erwin
Tim. Cahill
Jesse Powers
Jno. Armstrong

Privates
Jas. Kirk
Jno. Wilson
Solomon Askins
Thos. Gordon
Richd. Dixon

Privates
Elijah Oakley
James Capell, (or Caple)
Ewill Evans
James Sappington
Edward Wade

## 2ND COMPANY, 3RD REGIMENT.

Q. M. S.
William Forman

Serjts.
John H. Dorsey
Jno. Reeder
Jno. Lynch

Corpls.
William Lytle
Wm. Chatlin

Drummers
Jos. Follet
Jas. Collard
Thos. Atkinson
Aaron Perry

Privates
Peter Quidowney, (Equi-
  doroney)
Silas Frost
Jno. McLane
Peter French
Jno. Bowdy
Stephen Kimble
Wm. Bowden

Privates
Levin Thomas
Francis Reed
Wm. Simmonds
Saml. Chapple
Jno. Gorman
Charles Lego
Jno. McCall
Danl. McFetteridge
Oliver Denny
James Waddell
Richard Todd
Abraham Shockey
David Hatton
Andrew Flood
Matthias Dytch
Jery Fitzgerald
James Hayes
William Roe
Barney Dougherty
James Lynch
James Chard
James Hall
Teagle Tigner
James Tigner
Saml. Hurst
Robert Jones

Privates
Edwd. Tanner
James Cromwell
Archd. Kersey
Jas. Anderson
Neal McCowan
Feolix Snyder
James Crayton
Edward Evans
Andrew Travis
Lewis White
Michl. Pilkington
Wm. Broughton
John Kildare
Philip McDonald
John McDonald
Jno. Young
Francis Matthews
John Hudson
James Hudson
Richard Miles
John Hicken
Jos. McLane
Patrick Fleming
John Graham
John Boady

## 3RD COMPANY, 3RD REGIMENT.

Serjts.
Terrence Duffey
James Jackson
Saml. Filson, (Philson)
Bennett Mudd
Archd. Johnson

Corpls.
Thos. Polehouse
James Ashley

Privates
Jno. Deakins
Thos. Pinfold
Jno. Spyers
Timothy Lynch
Jno. Nicholson
Henry Evitt
Michl. Smith
Arthur Coffin
Willm. Mason

Privates
Jesse Furrow
Clement Harwood
Henry Lane
Elijah Hutt
George Diz
Leonard Holt
Richard Lane
Henry Reese
Jno. Shockles

26

Corpls.

Lazarus Higgs
Geo. Hamilton
Wm. Browning
Danl. Birmingham
Saml. Evans

Drummers

Jno. Jordan
Isaac Hill
Isaac Young
Richd. Jamison
Jno. Jones.
Michl. Smith

Privates

George Credo
Charles Hickey

Privates

Danl. Buckley
Jno. Durant
Francis Rogers
William Potter
Michael Downs
Richard Spyers
Benjamin Smith
Benjamin Gaither
Michael Madden
Jno. Anderson
Alex. Hughes
James Due
Philip Savoy
Francis Carnes
Stephen Fennell
John Hughes
Saml. Hussey

Privates

Jno. Turner
Thomas James
Thomas Berry
Charles Cooper
Charles Williams
Wm. Moorecraft
John Campbell
John Powell
James Jackson
Thomas Pattison
Saml. Harrison
Willm. Hamilton
John Haynes
Jacob Flowers
Francis McCann
John Thompson
Willm. Hancock

## 4TH COMPANY, 3RD REGIMENT.

Serjts.

Willm. Collis
Jno. Walker
Jno. Carson
Francis Duffey
Jacob Keyser

Corpls.

Jacob Knight
James Clements
Jno. Davis

Drummers

Edwd. Armstrong
Jno. Roach
Archd. Butt
Thos. Hutchcraft
Jno. McKay

Privates

Wm. Chapman
Jno. Wade
Jno. Blades
Dennis Downes
William Glory
Michael Doring
Thomas Jones
Thomas Woodland

Privates

Thomas Arthurs
John Malady
Benjamin Baulk
Zach. Robertson
Saml. Gray
Thomas Potts
Philip Graham
Thomas Hammond
William Turner
Jno. Smith
Jno. Davies Tulley
Jno. Ryon
Thomas Porter
Samuel Boswell
Patrick Reading
James Crisbury
Peter Richards
Allen Townsend
Wm. Marlow
Lucas Ives
William Newton
Alex. Steele
Jno. Hicks
Jos. Turner
Momus Leary
Wm. Whitmore

Privates

Jno. Johnson
Henry Tarman
Joseph Isaacs
Henry Frazier
James Steward
Wm. McPherson
James Lyles
Jno. Stonehunt
Abm. Manning
Roger Landers
Thos. B. Allum
George Linton
James Jones
Willm. Preator
Saml. Silk
Thos. Hickenbottom
Wm. Maddux
Wm. Stanley
Francis McGurrow
Dennis Disman
William Berry
Peter Carbury
Robt. Campbell
Edward Walter
George Campbell
Thomas Neall

## 5TH COMPANY, 3RD REGIMENT.

**Serjts.**

Saml. Shoemaker
Nichls. Nicholson
John Brady
James Brown

**Corpls.**

Jno. Moore
Jno. Clancey
Ralph Hagen
Charles Fullam

**Drummers**

Jno. Hannon
Jno. Morrison
Henry Ferns
Jno. Onions

**Privates**

Benj. Marsh
Charles Dean
Jno. Willin
William Wilson
Abraham Kettle
George Silver
Henry Fisher, Sr.
Adam Mushler
Jacob Caufman
Danl. Williams
Peter Coons

**Privates**

George Fleck
Jno. Eppinstall, (Eppin-
    stoole)
Jno. Flowers
Wm. Artman
Jos. Lewis
William Goodey
Henry Fisher, Jr.
Michl. Ritmire
Jno. Fennell
Jno. Holdson
Nichs. Hyner
Jno. Welty
Richard Jones
William Clover
Corns. Vaughan
William Craill
William Rider
Jos. Cox
Samuel Young
Nathl. Aldridge
Jno. McGlenn
Willm. Wheland
Thomas Tanner
John Follet
John Merry
Jos. Ferroll
Robert Eaton
Danl. Mann

**Privates**

James Wilson
Jno. Stoffell
Fredk. Stoffell
Jacob Detrow
Willm. Dawson
Lambert Goodey
James Hales
Dennis Creagon
Robert Folger
James Terry
Thomas Cullumber
Frederick Hioms
Henry Lynn
Robert Anderson
Charles Willett
John Gee
Jno. Wright
James Fisher
Jno. Flanagan
William Dytch
Jno. Curll
Andrew Rearside
Jno. Winslow
John Thompson
Dennis Tramell
William Taylor
John Fransey
Edward Mahawney, (Maho-
    ney

## 6TH COMPANY, 3RD REGIMENT.

**Serjts.**

George Holton
George Finlay
James Wood
Benjamin Ward

**Corpls.**

William Elburn
William Doncan
James Wilson
Isaac Henderson

**Drummers**

Henry Harris
Daniel Willis

**Drummers**

Thomas Clinton
William Copeland
James Bryan

**Privates**

William Aggis
Henry Emmes
William Harrison
Edward Scantlum
Levin Abott
Luke Osborne
William Taylor
Jacob Jefferies
Edward Bartlet

**Privates**

William Gudgeon
Smith Bragwell
James Chambers
Bennet George
Thomas Harris
Jno. Harris
Shadrach Sapp
Peter Hollowburn
Patrick Sullivan, (belong-
    ing to the Eastern
    Troops)
Peter Surkey, (belonging
    to the Eastern Troops)
James Sheppard
Jno. Burke

Privates
Richard Green
John Steward
John Cole
Philip McGlaskey
Jno. Smallwood
Jno. Anderson
Stephen Hancock
James Smith
David Wilton
Peter Cinquiad, (Cincuid, Kincade)

Privates
Thomas Johns
Abraham Reynolds
Jno. Starkey
Banks Webb
Isaac Davis
James Brannon
Absalom Scott
William Lyons
James Reynolds

Privates
Jno. Collins
Jacob Collins
Lawrence Simpson
Robert Carnes
Henry Burns
Notley Whitcomb
Edward Chambers
George Belfast

### 7TH COMPANY, 3RD REGIMENT.

Serjts.
John Newman
Wm. Needham
Jno. Neary
Wm. Martin
James Collins
Alex. Mackey

Corpls.
Jno. Biggs
Wm. Clements
Jno. Matthews

Drummers
Jno. McCauliff
Nichs. Elliott
Henry Burns
Philip Huston

Privates
Daniel Doncan
Jno. Harris, Sr.
Jas. Cockrall
James Evans
Jno. Thomas
William Brady
Thomas Wood
William Coe

Aquilla Deaver
John Milstead
John Young
Paul Richards
Thos. Bailey
Wm. Lynch
Benj. Gray, Serjt.
John Noble
Joseph Fowler

Privates
Joseph White
Richard Price
Thomas Adams
Kindall Cobb
Matthew Stainton
Richard Dalvin, (Delvin)
Richard Dimby
Jno. Pinder
Henry Williams
James Powell
Jos. McNamara
Andrew Haufman
Edwd. Appleton
Joshua Atkins
Jno. King
Emanuel Ebbs
John Walker
James Blancher
James Humphreys
Jno. Willis
William Porter
Jno. Lesley
James Needs
Solomon Green
James Scott
Thomas Clarke

Stafford Foysdoyle, (Foysdale)
Wm. Cutler
John Smith
Alex. Robertson
Benj. Williams
Charles McNabb, Serjt.
Richd. Fenwick,    "

Privates
John Collins
Nathan Ross
Wm. Mansfield
Michael Mondis
Edward Edes
Richard Farraby
Prestly Brewington
Thomas Jones
John Hurley
Wm. Guantley
Oliver Stephens
William Correll
James Bailey
John Keetch
Thos. Clements
Thos. Matthews
Isaac Graves
John Ranson
Jno. McNeall
Henry Hughes
Francis Burton
James Lawrence
James Davidson
Abm. Dougan
Francis Taylor
John Brewington

John Willin,    Serjt.
Gabriel Williams,  "
Peter McNaughton, "
Aquilla Chittham,  "
B. Fitzgerald,     "
Saml. Davis,       "
William Pitts
Wm. Rose, Serj. M.

### 4TH REGT. 10 SEPT., 1781.

Thos. Duffee
John Betsey
George Leseh
Nathl. Baley
Chas. Nabb
Thomas Elliott
Luke Griffith
Robt. Mitchell
Saml. Lynch
Thos. Foxall
Edw. Fincham
Wm. Lee
John Briley
John O'Conner
John Charles
John Taylor
Aaron Mitchell
Michael Hennessy
David Meadows
Timothy Donlon
Philip Welsh
Melby Christopher
Isaac Christopher
Wm. Bacchus
Chas. Gordon
John Watkins
John Dean

Aliad Melville
Moses Morleck
Robt. Blood
Thomas Davis
John Hudson
Heithcote Edwards
Geo. Carney
Cornish Friend
Cato Snowden
Andrew Bramble
Wm. Paul
Philip Knight
John A. Mildorph
Wm. Burgis
John Cleverdence
James Darnell
Edward Henesy
John Paxman
Daniel Murphey
Adam Weatherholt
Peter Hammond
Jacob Yeast
Wm. Tillwood
Chas. Wheeler
Godfrey Sullender
Wm. Donoho
John Loaness

John Stephens
John Willin
Wm. Cork
Wm. Whiticoe
Thos. Long
John Dobson
John Nelson
Thos. Burke
Walter Pruit
George Jones
Martin Rohrer
Fredk. Meyers
John Gothard
Hanry Rorer
Thomas James
Wm. Grant
Benj. Belcher
Robt. Smith
Jesse Locker
Pompey Hollis
Wm. Absalom
Igns. Smith
James Green
James McDaniel
Humphrey Wells
Wm. Welsh

John Dove, Serjt., Aug. 28th.        Wm. Stewart, Fifer, Aug. 28th.
Wm. Smith, Drum. "        "        Thos. Clinton, "        "        "

### 5TH REGT. 13 OCT., '81.

John Riley
George Parker
Edwd. Kirk
Thos. Fleming
Patk. Quinn
Joseph Fisher
Edwd. Riley
Jacob Adams
Roderick McKenny
Nehemiah Lanham
Zacha. Berry
Richard Hoggin
Jona. Sheppard

Smart Green
Jacob Keller
Thomas Calpin
Thomas Smith
James Driver
Jeremiah Dillen
Nehemiah Lingrell
George Welsh
Wm. Harper
Fredk. Smith
John Morris
Richd. Peplow

John McBryde, Drum.
John Murrant,        "
Danl. Howe, Fifer
John Brown,        Corpl.
Elijah Cockendale, "
Robt. Firth,        "
Wm. Marlow
Dennis Carty
Basil Shaw, Serjt.
Benj. Johnson, Aug 28th
Geo. Williams, Serjt.
Robt. Mahill, (or Hukell),
        Serjt.

Annapolis, 13th October, 1781. Received of Robt. Denny the sum of one pound two shillings & sixpence by each of us subscribers, of the

Bills of Credit emitted for defraying the expences of the present Campaign, in part of pay due us.

William Cox, late 2nd Regt.
William George, late 6th Regt.
Daniel O'Neall
William Moore
Richard Blandford                          These were prisoners and received £5
Thomas Richardson, late 5th Regt.          previous to this date.
Emanuel Allen, late 5th Regt.
Joseph Blaize, late 7th Regt.
Thomas Bird
Michael Clancey, late 5th Regt.

The following received from Robt. Denny such sums as were due them, October 13th, 1781.

| | | |
|---|---|---|
| Joseph Harper | Southard George | John Parks |
| Charles Horner | Thomas Jones | Richard Clarke |
| David Foxwell | Vincent Molen | James Underhill |
| William Justice | Walter Ferroll | John Armond |
| Christian Boss | William Camm | Benjamin Reed |
| John Faucett | Daniel Harden | Charles Syckle |
| Charles Davis | Thomas McKouff,(or McBruff) | Thomas Pettit |
| William Corsey | James Creighton | James Bowen |
| James Halloran | John Gordan | John Cannon |
| Edwd. Jackson | Wm. Batten | John Cole |
| Zachariah Mills | Franciss Dewiss | Joseph Neall |
| Isaac Nichols | John Gorman | Joseph McClain |
| John McDaniel | William Smith | Joseph Crouch |
| James McDaniel | | |

The following received from Robt. Denny pay due them.

Aug 13 '81 Lowrence Hurdle, 3rd Regt.    Oct 6 '81 James French
Jan  8 '82 Henry Lynn                     Mch 5 '82 Nelce Jones, 2nd Regt.
    18  "   Wm. Kaugh                        23  "   Robt. Taylor
    18  "   Wm. Douglass

The following received from Robert Denny pay due them.

LT. CLEMONS' CO. NOV. 2ND, 1781.

| | | |
|---|---|---|
| John Connelly | Amis Griffith | John Wilson |
| John Burn | John Toole | Harris Austin |
| Christr. Lambert | Jesse King | Timothy Langrell |
| Andw. Mullane | Nathl. Price | |

| | |
|---|---|
| Lieut. Batte | from Capt. Hall's Company. |
| Ensign Inglehart | from Capt. Sanders. |
| John Knighton | |
| Stephen Beard | |
| Richard Jones | |
| Jnothan Weeden | |
| William Onion | from Capt. Sanders. |
| Austin Atwell | |
| John Taymon | |
| Jeremiah Wells | |
| William Davis | |
| Aquila Linthicum | |
| Sabrit Journey | from Capt. Mulliken. |
| Cephas Benson | |
| John Elliott | |
| James Elliott | |
| Walter Dent | |
| Israel Pearce | from Capt. Watkins. |
| —— Sweney | |
| Richard Butler | from Capt. Hall. |
| Notley Sweeney | |

The Above list is handed to the Accotnt. by Major Higgins as of the Men for whom Dinner was furnished by M. Smith in April. They were draughts from Major Higgin's Battalion in Service of U. States.

---

Harford County, 11th December, 1781.

Sir :

Agreeable to Directions from the Lieut. Enclosed I transmit your Excellency, A Return of Recruits, Draughts &c, Agreeable to an Act Entitled an Act to procure Recruits, Also a Return of Substitutes & Draughts, Agreeable to an Act Entitled an Act to Raise Two Battalions of Militia—I should also have sent your Excellency an Account of the Balance due the State of the four Shilling Tax, but there is not yet as much Collected as has been paid to Recruits—and the Lieut. has thought it unnecessary to grant more Executions, as the Sheriff has not settled for, nor paid, what has been Already Granted, tho a long time in his hands. I am your Excellency's very Humble Servant

A. Crawford, Secy. L. H. County.

To his Excellency Thos. Sim Lee, Esq.

---

Return of Recruits, Substitutes & Draughts, raised in Harford County for the Two Battalions of Militia, Agreeable to an Act of Assembly in the Year 1781.

| NAMES OF SUBSTITUTES. | NAMES OF SUBSTITUTES. | NAMES OF SUBSTITUTES. |
|---|---|---|
| John Gordon | William Butler | Alex. Christie |
| Nathan Strong | James Keys | Thos. Monahon |
| John Usher | Wm. Truss | John Miles |
| John Morris | James Bond | Anguis McCreary |
| John Curl | George Todd | James Condren |
| Saml. Hodgkins | Peter Ratagan | Wm. Payne |
| Barachius Coop | John Sullivan | John Willard |
| William Bently | Samuel Scarborough, deserted | Thos. Ask |
| Edward Fincham | William Smith | James Silk |
| William Wright | Jeremiah Williamson | John Norris |
| Griffith Evans | John Shields | Robert Mitchell |

NAMES OF DRAUGHTS.                                        REMARKS.

| | |
|---|---|
| William Condron | |
| George O'Keil | |
| Horatio Coop | |
| Nathan Price | |
| John Offield | |
| John Dearmott | taken ill with the Flux          [Children |
| Aaron Grace | dischd., being poor & having a Wife & 5 |
| David Deaver | id    same having Wife & 7 Children |
| Negroe Tower | id    same having Wife & Children |
| Nathan Gallion | Infirm and Sickly |
| Edward Prigg | id |
| Richd. Greenland | id |
| Richard Kenly | id |
| Jona. West | poor, a Wife & Children to support |
| Joseph Johnson | id |
| Thos. Rhoads | id |
| Wm. Grafton | id |
| Nathan Johns | a Quaker & id but did not appear |
| Richd. Johns | id    son to the above |
| Isaac Henry | id    did not appear |
| Robt. Jones | never taken up |
| Nathan Brownly | id |
| Henry Russ | id |
| James McGaw | id |
| John McGaw | id |
| Wm. Major | id |
| James Bevard | id |
| Joseph Aikens | id |
| Henry Harrod | id |
| Thos. Ely | Quaker id |
| Wm. Judd | kept out of the way |
| Michael Rook | run |
| James Andrews | id |
| Wm. Gash | id |

A. Crawford, Secy. L. H. County.    11 Dec., 1781.

Return of Recruits, Substitutes and Draughts, raised in Harford County, Agreeable to an Act Entitled, An Act to procure Recruits, in the Year 1781.

| NAMES OF SUBSTITUTES. | TERM OF ENLISTMENT. | NAMES OF SUBSTITUTES. | TERM OF ENLISTMENT. |
|---|---|---|---|
| Oliver Denny | three years | John Overman | three years |
| Edward Appleton | "　　" | John Hutson | "　　" |
| John Oldham White | a very great imposter | Lawrence Hines | "　　" |
|  |  | William Newberry | "　　" |
| George Gardners | three years | John McCall | "　　" |
| John Pendall | "　　" | John Ranson | "　　" |
| John McClain | "　　" | Evan Thomas | "　　" |
| John Fulfit | "　　" | Patrick Mullen | "　　" |
| Thos. Sheredin | "　　" | James Hutson | "　　" |
| John Finnch | "　　" | James Cromwell | to the 10th Dec. |
| Philip McDonald | "　　" | Robert Jones | "　　　" |
| Neal McOwen | "　　" | John H. Dorsey | "　　　" |
| Wm. Coe | "　　" | Peter Wedoney | "　　　" |
| James Caple | "　　" | John O'Neal | "　　　" |
| Peter French | "　　" | John Thompson | "　　　" |
| John Willson | "　　" |  |  |

| DRAUGHTS. | TERM OF ENLISTMENT. | DRAUGHTS. | TERM OF ENLISTMENT. |
|---|---|---|---|
| James McNabb | to the 10th Dec. | Wm. Carlen | lame and unfit for duty |
| Benj. Culver | dischd. by Gov. & Council | Daniel Davey | not to be found |
| Wm. Cantlin | lame and unfit for duty | Danl. Douglas | not to be taken |
|  |  | Saml. McComas | run away |

A. Crawford, Secy. L. H. County.

11 Dec., 1781.

Dates and Terms of Enlistments of men inlisted in the 4th and 5th Regts. in 1781.

| NAMES. | WHEN ENLISTED. | REGIMENT. | TERM. | BY WHOM ENLISTED. |
|---|---|---|---|---|
| John Briley | July 29 '81 | Md. Line | War | Captain Lynn |
| Benj. Belcher | Aug 7 | 4th Regt. | do | do |
| John Betsworth | 11 | Md. Line | 3 years | do |
| Thos. Burke | 12 | 4th Regt. | do | do |
| Nathl. Bailey | 12 | do | do | do |
| Thos. Berry | 14 | do | do | do |
| Andrew Bramble | 17 | Md. Line | do | do |

| Names. | When Enlisted. | Regiment. | Term. | By Whom Enlisted. |
|---|---|---|---|---|
| John Baxter | Aug 23 | Md. Line | 3 years | Captain Lynn |
| Christian Boss | 28 | 5th Regt. | War | Lt. Sears |
| John Balor | Sept 1 | do | 3 years | do |
| Wm. Covey | Aug 3 | 4th Regt. | do | Lt. Crawford |
| Richd. Clarke | 11 | do | War | Capt. Lynn |
| John O'Connor | 17 | Md. Line | do | do |
| John Curll | 18 | do | 3 years | do |
| Thos. Calpin | 24 | do | do | do |
| John Cleverdence | 28 | do | do | do |
| Milbey Christopher | 29 | do | do | do |
| Isaac Christopher | 29 | do | do | do |
| John Callahan | Sept 1 | do | do | do |
| William Courcey | Oct 3 | 5th Regt. | do | Lt. Sears |
| John Cannon | Sept 1 | do | do | do |
| Arthur Coffin | May 5 | 3d Regt. | War | Capt. Trueman |
| Alex. Cockburne | 2 | do | 3 years | Col. Brice, Lt. A. A. Co. |
| John Deane | July 29 | Md. Line | War | Capt. Lynn |
| John Dobson | Aug 2 | 4th Regt. | do | do |
| James Driver | 4 | do | do | do |
| Thos. Duffee | 7 | Md. Line | 3 years | do |
| Timothy Donlan | 17 | do | do | do |
| Thos. Davis | 18 | 4th Regt. | do | do |
| Geo. Dawson | 21 | Md. Line | do | do |
| Jeremiah Dillon | Sept 10 | 5th Regt. | do | Lt. Sears |
| Walter Evans | Aug 15 | Md. Line | do | Capt. Lynn |
| Hethesale, (Hethcoat), Edwards | 25 | do | do | do |
| Jacob Flowers | 11 | do | do | do |
| Thomas Foxall | 14 | 3d Regt. | do | do |
| Edward Fincham | 15 | Md. Line | do | do |
| John Frazier | 31 | do | do | do |
| John Fawcitt,(Fosset) | Sept 1 | do | do | do |
| John Frederick | 11 | do | do | do |
| David Foxwell | 6 | do | do | do |
| Benj. Foard | 9 | 5th Regt. | do | Lt. Sears |
| Walter Ferroll | 12 | do | do | do |
| Wm. Frazier | 10 | do | do | do |
| John Gothard | Aug 6 | 4th Regt. | War | Capt. Lynn |
| Luke Griffith, (or Griffen) | 9 | Md. Line | do | do |
| Amos, (or Moses), Griffith | 26 | do | 3 years | do |
| Francis Gavon | Sept 11 | 5th Regt. | do | Lt. Sears |
| John Huffington | July 12 | Md. Line | do or War | Lt. Dorchester County |
| Richd. Herrington | 16 | do | 3 years | do |

| NAMES. | WHEN ENLISTED. | | REGIMENT. | TERM. | BY WHOM ENLISTED. |
|---|---|---|---|---|---|
| Levin Herrington | July | 16 | Md. Line | 3 years | Lt. Dorchester County |
| Edwd. Hennessy | | 29 | 4th Regt. | War | Capt. Lynn |
| Michael Hennessy | Aug | 8 | do | do | do |
| William Hamilton | | 9 | Md. Line | 3 years | Lt. Crawford |
| James Hayes | | 15 | do | do | Capt. Lynn |
| Pompey Hollis | | 16 | do | do | do |
| Joseph Harper | | 26 | do | do | do |
| William Harper | | 26 | do | do | do |
| Foster Hooper | | 26 | do | do | do |
| Charles Horner | Sept | 6 | do | do | do |
| James Holloren, (Halloran) | | 9 | 5th Regt. | do | Lt. Sears |
| John Jennings | Aug | 17 | Md. Line | do | Capt. Lynn |
| Edwd. Jackson | | 18 | do | do | do |
| Aaron Jester | | 22 | do | do | do |
| Wm. Justice | | 24 | do | do | do |
| Robt. Johnson | | 26 | do | do | do |
| William Jones | Sept | 14 | 5th Regt. | do | Lt. Sears |
| Philip Knight | Aug | 15 | 4th Regt. | do | Capt. Lynn |
| Thomas Kelly | Sept | 6 | Md. Line | War | do |
| Anthony Lewitz | Aug | 9 | do | 3 years | do |
| Thomas Long | | 12 | 4th Regt. | do | do |
| William Leary | | 14 | Md. Line | do | do |
| Thomas Lane | | 20 | do | do | do |
| Timothy Langrell | | 26 | do | do | do |
| David Meadows | July | 29 | do | do | do |
| Aaron Mitchell | | 29 | 4th Regt. | War | do |
| Moses Morelake, (Morleck) | | 30 | do | do | do |
| Aliad Melville | Aug | 4 | do | do | do |
| Michael McKnight | | 4 | do | 3 years | do |
| Alex. McCoy | | 8 | do | War | do |
| John Mifford, (Mofford) | | 11 | Md. Line | 3 years | do |
| Wm. Murphey | | 14 | do | do | do |
| John A. Mildorph | | 14 | do | War | do |
| Robert Mitchell | | 15 | do | 3 years | do |
| Daniel Murphey | | 16 | do | War | do |
| Martin Madden | | 21 | do | 3 years | do |
| Francis McCann | | 24 | do | do | do |
| John Morris | Sept | 1 | do | do | do |
| Hezekiah Massey | | 1 | do | do | do |
| Andrew Mullen | Dec | 10 | 5th Regt. | do | Lt. Sears |
| Vincent Molen | Sept | 10 | do | do | do |
| John McAffee | | 1 | do | do | do |

| NAMES. | WHEN ENLISTED. | | REGIMENT. | TERM. | BY WHOM ENLISTED. |
|---|---|---|---|---|---|
| Aaron Perry | July | 10 | 4th Regt. | War | Capt. Lynn |
| John Parks | Aug | 1 | do | do | do |
| Lodwick Pole | | 11 | do | do | do |
| John Paxman | | 25 | Md. Line | 3 years | do |
| Walter Prewitt, (Pruett) | | 29 | do | do | do |
| Nathan Price | | 30 | do | do | do |
| Thos. Pattison | June | 1 | 3d Regt. | War | Lt. Denny |
| Chas. Nabb | Aug | 12 | 4th Regt. | 3 years | Capt. Lynn |
| John Nelson | | 15 | do | do | do |
| John Riley | Sept | 8 | 5th Regt. | do | Lt. Sears |
| Benj. Ried, (Read) | | 6 | do | do | do |
| Charles Syckle, (Sickle) | July | 16 | Md. Line | do | Lt. Dorchester County |
| Thomas Smith | | 30 | 4th Regt. | War | Capt. Lynn |
| John Stennett | Aug | 4 | do | 3 years | do |
| William Scott | | 10 | Md. Line | do | do |
| John Sheffer, (Shiffer) | | 11 | 4th Regt. | do | do |
| Robt. Smith | | 13 | do | War | do |
| John Stephens | | 25 | Md. Line | 3 years | do |
| Godfrey Sullender | | 26 | do | do | do |
| Salady Stanley | Sept | 4 | do | do | do |
| Patrick Shields | | 25 | 5th Regt. | do | Lt. Sears |
| John Sloan | | 10 | do | do | do |
| John Taylor | Aug | 1 | 4th Regt. | War | Capt. Lynn |
| John Thompson | | 9 | do | do | do |
| Edwd. Tanner | | 13 | 3d Regt. | 3 years | do |
| Henry Tucker | | 17 | Md. Line | War | do |
| Wm. Tillwood | | 25 | do | 3 years | do |
| John Toole | Oct | 11 | 5th Regt. | War | Lt. Sears |
| James Underhill | Aug | 9 | 4th Regt. | 3 years | Capt. Lynn |
| John Watkins | | 3 | Md. Line | do | do |
| John Willin | | 4 | 4th Regt. | War | do |
| Philip Welsh | | 5 | do | 3 years | do |
| William Whitticoe, (Whittacar) | | 12 | Md. Line | do | do |
| John Winstanley | | 18 | do | do | do |
| James Williams | | 19 | do | do | do |
| Charles Wheeler | | 19 | do | do | do |
| Geo. Williams | | 27 | do | do | do |
| Humphrey Wells | | 27 | do | War | do |
| Richd. Williams | Sept | 4 | 4th Regt. | 3 years | do |

Additional Names to the above List From a Return of Men Inlisted in the Md. Line in 1781.

| NAMES. | WHEN ENLISTED. | REGT. | TERM. |
|---|---|---|---|
| Wm. Allen | 15 Aug | | Term not mentioned in |
| Peter Boughan | 1 " | | War        [Inlistment |
| Robt. Blood | 20 July | 5th | 3 yrs. |
| John Bailey | 29 " | | War |
| Peter Collins | 21 " | | 3 yrs. |
| John Campbell | 24 " | | " |
| Thos. Crampton | 14 Aug | 5th | " |
| James Collins | 2 May | | " |
| Wm. Cock | 13 July | | War |
| Wm. Dannahugh | 10 Aug | | 3 yrs. |
| Abraham Dogan | 19 July | | War |
| Thos. Dickenson | 23 " | | 3 yrs. |
| John Davis | 15 Nov | 5th | " |
| James French | 1 May | | "      Waggoner |
| Cornish Frend | 17 July | | War |
| Edward Fitcham | 15 Aug | | 3 yrs. |
| Wm. Grant | 22 " | | War |
| Vincent Gray | 11 Dec | | 3 yrs. |
| Peter Hammon | 9 Aug | | " |
| Danl. Holdman | 9 " | | " |
| Jesse Johnson | 18 July | | " |
| Geo. Karney | 18 " | 5th | " |
| Henry Korer | 9 Aug | | " |
| Martin Korer | —— | | " |
| Jesse Locker | 7 Sept | | " |
| Willm. Lee | 8 Aug | | " |
| Anthony Lewis | 9 " | 4th | " |
| John Lownas | 13 " | | " |
| Thomas Lam | 20 " | | " |
| Patrick Mellon | 12 July | | " |
| Fredk. Moyer | 8 Aug | | " |
| Alex. Montgomery | 8 " | | " |
| David Medes, (Meddis) | 29 July | | " |
| And. Mallone | 4 Sept | 5th | " |
| Henry Ritch | 18 July | | " |
| Geo. Roach | 6 Aug | | " |
| Willm. Roberts | 14 Dec | | " |
| Wm. Robertson | 14 " | | " |
| Wm. Smith | 1 Sept | | " |
| Wm. Smith | 3 Aug | | " |
| John Showman | 8 " | | " |
| Solomon Sullivant | 20 June | 5th | " |

| NAMES. | WHEN ENLISTED. | REGT. | TERM. |
|---|---|---|---|
| Lewis White | 12 Feb | 5th | War |
| Adam Weatherhold | 8 Aug | | 3 yrs. |
| Jacob Yeast | 11 " | | " |
| Aaron Jester, (or Tester) | 22 " | 4th | " |

"An Alphabetical List of discharged Soldiers of the two Battalions of Militia raised to serve in the Continental Army in the year 1781."

| COUNTY. | NAMES. | COUNTY. | NAMES. |
|---|---|---|---|
| | Adams, John | | Austin, Harris |
| St Mary's | Anderson, Bennett | St Mary's | Adams, Moses |
| | Alsey, William | St Mary's | Adams, William |
| Charles | Anderson, James | | Alsop, John |
| St Mary's | Adams, Ignatius | | Alsop, Joseph |
| | Anthony, John | | Atwell, Joseph |
| | Allender, Perry | | Alexander, John |
| | Arbor, or Auburgh, John | | Abbott, John |
| | | | |
| Charles | Brookes, Walter | | Baun, John |
| Charles | Beall, Barton | | Bussey, Samuel |
| | *Baker, George | St Mary's | Burris, Elisha |
| | *Baker, George | | Beggarly, David |
| | Beard, Frederick | Kent | Basnett, Nathaniel |
| | Bryan, Edward | Charles | Boswell, John |
| Charles | Brookes, Matthew | Charles | Butler, John |
| | Baldwin, Samuel | | Butler, Walter |
| | Bennett, Joshua | St Mary's | Brown, Joseph |
| | Beard, Richard | | Beswick, Joseph, |
| | Bridewell, Theodore | | voucher lost |
| | Beans, Joseph | | Barneclow, Charles |
| Worcester | Butler, William | | Barneclow, John |
| | Black, Aaron | Dorchester | Bramble, Andrew, |
| | Baker, Nathan | | Upper Battalion |
| Charles | Butler, Henry | Caroline | Baxter, John, voucher lost |
| St Mary's | Briscoe, Henry | | Bryan, Daniel |
| St Mary's | Bryan, Ignatius | Caroline | Baxter, Thomas |
| | Beard, Thomas | | Beaven, Thomas |
| | Burris, Robert | Dorchester | Briley, John, |
| | Benyan, Alexander | | Upper Battalion |
| | Brashears, John | Washington | Bringman, Martin |
| | Barnes, Thomas | | Bozeman, William |

* Probably different persons, as the amounts paid were not the same.

| COUNTY. | NAMES. | COUNTY. | NAMES. |
|---------|--------|---------|--------|
| St Mary's | Black, Moses | Washington | Bowen, James |
| | Burns, Timothy | | Brereton, William |
| | Bentley, William | | |
| | Chard, William | | Cheesely, James |
| | Cassady, James | | Cummings, Nathaniel |
| Washington | Cline, Nicholas | | Clash, Richard |
| Charles | Combes, William | Dorchester | Collins, Levy, or Levin, |
| Pr. George's | *Connolly, John | | Upper Battalion |
| | *Connolly, John | | Coop, Borachiah |
| | Coachman, John | Charles | Clements, Henry |
| | Curtis, Samuel | | Clements, John H. |
| | Crawford, Hugh | Charles | Clinckscales, Levy, |
| | Condon, William | | voucher lost |
| Caroline | Connor, Daniel | | Clarke, George, |
| Caroline | Connolly, Roger | | voucher lost |
| | Cheesely, Robert | | Coops, Horatio |
| Talbot | Chapman, Thomas | Charles | Clinckscales, William |
| Charles | Chunn, Launcelot | St Mary's | Curtis, Thomas |
| St Mary's | †Cole, Charles | | Canfield, Thomas |
| | †Cole, Charles | | Coves, William |
| | Croney, William | | Cregar, Michael |
| | Cruckley, Benjamin | | Carlile, Basil |
| | Carter, Edward | | Cromwell, James |
| Charles | Clements, John | | Clements, Henry |
| | Clements, Bennett | | Campbell, Allen |
| St Mary's | Dixon, Solomon | Anne Arundel | Davidson, James |
| | Dilman, John | | Deaver, Samuel |
| Charles | Davis, Jesse | | Dorsey, Henry |
| | Dunn, William | | David, Valentine |
| | Dobson, William | Charles | Davis, David |
| | Duvall, Samuel | | Dawson, Thomas |
| | Davis, Cornelius | Pr. George's | Duvall, Benjamin |
| | Duvall, Richard | Dorchester | Deane, John |
| | Deale, Henry | | Upper Battalion |
| Charles | Dunning, James | Caroline | Derochbroom, John |
| Charles | Dent, Samuel | | Dobson, Samuel |
| | Davis, Peter | | Devitt, Valentine |
| Dorchester | Dicks, John | | Duffey, Thomas |
| Dorchester | Davis, David, | | Donnelly, Patrick |
| | Lower Battalion | | Dorman, Major |
| Pr. George's | Davis, Caleb | | |
| | Eack, Adam | | Elliott, Mark |
| | Edge, Peter | Charles | Elgin, Harrison |

| COUNTY. | NAMES. | COUNTY. | NAMES. |
|---|---|---|---|
| Caroline | Emerton, Henry | Charles | Elgin, Hezekiah |
| St Mary's | Edwards, Stratton | | Everett, Elihu |
| | | | Eubanks, Thomas |
| | *Franklin, John | | Farding, Aaron |
| | *Franklin, John | | Fream, William |
| | Ford, William | Talbot | Faulkner, Isaac |
| | Frogget, Richard | Dorchester | Foxwell, Adam, |
| | Flechinger, Michael | | For the Corps |
| | Fitzgerald, John | Talbot | Foster, Nathan |
| | Fulton, James P. | | Fighter, George |
| Dorchester | Fetcher, Benjamin, | | Fitzgerald, Clement |
| | Lower Battalion | | Fickle, Isaac |
| | Fields, Charles | Kent | Frazier, Thomas |
| | †Finch, George | | Frazier, Henry |
| | †Finch, George | | Farr, Nicholas |
| | Febus, George | Talbot | Faulkner, Hynson |
| | Griffith, William | Queen Anne's | Greenage, Benjamin |
| Dorchester | Garner, Abell, | Dorchester | Goosetree, Absalom, |
| | Lower Battalion | | Lower Battalion |
| | Gearey, Samuel | | Green, Clement |
| Charles | Glasco, William | | Gentle, Stephen |
| St Mary's | Gough, Baptist | Kent | Griffith, James |
| St Mary's | Greenwell, John | | Gough, John Sparks |
| St Mary's | Gough, Charles | | Grant, Thomas |
| | Gilpin, Benjamin | | Gingle, George |
| | Gatton, Azariah | | Gillis, William |
| | Gillum, Thomas | | Gillis, Joseph |
| Dorchester | Greenwood, John, | | Grimes, Greenbury |
| | Upper Battalion | | Graham, George |
| Queen Anne's | Holland, John | Kent | Hall, William |
| | Hill, or Hall, James | Kent | Hickenbottom, James |
| | Hartshorne, Jonathan | | Henwick, or Hancock, |
| Washington | Hover, Daniel | | Elie |
| Washington | Hoskins, Joseph | | Hasley, Stephen |
| | Hecketon, Martin | | Hickman, Joshua |
| Queen Anne's | Harris, James | | Harey, or Harvey, Rich- |
| Washington | Haney, William | | ard |
| | Heck, Daniel | | Hogins, Jere |
| | Holtzman, Henry | | Hardy, Kinsey |
| | Hurd, Bennett | | Hunter, James |
| Kent | Herring, Daniel | St Mary's | Hazle, Edward |
| | Horne, George | | Hall, Thomas |

| County. | Names. | County. | Names. |
|---------|--------|---------|--------|
| Dorchester | Hubbard, Job | St Mary's | Howard, Ignatious |
| Talbot | Holt, John | Dorchester | Harper, Joseph, |
| Charles | Hudson, George | | Lower Battalion |
| St Mary's | Hubbard, or Herbert, | Dorchester | Harper, William, |
| | Jere | | Lower Battalion |
| St Mary's | Hazle, Jere | Dorchester | Horner, Charles, |
| | Haycock, Solomon | | For the Corps |
| | Hamilton, John | | Higden, Joseph |
| Dorchester | Harper, Henry, | | Hagan, Michael |
| | Lower Battalion | Charles | Hannon, Walter Warren |
| Dorchester | Hays, Richard, | | Hunter, William |
| | Lower Battalion | | Henninger, George |
| Caroline | Hudson, Hooper | | Holland, Charles |
| Queen Anne's | Hadley, Samuel | | Hamilton, Edward |
| | Hooper, Abraham | Dorchester | Hurst, Samuel |
| | Hughes, William | | |
| | | | |
| | Ijams, Vachel | Anne Arundel | Isleck, Pasco |
| Dorchester | Insley, Francis, | Dorchester | Insley, Joseph, |
| | For the Corps | | For the Corps |
| | | | |
| St Mary's | Jones, Cuthbert | | Jenkins, Edward |
| | Jenkins, Edward | | Jenkins, Joseph |
| Talbot | Jones, Thomas | St Mary's | Jarber, Peter |
| | Jones, Michael | St Mary's | Jarboe, Robert |
| Dorchester | Johnson, Frederick, | | Jefferson, Jestinian |
| | Upper Battalion | Dorchester | Johnson, Robert, |
| | Jackson, John | | For the Corps |
| | Jones, Samuel | | Jackson, Edward |
| Charles | Johnson, Nelson | | Jenkins, Philip |
| Charles | Johnson, Benjamin | | |
| | | | |
| | King, John | St Mary's | Kahill, Nathaniel |
| | Knowell, John | Kent | Kelly, Edward |
| | Knap, Nero | Kent | Kelly, John |
| Charles | King, Charles | | Kelly, James |
| St Mary's | Kirkpatrick, William | | Kettle, Thomas Gibson |
| | Kent, Isaac | | Kinnard, Benjamin |
| | Kibley, Joseph | | |
| | | | |
| Washington | Leatherman, Michael | Caroline | Longfellow, Gideon |
| Washington | Lyday, Simon | | Lee, William |
| | Leath, Alexander | | Lyons, John |
| | Long, Jonathan | | Lewis, Isaac |
| Caroline | Lavington, Garey, or | Kent | Lazenby, William John |
| | George | | Laceman, Lodwick |
| | Latham, Aaron | Pr. George's | Letman, John |

27

| County. | Names. | County. | Names. |
|---------|--------|---------|--------|
|  | Lancaster, Samuel |  | Linnington, John, |
| Queen Anne's | Longfellow, Arnold |  | voucher lost |
|  | Lockyer, Philip | Washington | Lewis, William |
| Charles | Lovely, or Lovelin, Wm. |  | Long, Jacob |
|  | Leath, John | Dorchester | Lingard, Nehemiah |
|  | *Miller, John |  | Muser, Francis |
|  | *Miller, John |  | McGuire, Nicholas |
|  | McIlvaine, Benjamin | Dorchester | Morgan, Thomas, |
| St Mary's | Mattingley, Ignatious |  | Lower Battalion |
| Washington | McLaughlin, Hugh |  | Merrick, William |
|  | Mahoney, Daniel |  | McCann, Marmaduke |
|  | Moore, William | Charles | Maddux, George |
|  | Myers, Philip | Charles | McNess, George |
| Dorchester | Madkin, John | Charles | McDonald, Charles |
| AnneArundel | Moffitt, Thomas | Dorchester | Meadows, David, |
| Charles | Montgomery, Ignatius |  | Upper Battalion |
|  | McGill, Thomas | Talbot | Morris, James |
| Talbot | Merrick, John |  | Miles, Jacob |
| St Mary's | Maddux, John |  | Massey, Hezekiah |
|  | †Morgan, Thomas, | St Mary's | Monarch, Edward |
|  | voucher lost |  | Meyer, John |
|  | †Morgan, Thomas | Charles | Maddux, Allison |
| Dorchester | McGraw, Leonard, (Levin), |  | McGraw, James, |
|  | For the Corps |  | voucher lost |
| Dorchester | ‡Murphey, William, |  | Moser, Michael |
|  | For the Corps | Frederick | McCray, James, |
|  | ‡Murphey, William |  | served from 7 Aug to |
| Dorchester | Meekins, Robert, |  | 10 Dec '81 |
|  | Lower Battalion |  | Murphey, Hezekiah |
| Caroline | Minor, or Minie, Levin |  | § Miller, George |
| Pr. George's | Marlow, Butler |  | § Miller, George |
|  | Mauledge, Samuel |  | McDonald, John |
|  | Marr, William |  | McDonald, James |
|  | McCartey, James | Dorchester | Morelake, Moses, |
|  | Manspiker, Henry |  | Upper Battalion |
|  | Morris, John |  | McConnell, Matthew |
| Charles | Miles, Nicholas |  | Malachi, Daniel |
|  | Murphey, William |  | McKim, Benjamin |
| Charles | Mudd, Hezekiah |  | Murray, Matthias |
|  | McGlamory, Elijah |  | McGlamory, John |
|  | Mure, Thomas |  | Matthiot, John |
|  | Martin, George |  | Morelache, Moses |
| St Mary's | Newton, Zachariah | St Mary's | Norris, Arnold |

* See previous note.    † See previous note.    ‡ See previous note.    § See previous note.

| COUNTY. | NAMES. | COUNTY. | NAMES. |
|---|---|---|---|
| St Mary's | Norris, Henry | | Nichols, Ace |
| | Nelson, John | Kent | Norris, Daniel |
| St Mary's | Norris, John | | Nagle, Richard |
| Dorchester | Navey, Matthew, | St Mary's | Norris, John |
| | Lower Battalion | Charles | Neale, William |
| | Needham, Michael | | |
| | | | |
| Dorchester | Owens, Thomas, | | Owens, Isaac |
| | Lower Battalion | | Onstrutt, George |
| Charles | Oliver, William | | Ogden, John |
| | Offutt, Nathaniel | | O'Neale, John |
| | Ogden, John | | O'Connor, John |
| | Odle, Rigden | | O'Neale, John |
| | O'Bryan, Joseph | | O'Kell, George |
| Kent | Ogelsby, Charles | | |
| | | | |
| Dorchester | Proctor, William, | St Mary's | Pike, William |
| | Lower Battalion | St Mary's | Payne, Ignatious |
| | Polston, Joseph | | Philpot, Thomas |
| Charles | Proctor, Henry | Charles | Posey, Zachariah |
| Queen Anne's | Penfold, George | Charles | Posey, Roger |
| | Paine, William | | Pugh, Humphrey |
| | Popham, Benjamin | | Platford, Edward |
| Kent | Perkins, John | St Mary's | Pratt, William |
| Kent | Pearce, John | | Proctor, Thomas |
| Kent | Pearce, Hugh | | Pronso, Jacob |
| | Pinter, Thomas | | Perkinson, Thomas |
| St Mary's | Payne, Barney | | Pardo, Benjamin |
| | | | |
| | Queener, John | | Queake, Manasses |
| | | | |
| | Robertson, Edward | Dorchester | Ross, Levin, |
| St Mary's | Risswick, Joseph | | Lower Battalion |
| Charles | Rollins, Elias | | Ross, George |
| | Right, or Wright, Elijah | | Rich, Vilet |
| | Roberts, Archibald | | Ratiken, Peter |
| | Richardson, Jonathan | Kent | Read, Peregrine |
| Dorchester | Roberts, William, | Dorchester | Rose, Joseph, |
| | Lower Battalion | | Upper Battalion |
| | Richards, Samuel | | Ridgely, Zephaniah |
| | Roberts, William | | Richards, Clement |
| | Robinson, Charles | | Rawlings, Solomon |
| | Ray, Benjamin | | Ridge, William |
| | Roberts, William | Pr. George's | Reston, Zedock |
| | | | Richardson, William |
| | | | |
| | Sax, Henry | Caroline | Smith, Nathan |

| County. | Names. | County. | Names. |
|---|---|---|---|
| | Seabrooke, Richard | | Scott, William |
| | Simmons, John | | Shepherd, John |
| Washington | Snyder, Frederick | | Smith, Emory |
| | Stitely, Frederick | | Souther, William |
| | Scott, Robert | Charles | Smoote, Matthew |
| Talbot | Start, Richard | | Smith, Ignatious |
| | Shine, or Shrine, Adam | Charles | Steward, Joshua |
| | Sadler, Thomas | St Mary's | Sute, John |
| | Snowden, Ned | | Sparks, Nimrod |
| | Starr, Obediah | | Shiffer, John |
| | Syass, James | Caroline | Smith, Richard |
| Charles | Steward, Ignatious | Talbot | Sherwood, Charles |
| Dorchester | Steward, David, | Washington | Smith, Lodwick |
| | Upper Battalion | | Silk, James |
| | Scott, Samuel | | Sollers, William |
| | Steele, John | Dorchester | Stanley, Salady, |
| | Skelly, John | | Upper Battalion |
| | Smith, John | | |
| | | | |
| St Mary's | Taney, Charles | Dorchester | †Taylor, James, |
| Talbot | Townsend, George | | Upper Battalion |
| | Tarman, Senr., Richard | | Tucker, George |
| | Tarman, Junr., Richard | | Tomlinson, Grove |
| | Taylor, Richard | | Tarr, Thomas |
| | Tennant, James | | Troy, Jeremiah |
| | *Taylor, Thomas | | Thompson, James |
| | *Taylor, Thomas | Kent | Thomas, Beal |
| Anne Arundel | Tidings, Caleb | Dorchester | Toll, Anthony |
| Kent | Thomas, Starling | | Turner, Junr., Solomon |
| Pr. George's | Tilley, Zachariah | | Taylor, Jacob |
| Dorchester | Tucker, Jacob, | | Tyler, Robert Bradley |
| | Lower Battalion | Dorchester | Thomas, Levin |
| Charles | †Taylor, James | | Taylor, Jason |
| | | | |
| Washington | Valentine, George | Dorchester | Vincent, Aaron, |
| | Valiant, Aaron | | Lower Battalion |
| | | | |
| | Weems, David | | Ward, John |
| | Willen, Charles | | Wright, Benjamin |
| Charles | Warrington, James | | Wallace, John |
| Charles | Wathen, Barton | | Woodward, James |
| | Wickert, Michael | | Welast, John |
| Washington | Wright, Thomas | St Mary's | Wise, Thomas |
| | Waggoner, Christopher | St Mary's | Winsett, Joseph |
| | Wood, Jeremiah | | Willard, John |
| | Wilson, Acquila | | Walls, George |

* See previous note.  † See previous note.

| County. | Names. | County. | Names. |
|---|---|---|---|
| Dorchester | Willis, John, | Pr. George's | Wood, James |
| | Lower Battalion | | Woodringer, Daniel |
| | Whitehook, Ezekiel | Pr. George's | Wood, Thomas |
| Charles | Wright, James | Charles | Warder, Jesse |
| Dorchester | Wheeler, John | | Wilson, Tobias |
| Dorchester | White, John, | Caroline | Williams, James |
| | Upper Battalion | Charles | Whitcombe, Notley |
| | Wilson, Joseph Crawford | | White, Henry |
| | | | |
| | Yeates, Thomas | | Young, William |
| | Yeates, Benjamin | | Young, Peter |

Received this 21st day of July, 1787, of the State of Maryland, Sundry Accounts for Pay of Militia serving in the Continental Army, in the year 1781, agreeable to the foregoing list, amounting to five thousand, five hundred and twenty-three pounds, seven shillings and four pence currency of the State of Maryland, which amounts I am to forward to the Commissioner of Army Accounts to be settled, agreeably to the Ordinance of Congress of the seventh of May last.

John White,
Commissioner of Accounts for the States of
Pennsylvania, Delaware and Maryland.

Maryd. Currency,
£5523··7··4
Equal to 14,728 88-90 dollars.

NOTE.—Names of Counties are inserted from other Rolls.

## MUSTER AND PAY ROLLS FOR 1782.

LIST OF DEFECTIVES FROM THE MARYLAND LINE, FROM JUNE, 1780, TO FEBY., 1782.

| NAMES. | DATES. | COUNTIES OF RESIDENCE. | NAMES. | DATES. |
|---|---|---|---|---|
| Zachariah Askey | 21 Sept '80 | Frederick | John Riding | 16 Aug '80 |
| Samuel Philips | " " | Cicil | James Nowland | " " |
| Edmund Collins | 6 Nov " | Frederick | John Hall | 15 Mch '81 |
| John McDaniel | 18 Aug " | do | Charles Close | " " |
| John Pound | " " | Harford | Joseph McDonald | Aug '80 |
| Robert Harmon | 10 July " | N. Carolina | Thomas Brown | |
| William Dixon | 5 " " | Prince Georges | Wm. Allman | July " |
| James Munks | 2 Oct " | Scicell | John Simmons | |
| Thomas Bulling | " " | Harford | John Eyre | May " |
| Francis King | June " | Washington | John Lenox | Oct " |
| Elias Smith | " " | Frederick | Thos. McDonald | |
| Reason Hanson | Aug " | Montgomery | Alex. Adamson | |
| Patrick Mullen | | Baltimore | John Pike | |
| Richard Ballod | | Annarundel | John Licety (?) | |
| William Roe | June " | Frederick | Patk. Murphy | " " |
| Michael Standley | " | do | Richd. Jacks | |
| Michael Rogers | " | Harford | John Lucas | Aug " |
| William Chambers | 14 Feb '81 | Frederick | John Simmons | " " |
| Benjamin Taylor | 10 Mch " | Harford | John Donovan | " " |
| William Moran | 6 " " | Prince Georges | Michl. Byrne | " " |
| Thomas Smith | 14 Feb " | Baltimore | Jno. Lester | " " |
| William Fuller | 26 Jan " | do | Robert Hudson | " " |
| Timo. Fitzgerald | 1 April " | do | John Heaton | " " |
| Thomas Simister | 4 May " | do | Michl. Gainsford | |
| Jno. Peter Fevott | " " | Frederick | Richard Goff | |
| William Pattern | " " | do | Francis Garrish | |
| William Durham | 7 " " | Harford | Edward Balf | |
| Leonard Boward | " " | Washington | Thomas Longdon | Oct '80 |
| Caleb Donnolly | 8 June " | Scicill | George Streett | Sept " |
| William Dunn | " " | do | James Stonely | July " |
| Michael Connolly | 2 July " | Baltimore | George Crosby | " " |
| Michael Connolly | " " | Annarundel | Thos. Williams | " " |
| James McDonald | 7 " " | Harford | Henry McAway | " " |
| Bartle Boome | 1 " " | Frederick | Edwd. Nichols | " " |
| Edward Purdy | 1 March " | Prince Georges | John Welsh | " " |
| James Kennedy | 15 " " | | Saml. Eyles | " " |
| Joshua Barrett | 16 Aug '80 | | John Miles | " " |

| NAMES. | DATES. | NAMES. | DATES. | COUNTIES OF RESIDENCE. |
|---|---|---|---|---|
| Alex. Montgomery | July '80 | Thomas Hatton | | |
| Michael Dease | " " | Willm. Rhodes | | |
| John Webster | " " | John Craig | | |
| Danl. Oldham | " " | John Hodges | | |
| John Church | " '81 | James Jarrett | | |
| Rowland Bates | Sept '80 | Joseph Butler | | |
| Joseph Walldram | " " | Chrisr. Flanery | | |
| Thos. Bryant | July " | Wm. Williams | Aug '80 | |
| Jno. Bartliff | Sept " | Willm. Downes | " " | |
| Jno. Lunn | July " | Laurence Craigen | | |
| Archibald Nichols | | Barnabas Doling | | |
| John Goldsborough | Sept " | Samuel Jones | | |
| John Fitzgerald | " " | Frs. Scroggy | " " | |
| Robert Gray | Mch '81 | Thos. Newland | " " | |
| Richd. Mansell | Oct '80 | John Brading | " " | |
| Joseph Wilmington | Mch '81 | Math. Skivington | July " | |
| Thos. Turner | Aug " | John Page | | |
| Joseph Nichols | " " | Pat. McGenalty | Aug " | |
| Robert Darling | Mch " | John Wills | 15 Mch '81 | |
| Danl. McIntire | Feb " | And. Marwood | Oct " | |
| James Glynn | " " | James Stuart | Feb " | |
| Jno. Pryor | " " | James Wigans | | |
| Timo. Murphey | 15 Mch " | Geo. Adamson | | |
| Robert Stewart | Feb " | Robt. Brown | May '80 | |
| Fredk. Flynn | 16 Aug '80 | Thos. Prudent | June " | |
| Michl. Griffin | June " | Jno. Thoroughgood | | Prince Georges |
| John Easton | | Thos. Pinkston | Sept '81 | Annarundle |
| Patk. Bermingham | 16 Aug " | Barnabas Maloy | May " | do |
| John Murphy | " " | Lawrence Carty | " " | Frederick |
| Matth. Spilliards | " " | John Bellamy | 15 Mch " | Baltimore |
| Timo. Shean | " " | Edwd. Hinks | Aug " | Annarundel |
| Thomas Dwier | June " | Peter Eamick | | Frederick |
| James Wheeler | | John Higgins | | Eastern Shore |
| Phil. Brissillton | | Andrew Bramble | 10 Oct " | |
| Thomas Eddis | | Moses Morelake | " " | |
| James Greene | | Godfrey Sollinder | " " | |
| John Taylor | 16 Aug '80 | Isaac Christopher | 15 " " | |
| Darby Dwyer | " " | Milby Christopher | " " | |
| Richd. Ellwood | " " | John Millford | 20 " " | |
| Peter Humman | 3 Nov '81 | Alex. Hughs | | |
| Robert Smith | " " | Jacob Flowers | | |
| Jno. Fincey (?) | " " | Benj. Smith | | |
| James Hays | " " | Willm. Baker | '81 | Baltimore |
| John Mildurph | " " | Michl. Connolly | 2 July '81 | Annarundle |
| James Greene | 6 " " | Jno. Alex. Mackey | 20 May " | Washington |

| NAMES. | DATES. | NAMES. | DATES. | COUNTIES OF RESIDENCE. |
|---|---|---|---|---|
| John Brittain | 20 Nov '81 | Isaac Beckett | 26 June '81 | Kent |
| Chas. Wheeler | 29 " " | John Slight | 15 Mch " | Annarundle |
| Willm. Tillwood | " " | Jas. Saunders | " " | Queen Anne's |
| John Frederick | | Saml. Furrough | " " | Dorcet |
| Robert Blood | | Jno. Holliday | " " | Kent |
| Adam Weatherholt | | Jacob Allen | " " | Frederick |
| James Gillin | | Thos. Collior | 25 April " | Annarundle |
| John Jessup | | John Reilly | " " | Queen Anne's |
| James Wilson | | James Hughs | | |
| Dennis Dolan | | Benj. Elliott | | |
| Michl. Ramler | | Wm. Pointer | | |
| John Dalton | | Alex. Scalls, (or Sealls) | | |
| John English | | Thos. Helphery | | |
| And. Humberry | | James Brown | | |
| Jerremiah Dilling | | James Smith | | |
| John Harmon | | Jno. Larose | | |
| Jas. Underhill | | Jno. Hackett | | |
| Willm. Stuart | | Robert Smith | | |
| Thos. Killpin | | Thos. Makrell | | |
| Jas. McDonald | | Jno. Amorsley | | |
| Vincent Molling | | Abraham Welsh | | |
| Richd. Paplow | | Wm. Mansfield | | |
| George Welsh | | Bernard Reilly | | |
| John McDonold | | Jno. Campbell | | |
| Danl. Buckley | | Jno. Powell | | |
| Jno. Arber | | Thos. James | | |
| Saml. Evans | | Thos. Berry | | |
| Willm. Mason | | John Dycus | | |

## NAMES OF THE DESERTERS FROM THE FIRST REGIMENT.

| | | | |
|---|---|---|---|
| James Shepperd | Deserted 11 Nov '81 | Isaac Henderson | Deserted 13 Dec '81 |
| Thomas Harris | do do | Ben. Thompson | do 23 do |
| Richd. Jeffers | do 18 do | | |

## REGIMENTS AND DATES OF DESERTION NOT KNOWN.

| | | |
|---|---|---|
| James Fennel | John Brown | Richard Miles |
| Willm. Mattock | James Kisk | Robt. Jones, (or Johes) |
| James Wilson | John Welch | Thos. Atkinson |
| Robt. Robertson | Wm. Jefferies | Wm. Brawton |
| Willm. English | James Navy | James Waddle |
| James Anderson | James Gardner | Richd. Todd. |
| Andrew Lloyd | Geo. Gardner | Henry Fisher |
| Jonathan Foster | Lewis White | James Fisher |
| John Avelman | Danl. McPatridge | Wm. Goody |
| St. Leger Neal | | |

VOLUNTARY ENLISTMENTS OF

| NAMES. | REGT. | TERM. | WHEN ENLISTED. | SWORN. |
|---|---|---|---|---|
| Zachariah Berry | 2nd Md. Regt. | three years | March 6th, 1782 | Mch 29th |
| Leavin Claridge | 3rd " | do | May 21st, " | |
| Daniel Howe | 4th " | do | Feb 23rd, " | Feb 23rd |
| Benjamin Burch | 4th " | do | Feb 14th, " | 25th |
| Jonathan Weaden | 4th " | do | April 3rd, " | 25th |
| William Marlow | 4th " | do | April 10th, " | 25th |
| John Brown | 4th " | do | May 18th, " | 23rd |
| John Riley | 6th " | do | Aug 26th, 1781 | Aug 26th '81 |

BACON'S BRIDGE, APL. 19TH, 1782.    PERSONS IN THE PROVOST.

| NAMES. | | | CONFINED BY |
|---|---|---|---|
| Murphey Shee | Md. Brigade | plundering | Capt. Trueman |
| Arthur Corbin | Q. M. Dept. | thief | Maj. Roxburgh |
| Fed. Smith | Md. Brigade | thief | Capt. Mills |

(From the Gist Papers.)

RETURN OF MEN OF THE MARYLAND LINE INLISTED IN 1782.

| NAMES. | WHEN INLISTED. | TERM. | REMARKS. |
|---|---|---|---|
| Benj. Popham | | 3 years | recruited by Cap. D. Lynn in |
| James Murphy | 6 Feb '82 | War | deserted 8 March [FrederickTown |
| Isaac McFadden | 16 | do | |
| Laurence Mushter | 16 | do | |
| Godfrey Wolfe | 18 | 3 years | deserted 8 March |
| Chas. Blundel | 21 | War | |
| Thos. Grant | 25 | do | deserted 15 March |
| Richd. Collins | 25 | do | deserted 20 March |
| Jesse Carter | 25 | do | |
| Richd. Jacks | 26 | 3 years | deserted 10 March |
| Elijah Smith | 28 | do | deserted 10 March |
| John Wilmore | 12 March | War | |
| Isaac Holland | 12 | do | |
| John Green | 15 | 3 years | time out 9 Jan '82, reinlisted |
| Thos., (or John), Philips | 1 April | do | |
| Benj. MaCall | 1 | do | |
| Wm. Dunn | 11 | do | |
| Chas. Love | 17 | War | |
| John Mifford | 18 | do | |
| Wm. Laurence | 20 | do | |

| NAMES. | WHEN INLISTED. | TERM. | REMARKS. |
| --- | --- | --- | --- |
| James Morris | 11 May | 3 years | |
| Isaac Date, (Deale) | 19 | do | |
| John Long | 26 | War | |
| Sylvester Gatton | 3 July | 3 years | |
| David McCullam | 20 | War | |
| Thomas Reynolds | 5 | 3 years | |
| Wm. Smith | 9 Aug | ——— | |
| Wm. Holland | 23 | 3 years | |
| Thos. Barber | 20 | War | |
| James Dawson | | do | |
| Edwd. Cantwell | 1 Sept | 3 years | |
| James Hunt | 11 | War | |
| Benj. Daniel | 7 | 3 years | |
| Jos. Pully | 15 | War | |
| John Brireck | 19 | do | |
| John Walker | 27 Aug | 3 years | reinlisted |
| James Burk | 13 | do | deserted 14 August |
| John Abraham | 22 Sept | do | do    returned 25 Dec |
| Wm. Cawood | 30 | do | |
| Francis Orbough, (or Osbough) | 1 Oct | do | |
| William Coleman | 7 | War | |
| Pat. Mayher | 8 | 3 years | |
| James Murray | 10 | do | |
| John McElroy | 10 | do | |
| Josiah Burgiss | 16 | do | |
| | | | |
| Joseph Overcreek | 1 Jan | War | recruited by Capt. John Agner |
| Patrick Nugent | 16 Feb | do | [Hamilton, 2 Regt. |
| Joseph Sharp | 25 | do | |
| John McDonald | 25 | do | |
| Thos. Glenn | 25 | do | deserted |
| James Veal | 28 | do | |
| Timo. Campbell | 1 March | do | |
| Thos. Wild | 2 | do | deserted |
| David Johnston | 5 | do | |
| Tobias Randles | 6 | do | |
| Edwd. Stone, (or Rone) | 6 | do | |
| Fredk. Wolveram | 6 | do | |
| John Bevard | 13 | do | |
| Wm. Norris | 13 | do | deserted |
| Saml. Powers | 13 | do | |
| Wm. Biddle | 13 | do | |

| NAMES. | WHEN INLISTED. | TERM. | REMARKS. |
|---|---|---|---|
| Timo. Burns | 16 March | War | |
| Benj. Houghton | 16 | do | |
| John Rogers | 18 | 3 years | |
| John Watson | 18 | War | deserted |
| Andw. Potter | 18 | do | |
| John Smith | 18 | do | |
| Saml. Hardcastle | 18 | 3 years | |
| Josiah Bay | 19 | do | deserted |
| John Merryman | 19 | do | deserted |
| John Donnald | 20 | War | |
| George McDonald | 20 | do | |
| James Brown | 20 | 3 years | |
| David Banks | 26 | War | |
| Richd. Burrows | 28 | do | |
| Wm. Harris | 26 | do | |
| James Carven | 25 | do | |
| Joseph Ward | 2 April | do | |
| Donald Cameron | 3 | do | |
| John Smith | 3 | do | |
| John Davis | 3 | do | |
| Jacob Scrivener | 3 | do | |
| Lewis Flash | 6 | do | |
| Isaac Carr | 6 | do | |
| Robert Deane | 7 | do | |
| Thos. Simmonds | 7 | do | |
| James Karnes | 10 | do | |
| John Underwood | 10 | do | |
| John Adams | 10 | do | |
| George Adams | 10 | do | |
| Isaac Burton | 11 | do | |
| Wm. Commott | 11 | do | |
| | | | |
| Alex. Wallace | 4 March | 3 years | recruited by Capt. Anderson, |
| Abraham Stoner | 13 | War | [4 Regt. |
| John Reid | 14 | do | |
| Joshua Cutmare | 20 | do | |
| Chrisr. Coye | 20 | do | |
| John Turner | 10 April | do | |
| John Pope | 11 | do | |
| Ezekiel Kidwell | 17 | 3 years | |
| John Cosby | 21 | War | |

| NAMES. | WHEN INLISTED. | TERM. | REMARKS. |
|---|---|---|---|
| Basil Newton | 16 March | 3 years | recruited by Capt. Jas. Sumervill |
| Wm. Dervin, (or Duvin) | 29 | do | |
| Benj. Asgurth | 14 April | do | |
| Wm. Dyke | 14 Aug | do | deserted a few days after Inlistment |
| Wm. Smith | 20 Feb | War | prov'd a Servt., claimed by his |
| Paul Gilmore | 1 March | 3 years | [Master and delivered |
| Thos. Billingham | 6 | do | |
| Wm. T. Bowling | 12 | do | |
| Roderick McKenny | 16 Feb | do | |
| Stephen Nicholson | 27 | do | |
| John McBride | 28 | do | |
| Wm. Batton | 10 March | do | |
| Wm. Marlow | 10 April | do | |
| Geo. Partner | 12 | do | |
| Danl. Howe | 14 | do | |
| Nicholas Walsh | 25 | do | |
| John Brown | 18 May | do | |
| John Gordon | 25 | do | |
| Francis Dewiss | 20 June | do | |
| Richd. Hogan | 15 Feb | do | |
| Thos. Carroll | 3 April | War | |
| Robt. Firth | 28 May | 3 years | |
| Edwd. Kirk | 12 April | do | |
| Dennis Carty | 14 Feb | War | |
| Joseph Neal | 14 | 3 years | |
| Wm. Johnston | 26 April | do | |
| Geo. Twinch | 2 | do | |
| Peirce Deacon | 10 | do | |
| Thos. Craig | 3 May | do | |
| Thos. Hill | 27 March | do | |
| John Trevis | 28 | do | |
| Wm. Wilson | 15 April | do | |
| James Dowden | 10 May | do | |
| Wm. Taylor | 2 April | do | |
| Isaac Johnson | 29 May | do | |
| Basil Shaw | 5 April | do | |
| Patrick Quynn | 27 Feb | do | |
| Thos. Fleming | 20 April | do | |
| Thos. McKinsey | 23 | do | |
| Jonath. Weedon | 3 | do | |
| Benj. Burch | 14 Feb | do | reinlisted. |
| | | | |
| Thos. Loveday | 17 March | 3 years | inlisted by Capt. R. Denny |
| Jacob Sheets | 19 June | War | |
| John Graham | 24 | 3 years | |

| NAMES. | WHEN INLISTED. | TERM. | REMARKS. |
|---|---|---|---|
| Zachariah Berry | 6 March | 3 years | inlisted by Major Roxburgh in Carolina |
| | | | |
| Joseph Jones | · 23 July | 3 years | Denny |
| John Connolly | 29 | do | do |
| | | | |
| John Alsop | 26 Feb | 3 years | inlisted by Lt. Roger Nelson, |
| Elisha Onsborn | 27 | do | [5 Regt. |
| George Rhodes | 10 March | do | |
| Martin Murphy | 14 | War | deserted 17 March |
| John Allen | 18 | 3 years | |
| Thos. Jones | 18 | do | deserted |
| Geo. Dadisman | 24 | do | |
| Wm. Fields | 18 | do | deserted |
| Thos. Hawkes | 1 April | War | |
| Jas. Murray | 1 | do | |
| Henry Barnes | 27 | 3 years | |
| Rob. Jones | 4 May | War | |
| Michael Griffith | 11 | do | |
| John Reese | 18 | do | deserted |
| Isaac Dall | 19 | do | |
| John Barrett | 12 July | do | |
| | | | |
| Jacob Mifford | 1 March | 3 years | inlisted by Capt. W. Lamar, 1 Regt. |
| David Love | 11 | War | |
| Nichos. Fitzgerald | 26 | do | |
| George Hoggert | 1 April | do | |
| James Smith | 6 | 3 years | deserted 7 Apl. |
| James McCray | 15 | do | |
| Joseph Clancey | 24 July | War | |
| John Johnson | 15 Aug | 3 years | |
| John McElroy | 9 Oct | do | |
| Wm. Layland | 14 | do | |
| Jacob Gibson | 17 | do | |
| James Gelmore | 19 | do | |
| Robt. Eaton | 19 | War | |
| Henry Philips | 19 | do | |

| NAMES. | WHEN INLISTED. | TERM. | REMARKS. |
|---|---|---|---|
| Alex. McGreger | 17 March | War | inlisted by Capt. Thos. B. Hugou |
| James Burk | 25 | 3 years | |
| James Scott | 29 | War | deserted |
| John Adams | 29 | do | |
| Phinehas Hervey | 3 April | do | |
| John Williams, 2d. | 6 | do | |
| John Pennington | 6 | do | |
| John Paul | 9 | do | deserted at Head of Elk |
| James Williams | 10 | do | |
| John Nicholson | 12 | do | |
| Thos. Quinney | 26 | 3 years | |
| James Morrison | 5 May | War | |
| Henry Clawson | 12 April | do | |
| Wm. Kent | 3 May | 3 years | |
| Alex. McCoy | 6 | War | |
| James Waters | 6 | do | |
| Michl. Dougherty | 5 | — | taken |
| John Gorman | 11 | War | |
| Robert Wright | 6 June | do | |
| John Torrey | 19 May | do | |
| Wm. Johnson | 12 June | do | |
| Danl. Newman | 23 | do | |
| Richd. Scotton | 24 | do | |
| Joseph Harper | | do | |
| Alex. Garrett | | do | |
| Jas. Middleton | 28 Aug | do | |
| Peter Dawson | 11 Sept | 3 years | |
| | | | |
| Barthw. Roche | 23 March | 3 years | by Capt. Clagget, 5 Regt. |
| Wm. Harrison | 8 May | do | |
| | | | |
| Basil J. Dorsey | 17 April | War | by Capt. J. A. Hamilton |
| Wm. Balentine | 22 | do | deserted |
| Randel Skly | 22 | do | |
| John Wilson, 2d. | 22 | do | |
| Chas. Davis | 23 | do | |
| Christn. Hanson | 25 | do | |
| John Bond | 1 May | do | |
| James Green | 1 | do | inl. by Capt. J. A. Hamilton, de- |
| Thos. Wilson | 2 | do | [serted |
| John Hanna | 3 | do | deserted, taken 23 Oct. |
| Wm. Hart | 7 | do | |

| NAMES. | WHEN INLISTED. | TERM. | REMARKS. |
|---|---|---|---|
| Christr. Reynor | 9 May | War | |
| Richd. Perkins | 9 | do | |
| Geo. Shingleborrough | 13 | do | |
| Christian Ernest | 14 | do | |
| Wm. Matthews | 19 | do | |
| John Ballast, (or Ballart) | 20 | do | |
| James Thompson | 21 | do | |
| John McDonald | 22 | do | |
| John Fairweather | 1 June | do | |
| Richd. Franklin | 1 | do | |
| Richd. Nabell | 4 | do | |
| James Loveless | 4 | 3 years | deserted |
| John Burgess | 12 | War | |
| John Lowe | 12 | do | |
| John McFarlin | 13 | do | |
| Thos. Hand | 15 | do | |
| Thos. Gritchard | 2 July | do | |
| John Sheppardson | 2 | do | |
| George Tate | 11 | 3 years | |
| John Bluefield | 30 | War | |
| Richd. Jennings | 13 Aug | do | |
| John Dougherty | — | do | |
| Saml. Mahew | 14 | do | |
| Richd. Burk | 16 | do | |
| Thos. Reynolds | | do | |
| John Ward | 20 | do | |
| John Welsh | | do | |
| John McDonald | | do | deserted |
| Peter Sprangle | 21 | do | |
| Thomas Channon | 24 | do | |
| Basil Wheeler | 4 Sept | do | |
| John Gray | 10 | do | |
| Philip Fraizer | | do | |
| Geo. Findleston | | do | |

| | | | |
|---|---|---|---|
| Arthur Boyes | 30 March | 3 years | inl. by Capt. J. Marbery, 3 Regt. |
| Geo. Tomlinson | 30 May | do | |
| Joseph Moseley | 19 Apl | War | |
| Roger Hagan | 29 | do | |
| Dyer Waters | 6 May | do | |
| Zachariah Moore | 18 June | do | |
| Danl. Skinner | 26 | do | |
| Isaac Jenkins | 12 Sept | do | |

| NAMES. | WHEN INLISTED. | TERM. | REMARKS. |
|---|---|---|---|
| Hillary Lanham | 13 Sept | War | |
| Hezekiah Moore | 15 | do | |
| Thomas Sturgis | 16 | do | |
| John Garrick | 21 | do | deserted |
| Geo. Chambers | 26 | do | |
| Rezin Lowe | 30 | do | |
| Danl. Hurley | 14 Oct | do | |
| | | | |
| Thos. McDowell | 5 Apl | War | inlisted by Lt.J.Hartshorn, 3 Regt. |
| Rob. McCleary | 25 | do | |
| John Maxwell | 13 | do | |
| John Smallwood | 29 | 3 years | |
| John Wilson | 6 May | War | |
| John Connolly | 9 | do | |
| Hugh Weer | 21 | do | |
| Wm. Selley | 21 | do | |
| Wm. Utie | 19 July | do | deserted 30 July |
| Alex. Christie | 14 May | 3 years | |
| Matthew Norris | 17 | do | |
| | | | |
| Alex. Boyes | 1 April | 3 years | inlisted by Lt. J. Sears, 5 Regt. |
| Peter Jackson | 2 | War | |
| John Crockett | 4 May | do | |
| Wm. Hutchman | 4 | do | never recd. nor chargd. in accts. |
| Michl. Stanley | 21 | 3 years | |
| John Hukill | 8 June | do | |
| Danl. Hukill | 8 | do | |
| John Nelson | 4 Aug | do | |
| John Moran | 8 | do | supposed reinlisted |
| Saml. Brady | 12 Sept | do | |
| | | | |
| Job Buley | 8 April | War | inl. by Capt.LilburnWilliams,3 Regt. |
| John Applead | 14 | do | |
| John White | 15 | do | |
| Thos. Alford | 15 | do | |
| Geo. Trice | 15 | 3 years | |
| John Vain | 15 | do | |
| Jeremiah Carter | 16 | do | |
| Danl. Campbell | 27 | War | |
| Brannick Meakins | 29 March | do | |
| Evan Willings | 27 April | do | |

| NAMES. | WHEN INLISTED. | TERM. | REMARKS. |
|---|---|---|---|
| Wm. Smallwood | 27 April | War | |
| John Greenwood | 27 | do | |
| Thos. Keyes | 24 | 3 years | |
| Joseph Rose | 8 | do | |
| Elijah Lyons | 24 | War | |
| Bennet Valient | 27 | 3 years | |
| Isaac Kent | 29 | War | |
| John Husk | 3 May | do | |
| Henry Winder | 3 | do | |
| Thos. Harding | 3 | do | |
| Arthur Pritchard | 3 | 3 years | |
| Danl. Sullinger | | do | |
| Thos. Hooper | | do | |
| John Elliot | | do | |
| Wm. Connelly | | War | |
| Levin Cleridge | | 3 years | |
| Wm. Powell | | War | |
| Joseph McCallister | | do | Capt. L. Williams |
| Wm. Henderson | | do | |
| Wm. Carey | | do | |
| James Coleman | | 3 years | |
| Francis Irsley | | do | |
| Chas. Missick | | do | |
| Willis Cotter | 7 Sept | War | |
| John Cotter | 7 | do | |
| Chas. Beachamp | 5 Aug | do | |
| Paris Owens | 14 Sept | 3 years | |
| Chas. Griffiths | 14 | do | |
| Edwd. Paul | 15 Aug | do | |
| Wm. Eagill | 22 Sept | do | |
| John Acock | 3 April | War | inl. by Lt. S. Hanson, 5 Regt. |
| Saml. Parramore, (or Palmore) | 10 | 3 years | inl. by Capt. R. Waters, 3 Regt. |
| Ephraim Marshall | 10 | do | deserted |
| Chas. Hall | 10 | do | |
| Chas. Parramore, (or Palmore) | 7 May | do | |
| Kemp Holder | 20 | War | |
| Cutler Jones | 31 | do | |
| John Wilson | 30 June | do | |
| Edwd. Edwards | 10 | do | |
| Oliver Blake | 7 May | 3 years | |

28

| NAMES. | WHEN INLISTED. | TERM. | REMARKS. |
|---|---|---|---|
| Thos. Whaley | | War | inl. by Capt. Perry Benson, 5 Regt. |
| John Murray | 17 May | 3 years | |
| | | | |
| John Beale | 15 April | 3 years | inl. by Lt. Fickle, 5 Regt. |
| Michl. McDevitt | 16 | do | |
| James Beale | 22 | do | |
| Wm. Hunter | 8 June | do | |
| Francis Reynard | 22 Aug | War | |
| John Williams | 3 Nov | 3 years | |
| Lewis McCuttough | 18 Aug | do | |
| John Steele | 2 Sept | War | |
| Jonas Crawford | 11 Nov | 3 years | |
| John Lee | 1 Dec | do | |
| | | | |
| James Roe | 22 June | 3 years | inlisted by Lt. Nathan Wright 3rd Regt. |
| Wm. Hill | 6 July | do | |
| Edwd. Shebrick, (or Shelrick) | 7 | do | |
| Whittington Guild | 9 | do | |
| Wm. Madden | 13 | War | |
| Durden O'Neil | 19 | 3 years | |
| Henry Gilpin | 20 | do | deserted |
| John Green | 12 | do | |
| Wm. Watkins | 1 June | do | |
| John Wilson | 1 Aug | do | |
| | | | |
| Wm. Deveraue | 9 April | 3 years | Capt. Jas. Ewing, 1 Regt. |
| | | | |
| Wm. Callaghan | 12 June | 3 years | Lt. Adam Jameson, 5 Regt. |
| Thos. Countess | 12 | do | |
| Thos. Hale | 15 | do | |
| Saml. Fisher | 1 July | War | |
| Isaac Doncan | 1 | do | |
| Thos. Leagar | 22 | do | |
| Henry Bradley | 23 | 3 years | |
| John Callaghan | 23 | War | |
| Danl. Stephens | 24 | do | |
| Richd. Reaves | 24 | do | |
| James Countess | | | Quere is not the Thos. Countess ? |
| John Coulter | 15 Oct | do | |

| NAMES. | WHEN ENLISTED. | TERM. | REMARKS. |
|---|---|---|---|
| Randolph Booth | 10 March | 3 years | Capt. Wm. Bruce, 5 Regt. |
| Edmund Wheatly | 12 | do | |
| Bennet Thompson | 1 April | do | |
| Elisha Sullivan | | | |
| Jas. Crosingbury, | 17 March | do | |
|    (or Coosingbury) | | | |
| Wm. Caldwell | 8 April | War | |
| | | | |
| John Sewell | 11 Aug | War | Lt. R. Denny, 5 Regt. |
| Thos. Richardson | 11 | do | |
| Henry Tibbett | 5 Sept | do | |
| Danl. Wilkins | 5 Oct | do | |
| Joseph Norman | 5 | War | |
| Hugh Roney | 17 June | do | |
| John Swails | 28 Sept | 3 years | |
| Geo. Warner | 28 Oct | War | |
| John Jordine | 12 Dec | do | |
| Thos. Wyndham | 14 Jan '83 | 3 years | |
| | | | |
| Wm. Gray | 9 Sept | 3 years | inl. by Lt. J. Lynn, 5 Regt. |
| Wm. Carlton | 7 | War | |
| Peter Fletcher | 9 | do | |
| Isaac Loyder | 28 Oct | 3 years | deserted |
| John Shields | 29 | War | |
| James Stephens | 8 | do | |
| Nicholas McCarlin, | 11 | do | |
|    (or McCaslin) | | | |
| John Stuart | 11 | do | |
| John Cooper | 1 | do | |
| | | | |
| Jeremiah Cypher | 30 Sept | War | inl. by Capt. John A. Hamilton |
| Michl. Kaine | 1 Oct | do | |
| Joseph Hudson | 1 | do | |
| Nichs. Perker | 1 | do | |
| Chas. Brutzill | 1 | do | |
| Wm. Laylan | 1 | do | deserted in Baltm. |
| John Layton | 3 | do | do    5 Oct |
| Jesse Wrinsile | 3 | do | do    do |
| John Messer | 3 | 3 years | |
| Wm. Belcher | 5 | War | |
| Jas. Poole | 5 | do | suppos'd reinlisted |
| Thos. Evans | 10 | do | ditto |

| NAMES. | WHEN ENLISTED. | TERM. | REMARKS. |
|---|---|---|---|
| Lodwick Chezloe | 10 Oct | War | |
| Wm. Frazier | 12 | do | |
| John Rigan | 12 | do | |
| Michl. Burns | 12 | do | |
| Thos. Lawyer | 14 | do | |
| James Morris | 14 | do | |
| Lewis Davis | 17 | do | |
| John Kelner | 18 | 3 years | |
| John Tully | 19 | War | |
| Patrick McDonough | | do | |
| John Adamson | | do | |
| Wm. Sowder | | do | |
| Peter Francis | | 3 years | |
| Thomas Hand | | War | supposed reinlisted |
| Saml. Crowell | | do | |
| Thos. Blake | | | |
| John Miller | | do | |
| | | | |
| James Reese | 21 Feb '82 | War | inl. by Maj. John Davidson, 5 Regt. |
| John Cleanscrote | 21 | 3 years | |
| Thos. Gordon | 25 March | do | |
| John Maxwell | 5 April | do | |
| Bennet Heard | 16 | do | |
| Thos. Wood | 25 | do | suppos'd reinlisted |
| Daniel Harris | 28 May | do | |
| John Smith | 10 July | do | |
| Michael Scott | 2 Nov | War | |
| Benj. Wright | 20 | do | |
| Geo. Baker | 29 Oct | 3 years | |
| James Barber | 30 Dec | War | |
| Saml. Davis | 8 Jan '83 | do | |
| James Sengo | | | |
| Wm. Watkins | 1 — | | |
| John Green | 12 July | | |
| John Wilson | 1 Aug | 3 years | |
| Wm. McNeue | | do | supposed reinlisted |
| | | | |
| John Hillam | 23 Nov | 3 years | Capt. D. Lynn, 4 Regt. |
| Dennis Bryan | 10 Dec | do | |
| Stephen Erlinger | 20 | War | |
| | | | |
| Colvert Mason, (alias Woodyard) | 30 Oct | 3 years | inl. by Gen. Smallwood |
| Wm. Harris | 2 Jan | War | |

## LIST OF SUNDRY SOLDIERS ENLISTMENTS FOR DURING THE WAR.

| NAMES. | WHEN ENLISTED. | TERM. | NAMES. | WHEN ENLISTED. | TERM. |
|---|---|---|---|---|---|
| Wm. Powell | 23 May '82 | War | Saml. Smith | 10 Apl '81 | 3 years |
| Parris Owens | 7 Sept " | 3 years | John Connally | 5 June " | " |
| Evan Willing | 27 Apl " | War | Wm. Harrison | 30 May " | " |
| Jno. Vaine | | 3 years | Nathan Homersly | 22 May " | " |
| Thos. Harding | 3 May " | War | Garett Welch | 15 March " | " |
| John Hursk | 3 May " | 3 years | Jas. Capels | 4 May " | " |
| Jere. Carter | 16 Apl " | " | Handy Handly | 7 March " | " |
| Thos. Hooper | 22 May " | " | Robert Robertson | 19 May " | " |
| Wm. Cary | 22 June " | " | Jacob Doyne | 10 Apl " | " |
| Jno. Pritchard | 8 March " | " | Aquilla Clements | 16 May " | " |
| Sammerset Downed, deserted 5 Oct '82 | 5 Oct " | War | Jas. Kirk | 19 May " | |
| | | | Elijah Oakly | 28 Apl " | " |
| Chs. Griffith | 14 Sept " | " | John Newberry | 7 Apl " | " |
| Jno. Cotter | 7 Sept " | " | Jas. Lowry | 14 June " | War |
| Willis Cotter | 7 Sept " | " | Chs. Beachem | 5 Aug '82 | " |
| Joseph McCallester | 28 May " | 3 years | James Coen | 26 March " | " |
| Job Bewley | 8 Apl " | War | Saml. Crowell | 6 Dec " | " |
| Wm. Connally | 7 May " | " | Wm. Hand | 12 Dec " | " |
| Danl. Sellinger | 26 June " | " | John Smith | 18 Feb " | " |
| Wm. Henderson | 28 May " | 3 years | John Smith | 3 Apl " | " |
| Walter B.Smallwood | 5 June '81 | " | Christr. Raynor | 9 May " | " |
| Nathl. Hawthorn | 20 July " | " | John Tulley | 19 Oct " | " |
| John Baneworth | 20 July " | " | John Welch | 20 Aug " | " |
| Thos. Gordon | 2 March " | " | | | |

An Acct. of Pay due the Non Commis'd Officers and Privates of the Maryland Line, from Jan'y 1st, 1782, to Jan'y 1st, 1783.

| NAME AND RANK. | WHEN COMMENCED. | WHEN LEFT SERVICE AND THE REASONS. | REMARKS. |
|---|---|---|---|

1 Co., 1 B. CAPT. JONA. SELLMAN. LT. NICH. GASSAWAY. ENSIGN HENRY BAKER.

| | | | |
|---|---|---|---|
| Jesse Simms | S. | All on | |
| George Childs | C. | 1 Jan '82 | |
| John Mills, 1st | C. | unless | |
| Wm. Dillon | C. | otherwise | furlough Maryd. |
| | | noted  dischd. 2nd May | |
| Thomas Gossage | D. | | |
| *James Bailey | D. | not heard of since June muster | |
| *Wm. Hamilton, 1st | D. | do | waiter in Md. |
| *Wm. Swan | D. | do | do |
| John Carr | P. | | |

| NAME AND RANK. | WHEN COMMENCED. | WHEN LEFT SERVICE AND THE REASONS. | REMARKS. |
|---|---|---|---|
| Richard Hall | P. | All on | |
| John Adams, 1st | P. | 1 Jan. '82 | |
| John Baley, 1st | P. | unless | |
| Peter Bocard | P. | otherwise | |
| Michl. Lollar | P. | noted | |
| Daniel Clancey | P. | | |
| John Ferrall | P. | | |
| Basil Brown | P. | | |
| *Andrew Fernen | P. | | on June muster not heard of since surplus roll |
| Thos. Canada | P. | | |
| John Brown | P. | | |
| Saml. Hamilton | P. | | |
| Nehemiah Hadder | P. | | |
| Wm. Lilley | P. | | |
| Patk. Mollihan | P. | | |
| John Goddard | P. | | |
| John Williams, 1st | P. | | |
| Robertson Ross | P. | | |
| Wm. Sterling | P. | | |
| Barney Lemmon | P. | | |
| Thomas Drudge | P. | | |
| Wm. Franklin | P. | | |
| Thomas Thomas | P. | | |
| James Crozier | P. | | |
| John B. Haislip | P. | | died 11 Sept '82 |
| Chas. Goldsbury | P. | | |
| *Benj. Stuard | P. | 1 Feb '82 | |
| Alex. Francis | P. | | |
| Peregrine Howard | P. | | |
| Richard Procter | P. | | |
| *Robert Taylor | P. | | not heard from since June muster |
| Saml. Harper | P. | | |
| Wm. Gates | P. | | |
| Edwd. Hammond | P. | | |
| Barney Wilson | P. | | |
| Noah Sayres, or Sears | P. | | |
| Thos. Thompson | P. | | waiter on Capt. Mr., Md. |
| William Peters | P. | | |
| Joseph Thompson· | P. | | |
| Cornelius McLochlin | P. | | |
| Edwd. Richardson | P. | | dischd. 14 July '82 |
| *——nce White | P. | | not heard of since June muster |
| Willm. Lynch | P. | | waiter, Maryd. |
| Aquilla Diver | P. | | ditto |

| NAME AND RANK. | WHEN COMMENCED. | WHEN LEFT SERVICE AND THE REASONS. | REMARKS. |
|---|---|---|---|
| ——— Richards | P. | All on | waiter, Maryd. |
| Thos. Baley | P. | 1 Jan '82 | ditto |
| *Isaac Henderson | P. | unless otherwise | not heard of since June muster | ditto |
| Jacob Blake, 1st | P. | noted | ditto | ditto |
| John Hancock | P. | | | |
| Frederick Wilmott | P. | | | |
| ———as Clark, 1st | P. | | | |
| ———el Calahan | P. | | | |
| John Osban | P. | | | |
| *Willm. Butler | P. | | not heard of since March muster | furlough, Md. |
| *Thos. Cardiff | P. | | do | do |
| *Saml. Trig | P. | | do | do |
| Jas. Thomas, Jr. | P. | | | |
| Jas. Thomas, Sr. | P. | | | sick, Camden |
| *Benton Harris | P. | | do | furlough, Md |
| Benj. Boyd | P. | | | |
| *John Turner | P. | | discharged | |
| *John Beal | P. | | ditto | |
| Wm. Kernal | P. | 1 Feb '82 | deserted 20 June '82 | |

2 CO., 1 B. CAPT. EDWARD PRALL. LT. WM. RAISIN. ENSIGN BASIL BURGESS.

| NAME AND RANK. | WHEN COMMENCED. | WHEN LEFT SERVICE AND THE REASONS. | REMARKS. |
|---|---|---|---|
| Thos. Windham | S. | | furlough, Md |
| Peter McNorton | S. | | |
| Wm. Martin | S. | died 30 Dec '82 | |
| Dennis Kelly | S. | | |
| Benj. Prior | C. | | |
| *Walter, or Martin, Mills | C. | | |
| Peter Smith | P., C. & S. | | promoted Corpl. 15 Mch '82, made [Serjt. 1 Oct '82 |
| John Martindale | D. | | waiter in Maryland |
| Dennis Dunning | D. | | |
| John McDonald | F. | | |
| *John McCormick | F. | not heard of since March muster | waiter in Maryland |
| Michael Clansey | F. | | |
| Joseph Hall | P. | | |
| Amos Green | P. | | |
| Francis Demar | P. | | |
| Chas. Scott | P. | | |
| Wm. Herrington | P. | | |
| Thos. Lewis | P. | dischd. 13 Jan '82 | |
| Abijah Buxton | P. | | |
| John Harrell | P. | | |

| Name and Rank. | | When Commenced. | When Left Service and the Reasons. | Remarks. |
|---|---|---|---|---|
| Abraham Garsener | P. | All on | | |
| Wm. Silkes | P. | 1 Jan '82 | | |
| Darby McLamar | P. | unless | | |
| David Cale | P. | otherwise | | |
| Alexander West | P. | noted | died 1 Nov '82 | |
| Thomas Glover | P. | | | |
| Wm. Clements | P. | | | |
| Stephen Fresh | P. | | | |
| Wm. Poling | P. | | | |
| Michael Miller | P. | | | |
| John Jackson | P. | | | |
| Ignatius Adams | P. | | | |
| Notley Tippet | P. | | | |
| Jonathan Fowler | P. | | | |
| Buto, (or Brito), Devo | P. | | transferred to Invalids 4 Apl '82 | |
| William Nailor | P. | | | |
| John Tucker | P. | | | [Guard |
| Benj. Gray | P. | | | on Gen. Small.'s |
| *Jonathan Millstead | P. | | | do    do |
| Wm. Dorch | P. | | | |
| Wm. Kews, or Hews | P. | | died 6 Dec '82 | |
| Wm. Joice, 1st | P. | | | |
| John Brookbank | P. | | | |
| John Irons | | | | |
| Jacob Flora | P. | | | |
| *Dennis Devine | P. | | not heard of since June muster | |
| Thos. Bird | P. | | discharged 13 Jan '82 | |
| John Bean | P. | | do    22 Jan '82 | |
| Nathan Peeke | P. | | disch'd 14 Nov '82 | |
| Wm. Clary | P. | | | |
| Francis Fairbrother | P. | | | |
| John Dyxson | P. | | | waiter in Maryland |
| Joseph Fowler | P. | | | waiter in Maryland |
| Francis Thompson | P. | | | |
| Edward Elliott | P. | | | waiter in Maryland |
| Thos. Evins | P. | | | |
| *John Luffer | P. | | not heard of since then furlough Maryland March muster land | |
| Chas. Robinson | P. | | | do    do |
| Simon Perry | P. | | | furlough  Maryland |
| *James Harris, 1st | P. | | ditto | then  do |
| Banks Webb | P. | | | furlough  Maryland |
| Stephen Preston | P. | | | do |
| John Anderson | P. | | | |

| NAME AND RANK. | WHEN COMMENCED. | WHEN LEFT SERVICE AND THE REASONS. | REMARKS. |
|---|---|---|---|
| Wm. Gughan, or Gudgeon | P. | All on 1 Jan '82 | Annapolis waiter |
| Michael Clarke, 1st | P. | unless | |
| Christopher Lamberts | P. | otherwise | |
| Joseph Isaacs, 1st | P. | noted | sick in W'm'sb'gh, N. C. March '82 |
| *John Nevitt, 1st | P. | not heard of since March muster | then sick in Wm's-burgh, N. Carolina |
| Laurence Simpson | P. | | sick in Virginia |
| Notley Witcomb | P. | | do |
| *Peter Richards | P. | not heard of since March muster | then sick as above |

3 CO., 1 B.   CAPT. WM. RIELEY.   LT. HENRY CLEMENTS.

| NAME AND RANK. | WHEN COMMENCED. | WHEN LEFT SERVICE AND THE REASONS. | REMARKS. |
|---|---|---|---|
| Levi Smith | S. | | |
| Abram Bowen | S. | | |
| George Haydon | S. | | |
| Thos. Sappington | S. | dischd. 12 Feb '82 | |
| John Wilkinson | S. | | |
| George Bateman | P. | dischd. 8 Jan '82 | |
| William Forman | S. | | |
| John Smith, 1st | C. | | |
| *John Lucas, 2d | C. | on June muster & surplus roll | |
| *George Scone | C. | not heard of since March muster | then furlough Maryland |
| *Joshua Taylor | C. | ditto | then prisoner War |
| John Hull | D. | | |
| Wm. Ferroll | D. | | |
| James Reynolds | D. | | reduced to private Jan '81 |
| Joseph Nabb | F. | | |
| *William Kelly | F. | not heard of since June muster | |
| Aaron Jones | P. | | |
| John Andrew | P. | | |
| Henry Gilby | P. | | |
| Jas. Allen | P. | | |
| Jas. Owens | P. | | |
| John Downy | P. | | |
| Perry Sullivan | P. | | |
| Wm. St. Clair | P. | | |
| Thos. Ayres | P. | | |
| Jas. Doyle | P. | | |
| Rigby Forster | P. | | |
| Thos. Gilham | P. | | |

| NAME AND RANK. | | WHEN COMMENCED. | WHEN LEFT SERVICE AND THE REASONS. | REMARKS. |
|---|---|---|---|---|
| William Hill | P. | All on | | |
| Benj. Loffman | P. | 1 Jan '82 | | |
| John Burnett | P. | unless | | |
| John Bantham | P. | otherwise | | |
| James Holmes | P. | noted | | promoted Corpl 1 Oct '82 |
| Paul Lappine | P. | | | |
| John Johnston, 3rd | P. | | | |
| John Hughes, 1st | P. | | | |
| John McCay, 2nd | P. | | | |
| Thomas Carney, | P. | | | |
| Anthony Wearver | P. | | | |
| Thos. Feimley | P. | | | |
| John Fullam | P. | | | |
| Alex. Downy | P. | | | |
| David Wilson | P. | | | |
| William Horney | P. | | | |
| John Mills | P. | | | |
| Cornelius Thompson | P. | | | |
| Thos. Bowser | P. | | | |
| John Gother | P. | | transferred Invalids, 25 Feb '82 | |
| John Hood | P. | | died 20 Dec '82 | |
| Jarvis Eccleston | P. | | | |
| Augustin Cann | P. | | | |
| Chas. Girdler | P. | | | |
| Wm. Civil | P. | | | |
| Solomon Summers | P. | | | |
| Stafford Fosdale | P. | | | |
| Samuel Richardson | P. | | | |
| George Jurnings, (or Jennings) | P. | | | |
| Wm. Sullivan | P. | | | |
| Mark Forster | P. | | | |
| Alex. Rutherford | P. | | dischd. 4 Jan '83 | made up to 31 Dec |
| *Jonas Graves | P. | | not heard of since June muster. | [and no longer |
| Anthony Burn | P. | | on June muster and surplus roll | |
| Roger Shorter | P. | | | |
| John Harris | P. | | | |
| Joseph Geier | P. | | | |
| *Dennis Murley | P. | | not heard of since June muster | |
| *Joseph Sidney | P. | | | |
| *George Saunders | P. | | | |
| *John Vallow | P. | | | waiter Col. Howard |

| NAME AND RANK. | WHEN COMMENCED. | WHEN LEFT SERVICE AND THE REASONS. | REMARKS. |
|---|---|---|---|
| *George Blackam | P. | All on | waiter Capt. Gibbons |
| *Abram Gamble | P. | 1 Jan '82 | furlough Mary'd |
| *Daniel Smith, 1st | P. | unless | ditto |
| *Robt. Pennington | P. | otherwise noted | not heard of since March muster | then ditto |
| *Thomas Ross | P. | | not heard of since March muster | then furlough Mary'd |
| *John Canahan | P. | | ditto | then taken prisoner 8 Sept '81 |
| *Basley Barrett | P. | | ditto | do  taken prisoner 8 Sept '81 |
| *Timothy Conner | P. | | ditto | do    do |
| James Pool | P. | | | do |
| *Wm. Woolcot | P. | | ditto | do  do 10 Feb '81 |
| *Wm. Terrot | P. | | ditto | do  do 25 Apl '81 |
| John Carroll, 2nd | P. | | | do |
| *James Bradshaw | P. | | ditto · | do  do |
| John Duhague | P. | | died 1 Dec '82 | |
| Valentine Clapper | P. | | | |
| Emanual Allen | P. | | | |
| George Dyce | P. | | | |
| *Samuel Griffith | S. | | not heard of since June muster | |

4 Co., 1 B.   Capt. John S. Belt.   Lt. Hezekiah Ford.
Ensign Francis Ware.

| | | | |
|---|---|---|---|
| Leonard Smith | S. | | |
| John Moore, 2nd | S. | | |
| Lawrence Brannan | S. | | |
| Humphry Becket | S. | | |
| James Kelly, 1st | S. | | |
| John Hamilton | C. | | |
| *Griffin Taylor | C. | not heard of since June muster. | wounded at Eautaw |
| Walter Howe | C. | | |
| Anthony Gohogan | D. | | |
| Hezekiah Carr | D. | | reduced 1 July '82 |
| John Scott | D. | | waiter in Maryland |
| Hezekiah, or Zachariah, Clark | F. | | reduced 1 July '82 |
| John Riggs | D. | | |
| John Ashmore | P. | | |
| *John Wood | P. | not heard of since June muster | |
| Willm. McGee | P. | | |
| Emanuel Farara | P. | | |
| Chas. McGee | P. | | |

| NAME AND RANK. | | WHEN COMMENCED. | WHEN LEFT SERVICE AND THE REASONS. | REMARKS. |
|---|---|---|---|---|
| George Foard | P. | All on | | |
| Austin Howard | P. | 1 Jan '82 | | |
| Christr. Seemore | P. | unless | | |
| Francis Hopkins | P. | otherwise | | |
| Michael Waltman | P. | noted | | |
| James Ruark | P. | | | |
| Edward Roberts | P. | | | |
| Dudley Lee | P. | | | |
| John Cragg | P. | | | |
| John Appleby | P. | | | |
| Luke Dempsey | P. | | | |
| Thos. Jones | P. | | | |
| Jacob Moses | P. | | | |
| Luke Carter | P. | | | |
| John Fransway, or Francois, | P. | | | |
| John McCay, 1st | P. | | dischd. 14 Feb '82 | |
| Wm. Derrington | P. | | | |
| Edward Irvine | P. | | | |
| John Gordan | P. | | | |
| Neal Peacock | P. | | | |
| John Lee, 1st | P. | | | |
| Thomas Evans, 2nd | P. | | | pro'd C. 1 Oct '82 |
| Richard Tasco | P. | | | |
| Travis Alby | P. | | | |
| Wm. Mitchell | P. | | | |
| *Alex. Bingley | P. | | not heard of since June muster | |
| John Lewin | P. | | | |
| John Wells | P. | | | |
| Joshua Pearce | P. | | | |
| Henry Crooke | P. | | Invalids 9 Apl '82 | |
| Michael Woolford | P. | | | |
| James Byass | P. | | | |
| John Jarvis | P. | | | |
| Perry Bantham | P. | | | Com'd Maryland |
| Benj. Johnson | P. | | not heard of since March muster | then ditto |
| Joseph Jenkins | P. | | | |
| John Buckley | P. | | | |
| John Love | P. | | | |
| *James Bluer | P. | | do | then furlough Maryland |
| John Walker, 1st | P. | | | |
| Nathaniel Sullivan | P. | | not heard of since June muster | |
| *James Sullivan | P. | | | |

| NAME AND RANK. | WHEN COMMENCED. | WHEN LEFT SERVICE AND THE REASONS. | REMARKS. |
|---|---|---|---|
| George Dixon | P. | All on | |
| Thomas King | P. | 1 Jan '82 | furlough Maryland |
| Francis Dunnington | P. | unless | |
| Samuel B. White | P. | otherwise | dischd. 24 Aug '82 furlough Md. |
| Philip Fisher | P. | noted | do |
| Lazarus Higgs | P. | | do |
| *William Snow | P. | not heard of since March muster | then furlough Md. |
| *Jas. McNamara | P. | ditto | ditto      ditto |
| Joseph Southall | P. | | |
| John Dyer | P. | | |
| Andrew Russell | P. | | |
| *Thomas Weston | P. | do | ditto      ditto |
| Chas. Bucklep | P. | | furlough Maryland |
| John Jones | P. | | ditto |
| Matthew Moore, 1st | P. | | |
| Joseph Quinn | P. | | ditto |
| James White | P. | | |
| *Andrew Miller | P. | not heard of since June muster | |
| Edward Evans | P. | | |

5 Co., 1 B.   CAPT. LLOYD BEALL.   LT. EDWARD M. SMITH.

| NAME AND RANK. | WHEN COMMENCED. | WHEN LEFT SERVICE AND THE REASONS. | REMARKS. |
|---|---|---|---|
| Stephen Fluharty | S. | | |
| Arthur McClain | S. | | |
| David Love | S. | | furlough |
| *James Scott | S. | not heard of since March muster | then ditto |
| Samuel Fillson | S. | | |
| Cuthbert Able | S. | | |
| Chas. McNabb | S. | | Asst. Forge Master sick in Va. |
| Samuel Davies, 1st | S. | dischd. by Col. Adams 1 Aug '82 | March muster |
| Wm. Bruff | C. | | promoted Sjt. 1 May '82 |
| Peter Stephens | C. | | Pris. 10 Apl '80 |
| John Falling | C. | | |
| Boston Medler | D. | | |
| Benj. Williams | D. | | |
| Edwd. Clancey | D. | | |
| Jesse Barnett | F. | | |
| Abram Stallions | F. | | |
| *Thos. Wingate | F. | not heard of since Mch muster | then Pris. War |
| Saml. Clarke | P. | | |
| Daniel Smith, 2d | P. | | |

| Name and Rank. | When Commenced. | When Left Service and the Reasons. | Remarks. |
|---|---|---|---|
| Zadock Whaley | P. | All on | |
| Wm. Quinton | P. | 1 Jan '82 | |
| Wm. Harnston | P. | unless otherwise | on June muster and surplus roll | found and disch'd Jan '83 |
| John Loveday | P. | noted | |
| Wm. Casey | P. | | |
| Alex. Ross | P. | | |
| Joseph Mattingby | P. | | |
| John Hadan | P. | | |
| Richard Taylor | P. | | |
| George Buck | P. | | |
| Peter Maguire | P. | | |
| Walter Hagan | P. | | |
| *Wm. Young | P. | not heard of since March muster | then Com'd |
| John Twiner | P. | | |
| Joshua Leister | P. | | |
| James Keiland | P. | | |
| Luke Sampson | P. | | |
| Fredk. Harty | P. | | |
| Leonard Hagan | P. | | time expired Jan '83 |
| John Blair | P. | | |
| Neal Morris | P. | | |
| Darby Crowley | P. | | |
| Joseph Blaze | P. | | |
| Michael Curtis | P. | | |
| John Ryan | P. | | |
| Robert Dunkin | P. | | |
| John Neighbours | P. | on June muster and surplus roll | |
| Absalom Fardo | P. | | |
| William Leakins | P. | | |
| George Devitt | P. | | |
| Elijah Pepper | P. | | |
| *Laurence Hurdle | P. | not heard of since March muster | then Com'd Maryland |
| John Mills | P. | | |
| Jacob Hunt | P. | | |
| Jas. McDonald | P. | | |
| Partrick Reiley | P. | | furlough |
| *Jas. Smith, 1st | P. | | waggoner in Md. |
| Wm. Niblett | P. | | |
| Richd. Gee | P. | | |
| *Danl. Hall | P. | ditto | transfer'd 23 March '82 |
| *Philip Sullivan | P. | ditto since June muster | |
| Wm. Taylor, 1st | P. | | |

| NAME AND RANK. | WHEN COMMENCED. | WHEN LEFT SERVICE AND THE REASONS. | REMARKS. |
|---|---|---|---|
| Wm. Mann | P. | All on | |
| Moses Foster | P. | 1 Jan '82 | |
| Willm. Cummings | P. | unless | Com'd Md |
| Peter Outhouse | P. | otherwise | do |
| Basil Norman | P. | noted | do |
| Chas. Simpkins | P. | | |
| Wm. Crail | P. | | |
| John Maxwell | P. | | |

1 Co., 2 B.  Capt. Alex. Trueman.  Lt. Jacob Crawford.  Ensign Skirvins.

| NAME AND RANK. | WHEN COMMENCED. | WHEN LEFT SERVICE AND THE REASONS. | REMARKS. |
|---|---|---|---|
| Stephen Price | S. | | |
| Jesse Jacobs | S. | | |
| Wm. Rose | S. | | |
| Robt. Taylor, 2nd | S. | | furlough in Md. Feb '82 |
| Peter Shugart | C. | deserted 2 July '82 | |
| John Thomas, 1st | C. | | |
| Robt. Sharpless | C. | | furlough Md. Feb '82 |
| James Maxwell | C. | | ditto |
| Danl. Warrior | D. | | |
| Alex. Stevenson | D. | | |
| James Greenwood | D. | | |
| Benj. H. Kerrick | F. | | |
| John Denoone | F. | | waiter to Lt. Rutledge, Md. |
| Thos. Cahoe, Jr. | F. | | ditto Lt. Lynn, ditto |
| Benj. Williams, 2nd | P. | | |
| Absalom Wright | P. | | |
| Michael Sours | P. | on June muster and surplus roll | |
| Saml. Young | P. | | promoted Corpl. 1 Apl '82 |
| Thomas McHandy | P. | died 28 Aug '82 | |
| Jas. Steward, 1st | P. | ditto 1 Dec '82 | |
| Joseph Kerrick | P. | ditto 27 do '82 | |
| Adam Rider | P. | | |
| George Mauntle | P. | | |
| Wm. Harris, 1st | P. | | |
| Darby Leneham | P. | | |
| John Mantle | P. | | |
| Michael McCann | P. | | |
| Thos. Sheridan | P. | | |
| Wm. George | P. | died 24 July '82 | |
| Mathias Dytch | P. | | |
| John Purdy | P. | | |
| Henry Purdy | P. | | |

| Name and Rank. | | When Commenced. | When Left Service and the Reasons. | Remarks. |
|---|---|---|---|---|
| John Hillary | P. | All on | died 27 Dec '82 | |
| Paul Grinnard | P. | 1 Jan '82 | | |
| George Taylor | P. | unless | | |
| Christopher Cusick | P. | otherwise | | |
| Wm. Stonestreet | P. | noted | | |
| Joseph Elliott | P. | | | |
| Michael Wiery | P. | | | |
| Isaac Grieves | P. | | | |
| Joseph Long | P. | | | |
| John Armstrong, 1st | P. | | | |
| Richd. Duvall | P. | | | |
| Nicholas Milburn | P. | | | promoted Corp. 1 [Apl '82 |
| Joseph Sloop | P. | | | |
| Harry Billip | P. | | | |
| John Stackhouse | P. | | | furlough Md. June ['82 |
| John Holliday | P. | | | |
| Jas. Devericks | P. | | | promoted S. 1 Oct ['82 |
| Walter B. Smallwood | P. | | | |
| *Henry David | P. | | not heard of since March muster | then sick in Virginia |
| *Jas. Neagle | P. | | ditto | ditto        ditto |
| *Richard Brockhill | P. | | ditto | ditto at Annapolis |
| *Asel Rockhold | P. | | ditto | ditto Artificer |
| Benj. Cleaver | P. | | | |
| George Bomgardner | P. | | | |
| Moses Graham | P. | | | |
| *Jacob Rowland | P. | | ditto | then waiter Lt. Jacobs Mary'd |
| *Thos. Kearnes | P. | | not heard of since March muster | then waiter to Gen. Gates |
| George Kelson | P. | | | |
| Jas. Nowell | P. | | | waiter Maj. Hardman, Md |
| Thos. Smith, 1st | P. | | | do        do |
| Stephen Owens | P. | | | do Lt. Lynn |
| John Lincoln | P. | | | do Capt. Smith |
| John Elliott | P. | | | |
| Nathan Speak | P. | | died 6 Oct | furlough Md. 2 Nov '80 |
| Jas. Burck | P. | | | do 24 Aug '81 |
| Thos. Cahoe, Senr. | P. | | | do 29 Dec '81 |
| Nicholas Welch | P. | | | do 20 Feb '82 |
| Jas. Sewell | P. | | | [8 Sept '81 |
| *Patrick Eagen | P. | | ditto | then prisoner War |
| *John Durough | P. | | ditto | then do 15 Mch '81 |
| John Hall | P. | | | |
| Benj. Mooren | P. | | died 2 Feb '82 | |

| NAME AND RANK. | WHEN COMMENCED. | WHEN LEFT SERVICE AND THE REASONS. | REMARKS. |
|---|---|---|---|
| 2 Co., 2 B. CAPT. THOS. MASON. LT. ZEDEKIAH MOORE. ENSIGN MALACHI BONHAM. | | | |
| Patrick Doran | S. | All on | |
| John Quick | S. | 1 Jan '82 | |
| Humphry Spencer | S. | unless | |
| Richd. Smith | S. | otherwise | ['82 |
| Wm. McNeal | S. | noted | furlough Md. Feb |
| *Saml. Wilson | S. | not heard of since March muster | then furlough Md. Feb '82 |
| Edwd. Suite | C. | died 24 July | |
| Bennet H. Clements | C. | | |
| Isaccher Mason | C. | | |
| Henry Nicholson | C. & P. | | reduced 19 Mch '82 |
| Thos. Hawson | D. | | ditto to private 1 July |
| Christopher McGraw | D. | | ['82 |
| Edward Holland | D. | | ditto |
| Daniel Bassett | F. | | reduced 1 Oct '82 |
| Fredk. Bennett | F. | | do   1 Feb '82 |
| Josias Alvey | P. | discharged 24 May | |
| John Ashberry | P. | | |
| Jas. Barber | P. | | |
| Jeremiah Brown | P. | | |
| John Branson | P. | | |
| Andrew Crummy | P. | | promoted Corpl. 1 Oct '82 |
| *Jacobus Debore | P. | not heard of since June muster | |
| George Dunkin | P. | | |
| *William Day | P. | on June muster & surplus roll | time expires in July '83 |
| John Ennis | P. | | |
| Enoch Ennis | P. | | |
| Willm. Fitzgerald | P. | | |
| Chas. Fitzgerald | P. | | |
| John Henly | P. | | deserted 4 Aug '82 |
| Peter Howard | P. | | |
| Willm. Hope | P. | | |
| Leonard Holt | P. | | |
| Benj. Kearns | P. | | |
| Levi Lord | P. | | |
| Francis Lang | P. | | |
| John Lee, 2nd | P. | | deserted 4 Aug '82 |
| Wm. Moore, 1st | P. | | |
| John Moore, 1st | P. | | |
| Richard Mitchell | P. | | |

| NAME AND RANK. | | WHEN COMMENCED. | WHEN LEFT SERVICE AND THE REASONS. | REMARKS. |
|---|---|---|---|---|
| Joseph Ray | P. | All on | | |
| Wm. Shirley | P. | 1 Jan '82 | | |
| Bennit Shirley | P. | unless | | |
| Bartholomew Thompson | P. | otherwise | | |
| Giles Thomas | P. | noted | | |
| Daniel Votier | P. | | deserted 1 July '82 | |
| Gabriel Williams | S. | | disch'd 6 Feb '83 | |
| 5 Co., 1 B. | | | | |
| Willm. Hurly | P. | | | |
| *Cuthbert Stone | P. | | not heard of since March muster | |
| *Barney Munro | P. | | ditto | then furlough Oct '81 |
| *Jeremiah Fitzgerald | P. | | ditto | then sick in Virginia |
| *Wm. Pringle | P. | | ditto | then prisoner War |
| Robt. Walker | P. | | | |
| Lazarus Harmar | P. | | | |
| Thos. Baker | P. | | | sick Maryland |
| *John Plumary | P. | | ditto | then ditto |
| *Laurence Whaland | P. | 1 Apl '82 | ditto | |
| Wm. Hillman | P. | | | |
| 2 Co., 2 B. | | | | |
| Walter Watson | P. | | | |
| Jesse Wright | P. | | | |
| Wm. Carter | P. | | | |
| Rhode Woodland | P. | | | |
| Job Sylvester | P. | | | |
| Thos. Cooper | P. | | died 1 Apl '82 | |
| John Smallwood, 1st | P. | | | |
| Francis Rogers | P. | | deserted 13 July '82 | Mch sick at George Town |
| *Richard Laine | P. | | not heard of since March muster | then sick at Wm's-burgh |
| Chas. White | P. | | | |
| Jacob Blake | P. | | | |
| Francis Freeman | P. | | | |
| Peter Bushell | P. | | | |
| Gabriel Brand | P. | | disch'd 12 Jan '82 | |
| Jeremiah French | P. | | | |
| James Corsey | P. | | deserted 10 Dec '82 | |
| William Jones, 1st | P. | | | |
| *John Anderson, 2nd | P. | | not heard of since March muster | then Gardner Gen. Smallwood, Md. |
| *Edward Laigg | P. | | ditto | then Waggoner Clot. Genl. |

| NAME AND RANK. | WHEN COMMENCED. | WHEN LEFT SERVICE AND THE REASONS. | REMARKS. |
|---|---|---|---|
| *Jas. Isaacs | P. | All on 1 Jan '82 unless otherwise noted    not heard of since June muster | then transferred to the Corps of Invalids about Sept., 1781. Col. Tootal has his papers |
| George Dyer | P. | Mr. Randall has discharge | |
| John Frawney | P. | | |
| Thos. Gadd | P. | | |
| Benj. Gilbert | P. | | |
| Wm. Hicks | P. | | |
| John Moore, 3rd | P. | disch'd 12 Jan '83 | furlough Md., Oct '81 |
| *Caleb Hailey | P. | not heard of since March muster | furlough Md., Feb '82 |
| Leonard Ennis | P. | | do |
| Lewis Cunningham | P. | | do |
| Walter Keech | P. | | do |
| John Matthews, 1st | P. | | do |
| James Smith, 2nd | P. | | |
| Henry Tucker | P. | transfer'd 29 March | |

3 Co., 2 B.    Capt. Saml. McPherson.    Lt. Wm. Smoot.

| NAME AND RANK. | WHEN COMMENCED. | WHEN LEFT SERVICE AND THE REASONS. | REMARKS. |
|---|---|---|---|
| Wm. Collis | S. | | |
| John Brady | S. | | |
| Richd. Wheelor | S. | | |
| *Luke Barnwell | S. | not heard of since March muster | then on furlough |
| Wm. Brathwaite | C. | | |
| Bartholomew Eshum | C. | | |
| John Head | D. | | |
| John Peany | D. | | |
| Andrew Garnett | F. | | |
| *Walter Little | F. | on June muster and surplus roll | |
| Equilla Pearse | P. | | |
| Philip Fitzpatrick | P. | | |
| Robert Shipley | P. | died 20 July '82 | |
| John Haney | P. | | |
| John Mick | P. | | |
| Wm. Goold | P. | | |
| Jas. Hair | P. | died 6 July '82 | |
| Hampton Coarsey | P. | | |
| Henry Green | P. | | |
| John Welch, 1st | P. | | |
| *Jas. Shotten | P. | not heard of since June muster | |

| Name and Rank. | | When Commenced. | When Left Service and the Reasons. | Remarks. |
|---|---|---|---|---|
| Jas. Jackson | P. | All on | | |
| Roger Landers | P. | 1 Jan '82 | | |
| Michael Lloyd | P. | unless | | |
| Chas. Cooper | P. | otherwise | | |
| Wm. Jenkins | P. | noted | | |
| Jas. Meason | P. | | | |
| John Gregory | P. | | | |
| Thos. Waite | P. | | | |
| Levi Burck | P. | | | |
| John Alby | P. | | | |
| Peter Melvin | P. | | | |
| Wm. Moore, 2nd | P. | | | |
| James Wilson, 1st | P. | | | |
| Danl. Bulgar | P. | | | |
| Jacob Game | P. | | | |
| John Robbins | P. | | | |
| John Buckhannan | P. | | | |
| Jas. Farrell | P. | | | |
| Abram Irvin | P. | | | |
| David Bramble | P. | | | |
| *George Riggs | P. | | | not heard of since June muster |
| Thos. Camphire | P. | | | |
| Wm. Purchace | P. | | | |
| Wm. Lee, 2nd | P. | | | |
| John Taylor, 1st | P. | | | |
| Adam Kipart | P. | | | |
| Jacob Knight | P. | | | |
| Wm. Laws | P. | | | |
| Michl. Casner | P. | | | |
| Richd. Blamford | P. | | | |
| Wm. Groves | P. | | | |
| *Nathan Cripps | P. | | | not heard of since June muster |
| Joseph Jones | P. | | | |
| Lambert Thompson | P. | | | |
| *Wm. Lucas | P. | | | killed Oct '82 |
| Callothil Carmile | P. | | | |
| Partrick Cavenough | P. | | | |
| Joseph Horsefield | P. | | | |
| Joseph Huskill | P. | | | |
| Richd. Biddle | P. | | | |
| James Shane | P. | | | |
| Robt. Farrell | P. | | | sick in Maryland with Capt Smith, Charles Town |
| John Romills | P. | | | waiter to Col. Williams |

| Name and Rank. | When Commenced. | When Left Service and the Reasons. | Remarks. |
|---|---|---|---|
| *John Moran | P. | All on 1 Jan '82 not heard of since March muster | then waiter to Lt. Jamison |
| Jas. Harris, 2nd | P. | unless | |
| Thos. Ashell, or Aspell | P. | otherwise noted. | waiter to Lt. Armstrong |
| Wm. Cutler | P. | | |
| Stephen Varlow | P. | | waiter to Maj. Davidson |
| Levin Button | P. | | ditto Dr. Haney |
| *Richard Lloyd | P. | ditto | then pris. War |
| *Chas. Burns | P. | ditto | ditto |
| *Richd. Downes | P. | ditto | ditto |
| *John McCowan | P. | ditto | ditto |
| *George Stevens | P. | not heard of since March muster | then pris. War |
| Solomon Britanham | P. | | |

4 Co., 2 B.   Lt. Wm. Adams.   Ensign John D. Carey.

| Name and Rank. | When Commenced. | When Left Service and the Reasons. | Remarks. |
|---|---|---|---|
| Terrence Duffee | S. | | |
| Francis Duffee | S. | | |
| Jesse Boswell | S. | | |
| Robert Scribner | S. | | |
| *Jas. Flack | S. | | furlough Maryland |
| Jas. Hagen | C. | | |
| *Edward White | C. | not heard of since March muster | then furlough Md. Jan '82 |
| Wm. Steward | D. | | |
| Wm. Prater | D. | | |
| George Steem | F. | | waiter in Md. |
| Wm. Moore, 3d | P. | | |
| John Summers | P. | | |
| Robert Clenehan | P. | | |
| *Abram Shockee | P. | on June muster & surplus roll | |
| Thos. Baire | P. | | |
| Wm. Rice | P. | | |
| *Dennis Downes | P. | not heard of since June muster | time expires 10 June '83 |
| William Glory | P. | | |
| Thos. Arthurs | P. | | |
| Jesse Powers | P. | | |
| *Alex. Steel | P. | not heard of since June muster | |
| Thos. Patterson | P. | | |
| Henry Evans | P. | | |
| Wm. McLochlin | P. | | |
| Aron Rawlings | P. | | furlough Md. Jan '82 |
| Benj. Gaither | P. | | |
| *Joseph Adams | P. | on June muster & surplus roll | |

| NAME AND RANK. | | WHEN COMMENCED. | WHEN LEFT SERVICE AND THE REASONS. | REMARKS. |
|---|---|---|---|---|
| Robert Straights | P. | All on | | |
| *Chas. Hickey | P. | 1 Jan '82 | on June muster & surplus roll | |
| *Edwd. Sheehee | P. | unless | not heard of since June muster | |
| Jas. Crasberry | P. | otherwise | | |
| John Newton, 1st | P. | noted | | |
| Thos. Porters | P | | | |
| Richd. Hays | P. | | | |
| John Brewer | P. | | died 7 July '82 | |
| Joseph Donohoo | P. | | | |
| Saml. Scott | P. | | | furlough Md '82 |
| Patrick Rowan | P. | | | |
| Wm. Jones, 2nd | P. | | | |
| *Joseph Martin | P. | | not heard of since June muster | |
| Edwd. Kearsy | P. | | | |
| John Lucas, 1st | P. | | | |
| *Joseph Points | P. | | not heard of since March muster | then waiter Maj. Giles, Md |
| John C. Harwood | P. | | | do Lt. Skinner, Va. |
| John Deakins | P. | | | |
| Jesse Furroughs | P. | | deserted 1 Apl '82 | |
| Edwd. Vickers | P. | | | |
| *Jeremiah Reed | P. | | not heard of since June muster | |
| John Sammon | P. | | | |
| *John Fulsom | P. | | ditto | |
| John Denson | P. | | | sick Camden |
| *Zachariah Prather | P. | | ditto | |
| Wm. Matthews | P. | | | |
| *John Butcher | P. | | ditto since March muster | then furlough Md. Jan '82. On pension |
| *Wm. Scaggs | P. | | ditto since June muster | |
| James Bigwood | P. | | | |
| James Barrow | P. | | trans'd Inv. 1 Apl '82 | |
| Richd. Kisby | P. | | | |
| Danl. Jarvis | P. | | | |
| John Housely | P. | | | |
| *Peter Henesy | P. | | not heard of since June muster | |
| John Shovell | P. | | | furlough Md. Jan '82 |
| *John Deskey | P. | | not heard of since March muster | then do |
| *George Holliday | P. | | ditto | do do |
| Wm. Chatland | P. | | | do |
| *Wm. Allender | P. | | ditto | then do |
| Thos. Bishop | P. | | | do |
| *George Collins | P. | | not heard of since June muster | |
| Zachariah Mills | P. | | | |
| Chas. Sickle | P. | | | |

| NAME AND RANK. | WHEN COMMENCED. | WHEN LEFT SERVICE AND THE REASONS. | REMARKS. |
|---|---|---|---|
| 5 Co., 2 B. | LT. THOS. PRICE. | ENSIGN THOS. BEATTY. | |
| Saml. F. Shoemaker | S. | All on | |
| Francis MaGauran | S. | 1 Jan '82 | Qr. Mr. Serjt. |
| Chas. Ronenberger | S. | unless | |
| Jacob Keyser | S. | otherwise | disch'd 13 Feb '82 |
| Moses McKinsey | C. | noted | reduced 10 Nov '82 |
| Joshua McKinsey | C. | | ditto |
| John Roach | C. | | reduced 1 May '82 |
| Jas. Ashley | C. | | |
| Benj. Cole | C. | | |
| George Silver | P. | | |
| Henry Fisher, 1st | P. | | |
| Adam Mushler | P. | | |
| Michl. Rhydmyer | P. | | |
| George Bough | P. | | |
| Owen Curly | P. | deserted 22 June '82 | |
| John Wade | P. | | |
| *John Malady | P. | not heard of since June muster | |
| Wm. Ryder | P. | | |
| Thos. Larmore | P. | | |
| Danl. Williams | P. | | |
| John Follet | P. | deserted 30 June '82 | |
| Cornelius Vaughan | P. | | |
| Michl. Hardman | P. | | |
| Chas. Jones | P. | | |
| *Jas. Tite | P. | not heard of since June muster | |
| Francis Karns | P. | | Inlisted in '78 in the German Regt. and was drafted in the line in '81 for the War |
| John Walker, 2nd | P. | | |
| John Shively | P. | deserted 19 Apl '82 | |
| Wm. Sillwood | P. | | promoted C. 1 Oct '82, reduced 27 Dec |
| Jas. Johnston | P. | deserted 19 Apl '82 | |
| Christopher Smith | P. | | |
| Nathan Aldridge | P. | | |
| John Stanton | P. | | |
| *Edwd. Wade | P. | not heard of since June muster | |
| Alex. Robinson | P. | | |
| Jas. Erwin | P. | | |
| Thos. Jones, 2nd | P. | | |
| Joseph McAtlee | P. | | |

| NAME AND RANK. | WHEN COMMENCED. | WHEN LEFT SERVICE AND THE REASONS. | REMARKS. |
|---|---|---|---|
| Saml. Harrison | P. | All on | died 2 Aug '82 | |
| Mathias Cyphert | P. | 1 Jan '82 | |
| Peter Cones | P. | unless | deserted 11 Feb '82 |
| Thos. Hutchcroft | P. | otherwise | |
| Richd. Haislip | P. | noted | |
| Nathan Hoursbury | P. | | deserted 20 July '82 |
| Luke Merryman | P. | | |
| John Wilson, 1st | P. | | |
| John Thompson | P. | | |
| Wm. Hancock | P. | | deserted 1 June '82 |
| John Nicholson | P. | | |
| *Henry Wilstock | P. | | not heard of since March muster | then on Com'd Va. |
| Jacob Coffman | P. | | deserted 1 July '82 |
| Danl. Kettle | P. | | |
| Samual Wright | P. | | died 20 Jan '82 | sick Fred'sburgh |
| Chas. Williams | P. | | |
| John Nevitt, 2nd | P. | | |
| Saml. Boswell | P. | | |
| Jesse McKinsey | P. | | |
| Abraham Kettle | P. | | |
| *Timothy Cahill | P. | | not heard of since June muster |
| Chas. Leago | P. | | | furloughed to Mary'd |
| Handy Handly | P. | | deserted 6 Nov '81 |
| *Michl. Downs | P. | | not heard of since March muster | then sick Wm's-burg, Va. |
| *Wm. Hamilton, 2nd | P. | | ditto | ditto      ditto |
| Arthur Coffins | P. | | |
| *Henry Ferns | P. | | ditto | then Hosp'l George Town, Md. |
| Francis Purcell | P. | | |
| John Haines | P. | | died 2 Feb '83 |
| John Fennell, 1st | P. | | | sick Annapolis |
| John Turner, 2nd | P. | | | do Baltimore |
| *Wm. Newberry | P. | | on June muster and surplus roll |

1 Co., 3 B.  CAPT. CHRISTIAN ORENDORF.  LT. JOHN T. LOWE.
ENSIGN SAML. B. BEALL.

| NAME AND RANK. | WHEN COMMENCED. | WHEN LEFT SERVICE AND THE REASONS. | REMARKS. |
|---|---|---|---|
| Michael Smith, 1st | S. | | |
| *Jacob Doyne | S. | 16 June '82 | |
| Benj. Ward | S. | | |
| George Finlay | S. | | |
| George Holton | S. | | |
| James Wood | S. | | on Command |

| NAME AND RANK. | WHEN COMMENCED. | | WHEN LEFT SERVICE AND THE REASONS. | REMARKS. |
|---|---|---|---|---|
| *James Clement | C. | All on | not heard of since June muster | |
| Bennit George | C. | 1 Jan '82 | dead 1 Oct '82 | |
| Saml. Gray | C. | unless | | |
| John D. Tulley | C. | otherwise | | reduced 1 Oct '82 |
| Archibald Butt | D. | noted | | transferred to N. C. Line 28 Apl '82 |
| *Henry Harris | D. | | not heard of since March muster | then sick at Wm's-burgh |
| Daniel Willis | F. | | | on furlough |
| *John Burke | P. | | not heard of since June muster | |
| Thos. Gordon, 1st | P. | | deserted 16 Apl '82 | |
| *Henry Connelly | P. | | not heard of since June muster | |
| Levin Abbott | P. | | | |
| Wm. Harrison, 1st | P. | | | |
| Richard Ariss | P. | | deserted 16 Apl '82 | |
| *Edwd. Scantlin | P. | | not heard of since June muster | |
| Matthew Carty | P. | | | |
| *Henry Enniss | P. | | ditto | |
| Jacob Collins | P. | | | |
| James Jones | P. | | | |
| *George Belfast | P. | | ditto | |
| John Starkey | P. | | | |
| Garrett Welch | P. | | | |
| John Smith, 2nd | P. | | on June muster and surplus roll | |
| Wm. Aggas | P. | | deserted 29 Apl '82 | |
| Barton Cecil | S. | | disch'd 13 Jan '82 | |
| Walter C. Davids | S. | | deserted 1 Jan '83 | |
| Jas. Chambers | P. | | | |
| Edwd. Furrener | P. | | | |
| John Cole | P. | | | |
| Thomas John | P. | | | |
| Oliver Stephens | P. | | | |
| Wm. Standley | P. | | | |
| Jas. Smith, 3d | P. | | | sick Annapolis |
| *Eccabut Golden | P. | | not heard of since March muster | then    ditto |
| Wm. Smith, 1st | P. | | | ditto |
| *John Steward, 1st | P. | | ditto | then    ditto |
| *Edwd. Bartlett | P. | | ditto | |
| | | | | then sick Wm'sburgh |
| Stephen Hancock | P. | | | ditto |
| Jas. Reynolds, 2nd | P. | | | |
| Jas. Brannin | P. | | | ditto |
| Robt. Carns | P. | | | ditto |
| Edwd. Mahoney | P. | | | ditto |

| NAME AND RANK. | | WHEN COMMENCED. | WHEN LEFT SERVICE AND THE REASONS. | REMARKS. |
|---|---|---|---|---|
| *John Holston | P. | All on | not heard of since | then sick |
| | | 1 Jan '82 | March muster | Wm'sburgh |
| *Peter Hollaby | P. | unless | ditto | ditto  ditto |
| *Abraham Reynolds | P. | otherwise | ditto | ditto  ditto |
| Chas. Murphy | P. | noted | | |
| James Wilson, 2d | P. | | | |
| *Wm. Dunkin | P. | | ditto | ditto  ditto |
| Thos. Perry | P. | | | |
| John Smallwood, 2d | P. | | | |
| Jacob Jeffers | P. | | | |
| Wm. Taylor, 2d | P. | | | |
| Benj. Baulk | P. | | | |
| Wm. McPherson | P. | | | |
| *Wm. Elbom | P. | | not heard of since | then sick |
| | | | March muster | Wm'sburg |
| *Leonard Turner | P. | | deserted | |
| *Ephraim Ganes | P. | | ditto | |

2 Co., 3 B.   Capt. Jas. W. Gray.  Lt. Rignal Hillary.   Lt. Philip Hill.
Ensign Basil Waring.

| NAME AND RANK. | | WHEN LEFT SERVICE AND THE REASONS. | REMARKS. |
|---|---|---|---|
| John Reeder | S. | | |
| John Lynch, 1st | S. | | |
| John Hamond Dorsey | S. | deserted 1 Jan '82 | |
| John Moore, 4th | C. | | |
| Wm. Little | C. | | |
| Peter French | C. | | |
| Wm. Wilison, 1st | C. | | promoted Sergt. |
| | | | 1 Oct '82 |
| John Morrison | D. | | |
| John Onians | D. | | |
| Jas. Cholard | F.& P. | | reduced 1 Apl '82 |
| John Graham | F. | | prisoner 1 May '82 |
| Michael Pilkerton | P. | | |
| Jacob Dudderow | P. | | |
| *John Flowers | P. | not heard of since June muster | |
| Wm. Dawson | P. | | |
| Frederick Jams | P. | | |
| Dennis Trammell | P. | | |
| John Gorman | P. | | |
| David Hatten | P. | | |
| *Charles Willet | P. | not heard of since June muster | |
| Levin Thomas | P. | | |
| Edward Chambers | P. | | |
| Edward Tanner | P. | | |
| Joseph Lewis | P. | | |

| NAME AND RANK. | WHEN COMMENCED. | WHEN LEFT SERVICE AND THE REASONS. | REMARKS. |
|---|---|---|---|
| Joshua Cox | P. | All on | |
| Wm. Glaver | P. | 1 Jan '82 | |
| *Wm. Roe, 3rd | P. | unless | not heard of since June muster |
| John Spears | P. | otherwise | |
| John Francis | P. | noted | |
| Wm. Taylor, 3rd | P. | | |
| John McCall | P. | | |
| *John Appingstall | P. | | not heard of since June muster |
| Chas. Dean | P. | | |
| Saml. Rudolph | P. | | deserted 15 Apl '82 |
| Barnaby Doherty | P. | | |
| Francis Reed | P. | | |
| Nehemiah Lingard | P. | | |
| James Tigner | P. | | |
| Wm. Simonds | P. | | |
| Wm. Goody | P. | | deserted 1 Jan '82 |
| Lambert Goody | P. | | |
| Saml. Hurst | P. | | |
| Philip Savoy | P. | | |
| John Bowdy | P. | | |
| *Henry Ferrence | P. | | not heard of since then sick at Hospital March muster Georgetown |
| Aaron Perry | P. | | deserted 1 Feb '82 [6 Sept '81 |
| Dennis Cragon | P. | | |
| *Archibald Kersey | P. | | not heard of since June muster |
| John Young, 2nd | P. | | Com'd Maryland |
| *Joseph McLain | P. | | not heard of since then Hospital March muster Annapolis Aug '81 |
| *Philip McDonald | P. | | ditto then ditto |
| James Carey | P. | | |
| Nicholas Free | P. | 18 Dec '82 | |
| James Hudson | P. | | Hospital Annapolis Aug '81 |
| John Hudson, 1st | P. | | ditto |
| John Murray, 1st | P. | | ditto |
| *Robert Tolgan | P. | | not heard of since then ditto March muster |
| John Clancey | P. | | made Corporal ditto Georgetown 6 Sept '81 |
| *Robert Eaton | P. | | not heard of since then ditto March muster |
| *Jas. Crumwell | P. | | ditto then ditto Wm'sburgh Oct '81 |
| Jas. Chard | P. | | ditto |
| *Jas. Lynch | P. | | ditto then ditto |

| NAME AND RANK. | | WHEN COMMENCED. | WHEN LEFT SERVICE AND THE REASONS. | REMARKS. |
|---|---|---|---|---|
| *Andrew Flood | P. | All on 1 Jan '82 | not heard of since June muster | |
| *Patrick Fleming | P. | unless otherwise | not heard of since March muster | then Wm'sburgh Oct '81 |
| *Oliver Denny | P. | noted | ditto | ditto   ditto |
| *Wm. Bowden | P. | | ditto | ditto   ditto |
| | | | | in Nov '81 |
| Jas. Creighton, Craighton | P. | | | ditto |
| John Gee | P. | | | ditto |
| *Peter Baker | P. | | ditto | then   ditto |
| John McLain | P. | | | ditto |
| *John Thompson | P. | | not heard of since June muster | |
| Henry Fisher, 2nd | P. | | | |
| Wm. Hartman | P. | | | |

|  | 3 Co., 3 B.   CAPT. BENJ. PRICE.   LT. JAS. WINCHESTER. | | | |
|---|---|---|---|---|
| Archibald Johnston | S. | | | |
| George Fields | S. | | | |
| Nicholas Nicholson | S. | | | |
| Theophilus Linsey | C. | | | |
| Joseph Pherson | C. | | | |
| John Cooper, 1st | P. | | | |
| Wm. Potter | C. | | | |
| George Hamilton | C. | | | reduced 1 Oct '82 |
| Peter Boyall | C. | | died 15 Jan '82 | sick W'msburg |
| John Hannon | F. | | | |
| Isaac Hill | F. | | | |
| Isaac Young | D. | | | |
| John Jones, 2d | D. & P. | | | reduced 1 Feb '82 |
| Benj. Smith | P. | | | |
| Joseph Austin | P. | | deserted 17 May '82 | |
| Wm. Wheylin | P. | | | |
| Nicholas Hyner | P. | | | |
| *Stephen Kimble | P. | | not heard of since June muster | |
| John McGlin | P. | | | |
| Henry Hughes | P. | | deserted 17 May '82 | |
| Zachariah Robertson | P. | | | |
| Thomas Clark, 2d | P. | | | |
| Jas. Knott | P. | | | |
| Benj. Marsh | P. | | | |
| John Armstrong, 2d | P. | | | |
| Levi Moody | P. | | died 15 Oct '82 | |
| Henry Townley | P. | | | |
| Patrick Kelly | P. | | deserted 17 May '82 | |
| Wm. Elkins | P. | | | |

| NAME AND RANK. | WHEN COMMENCED. | WHEN LEFT SERVICE AND THE REASONS. | REMARKS. |
|---|---|---|---|
| Jas. Philips | P. | All on | |
| Jeremiah Sullivan | P. | 1 Jan '82 | |
| Jas. Shepherd | P. | unless | |
| Joseph Cooley | P. | otherwise | disch'd 9 Jan '82 |
| Chas. Clements | P. | noted | promoted C. 1 Oct '82 |
| Richd. Spires | P. | | |
| Patrick Reed | P. | | deserted 17 May '82 |
| John Newton, 2d | P. | | |
| Richd. Dickson | P. | | died 27 Dec '82 |
| Patrick McKinsey | P. | | |
| John Smith, 3d | P. | | |
| *Thos. Allen | P. | | not heard of since then sick |
| | | | March muster  Annapolis 1 Jan '82 |
| Peter Carbury | P. | | ditto |
| George Linton | P. | | ditto |
| Jas. Stewart, 2d | P. | | Mch   ditto |
| Jas. Terry | P. | | do at Georgetown |
| John Lesley | P. | | ditto |
| John Holder | P. | | ditto |
| Thos. Tanner | P. | | died 3 Jan '82  do at W'msburgh |
| *John Durant | P. | | not heard of since  ditto |
| | | | June muster |
| *Benj. Shaw | P. | | not heard of since then   ditto |
| | | | March muster |
| *Wm. Turner | P. | | ditto   then  ditto |
| *John Keech | P. | | ditto   then  ditto |
| Thos. Jones, 3d | P. | | discharged  then  ditto |
| | | | 13 March '82 |
| Wm. Marlow | P. | | do prod. X Serjt. |
| | | | 1 Nov '82 |
| *Abraham Manhan, or | | | Mch sick at W'msburgh |
| Manning | P. | | to be made up |
| *Michael Downes | P. | | not heard of since then   ditto |
| | | | March muster |
| *James Lyles | P. | | ditto   then  ditto |
| John Stoffle | P. | | ditto |
| Robert Campbell | P. | | ditto |
| Jonathan Lewis | P. | | |
| Randolph Hoskins | P. | | disch'd 8 Jan '82 |
| *John Flanagan | P. | | not heard of since  sick Petersburgh |
| | | | June muster |
| David Relly | P. | | do Charlotte |
| John Smyth, 4th | P. | | ditto |
| John Brown, 2d | P. | | ditto |
| *John Patterson | P. | | ditto   ditto |

| NAME AND RANK. | | WHEN COMMENCED. | WHEN LEFT SERVICE AND THE REASONS. | REMARKS. |
|---|---|---|---|---|
| *Patrick Reading | P. | All on 1 Jan '82 | not heard of since March muster | then Smith at Annapolis |
| *Saml. Silk | P. | unless | ditto | then Armourer, do |
| John McNeal | P. | otherwise | | Waggoner |
| *Wm. Dych | P. | noted | not heard of since June muster | Artificer |
| John Fulford | P. | | | |
| *Henry Clark | P. | | ditto | |
| Edward Cosgrove | P. | | | |
| John Wise | P. | | deserted 4 May '82 | Boon's Hospl. 4 March '82 |
| Andrew Rereside | P. | | died 16 Dec '82 | ditto |
| John Hewlett | P. | | | ditto |
| Paul Rowwen | P. | | | look Genl. Gist |

4 Co., 3 B.   CAPT. FRANCIS REVELLEY.   LT. HENRY BALDWIN.

| NAME AND RANK. | | WHEN COMMENCED. | WHEN LEFT SERVICE AND THE REASONS. | REMARKS. |
|---|---|---|---|---|
| Timothy McMahon | S. | | | promoted S. Major 10 Jan '82 |
| James Collins | S. | | | |
| John Neary | S. | | | |
| John Newman | S. | | | |
| Wm. Clements | C. | | | |
| Danl. Brimugum | C. | | | reduced 1 Oct '82 |
| John McCaliff | D. | | | do 1 Apl '82 |
| Philip Huston | D. | | | |
| John Biggs | P. | | | |
| Joseph White | P. | | | |
| Thomas Matthews, 1st | P. | | | |
| Wm. Downes | P. | | | |
| John Carroll, 1st | P. | | disch'd 13 Jan '82 | |
| Richd. Dolvin | P. | | | |
| Henry Williams | P. | | | |
| Jas. Humphries | P. | | | |
| Wm. Porter | P. | | | |
| John Collins | P. | | | |
| Nathaniel Ross | P. | | | |
| John Hurly | P. | | | |
| Francis Taylor | P. | | | |
| Wm. Mansfield | P. | | | |
| William Brady | P. | | | |
| *Danl. Duncan | P. | | | pris. 11 Apl '82 |
| Elijah Hutt | P. | | | |
| Thomas Shortwill | P. | | deserted 9 Apl '82 | |
| *Thos. Crofford | P. | | | pris. 11 Apl '82 |
| Francis Burton | P. | | do 15 May '82 | |

| NAME AND RANK. | | WHEN COMMENCED. | WHEN LEFT SERVICE AND THE REASONS. | REMARKS. |
|---|---|---|---|---|
| John Matthews, 2d | P. | All on | disch'd 16 Feb '82 | |
| *John McRhea | P. | 1 Jan '82 | | |
| Ebram, Abram, Doogan | P. | unless | | |
| Nicholas Elliott | P. | otherwise | | pro. Fifer 1 Apl '82 |
| Christian Clore, (or Close) | P. | noted | died 1 Mch '82 | |
| Benj. Williams, 3d | P. | | | |
| Peter Equed Downey | P. | | | |
| John Carll, 1st | P. | | | |
| Jas. Bailess | P. | | | |
| Jeremiah Owens | P. | | | |
| Wm. Coe | P. | | | Waggoner |
| Guilford Miniky | P. | | | |
| Richd. Dunby | P. | | | |
| Thos. Adams | P. | | | Waggoner |
| Thos. Matthews | P. | | | Waggoner |
| Thos. B. Clements | P. | | | |
| John Harris, 2d | P. | | | |
| James Cougherin, or Cockerile | P. | | | |
| Jas. Evans | P. | | | |
| Thos. Jones, 4th | P. | | | |
| John Thomas, 2nd | P. | | | |
| Thos. Wood, 2nd | P. | | | |
| *Edward Appleton | P. | | not heard of since March muster | then on furlough Md., Jan '82 |
| *Emanual Eabbs | P. | | ditto | then on Comd. Annapolis, Jan '82 |
| *Edward Blake | P. | | ditto | then on Clothl. Genl. Guard |
| John King | P. | | | transf. 2 Regt. 4 Apl '82 |
| John Jordan | P. | | deserted 19 Apl '82 | |
| *George Cougheren | P. | | not heard of since March muster | then sick Petersburg |
| Solomon Green | P. | | | |
| Pressley Bruenton | P. | | | sick Peterbourough |
| Joseph McNamara | P. | | | Mch sick W'msburgh |
| *Wm. Gantley | P. | | ditto | ditto    ditto |
| Jas. Davidson | P. | | | |
| *Jas. Hays | P. | | ditto | ditto |
| Saml. Chappel | P. | | | sick W'msburgh |
| *Neal McCowen | P. | | not heard of since March muster | then ditto |
| John Kildare | P. | | | Mch do Georgetown |
| *Matthew Stanton | P. | | ditto | then do  Annapolis |

| NAME AND RANK. | | WHEN COMMENCED. | WHEN LEFT SERVICE AND THE REASONS. | REMARKS. |
|---|---|---|---|---|
| *John Nolen | P. | 21 Dec '82 | | |
| John Pendar | P. | | died 10 Nov '81 | sick W'msburgh |
| Alex. Steward | P. | All on | | Mch sick W'msburgh |
| *Thos. Blansher | P. | 1 Jan '82 unless | not heard of since Mch muster | then do Annapolis |
| John Willis | P. | otherwise | | ditto |
| John Ransom | P. | noted | | ditto |
| *Ezekial Taylor | P. | | ditto | then ditto |
| John Hickins | P. | | | ditto |
| *Francis Matthews | P. | | ditto | then ditto |
| Thos. Ellitt, 1st | P. | 10 Feb '82 | | |

1 Co., 4 B.　CAPT. WM. WILMOT.　LT. MARK MCPHERSON.

| NAME AND RANK. | | WHEN COMMENCED. | WHEN LEFT SERVICE AND THE REASONS. | REMARKS. |
|---|---|---|---|---|
| Thos. Edwards | S. | | | |
| Hugh McMillan | S. | | | |
| John Gwin | S. | | | |
| Wm. Needham | S. | | | on Command, Jan '82 |
| John Colein | S. . | | | |
| Chas. Harvey | S. | | trans. Invalids 10 Jan '83 | |
| George Bradley | C. | | died 31 Nov '82 | |
| *Richd. Fenwick | C. | | not heard of since March muster | then on furlough Md., and he must produce a Certificate of his doing duty after being furloughed or he will be Considered a deserter |
| Richd. Ferraby | C. | | | |
| Wm. Smyth, 2d | D. | | | pris. War in Charlestown 10 Dec '82 |
| John McKnight | D. | | | |
| Thos. Clinton | F. | | | |
| John Beach | D. | | died 15 Dec '82 | |
| Joseph Follett | F. | | died 25 July '82 | |
| Wm. Douglass | P. | | deserted 20 Nov '82 | Waiter Dr. [Brown, Md. |
| Peter Topping | P. | | | |
| Michael Callihorne | P. | | | |
| Jeremiah Rhodes | P. | | disch'd 17 Feb '82 | |
| John Hyde | P. | | | |
| Emmanuel Carthagena | P. | | | |
| John Crosby, 1st | P. | | died 24 July '82 | |
| Robinson Wood | P. | | | |
| Rueben Smith | P. | | | |
| John Kidd | P. | | | |

| NAME AND RANK. | | WHEN COMMENCED. | WHEN LEFT SERVICE AND THE REASONS. | REMARKS. |
|---|---|---|---|---|
| James Gray | P. | All on | | |
| Hugh Gaynor | P. | 1 Jan '82 | | |
| Wm. Carter, 2d | P. | unless | | Flying Hospl. N. Army |
| Joseph Johnson | P. | otherwise | | |
| Jas. Wood | P. | noted | | |
| Wm. Ingle | P. | | | |
| *Robert Lynch | P. | | not heard of since November muster | |
| Jeremiah Williams | P. | | | |
| *John Young, 1st | P. | | not heard of since June muster | |
| Adam Jamieson | P. | | | |
| Thos. Murphy | P. | | | |
| Isaac Holliday | P. | | | |
| *John Bellamy | P. | | ditto | |
| *Edward Freeman | P. | | ditto | |
| Elijah Smith | P. | | | |
| *Jas. Silver | P. | | ditto | |
| Daniel O'Quinn | P. | | | |
| John Berryman | P. | | | |
| Thos. Slade | P. | | | |
| Joseph Batts | P. | | | |
| Dennis Flannigan | P. | | Private, Artillery | |
| Henry Ramsden, Ramsey | P. | | | |
| John Vanzant | P. | | | furlough Md. |
| John Dunnigan | P. | | | Hospl. Camden |
| John Lynch, 2d | P. | | | |
| *Cornelius Murphy | P. | | not heard of since June muster | |
| Wm. Evans | P. | | | furlough Md. |
| Conrad Smith | P. | | | |
| *Joseph Whitehouse | P. | | not heard of since March muster | then prisoner War |
| Edward Evans | P. | | | Hospl. Camden |
| *John Linday | P. | | ditto | then furlough Md. |
| James Gath | P. | | | do |
| Matthew Moore, 2d | P. | | | Waggoner |
| Henry Redding | P. | | | do |
| *Jarvis Williams | P. | | ditto | then in Md. |
| *Robert Stacey | P. | | not heard of since June muster | |
| Joseph Roberts | P. | | | Mch waiter in Md. |
| Philip Bailey | P. | | | waiter Genl. Gist |
| Wm. Purcell | P. | | not heard of since March | then waiter to Col. Wms. |
| Edward Wright | P. | | | do to Dr. Smith, Savannah |
| Joseph Bautcheby | P. | | | Taylor, Charlotte |
| Wm. Pecker | P. | | | |

30

| NAME AND RANK. | | WHEN COMMENCED. | WHEN LEFT SERVICE AND THE REASONS. | REMARKS. |
|---|---|---|---|---|
| Evan Tumbleston | P. | All on | | |
| Thos. Wood, 1st | P. | 1 Jan '82 | | furlough Maryland |
| Christopher McAway | P. | unless | | Artificer |
| Michael Smith, 2d | P. | otherwise | | |
| *Edward Walter | P. | noted. | | |
| *Wm. Morecraft | P. | 15 Feb '82 | not heard of since March muster | ? |
| | | | | |
| Philip Graham | P. | | | |
| Asaph Colegate | P. | | | |
| Wm. Hedge | P. | | | |
| Michael Clark, 2d | P. | | | |
| Ralph Hope | P. | | | |
| *Henry Matthews | P. | | not heard of since March muster | then on Guard |

2 Co., 4 B. Capt. John Mitchell.   Lt. John McCoy.   Ensign Joseph Cross.

| NAME AND RANK. | | WHEN LEFT SERVICE AND THE REASONS. | REMARKS. |
|---|---|---|---|
| Thos. Duffee | S. | | |
| John Willing | S. | | |
| George Lash | S. | deserted 11 Apl '82 | |
| Kinsey Lanham | C. | died 20 Dec '82 | |
| Nathaniel, or Nathan, Price | C. | | promoted S. 1 March '83 |
| Chas. Nabb | C. | | sick W'msburg North Carolina |
| *Walter Evans | C. | not heard of since March muster | then ditto Virginia |
| Edward Henesy | P. | | |
| Frederick Myers, Myirs | P. | deserted 11 Apl '82 | |
| Cato Snowden | P. | | |
| Ignatius Smith | P. | died 20 Apl '82 | |
| Wm. Absalom | P. | | |
| *Richard Clark | P. | not heard of since June muster | then Armour Artificers |
| Thomas Long | P. | | |
| Aaron Mitchell | P. | | |
| Humphry Wells | P. | | |
| Joseph Jeans | S. | | |
| Levi Scott | F. | | |
| John Burns | P. | | |
| Timothy Langrel | P. | | |
| John Hudson, 2d | P. | | |
| George Jones | P. | | |
| Wm. Cork | P. | | |
| Daniel Mann | P. | | |
| Walter Prewit | P. | | |

| Name and Rank. | When Commenced. | When left Service and the Reasons. | Remarks. |
|---|---|---|---|
| Smart Greor | P. | All on | |
| John Taylor, 2d | P. | 1 Jan '82 | |
| Jas. Bowen | P. | unless | |
| Edward Fincham | P. | otherwise | not heard of since June muster |
| *Wm. Grant | P. | noted. | |
| John Dobson | P. | | |
| Amos Griffin | P. | | |
| Wm. Paul | P. | | |
| Francis McCann | P. | | |
| John Lonass | P. | died 2 Oct '82 | Waggoner |
| Alyard Melvin | P. | | |
| *Wm. Richardson | P. | time expires 1 Apl '82 | June do |
| John Briley, or Bailey | P. | | |
| Thos. Elliott, 2d | P. | | |
| Thos. Davies | P. | | |
| John Watkins | P. | | |
| Wm. Whittico | P. | | |
| Michael McKnight | P. | deserted 25 Apl '82 | |
| Saml. Green | P. | disch'd 9 Jan '82 | |
| John Nelson | P. | | Waggoner |
| Wm. Lee, 1st | P. | | do |
| Thos. Foxall | P. | | do |
| Heath C. Edwards | P. | | do |
| Jacob Yeast | P. | | do |
| Pompey Hollis | P. | died in 1783 | do |
| *John Charles | P. | disch'd 15 Mch '83 | |
| *John O'Conner | P. | not heard of since March muster | then sick Hospl. Virginia |
| *John Cuthart | P. | ditto | then do |
| John Cleverdence | P. | | do |
| *Wm. Bercus | P. | not heard of since June muster | do |
| *Wm. Donoho | P. | not heard of since March muster | then do |
| David Meadows | P. | | do W'msburg |
| George Carney | P. | | do |
| Wm. Burgess | P. | | |
| Timothy Donnelly | P. | deserted 15 Apl '82 | |
| Robt. Michael | P. | | |
| *John Stephens | P. | not heard of since March muster | then sick Hospl. in Virginia |
| *Jas. Darnell | P. | ditto | then do |
| Danl. Murphy | P. | | do |
| *Cornish Freind | P. | ditto | then do |

| NAME AND RANK. | | WHEN COMMENCED. | WHEN LEFT SERVICE AND THE REASONS. | REMARKS. |
|---|---|---|---|---|
| *John Poxman | P. | All on 1 Jan '82 | not heard of since March muster | then sick Hospl. Virginia |
| *Thos. Lane | P. | unless | ditto | then Petersburg |
| *Charles Gordon | P. | otherwise | ditto | do do |
| *Martin Rosah | P. | noted. | not heard of since June muster | then sick Hospl. |
| John Edwards | P. | | | N. Carolina |
| Wm. Fairburne | P. | | died 16 Mch '82 | refer to Gray for his death |
| Thos. Burk | P. | | | sick N. Carolina |
| John Betsworth | P. | | deserted 5 Apl '82 | |
| Luke Griffin | P. | | | sick S. Carolina |

3 Co., 4 B. Lt. Edmond Compton. Ensign Wm. Hanson.

| NAME AND RANK. | | WHEN COMMENCED. | WHEN LEFT SERVICE AND THE REASONS. | REMARKS. |
|---|---|---|---|---|
| Chas. Fulham | S. | | | |
| George Williams | S. | | | reduced 7 Apl '82 |
| John Walker, 3rd | S. | | | sick Maryland |
| Basil Shaw | S. | | | |
| Saml. Evans | C. | | | promoted Serjt. 7 Apl '82 |
| Wm. Browning | C. | | deserted 2 July '82 | |
| Nathan Harper | D. | | | |
| John T. West | F. | | on June muster & surplus roll | waited of Major Winder |
| Alex. Levi | P. | | | |
| Peter Degazoone | P. | | | |
| Patrick Dennison | P. | | | |
| Thos. Crampton | P. | | | |
| *Thos. Gray | P. | | on June muster not heard of since | promoted Corpl. 1 Apl '82 |
| Abraham Catchsides | P. | | | |
| Wm. Manly | P. | | | |
| Thos. Pender | P. | | | |
| Stephen Fennell | P. | | | |
| Thos. Pennifield | P. | | | |
| Henry Crane | P. | | | |
| Jacob Myers | P. | | | |
| John West | P. | | | |
| Jonathan Chubb, | P. | | | |
| Richard Wiley | P. | | | |
| Lambert Philips | P. | | | |
| John Blair | P. | | disch'd 15 Jan '82 | |
| Thos. Ellis | P. | | | |
| Wm. Cox | P. | | | |

| NAME AND RANK. | WHEN COMMENCED. | WHEN LEFT SERVICE AND THE REASONS. | REMARKS. |
|---|---|---|---|
| John McGinnis | P. | All on | |
| Thos. Wember | P. | 1 Jan '82 | |
| Thos. Butt | P. | unless | |
| Wm. Toland | P. | otherwise | |
| Henry Ostin | P. | noted. | |
| Patrick Reiley, 2d | P. | | |
| Thos. Buckley | P. | | |
| George Cragg | P. | | |
| Henry Mansfield | P. | | |
| Patrick Nowlan | P. | not heard of since June muster | died last of Aug '82 |
| Henry Rice, (or Reec) | P. | | |
| David Crady | P. | on June muster & surplus roll | waiter Col. Gunby Md. |
| Jas. Huitt | P. | | artificer |
| Joseph Burch | P. | | furlough Md. |
| Wm. Newton | P. | | |
| Danl. Bulkley | P. | | |
| *Danl. Crosby | P. | not heard of since June muster | furlough Maryland |
| Baruck Butt | P. | | waiter Md. |
| Wm. Conner | P. | | do |
| George Clark | P. | | furlough Md. |
| Thos. Wood, 3d | P. | | do |
| Wm. Priest | P. | | |
| John Jones, Senr., 3d | P. | | |
| *Nathan Wheelor | P. | ditto | |
| *George F—— (?) | P. | | ditto |
| Wm. King | P. | | |
| Thos. Harrison, 1st | P. | | June sick in Va. |
| John Whitcomb | P. | | |
| *Jas. Killegan | P. | not heard of since June muster | |
| Edward Dominick | P. | | |
| Jeremiah Mudd | P. | not heard of since March muster | then furlough '81 |
| John Shanks | P. | | do |
| *Thos. Smee | P. | ditto | then do |
| John Green, 2d | P. | | furlough, may be another of the same name |
| John Conaly | P. | | |
| Jas. West | P. | | |
| Aquilla Clements | P. | | |
| Elijah Oakley | P. | | Waggoner |
| *James Smith, 4th | P. | on June muster & surplus roll | do |
| Jas. Sappington | P. | | do |

| NAME AND RANK. | | WHEN COMMENCED. | WHEN LEFT SERVICE AND THE REASONS. | REMARKS. |
|---|---|---|---|---|

4 Co., 4 B.  CAPT. GEORGE, RICHARD, BIRD.  LT. JOHN BREVET. ENSIGN THOS. A. DYSON.

| NAME AND RANK. | | WHEN COMMENCED. | WHEN LEFT SERVICE AND THE REASONS. | REMARKS. |
|---|---|---|---|---|
| Aaron Spalding | S. | All on | | |
| John Carson | S. | 1 Jan '82 | | |
| Elijah Cockendall | C. | unless | died 18 July '82 | |
| Joseph Harper | P. & C. | otherwise | | promoted Corpl. |
| Joseph Fisher | P. | noted. | died 20 Nov '82 | [9 May |
| Christian Boss | P. | | | |
| Wm. Dickerson | P. | | deserted 14 July '82 | |
| Southy George | P. | | | |
| Jacob Kelly | P. | | | |
| John Blades | P. | | | |
| Walter Ferrall | P. | | | |
| Edward Jackson | P. | | | |
| Henry T——? | P. | | | |
| Thos. Gillon, (Gauser) | P. | | | |
| John Morant | P. | | deserted 14 July '82 | |
| John Nave | P. | | | |
| Wm. Harper | P. | | | |
| Frederick Smith | P. | | | |
| *Benj. Reed | P. | | not heard of since March muster | |
| Danl. Harding | P. | | deserted 14 July '82 | |
| Thos. Smith, 2d | P. | | | |
| Jas. Driver | P. | | | |
| Danl. Foxwell | P. | | | |
| Wm. Chapman | P. | | | |
| Isaac Nicholls | P. | | | |
| John Morriss | P. | | | |
| John Fossett | P. | | | |
| James Halleron | P. | | died 16 Dec '82 | |
| Edward Reiley | P. | | | |
| Wm. H. Savage | P. | | | |
| Murphy Shee | P. | | | |
| John Johnson, 1st | P. | | | |
| Jacob Adams, or Adamson | P. | | | |
| Thos. Richardson | P. | | | |
| Wm. Corsey | P. | | | |
| *Wm. Justice | P. | | not heard of since March muster | |
| *Charles Horner | P. | | not heard of since June muster | |
| Wm. Camm | P. | | | |
| *Basset McClary | P. | | not heard of since June muster | |
| Thos. Watson | P. | | | ⎧ of Capt. |
| Wm. Inglis | P. | | deserted previous to 1782 | ⎨ Sellman's |
| Wm. West | P. | | disch'd 13 Jan '82 | ⎩ Co. |

| NAME AND RANK. | | WHEN COMMENCED. | WHEN LEFT SERVICE AND THE REASONS. | REMARKS. |
|---|---|---|---|---|
| Benj. Fitzgerald | S. | All on | | |
| Wm. Pherson | P. | 1 Jan '82 | prisoner 1 May '82 | Capt. Prall's Co. |
| Solomon Barrett | P. | unless | | Rieley's Co. |
| *Joseph Turner | P. | otherwise | | |
| *John Hicks | P. | noted. | | |
| *Ralph Tawney | P. | | not heard of since March muster | said to be transferred from Sellman's Co. to 2d Regt. |
| Thos. Hammond | P. | | | |
| *Thos. Pott | P. | | ditto | |
| Allen Townshend | P. | | | |
| Wm. Willson, 2d | P. | | | Gray's Co. |
| Fredk. Stoffel | P. | | died 16 Jan '82 | Price |
| Benj. Belcher | F. | | | Mitchell |
| Jas. McDonald | D. | | | do |
| Robt. Bowen | D. | | | do |
| *George Kelty | P. | | | |
| *Wm. Holt | P. | | not mustered since | |
| *Wm. Roberts, 3d | P. | | | |
| Chas. Orms | P. | | | |
| John Wright | P. | | | |
| *Lawrence Simpson | P. | | | |
| *James Anderson | P. | 26 March '82 | | |
| John Knox | P. | 1 Apl '82 | transfd. from Pa. Line | |
| James Managa | P. | | | |
| *John Lashley | P. | | | |
| Elias Smith | P. | | | |
| James Dyer, 2d | P. | | disch'd 1 Sept '82 | |
| *Wm. Cook | P. | | | |
| *Chas. Wheelor | P. | | | |
| *Robt. Cornick | D. | | | |
| *Henry Jacobs | P. | | | |
| *Joseph Barton | P. | | | |
| *John McNally | P. | | | |
| *Saml. Wedge | P. | | | |
| *John Wiley | C. | (not stated) | | |
| *Henry Lawers | P. | (not stated) | | |
| Richd. Butler | P. | (not stated) | | served 12 months |
| Saml. Vermillion | P. | | | |
| *Richd. Price | S. | (not stated) | | |
| *George Pearce | P. | (not stated) | | |
| *John McCann | P. | | | |
| *John Delany | P. | (not stated) | | |
| James Due | P. | | | |
| *Henry Bradley | P. | 23 July '82 | | |

| NAME AND RANK. | | WHEN COMMENCED. | WHEN LEFT SERVICE AND THE REASONS. | REMARKS. |
|---|---|---|---|---|
| *Joshua Barrett | S. | All on | | |
| Lawrence Mesler | P. | 1 Jan '82 | | |
| *Danl. Holdman | P. | unless | | |
| *James Dawer | | otherwise noted | must produce a certificate | on Surplus Roll |
| Elijah Sullivan | | 3 May | to the end | do ⌠ not on any |
| *Danl. Stephens | | 24 July | ditto | do ⎹ previous |
| George Patrick | | | | do ⎹ roll |
| *Wm. Walker | | | | do ⌡ |

MUSE' Co.

| NAME AND RANK. | | WHEN COMMENCED. | WHEN LEFT SERVICE AND THE REASONS. | REMARKS. |
|---|---|---|---|---|
| Nathaniel Bailey | S. | | | on detacht. Nd. |
| John McDonald | S. | | | do |
| Wm. Smith | P. | 9 Aug '82 | | do |
| *Wm. Keough | P. | | deserted 23 Nov '82 | do |
| *John Cole | P. | | do 20 do | do |
| *John Sewall | F. | 11 Aug | do 20 do | do |
| *George Plumly | P. | | disch'd 31 Dec '82 | do |
| Benj. Burck | C. | | do 19 Jan '83 | do |
| Hezekiah Massey | P. | | do 31 Dec '82 | do |
| *Elijah Lyons | P. | 24 Apl | deserted from Head of Elk, 14 Nov '82 | do |
| *John Gardner | P. | | ditto 1 Jan '83 | |
| *Wm. Johnson, 1st | S. | | | |
| Robt. Harpin | S. | | | |
| Isaac Johnson | C. | | | |
| Evan Thomas | C. | | | |
| *Jas. Barron | C. | | | |
| Robt. Firth | P. | | | |
| *John Reed | P. | 14 March | | |
| *Danl. McCollum | P. | 20 July | | |
| *Lewis Flash | P. | 6 Apl | | |
| *John Rodgers | P. | 18 March | | |
| *Jeremiah Carter | P. | 16 Apl | | |
| *Roger Hogan | P. | 29 Apl | | |
| *Thos. McQuinney | | 28 Apl | | |
| *Francis Dewist | | | | |
| *Wm. Batton | | 10 Mch | | |
| *Thos. McKinsie | | 23 Apl | | |
| Wm. Griffin | F. | | disch'd 15 May '82 | |
| John Waller | | | 2d | |
| *Binneck Meakins | P. | 29 Mch | | |
| *Chas. Love | P. | 17 April | | |
| *John Pope | P. | 11 do | | |
| Wm. Devine | P. | reinlisted | | |

| NAME AND RANK. | WHEN COMMENCED. | WHEN LEFT SERVICE AND THE REASONS. | REMARKS. |
|---|---|---|---|
| *Thos. Hall | P. | 15 June | |
| *Patrick Quinn | P. | 27 Feb '82 | |
| Daniel Howe | P. | 1 Jan '82 | |
| Jas. Dowden | P. | 1 Jan '82 | |
| John Traverse | P. | 1 Jan '82 | |
| *Zachariah Berry | P. | 6 March | |
| *George Trice | P. | 15 April | |
| Edward Kirk | P. | 1 Jan '82 | |
| *Thos. Houseman | P. | (not stated) | |
| *Zadock Risden | P. | (not stated) | |
| *John Welch, 2d | P. | 1 Aug | |
| *Joseph Ward | P. | 2 April | |
| *John Gray | P. | 10 Sept | |
| *Wm. Patterson | P. | 30 May | |
| *Wm. Senah | P. | 26 July | |
| *Matthew Kelly | P. | (not stated) | |
| *George Tate | P. | 10 July | |
| Roderick McKinsie | P. | 16 Feb | |
| *Thos. Richardson, 2d | P. | 11 Aug | |
| Michael Standley | P. | 1 Jan '82 | |
| *Joseph Allen | S. | 18 March | |
| *Joseph Neal | S. | 1 Jan '82 | |
| *Basil Newton | P. | 16 March | |
| *Joseph Clancey | F. | 24 July | |
| *Thos. Ellison | C. | (not stated) | |
| *Christopher Hinson | C. | (not stated) | |
| *Isaac Dunkin | P. | 1 July | disch'd proper in '83 |
| Thos. Harris, 1st | P. | 1 Jan '82 | |
| Sylvester Gatten | P. | 2 July | |
| Wm. Hutchinson | P. | 1 Jan '82 | |
| Andrew Bramble | P. | do | |
| Selladay Standley | P. | do | |
| John Boody | P. | do | |
| John Baxter | P. | do | |
| *Wm. Powell | P. | not known | |
| *Jas. Williams | P. | 10 Apl | |
| *John Vane | P. | 5   do | |
| *John Lowe | P. | 12 June | |
| Levin Harrington | P. | 1 Jan '82 | |
| *Wm. Rice, or Rue | P. | do | |
| *Richd. Jennings | P. | 13 Aug | |
| *Jesse Locker | P. | 1 Jan '82 | |
| *Danl. Harness | P. | 28 May | |
| *John Swales | P. | 28 Sept | |
| *Wm. Madan | P. | 13 July | |

| Name and Rank. | | When Commenced. | When Left Service and the Reasons. | Remarks. |
|---|---|---|---|---|
| Solomon Sullivan | P. | 1 Jan '82 | | |
| Jas. Hunt | P. | 11 Sept | | |
| *Chas. Griffith | P. | 14  do | | |
| *John Conner | P. | (not stated) | | |
| *Peter Jackson | P. | 2 April | | |
| *Paris Owens | P. | 14 Sept | | |
| *Thomas Baxter | P. | 21 Aug | | |
| John Moore, 5th | P. | 1 Jan '82 | | |
| *Alex. McGregor | P. | 17 March | | |
| *Edward Paul | | 15 Aug | | |
| Jonathan Mahugh | P. | 1 Jan '82 | | disch'd 9 Jan '82, reinlisted |
| *John Willman | P. | (not stated) | | |
| *Jacob Mifford | P. | 1 March | | |
| *Whittington Gild | P. | 9 July | | |
| Richd. Harrington | P. | 1 Jan '82 | | |
| John Clineslaught | P. | do | | |
| *John Fairweather | P. | 1 June '82 | | |
| John Courts | P. | 1 Jan '82 | | |
| *Hugh Ware | P. | 21 May | | |
| *Wm. Cotter | P. | 7 Sept | | |
| Thos. Dickenson | P. | 1 Jan '82 | | |
| Isom Coleman | P. | do | | |
| *Wm. Holland | P. | 23 Aug | | |
| *James Kirk | P. | (not stated) | | |
| *Thos. Channon | P. | 24 Aug | | |
| *John Williams, 2d | P. | 6 Apl | | |

### 3RD COMPANY.

| Name and Rank. | | When Commenced. | When Left Service and the Reasons. | Remarks. |
|---|---|---|---|---|
| Richd. Huggins | S. | 1 Jan '82 | | |
| Aquilla Chitham | S. | do | | |
| *Thos. Craig | S. | 3 May | | |
| Stephen Nicholson | S. | 1 Jan '82 | | reinlisted in the field |
| Benj. Burch | S. | do | | |
| *Wm. Watkins | D. | do | | |
| *John Burgess | C. | 12 June | | |
| *Kemp Holden | C. | 20 May | | |
| Thos. White | C. | 1 Jan '82 | | |
| Benj. McCall | C. | 1 April | | |
| William Ayhun | P. | 1 Jan '82 | | |
| *James Bell | P. | 22 April | | |
| *Wm. Hunter | P. | 8 June | | |
| *Danl. Hukill | P. | 8 June | | |
| John White, 2d | P. | 15 April | to the end | |
| John Cannon | P. | 1 Jan '82 | | |
| *Chas. Palmore | P. | 7 May | | |

| NAME AND RANK. | | WHEN COMMENCED. | WHEN LEFT SERVICE AND THE REASONS. | REMARKS. |
|---|---|---|---|---|
| *Saml. Palmore | P. | 10 April | | |
| *Thos. Seego | P. | 22 July | | |
| *John Hukill | P. | 8 June | | |
| *George Daddisman | P. | 24 March | | |
| *John Beall, 2d | P. | 15 April | | |
| *Henry Barns | P. | 27  do | | |
| *Joseph Rose | P. | 8   do | | |
| *Chas. Mearick | P. | not known | | |
| John Shafer | P. | 1 Jan '82 | | |
| *Basil Dorsey | P. | 17 March | | |
| *Wm. Harris, 2d | P. | 2 Jan | | found as per discharge, dated 20 June, '83, from [Genl. Lincoln |
| *Thos. Harding | P. | 3 May | | |
| *Thos. McDowell | P. | 5 Apl | | |
| Robert Johnson | P. | 1 Jan '82 | | |
| *George Miller | P. | (not stated) | | |
| *Evans Willing | P. | 27 April | | |
| *Edward Roan | P. | 6 March | | |
| *John Greenwood | P. | 27 April | | |
| *Isaac Kent | P. | 29  do | | |
| *Wm. Smallwood | P. | 27  do | | |
| *Robert Dean | P. | 7   do | | |
| John Britton | P. | 1 Jan '82 | | |
| Richard Freeman | P. | do | disch'd 12 Jan '82 | |
| *Henry Windows | P. | 3 May | | |
| *Isaac Mitchell | P. | (not stated) | | |
| *Frederick Flinn | P. | (not stated) | | |
| *Wm. Connelly | P. | not known | | |
| *Matthew Daley | P. | (not stated) | | |
| *Edwd. Cantwell | P. | 1 Sept '82 | | |
| *John Willson, 2d | P. | 22 April | | |
| John Turner, 3d | P. | 1 Jan '82 | | |
| Isaac McFadon | P. | 16 Feb | | |

4TH COMPANY.

| Perry Evans | S. | 1 Jan '82 | | |
|---|---|---|---|---|
| Harris Austin | S. | do | | |
| *John Brown, 3d | S. | 18 May | | |
| *John Bond | S. | 1  do | | |
| John Davies, 1st | C. | 1 Jan '82 | promoted Corpl. 1 July '82 | |
| *Isaac Deale | C. | 19 May | | |
| Wm. Dunn | C. | 11 April | | |
| Isaac Holland | D. | 12 March | | |
| Joel Baker | P. | 1 Jan '82 | | |

| NAME AND RANK. | WHEN COMMENCED. | | WHEN LEFT SERVICE AND THE REASONS. | REMARKS. |
|---|---|---|---|---|
| *John Long | P. | 26 May | | |
| *Martin Bowles | P. | 1 Jan '82 | | |
| *Saml. Fisher | P. | 1 July | | |
| *Leonard Nable | P. | (not stated) | | |
| *Robert McClary | P. | 25 April | | |
| Benj. Donnelly, (or Daniel) | P. | 7 Sept | | |
| John Richardson | P. | 1 Jan '82 | | |
| Wm. Matthews, 2d | P. | 19 May | | |
| *Lawrence Pines | P. | (not stated) | | |
| *Jas. Silk | P. | (not stated) | | |
| John Bailey, 2d | P. | 1 Jan '82 | | |
| John Campbell, 2d | P. | do | | |
| *Joseph Cluley | P. | 5 April '82 | | |
| *John Cotter | P. | 7 Sept | | |
| Herculus Hutchings | P. | 1 Jan '82 | | |
| *Richd. Rivers | P. | 24 July | | |
| *John Nicholson | P. | 12 May | | |
| *Edward Burns | P. | 26 Sept | | |
| *Henry Frazer | P. | (not stated) | | |
| *Wm. Deverix | P. | 9 April | | |
| Wm. Marshall | P. | 1 Jan '82 | | |
| *Michael Keene | P. | 1 Oct | | |
| *Richard Burck | P. | 16 Aug | | |
| *Wm. Colin | P. | (not stated) | | disch'd properly |
| *Darden Orrell | P. | (not stated) | | [in 1783 |
| *Wm. Watkins, 2d | P. | 1 June | | |
| *Edward Shoebrook | P. | 1 July | | |
| *Danl. Wilkins | P. | 5 Oct | | |
| *Wm. Eagle | P. | 22 Sept | | |
| *Joseph McCollister | P. | not known | | |
| *Levin Claridge | P. | ditto | | |
| Robert Folger | P. | 1 Jan '82 | | |
| George Filleston | P. | do | | |
| *Thos. Countess | P. | 12 June | | |
| Jas. Kelly, 2d | P. | 1 Jan '82 | | |
| Benj. Worthington | P. | do | | 17 months service |
| *Richd. McDonald | P. | (not stated) | | |
| Barney Haney | P. | 1 Jan '82 | | |
| Jas. Hudson, 2d | P. | do | | |
| *Godfrey Fletcher | P. | (not stated) | died 1 Jan 1783 | |
| *John Acock | P. | 3 April | | |

FREDERICK DETACHMENT.

| John Philips | P. | 1 April '82 | | |
| John Barlow | P. | 1 April | to the end | |

| NAME AND RANK. | | WHEN COMMENCED. | WHEN LEFT SERVICE AND THE REASONS. | REMARKS. |
|---|---|---|---|---|
| Thos. Kettle | C. | All on | to the end, reduced 22 Feb '82 | |
| Domini Coines | P. | 1 Jan '82 | | |
| Neelee Jones | P. | unless | | |
| Enoch McClain | S. | otherwise | | |
| John Jordan, 2d, Clerk | P. | noted | | |
| P. Joseph Purdy | D. M. | | | |
| Jonathan Short | S. M. | | died 26 Oct '82 | |
| James Mead | D. M. | | | |
| *George Elms | F. M. | | | |
| *Chas. Blundell | P. | 21 Feb '82 | | |
| *Jesse Carter | P. | 25  do | | |
| *John Wilmore | P. | 12 March | | |
| *Wm. Lawrence | F. | 20 April | | |
| *James Morris | P. | 11 May | | |
| *Thos. Reynolds | P. | 5 July | | |
| *Thos. Barber | P. | 20 Aug | | |
| *James Dawson | P. | 1 Sept | to the end | |
| *Joseph Pully | P. | 15 do | | |
| *John Briruk | P. | 19 do | | |
| *Jas Burck, 2d | P. | 13 Aug | | |
| *John Abraham | P. | 22 Sept | | |
| *Wm. Caywood | P. | 30  do | | |
| *Francis Orbough | P. | 1 Oct | | |
| *Wm. Coleman | P. | 7 Oct | | |
| *Patrick Mayhorne | P. | | | |
| *Jas. Murray, 1st | P. | 10 Oct | | |
| *John McElroy | P. | 10 Oct | | |
| *Joseph Overcreek | P. | | | |
| *Patrick Nugent | P. | 16 Feb | | |
| *Joseph Sharp | P. | 25 Feb '82 | | |
| *J. Thos. Glinn | P. | 25 Feb | | |
| *James Neale | P. | 28 Feb | | |
| *Timothy Campbell | P. | 1 March | | |
| *David Johnson | P. | 5 March | | |
| *Tobyas Randalls | P. | 6 March | | |
| *Edward Stone | P. | 6 March | | |
| *Fredk. Wolveram | P. | 6 March | | |
| *John Bevard | P. | 13 March | | |
| *Saml. Powers | P. | 13 March | | |
| *Wm. Biddle | P. | 13 March | | |
| *Timothy Burns | P. | 16 March | | |
| *Benj. Houghton | P. | 16 March | | |
| *Andrew Potter | P. | 18 March | | |
| Jonathan Weedon | P. | | to the end | |
| *Saml. Hardcastle | P. | 18 March | | |

| NAME AND RANK. | | WHEN COMMENCED. | WHEN LEFT SERVICE AND THE REASONS. | REMARKS. |
|---|---|---|---|---|
| *John Donnold | P. | 20 March | | |
| *George McDonnald | P. | 20 March | | |
| *James Brown | P. | 20 March | | |
| *David Banks | P. | 26 March | | |
| *Richd. Burrows | P. | 28 March | | |
| *Jas. Carven | P. | 25 April | | |
| *Donald Cameron | P. | 3 April | | |
| *Jacob Scrivenor | P. | 3 April | | |
| *Isaac Carr | P. | 6 April | | |
| *Thos. Simonds | P. | 7 April | | |
| Robt. Legg | P. | 1 Jan | | |
| John Hackett | P. | 1 Jan | supposed to be settled with. In the Invalid Regt. | |
| Isaac Green | P. | 1 Jan | disch'd 15 Jan '82 | |
| *James Karns | P. | 10 April | | |
| *John Underwood | P. | 10 April | | |
| John Adams, No. 2 | P. | 1 Jan | | |
| *George Adams | P. | 10 Jan | | |
| *Isaac Burton | P. | 11 Jan | | |
| *Wm. Commett | P. | 11 Jan | | |
| *Alex. Wallace | P. | 4 March | | |
| *Abraham Stoner | P. | 13 March | | |
| *Joshua Cutmore | P. | 20 March | | |
| *Christopher Coy | P. | 20 March | | |
| *Ezekial Kidwell | P. | 17 April | | |
| *John Crosby, 2d | P. | 21 April | | |
| *Benj. Askew | P. | 14 April | | |
| *Paul Gilmore | P. | 1 March | | |
| *Thos. Billingham | P. | 6 March | | |
| *Wm. Bowling | S. | 12 March | | |
| *John McBride | P. | 1 Jan | | |
| *John Gordon, 2d | C. | 1 Jan | promoted Corpl. 22 Dec '82 | |
| *Thos. Carroll | P. | 3 April | | |
| *Dennis Carty | P. | 14 Feb | | |
| George Twinch | S. | 1 Jan | | |
| *Pierce Deacon | P. | 10 April | not heard of since | |
| Thos. Hill | C. | 1 Jan | | |
| Thos. Fleming | P. | 1 Jan | | |
| *Jas. Morrison | P. | 5 May | | |
| *Alex. McCoy | P. | 6 May | | |
| *Jas. Middleton | P. | 28 Aug | | |
| *John Adams, 3d | P. | 29 March | | |
| *Phineas Hervey, (or Hewey) | P. | 3 April | | |
| *John Pennington | P. | 6 April | | |

| Name and Rank. | | When Commenced. | When Left Service and the Reasons. | Remarks. |
|---|---|---|---|---|
| *Jas. Waters | P. | 6 April | | |
| *Robert Wright | P. | 6 June | | |
| *Henry Clawson | P. | 12 Apl | | |
| *Wm. Kent | P. | 3 May | | |
| *Michael Dougherty | P. | 5 May | | |
| *Peter Dawson | P. | 11 Sept | | [plus Roll |
| *Chas. Davis | P. | 23 April | must produce a certificate | on Sur- |
| *John German | P. | 11 May | | |
| *Alex. Garrett | P. | not known | | |
| *John Torrey | P. | 19 May | | |
| *Wm. Johnston, 2d | P. | 12 June | | |
| *Danl. Newman | P. | 23 June | | |
| *Richd. Scotten | P. | 24 June | | |
| *Wm. Harrison, 2d | P. | 8 May | | |
| *Christian Hanson | P. | 25 April | | |
| *Bartholomew Roach | P. | 23 March | | |
| *Randall Skly | P. | 22 April | | |
| *Thos. Wilsen | P. | 2 May | | |
| *John Hoina | P. | 3 May | | |
| *Wm. Hart | P. | 7 May | not heard of since | |
| *Thos. Hand | P. | 5 June | | |
| *Christian Reynor | P. | 9 May | | |
| *Richd. Perkins | P. | 9 May | | |
| *George Singleborough | P. | 13 May | | |
| *Christian Ernest | P. | 14 May | | |
| *John McDonald, 3d | P. | 22 May | | |
| Raphael Hagan | C. | 1 Jan | disch'd 30 April '82 by Col. Adams | |
| *John Ballast | P. | 20 May | | |
| *Josiah Burgess | P. | 16 Oct | | |
| *John Bluefield | P. | 30 July | | |
| *Richard Franklin | P. | 1 June | | |
| *Richard Nable | P. | 4 June | | |
| *John McFarlin | P. | 13 June | | |
| *Saml. Mahew | P. | 14 Aug | | |
| *Thos. Gritchard | P. | 2 July | | |
| *John Shephardson | P. | 2 July | | |
| *John Dougherty | P. | not known | | |
| *John Waid, 2d | P. | 20 Aug | | |
| *Peter Sprangle | P. | 21 Aug | | |
| *George Chambers | P. | 26 Sept | | |
| *John Connelly, 2d | P. | 9 May | | |
| *Alex. Christie | P. | 14 May | | |
| *Basil Wheelor | P. | 4 Sept | | |
| *Philip Frazier | P. | not known | | |
| *Arthur Boyes | P. | 30 March | | |

| Name and Rank. | | When Commenced. | When Left Service and the Reasons. | Remarks. |
|---|---|---|---|---|
| *George Tomlinson | P. | 30 May | | |
| *Joseph Moseley | P. | 19 April | | |
| *Dyer Waters | P. | 6 May | | |
| *Zachariah Moore | P. | 18 June | | |
| *Hezekiah Moore | P. | 15 Sept | | |
| *John Matwell, 2d | P. | 13 April | | |
| *Rezin Lowe | P. | 30 Sept | | |
| *Daniel Hurly | P. | 14 Oct | | |
| *John Wilson, 3d | P. | 6 May | | |
| *Daniel Skinner | P. | 26 June | | |
| *Thos. Sturges | P. | 16 Sept | | |
| *William Solley | P. | 21 May | | |
| *Isaac Jenkins | P. | 12 Sept | | |
| *John Wilson, 4th | P. | 30 June | | |
| *Thos. Wood, 4th | S. | 1 April | | |
| *Hillary Lanham | P. | 13 Sept | | |
| *Matthew Norris | P. | 17 May | | |
| *Thos. Loveday | P. | 17 March | not since heard of | |
| *Thos. Sheets | P. | 19 June | | |
| *Joseph Jones, 2d | P. | 23 July | | |
| *John Connelly, 3d | P. | 29 July | | |
| *John Alsop | P. | 26 Feb | | |
| *John Allen | P. | 18 March | | |
| *Elisha Osborn | P. | 27 Feb | | |
| *George Rhodes | P. | 10 March | | |
| *Thos. Hawkes | P. | 1 April | | |
| *Jas. Murray | P. | 1 April | | |
| *Robt. Jones | P. | 4 May | | |
| *Michael Griffith | P. | 11 May | | |
| *John Barrett, 1st | P. | 12 July | | |
| *Nicholas Fitzgerald | P. | 26 March | | |
| *John McElroy | P. | 9 Oct | | |
| *James McCray | P. | 15 April | | |
| *Wm. Layland | P. | 14 Oct | | |
| *Jas. Gilmore, 2d | P. | 19 Oct | | |
| *Jacob Gibson | P. | 17 Oct | | |
| *Henry Philips | P. | 19 Oct | | |
| *George Hoggart | P. | 1 April | | |
| *Jas. Thompson | P. | 21 May | | |
| *Wm. Henderson | P. | { not known } { 28 May '82 } | Col. Tootal | |
| *Jas. Coleman | P. | do | | |
| *Francis Irsley | P. | do | | |
| *Chas. Beauchamp | P. | 5 Aug | | |
| *Ephraim Marshall | P. | deserted | | |

| NAME AND RANK. | | WHEN COMMENCED. | WHEN LEFT SERVICE AND THE REASONS. | REMARKS. |
|---|---|---|---|---|
| *Chas. Hall | P. | 10 April | | |
| *Cotter Jones | P. | 31 May | | |
| *John Johnston, 2d | P. | 15 Aug | | |
| *Wm. Mead | P. | 1 Jan | | |
| *Thos. Whaley | P. | not known | | |
| *John Williams, 3d | P. | 3 Nov | | |
| *Edward Edwards | P. | 10 June | | |
| *Oliver Blake | P. | 7 May | | |
| *John Murray, 2d | P. | 17 May | | |
| *Michael McDevitt | P. | 16 Apl | | |
| *Lewis McCuttough, (or McCulloch) | P. | 18 Aug | | |
| *Francis Raynard | P. | 22 Aug | | |
| *John Steele | P. | 2 Sept | | |
| *John Lee, 3d | P. | 1 Dec | | |
| *Jonas Crawford | P. | 11 Nov | | |
| *Jas. Rowe | P. | 22 June | | |
| *Wm. Hill, 2d | P. | 6 July | | |
| *Henry Gilpin | P. | 20 July | deserted | |
| John Green, 1st | P. | 1 Jan | disch'd 9 Jan, reinlisted 12 July | |
| *Darden O'Neil | P. | 19 July | | |
| *John Wilson, 5th | P. | 1 Aug | | |
| *John Calahan | P. | 23 July | | |
| *Wm. Calahan | P. | 12 June | | |
| *Wm. Caldwell | P. | 8 April | | |
| *James Coosingbury | P. | 17 March | | |
| *Thos. Leagor | P. | 22 July | | |
| *Randolph Booth | P. | 10 March | | |
| *Edward Wheatly | P. | 12 March | | |
| *George Warner | P. | 28 Oct | | |
| *James Countess | P. | 20 Sept | | |
| *Benj., or Bennet, Thompson | P. | 1 April | | |
| *Henry Tibbett | P. | 5 Sept | | |
| *John Tordine | P. | 12 Dec | | |
| *Joseph Norman | P. | 5 Oct | | |
| *Hugh Roney | P. | 17 June | | |
| David Connor | P. | 1 Jan | | |
| *William Gray | P. | 9 Sept | | |
| *Wm. Carleton, or Carlin | P. | 7 Sept | | |
| *Peter Fletcher | P. | 9 Sept | | |
| *Wm. Frazier | P. | 12 Oct | | |
| *Peter Francis | P. | (not stated) | | |
| *John Shields | P. | 29 Oct | | |
| *Jas. Stephens | P. | 8 Oct | | |

31

| Name and Rank. | When Commenced. | When Left Service and the Reasons. | Remarks. |
|---|---|---|---|
| *John Stuart, 2d | P. | 11 Oct | |
| *Wm. Sowden | P. | 1 Oct | |
| *Nicholos McFarlin | P. | 11 Oct | |
| *John Messer | P. | 3 Oct | |
| *Jas. Morris, 2d | P. | 14 Oct | |
| *Patrick McDonough | P. | (not stated) | |
| John Miller | P. | 1 Jan | |
| *John Cooper, 2d | P. | 1 Oct | |
| *Jeremiah Cyphert | P. | 30 Sept | |
| *John Kelner | P. | 18 Oct | |
| *Joseph Hudson | P. | 1 Oct | |
| *Nicholas Pecker | P. | 1 Oct | |
| *Chas. Brutzill | P. | 1 Oct | |
| *Wm. Belcher | P. | 5 Oct | |
| *Michael Burns | P. | 12 Oct | |
| *Thos. Blake | P. | (not stated) | |
| *Chezloe Lodwick | P. | 10 Oct | |
| *Saml. Crowell | P. | (not stated) | |
| *John Rigan | P. | 12 Oct | |
| *Thos. Lawyers | P. | 14 Oct | |
| *Lewis Davies | P. | 17 Oct | |
| *John Tully, 2d | P. | 19 Oct | |
| *John Adamson | P. | (not stated) | |
| *John Crotchett | P. | 4 May | |
| *Danl. Campbell | P. | 27 April | |
| *Danl. Sullinger | P. | not known | |
| *John Husk | P. | 3 May | |
| *Thos. Hooper | P. | (not stated) | |
| *John Nelson, 2d | P. | 4 Aug | |
| Jeremiah Driskell | P. | 1 Jan '82 | |
| John Ferguson | P. | 1 Jan | disch'd 1 April |
| Jas. Curren | P. | 1 Jan | |
| *Saml. Brady | P. | 12 Sept | |
| *Job Buley | P. | 8 April | |
| *John Applead | P. | 14 April | |
| *John Alford | P. | 15 April | |
| *Thos. Keys | P. | 24 April | |
| *Bennet Valient | P. | 27 April | |
| *Arthur Pritchard | P. | 3 May | |
| *John Elliott | P. | not known | |
| *James Rose | P. | 21 Feb | |
| *Thos. Gorden | P. | 25 March | |
| *Bennet Heard | P. | 16 April | |
| *John Hillam | P. | 23 Nov | |
| *Michael Scott | P. | 2 Nov | |

| Name and Rank. | When Commenced. | When Left Service and the Reasons. | Remarks. |
|---|---|---|---|
| *Benj. Wright | P. | 20 Nov | |
| *Colvert Mason, alias Woodyard | | (not stated) | |
| *George Baker | P. | 1 Aug | |
| *Jas. Barber, 2d | P. | 30 Dec | |
| *Dennis Bryan | P. | 10 Dec | |
| *Stephen Erlinger | P. | 20 Dec | |
| *Dennis O'Bryan | P. | 11 Dec | |
| *George Bowers | P. | 12 June | |
| Henry Young | P. | 1 Jan | |
| George Parker | P. | 1 Jan | |
| James Lowry | P. | 1 Jan | |
| Jesse Suite (?) | S. | 1 Jan | |
| John Cusber (?) | D. | 1 Jan | |
| James Dyer, 1st | P. | 1 Jan | |
| John Martin | | 1 Jan | |
| Thos. Summers | | 1 Jan | |
| John M. Funner | P. | 1 Jan | |
| Isom, (or Asa), Moore | | 15 Sept | [old 7th Regt. |
| Joseph Murphy | P. | 1 Jan | prisoner 16 Aug '80 and returned, of the |
| Michael Casey | P. | 1 Jan | |
| James Grary | P. | 1 Jan | |
| Edwd. Gearish | P. | 1 Jan | disch'd 8 Aug |
| Richd. Mud | S. | 1 Jan | do   9 Jan '82 |
| Michael McGuire | | | do   9 Sept |
| Morris Neagle | P. | 1 Jan | |
| *Wm. Rodgers | P. | 1 Jan | entd. Gratuity |
| Saml. Street | F. | 1 Jan | |
| John Williams, 4th | P. | 1 Jan | disch'd 9 Jan '82 |
| Edwd. Wade | P. | 1 Jan | Genl. Guard |
| Wm. Robinson | P. | 14 Dec | |
| James Fisher | P. | 1 Jan | deserted 1 Jan '82 |
| Jesse Grace | P. | (not stated) | discharged previous to '82 |
| Peter Kincaid | P. | 1 Jan | died January '82 |

[A star prefixed to any name indicates that the length of service is not known. In all other cases it is to be understood that service was from date of enlistment to Dec. 31st, 1782, or to an earlier date given after the date of enlistment.]

## MUSTER AND PAY ROLLS FOR 1783.

Arrangement of the Maryland Line, January 1st, 1783.

| Names. | When Commissioned. | Names. | When Commissioned. |
|---|---|---|---|
| | FIRST REGIMENT. | | |
| Col. John Gunby | 17 April '77 | Lieut. Nicholas Gassaway | 1 Jan '80 |
| Lt. Col. Levin Winder | 3 June '81 | Phillip Hill | 9 May '78 |
| Major John Eccleston | 10 Dec '77 | Hezekiah Ford | 16 Aug '80 |
| Capt. Joseph Marbury | 1 Jan '77 | Arthur Harris | 26 Oct '79 |
| Jacob Brice | do | William Pendergast | 29 do do |
| John Smith,(late 6th) | do | William Raisin | 26 Jan '80 |
| Henry Gaither | 17 April do | Nathan Wright | 1 Jan '81 |
| Edward Oldham | 20 May do | John Sears | 1 do do |
| Walker Muse | 10 June do | John F. Lowe | 20 Jan '81 |
| John C. Jones | 20 Sept do | Samuel Edminston | 14 Mch do |
| Horatio Claggett | 10 Oct do | Robert Halkerston | 12 April do |
| Richard Anderson | 15 Nov do | Henry Clements | 25 do do |
| Lieut. John Lynn | 1 June '79 | Henry Gassaway | 25 do do |
| Wm. Adams | 8 do do | Francis Ware | Aug |
| Regnal Hillery, died | | Basil Burgess | 18 June '81 |
| 11 Aug '83 | 13 July do | Surg'on Richard Pendell | |
| Samuel Hanson | 1 Aug do | Mate Alexander Smith | |
| | SECOND REGIMENT. | | |
| Lt. Col. Commd. Peter Adams | 1 Aug '79 | Lt. Joshua Rutledge | 1 May |
| | | Thos. Rouse | |
| Major Henry Hardman | 22 May do | Walter Dyer | 15 Sept |
| Alexander Rox- | | John Brevill | 20 do |
| burgh | 7 April '80 | Thomas Boyd | 1 Jan '81 |
| Capt. John Gale | 10 Dec '77 | Mark McPherson | 1 do do |
| James W. Gray | 26 do do | Thos. A. Dyson | 8 Sept '81 |
| George Hamilton | 25 Jan '78 | Basil Warring | 25 Oct do |
| Percey Benson | 11 March | Malakiah Bonham | 12 Sept do |
| John Mitchell | 15 July '79 | John D. Carry | 16 Oct do |
| William Bruce | 1 Aug '79 | William Hanson | 25 do do |
| John Gassaway | 2 April '80 | Thomas Beatty | 8 Sept do |
| Lloyd Beal | 19 Feb '81 | Joseph Cross | 6 Nov do |
| Francis Reveley | 18 June | *Wm Goldsborough | '82 |
| Lt. Henry Baldwin | 11 Feb '81 | William Telson | 9 May do |
| Edmond Compton | 18 do | †Surg. Walter Warfield | |
| Benjamin Fickle | 19 do | Mate Wm. Watts | 15 Aug '81 |
| David Luckett | 7 April | | |

*On Arthur's resignation Spring of '82.        † To be found in Council Office.

| NAMES. | WHEN COMMISSIONED. | REMARKS. |
|---|---|---|
| | ARTILLERY. | |
| Capt.   William Brown | 22 Nov '77 | Promoted Major 31 Jan '81 |
| Richard Dorsey | 24 Nov '77 | |
| James Smith | 1 Nov '79 | |
| Capt. Lt. Ebenezer Finly | 24 Nov '77 | |
| James McFadden | 1 Nov '79 | |
| 1 Lt.   James Bagus | 3 Sept '79 | |
| 2nd Lt.  Clement Skerret | Feb '78 | |
| Nicholas Ricketts | Dec '77 | |
| Isaac Rawlins | 3 Sept '79 | |
| 1 Lt.   Robert Wilmot | 24 Nov '77 | deranged in '8b for want of men. |
| 2nd Lt.  Young Wilkinson | Mch '78 | Furloughed by Genl. Greene Apl '82, deranged for want of Command |
| John Cheevers | 3 Sept '78 | Furloughed by Genl. Greene 1780, deranged for want of Command |
| | | Copy   J. Howell, Jr. |

Arrangement of the Maryland Line in Five Regiments; promotions filled to January 1st, 1783.

| NAMES. | RANK. | WHEN COMMISSIONED. | PROMOTIONS. | CONTINUE OR RETIRE. |
|---|---|---|---|---|
| | | FIRST REGIMENT. | | |
| John Steward | Lt.Col.Comd. | 9 May '82 | Gen.Williamson's promotion, dead | continue |
| John Eccleston | Major | 10 Dec '77 | | do |
| Jona. Sillman | do | 9 May '82 | Col. Steward's promotion | retire |
| Edwd. Prall | Captain | 10 June '77 | | do |
| Wm. Riely | do | 15 Oct do | cont'e on Duty So.Army 'til Aug '83 | do |
| John S. Belt | do | 15 Dec do | | do |
| John Smith, (old 6th) | do | 1 April '78 | He took Capt.Orendorff's Rank and Orendorff his as settled by a board of Officers at the Southward | do |
| Lloyd Beal | do | 19 Feb '81 | | do |
| Thos. B. Hugou | do | 1 June do | | do |
| Francis Revelly | do | 18 do do | Capt. Armstrong's death | continue |

| NAMES. | RANK. | WHEN COMMISSIONED. | PROMOTIONS. | CONTINUE OR RETIRE. |
|---|---|---|---|---|
| James Winchester | Captain | 9 Feb '82 | Capt. Sillman's promotion, on duty with So. Army till Aug '83 | retire |
| Philip Reed | do | do | Capt. Bird's death Aug or Sept '82, not known which. Prisoner War | prisoner |
| John Hamilton | Lieut. | 1 June '79 | continued with Army to end of War | retire |
| Wm. Raison | do | 26 Jan '80 | | continue |
| Joshua Burgess  . | do | 14 Mch do | Prisoner War | retire |
| Hezh. Foard | do | 16 Aug do | | do |
| John T. Lowe | do | 20 Jan '81 | | do |
| Edwd. Miles Smith | do | 19 Feb do | | do |
| Saml. Edmiston | do | 14 Mch do | | do |
| John Trueman | do | 16 do do | Invalid, Prisoner War | do |
| Geo. Winchester | do | 1 June do | Lt. Carr's resignation, retire 1 Jan '83 | |
| Henry Hawkins | do | Ensn. 1 Aug do | Appt. Ensn. 1 Aug '81, a vacancy for Lt. 1 Sept '82 on Lt. Manger's promotion | do |
| Malakh. Bonham | do | do 4 Sept do | do Hardcastle's resignation 12 Sept '82, with Detachment 'til dismissed Main Army | |
| Chas. Skerving | do | | App. by G. Greene, vacancy 20 Nov '81 Lt. Richmond's prom. | |
| Richd. Pindell | Surgeon | | his Appt. to be found in Council Chamber | |
| Alex. Smith | Mate | | do | continue |
| Saml. Y. Keene | do | | App. by G. Greene tho' there is no vacancy. His appointment never confirmed by the State but continued on duty till 31 Mch '83 in ye S. Army | |

SECOND REGIMENT.

| John Gunby | Colonel | 17 Apl '77 | | |
| Levin Winder | Lt. Col. | 3 June '81 | Col. Howard's promotion | |

| NAMES. | RANK. | WHEN COMMISSIONED. | PROMOTIONS. | CONTINUE OR RETIRE. |
|---|---|---|---|---|
| Wm. D. Beal | Major | 6 Nov do | Major Dean's death | retire |
| Alex. Trueman | Captain | 1 Jan '77 | | do |
| Jona. Morris | do | 14 Apl do | Prisoner War | do |
| Walker Muse | do | 10 June do | | continue |
| Thos. Mason | do | 8 June '79 | | retire |
| John Gassaway | do | 2 Apl '80 | | continue |
| Adam Hoops | do | 16 Mch '81 | to receive pay to 4 Oct '81, entitled to Commutation. Prisoner of War | retire |
| Saml. McPherson | do | 25 Apl do | on duty in So. Army until June '83 | do |
| Christ. Richmond | do | 20 Nov do | Capt. Manger's death. Aid to G. Gates. On duty in the N. Army | do |
| Jacob Norris | do | 14 Nov '82 | Capt. Wilmot's death | do |
| Wm. Adams | Lieut. | 8 June '79 | | |
| Nich. Gassaway | do | 1 Jan '80 | | continue |
| Arthur Harris | do | 26 Oct '79 | | |
| Thos. Price | do | 11 Feb '80 | | retire |
| Zedekiah Moore | do | 10 Sept do | Dead | do |
| Mark McPherson | do | 1 Jan '81 | | do |
| Jacob Crawford | do | 20 Feb do | | do |
| Wm. Smoote | do | 16 Mar do | | do |
| Henry Baker | do | Ensn. 1 Aug do | A vacancy from 3 June '81 Lt. Dyer's prom. Duty So. Army 31 Mch '83 | |
| Edwd. Hamilton | do | do   do | Vacancy 8 Sept '81 Bruff's promotion | do |
| John Carey | do | do 4 Sept do | do 16 Oct Woolford's death | |
| *George Browne | do | | | |
| Walter Warfield | Surgeon | | to be found in Council Office | |
| Gerard Wood | Mate | 1 Aug '81 | on duty S. Army till 31 March '83 | do |

### THIRD REGIMENT.

| NAMES. | RANK. | WHEN COMMISSIONED. | PROMOTIONS. | CONTINUE OR RETIRE. |
|---|---|---|---|---|
| Peter Adams | Lt.Col.Com. | 1 Aug '79 | | |
| Henry Hardman | Major | 22 May do | | continue |
| Thos. Lansdale | do | 19 Feb '81 | on Detacht. No. Army 30 June | retire |

\* G. Brown appointed by Genl. Greene, a vacancy in the spring of '82 on Lt. Murdock's resignation—the date of Brown's appointm't not known.

| NAMES. | RANK. | WHEN COMMISSIONED. | PROMOTIONS. | CONTINUE OR RETIRE. |
|---|---|---|---|---|
| Joseph Marbury | Captain | 1 Jan '77 | | continue |
| Lilburn Williams | do | 17 April do | | retire |
| James W. Gray | do | 26 Dec do | | continue |
| Edward Spurrier | do | 21 May '79 | on Duty No. Detacht. | retire |
| Benjn. Price | do | 1 July do | on do So. Army, and arrived with troops from C. Town | do |
| Richard Waters | do | 7 April '80 | | do |
| Edward Dyer | do | 3 June '81 | Capt. Dobson's promotion | do |
| John A. Hamilton | do | 25 Oct do | Capt. Chesley's resignation | do |
| Gassaway Watkins | do | 15 May '82 | Capt. Orendorff's do | do |
| John Hartshorne | Lieut. | 21 May '79 | on Detachmt. No. Army, Adjt. | do |
| Rignal Hillary | do | 13 July do | | continue |
| Philip Hill | do | May '78 | Prisoner | do |
| Wm. Pendergrast | do | 29 Oct '79 | | |
| Henry Baldwin | do | 11 Feb '80 | | do |
| David Luckett | do | 7 April do | | |
| Walter Dyer | do | 15 Sept do | | |
| Nathan Wright | do | 1 Jan '81 | | |
| Basil Burgess | do | Ensn. 1 Aug '81 | Vacancy 18 June Revelly promoted | |
| Thomas Dyson | do | do do | do 8 Sept Lamar prom. | continue |
| Basil Waring | do | do do | do 25 Oct Hamilton prom. | |
| Wm. Goldsborough | do | '82 | do Spring of '82, Arthur's resign, date of Goldsborough's appmt. not known | |
| Levin Denwood | Surgeon | | in Council Office, on Duty So. Army | retire |
| Wm. Watts | Mate | 15 Aug '81 | | |

### FOURTH REGIMENT.

| NAMES. | RANK. | WHEN COMMISSIONED. | PROMOTIONS. | CONTINUE OR RETIRE. |
|---|---|---|---|---|
| Thomas Woolford | Lt. Col. Com. | 23 Oct '79 | Prisoner of War | retire |
| Alex. Roxburgh | Major | 7 April '80 | | continue |
| John Lynch | do | 8 Sept '81 | Major Dobson's death, Prisoner of War | retire |
| Jacob Brice | Captain | 1 Jan '77 | | |
| Henry Gaither | do | 17 April do | | |
| John C. Jones | do | 20 Sept do | | continue |
| Richd. Anderson | do | 15 Nov do | | |
| Geo. Hamilton | do | 25 Jan '78 | | do |
| David Lynn | do | 22 May '79 | | retire |
| John Mitchel | do | 15 July do | | continue |
| Jona. Gibson | do | 1 May '80 | Dead | retire |

| NAMES. | RANK. | WHEN COMMISSIONED. | PROMOTIONS. | CONTINUE OR RETIRE. |
|---|---|---|---|---|
| James Bruff | Captain | 8 Sept '81 | Capt. Lynch's promotion, Prisoner of War | half pay |
| Wm. P. Stoddart | Lieut. | 21 May '79 | | retire |
| Lavacher DeVauburn | do | Ensn. 10 Mch '77 | Date of promotion not known, gone to France | |
| *Isaac Hanson | do | 15 Dec '79 | Prisoner of War | do |
| Edward Compton | do | 18 Feb '80 | | continue |
| Joshua Rutledge | do | 1 May do | | do |
| John Brevet | do | 20 Sept do | | retire |
| John McCoy | do | 1 Jan '81 | | do |
| Rob. Halkerson | do | 12 Apl '81 | | |
| Henry Gassaway | do | 25 do do | | continue |
| Saml. B. Beal | do | Ensn. 1 Aug do | Vacancy Nath. Smith's resignation 4 July '81 | retire |
| Henly Chapman | do | do 4 Sept do | Vacancy 8 Sept Duval killed | |
| William Hanson | do | do do | do 25 Oct Boones resigned | continue |
| †William Tolson | do | | do 9 May '82 Winchester promoted | |
| William Kelty | Surgeon | | Prisoner of War | |
| Elisha Harrison | Mate | 15 Oct '81 | | |

FIFTH REGIMENT.

| NAMES. | RANK. | WHEN COMMISSIONED. | PROMOTIONS. | CONTINUE OR RETIRE. |
|---|---|---|---|---|
| John E. Howard | Lt. Col. Com. | 3 June 1781 | Col. Foard's death. | |
| John Davidson | Major | 1 Jan do | | retire |
| Benj. Brookes | do | 16 March do | | continue |
| John Smith, 3d | Captain | 1 Jan '77 | | do |
| Edward Oldham | do | 20 May do | | do |
| Horatio Clagget | do | 10 Oct do | | do |
| John Gale | do | 10 Dec do | | do |
| Perry Benson | do | 11 March '78 | | do |
| James Sumervill | do | 1 June '79 | | retire |
| Wm. Bruce | do | 1 Aug do | | continue |
| Wm. Lamar | do | 8 Sept '81 | Capt. Edgerly's death | |
| James Ewing | do | 6 Nov do | Capt. Beall's promotion | |
| John Lynn | Lieut. | 1 June '79 | | |
| Samuel Hanson | do | 1 Aug do | | continue |
| Thomas Rowse | do | 15 Sept do | | |
| Robt. Denny | do | 3 Jan '80 | | retire |
| Benj. Fickle | do | 19 Feb do | | |

* Omitted in arrangement of 1781 by being reported dead of his wounds in captivity—Cambden.

† Never received his appointment but was promised one and acted on the recruiting service, his situation is similar to Goldsborough's who was appointed.

| NAMES. | RANK. | WHEN COMMISSIONED. | PROMOTIONS. | CONTINUE OR RETIRE. |
|---|---|---|---|---|
| Thos. Boyd | Lieut. | 1 Jan '81 | | |
| John Sears | do | do  do | | continue |
| Henry Clements | do | 25 Apl do | | retire |
| Adam Jamison | do | 1 June do | | do |
| Francis Ware, Jr. | do | Ensn. | Vacancy some time in | |
| | | 1 Aug do | Aug on Lt. Lynn's resignation | |
| Thos. Beaty | do | do | Vacancy 8 Sept Lt. | |
| | | 4 Sept do | Goud killed | |
| Joseph Cross | do | 6 Nov 81 | do 6 Nov '81 Ewing promoted | |
| Ezekiel Haynie | Surgeon | 17 Jan '82 | | retire |
| John L. Elbert | Mate | 1 Jan do | | do |

## A List of Officers deranged in the Maryland Line 1 Jan., 1783.

| RANK. | NAMES. | WHEN COMMISSIONED. | REMARKS. |
|---|---|---|---|
| Lt. Col. | John Stewart | | Dead |
| Major | Jonathan Silman | 9 May '82 | |
| Captain | Edward Prall | 10 June '77 | |
| do | William Reiley | 15 Oct '77 | { continued on duty in S. Army till Aug |
| do | John S. Belt | 15 Dec '77 | |
| do | John Smith, (late 6th) | 1 Apl '78 | |
| do | Thomas B. Hugou | 1 June '81 | |
| do | James Winchester | 9 Feb '82 | { Continued on duty with ye S. Troops till Aug. When ye arrived at Annapolis, recd. pay for Feb, Mch & Apl |
| do | Phillip Reed | do  do | Prisoner of War |
| Lieut. | John Hamilton | 1 June '79 | |
| do | Henry Baker | Apd. Ens. 1 Aug '81 | { on duty till 31 Mch '83, S Army, entitd. to promtn. 3 June '81 |
| do | Edward Hamilton | do 8 Sept do | entitd. to promtn. 8 Sept '81 |
| S. Mate | Gerard Wood | 1 Aug '81 | on duty 31 Mch S. Army |
| Major | Thomas Lansdale | 19 Feb '81 | on duty Northern Army, paid |
| Captain | Lilbourne Williams | 17 Apl '77 | |
| do | Edward Spurrier | 21 May '79 | on duty Northn. Detachmt., paid |
| do | Benj. Price* | 1 July '79 | { on duty and arriv'd with Troops from C. Town, paid for Feb, Mch & Apl |

*Paid for Feb. Mch. & Apl.

| RANK. | NAMES. | WHEN COMMISSIONED. | REMARKS. |
|---|---|---|---|
| Captain | Richard Waters | 7 Apl '80 | • |
| do | Edward Dyer | 3 June '81 | |
| do | John A. Hamilton | 25 Oct '81 | |
| do | Gassaway Watkins | 13 May '82 | Promoted Capt. 13 May '82 |
| do | John Hartshorne | 21 May '79 | |
| Surgeon | Leven Denwood | | |
| Lt. Col. | Thomas Woolford | | Prisoner of war |
| Major | John Lynch | 8 Sept '81 | ditto |
| Captain | David Lynn | 22 May '79 | |
| do | John Gibson | 1 May '80 | Dead |
| do | James Bruff | 8 Sept '81 | Prisoner of War |
| Lieut. | Wm. T. Stoddard | 21 May '79 | |
| do | Levachee De Vaubrunn | | |
| do | Isaac Hanson | 15 Dec '79 | Prisoner of War |
| do | John McCoy | 1 Jan '81 | |
| do | Saml. B. Beal | 1 Aug '81 | |
| do | Henly Chapman | 4 Oct '81 | entitled to Lt. |
| Surgeon | William Kelty | | Prisoner of War |
| Mate | Elisha Harrison | | |
| Lt. Col. Comt. | John E. Howard | 3 June 81 | |
| Major | John Davidson | 1 Jan '81 | Subsisten— |
| do | Benjm. Brookes | | |
| Captain | James Summerville | | |
| do | William Lamar | | |
| do | James Ewing | | |
| Lieut. | Robert Denny | | |
| do | Adam Jameson | | |
| Surgeon | Ezekiel Haynie | | |
| Mate | John L. Elbert | | |

Copy   J. Howell, Jr.

Defective, the names of a Major, 7 Captains, 9 Lieutenants and a Surgeon being torn off.

Agreeable to a resolution of Congress bearing Date the 26th Day of May, 1783, the Bearer hereof, John Cole, private of the 1st Maryland Regiment, has leave of Absence until called upon by proper authority to join his Corps, or is finally discharged.  Given at Annapolis, 31st day of July, 1783.

Registered & Attested,                                J. Gunby, Col.
M. McPherson, Adjt.

Mathias Cyphert, private 1st Md. Regt., received the same leave as above, Aug 6th, 1783.

PRISONERS IN THE PROVOST, MAY 9TH, 1783.

| NAMES. | REGT. | CRIMES. | BY WHOM CONF'D. | WHEN CONF'D. |
|---|---|---|---|---|
| Wm. Potter, Corpl. | Md. | neglect of Duty | Capt. Paskie | |
| John Summers | " | desertion | | 2 May |
| John Sammon | " | ditto | | do |
| Wm. Harper | " | susp. of break'g in Q. M. Stores | Capt. Price | 7 do |
| Aaron Mitchell | " | ditto | | do |

J. W. Gray, Capt. Guard

[from the Gist Papers]

## PAY ROLL OF THE MARYLAND LINE FOR 1783.

[Imperfect, pages 1 and 2 missing.]

Unless otherwise stated service is from Jan. 1st to Nov. 15th, 1783.

| NAMES AND RANK. | | WHEN LEFT SERVICE AND THE REASONS. | REMARKS. |
|---|---|---|---|
| John McKay | P. | | |
| John Harris, 1st | P. | | |
| Daniel Brumigen | P. | deserted 2 May '83 | pardoned |
| John Hurley | P. | | |
| Peter Equedoroney | P. | | |
| Solomon Green | P. | | |
| James Evans | P. | | |
| Richard Dolvin | P. | | |
| James Humphries | P. | | |
| Thomas Elliott, 1st | P. | deserted 2 May '83 | pardoned |
| John Carrell, 2nd | P. | | |
| Samuel Richardson | P. | | |
| Nicholas Elliot | P. | | |
| George Jennings | P. | | |
| George Kelson | P. | | |
| Thomas Wood, 2nd | P. | | |
| Thomas Jones, 5th | P. | | |
| Thomas Carney | P. | | |
| Cornelius Thompson | P. | | |
| Joseph Sidney | P. | deserted 2 May '83 | Waggoner Artificers, pardoned |
| Paul Lapping | P. | | |
| James Bayless | P. | | |
| John Duhague | P. | dead previous to '83 | |
| John Lesslie | P. | | Artificers |
| John McCaliff | P. | | |
| James Davidson | P. | | |
| Francis Taylor | P. | | |
| John Hull | P. | | |
| John Fullham | P. | | |
| John Hood | P. | died 20 Dec '82 | |
| Charles Girdler | P. | | |
| William Brady | P. | | |
| John Bamtham | P. | | |

2ND COMPANY.  CAPT. WILMOT.

| | | | |
|---|---|---|---|
| Thomas Edwards | S. | | |
| Hugh McMillan | S. | | |

| NAMES AND RANK. | | WHEN LEFT SERVICE AND THE REASONS. | REMARKS. |
|---|---|---|---|
| John Gwyne | S. | | |
| John Colein | S. | | |
| Charles Harvey | S. | | |
| Nathan Price | C. | | promd. Serjt. 1 Mch '83 |
| Charles Nabb | C. | dischd. 14 Oct '83 | |
| Richard Ferreby | C. | | |
| Kirney Lahnnum | C. | died 20 Dec '82 | |
| John McKnight | F. | | |
| Peter Topping | P. | | |
| Emanuel Carthagene | P. | | |
| John T. West | P. | | |
| James Gray, 1st | P. | | |
| John Briley | P. | | |
| Joseph Johnson | P. | | |
| William Ingle | P. | | |
| Jeremiah Williams | P. | | |
| Joseph McAntee | P. | | |
| Adam Jamieson | P. | | |
| Thomas Slade | P. | | |
| John Lynch, 2nd | P. | | |
| Daniel O'Quinn | P. | | |
| Asaph Colegate | P. | | |
| John King | P. | | |
| Michael Callihorne | P. | | |
| Thomas Murphey | P. | | |
| John Kidd | P. | | |
| Hugh Gaynor | P. | | |
| Conrod Smith | P. | | |
| William Hedge | P. | | |
| William Carter | P. | | |
| Isaac Holliday | P. | died 30 Jan '83 | |
| John Dunnagan | P. | died 25 Jan '83 | |
| Michael Clark, 2nd | P. | | |
| John Hide | P. | | |
| John Berryman | P. | | |
| David Crady | P. | | |
| William Pecker | P. | deserted 2 May '83 | pardoned |
| Edward Evans | P. | | |
| Elijah Smith | P. | | |
| Henry Reeding | P. | | |
| Evans Tumblestone | P. | | |
| Matthew Moore | P. | | |
| Ralph Hope | P. | | |
| Christopher McCaway | P. | | Artificer |
| Henry Ramsey | P. | | |
| Edward Wright | P. | died 4 Mch '83 | |

| Names and Rank. | | When Left Service and the Reasons. | Remarks. |
|---|---|---|---|
| Philip Bailey | P. | died 20 Feb '83 | |
| Aaron Mitchell | P. | | |
| William Cork | P. | | |
| Daniel Mann | P. | deserted 30 Apl '83 | pardoned |
| Daniel Murphy | P. | | |
| Alyand Melvin | P. | | |
| Edward Henecy | P. | died 28 Apl '83 | |
| Southern George | P. | | |
| Thomas Richardson, 1st | P. | | |
| John Blades | P. | | |
| Jacob Adamson | P. | died 24 Mch '83 | |
| Walter Ferrill | P. | | |
| John Nave | P. | | |
| William Harper | P. | | |
| Daniel Foxwell | P. | | |
| John Morris | P. | | |
| John Fossett | P. | | |
| Murphy Shee | P. | died 28 Jan '83 | |
| William Camm | P. | | |
| Cato Snowden | P. | | |
| William Absalom | P. | | |
| Thomas Long | P. | | |
| Timothy Langrill | P. | | |
| John Lucas | P. | | |
| Thomas Matthews, 2nd | P. | | |
| James Due | P. | | |

3RD COMPANY.    CAPT. JOHN S. BELT.

| Francis Magauran | S. | | |
|---|---|---|---|
| Jesse Jacobs | S. | | |
| John Carson | S. | | |
| James Deverex | S. | | |
| William Rose | S. | deserted 29 Mch '83 | pardoned |
| James Ashley | C. | | |
| Nicholas Milbourne | C. | | |
| Samuel Young | C. | | |
| William Sillwood | P. | | |
| Daniel Warrier | D. | deserted 27 Apl '83 | pardoned |
| Alexander Stevenson | F. | | |
| Richard Dewall | P. | | |
| Benjm. Williams | P. | | |
| Michael McCann | P. | | |
| John Nicholson | P. | | |
| Thomas Davies, 1st | P. | | |
| John Wade | P. | deserted 15 Apl '83 | pardoned |
| Christopher Cusack | P. | | |

| NAMES AND RANK. | | WHEN LEFT SERVICE AND THE REASONS. | REMARKS. |
|---|---|---|---|
| James Steward | P. | died 3 June '83 | |
| Willm. Stonestreet | P. | | |
| Joshua McKinsay | P. | | |
| Paul Greenard | P. | | |
| John Holloday | P. | | |
| Thomas Hutchcraft | P. | | |
| Edward Fincham | P. | | |
| Thomas Burke | P. | | |
| James Erwin | P. | | |
| John Nevitt, 2nd | P. | | |
| John Wilson | P. | | |
| Charles Wheelor | P. | | |
| George Jones | P. | | |
| George Bough | P. | | |
| Daniel Kettle | P. | | |
| Abraham Kettle | P. | | |
| Moses McKinsey | P. | | |
| Wm. Cooke | P. | | |
| Cornelius Vaughan | P. | | |
| Matthias Dyche | P. | deserted 15 Apl '83 | pardoned |
| Michael Smith, 1st | P. | | |
| Francis McCann | P. | | |
| Thomas Larymore | P. | deserted 15 Apl '83 | pardoned |
| Absalom Wright | P. | ditto | pardoned |
| Francis Karns | P. | | |
| William Ryder | P. | | |
| William Whittico | P. | | |
| John Hall | P. | | |
| Thomas Foxall | P. | | |
| Walter B. Smallwood | P. | | |
| William Paul | P. | | |
| Robert Mitchell | P. | | |
| George Taylor | P. | | |
| Henry Billop | P. | | |
| John Thompson | P. | | |
| George Mauntle | P. | deserted 15 Apl '83 | pardoned |
| Samuel Baswell | P. | | |
| Elias Smith | P. | | |
| Charles Jones | P. | | |
| Arthur Coffins | P. | | |
| Richard Denby | P. | died 8 May '83 | |
| John Elcott, 1st | P. | deserted 29 Apl '83 | pardoned |
| Thomas Jones, 2nd | P. | | |
| John Stanton | P. | | |
| James Bowen | P. | | |
| Smart Greer | P. | | |

| NAMES AND RANK. | WHEN LEFT SERVICE AND THE REASONS. | REMARKS. |
|---|---|---|
| Michael Hartman | P. | |
| Benjm. Clever | P. | Artificer |
| Joseph Elliott | P. | |
| Thomas Elliotte, 2nd | P. | |
| George Bomgardner | P. | |
| Christopher Smith | P. | |
| Moses Graham | P. | |
| John Nelson, 1st | P. | |

4TH COMPANY.  CAPT. JAMES W. GRAY.

| John Reeder | S. & P. deserted 29 Apl '83 reduced 15 Jan '83, pardoned | |
| John Moore, 2nd | S. | |
| Humphrey Beckett | S.  deserted 29 Apl '83 | pardoned |
| James Kelley | S. & P. | reduced 22 Feb '83 |
| Lawrence Bromham | S. & P. | ditto   22 Feb '83 |
| John Hamilton | C. & S. | promoted Sjt. 1 Mch '83 |
| Walter Howe | C. & S. | do   do 1 Mch '83 |
| George Dixon | P. & C. | do   Corpl. 1 Mch '83 |
| Wm. Derrington | P. & C. | do   do   1 Mch '83 |
| Thomas Jones, 1st | P. & C. | do   do   1 Mch '83 |
| William Lytle | C. | |
| Samuel Gray | C. | |
| Anthony Gohegan | D.  deserted 30 Apl '83 | pardoned |
| Robert Cornick | F. | |
| Luke Carter | P. | |
| John Ashmore | P. | |
| John Craig | P. | |
| William McGee | P. | |
| George Ford | P. | |
| Christopher Seymore | P. | |
| Francis Hopkins | P. | |
| John Gordon, 1st | P. | |
| Neal Peacock | P. | |
| John Love | P. | |
| William Mitchell | P. | |
| Emanuel Farrara | P. | |
| Richard Tascow | P. | |
| Matthew Moore, 1st | P. | |
| Joseph Jenkins | P.  deserted 29 Apl '83 | pardoned |
| John Dyer | P. | |
| Joseph Southall | P. | |
| Hezekiah Carr | P. | |
| Zachariah Clark | P. | |
| John Fransway | P. | |
| John Lee | P. | |
| Richard Taylor | P.  dischd. 6 May | |

32

| NAMES AND RANK. | | WHEN LEFT SERVICE AND THE REASONS. | REMARKS. |
|---|---|---|---|
| John Wells | P. | | |
| Edward Irvin | P. | | |
| John Jarvis | P. | | |
| James Byas | P. | | |
| John Lewin | P. | | |
| Charles Ormes | P. | | |
| Charles McGee | P. | | |
| John Bulkley | P. | | |
| Dudley Lee | P. | | |
| Andrew Russell | P. | | |
| Edward Evins | P. | | |
| Luke Dempsey | P. | | |
| John Onians | P. | | |
| John Gorman | P. | | |
| Francis Reed | P. | | |
| Willm. Hartman | P. | | |
| Philip Savoy | P. | | |
| Edward Chambers | P. | | |
| Michael Pilkerton | P. | | |
| James Tigner | P. | | |
| Lambert Goody | P. | | |
| John Graham | P. | deserted 2 May '83 | pardoned |
| Matthew Carty | P. | | |
| Lewin Abbott | P. | deserted 29 Apl '83 | pardoned |
| Edward Forreignner | P. | | |
| Lawrence Simpson | P. | | |
| Thomas Johns | P. | deserted 29 Apl '83 | pardoned |
| William McPherson | P. | | |
| Thomas Perry | P. | | |
| James, or Jesse, Chambers | P. | | |
| Jacob Jeffers | P. | | |
| Charles Murphy | P. | | |
| John Cole | P. | | |
| *John D. Tally | P. | | prisoner 20 Dec '82 |
| Austin Howard | P. | | |
| John Appleby | P. | | |
| Michael Woolford | P. | | |
| Traverse Alvey | P. | deserted 29 Apl '83 | pardoned |
| Joshua Pierce | P. | | |
| James Thomas | P. | deserted 29 Apl '83 | pardoned |

### 5TH COMPANY.   CAPT. B. PRICE.

| | | | |
|---|---|---|---|
| Wm. A. Needham | S. | | |
| John Quick | S. | | |
| George Williams | S. | | |
| Charles Fulham | S. | | |

| NAMES AND RANK. | | WHEN LEFT SERVICE AND THE REASONS. | REMARKS. |
|---|---|---|---|
| Patrick Doran | S. & P. | | reduced to private 20 Jan '83 |
| James Greenwood | D. | | |
| Thomas Hawson | F. | | |
| Issachar Mason | P. | | |
| Frederick Bennet | P. | | |
| William Moore, 1st | P. | | |
| John Ashbury | P. | | |
| James Barber | P. | | |
| John Branson | P. | | |
| Daniel Bassett | P. | | |
| William Carter | P. | | |
| George Craggs | P. | | |
| James Driver | P. | | |
| Peter Degazoone | P. | | |
| Stephen Fennell | P. | | |
| John Frawney | P. | | |
| Thomas Gadd | P. | | |
| William Hope | P. | | |
| Edward Holland | P. | | |
| Benjamin Kearns | P. | deserted 30 Apl '83 | pardoned |
| James Knott | P. | | |
| Levi Lord | P. | | |
| Alexander Levi | P. | | |
| Francis Lang | P. | | |
| Henry Mansfield | P. | | |
| William Nuton | P. | | |
| Thomas Pendor | P. | | |
| Lambert Philips | P. | | |
| Joseph Rhea | P. | | |
| Partrick Reiley | P. | | |
| William Shirley | P. | | |
| Bennet Shirley | P. | | |
| Jesse Wright | P. | | |
| John West | P. | | |
| Thomas Wember | P. | | |
| Thomas Pennefield | P. | | |
| Richard Kisby | P. | | |
| George Duncan | P. | | |
| Henry Jacobs | P. | | drafted Artificer |
| William Hicks | P. | | |
| William Cox | P. | | |
| John Ennis | P. | | |
| Henry Nicholson | P. | | |
| John Moore, 1st | P. | | |
| Rhode Woodland | P. | | |
| Leonard Holt | P. | | |

| NAMES AND RANK. | | WHEN LEFT SERVICE AND THE REASONS. | REMARKS. |
|---|---|---|---|
| Enoch Ennis | P. | | |
| Thomas Ellis | P. | | |
| Abraham Catchsides | P. | | |
| Richard Wiley | P. | | |
| William Fitzgerald | P. | | |
| Charles Fitzgerald | P. | | |
| William Toland | P. | | |
| Joseph Fowler | P. | | |
| William Manley | P. | | |
| William Jones, 1st | P. | | |
| Thomas Butt | P. | | |
| Jacob Blake | P. | | |
| Francis Freeman | P. | | |
| Job Sylvester | P. | | |
| Charles White | P. | | |
| Edward Kersey | P. | | |
| Joseph Barton | P. | | |
| William Lee, 1st | P. | | |
| James Hewitt | P. | | drafted Artificer |
| Jeremiah French | P. | | |
| James Smith | P. | | |
| John Whitcomb | P. | discharged for inability 30 Apl '83 | |
| Peter Howard | P. | died 4 Feb '83 | |

6TH COMPANY.    CAPT. LLOYD BEALL.

| | | | |
|---|---|---|---|
| William Bruff | S. | | |
| Stephen Fluherty | S. | | |
| George Fields | S. | | |
| Charles McKnabb | S. | | |
| Samuel Filson | S. | | |
| Boston Medler | D. | | |
| Benjm. Williams | F. | | |
| Peter Stephens | C. | | |
| William Potter | C. | | |
| Robert Sharpless | C. | | |
| John Scott | D. | | |
| Charles Clements | C. | deserted 26 Apl '83 | pardoned |
| Joseph Pherson | C. | ditto | pardoned |
| Theophilus Linsday | C. | | |
| George Devit | P. | | |
| Samuel Clark | P. | | |
| Zedekiah, or Zadock, Whaley | P. | | |
| Alexander Ross | P. | | |
| George Buck | P. | | |
| Joshua Leister | P. | | |

| NAMES AND RANK. | | WHEN LEFT SERVICE AND THE REASONS. | REMARKS. |
|---|---|---|---|
| Robert Duncan | P. | | |
| Absalom Fardo | P. | | |
| Darby Crowley | P. | | |
| William Leakins | P. | | |
| John Knox | P. | | |
| John Ryan | P. | | |
| Elijah Pepper | P. | | |
| Neil Morriss | P. | | |
| John Loveday | P. | | |
| Joseph Blaze | P. | | |
| Michael Curtis | P. | | |
| Frederick Harty | P. | | |
| William Mann | P. | | |
| John McNelly | P. | | |
| William Quinton | P. | | |
| John Twiner | P. | | |
| Luke Sampson | P. | | |
| Moses Foster | P. | | Artificer |
| Richard Gee | P. | | |
| John Maxwell | P. | | |
| John Miles, or Mills | P. | | |
| Samuel Wedge | P. | | |
| Lazarus Harmer | P. | | |
| Charles Simpkins | P. | | |
| William Crail | P. | | |
| William Casey | P. | | |
| Peter McGuire | P. | | |
| Benjamin Mash | P. | | |
| Robert Campbell | P. | deserted 29 Apl '83 | pardoned |
| John Armstrong | P. | | |
| Henry Townley | P. | | |
| Richard Spires | P. | | |
| George Hamilton | P. | | promoted Corpl. 1 Mch '83 |
| John Hewlett | P. | | |
| Paul Rowan | P. | | |
| Edward Cosgrove | P. | | |
| William Elkins | P. | | |
| John Fulford | P. | | |
| John Jones, 2nd | P. | | |
| Andrew Rauside | P. | died previous to '83 | |
| John Smith, 4th | P. | | |
| William Whaling | P. | | |
| Richard Dixon | P. | died previous to '83 | |
| Thomas Clarke, 2nd | P. | | |
| Nicholas Hiner | P. | | |
| John McGlin | P. | | |

| Names and Rank. | | When Left Service and the Reasons. | Remarks. |
|---|---|---|---|
| John McNeal | P. | | |
| John Bowdy | P. | deserted 2 May '83 | pardoned |
| Nehemiah Lingard | P. | | |
| Samuel Hurst | P. | | |
| John Spires | P. | | |
| William Glover | P. | | |
| John Wrighte | P. | | |
| William Taylor, 1st | P. | | |
| Zachariah Robinson | P. | mustered in the 8th Company | |
| William Niblet | P. | | |
| William Hillman | P. | | |

### 7TH COMPANY. CAPT. SAMUEL McPHERSON.

| Names and Rank. | | When Left Service and the Reasons. | Remarks. |
|---|---|---|---|
| William Collis | S. | | |
| John Brady | S. | | |
| Robert Scrivenor, or Scribner | S. | died 15 Feb '83 | |
| Humphry Spencer | S. | | |
| Aaron Spalding | S. | | |
| William Braithwaite | C. | | |
| Bartholomew Essom | C. | | |
| John Head | D. | | |
| Andrew Garnett | F. | | |
| Richard Hayes | P. | | |
| Isaac Greaves | P. | | |
| Aquilla Pierce | P. | deserted 29 Apl '83 | pardoned |
| Philip Fitzpatrick | P. | | |
| John Haney | P. | | |
| William Goold | P. | | |
| Hampton Coarsey | P. | | |
| Henry Green | P. | | |
| Roger Landers | P. | | |
| John Welch, 1st | P. | | |
| Michael Lloyd | P. | | |
| Charles Cooper | P. | | |
| James Meason, Mason | P. | | |
| John Gregory | P. | | |
| Thomas Waite | P. | | |
| John Alby | P. | | |
| William Moore, 2nd | P. | | |
| Jacob Games | P. | | |
| John Robins | P. | | |
| John Buckhannan | P. | | |
| James Farrell | P. | | |
| David Bramble | P. | | |
| Luke Merryman | P. | | |

| NAMES AND RANK. | | WHEN LEFT SERVICE AND THE REASONS. | REMARKS. |
|---|---|---|---|
| Thomas Camphor | P. | | |
| William Purchace | P. | | |
| Adam Kiphart | P. | | |
| Jacob Knight | P. | | |
| William Laws | P. | | |
| Michael Casnor | P. | | |
| Richard Blansford | P. | | |
| James Harris | P. | deserted 1 May '83 | pardoned |
| John Dennison, or Denion | P. | | |
| William Glory | P. | | |
| John Summers | P. | | |
| Henry Ostin | P. | | |
| Henry Evans, or Evis | P. | | |
| Benjamin Gaither | P. | deserted 1 May '83 | pardoned |
| Robert Streets | P. | | |
| Joseph Donoho | P. | | |
| William Rice | P. | | |
| William Matthews | P. | deserted 1 May '83 | pardoned |
| Thomas Patterson | P. | ditto | pardoned |
| Thomas Bear | P. | | |
| John Sammon | P. | | |
| James Cresbury | P. | | |
| James Wilson, 1st | P. | deserted 17 April '83 | pardoned |
| Charles Siekle | P. | | |
| Abraham Irwine | P. | | |
| John Taylor | P. | deserted 17 Apl '83 | pardoned |
| Matthias Cyphert | P. | | |
| Peter Melvin | P. | | |
| Patrick Conavough | P. | to be altered name | |
| Daniel Bulger | P. | | |
| William Moore, 3d | P. | | |
| Thomas Porter | P. | | |
| Richard Biddle | P. | | |
| James Bigwood | P. | | |
| Daniel Jarvis | P. | | |
| Joseph Hewkill | P. | deserted 1 May '83 | pardoned |
| Solomon Brittenham | P. | | |
| Joseph Horsefield | P. | | Artificer |
| William Groves | P. | | |
| William Jones, 2nd | P. | | |
| Lambert Thompson | P. | | |
| Cathoel Carmile | P. | | |
| Patrick Rowing, or Rowan | P. | | |

8TH COMPANY.    CAPT. JAMES WINCHESTER.

| | | | |
|---|---|---|---|
| Peter McNortin | S. | | |
| Peter Smith | S. | | |

| NAMES AND RANK. | | WHEN LEFT SERVICE AND THE REASONS. | REMARKS. |
|---|---|---|---|
| Samuel Evans | S. | | |
| John Willing | S. | | |
| Benjm. Prior | C. | | |
| George Childs | C. | | |
| John Willey | C. | | |
| Thomas Gossage | F. | | |
| John Martindale | D | | |
| Richard Hall | P. | | |
| John Adams | P. | | |
| John Baley | P. | | |
| Peter Bocard | P. | | |
| Michael Lawler, or Loller | P. | | |
| Basil Brown | P. | | |
| Thomas Canady | P. | | |
| John Brown | P. | | |
| Samuel Hamilton | P. | | |
| William Lilley | P. | | |
| Patrick Molohon | P. | | |
| John Williams | P. | | |
| Thomas Thomas | P. | | |
| James Thomas, 2nd | P. | | |
| Charles Goldsbury | P. | | |
| Benjamin Steward | P. | | |
| Alexander Francis | P. | | |
| Peregrine Howard | P. | | |
| Richard Proctor | P. | | |
| Samuel Harper | P. | | |
| Edward Hammond | P. | | |
| Barney Wilson | P. | | |
| Samuel Calahan | P. | | |
| Henry Loyers, or Lawers | P. | | |
| William Pherson | P. | { mustered deserted 26 Apl in 7th Co. } | pardoned |
| Joseph Hall | P. | | |
| Amos Green | P. | | |
| Francis Demar | P. | deserted 27 Apl '83 | pardoned |
| William Herrington | P. | | |
| Abijah Buckstone | P. | | |
| Abraham Garsene | P. | | |
| William Sax, or Sikes | P. | | |
| Darby McLamar | P. | | |
| David Cale | P. | | |
| Stephen Fresh | P. | | |
| William Poland | P. | | |
| Michael Miller | P. | | |
| John Jackson | P. | | |

| Names and Rank. | | When Left Service and the Reasons. | Remarks. |
|---|---|---|---|
| Ignatius Adams | P. | | |
| Jonathan Fowler | P. | | |
| William Nailor | P. | | |
| William Joice | P. | | |
| John Brookbank | P. | | |
| John Irons | P. | | |
| Jacob Flora | P. | | |
| William Clary | P. | | |
| Samuel Vermillion | P. | | |
| John Anderson, 1st | P. | | |
| Garrard Welch | P. | | |
| Joshua Cox | P. | | |
| Charles Dean | P. | | |
| David Hatten | P. | died 9 Mch '83 | |
| Jacob Drudo, or Duddero | P. | | |
| William Dawson | P. | | |
| William Harrison | P. | | |
| William Stanley | P. | | |
| Noah Sears | P. | died 3 Apl '83 | |
| Frederick Wilmot | P. | | Artificer |
| Thomas Clark, 1st | P. | | |
| Benjamin Boyd | P. | | |
| John Osburn, or Osban | P. | | |
| Richard Butler | P. | | in Maryland |
| Francis Fairbrother | P. | | |
| John Carr | P. | died 25 Feb '83 | |
| Henry Bradley | P. | | |

9TH COMPANY.    CAPT. FRANCIS REVELLY.

| Names and Rank. | | When Left Service and the Reasons. | Remarks. |
|---|---|---|---|
| Stephen R. Price | S. | | |
| Chas. Runenberger | S. | | |
| John Lynch | S. | | |
| Archibald Johnson | S. | | |
| Samuel F. Shoemaker | S. | deserted 12 Jan '83 | |
| John Foldier, or Falling | C. | | |
| Andrew Crummy | C. | | |
| Thomas Evans, 2nd | P. | | |
| Benj. H. Kerrick | D. | | |
| Michael Clansey | F. | | |
| William Sullivan | P. | | |
| John Burnett | P. | deserted 26 Apl '83 | pardoned |
| George Pearce | P. | ditto | pardoned |
| Rigby Foster | P. | | |
| John McCall | P. | | |
| John Gee | P. | | |
| Daniel Smith, 2nd | P. | | |

| NAMES AND RANK. | | WHEN LEFT SERVICE AND THE REASONS. | REMARKS. |
|---|---|---|---|
| Edward Tanner | P. | deserted 26 Apl '83 | pardoned |
| *Edward Roberts | P. | | promoted Corpl. 1 Apl |
| Michael Waltman | P. | | ['83 |
| *James Ruarck | P. | | promoted Corpl. 1 Apl |
| William Roberts | P. | | ['83 |
| Charles Scott | P. | | |
| Robinson Ross | P. | | |
| John McCann | P. | deserted 2 May '83 | pardoned |
| John Harrell | P. | | |
| John Roach | P. | | |
| Joseph Long | P. | | |
| Joseph Sloop | P. | deserted 27 Apl '83 | pardoned |
| John Walker, 1st | P. | | |
| Nathan Aldridge | P. | | |
| Robert Clanahan | P. | | |
| William McGloughlin, or | | | |
| McLochlin | P. | | |
| James Sewall | P. | | |
| Zachariah Mills | P. | | |
| William Jenkins | P. | deserted 26 Apl '83 | pardoned |
| Daniel Buckley | P. | | |
| Patrick Dennison | P. | | |
| Jacob Myers | P. | | |
| Barrack Butt | P. | | |
| Henry Crane | P. | deserted 26 Apl '83 | pardoned |
| Richard Mitchell | P. | | |
| Bartholomew Thompson | P. | | |
| Amos Griffin | P. | | |
| James Wood, 2nd | P. | | |
| John Burns | P. | deserted 26 Apl '83 | pardoned |
| Isaac Nichols | P. | | |
| Joseph Botchabay | P. | | |
| Rueben Smith | P. | died 9 May '83 | |
| Richard Haislip | P. | | |
| John Taylor | P. | | |
| Henry Williams | P. | | |
| Benj. Williams, 3rd | P. | | |
| Abraham Dougan, or | | | |
| Doogan, | P. | | |
| Edward Vickers | P. | | |
| James Collierd, or Cholard | P. | | |
| James Crozier | P. | | |
| John Delany | P. | | |
| John Haiden, or Hadan | P. | | |
| James Jones | P. | | |
| Michael Weirey | P. | deserted 26 Apl '83 | pardoned |

| NAMES AND RANK. | | WHEN LEFT SERVICE AND THE REASONS. | REMARKS. |
|---|---|---|---|
| George Saunders | P. | | |
| Robert Taylor | S. | | |
| George Steem | F. | | |
| James Managa | | | |
| Thomas Gillon | | | |
| *James Keelan | P. | | |
| *Jacob Collins | P. | | |
| *Jacob Moses | P. | | |
| *Nehemiah Hader | P. | | |
| Henry Fisher, 2nd | P. | German Regiment | |
| Levi Burck | P. | drum'd out & dischd. 3 May '83 | |
| *James Jackson | P. | | |
| *Joseph Jones, 1st | P. | | |
| Alex. Rutherford | P. | dischd. 4 Jan '83 | |
| *Joshua Barrett | S. | | |
| John Armstrong, 1st | P. | formerly of the 5th Regt. | |
| *Daniel Holdman | P. | | |
| Thomas Bulkley | P. | | |
| Laurence Mesler | P. | | |
| *Thomas Windham | S. | | |
| David Middis | P. | | |
| *Thomas Smith, 1st | P. | | |
| Peter Outhouse | P. | | |
| *John Newton, 1st | P. | | |
| Thomas Crompton | P. | | |
| Simon Perry | P. | | |
| Jonathan Weedon | P. | died 13 Feb '83 | |
| Thomas Wood, 4th | S. | | |
| Charles Robinson | P. | | |
| Thomas Summers | | | |

## NORTHERN DETACHMENT.

### I.—CAPT. WALKER MUSE.   LIEUT. HENRY CHAPMAN.

| NAMES AND RANK. | | WHEN LEFT SERVICE AND THE REASONS. | REMARKS. |
|---|---|---|---|
| *Nathaniel Bailey | S. | | |
| *John McDonald | S. | | |
| William Johnson | S. | dischd. 22 Oct '83 | |
| Robert Harpin | S. | | |
| Daniel Willis | D. | | |
| Samuel Street | F. | deserted 29 Apl '83 | |
| Isaac Johnston | C. | dischd. 1 Oct '83 | |
| *Evan Thomas | C. | | |
| James Barron | C. | | |
| John Hudson | P. | | |
| Robert Firth | P. | | |
| *James Hudson | P. | | |
| *John Reed | P. | | |

| Names and Rank. | | When left Service and the Reasons. | Remarks. |
|---|---|---|---|
| *David McCollum | P. | | |
| John Smallwood | P. | deserted 20 June '83 | |
| *Lewis Flash | P. | | |
| John Turner | P. | | |
| John Rogers | P. | | |
| Jeremiah Carter | P. | | |
| James Brannon | P. | | |
| William Smith, 3rd | P. | | |
| Roger Hogan | P. | | |
| John Stackhouse | P. | dischd. 4 May '83 | |
| Thos. McQuinney | P. | | |
| Francis De Wist | P. | | |
| William Batton | P. | | |
| Thomas McKinzie | P. | | |
| *Samuel Chapel | P. | | |
| Edward Ellicott | P. | | |
| William Willion | P. | | |
| John Purdy | P. | dischd. 27 Jan '83 | |
| Benj. Burch | C. | do 19 do do | |
| Enoch McClain | S. | | |
| *Birnnick Meakins | P. | | |
| Charles Leago | P. | dischd. 1 Apl '83 | |
| *Charles Love | P. | | |
| *John Pope | P. | | |
| William Devin | P. | | |
| John Murray, 1st | P. | | |
| *Notley Tippet | P. | | |
| Thomas Hall | P. | | |
| Patrick Quinn | P. | | |
| Daniel Howe | P. | | |
| James Dowden | P. | | |
| John Traverse | P. | | |
| John Housely | P. | | |
| Zachariah Berry | P. | | |
| George Trice | P. | | |
| Edward Kirk | P. | | |
| *Thomas Houseman | P. | | |
| Zadock Risden | P. | | |
| John Welch, 2nd | P. | | |
| *Joseph Ward | P. | | |
| *John Gray | P. | | |
| William Patterson | P. | | |
| John Ransom | P. | | |
| *Banks Webb | P. | | |
| John Walker, 2nd | P. | | |
| Nicholas Welch | P. | | |

| NAMES AND RANK. | | WHEN LEFT SERVICE AND THE REASONS. | REMARKS. |
|---|---|---|---|
| William Senah | P. | | |
| Matthew Kelly | P. | | |
| George Tate | P. | | |
| Roderick McKinsie | P. | | |
| Thomas Richardson, 2nd | P. | not heard of 2 months past | |
| Michael Standley | P. | | |

### 2.—CAPT. HORATIO CLAGGETT.  LT. WALTER DYER.  ENSIGN HENRY HAWKINS

| | | | |
|---|---|---|---|
| David Love | S. | | |
| William Marlow | S. | to the End | |
| *Joseph Allen | S. | | |
| Joseph Neal | S. | reduced to Private 15 Nov '83 | |
| Dennis Dunning | D. | | |
| *Joseph Clancey | F. | | |
| *Thomas Ellison | C. | | |
| John Fennel, 1st | C. | | |
| *Christopher Hinson | C. | | |
| William Gudgeon | P. | | |
| *Preistly Bruington | P. | | |
| Isaac Dunkin | P. | dischd. 15 Nov | |
| Thomas Harris | P. | | |
| Sylvester Gatten | P. | | |
| John McClain | P. | | |
| William Hutchinson | P. | | |
| Andrew Bramble | P. | | |
| Selladay Standley | P. | | |
| John Boody | P. | | |
| Basil Newton | P. | | |
| William Conner | P. | | |
| John Baxter | P. | | |
| *William Powell | P. | | |
| James Newell | P. | | |
| *James Williams | P. | | |
| John Vane | P. | | |
| John Lowe | P. | | |
| *Levin Harrington | P. | | |
| William Rue | P. | to the End | |
| *Richard Jennings | P. | | |
| Jesse Locker | P. | | |
| *Aron Rawlings | P. | | |
| *Daniel Harness | P. | | |
| John Swales | P. | | |
| *William Madan | P. | | |
| *Solomon Sullivan | P. | | |
| *James Hunt | P. | | |
| Charles Griffith | P. | dischd. 1 May '83 | |

| NAMES AND RANK. | | WHEN LEFT SERVICE AND THE REASONS. | REMARKS. |
|---|---|---|---|
| John Hickings | P. | | |
| John Cleverdence | P. | | |
| *Peter Jackson | P. | | |
| Paris Owens | P. | | |
| *John Conner | P. | | |
| Thomas Baxter | P. | dischd. 24 Sept '83 | |
| John Moore, 5th | P. | | |
| *Alexander McGregor | P. | | |
| *John Willman | P. | | |
| Jacob Mifford | P. | | |
| *Whittington Gild | P. | | |
| Richard Harrington | P. | | |
| John Climeslaught | P. | | |
| *John Fairweather | P. | | |
| John Courts | P. | time expired 16 Apl '83 | |
| *Hugh Ware | P. | | |
| *Willan Colter | P. | | |
| *Thomas Dickerson | P. | | |
| *Samuel Scott | P. | dischd. 20 June '83 | |
| *Isom Coleman | P. | | |
| William Holland | P. | | |
| *James Kirk | P. | | |
| *James Pool | P. | | |
| *Thomas Channon | P. | | |
| John Williams, 2nd | P. | | |

### 3.—Capt. Edward Spurrier. Lt. Joshua Rutledge. Lt. Robert Halkerston.

| | | | |
|---|---|---|---|
| William McNeal | S. | | |
| Richard Hogins | S. | | |
| Aquilla Chitham | S. | | |
| Thomas Craig | S. | | |
| Stephen Nicholson | S. | | |
| Benjamin Burch | S. | dischd. 3 Nov '83 | |
| *William Watkins | D. | | |
| John Denoone | F. | | |
| *John Burgess | C. | | |
| *Kemp Holden | C. | | |
| Thomas White | C. | | |
| Benjamin McCall | C. | | |
| Thomas King | P. | | |
| William Ayhun | P. | | |
| *James Bell | P. | | |
| William Hunter | P. | | |
| *John Bell | P. | | |

| NAMES AND RANK. | | WHEN LEFT SERVICE AND THE REASONS. | REMARKS. |
|---|---|---|---|
| Daniel Hukell | P. | | |
| John Jones, Jr. | P. | | |
| John White | P. | | |
| John Cannon | P. | | |
| Charles Palmore | P. | | |
| *Thomas Scego | P. | | |
| John Hukill | P. | | |
| George Dadisman | P. | | |
| *Henry Barns | P. | | |
| Joseph Rose | P. | | |
| John Jones, Sr. | P. | | |
| John Smith, 3rd | P. | | |
| Charles Masseck | P. | dischd. 22 Oct '83 | |
| *John Stoffel | P. | | |
| John Shefar | P. | | |
| *Bassell Dorsey | P. | | |
| *Thomas Hardin | P. | | |
| *Thomas McDowell | P. | | |
| John Johnson, 1st | P. | | prom. Corpl. 1 May '83 |
| Robert Johnson | P. | | |
| *Henry Windows | P. | | |
| George Miller | P. | | |
| *Evans Willing | P. | | |
| *Edward Roan | P. | | |
| *John Greenwood | P. | | |
| *Isaac Kent | P. | | |
| *William Smallwood | P. | | |
| *Robert Dean | P. | | |
| John Britton | P. | | |
| *Isaac Mitchell | P. | | |
| Frederick Flinn | P. | | |
| William Connelly | P. | dischd. 16 July '83 | |
| Matthew Daley | P. | | |
| Edward Cantwell | P. | dischd. 24 Sept '83 | |
| John Willson, 2nd | P. | | |
| James Creighton | P. | | |
| John Dixson | P. | | |
| *Thomas Wood, 3rd | P. | | |
| John Turner, 3rd | P. | | |
| Christopher Rayner | P. | dischd. 10 Apl '83 | |
| *Isaac McFadon | P. | | |
| Edward Mahony | P. | not heard of | |

4.—Capt. Wm. Bruce.  Lieut. Thomas Rowse.

| | | | |
|---|---|---|---|
| Perry Evans | S. | | Certd. Lt. Gassaway. |
| John Walker, 3rd | S. | | |

| Names and Rank. | | When Left Service and the Reasons. | Remarks. |
|---|---|---|---|
| Harris Austin | S. | | |
| John Browne, 3rd | S. | Rawlings' Regt. | |
| *John Bond | S. | | reduced 1 Feb '82 |
| William Chatlin | C. | | |
| *John Davis | C. | | |
| James Maxwell | C. | | |
| Isaack Deal | C. | | |
| William Dunn | C. | | |
| *Isaac Holland | D. | | |
| Joel Baker | P. | | |
| *John Long | P. | | |
| Martin Bowles | P. | | |
| *Samuel Fisher | P. | | |
| Solomon Barret | P. | | |
| *Leonard Nable | P. | | |
| *Robert McClary | P. | | |
| Benj. Donelly | P. | | |
| John Richardson | P. | | |
| *John Green, 2nd | P. | | |
| William Matthews, 2nd | P. | | |
| *Lawrence Pines | P. | | |
| James Silk | P. | | |
| *John Bailey | P. | | |
| Joseph Cluley | P. | | |
| John Cotter | P. | | |
| Perry Bantham | P. | | |
| Herculus Hutchins | P. | | |
| Richard Rivers | P. | | |
| *John Nicholson | P. | | |
| *Edward Burns | P. | | |
| *Henry Frazer | P. | | |
| William Deveraux | P. | | |
| Stephen Owens | P. | | |
| William Marshall | P. | dischd. 3 Mch '83 | |
| Stephen Hancock | P. | | |
| *Michael Keen | P. | | |
| *Richard Burck | P. | | |
| *William Coulin | P. | | |
| Dorden Orrell | P. | | |
| James Burck, 1st | P. | | |
| George Carney | P. | | |
| William Watkins | P. | | |
| Edward Shoebrook | P. | | |
| *Lewis Cunningham | P. | time expired 22 July '83 | |
| John Smith, 2nd | | | |
| *Daniel Wilkins | P. | | |

| NAMES AND RANK. | | WHEN LEFT SERVICE AND THE REASONS. | REMARKS. |
|---|---|---|---|
| John Harris, 2nd | P. | | |
| Robert Ferrall | P. | | |
| William Eagle | P. | | |
| Joseph McCalister | P. | died 24 Mch '83 | |
| Levin Clarage | P. | | |
| *Robert Folger | P. | | |
| George Filliston | P. | | |
| *George Linton | P. | | |
| Thomas Countess | P. | | |
| James Kelly, 2nd | P. | dischd. 10 Apl '83 | |
| Benjm. Worthington | P. | | |
| *Richard McDonald | P. | | |
| Barney Haney | P. | War | |
| James Hudson | P. | | |
| James Terry | P. | | |
| *John Philips | P. | commenced 8 Mch | |
| *James Sullivan | P. | | |
| John Barlow | P. | | |
| Thomas Kettle | C. | | reduced 22 Feb '83 |
| Domini Coines,(or Conies) | P. | (when commenced not stated) | |
| George Bowers | P. | | |
| Thomas Baker | P. | | |
| Samuel Crowell | P. | | |
| James Gilmore | P. | | |
| Daniel Sullinger | P. | | |

INVALID COMPANY.

| | | | |
|---|---|---|---|
| Arthur McClain | S. | dischd. 10 Feb '83 | |
| John Auber | D. | | |
| Dennis Flanagan | P. | Private of Artillery | |
| Matthias Funner | P. | | |
| Joseph Batts | P. | | |
| John Cooper, 1st | P. | | |
| John Mick | P. | | |
| John Alsop | P. | | |
| Jonathan Lewis | P. | | |
| Giffard Miniky | P. | dischd. 16 Jan '83 | |
| John Martin | P. | | |
| Robert Carns | S. | | |
| John Brown, 2nd | S. | | |
| Abram Gamble | S. | | |
| John Matthews, 1st | C. | | |
| *Daniel Smith | C. | | |
| Henry Crooke | P. | | |
| *Christopher Lambert | P. | | |
| David Kelly | P. | | |

| NAMES AND RANK. | | WHEN LEFT SERVICE AND THE REASONS. | REMARKS. |
|---|---|---|---|
| James Smith, 3rd | P. | | promoted Corpl. 1 Oct '83 |
| Joseph Quinn | P. | | |
| John Shovell | P. | | |
| James Shane | P. | | |
| Patrick Reiley | P. | dischd. 3 Oct '83 | |
| William Evans | P. | | |
| John Shanks | P. | | |
| James Gath | P. | | |
| John Vanzant | P. | | |
| John Neighbours | P. | dischd. 1 Feb '83 | |
| Philip Fisher | P. | | |
| James Burck, 2nd | P. | | |
| Thomas Bishop | P. | | |
| John C. Harwood | P. | | waiting to Lt. Skinner, Virginia |
| Walter Keech | P. | dischd. 1 Aug '83 | |
| William Hurly | P. | | |
| Charles Bucklep | P. | | |
| Thomas Watson | P. | | |
| Joseph Burch | P. | | |
| David Conner | P. | | Joined 1 Oct '83 |

### LIEUT. BOHAM'S COMPANY.

| NAMES AND RANK. | | WHEN LEFT SERVICE AND THE REASONS. | REMARKS. |
|---|---|---|---|
| Benj. Ward | S. | dischd. 1 July '83 | |
| Terrence Duffee | S. | | |
| George Finlay | S. | | |
| Jesse Boswell | S. | time expired 1 June '83 | |
| Leonard Smith | S. | dischd. 26 July '83 | |
| Benjm. Fitzgerald | S. | | |
| Richard Smith | S. | time expires 1 June '83 | |
| Richard Wheelor | S. | dischd. 23 July '83 | |
| Jesse Simms | S. | dischd. 20 Mch '83 | |
| Thomas Duffee | S. | | |
| William Preist | S. | | |
| George Holton | S. | | reduced 1 June |
| John Moore, 4th | C. | | |
| James Hagan | C. | time expires 1 June '83 | |
| Joseph Harper | C. | | |
| Bennet Clements | C. | dischd. 23 July '83 | |
| James Mead | D. | | |
| John Riggs | D. | dischd. 6 May '83 | |
| Abram Stallions | D. | | |
| Alexander Stewart | P. | dischd. 1 Aug '83 | |
| Joseph Greir | P. | | |
| Christopher McGraw | D. | | |
| Philip Hueston | D. | | |
| Samuel Davies | F. | | |

| NAMES AND RANK. | | WHEN LEFT SERVICE AND THE REASONS. | REMARKS. |
|---|---|---|---|
| Isaac Young | F. | | |
| Edward Clancey | F. | | |
| John Peany | F. | | |
| William Chapman | P. | dischd. 17 July '83 | |
| Benjamin Smith | P. | do   1 Aug '83 | |
| John Newton, 2nd | P. | do   31 Jan '83 | |
| Elijah Hutt | P. | | |
| John McGinnis | P. | | |
| Jesse McKinsey | P. | dischd. 7 Aug '83 | |
| Thomas Matthews, 1st | P. | | |
| William Burgess | P. | dischd. 16 Aug '83 | |
| Alexander Robinson | P. | | |
| James Dawson | P. | | |
| James West | P. | | |
| Peter Bushell | P. | dischd. 1 May '83 | |
| John Young, 2nd | P. | | |
| Jacob Kelly | P. | | |
| John Barrett | P. | | |
| John Campbell, 2nd | P. | | |
| Daniel Clancey | P. | | |
| Adam Musler | P. | | |
| Levin Button | P. | | |
| Dennis Cragon | P. | Settled part in Invalids, dischd. 1 July '83 | |
| Philip Graham | P. | | |
| Richard Franklin | P. | | |
| Cuthbert Able | S. | dischd. 1 Feb '83 | |
| Edward Dominick | P. | do   1 July '83 | |
| Benj. Gilbert | P. | | |
| Thomas Smith, 2d | P. | | |
| James Cockerill, or Cougherin | P. | | |
| Levin Thomas | P. | | |
| James McDonald | P. | | |
| Barney Dougherty | P. | | |
| John Deakins | P. | | |
| John Edwards | P. | | |
| William Stirling, 1st | P. | | |
| Michael Smith, 2nd | P. | | |
| William Cummings | P. | | |
| William Cutler | P. | | |
| Robert Bowen | P. | | |
| Thomas Bailey | P. | | |
| William Lee, 2nd | P. | | |
| Adam Rider | P. | | |
| Isom, or Asa, Moore | P. | | |
| Wm. Taylor, 2nd, Sr. | P. | | |

| NAMES AND RANK. | | WHEN LEFT SERVICE AND THE REASONS. | REMARKS. |
|---|---|---|---|
| John Conley, 2nd | P. | | |
| Christian Boss | P. | | |
| Joseph White | P. | dischd. July '83 | |
| John Haycock, or Hancock | P. | | |
| Elisha Oakley | P. | | |
| Henry Rees, or —— | P. | | |
| William Mansfield | P. | | |
| William Taylor, 3rd, Jr. | P. | | |
| Patrick McKinsie | P. | | |
| Daniel Williams | P. | time expires 1 Apl '83 | |
| Frederick Iams | P. | dischd. 1 July '83 | |
| George Silver | P. | do   5 Sept '83 | |
| Giles Thomas | P. | do   25 July '83 | |
| John Tucker | P. | do   21 Feb '83 | |
| James Sappington | P. | | |
| William Franklin | P. | dischd. 28 July '83 | |
| John Nolan | P. | | |
| James Procter | P. | | |
| James Willson, 2d | P. | | |
| James Philips | P. | dischd. 1 Aug '83 | |
| Mark Foster | P. | | |
| Jacob Yeast | P. | to the End | |
| Edward Jackson | P. | | |
| Michael Clark | P. | | |
| William Prater | P. | | |
| **LIEUT. LYNN'S COMPANY.** | | | |
| Joseph Jeanes | S. | | |
| Dennis Kelly | S. | dischd. 1 Apl '83 | |
| Jeremiah Brown | S. | do   1 May '83 | |
| John Clancy | C. | Served 7 months and 16 days | |
| Wm. Clements | C. | dischd. 1 Aug '83 | |
| John Gorden, 2nd | C. | | |
| Benj. Belcher | F. | | |
| William Stewart | F. | | |
| Henry Fisher, 1st | P. | | |
| John Starkey | P. | | |
| James Greavy | P. | | |
| Daniel Stephens | P. | to the End | |
| Gabriel Williams | S. | dischd. 6 Feb '83 | |
| William Simonds | P. | do   1 July '83 | |
| Thomas Newman | P. | | |
| James Carey | P. | | |
| Nicholas Free | P. | | |
| James Reynolds | D. | | |
| George Clarke | P. | | |

| NAMES AND RANK. | | WHEN LEFT SERVICE AND THE REASONS. | REMARKS. |
|---|---|---|---|
| Joseph Lewis | P. | | |
| Charles Williams | P. | dischd. 27 Mch '83 | |
| Notley Whitcomb | P. | time expires 1 April '83 | |
| Benjm. Thompson | P. | | |
| William Downes | P. | | |
| James Shepherd | P. | | |
| Isaac Hill | P. | dischd. 11 Aug '83 | |
| Lazarus Higgs | P. | time expires 1 June '83 | |
| Allen Townshend | P. | | |
| Patrick Mayhorn | P. | | |
| William Snowden | P. | | |
| William Dorch | P. | dischd. 6 Aug '83 | |
| George Baker | P. | | |
| Thomas Sheridan | P. | | |
| Benjm. Askew | P. | | |
| John Mumford | P. | | |
| William Hand | P. | | |
| Nathan Harper | P. | | |
| Thomas Thompson | P. | | |
| John Abrams | P. | | |
| James Barber | P. | | |
| Thomas Wood, 1st | P. | | |
| Basil Shaw | S. | | |
| Thomas Clements | P. | dischd. 1 Aug '83 | |
| James Roe | P. | | |
| Nicholas Farr | P. | | |
| Thomas Evans, 1st | P. | | |
| Jesse Suite | S. | | |
| Jacob Doyne | S. | | |
| William Bowling | S. | | |
| Zachariah Moore | S. | | |
| Elisha Osborne | S. | | |
| Thomas Hill | C. | | |
| Thomas Fleming | C. | | |
| Christopher Coy | C. | | |
| Thomas Clinton | F. | | |
| William Lawrence | F. | | |
| Hugh Roney | P. | | |
| Stephen Preston | P. | | |
| Henry Tippett | P. | | |
| John Calahan | P. | | |
| Thomas Hammond | P. | | |
| George Chambers | P. | | |
| Thomas Sturges | P. | | |
| James Countess | P. | | |
| Peter Carberry | P. | | |

| NAMES AND RANK. | | WHEN LEFT SERVICE AND THE REASONS. | REMARKS. |
|---|---|---|---|
| Robert Walker | P. | | |
| John Cooper, 2nd | P. | | |
| Francis Purly | P. | | |
| Francis Ensly | P. | | |
| John Romills | P. | | |
| John Moore, 3rd | P. | dischd. 12 Jan '83 | |
| Thomas Billingham | P. | | |
| John Willis | P. | | |
| Leonard Ennis | P. | | |
| James Cowen | P. | | |
| William Coleman | P. | | |
| Cotter Jones | P. | | |
| Humphrey Wells | P. | | |
| Edward Wheatley | P. | | |
| Robert Wright | P. | | |
| Lewis McCullough | P. | | |
| Joseph Murphy | P. | | |
| John Johnson, 2nd | P. | | |
| James Morris | P. | | |
| Dennis O'Bryan | P. | | |
| George Blackham | P. | | |
| John McElroy | P. | | |
| Robinson Wood | P. | | |
| *Samuel Neville | P. | (when commenced not stated), deserted in 1780 and must produce a certificate from an Officer of his Service | |
| *John Hicks | P. | (when commenced not stated) | |
| John Connelly, 1st | P. | dischd. 1 Apl '83 | |
| James Wood | S. | | |
| *William Helmes | P. | (when commenced not stated) | |
| *Joseph Procter | P. | (when commenced not stated) | |
| *Peter Ryan | P. | commenced 24 Sept '83 | |
| *Thomas Petit | P. | (when commenced not stated) | |
| Jonathan Mayhugh | P. | | |
| William Howe | P. | commenced 1 Oct '83 | |
| Neilee Jones | P. | | |
| *John Johnston, 3rd | P. | dischd. 11 Aug '83 | |
| Michael Rhydmyer | P. | do    13 Feb '83 | |
| William Forman | S. | | |
| *Thomas Twinch | Q. M. S. | | |
| George Elms | F. M. | | |
| Timothy McMahon | S. | | |
| Joseph Purdy | D. M. | | |
| Barney Lemon | P. | dischd. 14 Apl '83 | |
| Abraham Manning | P. | | |
| Henry Young | P. | | |

| NAMES AND RANK. | WHEN LEFT SERVICE AND THE REASONS. | REMARKS. |
|---|---|---|
| John McBride | P. | |
| George Parker | P. | |
| John Green, 1st | P. | |
| Joseph McNamara | | dischd. 25 July '83 |
| *John Clancy, 2nd | P. | |
| James Lowry | P. | dischd. at Frederick in Nov '83 |
| Jacob Hunt | P. | |
| John Lincoln | P. | |
| Lawrence Simpson | P. | |
| John Wright | P. | |
| William Harris, 1st | P. | time expires 2 Feb '83 |
| George Twinch | S. | |
| Robert Legg | P. | |
| Joseph Overcreek | P. | |
| John Haynes | P. | died 2 Feb '83 |
| Edward Reiley | P. | dischd. 3 June '83 |
| Jesse Powers | P. | do　29 May '83 |
| Dennis Trammile | P. | do　31　do　do |
| Thomas Drudge | P. | died 10 Apl '83 |
| Francis Dunnington | P. | do　23　do　do |
| John Watkins | P. | do　26　do　do |
| Pompey Hollis | P. | do　28　do　do |
| Benjamin Cole | P. | dischd. 1 Apl '83 |
| James Reynolds, 2nd | P. | |
| James Rose | P. | |
| John Missell | P. | |
| *Stephen Olingan | P. | |
| *John Charles | P. | |
| Michael Sours | P. | dischd. 5 May '83 |
| Jeremiah Mudd | P. | do　1 Aug '83 |
| Benjamin Gray | P. | |
| John Christr. Miller | P. | |
| William King | P. | |
| Levi Scott | D. | |
| John Vallow | P. | |
| Walter Watson | P. | dischd. 1 Aug '83 |
| Benjm. Johnston | P. | |
| Jeremiah Driskill | | |
| William Gates | P. | dischd. 30 Mch '83 |
| William Moad | P. | |
| John Curl, 1st | P. | |
| Stephen Varlow | P. | |
| James White | P. | Invalided by the State 10 June '83 |
| Thomas Glover | P. | dischd. 14 Feb '83 |
| James Curren | P. | do　1 Mch '83 |
| Wm. Lynch | P. | |

| NAMES AND RANK. | | WHEN LEFT SERVICE AND THE REASONS. | REMARKS. |
|---|---|---|---|
| John Blair, 1st | P. | Invalided by the State 10 June '83 | |
| Aquilla Dever | P. | | |
| William Clements, 1st | | dischd. 31 July '83 | |
| Thomas Harrison, 1st | P. | | |
| John Waller | P. | | |
| James Dyer, 1st | P. | | |
| Basil Norman | P. | | |
| Thomas Cahoe, Sr. | | | |
| Thomas Cahoe, Jr. | | | |
| William Peters | P. | | |
| John Morrison | F. | | |
| John Ferral | P. | dischd. 14 Feb '83 | |
| John Mantle | P. | do        do        do | |
| Francis Thompson | P. | do    18 Apl  do | |
| John Hughes | P. | do    10 May do | |
| John Goddart | P. | do    26 Feb  do | |
| Walter Miles | C. | do     1 Apl   do | |
| Joseph Mattingley | P. | do     1 Feb   do | |
| John Mills | C. | do    14 Feb  do | |
| Henry Purdy | P. | do        do    do | |
| George Haydon | P. | do    23 do    do | |
| William Carlin | P. | do    15 Nov do | enlisted for War |
| Wm. Hamston | P. | do    31 Jan  do | |
| John Holder | P. | | |
| Walter Hagan | P. | dischd. 23 Feb '83 | |
| John Nary | P. | do    23 Mch do | time expires |
| Nicholas Nicholson | | do     1 Apl   do | ditto in April |
| Morris Neagle | | | |
| George Patrick | | dischd. 23 Mch '83 | |
| William Purcell | | | |
| William Rodgers | P. | | |
| Paul Richards | P. | | |
| Jos. Roberts | P. | | |
| Jeremiah Sullivan | | dischd. 12 Mch '83 | |
| Wm. Smith | D. | | |
| Ed. Wade, 2nd | P. | | |
| Jesse Barnet | F. | dischd. 1 Apl '83 | |
| John McDonald | F. | do     1 June '83 | |
| John Thomas, 2nd | | | |
| William Coe | P. | | |
| Thomas Adams | P. | | |
| John Biggs | P. | dischd. 1 July '83 | |
| John Francis | P. | | |
| James Chard | P. | dischd. 1 Aug '83 | |
| Oliver Stephens | P. | | |
| Benj. Baulk | | | |

| NAMES AND RANK. | | WHEN LEFT SERVICE AND THE REASONS. | REMARKS. |
|---|---|---|---|
| John Smallwood, 1st | | | |
| Wm. Corsey | P. | | |
| Jonathan Chubb | | dischd. 1 July '83 | |
| Joseph Isaacks | | | |
| Darby Lenehan | | dischd. 1 Feb '83 | time expires |
| Thomas Arthurs | | time expires 1 Apl '83 | |
| Elijah Sullivan | P. | | |
| John Kildee | | | |
| John Adams, 2nd | | | |
| George Dyer | P. | | |
| John Hannor | F. | | |
| William Robinson | P. | | |

M.

[A star prefixed to any name indicates that the length of service is not known. In all such cases, however, service began 1 Jan., '83, unless otherwise stated. Deserters, when pardoned, are credited with 10 months and 15 days service, the same as the other soldiers in this roll.]

MARYLAND ACTS—OCTOBER, 1780.

An ACT to settle and adjust the accounts of the troops of this state in the service of the United States, and for other purposes therein mentioned.

WHEREAS, from a variety of causes, the United States have not complied with their engagements heretofore made with their officers and soldiers (which has occasioned great and unavoidable difficulties and distresses in the service) to whose virtuous and disinterested exertions America is much indebted:

*Be it therefore enacted, by the General Assembly of Maryland,* That Zephaniah Turner be and is hereby appointed commissioner to settle and adjust the pay due to the officers and soldiers of the troops of this state, and the said commissioner is hereby empowered and directed to estimate, in specie, all sums of paper money received by the said officers and soldiers, on account of their pay or otherways, . . . . according to the value thereof at the time of the money received.

*And be it enacted,* That the said commissioner is hereby empowered and directed to give to the officers and soldiers aforesaid, to whom pay as aforesaid may be found due, . . . . one certificate or more, bearing interest from the date thereof, and specifying the sum due in specie.

*And be it enacted,* That the said commissioner shall in like manner settle and adjust the pay and accounts of all officers and soldiers who have fallen or died in the service, and their widows and children shall be entitled to such certificates.

*Be it enacted*, That the lands commonly called Talbot's, or New Connought Manor, in Caecil county, My Lady's Manor in Baltimore or Baltimore and Harford counties, and Monococy Manor in Frederick county, being British property, and seized and confiscated as such, . . . . shall be and are hereby set apart and burthened and charged with the payment of the money and interest aforesaid due on the said certificates, and the same shall be raised out of the said lands, by sales thereof, in such manner as the general assembly shall hereafter direct.

Depreciation Certificates, stopped at the Treasuries agreeable to Act of Assembly passed November Session, 1784.

| NAMES. | REGT. | FOR WHAT REASONS STOPPED. |
|---|---|---|
| Abel Arman | 7th | obtained by John Dove, in 1783, although Arman had deserted in July, 1780, order for the receipt supposed to be forged. |
| Edward Bailey | 1st | not mustered before Aug, 1780, therefore not entitled to Depreciation. |
| William Bramble | 2nd | was enlisted for nine months only, therefore not entitled to Depreciation. |
| John Burgess | Hartley's | received his Depreciation in Pennsylvania, see the letter of Mr. Nicholson, Comptroller of that State. |
| John Barbar | do | do          do |
| James Beall | do | do          do |
| John Coomy | Hazen's | obtained twice, first upon a Certificate in the Name John Kuny, the second on a discharge John Coomy, the same person meant. |
| Patrick Connally | 5th | was left out of the Rolls in the Year 1779, and never served afterwards, therefore not entitled to Depreciation. |
| John Cheshire | 2nd | obtained by perjury and forgery, some person unknown having sworn himself to be Cheshire, and signed his name as such in June, 1783, the real John Cheshire was killed in June, 1781. |
| John Callahan | 1st | he Deserted in the year 1778, therefore not entitled. |
| Michl. Connell | 2nd | obtained upon his own Oath in June, 1783, his Wife as supposing him dead, had obtained his Depreciation before. |
| William Dye | 4th | after serving one Year, was stopped in Maryland by his former Master, this part of his pay therefore stopped payment. |

| Names. | Regt. | For what Reasons Stopped. |
|---|---|---|
| John Edwards | 2nd | no such Man on any Musters. |
| Patk. Flemon | German | issued twice, the name being spelled differently in the Certificates by which Depreciation was issued. |
| Nathan Forster | 5th | issued twice, as supposing there were two of that name, but upon comparing with the Muster Rolls, there was but one of the Name. |
| John Francis | 1st | was not in Service until the year 1781, therefore not entitled to Depreciation. |
| Jereh. Farrell | Hartley's | see John Burgess and others of Hartley's Regt. |
| Alex. Grim | Rawlings' | is not upon the Musters of Rawlings' Regiment or any others of the Maryland Quota. |
| Joseph Hyner | Moylan's | he received his Depreciation in Pennsylvania, before his Application to this State, his final Settlement, which is Stopped, will however discharge part of this Depreciation. |
| Charles Howard | 3rd | obtained by Perjury and Forgery in 1783 by some person assuming the Name, Charles Howard having died in October, 1781. |
| Charles Hickey | 2nd | he does not appear by the Musters to have enlisted before the year 1781, therefore not entitled to Depreciation. |
| Th. Hewington | 7th | obtained by John Dove as Abel Arman's was, and stopped for the same reason. |
| Henry Ijams | 5th | is not on any Musters therefore not entitled. |
| Willm. Jones | Artillery | he deserted by Information of Major Brown, therefore not entitled. |
| Wm. Johnson | 5th | there is no such person on the Musters of the 5th Regt., there is a Wm. Johnson on the Rolls of the 2nd Regt. but neither of them entitled. |
| Patk. Lynch | 7th | issued twice by mistake. |
| Wm. Marquis | Hartley's | see John Burgess and others. |
| Dennis McCarty | Rawlings' | not upon the Musters of Rawlings' Regiment. |
| James McGuire | 3rd | received his Depreciation twice. |
| John Macam | 7th | rec'd by John Dove in 1783, Macam has not been in the army since Augt. 16th, 1780, is supposed to be dead, and his Father has administered and now claims the Pay, &c. |
| Timothy Mullen | 3rd | not regularly discharged not having appeared since August 1780, probably received by a person who assumed his name. |
| John Malcom | 2nd | no such Man on the Musters of the 2nd Regt., probably received by a person who assumed his name. |
| Alex. Mackay | Artillery | he deserted, therefore not entitled. |
| Nichs. Nicholls | 5th | stopped for the reasons given in the Auditor's Rept. |

| NAMES. | REGT. | FOR WHAT REASONS STOPPED. |
|---|---|---|
| George Phillips | 7th | George Phillips died in April, 1781, some person, assuming the name, received this in 1783. |
| Thos. Peacock | 7th | he was killed the 8th Sept., 1781, John Dove received his Depreciation as if alive, in June, 1783. |
| John Pennington | 3rd | not regularly mustered or discharged. |
| John Radley | 4th | he was hanged for exciting a Mutiny, this was rec'd in 1783 by some person assuming his name, the Widow of Radley now claims what was due to her husband. |
| Robt. Smith | German | he was a Recruit after August, 1780, and deserted in 1781. |
| Jas. Stillwell | 5th | not found on any of the Musters of the Maryland Quota of Continental Troops. |
| Jereh. Sullivan | 6th | not on any of the Musters of the Maryland Line. |
| Wm. Townsend | 7th | delivered to John Dove—another Wm. Townsend who was entitled had rec'd Depreciation, this man was not entitled. |
| Wm. Whipple | 7th | received by John Dove in the manner described in the case of Abel Arman. |
| George Wilson | 5th | issued twice, as supposing there were two of the same name, which, upon examination with the Musters did not turn out to be the Case. |
| Edward White | 2nd | ditto.          ditto.          ditto. |
| Richd. White | 1st | not found on any Musters. |

C. Richmond, Aud. Genl.

List of Certificates for Depreciation of Pay fraudulently obtained by Soldiers of the Seven Maryland Regiments.

List of Depreciation Certificates which have been fraudulently obtained, the payment of which is stopped at the Treasuries agreeable to an Act of the last Session of Assembly.    Auditor's Office, May 25th, 1785.

| DATE OF ISSUE. | NAMES. | DATE OF ISSUE. | NAMES. |
|---|---|---|---|
| 27 Oct '83 | Vendel Andrews | 27 Oct '83 | George Hyatt |
| 5 Dec " | William Basht | 27 Oct " | Philip Helter |
| 15 Oct " | James Calhoun | 27 Oct " | John Hart |
| 5 Dec " | Thomas Cammell | 5 Dec " | George Hartsell |
| 5 Dec " | Timothy Conn | 5 Dec " | Michael Hausman |
| 15 Oct " | Charles Charell | 8 Aug " | Michael Jackell |
| 27 Oct " | Frederick Charell | 5 Dec " | Nicholas Johnson |

| DATE OF ISSUE. | NAMES. | DATE OF ISSUE. | NAMES. |
|---|---|---|---|
| 27 Oct '83 | Peter Finley | 27 Oct '83 | Jacob Kaufman |
| 27 Oct " | Andrew Goar | 15 Oct " | William Kumius |
| 18 June " | John Hammersly | 27 Oct " | Nicholas Keyser |
| 18 June " | Henry Harris | 5 Dec " | Charles Kees |
| 22 Sept '81 | John Hickens, | 5 Dec " | William Kemp |
|  | stoppage taken off | 11 Sept '81 | Dennis McCarty |
| 7 Aug '83 | Jacob Levy | 21 Oct '83 | Anthony Miller |
| 5 Dec " | Nicholas Lines | 27 Oct " | John Miller |
| 5 Dec " | Henry Lane | 27 Oct " | Henry Mielberger |
| 11 Aug " | Thomas Peacock | 27 Oct " | John Moore |
| 23 June " | John Pickeron, | 15 Oct " | Fredk. Weiger |
|  | stoppage taken off | 27 Oct " | Michael Yewling |
|  | Certificate of Ser- | 5 Dec " | John Ziegler |
|  | vice having been | 13 June " | Charles Hickey |
|  | produced | 15 Oct " | George Hensell |
| 27 Oct " | Joshua Procter | 27 Oct " | Henry Hargrader |
| 15 Oct " | Peter Sigman | 5 Dec " | Valentine Shultz |
| 21 Oct " | Joseph Smith | 5 Dec " | George Shriver |
| 27 Oct " | Henry Spengell | 6 Mch '84 | Jacob Smith |
| 27 Oct " | John Shultz | 27 Oct '81 | Samuel Tindel, |
| 27 Oct " | James Smith |  | stoppage off |
| 27 Oct " | Nicholas Stover | 27 Oct '83 | Frederick Tawney |
| 5 Dec " | Peter Shrover |  |  |

C. Richmond, Aud. Genl.

## AN ACCOUNT OF ALL CERTIFICATES RECEIVED FROM JOHN WHITE, AJT. COMSR., BY OFFICERS AND SOLDIERS OF THE MARYLAND LINE.

| RANK. | NAMES. | SERVED BETWEEN 1 AUG 1780 AND 1 JAN 1782 | SERVED BETWEEN 1 JAN 1782 AND 1 JAN 1783 | SERVED BETWEEN 1 JAN AND 15 NOV 1783 | SERVED BETWEEN 15 NOV 1783 AND 10 JULY 1784 |
|---|---|---|---|---|---|
| [Major] | Alex'd'r Roxburgh | " | " | " | |
| [Surg. Mate] | Alexander Smith | " | " | " | |
| [Lieut.] | Thomas Boyd | " | " | " | " |
| [Lieut.] | Henry Hawkins | | " | | |
| [Lieut.] | John McCoy | " | " | | |
| [Capt.] | Thomas B. Hugon | " | " | | |
| [Lieut.] | Jacob Gramoth | | | | |
| Capt. | Edwd. Dyer | " | " | | |
| Major | Henry Dobson | " | | | |
| Capt. | John Hardman | | | | |
| Genl. | Mordecai Gist | " | " | " | |
| Lieut. | John G. Lowe | " | " | " | |
| " | Peter Hardcastle | " | | | |
| " | | | | | |
| " | Jacob R. Shoemaker | | | | |
| Surg. Mate | Wm. J. Smith | | | | |
| Lieut. | James Simms | " | | | |
| Surgeon | Richard Sappington | | | | |
| Surg. Mate | John Ross | | | | |
| Surgeon | Thomas Parren | | | | |
| Lieut. | Edwd. Moran | | | | |
| Ensign | Caleb Mason | " | | | |
| Surg. Mate | Elisha Hamson | " | | | |
| Ensign | Saml. Hamilton | | | | |
| " | David Greene | " | | | |
| Lieut. | Samuel Farmer | " | | | |
| " | Richd. Donovan | " | | | |
| " | John Carr | " | | | |
| " | John Boon | ' | | | |
| " | Charles Beaven | | | | |
| Capt. | Joseph Marbury | " | " | " | |
| Lieut. | Martin Shugart | " | | | |
| " | Nathan Smith | ' | | | |
| Capt. | Jonathan Gibson | " | " | | |
| " | John Hawkins | " | | | |
| " | George Hamilton | " | " | " | |

| RANK. | NAMES. | SERVED BETWEEN 1 AUG 1780 AND 1 JAN 1782 | SERVED BETWEEN 1 JAN 1782 AND 1 JAN 1783 | SERVED BETWEEN 1 JAN AND 15 NOV 1783 | SERVED BETWEEN 15 NOV 1783 AND 10 JULY 1784 |
|---|---|---|---|---|---|
| | OFFICERS WHOSE ACCOUNTS WERE SETTLED. | | | | |
| Capt. | George Armstrong | " | | | |
| " | Richard Anderson | " | " | " | |
| Lieut. | William Adams | " | " | " | |
| " | William Bruff | | " | " | |
| " | Thos. Beatty | | " | " | |
| " | Henry Baldwin | " | " | " | |
| Capt. | John Sprig Belt | " | " | | |
| Lieut. | Joshua Burgess | | " | | |
| Capt. | Lloyd Beall | " | " | " | |
| " | Joseph Burgess | | | | |
| Maj. | Benj. Brooks | " | " | | |
| Capt. | Richard Bird | " | " | | |
| Lieut. | Basil Burgess | " | " | " | |
| Capt. | Michael Boyer | " | | | |
| " | Charles Baltzell | " | | | |
| " | Jacob Brice | " | | " | |
| Lieut. | John Brevett | " | " | " | |
| Maj. | Wm. Dent Beall | " | " | | |
| Lieut. | Joseph Britten | | | | |
| Capt. | William Beatty | " | | | |
| Lieut. | Henry Baker | " | " | | |
| " | Malachi Bonham | " | " | " | |
| " | Saml. B. Beall | | " | | |
| Capt. | Perry Benson | | " | " | |
| Lieut. | William Bruce | " | " | " | |
| " | Henry Clements | " | " | " | |
| " | Joseph Cross | " | " | " | |
| " | Edmond Compton | " | " | " | |
| " | John Carey | " | " | | |
| " | Henry H. Chapman | | " | " | |
| " | Jacob Crawford | " | " | | |
| Capt. | Robert Chesley | " | | | |
| Lieut. | John Colegate | | | | |
| " | Walter Dyer | | " | " | |
| Surgeon | Willm. A. Dashiell | | | | |
| Maj. | John Davidson | " | " | | |
| " | John Deane | " | | | |
| Lieut. | Thomas A. Dyson | | " | " | |
| Capt. | Rezin Davis | | | " | |
| Lieut. | Isaac Duval | " | | | |
| Surgeon | Levin Denwood | " | " | " | |
| Lieut. | Robert Denny | " | " | | |

| RANK. | NAMES. | SERVED BETWEEN 1 AUG 1780, AND 1 JAN 1782 | SERVED BETWEEN 1 JAN 1782 AND 1 JAN 1783 | SERVED BETWEEN 1 JAN AND 15 NOV 1783 | SERVED BETWEEN 15 NOV 1783 AND 10 JULY 1784 |
|---|---|---|---|---|---|
| Lieut. | Saml. Edminston | " | " | " | |
| Lt. Col. | John Eccleston | " | " | " | |
| Lieut. | Elijah Evans | " | | | |
| Capt. | James Ewing | " | " | | |
| Dr. | John L. Elbert | | " | | |
| Capt. | Edward Edgerly | " | | | |
| Lieut. | Benj. Fickle | " | " | " | |
| " | Hezekiah Foard | " | " | " | |
| Lt. Col. | Uriah Forrest | " | | | |
| " " | Benj. Foard | " | | | |
| Lieut. | James Gould | " | | | |
| " | Nicholas Gassaway | " | " | " | |
| Capt. | John Gist | | | | |
| " | James W. Gray | " | " | " | |
| " | John Gale | " | " | " | |
| Col. | John Gunby | " | " | " | |
| Lieut. | Wm. Goldsborough | | | " | |
| " | Henry Gassaway | | | " | |
| Capt. | John Gassaway | | | " | |
| " | Henry Gaither | " | " | | |
| Lt. Col. | J. E. Howard | " | " | | |
| Maj. | Henry Hardman | " | " | | |
| Capt. | John A. Hamilton | " | " | | |
| Lieut. | Edward Hamilton | | " | | |
| " | Robt. Halkerson | " | " | " | |
| Capt. | Levin Handy | | | | |
| Lieut. | John Hartshorn | " | " | " | |
| " | Elihu Hall | " | | | |
| " | Arthur Harris | " | | " | |
| " | Rignal Hillary | | " | ' | |
| " | Philip Hill | " | " | " | |
| " | Samuel Hanson | " | " | " | |
| " | Willm. Hanson | | " | ' | |
| " | John Hamilton | " | " | | |
| " | Isaac Hanson | " | " | | |
| Col. | Josias C. Hall | " | | | |
| Doct. | Ezekiel Haynie | " | " | " | |
| Capt. | Adam Hoops | " | | | |
| Lieut. | George Jacobs | " | | | |
| " | Adam Jamison | | | | |
| Capt. | John C. Jones | " | " | " | |
| Surgeon | William Kilty | " | " | " | |
| " | Saml. Y. Keene | " | " | " | |
| Lieut. | John Lynn | | " | " | " |

| RANK. | NAMES. | SERVED BETWEEN 1 AUG 1780 AND 1 JAN 1782. | SERVED BETWEEN 1 JAN 1782 AND 1 JAN 1783. | SERVED BETWEEN 1 JAN AND 15 NOV 1783. | SERVED BETWEEN 15 NOV 1783 AND 10 JULY 1784. |
|---|---|---|---|---|---|
| Capt. | Henry Lyles | " | | | |
| " | Thos. H. Luckett | " | | | |
| Lieut. | David Luckett | | " | " | |
| Maj. | John Lynch | | " | | |
| Lieut. | Willm. Lemar | " | " | | |
| Capt. | David Lynn | " | " | " | |
| Maj. | Thos. Lansdale | " | " | " | |
| Capt. | James M. Lingan | " | " | | |
| " | Walker Muse | " | " | " | |
| " | Thos. Mason | " | " | | |
| Lieut. | John Maguire | | | | |
| " | David Morgan | | | | |
| Capt. | Christian Myers | | | | |
| Lieut. | Zedk. Moore | " | " | " | |
| " | Nicholas Mangers | " | | | |
| " | Lawrence Myers | | | | |
| " | Mark McPherson | " | " | " | |
| Capt. | Jonathan Morris | | " | " | |
| " | John Mitchell | " | " | " | |
| " | Saml. McPherson | " | " | " | |
| " | Jacob Norris | | " | " | |
| Ensign | John Nelson | " | | | |
| Capt. | Edward Oldham | " | " | " | |
| " | Christn. Orendorff | | " | | |
| " | Benj. Price | " | " | " | |
| Col. | Thomas Price | | | | |
| Lieut. | Thomas Price | " | " | " | |
| Surg. | Richard Pindell | " | " | " | |
| Lieut. | Willm. Pendergast | | | " | |
| Capt. | Edward Prall | " | " | | |
| Ensign | Jacob Reybold | | | | |
| Lieut. | Willm. Rasin | " | " | " | |
| Capt. | Willm. Reiley | " | " | " | |
| Lieut. | Joshua Rutledge | | | | |
| Capt. | Christr. Richmond | " | " | " | |
| Lieut. | Thomas Rown | " | " | " | |
| Capt. | Francis Revelly | " | " | " | |
| " | Phillip Reed | | " | " | |
| Lt. Col. | Nathl. Ramsey | | | | |
| Lieut. | Jas. Jno. Skinner | " | " | | |
| " | Edwd. M. Smith | " | " | | |
| Capt. | John Smith | | " | " | |
| " | James Somervill | " | " | | |
| " | Jonathan Sellman | " | " | | |

34

| RANK. | NAMES. | SERVED BETWEEN 1 AUG 1780 AND 1 JAN 1782. | SERVED BETWEEN 1 JAN 1782 AND 1 JAN 1783. | SERVED BETWEEN 1 JAN 1783 AND 15 NOV 1783. | SERVED BETWEEN 15 NOV 1783 AND 10 JULY 1784 |
|---|---|---|---|---|---|
| Lieut. | John Sears | " | " | " | |
| Capt. | Edward Spurrier | " | " | | |
| Lieut. | Willm. Smoot | " | " | | |
| Genl. | Willm. Smallwood | " | " | " | |
| Lieut. | Willm. Stoddard | " | " | | |
| Capt. | Joseph Smith | " | | | |
| " | John Smith, (6 Regt.) | " | " | | |
| " | Alex. Truman | " | " | | |
| Lt. Col. | Edward Tillard | | | | |
| Lieut. | James Toole | | | | |
| " | John Trueman | " | " | | |
| Capt. | A. Tannehill | | | | |
| Lieut. | Willm. Towson | | " | " | |
| Surg. Mate | William Watts | " | " | " | |
| Capt. | William Wilmott | " | " | | |
| Lieut. | William Woolford | " | | | |
| Capt. | Saml. T. Wright | | | | |
| Lt. Col. | Lodwick Weltner | " | " | | |
| Brig. Gen. | O. H. Williams | | " | | |
| Lieut. | Francis Ware | " | " | " | |
| Lt. Col. | Thos. Woolford | " | " | | |
| Lieut. | Nathan Wright | " | " | " | |
| Surgn. | Walter Warfield | " | " | " | |
| Lieut. | Basil Waring | | " | " | |
| " | George Winchester | " | " | | |
| Surg. | Gerard Wood | " | " | | |
| Capt. | James Winchester | " | " | " | |
| " | Richard Waters | " | " | | |
| Lt. Col. | Levin Winder | " | " | " | |
| Lieut. | Gassaway Watkins | | " | | |
| Capt. | Lilburn Williams | | " | | |

## PRIVATES.

| RANK. | NAMES. | REMARKS. | SERVED BETWEEN 1 AUG '80 AND 1 JAN '82. | SERVED BETWEEN 1 JAN '82 AND 1 JAN '83. | SERVED BETWEEN 1 JAN '83 AND 15 NOV '83. | SERVED BETWEEN 15 NOV '83 AND 10 JULY '84. |
|---|---|---|---|---|---|---|
| Private | Adam Adams | Dischd. 16 May '81 | " | | | |
| " | Ignatius Adams | | " | " | " | |
| " | George Abbott | " 24 May '81 | " | | | |
| " | John Alvey | | " | " | " | |
| " | Thos. G. Alvey | " 24 Apl '81 | " | | | |
| " | John Appleby | | " | " | " | |
| " | Danl. Anderson | Died 15 Apl '81 | " | | | |

| RANK. | NAMES. | REMARKS. | SERVED BETWEEN 1 AUG '80 AND 1 JAN '82. | SERVED BETWEEN 1 JAN '82 AND 1 JAN '83. | SERVED BETWEEN 1 JAN '83 AND 15 NOV '83. | SERVED BETWEEN 15 NOV '83 AND 10 JULY '84. |
|---|---|---|---|---|---|---|
| Private | James Allen | | " | " | " | |
| " | Thos. Ayres | | " | " | " | |
| " | Emanuel Allen | | " | " | " | |
| " | John Andrews | | " | " | " | |
| " | William Aythur | | " | " | " | |
| " | John Armstrong | | " | " | " | |
| " | John Ashmow | | " | " | " | |
| Serjt. | Cuthbut Able | Dischd. 1 Feb '83 | " | " | | |
| Corpl. | John Adams | | " | " | " | |
| Private | Thomas Arthur | Time expires 1 Apl '83 | " | " | | |
| Drum. | John Auber | Invalided | " | " | " | |
| Private | John Ashbury | | " | " | " | |
| " | John Armstrong, 2nd | | " | " | " | |
| " | Harris Austen | | " | " | " | |
| " | Thomas Adams | | " | " | " | |
| " | Josias Alvey | Dischd. 24 May '82 | " | " | | |
| " | James Ashley | | " | " | " | |
| " | Jacob Adams | Died 24 Mch '83 | " | " | | |
| " | William Absolom | [Dischd. 29 Nov '83] | " | " | " | |
| " | John Anderson | | | " | " | |
| " | Traverse Alvey | | | " | " | |
| " | Nathan Aldridge | | | | " | |
| " | Levin Abbott | | " | " | " | |
| " | John Adams, 2nd | | | " | " | |
| " | John Abrahams | | | " | " | |
| " | Benjamin Askew | | " | " | | " |
| " | John Alsop | [Dischd. 29 Nov '83] | " | " | | |
| Serjt. | Joseph Allen | | " | " | | |
| Private | James Anderson | | | | | |
| " | James Anderson | | | | " | |
| " | John Anderson | | | | | |
| Fifer | Daniel Basil | | " | " | " | |
| Private | John Baker | Dischd. 3 May '81 | " | | | |
| " | George Bateman | "   8 Jan '82 | " | " | | |
| " | John Brookbank | | " | " | " | |
| " | Levi Burk | "   May '83 | " | " | | |
| Serjt. | Thos. Buckley | | " | " | " | |
| Private | William Brooks | "   18 June '81 | " | | | |
| " | Joseph Burch | | " | " | " | |
| " | Thos. Bishop | [Dischd. 29 Nov '83] | " | " | " | |
| Corpl. | Wm. Braithwait | | " | " | " | |
| Private | Barrock Butt | | " | " | " | |
| " | Thomas Butt | | " | " | " | |
| " | Edward Butt | Died 15 Mch '81 | " | | | |

| Rank. | Names. | Remarks. | Served between 1 Aug '80 and 1 Jan '82. | Served between 1 Jan '82 and 1 Jan '83. | Served between 1 Jan '83 and 15 Nov '83. | Served between 15 Nov '83 and 10 July '84. |
|---|---|---|---|---|---|---|
| Fifer | Frederick Bennet | | " | " | " | |
| Private | Richd. Blansford | | " | " | " | |
| Fifer | Solomon Brittenham | | " | " | " | |
| Private | Levi Buttons | [Disch. 18 Sept '83] | " | " | " | |
| " | Levin Bramble | Died 13 July '81 | " | | | |
| " | John Blades | | " | " | " | |
| Corpl. | Thomas Brown | Killed 8 Sept '81 | " | | | |
| Private | John Brown, 1st | | " | " | " | |
| " | Richard Butler | | " | " | " | |
| " | John Barret, 1st | Dischd. 1 May '81 | " | | | |
| " | Thomas Barcklay | | " | " | " | |
| " | Basil Brown | | " | " | " | |
| " | George Brown | Dischd. 24 Apl '81 | " | | | |
| " | Zachariah Burck | " 12 " '81 | " | | | |
| Corpl. | Leonard Bean | " 12 " '81 | " | | | |
| Private | Gabriel Brand | " 12 Jan '82 | " | " | | |
| " | John Beane | " 22 " '82 | " | " | | |
| " | Thomas Bird | " 13 " '82 | " | " | | |
| " | Benjamin Boyd | | " | " | " | |
| " | John Blair | Dischd. 15 Jan '82 | " | " | | |
| " | Peter Bochard | | " | " | " | |
| " | Thomas Bailey | [Dischd.11 Aug '83] | " | " | " | |
| " | John Buckley | | " | " | " | |
| " | Joshua Barret | | " | " | " | |
| Corpl. | George Bradley | Died 31 Nov '82 | " | " | | |
| " | William Bruff | | " | " | " | |
| Private | Peter Bowler | Dischd. 1 May '81 | " | | | |
| " | Joseph Bautcheby | | " | " | " | |
| Fifer | Robert Bowen | | " | " | " | |
| Private | Philip Bailey | Died 20 Feb '83 | " | " | | |
| Drum. | John Beach | " 15 Dec '82 | " | " | | |
| " | John Buchanon | | " | " | " | |
| Private | Daniel Buckley | | " | " | " | |
| " | David Bramble | | " | " | " | |
| " | James L. Brass | | " | " | " | |
| " | John Burnet | | " | " | " | |
| " | Perry Bantham | | " | " | " | |
| Fifer | John Brent | Died 14 May '81 | " | | | |
| Private | George Blackham | [Disch. 11 Aug '83] | " | " | " | |
| " | James Barron | | " | " | " | |
| Serjt. | James Bailey | Died 27 Apl '81 | " | | | |
| Private | Abraham Bowen | | " | " | " | |
| " | John Bantham | | " | " | " | |
| " | Solomon Barrett | | " | " | " | |
| " | James Burk, 1st | [Dischd. 29 Nov '83] | " | " | " | |

| RANK. | NAMES. | REMARKS. | SERVED BETWEEN 1 AUG '80 AND 1 JAN '82. | SERVED BETWEEN 1 JAN '82 AND 1 JAN '83. | SERVED BETWEEN 1 JAN '83 AND 15 NOV '83. | SERVED BETWEEN 15 NOV '83 AND 10 JULY '84. |
|---|---|---|---|---|---|---|
| Serjt. | John Brown, 2nd | [Dischd. 29 Nov '83] | " | " | " | |
| Private | George Bowers | Died 1 May '81 | | | | |
| " | Henry Billup | | " | " | " | |
| " | Thomas Bear | | " | " | " | |
| " | George Bombgardiner | | " | " | " | |
| Corpl. | Benj. Burch, 2nd | Dischd. 19 Jan '83 | " | " | | |
| Private | Thomas Brady | "   24 June '81 | " | | | |
| " | Joseph Blaze | | " | " | " | |
| " | Joseph Botts | [Dischd. 29 Nov '81] | " | " | " | |
| Serjt. | Moses Barney | Dischd. 1 Aug '81 | " | | | |
| Private | Richard Boone | Died 15 Mch '81 | " | | | |
| " | Joshua Brown | Dischd. 23 Apl '81 | " | | | |
| " | Josiah Burgess | "   19 Apl '81 | " | | | |
| " | Humphrey Becket | | " | " | " | |
| " | Lawrence Bronham | | " | " | " | |
| " | George Brown | Dischd. 23 Apl '81 | " | | | |
| " | George Buck | | " | " | " | |
| " | Martin Bowles | | " | " | " | |
| " | Abijah Buxton | | " | " | " | |
| Fifer | Jesse Barnett | Dischd. 5 Aug '83 | " | " | " | |
| Private | Thomas Bowser | | " | " | " | |
| " | James Barber | [Dischd. 29 Nov '83] | " | " | " | |
| " | Daniel Bulger | | " | " | " | |
| Corpl. | Jesse Boswell | Time expires 5 Aug '83 | " | " | " | |
| Private | Joseph Barton | | " | " | " | |
| " | John Brewer | Died 17 July '82 | " | " | | |
| " | John Branson | | " | " | " | |
| " | Jeremiah Brown | Dischd. 1 Aug '83 | " | " | " | |
| " | Richard Biddle | | " | " | " | |
| " | James Bigwood | | " | " | " | |
| " | Peter Bushell | Dischd. 6 Sept '83 | " | " | " | |
| " | Thomas Baker | | " | " | " | |
| " | James Bailess | | " | " | " | |
| | John Berriman | | " | " | " | |
| | James Brannon | | | | | |
| | John Brion | Transd. Inv'ds Aug'81 | " | | | |
| | John Biggs | Died 1 July '83 | " | " | " | |
| | Jacob Blake | | " | " | " | |
| Corpl. | John Brown, 3rd | | " | " | " | |
| Serjt. | Benjamin Burch | Died 3 Nov '83 | " | " | " | |
| Private | Gassaway Braziers | Dischd. 28 Jan '81 | " | | | |
| " | George Bough | | " | " | " | |
| " | Samuel Boswell | | " | " | " | |
| " | William Battin | | " | " | " | |
| " | Zachariah Berry | Died 6 Mch '84 | " | " | " | " |

| RANK. | NAMES. | REMARKS. | SERVED BETWEEN 1 AUG '80 AND 1 JAN '82. | SERVED BETWEEN 1 JAN '82 AND 1 JAN '83. | SERVED BETWEEN 1 JAN '83 AND 15 NOV '83. | SERVED BETWEEN 15 NOV '83 AND 10 JULY '84. |
|---|---|---|---|---|---|---|
| Private | John Burns | | " | " | " | |
| " | Benjamin Bough | | " | " | " | |
| " | James Bryan | Killed 15 Sept '81 | " | | | |
| " | John Bowdy | | " | " | " | |
| " | John Boody | [Dischd. 18 Sept '83] | " | " | " | |
| " | John Britton | [Dischd. 29 Nov '83] | " | " | " | |
| " | Christian Boss | | " | " | " | |
| " | John Briley | | " | " | " | |
| " | Benjamin Belcher | | " | " | " | |
| " | Thomas Burck, 2nd | [Dischd. 29 Nov '83] | " | " | " | |
| Serjt. | Nathaniel Bailey | | " | " | " | " |
| Private | Andrew Bramble | | " | " | " | |
| " | John Baxter | | " | " | " | |
| " | John Bailey | | " | " | " | |
| " | William Burgess | Time expires 16 [Aug '83 | " | " | " | |
| " | Joel Baker | | " | " | " | |
| " | James Bowen | | " | " | " | |
| " | William Brady | | " | " | " | |
| " | George Belfast | | " | " | " | |
| " | Charles Buckley | [Dischd.29 Nov' 83] | " | " | " | |
| Serjt. | John Brady | | " | " | " | |
| Private | James Barrow | Trans. Inv'ds 1 Apl '82 | | | | |
| " | Archibald Butt | " to N. C. Line 28 [Apl '82 | | " | | |
| Corpl. | Peter Boyer | Died 15 Jan '82 | | " | | |
| " | Danl. Brumagum | | | | | |
| Private | Presstly Bruington | | | " | " | |
| " | John Blair, 1st | Invd. 10 June '83 | | " | " | |
| " | Henry Bradly | | | " | " | |
| Corpl. | John Burgess | | | " | " | |
| Private | James Bell | [Dischd. 31 Aug '83] | | " | " | |
| " | John Bell, 2nd | | | " | " | |
| " | Henry Barnes | | | " | " | |
| Serjt. | John Bond | | | " | " | |
| Private | Edward Burns | | | " | " | |
| " | Richard Burk | | | " | " | |
| " | John Barlow | | | " | " | |
| " | James Burk, 2nd | Invd. 15 Nov '83 | | " | " | |
| " | Thos. Bilingham | [Dischd. 29 Nov '83] | | " | " | |
| " | Wm. Boling | | | " | " | |
| " | John Barret, 1st | [Dischd. 15 Aug '83] | | " | " | |
| " | John Bailey, 2nd | | | " | " | |
| " | George Baker | | | " | " | |
| " | George Bowers | see back | " | " | " | |

| RANK. | NAMES. | REMARKS. | SERVED BETWEEN 1 AUG '80 AND 1 JAN '82. | SERVED BETWEEN 1 JAN '82 AND 1 JAN '83. | SERVED BETWEEN 1 JAN '83 AND 15 NOV '83. | SERVED BETWEEN 15 NOV '83 AND 10 JULY '84 |
|---|---|---|---|---|---|---|
| Private | Thomas Baxter | Died 24 Sept '83 | " | " | " | |
| " | James Barber, 2nd | | | | | " |
| " | James Blewer | Invd. 1 Mch '82 | " | " | | |
| " | John Butcher | " 1 Aug '82 | " | " | | |
| Drum. | James Bailey | Died 1 Aug '82 | | | " | |
| Private | Nathan Bateman | Killed 18 June '81 | " | | | |
| " | John Bennet | Invd. 15 Nov '82 | | | | " |
| | | | | | | |
| Private | William Clary | | " | " | " | |
| " | David Cole | | " | " | " | |
| " | John Carroll | Died 13 Jan '82 | " | " | | |
| Fifer | James Cholard | | " | " | " | |
| | Wm. Clements, 2nd | | " | " | " | |
| Private | Michael Cole | Died 16 Aug '81 | " | | | |
| " | Thomas Campher | | " | " | " | |
| " | Patk. Cavenough | | " | " | " | |
| Serjt. | William Cata | Died 18 June '81 | " | | | |
| Private | Hugh Cane | " 19 March '81 | " | | | |
| " | David Conner | [Dischd. 29 Nov '83] | " | " | " | |
| " | Morris Citizen | Died 15 May '81 | " | | | |
| " | Wm. Chatland | | " | " | " | |
| " | Wm. Cutler | [Dischd. 18 Sept' 83] | " | " | " | |
| Corpl. | John Campher | Killed 8 Sept '81 | " | | | |
| Private | Hampton Coursey | | " | " | " | |
| " | Wm. Conner, 1st | | " | " | " | |
| Corpl. | George Childs | | " | " | " | |
| Private | Daniel Clancy | [Dischd. 18 Sept '83] | " | " | " | |
| " | John Craig | | " | " | " | |
| Corpl. | Bartin Cicil | Died 13 Jan '82 | " | " | | |
| Private | Charles Clements | | " | " | " | |
| " | Luke Carter | | " | " | " | |
| " | John Clegget | Died 25 Apl '81 | " | | | |
| " | Thos. Clark, 1st | | " | " | " | |
| Drum. | Hezekiah Carr | | " | " | " | |
| Private | John Courts | Time expires 16 Apl ['83 | " | " | | |
| | | | | | | |
| " | Michael Clark, 2nd | | " | " | " | |
| Serjt. | John Colin | | " | " | " | |
| Private | Thos. B. Clements | Died 1 Aug '83 | " | " | " | |
| " | Wm. Carter, 2nd | | " | " | " | |
| " | Emanl. Carthagene | | " | " | " | |
| | Abrahm. Catchsides | | " | " | " | |
| Fifer | Thomas Clinton | [Dischd. 29 Nov '83] | " | " | " | |
| Private | Michael Callahan | | " | " | " | |
| " | Asaph Colegate | | " | " | " | |

| RANK. | NAMES. | REMARKS. | SERVED BETWEEN 1 AUG '80 AND 1 JAN '82. | SERVED BETWEEN 1 JAN '82 AND 1 JAN '83. | SERVED BETWEEN 1 JAN '83 AND 15 NOV '83. | SERVED BETWEEN 15 NOV '83 AND 10 JULY '84. |
|---|---|---|---|---|---|---|
| Private | Andrew Crummy | | " | " | " | |
| " | John Carr | Died 25 Feb '83 | " | " | | |
| Fifer | Robert Cormick | | " | " | " | |
| Private | John Carroll, 2nd | | " | " | " | |
| " | Charles Couch | Died 24 Aug '81 | " | | | |
| " | Augustin Cann | | " | " | " | |
| " | Thomas Carney | | " | " | " | |
| Fifer | Michael Clancey | | " | " | " | |
| Private | Thomas Cahoe, Sr. | | " | " | " | |
| Fifer | Thomas Cahoe, Jr. | | " | " | " | |
| Private | Benjamin Cleaver | | " | " | " | |
| " | Christopher Cusick | | " | " | " | |
| " | Robert Clanahan | | " | " | " | |
| " | William Cook | | " | " | " | |
| " | William Crail | | " | " | " | |
| " | Darby Crowley | | " | " | " | |
| Serjt. | John Cheshire | Killed 18 June '81 | " | | | |
| Private | William Casey | | " | " | " | |
| " | Adam Crow | Dischd. 28 Apl '81 | " | | | |
| " | Willm. Cummings | | " | " | " | |
| Serjt. | Aquilla Chitham | | " | " | " | |
| Corpl. | Owen Cavey | Died 16 Feb '81 | " | | | |
| Private | Ignatius Cumpton | " 13 Oct '81 | " | | | |
| " | James Curren | Dischd. 1 Mch '83 | " | " | | |
| " | Stephen Carr | Died 13 Oct '81 | " | | | |
| Fifer | Edward Clancey | [Dischd. 10 Sept '83] | " | " | " | |
| Private | John Cochren | Killed 15 Mch '81 | " | | | |
| Serjt. | William Collis | | " | " | " | |
| Private | Jonathan Chub | Dischd. 1 July '83 | " | " | " | |
| " | Wm. Chapman | [Dischd. 11 Sept '83] | " | " | | |
| " | Henry Crook | Time expires 1 May '83 Invalided | " | " | " | |
| " | William Cox | | " | " | " | |
| " | Henry Craine | | " | " | " | |
| " | George Clark | [Dischd. 7 Sept '83] | " | " | " | |
| " | Thomas Cooper | Died 1 April '82 | " | " | | |
| Corpl. | Bennet H. Clements | Dischd. 23 July '83 | " | " | " | |
| Private | James Casey | | " | " | " | " |
| " | Lewis Cuningham | | " | " | " | |
| " | Calothel Carmile | | " | " | " | |
| Fifer | David Crady | | " | " | " | |
| Private | Michael Casner | | " | " | " | |
| " | Samuel Callahan | | " | " | " | |
| " | John Cooper, 1st | [Dischd. 11 Aug '83] | " | " | " | |
| " | Wm. Clements, 1st | Dischd. 31 July '83 | " | " | " | |

| RANK. | NAMES. | REMARKS. | SERVED BETWEEN 1 AUG '80 AND 1 JAN '82. | SERVED BETWEEN 1 JAN '82 AND 1 JAN '83. | SERVED BETWEEN 1 JAN '83 AND 15 NOV '83. | SERVED BETWEEN 15 NOV '83 AND 10 JULY '84. |
|---|---|---|---|---|---|---|
| Private | Kendel Cobb | Died 10 Nov '81 | " | | | |
| " | Thomas Cannady | | " | " | " | |
| " | John Clancy, 2nd | [Dischd. 11 Aug '83] | | | " | |
| " | Valentine Clapper | | " | " | " | |
| " | Charles Cooper | | " | " | " | |
| " | George Coins | | " | " | " | |
| " | Benjamin Cole | Dischd. 1 Apl '83 | " | " | | |
| " | John Connelly, 1st | " 1 Apl '83 | " | " | | |
| " | Isom Coleman | | " | " | " | |
| " | Wm. Carter, 1st | | " | " | " | |
| " | James Crozier | | " | " | " | |
| " | Peter Carberry | Invalided 15 Nov '83 | " | " | " | |
| " | Saml. Chappell | | " | " | " | |
| " | Michael Curtis | | " | " | " | |
| " | John Cole, 1st | | " | " | " | |
| " | Jacob Collins | | " | " | " | |
| " | James Chambers | [Dischd. 29 Nov '83] | " | " | " | |
| " | John Carson | | " | " | " | |
| " | John Collins | | " | " | " | |
| " | Thomas Clark, 2nd | | " | " | " | |
| " | John Curl | | " | " | " | |
| " | John Cleverdence | | " | " | " | |
| " | Arthur Coffins | | " | " | " | |
| " | Joshua Cox | [Dischd. 29 Nov '83] | " | " | " | |
| " | Edward Chambers | [Dischd. 29 Nov '83] | " | " | " | |
| " | James Chard | Dischd. 1 Aug '83 | " | " | " | |
| " | James Cochran | [Dischd. 29 Nov '83] | " | " | " | |
| " | John Cannon | | " | " | " | |
| " | Thomas Compton | | " | " | " | |
| Serjt. | James Collins | [Dischd. 29 Nov '83] | " | " | " | |
| Private | William Cork | | " | " | " | |
| " | George Carney | [Dischd. 29 Nov '83] | " | " | " | |
| " | Robert Carns | [Dischd. 29 Nov '83] | " | " | " | |
| " | Mathias Cyphart | | " | " | " | |
| Corpl. | James Clements | | " | " | " | |
| Private | William Coe | | " | " | " | |
| Corpl. | Elijah Cockendall | Died 18 July '82 | " | " | | |
| Private | John Crosby, 1st | " 24 July '83 | " | " | | |
| " | James Crasberry | | " | " | " | |
| " | William Camm | | " | " | " | |
| Fifer | Zachariah Clark | | | " | " | |
| Private | Samuel Clark | | " | " | | |
| " | Matthew Carty | | | " | " | |
| " | Michael Clark, 1st | [Dischd. 18 Sept '83] | | " | " | |
| " | Dennis Cragan | [Dischd. 18 Sept '83] | " | " | " | |

| RANK. | NAMES. | REMARKS. | SERVED BETWEEN 1 AUG '80 AND 1 JAN '82. | SERVED BETWEEN 1 JAN '82 AND 1 JAN '83. | SERVED BETWEEN 1 JAN '83 AND 15 NOV '83. | SERVED BETWEEN 15 NOV '83 AND 10 JULY '84. |
|---|---|---|---|---|---|---|
| Private | James Craighton | [Dischd. 29 Nov '83] | | | " | " |
| " | Robert Campbell | | | " | " | " |
| " | Edward Cosgrove | | | " | " | " |
| " | Joseph Cooley | Dischd. 9 Jan '82 | " | " | | |
| " | Jeremiah Carter | | | " | " | " |
| Fifer | Joseph Clancey | | | " | " | |
| Private | William Cotter | | | " | " | |
| " | Thomas Channon | | | " | " | |
| Serjt. | Thomas Craig | | " | " | " | |
| Private | Edward Cantwell | Dischd. 24 Sept '83 | | " | " | |
| " | John Campbell, 2nd | [Dischd. 7 Sept '83] | " | " | " | |
| " | Joseph Cluly | [Dischd. 29 Nov '83] | | " | " | |
| " | John Cotter | [Dischd. 7 Sept '83] | | " | " | |
| " | Thomas Countiss | | | " | " | |
| " | William Coleman | [Dischd. 23 Sept '83] | | " | " | |
| " | George Chambers | [Dischd. 7 Sept '83] | | " | " | |
| " | John Connelly, 2nd | | " | " | " | |
| " | John Callahan | | | " | " | |
| " | James Countiss | | | " | " | |
| " | Willm. Carlin | | | " | " | |
| " | John Cooper, 2nd | | | " | " | |
| " | Christopher Coy | [Corpl., Dischd. 12 Aug '83] | " | " | | |
| " | Michael Cary | | | " | | |
| " | John Clineslought | | | " | " | " |
| " | John Conner | | | | " | |
| " | Wm. Connelly | | | | " | " |
| " | Levin Clarage | | | " | " | |
| " | Samuel Crowell | | | | " | |
| Corpl. | John Clancey, 2nd | [Dischd.16 Aug '83] | " | " | " | |
| Private | James Coen | [Dischd.12 Aug '83] | | | " | |
| " | John Charles | Dischd. 15 Mch '83 | " | " | | |
| " | William Colin | | | | " | |
| " | William Coursey | | " | " | " | |
| " | Patrick Connor | Invalided 1 Oct '81 | " | | | |
| " | James Crawford | | " | " | " | |
| " | Willm. Civill | Died on 15 June '83 on Jas. Isld. | " | " | " | |
| " | Timothy Cahill | | " | " | | |
| " | Christian Close | Died 1 Mch '82 | | " | | |
| " | Jacob Carnant | " 15 Sept 81 | " | | | |
| " | John Carter | Killed 8 Sept '81 | " | | | |
| " | Owen Coffield | | | | " | |
| " | George Collins | Dischd. 15 June '81 | " | | | |
| " | Byan Carroll | " 1 June '83 | | | " | |
| " | Michael Coyle | " 1 June '81 | " | | | |

| RANK. | NAMES. | REMARKS. | SERVED BETWEEN 1 AUG '80 AND 1 JAN '82. | SERVED BETWEEN 1 JAN '82 AND 1 JAN '83. | SERVED BETWEEN 1 JAN '83 AND 15 NOV '83. | SERVED BETWEEN 15 NOV '83 AND 10 JULY '84. |
|---|---|---|---|---|---|---|
| Private | Edward Cain | Invalided 15 Nov '83 | | | " | |
| " | Joseph Crouch | | | | " | |
| " | Thomas Cardiff | Invalided | | | " | |
| Serjt. | Charles Dawkins | Dischd. 5 Apl '81 | " | | | |
| Drum. | Dennis Dunning | | " | " | " | |
| Private | John Dixon | | " | " | " | |
| " | Francis Demar | | " | " | " | |
| " | William Dorch | Dischd. 6 Aug '83 | " | " | " | |
| " | Henry Dixon | " 8 Feb '81 | " | | | |
| " | John Denson | | " | " | " | |
| " | George Dixon | | " | " | " | |
| Corpl. | Willm. Dillon | Dischd. 2 May '82 | " | " | | |
| Private | John Dyer | | " | " | " | |
| " | Aquilla Deaver | | " | " | " | |
| " | Luke Dimpsey | | " | " | " | |
| " | Thomas Drudge | Died 10 Apl '83 | " | " | | |
| " | John Donovan | | " | | | |
| " | William Downs | [Dischd. 9 Sept '83] | " | " | " | |
| " | Thomas Doyle | Dischd. 4 Feb '81 | " | | | |
| " | Peter Degagoone | | " | " | " | |
| Corpl. | James Daffin | Dischd. 5 Apl '81 | " | | | |
| Serjt. | Edmund Dougherty | Died 15 Jan '81 | " | | | |
| Private | Francis Dunnington | " 23 Apl '83 | " | " | | |
| " | James Doyle | | " | " | " | |
| " | John Duhague | Died 1 Dec '82 | " | " | | |
| " | John Downey | | " | " | " | |
| " | Elijah Deane | Dischd. 31 May '81 | " | | | |
| " | Robert Davis | " 1 May '81 | " | | | |
| " | Richard Duvall | | " | " | " | |
| Serjt. | Patrick Doran | | " | " | " | |
| Drum. | John Denoon | | " | " | " | |
| Private | James Devericks | | " | " | " | |
| " | George Dewitt | | " | " | " | |
| " | Robert Dunken | | " | " | " | |
| Serjt. | Samuel Denny | Dischd. 2 Mch '81 | " | | | |
| " | Samuel Davis | | " | " | " | |
| Private | James Dyer | | " | " | " | |
| " | John Delany, (or Delanaway) | | " | " | " | |
| " | Mathias Dyche | | " | " | " | |
| " | John Deakins | [Dischd. 12 Aug '83] | " | " | " | |
| " | Edward Domonick | Dischd. 1 July '83 | " | " | " | |
| " | Joseph Donoho | | " | " | " | |
| " | James Davidson | | " | " | " | |
| " | William Deaver | Dischd. 7 Mch '82 | " | " | | |

| RANK. | NAMES. | REMARKS. | SERVED BETWEEN 1 AUG '80 AND 1 JAN '82 | SERVED BETWEEN 1 JAN '82 AND 1 JAN '83 | SERVED BETWEEN 1 JAN '83 AND 15 NOV '83 | SERVED BETWEEN 15 NOV '83 AND 10 JULY '84. |
|---|---|---|---|---|---|---|
| Private | James Due | | " | " | " | |
| " | William Devine | | " | " | " | |
| " | James Dyer, 2nd | Dischd. 1 Sept '82 | " | " | | |
| " | John Donogan | Died 25 Jan '83 | " | " | | |
| " | John Davis, 1st | | " | " | " | |
| " | William Dawson | [Dischd. 29 Nov '83] | " | " | " | |
| " | Barnaba Dougharty | Invalided 3 Nov '83 | " | " | " | |
| " | Jacob Duddera | [Dischd. 29 Nov '83] | " | " | " | |
| " | Terrance Duffee | [Serjt., Dischd. 29 Nov '83] | " | " | " | |
| " | John Deane | Died 15 Dec '81 | " | | | |
| " | John Dobson | | " | " | " | |
| " | James Driver | | " | " | " | |
| Serjt. | Thomas Duffee | | " | " | " | |
| Private | Thomas Davis, 1st | [Dischd. 29 Nov '83] | " | " | " | |
| " | Abraham Dugan | | " | " | " | |
| " | Thomas Dickeson | | " | " | " | |
| " | Charles Deane | | " | " | " | |
| " | Richard Dolvin | | " | " | " | |
| " | Richard Dunby | Died 8 May '83 | " | " | " | |
| | Willm. Derrington | | " | " | " | |
| " | James Dawson | [Dischd. 18 Sept '83] | " | " | " | |
| " | George Dunken | | | | " | |
| " | Patrick Dennison | | " | " | " | |
| " | Joseph Deford | Dischd. 8 Mch '81 | " | | | |
| " | George Dice | | " | " | " | |
| " | Alexander Downey | | " | " | " | |
| " | Richard Dixon | Died 27 Dec '82 | " | " | | |
| " | Francis Dewist | [Dischd. 1 Sept '83] | " | " | " | " |
| " | James Dowden | | " | " | " | " |
| " | Buto Devo | Invd. 4 Apl '82 | " | " | | |
| Serjt. | Francis Duffee | | | " | | |
| " | Jacob Doyle, (or Doyne) | | | " | " | |
| Private | Isaac Dunken | | | " | " | |
| " | George Dadisman | | | " | " | |
| " | Basil Dorsey | | | " | " | |
| " | Robert Dean | | | " | " | |
| Corpl. | Isaac Deale | [Dischd. 29 Nov '83] | | " | " | |
| " | William Dunn | | | " | " | |
| Private | Benj. Donnelly | [Dischd. 29 Nov '83] | | " | " | |
| " | Wm. Devericks | | | " | " | |
| " | Matthew Doley | | | | " | |
| Fifer | Samuel Davis | | | | " | |
| Private | Jeremiah Driscoll | | | | | |
| " | George Dyer | | " | " | " | |
| " | John Dent | Invalided 1 Apl '83 | " | " | | |

| RANK. | NAMES. | REMARKS. | SERVED BETWEEN 1 AUG '80 AND 1 JAN '82. | SERVED BETWEEN 1 JAN '82 AND 1 JAN '83. | SERVED BETWEEN 1 JAN '83 AND 15 NOV '83. | SERVED BETWEEN 15 NOV '83 AND 10 JULY '84. |
|---|---|---|---|---|---|---|
| Serjt. | John Dove | Dischd. 31 Jan '83 | " | " | | |
| Private | Benj. Dominick | Killed 8 Sept '81 | " | | | |
| " | James Dennison | Dischd. 26 July '82 | | " | | |
| " | Richard Downs | Dischd. 25 Apl '81 | " | | | |
| " | Pearce Deacon | Died 1 Nov '82 | | " | | |
| " | William Day | Dischd. 22 July '83 | | | " | |
| " | John Davis | Died 12 Aug '82 | | " | | |
| " | James Davidson | Dischd. 20 Apl '81 | " | | | |
| " | Thomas Dutton | Killed 8 Sept '81 | " | | | |
| " | Charles Davis | | | | " | |
| | | | | | | |
| Private | Henry Evis | | " | " | " | |
| " | Edward Ellicot | | " | " | " | |
| Serjt. | Peregrine Evins | | " | " | " | |
| Corpl. | Bartholomew Esom | | " | " | " | |
| Fifer | Michael Ellis | Dischd. 6 June '81 | " | | | |
| Private | Thomas Evans, 2nd | | | " | " | |
| " | Thomas Elliot, 2nd | | " | " | " | |
| " | William Ellis | Killed 26 June '81 | " | | | |
| " | Edward Evans, 1st | | " | " | " | |
| " | William Evans | Invalided 15 Nov '83 | " | " | " | |
| Serjt. | Thomas Edwards | | " | " | " | |
| Private | Jarvis Eccleston | | " | " | " | |
| " | Joseph Ellicot | | " | " | " | |
| F. M. | George Elins | | " | " | " | |
| Private | John Elliot, 1st | | " | " | " | |
| Serjt. | Edward Evans, 2nd | | " | " | " | |
| Private | William Elkins | | " | " | " | |
| " | Thomas Ellis, 1st | | " | " | " | |
| " | Enoch Ennis | | " | " | " | |
| " | Leonard Ennis | | " | " | " | |
| " | John Ennis | | " | " | " | |
| " | John Edwards | [Dischd. 18 Sept '83] | " | " | " | |
| " | Peter Equidowney | [Dischd. 29 Nov '83] | " | " | " | |
| " | James Evans | | " | " | " | |
| " | Thomas Elliott, 1st | [Dischd. 29 Nov '83] | " | " | " | |
| Corpl. | Samuel Evans | | " | " | " | |
| Private | Thomas Evans, 1st | [Dischd. 24 Sept '83] | " | " | " | |
| " | James Ervine | | | " | " | |
| Fifer | Nicholas Ellicott | | | " | " | |
| Private | William Eagle | | | | " | |
| Corpl. | Thos. Ellison, (or Allison) | | | | " | |
| Private | Francis Ensley | | | | " | |
| " | Heathcoat Edward | | | | " | |
| " | Emanuel Ebbs | | " | " | " | |

| RANK. | NAMES. | REMARKS. | SERVED BETWEEN 1 AUG '80 AND 1 JAN '82. | SERVED BETWEEN 1 JAN '82 AND 1 JAN '83. | SERVED BETWEEN 1 JAN '83 AND 15 NOV '83. | SERVED BETWEEN 15 NOV '83 AND 10 JULY '84. |
|---|---|---|---|---|---|---|
| Private | Mcl. Evans | Dischd. 25 Oct '81 | " | | | |
| " | Thomas Ellison | "    1 Jan '83 | | | " | |
| Serjt. | John Edwards | "    1 June '81 | " | | | |
| Private | Jacob Flora | | | " | " | " |
| " | Francis Fairbrother | | | " | " | " |
| " | John Fransway | | | " | " | " |
| " | Stephen Fresh | | | " | " | " |
| " | Joseph Fowler | | | " | " | " |
| " | William Fisher | Dischd. 21 May '81 | " | | | |
| " | Jonathan Fowler | Died Sept '83 | | " | " | " |
| " | George Filleson | Invalided 6 June '83 | " | " | " | |
| " | Henry Fisher, 2nd | | | " | " | " |
| " | James Farrell | | | " | " | " |
| " | James Fitzgerald | Dischd. 3 Apl '81 | " | | | |
| " | Francis Freeman | | | " | " | " |
| " | John Ferguson | Dischd. 1 Apl '82 | " | " | | |
| " | Edward Furrener | | | " | " | " |
| " | James Foster | Died 30 June '81 | " | | | |
| " | Alexander Francis | | | " | " | " |
| " | Richard Freemane | Dischd. 12 Jan '82 | " | " | | |
| " | William R. Franklin | "    28 July '83 | " | " | " | |
| " | John Farrell | "    14 Feb '83 | " | " | | |
| " | Richard Farraby | | | " | " | " |
| " | Frederick Flinn | | | " | " | " |
| " | Stafford Fosdale | | | " | " | " |
| " | Peter Fountain | Dischd. 15 May '81 | " | | | |
| Drum. | Benjamin Folliot | Died 17 June '81 | " | | | |
| Private | Rigby Foster | | | " | " | " |
| Serjt. | William Foreman | | | " | " | " |
| Drum. | William Farrell | | | " | " | " |
| Private | John Fulham | | | " | " | " |
| " | Edward Flowers | Died 1 June '81 | " | | | |
| " | Mark Foster | [Dischd. 7 Sept '83] | | " | " | " |
| Serjt. | Benj. Fitzgerald | [Dischd. 11 Sept '83] | | " | " | " |
| Private | Absalom Fardo | | | " | " | " |
| " | John M. Funner | Invalided 15 Nov '83 | | " | " | " |
| " | Doras Filmot | Dischd. 5 May '81 | " | | | |
| " | Nicholas Fitzgerald | "    2 May '81 | " | | | |
| " | Moses Foster | | | " | " | " |
| Serjt. | Saml. Filson | | | " | " | " |
| " | Stephen Fluharty | | | " | " | " |
| Private | Dennis Flanagan | [Dischd. 29 Nov '83] | | " | " | " |
| " | Emanl. Farrara | | | | | |
| " | Philip Fisher | Invalided. [Dischd. 29 Nov '83] | | " | " | " |

| Rank. | Names. | Remarks. | Served between 1 Aug '80 and 1 Jan '82. | Served between 1 Jan '82 and 1 Jan '83. | Served between 1 Jan '83 and 15 Nov '83. | Served between 15 Nov '83 and 10 July '84. |
|---|---|---|---|---|---|---|
| Private | John Folling | | " | " | " | |
| " | Robert Farrell | | " | " | " | |
| Corpl. | Peter Farrell | Died 18 June '81 | " | | | |
| Private | Jeremiah French | | " | " | " | |
| | Philip Fitzpatrick | [Dischd. 29 Nov '83] | " | " | " | |
| " | Charles Fitzgerald | | " | " | " | |
| " | Willm. Fitzgerald | | " | " | " | |
| " | John Frawney | | " | " | " | |
| Serjt. | George Finlay | | | | " | |
| Private | John Francis | | " | " | " | |
| " | Robert Folger | | " | " | | |
| Corpl. | Peter French | | " | " | " | |
| Private | Thomas Foxall | | " | " | " | |
| " | Edward Fincham | | " | " | " | |
| " | John Fosset | [Dischd. 29 Nov '83] | " | " | " | |
| " | Walter Ferrall | | " | " | " | |
| " | Daniel, (David), Foxall | | " | " | " | |
| " | Stephen Fennell | | " | " | " | |
| " | George Ford | | " | " | " | |
| " | John Fulford | | " | " | " | |
| Serjt. | George Fields | | " | " | " | |
| Private | Robert Firth | | " | " | " | " |
| " | Thomas Fleming | | " | " | | |
| " | Joseph Fisher | Died 20 Nov '82 | " | " | " | |
| " | John Fennel | | " | " | " | |
| Corpl. | Charles Fulham | | " | | | |
| Private | John Franklin | Dischd. 4 Mch '81 | " | | | |
| " | Joseph Folliet | Died 25 July '82 | " | " | | |
| " | Thomas Frumley | | | " | " | |
| " | Lewis Flash | | | " | " | |
| " | John Fairweather | | | " | " | |
| " | Samuel Fisher | | | " | " | |
| " | Richard Franklin | [Dischd. 18 Sept '83] | | " | " | |
| " | Nicholas Free | [Dischd. 29 Nov '83] | | | " | |
| " | Henry Frazier | | " | " | " | |
| " | Henry Fisher, 1st | | | | " | |
| " | Nicholas Farr | | | | | |
| " | William Fairbourn | Died 16 Mch '82 | " | " | | |
| Serjt. | James Flack | Dischd. 28 Apl '82 | " | " | | |
| Private | Jeremiah Fitzgerald | Died 1 Aug '82 | | " | | |
| " | Richard Fenwick | | | | " | " |
| " | Andrew Ferneen | | | | " | |
| " | James French | Enlisted in '82 | | | " | |
| Serjt. | Benjamin Gray | | " | " | " | |
| Private | Amos Green | | " | " | " | |

| RANK. | NAMES. | REMARKS. | SERVED BETWEEN 1 AUG '80 AND 1 JAN '82. | SERVED BETWEEN 1 JAN '82 AND 1 JAN '83. | SERVED BETWEEN 1 JAN '83 AND 15 NOV '83. | SERVED BETWEEN 15 NOV '83 AND 10 JULY '84. |
|---|---|---|---|---|---|---|
| Private | Abraham Garsene | | " | " | " | |
| " | Sylvester Gatting | Dischd. 4 Sept '81 | | | | |
| " | Samuel Green, | " 9 Jan '82 | " | " | | |
| " | John Greene, 1st | | " | " | " | |
| Fifer | William Griffin | Dischd. 15 May '82 | " | " | | |
| Private | Thomas Glover | " 14 Feb '83 | " | " | | |
| Fifer | Andrew Garnet | [Dischd. 29 Nov '83] | " | " | " | |
| Private | William Gold | | " | " | " | |
| " | Mark Griffin | Dischd. 15 Jan '81 | " | | | |
| " | Nathan Griffin | " 15 Jan '81 | " | | | |
| " | Reuben Gooster | " 27 Dec '81 | " | | | |
| " | Henry Green | | " | " | " | |
| Drum. | Thomas Gossage | | " | " | " | |
| " | Anthony Geohagan | | " | " | " | |
| Private | Jesse Grace | Dischd. 17 April '81 | " | | | |
| " | John Gibson | " 25 April '81 | " | | | |
| " | Isaac Green | " 15 Jan '82 | " | " | | |
| " | William Glascow | " 12 April '81 | " | | | |
| " | Charles Goldsborough | | " | " | " | |
| Drum. | John Gorden, 1st | | " | " | " | |
| Private | William Gates | Dischd. 30 Mch '83 | " | " | | |
| " | John Goddard | " 26 Feb '83 | " | " | | |
| " | Hugh Gainor | | " | " | " | |
| " | James Garth | | " | " | " | |
| Serjt. | John Given | | " | " | " | |
| Private | James Gray, 1st | | " | " | " | |
| " | John Gorman, 1st | | " | " | " | |
| " | Thomas Gillen | | " | " | " | |
| " | Henry Gilby | | " | " | " | |
| " | Abraham Gamble | | " | " | " | |
| Drum. | James Greenwood | | " | " | " | |
| Private | Moses Graham | | " | " | " | |
| " | Isaac Graves | | " | " | " | |
| " | Edward Garish | Dischd. 8 Aug '82 | " | " | | |
| " | Paul Grinard | | " | " | " | |
| " | Richard Gee | | " | " | " | |
| " | Samuel Gerry | Dischd. 28 April '81 | " | | | |
| " | Joseph Gorden | " 1 May '81 | " | | | |
| " | Henry Goldsborough | Died 17 June '81 | " | | | |
| " | John Gordon, 2nd | | " | " | " | |
| " | William Glory | | " | " | " | |
| " | William Groves | | " | " | " | |
| Serjt. | John Green, 2nd | | " | " | " | |
| Private | Benj. Gilbert | | " | " | " | |
| " | Thomas Gadd | | " | " | " | |

| Rank. | Names. | Remarks. | Served between 1 Aug '80 and 1 Jan '82. | Served between 1 Jan '82 and 1 Jan '83. | Served between 1 Jan '83 and 15 Nov '83. | Served between 15 Nov '83 and 10 July '84. |
|---|---|---|---|---|---|---|
| Private | Philip Graham | [Dischd. 29 Nov '83] | " | " | " | |
| " | Bennet George | Died 1 Oct '82 | " | " | | |
| " | Lambert Goody | | " | " | " | |
| " | John Gee | | " | " | " | |
| " | Amos Griffith | | | " | " | |
| Fifer | John Graham | | " | " | " | |
| Private | Charles Girdler | | " | " | " | |
| " | Thomas Gilham | | " | " | " | |
| " | William Glover | [Dischd.29 Nov '83] | | | | |
| " | Solomon Green | | " | " | " | |
| " | Charles Goff | Dischd. 21 Jan '81 | " | | | |
| " | John Gregory | | " | " | " | |
| " | James Gravey | [Dischd. 7 Sept '83] | " | " | " | |
| " | William Greenage | Dischd. 18 May '81, reinlisted | " | | " | |
| " | Smart Greer | | " | " | " | |
| " | Samuel Gray | | " | " | " | |
| " | William George | Died 24 July '82 | " | " | | |
| " | Southy George | | " | " | " | |
| " | Joseph Greer | | " | " | " | |
| " | William Gudgeon | [Dischd.29 Nov '83] | " | " | | |
| " | John Gother | Invd. 25 Feb '82 | " | " | | |
| " | Jacob Games | | | " | " | |
| " | Benjamin Gater | | | " | " | |
| " | John Gray | | | " | " | |
| " | Sylvester Gatting | | " | " | " | |
| " | Chas. Griffith | | | " | " | |
| " | Whittington Gild | | | " | " | |
| " | John Greenwood | | | " | " | |
| " | James Gilmore, 2nd | | | " | " | |
| " | William Gallispie | Dischd. 1 Oct '83 | " | | | |
| " | John Gnatzinger | " 29 Mch '81 | " | | | |
| " | Marshall Galloway | | " | " | " | |
| " | James Goodwin | | " | " | " | |
| " | William Grant | | " | " | " | |
| " | Vincent Gray | | | | " | |
| " | Michael Grosh | Dischd. 4 Mch '81 | " | | | |
| " | Robert Gilhampton | Died 1 Oct '81 | " | | | |
| | Thomas Gray | " 15 Oct '82 | | " | | |
| Private | William Harrington | | " | " | " | |
| Corpl. | Ralph Hagan | Dischd. 30 April '82 | " | " | | |
| Drum. | John Head | | " | " | " | |
| Private | John Hughs, 1st | Dischd. 10 May '83 | " | " | | |
| " | Richard Harper | " 19 Mch '81 | " | | | |

35

| Rank. | Names. | Remarks. | Served between 1 Aug '80 and 1 Jan '82. | Served between 1 Jan '82 and 1 Jan '83. | Served between 1 Jan '83 and 15 Nov '83. | Served between 15 Nov '83 and 10 July '84. |
|---|---|---|---|---|---|---|
| Private | Thomas Harrison | | | " | " | " |
| " | James Hill | Dischd. 15 Jan '81 | " | | | |
| " | John Haney | | " | " | " | |
| " | Joseph Horsfield | | " | " | " | |
| Serjt. | George Hagarthy | Killed 15 Mch '81 | " | | | |
| Private | John Howard | Dischd. 25 Feb '81 | " | | | |
| " | Joseph Huckell | | " | " | " | |
| " | James Hare | Died 6 July '82 | " | " | | |
| Drum. | Vachel Hays | Killed 8 Sept '81 | " | | | |
| Private | John Hood | Killed 15 Mch '81 | " | | | |
| " | Barney Haney | [Dischd. 11 Sept '83] | " | " | " | |
| " | Samuel Hughs | Killed 15 Mch '81 | " | | | |
| " | John Homes | Dischd. 30 Apl '81 | " | | | |
| " | Henry Horley | "    23 Apl '81, reinlisted | " | | " | |
| " | Austin Howard | | " | " | " | |
| " | Richard Hall | | " | " | " | |
| " | Edward Harley | Dischd. 25 Apl '81 | " | | | |
| " | William Harris | "    22 Jan '81 | " | | | |
| Corpl. | Josias Harris | "    25 Apl '81 | " | | | |
| Private | Elias Hardy | "    25 Apl '81 | " | | | |
| " | John Hamilton | | " | " | " | |
| " | Peregrine Howard | | " | " | " | |
| Serjt. | Cornelius Howard | Died 1 Oct '81 | " | | | |
| Private | John B. Haislip | "  11 Sept '82 | " | " | | |
| Drum. | Isaac Hill | Dischd. 11 Aug '83 | " | " | " | |
| Serjt. | Charles Harvey | | " | " | " | |
| Private | John Hide | | " | " | " | |
| " | John Howell | Dischd. 21 Jan '81 | " | | | |
| " | William Howe | "  2 July '81 | " | | | |
| " | Isaac Holliday | Died 30 Jan '83 | " | " | | |
| " | Jacob Hines | Dischd. 1 May '81 | " | | | |
| " | Nathaniel Hull | "  15 Jan '81 | " | | | |
| Serjt. | Robert Harpham | | " | " | " | |
| Private | Thomas Harris, 1st | [Dischd. 29 Nov '83] | " | " | " | |
| " | Henry Hines | Dischd. 30 Apl '81 | " | | | |
| " | Francis Hopkins | | " | " | " | |
| " | John Holder | | " | " | " | |
| " | John Harris, 1st | | " | " | " | |
| " | Zadock Harvey | Dischd. 1 May '81 | " | | | |
| " | William Horney | | " | " | " | |
| Drum. | John Hull | | " | " | " | |
| Private | Charles Hill | Dischd. 21 Apl '81 | " | | | |
| " | John Holliday | | " | " | " | |
| " | John Housley | | " | " | " | |

| RANK. | NAMES. | REMARKS. | SERVED BETWEEN 1 AUG '80 AND 1 JAN '82. | SERVED BETWEEN 1 JAN '82 AND 1 JAN '83. | SERVED BETWEEN 1 JAN '83 AND 15 NOV '83. | SERVED BETWEEN 15 NOV '83 AND 10 JULY '84. |
|---|---|---|---|---|---|---|
| Corpl. | John Hall, 2nd | | " | " | " | |
| Private | William Harris, 1st | Time expires 2 Feb '83 | " | " | | |
| " | Nicholas Heisler | Dischd. 24 Apl '81 | " | | | |
| " | Jacob Hunt | [Dischd. 11 Sept '83] | " | " | " | |
| " | Frederick Harty | | " | " | " | |
| " | Thomas Hoy | Dischd. 25 Apl '81 | " | | | |
| " | William Hurley | [Dischd. 29 Nov '83] | " | " | " | |
| " | Leonard Hagan | Died 17 Dec '82 | " | " | | |
| " | Walter Hagan | Dischd. 23 Feb '83 | " | " | | |
| " | Randolph Hoskins | "     8 Jan '82 | " | " | | |
| " | John Hulet | | " | " | " | |
| " | William Hughes | Died 6 Dec '82 | " | " | | |
| " | John Harrell | | " | " | " | |
| " | Joseph Hall | | " | " | " | |
| " | John Haden | | " | " | " | |
| " | William Hillman | | " | " | " | |
| " | John Higgins | Killed 14 June '81 | " | | | |
| Corpl. | Lazerous Higgs | Time expires 1 June '83 | " | " | " | |
| Private | Walter Howe | | " | " | " | |
| " | John Hare | Died 27 May '81 | " | | | |
| Drum. | Edward Holland | | " | " | " | |
| Corpl. | James Hagan | Time expires 1 June '83 | " | " | " | |
| Private | Peter Howard | Died 4 Feb '83 | " | " | | |
| " | William Hicks | | " | " | " | |
| " | George Hamilton | | " | " | " | |
| Drum. | Philip Huston | [Dischd. 12 Aug '83] | " | " | " | |
| Private | Nathan Harper | [Dischd. 11 Aug '83] | " | " | " | |
| " | Samuel Hamilton | | " | " | " | |
| " | Samuel Harper | | " | " | " | |
| " | Lazarous Harman | | " | " | " | |
| " | Nehemiah Hadder | | " | " | " | |
| " | Edward Hammond | | " | " | " | |
| " | John Hancock | | " | " | " | |
| " | Elijah Hutt | [Dischd. 29 Nov '83] | " | " | " | |
| " | Ralph Hope | | " | " | " | |
| " | William Hill, 1st | | " | " | " | |
| " | John Hood, 2nd | Died 20 Dec '82 | " | " | | |
| " | James Hewitt | | " | " | " | |
| " | John Hillary | Died 27 Dec '82 | " | " | | |
| " | John S. Hunt | "     3 Dec '81 | " | | | |
| " | James Harris, 2nd | | " | " | " | |
| Corpl. | George Hadan | Dischd. 23 Feb '83 | " | " | | |

| RANK. | NAMES. | REMARKS. | SERVED BETWEEN 1 AUG '80 AND 1 JAN '82. | SERVED BETWEEN 1 JAN '82 AND 1 JAN '83. | SERVED BETWEEN 1 JAN '83 AND 15 NOV '83. | SERVED BETWEEN 15 NOV '83 AND 10 JULY '84. |
|---|---|---|---|---|---|---|
| Private | Thomas Hawson | | " | " | " | |
| " | Stephen Hancock | | " | " | " | |
| " | John Hickens | | " | " | " | |
| " | Daniel Howe | | " | " | " | " |
| Serjt. | Richard Huggins | [Dischd. 29 Nov '83] | " | " | " | |
| Private | Thomas Hill | | " | " | " | " |
| " | William Hope | | " | " | " | |
| " | John Hurley | | " | " | " | |
| " | Leonard Holt | | " | " | " | |
| " | Nicholas Hiner | | " | " | " | |
| | Richard Harrington | | " | " | " | |
| " | Levin Harrington | | " | " | " | |
| " | Edward Henesee | Died 28 Apl '83 | " | " | | |
| " | Pompey Hollis | " 28 Apl '83 | " | " | | |
| " | James Homes | 1st Regt. | | | | |
| " | Joseph Harper | | | " | " | |
| " | William Harper | [Dischd. 29 Nov '83] | " | " | " | |
| " | James Halloron | Died 16 Dec '82 | " | " | | |
| " | Daniel Holoman | | " | " | " | |
| " | John Hudson, 1st | | " | " | " | |
| " | Samuel Hurst | [Dischd. 29 Nov '83] | " | " | " | |
| " | James Hudson, 1st | | " | " | " | |
| " | John Hawes | Died 2 Feb '83 | " | " | | |
| " | David Hatten | " 9 Mch '83 | " | " | | |
| " | William Hamston | " 31 Jan '83 | " | " | | |
| Serjt. | Thomas Harrison, 2nd | Dischd. 1 July '81 | " | | | |
| Private | William Hedge | | " | " | " | |
| " | William Hutcheson | | " | " | " | |
| " | William Harrison, 1st | | " | " | " | |
| " | Michael Hartman | | " | " | " | |
| " | Richard B. Haselip | | " | " | " | |
| " | Thomas Hutchcroft | | " | " | " | |
| " | Richard Hays | | " | " | " | |
| Serjt. | George Holton | Dischd. 5 Apl '84 | " | " | " | " |
| Private | William Hartman | [Dischd. 29 Nov '83] | " | " | " | |
| " | James Humphrys | [Dischd. 29 Nov '83] | " | " | " | |
| " | Samuel Harrison | Died 2 Aug '82 | " | " | | |
| " | John C. Harwood | | | " | " | |
| " | John Harris, 2nd | | " | " | " | |
| " | John Hicks | | | " | " | |
| " | Thomas Hammond | [Dischd.29 Nov '83] | " | " | " | |
| " | Roger Hogan | [Dischd. 29 Nov '83] | | " | " | |
| " | Thomas Hall | | | " | " | |
| " | Daniel Harness | | | " | " | |
| " | James Hunt | | | " | " | |

| RANK. | NAMES. | REMARKS. | SERVED BETWEEN 1 AUG '80 AND 1 JAN '82. | SERVED BETWEEN 1 JAN '82 AND 1 JAN '83. | SERVED BETWEEN 1 JAN '83 AND 15 NOV '83. | SERVED BETWEEN 15 NOV '83 AND 10 JULY '84. |
|---|---|---|---|---|---|---|
| Private | William Holland | | | " | " | |
| Corpl. | Kemp Holden | | | " | " | |
| Private | William Hunter | | | " | " | |
| " | Daniel Hukill | | | " | " | |
| " | John Hukill | | | " | " | |
| " | Thomas Harding | | | " | " | |
| Drum. | Isaac Holland | | | " | " | |
| Private | Herculas Hutchings | [Dischd. 29 Nov '83] | " | " | " | |
| " | James Hudson | | | " | " | " |
| " | Thomas Houseman | | | | " | |
| Corpl. | Christopher Hinson | | | " | " | |
| Private | William Hand | | | | " | |
| Fifer | Benjamin Harrison | | | | | |
| Private | John Hannon | | " | " | " | |
| " | Charles Hickey | | " | " | " | |
| " | John Hutson, 2nd | | " | " | " | |
| " | Caleb Hailey | Invalided 15 Nov '83 | " | " | " | |
| " | John Holston | | " | " | " | |
| " | Samuel Hughes | Invalided 1 Apl '81 | " | | | |
| " | William Harris, 2nd | 6 Regt. | | " | " | " |
| Drum. | William Hamilton | | " | " | | |
| Private | Daniel Hall | Invalided 1 Mch '82 | " | " | | |
| Drum. | Henry Harris | Depreciation wrong | " | " | " | |
| Private | Lawrence Hurdle | | | | " | " |
| " | Peter Hammond | Dischd. 5 July '82 | | " | | |
| " | Burton Harris | Died of his wounds '84 | | | " | |
| | | | | | | |
| Private | William Joice, 1st | | | " | " | " |
| Serjt. | Archibald Johnson | | | " | " | " |
| Private | Edward Irvine | [James (?) Dischd. 29 Nov '83] | | " | " | " |
| " | Joseph Jenkins | | | " | " | " |
| " | Henry Jacobs | | | " | " | " |
| " | Nealy Jones | | | " | " | " |
| " | Joseph Jones, 1st | | | " | " | " |
| " | Robert Joshson | Dischd. 19 Mch '81 | " | | | |
| Serjt. | James Jackson | | " | " | " | |
| Corpl. | David Jones | Died 15 Jan '81 | " | | | |
| Fifer | Benj. Johnson | | " | " | " | |
| Private | Thomas Jones, 1st | | " | " | " | |
| " | Thomas Jones | Dischd. 25 Apl '81 | " | | | |
| " | Zachariah Jacobs | "    1 June '81 | " | | | |
| " | Joseph Johnson | | " | " | " | |
| " | Adam Jenison | | " | " | " | |
| " | John Johnson | Died 15 Jan '81 | " | | | |

| RANK. | NAMES. | REMARKS. | SERVED BETWEEN 1 AUG '80 AND 1 JAN '82. | SERVED BETWEEN 1 JAN '82 AND 1 JAN '83. | SERVED BETWEEN 1 JAN '83 AND 15 NOV '83. | SERVED BETWEEN 15 NOV '83 AND 10 JULY '84. |
|---|---|---|---|---|---|---|
| Private | William Joice, 2d | Killed 8 Sept '81 | " | | | |
| " | John Johnson, 1st | [Dischd. 29 Nov '83] | " | " | " | |
| " | William Ingles | Engle | " | " | " | |
| " | Aaron Jones | | " | " | " | |
| Serjt. | Thomas Jones, 3d | Dischd. 13 Mch '82 | " | " | | |
| " | Jesse Jacobs | | " | " | " | |
| Private | Daniel Jarvis | quere if not Danl. Javins | " | " | " | |
| Serjt. | Joseph Jeans | | " | " | " | |
| Private | John Jones, Sr., 3rd | | " | " | " | |
| " | John Johnson, 3rd | Dischd. 11 Aug '83 | " | " | " | |
| " | William Jones, 1st | | " | " | " | |
| " | William Jones, 2nd | | " | " | " | |
| " | Jacob Jeffers | [Dischd. 29 Nov '83] | " | " | " | |
| " | Thomas John | | " | " | " | |
| " | Robert Johnson | | " | " | " | |
| " | John Jones, 2nd | | " | " | " | |
| " | Edward Jackson | | " | " | " | |
| " | Frederick Iiams | | " | " | " | |
| " | William Jenkins | | " | " | " | |
| " | John Jones, 1st | | " | " | " | |
| " | George Jenings | | " | " | " | |
| " | John Jackson | | " | " | " | |
| " | Joseph Isaacs | | " | " | " | |
| " | Abraham Irvine | | " | " | " | |
| " | John Jarvis | | " | " | " | |
| " | Isaac Johnson | Dischd. 1 Oct '83 | " | " | " | |
| " | Thomas Jones, 2nd | | " | " | " | |
| Serjt. | William Johnson | Dischd. 22 Oct '83 | " | " | " | |
| Private | Charles Jones | | " | " | " | |
| " | George Jones | [Dischd. 29 Nov '83] | " | " | " | |
| " | Thomas Jones, 4th | | " | " | " | |
| " | John Irons | | " | " | " | |
| " | James Jones | | | " | | |
| " | John Jorden, 2nd | | | | | |
| " | Richard Jenings | | | " | " | |
| " | Peter Jackson | | | " | " | |
| " | John Johnson | | | " | " | |
| " | Cotter Jones | [Dischd.12 Aug '83] | | " | " | |
| " | James Isaacs | Invalided 15 Sept '83 | " | " | " | |
| Serjt. | William Johnston | Dischd. 16 May '81 | " | | | |
| " | Robert Isabel | "   4 July '82 | | " | | |
| Private | William Justice | | | | " | |
| Serjt. | Dennis Kelly | Dischd. 1 Apl '83 | " | " | | |
| Private | Thomas King | | " | " | " | |

| RANK. | NAMES. | REMARKS. | SERVED BETWEEN 1 AUG '80 AND 1 JAN '82. | SERVED BETWEEN 1 JAN '82 AND 1 JAN '83. | SERVED BETWEEN 1 JAN '83 AND 15 NOV '83. | SERVED BETWEEN 15 NOV '83 AND 10 JULY '84. |
|---|---|---|---|---|---|---|
| Private | Adam Keephart | | " | " | " | |
| " | Jacob Knight | | " | " | " | |
| " | Edward Killman | Dischd. 24 May '81 | " | | | |
| " | James Kelly, 2nd | " 10 Apl '83 | " | " | | |
| " | John Knoc, 1st | Died in '82 | " | | | |
| " | John Kidd | | " | " | " | |
| " | John King | | " | " | " | |
| " | William King | | " | " | " | |
| " | David Kelly | | " | " | " | |
| " | John King | Dischd. 25 Apl '81 | " | | | |
| Corpl. | Joseph Kerrick | Died 27 Dec '82 | " | " | | |
| Private | George Kelson | | " | " | " | |
| " | Michael Kernon | Dischd. 18 May '81 | " | | | |
| " | Benj. H. Kerrick | | " | " | " | |
| " | William Kindle | Dischd. 25 Apl '81 | " | | | |
| " | Francis Kitely | Died 25 Apl '81 | " | | | |
| Corpl. | James Kelly, 1st | | " | " | " | |
| Private | James Keeland | | " | " | " | |
| " | John Kildee | | " | " | " | |
| " | Richard Kisby | | | | " | |
| " | Walter Keech | Dischd. 1 Aug '83 | " | " | " | |
| " | Jacob Kelly | [Dischd. 21 Aug '83] | " | " | " | |
| " | Thomas P. Kettle | | " | " | " | |
| " | Benjamin Karns | | " | " | " | |
| " | Edward Kearsey | | " | " | " | |
| " | James Knot | | " | " | " | |
| " | Edward Kirk | | " | " | " | " |
| " | Francis Kearns | | " | " | " | |
| " | Daniel Kettle | | " | " | " | |
| " | Jacob Kiser | Dischd. 13 Feb '82 | " | " | | |
| " | Abraham Kettle | | " | " | " | |
| " | Peter Kincade | Died 1 Jan '82 | " | | | |
| " | George Kelty | | | " | | |
| " | Matthew Kelly | | " | " | " | |
| " | Isaac Kent | | | " | " | |
| " | Michael Keene | | | " | " | |
| " | James Kirk | | | | " | |
| " | John Knox, 2nd | | | " | " | |
| " • | Stephen Kamble | Died 1 Sept '82 | " | " | | |
| Serjt. | William Kello | Killed 15 Mch '81 | " | | | |
| Private | James Killegan | | | | " | |
| " | Nathaniel Knott | | | | " | |
| Private | Jonathan Lewis | | " | " | " | |
| " | Michael Lloyd | [Dischd. 29 Nov '83] | " | " | " | |

| RANK. | NAMES. | REMARKS. | SERVED BETWEEN 1 AUG '80 AND 1 JAN '82. | SERVED BETWEEN 1 JAN '82 AND 1 JAN '83. | SERVED BETWEEN 1 JAN '83 AND 15 NOV '83. | SERVED BETWEEN 15 NOV '83 AND 10 JULY '84. |
|---|---|---|---|---|---|---|
| Private | William Letman | Killed 8 Sept '81 | " | | | |
| " | William Laws | | " | " | " | |
| " | Roger Landers, (Sanders?) | | " | " | " | |
| " | John Lucas, 1st | | " | " | " | |
| " | George Laws | Died 22 Jan '81 | " | | | |
| " | Benj. Loffman | | " | " | " | |
| " | Levi Lord | | " | " | " | |
| " | William Lee | Died 15 Sept '81 | " | | | |
| " | Henry Laws | | " | " | " | |
| " | William Little | Died 1 Aug '83 | " | " | " | |
| " | William Linch | | " | " | " | |
| " | John Love, 1st | | " | " | " | |
| " | John Lee, 1st | | " | " | " | |
| " | Thomas Lewis | Dischd. 13 Jan '82 | " | " | | |
| " | Michael Loller | | " | " | " | |
| " | John Linday | | " | | | |
| " | John Lynch, 2nd | | " | " | " | |
| " | Alexander Levi | | " | " | " | |
| " | Robert Legg | [Dischd. 29 Nov '83] | " | " | " | |
| " | Barney Lemmon | Dischd. 14 Apl '83 | " | " | | |
| " | John Linken | [Dischd. 26 Oct '83] | " | " | " | |
| " | Joseph Long | | " | " | " | |
| " | John Lowry | Dischd. 28 Apl '81 | " | | | |
| " | Joshua Liester | | " | " | " | |
| " | William Leakins | | " | " | " | |
| Serjt. | David Love | | " | " | " | |
| Private | John Loveday | Died Aug '83 | " | " | " | |
| " | John Lewin | | " | " | " | |
| " | Francis Lang | | " | " | " | |
| " | Christopher Lambert | | " | " | " | |
| " | George Linton | | " | " | " | |
| " | Paul Lapine | | " | " | " | |
| " | Dudley Lee | | " | " | " | |
| " | William Lucas | Killed 1 Oct '82 | " | " | | |
| " | Theopilus Lindsay | | " | " | " | |
| Serjt. | John Lomax | Dischd. 6 Jan '81 | " | | | |
| Private | Darby Lanahan | " 1 Feb '83 | " | " | | |
| " | Thomas Laramore | | " | " | " | |
| " | Charles Leago | Dischd. 1 Apl '83 | " | " | | |
| Serjt. | Jacob Lowe | " 21 Feb '81 | " | | | |
| Private | Kinsey Lanham | Died 20 Dec '82 | " | " | | |
| " | Joseph Lewis, 2nd | [Dischd .29 Nov '83] | " | " | " | |
| " | John Lynch, 3rd | | " | " | " | |
| " | John Lestley | lives in Georgetown | " | " | " | |
| " | William Lee, 2nd | [Dischd. 7 Sept '83] | " | " | " | |

| RANK. | NAMES. | REMARKS. | SERVED BETWEEN 1 AUG '80 AND 1 JAN '82. | SERVED BETWEEN 1 JAN '82 AND 1 JAN '83. | SERVED BETWEEN 1 JAN '83 AND 15 NOV '83. | SERVED BETWEEN 15 NOV '83 AND 10 JULY '84. |
|---|---|---|---|---|---|---|
| Private | Thomas Long | [Dischd. 29 Nov '83] | " | " | " | |
| " | John Lonass | Died 2 Oct '82 | " | " | | |
| " | Nehemiah Lingard | [Dischd. 29 Nov '83] | " | " | " | |
| " | Timothy Langrill | | " | " | " | |
| " | Jesse Locker | | " | " | " | |
| " | William Little | | " | | | |
| " | William Lee, 1st | | | " | " | |
| " | John Lashly | supposed John Lessley | | " | | |
| " | Charles Love | | | " | " | |
| " | John Lowe | | | " | " | |
| " | John Long | | | " | " | |
| Fifer | William Lawrence | [Dischd. 23 Sept '83] | | " | " | |
| Private | James Lowrey | [Dischd. 9 Sept '83] | | " | " | |
| Serjt. | Theophilus Lomax | | " | " | " | " |
| Private | Edward Legg | | | | " | |
| Drum. | Thomas Loveday | | | | " | |
| Private | Zachariah Lyles | Died 18 June '81 | " | | | |
| " | Dennis Leary | | | | " | |
| Private | Michael Miller | | " | " | " | |
| " | John Majors | Dischd. 15 Feb '81 | " | | | |
| " | Darby Maclamar | | " | " | " | |
| Serjt. | Richard Mudd | Dischd. 9 Jan '82 | " | " | | |
| F. M. | John Martindale | | " | " | " | |
| Serjt. | Peter McNorton | [Dischd. 29 Nov '83] | " | " | " | |
| Fifer | John Morrison | | " | " | " | |
| Corpl. | Walter Miles | Dischd. 1 Apl '83 | " | " | | |
| Private | Gilford Minike | " 16 Jan '83 | " | " | | |
| " | William Maglocklin | | " | " | " | |
| Drum. | Christopher Magraw | | " | " | " | |
| Private | James Mason | | " | " | " | |
| " | William Moore, 1st | | " | " | " | |
| " | William Mann, 2nd | Dischd. 19 Mch '81 | " | | | |
| " | James Magraw | " 15 Feb '81 | " | | | |
| Corpl. | Frederick C. Miles | " 1 May '81 | " | | | |
| Private | Richard Mitchell | | " | " | " | |
| " | William Moore, 2nd | | " | " | " | |
| " | John Martin, 1st | | " | " | " | |
| " | Cornelius Maglocklin | | " | " | " | |
| Serjt. | Charles Murphy | | " | " | " | |
| Private | William Macall | | " | " | " | |
| " | Charles McGee | | " | " | " | |
| " | John Morris | Dischd. 10 June '81 | " | | | |
| " | Valentine Murray | " 19 June '81 | " | | | |
| " | John Matthews, 1st | Invalided 15 Nov '83 | " | " | " | |

| RANK. | NAMES. | REMARKS. | SERVED BETWEEN 1 AUG '80 AND 1 JAN '82. | SERVED BETWEEN 1 JAN '82 AND 1 JAN '83. | SERVED BETWEEN 1 JAN '83 AND 15 NOV '83. | SERVED BETWEEN 15 NOV '83 AND 10 JULY '84. |
|---|---|---|---|---|---|---|
| Private | Jonathan Mahugh | Dischd. 9 Jan '82 | " | " | | |
| " | Matthew Moore, 1st | | " | " | " | |
| Corpl. | John Mills, 1st | Dischd. 14 Apl '83 | " | " | | |
| Private | William Mitchell | | " | " | " | |
| " | John McCann | | " | " | " | |
| " | Jacob Moses, 1st | | | | " | |
| " | Patrick Mahorn | | " | " | " | |
| " | Matthew Moore, 2nd | | " | " | " | |
| " | Humphrey Menchen | Died 15 July '81 | " | | | |
| " | Thomas Murphy | | " | " | " | |
| " | Christopher McAway | | " | " | " | |
| " | James Mathias | Dischd. 3 Apl '81 | " | | | |
| Serjt. | Hugh McMillen | | " | " | " | |
| D. M. | James Mead | | " | " | " | |
| Private | Benj. McHaffe | Killed 18 June '81 | " | | | |
| " | John McCay | | " | " | " | |
| " | William Marshall | Dischd. 3 Mch '83 | " | " | | |
| " | George Mantle | | " | " | " | |
| " | Robert Matthews | Dischd. 10 May '81 | " | | | |
| " | Thomas McCernon | " 1 Feb '81 | " | | | |
| Serjt. | John Mantle | " 14 Feb '83 | " | " | | |
| Private | Benj. Moran | Died 2 Feb '82 | " | " | | |
| " | Michael McCann | | " | " | " | |
| Corpl. | James Maxwell | | " | " | " | |
| Private | William Moore, 3rd | | " | " | " | |
| " | John Martin, 2nd | Killed 15 Feb '81 | " | | | |
| " | William Matthews, 1st | | | | " | |
| Drum. | Boston Medler | | " | " | " | |
| Private | William Mann, 1st | | " | " | " | |
| " | John Moore, 1st | [Dischd. 29 Nov '83] | " | " | " | |
| " | Christopher Miers | Died 13 Oct '81 | " | | | |
| " | John McGlochlin | " 1 Mch '81 | " | | | |
| " | Andrew Moore | " 15 Mch '81 | " | | | |
| Serjt. | Charles McNabb | | " | " | " | |
| Private | James Managa | | " | " | " | |
| " | Joseph Murphy | | " | " | " | |
| " | Peter McGuire | | " | " | " | |
| " | John McNelley | | " | " | " | |
| Serjt. | Enoch McLane | | " | " | " | |
| Private | John Maxwell, 1st | | " | " | " | |
| " | William Moad | | " | " | " | |
| " | John Mick, (Meek) | [Dischd. 29 Nov '83] | " | " | " | |
| " | Neale Morris | | " | " | " | |
| " | John Mills, 2nd | | " | " | " | |
| " | Joseph Mattingly | Dischd. 1 Feb '83 | " | " | | |

| RANK. | NAMES. | REMARKS. | SERVED BETWEEN 1 AUG '80 AND 1 JAN '82. | SERVED BETWEEN 1 JAN '82 AND 1 JAN '83. | SERVED BETWEEN 1 JAN '83 AND 15 NOV '83. | SERVED BETWEEN 15 NOV '83 AND 10 JULY '84. |
|---|---|---|---|---|---|---|
| Serjt. | Arthur McLain | Dischd. 10 Feb '83 | " | " | | |
| Private | Nicholas Milburn | | " | " | " | |
| Corpl. | William Martin | Died 31 Dec '82 | " | " | | |
| " | William McNeal | | " | " | " | |
| Serjt. | Samuel McConnel | Dischd. 9 June '81 | " | | | |
| Private | Joseph McNamara | Dischd. 25 July '83 | " | " | " | |
| " | James McDonnald | [Dischd. 9 Sept '83] | " | " | " | |
| Corpl. | Thomas Matthews, 1st | | " | " | " | |
| Private | Timothy McLamar | Killed 18 June '81 | " | | | |
| " | John McGinnis | [Dischd. 29 Nov '83] | " | " | " | |
| Serjt. | Jeremiah Mudd | Dischd. 1 Aug '83 | " | " | " | |
| Corpl. | Issacher Mason | | " | " | " | |
| Private | John Matthews, 2nd | Dischd. 16 Feb '82 | " | " | | |
| " | William Manley | | " | " | " | |
| " | Henry Mansfield | | " | " | " | |
| " | John Moore, 2nd | | " | " | " | |
| " | John C. Miller | | " | " | " | |
| " | Michael McGower | Killed 8 Sept '81 | " | | | |
| " | Jacob Myers | | | " | " | " |
| " | Joseph McAtlee | Died Aug '83 | " | " | " | |
| " | Jesse McKinsey | [Dischd. 9 Aug '83] | " | " | " | |
| " | Roderick McKinsey | | " | " | " | " |
| " | John McNeal | [Dischd. 29 Nov '83] | " | " | " | |
| " | John Moore, 4th | | " | " | " | |
| " | Adam Musler | | " | " | " | " |
| " | John McCall | | " | " | " | |
| " | David Meadows | | " | " | " | " |
| " | Aaron Mitchell | | " | " | " | |
| " | Aliard Melvin | | " | " | " | |
| " | Robert Mitchell | [Corpl., Dischd. 29 Nov '83] | " | " | " | |
| " | Daniel Murphy | | " | " | " | |
| " | Francis McCann | [Dischd. 29 Nov '83] | " | " | " | |
| " | John Morris, 2nd | | " | " | " | |
| " | John Mills, 3rd | | " | " | " | |
| " | John Moore, 3rd | Dischd. 12 Jan '83 | " | " | | |
| " | John Murray, 1st | | " | " | " | |
| Serjt. | John McDonald | | " | " | " | |
| Fifer | John McNight | | " | " | " | |
| Private | Edward Mahony | | " | " | " | |
| Corpl. | James Murphy | Invalided 10 July '81 | " | was dischd. from Invalids 16 Jan '80 | | |
| Private | George McCauley | Dischd. 28 Jan '81 | " | | | |
| " | Thomas McCauley | "     28 Jan '81 | " | | | |
| " | Hezekiah Massey | "     31 Dec '82 | " | " | | |

| RANK. | NAMES. | REMARKS. | SERVED BETWEEN 1 AUG '80 AND 1 JAN '82. | SERVED BETWEEN 1 JAN '82 AND 1 JAN '83. | SERVED BETWEEN 1 JAN '83 AND 15 NOV '83. | SERVED BETWEEN 15 NOV '83 AND 10 JULY '84. |
|---|---|---|---|---|---|---|
| Private | Benjamin Marsh | | " | " | " | |
| " | John McCoy, 1st | Dischd. 14 Feb '82 | " | " | | |
| Serjt. | William Marlow | | " | " | " | |
| " | Timothy McMahon | Died June '83 | | " | " | |
| Fifer | John McDonald | Dischd. 1 June '83 | " | " | " | |
| Private | Luke Merryman | | " | " | " | |
| Drum. | John McCaliff | [Dischd. 29 Nov '83] | " | " | " | |
| Private | William Mansfield | [Dischd. 29 Nov '83] | " | " | " | |
| " | Michael McGuire | Dischd. 9 Sept '82 | " | " | | |
| " | John Maglin | [Dischd. 29 Nov '83] | " | " | " | |
| " | Daniel Mann | | " | " | " | |
| " | Peter Melvin | | " | " | | |
| " | John McClaine | [Dischd. 7 Sept '83] | " | " | | |
| " | John Moore, 5th | | " | " | | |
| " | Thomas Matthews, 2nd | [Dischd. 11 Sept '83] | " | " | " | |
| " | Joshua McKinsey | | " | " | " | |
| " | Moses McKinsey | | " | " | " | |
| Serjt. | Francis McGauran | | " | " | " | |
| Private | Thomas Mahony | Died 3 Apl '81 | " | | | |
| " | Stephen McGraw | " 19 Mch '81 | " | | | |
| " | Jacob Moses, 2nd | " 15 Mch '81 | " | | | |
| " | Patrick McKinsey | | " | " | " | |
| " | John McBride | | " | " | " | |
| " | Thomas McKinsey | | " | " | " | |
| " | Thomas Mahoney | Died 28 Aug '82 | " | " | | |
| " | Zachariah Mills | | " | " | " | |
| " | Abraham Maning | | " | " | " | |
| " | Patrick Molohon | | | " | " | |
| " | William McPherson | | | " | " | |
| " | Levi Moody | Died 15 Oct '82 | | " | | |
| " | Lawrence Mesler | | | " | " | |
| " | Thomas McHandy | Died 28 Aug '82 | | " | | |
| " | Daniel McCollom | | " | " | " | |
| " | Thomas McQuinny | | " | " | " | |
| " | Bennet Meakins | | " | " | " | |
| " | William Madden | | " | " | " | |
| " | Alexander McGrigger | | " | " | " | |
| " | Jacob Mifford | | " | " | " | |
| Corpl. | Benjamin McCaull | | " | " | " | |
| Private | Thomas McDowell | | " | " | " | |
| " | Isaac McFaddon | | " | " | " | |
| " | Robert McClary | | " | " | " | |
| ' | William Mathews, 2nd | | " | " | " | |
| " | James Morris, 1st | [Dischd. 29 Nov '83] | " | " | " | |
| " | John McElroy | [Dischd. 29 Nov '83] | " | " | " | |

| RANK. | NAMES. | REMARKS. | SERVED BETWEEN 1 AUG '80 AND 1 JAN '82. | SERVED BETWEEN 1 JAN '82 AND 1 JAN '83. | SERVED BETWEEN 1 JAN '83 AND 15 NOV '83. | SERVED BETWEEN 15 NOV '83 AND 10 JULY '84. |
|---|---|---|---|---|---|---|
| Private | Zachariah Moore | [Serjt., Dischd. 7 Sept '83] | | " | " | |
| " | Lewis McCullough | | | " | " | |
| " | Isom Moore | | | " | " | |
| " | Charles Messick | Died 22 Oct '83 | | | " | |
| " | George Miller | | | " | " | |
| " | Isaac Mitchell | | | " | " | " |
| " | Joseph McCollester | Died 24 Mch '83 | | " | | |
| " | Richard McDonald | | | | " | |
| " | John Munford | | | | " | |
| " | John Misseral | | | | " | |
| " | John Moran | | | | | |
| " | Thomas Mec | | " | " | " | |
| " | John Milstead | | " | " | " | " |
| " | Thomas Maloney | Wounded 15 Mch '81 | " | | | |
| " | Nicholas McNamara | | | | " | |
| Serjt. | Bennet Mudd | Dischd. 6 Nov '81 | " | | | |
| Serjt. | Nicholas Nicholson | Dischd. 1 Apl '83 | " | " | | |
| " | John Navey | "        23 Mch '83 | " | " | | |
| Corpl. | Henry Nicholson | | " | " | " | |
| Serjt. | Stephen Nicholson | | " | " | " | |
| Private | William Newton | | " | " | " | |
| " | Morris Neigle | | " | " | " | |
| " | Asabel Nichols | Dischd. 10 Apl '81 | " | | | |
| " | Richard Neilson | Died 15 Mch '81 | " | | | |
| Serjt. | William A. Needham | | " | " | " | |
| Fifer | Joseph Nabb | | " | " | " | |
| Private | William Nailor | | " | " | " | |
| Fifer | James Newell | | " | " | " | |
| Private | Isaac Nichols | | " | " | | |
| " | John Neighbours | Dischd. 1 Feb '83 | " | " | | |
| " | Basil Norman | | " | " | " | |
| " | William Niblet | | " | " | " | |
| " | John Newton, 1st | | " | " | " | |
| " | Charles Nabb | | " | " | " | |
| " | John Nelson | | " | " | " | |
| " | John Newton, 2nd | Dischd. 1 Feb '83 | " | " | | |
| " | Patrick Noland | Died 1 Sept '82 | " | " | | |
| " | Michael Noland | Dischd. 1 Mch '81 | " | | | |
| " | John Nevit, 2nd | [Corpl., Dischd. 29 Nov '83] | " | " | " | |
| " | Joseph Neal | [Dischd. 29 Nov '83 | " | " | " | |
| " | John Nicholson | | " | " | " | |
| " | John Nave | | " | " | " | |
| " | John Noland | | | | " | " |

| Rank. | Names. | Remarks. | Served Between 1 Aug '80 and 1 Jan '82. | Served Between 1 Jan '82 and 1 Jan '83. | Served Between 1 Jan '83 and 15 Nov '83. | Served Between 15 Nov '83 and 10 July '84. |
|---|---|---|---|---|---|---|
| Private | Basil Newman | [Newton, Dischd. 29 Nov '83] | | " | " | |
| " | John Nicholson | | | " | " | |
| " | Leonard Nable | | | " | " | |
| " | Thomas Newman | [Dischd. 9 Sept '83] | | | " | |
| " | Thomas Neale | Died 15 Mch '81 | " | | | |
| | | | | | | |
| Private | Leonard Outerbridge | Dischd. 25 Apl '81 | " | | | |
| " | John Osborn | | " | " | " | |
| " | Joseph Overcreek | [Dischd. 29 Nov '83] | " | " | " | |
| " | Daniel O'Quinn | | " | " | " | |
| " | Samuel Oram | Died 1 Sept '81 | " | | | |
| " | Stephen Owens | | " | " | " | |
| " | James Owens | | " | " | " | |
| " | Charles Orms | | " | " | " | |
| " | Henry Osten | | " | " | " | |
| " | John O'Bryan | Died 25 April '81 | " | | | |
| Fifer | John Onions | | " | " | " | |
| Private | Peter Outhouse | [Dischd. 29 Nov '83] | " | " | " | " |
| " | Elijah Oakley | | | " | " | |
| " | Dennis O'Bryan | | | " | " | |
| " | Paris Owens | | | " | " | |
| " | Elisha Osborn | [Dischd. 29 Nov '83] | | " | " | |
| " | Dorden Orrell | | | | " | |
| " | Stephen Olinger | | | " | | |
| " | Samuel Owens | | | | " | " |
| | | | | | | |
| Private | George Parker | | " | " | " | |
| Serjt. | Nathan Peak | Dischd. 14 Nov '82 | " | " | | |
| Private | William Poland | | " | " | " | |
| " | Simon Perry | | " | " | " | |
| " | William Pherson | | " | " | " | |
| " | John Pickering | Killed 18 June '81 | " | | | |
| " | Henry Phillips | Dischd. 1 May '81 | " | | | |
| | Cupid Plummer | " 27 May '81 | " | | | |
| | Obediah Plummer | " 27 May '81 | " | | | |
| Drum. | Aquilla Pierce | | " | " | " | |
| Corpl. | William Purchase | | " | " | " | |
| Drum. | John Peany | [Dischd. 29 Nov '83] | " | " | " | |
| Private | George Patrick | Dischd. 23 Feb '83 | " | " | | |
| " | Stephen Preston | [Dischd. 11 Aug '83] | " | " | " | |
| " | Richard Proctor | | " | " | " | |
| " | William Peters | | " | " | " | |
| " | William Pursell | | " | " | " | |
| " | William Prior | Died 15 Feb '81 | " | | | |

| RANK. | NAMES. | REMARKS. | SERVED BETWEEN 1 AUG '80 AND 1 JAN '82. | SERVED BETWEEN 1 JAN '82 AND 1 JAN '83. | SERVED BETWEEN 1 JAN '83 AND 15 NOV '83. | SERVED BETWEEN 15 NOV '83 AND 10 JULY '84. |
|---|---|---|---|---|---|---|
| Private | William Pecker | | “ | “ | “ | |
| Drum. | Joseph Purdy | | “ | “ | “ | |
| Private | James Pool | | “ | “ | “ | |
| “ | Gabriel Peters | Dischd. 8 Apl '81 | “ | | | |
| “ | George Pierce | | “ | “ | “ | |
| Serjt. | Stephen Price | | “ | “ | “ | |
| Private | John Purdy | Dischd. 22 Jan '83 | “ | “ | | |
| “ | Henry Purdy | “ 14 Feb '83 | “ | “ | | |
| “ | George Philips | Died 15 Apl '81 | “ | | | |
| “ | Neale Peacock | | “ | “ | “ | |
| Serjt. | John Peace | Dischd. 28 Apl '81 | “ | | | |
| Private | Elijah Pepper | | “ | “ | “ | |
| “ | Thomas Peacock | Killed 8 Sept '81 | “ | | | |
| “ | Jesse Powers | Dischd. 19 July '83 | “ | “ | “ | |
| “ | Thomas Phipps. | “ 4 May '81 | “ | | | |
| “ | Samuel Pheasent | “ 8 Mch '81 | “ | | | |
| “ | John Pope | | | “ | “ | |
| “ | James Philips | Dischd. 1 Aug '83 | “ | “ | “ | |
| “ | Thomas Pender | | “ | “ | “ | |
| “ | Thomas Pennyfield | | “ | “ | “ | |
| “ | Lambert Philips | | “ | “ | “ | |
| “ | George Plumley | Dischd. 31 Dec '82 | “ | “ | | |
| “ | Thomas Patterson | | “ | “ | “ | |
| “ | Nathaniel Price [Serjt] | [Dischd. 29 Nov '83] | “ | “ | “ | |
| “ | Thomas Perry | | “ | “ | “ | |
| Corpl. | William Priest | [Dischd. 29 Nov '83] | | | “ | |
| Private | Joshua Pierce | | “ | “ | “ | |
| | Michael Pilkerton | | “ | “ | “ | |
| Corpl. | Joseph Pherson | | “ | “ | “ | |
| Fifer | William Prater | [Dischd. 29 Nov '83] | “ | “ | “ | |
| Private | William Paul | | “ | “ | “ | |
| “ | Thomas Porter | | “ | “ | “ | |
| “ | Robert Pennington | | | “ | “ | |
| “ | William Patterson | | | “ | “ | |
| “ | Charles Palmore | | | “ | “ | “ |
| “ | Samuel Palmer | | | “ | “ | “ |
| “ | John Philips | | | “ | “ | |
| Corpl. | Benjamin Prior | | | “ | “ | “ |
| “ | William Potter | | | “ | “ | |
| Private | William Porter | ᵗ. | “ | “ | “ | |
| “ | William Powell | | | “ | “ | |
| “ | Lawrence Pines | | | | “ | |
| “ | Joseph } James } Proctor | [Dischd. 29 Nov '83] | | “ | “ | |
| “ | Francis Pursley | [Dischd. 29 Nov '83] | | “ | “ | |

| RANK. | NAMES. | REMARKS. | SERVED BETWEEN 1 AUG '80 AND 1 JAN '82. | SERVED BETWEEN 1 JAN '82 AND 1 JAN '83. | SERVED BETWEEN 1 JAN '83 AND 15 NOV '83. | SERVED BETWEEN 15 NOV '83 AND 10 JULY '84. |
|---|---|---|---|---|---|---|
| Corpl. | Samuel Perry | | | | | |
| Private | Thomas Proctor | | | | | |
| " | William Pagram | | " | " | " | |
| " | Thomas Pettit | [Dischd. 29 Nov '83] | " | " | " | " |
| " | Arthur Pritchet | | | | " | |
| " | Thomas Polhouse | Dischd. 4 Nov '81 | " | | | |
| Serjt. | John Quick | | " | • | " | " |
| Private | Joseph Quinn | Invalided 15 Nov '83 | " | " | " | |
| " | William Quinton | | " | " | " | |
| Private | Patrick Quynn | [Dischd. 29 Nov '83] | " | " | " | |
| " | William Rowles | Dischd. 1 May '81 | " | | | |
| " | William Rogers | Invalided 15 Nov '83 | " | " | " | |
| " | William Roberts, 1st | Dischd. 15 May '81 | " | | | |
| " | Charles Robinson | Invalided 15 Nov '83 | " | " | " | |
| Drum. | William Roberts, 3rd | | " | " | " | |
| Private | Joseph Rhea | | " | " | " | |
| " | Patrick Rowan | | " | " | " | |
| " | Andrew Riggs | Dischd. 10 Feb '81 | " | | | |
| " | Edward Richardson | "        14 July '82 | " | " | | |
| " | Paul Richards | | " | " | " | |
| " | John Rock | Dischd. 2 May '81 | " | | | |
| " | William Rock | "        2 May '81 | " | | | |
| " | Jeremiah Rhodes | "        17 Feb '81 | " | " | | |
| " | Adam Rains | "        24 May '81 | " | | | |
| " | James Reily | Killed 17 Jan '81 | " | | | |
| " | John Robinson | Dischd. 1 May '81 | " | | | |
| " | Edward Roberts | | " | " | " | |
| " | James Ruark | | " | " | " | |
| " | John Richardson | | " | " | " | |
| " | Henry Redding, Sr. | | " | " | " | |
| " | Henry Ramsey | | " | " | " | |
| " | Robart Richardson | Dischd. 15 Feb '81 | " | | | |
| " | Joseph Roberts | | " | " | " | |
| " | Thomas Redman | Dischd. 1 Apl '81 | " | | | |
| " | Benedict Reynolds | "        28 July '81 | " | | | |
| " | Bennet Rawlings | "        18 June '81 | " | | | |
| Drum. | James Reynolds, 1st | | " | " | " | |
| | Thomas Richardson, 1st | | " | " | " | |
| Private | Robert Rice | Dischd. 26 Apl '81 | " | | | |
| " | William Rice | | " | " | " | |
| " | Alexander Ross | | " | " | " | |
| " | Patrick Riely, 1st | [Dischd. 3 Oct '83] | " | " | " | |
| Fifer | John Riggs | [Dischd.18 Sept '83] | " | " | " | |
| Private | Henry Reese | | " | " | " | |

| RANK. | NAMES. | REMARKS. | SERVED BETWEEN 1 AUG '80 AND 1 JAN '82. | SERVED BETWEEN 1 JAN '82 AND 1 JAN '83. | SERVED BETWEEN 1 JAN '83 AND 15 NOV '83. | SERVED BETWEEN 15 NOV '83 AND 10 JULY '84. |
|---|---|---|---|---|---|---|
| Private | Andrew Russell | | " | " | " | |
| Serjt. | Charles Reynolds | Died 15 July '81 | " | | | |
| Private | Patrick Reily, 2nd | | " | " | " | |
| " | John Robins | | " | " | " | |
| " | Aaron Rawlings | | " | " | " | |
| Serjt. | John Reeder | | " | " | " | |
| Private | Charles Riddle | Died 15 June '81 | " | | | |
| " | John Romills | | " | " | " | |
| " | Robinson Ross | | " | " | " | |
| " | James Reynolds, 2nd | [Dischd. 9 Sept '83] | " | " | " | |
| " | Francis Reed | | " | " | " | |
| " | Alexander Robinson | | " | " | " | |
| " | Zachariah Robinson | | " | " | " | |
| " | Samuel Richardson | | " | " | " | |
| " | John Ryan | | | | " | |
| " | Adam Rider | | | | " | |
| " | Christopher Ronemberger | | " | " | " | |
| " | Michael Rhydmyer | Dischd. 13 Feb '83 | " | " | | |
| " | John Roach | | " | " | " | |
| " | William Rider | | " | " | " | |
| " | John Ransom | | " | " | " | |
| " | Paul Roan | | " | " | " | |
| " | William Rue | | " | " | " | |
| " | Horatio Roberts | Died 1 Mch '81 | " | | | |
| " | Edward Riely | Dischd. 3 June '83 | " | " | " | |
| " | Alex. Rutherford | " 1 Jan '83 | " | " | | |
| " | William Richardson | " 1 Apl '82 | " | | | |
| Serjt. | William Rose | | " | " | | |
| Private | Andrew Reveside | Died 16 Dec '82 | " | | | |
| " | Nathaniel Ross | | | " | " | |
| " | John Reed | | | " | " | |
| " | John Rodgers | | | " | " | |
| " | Thomas Richardson, 2nd | | | " | " | |
| " | Joseph Rose | | | " | " | |
| " | Richard Rivers | | | " | " | |
| " | James Roe | [Dischd. 29 Nov '83] | | " | " | |
| " | Hugh Roney | [Dischd. 11 Aug '83] | | " | " | |
| " | James Rose | | | " | | |
| " | Christopher Raynor | Dischd. 10 Apl '83 | | " | | |
| " | Zadock Risden | [Dischd. 18 Sept '83] | | " | " | " |
| " | Edward Rowan | | | | " | " |
| " | Christopher Reed | Dischd. 1 Jan '81 | | " | " | " |
| " | William Robinson | | | | " | |
| " | George Riggs | | | | " | |
| " | Michael Redman | | | | | |

36

| RANK. | NAMES. | REMARKS. | SERVED BETWEEN 1 AUG '80 AND 1 JAN '82. | SERVED BETWEEN 1 JAN '82 AND 1 JAN '83. | SERVED BETWEEN 1 JAN '83 AND 15 NOV '83. | SERVED BETWEEN 15 NOV '83 AND 10 JULY '84. |
|---|---|---|---|---|---|---|
| Private | James Ryan, (Peter ?) | [Dischd. 29 Nov '83] | " | " | " | |
| Serjt. | John Radery | Shot 1 Sept '81 | " | | | |
| Serjt. | Peter Smith | | " | " | " | |
| Private | William Smith | Dischd. 18 June '81 | " | | | |
| " | Thomas Saunders | "   1 Aug '81 | " | | | |
| " | William Sikes | | " | " | " | |
| " | William Smith | Dischd. 8 Feb '81 | " | | | |
| " | Charles Scott | | " | " | " | |
| " | John Snelling | Dischd. 2 Aug '81 | " | | | |
| " | John Smith, 2nd | | " | " | " | |
| Serjt. | Humphry Spencer | | " | " | " | |
| " | Jesse Suit | [Dischd. 11 Sept '83] | " | " | " | |
| Private | John Salmon | | " | " | " | |
| " | James Shane | [Dischd. 29 Nov '83] | " | " | " | |
| " | John Shovel | | " | " | " | |
| | Anthony Smith | Dischd. 1 Apl '81 | " | | | |
| Serjt. | Robert Scribner | Died 15 Feb '83 | " | " | | |
| Private | David Smith | Dischd. 1 Mch '81 | " | | | |
| Serjt. | Aaron Spalding | | " | " | " | |
| Private | Thomas Stokes | Killed 8 Sept '81 | " | | | |
| " | Noah Sears | Died 3 Apl '83 | " | " | | |
| " | James Smith, 2nd | 3rd Regt. | " | " | " | |
| Corpl. | John Smith, 4th | | " | " | " | |
| Private | Leonard Swan | Dischd. 1 May '81 | " | | | |
| Drum. | John Scott | | " | " | " | |
| Corpl. | Jesse Simms | Dischd. 20 Mch '83 | " | " | | |
| Drum. | William Smith, 2nd | | " | " | " | |
| Private | Conrod Smith | | " | " | " | |
| " | Thomas Slade | | " | " | " | |
| " | Thomas Smith | Dischd. 13 May '81 | " | | | |
| " | James Stewart, 2nd | Died June '83 | " | " | " | |
| " | Reubin Smith | Died 9 May '83 | " | " | " | |
| " | Elijah Smith | | " | " | " | |
| " | William Sinclair | | " | " | " | |
| " | Andrew Stewart | Dischd. 1 Aug '81 | " | | | |
| Serjt. | Levi Smith | | " | " | " | |
| Private | Daniel Smith, 1st | | " | " | " | |
| " | William Sullivan | | " | " | " | |
| Corpl. | John Smith, 1st | | " | " | " | |
| Private | Perry Sullivan | | " | " | " | |
| Serjt. | Thomas Sappington | Dischd. 12 Feb '82 | " | " | | |
| Private | Roger Shorter | | " | " | " | |
| Corpl. | William Sharp | Dischd. 1 Mch '81 | " | | | |
| Private | Solomon Summers | | " | " | " | |

| RANK. | NAMES. | REMARKS. | SERVED BETWEEN 1 AUG '80 AND 1 JAN '82. | SERVED BETWEEN 1 JAN '82 AND 1 JAN '83. | SERVED BETWEEN 1 JAN '83 AND 15 NOV '83. | SERVED BETWEEN 15 NOV '83 AND 10 JULY '84. |
|---|---|---|---|---|---|---|
| Private | George Saunders | | " | " | " | |
| Corpl. | Robert Sharpless | | " | " | " | |
| Drum. | Alexander Stevenson | | " | " | " | |
| Private | John Summers | | " | " | " | |
| " | William Stonestreet | | " | " | " | |
| " | William Simmonds | Dischd. 1 July '83 | " | " | " | |
| " | Joseph Sloop | | " | " | " | |
| " | James Sewall | [Dischd. 29 Nov '83] | " | " | " | |
| " | Thomas Smith, 1st | | " | " | " | |
| " | Michael Standley | | " | " | " | |
| " | George Steem | | " | " | " | |
| " | John Stackhouse | Dischd. 4 May '83 | " | " | | |
| " | Michael Sours | " 6 May '83 | " | " | | |
| " | James Smith, 3rd | 7th Regt. | " | " | " | |
| " | Charles Simpkins | | " | " | " | |
| Drum. | Abraham Stallions | | " | " | " | |
| Private | Aquilla Smith | Dischd. 2 June '81 | " | | | |
| Corpl. | Peter Stephens | | " | " | " | |
| " | Daniel Smith, 2nd | | " | " | " | |
| " | William Sly | Dischd. 1 May '81 | " | | | |
| Private | Jeremiah Sullivan | " 12 Mch '83 | " | " | | |
| " | Christopher Seymore | | " | " | " | |
| " | James Sullivan | | " | " | " | |
| " | John Smith, 3rd | [Dischd. 29 Nov '83] | " | " | " | |
| " | Leonard Smith | Dischd. 26 July '83 | " | " | " | |
| " | John Shanks | Invalided 15 Nov '83 | " | " | " | |
| " | Bennet Shirley | | " | " | " | |
| " | John Smallwood, 2nd | | " | " | " | |
| Serjt. | Richard Smith | Dischd. 1 June '83 | " | " | " | |
| Private | Alexander Stewart | " 1 Aug '83 | " | " | " | |
| " | Samuel Scott | " 20 June '83 | " | " | " | |
| " | Job Sylvester | | " | " | " | |
| Drum. | Levi Scott | | " | " | " | |
| Private | Robert Streets | | " | " | " | |
| " | William Stirling | [Dischd. 11 Aug '83] | " | " | " | |
| " | Benjamin Smith | Dischd. 1 Aug '83 | " | " | " | |
| " | John Smallwood, 1st | | " | " | " | |
| " | John Starkey | [Dischd. 18 Sept '83] | " | " | " | |
| " | James Shepherd | | " | " | " | |
| " | James Stewart, 1st | Died 1 Dec '82 | " | " | | |
| " | John Spires | [Dischd. 29 Nov '83] | " | " | " | |
| " | Charles Sickle | | " | " | " | |
| " | Solomon Sollovan | | " | " | " | |
| " | Richard Spires | | " | " | " | |
| " | John Shefer | | " | " | " | |

| Rank. | Names. | Remarks. | Served between 1 Aug '80 and 1 Jan '82. | Served between 1 Jan '82 and 1 Jan '83. | Served between 1 Jan '83 and 15 Nov '83. | Served between 15 Nov '83 and 10 July '84. |
|---|---|---|---|---|---|---|
| Private | Thomas Smith, 2nd | | " | " | " | |
| " | Salady Standly | [Dischd. 29 Nov '83] | " | " | " | |
| " | Luke Samson | | " | " | " | |
| " | John Smith | Died 15 July '81 | " | | | |
| " | Thomas Summers | | " | " | " | |
| " | Nathan Speake | Died 6 Oct '82 | " | " | | |
| " | William Silwood | | " | " | " | |
| " | Benj. Steward | | " | " | " | |
| " | Lawrence Simpson | [Dischd. 29 Nov '83] | " | " | " | |
| Drum. | William Steward | [Fifer, Dischd. 9 Sept '83] | " | " | " | |
| Private | George Silver | Dischd. 8 Mch '83 | " | " | | |
| " | John Stoffee | | " | " | " | |
| " | Frederick Stoffee | Died 16 Jan '82 | " | " | | |
| " | Joseph Smith | Dischd. 13 Aug '81 | " | | | |
| " | Philip Savoy | | " | " | " | |
| Fifer | Samuel Street | | " | " | " | |
| Private | Joseph Sidney | | " | " | " | |
| " | Elias Smith | | " | " | " | |
| " | Michael Smith, 2nd | | " | " | " | |
| " | Christopher Smith | | " | " | " | |
| " | Michael Smith, 1st | | " | " | " | |
| " | Samuel F. Shomaker | [Dischd. 15 Aug '83] | " | " | " | |
| " | John Stanton | | " | " | " | |
| " | Oliver Stephens | | " | " | " | |
| " | Caio Snowden | [Dischd. 29 Nov '83] | " | " | " | |
| Serjt. | Basil Shaw | [Dischd. 29 Nov '83] | " | " | " | |
| Corpl. | Edward Suit | Died 24 July '82 | " | " | | |
| Private | Murphy Shee | " 28 Jan '83 | " | " | | |
| " | Thomas Seondrick | | " | " | " | |
| " | Robert Shipley | Died 20 July '82 | " | " | | |
| " | Joseph Southall | | | | | |
| " | Thomas Sheriden | Time expires 26 Mch'84, to serve out for Thos. Duffy | | | | |
| | Walter B. Smallwood | | " | " | " | |
| " | William Shirley | Died 12 June '83 | | " | " | |
| " | William Standly | | " | " | " | |
| " | Ignatius Smith | Died 20 Apl '82 | | " | | |
| | James Sappington | [Dischd. 29 Nov '83] | " | " | " | |
| Serjt. | Jonathan Short | Died 26 Mch '82 | " | " | | |
| Private | Elijah Sullivan | | | " | " | |
| " | Daniel Stevens | [Dischd. 7 Sept '83] | | " | " | |
| | William Smith, 3rd | | | " | " | |

| RANK. | NAMES. | REMARKS. | SERVED BETWEEN 1 AUG '80 AND 1 JAN '82. | SERVED BETWEEN 1 JAN '82 AND 1 JAN '83. | SERVED BETWEEN 1 JAN '83 AND 15 NOV '83. | SERVED BETWEEN 15 NOV '83 AND 10 JULY '84. |
|---|---|---|---|---|---|---|
| Private | William Sena | | | " | " | |
| " | John Swails | | | " | " | |
| " | Thomas Sergo | | | " | " | |
| " | William Smallwood | | | " | " | |
| " | Thomas Sturgess | [Dischd. 11 Aug '83] | | | " | |
| ' | William Sewell | | | | " | |
| " | James, or Saml., Silk | | | | " | |
| " | Daniel Sullinger | | | " | " | |
| Serjt. | Josiah Smith | Died 15 July '81 | " | | | |
| Private | James Smith, 1st | Invalided 15 July '82 | " | " | | |
| " | Jacob Standley | "    1 Nov '83 | " | " | " | |
| " | William H. Savage | | " | " | " | |
| " | James Scott | | " | " | " | " |
| Corpl. | Charles Scondrick | Died 1 July '81 | " | | | |
| | Frederick Smith | | | " | " | |
| Private | Abraham Stockee | Died 1 Nov '82 | " | " | | |
| Corpl. | George Scone | • | " | " | " | |
| Private | William Sizeland | | | | " | |
| " | Edward Shoebrook | | | " | " | |
| " | William Snowden | [Dischd. 7 Sept '83] | | " | " | |
| Serjt. | Joseph H. Spencer | | | | " | " |
| Private | John Smithird | Dischd. 20 Apl '81 | " | | | |
| | William Smith | Killed 3 June '83 | | " | | |
| Private | Edward Timms | Dischd. 10 July '81 | " | | | |
| " | William Taylor, 1st | [Dischd. 18 Sept '83] | " | " | " | |
| " | John Tucker | Dischd. 21 Feb '83 | " | " | | |
| " | Notley Tippet | | | " | " | " |
| " | William Toland | | | " | " | " |
| " | Lambert Thompson | | | " | " | " |
| | Bartholomew Thompson | | | " | " | " |
| " | John Taylor, 1st | | | " | " | " |
| " | Peter Tippet | Died 15 Dec '81 | " | | | |
| " | James Thomas, Jr., 2nd | | | " | " | " |
| " | John Turner, 3rd | | | " | " | " |
| " | Richard Tasco | | | " | " | " |
| " | Henry Townley | | | " | " | " |
| " | Thomas Thompson | | | " | " | " |
| " | John Trusty | Died 17 July '81 | " | | | |
| " | Peter Topping | | | " | " | " |
| " | Dennis Trammill | Dischd. 31 May '83 | " | " | " | |
| " | John Taylor, 2nd | | " | " | " | |
| " | Evan Tumbleston | | " | " | " | |
| " | Cornelius Thompson | | " | " | " | |

| Rank. | Names. | Remarks. | Served between 1 Aug '80 and 1 Jan '82. | Served between 1 Jan '82 and 1 Jan '83. | Served between 1 Jan '83 and 15 Nov '83. | Served between 15 Nov '83 and 10 July '84. |
|---|---|---|---|---|---|---|
| Serjt. | Robert Taylor, 2nd | | " | " | " | |
| Private | George Taylor | | " | " | " | |
| " | William Taylor, 2nd | | " | " | " | |
| " | William Townsend | Dischd. 24 Apl '81 | " | | | |
| " | John Twiner | | " | " | " | |
| " | Samuel Taylor | Died 15 June '81 | " | | | |
| " | Richard Taylor | Dischd. 6 May '83 | " | " | " | |
| " | Francis Thompson | " 18 Apl '83 | | " | | |
| " | Solomon Turner | " 12 May '81 | " | | | |
| " | Thomas Tanner | Died 3 Jan '82 | " | | | |
| " | James Terry | [Dischd. 23 Sept '83] | " | " | " | |
| " | Giles Thomas | Dischd. 25 July '83 | " | " | " | |
| " | William Taylor, Jr., 3rd | | " | " | " | |
| Serjt. | James Thomas, Sr. | | " | " | " | |
| " | Allen Townsend | | " | " | " | |
| " | Levin Thomas | | " | " | " | " |
| " | James Tigner | | " | " | " | |
| | John Thompson, 1st | | " | " | " | |
| " | Edward Tanner | | " | " | " | |
| " | Thomas Thomas | | " | " | " | |
| " | John D. Tully | | " | " | | |
| " | John Thomas, 2nd | | " | " | " | |
| Serjt. | George Twinch | [Dischd. 29 Nov '83] | " | " | " | |
| Private | John Traverse | Deserted in '84 | " | " | " | " |
| Corpl. | Peter Teban | | | | | " |
| Private | Henry Tucker | Invalided 29 Mch '82 | " | " | | |
| " | John Turner, 2nd | | | " | " | |
| " | Francis Taylor | | | " | " | |
| | Benjamin Thompson | | | " | " | |
| " | Evan Thomas | | | " | " | |
| " | George Trice | | | " | " | |
| " | George Tate | | | " | " | " |
| " | Henry Tippet | [Dischd. 11 Aug '83] | | " | " | |
| M. S. | Thomas Twinch, 2nd | | | | " | |
| Private | Samuel Taylor | | | | | |
| " | John Thomas, 1st | | " | " | " | |
| " | James Tite | Died 1 Oct '82 | " | " | | |
| " | Samuel Tindell | Invalided 15 Aug '83 | " | " | " | |
| | Samuel Trig | Dischd. 18 Mch '82 | | " | | |
| " | John Timlon | " 28 Apl '81 | " | | | |
| " | Dennis Terney | | | | " | " |
| " | Joseph Thompson | | | | " | |
| " | Christopher Touch-stone | Died 8 Sept '81 | " | | | |
| " | Anthony Tucker | Killed 8 Sept '81 | " | | | |

| RANK. | NAMES. | REMARKS. | SERVED BETWEEN 1 AUG '80 AND 1 JAN '82. | SERVED BETWEEN 1 JAN '82 AND 1 JAN '83. | SERVED BETWEEN 1 JAN '83 AND 15 NOV '83. | SERVED BETWEEN 15 NOV '83 AND 10 JULY '84. |
|---|---|---|---|---|---|---|
| Private | John Vane | | | " | " | " |
| " | Cornelius Vaughan | | " | " | " | |
| " | William Vaughan | Dischd. 8 May '81 | " | | | |
| " | John Vincent | Died 25 Apl '81 | " | | | |
| " | Stephen Varlow | | " | " | " | |
| " | Samuel Vermillion | | " | " | " | |
| " | George Vernon | . Killed 8 Mch '81 | " | | | |
| " | Edward Vickers | | " | " | " | |
| " | John Vanzant | Invalided 15 Nov '83 | " | " | " | |
| " | John Varlow | | " | " | " | |
| | | | | | | |
| Private | John Willing | | " | " | " | |
| " | John Wade, 1st | | " | " | " | |
| " | Thomas Woolford | Dischd. 9 Nov '81 | " | | | |
| " | Edward Wade, 2nd | | " | " | " | |
| " | William Whaland | | " | " | " | |
| " | John Willis | [Dischd. 29 Nov '83] | " | " | " | |
| " | John Waller | | | | | |
| " | Jonathan Weedon | Died 13 Feb '83 | " | " | | |
| " | Thomas Wood | Dischd. 28 Jan '81 | " | | | |
| | Daniel Williams | "    1 Apl '83 | " | " | | |
| " | Nicholas Welch | | " | " | " | |
| | Benjamin Williams, 3rd | | " | " | " | |
| " | Thomas Wood, 3rd | | " | " | " | |
| Serjt. | Thomas Windham | | | | | |
| Private | Henry Williams | | " | " | | |
| " | John Williams | Dischd. 9 Jan '82 | " | " | | |
| " | George Ward | "    10 May '81 | " | | | |
| " | John Walker, Jr., 2nd | | " | " | " | |
| Fifer | John T. West | | " | " | " | |
| Private | Alexander West | Died 1 Nov '82 | " | " | | |
| " | Jonathan White | Invalided 13 Sept '81 | " | | | |
| " | Jesse Wright | | " | " | " | |
| " | John Welsh, 1st | [Dischd. 18 Sept '83] | " | " | " | |
| Fifer | David Williams | Dischd. 12 Apl '81 | " | | | |
| Private | William Wheatly | "    20 Apl '81 | " | | | |
| | Andrew Windgate | "    1 May '81 | " | | | |
| " | Thomas Wood, 1st | | " | " | " | |
| " | James Wilson, 1st | | " | " | " | |
| " | Thomas Wimber | | " | " | " | |
| " | York Waters | Dischd. 4 June '81 | " | | | |
| " | Thomas Wate | | " | " | " | |
| " | Robert Walker | [Dischd. 9 Sept '83] | " | " | " | |
| " | Michael Woolford | | " | " | " | |
| " | Frederick Willmott | | " | " | " | |

| RANK. | NAMES. | REMARKS. | SERVED BETWEEN 1 AUG '80 AND 1 JAN '82. | SERVED BETWEEN 1 JAN '82 AND 1 JAN '83. | SERVED BETWEEN 1 JAN '83 AND 15 NOV '83. | SERVED BETWEEN 15 NOV '83 AND 10 JULY '84. |
|---|---|---|---|---|---|---|
| Private | Thomas Watson | [Dischd. 29 Nov '83] | " | " | " | |
| " | Samuel B. White | Dischd. 24 Aug '82 | " | " | | |
| " | William Wilson | Died 15 Mch '81 | " | | | |
| | George Windham | Dischd. 25 Apl '81 | " | | | |
| " | William West | "    13 Jan '82 | " | " | | |
| " | John Williams, 1st | | " | " | " | |
| " | Barney Wilson | | " | " | " | |
| " | William Wilkeson | Dischd. 1 Mch '81 | " | | | |
| " | Charles Williams, 1st | "    20 Aug '83 | " | " | " | |
| " | Robertson Wood | | " | " | " | |
| " | Thomas Wood, 2nd | [Dischd. 29 Nov '83] | " | " | " | |
| " | Edward Wright | Died 4 Mch '83 | " | " | | |
| Corpl. | Jeremiah Williams | | " | " | " | |
| Private | James Wood, 2nd | | " | " | " | |
| Drum. | Daniel Willis | | " | " | " | |
| Private | George Wilson | Dischd. 5 May '81 | " | | | |
| " | David Wilson | | " | " | " | |
| Serjt. | John Wilkeson | | " | " | " | |
| Drum. | Daniel Warrior | | " | " | " | |
| Private | Jonathan Windal | Dischd. 1 Apl '81 | " | | | |
| Fifer | Michael Wiery | | " | " | " | |
| | Benj. Williams, 2nd | | " | " | " | |
| " | Absalom Wright | | " | " | " | |
| " | Michael Wiser | Dischd. 1 June '81 | " | | | |
| Private | William Wilson, 2nd | | " | " | " | |
| " | Notley Whitcomb | Dischd. 1 Apl '81 | " | " | | |
| " | Samuel Wedge | | " | " | " | |
| " | William Wedge | Dischd. 15 Mch '81 | " | | | |
| " | James White | Invd. 10 June '83 | " | " | " | |
| " | Michael Waltman | | " | " | " | |
| Serjt. | Gabriel Williams | Dischd. 6 Feb '83 | " | " | | |
| Private | John Wells | | " | " | " | |
| " | Richard Wiley | | " | " | " | |
| " | John Wilson, 1st | [Dischd. 29 Nov '83] | " | " | " | |
| Corpl. | Richard Wheeler | Dischd. 23 July '83 | " | " | " | |
| Private | Rhode Woodland | | " | " | " | |
| " | John Whitcomb | Dischd. 7 Jan '83 | " | " | | |
| " | Walter Watson | "    1 Aug '83 | " | " | " | |
| Serjt. | John Walker, 3rd | | " | " | " | |
| Private | Banks Webb | | " | " | " | |
| " | John West, 2nd | | " | " | " | |
| Drum. | William Watkins | [Dischd. 29 Nov '83] | " | " | " | |
| Private | James Wilson, 2nd | [Dischd. 29 Nov '83] | " | " | " | |
| " | Charles Wheeler [Corpl., Dischd. 29 Nov '83] | | " | " | " | |
| Serjt. | George Williams | | " | " | " | |

| RANK. | NAMES. | REMARKS. | SERVED BETWEEN 1 AUG '80 AND 1 JAN '82. | SERVED BETWEEN 1 JAN '82 AND 1 JAN '83. | SERVED BETWEEN 1 JAN '83 AND 15 NOV '83. | SERVED BETWEEN 15 NOV '83 AND 10 JULY '84. |
|---|---|---|---|---|---|---|
| Private | Humphry Wells | [Dischd. 11 Aug '83] | " | " | " | |
| " | William Wilson, 1st | [Serjt., Dischd. 29 Nov '83] | " | " | " | |
| " | James West | [Dischd. 29 Nov '83] | " | " | " | |
| Serjt. | James Wood, 1st | | " | " | " | |
| " | Benjamin Ward | Dischd. 1 July '83 | " | " | " | |
| Private | John Willing | Died 15 Dec '81 | " | | | |
| " | Philip Welch | " 1 Dec '81 | " | | | |
| " | John Wright | [Dischd. 29 Nov '83] | " | " | " | |
| " | Joseph White | Dischd. 1 July '83 | " | " | " | |
| " | Zadock Whaley | | " | " | " | |
| " | Anthony Weaver | | " | " | " | |
| Drum. | Benj. Williams, 1st | | " | | | |
| Private | John Wilkeson | Died 15 Jan '81 | " | | | |
| " | William Whitteco | | " | " | " | |
| " | Samuel Wright | Died 20 Jan '82 | " | " | | |
| " | Charles White | | | " | " | |
| " | John Walker, 1st | [Dischd. 29 Nov '83] | " | " | " | |
| " | Garret Welch | | | " | " | |
| " | John Welch, 2nd | | " | " | " | |
| " | Joseph Ward | | | " | " | |
| " | James Williams | | " | " | " | |
| " | Hugh Ware | | | " | " | |
| " | John Williams, 2nd | | | " | " | |
| " | John White, 2nd | | | " | " | |
| " | Henry Windows | | | " | " | |
| " | Evan Willing | | | " | " | |
| " | John Wilson, 2nd | | | " | " | |
| | William Watkins, 2nd | | | " | " | |
| " | Daniel Wilkins | | | " | " | |
| " | Benjamin Worthington | | | " | " | |
| " | Robert Wright | [Dischd. 11 Aug '83] | | " | " | |
| " | Edward Wheatly | | | " | " | |
| " | Thomas Wood, 4th | | | " | " | |
| " | John Wilmore | | | | " | |
| Corpl. | John Wiley | | | | " | |
| Private | John Wilman | | | | " | |
| " | Thomas White | | | | | |
| " | John Watkins | Died 26 Apl '83 | " | | | |
| " | George Watson | " 4 July '81 | " | | | |
| Serjt. | Samuel Wilson | Invalided 12 Oct '82 | " | " | " | |
| Private | Edward Walter | | " | " | " | |
| " | Calvert Woodward, (Mason) | | " | " | " | |
| " | Sylvester Wheatley | Dischd. 1 July '81 | " | | | |
| " | Charles Willet | Died 19 Sept '82 | | " | | |
| " | Jarvis Williams | | " | " | " | " |

| RANK. | NAMES. | REMARKS. | SERVED BETWEEN 1 AUG '80 AND 1 JAN '82. | SERVED BETWEEN 1 JAN '82 AND 1 JAN '83. | SERVED BETWEEN 1 JAN '83 AND 15 NOV '83. | SERVED BETWEEN 15 NOV '83 AND 10 JULY '84. |
|---|---|---|---|---|---|---|
| Private | Samuel Young | | " | " | " | |
| Corpl. | John Young, 2nd | | " | " | " | |
| Private | Godfrey Young | Invd. 23 Oct '80 | " | | | |
| " | Jacob Yeast | | " | " | " | |
| " | Henry Young | | " | " | " | " |
| " | Isaac Young | [Dischd. 2 Aug '83] | | " | " | " |
| " | John Young | [Dischd. 18 Sept '83 | | | " | |

### HAZENS.

| | NAMES. | | | | | |
|---|---|---|---|---|---|---|
| | John Ryan | | " | " | " | " |
| | Charles March | | " | " | " | " |
| | Harvey Burns | | " | " | " | " |
| | John Dugan | | " | | | |
| | James McEntire | | " | " | " | " |
| | Thomas Deavond | | " | " | " | " |
| | William Dooley | | " | | | |
| | Benjamin Willson | | " | | | |
| | William Deacon | | " | " | " | " |
| | Nehemiah Barns | | " | " | " | " |
| | William Duly | | " | " | " | " |
| | William Perkins | | " | " | " | " |
| | John Crany | | " | " | " | |
| | Joseph Lewis | | " | " | " | |
| | Michael Fitzgerald | | " | " | " | |

### INVALIDS.

| | NAMES. | | | | | |
|---|---|---|---|---|---|---|
| | James Dyer | | " | | | |
| | James Dwire | | " | | | |
| | John Smith | | " | | | |
| | Michael McGuire | | " | " | | |
| | John Saunders | | " | " | | |
| | Valentine Smith | | " | " | | |
| | John Willis | | " | " | " | |
| | Paul Dugan | | " | | | |
| | Michael Duffee | | " | | | |
| | John O'Brion | | " | | | |
| | Robert Poneston | | " | | | |
| | John Howard | | " | | | |
| | Jacob Lyons | | " | | | |
| | John Brown | | " | | | |
| | Thomas Evans | | " | | | |

NOTE.—Information in brackets is taken from a Register of Maryland Troops Discharged at the Post of Frederick Town.

## ARTILLERY ROLLS.

The Enrolment of the First Company of Matrosses In the Province of Maryland, Commanded by Capt. Nathaniel Smith, Lt. Wm. Woolsey, Lt. Alex. Fornivall, Lt. George Keepott.*

| DATE OF ENLISTMENT. | NAMES. | WHERE BORN. | HEIGHT. | OCCUPATION. | AGE. |
|---|---|---|---|---|---|
| | Serjeants | | | | |
| Jan 24th '76 | Wm. Cornwall | In the parish Armagh, Ireland | 5.10 | Joyner | 30 |
| | Samuel Chester | Shrewsbury, Eng. | 5.6 | Breeches Maker | 26 |
| | John Lemon | North of Ireland | 5.7¾ | Brick Maker | 26 |
| | John Hall | Pennsylvania | 5.6 | Brick Layer | 22 |
| | Corporals | | | | |
| | Wm. Godman | Fredk. Co., Md. | 5.8 | Labourer | 21 |
| | Geo. Litzinger | Maryland | 5.8¼ | Brick Layer | 21 |
| | Isaac James | Philadelphia | 5.9½ | Taylor | 27 |
| | Alex. Craig | Ireland | 6.0 | Labourer | 20 |
| | Fifer | | | | |
| | Marmadk. Grant | Dublin | 5.4 | Cane Maker | 20 |
| | Drummer. | | | | |
| | Henry Kelleher | Cork, Ireland | 5.8 | Taylor | 18 |
| | John Power | Ireland | 5.8 | Brick Layer | 36 |
| | John Clarke | North Ireland | 5.8 | Glover | 21 |
| | Hugh Martin | Pennsylvania | 5.7¾ | Tanner & Currier | 23 |
| | Robt. Tool | County Kerry, Ireland | 6.1½ | Labourer | 28 |
| | David Garrison | West New Jersey | 5.5 | Brick Layer | 30 |
| | George Rees | Germany | 5.7 | Rope Maker | 23 |
| | Philip Sitzley | Pennsylvania | 5.7 | Breeches Maker | 30 |
| | Henry Rees | Germany | 5.11 | Wever | 38 |
| | Samuel Thompson | Nanticoke, Md. | 5.8½ | Shoe Maker | 21 |
| | Thos. Conner | Ireland | 5.8¼ | Hatter | 19 |
| | Nathl. Aldrich | Elk Ridge, Md. | 5.8¼ | | 21 |
| | John Houlton | Philadelphia | 6.0⅜ | Plasterer | 19 |
| | Jno. Cunningham | Charles Town, Md. | 6.0 | Labourer | 23 |
| | Robert Mitchel | Charles Town, " | 5.6 | Sadler | 22 |
| | Joel Bennett | West New Jersey | 5.7½ | Shoe Maker | 22 |
| | Freeman Newman | Dublin, Ireland | 5.5 | Labourer | 21 |

* This Company was raised in accordance with the Resolves of the Maryland Convention of December, 1775, see page 4.

| Date of Enlistment. | Names. | Where Born. | Height. | Occupation. | Age. |
|---|---|---|---|---|---|
| Jan 24th '76 | Alex. McMullen | North Ireland | 5.6¾ | Tanner | 23 |
| | John Schley | Bucks Co., Penna. | 5.10¼ | Brick Maker | 26 |
| | Barney Quinn | Dublin, Ireland | 5.8 | Labourer | 21 |
| | James Badley | Dublin, " | 5.5½ | Gardner | 22 |
| | James Roney | Leinst'r, " | 5.7 | Breeches Maker | 23 |
| | Willm. Forbes | Ireland | 5.4 | Wever | 25 |
| | Hugh McDowell | Newry, Ireland | 5.5¼ | Black Smith | 28 |
| | Roger O'Donnald | Donegal, " | 5.7 | Labourer | 28 |
| | Richd. Wilkinson | Dublin, " | 5.6¾ | Sailor | 30 |
| | John Gormon | Munster, " | 5.7¼ | Pump Borer | 22 |
| Jan 25th | Philip Jones | Maryland | 5.7 | Brick Layer | 21 |
| | Robert Brett | Maryland | 5.6½ | Taylor | 24 |
| | John Videon | Kent, England | 5.7¾ | Baker | 23 |
| | James Jack | Glasgo | 5.4 | Wever | 24 |
| | Edward Barrey | Ireland | 5.5½ | Silk Wever | 33 |
| Jan 25th | John Burke | County Kerry, Ireland | 5.6½ | Labourer | 30 |
| | John Pearson | Pennsylvania | 6.0 | Brick Layer | 30 |
| | John Turner | Nottingham, England | 5.7 | Sawyer | 28 |
| | Luke Gardiner | Killarney, Ireland | 5.9 | Barber | 22 |
| | David Walsh | Cork, Ireland | 5.8 | Cooper | 23 |
| | Danl. Donoghue | Cork, " | 5.7 | Plaisterer | 22 |
| Jan 27th | George Cooper | England | 5.8¼ | Labourer | 20 |
| | John Curties | Bucks Co., Pa | 5.5 | " | 33 |
| | Martin Gutro | Nova Scotia | 5.8¾ | " | 28 |
| | John Howard | Maryland | 5.11 | " | 27 |
| | Thos. Mahoney | Ireland | 5.7 | " | 25 |
| | James Barrey | | 5.10¼ | | 33 |
| | John Carroll | Limer'k, Ireland | 5.6¼ | Butcher | 30 |
| | Heart Dick | Scotland | 5.7½ | Baker | 23 |
| Jan 27th | Thos. Smith | Maryland | 5.6¾ | Carpenter | 20 |
| | Richd. Bourk,(Burke) | Ireland | 5.7¼ | Butcher | 22 |
| Jan 28th | David White | Dublin, Ireland | 5.5¼ | Wever | 30 |
| | Thos. Pearson | Philadelphia | 5.5½ | Brick Layer | 28 |
| | Robt. Thompson | Maryland | 5.9 | Labourer | 33 |
| | James Mathies | W. New Jersey | 5.8½ | " | 24 |
| | Andrew Shrike | Pennsylvania | 5.6¾ | Turner | 17 |
| | John Bradey | Dublin, Ireland | 5.6½ | Plaisterer | 21 |
| | Edmund Walsh | Cork, " | 5.6½ | Labourer | 25 |
| | Wm. Colbertson | Cork, " | 5.5 | " | 30 |
| | Wm. Ellis | Portsmouth, England | 5.5½ | " | 36 |
| | Peter Richards | Nova Scotia | 5.9 | " | 23 |
| | Henry Carroll | West of Ireland | 5.5 | Breeches Maker | 21 |
| | Willm. Read | Warwickshire, Eng. | 5.7½ | Stocking Wever | 30 |
| | Robert Foster | England | 5.7¼ | Brick Layer | 23 |
| Jan 30th | Benj. Spencer | Pennsylvania | 5.5½ | Brick Layer | 30 |

| Date of Enlistment. | Names. | Where Born. | Height. | Occupation. | Age. |
|---|---|---|---|---|---|
| Jan 30th '76 | Joseph Bear | Nova Scotia | 5.6½ | Labourer | 28 |
| | Joseph Wilkes | England | 5.6½ | " | 32 |
| | Benj. Jones | Maryland | 5.6¾ | Brick Layer | 30 |
| Jan 31st | David Thomas | Gloucestershire, Eng. | 5.7¼ | Brick Layer | 37 |
| | Jacob Boger, (Booger) | Pennsylvania | 5.5¾ | Carpenter | 20 |
| | Felix Branagin | Armagh, Ireland | 5.6¾ | Labourer | 33 |
| | James Scott | Antrim, " | 5.9¼ | Shoe Maker | 35 |
| | Timothy Donnovin | Cork, " | 5.4½ | Labourer | 26 |
| | Thomas Neilson | Tyrone, " | 5.7½ | Carpenter | 24 |
| | Jas. Henrickson | Maryland | 5.6¼ | Labourer | 26 |
| | Martin Cunden | Waterf'd, Ireland | 5.7½ | Drayman | 21 |
| | Patk. Shaughness | Dublin, " | 5.7 | Breeches Maker | 21 |
| | William Foard | Cecil Co., Md. | 5.7½ | Labourer | 18 |
| | Jas. McFadon | Ireland | 6.1 | " | 20 |
| | Timo. Murphey | Dublin, Ireland | 5.4½ | " | 20 |
| | Anthony Barns | Virginia | 5.6 | Shoe Maker | 21 |
| | David Moroney | Cork, Ireland | 5.9 | Brick Layer | 22 |
| Feb 1st | John Handlen | Dublin, " | 5.5 | Taylor | 28 |
| | Anthony Selister | Nova Scotia | 5.4 | Labourer | 37 |
| | John Philips | Dublin, Ireland | 5.6½ | " | 20 |
| Feb 3rd | John Conly, (Connolly) | Athlone, " | 5.6½ | Shoe Maker | 26 |
| | John Wilkins | South Carolina | 5.9 | Labourer | 33 |
| | James Brooks | North of England | 5.5½ | Weaver | 23 |
| | Richard Pitsland | South Carolina | 5.7 | Labourer | 27 |
| | Jno. Richardson | Pennsylvania | 5.8¼ | Carpenter | 23 |
| | Thos. Robinson | Harford Co., Md. | 6.0 | Black Smith | 21 |
| | Chas. Cloes | Antrim, Ireland | 5.7 | Labourer | 19 |
| | Francis Dushield | Nova Scotia | 5.9¾ | Brick Layer | 23 |
| | John Forrester | Maryland | 5.8½ | Labourer | 28 |
| | Alex. Forrester | Maryland | 5.5 | " | 30 |
| | Cornelius Forrester | Maryland | 5.10¾ | " | 21 |

Baltimore, 19 February, 1776.
the above Company Examined and passed by

M. Gist

M.

## Nathan Smith's Company.

June 29th, 1776.

| Rank. | Names. | Remarks. |
|---|---|---|
| Serjts. | Wm. Cornwall | present |
| | —el Chester | " |
| | John Hall | " |
| | James McFadon | " |

| RANK. | NAMES. | REMARKS. |
|-------|--------|----------|
| Corpls. | Wm. Godman | present |
|  | George Littsinger | " |
|  | Alex. Craige | " |
|  | Young Wilkinson | " |
| Fifer | Marmaduke Grant | " |
| Drum. | Henry Keleher | " |
|  | David Garritson | " |
|  | John Houlton | absent on Guard |
|  | John Cunningham | present |
|  | John Pearson | absent on Guard |
|  | Thomas Robinson | present |
|  | Nicholas Ricketts | " |
|  | John Howard | " |
|  | Saml. Thompson | " |
|  | Corns. Forrester | ' |
|  | James Barry | " |
|  | James Rice | ' |
|  | John Shley | ' |
|  | Fran. DeShields | " |
|  | Robert Thompson | " |
|  | Luke Gardiner | " |
|  | Peter Richards | " |
|  | David Moroney | " |
|  | John Wilkins | " |
|  | Martin Gutro | sick in Barracks |
|  | Thomas Connor | present |
|  | James Mathias | " |
|  | John Forrester | " |
|  | Nathaniel Aldridge | " |
|  | George Cooper | " |
|  | John Power | " |
|  | John Clarke | " |
|  | Barney Quinn | " |
|  | David Walsh | " |
|  | Hugh Martin | " |
|  | John Vidon | " |
|  | Martin Conden | " |
|  | ——el Bennett | " |
|  | Thomas Nelson | " |
|  | Richard Burke | " |
|  | ——m Reed | " |
|  | —— Dick | " |
|  | ——vid Thomas | " |
|  | John Gorman | " |
|  | Thomas Mahony | " |
|  | John Turner | " |

| RANK. | NAMES. | REMARKS. |
|---|---|---|
| | Henry Rees | present |
| | Richd. Pitsland | " |
| | ———oney | " |
| | R—— ODonnell | " |
| | —— Cloes | " |
| | —— Sitsler | " |
| | —— Jones | " |
| | Ro—— Toole | " |
| | Da—— Donahue | " |
| | P——k Shaughness | " |
| | Richd. Wilkinson | " |
| | Alex. McMullen | " |
| | Phelix Branagan | " |
| | Thomas Smith | " |
| | Andrew Shriek | " |
| | Benj. Jones | " |
| | John Troy | |
| | John Connolly | sick in the Hospital |
| | John Philips | present |
| | Joseph Wilkes | " |
| | Edward Walsh | " |
| | John Brady | " |
| | John Carroll | " |
| | Robert Britt | " |
| | James Henrickson | " |
| | Anthony Barnes | " |
| | Robert Mitchell | " |
| | Jacob Boager | " |
| | William Ellis | " |
| | Benj. Spencer | dead or deserted, 18th Inst |
| | Edward Barry | present |
| | Hugh McDowell | " |
| | Thomas Pearson | " |
| | James Bradley | " |
| | David Whyte | " |
| | George Rees | " |
| | Alex. Forrester | " |
| | John Hanlon | " |
| | John Curtis | " |
| | Freeman Newman | " |
| | Wm. Culbertston | " |
| | Henry Carroll | " |
| | Timothy Murphy | " |
| | Anthony Silister | sick in barracks |
| | Timothy Donovan | present |
| | Ja——es Jack | " |

| RANK. | NAMES. | REMARKS. |
|---|---|---|
| | William Forbes | present |
| | Frans. MaGauran | " |
| | James Scott | dead or deserted, 13th Inst |
| | Benjamin Todd | present |
| | Fredk. Pine | " |
| | William Delany | " |

Whetstone Point, Sept. 7th, 1776.

FIRST COMPANY OF MATROSSES.

| | |
|---|---|
| Capt. Nathaniel Smith. | Present. |
| Lieutenant Alex. Furnivall. | " |
| Lieutenant N. Ruxton Moore. | " |
| Lieutenant Richd. Dorsey. | " |

| RANK. | DAY OF INLISTMENT. | NAMES. | REMARKS. | |
|---|---|---|---|---|
| Serjeants | Jan 26 | Wm. Cornwall | Present | |
| | | Saml. Chester | Absent | On Furlough 7th |
| | | Jno. Hall | Present | |
| | | Jas. McFadon | " | |
| Corporals | | Wm. Godman | " | |
| | | Geo. Litsinger | " | |
| | | Alex. Craige | " | |
| | | Young Wilkinson | " | |
| Drum | | Henry Kelliher | " | |
| Fife | | Marmaduke Grant | " | |
| | | David Garrison | " | |
| | | Jno. Holton | " | |
| | | Jno. Pearson | " | |
| | May 29 | Benj. Todd | Absent | On furlough 5th |
| | Jan 26 | Thos. Robinson | Sick | In the Hospital |
| | | Nichs. Ricketts | Present | |
| | | John Howard | " | |
| | | Saml. Thompson | " | |
| | | Corns. Forrester | " | |
| | | Jas. Barry | " | |
| | Apl 3 | Jas. Rice | " | |
| | Jan 26 | Jno. Shly | Sick | In Hospital |
| | | Frans. de Shields | Prest. | |
| | May 29 | Wm. Delany | " | |
| | Jan 26 | Robt. Thompson | " | |
| | | Luke Gardiner | " | |
| | | Peter Richards | " | |

| RANK. | DAY OF INLISTMENT. | NAMES. | REMARKS. |
|---|---|---|---|
| | | David Maroney | Sick    In Town |
| | | Jno. Wilkins | Present |
| | May 29 | Fredk. Pine | " |
| | Jan 26 | Martin Gutro | " |
| | | Thos. Connor | " |
| | | Jas. Mathias | " |
| | | Jno. Forrester | " |
| | | Nathan Aldridge | " |
| | | Geo. Cooper | " |
| | | Jno. Power | " |
| | | Jno. Clarke | " |
| | | Barny Quinn | " |
| | | David Welsh | " |
| | | Hugh Martin | " |
| | Aug 5 | Jno. Vidon | " |
| | Jan 26 | Leaven Dorsey | " |
| | | Martin Condon | " |
| | | Thos. Nelson | " |
| | | Richd. Burke | " |
| | | Wm. Read | " |
| | Aug 5 | Jno. Ring | " |
| | Jan 26 | Davd. Thomas | " |
| | | Jno. Gorman | " |
| | Aug 31 | Matthew Kelly | " |
| | Jan 26 | Jno. Turner | " |
| | | Richd. Pitsland | " |
| | | Jas. Roney | " |
| | | Roger O'Donnald | " |
| | | Charles Cloes | " |
| | | Philip Sitzler | " |
| | | Philip Jones | " |
| | | Robert Toole | " |
| | | Danl. Donohou | " |
| | | Patrick Shockness | " |
| | July 2 | Stephen Fennell | " |
| | Jan 26 | Richd. Wilkinson | " |
| | | Alex. McMullon | " |
| | | Felix Branagan | " |
| | | Thos. Smith | " |
| | | Andw. Shrake | " |
| | | Benj. Jones | " |
| | | Jno. Phillips | Sick    In Hospital |
| | | Joseph Wilkes | Present |
| | | Edmund Welsh | " |
| | | Jno. Brady | " |

37

| RANK. | DAY OF INLISTMENT. | NAMES. | REMARKS. | |
|---|---|---|---|---|
| | | Jno. Carroll | Absent | In Town |
| | | Robt. Brett | " | On Guard |
| | June 20 | Thos. Wilson | " | |
| | May 16 | Fras. MaGauran | Present | |
| | Jan 26 | Anthy. Barnes | " | |
| | | Robt. Mitchell | " | |
| | | Jacob Boger | " | |
| | | Wm. Ellis | " | |
| | | Hugh McDole | " | |
| | | Thos. Pearson | " | |
| | | Jno. Curtis | Absent | On Guard |
| | | Jas. Bradley | Present | |
| | | Davd. White | " | |
| | | Geo. Rees | Absent | On furlough Aug 31st |
| | | Alex. Forrester | Present | |
| | | Jno. Handlen | " | |
| | | Jno. Curtis | " | |
| | | Freeman Newman | " | |
| | | Wm. Culbertson | " | |
| | | Henry Carroll | " | |
| | | Tim Murphy | Sick | In Hospital |
| | | Anthy. Selister | Present | |
| | | Tim Donnavan | " | |
| | July 23 | Bartho. Donohou | " | |
| | Jan 26 | Jas. Jack | " | |
| | | Wm. Forbes | " | |
| | | Jas. Fox | Absent | On Guard |
| | | Ed. Barry | Present | |

Return of Capt. Nathaniel Smith's Matross Company.

Nathl. Smith.

## COMPANY OF MATROSSES STATIONED AT ANNAPOLIS.

Capt. John Fulford, commissioned Feb. 9th, 1776 *
1st Lt. Thomas Goldsmith *
    William Brown, commissioned July 5th, 1776 *
2nd Lt. Felix Lewis Baron Massenbach, commissioned Feb. 20th, 1776 *
    Nicholas Ruxton Moore, commissioned March 23rd, 1776,* vice Massen-
        bach resigned
    William Campbell, commissioned July 15th, 1776 *
3rd Lt. Nicholas Ruxton Moore, commissioned March 1st, 1776 *
    William Campbell, commissioned March 23rd, 1776 *
    Adam Berthaud, commissioned July 17th, 1776 *

* See Md. Archives vol. XI, pgs. 145, 169, 550, 173, 279, 196 and vol. XII, pgs. 47, 62.

RESOLVES OF THE MARYLAND CONVENTION 23 OCTOBER, 1776.

" *Resolved,* That three companies of artillery, each company to consist of ninety-two privates, four serjeants, four corporals, one drummer, and one fifer, commanded by one captain, one captain-lieutenant, and two lieutenants, be immediately raised ; one of the said companies to be stationed at Baltimore town, and the remaining two companies to be stationed at the city of Annapolis.   That the non-commissioned officers and privates be enlisted in the service of this state for the war : . . . . . and they shall not be compelled to march to any place out of this state."

MARYLAND ACTS—JUNE, 1777.

" An ACT to reinforce the *American* army.

*And be it enacted,* That the governor and the council be empowered to order any part of any of the artillery companies raised for the immediate defence of this state, not exceeding sixty-six privates, under officers proper for such a number of artillerists, to march with all expedition to the city of *Philadelphia*, there to obey the orders of congress, or of his excellency general *Washington*, and to remain in the continental service during this campaign, or so long as the commander in chief shall require their service, unless the exigencies of this state should require their recal by the governor and the council."

RESOLVES OF CONTINENTAL CONGRESS, 20 OCTOBER, 1777.

" *Resolved,* That the governor and council of Maryland be informed that the artillery regiments in the service of the United States have suffered so much in the late engagements, that there are not a sufficient number to do the duty of artillery-men in the army, and therefore that the government of that state be earnestly requested to order the companies of matrosses in the service of the state of Maryland to join the army immediately, and that the said companies shall be ordered to return whenever the government of that state shall require it."

A COMPANY OF MATROSSES AT ANNAPOLIS.

Capt. Thomas Watkins  
1st Lt. Levin Lawrence  
2nd Lt. Thomas Todd  
3rd Lt. John Iiams, Jr.

Officers elected  
by the Convention  
of Maryland  
Oct. 26th, 1776.*

* See Proceedings of the Convention, pg. 288.

Annapolis, December 12th, 1776.

A Return of Sundries wanting for the Recruits for the Artillery at Annapolis.

| | | |
|---|---|---|
| John Fitzjarrold | Joseph Tucker | John Carrall |
| James Simmons | Elisha Talbott | John Orber |
| Timothy Kennedy | William Nichols | Henry Scott |
| Partrick Coursey | John Folks | John Boyle |
| Anthony Murphy | James Clarke | John Saunders |
| Thomas Condram | James Cole | John King, Jr. |
| Wm. Pritchett | William Powell | Phillip Obrian |
| Joseph Duvall | William Poland | John Burgess |
| Thomas Fanning | Joseph Bryan | James Lawson |
| Andrew Keith | Joseph Deale | John Reynolds |
| William Brady | William Hoharo | Joseph Smith |
| Michael Clansey | Denniss Myhan | Robert Moree |
| Saml. Q. Winser | John Wells | James Moree |
| Zekiel Harris | John Lamb | |

41 blankets, 41 coats, 41 vests, 35 breeches, 39 hats, 34 pair of shoes and 38 pair of stockings wanted for the above recruits.

James John Skinner,

Serjt. Captn. Fulford.

MUSTER ROLL OF CAPT. FURNIVAL'S COMPANY OF ARTILLERY.

3D COMPY. OF MATROSSES.

| Date of Commission | { | Nov. 5th, 1776 | Alex. Furnival, Capt. | |
|---|---|---|---|---|
| | | | Saml. Gerock, 1st Lieut. | Fever |
| | | | Robt. Willmott, 2nd " | On Furlow |
| | | | Saml. Sadler, 3rd " | |

| RANK. | NAMES. | | CAUSE OF ABSENCE. |
|---|---|---|---|
| Serjt. | Willm. Cornwall | sick | |
| " | Willm. Day | present | Reduced to a priv. Sent. |
| " | Richd. Lewis | sick | |
| " | Nath. Thomas | absent | On Furlow |
| Corpl. | Jno. Mahoney | present | |
| " | Jno. Wheeler | absent | On Furlow till 19th Ins. |
| " | Jeremh. Sullivan | present | |
| " | Danl. Rodden | sick | Putrid Fever |
| Drum. | Thos. Williams | present | |
| | Dennis Flanagan | " | |
| | Jno. Taylor | " | |
| | Jno. Yellum | sick | Convalescent |

| RANK. | NAMES. | | CAUSE OF ABSENCE. |
|---|---|---|---|
| | Jno. Quin | present | |
| | Jno. Sandle | " | |
| | Howell Lewis | " | |
| | Bryan Farral | " | |
| | Corns. Carney | sick | Agae Fever |
| | Richd. Wheelen | present | |
| | Jno. Fitzpatrick | " | |
| | Jno. Fitzgerrald | deceased | Oct 15th |
| | Robert Craig | present | |
| | Danl. Neal | " | |
| | John Kendercline | sick | Shoulder bruised by Accident at [Camp |
| | Thos. Glessin | present | |
| | Phillip Masterson | " | |
| | Adam Myers | " | |
| | Saml. Lambart | " | |
| | Michael O'Conner | " | |
| | Robert Karr | sick | Burnt Arm at Camp |
| | John O'Donnell | present | |
| | Mathew McMahone | " | |
| | Saml. Coyl | absent | Prisoner in Balto. Goal |
| | Thomas York | present | |
| | Jno. Garrity | " | |
| | Thos. Yates | sick | Sore leg |
| | Jno. White | present | |
| | Thos. Price | " | |
| | Zephaniah White | " | |
| | Wm. Grimes | " | |
| | Thos. Randle | " | |
| | Jno. Ginnivan | " | |
| | Willm. Wade | sick | Flux |
| | Willm. Richardson | absent | Wounded by Accident |
| | John Stonehouse | deserted | Sept 20th |
| | John Bryan | present | |
| | Willm. McNamarra | deserted | Sept 29th |

The Above is an Exact Return of my Company taken Nov. 17th, 1777.

Alex. Furnival, Captn. Artillery.

A REPORT OF CAPT. RICHARD DORSEY'S COMPANY OF ARTILLERY.

Richard Dorsey, Capt.     Ebenezar Finley, 1st Lt.     Wm. Judah, 2nd Lt.

| | | | | |
|---|---|---|---|---|
| Young Wilkinson, Serjt. | on furlow | Andrew Shrink | present |
| Nicholas Ricketts | do | present | Benj. Jones | " |
| Alex. Craige | do | " | Joseph Wilks | " |
| John Curtis | do | " | Edmd. Walsh | " |

| | | |
|---|---|---|
| Ths. Pearson | Corpl. | present |
| Sam. Thomson | " | " |
| Jas. Hendrickson | " | " |
| Henry Kelliher | Drum. | " |
| John Pearson | | " |
| Ths. Robinson | | sick |
| Cornelius Forrester | | " |
| James Barry | | present |
| James Rid | | " |
| Edwd. Coughlan | | . " |
| John Sly | | sick |

Wm. Delany, in Gaol on Susspion of House Breaking

| | | |
|---|---|---|
| Robt. Thompson | | " |
| Peter Richards | | " |
| David Marony | | " |
| John Wilkins | | " |
| Fred. Pine | | " |
| Ths. Connor | | " |

James Mathias, in Gaol for House Breaking

| | | |
|---|---|---|
| George Cooper | | " |
| John Power | | sick |
| John Clark | | present |
| David Walsh | | " |
| Martin Condon | | " |
| Richard Burke | | " |
| Wm. Reed | | " |
| Mathew Kelly | | " |
| John Turner | | " |
| Joel Bennett | | " |

Richd. Pitsland, sick in the Country with Bilious Fever

R—— O'D——l,    "

[Nos. 28 to 32 are torn off and Nos. 27 and 33 are partly torn off.]

| | | |
|---|---|---|
| —— Shoughnesey (?) | | present |
| Stephen Fennell | | " |
| Richard Wilkinson | | " |
| Alex. McMullain | | " |
| Thomas Smith | | " |

| | |
|---|---|
| John Brady | present |
| Robert Britt | " |
| Alex. Blake | " |
| Anthony Barnes | " |

Robert Mitchell, in Goal for House Breaking

Edwd. Barry    "

James Bradly, in Goal for House Breaking

David White    "

Alex. Forrester, sick in the Country with Fevers

| | |
|---|---|
| John Handlen | " |
| Freeman Newman | " |
| Wm. Culbertson | " |
| Henry Carrol | " |
| Timothy Murphy | " |
| Timothy Dunnavin | " |

[One, No. 57, torn off]

| | |
|---|---|
| Will (?) Forbes | " |
| Hugh McDowell | sick |
| Saml. Chester | present |
| John Curtis | " |
| Ths. Nelson | " |
| Wm. Whittom | " |
| John Akerly | sick |
| John Cockerton | present |
| Thos. Grainger | " |

Wm. Clark, in Goal for House Breaking

| | |
|---|---|
| John Jarvis | " |
| John Howard | " |
| George Letzinger | " |

1 Captain
2 Lieutenants
4 Serjeants
3 Corporals
1 Drummer
56 Effective Privates
8 Sick
1 On Furlow

Nov. 17th, 1777.

The Above is a True State of my Company.

Richd. Dorsey, Capt. Artillery.

## A Return of Capt. William Marbury's Company of Artillery.

| | | |
|---|---|---|
| Thomas McNear | Hezekiah Wayman | John T. Shaaff |
| John Sands | William James | James P. Maynard |
| John Bond | William Johnson | Daniel Murray |
| Christopher Hohne | Henry Smith | Francis T. Clemments |
| Edward Roberts | John Barber | Arthur Shaaff |
| Patrick Dunn | Jesse Lewis | Isaac Holland |
| William Grant | Francis Welsh | John Welsh |
| Danl. Wells, Jr. | Robert Lusby | Edward Pryse |
| William Glover | Richard Dorsey | Henry Johnson |
| William Taylor | Jonathan Rawlings | Henry Syble |
| Thomas Hewitt | William Robertson | Edward Holland |
| Jesse Ray | Andrew Williams | James Bright |
| John Thompson | John Williams | Robert Parker |
| Thomas Chalmers | John Callahan | John Sullivan, Jr. |
| John Keith | Richard Harwood, of Thomas | Richard Dawes |

Muster Roll of Capt. William Brown's Company in the Regt. of Artillery in the Service of the United States of America, Commanded by Col. Charles Harrison, for November, 1778.

Commissioned, {
William Brown, Captain.  Absent with Leave of Gen. Knox.
James Smith, Capt. Lieut.
James McFadon, 1st Lieut.
Clement Skerritt, 2nd Lieut.
Alex. Neilson, 2nd Lieut.
}

| APPOINTED. | NAMES. | APPOINTED. | NAMES. |
|---|---|---|---|
| | | Serjeants | |
| 1777, Nov 22 | John Stapples | 1777, Nov 22 | Thomas Barber |
| " | James Adams | " | Patrick Corcoran |
| " | Henry Slack | " | Charles Stewart |
| | | Bombardiers | |
| " | Michael Hawk | | William Jones |
| | Thomas Conderall | | William Heany |
| | Michael O'Brian | | |
| | | Drummer | |
| " | James Brooks | | |
| | | Corporals | |
| " | Arthur Carnes | | John Ratcliff |
| | Tamlin Spencer | | Thomas Fanning |
| | Matthew Adams | | |

| APPOINTED. | NAMES. | REMARKS. |
|---|---|---|
| | Gunners | |
| 1777, Nov 22 | Phillip O'Brian | On Comd. with Capt. Brown |
| " | John Vaughan | |
| " | John Connelly | |
| " | Benj. Patman | Reduced to Matross, 1 Dec |
| | James Royston | |
| | Fifer | |
| | David Younge | |

| INLISTED. | NAMES. | REMARKS. |
|---|---|---|
| | Matrosses | |
| 1777, Nov 22 | John Burke | Joined 7 Nov |
| | Isaac Burton | |
| | George Baker | |
| | William Connelly | |
| | Robt. Campbell | |
| | Timothy Connelly | Joined 5 Dec |
| | Patrick Coursey | |
| | John Carrell | |
| | Thomas Carter | |
| | James Coale | |
| | James Clarke | |
| | Hugh Champlin | |
| | James Compton | Joined 21 Dec |
| | William Davis | |
| | John Evans | |
| | John Fitzgerald, Sr. | |
| | John Fitzgerald, Jr. | Sick Bedford, 30 Aug |
| | John Foalks | |
| | James Ford | |
| | Charles Groom | |
| | Mark Goldsbury | |
| | Jonathan Gill | |
| | Ignatius Griffin | |
| | Danl. Heavey | |
| | Henry Higgs | |
| | John Head | |
| | Michael Hughs | [23 Nov |
| | Wm. Hickinson | Joined 15 Nov. Sent to Hosptl. N. Windsor, |
| 1777, Nov 22 | Edward Jeffirson | Sick Bedford, 30 Aug |
| | William Johnston | On Comd. with Artificers |
| | Francis Johnston | |
| | Petter Lawrence | Comd. for Col. Duply |
| | Joh ——— | |

| INLISTED. | NAMES. | REMARKS. |
|---|---|---|
| | Matrosses | |
| | John Lynch | |
| | James Moree | |
| | Charles Murritt | Sick Yellow Springs, 26 May |
| 1778, May 8 | Henry Magen | |
| 1777, Nov 22 | Chas. McGloghlan | |
| | Mays Nevin | |
| | Benj. Patman | Joined as Matross, 1 Dec |
| | Joseph Poague | |
| | Francis Popham | |
| | Saml. Popham | |
| | John Rhoads | |
| | Petter Robinson | |
| | John Reynolds | |
| | Darbey Spilcey | |
| 1778, Jan 5 | Thomas Smith | |
| 1777, Nov 22 | Charles Sutton | |
| | Robert Smith | |
| | John Slack | |
| | John Saunders | |
| | Reuben Scott | |
| | James Tayler | |
| | James Whailing | |
| | James Walsh | |

[All in the above Roll enlisted for 3 years.]

Pluckimin, 23rd December, 1778. Mustered then Capt. Wm. Brown's Company as Specified in the Above Roll.

Samuel F. Parker, D. C. M.

### PROOF OF EFFECTIVES.

| | Capt. | Cn. Lt. | 1st Lt. | 2 Lts. | Sgts. | Cpls. | Bomds. | Gunners. | Drummer. | Fifer. | Matrosses. |
|---|---|---|---|---|---|---|---|---|---|---|---|
| Present | | 1 | 1 | 2 | 6 | 5 | 5 | 3 | 1 | 1 | 50 |
| Absent | 1 | | | | | | | 1 | | | 6 |
| Totals | 1 | 1 | 1 | 2 | 6 | 5 | 5 | 4 | 1 | 1 | 56 |

We do swear that the within Muster Roll is a True State of the Company without fraud to these United States or to any Individual, According to the Best of Our Knowledge.

James Smith, Capt. Lieut.<br>Clement Skerrett, Lieut.

Sworn Before me at Pluckemin this 23rd day of December, 1778.

T. Knox, M. G. Artillery.

MARYLAND ACTS—JULY, 1779.

"An ACT relating to the officers and soldiers of this state in the American army, and other purposes therein mentioned.

. . . . . . . . . . .

*And be it enacted*, That the matrosses in the city of Annapolis and Baltimore-town, who are effective, shall be incorporated into one company, and sent as soon as may be to camp, and shall hereafter be considered as part of the quota to be found by this state, . . . . and the governor and council may select and appoint a proper number of officers to command such company, out of the most capable of the present officers, . . . . and the governor and council are requested to recommend such of them as remain to his excellency general Washington, to be provided for, and they shall continue in the pay of this state until they shall be taken into the continental service."

RESOLVES OF THE MARYLAND ASSEMBLY 9 MAY, 1780.

"*Resolved*, That the three companies of artillery belonging to this state in the continental army, commanded by Captains Brown, Dorsey and the late Captain Gale, be incorporated with and annexed to the regiment commanded by colonel Harrison, of the Virginia corps of artillery, or to some other in the continental Army.

*Resolved*, That the same be formed into four companies, with proper officers belonging to this state to command them, and that the governor and council be requested to communicate the above resolutions to congress as soon as may be, that the same may be carried into immediate effect and execution."*

Pay Roll of the 2nd & 3d Companies of Maryland Artillery, Incorporated, for Aug., Sept., Oct., Nov. & Dec., 1780.

| NAMES. | REMARKS. | NAMES. | REMARKS. |
|---|---|---|---|
| Capt. James Smith | promoted from a Capt. Lt. and rec'd 4 mos. pay as such | Fifers Thos. Tyack | returned from No. Caro. Regt. |
|  |  | Elisha Redman |  |
|  |  | Peter Davis |  |
|  |  | Thomas Potter |  |

* For the results of the incorporation of the Maryland Artillery Companies with Harrison's Virginia Artillery see page 596.

| NAMES. | REMARKS. | NAMES. | REMARKS. |
|---|---|---|---|
| Capt. Lt. | | Matrosses | |
| Ebenr. Finley | | William Hutton | |
| | | Andrew Shrink | |
| 1st Lts. | | John Sandall | |
| Robt. Willmott | | Thomas Bowler | |
| James Baques | | Edward Berry | |
| | | Bennit Railey | |
| 2nd Lts. | | Thos. Redman | |
| Nichs. Ricketts | | Daniel Rodden | |
| Young Wilkinson | | Willm. Grimes | |
| Isaac Rawlings | | John Prout | |
| John Cheever | | Jacob Owings | deceased 19 Nov '81, paid widow 1 mo. |
| Sergeants | | | |
| Jesse Thompson | | Thomas Randall | |
| Wm. Rawlings | | John Ireland | |
| David Welsh | | Danl. Neale | |
| Wm. Cornwall | | John Clarke | |
| Saml. Carter | | Thomas Gleeson | |
| | | Peregrine Askew | |
| Corpls. | | Hugh McDowell | |
| James Hutton | | Benedict Johnson | lost his leg |
| Rawleyh Spinks | deceased 28 Nov '81 | Michael Connor | |
| | | Philip Martuson | |
| Bombrs. | | John Brady | |
| James Hammond | | James Neale | discharged Sept '82 |
| Willm. Allen | | John Smith | " " " |
| | | John Stanley | deceased 24 Apl '83 |
| Gunners | | | |
| Philip Jones | | John Compton | " 1 July '83 |
| Willm. Dixon | | Cornelius Harling | " 8 June '83 |
| Dennis McCormack | discharged Sept '82 | Michael O'Ferrell | " 23 Feb '83 |
| | | John Payne | " 22 May '83 |
| Drummer | | | |
| Thos. Williams | | | |

For the Arrangement of the Artillery Jan. 1st, 1781, and Jan. 1st, 1783, see pages 365 and 477.

Roll and Muster of the 1st Company of Maryland Artillery from Jan. 1st to Mch. 31st, 1782.   [All Enlisted for the War.]

| NAMES. | REMARKS. | NAMES. | REMARKS. |
|---|---|---|---|
| Capt. | | | |
| William Browne | | Matrosses | |
| | | Isaac Burton | |
| 1st Lieut. | | Arthur Carnes | |
| James McFadon | | Hugh Champlin | |
| | | John Fitzgerrald | |
| Serjeants | | Jonathan Gill | |
| Henry Slack | | Henry Higgs | Commd. Light |
| Charles Stewart | | | Infantry |
| John Slack | Commd. Military Stores | | |
| | | Daniel Heavey | |
| John Vaughan | | Francis Johnston | |
| Charles Sutton | | Robert Livingston | |
| | | Joshua Lovley | |
| Corporals | | John Sellman | |
| Michael Hawke | | William Stalker | |
| Thomas Condran | | Robert Smith | |
| James Royston | | David Young | |
| John Ratcliffe | Commd. Military Stores | Mark Goldsbury | |
| | | Reuben Scott | Commd. Light Infantry |
| Thomas Fanning | | | |
| Thomas Browne | | Timothy Connelly | |
| | | William Davis | |
| Bombardiers | | Charles Groome | |
| Michael O'Brian | | John Head | Commd. Forage Waggon |
| Phillip O'Brian | | | |
| | | Charles Murritt | |
| Gunners | | John Reynolds | |
| James Walsh | | Peter Lawrence | |
| James Moree | Comd. Light Infantry | John Evans | Commd. Military Stores |
| | | | |
| James Whailing | | Joseph Poague | |
| Peter Mayner | | Thomas Smith | |
| | | Charles Sutton | Promoted to Serjt. 1 Jan |
| Matrosses | | | |
| Thomas Browne | Promoted Corpl. 1 Jan | James Symonds | |
| | | Robert Myers | Sick Camden 6 Dec |

I certifie the above Roll to be the true state of said Company, Camp near Bacon's Bridge, So. Carolina, 5th April, 1782.

W. Brown, Capt. Artillery.

## FREDERICK GERMAN ARTILLERY.

Serjt.
Fredk. Grammer
Jona. Pinkney
Thos. McNier
John Sands

Corpl.
John Bond
Alex. Thompson
Chrs. Hohne
Edwd. Roberts

Gunrs.
Edward Roper
John Kerr
Patrick Dunn
James Elliott
Willm. Grant
Willm. Sifton

Bomb.
Caleb Marriott
Danl. Wells, Jr.
Willm. Glover
Willm. Tayler
Thomas Hewit
John Woolfit

Bomb.
James McDonnall
Gideon Kent
Henry Johnson
Samuel Lusby
John May
Elijah Pennington
Richard Flimming
Jesse Ray
James Sears
John Thompson
David Biggs
Thomas Lusby
Thomas Chalmers
John Keith
Hezekiah Wayman
Willm. Phelps
Willm. Perdue
Willm. James
John Barry
Willm. Johnson
Robert Nicols
Henry Smeth
John Barber
Joseph Gest
Jesse Lewis
Henry Wood
M.

Bomb.
Francis Welsh
John Gordon
Robert Lusby
Richd. Dorsey
Jona. Raullings
Willm. Robeson
Willm. Madcafe
John Edwill
W. Barns
Jos. Burneston
Edwd. Lusby
Andrew Williams
John McNier
John Williams
John Callahan
Richd. Harwood, of Thos.
John T. Shaaff
James P. Maynard
Daniel Murray
Francs. T. Clements
Arthur Shaaff
John Keeth
John Thompson
Joseph Gist

### ARTILLERY MEN.

James Welch
Henry Higgs
Hugh Champlin

Peregrine Askew
Thomas Bowler
Charles Groome

Joseph Poogue
Robert Campbell
Thomas Larymore

### INFANTRY.

Steven Hancock
Thomas Clarke
Joshua Lister

Robert Statia
Richd. Haslip
Emanuel Carthegene

John McDaniel
Peter McGuire
J. Smith

December 23rd, 1783.    A Sargent and Corpral and Six Men.

I Hope that you Will Generrel Smallwood that you Wood Be So Good has to Be Stoo a Litel monney.

Han. Hus.

                                     Decem ................
Account of Expences of Seventeen ...................................................
Great Guns, by order of the Governor...................... ....... ...
the Entertainment given to Gen ...... . ...................... ..............
    17 Men per List, to be paid by .. ............. ......... ..............
Auditors Office 12th January, 1784
         Passed for Four pounds f ...................................... .........,
    Receipt for 17 soldiers, Guards

[Entertainment of General Washington at Annapolis at the time he resigned his Commission.]

---

### RESOLVES OF CONTINENTAL CONGRESS 15 MAY, 1778.

"*Resolved, unanimously*, That every non-commissioned military officer and soldier, who hath inlisted, or shall inlist, into the service of these states, for and during the war, and shall continue therein to the end thereof, shall be entitled to receive the further reward of 80 dollars at the expiration of the war."

---

A List of the Noncommissioned and Privates of the Maryland Artillery, who were entitled to the Gratuity of Eighty Dollars as allowed by Act of Congress of May 15th, 1778, and settled by Jno. White, Esquire, late Commissr.'s Assistant for Settling the Accounts of the Army for Maryland.

| | | |
|---|---|---|
| Henry Slack, Serjt | Robert Smith | Elisha Redman |
| Charles Stewart " | David Young | Thomas Potter |
| John Slack " | Mark Goldsbury | Michael Conner |
| John Vaughan " | Reuben Scott | William Grimes |
| Charles Sutton " | Timothy Connelly | John Ireland |
| Thomas Brown " | Charles Groom | Philip Masterson |
| Michael Hawke, Corpl. | John Head | John Prout |
| Thomas Condran " | Charles Muirett | Daniel Neal |
| James Roystan " | Peter Lawrence | Bennit Rieley |
| Philip O'Bryan " | John Evans | Andrew Sprink |
| Michael O'Bryan | Thomas Smith | Thomas Bowler |
| James Welch | James Simonds | John Brady |
| James Moree | Robert Myers | Danl. Rawdon |
| James Whaling | Jesse Thompson, Serjt. | Thomas Gleeson |
| Peter Maynor | William Rawlings " | Edward Berry |
| Isaac Burton | James Hutton " | Perry Askey |
| Arthur Carnes | William Cornwell " | Samuel Carter, Serjt. |
| Hugh Champlin | David Welch | Benedict Johnson |

| | | |
|---|---|---|
| John Fitzgerald | James Hammond, Corpl | Thomas Redman |
| Jonathan Gill | William Hutton " | Thomas Randall |
| Henry Higgs | William Dixon | John Sandall |
| Daniel Havey | William Allen | Hugh McDowell |
| Robert Levingston | John Clark | Francis Johnston |
| Joseph Pogue | Thomas Williams | Richard Lewis, Serjt. |
| John Stillman | Thomas Tyack | William Davies |
| William Stalker | Peter Davies | Philip Jones |

List of Non Commissioned Officers and Privates of the Maryland Artillery who received the Gratuity of Congress for serving to the End of the War      rec'd from

J. Howell, Esq., Paymr. Genl.

Dec. 5th, 1788.

Return of Certificates issued to the NonCommissioned Officers &c, of the Corps of Maryland Artillery late commanded by Major Brown, taken from the Register of John White, Esquire, Asst. Commissr. of Army Accounts for the State of Maryland.

| | | | | | |
|---|---|---|---|---|---|
| Henry Slack | Serjt. | John Sandall | M. | Rawling Spinks | M. |
| Charles Stewart | " | Edward Berry | " | William Hellin | " |
| John Slack | " | Isaac Burton | " | Thomas Redman | " |
| John Vaughan | " | Arthur Carnes, Corpl. & M. | | James McGowen | " |
| Charles Sutton | " | Hugh Champlin, Jr. | M. | Timothy Donovan | " |
| Michael Hawke | Corpl. | John Fitzgereld, Jr. | " | John Wheeler | " |
| Thomas Condron | " | Jonathan Gill | " | Frederick Eyen | " |
| James Roystan | " | Henry Higgs | " | John Howard | " |
| John Ratcliffe | " | Daniel Havey | " | Jonas Philips | " |
| Thomas Fanning | " | Francis Johnston | " | William Davies | " |
| Thomas Brown | Serjt. | Robert Livingston | " | Charles Groom | " |
| Michael O'Bryan | B. | Joshua Lovely | " | John Head | " |
| James Welch | " | John Sillman | " | Charles Muiret | " |
| Phillip O'Bryan | Corpl. | William Stalker | " | John Reynolds | " |
| James Moore | Gun. | Robert Smith | " | Peter Laurence | " |
| James Whaling | " | David Young | " | John Evans | " |
| Peter Maynor | Fifer | Mark Goldsbury | " | Joseph Pogue | " |
| Samuel Carter | Serjt. | Reuben Scott | " | Thomas Smith | " |
| Richard Lewis | " | Timothy Conolly | " | James Simonds | " |
| James Hammond | Corpl. | Benedict Johnson | " | Robert Myers | " |
| William Hutton | " | John Paine | " | Thomas Brown | " |
| Dennis McCormick | " | Thomas Bowler | " | James Welch | " |
| William Hallin | B. | John Compton | " | Jesse Thompson | Serjt. |
| William Dixon | " | John Standley, Jr. | " | William Rawlings | " |
| John Clark | G. | John Brady | " | James Hutton | " |

| | | | | | | |
|---|---|---|---|---|---|---|
| Thomas Williams | D. | Philip Jones | M. | William Cornwall | Serjt. |
| Elisha Redman | " | Hugh McDowell | " | James Hendrickson | M. |
| Thomas Potter | F. | John Smith | " | William Willthon | " |
| Peter Davies | D. | Daniel Rawdon | " | John Pearson | " |
| Perry Askey | M. | Thomas Tyack | F. | John Turner | " |
| Michael Conner | " | David Welch | Serjt. | James Berry | " |
| Thomas Gleeson | " | Thomas Barber, | " | David White | " |
| William Grimes | " | died in Virginia | | Jacob Owens, | " |
| Cornelius Harling | " | John Connelly, | M. | died | |
| John Ireland | " | dischd. at Pow' Pow | | John Quinn, | " |
| Philip Masterson | . " | Robert Campbell | " | dischd. in 1781 | |
| James Neil | " | Michael Hughes | " | James Clark | " |
| Michael O'Farol | " | Edward Henesey, | " | William Allen | " |
| Daniel Neil | " | infantry afterwards | | | |
| John Prout | " | Peter Maynor, Sr., | " | | |
| John Redman | " | died | | | |
| Thomas Randall | " | Francis Popham, | " | | |
| Bennet Reily | " | killed | | | |
| Andrew Shrink | " | Thomas Stanley | " | | |

Amount of pay for the Year 1782......................................Dols.   9189.83
"   from 1 Aug to 1 Jan '82 ...... ........ ..................   9750.80
"   for Gratuity ............. .................... ..............   6240.00
"   for 1783 . ................ ......................................   4489.20

29,670.03

Total amount received by Major W. Brown for the Non Commissd. & Privates of the Artillery late under his command, twenty nine thousand six hundred & seventy dollars & $\frac{3}{100}$ pts., which agrees with his Receipts.

Joseph Howell, Jr., Comiss.

Chrisr. Richmond, Esquire,
    Aud. General for Maryland
Entered in List of those entitled to Land.

# ROLLS OF MARYLAND MEN IN LEE'S DRAGOONS.

## CAPT.-MAJOR-LT. COL. HENRY LEE

Henry Lee was commissioned Captain of a Company of Virginia Dragoons June 18th, 1776. This Company was attached to the 1st Continental Dragoons March 31st, 1777.

### RESOLVES OF CONTINENTAL CONGRESS 7 APRIL, 1778.

"*Resolved*, That captain H. Lee be promoted to the rank of major-commandant; that he be empowered to augment his present corps by inlistment to two troops of horse, to act as a separate corps."

### RESOLVES OF CONTINENTAL CONGRESS 28 MAY, 1778.

"*Resolved*, That major Henry Lee's corps of partizan light dragoons consist of three, instead of two, troops."

### RESOLVES OF CONTINENTAL CONGRESS 13 JULY, 1779.

"*Resolved*, That capt. M'Lane's company, now attached to the Delaware regiment, and the dismounted dragoons belonging to major Lee's partizan corps, be formed into a fourth troop and added to the corps: this troop to be commanded by capt. M'Lane, and to serve on foot."

### RESOLVES OF CONTINENTAL CONGRESS 14 FEBRUARY, 1780.

"*Resolved*, That recruiting money be furnished to major Lee, to enable him to inlist seventy privates, to serve as dismounted dragoons in addition to those now in the corps; the whole to be formed into three troops."

### RESOLVES OF THE MARYLAND ASSEMBLY 11 APRIL, 1780.

"*Resolved*, That the officers and soldiers raised in this state, and now in colonels Hazen's, Spencer's, Gist's and major Lee's corps, be entitled to receive the same privileges, bounties, and cloathing, that the officers in the line have or are entitled to receive under the resolution of the 4th of December, 1778, and the act of assembly, entitled, An act relating to the officers and soldiers of this state, in the American army, and other purposes therein mentioned, passed at a session of assembly, begun and held at the city of Annapolis, on Thursday the 22d day of July, in the year 1779." *

* Also see pages 596 and 597.

RESOLVES OF CONTINENTAL CONGRESS 21 OCTOBER, 1780.

" Resolved, . . . . . . . . . . . . That there be 2 partizan corps, consisting of 3 troops of mounted and 3 of dismounted dragoons, of 50 each, one of which corps to be commanded by col. Armand, and the other by major Lee, and officered by appointment of the commander in chief, with the approbation of Congress: and that the commander in chief be authorized to direct a mode for completing, recruiting and supplying the said corps."

RESOLVES OF CONTINENTAL CONGRESS 6 NOVEMBER, 1780.

" *Resolved*, That the partizan corps commanded by major Lee in future have two field officers, a lieutenant-colonel and a major.

*Resolved*, That major Lee be, and hereby is, promoted to the rank of lieutenant-colonel of cavalry in the army of the United States, retaining the command of his present corps."

A Roll of Men enlisted in the Partizan Cavalry under the command of Major Henry Lee, out of Cecil County, June, 1778.

| | |
|---|---|
| John Germain Thomas | Jesse Crasby |
| James Wallace | Thomas Owins |
| Thomas Manly | Jos. Owins |
| Daniel Williamson | Christopher Rutledge |
| William Richardson | George Hill |
| John Ward | John Cummins |
| William Richardson, (miller) | Jos. Hemphill |
| Michael Rudulph | Jnonath Short |
| Thomas Broom | Abiah Hukill |
| Robert Crouch | George Boice |

Sir :—Above you have a return of Men enlisted by me in the Partizan Cavalry, it has not been in my power owing to the absence of some of our Non Comd. Officers, to make a return e'er this, all the above men were enlisted out of yr. County.

I am, Sr. yr. very hbl. srvt.

John Rudulph,<br>L. P. L. D.

A Pay Roll for a Detachmt. of Dragoons of Lt. Col. Henry Lee's Legion, belonging to the State of Maryland, for the months of Aug., Sept., Oct., Nov. and Dec., 1780. [All paid for five months, except

Arch. Gordon, 2 months, and John Manly, not paid, being advanced and the time uncertain when.]

| NAMES. | RANK. | NAMES. | RANK. |
|---|---|---|---|
| Michael Rudulph | Capt. | John J. Thomas | Privates |
| David Henderson | Serjt. | George Hill | |
| John Manly | | Robert Crouch | |
| | | Abiah Hukill | |
| William French | Beuglers | John Bennet | |
| Jesse Crasbey | | Samuel Tenkins | |
| | | John Kinard | |
| Samuel Thompson | Privates | James Arrants | |
| Christ. Rutledge | | James Veazey | |
| Joseph Owens | | William Dowdle | |
| Joseph Hemphill | | John Towlin | |
| Richard Basset | | George Boice | |
| James McCracken | | John Howard | |
| Joshua Harvey | | Arch. Gorden | |
| Willm. Chesnut | | Abrahm. Sutton | Fife Major. |

Michl. Rudulph,
Capt. Lee's Legion.
Oct 4th, 1783.

A Return of Dragoons who have served in Lieut. Col. Henry Lee's Legion, belonging to the State of Maryland.

| NAMES. | COMMENCEMENT OF PAY. | NAMES. | COMMENCEMENT OF PAY. |
|---|---|---|---|
| Thomas Broom | 7th Aprril, 1778 | William French | 7th Apl., '78 Bugler |
| George Hill | " | Jessee Crasby | "      " |
| John Manly | " | David Henderson, | 1st Jan., 1779 |
| Christopher Rutledge | " | Promoted Serjeant, 1st Apl., '80 | |
| Joseph Owens | " | Johsua Harvey | 1st Jan., 1779 |
| Joseph Hemphill | " | William Chisnut | " |
| Richard Bassett | " | Samuel Tenkins | |
| James McCracken | " | James Arrants | 8th March, 1780 |
| John Jerman Thomas | " | James Veazey | " |
| Robert Crouch | " | William Dowdle | 12th March, 1780 |
| Abiah Hukill | " | John Towlin | 16th March, " |
| John Kinard | " | John Howard | 1st April, " |
| John Bennet | " | John Johnson | 10th July, 1780 |
| George Boice | " | | |

There are several Men, who are entitled to have their Depreciation Accts. settled, whose Names are not entered above.

M. Rudulph

Return of Sundry Soldiers of Lee's Legion by Capt. Michl. Rudolph in October, 1783.

I do hereby certify that the bearer hereof John McColla Served three years in the 4th regt. Light Dragoons, as a private, and that he was a Citizen of the State of Maryland, and has been returned as one of its Soldiers. Nor has he received any consideration for the depreciation of his pay during the term of his Service, which commenced 10th April, 1777.

David Hopkins,

28th Sept., 1785.           Late Major Light Dragoons.*

I do certify that the bearer hereof, James McCrackin, (McCracking), a dragoon of the Partizan Legion, Commanded by Lieut. Col. Henry Lee, belonging to the State of Maryland has pay due him for his service in the Legion, from the first day of April, 1780, to this date, deducting one Months pay rec'd in cloathing.

Given this 20th Aug., 1783

Michl. Rudulph,

Capt., Lee's Legion.

Same to John Kinkead, (Kincaid), of Delaware.

By Virtue of the Orders of the Honble. Major Genl. Green, John Wisham, the Bearer hereof, Belonging to the Third Troop of the Partizan Legion, Commanded by Lieut. Col. Henry Lee, has Leave of Absence till called for, and then to repair to such rendezvous as shall be appointed in the State of Maryland, under pain of being considered and treated as a Deserter, the said Summons being published in the Maryland Newspapers three Weeks successively, to be considered as sufficient Notice. Given under my Hand this 17th Day of June, 1783.

Jos. Eggleston,

Ma. Comg., Lee's Legion.

Same to John Manly, George Boice and Robert Crouch of the Second Troop June 12th, 1783, George Hill of the Second Troop June 19th, 1783, and Jessey Cosby of the First Troop and William French of the Third Troop June 28th, 1783. Also the same to Thomas Broom of the First Troop March 20th, 1784, and William Dowdle of the Second Troop March 30th, 1784, signed by James Armstrong, Capt. 1st Troop.

---

* This has been accidentally misplaced.  John McColla belonged to Moylan's (see page 599).

Agreeable to a resolution of Congress, bearing date the 26th day of May, 1783, the bearer hereof Archibald Gordon a Soldier (Was of Lt. Col. Henry Lee's Legion) belonging to the State of Maryland has leave of absence untill called upon by proper authority to join his Corps, or is finally discharged.

Given at the Head of Elk in Mary Ld. this 26th Aug., 1783.

> Michael Rudulph,
> Capt., Lee's Legion.

---

Sir—Please pay to Archibal Gordan my pay Due me as a Soldier in the Partizan Legion, and his Receipt Shall be good for the Same.

> Sir I am yours
> Abiah Hukill
> Christopher Rutledge
> Robert Crouch

I do authorize and appoint David Henderson to receive and settle the above Order from Abih. Hukill in favour of me.  Given this 12th Sept., 1783                              Archibald Gordon.

Michl. Rudulph, Capt., Lee's Legion.

---

> Cecil County 7th Novem., 1785.

Sir—Please to Settle with the Bearer, Mr Tobias Rudulph, what's Due to me On your Books for my Services as a Soldier in Col. Henry Lee's Legion as my furlow will shew and Remit it to me by him

> and you will Oblige Sr. yours &c
> Archibald Gordon.

Capt. White Or any Other ⎫
  Officer that hath the   ⎬
  Settling said Accts.    ⎭

> Called John Gordon

---

Power of Attorney from Abiah Hukins to David Henderson to collect all sums due from the United States to Hukins for his services in Lt. Col. Lee's Partizan Legion.

Same from William Dowdle to Thomas Broom, April 10th, 1784.

Sir : —Please Pay Unto Mr. Henry Robinson the Sum or Sums of money wich may Be Due on finall Setlement with John Kinkead and his Receipt Shall Be your Discharge for the same from Sir your
Humble Servt.

Elk, May 31st, 1785.                                        Wm. Hugg.

To the Agent for Col. Lee's Legion for State Maryland.

Same for pay due William Dowdle, assigned by him to Thomas Broom, signed T. Broom, May 30th, 1785.

---

Auditor's Office, 23rd April, '87.

I do certify That there is due from the State of Maryland to James Gillis' Admor. £18. 15s. due to the said Gillis as Trumpeter in Col. Lee's Legion, from Aug. 1st, 1780, to Jan. 1st, 1781.

C. Richmond, Aud. Genl.

---

Auditor's Office, 23rd April, '87.

I do certify That there is due from the State of Maryland to William Crookshank's Admix. £15. 12s. and sixpence for pay as Trooper in Col. Lee's Legion, from Aug. 1st, 1780, to Jan. 1st, 1781.

C. Richmond, Aud. Genl.

Same to the Administrator of Jonathan Short's estate.

# ROLLS OF MARYLAND MEN IN PULASKI'S AND ARMAND'S LEGIONS.

### BRIGADIER GENERAL COUNT PULASKI

#### RESOLVES OF CONTINENTAL CONGRESS 15 SEPTEMBER, 1777.

" *Resolved,* That a commander of the horse be appointed with the rank of a brigadier ; the ballots being taken, count Pulaski was elected."

#### RESOLVES OF CONTINENTAL CONGRESS 28 MARCH, 1778.

" *Resolved,* That count Pulaski retain his rank of brigadier in the army of the United States, and that he raise and have the command of an independent corps to consist of 68 horse, and 200 foot, the horse to be armed with lances, and the foot to be equipped in the manner of light infantry: the corps to be raised in such way and composed of such men as general Washington shall think expedient and proper ; and if it shall be thought by general Washington that it will not be injurious to the service, that he have liberty to dispense, in this particular instance, with the resolve of Congress against enlisting deserters."

#### RESOLVES OF CONTINENTAL CONGRESS 6 APRIL, 1778.

" *Resolved,* . . . . . . That, if any of the states in which brigadier Pulaski shall recruit for his legion, shall give to persons inlisting in the same for three years, or during the war, the bounty allowed by the state in addition to the continental bounty, the men so furnished not being the inhabitants of any other of the United States, shall be credited to the quota of the state in which they shall be inlisted."

#### RESOLVES OF THE ASSEMBLY OF MARYLAND 21 APRIL, 1778.

" *Resolved,* That the governor and council be authorized and empowered to assist brigadier-general Pulaski in recruiting for his legion ; and that all persons enlisting in the same (not being inhabitants of any other of the United States) for three years or during the war, shall be allowed the bounty given by act of assembly to soldiers enlisting for three years or during the war, and shall be credited to the proportion of the county where such recruits shall have last resided ; and such recruits shall not be subject to be draughted under the late act for procuring troops for the American army. That the said recruits be passed by the lieutenant of the county wherein they shall be enlisted, who shall keep an account of all such recruits."

" *Resolved,* That all the men, inhabitants of these states, who shall be recruited in the corps of gen. Pulaski, and colonel Armand, in any of the United States, shall be credited to the quota of the state in which they shall be inlisted, they not being inhabitants of any other of the United States.

*Resolved,* That brigadier general Pulaski and col. Armand, make returns to the board of war of the recruits they shall inlist; and in such returns the places of nativity and settlement, and the state wherein they were inlisted shall be particularly mentioned; and the board are hereby directed to transmit to the respective states, the names and numbers of such persons, inhabitants thereof, as shall be so inlisted."

" *Resolved,* That Congress approve the mode suggested by the commander in chief, of incorporating the remainder of the men of the late brigadier general Pulaski's legion, and as many of the officers as there are vacancies for, into colonel Armand's corps; and that a return be made to the board of war of the deficiency of that corps, that measures may be taken to complete it according to the late establishment; and that lieutenant-colonel Lee make a return of the deficiency of his corps, for the same purpose."

A List of Recruits Enlisted in Pulaski's Legion, Balto.

| | | |
|---|---|---|
| Edward Dannally | William Rolph | William Trugard |
| Roger Owings | John Collins | |
| Henry Kent | Bryan Dallam (?) | |

This is to Certifie that I have Pas'd the Seven recruits & Substitutes above mentioned Enlisted by Capt. De Segond. General Polaskie's Legion, April 29th, 1778.

And. Buchanan, Lt. Col.

To the Counceal

I should have sent to you the certificat of the other men if Mr. Buckanon your lieutenant, was came in town since the 29 of April that he hath pas'd the seven above. I call for him many times I never met him, as soon as he will make his appeareance in town I'll present them and I'll send you his pass.

De Segond deLaplan.

Thomas Bond, enlisted in Baltimore May 8th, 1778, by Capt. Siggond for Count Pulaski's Legion.

Money advanced for General Pulaski's Legion since the 10th day of April til the 12th of May, 1778.

| NAMES. | WHEN ENLISTED. | NAMES. | WHEN ENLISTED. |
|---|---|---|---|
| Edward Dannaly | April 10 | Nicholas Ryland | May 8 |
| Roger Owings | 27 | Thomas Hoult | 9 |
| John Cain | May 4 | Charles Daemon | 10 |
| John Collins | April 28 | James Carter | 11 |
| Henry Kent | 22 | Philop Beaty | 11 |
| William Rolph | 22 | John Tedford | 12 |
| John Price | May 6 | William Trugard, deserter | 22 |
| Peter Neguire | 8 | William Herlity | 6 |
| Thomas Bond | 8 | | |
| | £201.5.0. | | |

Affidavits of Benjamin Prior and Notley Tippett that they, in the company of Joseph Smith, enlisted in Count Pulaski's Legion, sometime in the month of July, 1779, being then in Charles Town, S. C. Said Smith is now before Richard Barnes, Lt. of St. Mary's County, taken up as a deserter.

Sworn to before Jeremiah Jordon.

St. Mary's County, July 26th, 1780.

## ARMAND'S LEGION

Colonel Armand, Marquis De La Rouerie, commissioned 10 May, 1777.

### RESOLVES OF CONTINENTAL CONGRESS 10 MAY, 1777

" *Resolved*, That Mons. Armand have a commission, with the rank of colonel, and that he be directed to repair to general Washington."

### RESOLVES OF CONTINENTAL CONGRESS 25 JUNE, 1778.

" *Resolved*, That the independent corps raised by col. Armand, in consequence of general Washington's permission, be taken into continental pay. That general Washington be authorised to officer this corps with such foreign and other officers of merit as at present hold commissions, and who are not already and can not be annexed to other corps on the proposed arrangement of the army:

That if any of the States shall think proper to allow the non-commissioned officers and privates, who have or shall enlist in col. Armand's corps, the bounty allowed by them respectively, in addition to the continental bounty, the men so engaged shall be credited as part of the quota of the state who shall allow the additional bounty."

### RESOLVES OF CONTINENTAL CONGRESS 21 JUNE, 1779.

"*Resolved*, That the non-commissioned officers and privates of the intended corps of German volunteers be transferred to the corps commanded by colonel Armand."

### RESOLVES OF CONTINENTAL CONGRESS 23 FEBRUARY, 1780.

"*Resolved*, That the remains of the legion of the late count Pulaski be incorporated with the corps of colonel Armand, marquis de la Rouerie, in such manner as the commander in chief of the southern army shall think proper : the united corps to be formed into a legion to be commanded by colonel Armand."

### RESOLVES OF CONTINENTAL CONGRESS 26 MARCH, 1783.

"*Resolved*, That in consideration of the merit and services of colonel Armand, he be promoted to the rank of brigadier-general, retaining the command of his present corps."

A Return of the Men belonging to the State of Maryland, who served in the First Partizan Legion, commanded by Brigadier General Armand, Marquis de la Rouerie, discharged Nov. the 15th, 1783.

| NAMES AND RANK. | WHAT YEAR ENLISTED. | NAMES AND RANK. | WHAT YEAR ENLISTED. |
|---|---|---|---|
| Serjeant. | | Privates. | |
| William Seth | 1778 | Dennis Lowe | 1782 |
| Corporals. | | Benjamin Carlisle | 1782 |
| Joseph Higdon | 1781 | Benjamin Gilpin | 1782 |
| John Higdon | 1782 | Edward Jenkins | 1782 |
| Trumpeter. | | George Tucker | 1782 |
| Joseph Herold | 1782 | Farrier. | |
| Privates. | | Thomas Aspell, Draughted | 1780 |
| Edward Donnally | 1779 | Privates. | |
| William Bennister | 1782 | Bernard Thompson | 1782 |
| Farrieres. | | Philip McDad | 1782 |
| Nathaniel Mason | 1782 | Jacob Ortner | 1782 |
| Peter Teams | 1778 | Michael Eckhart | 1782 |
| Corporal. | | Frederick Stein | 1782 |
| Bazil Lowe | 1782 | Joseph Chalupetzky | 1782 |

| NAMES AND RANK. | WHAT YEAR ENLISTED. | NAMES AND RANK. | WHAT YEAR ENLISTED. |
|---|---|---|---|
| Privates. | | Privates. | |
| Matthias Murray | 1781 | Jasper Shomig | 1782 |
| Bazil Carlisle | 1781 | Anthony Ulrich | 1782 |
| William Davis | 1781 | Jacob Bartling | 1782 |
| John Steel | 1782 | John Mate | 1782 |
| Robert Henwood | 1782 | George Young | 1782 |
| James Lowman | 1778 | Frederick Klein | 1782 |
| Clement Green | 1781 | John Fair | 1782 |
| | | James McDonald | 1778 |

Godfried Swartz, Adjutant of the Legion.

Armand, Mqis. de la Rouerie.

## ROLLS OF MARYLAND MEN IN VARIOUS OTHER CORPS NOT BELONGING TO MARYLAND.

### RESOLVES OF CONTINENTAL CONGRESS 27 DECEMBER, 1776.

"*Resolved*, That general Washington shall be, and he is hereby, vested with full, ample, and complete powers to raise and collect together, in the most speedy and effectual manner, from any or all of these United States, 16 battalions of infantry, in addition to those already voted by Congress; to appoint officers for the said battalions of infantry; to raise, officer, and equip 3000 light horse; three regiments of artillery, and a corps of engineers, and to establish their pay; to apply to any of the states for such aid of the militia as he shall judge necessary; . . . to displace and appoint all officers under the rank of brigadier-general, and to fill up all vacancies in every other department in the American army."

### HOUSE OF DELEGATES, ASSEMBLY OF MARYLAND, 7 JANUARY, 1782.
#### COMMITTEE REPORT.

" THE committee, appointed to enquire the number of recruits wanting to complete the quota of this state, &c. beg leave to report . . . . . . that three companies of artillery (nearly full) belonging to this state, have been incorporated with colonel Harrison's regiment of Virginia artillery; and your committee are of opinion, that the said companies, in justice to this state, ought to have been attached to her line of infantry, and that the said regiment ought to be kept up by Virginia and this state, and that the promotion to vacancies ought to be extended in common to the officers so incorporated, agreeable to their rank and pretentions; but your committee are informed that although the said regiment now consists almost entirely of the men of the companies of this state, yet they are commanded by Virginia officers, and the former officers of the said companies belonging to this state are forced to retire from the service on half pay.  Your committee are of opinion, that this matter ought to be represented to congress:

Your committee beg leave further to report as their opinion, that this state has been materially injured, by permitting corps of other lines, and of the additional sixteen regiments, to recruit within this state, as will appear by the following list of companies enlisted in this state, for the following corps of artillery, cavalry, and infantry, to wit:  Colonel Hazen's regiment, 2 companies; Hartley's, 3 ; Gist's, 2 ; Grayson's, 2 or 3 ; Rifle, 4 ; officers discharged by colonel Brodhead at Fort Pit, and the men incorporated with Brodhead's regiment of Pennsylvania troops, but some of them have since deserted and joined the Maryland line; German, 4, now attached to the Maryland line about one company, desertion and term of service expiring must account for the remainder; Foreman's, 2 or 3, attached to the Jersey troops ; Patten's, 2, attached to the Pennsylvania line; artillery, 3, incorporated with Harrison's Virginia regiment ; Moylan's horse, 3 ; Baylor's horse, 1 ; Pulaski's, 1 or 2 ; Lee's, 1 or 2.  In all 30 or 34 companies.

Your committee are informed, that many of the men in the said companies were enlisted for the war, and now remain in such of the above corps as have been continued on the establishment, and others of the reduced corps are now attached to the line of the state in which they have respectively served ; and your committee are of opinion, that congress should be requested to order, that all the men, now in service, raised in this state for any of the above companies, be returned and annexed to the line of this state."

---

### 2ND CANADIAN OR HAZEN'S

#### COL. MOSES HAZEN, COMMISSIONED 22 JANUARY, 1776.

This Regiment was intended to be raised in Canada and for some time was called the 2nd Canadian.  Later it was recruited in the United States.  It was also called ' Congress Own.'

---

### RESOLVES OF CONTINENTAL CONGRESS 19 APRIL, 1781

" *Resolved,* That it be, and hereby is recommended to the states of Rhode-Island and Providence Plantations, New-York, New-Jersey, Pennsylvania, Delaware, Maryland and Virginia, to make good the depreciation of the monthly pay of the officers and soldiers belonging to colonel Moses Hazen's regiment that are considered as a part of the quota of the respective states aforesaid, in the same manner they have made good the depreciation to the officers and soldiers in the battalion belonging to the lines of those states respectively."

---

Non-commissioned Officers and Privates of Col. Hazen's Regiment, belonging to the State of Maryland.

### CAPT. POPHAM'S COMPANY.
Daniel Keith, Private

### CAPT. HERON'S COMPANY.

Harvey Burnes, Private
James Hayton    do

David Kennedy, Private
Thomas McGee    do

### LATE CAPT. BURNES'S COMPANY.

John McColgain, Drum.
Willm. Brown, Private
James Duncan    do
John Dugan    do

Massy Fluart,    Private
John Kuny, (Coony) do
Chas. March    do
Edward White    do

### CAPT. CARLILE'S COMPANY.

John Ryan, Serjt.
Thomas Capen (assigned his depreci-
    ation money March 23rd, 1781)
Wm. Douly, Corpl.
Geo. McDonald, Drum.
Nehemiah Barnes, Private
John Batten    do
William Deacons    do
Thomas Deavour    do
Samuel Frazer    do

James Hopkins,    Private
Martin Mulloy    do
James M'Intire, (McIntier) do
George Somerville,    do
    (assigned his depreciation
    money March 12th, 1781)
William Smith,    Private
Francis Tycont    do
Edward Wall    do

### CAPT. WHITE'S COMPANY.
Christopher Nash

### CAPT. MUNSON'S COMPANY.
Bartholomew Sheridan, Serjt.

### CAPT. PRY'S COMPANY.

James Edes, Private

James Flood, Private

Wm. Perkins, Private

### CAPT. TAYLOR'S COMPANY.

Michael Anderson, Private
John Collins,    do    —Carlile
    (assigned his depreciation money
    March 15th, 1781)

Hugh Conolly,    Private
Saml. Richardson,  do
Benjamin Wilson    do

N. B.—John Durbin (from Capt. Carlile's Co.) Prisoner of War, not mentioned in the Body of this List.

## Return of Hazen's Regiment, 1783.

### HARTLEY'S.

RESOLVES OF CONTINENTAL CONGRESS 16 DECEMBER, 1778.

"*Resolved*, That col. Hartley's regiment and the four independent companies raised in the state of Pennsylvania, commanded by captains

Doyle, Wilkie, Steel and Calkerwood, and also the remains of col. Patton's regiment, except capt. M'Lane's company, be incorporated into one regiment, and added to the Pennsylvania line, as an eleventh regiment, and that capt. M'Lane's company be annexed to the Delaware regiment."

---

COL. THOMAS HARTLEY, COMMISSIONED 1 JANUARY, 1777.
COL. JOHN PATTON, COMMISSIONED 11 JANUARY, 1777.

These were 2 of the Additional 16 Regiments. Hartley's was transferred to the Pennsylvania Line and designated the Eleventh Pennsylvania, the original Eleventh Pennsylvania having been disbanded 1 July, 1778. Patton's was broken up 13 January, 1779, and attached to Hartley's, except capt. McClean's Company, which was attached to the Delaware Line.

HARTLEY'S REGIMENT, Aug. 1st, 1780–Jan. 1st, 1781.

| | | | |
|---|---|---|---|
| Corpl. | John Burgess, no five months Pay | Pt. | George Miller |
| | Gassaway Brashears | Pt. | Thomas McCallo |
| Serjt. | John Barber | Pt. | George McCallo |
| | James Beall | | Ben Marshall, no 5 mos. |
| | James Doren | | Wm. Marquess |
| Serjt. | Jeremiah Ferrall | | Corpl. Matthew Pearson |
| Pt. | James Farwell | Pt. | Thomas Wood |
| Serjt. | John McDaniel | | |

MOYLAN'S.

COL. STEPHEN MOYLAN, COMMISSIONED 8 JANUARY, 1777.

4th Regiment of Light Dragoons, raised in Pennsylvania in 1777.

Aug. 1st, 1780–Jan. 1st, 1781.
Joseph Hyner, 5 mos.*

COL. NATHL. GIST'S REGT. OF RANGERS.

Col. Nathaniel Gist, commissioned 11 January, 1777.
Col. William Grayson, commissioned 11 January, 1777.
Col. Charles M. Thruston, commissioned January, 1777.

These were 3 of the Additional 16 Regiments and were consolidated as Gist's, 22 April, 1779.

* Also see John McColla, page 588.

Muster Roll of Capt. John Gist's Co., in Col. Nathl. Gist's Regt. of Rangers in the Service of the United States of America, Attached to the Third Maryland Regt., Commanded by Col. Mordicai Gist, for the Month of February, 1778.

| | | | |
|---|---|---|---|
| Capt.   John Gist, | Commissioned March 9th, 1777. | | |
| 1 Lieut. John Toomy, | "   April 10th, 1777. | | |
| 2 Lieut. Richard Chinowith, | "   April 6th, 1777, | { absent Contrary to Orders, gone to Maryland | |
| Ensign  George Winchester | "   April 8th, 1777, | { on Command in Md. Since Sept. last | |

| NAMES AND RANK. | TIME. | REMARKS. | NAMES AND RANK. | TIME. | REMARKS. |
|---|---|---|---|---|---|
| Serjt. | | | Privates | | |
| Matthew McHugh | 3 yrs. | Confin'd | Paul Duggan | 3 yrs | Sick in |
| Corpl. | | M. Guard | | | Hospl. |
| Edward Joice | War | | Danl. Brion | " | " " |
| Drum. & Fife. | | | | | |
| Michl. Smith | 3 yrs. | Sick in | James Ward | " | " " |
| | | Hospl. | Jerry Coholen | " | " " |
| Privates | | | John Sponsellor | War | " " |
| John Connelly | War | | David Dean | 3 yrs | " " |
| William Rian | 3 yrs | | Nathan Chambers | " | " " |
| John Lewin | " | | James Homes | " | " " |
| Thomas Watson | " | | David Norton | " | " " |
| William Knowles | " | | William Mays | War | " " |
| Walter Hartley | War | On Picquet | Michael Madden | 3 yrs | " " |
| William Welch | " | | Nicholas Shire | War | |
| Joseph Lovett | " | | John Dobson | 3 yrs | Deserted |
| Thomas Carroll | 3 yrs | | | | 29 Jan |
| Archd. Bartlett | " | | Christr. Hughs | " | " " |
| William Harris | War | | John Loyd | " | " " |
| Daniel Spratt | " | On Fur- | Isaac Bush | " | " " |
| | | lough | Timothy Sulivan | " | " " |

Wilmington, March 17th, 1778, Mustered Capt. John Gist's Company, as Specified in the Above Roll.

A. Horton, D. M. M.

CAPT. JOSEPH SMITH, N. GIST'S REGT.

Pay due from August 1st, 1780, to January 1st, 1781     £75.
Dec. 6th, 1784, Contents Rec'd.

Joseph Smith, Capt.

## List of Non Commissioned Officers & Privates of Col. Grayson's Regiment.

| NAMES AND RANK. | WHEN ENLISTED. | NAMES AND RANK. | WHEN ENLISTED. |
|---|---|---|---|
| | LATE CAPT. MOORE'S COMPANY. | | |
| Serjts. | | Privates | |
| Thomas Snead | Mch  4 '77 | James Johnston | Apl  3 |
| Sherwood Vaughan | 4 | George Tombleson | Mch  8 |
| Edward Harvie | June  5 | John Swepston | 4 |
| Corpl. | | Joseph Wilson | 6 |
| John Robertson | | Daniel White | |
| Drum. | | John Woster, (or Woter) | 14 |
| Hazle Williams | Mch 18 | Robt. McAdams | 30 |
| Corpls. | | Peter Carberry | 10 |
| John Sale | 4 | John Winn | Apl 25 |
| Robt. Oglesby | 10 | Elisha Derenton | Mch  7 |
| Fifer | | Thomas Curtis | Feb  8 |
| Thomas Griffin | 10 | Christr. Obrion | Apl  9 |
| Privates | | George Lambert | Mch 29 |
| John Tinsley | 4 | Charles George | Sept 30 |
| Thomas Gordon | May 11 | John Turnbull | |
| Thomas Carroll | Feb 14 | Thomas Miller | Apl 23 |
| Wm. Hitchcox | Jan  7 | Charles Ward | |
| | LIEUT. DREW. | | |
| Serjts. | | Privates | |
| Edward Rinker | Mch 10 | Luke Metheny | Mch  7 |
| John Spitsfathom | Feb 14 | John Gratage | July 23 |
| Durit Cary | July 20 | Timothy Kelley | 14 |
| Corpls. | | William Crosby | Feb 27 |
| Gilbert Been | Mch 10 | Thomps. Flood | Mch  7 |
| Luke Oneal | July 22 | John Maruny | May 26 |
| Chas. Melton | Jan 17 | Jesse Rinker | July 16 |
| Privates | | Peter Kittare, or (Kintare) | May 20 |
| Isaac Artes | May  8 | Willm. Nurse | June  6 |
| Caleb Balden | Mch 14 | Henry Orum | Apl  4 |
| Thomas Hopewell | Apl  5 | Saml. Johnston | |
| John Kirk | Oct 11 | Daniel Gilder | Sept 15 |
| William Haley | Apl  1 | Francis Ravenscroft | Apl  5 |
| Saml. Batterton | July 13 | Waitman Reenals | Mch 26 |
| Richd. Perrell | May 13 | John McDonnell | May |
| Jas. Thompson | 25 | | |

| NAMES AND RANK. | WHEN ENLISTED. | NAMES AND RANK. | WHEN ENLISTED. |
| --- | --- | --- | --- |

## LATE GRANT.

| Serjts. | | Privates | |
| --- | --- | --- | --- |
| Hezekiah Bready | | Anderson Briant | |
| Perigrine Bready | | Morris Minisham | |
| Corpl. | | William Foster | |
| Joseph Bready | | William Knighton | |
| Privates | | James Rains | |
| Benjamin Dawson | | Joseph West | |
| Jesse Davis | | Andrew Killgrest | |
| Jaby Friar | | Michael Moody | |
| Henry Rains | | | |

## ENSIGN KIRK.

| Serjts. | | Privates | |
| --- | --- | --- | --- |
| Alexander Ratrey, (or Ratsey) | | Smith Tompson | |
| Corpl. | | Owen Kelley | |
| Joseph Smith | | Patrick Boyd | |
| Privates | | Andrew Laiswell | |
| William Gillaspy | | Richard Spindles | |
| Hugh McGlochlin | | John Williams | |
| Ambrose Jones | | | |

## LIEUT. BELL.

| Serjts. | | Privates | |
| --- | --- | --- | --- |
| Patrick Shannon | | Thomas Conway | Apl 5 |
| James Tate | Mch 8 | Abel Armstrong | Mch 28 |
| Thomas Chapman | | William Kingors | |
| Sampson Archer | May 1 | James Shields | 22 |
| Corpls. | | George Weefield | Apl 5 |
| David Chambers | Mch 17 | James Obrien | |
| John Stevens | Apl 4 | Jos. Lee Bullock | Mch 17 |
| John Mitchell | Mch 17 | Ronsey Merritt | |
| Drums. | | James Lockhart | July 25 |
| Wm. McGowen | | Bartho. Reagon | |
| Fifer | | John Lock | May 4 |
| John Brown | | Ludwick Miller | |
| Privates | | Thomas Foster | Mch 17 |
| James Wilson | Mch 22 | Gordon Kelley | Apl 3 |
| William Shull | June 4 | Martin Sutton | July 25 |
| John Forchano | July 25 | James Strickland | Mch 17 |
| Dennis McKinnis | | Joseph Kenny | 17 |
| Joseph Hood | | Joseph Hays | 17 |
| John Monday | Mch 10 | George Jones | July 30 |
| Michael McMasters | 28 | | |

| NAMES AND RANK. | WHEN ENLISTED. | NAMES AND RANK. | WHEN ENLISTED. |
|---|---|---|---|

### ENSIGN TRIPLETT.

| Serjts. | | Privates | |
|---|---|---|---|
| Patrick Coleman | | Dennis Shea | June 30 |
| Alex. Munroe | Feb 13 | Wm. I. Conner | Apl 19 |
| Corpls. | | William Jacoe | Mch 15 |
| John Hillard | Mch 21 | John Jacoe | Apl 1 |
| Wm. Mitchell | 1 | Thomas Johnson | |
| Privates | | Benj. Atthea | Mch 11 |
| James Taylor | 8 | Jeffery Basdill | 1 |
| Francis Rogers | Feb 25 | John Parrot | July 4 |
| Daniel Chumley | Apl 15 | James Solomon | May 13 |
| Charles Hagan | Feb 20 | Peter Pool | Apl 16 |
| George Gordon | June 24 | Thomas Atthea | 14 |

A List of Officers and Soldiers of Col. Grayson's Regt. to whom Depreciation and other Advances have been paid by the State of Maryland on Account of the United States.

| ISSUED. | TO WHOM. | DEPRECIATION SUMS. | PAY FROM 1 AUG. '80 TO 1 JAN. '81. | TIME TO WHICH DEPRECIATION WAS PAID. |
|---|---|---|---|---|
| 15 Aug '82 | Peter Carbury, Pt., reinlisted £74.12.16 in the Maryland Line | | £12.8.4 | 18 May '80 |
| 7 Nov '82 | Matw. Coffer | 78.18.1 | 12.10.0 | 1 Aug '80 |
| 6 Oct '83 | Nehemiah Crawford, Sergt. | 88.2.4 | | 10 Mch '80 |
| 20 Nov '83 | Owen Coffield, Pt. | 81.15.4 | 12.10.0 | 1 Aug '80 |
| 14 Aug '83 | Wilson Gray | 74.17.8 | | 1 June '80 |
| 22 Aug '82 | Thomas Harrison, Sergt. | 103.3.11 | 18.15.0 | 20 Apl '80 |
| 6 Oct '83 | John Howard, Pt. | 80.15.0 | 18.15.0 | 1 Aug '80 |
| 26 May '83 | Jacob Johnson, Corpl. | 83.19.6 | | 1 Aug '80 |
| 20 July '82 | Joshua Power, Pt. | 77.14.10 | | 8 June '80 |
| 12 Feb '82 | George Speak, Corpl. | 88.8.11 | 13.15.0 | 1 Aug '80 |
| 23 Aug '82 | Aaron Simmons, Pt. | 77.1.5 | 12.10.0 | 18 July '80 |
| 6 Oct '83 | Hezekiah Speake | 72.3.2 | | 10 Mch '80 |
| 9 Oct '83 | William Speake | 77.5.2 | | 1 Aug '80 |
| 27 Apl '84 | John Willis | 73.9.0 | 12.10.0 | 11 Apl '80 |

### BAYLOR'S DRAGOONS

COL. GEORGE BAYLOR, COMMISSIONED 8 JANUARY, 1777.
LT. COL. WILL. WASHINGTON, COMMISSIONED 20 NOVEMBER, 1778.

3rd Regiment of Light Dragoons, raised in Virginia in 1777. Consolidated, as Baylor's, with Bland's 1st Regt. 9 November, 1782.

### Forman's

#### Col. David Forman, commissioned 12 January, 1777.

One of the Additional 16 Regiments. It was never fully completed and 1 July, 1778, was disbanded and officers and men transferred mainly to the New Jersey Line.

---

### Spencer's

#### Col. Oliver Spencer, commissioned 15 January, 1777.
#### Col. William Malcolm, commissioned 30 April, 1777.

These were 2 of the Additional 16 Regiments. They were consolidated as Spencer's, 22 April, 1779.

---

### 8th Pennsylvania

#### Resolves of Continental Congress—15 July, 1776.

"*Resolved*, That the battalion for the defense of the western frontiers, be raised in the counties of Westmoreland and Bedford, in the following proportions, to wit: seven companies in Westmoreland, and one company in Bedford."

---

#### Col. Daniel Brodhead, commissioned 29 September, 1776.

This Regiment was raised for the defence of the frontier. Capt. Moorhead's Independent Company was attached to this Regiment.

Some Maryland troops were sent to Fort Pitt and Col. Brodhead tried to increase his Regiment, at Maryland expense, by discharging Maryland officers and enrolling the men in his own Regiment. Many of these men deserted him and returned to the Maryland Line.

---

### Washington's Guards

Circular Letter sent to Col. Alexander Spottswood and three other Colonels by General Washington.*

Morristown, 30 April, 1777.

Sir,

I want to form a company for my guard. In doing this I wish to be extremely cautious, because it is more than probable, that, in the

---

* Sparks' Writings of George Washington, Vol. IV, pg. 407.

course of the campaign, my baggage, papers, and other matters of great public import, may be committed to the sole care of these men. This being premised, in order to impress you with proper attention in the choice, I have to request, that you will immediately furnish me with four men of your regiment; and, as it is my farther wish, that this company should look well and be nearly of a size, I desire that none of the men may exceed in stature five feet ten inches, nor fall short of five feet nine inches, sober, young, active, and well made. When I recommend care in your choice, I would be understood to mean men of good character in the regiment, that possess the pride of appearing clean and soldier like. I am satisfied there can be no absolute security for the fidelity of this class of people, but yet I think it most likely to be found in those who have family connexions in the country. You will therefore send me none but natives, and men of some property, if you have them. I must insist, that, in making this choice, you give no intimation of my preference of natives, as I do not want to create any invidious distinction between them and the foreigners. I am, yours &c.

---

CALEB GIBBS, COMMISSIONED CAPTAIN AND COMMANDER OF WASHINGTON'S GUARDS 12 MARCH, 1777, COMMISSIONED MAJOR 29 JULY, 1778.

---

I hereby Certify that the after mentioned men joined the Commander in Chief's Guard at the different periods rit against their Names & that they have not drawn any pay in said Corps since their joining.

| | | |
|---|---|---|
| James McDonald, | Formerly of 7th Md. Regt. | Jan 1st, '81. |
| Edward Wade, (Weed) | "    " 3rd "    " | May 15th, '81. |
| John Dent, | "    " 3rd "    " | Apl 11th, '80. |
| Jere. Driskill, | "    " 4th "    " | Apl 11th, '80 |
| Thomas Gillen, | "    " 5th "    " | July, '80. |

W. Colfax, Lt. Comt.,
Commd. in Chief's Guard.

Hd. Qurs., Head of Elk, 7th Sept., 1781.

## MISCELLANEOUS NAVAL ROLLS.

A List of the Officers and Men on Board the Ship Defence the 19th of September, Anno Dom. 1776, George Cook, Commander.

1st Lieut.
Henry Auchentick
2ndLieut.
John Burnell
Master
James Cordray
Chief Mate
John Hale
2nd Mate
Nathnl. Cooper
3rd Mate
Levin Langle
Midshipmen
Peter Sharp
James Rownds
Archibald Douglass
William Carter
Capt. Clerk
Francis Muir
Quartermasters
James Hasty, Disrated
Oct. 23rd
John Wright
James Falconer
Chas. Chamberlane
Boatswains
Anthony Hanson
Benjamin Simpson
John Barr
Yeoman
James Hawkins
Gunner
John Berryman
Gunner's Mate
Henry Rentford
Yeoman
William Piercey
Qr. Gunner
James Arne
Armourer
Mathew Murray

Able Seamen
James Hagan
Joseph Walpole
James Giffard
James Allen
Wm. Partus
Colin Brown
John Valiant
Wm. Gaggen
Dennis Larkins
Thomas Howard
William Hurburt
Christr. Short
Alex. Nicholson
David Primrose
Willm. King
John Knight
Henry Carberry
Wm. Fleming
John Crapper
Ordinary Seamen
Joseph Jones
Hoshier Cole
Henry Gilbert
Thomas Gilbert
Robert Fosset
Dennis Foloue
Richard Sutton
Patrick Cole
Charles Blunt
Daniel Nevin
Robert Hope
Thomas Green
James Barry
John McIntyre
Samuel Wolf
James Bradford
William Trott
Joshua Ozier
Lynn Sarmer
James Collins

Surgeon's Mate
Samuel Church
Purser
Francis Muir
Capt. Marines
Garret Brown
1st Lieut.
Thomas Walker
2nd Lieut.
Joseph Smith
3rd Lieut.
William Morris
Sergeants
William Radford
Vachel Yates
Michael Craig
Wm. DeCourcey
Drummer
Thomas Roberts
Corporals
William Matthews
Alexander Stanton
Privates
Ezekiel Disney
Robert Conner
Michael Conway
William Bishop
William Grantham
John Schea
Charles McNealis
Simon Trainer
William Askins
John Squible
William Judges
John Power
Benjamin Sutton
John Garvey
Morgan Murphy
James Cadey
Conrad McGuire
John Grant

Master at Arms
George Rowen
    Carpenter
Wm. Beauchamp
    Carpenter's Mate
William Prince
    Carpenter's Crew
Alex. Cummings
Wm. Howard
Nathan Ross
    Cooper
Joseph Dunbar
    Ship Steward
Joseph Burge
    Cabin Steward
Fran. Jackquelin
    Cook
James Gaggen
    Armourer's Mate
James Greer
    Able Seamen
Fran. Hurburt
Alex. Duffey, Rated Qr.
    Master Oct. 23rd

Ordinary Seamen
James Green
Thomas Moore
Abel Mason
Richard Cockey
Samuel Wilson
Joseph Dennis
John McKennie
Benjamin Thompson
Jacob Sutton
John Vaughan
Abram Strong
Moses Scott
Timothy Kelly
John Smyley
Bazil Smith
Robert McDonald
John Davis
William Adair
    Cabin Boys
Thomas Buckley
James Brown
    Surgeon
Nathan Dorsey

Privates
Barth. Deloray
Thomas Crow
John Donavin
Moses Greer
Robert Wilmott
Henry Carr
William Porter
John Lemmon
Edward Gibbons
William Sohan
James Armstrong
John Wilson
William Huggard
James McGill
Philip Handly
Waltely Masters
Barny McManus
William Davis
James Smith
    Loblolly Boy
Clement Tossuir

---

May 2nd, 1777.

William Paddison, Captain of the armed Schooner Dolphin.

---

Pay Roll of Capt. Robert Conway's Crew of Sailors on Board the Sloop Molly belonging to the State of Maryland, untill the 15th June, 1777.

| MEN'S NAMES. | TIME OF ENTRY. | | WHEN DISCHARGED. | |
|---|---|---|---|---|
| Robert Conway, Capt. | Feb | 1 | | |
| Joseph Conway, Lieut. | Mar | 9 | | |
| Wm. Thomas, Pilot | | 4 | June | 4 |
| Levi Thomas, Midshipman | | 5 | | 5 |
| Francis Boatswain, Boatswain | Apl | 11 | | |
| John Kelly, Gunner | Feb | 19 | June | 10 |
| Manuel Anthony, Mate | Apl | 24 | | |
| William Culpepper, Carpr. | | 26 | | |
| Jas. McDonald, Steward | Feb | 24 | June | 7 |
| Tobias Zimmerman, Master at Arms | | 28 | | 4 |
| John Lamond | | 5 | | |

| MEN'S NAMES. | TIME OF ENTRY. | | WHEN DISCHARGED. | |
|---|---|---|---|---|
| John Traner | Feb | 5 | | |
| Peter Packman | | 24 | June | 5 |
| Henry Grimfeild | | 24 | | 8 |
| Darby Melony | | 25 | | 9 |
| Jeremiah Clifford | | 26 | | 3 |
| William Burnhouse | Mar | 3 | | 15 |
| William Brown | | 3 | | 3 |
| John Price | | 3 | | 3 |
| Joseph Wheatcock | | 4 | | 4 |
| Joseph Bullock | | 5 | | 10 |
| John Hurst | | 11 | | |
| William Tignor | | 12 | June | 4 |
| Augustine Auger | Apl | 11 | | |
| Michael Anthony | | 22 | | |
| Manl. Davis | | 22 | | |
| Manl. Anthony | | 22 | | |
| Manl. Dicamon | | 24 | | |
| John Hicnarl | | 24 | | |
| John Jones | | 26 | | |
| John Johns | | 30 | | |
| John Ecloes | | 30 | | |
| Jacob Gonsac | | 30 | | |
| Mather Tindar | | 30 | | |
| Manl. Firnano | May | 2 | | |
| Bravo Bilbo | | 13 | | |

Oct. 18th, 1777.

Geo. Keith Elphinstone, Captain of the Perseus.

MARYLAND ACTS—OCT., 1780.

An ACT for the defence of the bay

"*Be it enacted, by the General Assembly of Maryland,* That the governor and council be authorised and requested to purchase (or cause to be built) and fitted with sails and oars, and manned as soon as possible, four large barges or row-boats, capable of carrying swivels and twenty five men at least; and that the governor and council be also authorised and requested to purchase (or cause to be built) as soon as possible, one galley, capable of carrying two eighteen and two nine pounders, with swivels; and one sloop or schooner, capable of carrying ten four pounders, and procure them to be well found, fitted, armed, and manned.

*And be it enacted,* That the governor and council be authorised and requested to appoint and commission a proper number of brave, experienced, and able seamen and officers, to command the said galley and sloop or schooner

*And be it enacted,* That a company of one hundred men be immediately raised to serve as marines on board the said galley and sloop or schooner, and occasionally on board the said barges or row-boats ; and that the governor and council be authorised and requested to appoint and commission one captain and two lieutenants to command the said company of marines, and to direct such officers to procure by enlistment as soon as possible, the said number of healthy able bodied men, including two sergeants and two corporals, to serve in such company for the term of three years, unless sooner discharged.

*And be it enacted,* That if any officer, soldier, or marine, shall lose a limb, or be otherwise maimed or hurt, so as to be rendered incapable of procuring a livelihood, such officer, soldier, or marine, shall be entitled to receive the same provision and support as is or shall hereafter be established by this state for its officers and soldiers in the service of the United States.''

MARYLAND ACTS—MAY, 1781.

A Supplement to the act for the defense of the bay.

"*Be it enacted, by the General Assembly of Maryland,* That for the immediate defense of the bay, . . . . the governor and council be authorised and empowered to purchase, at such price as they may think reasonable, the galley now in Baltimore-town, . . . . if on examination by such proper person as they may appoint, she shall be found to be sound and fit for the service, . . . . . . . and that they have power to contract for the building another galley, agreeable to the act of assembly of the last session, and cause her to be completely fitted and manned at the public expense ; both of which gallies to be employed in such manner as the governor and council shall from time to time direct, for the defense of our bay and the protection of the trade thereof;

*Be it enacted,* That the Governor and Council be authorised and empowered to contract for any number of barges, not exceeding eight, that they may think necessary for the defense of this bay, and to cause them to be completely fitted and manned."

A Pay List for the Barge Intreped, 1781.

| MONTH OF ENTRY. | DAY. | MENS NAMES. | QUALITY. | TIME PAYED UP TO. |
|---|---|---|---|---|
| June | 1 | Wm. Barns | Lieut. | July 14 |
| | 14 | Oakely Haddaway | " | " " |

Pay Roll of Part of the Crew Belonging to the Barge Intrepid in 1781.

| | | |
|---|---|---|
| Waterman | Chas. Price | Philem. Horney |
| Jos. Dawson | Peter Pickering | Robt. Spedding |
| Gunner | Nicholas Sherwood | Robt. Burch |
| Richard Eaton | David Robinson | Jesse Burkett |
| Watermen | Solo. Holmes | Alex. Cray |
| John Cook | Danl. M'Giney | Danl. Cork |
| John Sommers | Spedden Oram | David Robinson |
| Thomas Laruden | Jas. Holt | 2nd Lt. |
| Henry Powell | Levin Jacobs | Elliott Shanahan |

[3 months pay due to all except Cook and Laruden 1 month's pay. Shanahan's time is not given.]

July 14th, 1781. A Pay Roll for the Barge Terable.

| MONTH OF ENTRY. | DAY. | MENS NAMES. | QUALITY. | TIME PAY'D UP TO. | | WAGES IN HARD MONEY. | |
|---|---|---|---|---|---|---|---|
| June | 1 | John Ball | Lieut. | July 14 | 7. | 6. | 8. |
| | 1 | Danl. Caulk | Seaman | 14 | 4. | 8. | 0. |
| | 7 | Nathan Porter | Gunner | 14 | 4. | 8. | 8. |
| | 13 | Joseph Reddish | Seaman | 14 | 2. | 11. | 8. |

Errors Excepted, John Ball.

July 10th, 1782—August 2nd, 1782.
Oakley Haddaway, Lieutenant of the Barge Terrible

1782. Dr. The State of Maryland

In Acct. with Joseph Handy.

May 1st. To my pay as Lieut on board the Barge Protector from June 12th, '81, to this day, 10 mo. 18 days @ £13. 10 pr. mo. . . . . . . . £143. 2. 0

Nov. 12th. By Cash . . . . . £33. 15. 0
By Balance . . . . £109. 7. 0

Annapolis, August 5th, 1782. £143. 2. 0

Excepted      Joseph Handy.

The State of Maryland to Edward Spedden, Gentleman, Greeting.

Be it known that We reposing especial trust and Confidence in your Patriotism valour Conduct and Fidelity, do by these presents constitute and appoint you to be Second Lieutenant of the Barge Fearnought in the Service of this State, fitted out for repelling every hostile invasion thereof, and for the Defence of our Liberties. You are therefore carefully and diligently to discharge the Duty of Second Lieutenant of the said Barge by doing and performing all manner of things thereunto belonging, according to the rules and Discipline of War, and the usage of the Sea, and the Instructions which may from Time to Time be given you. And we do strictly charge and require all Officers, Seamen, Marines, and others under your Command, to be Obedient to your Orders as Second Lieutenant of the said Barge and you are to observe and follow all such Orders and Directions which you shall receive from the Supreme Executive Power of this State. This Commission to be in force until Lawfully revoked. Given at Annapolis in Council this 23rd Day of May, A. D. 1782.

### ROLL OF THE BARGE FEARNOUGHT. CAPT. SPEDDING.

| THE NAMES OF MEN ENLISTED FOR THE BARGE "FEARNOUGHT." | TIME OF INLISTMENT. | LAST PLACE OF RESIDENCE AND PLACE OF THEIR BIRTH. | | STATURE. | COMPLECTION. |
|---|---|---|---|---|---|
| Robert Burch | 27 May | Talbot County | | 5.5 | Dark |
| Wm. L. Merrick | 27 | " | " | 5.5 | " |
| George Willson | 27 | Caroline County | | 5.8 | Fair |
| Thomas Moore | 27 | " | " | 5.11 | " |
| John Shipperd | 28 | Talbot | " | 5.6 | " |
| Thos. Shenin | 28 | " | " | 5.8 | " |
| John Stuart | 28 | " | " | 5.6 | Dark |
| Henry Buckly | 28 | " | " | 5.9 | Fair |
| Levi Neighbours | 28 | " | " | 5.7 | " |
| Thos. Ewbanks | 28 | " | " | 6.0 | " |
| John Jacobs, Jr. | 28 | " | " | 5.6 | Dark |
| Thos. Chapman | | " | " | | " |
| James Fleming | 28 | " | " | 5.11 | Fair |
| Zadok Harvey | 29 | Caroline | " | 5.10 | Dark |
| Chas. Price | 29 | Talbot | " | 5.10 | Fair |
| Richard Eaton | 29 | " | " | 6.0 | Dark |
| Wm. Lee | 29 | " | " | 6.2 | Fair |
| Wm. Low | 30 | " | " | 5.7 | " |
| Thos. Perry | 1 June | Caroline | " | 5.6 | " |
| Henry Perry | 1 | " | " | 5.6 | " |

| The Names of Men Enlisted for the Barge "Fearnought." | Time of Inlistment. | Last Place of Residence and Place of Their Birth. | Stature. | Complection. |
|---|---|---|---|---|
| Joseph Bush | 1 June | Talbot County | 5.10½ | Dark |
| Nehemiah Beckwith | 1 | Dorset " | 5.7 | " |
| David Davis | 1 | " " | 5.11 | " |
| James Frazier | 1 | " " | 5.9 | " |
| Wm. Frazier | 1 | " " | 5.10 | " |
| John Thomas, Jr. | 1 | " " | 5.5½ | " |
| Saml. Abbet | 1 | Talbot " | 5.11 | Fair |
| George Price | 1 | " " | 5.5 | " |
| Sails Canner | 1 | " " | 5.10 | Dark |
| Thos. Richardson | 2 | " " | 5.10 | Fair |
| Emmory Collins | 2 | Caroline " | 5.6 | Dark |
| Saml. Farrow | 4 | " " | 5.8 | Fair |
| Jacob Jackson | 4 | Queen Ann's County | 5.5 | Dark |
| Henry Powel | 4 | Caroline " | 5.8½ | " |
| James Neighbours | 4 | Talbot " | 5.5 | Fair |
| James Crouch | 5 | " " | 5.5 | Dark |
| Rich. Ewbanks | 11 | " " | 5.10 | Fair |
| James Collins | 11 | Caroline " | 6.1 | " |
| William Murphy | 12 | " " | 5.9 | Dark |
| William Rumble | 15 | " " | 5.9 | " |
| John Thomas | 16 | Dorset " | 5.7 | " |
| John Wheelor | 1 | " " | 5.10 | " |
| William Willby | 30 | " " | 6.4 | Fair |
| William Navy | 10 | " " | 5.8 | Dark |
| John Frazier | 7 July | " " | 6.1 | " |
| Rich. Smith | 22 | { Baltimore Town, born in Balto. County | 5.8 | Fair |
| Gideon Gambrel | 15 June | Caroline County | 5.7 | " |
| Daniel Oneal | 26 July | { Annapolis, born in New England | 5.10 | Dark |
| George Gore | 26 | { Annapolis, born in New England | 5.8 | " |
| John Faris, (or Fanis) | 29 | Talbot County | | |

[Each was paid £3 bounty except Richard Eaton, John Thomas and George Gore, who were paid £3.15.

Each enlisted for one year except William Navy and George Gore, who enlisted to Jan. 1st, 1783.]

A Pay Roll of the Officers and Men of the Barge Fearnought, Capt. Levin Spedden.

| Officers' and Men's Names and Station. | Pay Per Month. | Officers' and Men's Names and Station. | Pay Per Month. |
|---|---|---|---|
| Captain | £15 | Boatswn. | 5. 12. 6 |
| Levin Spedden | | George Wilson | |
| 1st Lieut. | 10 | Gunner | 5. 12. 6 |
| Zadock Botfield | | Jacob Jackson | |
| 2nd Lieut. | 10 | Steward | 3. 15. 0 |
| Edward Spedden | | Samuel Abbot | |
| Privates, £3 each per month | | Privates | | Privates |
| John Frazier, (for 1 year, Furld.) | | Joseph Valliant, (absent) | | Nehem. Beckwith, (absent) |
| William Lee, (absent) | | John Jacobs | | Henry Powel, (in Flying Fish) |
| William Frazier | | Thomas Chapman | | Thos. Perry, (in Flying Fish) |
| Thomas Moore | | William Rumble | | John Thomas, Jr., (in Flying Fish) |
| Zadock Harvey | | Thomas Ewbanks | | Richd. Eaton, (absent) |
| William Merrick | | James Collins | | John Thomas |
| Gideon Gambrel | | Emory Collins | | James Neighbours |
| William Willowby | | Henry Perry, (in Flying Fish) | | David Davis |
| George Price | | John Steward | | James Frazier |
| Charles Price | | Joseph Bush | | Joseph Christian |
| John Shepherd | | William Low | | |
| Samuel Farrow | | William Navy | | |
| John Weaver | | John Wheeler | | |
| Thos. Richardson | | James Barnes, (paid off) | | |

[Pay commenced 21st Sept. '82, for all except Joseph Christian, whose pay commenced Nov. 15th, '82.
Each was paid for 2 Months and pay was due to Jan. 1st, 1783.]

Annapolis, Saturday, Dec., 1782.

Gentlemen

As you have suspended me from officiating the duty of Lt. on board the Barge Fearnought, I think It a hard case that I have not had a hearing in my own defence, as there is so many false reports propogated to my prejudice, in respect of my Conduct on that day in the action with the British Barges, Sincerely was this. I was Stationed at the bow Gun a 6lber. when we came into Action the first fire bursted, as much as Two feet of the uper part of the Muzzle blew of. I immediatly acquainted the Capt. of the Misfortune his answer was try her again my Answer was here is at It then and accordingly fired two rounds Shot & Two rounds Grape before the Comodore's Barge had blew up & It's said that I Contradicted his Orders when he gave Orders to board the British Barge then Nearly Along side the Comodore's Barge. I affirm on the word of a man that I did not hear the Orders given being at too great a distance & the men in Confusion but Expected as the men had their Oars out that we was to try to board the British Barge & try to save some of the Comodore's men if possible that was blown Overboard. I saw our men Confused in rowing some giving way a Head & Others backing water I called to them & told them to give way all together & not to be so Confused and as for leaving my Station I never left It till we where Oblidged to make our retreat & all Sails Set. Then I went Aft & told the boy at the Helmn to let me have the Helmn as I thought I could Steer better myself. & If Capt. Speddin wanted me forward I would gone at the first word.

I am, Gentlemen

Yr. Hble. Servt. tho' in Disgrace.
Zadok Botfield.

November the 26th Day, 1783.

Pleas to pay untow John Dawson Six Dolors being Dew me for Sarvis in the Barge ferenot Comemand by Captan Speden is Recat Shal be Good a Genst yours Umbel Servent

his
Zadock + Herey.
mark

to Mist. Jonson.

1782.   Pay Roll to the Schooner Flying Fish from Sept. 19th to Dec. 19th, '82.

| TIME COMMENCED. | NAME AND STATION. | AMOUNT DUE. |
|---|---|---|
| Sept. 19th | Daniel Bryan, (Brian), Captain | £45.  0.0 |
| Oct. 19th | George Grason, Lieut. | 20.  0.0 |
| Sept. 19th | James Joiner, Private | 9.  0.0 |
| ditto | William House, ditto | 9.  0.0 |
| ditto | William Dixon, ditto | 9.  0.0 |
| Oct. 4th | Wm. Bud,        ditto | 7.10 0 |
| | | £99.10.0 |

E. Excepted.

Daniel Bryan.

## SAILORS ENLISTED BY CAPT. BRYAN.

William Wood, Lt.
Thomas Birch, Lt.
John Smith, Gunner
William Warner, Steward
John Hudson, Carpenter
Luke Young, Gun.Capt.Fr.
Wm. Dyer, Private
B·rney Casey
Charles Jones
John Hardy, Boatswain
James Downing, Private
John Anthony
Emanual Roduger
Antonio Cocoanat, (or
  Coroanat)
Alexander McMullen
Joseph Ganney
Joseph Ramon

Robert Collins
Benito Losada
Modesto d Asoan
Antonio Cadenay
John Mitchell
John Maxwell
Andrew Boyd
Edward Russum
David Lowny
Charles Riggs
James McGwin,
  (or McGwire)
Peter Hardy
John Caine
John White
John Peters
John Robinson

Owen Cunningham
Edward Connolly
William House
Solomon Boone
David Wallace
William Swan
Ebin Brown
Michael Fischer
Henry Shepherd
Michael Sullivane
James Pennington
Blagdon Abbutt
John Armstrong
Lawrence Simons
John Robins
Joseph Valliant
William Dunn

## CAPT. FRAZIER.

Lieut. Botfield
Lt. Wm. Byus
John Frazier

Philn. Caldwell
John Wheeler
Nehem. Beckwith

William Frazier
Thomas Walker

## CAPT. O. DELISLE's CREW.

Lt. George Mignot
Lt. John Yeaton
Gasper Low
Thomas Johnson
Richard Murray, (or
  Munay)
Emanual Antony
John Gellard
William Heyton

James Kerr
James McConn
Silas Coolidge
Thomas English
William Roiley
Henry Simpson
Richard Turner
Thomas Flint

Joshua Nicholas
Antony Argers
Samuel Phill
Charles Stoker
John Thomas
Richard Johnson
John Hergrears
Anthony Dyes

## A LIST OF MEN BLOWN UP IN THE BARGES.

William Lowe, Lieut.
Patrick Long, Gunner,
  died of his wounds.
James Raynolds
John Kirby,
  died of his wounds.

George Brumwell
Joseph Sewull
William Sewell
William Blake
John Raynolds
Charles Spencer

John Scott
Nathl. Grace
Joseph Riddish
James Spencer
Ralph Dawson
Robt. Harrison

## ROLLS OF ESCAPED AND EXCHANGED PRISONERS.

Return of Maryland Officers exchanged from the 24th March, 1777.

| | | | |
|---|---|---|---|
| Ensign | James Fernandez | 1st Md. Regt. | March 24th 1777 |
| | William Coats | 1st Md. Regt. | ditto |
| Lieut. | D. Courcy | Smallwood's Regt. | Sept 27th '77 |
| | Ely Dorsey | 2nd Md. | ditto |
| Major | Otho H. Williams | Rifle Regt. | Jan 16th '78 |
| Lieut. | Edward Duvall | 2d Md. | April 20th '78 |
| | Hatch Dent | 1st Md. | ditto |
| | Walter Muse | 1st Md. | ditto |
| | Saml. Wright | 2nd Md. | ditto |
| | Edward Prall | 1st Md. | ditto |
| Capt. | John Dean | 5th Md. | Aug 26th '78 |
| | Abraham Shepherd | Md. Cont'l | ditto |
| | Henry Hardman | 6th Md. | ditto |
| Lieut. | John Gale | Md. Cont'l, 2nd Regt. | Oct 12th '78 |
| Lt. Col. | Ramsey | Md. Cont'l | Oct 25th 1780 |
| Major | Edward Tillard | Md. Cont'l | ditto |
| Lieut. | Thos. H. Lucket | Md., Rawlings | ditto |
| Cornet | Peregrine Fitzhugh | Baylor's | ditto |
| Lieut. | James Lingan | Rawlings' | ditto |
| | Thomas Warman | Rawlings' | ditto |
| | Christian Orendorff | Flying Camp | ditto |
| Ensign | Reg. Hillery | Cont'l | ditto |
| | John Levash | Cont'l | ditto |
| | Thomas Rouse | Cont'l | ditto |
| | Elihu Hall | 1st Md. | ditto |
| Lieut. | Kelty | | ditto |
| Col. | Luke Mabury | Militia | Sept 3rd 1781 |
| Ensign | H. Beddinger | Rawlings' | Oct 25th 1780 |
| | Rezin Davies | Rawlings' | ditto |
| | Edward Smith | Rawlings' | ditto |

We whose Names are hereto Subscribed, being exchanged Prisoners from Charles Town, do acknowledge to have received of Lt. Robert Denny 5 Pounds Specie each, on Account.     September 3rd, 1781.

| | | | |
|---|---|---|---|
| Law. Brennan | 7th Regt. | Thomas Allison | 1st Regt. |
| Jesse Jacobs | 6th " | Roger O'Donald | Artillery |
| Robt. Harpham | 4th " | John Ferguson | 2nd Regt. |
| Matthew McMahon | Artillery | John Jones | 2nd " |
| Benj. Peirce Beech | 5th Regt. | John Smith | 3rd " |
| Benj. Burch | 6th " | Peter Caldwell | 6th " |
| William Moore | 2nd " | Danl. O'Neal | Artillery |
| Thomas Bird | 3rd " | | |

The following Exchanged Prisoners each received the sum of 5 pounds from Robert Denny. 1781–1782.

| | | | | |
|---|---|---|---|---|
| Dec 3 1781 | Henry Flannagan, exchanged prisoner from South Carolina | Jan 17 1782 | John Linday, exchanged prisoner from Charles Town | |
| Nov 26 | Thomas Wood, ditto from Charles Town | Aug 24 1781 | Stephen Preston, 3d Regt. | ditto |
| Mch 13 1782 | Nathl. Wheeler, ditto and in distress | Feb 4 1782 | George Findleson | ditto |
| | | " | Patrick Connor | ditto |
| Dec 19 1781 | James Garth | Oct 8 1781 | Thomas Cardiff | ditto |
| Aug 1 | James Barren, 5th Regt. | 10 | John Wills | ditto |
| " | Jos. Overcreek, 3d Regt. | 9 | Saml. Carter | ditto |
| Sept 18 | William Griffin, 1st Regt. | Feb 21 1782 | Thomas Smee, exchanged prisoner & badly wounded | |
| 25 | Thomas James, 7th Regt. | | | |
| 26 | Daniel Willis, 5th Regt. | Aug 1 1781 | Benton Harris, 1st Regt. | |
| 28 | Robt. Pennington, 1st Regt. | " | George Scone, 5th Regt. | |
| | | " | James Currin, 7th Regt. | |
| " | Abraham Gamble, 1st Regt. | " | John Brent, 5th Regt. | |
| | | " | John Lowry, 7th Regt. | |
| 29 | Thos. King, 1st Regt. | " | Willm. Deaver, 3d Regt. | |
| " | Jona. White, 1st Regt. | " | Joseph Smith, 1st Regt. | |
| " | Michael Cole, 1st Regt. | " | Willm. Sly, 7th Regt. | |
| " | James Clark, Brown's Artly. | " | Dennis Tearnan, 7th Regt. | |
| | | " | Emanuel Allen, 5th Regt. | |
| Oct 2 | Silvester Gatton, 1st Regt. | " | Edward Kain, 4th Regt. | |
| 24 | Aaron Winfrey, Extra Regt., exchanged prisoner from Charles Town | " | Willm. Pegrim, 2nd Regt. | |
| | | " | John Martin, 2nd Regt. | |
| | | " | Thos. Saunders, 1st Regt. | |
| " | William King, 4th Regt., exchanged prisoner from Charles Town | " | John Holmes, 3rd Regt. | |
| | | " | Wm. Ashwell, 7th Regt. | |
| | | " | Wm. Fairbairn, 3rd Regt. | |
| Aug 2 | Dennis Flanagan, Dorsey's Artly. | " | Wm. Marshall, 5th Regt. | |
| | | 20 | Joseph Blaize, 7th Regt. | |
| " | Rich. Wilkinson, Dorsey's Artly. | Nov 2 | Thomas Barkley, exchanged prisoner from Charles Town | |
| Dec 5 | Mathias Funner, (Fanner) | | | |
| 20 | Thomas Bishop | Aug 15 | Saml. Tindale, 3rd Regt. | ditto |
| Aug 29 | Wm. Wallkird, exchanged prisoner from Charles Town | Oct 6 | John Howard, Artillery | ditto |
| 1 | Robt. Ferroll, 2nd Regt. | 11 | Rich. Blandford, 2nd Regt. | ditto |
| " | Robert Rankin, 5th Regt. | | | |
| 20 | John Courts, 3rd Regt. | 17 | James Smith, prisoner from Chs. Town | |
| " | Michael Clancey, 5th Regt. | 25 | John Chivel, received £ 21.00. | |
| " | Thos. Richardson, 5th Regt. | Apl 15 1782 | Robert Sharpless, exchanged prisoner and wounded. | |
| " | William George, 6th Regt. | | | |
| " | William Cox, 2nd Regt. | | | |

40

## RETURN OF INVALIDS.

### A Sick Return, November 17th, 1777.

| MEN'S NAMES. | COMPANY. | DISORDER. |
|---|---|---|
| Stephen Fennell | Capt. Dorsey | Convalescent |
| Hugh McDowell | do | Bilious Fever |
| John Poore | do | Sore Leg |
| John Sly | do | Peupneumony |
| Sargt. Cornwall | do | Convalescent |
| John Ackerly | do | Convalescent |
| Cornelius Forester | do | Rheumatism |
| Thomas Robertson | do | Intermittent Fever |
| Robert Carr | Furnavil | Sore Arm |
| Thomas Yates | do | Sore Leg |
| Daniel Rodden | do | Putrid Fever |
| John Jellom | do | Convalescent |

G. Gale, Surgeon.

### CONTINENTAL HOSPITAL RETURNS, 1777–1778.*

A List of the Soldiers in the Court House Hospital at Reading Nov. 17, 1777.*

| Wm. Jeffries | 5th Maryland | William Cofferoth | 7th Maryland |
|---|---|---|---|
| John Barber | 3rd Maryland | Charles Major | do |
| Henry Tom | Col. Weltner's | Coonrod Cofferoth | do |
| Nicholas Nichols | 5th Maryland | Christopher Reed | do |
| Wm. Donaldson | 7th Maryland | Thomas Young | do |
| Francis Mitchel | do | Wm. Markwelch | do |

A List of Soldiers in the Brick House Hospital at Reading, Nov. 17th, 1777.*

| John Hunt | 6th Maryland | Samuel Huggins | 6th Maryland |
|---|---|---|---|

"A List of the Sick in the Potter's Shop at Reading, Nov. 17." *

| Gilber Allen | 5th Maryland | Wm. Pinkfield & wife | 5th Maryland |
|---|---|---|---|
| Zadock Woods | do | Thomas Oliphant | do |
| Saml. Kennedy | do | David Kelly & wife | do |
| Thos. Fenitree & wife | do | | |

*Taken from the Pennsylvania Magazine of History and Biography, April, 1899, pages 38-50.

A Return of the Sick sent from Robinson's to New Windsor.*

John Danster                4th Maryland                Norwood's Co.

Sir.
    Please to receive into Hospital Richard Stids of Capt. Godman's Company belonging to the 4th Maryland Regt. & John Cornish of Capt. Eccleston's Company belonging to the 2d Maryland Regiment.
                    John Ross, Asst. Surg.
                        25th Novem., 1778.*

To Dr. Allison
    Superintending the Hospitals
    New Windsor

A Return of Sick of the 6th Maryland Regt. commanded by Col. Otho H. Williams.*

| | | |
|---|---|---|
| Robert Body | Capt. Beall's Co. | Fever |
| John Holiday | do | do |
| George Thomas | do | do   Putrid |

Sir
    Please to receive to ye Hospital the above sick.
                    W. Warfield, A. S.
                        6th M. Regt.
To the Hospital Surgeon        Nov. 25, 1778.
    at Newburg.

                    Newburgh, 28th Nov., 1778.
Sir
    You'l be kind enough to Receive into the Hospital the Following Soldiers of a Detachmt. under my Command, who for want of a Doctor are likely to Continue in a bad Situation if not Received.   Your Compliance will be highly Acknowledged by Sir
                Your Most Hhble. Servt.
            J. Brice, Capt. Comdt. of a Detachmt.
                    of the 1st Maryland Bg.*

To the Superintendt. of the Hospital
    at New Windsor.

| | | |
|---|---|---|
| John Sullivan | Capt. Brooks' Co. | 3rd Regt. Md. |
| James Foster | do | do |
| John Owens | late C. Hindman's | do |
| Owen Corkran | Capt. Brice | do |
| Daniel Claney | do | do |

* See note on page 618.

Sir                              Newburgh, 1st Decmbr., 1778

Be kind enough to Receive into the Hospital William Ross of the 6th Maryland Regiment.

I am Sir your most Hhble. Servt.

J. Brice, Capt. Comdt. of a
Detachment of Maryd. Bg.*

To the Superindt.
of New Windsor.

---

Sir                              Newburgh December 1, 1778.

Be pleased to Receive into the Hospital Benj. Moore of the Sixth Maryland Regiment whose situation requires Assistance.

I am Sir your Most Humble Servt.

Lud. Weltner, Lt. Col.*

To the Superindt. of the Hospital
at New Windsor.

---

A Return of Sick of the 6th Maryland Regt. Commanded by Col. Williams, Dec. the 7th, 1778.*

| | | |
|---|---|---|
| Samuel English | Lieut. Williams' Co. | Putrid Fever |
| Peter Woolf | do        do | Intert. Fever |
| Pat. Trainer | Capt. Ghireliu's do | Infat. |
| Willm. Chambers | do     do | do |

Hospital Surgeon at New Windsor.              W. Warfield, A. S.

---

A Return of the Sick of the Second Maryland Regiment sent to the Hospital at New Windsor commanded by Lieut Col. Woolford, December 7, 1778.*

| | | |
|---|---|---|
| John Wall | Capt. Anderson's Co. | Fever Inflam. |
| Patrick Fenesick | Capt. Davidson's do | Fever Remit. |
| Saml. Hughes | do | Rheumat. |

James McCallmont, Surgn.

* See note on page 618.

A Return of the Sick 7th Maryland Regiment Col. Gunby, Gen. Smallwood's Brig.*

| Nichs. Carr | Capt. Bayle's Co. | Putrid Fever |
| Darby Crowley | do | do |
| Wm. Hopkins | Capt. Grosh | Interm. Fever |
| Ed. Fennile | Capt. Morris | do |

H. Tabbs, Surgn.

F. Allison, Esq.
Senr. Surgeon G. Hospital New Windsor.

---

A Return of the Sick in the 5th Maryland Regiment Commanded by Col. William Richardson, to be sent to the Hospital at New Windsor.*

| Moses Cook | Lynch's Co. | Diarrhea |
| Robert Bromwell | Dean's do | Bilious fever |
| William Arnett | do do | Int. fever |
| James Hawkins | do do | do |
| Thos. Hinds | Emory's do | Jaundice |
| Thos. Greenwich | do do | Cough |
| Wm. Samuel | Richardson's do | Convalescent |
| Peter Kincaid | Hamilton's do | Bilious fever |
| Joseph Peters | Lynch's Orderly | |

William Kilty, Surgeon
5th Maryland Regt.

Chester, Dec. 8, 1778.

---

A Return of Cloaths etc, 3rd Maryland.*

| Daniel Lingist | Capt. Bailey | David Lawler | Capt. Marborough |
| Joseph Cronch | do Brice | Thos. Wright | do Hindman |
| Thos. Cowin | do do | Michl. Gownan | do Smith |

Jacob Lyon,
Sergeant.

Dec. 10, 1778.

*See note on page 618.

A List of the Sick of the 2nd Maryland Brigade April 21st, 1779.

| NAMES. | REGT. | HOSPITAL. |
| --- | --- | --- |
| John Taylor | 4th Md. | |
| Jas. Fitzgerald | ditto | |
| Dennis Carroll | ditto | |
| Thos. Davis | 2nd Md. | { Summerset Court- |
| Nathl. Griffin | ditto | House |
| John Holladay | 6th Md. | |
| Wm. Merl | ditto | |
| John Toof | ditto | |
| Mark Griffin | 2nd Md. | |

Chas. Dabney, Lieut-Col.

[From the Gist Papers.]

## RESOLVES OF CONTINENTAL CONGRESS 20 JUNE, 1777.

"*Resolved*, That a corps of invalids be formed, consisting of eight companies, each company to have one captain, two lieutenants, two ensigns, five serjeants, six corporals, two drummers, two fifers, and one hundred men. This corps to be employed in garrison, and for guards in cities and other places, where magazines or arsenals, or hospitals are placed; as also to serve as a military school for young gentlemen, previous to their being appointed to marching regiments; for which purpose, all the subaltern officers, when off duty, shall be obliged to attend a mathematical school, appointed for the purpose, to learn geometry, arithmetic, vulgar and decimal fractions, and the extraction of roots; and that the officers of this corps shall be obliged to contribute one day's pay in every month, and stoppages shall be made of it accordingly, for the purpose of purchasing a regimental library of the most approved authors on tactics and the petite guerre: That some officers from this corps be constantly employed in the recruiting service in the neighborhood of the places they shall be stationed in; that all recruits so raised shall be brought into the corps and drilled, and afterwards draughted into other regiments as occasion shall require.

Congress proceeded to the election of a colonel of the said corps of invalids; and, the ballots being taken,

Lewis Nicola, esq. was elected."

A Return of Invalids belonging to the Maryland Line, now in the Service at the Garrison of Philadelphia, June 19th, 1781.

| NAMES. | REGIMENT. | TRANSFERRMENTS. |
| --- | --- | --- |
| Thomas Adams | 3d Maryland | 27 July 1780 |
| Lawrance Brooks, Serjt. | 5th " | 13 October 1778 |
| Timothy Brennan | 6th " | 5 May 1779 |
| Benjamin Cheshire | 3d " | 7 February 1780 |
| William Collier | 3d " | 25 April 1780 |
| James Connor | 5th " | 24 July 1780 |
| Micheal Duffey | 3d " | 1 August 1778 |
| Walter Chas. Davids, Serjt. | 3d " | 30 September 1778 |
| Barns. Dougherty | 5th " | 8 September 1779 |
| James Desire | 3d " | 22 April 1780 |
| Robert Freemoult | 3d " | 6 October 1778 |
| Edward Franklin | 2nd " | 24 July 1777 |
| John Hackett | 4th " | 2 June 1779 |
| Richard Jenkins | 3d " | 2 September 1778 |
| William Keymer | 3d " | 19 October 1778 |
| James Lipscomb, Serjt. | 3d " | 19 October 1778 |
| Jacob Lyons, Serjt. | 3d " | 1 June 1779 |
| Daniel Longist | 3d " | 24 April 1780 |
| John McDonald | 3d " | 21 June 1779 |
| John Murray | 3d " | 7 February 1780 |
| John Nulan | 3d " | 26 January 1779 |
| Joseph Polemus | 4th " | 27 May 1778 |
| James Sherridan | 3d " | 27 October 1778 |
| John Schwager, Serjt. | 3d " | 13 October 1778 |
| Jacob Shandley | 7th " | 2 November 1779 |
| John Saunders | 3d " | 14 July 1779 |
| Valentine Smith | 1st " | 22 April 1780 |
| William Tutone | 2nd " | 8 May 1779 |
| Godfrey Young | 6th " | 23 October 1780 |
| Luke Burns | 1st " | 22 April 1780 |
| Dennis Cregannon | 1st " | 22 April 1780 |
| Thomas Hunt | 7th " | 15 March 1780 |
| Thomas Bond, Serjt. | Pulaski's | 25 February 1779. Promoted Serjt. 15 Feb., 1780 |

Serjt. Brooks was discharged from the 5th, the 13th October, '78, but his discharge being contrary to Genl. Washington's order it was taken from him and he ordered to do duty in the Invalid Regt. by the Board of War, in which station he still continues & is returned as belonging to the quota of the State of Maryland.

                                        Lewis Nicola, Col. Inv.

I certify that the men mentioned in within list were all transferred from the line of the State of Maryland State into the Invalid Regt. under my command and still continue therein & are returned as belonging to the quota of that State.   Philadelphia, 3 July, 1781.

Lewis Nicola, Col. Inv.

I certify that Thomas Bond of Count Pulaski's Legion joined the Invalid Regt. the 25th day of February, 1779, was appointed a Corporal therein 1st June, 1779, & promoted to a Serjeant 15th January, 1781, in which station he has continued ever since.

Lewis Nicola, Col. Inv.

Philadela. 28th June, 1781.

I do Certify that Thomas Bond was inlisted a Soldier by Capt. Siggond in Baltimore for Genl. Count Pulaski's Legion, May 8th, 1778, & was transfered to join the Invalid Regiment Feby. 25th, 1779, not being fit for Camp duty.   Henry Becker, Capt.

June 28th, 1781.   Light Dragoons.

James Murphy, of Queen Ann's County, enlisted in the 5th Md. Regt. in 1777, and was transferred to the Invalid Regt., (having lost a leg), from which he was discharged by Col. Lewis Nicola, Jan. 17th, 1780. He was referred by the Council of Maryland Oct 14th, 1785, as a pensioner under the Act of Oct., 1778, to the Orphans' Court of Queen Ann's County.

MARYLAND ACTS—OCTOBER, 1778.

An ACT for the relief of disabled and maimed officers, soldiers, marines, and seamen.

"*Be it enacted, by the General Assembly of Maryland*, That every commissioned officer, non-commissioned officer, and private soldier, who have or shall lose a limb, or have been or shall be so disabled in the service of the United States of America, as to render him incapable of getting a livelihood, and who, at the time of entering into the service of the said United States, was or shall be enlisted or recruited by this state, shall receive during his life, or the continuance of such disability, the one half of his monthly pay, from and after the time that his pay as an officer or soldier ceases.   And that every commander of any ship of war or armed vessel, commissioned officer, warrant officer, marine, or seaman, belonging to the United States of America, who have or shall lose a limb, or have been or shall be otherwise so disabled in the service of the said States, as to be rendered incapable of getting a livelihood, and who, at the time of engaging in the said service, was or shall be enlisted or recruited by this state, shall receive during his life, or continuance of such disability, the one half of his monthly pay, from and after the time that his pay as an officer, or marine, or seaman, ceases.

*And be it further enacted,* That every commissioned officer, non-commissioned officer, and private soldier, in the army, and every commander, commissioned officer, warrant officer, marine, or seaman, of any of the ships of war or armed vessels belonging to the United States of America, who have been or shall be wounded in any engagement, so as to be rendered incapable of serving in the army or navy, though not totally disabled from getting a livelihood, and who at the time of entering into the service of the said States, was or shall be enlisted or recruited by this state, shall receive such monthly sum as shall be adjudged adequate by the justices of the orphans court of the county in which such commissioned officer or private soldier of the army, or commander, commissioned officer, warrant officer, or seaman, of the navy, shall reside ; provided the same doth not exceed his half pay.

*And be it enacted,* That . . . . . the justices of the said courts are hereby enjoined to cause due entries to be made in their proceedings, of the name or names of all persons to whom drafts or orders shall be given in pursuance of this act ; also of their places of residence, in what regiment or company they served, the engagement or action in which they received their wound, and the sums alloted them ; also of the death of such disabled person, or ceasing of such allowance.

*And be it further enacted,* That all such officers and soldiers, who may be entitled to the provisions under this act, and shall be found to be capable of doing guard or garrison duty, may be formed into a corps of invalids, and subject to the said duty ; and all officers, marines, and seamen, of the navy, who shall be entitled to the same provision, and shall be found capable of doing any duty on board the navy, or any department thereof, shall be liable to be so employed."

A Muster Roll of the Invalids and Recruits of the Garrison At Fort Whetstone Point.

| MENS NAMES. | TIME OF APPOINTMENT & INLISTMENT. | REMARKS. |
| --- | --- | --- |
| Saml. Swan, Serjt. | Appointed Oct 6th 1779 | Discharged Nov 19th 1780 |
| Benjamin Jones | Left as Inv. Sept 15th 1779 | "  May 8th 1781 |
| William Richardson | "   "   "   "   "   " | "   "   "   " |
| Joseph Wilks | Left Sick Sept 15th 1779 | Claimed by Lieut. Saml. Saddler as Fit for Duty Dec 23rd 1779 |
| William Robinson | Inlisted Sept 23rd 1779 | Discharged Jan 27th 1780 |
| Peter Decamp | "   "   28th 1779 | Deserted from Recruiting Officer |
| Dominick Sara | "   "   "   " | ditto      ditto |
| Peter Laci | "   "   "   " | ditto      ditto |
| John Granada | "   "   "   " | Deserted Dec 1st 1779 |
| Samuel Powell | "   Oct 2nd 1779 | "  Abt. the Last of Nov 1779 |
| Thomas Acres | "   "  4th  " | Discharged Jan 27th 1780 |
| Daniel Mathews | "   "   "   " | Deserted Oct 12th 1779 |
| Thomas Hooper | "   "  21st  " | Discharged Jan 27th 1780 |
| Thomas Gillard | "   Nov 15th 1779 | "   "   "   "   " |
| Samuel True | "   Dec 7th 1779 | "   "   "   "   " |

Proof of the Above Muster Roll.

Present.

| | | |
| --- | --- | --- |
| Deserted and one taken away by Lt. S. Saddler | | 7 privates |
| Discharged by Order of the Governor & Council | 1 serjt. | 7  " |
| Total | 1 serjt. | 14  " |

Geo. P. Vreeportz.

Baltimore, May 8th, 1781.

Detachment of Md. Troops at the Garrison of Whetstone Point.

| REGT. | NAMES. | REGT. | NAMES. |
| --- | --- | --- | --- |
| 2nd | Jas. Jackson, Serjt. | Extra | John Deakins |
| 4th | Peter McNaughton | " | John Anderson |
| 4th | John Colin, Serjt. | " | Thos. Pennifield |
| " | Jos. Fawlit, Fifer | " | Wm. Glorey |
| " | Wm. Smith, Drum. | " | Dennis Donans |
| " | John Moore | " | John Turnstil |
| " | Peter Blang | " | Wm. Chapmon |
| " | Henry Hughes | " | David Brien |
| Extra | Lazaris Higgs | " | Jesse O'Furra |
| " | James Brown | " | Jessey King |

| REGT. | NAMES. | REGT. | NAMES. |
|---|---|---|---|
| Extra | John Jones | 4th | Mathew Kelley |
| " | Patrick Smith | Extra | Wm. Masson |
| " | George Daw | " | James Woodword |
| " | James Wilson | " | Thos. Porter |
| " | Elexander Steward | " | Edwd. Taylor |
| " | John Johnston | " | George Gilword |
| " | Joseph McItee | " | Jessey McCarty |
| " | Steaven Fennil | " | Mitchal Doring |
| " | Thos. Artis | " | James White |

Jno. Hamilton, Capt. Lt.

[From the Gist Papers.]

The following wounded soldiers each received the sum of 5 pounds from Robert Denny, 1782.

Mch  5   Nelce Jones, a wounded soldier of the 2nd Md. Regt.
Mch 23   Robert Taylor, a wounded soldier in distress from the Southward.

Annapolis, June 25th, 1790.

Sir

I enclose returns of the invalid pensioners paid by this State, and I regret that they have been so long delayed which was owing to many of the returns being imperfect; indeed, although we have sent to many of the Counties to get the returns more perfect, they are not so complete as I would wish.

I think proper to make some remarks on the return of officers, and request that you will inform me which of them, (if any) are excluded from the half pay of the United States by the Acts of the late or present Congress, that I may communicate it to the legislature of this State, for them to determine whether they will continue the pensions to those who are rejected by the United States.

Perry Benson, James Bruff, Richard Anderson, John Trueman, John Lynn, James Ewing and James Somervill, have received their 5 years commutation from the United States, and under a particular law of this State made expressly for their relief have received half pay.

Jehu Bowen was wounded at German Town and afterwards resigned, but as the disability occasioned by his wounds still continued, the Legislature upon application passed a law putting him on a footing, as to his half pay, with other officers.. He has not received commutation.

Rignal Hillary and John Levasche died in the service, their widows have received pensions equal to the half pay of their husbands, under the laws of this State which I believe is provided for by Acts of the late Congress.

John Hoskin Stone was wounded and resigned, but was afterwards put on the half pay establishment by a law of this State.

Uriah Forrest lost his leg in the action of German Town and resigned the 23rd of Feb., 1781, as will appear by the votes and proceedings of Congress. The State of Maryland advanced him a sum of money equal to seven years half pay of a Lt. . . . . . . . . . . . . . . . .

[Torn off.]

Return of Invalid Pensioners in Charles County.

| NAMES. | RANK. | AGE. | CORPS. | COMMANDERS' NAMES. | CAUSE OF DISABILITY. | WHEN DISABLED. | WHERE DISABLED. | PLACE OF RESIDENCE. TOWN & COUNTY. | WHEN PENSION COMMENCED. | WHEN PENSION CEASED AND REASONS. | ALLOWANCE PER MONTH. | WHOLE AMOUNT PAID. | EXACT TIME TO WHICH THE PENSION HAS BEEN PAID. |
|---|---|---|---|---|---|---|---|---|---|---|---|---|---|
| ..orrison | Soldier | 44 | 1 Md. Regt. | | Wounded in the hand & head | 16 Aug 1780 | Camden | Charles Co. | 17 Nov 1780 | | 1.5.4¼ | 136.17.6 | 17 Sept 1789 |
| ..rtindale | Fifer | 27 | do | | Burn on his left hand | 28 Feb 1783 | James Island | do | 15 Nov 1783 | | 1.7.6 | 94.18.6 | 15 Aug 1789 |
| ..illard | Soldier | 26 | do | | Lost his left Arm | | Little York | do | 10 Dec 1781 | | 1.5.4¼ | 116.6.2 | 10 Aug 1789 |
| ..anders | do | 52 | do | John H. Stone, Col. | Wound on the hand & head | 16 Aug 1780 | Camden | do | 29 July 1781 | | 1.5.4¼ | 122.8.11½ | 29 Aug 1789 |
| ..Perry | do | | do | | Cause of disability unknown | | | do | 15 Nov 1783 | Removed out of the State Oct 1786 | 1.5.4¼ | 41.16.5½ | 15 Aug 1786 |
| ..ckannan | Drummer | | do | | Wound on the knee | Sometime in 1782 | North Carolina | do | 15 Nov 1783 | Died sometime in 1785 | 1.7.6 | 24.15.0 | 15 May 1785 |
| ..Green | Soldier | 50 | do | | Rheumatic pains | Can't get information when nor where disabled | | do | 11 Jan 1780 | | 1.5.4¼ | 148.5.7½ | 11 Oct 1789 |
| ..h Mudd | Sergeant | 30 | 2 Md. Regt. | John Gunby, Col. | Lost his left Arm | 17 June 1781 | 96th South Carolina | Pr.Geo. Co. | 5 Aug 1783 | | 1.17.6 | 131.5.0 | 5 June 1789 |

John Muschett, Regr. of Wills, Charles County.

Return of Invalid Pensioners

| NAMES. | RANK. | AGE. | CORPS. | | CAUSE OF DISABILITY. | WHEN DISABLED AND WHERE. |
|---|---|---|---|---|---|---|
| Abraham Gambell | Private | Abt. 30 yrs. | 1st Md. Regt. Commander unknown | As appears per Capt. Perry Benson's Cert. | Wounded through the shoulder | 25 April 1781 at battle of Camden |
| Henry Clarage | do | Unknown | 2nd Md. Regt. Col. Otho Williams | Per Col. William's Certificate | Wounded in the left arm & discharged from the Genl. Hosptl. of the Southern Army | |

Return of Invalid Pensioners

| PENSIONERS NAMES. | RANK. | MILITIA. | CONTINENTAL. | | WHERE DISABLED. |
|---|---|---|---|---|---|
| John Snider | Corporal | Flying Camp | | | White Plains |
| Samuel Hennis | Private | Militia | | | White Horse |
| "          " | " | " | | | "        " |
| John Brown | Sergeant | | 6 Regt. | | Camden |
| John Meek | Private | | 7 " | | Guilford Ct. House |
| Philip Fisher | " | | 1 " | | Guilford Ct. House |
| Henry Crook | " | | 1 " | | Guilford Ct. House |
| James Shean | " | | 2 " | | Monmouth |
| David Conner | " | | 2 " | | Disabled by Sickness |
| Charles Buchlup | " | | 1 " | | Eutaw Springs |
| Thos. Bishop | " | | 2 " | | Guilford Ct. House |
| John Auber | Sergeant | | 2 " | | Eutaw Springs |
| James Smith | Private | | 2 " | | Camden |
| John Alsop | " | | 7 " | | Barges |
| Robert Kerns | Sergeant | | 2 " | | York |
| James Burk | Private | | 2 " | | Cowpens |
| James Garth | " | | 4 " | | Ninety Six |
| Michael Waltman | " | | 1 " | | Guilford Ct. House |
| Christr. Lambert | " | | 3 " | | Disabled by Fire |
| Luke Sanson | " | | 1 " | | Guilford Ct. House |
| Peter Cunningham | " | | 7 " | | South Carolina |
| Paul Hagarty | " | | 1 " | | Brandy Wine |
| John Trisner | " | | 7 " | | German Town |
| Edward Rose | " | Militia | | | Jersey |
| John Shovell | " | | 6 " | | Camden |
| John Gombare | " | Flying Camp | | | York Island |

## in Dorchester County.

| PLACE OF RESIDENCE. | WHEN PENSION COMMENCED. | WHEN PENSION CEASED AND REASONS. | ALLOWANCE PER MONTH. | WHOLE AMOUNT PAID. | EXACT TIME TO WHICH THE PENSION HAS BEEN PAID UP. |
|---|---|---|---|---|---|
| Dorchester County | 13 Apl 1785 | Ceased 13 Oct 1785 no further application being made | Ten Shillings | Three Pounds | to the 13th October 1785 |
| Dorchester County | 23 June 1785 Ceased 23 Sept 1785 | | Ten Shillings | Thirty Shillings | to the 23rd Sept 1785 |

Certified per Jno. Goldsborough,
Regr. Wills for Dorchester County.
Dec. 1st, 1789.

## in Frederick County.

| WHEN PENSION COMMENCED. | ALLOWANCE PER MONTH. | WHEN PENSION CEASED. | CAUSE OF PENSION CEASING. | AMOUNT. |
|---|---|---|---|---|
| Dec 1 1776 | 27/6 | Nov 1 1789 | | 213 2 6 |
| Sept 20 1777 | 25/ | Sept 20 1782 | | 75 0 0 |
| Sept 20 1782 | 12/6 | Nov 1 1789 | | 53 6 8 |
| Nov 29 1783 | 37/6 | Mch 29 1786 | removed or dead | 52 10 0 |
| " " " | 25/ | Nov 1 1789 | | 88 16 6 |
| " " " | 25/ | " " " | | 88 16 6 |
| " " " | 25/ | Mch 29 1784 | removed or supposed dead | 5 0 0 |
| " " " | 25/ | April 29 1787 | dead | 51 5 0 |
| " " " | 25/ | Mch 29 1784 | dead | 5 0 0 |
| " " " | 25/ | Nov 1 1789 | | 88 16 6 |
| " " " | 25/ | " " " | | 88 16 6 |
| " " " | 37/6 | Mch 6 1788 | dead | 96 1 10½ |
| " " " | 25/ | Nov 1 1789 | | 88 16 6 |
| " " " | 25/ | " " " | | 88 16 6 |
| " " " | 37/6 | " " " | | 133 3 4 |
| Feb 10 1784 | 25/ | Mch 10 1788 | dead | 61 5 0 |
| Nov 29 1783 | 25/ | Nov 1 1789 | | 88 16 6 |
| Mch 29 1784 | 25/ | " " " | | 83 16 6 |
| Nov 29 1783 | 25/ | " " " | | 88 16 6 |
| Nov 16 1783 | 25/ | Oct 16 1785 | dead | 28 15 0 |
| Sept 29 1784 | 25/ | Mch 29 1789 | removed or supposed dead | 67 10 0 |
| Dec 27 1784 | 25/ | Nov 1 1789 | | 72 12 6 |
| April 12 1785 | 25/ | " " " | | 68 5 0 |
| April 24 1786 | 12/6 | Oct 24 1788 | removed or supposed dead | 18 15 0 |
| Mch 29 1786 | 25/ | Nov 1 1789 | | 53 16 6 |
| June 9 1788 | 25/ | " " " | | 20 18 9 |
| | | | | 1870 15 7½ |

George Murdoch, Regr. Wills,
Frederick County.

Return of Invalid Pensioners

| NAMES. | RANK. | CORPS. | PLACE OF RESIDENCE. | WHEN PENSION COMMENCED. |
|---|---|---|---|---|
| John Davis, (down County) | Private | Continental | Chester Town | in 1781 |
| James Carmicheal | " | 1 Md Regt. " | Kent Co. | in 1781 |
| Robert Sharpless | Corporal | " | Chester Town | in 1785 |
| John Davis, (up County) | Private | 6 " " " | Chester Town at this time | in 1785 |
| Hugh McClean | " | 1 " " " | | in 1785 |
| George Second | Corporal | " | Kent Co. | in 1786 |
| Daniel Smith | Private | " | " " | in 1786 |
| John Lynch | Corporal | " | " " | in 1786 |

Return of Invalid Pensioners

| NAMES. | AGE. | CORPS. | CAUSE OF DISABILITY. | WHEN DISABLED. | WHERE DISABLED. |
|---|---|---|---|---|---|
| James Murphey | 35 | 1 Md. Regt. | Lost one Legg | Aug 27, 1776 | Long Island |
| James White | | | | | |
| John Blair | | | | | |
| James Current | | | | | |
| Christr. Reed | | | | | |
| William Hurley | | | | | |
| Saml. B. White | 30 | 1 Md. Regt. | Disabled in the body | April 25, 1781 | Camden |

## in Kent County.

| WHEN PENSION CEASED AND REASONS. | ALLOWANCE PER MONTH. | WHOLE AMOUNT PAID. | EXACT TIME TO WHICH THE PENSION HAS BEEN PAID. |
|---|---|---|---|
| died in 1790 | 25/ | £300 curry. & £114 10 specie | 22 Oct 1789 |
| died in 1785 | 25/ | £56 5 0 currency & £52 10 specie | |
| struck off Nov. 9th, 1789, Court thinking him able to labor and a great Drunkard | 27/6 | £72 3 9 specie | |
| | 25/ | £67 10 specie | 22 Oct 1789 |
| struck off Oct. 22nd, 1789. Court thought him able bodied at this Time | 25/ | £67 10 specie | 22 Oct 1789 |
| allowed only £8.5 the last Order and were of opinion he ought not be allowed in future | 27/6 | £53 12 6 specie | Aug 1789 |
| | 25/ | £45 specie | 18 Jan 1789 |
| | 27/6 | £33 specie | 28 Aug 1789 |

John Nicholson, Regr. of Wills for Kent County.

## in Montgomery County.

| PLACE OF RESIDENCE. | WHEN PENSION COMMENCED. | WHEN & WHY PENSION CEASED. | ALLOWANCE PER MONTH. | WHOLE AMOUNT PAID. | EXACT TIME TO WHICH THE PENSION HAS BEEN PAID UP. |
|---|---|---|---|---|---|
| Montgomery County | April 10, 1781 | died Aug, 1789 | 25/ | £123 15 0 | 10 July 1789 8 yrs 3 mos |
| | June 10, 1783 | | 25/ | 95 16 8 | 1 Nov 1789 6 yrs 4 mos 21 days |
| | June 10, 1783 | | 25/ | 95 16 8 | 1 Nov 1789 6 yrs 4 mos 21 days |
| | Dec 20, 1783 | | 25/ | 87 18 4 | 1 Nov 1789 5 yrs 10 mos 10 days |
| | Aug 20, 1784 | | 25/ | 77 18 4 | 1 Nov 1789 5 yrs 2 mos 10 days |
| | Dec 14, 1784 | | 25/ | 73 2 6 | 1 Nov 1789 4 yrs 10 mos 17 days |
| Montgomery County | June 9, 1789 | | 25/ | 5 18 4 | 1 Nov 1789 4 mos 22 days |

Samuel Turner, Regr. Wills,
Montgomery County.

Return of Invalid Pensioners

| Names. | Rank. | Corps. | Commander. | Cause of Disability. | When Disabled. | Where Disabled. |
|---|---|---|---|---|---|---|
| Jonathan White | Private | 1 Md. Regt. | Genl. Wm. Smallwood | | 25 April 1781 | Cambden |
| Owen Coffield | ditto | | Col. Grayson | | | |
| Joseph Greer | | | | Lost a leg at the Siege of 96 | | |
| John Bean | | 3 Md. Regt. | | | | Cambden |
| Wm. Tuel, per his widow | ditto | | Capt. Horatio Clagett | Killed | 4 Oct 1777 | German Town |
| Joseph Shirtley, per his widow | ditto | | Col. Thos. Williams | Killed | 4 Oct 1777 | German Town |

Prince Georges County, to wit,

I Samuel Tyler, Register of the Orphans Court in and for the County aforesaid, do
Books of the Orphans' Court, in and for said County, concerning the Invalid Soldiers allowed
In Testimony whereof I have hereunto set my hand & Affixed the public seal of said

[Seal.]

Return of Disabled Soldiers who have been Allowed by the

| Names. | Rank. | Regiment. |
|---|---|---|
| John Lowrie | Private Soldier | Seventh |
| Nathaniel Wheeler | Private Soldier | Second |

## in Prince George's County.

| PLACE OF RESIDENCE. TOWN AND COUNTY. | WHEN PENSION COMMENCED. | WHEN PENSION CEASED AND REASONS. | STRUCK OFF THE LIST AND REASONS. | ALLOWANCE PER MONTH. | WHOLE AMOUNT PAID. | EXACT TIME TO WHICH THE PENSION HAS BEEN PAID. |
|---|---|---|---|---|---|---|
| near Uper Marlboro, Prince Georges Co. | 29 Sept 1781 | | | 25/ | £117 10 | |
| do    do | 15 Nov 1783 | | | 25/ | 56  5 | |
| | 15 Nov 1783 | dead | | 25/ | 52 10 | 15 May 1787 |
| | | | | | 40  0 | in full for his wounds |
| | | | | | 415 0 curry. & 68 5 real } | 31 July 1784 |
| | 6 June 1778 | | 14 Aug 1781 | | 320 0 curry. & 110 0 real } | Oct 1781 |

hereby Certify that the within is a true Abstract of the proceedings, taken from the Minute pension by the worshipfull Justices of said Court.
Office this Twentieth day of January, Anno Domini Seventeen Hundred and Ninety.

Samuel Tyler,
Register of Wills for Prince G. County.

## Orphans Court of Somerset County on Account their half pay etc.

| ACTION THEY WERE WOUNDED. | TIME OF BEGINNING THEIR HALF PAY. | TO WHAT TIME SETTLED WITH. | WHOLE AMOUNT, |
|---|---|---|---|
| Camden | From the time his full pay ceased | 13 July 1784 | |
| Eutaw Spring | 1 Jan 1783 | 1 Dec 1784 | £43 2 6 |

Somerset County, December 20th, 1784.
Esme Bayly, Regr. Wills, S. C.

# APPENDIX

# APPENDIX.

After the most of the volume was in type, certain muster rolls were secured by the Maryland Historical Society at an auction sale of manuscripts in New York City. These are printed in an appendix, as they were procured too late to be inserted in their proper chronological order. In addition to these, the appendix contains a list of militia who served in 1777, which was found among the papers deposited by the Johns Hopkins University, a list of the Select Militia of 1781, enlisted from Frederick County, and a roll of the crew of the Ship Defence, compiled by Mr. Philip D. Laird, from papers in the Land Office. It has seemed best to include all available rolls in this volume, so the muster rolls of the Flying Camp Companies, and the Eastern Shore Militia Companies ordered to Virginia, first printed in Volume XII of the Archives of Maryland, are reprinted in this appendix.

## EARLY AND INDEPENDENT COMPANIES.

### FIFTH COMPANY OF THE FIRST BATTALION.*
#### CAPTAIN NATHANIEL RAMSEY.

| | | |
|---|---|---|
| Capt. Nathl. Ramsey present | 2nd Lieut. Daviot Plunket | present |
| 1st Lieut. Levin Winder do | Ensign Walker Muse | do |

| RANK. | DATE OF ENLISTMENT. | NAMES. | CAUSE OF ABSENCE. | |
|---|---|---|---|---|
| Serjt. | | John Gassaway | present | |
| do | | Francis Revely | do | |
| do | | Edward Sinclair | do | |
| do | | John Brady | sick | in Hospital |
| Corpl. | | Joseph Dixon | present | |
| do | | John Bruce | do | |
| do | | Alex. McConaughey | do | |
| do | | Edwd. Ford | absent | on Furlough 8th Inst. |
| Drum | | James Murphey | present | |
| Fife | | John Harris, (hired) | do | |

* See page 13.

| RANK. | DATE OF ENLISTMENT. | NAMES. | | CAUSE OF ABSENCE. |
|---|---|---|---|---|
| Privates | | David Congleton | absent | on Guard |
| | | Thomas Brewer | present | |
| | | George Horner | do | |
| | May 18th '76 | John Callenan | do | |
| | | Ezekiel Pearce | do | |
| | May 29th | John Burgess | absent | on Guard |
| | | Charles Turner | present | |
| | | John Marr | dischd. | 18th Inst. |
| | | Thomas Hunter | present | |
| | | Richard Cheaney | do | |
| | | Godfrey Gash | do | |
| | | James Hogg | do | |
| | | Willm. Basford | sick | in Hospital |
| | | Willm. Marr | present | |
| | | Isaac Buttrim | absent | on Guard |
| | | Mathew Neeley | present | |
| | | James Mutton | do | |
| | | Thomas Reed | do | |
| | | Alex. McMunn | do | |
| | | Nicholas Marr | do | |
| | | Saml. Elliott | do | |
| | | Philip Harley | do | |
| | | [Torn off.] | | |

| Present on Duty | | Sick | Discharged |
|---|---|---|---|
| 1 Captain | 3 Corporals | 1 Serjeant | 6 Privates |
| 2 Lieutenants | 1 Drummer | 4 Privates | Absent |
| 1 Ensign | 1 Fifer | Deserted | 1 Corporal |
| 3 Serjeants | 54 Privates | 1 Private | |

M

## EIGHTH COMPANY OF THE FIRST BATTALION.*
### CAPTAIN SAMUEL SMITH.

| 1776 | | 1776 | |
|---|---|---|---|
| Jan 13 | John Fletcher | Jan 23 | Alexander Shaw |
| | Francis Hiltrhimer | | John Snyder |
| 15 | William Arnold | | Patrick Costigin |
| 18 | James Kelly | | Obadiah Stillwill |
| | William Corbin | | Aquilla Taylor |
| | Charles Simms | 24 | Nathan Bleak |

* See page 17.

1776

Jan 20  James Daly
   23   Geo. Edmondstone
        William Wetstet, (or Welstet)
        John Lorah
        Joseph Grey
        Robert Westbay
        Fredk. Hambright

1776

Jan 24  George Bennett
        Martin Wheelan
        David Smith
        Michael Casy
        John Edwards
        Jacob Flori
        [Torn off.]

M

## 2ND INDEPENDENT COMPANY.  [Somerset County.] *
### CAPTAIN JOHN GUNBY.

| DATE. | NAME. | REMARKS. |
|---|---|---|
| | [A large number of names torn off.] | |
| Mch | Wm. Matthews | sick in Barracks |
| 2nd | John Tull | present |
| 4th | Pressly Brewenton | sick in Barracks |
| | Thomas Parramore | present |
| | Wm. Craig | do |
| 8th | John Cooksey | do |
| 9th | Henry Chessey | sick in Barracks |
| | John Reed | present |
| | Nehemiah Knight | do |
| 12th | Patrick Philips | sick at Princess Anne |
| 14th | James Holder | deserted 24th June |
| 20th | Abraham Ervin | sick in Barracks |
| Apl 5th | Solomon Tull | present |
| 8th | George Finch | do |
| | Henry Clarke | do |
| 9th | John Holder | do |
| | John Chittam | do |
| | Wm. Williams | do |
| | Philip King | do |
| 15th | Joshua Gordey | do |
| 19th | Francis Figgen | do |
| May 1st | Thomas Adams | deserted 24th June |
| 14th | Jonathan Brown | present |
| 15th | Wm. North | sick at Princess Anne |
| 22nd | Elisha Taylor | present |
| 28th | Richd. Trane Weatherly | do |
| 29th | Willy Clarke | do |
| June 12th | John Mitchell | sick at Princess Anne |
| 26th | Obadiah Summers | present |

* See page 20.

| DATE. | NAME. | REMARKS. |
|-------|-------|----------|
| July 4th | Wm. Jones | deserted 9th Inst. |
| 15th | James Townsend | dischd. 21st Inst. |
| 26th | William Stockwell | present |
| Aug 1st | John Dowse | sick in Barracks |
| 6th | Richardson Moss | present |
| 13th | Thomas Power | do |

| 1 Captain | 4 Corporals | Privates | |
|-----------|-------------|----------|--|
| 3 Lieutenants | 1 Drummer | 62 On Duty | 16 Sick |
| 4 Serjeants | 1 Fifer | 10 Deserted | 1 Discharged |

G. Duvall, Muster Master

Cambridge, Aug. 21st, 1776.

I hereby certify that the Second Independent Company under my Command was this Day Mustered by Charles Wallace Howard. The above is a true Copy of the Muster Roll of said Company.

The persons who were not present at said Muster were absent for the Causes mentioned opposite to their respective Names in said Muster Roll and no other.

Jno. Gunby.

M

## 6TH INDEPENDENT COMPANY. [Dorchester County.]*
### CAPTAIN THOS. WOOLFORD.

| DATE. | NAME. | REMARKS. |
|-------|-------|----------|
| | [A few names torn off.] | |
| Jan 27th | John Murphy | present |
| 29th | Jacob Hustone | do |
| do | Edward Flin | do |
| do | William Kimplin | do |
| Feb 1st | Patrick Farren | do |
| do | William Cole | do |
| 2nd | Laurence Hughes | do |
| 4th | Laurence Fitzpatrick | do |
| do | Barney Maloy | do |
| do | William Thom | do |
| do | Samuel McCracking | do |
| 8th | Daniel Norriss | do |
| do | Samuel Roans | do |

* See page 25.

| DATE. | NAME. | REMARKS. |
|---|---|---|
| Feb 15th | George Nut | present |
| do | William Lee | do |
| 26th | John Malone | do |
| do | Joseph Read | do |
| Mch 2nd | Hugh Kelly | do |
| do | Michael Connar | do |
| do | Daniel Brophy | do |
| 7th | John Welsh | do |
| Feb 20th | Edward Hodson | do |
| do | Nathan Wright | do |
| do | Edmund Garoughty | sick up at his Mothers |
| 23rd | John Dunn | present |
| | Deweast Downing | do |
| | Jonathan Price | sick at John Greenwood's |
| Mch 21st | Ephraim Wheelar | present |
| 11th | Patrick Rack | do |
| 12th | John Basset | do |
| Feb 20th | Thomas Grayham | do |
| do | Luke Cox | do |
| do | Solomon Tylor | do |
| do | Thomas Bayley | do |
| do | Robert Ruarke | do |
| do | William Smith | do |
| do | Matthew Hayward | do |
| do | Charles Foxwell | do |
| do | Samuel North | do |
| do | Miles Shehern | do |
| do | Caleb Joy | do |
| do | Daniel Linch | do |
| do | William Man | do |
| do | Phillip Hodge | do |
| 23rd | William Dingle | do |
| do | Francis Noble | do |
| do | John Hayward | do |
| do | John Caffey | do |
| do | Edward Hardekin | do |
| 26th | Matthew Colbert | do |
| Mch 2nd | James Sherren | do |
| 4th | William Delihay | do |
| do | Peter Taylor | do |
| do | Thomas Harrison | do |
| 5th | Edward Williams | do |
| 4th | William Kellinough | do |
| 9th | Thomas Saunders | sick at his Father's |
| 14th | Isaac Southard | present |
| Feb 24th | Levin Prichard | do |

| DATE. | NAME. | REMARKS. | |
|---|---|---|---|
| Feb 24th | Joseph Staplefort | present | |
| do | Spencer Saunders | do | |
| do | Perry Harrison | dischd. by M. Gist 25th Inst. | |
| 25th | John Noble | present | |
| 26th | Richardson Gamble | do | |
| Mch 1st | James Sulivan | do | |
| do | Patrick Caton | do | |
| 7th | John Heron | do | |
| 14th | Patrick Connerly | do | |
| 15th | Richard Frazier | do | |
| do | Dennis Devine | do | |
| 19th | William Hale | do | |
| 21st | Hooper Elliot | do | |
| 28th | John Martin, D. C. | do | |
| do | Thomas Hayard | do | |
| do | James Andrew | do | |
| Apl 1st | Saml. Spencer | do | |
| 8th | William Hays | do | Total |
| do | James Urey | do | 1 Captain |
| 10th | Jeremiah Andrew | do | 3 Lieutenants |
| May 2nd | Robert Skinner | do | 4 Serjeants |
| do | James Haney | do | 4 Corporals |
| 9th | Thomas Hart | do | 1 Fifer |
| Apl 4th | Richard Burt | do | 89 Privates |

True Copy from the original Muster Roll of my Company.

Thos. Woolford.

M      G. Duvall, Muster Master.

## EASTERN SHORE MILITIA COMPANIES ORDERED TO VIRGINIA.

### RESOLVES OF CONTINENTAL CONGRESS—8 JANUARY, 1776.

" *Resolved*, That the convention or committee of safety of Maryland, be requested to order three companies of the minute-men in the service of that colony, to march immediately from thence to the counties of Accomack and Northhampton, in Virginia, instead of the forces that were directed to go thither from Pennsylvania, and to lay before Congress the accounts of their subsistence and pay, which shall be paid out of the continental treasury."

### RESOLVES OF THE MARYLAND CONVENTION—15 JANUARY, 1776.

"*Resolved*, That the minute company in Dorchester county commanded by captain Joseph Robson, and the minute company in Queen Anne's county commanded by captain James Kent, and the minute company in Kent county commanded by captain William Henry, immediately march to Accomac and Northampton counties in Virginia, to the assistance of the inhabitants there ; and that if any of the men belonging to either of the said companies cannot go on this occasion, then the full number to be made up of such volunteers as may offer for this particular service."

From the records of the Council of Safety, see Md. Archives, Vol. XI, it does not appear that Capt. Robson's Company marched.

A List of the Minute Company that march'd from Queen Anns County, Maryland the 3d Feby., 1776.*

James Kent, Capt.
Thomas Tillotson, 1st Lieut.
John Charris 2nd Lieut.

John Dames, Ensign
James Browne, Surgeon

Sergts.
George Findley
Ephraim Wyn Story
Philemon Davis
Samuel Copper

Corporals
John Jackson
Thomas Meridith Bryon
Thomas Freshwater, Drumr.
John Findley, Fifer.

William Stinson
Matthew Mason
Edward Wright
John Hawkins
James Clayland
Solomon Pratt
Samuel Seeney
John Hargadine
Barnaba Sinnott
Joseph Elliott
John Godwin
Charles Scrivenor
Christopher Yewell
John Keene
Thomas Meridith
Jonathan Gibson
Joseph Wright
John Kent
Thomas Harriss
William Middleton
William Holding
William Roe

Samuel Earle
Edward Taylor
Perigrine Ashford
William Briggs
Edward Downes
Robert Dawson
William Morgan
Richard Emory
Robert Love
John Lloyd
Henry Coursey
John Carman
Edward Harriss
John Thomas
Saml. Wright Thomas
Robert Wright
William Wilson Emory
Thomas Mayson
William Robinson
Benj. Blunt
Walter Meeds
William Larry

James Browne
Edward Tryall
William Tarr
Samuel White
James Harriss
Nathl. Tucker
William Bruff
John Smith
Thomas Lane Emory
Christopher Jackson
William Scott
Robert Russum
John Burnett
Richard Wickes
William Deford
James Gould Sparks
John Emory Hall
Samuel Boulsover
James Clayland, Jr.
Jacob Gibson
Richard Bruff
Gideon Emory

N. B.—John Kent was wounded the 6th Feby. and has not been able to join the Company since, William Middleton, William Roe, and John Findley, left the Compy. 1st March.

James Kent.

*Archives of Md., Vol. XI, page 194.

A List of the Minute Company from Kent County under the Command of William Henry, who marched from said County 29th January, 1776, and now stationed in Northampton County, Verginia.*

| | Serjts. | Corpls. | Drumr. |
|---|---|---|---|
| William Henry, Capt. | | | |
| John Hyland } Lieuts. | Enos Reves | John Day | Joseph Purden |
| G. W. Forester | Wm. Sprot | Robt. Gay | |
| William Clarke, Ensign | Geo. Vansant | Jas. Henry | Fifer |
| William Tillotson, Surgeon | Chas. Irons | Garret Vansant | Wm. ——— |
| Robert Campbell, Adjutant | | | |

| | | |
|---|---|---|
| John Bond | William Haley | Benedict Penington |
| Stephen Boddy | John Hurt | Matthew Richardson |
| Benj. Brockson | James Hurt | Sampson Redgrave |
| Henry Bostick | Peter Justice | Thos. Read |
| Lambert Boyer | William Johnson | John Richardson |
| John Burnsides | Nathl. Knock | Jacob Richardson |
| · Henry Clarke | David Keain | Thos. Sewell |
| Edward Clayton | Francis Lemon | Thos. Sapington |
| James Campher | Geo. Littles, Sr. | John Stephenson |
| John Cole | Geo. Littles, Jr. | Benj. Stoops |
| John Cry | John Miller | John Stoops |
| Isaac Cornelius | John McGowan | Marlow Taylor |
| William Davis | William Miers | Wm. Peregr. Thrift |
| Samuel Davis | Enoch Massy | John Vansant |
| Samuel Eades | Nathl. McClelland | Christr. Vansant |
| Isaac Freeman | John Massey | Benj. Vansant |
| Daniel Fergusson | Saml. Money | Jas. Wilson, Sr |
| Abraham Freeman | Joseph Newsom | John Wilson |
| Salethiel Freeland | John Nowland | Jas. Wilson, Jr. |
| Lambert Flowers | Richd. Nab | William Wilson |
| Benj. Garland | Wm. Petegrew | John Wilmer |
| James Greedy | Chas. Phillipshill | James Woodland |
| Oliver Gallop | Andw. Park | Robert Young |
| William Gray | | |

Given under my hand at Head Quarters,
29th Feby., 1776.

William Henry.

---

FLYING CAMP MILITIA.

---

### Capt. John Oglevee's Company.†

We the Subscribers, do hereby Enroll our Selves to serve, as Militia of Maryland, in the Middle Department, that is to say, from this Province to New York inclusive, untill the first day of December next, unless sooner discharged by the

Honorable Congress, according to the Resolution of the Convention of Maryland held at Annapolis the 21st day of June, 1776.

Capt. John Oglevee
1st Lieut. Joseph Tanner
2nd Lieut. Elisha Rodgers
Ensign James Boggs
Wm. Tilyard
Thomas Ramsey
Eliot Williams
Oliver Bing
William Smith
Benj. McMahon
James McKibbin
John Jameson
George Glass
William Strean
George Cunningham
William Brisland
James M. Clenshey
William Brison
Andrew Thompson
James Morrow
Samuel Bing

James Hasson
Daniel McGuffin
Alex. Thompson
John Sands
James Connor
William Duffield
John Johnson
Matthew McDowell
Benj. Hasson
Michael Askin
James Clendenin, (a lad), Drummer
Alexander Armstrong
Pattrick Donneley
Matthew Morgan
John Phillips
James Wright
George Day
William Bean
Carbery Cuningham

Daniel Robinson
George McClelland
David Morrison
William Mullen
Hugh McDowell
James Perry
John Minor
Thomas King
Elisha Gatchel
James Hindman
Benj. Moody
George Robinson
Saml. Thompson
Alex. Simpson
Josiah Porterfield
William Jameson
James Stevenson
Thomas Newell
William Johnson
James Welch

July the 25th, 1776:  The within and above men were viewed and are able bodied effective men.

Charles Rumsey.

## CAPT. RICHARD SMITH'S COMPANY.*

List of non commissioned officers and privates enrolled into a company of Militia for the service of the Flying Camp, under Captain Richard Smith, Lieuts. Walter White and Thomas Hayes and Ensign Thomas Sprigg, commencing the 19th of Sept., 1776, to each of whom the bounty money and one month's pay has been advanced at that time and at several dates since, as pr. List now in possession of
Oct. 15th, 1776.                                          Richd. Smith, Capt.

Levi Hayes
Henry Clagett
John Patrick
Matthias Hemstone
Andrew Hughes
Jesse Harris
William Summers
Joseph Lewis
John Davies

Jacob Irissler
William Veal Steuart
Michael Clancy
James Long
Charles Steuart
John Nolland
Nicholas Rodes
Alex. Mason
John Hennes

Robert Muckleroy
William Pollard
Jacob Hesse
William Preston
Thomas Fanning
Ezekiel Harris
John Gibson
William Sutton
John Harriss

* Archives of Md., Vol. XII, pages 352-3.  See page 74.

| | | |
|---|---|---|
| John Smith | Thos. Hays | John Fitzgerrald |
| Alexander Read | George Windom | John Carroll |
| Matthew Read | Peter Night | John Burgess |
| William Norris, (son of Benj.) | William Madden | Jeremiah Leitch |
| William Wallace | Henry Atcheson | Dennias Mannan |
| Levin Hayes | Andrew Keath | Nicholas Rodes, Jr. |
| John Raynolds | Samuel Queen Windsor | Zepheniah Wallace |
| Herbert Alex. Wallace | John Bennett | William Pruett |
| Robert Moore | John Hinton | James Jordan |
| Henry Kuhnes | William Johnston | Robert Robinson |
| Anthony Murphy | John Bowen | |

## CAPT. ROBT. HARRIS' COMPANY OF FLYING CAMP MILITIA.*

Philadelphia, 9th Nov., 1776.

| DATE 1776. | MEN'S NAMES. | DATE 1776. | MEN'S NAMES. |
|---|---|---|---|
| Sept 16th | James Coop | Sept 21st | Richd. Hopkins |
| " | Mathw. McElhany | " | Wm. Chambers |
| " | Joshua James | " | Patrick Nowlan |
| " | Jno. Chance | Oct 4th | Wm. Crook |
| " | James Trene | " | Jas. Watson |
| " | Levi Low | " | Robt. Armstrong |
| " | Wm. Feely | " | Michael Daugherty |
| " | Alex. Stevenson | 5th | Jas. Donnaly |
| " | Robt. Hannah | " | Matthew Criswell |
| " | Gregory White | 16th | Edmd. Daugharty |
| 18th | Robert Gordon | 19th | Jonn. Smith |
| 21st | James Bull | Sept 16th | Zebedee Hicks |
| " | James Harris | " | Horatio Coop |
| " | Wm. Hall | 25th | Richard Jordan |
| 28th | Jas. Blaney | Oct 4th | Jno. Haig |
| " | Christopher Fort | " | Gyks Hodges |
| Oct 15th | Wm. Lattimore | 16th | James Rigden |
| " | Francis Gibson | 17th | Jas. Witgurs |
| " | Jno. Davidson | 18th | Benj. Wailey |
| 16th | Davd. Armstrong | 20th | Thos. Capen |
| " | Barnet Rain | " | David McCullough |
| " | Thos. Roads | Sept 27th | Able Green |
| " | Jno. Cook | Oct 1st | Mathw. Skel |
| " | Jno. Bush | 2nd | Chas. Anderson |
| 17th | Wm. Cook | 3rd | David Campbell |
| " | Alex. Thomson | " | Thomas Stewart |
| 19th | Hugh Hutson | " | Wm. Kirk Patrick |
| " | Wm. Jordan | 6th | Joseph Steel |

*Archives of Md., Vol. XII, pages 435-6.  See page 74.

| DATE 1776. | MEN'S NAMES. | DATE 1776. | MEN'S NAMES. |
|---|---|---|---|
| Sept 26th | Wm. Cuthbert | Oct 6th | Jno. Orr |
| " | Jas. Munday | " | Jno. Patrick |
| " | Joseph Sanders | " | Jno. Pain |
| 25th | Jno. Armstrong | 7th | Jno. Taylor |
| 28th | Jona. Eddy | 9th | Joseph Dueberry |
| 29th | John Baker | 7th | Jas. Miller |
| " | Jno. Lattimore | " | Jessy Logan |
| " | Aquilla Dunham | " | Robt. Spencer |
| Oct 1st | Edwd. Morgan | " | Griffith Evans |
| " | David Wary | | |

## MARYLAND MILITIA IN CONTINENTAL SERVICE IN 1777.

### RESOLVES OF CONTINENTAL CONGRESS 9 DECEMBER, 1776.

" *Resolved,* That expresses be immediately sent to the committees of the counties of Cœcil, Baltimore, Hartford, and Frederick, in Maryland, requesting that they apply, without delay, to the militia of their respective counties, and send forward, immediately, for the defence of the city of Philadelphia, and the reinforcement of general Washington's army, as many troops as possible, informing the said committees that some assistance, in the way of arms, may be furnished here, to such as have no arms to bring with them."

### RESOLVES OF CONTINENTAL CONGRESS 21 JANUARY, 1777.

" *Resolved,* That it be recommended to the council of safety of Maryland, to request the militia of Hartford, Baltimore, Cœcil, and such other counties of their state as they shall think proper, to march, as soon as possible, to reinforce general Washington, giving directions that each company consist of not less than 36 privates, under the command of two commissioned officers, and that a field-officer take the command of every four companies."

A large number of men marched under the Resolves of Dec. 9th, 1776, especially from Frederick, Baltimore and Harford Counties, but no rolls of these companies, giving date of service, can be found. Johnson's and Buchanan's entire divisions were ordered out.

42

RESOLVES OF CONTINENTAL CONGRESS 19 APRIL, 1777.

" *Resolved*, That the gov. of the state of Maryland be authorized to detain the weakest continental battalion raised in the state of Maryland, till a further order of Congress; and that it be recommended to the executive authority of the state of Maryland, forthwith, to embody 300 of the militia of the said state, and to the executive authority of the state of Delaware, 100 of their militia, the said militia to co-operte with the battalion of continental troops, to obey the officer commanding the same, and to continue in service so long as the joint executive authorities of the states of Delaware and Maryland shall think necessary."

RESOLVES OF CONTINENTAL CONGRESS 1 MAY, 1777.

" Congress being informed, that governor Johnson has, in pursuance of the resolution of Congress, of April 19th, for the purposes therein expressed, detained colonel Richardson's battalion, two companies of which are now in Philadelphia on their way to general Washington:

*Resolved*, That the said companies proceed to the army, and that governor Johnson be empowered to replace them, by detaining two companies of the weakest Maryland battalion remaining in that state."

Roll of Capt. Robert Wrights Company of Militia, in the Service of the United States by a Resolution of Congress, under the command of Col. Wm. Richardson.　Aug. and Sept., 1777.

| Commissioned | | Warranted | |
|---|---|---|---|
| July 7th '77 | | | May 27th Capt. Robert Wright |
| June 19th '77 | | | 29th Lieut. John Kent, Jr., resigned Oct 10th |
| | | | 29th Lieut. Edward Thomas |
| July 7th '77 | | | 27th Ensign Thomas Clymer |

| RANK. | APPOINTED. | NAMES. | REMARKS. |
|---|---|---|---|
| Serjeant | June 4th '77 | Nathl. Wright | Sick in Hospital Sept |
| " | May 31st | Wm. Roe | |
| " | June 31st | Thos. Jackson | Sick in Quarters Aug. Deserted Sept 3rd |
| " | July 19th | John Cairey | |
| Corporal | May 31st | John Burnett | Enlisted in another Company Sept |
| " | June 1st | Thos. Covington | |
| " | May 31st | John Lloyd | |
| " | June 17th | Jas. Meredith | Sick in Quarters Aug |

| RANK. | APPOINTED. | NAMES. | REMARKS. |
|---|---|---|---|
| Drum & Fife | July 19th | Thomas Yoe | Enlisted in another Company Sept |
| Privates | Enlisted June 7th | Jacob Seth | Dischd. Aug 15th |
| | 7th | Charles Seth | |
| | May 31st | John Gormon | Enlisted in another Company Sept |
| | June 7th | John Davis | |
| | 7th | John Jeffers, (Geffers) | Sick in Hospital Aug and Sept |
| | 7th | Christr. Green | Dischd. Sept 1st '77 |
| | 7th | Peter Green | Dischd. Sept 1st '77 |
| | 7th | John Thom, (or Thorn) | Missing Oct 4th '77 |
| | 8th | Wm. Davis | Dischd. Sept 1st '77 |
| | 30th | Thos. Delanaway | Dischd. Sept 1st '77 |
| | 30th | Elias Jeffers | Deserted July 23rd |
| | 30th | Wm. Morgan | Dischd. Sept 1st |
| | 6th | Chas. Hands | Never joined Company. Dischd. Oct 7th |
| | July 7th | John Chase | Dischd. by Civil power |
| | June 10th | Chas. Walker | |
| | 17th | Thos. Griffith | |
| | 21st | Wm. Gray | Enlisted in another Company Sept |
| | 16th | John Collins | Deserted Aug 5th, brought back 14th, Sick. Discharged    [Sept 29th |
| | July 21st | Moses Ashford | |
| | June 26th | Nathaniel Baley, (Bailey) | |
| | July 6th | Bazil Jeffers | |
| | June 30th | Henry Weeden | Dischd. by Civil power |
| | July 1st | Wm. Price | Deserted Sept 12th |
| | 4th | Thos. Roe | Dischd. Aug 10th |
| | June 2nd | Wm. Pinfield | Enlisted in another Company Sept |
| | 2nd | Thos. Hall | Enlisted in another Company Sept |
| | July 19th | Saml. Wilkinson, (Wilkerson) | Deserted Sept 12th |
| | June 12th | Simon Rice | Deserted July 27th |
| | July 30th | Matthew B. Chambers | Enlisted in another Company Sept |
| | June 11th | Solo. Scott | Deserted Sept 12th |
| | July 3d | Philn. Davis | Enlisted in another Company Sept |

Mustered Sept. 1st by Robt. Harrison,  D. M. Master.
Mustered Oct. 15th by A. Horton, D. M. M.

RESOLVES OF CONTINENTAL CONGRESS 22 AUGUST, 1777.

"*Resolved*, That it be earnestly recommended to the state of Maryland, immediately to call out not less than 2000 select militia, to repel the expected invasion of the states of Pennsylvania, Delaware and Maryland; and that 1250 of the militia on the Western-shore of Maryland, repair, as soon as possible, to Baltimore and Hartford towns; that 750 of the militia on the Eastern-shore, repair as soon as possible, to Georgetown, on Sassafras, there to await the directions of general Washington:

That the militia requested from the states aforesaid, be in the pay of the continent to the 30th November next, unless sooner discharged by Congress, or the commander in chief:

That general Washington be directed to order brigadier-general Smallwood and colonel Gist, to repair immediately to the state of Maryland, to arrange, march and command the militia required of that state."

A large number of men marched under these Resolves, especially from Baltimore County, but no rolls can be obtained showing date of service. These troops were present at Paoli and Germantown. Capt. Cox, captain of a Baltimore militia company, was killed at Germantown. Maryland furnished more than 4000 militia during the years 1776 and 1777. They numbered about 1900 at Paoli and more than 1000 at Germantown.

It is, perhaps, not saying too much to state that almost the entire militia of Frederick and Baltimore Counties were in service at sometime during this year. The loss of these rolls causes the most serious gap in the Maryland records.

## SELECT MILITIA OF 1781.

A List of Substitutes and Draughts raised in Frederick County under An Act to raise two Battalions of Militia, passed May Session, 1781.*

### SUBSTITUTES.

| | | |
|---|---|---|
| William Dunn | Stephen Haffley | Frederick Stiteley |
| John Deilman | Nicholas Maguire | Christian Waggoner |

* This Roll was presented to the Maryland Historical Society by Mr. Douglas H. Thomas, May 8th, 1899.

Aaron Farthing
Henry Clements
James Bowen
Adam Eck
Thomas Burch
Gilbert Smith
Pompey Colless
Robert Johnson
James Morris
Thedy Donlon
William Hamilton
John Shiffer
Thomas Canfield
John Oneill
Peter Edge
John Allsop
William Fream
Geo. Lodo. Fitcher
William Richardson
Valentine Dewitt
Benjamin Yeates
Menasses Queah
George Becker
John Ogdon
John Betsworth
Jacob Flower
George Miller
Richard Nagle
Jacob Ligamire

John Baum
John Haynes
Lodowick Pole
John Mefford
George Lesh
Henry White
John Frederick
Archibald Roberts
Francis Moser
Michael Moser
Solomon Rawlings
John Lenegen
Joseph Alsop
William Hunter
Gilbert Hunt
John Alexander
John Wilhite
George Hyringer
James Hamilton, Jr.
James Stokes
John Harbough
Henry McGarey
George Dytch
John Casey
William Burgess
Walter Farrell
Thomas Houston
John Morriss
Frederick Beard

John Franklin
Martin Hecketorn
William Ridge
Edward Robinson
Henry Young
John Neave
John Moore
John Miller
Shadrick West
Daniel Hack
Thomas Parkinson
William Dobson
Solomon Turner, Jr.
John Helmes, dischd. by
    Gen. Smallwood
Henry Holtzman
Peter Butler
John Miller
Philip Koontz
Murphy Shee
John Brown
John Qu——
John Neav——
Charles Hammond
Daniel Mehoney
James Bu——
Thomas Da——
Henry Hardman
Patrick Don——

### DRAUGHTS.

Richard Seebrucks
Samuel Dobson
Edward Bryan
James Ogle
Adam Strine

Adam Souder
John Miller, (Major)
Peter Hartsoke
Christopher Scaggs

William Forquer
Michael Fleckinger
William Moore
Philip Myer

Benjn. Rice, appeared ready to march after Siege of York
William Scaggs, marched with Cattle to Fredericksburg

P. Thomas, Lt. Frederick County.

[All in the above Roll enlisted until the 10th of December, 1781. All marched
to Annapolis unless otherwise noted.]

## NAVAL ROLLS.

### THE SHIP DEFENCE.

#### The Ship's Company.

|   | |
|---|---|
|   | Adair, William, Armorer, Jan 11 to Oct 22, 1777; Armorer's Mate, Oct 22 to Dec 31, 1777. |
| B. | Allen, James, Quartermaster Jan 11 to May 18, 1777. |
| B. | Allen, Richard, Marine, March 30 to Dec 31, 1777. |
| + | Arm, ——, Quartermaster. |
| + | Arm, James, Ordinary Seaman. |
| + | Armstrong, James, Marine. |
| + | Askins, William, Marine. |
| B. + | Aubre, John, —— Apl 1 to July 25, 1777. |
|   | Auchenleck, ——, Lieutenant. |
| B. | Barnes, Henry, May 29 to July 27, 1777. |
| + | Barr, John, Coxswain. |
|   | Barrance, James, —— July 5 to Sept 22, 1777. |
|   | Barrett, John, —— Jan 25 to Dec 31, 1777. |
| + | Beachum, Wm., Carpenter's Mate. |
| B. | Bennett, George, —— May 19 to July 23, 1777. |
| B. | Benton, Thomas, Carpenter, Feb 11 to July 26, 1777. |
| + | Berry, James, Marine. |
|   | Berryman, John, Gunner, Jan 13 to Dec 31, 1777. |
| B. | Bird, Samuel, Marine, Apl 2 to Nov 7, 1777. |
| + | Birmingham, Christopher, Captain of Tender. |
| B. | Biscoe, Mackie, —— May 19 to June 1, 1777. |
| + | Bishop, William, Marine. |
|   | Blake, John, Boatswain, Jan 13 to June 17, 1777; Quartermaster, June 17 to Dec 31, 1777. |
|   | Blackman, Stephen, Seaman, Jan 11 to Dec 31, 1777. |
| B. | Blithen, John, Corporal of Marines, May 12 to Aug 31, 1777. |
| + | Blunt, Charles, Marine. |
|   | Bond, Nathaniel, Midshipman ——; Purser, Apl 15 to Dec 31, 1777. |
| + | Bradford, James, Ordinary Seaman. |
| + | Bradford, William, Sergeant of Marines. |
| B. | Brady, Michael, —— June 20 to July 25, 1777. |
| B. | Braithwaite, John, Marine, Apl 28 to Dec 11, 1777. |
|   | Briscoe, James, Marine, Oct 23 to Dec 31, 1777. |
|   | Bromfield, Thomas, Captain of Marines, Apl 25 to Oct 15, 1777. |
| B. | Brooks, Thomas, —— May 21 to June 28, 1777. |
| + | Brown, Colin, Sailor. |
| + | Brown, Garrett, Captain of Marines. |
| B. | Brown, Joseph, —— Feb 17 to March 16, 1777. |

B.    Brumicum, John, Seaman, May 29 to June 7, 1777.
+    Buckley, Thomas, Marine.
B.    Bunyan, John, Mate, May 24 to Aug 15, 1777 ; Chief Mate, Aug 15 to Dec
         31, 1777.
      Burge, Joseph, Steward, Jan 11 to Apl 21, 1777.
+    Burnell, John, Master.
B.    Butler, James, ——— March 6 to June 1, 1777.
      Campbell, James, ——— Jan 28 to July 15, 1777.
      Campbell, John, ——— Jan 28 to Dec 31, 1777.
+    Carr, Henry, Marine.
B.    Carmen, John, Sergeant of Marines, June 1 to Nov 22, 1777.
      Carter, William, ——— May 1 to Aug 15, 1777.
+    Chamborlam, Charles, Sailor.
B.    Champion, George, Boatswain's Yeoman, Feb 26 to Dec 31, 1777.
B.    Cheshire, Benjamin, Marine, May 25 to Dec 31, 1777.
      Chevier, John, Midshipman, Nov 1 to Dec 31, 1777.
      Childs, Cud., Marine, June 1 to Dec 31, 1777.
B.    Clark, James, Marine, July 1 to Dec 31, 1777.
      Clegness, John Francis, Surgeon's Mate, Feb 10 to Dec 31, 1777.
B.    Cockerton, Robert, Cabin Steward, April 28 to Dec 31, 1777.
+    Cockey, Richard, Marine.
+    Cody, James, Marine.
      Coe, Job, Corporal of Marines, Jan 29 to Dec 31, 1777.
+    Cole, Patrick, Marine.
+    Colins, James, Marine.
B.    Colson, (or Coulston), John, Marine, Jan 30 to Dec 31, 1777.
B.    Compton, John, Marine, March 3 to Dec 31, 1777.
+    Conner, Robert, Marine.
      Cook, George, Lieut., Sept 12 to Nov 15, 1776.   Captain, Nov 15, 1776, to
         Dec 31, 1777.
+    Cookson, John, Sailmaker.
      Cooper, Nathaniel, Second Mate, Jan 11 to June 1, 1777.
      Corbet, Patrick, Yeoman, Jan 13 to June 1, 1777 ; Marine, June 1 to Oct
         15, 1777.
      Cordray, James, Second Mate.
      Cornaflean, William, Midshipman, Sept 4 to Sept 22, 1777 ; Clerk, Sept 22
         to Dec 31, 1777.
+    Costillo, Thomas, Marine.
+    Crapper, John, Sergeant of Marines.
B.    Cratcher, Matthew, Marine, July 28 to Oct 1, 1777.
      Crawley, James, Marine, Oct 23 to Dec 31, 1777.
+    Cron, Thomas, Marine.
B.    Crosley, (or Crossley), William, Marine, Mch 16 to Dec 31, 1777.
B.    Cummings, Alexander, Marine ———; Carpenter's Yeoman, Feb 17 to Dec
         31, 1777.
B.    Cunningham, Thompson, Boatswain's Mate, July 31 to Dec 31, 1777.
B.    Daefney, John, Seaman, Aug 9 to Sept 6, 1777.
+    Davis, John, Corporal of Marines.
+    Davis, William, Marine.

+　　　Delong, Bartholomew, Marine.

　　　　Dennis, Joseph, ——— Jan 25 to April 9, 1777.

　　　　Dicks, Daniel, ——— Jan 18 to April 12, 1777.

　　　　Dickson, John, Seaman, Sept 1 to Dec 26, 1777.

+　　　Disney, Ezekiel, Sr., Ordinary Seaman.

+　　　Disney, Ezekiel, Jr., Marine.

+　　　Donavin, John, Marine.

　　　　Dorsey, Joseph, Marine, Oct 23 to Dec 31, 1777.

+　　　Dorsey, Richard, Midshipman.

+　　　Douglas, Archibald, Tender's Crew.

　　　　Douglass, William, Midshipman, Mch 13 to Apl 3, 1777.

　　　　Driskill, John, Seaman.

B.　　Dunbar, Joseph, Cooper, Jan 11 to Dec 31, 1777.

B.　　Durdin, Thomas, ——— Mch 6 to Dec 31, 1777.

　　　　Evans, Robert, ——— Aug 1 to Oct 31, 1777.

B.　　Fall, Patrick, ——— Jan 11 to May 18, 1777.

B.　　Farrajara, John, Midshipman, Aug 9 to Sept 8, 1777.

B.　　Fear, Ignatius, Gunner's Mate, May 28 to Sept 20, 1777.

B.　　Fenton, Cornelius, Marine, April 1 to Dec 31, 1777.

　　　　Fenwick, Richard, Marine, Oct 23 to Dec 31, 1777.

B.　　FitzJeffrys, Aaron, ——— June 21 to July 15, 1777.

B.　　Flannagan, John, ——— June 17 to June 29, 1777.

+　　　Flemming, John, Sergeant of Marines.

+　　　Flemming, William, Sergeant of Marines.

　　　　Foster, William, ——— March 27 to June 1, 1777.

B.　　Fowler, Joseph, Boy, May 19 to Dec 31, 1777.

　　　　Franceway, John, Marine, Jan 25 to Dec 31, 1777.

B.　　Gagan, (Gaggen, Glagging), James, Cook, Feb 20 to Dec 31, 1777.

+　　　Gaggen, William, Ordinary Sailor.

　　　　Gaither, Joseph, Clerk, Mch 18 to June 1, 1777.

B.　　Gardner, (or Garner), Clement, Marine, May 22 to Dec 31, 1777.

B.　　Gardner, Thomas, ——— May 22 to July 7 1777.

B.　　Garey, John, Marine, May 26 to Aug 15, 1777.

　　　　Gibson, Joshua, Marine, May 22 to Dec 31, 1777.

+　　　Gibbons, Edward, Marine.

+　　　Gilby, Henry, Ordinary Sailor.

+　　　Gilby, Thomas, Ordinary Sailor.

+　　　Gilford, James, Ordinary Sailor.

B.　　Gillis, Thomas, Third Mate, June 3 to Nov 25, 1777.

　　　　Goldsbury, John, Marine, Oct 23 to Nov 15, 1777.

　　　　Goldsbury, Stephen, Marine, Oct 23 to Nov 15, 1777. " Disch'd, being unfit for duty."

+　　　Gordon, Isaac Mount, Sergeant of Marines.

　　　　Grant, John, Carpenter's Mate, Jan 14 to Dec 31, 1777.

+　　　Grantham, William, Marine.

B.　　Green, James, Midshipman, June 24 to July 29, 1777.

+　　　Greer, James, Marine.

+　　　Greer, Moses, Marine.

B.　　Gullehan, John, ——— Mch 31 to July 15, 1777.

| | |
|---|---|
| B. | Hagan, (Hagans), Charles, Cooper's Mate, Feb 12 to Dec 31, 1777. |
| + | Hall, John, Third Mate. |
| + | Hall, Stephen, Mate. |
| B. | Hall, William, ——— May 26 to July 28, 1777. |
| + | Haly, Oliver, Marine. |
| + | Hambleton, Charles, Sergeant of Marines. |
| + | Hamer, (Harmer), John, " Taylor," Oct 10 to Dec 31, 1777. |
| + | Hanson, John, Midshipman. |
| B. | Harbest, (Harbert), Thomas, Marine, Jan 15 to Nov 15, 1777. |
| + | Harbert, William, Sailor. |
| B. | Harding, Richard,——— June 18 to June 29, 1777. |
| B. | Harper, Daniel, Boatswain, June 1 to Nov 24, 1777. |
| | Harris, William, Armorer, Feb 15 to Apl 13, 1777. |
| + | Hartie, James, Quarter Master. |
| B. | Havard, William, Seaman, Mch 6 to Dec 31, 1777. |
| B. | Havers, John, Cooper's Crew, June 19 to Dec 31, 1777. |
| B. | Hawkins, James, Midshipman, Mch 1 to Aug 15, 1777; with Ship's Tender, Aug 15 to Nov 15, 1777; Skipper, Nov 15 to Nov 24, 1777. |
| + | Henry, James, Marine. |
| + | High, George, Ordinary Sailor. |
| + | Hogan, James, Ordinary Sailor. |
| + | Hope, Robert, Ordinary Sailor. |
| B. | Hopewell, Thomas, Midshipman, May 15 to Dec 31, 1777. |
| B. | Hopkins, Roger, ——— Apl 28 to July 21, 1777. |
| | Hosier, Joshua, Seaman, Jan 23 to Dec 31, 1777. |
| B. | Howard, Thomas, Midshipman, Feb 2 to Dec 31, 1777. |
| | Howard, William, Carpenter's Mate, Aug 15 to Dec 31, 1777. |
| + | Howard, William, Marine. |
| B. | Hudson, William, Seaman, June 24 to Dec 31, 1777. |
| + | Huggard, William, Marine. |
| | Huggins, William, Marine, Sept 6 to Dec 31, 1777. |
| B. | Humphreys, Lewis, ——— June 25 to July 15, 1777. |
| + | Hurbert, Francis, Boatswain's Mate. |
| | Hurst, Cuthbert, (or Hurst, Catwood), ——— June 27 to Dec 31, 1777. |
| + | Hyndson, Anthony, Boatswain. |
| + | Jackelen, Francis, Marine. |
| + | Jennett, Green, Marine. |
| | Jerrial, John, Marine, June 8 to Aug 4, 1777. |
| | Johns, Aquilla, Lieutenant. |
| B. | Johnson, Horsford, Marine, Apl 28 to Dec 16, 1777. |
| | Johnson, John, Seaman, Jan 11 to March 3, 1777. |
| + | Jones, Joseph, Marine. |
| | Jones, Nathan, ——— Jan 25 to May 13, 1777. |
| | Jordan, Samuel, Corporal of Marines, Oct 22 to Dec 31, 1777. |
| | Jourdan, (Jorden), Jeremiah, ——— Jan 23 to Dec 31, 1777. |
| | Jourdan, (Jorden), John, Sergeant of Marines, Jan 23 to Dec 31, 1777. |
| + | Judges, William, Ordinary Sailor. |
| + | Kenderdine, John, Marine. |
| + | King, William, Ordinary Sailor. |

B.    Kinsey, Thomas, Midshipman, Apl 9 to Dec 31, 1777.
B.    Kirk, Daniel, Marine, May 28 to Dec 31, 1777.
+    Knight, John, Marine.
B.    Land, William, Marine, Apl 2 to Dec 21, 1777.
+    Langrale, Levin, Sailor.
     Larkan, Dennis, Seaman.
B.    Lawrence, Joshua, Seaman, July 2 to Dec 31, 1777.
B.    Lee, (Leigh), Christopher, Marine, May 20 to Dec 31, 1777.
B.    Leigh, William, Surgeon's Mate.
+    Lemmon, John, Marine.
B.+    Leury, John, ———.
B.    Lilburn, (Lilbon), Walter, Midshipman, May 22 to Nov 24, 1777.
     Little, John, Seaman, Sept 20 to Dec 31, 1777.
+    Loyal, John, Marine.
     Luke, Folius, ——— Jan 25 to Mch 31, 1777.
+    Lux, Robert, Midshipman.
     Lusby, Henry, Midshipman, Oct 15 to Nov 13, 1777 ; Lieutenant of Marines,
        Nov 13 to Dec 31, 1777.
     McAdams, John, Armorer, Oct 22 to Dec 31, 1777.
B.    McCarty, Florence, Seaman, June 25 to Dec 16, 1777.
B.    McClenan, (McCleland), Robert, Marine, June 26 to Dec 31, 1777.
B.    McCoy, George, ——— April 1 to Dec 31, 1777.
+    McDonald, Robert, Ordinary Sailor.
+    McGill, James, Marine.
     McLaughlan, Mark, Carpenter, Aug 5 to Dec 31, 1777.
+    McNealis, Charles, Marine.
B.    Maddox, John, Marine, June 3 to Oct 15, 1777.
+    Mason, Abel, Ordinary Sailor.
B.    Massey, Henry Lee, Midshipman, May 10 to Dec 31, 1777.
+    Masters, Watterly, Marine.
     Matthews, John, Sweeper, Jan 25 to Dec 31, 1777.
+    Matthews, Wm., Corporal of Marines.
     Medley, Enoch, Seaman, Oct 23 to Dec 31, 1777.
     Mercer, Stephen, ——— Jan 13 to April 21, 1777.
B.    Miller, Philip, Seaman, Jan 15 to Oct 1, 1777.
B.    Miller, William, Ship's Steward, June 2 to July 11, 1777 ; Seaman, July 11 to
        Oct 15, 1777 ; Gunner's Yeoman, Oct 15 to Dec 31, 1777.
B.    Mills, Jonathan, ——— May 22 to July 23, 1777.
B.    Montgomery, John, Ship's Tender, June 7 to Dec 31, 1777.
B.    Moore, Thomas, Ordinary Sailor.
     Moore, John, Marine, May 10 to Dec 31, 1777.
+    Moores, James R., Purser.
+    Morris, Wm., Lieutenant of Marines.
+    Murphy, Samuel, Marine.
+    Murray, Matthew, Marine.
     Murphy, Morgan, Marine, Jan 13 to Mch 23, 1777.
     Nagill, (Nagale), Michael, Marine, Oct 8 to Nov 26, 1777.
B.    Nash, Thomas, Boatswain's Mate, Apl 28 to Aug 15, 1777 ; Marine, Aug 15
        to Dec 11, 1777.

Nesbit, Thomas, Seaman, Nov 15 to Dec 31, 1777.

Neven, Daniel, Ordinary Seaman.

Nichols, Walter, ——— Jan 16 to Aug 15, 1777 ; Quarter Gunner, Aug 15 to Dec 31, 1777.

Nicholson, Alex., Sailor, Jan 11 to Aug 15, 1777 ; Quarter Master, Aug 15 to Dec 11, 1777.

\+ Nicholson, James, Captain.

\+ Nicholson, John, Lieutenant.

B. Palmer, Thomas, Marine, May 29 to Dec 31, 1777.

B. Parsons, William, Marine, Apl 28 to Dec 31, 1777.

B. Peres, Anthony, Seaman, Aug 9 to Sept 6, 1777.

Peters, Nicholas, Marine.

Piercy, William, Midshipman, Jan 13 to Dec 31, 1777.

Pike, John, Marine, Jan 21 to Dec 31, 1777.

Poland, (Polland), William, Marine, Apl 1 to Dec 31, 1777.

\+ Porter, William, Marine.

\+ Porter, William, Sailor.

\+ Power, John, Marine.

B Powlet, Severn, ——— June 3 to July 23, 1777.

Prew, William, Ship's Steward, July 9 to Dec 31, 1777.

B. Price, Henry, Marine, May 21 to Dec 31, 1777.

\+ Primrose, David, Sailor.

\+ Prince, William, Marine.

B. Quay, James, Ordinary Seaman, April 1 to Dec 31, 1777.

Ragan, Roderick, Marine, Aug 12 to Oct 7, 1777.

B. Ready, James, Marine, May 10 to Dec 17, 1777.

B. Ready, Lawrence, Marine, May 10 to Dec 17, 1777.

Rentford, Henry, Sailor, Feb 1 to Mch 11, 1777.

B. Richardson, Alexander, ——— Feb 15 to May 15, 1777.

\+ Riley, Michael, Marine.

\+ Riley, Tim, Ordinary Sailor.

\+ Roberts, Thomas, Marine.

Robertson, George, Surgeon, May 20 to Dec 31, 1777.

Robertson, William, Captain's Clerk, Feb 10 to Mch 26, 1777.

Rogers, John, 2nd Lieut. of Marines, Mch 11 to Dec 31, 1777.

Ross, George, 1st Lieut. of Marines, Mch 18 to Dec 31, 1777.

\+ Ross, Nathan, ———.

Rowe, John, ——— Jan 16 to July 23, 1777.

\+ Rowen, George, Master at Arms.

\+ Rowns, James, Midshipman.

B. Scone, Charles, ——— March 6 to June 30, 1777.

\+ Scott, Mores, Marine.

B. Seagreave, Patrick, ——— May 21 to July 28, 1777.

Seea, John, Marine.

B. Sency, William, ——— Apl 28 to Aug 15, 1777.

Sermon, Leonard, ——— Jan 23 to Apl 11, 1777.

\+ Sharp, Peter, Midshipman.

\+ Short, Christopher, Sailor.

\+ Simpson, Benj., Boatswain's Mate.

|   | |
|---|---|
|   | Skiffington, Roger, Marine, Jan 20 to Dec 31, 1777. |
| + | Slaymaker, John, Lieutenant. |
|   | Skinner, Francis, Prize Master, Sept 15 to Dec 31, 1777. |
|   | Smith, James, Marine, Oct 22 to Dec 31, 1777. |
| + | Smith, John Addison, Gunner. |
| + | Smith, Joseph, Lieutenant of Marines. |
| + | Sohan, William, Marine. |
| B. | Sommers, Jacob, ——— April 3 to Oct 15, 1777. |
| B. | Sommers, John, Quarter Master, Feb 15 to Dec 11, 1777. |
| + | Squib, John, Marine. |
| B. | Stanton, Alexander, Armorer, Jan 11 to Aug 15, 1777; Master at Arms, Aug 15 to Dec 31, 1777. |
| B. | Stiles, Solomon, Pilot, May 22 to Dec 31, 1777. |
| + | Strong, Abram, Marine. |
| B. | Sullivan, Bright, Sailmaker, July 15 to Dec 31, 1777. |
| + | Sutton, Benjamin, Marine. |
| + | Sutton, Jacob, Marine. |
| + | Sutton, Richard, Marine. |
|   | Swailes, Robert, Marine, Oct 23 to Dec 31, 1777. |
| + | Thompson, George, Sailor. |
|   | Thompson, John, ——— Jan 11 to Mch 1, 1777. |
| + | Tooloe, Dennis, Marine. |
| + | Topet, Robert, Marine. |
| + | Trainer, Simon, Marine. |
| + | Tregashes, Jacob, Armorer. |
| + | Trot, William, Ordinary Sailor. |
| + | Turnbull, C. George, Captain. |
| + | Tyler, Littleton, Carpenter. |
|   | Vansickle, Gilbert, Seaman, Jan 28 to June 1, 1777. |
| B. | Vaughan, Abraham, Marine, Aug 3 to Nov 19, 1777. |
| + | Vaun, John, Marine. |
|   | Walker, Samuel, Master, Apl 22 to Dec 31, 1777. |
| + | Walker, Thomas, Lieutenant of Marines. |
|   | Walter, Levin, ——— Jan 21 to June 1, 1777. |
| + | Ward, John, Marine. |
| + | Watpole, Joseph, Sailor. |
| B. | Watson, James, ——— June 23 to Aug 15, 1777; Capt. After Guard, Aug 15 to Nov 23, 1777. |
| B.+ | Wharton, Revel, ———. |
| B. | Wheeler, Benj., Marine, June 7 to Dec 31, 1777. |
|   | White, Benj., Seaman, Sept 20 to Dec 31, 1777. |
| B. | White, Peter, Seaman, Aug 9 to Nov 2, 1777. |
| B. | Williams, Francis, Cook's Mate, Feb 11 to Dec 31, 1777. |
| B. | Williams, John, Marine, Apl 28 to Dec 31, 1777. |
| B. | Williams, Marshall, Seaman, Jan 21 to Mch 21, 1777. |
| + | Wilson, John, Corporal of Marines. |
| B. | Woods, Benj., Mate, June 20 to Aug 15, 1777; 2nd Mate, Aug 15 to Dec 28, 1777. |
| + | Wright, John, Seaman. |

+    Wright, John, Quarter Master.
B.    Yates, Richard, Boatswain's Mate, Apl 28 to Dec 8, 1777.
      Yates, Vachel, Sergeant of Marines, ———; Lieut. of Marines, Feb 15 to Oct 15, 1777 ; Capt. of Marines, Oct 15 to Dec 15, 1777.

Compiled from Papers in the Land Office of Maryland by Philip D. Laird, 1896, and presented by him to the Maryland Historical Society.

It is compiled alphabetically from four Accounts of Seamen's Wages,—one from September 12, 1776, to August 15, 1777; one from August 15 to October 15, 1777; one from October 15 to November 15, 1777; one from November 15 to December 31, 1777— and from a List of Officers and Men, without date, which is manifestly prior to the dates of the pay accounts. The names in the list, where they are in addition to those in the pay accounts, are indicated by the mark +. The letter B., in the margin, indicates those who received bounty, the information being derived from two accounts of "Bounties paid by the Ship Defence," amounting, in the aggregate, to £630. The time of service is not given in all cases, in the pay accounts, and in a number of instances the rank is omitted. As far as possible dates of promotion are given.

---

## HARFORD COUNTY PENSIONERS.*

List of the names of maimed Soldiers entitled to half pay under the Act of October Session, 1778.

| | | |
|---|---|---|
| Joseph Botts. | Frederick Ire. | James Smith. |
| James Burk. | James Isaacs. | William Ely. |
| James Brewer. | Daniel Keith. | John Shaw, Sergt. |
| John Butcher. | Macnamara, (sic.) | Samuel Tyndall. |
| John Dent, Corpl. | Thomas McGee. | William Fulton. |
| James Dyre. | John Mathews, Corpl. | Samuel Wilson, Sergt. |
| Michael Duffy. | James O'Hara. | John Vanzant. |
| William Evans. | James Pope. | Richard Wilkinson. |
| George Finleyson. | Christopher Reynol. | Joseph Quinn. |
| Caleb Hazel. | Valentine Smith. | John Lowery. |
| John Howard. | | Edward Cain. |
| James Scott. | | |

Allowances for the support of the families of Soldiers enlisted in the Continental Army, 1777–1780.

| | | |
|---|---|---|
| Richard Crosby. | Edward Evans. | Michael Coaleman. |
| James McCarty. | James Kelly. | Wm. Hendersides. |
| Wm. Murphy. | Wm. Lytle. | |

Sept. 1778, a commission was appointed 'to take the deposition of Joseph Barnes, a Soldier' in a suit pending.

* Extracts, from the 'Proceedings of the Orphans Court of Harford County, 1784–1803' and the 'Records of the County Court of Harford County, 1777–1780' made by Dr. G. W. Archer.

# INDEX.